The American Journey

A History of the United States

Teaching and Learning Classroom Edition

Brief Third Edition

Combined Volume

David Goldfield

Carl Abbott

Virginia DeJohn Anderson

Jo Ann E. Argersinger

Peter H. Argersinger

William L. Barney

Robert M. Weir

PEARSON

Prentice
Hall

Upper Saddle River, New Jersey 07458

Library of Congress C̸ oging-in-Publication Data

The American Jour̸ a history of the United States / David Goldfield ... [et al.],—Brief 3rd ed.
   p. cm.   ̸me."
   "Combine̸graphical references and index.
   Includes ̸93-7
   ISBN 0-̸es   History.   I. Goldfield, David R., 1944–
   1. Uni̸ 2004
   E178.̸
   973—

2003066029

̸irector: Charlyce Jones Owen
VP, E̸tor: Charles Cavaliere
Exe̸tor: Emsal Hasan
Ass̸istant: Shannon Corliss
E̸ief, Development: Rochelle Diogenes
̸dia Editor: Deborah O'Connell
̸elopment Editors: Roberta Meyer, Gerald Lombardi
̸ctor of Production
̸anufacturing: Barbara Kittle
̸g Editor: Joanne Riker
̸tion Editor: Randy Pettit
̸ction Assistant: Marlene Gassler
̸ss and Manufacturing Manager: Nick Sklitsis
̸press and Manufacturing Buyer: Tricia Kenny
̸irector of Marketing: Beth Mejia
Executive Marketing Manager: Heather Shelstad
Creative Design Director: Leslie Osher

Interior and Cover Designer: Anne DeMarinis
Manager, Production, Formatting and Art: Guy Ruggiero
Cartographer: CartoGraphics
Electronic Artists: Maria Piper, Mirella Signoretto,
   Rosemary Ross, Bruce Killmer, Carey Davies
Director, Image Resource Center: Melinda Reo
Interior Image Specialist: Beth Boyd Brenzel
Color Scanning Services: Joe Conti, Cory Skidds,
   Greg Harrison, Rob Uibelhoer, Ron Walko
Cover Image Specialist: Karen Sanatar
Image Permission Coordinator: Craig Jones
Photo Researcher: Kathy Ringrose
Compositor: Preparé, Inc.
Printer/Binder: Von Hoffmann Corporation
Cover Printer: The Lehigh Press, Inc.
Cover Art: Sitting Bull, Bettmann/Corbis/Bettmann

Credits and acknowledgments borrowed from other sources and reproduced, with permission, in this textbook appear on appropiate page within text (or on page C-1)

Pearson Education Ltd., London
Pearson Education Australia Pty., Limited, Sydney
Pearson Education Singapore, Pte., Ltd.
Pearson Education North Asia Ltd., Hong Kong

Pearson Education Canada, Ltd., Toronto
Pearson Educación de Mexico, S.A. de C.V.
Pearson Education — Japan, Tokyo
Pearson Education Malaysia, Pte., Ltd.

10 9 8 7 6 5 4 3 2

ISBN 0-13-150093-7
NASTA   ISBN 0-13-119433-X

BRIEF CONTENTS

1 Worlds Apart 2

2 Transplantation 1600–1685 30

3 The Creation of New Worlds 56

4 Convergence and Conflict 80

5 Imperial Breakdown 1763–1774 108

6 The War for Independence 1774–1783 132

7 The First Republic 1776–1789 166

8 A New Republic and the Rise of Parties 1789–1800 194

9 The Triumph and Collapse of Jeffersonian Republicanism 1800–1824 216

10 The Jacksonian Era 1824–1845 240

11 Slavery and the Old South 1800–1860 264

12 The Market Revolution and Social Reform 1815–1850 350

13 The Way West 1815–1850 324

14 The Politics of Sectionalism 1846–1861 350

15 Battle Cries and Freedom Songs: The Civil War 1861–1865 378

16 Reconstruction 1865–1877 414

17 A New South: Economic Progression and Social Tradition 1877–1900 439

18 Industry, Immigrants, and Cities 1870–1900 468

19 Transforming the West 1865–1890 496

20 Politics and Government 1877–1900 524

21 The Progressive Era 1900–1917 546

22 Creating an Empire 1865–1917 578

23 America and the Great War 1914–1920 602

24 Toward a Modern America the 1920s 628

25 The Great Depression and the New Deal 1929–1939 654

26 World War II 1939–1945 684

27 The Cold War at Home and Abroad 1946–1952 712

28 The Confident Years 1953–1964 736

29 Shaken to the Roots 1965–1980 760

30 The Reagan Revolution and a Changing World 1981–1992 792

31 Complacency and Crisis 1993–2003 820

CONTENTS

AMERICAN VIEWS   xvi

FROM THEN TO NOW   xvii

MAPS   xvii

OVERVIEW TABLES   xix

ABOUT THE AUTHORS   xx

PREFACE   xxi

STUDENT TOOL KIT   xxvii

1 WORLDS APART 2

Voices from the American Journey:
  Moctezuma   4

DIFFERENT WORLDS   4
  Native American Societies Before 1492   6
  Cultural Perceptions and Misperceptions   11
  West African Societies   12
  Western Europe on the Eve of Discovery   16

CONTACT   18
  The Lure of Discovery   18
  Christopher Columbus   19
  Spanish Conquest and Colonization   20
  The Columbian Exchange   23

COMPETITION FOR A CONTINENT   24
  Early French Efforts in North America   24
  English Attempts in the New World   25

CONCLUSION   28

SUMMARY   28   REVIEW QUESTIONS   29

KEY TERMS   29   WHERE TO LEARN MORE   29

2 TRANSPLANTATION, 1600–1685 30

Voices from the American Journey:
  Thomas Dudley   32

THE FRENCH IN NORTH AMERICA   33
  The Development of New France   33
  The Fur Trade   34

ENGLISH SETTLEMENT IN THE CHESAPEAKE   34
  The Ordeal of Early Virginia   35
  The Importance of Tobacco   37
  Maryland: A Refuge for Catholics   39

THE FOUNDING OF NEW ENGLAND   40
  The Pilgrims and Plymouth Colony   40
  Massachusetts Bay Colony
    and Its Offshoot   41
  Families; Farms; and Communities
    in Early New England   43

COMPETITION IN THE CARIBBEAN   45
  Sugar and Slaves   45
  A Biracial Society   45

THE PROPRIETARY COLONIES   46
  Early Carolina   48
  Pennsylvania:
    The Dream of Tolerance and Peace   50

THE DUTCH OVERSEAS EMPIRE   51
  The West India Company and New Netherland   51
  New Netherland Becomes New York   52

CONCLUSION   53

SUMMARY   54   REVIEW QUESTIONS   54

KEY TERMS   55   WHERE TO LEARN MORE   55

3 THE CREATION OF NEW WORLDS 56

Voices from the American Journey:
  Olaudah Equiano   58

INDIANS AND EUROPEANS   59
  Indian Workers in the Spanish
    Borderlands   59
  The Web of Trade   60
  Displacing Native Americans in the English
    Colonies   61
  Bringing Christianity to Native Peoples   62
  After the First Hundred Years:
    Conflict and War   64

AFRICANS AND EUROPEANS   68
  Labor Needs and the Turn to Slavery   68
  The Shock of Enslavement   71
  African-American Families and Communities   72
  Resistance and Rebellion   74

European Laborers in North America 75
  A Spectrum of Control 75
  New European Immigrants 76

Conclusion 77

Summary 78   Review Questions 78

Key Terms 79   Where To Learn More 79

4

Convergence and Conflict 80

Voices from the American Journey:
  George Washington 82

Economic Development
and Imperial Trade
in the British Colonies 83
  The Regulation of Trade 83
  The Colonial Export Trade and the Spirit
    of Enterprise 84
  The Import Trade and Ties of Credit 86
  Becoming More Like England 87

The Transformation of Culture 88
  Goods and Houses 88
  Shaping Minds and Manners 89
  Colonial Religion and the Great Awakening 90

The Colonial Political World 93
  The Dominion of New England and the Limits
    of British Control 93
  The Legacy of the Glorious Revolution 94
  Diverging Politics in the Colonies
    and Great Britain 95

Expanding Empires 97
  British Colonists in the Backcountry 97
  The Spanish in Texas and California 98
  The French Along the Mississippi
    and in Louisiana 99

A Century of Warfare 100
  Imperial Conflict and the Establishment of an
    American Balance of Power,
    1689–1738 100
  King George's War Shifts the Balance,
    1739–1754 102
  The French and Indian War, 1754–1760: A
    Decisive Victory 102
  The Triumph of the British Empire, 1763 104

Conclusion 105

Summary 105   Review Questions 106

Key Terms 107   Where to Learn More 107

5

Imperial Breakdown, 1763–1774 108

Voices from the American Journey:
  Eliza Farmer 110

Imperial Reorganization 111
  British Problems 112
  Dealing with the New Territories 112

Indian Affairs 114
  Curbing the Assemblies 115
  The Sugar and Stamp Acts 116

American Reactions 116
  Constitutional Issues 117
  Taxation and the Political Culture 117
  Protesting the Taxes 118

The Aftermath of the Stamp Act Crisis 119
  A Strained Relationship 119
  Regulator Movements 120

The Townshend Crisis 121
  Townshend's Plan 121
  American Boycott 121
  The Boston Massacre 122
  The "Quiet Period" 123
  The Boston Tea Party 124
  The Intolerable Acts 124

The Road to Revolution 125
  American Response to the Intolerable Acts 125
  The First Continental Congress 125
  The Continental Association 127
  Political Divisions 127

Conclusion 128

Summary 129   Review Questions 130

Key Terms 130   Where to Learn More 130

6

The War for Independence, 1774–1783 132

Voices from the American Journey:
  John Laurens 134

The Outbreak of War and the Declaration of
Independence, 1774–1776 135
  Mounting Tensions 135
  The Loyalists' Dilemma 136

British Coercion and Conciliation   136
The Battles of Lexington and Concord   136
The Second Continental Congress,
    1775–1776   137
Commander in Chief George Washington   137
Early Fighting   138
Independence   138
Republicanism   142

THE COMBATANTS   142
Professional Soldiers   142
Women in the Contending Armies   145
African-American and Native-American
    Participation in the War   145

THE WAR IN THE NORTH, 1776–1777   147
The British Army Hesitates   147
The Year of the Hangman   147

THE WAR WIDENS, 1778–1781   149
The United States Gains an Ally   149
Fighting on the Frontier and at Sea   150
The Land War Moves South   152
American Counterattacks   152

THE AMERICAN VICTORY, 1782–1783   155
The Peace of Paris   156
The Components of Success   156

WAR AND SOCIETY, 1775–1783   158
The Women's War   158
Effect of the War on African Americans and
    Native Americans   158
The Price of Victory   160

CONCLUSION   160

SUMMARY   161   REVIEW QUESTIONS   162

KEY TERMS   162   WHERE TO LEARN MORE   163

VISUALIZING THE PAST
The Rattlesnake as a National Symbol   164

7
THE FIRST REPUBLIC,
1776–1789   166

Voices from the American Journey:
    William Shepard   168

THE NEW ORDER OF REPUBLICANISM   169
Defining the People   169
The State Constitutions   172
The Articles of Confederation   174

PROBLEMS AT HOME   175
The Fiscal Crisis   175
Economic Depression   176
The Economic Policies of the States   177
Congress and the West   179

DIPLOMATIC WEAKNESSES   181
Impasse with Britain   182
Spain and the Mississippi River   183

TOWARD A NEW UNION   183
The Road to Philadelphia   184
The Convention at Work   184
Overview of the Constitution   186
The Struggle over Ratification   188

CONCLUSION   190

SUMMARY   191   REVIEW QUESTIONS   192

KEY TERMS   192   WHERE TO LEARN MORE   193

8

A NEW REPUBLIC
AND THE RISE OF PARTIES,
1789–1800   194

Voices from the American Journey:
    William Maclay   196

WASHINGTON'S AMERICA   197
The Uniformity of New England   197
Mid-Atlantic Pluralism   198
The Slave South and Its Backcountry   198
The Growing West   199

FORGING A NEW GOVERNMENT   201
"Mr. President" and the Bill of Rights   201
Departments and Courts   202
Revenue and Trade   203
Hamilton and the Public Credit   203
Reaction and Opposition   204

THE EMERGENCE OF PARTIES   205
The French Revolution   205
Securing the Frontier   207
The Whiskey Rebellion   208
Treaties with Britain and Spain   208
The First Partisan Election   210

THE LAST FEDERALIST ADMINISTRATION   210
The French Crisis and the XYZ Affair   211
Crisis at Home   211
The End of the Federalists   212

CONCLUSION   213

SUMMARY   214   REVIEW QUESTIONS   215

KEY TERMS   215   WHERE TO LEARN MORE   215

9

THE TRIUMPH AND COLLAPSE OF JEFFERSONIAN REPUBLICANISM, 1800–1824 216

Voices from the American Journey:
Rosalie Calvert 218

JEFFERSON'S PRESIDENCY 219
Reform at Home 219
The Louisiana Purchase 220
Florida and Western Schemes 220
Embargo and a Crippled Presidency 223

MADISON AND THE COMING OF WAR 224
The Failure of Economic Sanctions 224
The Frontier and Indian Resistance 225
Decision for War 226

THE WAR OF 1812 226
Setbacks in Canada 229
Western Victories and British Offensives 229
The Treaty of Ghent and the Battle of New Orleans 230

THE ERA OF GOOD FEELINGS 231
Economic Nationalism 231
Judicial Nationalism 232
Toward a Continental Empire 232

THE BREAKDOWN OF UNITY 233
The Panic of 1819 233
The Missouri Compromise 235
The Election of 1824 237

CONCLUSION 237

SUMMARY 238   REVIEW QUESTIONS 238

KEY TERMS 239   WHERE TO LEARN MORE 239

10

THE JACKSONIAN ERA, 1824–1845 240

Voices from the American Journey:
Benjamin B. French 242

THE EGALITARIAN IMPULSE 243
The Extension of White Male Democracy 243
The Popular Religious Revolt 244
The Rise of the Jacksonians 246

JACKSON'S PRESIDENCY 247
The Jacksonian Appeal 248
Indian Removal 249
The Nullification Crisis 251
The Bank War 253

VAN BUREN AND HARD TIMES 254
The Panic of 1837 254
The Independent Treasury 255
Uproar over Slavery 256

THE RISE OF THE WHIG PARTY 256
The Party Taking Shape 256
Whig Persuasion 257
The Election of 1840 258

THE WHIGS IN POWER 259
Harrison and Tyler 259
The Texas Issue 260
The Election of 1844 261

CONCLUSION 261

SUMMARY 262   REVIEW QUESTIONS 263

KEY TERMS 263   WHERE TO LEARN MORE 263

11

SLAVERY AND THE OLD SOUTH, 1800–1860 264

Voices from the American Journey:
Hannah Crafts 266

THE LOWER SOUTH 267
Cotton and Slaves 267
The Profits of Slavery 268

THE UPPER SOUTH 270
A Period of Economic Adjustment 270
The Decline of Slavery 272

SLAVE LIFE AND CULTURE 272
Work Routines and Living Conditions 273
Families and Religion 274
Resistance 275

FREE SOCIETY 277
The Slaveholding Minority 278
The White Majority 280
Free Black People 281

THE PROSLAVERY ARGUMENT 282

CONCLUSION 285

SUMMARY 285   REVIEW QUESTIONS 286

KEY TERMS 286   WHERE TO LEARN MORE 286

12

THE MARKET REVOLUTION AND SOCIAL REFORM, 1815–1850 288

Voices from the American Journey:
  Angelina Grimké 290

INDUSTRIAL CHANGE AND URBANIZATION 291
  The Transportation Revolution 292

CITIES AND IMMIGRANTS 295
  The Industrial Revolution 297
  Growing Inequality and New Classes 301

REFORM AND MORAL ORDER 306
  The Benevolent Empire 306
  The Temperance Movement 307
  Women's Roles in Reform 308
  Backlash Against Benevolence 310

INSTITUTIONS AND SOCIAL IMPROVEMENT 310
  School Reform 311
  Prisons, Workhouses, and Asylums 312
  Utopian Alternatives 313

ABOLITIONISM AND WOMEN'S RIGHTS 315
  Rejecting Colonization 315
  Abolitionism 316
  The Women's Rights Movement 317
  Political Antislavery 320

CONCLUSION 321

SUMMARY 321   REVIEW QUESTIONS 322

KEY TERMS 322   WHERE TO LEARN MORE 323

13

THE WAY WEST, 1815–1850 324

Voices from the American Journey:
  George Catlin 326

THE AGRICULTURAL FRONTIER 327
  The Crowded East 327
  The Old Northwest 329
  The Old Southwest 331

THE FRONTIER OF THE PLAINS INDIANS 333
  Tribal Lands 333
  The Fur Traders 335
  The Oregon Trail 336

THE MEXICAN BORDERLANDS 338
  The Peoples of the Southwest 338
  The Americanization of Texas 339
  The Push into California and the Southwest 342

POLITICS, EXPANSION, AND WAR 343
  Manifest Destiny 343
  The Mexican War 344

CONCLUSION 346

SUMMARY 348   KEY TERMS 349

WHERE TO LEARN MORE 349

14

THE POLITICS OF SECTIONALISM, 1846–1861 350

Voices from the American Journey:
  Harriet Beecher Stowe 352

SLAVERY IN THE TERRITORIES 353
  The Wilmot Proviso 353
  The Election of 1848 354
  The Compromise of 1850 355
  Response to the Fugitive Slave Act 357
  Uncle Tom's Cabin 358
  The Election of 1852 359

POLITICAL REALIGNMENT 359
  Young America's Foreign Misadventures 360
  Stephen Douglas's Railroad Proposal 360
  The Kansas-Nebraska Act 360
  "Bleeding Kansas" 361
  Know-Nothings and Republicans:
    Religion and Politics 361
  The Election of 1856 362
  The Dred Scott Case 363
  The Lecompton Constitution 364
  The Lincoln-Douglas Debates 364

THE ROAD TO DISUNION 365
  North-South Differences 366
  John Brown's Raid 367
  The Election of 1860 368
  Secession Begins 369
  Presidential Inaction 371
  Peace Proposals 371
  Lincoln's Views on Secession 371
  Fort Sumter: The Tug Comes 373

CONCLUSION 375

SUMMARY 375   REVIEW QUESTIONS 376

KEY TERMS 376   WHERE TO LEARN MORE 377

15

BATTLE CRIES AND FREEDOM SONGS: THE CIVIL WAR, 1861–1865 378

Voices from the American Journey:
Sullivan Ballou 380

MOBILIZATION, NORTH AND SOUTH 381
War Fever 381
The North's Advantage in Resources 383
Leaders, Governments, and Strategies 384

THE EARLY WAR, 1861–1862 385
First Bull Run 385
The War in the West 385
Reassessing the War:
The Human Toll 386
The War in the East 388

TURNING POINTS, 1862–1863 388
The Naval War and Diplomatic War 389
Antietam 390
Emancipation 390
From Fredericksburg to Gettysburg 393
Vicksburg, Chattanooga,
and the West 393

WAR TRANSFORMS THE NORTH 397
Wartime Legislation and Politics 397

CONSCRIPTION AND THE DRAFT RIOTS 398
The Northern Economy 398
Northern Women and the War 399

THE CONFEDERACY DISINTEGRATES 400
Southern Politics 400
The Southern Economy 400
Southern Women and the War 401

THE UNION PREVAILS, 1864–1865 401
Grant's Plan to End the War 402
The Election of 1864
and Sherman's March 405
The Road to Appomattox and the Death
of Lincoln 406

CONCLUSION 407

SUMMARY 409   REVIEW QUESTIONS 410
KEY TERMS 411   WHERE TO LEARN MORE 411

VISUALIZING THE PAST
The Civil War 412

16

RECONSTRUCTION, 1865–1877 414

Voices from the American Journey:
T. Thomas Fortune 416

WHITE SOUTHERNERS AND THE GHOSTS
OF THE CONFEDERACY, 1865 417

MORE THAN FREEDOM:
AFRICAN-AMERICAN ASPIRATIONS IN 1865 418
Education 418
"Forty Acres and a Mule" 419
Migration to Cities 420
Faith and Freedom 420

FEDERAL RECONSTRUCTION, 1865–1870 421
Presidential Reconstruction, 1865–1867 422
Congressional Reconstruction, 1867–1870 425
Southern Republican Governments,
1867–1870 426

COUNTER-RECONSTRUCTION, 1870–1874 428
The Uses of Violence 428
The Failure of Northern Will 429
Liberal Republicans and the Election of 1872 430

REDEMPTION, 1874–1877 430
The Democrats' Violent Resurgence 430
The Weak Federal Response 431
The Election of 1876 and the Compromise
of 1877 431
The Memory of Reconstruction 431

THE FAILED PROMISE OF RECONSTRUCTION 432
Sharecropping 432
Modest Gains and Future Victories 433

CONCLUSION 435

SUMMARY 435   REVIEW QUESTIONS 436
KEY TERMS 437   WHERE TO LEARN MORE 437

17

A NEW SOUTH: ECONOMIC PROGRESSION AND SOCIAL TRADITION, 1877–1900 439

Voices from the American Journey: Anna J.
Cooper 441

THE NEWNESS OF THE NEW SOUTH 441
An Industrial and Urban South 442

The Limits of Industrial and Urban Growth   444
Farms to Cities: Impact on Southerners   446

THE SOUTHERN AGRARIAN REVOLT   448
Cotton and Credit   448
Southern Farmers Organize, 1877–1892   449
Southern Populists   451

WOMEN IN THE NEW SOUTH   452
Church Work Preserving Memories   453
Women's Clubs   454

SETTLING THE RACE ISSUE   454
The Fluidity of Southern Race Relations,
1877–1890   454
The White Backlash   455
Lynch Law   456
Segregation by Law   456
Disfranchisement   458
A National Consensus on Race   459
Response of the Black Community   461

CONCLUSION   464

SUMMARY   465   REVIEW QUESTIONS   466

KEY TERMS   466   WHERE TO LEARN MORE   467

18

INDUSTRY, IMMIGRANTS, AND CITIES, 1870–1900   468

Voices from the American Journey:
Mary Antin   470

NEW INDUSTRY   471
Inventing Technology: The Electric Age   472
The Corporation and Its Impact   474
The Changing Nature of Work   475
Child Labor   477
Working Women   478
Responses to Poverty and Wealth   479
Workers Organize   481

NEW IMMIGRANTS   483
Old World Backgrounds   484
The Neighborhood   485
The Job   486
Nativism   487
Roots of the Great Migration   489

NEW CITIES   490
Centers and Suburbs   491
The New Middle Class   493

CONCLUSION   495

SUMMARY   496   REVIEW QUESTIONS   496

KEY TERMS   496   WHERE TO LEARN MORE   497

19

TRANSFORMING THE WEST, 1865–1890   496

Voices from the American Journey:
Andrew J. Russell   498

SUBJUGATING NATIVE AMERICANS   499
Tribes and Cultures   499
Federal Indian Policy   501
Warfare and Dispossession   501
Life on the Reservation: Americanization   503

EXPLOITING THE MOUNTAINS: THE MINING
BONANZA   507
Rushes and Mining Camps   507
Labor and Capital   509

EXPLOITING THE GRASS: THE CATTLE KINGDOM   510
Cattle Drives the Cow Towns   510
Rise and Fall of Open-Range Ranching   511
Cowhands and Capitalists   512

EXPLOITING THE EARTH: HOMESTEADERS
AND AGRICULTURAL EXPANSION   513
Settling the Land   513
Home on the Range   515
Farming the Land   515

CONCLUSION   517

SUMMARY   517   REVIEW QUESTIONS   518

KEY TERMS   518   WHERE TO LEARN MORE   519

VISUALIZING THE PAST
Mythologizing the "Wild West"   520

20

POLITICS AND GOVERNMENT, 1877–1900   522

Voices from the American Journey:
Horace and William H. Taft   524

THE STRUCTURE AND STYLE OF POLITICS   525
Campaigns and Elections   525
Partisan Politics   526
Associational Politics   527

THE LIMITS OF GOVERNMENT   530
The Weak Presidency   530
The Inefficient Congress   531
The Federal Bureaucracy and the Spoils System   531
Inconsistent State Government   531

PUBLIC POLICIES AND NATIONAL
ELECTIONS   532
   Civil Service Reform   532
   The Political Life of the Tariff   533
   The Beginnings of Federal Regulations   534
   The Money Question   535
THE CRISIS OF THE 1890S   536
   Agricultural Protest   536
   The People's Party   537
   The Challenge of the Depression   539
   The Battle of the Standards
     and the Election of 1896   542
CONCLUSION   543
SUMMARY   544   REVIEW QUESTIONS   545
KEY TERMS   545   WHERE TO LEARN MORE   545

21
THE PROGRESSIVE ERA, 1900–1917   546

Voices from the American Journey:
  Inez Milholland   548
THE FERMENT OF REFORM   550
   The Context of Reform: Industrial
     and Urban Tensions   550
   Church and Campus   551
   Muckrakers   553
   The Gospel of Efficiency   553
   Labor's Demand for Rights   553
   Expanding the Women's Sphere   554
TRANSATLANTIC INFLUENCES   555
   Socialism   555
   Opponents of Reform   556
REFORMING SOCIETY   556
   Settlement Houses and Urban Reform   557
   Protective Legislation for Women
     and Children   557
   Reshaping Public Education   559
   Challenging Gender Restrictions   559
   Reforming Country Life   560
   Social Control and Moral Crusades   562
   For White People Only?   563
REFORMING POLITICS AND GOVERNMENT   564
   Woman Suffrage   564
   Electoral Reform   564
   Municipal Reform   565
   Progressive State Government   566

THEODORE ROOSEVELT AND THE PROGRESSIVE
PRESIDENCY   566
   TR and the Modern Presidency   567
   Roosevelt and Labor   567
   Managing Natural Resources   568
   Corporate Regulation   568
   Taft and the Insurgents   571
WOODROW WILSON AND PROGRESSIVE REFORM   572
   Election of 1912   572
   Implementing the New Freedom   573
   The Expansion of Reform   574
CONCLUSION   575
SUMMARY   575   REVIEW QUESTIONS   576
KEY TERMS   576   WHERE TO LEARN MORE   577

22

CREATING AN EMPIRE, 1865–1917   578

Voices from the American Journey:
  Major-General Leonard Wood   580
THE ROOTS OF IMPERIALISM   581
   Ideological Arguments   581
   Strategic Concerns   582
   Economic Designs   583
FIRST STEPS   585
   Seward and Blaine   585
   Hawaii   586
   Chile and Venezuela   587
THE SPANISH-AMERICAN WAR   588
   The Cuban Revolution   588
   Growing Tensions   589
   War and Empire   590
   The Treaty of Paris   591
IMPERIAL AMBITIONS: THE UNITED STATES
AND EAST ASIA, 1899–1917   592
   The Filipino-American War   593
   China and the Open Door   593
   Rivalry with Japan and Russia   594
IMPERIAL POWER: THE UNITED STATES
AND LATIN AMERICA,
1899–1917   595
   U.S. Rule in Puerto Rico   595
   Cuba as a U.S. Protectorate   596
   The Panama Canal   597
   The Roosevelt Corollary   598
   Dollar Diplomacy   598
   Wilsonian Interventions   599

CONCLUSION 600

SUMMARY 600   REVIEW QUESTIONS 601

KEY TERMS 601   WHERE TO LEARN MORE 601

23

AMERICA AND THE GREAT WAR, 1914–1920 602

Voices from the American Journey:
   Ray Stannard Baker 604

WAGING NEUTRALITY 605
   The Origins of Conflict 605
   American Attitudes 606
   The Economy of War 607
   The Diplomacy of Neutrality 607
   The Battle over Preparedness 609
   The Election of 1916 609
   Descent into War 610

WAGING WAR IN AMERICA 611
   Managing the War Economy 611
   Women and Minorities, New Opportunities, Old
      Inequalities 612
   Financing the War 613
   Conquering Minds 613
   Suppressing Dissent 614

WAGING WAR AND PEACE ABROAD 617
   The War to End All Wars 617
   The Fourteen Points 619
   The Paris Peace Conference 619

WAGING PEACE AT HOME 620
   Battle over the League 620
   Economic Readjustment and Social Conflict 621
   Red Scare 623
   The Election of 1920 624

CONCLUSION 625

SUMMARY 625   REVIEW QUESTIONS 626

KEY TERMS 626   WHERE TO LEARN MORE 627

24

TOWARD A MODERN AMERICA, THE 1920S 628

Voices from the American Journey:
   Upton Sinclair 630

THE ECONOMY THAT ROARED 632
   Boom Industries 632
   Corporate Consolidation 634
   Open Shops and Welfare Capitalism 634
   Sick Industries 635

THE BUSINESS OF GOVERNMENT 635
   Republican Ascendancy 635
   Government Corruption 636
   Coolidge Prosperity 636
   The Fate of Reform 637

CITIES AND SUBURBS 637
   Expanding Cities 638
   The Great Black Migration 639
   Barrios 639
   The Road to Suburbia 640

MASS CULTURE IN THE JAZZ AGE 640
   Advertising the Consumer Society 640
   Leisure and Entertainment 641
   The New Morality 641
   The Searching Twenties 642

CULTURE WARS 642
   Nativism and Immigration Restriction 642
   The Klu Klux Klan 643
   Prohibition and Crime 644
   Old-Time Religion and the Scopes Trial 645

A NEW ERA IN THE WORLD? 647
   War Debt and Economic Expansion 647
   Rejecting War 647
   Managing the Hemisphere 648

HERBERT HOOVER AND THE FINAL TRIUMPH
OF THE NEW ERA 648

CONCLUSION 649

SUMMARY 649   REVIEW QUESTIONS 650

KEY TERMS 651   WHERE TO LEARN MORE 651

VISUALIZING THE PAST
Advertising and the Modern Woman 652

25

THE GREAT DEPRESSION AND THE NEW DEAL, 1929–1939 654

Voices from the American Journey:
   Carlotta Silvas Martine, Eunice Langdon,
   and Meridel LeSeur 656

HARD TIMES IN HOOTERVILLE 658
   Crash! 658
   The Depression Spreads 659

"Women's Jobs" and "Men's Jobs" 660
Families in the Depression 660
"Last Hired, First Fired" 661
Protest 661

HERBERT HOOVER AND THE DEPRESSION 661
The Limits of Voluntarism 662
Repudiating Hoover: The 1932 Election 663

LAUNCHING THE NEW DEAL 664
Action Now! 665
Creating Jobs 666
Helping Some Farmers 667
The Flight of the Blue Eagle 667
Critics Right and Left 667

CONSOLIDATING THE NEW DEAL 669
Lifting Up and Weeding Out 669
Expanding Relief 670
The Roosevelt Coalition
    and the Election of 1936 670

THE NEW DEAL AND AMERICAN LIFE 672
Labor on the March 672
Women and the New Deal 673
Minorities and the New Deal 674
The New Deal: North, South, East, and West 675
The New Deal and Public Activism 676

EBBING OF THE NEW DEAL 677
Challenging the Court 677
More Hard Times 677
Political Stalemate 678

GOOD NEIGHBORS AND HOSTILE FORCES 678
Neutrality and Fascism 679
Ebbing Toward Involvement 680

CONCLUSION 681

SUMMARY 681   REVIEW QUESTIONS 682

KEY TERMS 683   WHERE TO LEARN MORE 683

26
WORLD WAR II, 1939–1945 684
Voices from the American Journey: Enrico Fermi 686

THE DILEMMAS OF NEUTRALITY 687
The Roots of War 687
Hitler's War in Europe 688
Trying to Keep Out 688
Edging Toward Intervention 690
The Brink of War 691
December 7, 1941 692

HOLDING THE LINE 692
Stopping Germany 692
The Survival of Britain 693
Retreat and Stabilization in the Pacific 693

MOBILIZING FOR VICTORY 695
Organizing the Economy 695
The Enlistment of Science 696
Men and Women in the Military 696
The Home Front 697
New Workers 698
Clashing Cultures 699
Internment of Japanese Americans 699
The End of the New Deal 702

WAR AND PEACE 702
Gathering Allied Strength 702
Turning the Tide in Europe 703
Operation OVERLORD 703
Victory and Tragedy in Europe 705
The Pacific War 705
Searching for Peace 707

CONCLUSION 708

SUMMARY 710   REVIEW QUESTIONS 710

KEY TERMS 711   WHERE TO LEARN MORE 711

27
THE COLD WAR AT HOME AND ABROAD, 1946–1952 712
Voices from the American Journey:
Bernadette Wheeler 714

LAUNCHING THE GREAT BOOM 715
Reconversion Chaos 715
Economic Policy 715
The GI Bill 716
Assembly-Line Neighborhoods 716
Steps Toward Civil Rights 717
Consumer Boom and Baby Boom 718

TRUMAN, REPUBLICANS, AND THE FAIR DEAL 719
Truman's Opposition 719
Whistle-Stopping Across America 720
Truman's Fair Deal 721

CONFRONTING THE SOVIET UNION 721
The End of the Grand Alliance 722
The Truman Doctrine and
    the Marshall Plan 723
Soviet Reactions 724
American Rearmament 724

COLD WAR AND HOT WAR 725
The Nuclear Shadow 725
The Cold War in Asia 726
NSC-68 and Aggressive Containment 727
War in Korea, 1950–1953 727

The Politics of War   728

THE SECOND RED SCARE   730
   The Communist Party and the Loyalty
      Program   730
   Naming Names to Congress   730
   Subversion Trials   732
   Senator McCarthy on Stage   732
   Understanding McCarthyism   733

CONCLUSION   733

SUMMARY   734   REVIEW QUESTIONS   735
KEY TERMS   735   WHERE TO LEARN MORE   735

28

THE CONFIDENT YEARS,
1953–1964   736

Voices from the American Journey:
   Melba Pattillo   738

A DECADE OF AFFLUENCE   739
   What's Good for General Motors   739
   Reshaping Urban America   740
   Comfort on Credit   741
   The New Fifties Family   741
   Inventing Teenagers   742
   Turning to Religion   742
   The Gospel of Prosperity   743
   The Underside of Affluence   744

FACING OFF WITH THE SOVIET UNION   744
   Why We Liked Ike   744
   A Balance of Terror   745
   Containment in Action   745
   Global Standoff   747

JOHN F. KENNEDY AND THE COLD WAR   748
   The Kennedy Mystique   748
   Kennedy's Mistakes   748
   Getting into Vietnam   749
   Missile Crisis: A Line Drawn in the Waves   750
   Science and Foreign Affairs   751

RIGHTEOUSNESS LIKE A MIGHTY STREAM: THE
STRUGGLE FOR CIVIL RIGHTS   752
   Getting to the Supreme Court   752
   Deliberate Speed   752
   Public Accommodations   753
   The March on Washington, 1963   754

"LET US CONTINUE"   754
   Dallas, 1963   754
   War on Poverty   755
   Civil Rights, 1964–1965   755
   War, Peace, and the Landslide of 1964   757

CONCLUSION   758

SUMMARY   758   REVIEW QUESTIONS   759
KEY TERMS   759   WHERE TO LEARN MORE   759

29

SHAKEN TO THE ROOTS,
1965–1980   760

Voices from the American Journey:
   Buzz Aldrin and Neil Armstrong   762

THE END OF CONSENSUS   763
   Deeper into Vietnam   763
   Voices of Dissent   765
   New Left and Community Activism   766
   The Feminist Critique   767
   Youth Culture and Counterculture   768
   Sounds of Change   768
   Communes and Cults   769

CITIES UNDER STRESS   769
   Diagnosing an Urban Crisis   770
   Racial Rioting   770
   Minority Separatism   771
   Suburban Independence:
      The Outer City   772

THE YEAR OF THE GUN, 1968   773
   The Tet Offensive   773
   LBJ's Exit   774
   Red Spring   774
   Violence and Politics   775

NIXON AND WATERGATE   776
   Getting Out of Vietnam,
      1969–1975   776
   Nixon and the Wider World   777
   Courting Middle America   778
   Oil, OPEC, and Stagflation   778
   Americans as Environmentalists   779
   From Dirty Tricks to Watergate   779
   The Ford Footnote   782

JIMMY CARTER: IDEALISM AND FRUSTRATION
IN THE WHITE HOUSE   783
   Carter, Energy, and the Economy   783
   Closed Factories and Failed Farms   783
   Building a Cooperative World   784
   New Crises Abroad   784

CONCLUSION   785

SUMMARY   786   REVIEW QUESTIONS   787
KEY TERMS   787   WHERE TO LEARN MORE   787

VISUALIZING THE PAST
Iconic Images of the Vietnam Era   **788**

30

THE REAGAN REVOLUTION AND A CHANGING WORLD, 1981–1992   790

Voices from the American Journey:
Celia Noup   793

REAGAN'S DOMESTIC REVOLUTION   794
    Reagan's Majority   794
    The New Conservatism   795
    Reaganomics: Deficits and Deregulation   796
    Crisis for Organized Labor   797
    An Acquisitive Society   798
    Poverty amid Prosperity   798

CONSOLIDATING THE REVOLUTION: GEORGE H.W. BUSH   800

THE SECOND (SHORT) COLD WAR   802
    Confronting the USSR   802
    Risky Business: Foreign Policy Adventures   803
    Embracing Perestroika   804
    Crisis and Democracy in Eastern Europe   804
    The First Persian Gulf War   805

GROWTH IN THE SUNBELT   806
    The Defense Boom   807
    New Americans   808
    Old Gateways and New   809
    The Graying of America   810

VALUES IN COLLISION   810

NEW MEANINGS FOR AMERICAN FAMILIES   811
    The Feminist Critique   811
    Women's Rights and Public Policy   812
    Coming Out   813
    Churches in Change   814
    Culture Wars   815

CONCLUSION   817

SUMMARY   818   REVIEW QUESTIONS   818

KEY TERMS   819   WHERE TO LEARN MORE   819

31

COMPLACENCY AND CRISIS, 1993–2003   820

Voices from the American Journey:
John McNamara   822

THE POLITICS OF THE CENTER   823
    Political Generations   823
    Policing the World   824
    Clinton's Neoliberalism   825
    Contract with America and the Election of 1996   825
    The Dangers of Everyday Life   826
    Morality and Partisanship   827

A NEW ECONOMY?   828
    The Prosperous 1990s   829
    The Service Economy   829
    The High-Tech Sector   829
    An Instant Society   832
    In the World Market   833

BROADENING DEMOCRACY   833
    Americans in 2000   833
    Women from the Grass Roots to Congress   834
    Minorities at the Ballot Box   835
    Rights and Opportunities   837

EDGING INTO A NEW CENTURY   838
    The Election of 2000   838
    Reaganomics Revisited   839
    Downsized Diplomacy   840

PARADOXES OF POWER   841
    Security and Conflict   841
    Iraq and Conflicts in the Middle East   844

CONCLUSION   844

SUMMARY   845   KEY TERMS   846

REVIEW QUESTIONS   846   WHERE TO LEARN MORE   846

APPENDIX   A-1–A22

GLOSSARY   G-1–G15

CREDITS   C-1–C2

INDEX   I-1–I33

CD-ROM DOCUMENT   CD-1–CD5

FOR SUGGESTED READINGS, GO TO:
www.prenhall.com/goldfield

AMERICAN VIEWS

Chapter 1   Cabeza de Vaca Among the Indians (1530)   5

    2   Miantonomo's Plea for Indian Unity (1642)   53

    3   Mary Rowlandson Among the Indians   66

    4   Boston Celebrates a New King (August 1727)   96

    5   Social Status and the Enforcement of the Nonimportation Movement   122

    6   A British Woman Observes an American Militia Exercise in 1775   146

    7   A French Observer Describes a New Society   170

    8   Little Turtle Defends the Miami Lands   209

    9   Federalist Antiwar Resolutions   227

   10   Memorial and Protest of the Cherokee Nation, 1836   252

   11   A Letter from an Escaped Slave to His Former Master   278

   12   Appeal of a Female Abolitionist   318

   13   A Mexican View of the Texans in 1828   341

   14   Lincoln on Slavery   374

   15   A Soldier Promotes the Union Cause   391

   16   Mississippi's 1865 Black Codes   423

   17   Robert Smalls Argues Against Disfranchisement   460

   18   Tenement Life   480

   19   Zitkala-Sa's View of Americanization   504

   20   A Populist Views American Government   540

   21   Mother Jones and the Meaning of Child Labor in America   560

   22   An Imperialist Views the World   584

   23   Mobilizing America for Liberty   616

   24   The Cult of Business   633

   25   An Ohio Mayor on Unemployment and Relief   664

   26   The Internment of Japanese Americans in 1942   700

   27   Deciding on a Nuclear Arms Race   726

   28   Two Presidents Assess the Implications of the Cold War   750

   29   Grassroots Community Action   780

   30   The Religious Imperative in Politics   816

   31   Creating and Working in the New Economy   830

FROM THEN TO NOW

Chapter 1 The Disappearance of Cod off the Grand Banks 27

3 The Legacy of Slavery 70

6 The American Revolution and the Teaching of American History 159

8 Hamilton's Legacy and the National Debt 206

9 The Lewis and Clark Expedition in Their World and Ours 236

11 The Economic Legacy of Slavery 284

12 Immigration: An Ambivalent Welcome 298

13 Manifest Destiny and American Foreign Policy 345

14 Religion and Politics 370

15 Gettysburg 396

16 African-American Voting Rights in the South 434

17 The Confederate Battle Flag 463

19 The Legacy of Indian Americanization 505

20 Political Parties 528

21 The Environmental Movement 570

24 The Culture Wars 646

25 Social Security 671

26 Nuclear Weapons 709

30 Women and Work in American Offices 814

31 Loyalty in 2001 and 1917 842

MAPS

*Denotes Interactive Map Explorations

*1–1 North American Culture Areas, c. 1500 8

*1–2 West Africa and Europe in 1492 13

1–3 Spanish, English, and French Settlements in North America in the Sixteenth Century 21

*2–1 New France, c. 1650 33

*2–2 English and Dutch Mainland Colonies in North America, c. 1655 35

*2–3 English North American Colonies, c. 1685 47

3–1 Spanish and French Missions in North America (A, B, & C) 63

*3–2 African Origins of North American Slaves, 1690–1807 71

*3–3 Ethnic Distribution of Settler Population in British Mainland Colonies, c. 1755 77

*4–1 Anglo-American Transatlantic Commerce 85

*4–2 European Empires in North America, 1750–1763 105

*5–1 Colonial Settlement and the Proclamation Line of 1763 113

*6–1 The Battles of Lexington and Concord 137

6–2 Early Fighting, 1775–1776 139

*6–3 The War in the North, 1776–1777 148

*6–4 The War on the Frontier, 1778–1779 151

*6–5 The War in the South, 1778–1781 153

*6–6 North America after the Peace of Paris, 1783 157

*7–1 Land Ordinance of 1785 180

*8–1   Indian Land Cessions, 1784–1800   200

*8–2   The Election of 1800   213

*9–1   The Louisiana Purchase and the Lewis and Clark Expedition   221

*9–2   The War of 1812   228

*9–3   The Missouri Compromise of 1820 and Territorial Treaties with Britain and Spain, 1818–1819   234

9–4   The Election of 1824   237

*10–1   Indian Removals   250

10–2   The Election of 1840   259

*11–1   The Spread of Slavery: New Slave States Entering the Union, 1800–1850   270

*11–2   Cotton and Other Crops in the South, 1860   271

*12–1   The Transportation Revolution   293

12–2   The Growth of Cities   (A & B)   302, 303

*13–1   The Westward Shift of the United States Population, 1790–1850 (A, B, & C)   328

*13–2   Western Overland Trails   336

*13–3   Texas and Mexico after the Texas Revolt   340

*13–4   The Mexican War   347

*14–1   The Compromise of 1850   357

*14–2   The Election of 1860   369

15–1   From the First Bull Run to Antietam: The War in the East, 1861–1862   386

15–2   The War in the West, 1861–1862   387

15–3   From Fredericksburg to Gettysburg: The War in the East, December 1862–July 1863   393

15–4   The Battle of Gettysburg, July 1–3, 1863   394

15–5   Vicksburg and Chattanooga: The War in the West, 1863   395

15–6   Grant and Lee in Virginia, 1864–1865   403

15–7   The Atlanta Campaign and Sherman's March, 1864–1865   404

16–1   Congressional Reconstruction, 1865–1877   425

17–1   Railroads in the South, 1859 and 1899   446, 447

*18–1   Patterns of Immigration, 1820–1914   484

*18–2   The Growth of America's Cities, 1880–1900   491

19–1   Economic Development of the West: Railroads, Mining, and Cattle, 1860–1900   507

*20–1   The Two-Party Stalemate of the Late Nineteenth Century   526

*20–2   The Election of 1896   543

21–1   The growth of National Forests and National Parks   569

22–1   United States Expansion in the Pacific, 1867–1899   586

*22–2   The Spanish-American War   591

*22–3   The United States in the Caribbean   596

23–1   The Election of 1916   610

23–2   The Western Front, 1918   618

24–1   Population Shifts, 1920–1930   638

25–1   The Dust Bowl   670

25–2   The Tennessee Valley Authority   676

26–1   Axis Europe, 1941, on the Eve of Hitler's Invasion of the Soviet Union   689

*26–2   World War II in the Pacific, from Pearl Harbor to Midway   694

*26–3   World War II in Europe, 1942–1945   704

*26–4   World War II in the Pacific, 1942–1945   706

*27–1   The Election of 1948   721

*27–2   The Korean War   728

*28–1   U.S. Intervention Around the Caribbean since 1954   747

*28–2   The Election of 1960   749

*29–1   The War in Vietnam   764

30–1   Election of 1980   794

30–2   Fast-Growing and Shrinking Metropolitan Areas, 1900–2000   807

31–1   Election of 1992   824

*31–2   Women as Business Owners, 1997   836

31–3   The Election of 2000   839

OVERVIEW TABLES

Chapter 1 The Columbian Exchange 23

2 English Colonies in the Seventeenth Century 49

4 British Imperial Trade Regulations, 1651–1733 84

4 The Colonial Wars, 1689–1763 101

5 New Restraints and Burdens on Americans, 1759–1774 126

6 Important Battles of the Revolutionary War 154

7 The Articles of Confederation and the Constitution Compared 187

7 Federalists versus the Antifederalists 189

8 Federalist Party versus Republican Party 207

9 Territorial Expansion Under the Republicans 232

10 The Second Party System 257

11 Structure of Free Society in the South, c. 1860 277

12 The Reform Impulse 309

12 Types of Antislavery Reform 315

13 Westward Expansion and the Growth of the Union, 1815–1850 332

14 South and North Compared in 1860 366

14 The Emerging Sectional Crisis 372

15 Major Battles of the Civil War, 1861–1865 408

16 Contrasting Views of Reconstruction: President and Congress 424

18 Workers Organize 483

19 Government Land Policy 513

20 Arguments in the Tariff Debates 534

21 Major Progressive Organizations and Groups 551

21 Major Laws and Constitutional Amendments of the Progressive Era 551

22 Rationales for Imperialism 582

23 Major Government Wartime Agencies 612

24 Issues in the Culture Wars of the 1920s 644

25 Major Laws of the Hundred Days 666

26 The Decision to Use the Atomic Bomb 708

27 The Second Red Scare 731

31 Presidential Impeachment 828

ABOUT THE AUTHORS

DAVID GOLDFIELD received his Ph.D. in history from the University of Maryland. Since 1982 he has been Robert Lee Bailey Professor of History at the University of North Carolina in Charlotte. He is the author or editor of thirteen books on various aspects of southern and urban history. Two of his works—*Cotton Fields and Skyscrapers: Southern City and Region, 1607-1980* (1982) and *Black, White, and Southern: Race Relations and Southern Culture, 1940 to the Present* (1990)—received the Mayflower Award for nonfiction and was nominated for the Pulitzer Prize in history. His most recent book is *Still Fighting the Civil War: The American South and Southern History* (2002). When he is not writing history, Dr. Goldfield applies his historical craft to history museum exhibits, voting rights cases, and local planning and policy issues.

CARL ABBOTT is a professor of Urban Studies and planning at Portland State University. He taught previously in the history departments at the University of Denver and Old Dominion University, and held visiting appointments at Mesa College in Colorado and George Washington University. He holds degrees in history from Swarthmore College and the University of Chicago. He specializes in the history of cities and the American West and serves as co-editor of the *Pacific Historical Review*. His books include *The New Urban America: Growth and Politics in Sunbelt Cities* (1981, 1987), *The Metropolitan Frontier: Cities in the Modern American West* (1993), *Planning a New West: The Columbia River Gorge National Scenic Area* (1997), and *Political Terrain: Washington, D.C. from Tidewater Town to Global Metropolis* (1999). He is currently working on a comprehensive history of the role of urbanization and urban culture in the history of western North America.

VIRGINIA DeJOHN ANDERSON is Associate Professor of History at the University of Colorado at Boulder. She received her B.A. from the University of Connecticut. As the recipient of a Marshall Scholarship, she earned an M.A. degree at the University of East Anglia in Norwich, England. Returning to the United States, she received her A.M. and Ph.D. degrees from Harvard University. She is the author of *New England's Generation: The Great Migration and the Formation of Society and Culture in the Seventeenth Century* (1991) and several articles on colonial history, which have appeared in such journals as the *William and Mary Quarterly* and the *New England Quarterly*. She is currently finishing a book entitled *Creatures of Empire: People and Animals in Early America*.

JO ANN E. ARGERSINGER received her Ph.D. from George Washington University and is Professor of History at Southern Illinois University. A recipient of fellowships from the Rockefeller Foundation and the National Endowment for the Humanities, she is a historian of social, labor, and business policy. Her publications include *Toward a New Deal in Baltimore: People and Government in the Great Depression* (1988) and *Making the Amalgamated: Gender, Ethnicity, and Class in the Baltimore Clothing Industry* (1999).

PETER H. ARGERSINGER received his Ph.D. from the University of Wisconsin and is Professor of History at Southern Illinois University. He has won several fellowships as well as the Binkley-Stephenson Award from the Organization of American Historians. Among his books on American political and rural history are *Populism and Politics* (1974), *Structure, Process, and Party* (1992), and *The Limits of Agrarian Radicalism* (1995). His current research focuses on the political crisis of the 1890s.

WILLIAM L. BARNEY is Professor of History at the University of North Carolina at Chapel Hill. A native of Pennsylvania, he received his B.A. from Cornell University and his M.A. and Ph.D. from Columbia University. He has published extensively on nineteenth century U.S. history and has a particular interest in the Old South and the coming of the Civil War. Among his publications are *The Road to Secession* (1972), *The Secessionist Impulse* (1974), *Flawed Victory* (1975), *The Passage of the Republic* (1987), and *Battleground for the Union* (1989). He is currently finishing an edited collection of essays on nineteenth-century America and a book on the Civil War. Most recently, he has edited *A Companion to 19th-Century America* (2001) and finished *The Civil War and Reconstruction: A Student Companion* (2001).

ROBERT M. WEIR is Distinguished Professor of History Emeritus at the University of South Carolina. He received his B.A. from Pennsylvania State University and his Ph.D. from Case Western Reserve University. He has taught at the University of Houston and, as a visiting professor, at the University of Southampton in the United Kingdom. His articles have won prizes from the Southeastern Society for the Study of the Eighteenth Century and the *William and Mary Quarterly*. Among his publications are *Colonial South Carolina: A History*, *"The Last of American Freemen": Studies in the Political Culture of the Colonial and Revolutionary South*, and, more recently, a chapter on the Carolinas in the new *Oxford History of the British Empire* (1998).

PREFACE

The path that led us to *The American Journey* began in the classroom with our students. Our goal is to make American history accessible to students. The key to that goal—the core of the book—is a strong clear narrative. American history is a compelling story and we seek to tell it in an engaging, forthright way. But we also provide students with an abundance of tools to help them absorb that story and put it in context. We introduce them to the concerns of the participants in America's history with primary source documents. The voices of contemporaries open each chapter, describing their own personal journeys toward fulfilling their dreams, hopes, and ambitions as part of the broader American journey. These voices provide a personal window on our nation's history, and the themes they express resonate throughout the narrative.

But if we wrote this book to appeal to our students, we also wrote it to engage their minds. We wanted to avoid academic trendiness, particularly the restricting categories that have divided the discipline of history over the last twenty years or so. We believe that the distinctions involved in the debates about multiculturalism and identity, between social and political history, between the history of the common people and the history of the elite, are unnecessarily confusing.

What we seek is integration—to combine political and social history, to fit the experience of particular groups into the broader perspective of the American past, to give voice to minor and major players alike because of their role in the story we have to tell.

APPROACH

In telling our story, we had some definite ideas about what we might include and emphasize that other texts do not—information we felt that the current and next generations of students will need to know about our past to function best in a new society.

Chronological Organization   A strong chronological backbone supports the book. We have found that the jumping back and forth in time characteristic of some American history textbooks confuses students. They abhor dates but need to know the sequence of events in history. A chronological presentation is the best way to be sure they do.

Geographical Literacy   We also want students to be geographically literate. We expect them not only to know what happened in American history, but where it happened as

well. Physical locations and spatial relationships were often important in shaping historical events. The abundant maps in The American Journey—all numbered and called out in the text—are an integral part of our story.

Regional Balance   *The American Journey* presents balanced coverage of all regions of the country. In keeping with this balance, the South and the West receive more coverage in this text than in comparable books.

Point of View   *The American Journey* presents a balanced overview of the American past. But "balanced" does not mean bland. We do not shy away from definite positions on controversial issues, such as the nature of early contacts between Native Americans and Europeans, why the political crisis of the 1850s ended in a bloody Civil War, and how Populism and its followers fit into the American political spectrum. If students and instructors disagree, that's great; discussion and dissent are important catalysts for understanding and learning.

Religion   Nor do we shy away from some topics that play relatively minor roles in other texts, like religion. Historians are often uncomfortable writing about religion and tend to slight its influence. This text stresses the importance of religion in American society both as a source of strength and a reflection of some its more troubling aspects.

Historians mostly write for each other. That's too bad. We need to reach out and expand our audience. An American history text is a good place to start. Our students are not only our future historians, but more important, our future. Let their American journey begin.

FEATURES OF THE TEXT

The American Journey Teaching and Learning Classroom Edition includes an array of features designed to make American history accessible to students. It provides more learning tools than any other U.S. history text.

- The **Student Tool Kit** that follows this preface helps students get the most out of the text and its features. It introduces students to key conventions of historical writing and it explains how to work with maps, documents, and visuals.

- **Single-Column Design** allows for a clean, easy-to-read narrative. Ample space in the margins allows for strategic placement of pedagogy.

- A new feature, **Voices from the American Journey**, opens each chapter. Consisting of letters, diary entries, and other first-hand accounts, these voices highlight the personal dimension of the American journey and show students the wealth and variety of experiences that make up this country's history. From Olaudah Equiano's narrative of his forced journey to Virginia as a slave, to the ultimate journey Sullivan Ballou made during the Civil War defending the Union, to Cambodian refugee Celia Noup's harrowing journey to California where she took her place as one of the thousands of new immigrants who are reshaping the face of our nation, "Voices from the American Journey" set the stage for the key themes that are explored in each chapter.

- **Visualizing the Past** essays, found at the end of selected chapters, analyze important aspects of U.S. History through photographs, fine art, sculpture, woodcuts, and advertisements. Focus questions and a running narrative guide students through a careful examination of the historical implication of each topic in question.

- The **American Views** box in each chapter contains a relevant primary source document. Taken from letters, diaries, newspapers, government papers, and other sources, these bring the people of the past and their concerns vividly alive. An introduction and prereading questions relate the documents to the text and direct students' attention to important issues. New "American Views" include the internment of Japanese Americans in Chapter 26 and working in the New Economy in Chapter 31.

- **America's Journey: From Then to Now**, found in more than half the chapters, relates important issues and events in each chapter to the issues and events of today, letting students see the relevance of history to their lives. Several are new to this edition. Examples include, "The Disappearance of Cod off the Grand Banks" (Chapter 1) and "Loyalty in 2001 and 1917" (Chapter 31).

- **Chapter-opening Questions** ask students to consider carefully the main issues addressed in the narrative.

- **Overview Tables** summarize complex issues.

- **Quick Reviews**, found at key places in the margins of each chapter, encourage students to review important concepts before moving on.

- Chapter **Chronologies** help students build a framework of key events.

- **Third-level subheads**, new to the Third Edition, highlight key topics in the narrative and make them more accessible for study and review. In the sections on social history,

for example, these headings help highlight the roles of women and minorities in the American journey.

- **Key Terms** are highlighted within each chapter and defined in a running marginal **Glossary**. The end of each chapter includes a list of key terms and relevant page numbers.

- Chapter **Review Questions,** organized by key subtopics in each chapter, help students review material and relate it to broader themes.

- A **Bibliography** at the end of the text directs interested students to further information about the subject of the chapter.

- **Where To Learn More** sections, found at relevant places in the margin, and listed at the end of each chapter, describe important historical sites (both real and virtual) that students can visit to gain a deeper understanding of the events discussed in the chapter.

- Abundant **maps** help students understand the spatial dimension of history. The topographical detail in many of the maps helps students understand the influence of geography on history.

- **Illustrations** and **photographs**—tied to the text with detailed captions—provide a visual dimension to history.

CHANGES TO THE THIRD EDITION
ORGANIZATION

- To make the text even more accessible to students—and to better match the teaching calendars of many institutions—the number of chapters in the Third Edition has been reduced from thirty-three to thirty-one.

- The chapters on urbanization and social change and reform movements in the antebellum period have been combined into a new chapter, "The Market Revolution and Social Reform" (Chapter 12). The chapter focuses on economic changes and industrialization as well as the connections between these forces and reform movements. Chapter 11, "Slavery and the Old South," now precedes this chapter.

- The Civil War is now treated in a single chapter (Chapter 15).

- The Eighties is now examined in an entirely revamped Chapter 30, "The Reagan Revolution and a Changing World."

- An all-new final chapter "Complacency and Crisis," examines America at the millennium and after September 11, 2001.

Taken together, these organizational changes make *The American Journey* an even more effective textbook for both students and instructors.

SUPPLEMENTARY INSTRUCTIONAL MATERIALS

The American Journey comes with an extensive package of supplementary print and multimedia materials for both instructors and students.

PRINT SUPPLEMENTS

Instructor's Resource Binder

This innovative, all-in-one resource organizes the instructor's manual, the Test-Item File, and the transparency pack by each chapter of *The American Journey* to facilitate class preparation. The Instructor's Resource Binder also includes an **Instructor's Resource CD-ROM**, which contains all of the maps, graphs, and illustrations from the text in easily downloadable electronic files.

Prentice Hall Test Generator

Suitable for both Windows and Macintosh environments, this commerical-quality, computerized test-management program allows instructors to select items from the test-item file and design their own exams.

History Notes (Volumes I and II)

Replacing a traditional study guide, History Notes provides students with practice tests, map exercises, and How? When? Where? Questions for each chapter of *The American Journey*. Each copy of the T.L.C. edition comes bundled with History Notes.

Retrieving the American Past: A Customized U.S. History Reader, 2004 Edition

This collection of documents is an on-demand history database written and developed by leading historians and educators. It offers eighty-six compelling modules on topics in American history, such as "Women on the Frontier," "The Salem Witchcraft Scare," "The Age of Industrial Violence," and "Native American Societies, 1870–1995." Approximately thirty-five pages in length, each module includes an introduction, several primary documents and secondary sources, follow-up questions, and recommendations for further reading. Instructor-originated material, including other readings and exercises, can be incorporated. Contact your local Prentice Hall representative for more information about this exciting custom-publishing option.

American Stories: Biographies in United States History

This two-volume collection of sixty-two biographies in United States history is free when packaged with *The American Journey*. Introductions, pre-reading questions, and suggested resources enrich this new supplement.

Prentice Hall and Penguin Bundle Program

Prentice Hall is pleased to provide adopters of *The American Journey* with an opportunity to receive significant discounts when copies of the text are bundled with Penguin titles in American history. Contact your local Prentice Hall representative for details.

MULTIMEDIA SUPPLEMENTS

Companion Website

Available at **http://www.prenhall.com/goldfield** *The American Journey Companion Website* offers students multiple choice, true-false, essay, identification, map labeling, and document questions based on material from the text, organized by the primary subtopics in each chapter. Additionally, the *Companion Website* provides numerous interactive maps tied to the text, source documents, and other interactive modules related to the content in each chapter. The Faculty Module contains materials for instructors, including the entire instructor's manual in PDF file, and downloadable presentations with maps, charts, graphs, summary tables, and illustrations.

U.S. History Documents CD-ROM

Bound in every new copy of *The American Journey*, and organized according to the main periods in American history, the U.S. History Documents CD-ROM contains over 300 primary sources in an easily-navigable PDF file. Each document is accompanied by essay questions that allow students to read important sources in U.S. history via the CD-ROM and respond online via a dedicated website.

Exploring America CD-ROM

The new *Exloring America CD-ROM* features thirty-one interactive learning activities that drill down to explore the impact of key episodes and developments in United States history, including such topics as industrialization, immigration, the women's suffrage movement, the Harlem Renaissance, the American Indian Movement, and globalization.

Evaluating Online Sources with Research Navigator, 2003 Edition

This brief guide focuses on developing critical thinking skills necessary to evaluate and use online sources. It provides a brief introduction to navigating the Internet with comprehensive references to History web sites. It also provides an access code and instruction on using Research Navigator, a powerful research tool that provides access to three exclusive databases of reliable source material: ContentSelect Academic Journal Database, *The New York Times* Search by Subject Archive, and Link Library.

OneKey

OneKey lets you in to the best teaching and learning resources all in one place. OneKey for *The American Journey* is all your students need for out-of-class work conveniently organized by chapter to reinforce and apply what they've learned in class and from the text. Among the resources available for each chapter are: a complete media-rich, interactive e-book version of *The American Journey*, quizzes organized by the main topics of each chapter, primary source documents, map labeling and interactive map quizzes. OneKey is all you need to plan and administer your course. All your instructor resources are in one place to maximize your effectiveness and minimize your time and effort. Instructor material includes: images and maps from *The American Journey*, hundreds of documents, video and audio clips, interactive learning activities, and PowerPoint presentations.

Prentice Hall History Resource Center

This site offers a rich array of hundreds of historical sources in textual, visual, or audio-visual format. All were carefully selected by history professors as particularly relevant to the United States survey course. Interactive Maps present historical transformations in a clear and compelling way. Learning Activities offer in-depth explorations of important topics. The Prentice Hall History Resource Center also includes a comprehensive glossary of terms and Best of the Web links for additional study.

ACKNOWLEDGMENTS

We would like to thank the reviewers whose thoughtful and often detailed comments helped shape this and the previous editions of *The American Journey*:

Joseph Adams, *Saint Louis Community College*
David Aldstadt, *Houston Community College*
William Allison, *Weber State University*
Janet Allured, *McNeese State University*
Tyler Anbinder, *George Washington University*
Michael Batinski, *Southern Illinois University*
Michael Bellesiles, *Emory University*
Eugene Berwanger, *Colorado State University*
Terry Bilhartz, *Sam Houston State University*
Fred Blue, *Youngstown State University*
Eric J. Bolsteri, *University of Texas at Arlington*
Charles Bolton, *University of Arkansas at Little Rock*
James Bradford, *Texas A&M University*
Michael Bradley, *Motlow State Community College*
Henry William Brands, *Texas A&M University*
Neal Brooks, *Essex Community College*
Richard Brown, *University of Connecticut*
Tom Bryan, *Alvin Community College*
Randolph Campbell, *University of North Texas*

Dale Carnagey, *Blinn College*
E. Wayne Carp, *Pacific Lutheran University*
JoAnn Carpenter, *Florida Community College*
David Castle, *Ohio University, Eastern Campus*
Andrew Cayton, *Miami University*
Bill Cecil-Fronsman, *Washburn University*
John Chalberg, *Normandale Community College*
Myles Clowers, *San Diego City College*
David Conrad, *Southern Illinois University*
William Corbett, *Northeastern State University*
Robert Cray, *Montclair State College*
Richard Crepeau, *University of Central Florida*
Samuel Crompton, *Holyoke Community College*
Gilbert Cruz, *Glendale Community College*
Light T. Cummins, *Austin College*
Paul K. Davis, *University of Texas at San Antonio*
Eugene Demody, *Cerritos College*
Joseph Devine, *Stephen F. Austin State University*
Donald Dewey, *California State University*
Leonard Dinnerstein, *University of Arizona*
Dean Dunlap, *Rose State College*
Marvin Dulaney, *University of Texas at Arlington*
Jonathan Earle, *University of Kansas*
Leflett Easley, *Campbell University*
Iris Engstrand, *University of San Diego*
Robin Fabel, *Auburn University*
Jay Fell, *University of Colorado*
Nancy Gabin, *Purdue University*
Scott Garrett, *Paducah Community College*
Marilyn Geiger, *Washburn University*
George Gerdow, *Northeastern Illinois University*
Gerald Ghelfi, *Rancho Santiago College*
Louis Gimelli, *Eastern Michigan University*
James Goode, *Grand Valley State University*
Gregory Goodwin, *Bakersfield College*
Laura Graves, *South Plains College*
Ralph Goodwin, *East Texas State University*
Robert Greene, *Morgan State University*
Mark Grimsley, *Ohio State University*
Ira Gruber, *U.S. Military Academy*
Harland Hagler, *University of North Texas*
Steve Haley, *Shelby State Community College*
Gwendolyn Hall, *Rutgers University*
Timothy D. Hall, *Central Michigan University*
David Hamilton, *University of Kentucky*
Joe Hapak, *Moraine Valley Community College*
Ronald Hatzenbuchler, *Idaho State University*
David G. Hogan, *Heidelberg College*
Alfred Hunt, *SUNY Purchase*
John Ingham, *University of Toronto*
Priscilla Jackson-Evans, *Longview Community College*
Donald Jacobs, *Northeastern University*

Frederick Jaher, *University of Illinois*

John Johnson, *University of Northern Iowa*

Wilbur Johnson, *Rock Valley College*

Juli Jones, *St. Charles Community College*

Yvonne Johnson, *Central Missouri State University*

Yasuhide Kawashima, *University of Texas at El Paso*

Joseph E. King, *Texas Tech University*

Gene Kirkpatrick, *Tyler Junior College*

Lawrence Kohl, *University of Alabama at Tuscaloosa*

Michael Krenn, *University of Miami*

Michael Krutz, *Southeastern Louisiana University*

Robert LaPorte, *North Texas University*

Armand LaPotin, *SUNY Oneonta*

John LaSaine, *University of Georgia*

Bryan LeBeau, *Creighton University*

J. Edward Lee, *Winthrop University*

Mark Leff, *University of Illinois, Urbana-Champaign*

Richard Lowe, *University of North Texas*

Ed Lukes, *Hillsborough Community College*

Leo Lyman, *Victor Valley College*

Scott Martin, *Bowling Green State University*

Ronald McArthur, *Atlantic Community College*

Donald McCoy, *University of Kansas*

David McFadden, *Fairfield University*

Gerald MacFarland, *University of Massachusetts*

Thomas McLuen, *Spokane Falls Community College*

Peter C. Mancell, *University of Kansas*

Norman Markowitz, *Rutgers University*

Frank Marmolejo, *Irvine Valley College*

James Matray, *New Mexico State University*

Karen Miller, *Oakland University*

Otis Miller, *Belleville Area College*

Nancy Smith Midgette, *Elon College*

Worth Robert Miller, *Southwest Missouri State University*

Timothy Morgan, *Christopher Newport University*

Christopher Moss, *University of Texas at Arlington*

Harmon Mothershead, *Northwest Missouri State University*

Benjamin Newcomb, *Texas Technological University*

Elizabeth Nybakken, *Mississippi State University*

Colleen O'Connor, *San Diego Mesa College*

William Paquette, *Tidewater Community College*

Chris Padgett, *Weber State University*

David Parker, *Kennesaw State College*

Peggy Pascoe, *University of Utah*

Christopher Phillips, *Emporia State University*

Thomas L. Powers, *University of South Carolina, Sumter*

Kay Pulley, *Trinity Valley Community College*

Norman Raiford, *Greenville Technical College*

John Rector, *Western Oregon State University*

Thomas C. Reeves, *University of Wisconsin, Parkside*

Gary Reichard, *Florida Atlantic University*

Joseph Reidy, *Howard University*

Ronald Reitvald, *California State University, Fullerton*

Howard Rock, *Florida International University*

Hal Rothman, *University of Nevada, Las Vegas*

Richard Sadler, *Weber State University*

Henry Sage, *Northern Virginia Community College, Alexandria*

Bufford Satcher, *University of Arkansas at Pine Bluff*

Sandra Schackel, *Boise State University*

Michael Schaller, *University of Arizona*

Dale Schmitt, *East Tennessee State University*

Ronald Schultz, *University of Wyoming*

Nancy Shoemaker, *University of Connecticut*

Rebecca Shoemaker, *Indiana State University*

Frank Siltman, *U.S. Military Academy*

David Sloan, *University of Arkansas*

J.B. Smallwood, *University of North Texas*

Sherry Smith, *University of Texas at El Paso*

Kenneth Stevens, *Texas Christian University*

William Stockton, *Johnson County Community College*

Mark Summers, *University of Kentucky*

William Tanner, *Humbolt State University*

Quintard Taylor, *University of Oregon*

Emily Teipe, *Fullerton College*

Frank Towers, *Clarion University*

Paula Trekel, *Allegheny College*

Stanley Underal, *San Jose University*

Andrew Wallace, *Northern Arizona University*

Harry Ward, *University of Richmond*

Ken Weatherbie, *Del Mar College*

Stephen Webre, *Louisiana Tech University*

Edward Weller, *San Jacinto College, South*

Michael Welsh, *University of Northern Colorado*

James Whittenberg, *College of William and Mary*

Brian Wills, *Clinch Valley Community College*

John Wiseman, *Frostburg State University*

James Woods, *Georgia Southern University*

Mark Wyman, *Illinois State University*

Neil York, *Brigham Young University*

William Young, *Johnson County Community College*

Nancy Zen, *Central Oregon Community College*

All of us are grateful to our families, friends, and colleagues for their support and encouragement. Jo Ann and Peter Argersinger would like in particular to thank Anna Champe, Linda Hatmaker, and John Willits; William Barney thanks Pamela Fesmire and Rosalie Radcliffe; Virginia Anderson thanks Fred Anderson, Kim Gruenwald, Ruth Helm, Eric Hinderaker, and Chidiebere Nwaubani; and David Goldfield thanks Frances Glenn and Jason Moscato. Jim Miller, Sylvia Mallory, and Sally Constable played key roles in the book's inception and initial development.

Finally, we would like to acknowledge the members of our Prentice Hall family. They are not only highly competent professionals but also pleasant people. We regard them with affection and appreciation. None of us would hesitate to work with this fine group again. We would especially like to thank our editorial team: Charles Cavaliere, executive editor, and Roberta Meyer, senior development editor, for their creativity and skill in crafting the plan for the fourth edition, and for helping us to execute it. Charlyce Jones Owen, vice president and editorial director for the Humanities, who organized her team flawlessly; Heather Shelstad, executive marketing manager, and Beth Meija, marketing director, whose creative and informed marketing strategies demonstrated a unique insight into the textbook market; Anne DeMaranis, designer, and Leslie Osher, creative design director; Joanne Riker and Randy Pettit for keeping the production on schedule; Rochelle Diogenes, editor in chief for development, for ensuring that the book had the developmental resources it needed; Nick Sklitsis, manufacturing manager, Tricia Kenny, manufacturing buyer, and Yolanda deRooy, president of Prentice Hall's Humanities and Social Sciences division, who had the good sense to let her staff run with this book.

DG

CA

VDJA

JEA

PHA

WLB

RMW

STUDENT TOOL KIT

When writing history, historians use maps, tables, graphs, and visuals to help their readers understand the past. What follows is an explanation of how to use the historian's tools that are contained in this book.

TEXT

Whether it is a biography of George Washington, an article on the Civil War, or a survey of American history such as this one, the text is the historian's basic tool for discussing the past. Historians write about the past using narration and analysis. Narration is the story line of history. It describes what happened in the past, who did it, and where and when it occurred. Narration is also used to describe how people in the past lived, how they passed their daily lives and even, when the historical evidence makes it possible for us to know, what they thought, felt, feared, or desired. Using analysis, historians explain why they think events in the past happened the way they did and offer an explanation for the story of history. In this book, narration and analysis are interwoven in each chapter.

STUDY AIDS

A number of features in this book are designed to aid in the study of history. Each chapter begins with **Questions**, organized by the main subtopics of each chapter, that encourage careful consideration of important themes and developments. Each question is repeated at the appropriate place in the margin of the text (see example below). A **Conclusion** and **Summary** at the end of each chapter puts the subject of the chapter in the broader perspective of U.S. history. All of these study aids can be used to review important concepts.

PROBLEMS AT HOME

Neither prosperity nor political stability accompanied the return of peace in 1783. The national government struggled to avoid bankruptcy, and in 1784, an economic depression struck the country. As fiscal problems deepened, creditor and debtor groups clashed angrily in state legislatures. The only solid accomplishment of the Confederation Congress during this troubled period was to formulate an orderly and democratic plan for the settlement of the West.

WHAT WERE the weaknesses of the United States after the Revolution?

MAPS

Maps are important historical tools. They show how geography has affected history and concisely summarize complex relationships and events. Knowing how to read and interpret a map is important to understanding history. Map 5–1 from Chapter 5 shows the British colonies on the eastern seaboard of North America in 1763, about twelve years before the American Revolution. It has three features

MAP EXPLORATION

To explore an interactive version of this map, go to
http://www.prenhall.com/goldfield/map5.1

MAP 5–1

Colonial Settlement and the Proclamation Line of 1763   This map depicts the regions claimed and settled by the major groups competing for territory in eastern North America. With the Proclamation Line of 1763, positioned along the crest of the Appalachian Mountains, the British government tried to stop the westward migration of settlers under its jurisdiction and thereby limit conflict with the Indians. The result, however, was frustration and anger on the part of land-hungry settlers.

WHY DO you suppose the Proclamation Line of 1763 was positioned along the crest of the Appalachian Mountains?

to help you read it: a **caption**, a legend, and a scale. The caption explains the historical significance of the map. Here the caption tells us that in 1763 the British government sought to restrict colonial settlement west of the Appalachian Mountains to prevent conflict between colonists and Indians. Colonial frustration with this policy contributed to the outbreak of the American Revolution.

The **legend** and the **scale** appear in the lower right corner of the map. The legend provides a key to what the symbols on the map mean. The solid line stretching along the Appalachian Mountains from Maine to Georgia represents the Proclamation Line of 1763. Cities are marked with a dot, capitals with a star, and forts by a black square. Spanish territory west of the Mississippi River is represented in blue; territory settled by Europeans is represented in green. The scale tells us that 7/8ths of an inch on the map represents 300 miles (about 480 kilometers) on the ground. With this information, estimates of the distance between points on the map are easily made.

The map also shows the topography of the region—its mountains, rivers, and lakes. This helps us understand how geography influenced history in this case. For example, the Appalachian Mountains divide the eastern seaboard from the rest of the continent. The mountains obstructed colonial migration to the west for a long time. By running the Proclamation Line along the Appalachians, the British hoped to use this natural barrier to separate Indians and colonists.

A **critical-thinking** question asks for careful considersation of the spatial connections between geography and history.

MAP EXPLORATIONS

Many of the maps in each chapter are provided in a useful interactive version on the text's Companion Website. These maps are easily identified by a bar along the top that reads "Map Explorations." An interactive version of Colonial Settlements and the Proclamation Line of 1763 can be found at **www.prenhall.com/goldfield/map5.1**. The interactive version of this particular map provides an opportunity to pan over an enlarged version of the territory in question. Cities, forts, settlements, and terrain are shown in detail. By moving the cursor north, south, east, or west one can gain a bird's-eye view of the entire region.

ANALYZING VISUALS

Visual images embedded thoughout the text can provide as much insight into our nation's history as the written word. Within photographs and pieces of fine art lies emotional and historical meaning. Captions also provide valuable information, such as in the example below. When studying the image, consider questions such as: "Who are these people?"; "How were they feeling?"; "What event motivated this photograph or painting?"; and "What can be learned from the backdrop surrounding the focal point?" Such analysis allows for a fuller understanding of the people who lived the American journey.

VISUALIZING THE PAST

These essays, found at the end of selected chapters, analyze important aspects of U.S. history through photographs, fine art, sculpture, woodcuts, and advertisements. Focus questions and a running narrative provide a careful examination of the historical implications of each topic in question.

OVERVIEWS

The Overview tables in this text are a special feature designed to highlight and summarize important topics within a chapter. The Overview table shown here, for example, summarizes the purpose and significance of the major laws and constitutional amendments passed during the Progressive Era.

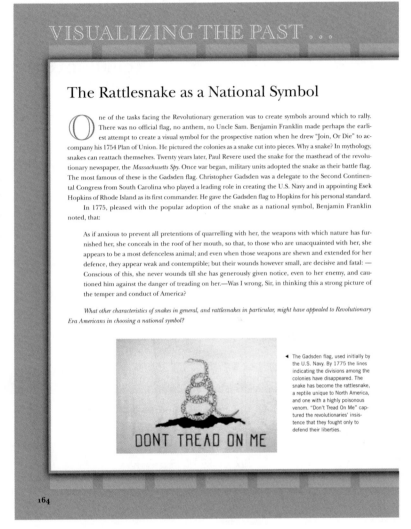

VISUALIZING THE PAST . . .

The Rattlesnake as a National Symbol

One of the tasks facing the Revolutionary generation was to create symbols around which to rally. There was no official flag, no anthem, no Uncle Sam. Benjamin Franklin made perhaps the earliest attempt to create a visual symbol for the prospective nation when he drew "Join, Or Die" to accompany his 1754 Plan of Union. He pictured the colonies as a snake cut into pieces. Why a snake? In mythology, snakes can reattach themselves. Twenty years later, Paul Revere used the snake for the masthead of the revolutionary newspaper, the *Massachusetts Spy*. Once war began, military units adopted the snake as their battle flag. The most famous of these is the Gadsden flag. Christopher Gadsden was a delegate to the Second Continental Congress from South Carolina who played a leading role in creating the U.S. Navy and in appointing Esek Hopkins of Rhode Island as its first commander. He gave the Gadsden flag to Hopkins for his personal standard.

In 1775, pleased with the popular adoption of the snake as a national symbol, Benjamin Franklin noted, that:

As if anxious to prevent all pretentions of quarrelling with her, the weapons with which nature has furnished her, she conceals in the roof of her mouth, so that, to those who are unacquainted with her, she appears to be a most defenceless animal; and even when those weapons are shewn and extended for her defence, they appear weak and contemptible; but their wounds however small, are decisive and fatal: — Conscious of this, she never wounds till she has generously given notice, even to her enemy, and cautioned him against the danger of treading on her.—Was I wrong, Sir, in thinking this a strong picture of the temper and conduct of America?

What other characteristics of snakes in general, and rattlesnakes in particular, might have appealed to Revolutionary Era Americans in choosing a national symbol?

◄ The Gadsden flag, used initially by the U.S. Navy. By 1775 the lines indicating the divisions among the colonies have disappeared. The snake has become the rattlesnake, a reptile unique to North America, and one with a highly poisonous venom. "Don't Tread On Me" captured the revolutionaries' insistence that they fought only to defend their liberties.

DONT TREAD ON ME

164

OVERVIEW

MAJOR LAWS AND CONSTITUTIONAL AMENDMENTS OF THE PROGRESSIVE ERA

Legislation	Effect
New York Tenement House Law (1901)	Established a model housing code for safety and sanitation
Newlands Act (1902)	Provided for federal irrigation projects
Hepburn Act (1906)	Strengthened authority of the Interstate Commerce Commission

The Fur Trade

◆ Fur traders were critical to New France's success.

◆ New France was ruled by royal appointees.

◆ *Coureurs de bois*: independent fur traders living among the Indians.

QUICK REVIEWS

The quick reviews, placed at key locations in the margins of each chapter, provide pinpoint summaries of important concepts.

CHRONOLOGIES

Each chapter includes a Chronology, a list of the key events discussed in the chapter arranged in chronological order. The chronology for Chapter 16 lists the dates of key events during the Reconstruction era from 1865 to 1877. Chronologies provide a review of important events and their relationship to one another.

CHRONOLOGY

1863	Lincoln proposes his Ten Percent Plan.	1871	Congress passes Ku Klux Klan Act.
1864	Congress proposes the Wade Davis Bill.	1872	Freedmen's Bureau closes down. Liberal Republicans emerge as a separate party. Ulysses S. Grant is reelected.
1865	Sherman issues Field Order No. 15. Freedmen's Bureau is established. Andrew Johnson succeeds to the presidency, unveils his Reconstruction plan. Massachusetts desegregates all public facilities. Black people in several Southern cities organize Union Leagues. Former Confederate states begin to pass black codes.	1873	Severe depression begins. Colfax Massacre occurs. U.S. Supreme Court's decision in the *Slaughter-house* cases weakens the intent of the Fourteenth Amendment. Texas falls to the Democrats in the fall elections.

PRIMARY SOURCE DOCUMENTS

Historians find most of their information in written records and original documents that have survived from the past. These include government publications, letters, diaries, newspapers—whatever people wrote or printed, including many private documents never intended for publication. Each chapter in the book contains a feature called American Views—a selection from a primary source document. The example shown here is a letter from a Union soldier fighting during the Civil War. Each American Views feature begins with a brief introduction followed by several questions—for discussion or written response—on what the document reveals about key issues and events.

In addition, each chapter begins with Voices from the American Journey, a brief firsthand account from an individual that powerfully recounts the personal journey he or she took in their lives. Each of these "voices" relates to the themes that follow in the chapter. For example, in Chapter 18 is an excerpt from a letter written by Mary Antin, a Russian-Jewish immigrant who came to America at the turn of the last century.

◆ AMERICAN VIEWS ◆

A SOLDIER PROMOTES THE UNION CAUSE

S oldiers wrote their thoughts down in diaries, in letters to their families, and, as in the case here of D. Beardsley, from Tompkins County, New York, to newspapers. Morale faltered in both the civilian and military ranks on both sides during the Civil War as this excerpt indicates. At the same time, Beardsley is buoyed by the sense of mission brought about by Abraham Lincoln's Emancipation Proclamation, which took effect one month before this letter.

DEMOCRATIC SOCIETIES have to balance civil liberties with the necessity of carrying on a war. What does this soldier think about where the balance ought to occur? The writer refers to "desertion" in the ranks. Why was there a morale problem in the Union armies in February 1863? How does this soldier hope the Emancipation Proclamation will affect the war effort in the North?

I having the honor of being a volunteer from old Tompkins County, and also fighting under the same banner and for the same principles that Washington did—still holding to my priviledges [sic] as a citizen of the United States, I think it will not be out of place for me to speak a few words through your columns, to the good people of my native county. . . .

If our Government would have no rebellion, she must pluck the tares of rebellion from the heart of the nation; and if we would have this rebellion crushed, we must cease to have traitors in power. Let that class in the Northern States, who would kiss the red hand of treason for a momentary peace, remember that the hand will be no less red by the kiss, or the blow no less sure by the pause; and I would humbly beg the people of the North, in the name of a soldier for the Union, that they will, in this dark and trying hour of our country's history, give us their undivided support, first, by stripping all power from the traitors at home, and then by their repentant prayers for our success in battles. . . . A few have deserted, and may God have mercy upon them. Let them go, their *blood* is altogether too poor to enrich the soil of worn out Virginia. We want the blood of patriots to make it bring forth the fruits of freedom. . . . We hope that in future the people and the army will become more pure, and work with a nobler purpose of heart. The first step toward this reformation has already been taken. We begin to see that all men have rights, whether white or black, and we hope that when the smoke of battle shall have cleared away, that the bright sun of peace will shine upon a truly free people.

Source: D. Beardsley, "Co. K, 137th Reg't, N.Y. Vols" that appeared in the *Ithaca Journal*, March 3, 1863; dated February 16, 1863 and written from Acquia Landing, Virginia.

United States History Documents CD-ROM

Bound into every new copy of this textbook is a free U.S. History Documents CD-ROM. This is a powerful resource for research and additional reading that contains more than 300 primary source documents central to U.S. History. Each document provides essay questions that are linked directly to a website where short-essay answers can be submitted online or printed out. Particularly relevant or interesting documents are called out at appropriate places in the margin of each chapter. A complete list of documents on the CD-ROM is found at the end of the text.

18–5
Address by George Engel, Condemned Haymarket Anarchist (1886)

From Then to Now

The feature called From Then to Now connects events and trends in the past to issues that confront Americans today, illustrating the value a historical perspective can contribute to our understanding of the world we live in. The example here, from Chapter 30, compares the roles of women in the American workforce today to those before the Civil War and at the turn of the century.

FROM THEN TO NOW
Women and Work in American Offices

At the end of the twentieth century, women filled the majority of America's office-based jobs. More women than men worked as office managers, receptionists, library administrators, bank tellers, travel agents, administrative assistants, insurance agents, bookkeepers, and other desk-and-computer occupations.

In 1997, women made up 46 percent of the American labor force. Seven out of ten of these women worked in professional, managerial, technical, administrative support, and sales positions. They ranged from corporate CEOs and college professors to clerks in state motor vehicle offices and the voices that take your orders and reservations when you dial 800.

This employment pattern, which most Americans now take for granted, is the product of 140 years of gradual change that began with, and was triggered by, the Civil War. Before the Civil War, American women found employment as domestic servants, sometimes as mill operatives, and increasingly as schoolteachers, but not as office workers. Clerks were men—sometimes settled into lower-status white-collar careers and sometimes learning a business from the inside before rising into management. Their jobs consisted of copying letters and documents by hand, tracing orders and correspondence, and keeping financial records.

The Civil War, however, sharply increased the flow of government paperwork while diverting young men into military service. The U.S. Treasury Department in Washington responded in 1862 by hiring women to sort and package federal bonds and currency. Treasury officials fretted about the moral implications of mixing men and women in offices but overcame these concerns when they found that women were both cheap and reliable workers. By 1870, several hundred women worked in Washington's federal offices, enough for a character in a novel about the Hayes administration (1877–1881) to comment that he could learn from a glance to "single out the young woman who supported her family upon her salary and the young woman who bought her ribbons with it; the widow who fed half-a-dozen children."

As the national economy grew in the late nineteenth century, it generated ever-increasing flows of information. New technologies such as telephones and typewriters routinized clerical work. These trends increased the need for desk workers, a need largely filled by middle-class women, whose literacy was often guaranteed by the high school diplomas that went disproportionately to women in the later nineteenth century. As women workers filled new downtown skyscrapers, the central districts of large cities lost some of their rough edges and grew more respectable as centers of shopping and entertainment.

By 1900, the division of labor that would characterize the first half of the twentieth century was in place. Women comprised 76 percent of the nation's stenographers and typists and 29 percent of its cashiers, bookkeepers, and accountants. For the most part, however, they occupied the lower echelons of the office hierarchy. It was men who determined what was to be said; women who transcribed, transmitted, recorded, and filed their messages. Only in recent decades have women begun successfully to challenge that established order.

Review Questions, Where to Learn More, and Additional Study Resources

At the end of each chapter review questions reconsider the main topics. The section called Where to Learn More lists important historical sites and museums and related Websites (which are also found at appropriate places in the margins of the text) that provide first-hand exposure to historical artifacts and settings. The URL for the Companion Website ™ is also found at the end of each chapter; this is an excellent resource for additional study aids.

WHERE TO LEARN MORE

The Underground Railroad Freedom Center, Cincinnati, Ohio
www.undergroundrailroad.org

REVIEW QUESTIONS

1. What do Eliza Farmar's letters tell us about the crisis over dutied tea in 1773 and 1774? What makes her increasingly sympathetic to the colonial position?

2. How did the British victory in the French and Indian War affect the relations between Native Americans and white settlers? Between British authorities and Americans?

3. How did the expectations of American and British authorities differ in 1763? Why were new policies offensive to Americans?

4. How was stationing British troops in America related to British taxation of the colonists? Why did the colonists object to taxation by Parliament?

5. How did Americans oppose the new measures? Who participated in the various forms of resistance? How effective were the different kinds of resistance?

6. What led to the meeting of the First Continental Congress? What did the Congress achieve?

WHERE TO LEARN MORE

Charleston, South Carolina. Many buildings date from the eighteenth century. Officials stored tea in one of them—the Exchange—to prevent a local version of the Boston Tea Party. The website for Historic Charleston, **http://www.cr.nps.gov/nr/travel/charleston**, provides a map, a list of buildings, and information about them.

GLOSSARY/KEY TERMS

Significant historical terms are called out in heavy type throughout the text, defined in the margin, and listed at the end of each chapter with appropriate page numbers. These are listed alphabetically and defined in a glossary at the end of the book.

KEY TERMS

Boston Massacre (p. 122)
Boston Tea Party (p. 124)
British Constitution (p. 117)
Cherokee War (p. 114)
Coercive Acts (p. 125)
Committees of correspondence (p. 124)
Continental Association (p. 127)
Currency Act (p. 116)
Declaration of Rights and Grievances (p. 119)

Declaratory Act (p. 119)
First Continental Congress (p. 125)
Intolerable Acts (p. 125)
Nonimportation movement (p. 118)
Parson's Cause (p. 115)
Pontiac's Rebellion (p. 114)
Proclamation Line (p. 113)
Proclamation of 1763 (p. 112)
Quartering Acts (p. 113)
Quebec Act (p. 125)
Regulators (p. 120)

Sons of Liberty (p. 118)
Stamp Act (p. 116)
Stamp Act Congress (p. 119)
Sugar Act (p. 116)
Suffolk Resolves (p. 127)
Tea Act of 1773 (p. 124)
Tories (p. 128)
Townshend Duty Act (p. 121)
Whigs (p. 128)
Writs of assistance (p. 117)

The American Journey

A History of the United States

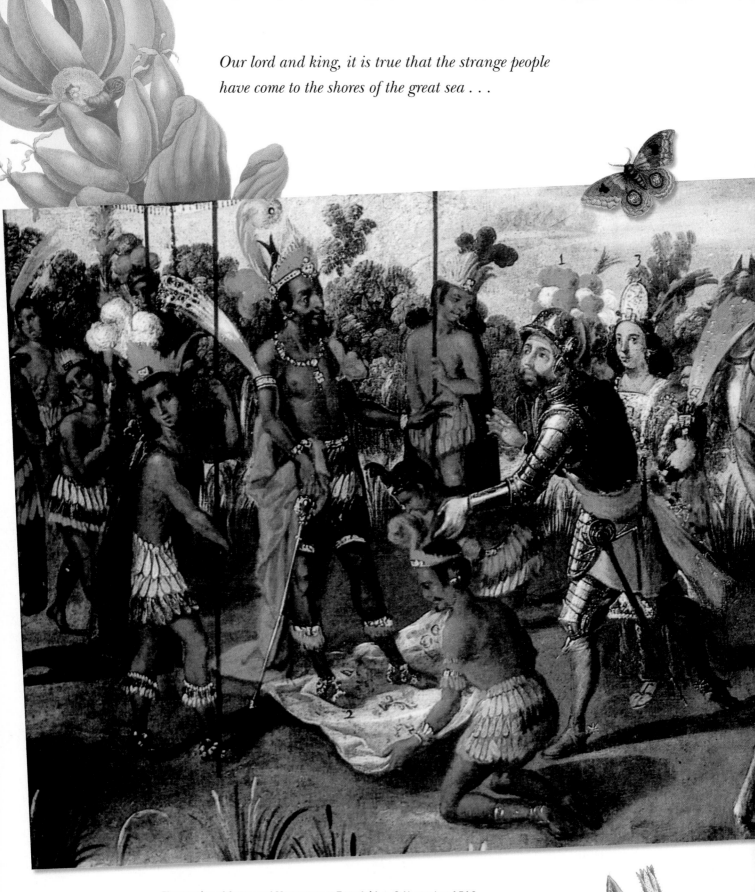

Our lord and king, it is true that the strange people
have come to the shores of the great sea . . .

The meeting of Cortes and Montezuma at Tenochtitlan, 8 November 1519.

1

WORLDS APART

WHAT WAS life like
for Native Americans prior to 1492?

WHAT BENEFITS to European princes,
merchants, and traders did exploration provide?

HOW DID the French, English,
and Spanish fare in their early efforts
in the New World?

WHAT WERE the consequences
of contact between the Old and New Worlds?

After a journey of over two hundred miles, the exhausted man arrived in the grand city of Tenochtitlán. He had hurried from the Gulf Coast with news for the Aztec leader, Moctezuma.

Our lord and king, forgive my boldness. I am from Mictlancuauhtla. When I went to the shores of the great sea, there was a mountain range or small mountain floating in the midst of the water, and moving here and there without touching the shore. My lord, we have never seen the like of this, although we guard the coast and are always on watch.

[When Moctezuma sent some officials to check on the messenger's story, they confirmed his report.]

Our lord and king, it is true that strange people have come to the shores of the great sea. They were fishing from a small boat, some with rods and others with a net. They fished until late and then they went back to their two great towers and climbed up into them. . . . They have very light skin, much lighter than ours. They all have long beards, and their hair comes only to their ears.

Miguel Leon-Portilla, *The Broken Spears: The Aztec Account of the conquest of Mexico* (Boston, 1962).

IMAGE KEY

for pages 2–3

a. Banana blossom.
b. The meeting of Cortes and Montezuma Tenochtitlan, 8 November 1519.
c. Pyramid of Kukulcan at Chichen Itza.
d. The coastal Algonquian village of Secoton.
e. Dutch colonial officer Peter Minuit purchases Manhattan Island from Man-a-hat-a Native Americans.
f. John White finding no trace of the colony of Roanoke on his return to Virginia in 1590.
g. Aztec Indians, with smallpox contracted from the Spaniards, ministered to by a medicine man.

MOCTEZUMA RECEIVED NEWS, like the messenger's initial report, filled with foreboding. In Aztec religion, omens and prophecies were thought to foreshadow coming events. Several unusual omens had recently occurred—blazing lights in the sky, one temple struck by lightning and another that spontaneously burst into flames, monstrous beings that appeared and vanished. Now light-skinned strangers were offshore. Magicians warned that trouble lay ahead.

The messenger's journey to Tenochtitlán occurred in 1519. The "mountains" he saw were the sails of European ships, and the strange men were Spanish soldiers under the command of Hernán Cortés. Like Columbus's voyage to the Caribbean in 1492, Cortés's arrival in Mexico is often considered a key episode in the European discovery of the "New World." But we might also view the messenger's entry into the Aztec capital as announcing the native Mexicans' discovery of a New World to the east, from which the strangers must have come. Neither the Aztecs nor the Spaniards could have foreseen the far-reaching consequences of these twin discoveries. Before long, Native Americans, Africans, and Europeans—who had previously lived worlds apart would come together to create a world that was new to all of them.

Section 1: pg 4-18

DIFFERENT WORLDS

WHAT WAS life like for Native Americans prior to 1492?

The New World reflected the diverse experiences of the peoples who built it. Improving economic conditions in the fifteenth and early sixteenth centuries propelled Europeans overseas to seek new opportunities for trade and settlement. Spain, Portugal, France, and England competed within Europe, and their conflict carried over into the Americas. Native Americans drew upon their familiarity with the land and its resources, their patterns of political and religious authority, and their systems of trade and warfare to deal with the European newcomers. Africans were brought to the Americas by the Europeans to work as slaves. They too would draw on their cultural heritage to cope with a new land and a harsh life.

⬦ AMERICAN VIEWS ⬦

Cabeza de Vaca Among the Indians (1530)

lvar Núñez Cabeza de Vaca came to the New World in 1527 in search of riches, not suffering. But the Spanish expedition of which he was a member met disaster shortly after it arrived in Florida on a mission to conquer the region north of the Gulf of Mexico. Of an original group of three hundred soldiers, only Cabeza de Vaca and three other men (including one African slave) survived by walking thousands of miles overland from the Gulf Coast to northern Mexico. This eight-year-long ordeal tested their wits and physical endurance. Instead of entering Indian villages as proud conquistadors, Cabeza de Vaca and his companions encountered native peoples from a position of weakness. To survive, they had to adapt to the ways of the peoples across whose land they passed. After Cabeza de Vaca made it back to Mexico City, he described his experiences in a report to the king of Spain. This remarkable document offers vivid descriptions of the territory extending from northern Florida to northern Mexico and the many peoples who inhabited it. It also reveals much about Cabeza de Vaca himself and the changes he made to survive.

WHILE LIVING among the Capoques, what sort of work did Cabeza de Vaca have to do, and why? Why did Cabeza de Vaca decide to become a merchant? What advantages did this way of life offer him? Why did the Indians welcome Cabeza de Vaca into their communities, even though he was a stranger?

I had to stay with the Capoques more than a year. Because of the hard work they put me to, and their harsh treatment, I resolved to flee to the people of Charruco in the forests of the main. . . . My life had become unbearable. In addition to much other work, I had to grub roots in the water or from underground in the canebrakes. My fingers got so raw that if a straw touched them they would bleed. The broken canes often slashed my flesh; I had to work amidst them without benefit of clothes.

So I set to contriving how I might transfer to the forest-dwellers, who looked more propitious. My solution was to turn to trade.

[Escaping to Charruco about February 1530,] I did my best to devise ways of making my traffic profitable so I could get food and good treatment. The various Indians would beg me to go from one quarter to another for things they needed; their incessant hostilities made it impossible for them to travel cross-country or make many exchanges.

But as a neutral merchant I went into the interior as far as I pleased. . . . My principal wares were cones and other pieces of sea-snail, conchs used for cutting, sea-beads, and a fruit like a bean [from mesquite trees] which the Indians value very highly, using it for a medicine and for a ritual beverage in their dances and festivities. This is the sort of thing I carried inland. By barter I got and brought back to the coast skins, red ochre which they rub on their faces, hard canes for arrows, flint for arrowheads, with sinews and cement to attach them, and tassels of deer hair which they dye red.

This occupation suited me; I could travel where I wished, was not obliged to work, and was not a slave. Wherever I went, the Indians treated me honorably and gave me food, because they liked my commodities. They were glad to see me when I came and delighted to be brought what they wanted. I became well known; those who did not know me personally knew me by reputation and sought my acquaintance. This served my main purpose, which all the while was to determine an eventual road out.

Source: Cyclone Covey, ed., *Cabera de Vaca's Adventures in the Unknown Interior of America*, pp. 66–67. Reprinted by permission of Scribner, a Division of Simon & Schuster. © 1961 by Macmillan Publishing Company.

NATIVE AMERICAN SOCIETIES BEFORE 1492

Convinced that he had landed in the East Indies in 1492 Columbus called the people he met *indios*. His error is preserved in the word *Indian*, used by Europeans to identify the original inhabitants of the two American continents.

By 1492, the continents of North and South America had been inhabited for a long time—estimates range from 15,000 to 50,000 years. The human population of the two continents may have been as high as 70 million—nearly equal to the population of Europe at that time, most of them south of what is now the border between the United States and Mexico. These people belonged to hundreds of groups, each with its own language or dialect, history, and way of life.

The first Americans were nomadic hunters from Siberia who probably came in several waves across a land bridge that once connected Siberia and Alaska. Some may have arrived from Asia as recently as 8,000 years ago. They and their descendants gradually ranged southward and eastward, spreading throughout North and South America.

The earliest Americans, whom archaeologists call *Paleo-Indians,* traveled in small bands, tracking and killing mammoths, bison, and other large game. Paleo-Indians were resourceful hunters who crafted sharp stone points for their spears. Their efficiency may have led to overhunting for by 9000 B.C. mammoths, mastodons, and other game had become extinct. The world's climate also grew warmer, turning grasslands into deserts and reducing the animals' food supply, hastening their disappearance. This meant that humans had to find other food sources.

Between roughly 8000 B.C. and 1500 B.C.—what archaeologists call the *Archaic* period—Indians adapted to regional environments, learning to use local resources efficiently. Gradually, populations grew, and people began living in larger villages. Men did most of the hunting and fishing. Women remained closer to home, gathering and preparing wild plant foods and caring for children. Each group made the tools it used, with men carving fishhooks and arrowheads and women making bone needles and baskets.

Archaic Indians also collected local nonfood resources, including rocks, shells, and bones. They fashioned goods from these materials and traded them with other peoples, sometimes hundreds of miles away. At Indian Knoll, in western Kentucky, archaeologists have found copper from the Great Lakes area and shells from as far away as the Gulf of Mexico. Ideas as well as goods circulated among Archaic Indian peoples. Across the continent, human burials became more elaborate, suggesting that ideas about death and the afterlife passed between groups. Bodies might be wrapped in woven mats or cloths, and the deceased's personal possessions were often placed in the grave.

Near the end of the Archaic period, some groups began farming. Around 5000 B.C., the people of southern Mexico started raising an ancient type of maize, or corn. At first, farming supplemented a diet still largely dependent on hunting and gathering, but agriculture gradually became more widespread. In addition to maize, the main crop in both South and North America, farmers in Mexico, Central America, and the Peruvian Andes learned to cultivate peppers, beans, pumpkins, squash, avocados, sweet and white potatoes (native to the Peruvian highlands), and tomatoes. Mexican farmers also grew cotton. Maize and bean cultivation spread from Mexico in a wide arc to the north and east. Peoples in what is now the southwestern United States began farming between 1500 and 500 B.C., and by A.D. 200, farmers tilled the soil in present-day Georgia and Florida.

Wherever agriculture took hold, populations grew, since farming produced a more secure food supply than hunting and gathering. Permanent villages ap-

Paleo-Indians

Archaic Indians

QUICK REVIEW

The Earliest Americans

● Paleo-Indians were resourceful hunters.

● During the Archaic period Indians adapted to regional environments.

● Farming began near the end of the Archaic Period.

peared as farmers settled near their fields. In central Mexico, agriculture eventually sustained the populations of large cities. Trade in agricultural surpluses flowed through exchange networks. In many Indian societies, women's status improved because of their role as the principal farmers. Specialized craftworkers produced pottery and baskets to store harvested grains. Even religious beliefs and practices reflected the centrality of farming. In describing the origins of their people, Pueblo Indians of the Southwest compared their emergence from the underworld to a maize plant sprouting from the earth.

Despite their diversity, certain generalizations can be made about societies that developed within broad regions, or *culture areas* (see Map 1–1, p. 8). Throughout the North and West, Indians did not adopt agriculture. In the challenging environment of the Arctic and Subarctic, small nomadic bands moved seasonally to fish, follow game, and, in the brief summers, gather wild berries. Far to the north, Eskimos and Aleuts hunted whales, seals, and other sea mammals. Further inland, the Crees and other peoples followed migrating herds of caribou and moose. Northern peoples fashioned tools and weapons of bone and ivory, clothing and boats from animal skins, and houses of whalebones and hides or blocks of sod or snow.

Along the Northwest Coast and Columbia River Plateau, abundant resources supported one of the most densely populated areas of North America. With rivers teeming with salmon and other fish and forests full of game and edible plants, people prospered without agriculture. Among groups like the Kwakiutls and Chinooks, extended families lived in large communal houses located in villages of several hundred people.

Farther south, in present-day California, hunter-gatherers lived in smaller villages, several of which might be led by the same chief. These settlements usually adjoined oak groves, where Indians gathered acorns. To protect their access to this important food, chiefs and villagers vigorously defended their territorial claims to the oak groves.

Small nomadic bands in the Great Basin, where the climate was warm and dry, lived in caves and rock shelters. Shoshone hunters captured antelope in corrals and trapped small game, such as squirrels and rabbits. In present-day Utah and western Colorado, Utes hunted elk, bison, and mountain sheep and fished in mountain streams. Women gathered pinyon nuts, seeds, and wild berries. In hard times, people ate rattlesnakes, horned toads, and insects. They celebrated whenever food was plentiful and urged religious leaders to seek supernatural help when starvation loomed.

Mesoamerica, the birthplace of agriculture in North America, extends from central Mexico into Central America. A series of complex, literate, urban cultures emerged in this region, beginning around 1200 B.C. with the Olmecs, who flourished on Mexico's Gulf Coast until 400 B.C. The Olmecs and other early Mesoamerican peoples built cities featuring large pyramids, developed religious practices that included human sacrifice, and devised calendars and writing systems.

Mayan civilization followed, reaching its greatest glory between about A.D. 150 and 900 in the southern Yucatán, creating Mesoamerica's most advanced writing and calendrical systems and developing a sophisticated mathematics that included the concept of zero. The Mayans of the southern Yucatán suffered a decline after 900, but there were still many thriving Mayan centers in the northern Yucatán in 1492. The great city of Teotihuacán dominated central Mexico from the first century to the eighth century A.D. and influenced much of the rest of Mesoamerica through trade and conquest.

Some two hundred years after the fall of Teotihuacán, the Toltecs, a warrior people, rose to prominence, dominating central Mexico from about 900 to 1100.

QUICK REVIEW

Mesoamerica

◆ Mesoamerica was the birthplace of agriculture in North America.

◆ Olmecs were the first literate urban culture in the region.

◆ Mayan civilization reached its height between A.D. 150 and 900.

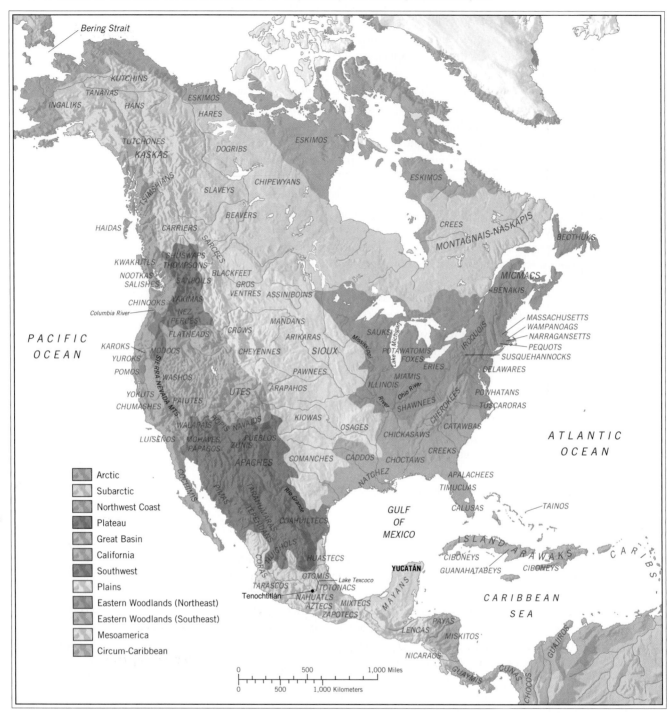

MAP 1–1

North American Culture Areas, c. 1500   Over the course of centuries, Indian peoples in North America developed distinctive cultures suited to the environments in which they lived. Inhabitants of each culture area shared basic patterns of subsistence, craftwork, and social organization. Most, but not all, Indian peoples combined farming with hunting and gathering.

WHAT DOES this map tell you about the role different geographic regions in the Americas played in determining the type of culture (social organization, hunting, farming, etc.) the inhabitants of those regions developed?

In the wake of the Toltec collapse, the **Aztecs**, another warrior people, migrated from the north into the Valley of Mexico and built a great empire that soon controlled much of Mesoamerica. The Aztec capital, Tenochtitlán, was a city of great plazas, broad avenues, magnificent temples and palaces, ball courts, and busy marketplaces. Built on islands in the middle of Lake Texcoco, it was connected to the mainland by four broad causeways. In 1492, Tenochtitlán was home to some 200,000 people, one of the largest cities in the world at the time.

In the great pyramid in Tenochtitlán, Aztec priests sacrificed human victims—by cutting open their chests and removing their still-beating hearts—to offer to the gods to prevent them from destroying the earth. Hundreds, even thousands, of victims died in ceremonies that sometimes lasted for days.

Aztec culture expanded through continuous military conquest, driven by a quest for sacrificial victims and for wealth in the form of tribute payments of gold, food, and handcrafted goods. Neighboring peoples hated the Aztecs and submitted to them out of fear. With a powerful ally to lead them, they would readily turn on their overlords and bring the empire down.

Native societies emerging north of Mexico shared certain characteristics with those of Mesoamerica. The introduction of a drought-resistant type of maize (probably from Mexico) into the desert Southwest in 400 B.C. enabled a series of cultures to develop. Beginning about 300 B.C., the Hohokams settled in southern Arizona, eventually building permanent villages of several hundred people. Substantial harvests of beans, corn, and squash, watered by a complex system of canals, fed Hohokam villagers. In large communities, inhabitants built ball courts similar to those found in Mexico. Artisans wove cotton cloth and made goods reflecting Mesoamerican artistic styles out of shell, turquoise, and clay. Extensive trade networks linked the Hohokams to places as far away as California and Mexico. Their culture endured for over a thousand years and then disappeared mysteriously by 1450.

Beginning around A.D. 1, the Anasazis (their name is Navaho for "ancient alien ones") settled where the borders of present-day Colorado, Utah, Arizona, and New Mexico meet. They gradually adopted agriculture, first adding maize and later beans and squash to a diet of wild foods. Scarce rainfall, routed through dams and hillside terraces, watered the crops.

The Anasazis originally lived in villages on mesas or canyon floors. Their dwellings included special rooms, or *kivas,* for religious ceremonies. The largest communal dwelling, Pueblo Bonito in New Mexico's Chaco Canyon, covered three acres and contained 650 to 800 rooms, housing about 1,200 people. Pueblo Bonito may have been the center of Anasazi society from about A.D. 900 to 1100.

After around 1200, the Anasazis began carving multistoried houses into canyon walls. These were not easy places in which to live, and they could be reached only by difficult climbs up steep cliffs and along narrow ledges. Archaeologists suggest that warfare and climate change forced the Anasazis into these homes. Around 1200, a colder climate reduced food supplies, and food scarcity may have encouraged violence. The Anasazis may have moved to the cliff dwellings for protection. By 1300, most Anasazi survivors had dispersed to villages along the Rio Grande.

The Pueblo peoples of the Southwest, including the Hopis and Zunis, are descendants of the Anasazis. In 1492, many lived in large communal dwellings in permanent villages (*pueblo* is the Spanish word for "village"). Pueblo men did most of the farming, and in religious rituals all Pueblos prayed to the gods for rain for the all-important harvest.

The Great Plains of the continent's interior were much less densely settled than the desert Southwest. Scattered villages of Mandans, Pawnees, and other groups clung

WHERE TO LEARN MORE

Mesa Verde National Park,
Colorado
www.mesa.verde.national-park.com

Aztecs   A warrior people who dominated the Valley of Mexico from 1100–1521.

CHRONOLOGY

c. 40,000–8,000 B.C.	Ancestors of Native Americans cross to Americas.	1492	End of *reconquista* in Spain. Christopher Columbus's first voyage.
c. 10,000–9000 B.C.	Paleo-Indians expand through the Americas.	1494	Treaty of Tordesillas.
c. 9000 B.C.	Extinction of large land mammals in North America.	1497	John Cabot visits Nova Scotia and Newfoundland.
c. 8000–1500 B.C.	Archaic Indian era.	1497–1499	Vasco da Gama sails around Africa to reach India.
c. 3000 B.C.	Beginnings of agriculture in Mesoamerica.	1517	Protestant Reformation begins in Germany.
c. 1500 B.C.	Earliest mound-building culture begins.	1519–1521	Hernán Cortés conquers the Aztec empire.
c. 500 B.C.–400 A.D.	Adena-Hopewell mound-building culture.	1532–1533	Francisco Pizarro conquers the Inca empire.
c. 700–1600 A.D.	Rise of West African empires.	1534–1542	Jacques Cartier explores eastern Canada for France.
c. 900	First mounds built at Cahokia. Anasazi expansion.	1540–1542	Coronado explores southwestern North America.
c. 1000	Spread of Islam in West Africa.	1542–1543	Roberval's failed colony in Canada.
c. 1000–1500	Last mound-building culture, the Mississippian.	1558	Elizabeth I becomes queen of England.
c. 1290s	Anasazi dispersal into smaller pueblos.	1565	Spanish establish outpost at St. Augustine in Florida.
1400–1600	Renaissance in Europe.	1560s–1580s	English renew attempts to conquer Ireland.
1430s	Beginnings of Portuguese slave trade in West Africa.	1587	Founding of "Lost Colony" of Roanoke.
		1598	Spanish found colony at New Mexico.

to tree-lined rivers. Women raised crops and gathered wild plants for food and medicine. Men hunted bison, whose skin and bones were used for clothing, shelter, and tools. Plains Indians moved frequently, seeking more fertile land or better hunting.

The spread of agriculture transformed native societies in the Eastern Woodlands, a vast territory extending from the Mississippi Valley to the Atlantic seaboard. Farming first appeared around 2500 B.C. but was not firmly established until about A.D. 700. As agriculture spread, several "mound-building" societies—named for the large earthworks their members constructed—developed in the Ohio and Mississippi Valleys. The oldest flourished in Louisiana between 1500 and 700 B.C. Members of the Adena-Hopewell culture, which appeared in the Ohio Valley between 500 B.C. and A.D. 400, built hundreds of mounds, often in the shapes of humans, birds, and serpents. Most mounds were grave sites, where people were buried with valuable goods, many obtained through long-distance trade.

The last mound-building culture, the Mississippian, emerged between 1000 and 1500 in the Mississippi Valley. One of the largest cities was **Cahokia**, located on the Mississippi River across from present-day St. Louis. By 1250, Cahokia, the largest city north of Mexico, had perhaps thirty thousand residents, making it about the same size as medieval London. Its central feature was a 100-foot-high mound, the world's largest earthwork. Cahokia dominated the Mississippi Valley, but numerous other towns, some with hundreds or thousands

WHERE TO LEARN MORE

Cahokia Mounds State Historic Site, Collinsville, Illinois
www.siue.edu/CAHOKIAMOUNDS

Cahokia   One of the largest urban centers created by Mississippian peoples, containing 30,000 residents in 1250.

of residents, dotted the Woodlands region, linked by trade networks. Powerful chiefs, thought to be related to the sun, dominated these communities.

Mississippian culture began to decline in the thirteenth century. Food shortages and warfare drove people from the great cities into the countryside. Elements of Mississippian culture survived among dispersed Woodlands people, particularly methods of maize and bean agriculture. By 1492, although the large cities of the Mississippian era had disappeared, Woodlands Indians maintained long-distance trade links throughout the region, with such precious goods as copper, shell beads, and pearls passing among groups.

This artist's rendering, based on archaeological evidence, suggests the size and magnificence of the Mississippian city of Cahokia. By the thirteenth century, it was as populous as medieval London and served as a center of trade for the vast interior of North America.

Cahokia Mounds State Historic Site.

The Caribbean islanders whom Columbus first encountered descended from ancient cultures. Ancestors of the Tainos probably came from what is now Venezuela. The Guanahatabeys of western Cuba originated in Florida, and the Caribs of the easternmost islands moved from Brazil's Orinoco Valley. Island peoples began farming perhaps in the first century A.D. on clearings made in the tropical forests. Canoes carried trade goods throughout the Caribbean, as well as Mesoamerica and coastal South America.

By 1492, as many as 4 million people may have inhabited the Caribbean islands. Powerful chiefs ruled over villages, conducted war and diplomacy, and distributed food and other goods obtained as tribute from villages. Elite islanders were easily recognized by their fine clothing, bright feather headdresses, and golden ear and nose ornaments—items that eventually attracted European visitors' attention.

Long before 1492, North America had witnessed centuries of dynamic change. Populations grew and spread across thousands of miles of territory. Farmers developed new varieties of essential food plants. Empires rose and fell. Large cities flourished and disappeared. People formed alliances with trading partners and warred with groups who refused to trade. Because their histories have been preserved in oral traditions and archaeological evidence rather than written documents, they are less distinct, but no less real, than the Europeans whom they would soon meet.

CULTURAL PERCEPTIONS AND MISPERCEPTIONS

Misunderstandings inevitably arose between Indians and Europeans when such dissimilar peoples encountered each other for the first time. Even simple transactions had unexpected results. When Columbus showed swords to the Tainos, for example, "they took them by the edge and through ignorance cut themselves" because they had never seen metal weapons. Similarly, French explorers choked when they tried to smoke unfamiliar Iroquois tobacco, which tasted, one of them reported, like "powdered pepper."

[Handwritten margin note: ① what are some misconceptions of Native Americans when the Europeans encountered them in mid-late 1400's?]

Many misunderstandings, however, had far graver consequences for the outcome of the encounter. Each group struggled to understand the strange behavior and customs of the other. Europeans usually decided that native practices were not just different from their own but inferior. Indians doubtless felt the same about European practices but their opinions were rarely recorded.

Religious differences were the hardest to reconcile. Seeing no churches or recognizable religious practices among the Tainos, Columbus wrote, "I do not detect in them any religion." His comment derived from his own Christian background. Christian Europeans worshiped one God in an organized church led by trained priests. They preserved their religious traditions in a written bible. Most Indians, however, believed in a variety of gods. They considered nature itself to be sacred and understood certain beings, including plants, animals, and stars, to possess spiritual powers. Indians living north of Mexico preserved religious beliefs through oral traditions, not in writing. Their religious leaders performed ceremonies that mediated between the human and spiritual worlds. Europeans, however, thought that these men were magicians or even witches. They assumed that Indians worshiped the devil and insisted that they adopt Christianity. In the face of this demand, many native peoples doubtless shared the opinion voiced by some Iroquois: "We do not know that God, we have never seen him, we know not who he is."

Europeans also disapproved of the relative equality of men and women they observed among some Native American peoples. Europeans believed that men were naturally superior to women and should dominate them. But in North America they encountered female rulers among the Wampanoags and Powhatans and learned that among groups such as the Hurons, women helped select chiefs. They found that many Indian societies, including the Pueblos, Hurons, and Iroquois, were *matrilineal*; that is, they traced descent through the mother's family line instead of the father's, as Europeans did.

In most Indian societies, men cleared the fields, but women planted and harvested the crops. Women also prepared food, cared for children, made clothing and baskets, carried burdens, and, in some regions, broke down, transported, and reassembled shelters when villages changed location. Europeans, who came from a society in which men did most agricultural work, thought that Indian women lived "a most slavish life." Misjudging the importance of Indian men's roles as hunters and warriors, Europeans scorned them as lazy husbands. Such confusion worked both ways. Massachusetts Indians ridiculed English husbands "for spoiling good working creatures" because they did not send their wives into the fields.

The ultimate source of conflict between Indians and Europeans was the intention of the Europeans to dominate the land. Within three days of his arrival in America, Columbus announced his intention "not to pass by any island of which I did not take possession" and soon speculated on the possibility of enslaving Indians. Native peoples everywhere challenged European claims to possession of their lands and resisted European attempts at domination.

WEST AFRICAN SOCIETIES

Many Europeans followed Columbus's lead in exploring what they soon realized was not Asia after all. Yet in the three centuries after 1492, fully six out of seven people who crossed the Atlantic to the Americas were not Europeans but Africans, the vast majority of whom arrived as slaves. Most came from West Africa, and like the inhabitants of North America or Europe, they belonged to many different ethnic groups, each with its own language and culture (see Map 1–2).

In 1492, Timbuktu, with a population of perhaps seventy thousand, was one of the greatest cities in West Africa. Located on the Niger River, the flourishing com-

[Handwritten margin notes: ✱ matrilineal; ② what goals did Europeans have that proved to be a source of conflict between N.A's + Europeans?; ✱ Timbuktu]

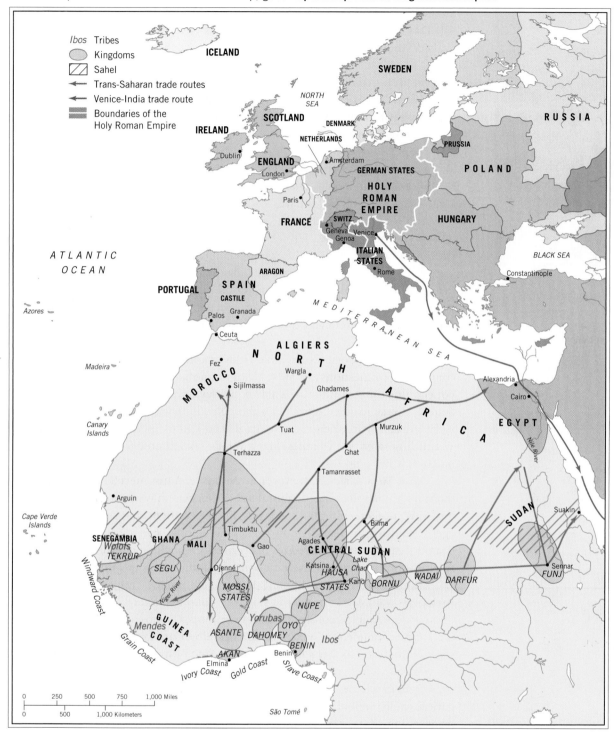

MAP 1–2

West Africa and Europe in 1492   Before Columbus's voyage, Europeans knew little about the world beyond the Mediterranean Basin and the coast of West Africa. Muslim merchants from North Africa largely controlled European traders' access to African gold and other materials.

HOW WERE the routes taken by European and North African traders conducive to the slave trading of the sixteenth, seventeenth, and eighteenth centuries? From what you can see on this map, do you suppose that (in addition to the trading of gold and other materials) the early trading of slaves was also somewhat regulated by North African Muslims?

⊛Songhai empire.

Craftsman from the West African kingdom of Benin were renowned for their remarkable bronze sculptures. This intricate bronze plaque depicts four African warriors in full military dress. The two tiny figures in the background may be Portuguese soldiers, who first arrived in Benin in the late fifteenth century.

Benin bronze plaque. National Museum of African Art, Smithsonian Institution, Washington, D.C., U.S.A. Aldo Turino, Art Resource, N.Y.

⊛patrilineal

(?) Describe life in western Africa.
— economy/agriculture
— religion
— gender relationships

mercial metropolis was the seat of the powerful Songhai empire ruled by Sunni Ali. The city was a center of trade as well as government. A visitor in 1526 described Timbuktu's busy streets lined with "shops of artificers and merchants, and especially of such as weave linen and cotton cloth," and reported—with some exaggeration—that the inhabitants "are exceeding rich."

The Songhai empire was only the latest in a series of powerful states to develop in western Sudan, the vast plain lying south of the arid Sahara. This large and wealthy empire emerged around 1450, dominating the Sudan until it fell to a Moroccan invasion in 1591. Large empires did not appear in coastal West Africa, although the Asante, Dahomey, Oyo, and Bini kingdoms there grew to be powerful. Other coastal peoples, such as the Mendes and Ibos, lived in autonomous villages where all adult males participated in making decisions.

In the vast grasslands of the Sudan, people raised cattle and cultivated millet and sorghum. In the 1500s, European visitors introduced varieties of Asian rice, which soon became another important crop. On the coast—where rain falls nearly every day—people grew yams, bananas, and various kinds of beans and peas in forest clearings. They also kept sheep, goats, and poultry.

West Africans were skilled artisans and particularly fine metalworkers. Smiths produced intricate bronze sculptures, designed distinctive miniature gold weights, and forged weapons.

Complex trade networks linked inland and coastal states, and long-distance commercial connections tied West Africa to southern Europe and the Middle East. For centuries, mines in the area of present-day Guinea and Mali produced tons of gold each year, which was exchanged for North African salt, a rare commodity in West Africa. North African merchants also bought pepper, leather, and ivory. The wealth generated by this trans-Saharan trade contributed to the rise of the Songhai and earlier empires.

Most West Africans, however, were farmers, not merchants. West African men and women shared agricultural tasks. Men generally prepared fields for planting, while women cultivated the crops, harvested them, and dried grain for storage. Men also hunted and, in the grassland regions, herded cattle. Women in the coastal areas owned and cared for other livestock, including goats and sheep. West African women regularly traded goods, including their crops, in local markets.

Family connections helped define each person's place in society. West Africans emphasized not only ties between parents and children but also those linking aunts, uncles, cousins, and grandparents. Groups of families formed clans that further extended an individual's kin ties. Most clans were *patrilineal*—tracing descent through the father's line—but some (including the Akans and Ibos) were matrilineal.

Religious beliefs magnified the powerful influence of family on African life. Africans believed that their ancestors acted as mediators between the worlds of the living and the dead. Families held elaborate funerals, which helped keep the memory of ancestors alive for younger generations.

West Africans worshiped a supreme being and several subordinate deities. West Africans, like Native Americans, believed that the gods often sent spirits to speak to people. And like Native American priests who mediated between the human and spirit worlds, West African medicine men and women provided protection against evil spirits and sorcerers. Religious ceremonies took place in sacred places often near water—but not in buildings that Europeans recognized as churches. And like the Indians, West Africans preserved their faith through oral traditions.

Islam began to take root in West Africa around the eleventh century, probably introduced by Muslim traders from North Africa. By the fifteenth century, the

Located in Djenné, Mali, this massive mosque, made of sun-hardened mud, dates from the fourteenth century. At that time, Djenné prospered as a center of trade and Islamic learning.

James Stanfield, National Geographic Image Collection.

cities of Timbuktu and Djenné had become centers of Islamic learning. Even so, most West Africans probably retained traditional religious beliefs and practices.

Before the fifteenth century, Europeans knew little about Africa beyond its Mediterranean coast. Spain, much of which had been subject to Islamic rule before 1492, had stronger ties to North Africa than most of Europe, but Christian merchants from other European lands had also traded for centuries with North Africans. When stories of West African gold reached the ears of European traders, they tried to move deeper into the continent, but they encountered powerful Muslim merchants intent on monopolizing the gold trade.

The kingdom of Portugal, eager to expand its trade, sought in the early fifteenth century to circumvent this Muslim monopoly. In 1415, Portuguese forces conquered Ceuta in Morocco and gained a foothold on the continent. Portuguese mariners gradually explored the West African coast, establishing trading posts along the way to exchange horses, clothing, wine, lead, iron, and steel for African gold, grain, animal skins, cotton, pepper, and camels.

By the 1430s, the Portuguese had discovered perhaps the greatest source of wealth they could extract from Africa—slaves. Slavery had long been a part of West African society. African law made land available to anyone willing to cultivate it—provided that no one else was using the same plot—and the possession of a large labor force to work the land became the principal means to wealth. Some people became slaves as punishment for crime, but most slaves were captured in raids into neighboring territories, a regular feature of African life.

Most slaves worked at a variety of tasks for their owners. Many labored more or less independently as farmers, producing surplus crops for their masters. Some rulers acquired female slaves to serve as wives, concubines, or workers. Powerful Sudanese rulers employed large numbers of slaves as bureaucrats and soldiers, rewarding them for loyal service with good treatment and, occasionally, freedom.

Europeans who observed African slaves' relative freedom and variety of employment often concluded that slaves in Africa were "slaves in name only." Slavery in Africa was not necessarily a permanent status and did not automatically apply to the slaves' children. European purchasers of African slaves generally treated them much more harshly. Slavery became even more oppressive as it developed in the Americas.

WESTERN EUROPE ON THE EVE OF DISCOVERY

When Columbus sailed from Spain in 1492, he left a continent recovering from the devastating disease and warfare of the fourteenth century and about to embark on the devastating religious conflicts of the sixteenth century. Between 1337 and 1453, England and France had exhausted each other in a series of conflicts known as the Hundred Years' War. And between 1347 and 1351, an epidemic known as the *Black Death* (bubonic plague) killed perhaps a third of all Europeans, with re-sults that were felt for more than a century.

The plague left Europe with far fewer workers, but the survivors learned to be more efficient, adopting labor-saving techniques to increase productivity. Metalworkers, for instance, built larger furnaces with huge bellows driven by water power. Shipbuilders redesigned vessels with steering mechanisms that could be managed by smaller crews. Innovations in banking, accounting, and insurance also fostered economic recovery.

By 1500, Europe had a stronger, more productive economy than ever before, but not everyone prospered equally. In parts of England, France, Sweden, and the German states, peasants and workers rebelled against the propertied classes. Protests grew from the workers' desire to protect their improving economic fortunes. They did not want to see their rising wages eaten up by higher rents and taxes.

In some parts of Europe, economic improvement encouraged an extraordinary cultural movement known as the *Renaissance*—a "rebirth" of interest in the classical civilizations of ancient Greece and Rome. The Renaissance originated in the city–states of Italy, where a prosperous and educated urban class promoted learning and artistic expression. Wealthy townspeople joined princes in becoming patrons of the arts, offering financial support to numerous painters, sculptors, architects, writers, and musicians.

European states were hierarchical, with their populations divided into fairly rigid classes. Monarchs stood at the top of society. Just below were the aristocrats, who, along with the royal family, dominated government and owned most of the land. Next came prosperous gentry families, independent landowners, and, at the bottom, landless peasants and laborers.

Most of Europe's people were peasant farmers. Peasant men did most of the heavy field work, while women helped at planting and harvest time and cared for children, livestock, and the household. The economic recovery after the Black Death brought prosperity to some families, but crop failures and disease could often cause great suffering in villages and towns.

European society was *patriarchal,* with men dominating political and economic life. Men also controlled the Catholic Church. Inheritance was patrilineal, and only men could own property.

By the end of the fifteenth century, after more than a hundred years of incessant conflict, a measure of stability had returned to Western Europe. Ferdinand and Isabella of Spain, Louis XI of France, and Henry VII of England successfully asserted royal authority over their previously fragmented realms, creating strong state bureaucracies to control political rivals. They gave special trading privileges to merchants to gain their support, creating links that would later prove important in financing overseas expeditions.

The consolidation of military power went hand in hand with the strength-

---

QUICK REVIEW

European Society

- European states were hierarchical.
- Most Europeans were peasant farmers.
- European society was patriarchal.

ening of political authority. Portugal developed a strong navy to defend its seaborne merchants. Louis XI of France commanded a standing army, and Ferdinand of Spain created a palace guard to use against potential opponents. Before overseas expansion began, European monarchs exerted military force to extend their authority closer to home. Louis XI and his successors used warfare and intermarriage with ruling families of nearby provinces to expand French influence. In the early sixteenth century, England's Henry VIII sent soldiers to conquer Ireland. And the Spain of 1492 was forged from the successful conclusion of the *reconquista* ("reconquest") of territory from Muslim control.

Even as these rulers sought to unify their realms, religious conflicts began to tear Europe apart. For more than a thousand years, Catholic Christianity had united western Europeans in one faith. By the sixteenth century, the Catholic Church had accumulated enormous wealth and power. The pope wielded influence not only as a spiritual leader but also as the political ruler of parts of Italy. The church owned considerable property throughout Europe. Many Christians, especially in northern Europe, began to criticize the worldliness of the popes and the church itself for corruption, abuse of power, and betrayal of the legacy of Christ.

In 1517, a German monk, Martin Luther, invited open debate on these issues, asserting that the church had become too insistent on the performance of good works, such as charitable donations or other actions intended to please God. He called for a return to what he understood to be the purer practices and beliefs of the early church, emphasizing that salvation came not by good deeds but only by faith in God. With the help of the newly invented printing press, his ideas spread widely, inspiring a challenge to the Catholic Church that has come to be called the **Reformation**.

When the church refused to compromise, Luther and other critics formed their own religious organizations, emphasizing the relationship between God and the individual believer. Luther urged people to take responsibility for their own spiritual growth by reading the Bible, which he translated for the first time into German. What started as a religious movement, however, quickly acquired an important political dimension.

Sixteenth-century Germany was a fragmented region of small kingdoms and principalities that were officially part of the Holy Roman Empire. Many German princes supported Luther for both spiritual and secular reasons. When the Holy Roman Empire under Charles V (who was also king of Spain) tried to silence them, the reformist princes protested. From that point on, these princes—and all Europeans who supported religious reform—became known as **Protestants.**

The Protestant movement took a more radical turn under the influence of the French reformer John Calvin, who emphasized the doctrine of **predestination.** Calvin maintained that an all-powerful and all-knowing God chose at the moment of creation which humans would be saved and which would be damned. Each person's fate is thus foreordained, or predestined, by God, although we cannot know our fate during our lifetimes. Good Calvinists struggled to behave as God's chosen, continually searching their souls for evidence of divine grace.

Calvin founded a religious community consistent with his principles at Geneva, a Swiss city–state near the French border. From Germany and Geneva the Protestant Reformation spread to France, the Netherlands, England, and Hungary. In succeeding years, other Protestant groups formed, split, and split again, increasing Europe's religious fragmentation. The new religious ideas particularly interested literate city dwellers, while peasants adopted the new ideas more slowly.

The Reformation addressed spiritual needs that the Catholic Church had left unfulfilled, but it also fractured the religious unity of western Europe and spawned

Reconquista   The long struggle (ending in 1492) during which Spanish Christians reconquered the Iberian peninsula from Muslim occupiers.

Reformation   Martin Luther's challenge to the Catholic Church, initiated in 1517, calling for a return to what he understood to be the purer practices and beliefs of the early church.

Protestants   All European supporters of religious reform under Charles V's Holy Roman Empire.

Predestination   The belief that God decided at the moment of Creation which humans would achieve salvation.

a century of warfare unprecedented in its bloody destructiveness. Protestants fought Catholics in France and the German states. Popes initiated a "Counter Reformation," intended to strengthen the Catholic Church. Europe thus fragmented into warring camps just at the moment when Europeans were coming to terms with their discovery of America.

section 2: pg 18-24

CONTACT

Portugal, Spain, France, and England competed to establish footholds on other continents in an intense scramble for riches and dominance. The success of these early endeavors was a reflection of Europe's prosperity and a series of technological breakthroughs that enabled its mariners to navigate beyond familiar waters. By 1600, Spain had emerged as the apparent winner among the European competitors for New World dominance. Its astonishingly wealthy empire included vast territories in Central and South America.

THE LURE OF DISCOVERY

Most Europeans, busy making a living, cared little about distant lands. But certain princes and merchants anticipated spiritual and material benefits from voyages of discovery. The spiritual advantages included making new Christian converts and blocking Islam's expansion. On the material side, the voyages would contribute to Europe's prosperity by increasing trade.

Merchants especially sought access to Asian spices like pepper, cinnamon, ginger, and nutmeg that added interest to an otherwise monotonous diet and helped preserve certain foods. But the overland spice trade—and the trade in other luxury goods such as silk and furs—spanned thousands of miles, involved many middlemen, and was controlled at key points by Muslim merchants. One critical center was Constantinople, the bastion of Christianity in the eastern Mediterranean. When it fell to the Ottomans—the Muslim rulers of Turkey—in 1453, Europeans feared that caravan routes to Asia would be disrupted. This encouraged merchants to turn westward and seek alternate routes. Mariners ventured farther into ocean waters, hoping to sail around Africa and chart a sea route to Asia.

Ocean voyages required sturdier ships and more reliable navigational tools. In the early fifteenth century, Prince Henry of Portugal, excited by the idea of overseas discovery, sponsored the efforts of shipbuilders, mapmakers, and other workers to solve these practical problems. Iberian shipbuilders perfected the caravel, a ship whose narrow shape and steering rudder suited it for ocean travel. Ship designers combined square sails (good for speed) with triangular "lateen" sails, which increased maneuverability. Two Arab inventions—the magnetic compass and the astrolabe (which allowed mariners to determine their position in relation to a star's known location in the sky)—gained popularity among European navigators. As sailors acquired practical experience on the high seas, mapmakers recorded their observations of landfalls, wind patterns, and ocean currents.

Portugal's Bartolomeu Días reached the southern tip of Africa in 1488. Eleven years later, Vasco da Gama brought a Portuguese fleet around Africa to India, opening a sea route to Asia. These initiatives gave Portugal a virtual monopoly on Far Eastern trade for some time.

The new trade routes gave strategic importance to the islands that lie in the Atlantic off the west coast of Africa and Europe. Spain and Portugal vied for control of the Canary Islands, located 800 miles southwest of the Iberian peninsula. Spain eventually prevailed in 1496 by defeating the islands' inhabitants. Portugal

---

(margin annotation) ?

WHAT BENEFITS to European princes, merchants, and traders did exploration provide?

(handwritten margin note) What technological advances made exploration possible?

QUICK REVIEW

Discovery and Exploration

- Europeans sought access to Asian spices.
- Technological innovations made longer sea voyages possible.
- State sponsorship funded voyages of exploration.

Advances in ship design, including the development of the caravel pictured in this fifteenth-century woodcut, made transoceanic voyages possible. The arrangement of sails allowed the caravel to catch the trade winds and move more quickly across the high seas.

The Granger Collection, New York.

(handwritten note at bottom) ⊛ Bartolomeu Dias   ⊛ Vasco da Gama

acquired Madeira and the Cape Verde Islands, along with a set of tiny islands off Africa's Guinea Coast.

Sugar, like Asian spices, commanded high prices in Europe, so the conquerors of the Atlantic islands began to cultivate sugar cane on them on large plantations worked by slave labor. In the Canaries, the Spanish first enslaved the native inhabitants. When disease and exhaustion reduced their numbers, the Spanish brought in African slaves, often purchased from Portuguese traders.

These island societies, in which a small European master class dominated a much larger population of native peoples or imported African slaves, were to provide a model for Spain's and Portugal's later exploitation of their American colonies. As early as 1494, Christopher Columbus wrote to Ferdinand and Isabella of Spain to suggest that Caribbean islanders could be sold as slaves in order to cover the costs of exploration.

CHRISTOPHER COLUMBUS

Columbus was not the first European to believe that he could reach Asia by sailing westward. The idea developed logically during the fifteenth century as mariners gained knowledge and experience from their exploits in the Atlantic and around Africa. Columbus himself may have gained valuable experience on a voyage to Iceland. He also read widely in geographical treatises and paid close attention to the stories and rumors that circulated among mariners.

Most Europeans knew that the world was round, but most also scoffed at the idea of a westward voyage to Asia, believing that it would take so long, it would exhaust any ship's supplies. Columbus's confidence that he could make the voyage grew from a mistaken calculation of the earth's circumference as 18,000 (rather than 24,000) miles, which led him to conclude that Asia lay just 3,500 miles west of the Canary Islands. Columbus first sought financial support from the king of Portugal, whose advisers warned him that he would starve at sea before reaching Asia. Undaunted, he turned to Portugal's rival, Spain.

Columbus tried to convince Ferdinand and Isabella that his plan suited Spain's national goals: Spain could grow rich from Asian trade, send Christian missionaries to Asia (a goal in keeping with the religious ideals of the *reconquista*), and perhaps enlist the Great Khan of China as an ally in the long struggle with Islam. If he failed, the "enterprise of the Indies" would cost little. The Spanish monarchs nonetheless kept Columbus waiting nearly seven years—until 1492, when the last Muslim stronghold at Granada fell to Spanish forces—before they gave him their support.

After thirty-three days at sea, Columbus and his men made landfall. Although puzzled not to find the fabled cities of China or Japan, they still believed they had reached Asia. Three more voyages, between 1493 and 1504, however, failed to yield clear evidence of an Asian landfall or substantiate Columbus's reports of "great mines of gold and other metals" and spices in abundance.

Obsessed with the wealth he had promised himself and others, Columbus and his men turned violent, sacking the villages of Tainos and Caribs and demanding tribute in gold. The Spanish forced native gangs to pan rivers for the precious nuggets. Dissatisfied with the meager results, Columbus sought to enslave islanders, a desperate attempt to show that the Indies could yield a profit. Queen Isabella initially opposed the enslavement of people she considered to be new Spanish subjects. Within thirty years of Columbus's first voyage, however, Spanish exploitation of native labor had brought the populations of many Caribbean islands close to extinction.

Columbus died in Spain in 1506, still convinced he had found Asia. What he had done was to set in motion a process that would transform both sides of the Atlantic. It would eventually bring wealth to many Europeans and immense suffering to Native Americans and Africans.

QUICK REVIEW

Christopher Columbus
- Most Europeans knew the earth was round.
- Columbus convinced the Spanish monarchs to support his voyage.
- Columbus died in 1506 still believing he had found Asia.

Christopher Columbus by Italian artist Sebastiano del Piombo. The explorer is dressed in the finery of a prosperous Italian Renaissance gentleman including a tricorn hat and sumptuous mantle. 1519 oil on canvas.

Ewing Galloway, Index Stock Imagery, Inc.

(handwritten margin notes)

⊛ conquistadors

⊛ Juan Ponce de Leon

W WHERE TO LEARN MORE

★ St. Augustine, Florida
www.augustine.com

⊛ Hernán Cortés

⊘ How does small pox play a role in the Spanish conquest of America?

⊛ Moctezuma
⊛ Francisco Pizarro

SPANISH CONQUEST AND COLONIZATION

Of all European nations, Spain was best suited to take advantage of Columbus's discovery. Its experience with the *reconquista* gave it both a religious justification for conquest (bringing Christianity to nonbelievers) and an army of seasoned soldiers—*conquistadores*. In addition, during the *reconquista* and the conquest of the Canary Islands, Spain's rulers had developed efficient techniques for controlling newly conquered lands that could be applied to New World colonies.

The Spanish first established outposts on Cuba, Puerto Rico, and Jamaica (see Map 1–3, p. 21). The conquistadores, who were more interested in finding gold and slaves than in creating permanent settlements, attacked Taino and Carib villages and killed or captured the inhabitants. By 1524, the Tainos had all but died out; the Caribs survived on more isolated islands until the eighteenth century. Spanish soldiers then ventured to the mainland. Juan Ponce de León led an expedition to Florida in 1513. In that same year, Vasco Núñez de Balboa arrived in Central America, crossing the isthmus of Panama to the Pacific Ocean.

In 1519, Hernán Cortés led a force of six hundred men to the coast of Mexico. "I and my companions," he declared, "suffer from a disease of the heart which can be cured only with gold." By 1521, Cortés and his men had conquered the powerful Aztec empire. The Spanish soldiers also discovered riches beyond their wildest dreams. They "picked up the gold and fingered it like monkeys," reported one Aztec witness. They were "transported by joy, as if their hearts were illuminated and made new."

The swift, decisive Spanish victory over a more numerous enemy depended on several factors. Spanish guns and horses often enabled them to overwhelm larger groups of Aztec foot soldiers armed with spears and wooden swords edged with obsidian. Cortés also benefited from divisions within the Aztec empire, acquiring indispensable allies among subject Indians who resented Aztec domination. Cortés led only six hundred Spanish soldiers but eventually gained 200,000 Indian allies eager to throw off Aztec rule.

An even more significant contribution to this quick victory was the fact that Indians lacked resistance to European diseases. One of Cortés's men was infected with smallpox, which soon devastated the native population. Nearly 40 percent of the inhabitants of central Mexico died of smallpox within a year. Other diseases followed, including typhus, measles, and influenza. By 1600, the population of Mexico may have declined from over 15 million to less than a million people.

Aztec society and culture collapsed in the face of appalling mortality. One survivor recalled, "The sick were so utterly helpless that they could only lie on their beds like corpses, unable to move their limbs or even their heads. . . . If they did move their bodies, they screamed with pain." Early in their bid to gain control of the Aztec empire, the Spanish seized Moctezuma, the Aztec king, and eventually put him to death. His successor died of disease less than three months after gaining the throne.

In 1532, Francisco Pizarro and 180 men discovered the Inca empire high in the Peruvian Andes. Taking advantage of a civil war within the empire following its ruler's death, the Spaniards captured Cuzco, the Inca capital, and established a new one at Lima.

By 1550, Spain's New World empire extended from the Caribbean through Mexico to Peru. It was administered from Spain by the Council of the Indies. The council aimed to project royal authority into every village in New Spain in order to maintain political control and extract as much wealth as possible from the land and its people.

For more than a century, Spanish ships crossed the Atlantic carrying seemingly limitless treasure from the colonies. The colonial rulers subjected the native inhabitants of New Spain to compulsory tribute payments and forced labor.

MAP 1–3

Spanish, English, and French Settlements in North America in the Sixteenth Century By the end of the sixteenth century, only Spain had established permanent settlements in North America. French outposts in Canada and at Fort Caroline, as well as the English settlement at Roanoke, failed to thrive. European rivalries for North America, however, would intensify after 1600.

BASED ON this map, what factors might help to explain why Spain was more successful in the establishment of permanent settlements before 1600 than either France or England? Do you think geographic location (climate, terrain, etc.) may have played a role?

Smallpox wreaked havoc among Native Americans who lacked biological resistance to European diseases. This drawing by Aztec illustrators shows Aztec victims of a smallpox epidemic that struck Tenochtitlán in 1520. Historians estimate that up to 40 percent of the population of central Mexico died within a year. This catastrophic decline weakened the Aztecs' ability to resist the Spanish conquest of their land.

The Granger Collection, New York.

(handwritten notes in margin):
⊛ Hernán de Soto.
⊛ Francisco Vasquez de Coronado.
⊛ St. Augustine.

1–5
Bartolomé de las Casas,
"Of the Island of Hispaniola"
(1542)

(handwritten notes in margin):
⊛ Bartolomé de las Casas.
⊛ Black Legend.

Tens of thousands of Indians toiled in silver mines in Peru and Bolivia and on sugar plantations in the Caribbean. When necessary, Spaniards imported African slaves to supplement a native labor force ravaged by disease and exhaustion.

The desire for gold eventually lured Spaniards farther into North America. In 1528, an expedition to Florida ended in the deaths of nearly all Spanish intruders when they provoked an attack by Apalachee Indians [see American Views, "Cabeza de Vaca among the Indians (1530)" p. 5]. In 1539, Hernán de Soto led an expedition from Florida to the Mississippi River. Along the way, the Spaniards harassed native peoples, demanding provisions, burning villages, and capturing women to be servants and concubines. They also exposed the Indians to deadly European diseases. The expedition kept up its rampage for three years, turning toward Mexico only after de Soto died in 1542. In these same years, Francisco Vásquez de Coronado led three hundred troops on an equally destructive expedition through present-day Arizona, New Mexico, and Colorado on a futile search for gold and precious stones.

The failure to find gold and silver halted the Spanish attempt to extend their empire to the north. By the end of the sixteenth century, they maintained just two precarious footholds north of Mexico. One was at St. Augustine, on Florida's Atlantic coast. Founded in 1565, this fortified outpost served as a naval base to defend Spanish treasure fleets from raids by English and French privateers. The other settlement was located far to the west in what is now New Mexico. Juan de Oñate, on a futile search for silver mines, claimed the region for Spain in 1598 and proceeded to antagonize the area's inhabitants. Having earned the enmity of the Pueblo people—astonishing even his own superiors with his brutality—Oñate barely managed to keep his tiny colony together.

The conquistadores' bloody tactics aroused protest back in Spain. The Indians' most eloquent advocate was Bartolomé de Las Casas, a Dominican priest shamed by his own role (as a layman) in the conquest of Hispaniola. Las Casas wrote *In Defense of the Indians*, including graphic descriptions of native sufferings. Instead of eliciting Spanish reforms, however, his work inspired Protestant Europeans to create the "Black Legend," an exaggerated story according to which a fanatical Catholic Spain sought to spread its control at any cost.

Meanwhile, between 1500 and 1650, an estimated 181 tons of gold and 16,000 tons of silver were shipped from the New World to Spain, making it the richest and most powerful state in Europe. But this influx of American treasure had unforeseen consequences that would soon undermine Spanish predominance.

In 1492, the Spanish crown expelled from Spain all Jews who refused to become Christians. The refugees included many leading merchants who had contributed significantly to Spain's economy. The remaining Christian merchants, now awash in American riches, saw no reason to invest in new trade or productive enterprises that might have sustained the economy once the flow of New World treasure diminished. As a result, Spain's economy eventually stagnated.

OVERVIEW

THE COLUMBIAN EXCHANGE

	From Old World to New World	From New World to Old World
Diseases	Smallpox, measles, plague, typhus, influenza, yellow fever, diphtheria, scarlet fever	Syphilis
Animals	Horses, cattle, pigs, sheep, goats, donkeys, mules, black rats, honeybees, cockroaches	Turkeys
Plants	Wheat, sugar, barley, coffee, rice, dandelion and other weeds	Maize, beans, peanut, potato, sweet potato, manioc, squash, papaya, guava, tomato, avocado, pineapple, chili pepper, cocoa, apples, peaches, pears, plums

Source: Adapted from Alfred Crosby Jr., *The Columbian Exchange: Biological and Cultural Consequences of 1492* (1972).

The flood of American gold and silver also inflated prices throughout Europe, hurting workers, whose wages failed to rise as fast, and aristocrats, dependent on fixed rents from their estates. Most damaging, Spain's monarchs wasted their American wealth fighting expensive wars in Europe that ultimately only weakened the nation. By 1600, some disillusioned Spaniards were arguing that the conquest had brought more problems than benefits to their country.

THE COLUMBIAN EXCHANGE

Spain's long-term economic decline was just one of many consequences of the conquest of the New World. In the long run, the biological consequences of contact—what one historian has called the **Columbian exchange**—proved to be the most momentous (see the overview table "The Columbian Exchange").

The most catastrophic result of the exchange was the exposure of Native Americans to Old World diseases. Epidemics of smallpox, measles, typhus, and influenza struck Native Americans with great force, killing half, and sometimes as much as 90 percent, of the people in communities exposed to them. The only American disease to infect the Old World was syphilis, which appeared in Spain just after Columbus returned from his first voyage.

The Columbian exchange also introduced Old World livestock to the New World. Columbus brought horses, sheep, cattle, pigs, and goats with him on his second voyage in 1493. Native Americans had few domesticated animals and initially marveled at these large beasts. However, with few natural predators to limit their numbers, livestock populations boomed in the New World, competing with native mammals, such as bison, for good grazing. The use of horses also often gave European soldiers a decisive military advantage in conflicts with Indians.

But the introduction of European livestock created opportunities for Yaquis, Pueblos, and other peoples in the American Southwest, who began to raise cattle and sheep. By the eighteenth century, Plains Indians had not only adopted horses but also become exceptionally skilled riders. The men found it much easier to hunt buffalo on horseback than on foot, and the women valued horses as beasts of burden.

1–9
The Columbian Exchange (1590)

ⓐ Columbian Exchange.
ⓟ Describe the significance of the columbian Exchange on the world?

Columbian exchange The transatlantic exchange of plants, animals, and diseases that occurred after the first European contact with the Americas.

European ships carried unintentional passengers as well, including the black rat and honeybees, both previously unknown in the New World. Ships also brought weeds such as thistles and dandelions, whose seeds were often embedded in hay for animal fodder.

Europeans brought a variety of seeds and plants in order to grow familiar foods. Columbus's men planted wheat, chickpeas, melons, onions, and fruit trees on Caribbean islands. European plants did not always fare well, at least not everywhere in the New World, so Europeans learned to cultivate native foods, such as corn, tomatoes, squash, beans, and potatoes, as well as nonfood plants such as tobacco and cotton. They carried many of these plants back to Europe, enriching Old World diets with new foods.

(handwritten) ⊛ Treaty of Tordesillas. Section 3 · pg 24–27.

COMPETITION FOR A CONTINENT

HOW DID the French, English, and Spanish fare in their early efforts in the New World?

In 1494, the pope resolved the conflicting claims of Portugal and Spain for New World territory with the **Treaty of Tordesillas.** The treaty drew a north-south line approximately 1,100 miles west of the Cape Verde Islands. Spain received all lands west of the line, while Portugal held sway to the east. This limited Portugal's New World empire to Brazil, where settlers followed the precedent of the Atlantic island colonies and established sugar plantations worked by slave labor. But the treaty also protected Portugal's claims in Africa and Asia, which lay east of the line.

France and England, of course, rejected the papal grant of the Western Hemisphere to Spain and Portugal. Initially, domestic troubles—largely sparked by the Protestant Reformation—distracted the two countries from the pursuit of empire. By the close of the sixteenth century, both France and England insisted on their rights to New World lands, but neither had created a permanent settlement to support its claim.

EARLY FRENCH EFFORTS IN NORTH AMERICA

France was a relative latecomer to New World exploration. Preoccupied with European affairs, France's rulers paid little attention to America until news of Corté's exploits in Mexico arrived in the 1520s.

In 1524, King Francis I sponsored a voyage by Giovanni de Verrazano, an Italian navigator, who mapped the North American coast from present-day South Carolina to Maine. During the 1530s and 1540s, the French mariner Jacques Cartier made three voyages in search of rich mines to rival those of Mexico and Peru. He explored the St. Lawrence River up to what is now Montreal, hoping to discover a water route through the continent to Asia (what came to be called the Northwest Passage). On his second voyage, in 1535, he and his crew almost froze to death and suffered from scurvy, a disease caused by a lack of Vitamin C. Some of the men survived because the Iroquois showed them how to make a vitamin-rich concoction of boiled white cedar needles and bark.

On his third voyage, in 1541, Cartier was to serve under the command of a nobleman, Jean François de la Rocque, sieur de Roberval, who was commissioned by the king to establish a permanent settlement in Canada. Unable to recruit colonists, he finally set sail in 1542, taking convicts as settlers. Cartier had sailed ahead, gathered samples of what he thought were gold and diamonds, and returned to France without Roberval's permission.

Roberval's expedition was poorly organized, and his cruel treatment of the convicts provoked several uprisings. The Iroquois, suspicious of repeated French intrusions on their lands, saw no reason to help them. A year after they arrived in Canada, Roberval and the surviving colonists were back in France. Their return

Treaty of Tordesillas Treaty negotiated by the pope in 1494 to resolve the territorial claims of Spain and Portugal.

coincided with news that the gold brought back by Cartier was iron pyrite (fool's gold) and the diamonds were quartz crystals.

Disappointed with their Canadian expeditions, the French made a few brief forays to the south, establishing outposts in what is now South Carolina in 1562 and Florida in 1564. They soon abandoned the Carolina colony (though not before the starving settlers resorted to cannibalism), and Spanish forces captured the Florida fort. Then, back in France, civil war broke out between Catholics and Protestants. Renewed interest in colonization would have to await the return of peace at home.

ENGLISH ATTEMPTS IN THE NEW WORLD

The English were quicker than the French to stake a claim to the New World but no more successful at colonization. In 1497, King Henry VII sent John Cabot, an Italian mariner, to explore eastern Canada on England's behalf, but neither Henry nor his wealthier subjects would invest the funds necessary to follow up on Cabot's discoveries.

The lapse in English activity in the New World stemmed from religious troubles at home. Between 1534 and 1558, England changed its official religion several times. King Henry VIII took up the Protestant cause when the pope refused to annul his marriage to Catherine of Aragon. In 1534, Henry declared himself the head of a separate Church of England and seized the Catholic Church's English property. But in 1553, Mary—daughter of the spurned Catherine of Aragon—became queen and tried to bring England back to Catholicism. She had nearly three hundred Protestants burned at the stake for their beliefs (earning her the nickname "Bloody Mary"), and many others went into exile in Europe.

After Mary's death in 1558, her half-sister Elizabeth, a committed Protestant, became queen, restoring Protestantism as the state religion, bringing stability to the nation, and renewing England's interest in the New World. She and her subjects saw colonization not only as a way to gain wealth and political advantage but also as a Protestant crusade against Catholic domination.

England's first target for colonization, however, was not America but Ireland. Located less than sixty miles west of England and populated by Catholics, Ireland threatened to become a base from which Spain or another Catholic power might invade England. Elizabeth launched a series of brutal expeditions that destroyed Irish villages and slaughtered the inhabitants. Several veterans of these campaigns later took part in New World colonization and drew on their Irish experience for guidance.

The English transferred their assumptions about Irish "savages" to Native Americans. Englishmen in America frequently observed similarities between Indians and the Irish. "The natives of New England," noted one Englishman, "are accustomed to build their houses much like the wild Irish." When Indians resisted conquest, the English recalled the Irish example, claiming that native "savagery" required brutal suppression.

The Irish experience also influenced English ideas about colonial settlement. English conquerors set up "plantations" surrounded by palisades on seized Irish lands, importing Protestant tenants from England and Scotland to farm the land. Native Irish people were excluded. English colonists in America followed this precedent when they established plantations that separated English and native peoples.

Sir Humphrey Gilbert, a notoriously cruel veteran of the Irish campaigns, composed a treatise to convince Queen Elizabeth to support New World colonization. The queen authorized several exploratory voyages, including Martin Frobisher's three trips in 1576–1578 in search of the Northwest Passage to Asia. Frobisher failed to find the elusive passage and sent back shiploads of glittering ore that proved to be fool's gold. Elizabeth had better luck in allowing privateers, such as John Hawkins and Francis Drake, to raid Spanish ships and New World ports for gold and silver.

 1–10
Thomas Harriot, The Algonquian Peoples of the Atlantic Coast (1588)

Meanwhile, Gilbert continued to promote New World settlement, arguing that it would increase England's trade and provide a place for the nation's unemployed people. Like many of his contemporaries, Gilbert believed that England's "surplus" population threatened social order. The population was indeed growing, and economic changes often made it difficult for people to support themselves. Gilbert suggested offering free land in America to English families willing to emigrate.

In 1578, Gilbert received permission to set up a colony along the North American coast. It took him five years to organize an expedition to Newfoundland, which he claimed for England. After sailing southward seeking a more favorable site for a colony, Gilbert headed home, only to be lost at sea during an Atlantic storm. His half-brother, Sir Walter Raleigh (another veteran of the Irish wars), immediately took up the cause of English colonization.

In 1585 Raleigh sent men to build a settlement on Roanoke Island off the Carolina coast. Most colonists were soldiers fresh from Ireland who refused to grow their own food, insisting that the Roanoke Indians should feed them. When the local chief, Wingina, organized native resistance, they killed him. Eventually, the colonists, disappointed not to have found gold or precious stones and exhausted by a harsh winter, returned to England in 1586.

Two members of these early expeditions, however, left a more positive legacy. Thomas Hariot studied the Roanoke and Croatoan Indians and identified plants and animals in the area, hoping that some might prove to be profitable commodities. John White drew maps and painted a series of watercolors depicting the natives and the coastal landscape. When Raleigh tried once more, in 1587, to found a colony, he chose White to be its leader.

This attempt also failed. The ship captain dumped the settlers—who, for the first time, included women and children—on Roanoke Island so that he could pursue Spanish treasure ships. White waited until his granddaughter, Virginia Dare (the first English child born in America), was safely born and then sailed to England for supplies. But the outbreak of war with Spain delayed his return for three years. Spain had gathered an immense fleet to invade England, and all English ships were needed for defense. Although England defeated the Armada in 1588, White could not obtain a relief ship for Roanoke until 1590.

White found the colony deserted. Digging through the ruins of the village, he found "my books torn from the covers, the frames of some of my pictures and Maps rotten and spoiled with rain." He also saw the word *CROATOAN* carved on a post and assumed that the colonists had moved to nearby Croatoan Island. But bad weather prevented him from searching there. For years, English and Spanish mariners reported seeing white people along the coast of Chesapeake Bay. But no Roanoke colonists were ever found.

England's interest in colonization did not wane. In 1584, Richard Hakluyt had aroused enthusiasm for America by writing the "Discourse of Western Planting" for the queen and her advisors. He argued that England would prosper from the expansion of trade and the sale of New World commodities. Once the Indians were civilized, Hakluyt added, they would eagerly purchase English goods. Equally important, England could plant Protestant Christianity in the New World and prevent the power of "the Spanish king from flowing over all the face . . . of America."

Hakluyt's arguments fired the imaginations of many people, and the defeat of the Spanish Armada emboldened England to challenge Spain's New World dominance. The experience of Roanoke should have tempered that enthusiasm. The colony's fate underscored the need for adequate funding, the unsuitability of soldiers as colonists, and the need to maintain good relations with the Indians. But the English were slow to learn these lessons. As it was, the sixteenth century ended with no permanent English settlement in the New World.

FROM THEN TO NOW
The Disappearance of Cod off the Grand Banks

Not long after John Cabot returned from his voyage to America in 1497, rumors began to swirl in port towns and European capitals alike. The Italian mariner who had sailed on behalf of England, it was said, had discovered astonishingly rich fishing grounds. One envious diplomat reported to the duke of Milan that Cabot and his men had caught enormous numbers of cod simply by dropping weighted baskets into the sea. As it happened, Basque fishermen sailing from ports in northern Spain and south-western France already knew about these fishing grounds. But Cabot's discovery spread the news and soon fishermen from all over western Europe scrambled to capture some of the bounty for themselves. By the 1550s, over a hundred ships a year traveled from French ports alone to fish in the waters of the Grand Banks off the coasts of Newfoundland and Labrador.

In 1994, on the eve of the five-hundredth anniversary of Cabot's historic voyage, Brian Tobin, a Canadian fisheries minister, reported that cod had become so scarce in the Grand Banks that fishing was no longer commercially viable. He announced that a moratorium on Atlantic cod fishing, first declared in 1992, would have to be extended. This measure was the latest in a series of efforts to address the decline in the cod population. In 1977, Canada's government had prohibited foreign fishing vessels from working within 200 miles of the Canadian coast. Nine years later, foreign boats fishing just beyond the 200-mile limit were no longer allowed to visit the city of St. John's in Newfoundland for repairs and supplies. Although these measures were designed mainly to protect Canadian fisheries from competition rather than to address issues of conservation, they clearly recognized that a valuable resource was in grave danger.

How had such abundant codfish stocks declined so dramatically? Ecological and historical factors combined to produce this result. Cod prefer to swim near the ocean floor in shallow waters, and migrate to even shallower places rich in plankton and krill—such as the Grand Banks—when they are ready to spawn. These locations are particularly vulnerable to climatic change, and that in turn affects the cod. Ten years after Canada declared the moratorium on fishing, cod populations on the Grand Banks have yet to rebound. Some scientists speculate that the depletion of the Earth's ozone layer may be allowing ultraviolet rays to penetrate shallower ocean waters, killing off young cod at a high rate.

Centuries of fishing have also taken their toll. Cabot's voyage sparked tremendous interest in the Grand Banks fisheries. By the middle of the sixteenth century, 60 percent of all the fish eaten in Europe was cod, and most of it came from the Grand Banks region. English and French fishing enterprises found particularly lucrative markets in Mediterranean countries, whose primarily Catholic populations had to abstain from eating meat on Fridays and during the six weeks of Lent because of religious restrictions. By the eighteenth century, New England colonists, plying the waters off their own coast as well as near the Grand Banks, had initiated a thriving trade with the West Indies, where planters purchased relatively cheap salted cod to feed their slaves. After the Revolution, victorious Americans insisted that Great Britain recognize their "right to take fish of every kind on the Grand Bank." This provision became part of the 1783 Treaty of Paris, testifying to the continued significance of the fishing industry.

Economic competition also encouraged technological developments: By the early nineteenth century, most fishermen had switched from using handlines—single baited hooks fastened to a weight and dropped in the water—to longlines, consisting of ropes anywhere from half a mile to four or more miles long, with baited hooks attached every three feet or so. Gill nets, positioned just above the ocean floor to catch "ground feeders" like cod, eventually made enormous catches possible. These changes, combined with the transition from sailing vessels to boats using first steam power and then diesel fuel, spelled doom for the once-plentiful supplies of cod on the Grand Banks.

Experts differ on whether cod populations can recover. In addition to the possible effects of climatic change, cod continue to be threatened by overfishing. In February of 2002, Canadian officials investigated reports of foreign boats ignoring the moratorium on cod and infringing on the 200-mile limit. The long-term legacy of John Cabot's voyage may well be the disappearance of the resource that drew him and so many early European adventurers to North America in the first place.

CONCLUSION

WHAT WERE the consequences of contact between the Old and New Worlds?

After Columbus's first voyage, Europeans, eager for wealth and power, came by the thousands to a continent that just a hundred years earlier they had not dreamed existed. Africans came in even greater numbers to the Caribbean, Mexico, and Brazil, forced to labor for white masters in unfamiliar lands. In many parts of the Americas, native peoples encountered white and black strangers whose presence often destroyed their accustomed ways of life.

In 1600 only Spain had established North American colonies. Though its New World dominance seemed secure, even Spain had struggled to expand north of Mexico. Virtually the entire continent north of the Rio Grande remained firmly in Indian hands. Except in Mexico and the Caribbean, Europeans had merely touched the continent's shores. In 1600, native peoples still greatly outnumbered European and African immigrants. The next century, however, brought powerful challenges both to native control and to the Spanish monopoly of settlement.

SUMMARY

Native American Societies Before 1492 On the eve of contact, Native American societies were coexisting much as they had over the centuries before, having developed distinctive cultures based on the regions in which they lived. As many Native American societies continued in their development of agriculture, others concentrated on fishing and tracking game. Mayan and Aztec societies were among a series of complex, literate, urban cultures making up Mesoamerican civilizations from central Mexico into Central America.

West African Societies West African societies, although they had developed trade networks with Europe and the Middle East, still consisted mostly of farmers, not merchants. Family connections helped define each person's place in society, and religious beliefs magnified the powerful influence of family on African life. Though slavery was not yet a major source of export, slavery had long been a part of West African society.

Western Europe on the Eve of Exploration In Western Europe, recovery from the Hundred Years' War and the Black Death meant a redefinition of labor and productivity. In some parts of Europe, economic improvement encouraged an extraordinary movement known as the Renaissance—a "rebirth" of interest in the classical civilizations of Greece and Rome. European society was patriarchal, with men dominating political and economic life. And, by the end of the fifteenth century, after more than one hundred years of incessant conflict, a measure of stability had returned to Western Europe.

Contact Portugal, Spain, France, and England were competing to establish footholds on other continents in an intense scramble for riches and dominance as the fifteenth century came to a close. Explorers like Columbus and Ponce de Leon crossed the Atlantic in search of new lands. The dawn of European exploration changed both sides of the Atlantic forever.

Competition for a New Continent In 1494, the pope resolved the conflicting claims of Portugal and Spain for New World territory with the Treaty of Tordesillas. France and England, of course, rejected the grant and insisted on their rights to New World land. Although the English were quicker than the French to stake a claim to the New World, neither was very successful at early colonization. However, England's interest in colonization did not wane, and, although the sixteenth century ended with no permanent English settlement in the New World, such a settlement was not far away.

REVIEW QUESTIONS

1. How did the Aztecs describe the Spanish ships off the coast of Mexico to Moctezuma? What details most captured their attention?

2. What were the similarities and differences between men's and women's roles in Native American, West African, and European societies? How did differences lead to misunderstandings?

3. Many of the first European colonizers in North America were military veterans. How did this affect their relations with Indian peoples?

4. Why did Spain so quickly become the dominant colonial power in North America? What advantages did it enjoy over France and England?

5. How did religion affect early European overseas colonization? Did religious factors encourage or interfere with European expansion?

KEY TERMS

Aztecs   (p. 9)
Cahokia   (p. 10)
Columbian exchange   (p. 23)

predestination   (p. 17)
Protestants   (p. 17)
reconquista   (p. 17)

Reformation   (p. 17)
Tordesillas, Treaty of   (p. 24)

WHERE TO LEARN MORE

🛡 **Cahokia Mounds State Historic Site, Collinsville, Illinois.** This site, occupied from A.D. 600–1500, was the largest Mississippian community in eastern North America. It now includes numerous exhibits, and archaeological excavations continue in the vicinity. The website, **www.siue.edu/CAHOKIAMOUNDS**, contains information and photos of archaeological excavations, as well as a link to a virtual tour.

🛡 **Mashantucket Pequot Museum, Mashantucket, Connecticut.** This tribally owned and operated complex offers a view of eastern Woodlands Indian life, focusing on the Pequots of eastern Connecticut. Exhibits include dioramas, films, interactive programs, and a reconstructed sixteenth-century Pequot village. The homepage for the Mashantucket Pequot Museum and Research Center is: **www.mashantucket.com**

🛡 **Mesa Verde National Park, Colorado.** Occupied by Ancestral Puebloan peoples as early as A.D. 550, the area contains a variety of sites, from early pithouses to spectacular cliff dwellings. The official National Park webpage for Mesa Verde is **www.nps.gov/meve.** Information on individual houses and sites within the park, plus travel and lodging information can be found at: **www.mesa.verde.national-park.com**

🛡 **St. Augustine, Florida.** Founded in 1565, St. Augustine is the site of the first permanent Spanish settlement in North America. Today the restored community resembles a Spanish colonial town, with narrow, winding streets and seventeenth- and eighteenth-century buildings. The site also contains the restored Castillo de San Marcos, now a national park. The official website for Historic St. Augustine, **www.oldcity.com/his2.html**, provides considerable information about the origins and development of the Spanish settlement.

 For additional study resources for this chapter, go to:
www.prenhall.com/goldfield/chapter1

These seventeen ships . . . made a long, a troublesome, and costly voyage . . . with contrary winds after they set sail, and so scattered with mists and tempests that few of them arrived together . . .

Map of New Netherland; detail from map entitled "Novi Belgii . . ." showing a view of New Amsterdam by Nicholas J. Visscher, c. 1655.

Ætatis suæ 21 Aᵒ. 1616.

Matoaks als Rebecka daughter to the mighty Prince
Powhatan Emperour of Attanoughkomouck als Virginia
converted and baptized in the Christian faith and
Wife to the Worll Mr Tho. Rolff.

2

TRANSPLANTATION
1600–1685

WHAT ROLE did the fur trade
and fur traders play in the success
of French colonies?

HOW DID the English colonies in and around
Jamestown of the early seventeenth century differ from
those in New England later in that same century?

WHY WAS tobacco so
important to the economies
of the Southern colonies?

WHAT ROLE did religion
play in the establishment of
the New England colonies?

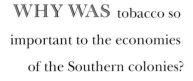

HOW WERE the Dutch
able to successfully establish New Netherland
along the eastern seaboard of America?

HOW WERE the societies of
the West Indies and Carolina different from
societies in other parts of North America?

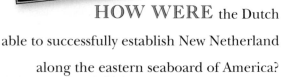

Canoe, five Naviculæ
e corticibus arborum.

Boston in New England
March 28, 1631

To the Right Honorable my very good lady, the Lady Bridget, Countess of Lincoln, Madam:

I have . . . thought fit to commit to memory our present condition and what hath befallen us since our arrival here. . . . [I] must do [so] rudely, having yet no table nor other room to write in than by the fireside upon my knee in this sharp winter. . . .

[In] April 1630 we set sail from old England with four good ships. And in May following, eight more followed, two having gone before in February and March and two more following in June and August, besides another set out by a private merchant. These seventeen ships arrived all safe in New England for the increase of the plantation here this year 1630, but made a long, a troublesome and costly voyage, being all windbound long in England and hindered with contrary winds after they set sail, and so scattered with mists and tempests that few of them arrived together. . . .

[Once we disembarked in mid-June, after more than nine weeks at sea] we began to consult of the place of our sitting down, for Salem, where we landed, pleased us not. And to that purpose some were sent to the Bay to search up the rivers for a convenient place. . . . [We] found a place . . . three leagues up Charles river, and thereupon unshipped our goods into other vessels and with much cost and labor brought them in July to Charlestowne, but there receiving advertisements by some of the late arrived ships from London and Amsterdam of some French preparations against us . . . we were forced to change counsel and for our present shelter to plant dispersedly. . . . This dispersion troubled some of us, but help it we could not. . . . The best counsel we could find out was to build a fort to retire to, in some convenient place, if an enemy pressed thereunto, after we should have fortified ourselves against the injuries of wet and cold.

Everett Emerson, ed., *Letters from New England: the Massachusetts Bay Colony,* 1629–1638 (Amherst, 1976).

IMAGE KEY
for pages 30–31

a. Several sugarcane stems.
b. Map of New Netherland showing a view of New Amsterdam.
c. Beaver
d. Matoaka, or Pocahontas (c. 1595 – 1617, the daughter of Native American Chief Powhatan, after her conversion to Christianity and marriage to settler John Rolfe under the new name Rebecca.
e. A tattered historical beaver hat from 1620.
f. Native American exchanges fur pelt for Western goods.
g. Tobacco plant.
h. John Winthrop, 1588 – 1649.
i. New Amsterdam traders bargaining with a view of trade transportation in the background.
j. African slaves working in a sugar mill in Brazil.

THOMAS DUDLEY, the man who wrote this letter, was 54 years old when he moved with his family to New England. Thomas and his wife Dorothy had six children ranging in age from 9 to 25 years old. Dudley had prospered in England by working as a steward for local aristocrats, including the Countess of Lincoln to whom he addressed his letter. A man of talent and education, he had been chosen as deputy governor of the new colony of Massachusetts and worried that it might not survive its first months.

The Countess of Lincoln, could not help but sense the contrast between her comfortable situation and the hardships Dudley endured. Neither could she miss this preoccupation with the French, who had established a colony in Canada. Remote as they were from Europe, the English colonists worried more about Old World enemies than about the Indians whose lands they now occupied.

The Dudleys ended up in Newtown (now Cambridge) and prospered. Thomas Dudley served four terms as governor and accumulated a large estate.

[handwritten: ⊛ Thomas Dudley]

He died in July 1653 at the age of 76, an unusually long life span for the seventeenth century. But Dudley could not have predicted such a happy outcome in the first difficult months following his voyage to America. His journey took place at a time of increased rivalry among European nations for New World territory. England's greatest adversaries were France and the Netherlands. Each nation scrambled to claim pieces of the North American mainland and islands in the Caribbean, hoping to match Spain's earlier success. As Thomas Dudley's letter suggests, this international race for overseas possessions was never far from colonists' minds.

2–2
Samuel de Champlain's Battle with the Iroquois, July 1609

[handwritten: section 1 pg. 33–34]

[handwritten: ✱ St. Lawrence River]

THE FRENCH IN NORTH AMERICA

The economic base of France's New World empire, known as New France, was the fur trade, which depended more on the control of waterways and alliances with Indians than on the occupation of land.

The focus of the French colony was the St. Lawrence River, which provided access to a vast interior populated by an abundance of beavers and by Indian peoples eager for trade. Because of its emphasis on the fur trade rather than extensive settlement, New France's population grew slowly in the seventeenth century. Its few, scattered villages were linked as closely to their Indian neighbors as to each other.

WHAT ROLE did the fur trade and fur traders play in the success of French colonies?

[handwritten: —N.A.; —population growth?]

THE DEVELOPMENT OF NEW FRANCE

As we saw in Chapter 1, French efforts to found American colonies in the late sixteenth century ended in failure, but French fishermen continued to visit the Newfoundland coast. Setting up frames onshore to dry their catch, they met Indians with furs to trade for European goods. The already strong market for furs in Europe soon expanded dramatically as broad-brimmed beaver fur hats became fashionable.

Once it was clear that a profit could be made in Canada, France's interest revived. French kings sold exclusive trading rights to merchants willing to set up outposts in Canada. But to succeed, the merchants needed to bring farmers to New France to produce food and other supplies for the traders.

Quebec, organized in 1608 by Samuel de Champlain, was the first permanent French settlement in Canada (see Map 2–1). It was inhabited for its first two decades by only a few dozen settlers. Thereafter, efforts to recruit colonists to New France intensified, and French Jesuits—members of a Catholic religious order founded during the Counter Reformation—sent missionaries to convert the Indians. In 1642, Montreal was founded as a religious and commercial center, and by the 1650s, the Jesuits claimed thousands of Indian converts, many of whom lived in native Christian communities.

By 1700, New France had about fifteen thousand settlers, less than 7 percent of the number of English colonists in mainland North America that same year. One observer reported that "if they are the least inclined to work," immigrants could prosper in Canada. Colonists generally lived in sturdier houses, enjoyed a better diet, and paid lower taxes than their relatives back home. They acquired land to pass on to their children with an ease that French

MAP EXPLORATION
To explore an interactive version of this map, go to
http://www.prenhall.com/goldfield2/map2.1

MAP 2–1
New France, c. 1650   By 1650, New France contained a number of thinly populated settlements along the St. Lawrence River Valley and the eastern shore of Lake Huron. Most colonists lived in Quebec and Montreal; other sites served mainly as fur-trading posts and Jesuit missions to the Huron Indians.

WHAT DOES this map tell you about the geographic location of many of the early French colonies in Canada? What do you think were among the critical geographic factors in the decisions France made in colonizing Canada?

[handwritten: ⊛ Quebec   ⊛ Samuel de champlain]

(?) *what major religion was practiced in New France?*

peasants could only envy. However, few French people moved to North America, and almost three out of four of those who did eventually returned to France.

Accounting for this reluctance to emigrate was Canada's reputation as a distant and inhospitable place. Rumors about frigid winters and surprise Indian attacks circulated among French peasants and villagers. In addition, the government required prospective settlers to be Catholic, reducing the pool from which they could be drawn.

Most settlers were sponsored by the government or by employers who paid their passage in return for three years of labor. Those who completed their terms of service received land. Most settlers were young men eager to marry and raise children to help them farm. But as late as 1666, only one out of three French settlers was female. Some young Frenchmen married Indian women. Others found brides from among the female orphans whom the French government paid to go to Canada in an attempt to remedy the sexual imbalance. Most young men, however, chose to go home to France.

THE FUR TRADE

Fur traders, not settlers, determined the colony's success. Furs were an ideal commodity—light, easy to transport, and very profitable. For the French, at least, the fur trade was also not very hard work. Indians, not Frenchmen, trapped the beavers, prepared the skins, and carried them from the interior to trading posts. French traders paid for the pelts with such goods as axes, knives, metal pots, and glass beads.

(?) *who actually trapped fur?*

The Indians understood trade as part of a broader process of alliance that involved the exchange of gifts and mutual military assistance. When Champlain approached the Hurons for trade, they insisted that the French agree to help them fight the Iroquois. By becoming Huron allies, the French acquired Iroquois enemies. Thereafter the security of the colony depended on the ability of its governors to handle delicate diplomatic relations with the Indians.

Beginning in 1663, the colony was ruled by a governor and an intendant, both royal appointees who in turn appointed several lesser officials. New France's settlers never developed institutions of self-government as English colonists did. The king also insisted on a strong military force to protect the colony from attack by Indian enemies or European rivals. He ordered the construction of forts and sent several companies of professional soldiers.

(X) HURON
(X) Iroquois
(X) coureur de BOIS

Yet colonial officials disobeyed orders from France when it suited them. Even though instructions from Paris prohibited westward expansion, the *intendant* in Quebec allowed explorers to move inland. By the 1670s, French traders and missionaries had reached the Mississippi River, and in 1681–1682, Robert, sieur de La Salle, followed it to the Gulf of Mexico, claiming the entire river valley (which he named Louisiana in honor of King Louis XIV) for France. Scores of independent fur traders, known as **coureurs de bois** ("woods runners"), roamed the forests, living and trading among the Indians there.

(X) RoBert de La Salle

coureur de bois French for "woods runner," an independent fur trader in New France.

section 2: pg. 34 – 37.

ENGLISH SETTLEMENT IN THE CHESAPEAKE

When the English again attempted to settle in America in 1607, they chose the lower Chesapeake Bay region. The new settlement, Jamestown, eventually developed into the prosperous colony of Virginia. The reason for Virginia's success was an American plant—tobacco—that commanded good prices from European consumers. Tobacco also underlay the economy of a neighboring colony, Maryland, and had a profound influence on the development of Chesapeake society.

(X) Jamestown.   (X) tobacco

THE ORDEAL OF EARLY VIRGINIA

In 1606, several English merchants, convinced that they could succeed where others had failed, petitioned King James I for a charter incorporating two companies, the *Virginia Company* and the *Plymouth Company,* to attempt New World settlement. James I issued a charter granting the companies two tracts of land along the mid-Atlantic coast. These **joint-stock companies** sold shares to investors (who expected a profit in return) to raise money for colonization.

On a peninsula about 50 miles up a river they named the James, in honor of their king, 104 colonists, all men, built a fortified settlement they called Jamestown (see Map 2–2). They immediately began searching for gold and exploring the James in search of the Northwest Passage to Asia. All they found were disappointment and suffering. The swampy region was a perfect breeding area for malarial mosquitoes and parasites carrying other diseases. The settlers neglected to plant crops, and their food supplies dwindled. By January 1608, only thirty-eight of them were still alive.

The colony's governing council turned to Captain John Smith for leadership. Just 28 years old, Smith had fought against Spain in the Netherlands and the Ottomans in Hungary. He imposed military discipline on Jamestown, organizing settlers into work gangs and decreeing that "he that will not worke shall not eate." His high-handed methods revived the colony but antagonized certain settlers. When a gun-powder explosion wounded Smith in 1609 and forced him to return to England, his enemies had him replaced as leader.

Once again, the colony nearly disintegrated. New settlers arrived, only to die of disease and starvation. Of the five hundred people in Jamestown in the autumn of 1609, just sixty remained alive by the spring of 1610—some of whom survived only by eating their dead companions. Facing financial ruin, company officials back in England tried to conceal the state of the colony. They reorganized the company twice and sent more settlers, including glassmakers, wine-growers, and silkmakers, in a desperate effort to find a marketable product. They experimented with harsh military discipline, with a legal code—the *Lawes Divine, Morall and Martiall*—that prescribed the death penalty for offenses as trivial as swearing or killing a chicken. When it became clear that such severity discouraged immigration, the company tried more positive inducements.

The first settlers had been expected to work together in return for food and other necessities. With no profits forthcoming, governors began assigning small plots of land to colonists who finished their terms of service to the company. In 1616, the company instituted the **headright system,** giving 50 acres to anyone who paid his own way to Virginia and an additional 50 for each person (or "head") he brought with him.

In 1619, three other important developments occurred. The company began transporting women to Virginia to become wives for planters and induce them to stay in the colony. It was also the year in which the first Africans arrived in Virginia, and the company created the first legislative body in English America, the

Joint-stock company Business enterprise in which a group of stockholders pooled their money to engage in trade or to fund colonizing expeditions.

headright system Instituted by the Virginia Company in 1616, this system gave fifty acres to anyone who paid his own way to Virginia and an additional fifty for each person (or "head") he brought with him.

MAP EXPLORATION

To explore an interactive version of this map, go to
http://www.prenhall.com/goldfield2/map2.2

MAP 2–2

English and Dutch Mainland Colonies in North America, c. 1655
Early English colonies clustered in two areas of the Atlantic seaboard—New England and the Chesapeake Bay. Between them lay Dutch New Netherlands, with settlements stretching up the Hudson River. The Dutch also acquired territory at the mouth of the Delaware River in 1655 when they seized a short-lived Swedish colony located there.

ON THE BASIS of this map, what about the geographic location of Dutch colonies was ideal for Dutch colonists? What about their locations might have been problematic?

CHRONOLOGY

1603–1625	James I reigns as king of England.
1607	Founding of English colonies at Jamestown and Sagadahoc.
1608	Establishment of French colony at Quebec.
1619	First Africans arrive in Jamestown. Virginia's House of Burgesses meets for the first time.
1620	Founding of Plymouth Colony in New England. Mayflower Compact signed.
1620s	Tobacco boom in Virginia.
1624	Dutch found colony of New Netherlands.
1625	Virginia becomes a royal colony. Fort Amsterdam founded.
1625–1649	Charles I reigns as king of England.
1627	English colony at Barbados founded.
1630	Massachusetts Bay Colony founded.
1630–1642	Great Migration to New England.
1634	Lord Baltimore (Cecilius Calvert) founds proprietary colony of Maryland.
1635–1636	Roger Williams banished from Massachusetts, founds Providence, Rhode Island.
1637	Anne Hutchinson banished from Massachusetts. Pequot War.
1638	New Haven colony founded.
1640s	Sugar cultivation and slavery established in West Indies.
1642–1660	English Civil War and Interregnum.
1649	Maryland's Act for Religious Toleration.
1660	Charles II restored to English throne; reigns until 1685.
1663	Founding of Carolina colony.
1664	New Netherlands conquered by the English, becomes New York. New Jersey established.
1673	French explorers reach the Mississippi River.
1681	Founding of Pennsylvania.

QUICK REVIEW

Powhatan, Indian Leader

- Chief of a confederacy of about thirty tribes.
- Besieged Jamestown when colonists began stealing corn.
- Instructed in English manners and religion by John Rolf.
- Father of Pocahontas.

House of Burgesses   The legislature of colonial Virginia. First organized in 1619, it was the first institution of representative government in the English colonies.

House of Burgesses, setting a precedent for the establishment of self-government in other English colonies. Landowners elected representatives to the House of Burgesses, which, subject to the approval of the company, made laws for Virginia.

The settlers were still unable to earn the company a profit. To make things worse, the headright system expanded English settlement beyond Jamestown, straining the already tense relations with the Indians.

The English settlement was in the heart of territory ruled by the Indian leader Powhatan, then at the peak of his power and chief of a confederacy of about thirty tribes with some fourteen thousand people. After an initial skirmish with English soldiers, he sent gifts of food, assuming that by accepting the gifts, the colonists acknowledged their dependence on him. Further action against the settlers seemed unnecessary, since they seemed fully capable of destroying themselves.

However, armed colonists began seizing corn from Indian villages whenever the natives refused to supply it. During one raid in 1609, John Smith held a pistol to the chest of Opechancanough, Powhatan's younger brother, until the Indians ransomed him with corn. Protesting that the English came "to invade my people and possess my Country," Powhatan besieged Jamestown and tried to starve the colony to extinction. The colony was saved by reinforcements from England. War with the Indians continued until 1614, when the colonist John Rolfe married Pocahontas, Powhatan's daughter. Pocahontas had briefly been held captive by the English during the war and had been instructed in English manners and religion by Rolfe. Sent to negotiate with Powhatan in the spring of 1614, Rolfe asked him for his daughter's hand. Powhatan gave his consent, and Pocahontas—baptized in the Church of England and renamed Rebecca—became Rolfe's wife.

Pocahontas died on a trip to England in 1617, severing the tie between her family and the English. Powhatan died in 1618, and Opechancanough succeeded him as chief. Still harboring intense resentment against the English, the new chief made plans to retaliate against them. Early in the morning on March 22, 1622, hundreds of Indian men traveled to the scattered English settlements, as if they meant to visit or trade. Instead they attacked the unsuspecting colonists, killing 347 by the end of the day—more than one-fourth of the English population.

[handwritten margin note: war between NA + English settlers]

The English gathered to plot revenge. They struck at native villages, killing the inhabitants and burning cornfields. At peace talks held in April 1623, the English served poisoned wine to their enemies, killing two hundred more. During nine years of war, the English treated the Indians with a ferocity that recalled their earlier subjugation of the Irish.

Economic activity ceased as settlers retreated to fortified garrisons. The Virginia Company went bankrupt. A royal commission investigating the 1622 surprise attack was shocked to discover that nearly ten times more colonists had died from starvation and disease than at the hands of Indians. King James had little choice but to dissolve the company in 1624 and Virginia became a royal colony the following year. Now the king chose the colony's governor and council, and royal advisors monitored its affairs.

[handwritten margin note: Royal colony status.]

[handwritten note: section 3: pg 37–39]

The Importance of Tobacco

In their search for a marketable product, settlers had begun growing tobacco after 1610. Initially expensive, it became popular among wealthy European consumers. The first cargo of Virginia-grown tobacco arrived in England in 1617 and sold at a highly profitable 3 shillings-per pound.

Settlers immediately planted tobacco everywhere—even in the streets of Jamestown. Company officials, unwilling to base the colony's economy on a single crop, tried to restrict annual production. After company rule ended, tobacco planting surged.

Between 1627 and 1669, annual tobacco exports climbed from 250,000 pounds to more than 15 million pounds. As the supply grew, the price per pound plunged from 13 pence in 1624 to a mere penny in the late 1660s, where it remained for the next half century. The only way colonists could compensate for falling prices was to grow even more, pushing exports to England to more than 20 million pounds by the late 1670s.

[handwritten margin note: 250,000 → 15 mil.]

[handwritten margin note: overproduced tobacco → lower price.]

Tobacco shaped nearly every aspect of Virginia society, from patterns of settlement to the recruitment of colonists. Planters scrambled to claim lands near navigable rivers so that ships could easily reach their plantations and carry their crops to market. As a result, the colonists dispersed across the countryside instead of gathering in towns. People settled, one governor wrote, wherever "a choice veine of rich ground invited them, and further from neighbours the better." Colonists competed to produce the biggest and best crop and get it to market the fastest, hoping to enjoy even a small price advantage over everyone else.

The key to success was to control a large labor force. Tobacco kept workers busy nine months of the year. Planters sowed seeds in the early spring, transplanted seedlings a few weeks later, and spent the summer pinching off the tops of the plants (to produce larger leaves) and removing worms. After the harvest, the leaves were "cured"—dried in ventilated sheds—and packed in large barrels. During the winter, planters cleared and fenced more land and made barrels for next year's crop. Working on his own, one planter could tend two thousand plants, which yielded about 500 pounds of cured tobacco.

To make a profit, planters needed help. They turned to England, importing thousands of **indentured servants,** or contract workers, who agreed to a fixed term

[handwritten margin note: ☆ indentured servants.]

QUICK REVIEW

Tobacco
- 1617: Virginia-grown tobacco arrives in England.
- 1669: tobacco exports reach 15 million pounds annually.
- A large labor force: key to tobacco farming.

[handwritten margin note: ⑦ What are some effects of the popularity of tobacco?]

indentured servants   Individuals who contracted to serve a master for a period of four to seven years in return for payment of the servant's passage to America.

"freedom dues"

? Describe conditions under which some indentured servants live.

? Why was population growth so slow?

of labor, usually four to seven years, in exchange for free passage to Virginia. The master provided food, shelter, clothing, and, at the end of the term of service, "freedom dues" paid in corn and clothing. Between 1625 and 1640, an estimated one thousand or more indentured servants arrived each year. Some were orphans; others were condemned criminals given a choice between execution and transportation to Virginia. Most, however, came from the ranks of England's unemployed, who emigrated in hopes of "bettering their condition in a Growing Country."

Most found such hopes quickly dashed. Many servants died from disease, and some, occasionally, from mistreatment. Richard Price beat his servant, Endymion Inleherne, for "being a common runaway and one that did use to feign himself sick" so severely that the young man died. A jury refused to charge Price with murder, reasoning that Inleherne deserved punishment and Price had not intended to kill him. The courts (administered by masters) usually favored masters' authority over servants' rights.

For every ex-servant who became a landholder, dozens died in poverty. Many ex-servants could find farms only in parts of the colony less suitable for tobacco cultivation and more vulnerable to Indian attack.

Because of their labor needs, masters favored young men in their teens and twenties as indentured servants, importing three or four times as many of them as women. As a result, Virginia's population in the seventeenth century was overwhelmingly young and male. Many free male servants found that marriage was as remote a possibility as landownership. John Rolfe's union with Pocahontas was one of only three English-Indian marriages recorded in seventeenth-century Virginia.

Population growth was further slowed because servants could not marry until their indentures were completed. Many men were already in their thirties when they married, usually to women in their early twenties. Older couples had fewer children than younger couples would have had. Few colonists lived past 50, and many of their offspring died young. Children who survived had usually lost one or both parents by the time they reached adulthood.

Surviving spouses often remarried a widow or widower with children, creating complex households with stepparents and half-brothers and half-sisters. Widows controlled property left to them by their husbands, assuming the normally male responsibility of managing estates for their children's benefit. A widow tried to choose a new spouse wisely, for he would manage the property that the children of her first marriage would inherit.

The number of settlers rose from about 2,500 in 1630 to 21,000 in 1660, thanks to the demand for indentured servants. When Opechancanough launched another raid in 1644 that killed nearly five hundred colonists, it had a far less devastating effect than his attack of 1622 because the settler population had grown so much and now outnumbered the Indians.

Some settlers acquired large estates and grew wealthy from the labor of indentured servants tilling their tobacco fields. Others, cultivating small land-holdings or renting plots from more successful colonists, grew just-enough food to survive and as much tobacco as they could manage. But even the most successful settlers, investing every penny of profit in labor and land, lived under quite primitive conditions.

Early colonial dwellings were often no larger than 16 by 20 feet, with one or two rooms. Poor settlers slept on the floor on straw mat-

Virginia-grown tobacco found a ready market among European consumers such as this contemplative smoker. As tobacco prices declined during the seventeenth century due to increased production, even people of modest means could take up the habit of smoking.

Arents Collection, The New York Public Library, Astor, Lenox, and Tilden Foundation.

? Describe the colonial dwelling.

tresses and had few other furnishings. Rich planters owned more goods, though often of poor quality. In 1655, for instance, William Brocas, a prominent colonial official, owned "a parcell of old hangings, very thin and much worn"; seven chairs, "most of them unusefull"; and seven guns, "most unfixt."

MARYLAND: A REFUGE FOR CATHOLICS

Encouraged by Virginia's success, King Charles I in 1632 granted 10 million acres of land north of Chesapeake Bay to the nobleman Cecilius Calvert, Lord Baltimore. Unlike Virginia, which was founded by a joint-stock company, Maryland was a **proprietary colony**—the sole possession of Calvert and his heirs. They owned all the land, which they could divide up as they pleased, and had the right to set up the colony's government.

Calvert, who was Catholic, intended Maryland to be a refuge for others of his faith. English Catholics were a disadvantaged minority. They paid double taxes, could not worship in public, hold political office, or send their children to universities. In Maryland, Calvert wanted Catholic colonists to enjoy economic and political power. He intended to divide the land into manors—large private estates like those of medieval England—and distribute them to wealthy Catholic friends. These manor lords would live on rents collected from tenant farmers, hold the most important governmental offices, and run their own law courts.

Calvert died before settlement began, and his plans unraveled. The majority of colonists, who began arriving in 1634, were Protestants who despised Catholics. Refusing to live as tenants on Catholic estates, they claimed land of their own—a process that accelerated after 1640, when Maryland adopted a headright system like Virginia's as a way to recruit settlers.

Maryland's problems intensified when civil war broke out in England in 1642. Charles I, who became king in 1625, clashed with Protestants who called for further reform of the Church of England. He also antagonized many government leaders by dissolving Parliament in 1629 and ruling on his own for eleven years. Needing funds to suppress a rebellion in Scotland in 1640, however, Charles was forced to recall Parliament, which quickly turned against him. Both king and Parliament recruited armies and went to war in 1642. Parliamentary forces triumphed, and in 1649, they executed Charles. For the next decade, Oliver Cromwell, a general, ruled until his death in 1658. His son, Richard, proved an inept successor, and in 1660 a group of army officers invited Charles's exiled son to accept the throne.

During the 1640s and 1650s, Maryland Protestants took advantage of the upheaval in England, contesting the Calverts' control of the colony. To pacify them, Calvert's son Cecilius established a legislature, assuming that Protestants would dominate the elective lower house while he could appoint Catholics to the upper house. In 1649, Calvert also approved the **Act for Religious Toleration,** the first law in America to call for freedom of worship for all Christians, but the Protestant majority continued to resist Catholic political influence, at one point passing a law that prohibited Catholics from voting.

Instead of the peaceful Catholic refuge Calvert intended, Maryland soon resembled neighboring Virginia. Its settlers raised tobacco and imported as many indentured servants as possible. Because Maryland initially provided former servants with 50 acres of land, more became landholders than in Virginia. As in Virginia, however, economic opportunity diminished after 1660 when the price of tobacco dropped. Maryland's settlers enjoyed more peaceful relations with the Indians among whom they settled than Virginians had, but they fought intensely among themselves.

WHERE TO LEARN MORE

Jamestown Settlement, near Williamsburg, Virginia
www.apva.org

WHERE TO LEARN MORE W

St. Mary's City, Maryland
www.somd.com

Proprietary colony A colony created when the English monarch granted a huge tract of land to an individual or group of individuals, who became "lords proprietor."

Act for Religious Toleration The first law in America to call for freedom of worship for all Christians.

Section 4: pg. 40-45.

THE FOUNDING OF NEW ENGLAND

WHAT ROLE did religion play in the establishment of the New England colonies?

⊛ Plymouth Colony

⊛ Anglican Church

⊛ Puritans.

⊛ John Calvin.

⊛ Separatists

The first English attempt to settle the northeastern coast of North America was a miserable failure. In 1607, the Plymouth Company sent a group of settlers who abandoned their settlement in present-day Maine the next summer. But English explorers and fishermen continued to visit New England, among them John Smith, who in 1616, published his book extolling its virtues as a site for colonization.

Six colonies appeared in the region between 1620 and 1640, settled by thousands of people troubled by religious, political, and economic upheavals in England. The society these settlers created differed markedly from the one developing in the Chesapeake—not least of all in the absence of significant Indian opposition. Between 1616 and 1618 a terrible epidemic swept through coastal New England, killing up to 90 percent of the Indians living there. The devastated survivors were unable to prevent the encroaching English from building towns where their villages had once stood.

THE PILGRIMS AND PLYMOUTH COLONY

Plymouth Colony, the first of the New England settlements, was founded in 1620. Its origins lay in religious disputes that had plagued England since the late sixteenth century. Most of Queen Elizabeth's subjects approved of her efforts to keep England a Protestant nation, but some believed that she had not rid the Church of England of Catholic practices. The enemies of these reformers, ridiculing them for wanting to purify the Church of England (or **Anglican** Church) of all corruption, called them **Puritans.**

Following the doctrine of predestination taught by John Calvin, English Puritans believed in an all-powerful God who, at the moment of Creation, had determined which humans would be saved and which would be damned. The centerpiece of their spiritual life was conversion: the transforming experience that occurred when individuals felt the stirrings of grace in their souls and began to hope that they were among the saved. Those who experienced conversion were considered saints and acquired new strength to live godly lives.

Puritans rejected the *Book of Common Prayer*, which regulated Anglican worship, insisting that ministers should pray from the heart and preach from the Bible. They objected when Anglican clergy wore rich vestments that set them apart from ordinary Christians. And they objected to any church organization above the level of individual congregations, seeing no need for bishops and archbishops. But what they hated most of all about the Anglican Church was that anyone could be a member. Puritans believed that everyone should attend church services, but they wanted church membership—which conferred the right to partake in the Lord's Supper, or communion—to be limited to saints.

Puritans thus insisted on further reform. Elizabeth and the rulers who followed her disagreed and tried to silence them. Some Puritans, known as **separatists,** were convinced that the Church of England would never change and left it to form their own congregations.

One such group, mainly artisans and middling farmers from the village of Scrooby, in Nottinghamshire, left England in 1607–1608, settling for more than a decade in Holland. There they worshiped in peace, but many struggled to make a living and feared that their children were being tempted by the worldly pleasures of Dutch city life. Some Scrooby separatists gained the backing of the Plymouth Company for a move to America. Called **Pilgrims** because they thought of themselves as spiritual wanderers, they were joined by other separatists and by non-

Anglican   Of or belonging to the Church of England, a Protestant denomination.

Puritans   Individuals who believed that Queen Elizabeth's reforms of the Church of England had not gone far enough in improving the church. Puritans led the settlement of Massachusetts Bay Colony.

Separatists   Members of an off-shoot branch of Puritanism. Separatists believed that the Church of England was too corrupt to be reformed and hence were convinced they must "separate" from it to save their souls.

Pilgrims   Settlers of Plymouth Colony, who viewed themselves as spiritual wanderers.

⊛ Pilgrims

separatist "strangers" hired to help get the colony started. In all, 102 men, women, and children set sail on the *Mayflower* in September 1620.

After a long and miserable voyage, they landed near Massachusetts Bay. Because this was about 200 miles north of the land their charter permitted them to settle, some of the "strangers" claimed that they were no longer legally bound to obey the expedition's separatist leaders. The leaders responded by drafting the *Mayflower Compact,* which became the first document to establish self-government in North America, and urging all adult males to sign it.

The Pilgrims settled at Plymouth, the site of a Wampanoag village recently depopulated by disease, where they found abandoned cornfields, Indian graves, and baskets of corn buried underground. Even with this corn, nearly half of the Pilgrims died of starvation and disease that first winter.

Two English-speaking natives, Squanto and Samoset, emerged from the woods the next spring and approached the Pilgrims on behalf of Massasoit, the Wampanoag leader. The Wampanoags thought the Pilgrims might be useful allies against Wampanoag enemies, such as the Narragansetts, who had escaped the recent epidemics.

In 1621, the Wampanoags and the Pilgrims signed a treaty of alliance. The Pilgrims assumed that Massasoit had submitted to the superior authority of King James, whereas Massasoit assumed that the agreement treated himself and the English king as equal partners. Despite frequent disputes caused by English assertion of authority over the Wampanoags, the two groups enjoyed relatively peaceful relations for nearly half a century.

The Indians taught the English how to plant corn and traded corn with them for manufactured goods. The Pilgrims also exchanged corn with other Indians to the north for furs, which they shipped back to England to help pay off their debts to English investors. In the autumn of 1621, Indians and Pilgrims gathered for a feast celebrating the settlers' first harvest—an event Americans still commemorate as the first Thanksgiving.

Plymouth remained small, poor, and weak. It never had more than seven thousand settlers and never produced more than small shipments of furs, fish, and timber to sell in England. It took the Pilgrims more than twenty years to repay their English creditors. Yet because of the idealistic visions of the founders of Plymouth Colony, who saw in the New World a chance to escape religious persecution and create peaceful communities and pure churches, it has become an important symbol in American history.

MASSACHUSETTS BAY COLONY AND ITS OFFSHOOTS

The Puritans who settled Massachusetts shared many of the Pilgrims' beliefs, but they insisted that the Anglican Church *could* be reformed and so were not separatists. They went to New England to create godly churches to serve as models for English reform. And England, they believed, was in more desperate need of reformation than ever.

Charles I, who became king in 1625, opposed Puritans more forcefully than his father had and supported changes in Anglican worship that recalled Catholic practices. England at the time also suffered from economic troubles that many Puritans saw as signs of God's displeasure with their country.

In 1629, a group of Puritan merchants received a royal charter for a joint-stock enterprise, the Massachusetts Bay Company, to set up a colony north of Plymouth. They chose John Winthrop, a prosperous Puritan lawyer, as their leader. In the spring of 1630, a fleet of eleven ships carried about a thousand men, women, and children across the Atlantic.

QUICK REVIEW

The Pilgrims

♦ Plymouth Colony founded in 1620.

♦ Puritans wanted reform of the Church of England.

♦ Pilgrims were separatists who believed the Church of England could not be reformed.

Wampanoag

QUICK REVIEW

Mayflower Compact

♦ Mayflower Compact signed in 1620.

♦ Established self-government in North America.

♦ Pilgrim leaders urged all adult males to sign the compact.

1621: 1st Thanksgiving

WHERE TO LEARN MORE **W**

Plimouth Plantation, Plymouth, Massachusetts
http://pilgrims.net/plimouthplantation/vtour

John Winthrop.

John Winthrop (1588–1649) served as the Massachusetts Bay Colony's governor for most of its first two decades. Throughout his life, Winthrop—like many fellow Puritans—struggled to live a godly life in a corrupt world.

Courtesy American Antiquarian Society.

Before Winthrop's ship landed, he preached a lay sermon, called "A Model of Christian Charity," to his fellow passengers, reminding them of their goal "to do more service to the Lord." They should "love one another with a pure heart" and place the good of all above private ambitions. Winthrop argued that the Lord had made them his chosen people, and that as a result, "we shall be as a city upon a hill, the eyes of all people are upon us." If they failed to live up to God's expectations, he would punish them. With this mingled encouragement and threat, the emigrants soon landed and founded Boston and six adjoining towns.

Winthrop described the settlers' mission in New England as a **covenant,** or contract, with God, binding them to meet their religious obligations in return for God's favor. The settlers also created covenants when they founded towns and churches, agreeing to live together in peace. The desire for peace and purity could breed intolerance. Settlers scrutinized their neighbors for signs of unacceptable behavior. But the insistence on convenants and conformity also created a remarkably stable society, far more peaceable than Virginia's.

That stability was enhanced by the development of representative government. The *General Court,* which initially included only the shareholders of the joint-stock company, was transformed into a twohouse legislature. Freemen—adult males who held property and were church members—had the right to elect representatives to the lower house, as well as 18 members (called "assistants") to the upper house. They also chose a governor and a deputy governor.

Between 1630 and 1642, at least thirteen thousand settlers came to New England and established dozens of towns. The progress of settlement was generally untroubled in coastal Massachusetts, but when colonists moved into the Connecticut River Valley, tensions with Indians grew rapidly. These erupted in 1637 in the brief, tragic conflict called the **Pequot War.**

English settlers from Massachusetts first arrived in the Connecticut Valley in the mid-1630s. Dutch traders already in the region had been dealing exclusively with the Pequot Indians as partners. In 1633, however, they invited other Indian groups to trade with them. The Pequots, suffering terribly from a recent smallpox epidemic, resented losing their special trading rights and began fighting the Dutch. Initially, they saw the English settlers as potential allies against the Dutch. But when the settlers demanded Pequot submission to English authority as the price of an alliance, they turned against them too.

The English settlers formed alliances with the Narragansetts and Mohegans, who were both rivals of the Pequots. In May 1637, English forces surrounded a Pequot village inhabited mainly by women and children, located on the Mystic River. They set it ablaze and shot anyone who tried to escape. Between three hundred and seven hundred Pequots died, a toll that shocked the settlers' Indian allies, who protested that English-style warfare was "too furious, and slays too many men." [See American Views, "Miantonomo's Plea for Indian Unity (1642)".] After the surviving Pequots had fled or been sold into slavery, many more settlers moved to Connecticut, which soon declared itself a separate colony. In 1639, the settlers adopted the *Fundamental Orders,* creating a government similar to that of Massachusetts, and the English government granted them a royal charter in 1662.

Massachusetts spun off other colonies as its population expanded in the 1630s and dissenters ran afoul of its intolerant government. Puritan leaders tried to suppress unorthodox religious opinions whenever they emerged, for fear that God would interpret their failure to do so as a breach of their covenant with him. Some dissenting colonists, however, refused to be silenced.

Roger Williams was one such irrepressible dissenter. Williams was a separatist minister who declared that because Massachusetts churches had not reject-

covenant A contract with God, binding settlers to meet their religious obligations in return for God's favor.

Pequot War Conflict between English settlers and Pequot Indians over control of land and trade in eastern Connecticut.

ed the Church of England, they shared its corruption. He argued for the separation of church and state, and also attacked the Massachusetts charter, insisting that the king had no right to grant Indian lands to English settlers.

Williams was an immensely likable man—even Governor Winthrop remained on friendly terms with him, but the General Court sentenced him to banishment, intending to ship him back to England. In the winter of 1635, Williams slipped away with a few followers and found refuge among the Narragansett Indians, from whom he purchased land for the village of Providence, founded in 1636. More towns soon sprang up nearby when a new religious crisis, provoked by a woman named Anne Hutchinson, sent additional refugees to Rhode Island from Massachusetts.

Anne Hutchinson arrived in Boston from England with her husband and seven children in 1634. Welcomed by the town's women for her talents as a midwife, she also began to hold religious meetings in her house, where she denounced several ministers.

Many people, including prominent Boston merchants, flocked to Hutchinson's meetings. But her critics believed her to be a dangerous *antinomian* (someone who claimed to be free from obedience to moral law) because she seemed to maintain that saints were accountable only to God and not to any worldly authority. Her opponents also objected to her teaching of mixed groups of men and women, a breach of normal gender roles. Colony magistrates arrested her and tried her for sedition—that is, for advocating the overthrow of the government.

During her trial, Hutchinson mounted a lively defense. In the end, however, the court found her guilty and banished her from the colony. With many of her followers, she moved to Rhode Island, where Roger Williams had proclaimed a policy of religious toleration.

At the height of the Hutchinson controversy, a group of zealous Puritan emigrants led by the Reverend John Davenport departed Boston to found New Haven in 1638. Davenport's efforts to impose perfect Puritan conformity in his colony made Massachusetts seem easygoing in comparison. But New Haven failed to thrive, and in 1662, the poor, intolerant, and isolated colony was absorbed into Connecticut.

FAMILIES, FARMS, AND COMMUNITIES IN EARLY NEW ENGLAND

"This plantation and that of Virginia went not forth upon the same reasons," declared one of Massachusetts's founders. Virginians came "for profit," whereas New Englanders emigrated to bear witness to their Puritan faith. Unlike the unmarried young men who moved in great numbers to Virginia, most New Englanders settled with their families.

The average family in early New England had seven or eight children. Because women and men arrived in nearly equal numbers, young adults easily found spouses and produced more children. Thus the population continued to grow rapidly even when immigration slowed after 1642, so that by 1660, New England's settlers numbered more than 33,000.

New Englanders were largely spared from the diseases that ravaged Virginia's settlers and devastated Indian populations. It seemed a "marvelous providence of God" to Plymouth's Governor Bradford that many settlers made it to their seventies and eighties when few of England's adults lived past 60. Longevity strengthened economic security as well as emotional ties. Fathers lived long enough to build prosperous farms to pass along to their sons. And they accumulated herds of livestock and stores of household goods to give to their daughters when they married.

2–7
The Trial of Anne Hutchinson (1638)

Unlike Chesapeake colonists, who spread out on tobacco lands near navigable rivers, New Englanders clustered in towns. The Massachusetts government strongly encouraged town formation by granting land to groups of families who promised to settle together. The families divided the land among themselves, allotting each family a farm of sufficient size to support all its members. People who had had higher social standing in England received larger farms than those of lower standing. Land that the original families could not yet farm was held "in common" to be distributed to their children as they grew up. Settlers and their children generally remained in their chosen towns for the rest of their lives.

Towns—usually made up of fifty to a hundred families—provided the context for religious, political, and economic activity. The importance Puritans placed on worship with fellow Christians helped promote community feeling. Every Sunday, townspeople gathered at the meetinghouse to listen to the minister preach God's word. At other times, the meetinghouse served as a town hall, where men assembled to discuss matters ranging from local taxes to making sure that everyone's fences were mended. Townsmen tried to reach decisions by consensus in order to preserve harmony. To oversee day-to-day local affairs, men chose five to seven of their most trusted neighbors to serve as selectmen.

Economic life likewise centered on the town. New England's stony soil and short growing season offered few ways to get rich, but most people achieved a modest prosperity. Farmers grew corn and other foods and raised livestock. Their goal was to achieve what they called *competency*—the possession of enough property to ensure their families' economic independence.

Maintaining competency was a family affair. New England farmers relied on their wives and children for labor. Women cared for children, cleaned, cooked, sewed and mended, milked cows, and tended poultry. Many farmwives made butter and cheese, brewed beer, preserved fruits and vegetables, salted meat, spun yarn, and wove cloth. Although they generally did not perform heavy agricultural work, women helped with planting and harvesting crops and tended gardens near their houses. If their husbands worked as merchants or craftsmen, wives might also help out in the shop.

Children began work shortly after their fifth birthday. Older siblings cared for younger ones, fetched tools, and minded cattle. Around age 10, girls began learning more complicated housekeeping skills from their mothers, and boys received instruction from their fathers in such tasks as plowing, cutting hay and wood, and caring for livestock. Many children in their early teens performed tasks little different from adult duties.

No family could produce all the goods that it needed, so New Englanders regularly traded with their neighbors. A skilled carpenter might erect a house in return for barrels of salted beef. Men with several sons sent them to help neighbors whose children were too young to work. Midwives delivered babies in return for cheese or eggs. Women nursed sick neighbors, whom they might one day call on for similar help. These sorts of transactions allowed most New Englanders to enjoy a fairly comfortable life.

Without a staple crop like tobacco, New England prospered by exploiting a variety of resources, developing a diversified economy that was less vulnerable to depression than Virginia's. Farmers sent livestock and meat to merchants to be marketed abroad. Fishermen caught thousands of pounds of cod, haddock, and other fish to be sold in Europe. Some of the region's timber found its way abroad, but most of it ended up in shipyards. New Englanders became such skilled shipbuilders and seafaring merchants that by the 1670s, London merchants complained about

(handwritten margin notes:)
? Describe New England towns.

? Describe N. England economic status?

? What was it like for New England children?

competition from them. England itself had little use for the dried fish, livestock, salted meat, and wood products that New England vessels carried, but enterprising merchants found exactly the market they needed in the West Indies.

Section 5: pg 45 – 46

COMPETITION IN THE CARIBBEAN

The Spanish claimed all Caribbean islands by right of Columbus's discovery, but during the early seventeenth century, French, Dutch, and English adventurers defied them. France eventually retained Guadaloupe, Martinique, Haiti (which the French called Saint Dominque), and several smaller islands. The Dutch had Aruba, Curaçao, St. Martin and St. Eustasius. The English occupied Antigua, Barbados, Montserrat, Nevis, and St. Christopher; in 1655, they conquered the Spanish-held island of Jamaica. The West Indies soon became the jewel of England's empire, producing vast wealth from the cultivation of sugar. Caribbean planters created a society totally unlike any of the mainland colonies—not least of all because their prosperity depended on the exploitation of African slaves.

SUGAR AND SLAVES

The first English colonists who came to the West Indies in the 1630s raised tobacco and imported indentured servants to work their fields. By that time, however, tobacco fetched low prices. Moreover, the disease environment of the West Indies proved even harsher than that of the Chesapeake, and settlers died in great numbers.

P) What was the new cash crop of the Caribbean islands?

But by the 1640s, a Barbados planter boasted of "a great change on this island of late from the worse to the better, praised be God." That change was a shift from tobacco to sugar cane. Many sugar planters grew wealthy. In 1646, a 500-acre plantation on Barbados sold for £16,000—more than the whole island had been worth just a few years before. On average, the estate of a Caribbean sugar planter was worth four times as much as a prosperous Chesapeake plantation.

P) How did sugar change the landscape of the West Indies?

Sugar rapidly transformed the West Indies. Planters deforested whole islands to raise sugar cane. They stopped planting food crops and raising livestock—thereby creating a demand for lumber and provisions that boosted New England's economy.

The sugar boom also led to a scramble for labor. Planters continued to import white indentured servants, including some kidnapped English and Irish youths, but soon turned to African slaves. Africans were already used to agricultural work in a tropical climate. And the English would not have to enslave any Africans themselves; they could simply import people who had already been enslaved by other Africans and sold to Dutch or Portuguese traders. The planters' choice has been called an "unthinking decision," but it had an enormous impact on English colonial life, first in the islands and then on the mainland.

P) How did sugar change the need for labor?

A BIRACIAL SOCIETY

The West Indies had the first biracial plantation society in the English colonial world. By 1700, more than 250,000 slaves had been imported into the region, quickly becoming the most numerous segment of its population. Slaves lived in wretched conditions, underfed, poorly dressed, and housed in rough huts. They labored six days a week from sunrise to sunset—except at harvest time, when they toiled seven days a week in round-the-clock shifts. Masters considered them property, often branding them like livestock and hunting them with bloodhounds when they ran away.

1st biracial plantation society

1700 : 250,000 slaves.

P) Describe the status of slaves.
— living conditions
— legal status

In this seventeenth-century drawing, African slaves are shown toiling in a Brazilian sugar mill. Similar scenes prevailed on Barbados and other Caribbean colonies dominated by sugar production.

The Granger Collection, New York.

Laws declared slavery to be a lifelong condition that passed from slave parents to their children. Slaves had no legal rights and were under the complete control of their masters. Only rarely would masters who killed slaves face prosecution, and those who did and were found guilty were subject only to fines. Slaves, in contrast, could be whipped, branded, or maimed for stealing food or harboring a runaway compatriot. Serious crimes such as murder or arson brought execution without trial. Slaves who rebelled were burned to death.

When masters began to import African women as well as men—hoping to create a self-reproducing labor force—slaves formed families and preserved at least some African traditions. They gave their children African names (although masters often gave them English names as well). They celebrated with African music and worked to the rhythm of familiar songs. They performed West African funeral rituals, often burying their dead with food and other goods to accompany them on the journey to the afterlife.

Some planters, profiting handsomely from their slaves' toil, lived better than many English gentlemen, dwelling in large houses, with fine furnishings. But sugar production required a heavy investment in land, slaves, mills, and equipment. As great planters took vast amounts of land for themselves, freed servants and small farmers struggled to survive. After 1650, some poorer white colonists headed for the mainland. They were joined by planters looking for a place to expand their operations once most of the good land on the islands had been brought under cultivation.

section 6: pg 46-51

THE PROPRIETARY COLONIES

The initial burst of English colonization ended in 1640 when England tottered on the brink of civil war. With the accession of Charles II to the English throne in 1660, however, interest in North American colonies revived. Charles II rewarded the supporters who had remained loyal to him during his long exile in France with huge tracts of American land. Four new colonies—Carolina, Pennsylvania, New Jersey, and New York—resulted from such grants during his reign (1660–1685) (see Map 2–3). All were proprietary colonies, essentially

MAP EXPLORATION
To explore an interactive version of this map, go to
http://www.prenhall.com/goldfield2/map2.3

MAP 2–3

English North American Colonies, c. 1685   After the restoration of Charles II in 1660, several large proprietary colonies joined earlier English settlements in New England and the Chesapeake. By 1685, a growing number of English settlers solidified England's claim to the Atlantic coast from Maine (then part of Massachusetts Bay Colony) to the southern edge of Carolina.

EXPLAIN WHY, on the basis of this map, England had such an early stronghold on North America? Why was it difficult by the mid-1680s for other European countries to establish colonies in the New World?

the private property of the people to whom they had been given. Carolina and Pennsylvania, like the earlier proprietary colony of Maryland, provided their owners the chance to test idealistic social visions. The origins of New York and New Jersey as English colonies, in contrast, lay not in proprietary visions of social harmony but in the stern reality of military conquest (see the overview table "English Colonies in the Seventeenth Century").

EARLY CAROLINA

In 1663, Charles II granted a group of supporters an enormous tract of land stretching from southern Virginia to northern Florida. The proprietors, who included several Barbados planters, called their colony Carolina, after the Latin form (Carolus) of the king's name. They envisioned it growing into a prosperous, orderly society.

One of the proprietors, Anthony Ashley Cooper, working closely with his secretary, John Locke, devised the **Fundamental Constitutions of Carolina,** a plan to ensure the stability of the colony by balancing property ownership and political rights. It called for the creation of a colonial aristocracy, who would own two-fifths of the land and wield extensive political power. Below them, a large class of freeholders would own small farms and elect representatives to an assembly. At the bottom of the social order would be slaves.

This plan never went into effect. People moved in from Virginia and the West Indies and settled where they pleased. They even voted in the assembly to reject the Fundamental Constitutions. When English traders first appeared, eager to buy deerskins, many Indians had welcomed them. But they grew hostile when some traders began selling guns to some tribes in exchange for captives from rival tribes who were sold as slaves to the West Indies. Resentments deepened as settlers moved onto native lands.

The colonists at first raised livestock to be sold to the West Indies. But the introduction of rice in Carolina in the 1690s transformed the settlers' economy, making it, as one planter noted, "as much their staple Commodity, as Sugar is to Barbadoes and Jamaica, or Tobacco to Virginia and Maryland." West African slaves probably introduced rice cultivation in Carolina. Ironically, the profits earned from rice persuaded Carolina planters to invest even more heavily in slave labor.

By 1708, there were more black slaves than white settlers in the colony, and two decades after that, black people outnumbered white people by two to one. Rice farming required a substantial investment in land, labor, and equipment, including dikes and dams for flooding fields. Those who could afford such an investment set themselves up as planters in Carolina's coastal rice district, acquiring large estates and forcing poorer settlers to move elsewhere.

Some of these dislocated men went to the northern part of Carolina, where the land and climate were unsuited to rice. There they raised tobacco and produced pitch, tar, and timber products from the region's pine forests. So different were the two regions that the colony formally split into two provinces—North and South Carolina—in 1729.

South Carolina rice planters became some of the wealthiest colonists on the mainland. But their luxurious style of life came at a price. As Carolina began to look "more like a negro country than like a country settled by white people," planters dreaded the prospect of slave rebellion. To avert this nightmare, they enacted **slave codes** as harsh as those of the sugar islands. Carolina would not be the harmonious colony that John Locke and Cooper had envisioned. It evolved instead into a racially divided society founded on the oppression of a black majority and permeated by fear.

Fundamental Constitutions of Carolina A complex plan for organizing the colony of Carolina, drafted in 1669 by Anthony Ashley Cooper and John Locke.

Slave codes A series of laws passed mainly in the southern colonies in the late seventeenth and early eighteenth centuries to define the status of slaves and codify the denial of basic civil rights to them.

OVERVIEW

ENGLISH COLONIES IN THE SEVENTEENTH CENTURY

Colony	Date of Founding	Established Religion	Economy	Government
Virginia	1607	Anglican	Tobacco	Royal (after 1625)
Plymouth	1620	Puritan	Mixed farming	Corporate
St. Christopher	1624	Anglican	Sugar	Royal
Barbados	1627	Anglican	Sugar	Royal
Nevis	1628	Anglican	Sugar	Royal
Massachusetts (including present-day Maine)	1630	Puritan	Mixed farming, fishing, shipbuilding	Corporate
New Hampshire	1630 (first settlement, annexed to Mass. 1643–1679; royal colony after 1679)	Puritan	Mixed farming	Corporate (royal after 1679)
Antigua	1632	Anglican	Sugar	Royal
Montserrat	1632	Anglican	Sugar	Royal
Maryland	1634	None (Anglican after 1692)	Tobacco	Proprietary
Rhode Island	1636	None	Mixed farming	Corporate
Connecticut	1636	Puritan	Mixed farming	Corporate
New Haven	1638	Puritan	Mixed farming	Corporate
Jamaica	1655 (captured from Spanish)	Anglican	Sugar	Royal
Carolina	1663	Anglican	Rice	Proprietary
New York	1664 (captured from Dutch)	None	Mixed farming, furs	Proprietary (royal after 1685)
New Jersey	1664	None	Mixed farming	Proprietary
Pennsylvania	1681	None	Wheat, mixed farming	Proprietary

[handwritten margin notes: ⊗ William Penn; ⊗ Society of Friends/Quakers; ? How do Quakers differ from Anglican church.]

No colonial proprietor was more idealistic than William Penn, shown here in a portrait made in about 1698 by Francis Place. Penn wanted Pennsylvania to be a place of peace, prosperity, and religious toleration—especially for his fellow Quakers. The colony eventually became an economic success but failed to achieve the social harmony that Penn had wanted.

AP/Wide World Photos.

[handwritten margin note: ⊗ Holy experiment]

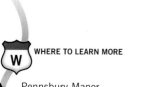

WHERE TO LEARN MORE

Pennsbury Manor,
Morrisville, Pennsylvania
www.pennsburymanor.org

[handwritten margin note: ⊗ Frame of Government]

Quakers   Members of the Society of Friends, a radical religious group that arose in the mid-seventeenth century. Quakers rejected formal theology, focusing instead on the Holy Spirit that dwelt within them.

Frame of Government   William Penn's constitution for Pennsylvania which included a provision allowing for religious freedom.

PENNSYLVANIA: THE DREAM OF TOLERANCE AND PEACE

William Penn put his own utopian plans into action in 1681, when Charles II granted him a huge tract of land north of Maryland as payment for a royal debt owed to Penn's father. Penn intended his colony to be a model of justice and peace, as well as a refuge for members of the Society of Friends, or **Quakers,** a persecuted religious sect to which Penn himself belonged.

Like the separatists, Quakers abandoned the Church of England as hopelessly corrupt, but they went even further in their beliefs. Rejecting predestination, they maintained that every soul had a spark of grace and that salvation was possible for all who heeded that "Inner Light." They rejected trained clergy and elaborate church rituals. Instead of formal religious services, Quakers held meetings in silence until someone, inspired by the Inner Light, rose to speak.

Quaker beliefs had disturbing social and political implications. Quakers granted women spiritual equality with men, allowing them to preach, hold separate prayer meetings, and exercise authority over "women's matters." Arguing that social distinctions were not the work of God, Quakers refused to remove their hats in the presence of those of higher social class. And instead of the formal *you*, Quakers addressed superiors with the informal *thee* and *thou.* Because their faith required them to renounce the use of force, Quakers also refused to perform military service.

When English authorities began harassing Quakers, William Penn (who was himself jailed briefly) conceived his plan for a New World "holy experiment," a harmonious society governed by brotherly love. Using his father's connection with the king, he acquired the land that became Pennsylvania ("Penn's Woods") and recruited settlers from among Europe's oppressed peoples and persecuted religious sects. By 1700, about 18,000 emigrants had left England, Wales, Scotland, Ireland, and various German provinces for the new colony.

Many came in families and settled in an area occupied by the Delaware Indians, whose numbers had recently been reduced by disease and warfare. The "holy experiment" required colonists to live "as Neighbours and friends" with the Indians as well as with one another. Penn paid Indians for land and regulated trade. As long as he remained in control of the colony, relations between the settlers and the Indians were generally peaceful—so much so that refugee Indians from nearby colonies moved into Pennsylvania. Relations between Penn and the settlers, however, were less cordial.

In the **Frame of Government,** his constitution for Pennsylvania, Penn remained true to his Quaker principles with a provision allowing for religious freedom. But true to his aristocratic origins, he designed a legislature with limited powers and reserved considerable authority for himself. When Penn returned to England after a brief stay in the colony (1682–1684), the governor and council—both appointed by Penn—fought with elected members of the assembly. Penn's opponents—many of whom were fellow Quakers—objected to his proprietary privileges, including his control of foreign trade and his collection of fees from landholders. Settlers on the lower Delaware River gained autonomy for themselves with their own legislature, in effect creating an unofficial colony that later became Delaware.

Settlers continued to fight among themselves, and with Penn's heirs, after his death. A flood of increasingly aggressive immigrants undermined peaceful relations with the Indians, forcing many natives to abandon their homelands and move west.

By 1720, Pennsylvania's ethnically and religiously diverse population numbered more than thirty thousand. The colony had some of the richest farmland along the Atlantic coast and was widely known as the "best poor man's country in the world." Growing wheat and other crops, the settlers lived mostly on scattered farms rather than in towns. From the busy port of Philadelphia, ships carried much of the harvest to markets in the West Indies and southern Europe. Penn's "holy experiment" in social harmony may have failed, but as a thriving colony, Pennsylvania succeeded handsomely.

Section 7: pg 51 - 53

THE DUTCH OVERSEAS EMPIRE

Small but densely populated, the Dutch Republic joined the scramble for empire in the early seventeenth century. The Northern Provinces, sometimes known as Holland, had declared their independence from Spain in 1581. The new republic, dominated by Protestants, was intent on challenging Catholic Spain's power for religious as well as political reasons in the New World as well as the Old. More than any other factor, however, the desire for profit drove the Dutch quest for colonies.

THE WEST INDIA COMPANY AND NEW NETHERLAND

The Dutch Republic served as a major center of world trade. Thousands of Dutch ships plied the world's oceans and the republic's earnings from foreign trade may have surpassed those of the rest of Europe combined. This commercial vitality provided the context for overseas expansion.

The first instrument of colonial dominance was the Dutch East India Company, founded in 1602. Eager to reap profits from spices and other exotic goods, the Company challenged what had until then been a virtual Portuguese monopoly of Asian trade. Its first success was the capture of the Spice Islands (now Indonesia and East Timor), followed by the takeover of Batavia (Jakarta), Ceylon (Sri Lanka), and Sumatra. The Company established trading posts on the Gold Coast of West Africa, where it competed with the Portuguese in the slave trade, and at the Cape of Good Hope on Africa's southern tip. Its far-flung commercial net eventually encompassed parts of India and Formosa (Taiwan). These possessions sealed Dutch trading predominance for decades to come.

The Dutch next set their sights on the Americas, creating the West India Company in 1621. Its claim to the Connecticut, Hudson, and Delaware valleys stemmed from the 1609 voyage of Henry Hudson, an Englishman sailing for the Dutch, who discovered the river that bears his name.

The first permanent Dutch settlers on mainland North America arrived in 1624 to set up a fur-trading post at Fort Orange (now Albany). Two years later, a company of Protestant refugees established New Amsterdam on Manhattan Island. The Hudson River corridor between these two settlements became the heart of the New Netherland colony. Like New France, its economic focus was the fur trade. Dutch merchants forged ties with the Iroquois, who brought furs to exchange for European tools and weapons.

In the 1630s, to help supply colonial traders, the West India Company offered large landed estates (called patroonships) to wealthy Dutchmen who would be responsible for populating them with tenant farmers. The plan never really worked, and at its peak, New Netherland's colonists only numbered about ten thousand.

What they lacked in numbers the colonists made up for in divisiveness. New Netherland became a magnet for religious refugees from Europe, as well as a

---

HOW WERE the Dutch able to successfully establish New Netherland along the eastern seaboard of America?

2–8
A Jesuit Priest Describes New Amsterdam (1642)

[handwritten marginal notes:]
① Describe the
- society makeup
- religion
- economy
of Pennsylvania.

⊛ Dutch East India Company

⊛ Henry Hudson.

⊛ New Amsterdam.

destination for Africans acquired through the slave trade. Ethnic differences hindered a sense of community. Among the colony's Dutch, German, French, English, Swedish, Portuguese, and African settlers were Calvinists, Lutherans, Quakers, Catholics, Jews, and Muslims.

The West India Company, more interested in making money than keeping order, dispatched inept governors who provoked conflict with Indians. Although colonists maintained good relations with their Iroquois trading partners on the upper Hudson River, they had far less friendly dealings with Algonquian peoples around New Amsterdam. In one gruesome incident in 1645, Governor Willem Kieft ordered a massacre at an encampment of Indian refugees who had refused to pay tribute. A horrified Dutch witness described Indian children being "thrown into the river, and when the fathers and mothers endeavored to save them, the soldiers would not let them come on land, but made both parents and children drown." He saw victims "with their hands, some with their legs cut off, and some holding their entrails in their arms." Ten years later, Governor Peter Stuyvesant antagonized Susquehannock Indians along the Delaware River by seizing a small Swedish colony where the Susquehannocks had traded.

Such actions provoked retaliatory raids by the Indians, further weakening the colony. Though profitable, the fur trade did not generate the riches to be found in other parts of the Dutch empire. By the 1650s and 1660s, New Netherland looked like a poor investment to company officials in Europe.

New Netherland Becomes New York

⊛ Duke of York.

The proprietary colonies of New York and New Jersey were carved out of the Dutch colony of New Netherland. Competition between the English and the Dutch had generated two Anglo-Dutch wars, first in 1652–1654, and again in 1665–1667. In the New World, tensions were heightened by the presence of English colonists on Long Island, which the Dutch claimed for themselves.

In 1664, Charles II brought matters to a head by claiming that since the site of New Netherland lay within the bounds of the original charter of Virginia, the land belonged to England. He granted the territory to his brother James, Duke of York, who sent ships to Long Island to back up England's claim. Their arrival provoked a rebellion by the island's English colonists, leading the Dutch governor, Peter Stuyvesant—who commanded just 150 soldiers—to surrender without firing a shot.

The Duke of York became proprietor of this new English possession, which was renamed New York. James immediately created another colony, New Jersey, when he granted some of the land to a group of his supporters.

New York, which James retained for himself, included the port of New York City (the former New Amsterdam) and the Hudson Valley with its fur trade. James, who succeeded his brother to the English throne in 1685, encouraged Dutch colonists to remain and promoted immigration from England. By 1700, the settlers numbered twenty thousand.

This engraving depicts New Amsterdam in 1643 as a bustling port. The figures of African laborers in the foreground attest to the importance of slavery in the Dutch colonial city, where perhaps a quarter of the residents had been born in Africa.

Corbis / Bettmann.

• AMERICAN VIEWS •

MIANTONOMO'S PLEA FOR INDIAN UNITY (1642)

*U**ntil European colonization, the native inhabitants of North America never thought of themselves as one people, any more than the inhabitants of Europe considered themselves "Europeans." Miantonomo, a Narragansett living in Rhode Island, was one of the first native leaders to call for a unified response to English intrusion. With the gruesome lessons of the Pequot War fresh in his mind, he urged the Montauks of Long Island to join the Narragansetts in opposing the settlers. His appeal, recorded by Lion Gardiner, an English officer during the Pequot War, was in vain. Captured by the English and convicted of the murder of an Indian, Miantonomo was turned over to a Mohegan rival for execution.*

HOW DID Miantonomo describe Indian life before the arrival of the English? What changes occurred as a result of their settlement?

Brothers, we must be as one as the English are, or we shall all be destroyed. You know our fathers had plenty of deer and skins and our plains were full of game and turkeys, and our coves and rivers were full of fish.

But, brothers, since these Englishmen have seized our country, they have cut down the grass with scythes, and the trees with axes. Their cows and horses eat up the grass, and their hogs spoil our bed of clams; and finally we shall all starve to death; therefore, stand not in your own light, I ask you, but resolve to act like men. All the sachems both to the east and the west have joined with us, and we are resolved to fall upon them at a day appointed, and therefore I come secretly to you, [be]cause you can persuade your Indians to do what you will.

Source: Steven Mintz, ed., *Native American Voices: A History and Anthology* (1995), pp. 84–85. Reprinted with permission of Brandywine Press.

CONCLUSION

D uring the seventeenth century, France, the Netherlands, and England competed for land and trade in North America, with France and England gaining colonies on the mainland and all three joining Spain in the Caribbean. New France's small and scattered settlements clung to the St. Lawrence River Valley. The profits from the fur trade encouraged the French to maintain friendly relations with their Indian allies and ensured that French kings would monitor the colony's affairs and invest in its defense. English kings granted charters—sometimes to joint-stock companies (Virginia, Plymouth, Massachusetts), sometimes to proprietors (Maryland, Carolina, New York, New Jersey, Pennsylvania)—and let the colonies develop more or less on their own.

English settlers adjusted to different environments, developed different economies and labor systems, and worshiped in different churches. In South Carolina, New York, Pennsylvania, the West Indies, most settlers were not even of English origin. What held these colonies together was an overlay of common English institutions of government. By the mid-1680s, all the colonies had legislatures that provided for self-government and laws and judicial institutions based on English models.

The planting of French, Dutch, and English colonies not only ended Spain's monopoly of settlement in North America but also challenged the Indians' hold on the continent. Native peoples had to deal with a rising tide of settlers and often to choose sides between European antagonists. Transplanted Europeans adapted too, not only in their dealings with native peoples but also in finding and controlling the

HOW WERE the biracial societies of the West Indies and Carolina different from societies in other parts of North America?

supply of laborers they needed to make their colonies prosper. For English colonists this meant the widespread adoption of slavery. For millions of Africans, the result was forced migration to the New World.

SUMMARY

The French in North America   Although French efforts to found American colonies in the late sixteenth century ended in failure, French fisherman continued to visit the Newfoundland coast. As a result, the French did begin to establish colonies in the early seventeenth century. Quebec, organized by Samuel de Champlain, was the first permanent French settlement in Canada. By 1700, New France had about fifteen thousand settlers.

English Settlement in the Chesapeake   When the English again attempted to settle in America in 1607, they chose the lower Chesapeake Bay region. The new settlement, Jamestown, eventually developed into the prosperous colony of Virginia. It didn't take long before tobacco became the staple crop of this region, supplying much of Western Europe while providing an important source of economy to the Chesapeake Bay area colonies.

The Founding of New England   Six English colonies appeared in the New England region between 1620 and 1640. The Pilgrims founded Plymouth in 1620, and, before long, the Massachusetts Bay colony and its offshoots comprised a populous region. The average family in New England had seven or eight children. Unlike Chesapeake colonists who spread out on tobacco lands near navigable rivers, New Englanders clustered in towns, which provided the context for religious, political, and economic activity.

Competition in the Caribbean   The Spanish claimed all Caribbean islands by right of Columbus's discovery, but during the early seventeenth century, French, Dutch, and English adventurers defied them. The first English colonists who came to the West Indies in the 1630s raised tobacco and imported indentured servants to work their fields. Sugar rapidly transformed the West Indies, and with its boom came the need for labor. Slave labor in the West Indies soon created a biracial society.

The Proprietary Colonies   With the accession of Charles II to the English throne in 1660, interest in North American colonies revived. In 1663, Charles II granted a group of supporters a track of land from southern Virginia to northern Florida. The proprietors called their colony Carolina. By 1708, there were more black slaves than white settlers in the colony. As Carolina continued to grow, William Penn started a colony just north of there. Penn's Quaker beliefs became entrenched in the fabric of the new colony, and his Frame of Government (Penn's constitution for Pennsylvania) included a provision allowing for religious freedom.

The Dutch Overseas Empire   Small but densely populated, the Dutch Republic joined the scramble for empire in the early seventeenth century. The first permanent Dutch settlers on mainland North America settled at Fort Orange (now Albany) in 1624. Two years later, a company of Protestant refugees established New Amsterdam on Manhattan Island. The Hudson River corridor between these two settlements became the heart of the New Netherland colony.

REVIEW QUESTIONS

1. Comparing French, Dutch, and English colonies, which ones attracted the most settlers, and which the fewest? How did these differences in emigration affect the various colonies' development?

2. Which English settlements were proprietary colonies? Did they share any common characteristics? What plans did the various proprietors have for their colonies?

3. Religion played a major role as a motive for settlement in both Massachusetts and Pennsylvania. What were the religious beliefs of the settlers in each colony, and how did those beliefs help shape each colony's development?

4. The Chesapeake, the West Indies, and Carolina were all colonies dependent upon staple crops. What were those staple crops? In what ways did staple crop agriculture shape society in each region?

KEY TERMS

Act for Religious Toleration   (p. 39)
Anglican   (p. 40)
coureur de bois   (p. 34)
covenant   (p. 42)
Frame of Government   (p. 50)
Fundamental Constitutions of Carolina   (p. 48)

headright system   (p. 35)
House of Burgesses   (p. 36)
indentured servants   (p. 37)
joint-stock company   (p. 35)
Pequot War   (p. 42)
Pilgrims   (p. 40)

proprietary colony   (p. 39)
Puritans   (p. 40)
Quakers   (p. 50)
separatists   (p. 40)
slave codes   (p. 48)

WHERE TO LEARN MORE

Jamestown Settlement, near Williamsburg, Virginia. Site includes replicas of first English passenger ships to Virginia, a reconstructed Powhatan Village, the recreated James Fort, and galleries with Indian and English artifacts. Visitors can also see archaeological excavations of site of the actual James Fort, as well as sample artifacts recovered from the area. For updated information about archaeological excavations at Jamestown, see **www.apva.org**. At **http:jeffersonvillage.virginia.edu**, you can take a virtual tour of the Jamestown settlement.

St. Mary's City, Maryland. Visitors to this site of the first permanent settlement under the Calvert family may tour the area and view exhibits and living history programs that describe life in early Maryland. The website **www.somd.com** contains information about the historic site of St. Mary's City and has links to a virtual tour of the area.

Plimoth Plantation, Plymouth, Massachusetts. A living history museum, Plimoth Plantation recreates colony life in the year 1627. There are reproductions of the English village and a Wampanoag settlement. Visitors may also see a replica of the Mayflower. For a virtual tour, go to **pilgrims.net/plimothplantation/vtour**. Information on Pilgrims and early years of the colony can be found at: **pilgrims.net/plymouth/history**

Pennsbury Manor, Morrisville, Pennsylvania. A reconstruction of William Penn's seventeenth-century plantation, this site includes furnished buildings and restored gardens. There are also guided tours and demonstrations of colonial crafts. Both **www.bucksnet.com/pennsbury** and **www.pennsburymanor.org** provide information about William Penn, the historic site, and various activities at the manor.

 For additional study resources for this chapter, go to:
www.prenhall.com/goldfield/chapter2

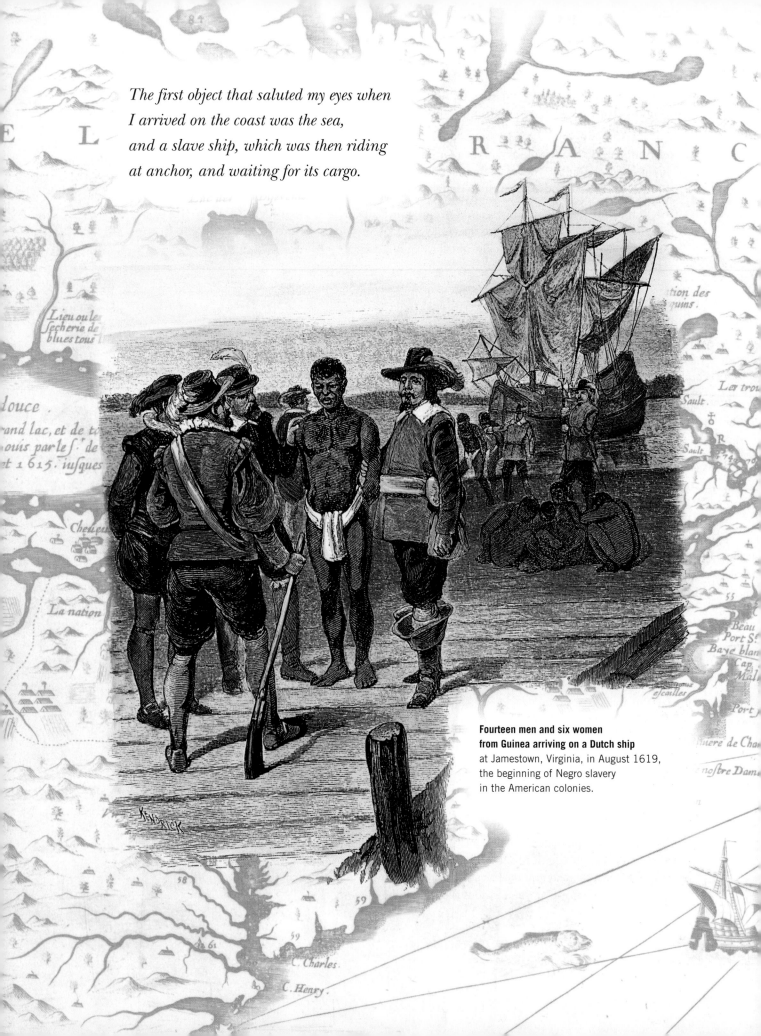

The first object that saluted my eyes when I arrived on the coast was the sea, and a slave ship, which was then riding at anchor, and waiting for its cargo.

Fourteen men and six women from Guinea arriving on a Dutch ship at Jamestown, Virginia, in August 1619, the beginning of Negro slavery in the American colonies.

3

THE CREATION OF NEW WORLDS

WHAT FACTORS shaped the character of the relationship between Native Americans and Europeans?

WHO WERE the first slaves in North America and what role did they play in early American colonies?

WHAT EFFECT did the development of African American families and communities have on slaves and slave owners?

WHAT FACTORS motivated European immigrants to make the long journey to North America during the seventeenth and eighteenth centuries?

IMAGE KEY

for pages 56–57

a. White Hills Map by John Foster, 1677, woodcut. America's first map.
b. 14 men and 6 women from Guinea arriving on a Dutch ship at Jamestown, Virginia in August 1619, the beginning of slavery in the American colonies.
c. Model of the slave ship Brookes, showing plan view of slave positions.
d. Jesuit missionary baptizing an Indian in New France.
e. "To be sold, a cargo of ninety-four prime, healthy Negroes."
f. The Old Plantation, showing slaves at work.
g. Chronicles of Michoacan; detail of manuscript.

The freed slave Olaudah Equiano appears in this 1780 portrait by an unknown artist. After purchasing his freedom, Equiano wrote a vivid account of his capture in Africa and his life in slavery. One of the first such accounts to be published (in 1789), this narrative testified to slavery's injustice and Equiano's own fortitude.

"Portrait of a Negro Man, Olaudah Equiano," 1780s (previously attributed to Joshua Reynolds) by English School (18ᵗʰ c.). Royal Albert Memorial Museum, Exeter, Devon, UK. Bridgeman Art Library, London/New York.

One day [in 1756], when all our people were gone out to their work as usual, and only I and my sister were left to mind the house, two men and a woman got over our walls, and in a moment seized us both; and without giving us time to cry out, or to make any resistance, they stopped our mouths and ran off with us into the nearest wood. Here they tied our hands, and continued to carry us as far as they could. . . . Thus I continued to travel, both by land and by water, through different countries and various nations, till at the end of six or seven months after I had been kidnapped, I arrived at the sea coast. . . .

The first object that saluted my eyes when I arrived on the coast was the sea, and a slave ship, which was then riding at anchor, and waiting for its cargo. These filled me with astonishment, that was soon converted into terror, which I am yet at a loss to describe. . . . I was immediately handled and tossed up to see if I was sound, by some of the crew; and I was now persuaded that I had got into a world of bad spirits, and that they were going to kill me. Their complexions too, differing so much from ours, their long hair, and the language they spoke, which was very different from any I had ever heard, united to confirm me in this belief. . . . I asked . . . if we were not to be eaten by those white men with horrible looks, red faces, and long hair. . . .

In a little time after, amongst the poor chained men, I found some of my own nation. . . . They gave me to understand we were to be carried to these white people's country to work for them. . . . [Many weeks later] we were landed up a river a good way from the sea, about Virginia county, where we saw few of our native Africans, and not one soul who could talk to me.

Olaudah Equiano, *The Interesting Narrative of the Life of Olaudah Equiano,* or Gustavus Vassa, the African.

Ⓧ Olaudah Equiano.

OLAUDAH EQUIANO, born in 1745 in the African kingdom of Benin, was only a boy when his terrifying journey to America began. The son of an Igbo chief, he was caught in the web of the expanding transatlantic slave trade. Slavery had spread from England's Caribbean colonies to dominate the Chesapeake settlements as well.

At the same time, North American Indian peoples, faced with a flood of immigrants from Europe and Africa, employed adaptation, co-existence, diplomacy, and resistance to assert their claims to land and their right to participate in the events and deliberations that affected their lives as much as those of colonists. The America to which Olaudah Equiano had been forcibly transported remained a place where Indian voices had to be heeded.

Equiano's journey did not end in Virginia. Over the next quarter-century, he visited nearly every part of England's empire and beyond. He worked as the servant of a naval officer, a barber, a laborer, and an overseer until he could purchase his own freedom. His extraordinary career bore witness to the emergence of an international market for laborers, which—like slavery and Indian relations—shaped the development of North America. Thousands of people from England, Scotland, Ireland, and Germany sought their fortunes in America. The interactions of Indians, Africans, and Europeans created not one but many New Worlds.

CHRONOLOGY

1440s	Portuguese enter slave trade in West Africa.	**1680**	Pueblo Revolt in New Mexico.
c. 1450	Iroquois form Great League of Peace and Power.	**1680s**	Second phase of Beaver Wars begins.
1610–1614	First war between English settlers and Powhatan Indians.	**1690s**	Shift from white indentured servants to black slaves as principal labor force in the Chesapeake.
1619	First Africans arrive in Virginia.	**1701**	Iroquois adopt policy of neutrality toward French and English.
1622–1632	Second war between English settlers and Powhatan Indians.	**1711–1713**	Tuscarora War in Carolina.
1637	Pequot War in New England.	**1713**	Beginnings of substantial Scottish, Scots-Irish, and German immigration to colonies.
1640s	Slave labor begins to dominate in the West Indies. First phase of the Beaver Wars.	**1715–1716**	Yamasee War in Carolina.
1651	First "praying town" established at Natick, Massachusetts.	**1720s**	Black population begins to increase naturally in English mainland colonies.
1661	Maryland law defines slavery as lifelong, inheritable status.	**1732**	Georgia established.
1670	Virginia law defines status of slaves.	**1739**	Stono Rebellion in South Carolina.
1675–1676	King Philip's War in New England.	**1741**	Slave conspiracy discovered in New York City.
1676	Bacon's Rebellion in Virginia.	**1750**	Slavery legalized in Georgia.
		1760–1775	Peak of European and African immigration to English colonies.

Section 1: pg 59-60

INDIANS AND EUROPEANS

Although, by 1750, European colonists and African slaves together outnumbered Indians north of the Rio Grande, Native Americans continued to dominate much of the continent. The colonists remained clustered along the coasts and had yet to make significant movement into the interior. Some native peoples had scarcely seen any colonists. Indians living along the northern Pacific coast, for instance, met their first white men—Russian fur traders—only in the 1740s. By this time, the Pueblos of the Southwest, the Hurons of Canada, and the Algonquians of the Atlantic seaboard had more than a century's experience with European colonists.

The character of the relationship between Indians and Europeans depended on more than relative population size and the length of time they had been in contact. It was also shaped by the intentions of the newcomers—whether they came to extract resources, to trade, to settle, or to gain converts—and the responses of particular Native American groups intent on preserving their cultures. The result was a variety of regionally distinctive New World communities.

WHAT FACTORS shaped the character of the relationship between Native Americans and Europeans?

INDIAN WORKERS IN THE SPANISH BORDERLANDS

More than any other European colonists, the Spanish sought direct control over Indians. Their ability to marshal Indian workers for Spanish gain depended on the existence of sizable Indian communities and Spanish military force. In North America outside of Mexico itself, these conditions could be found in New Mexico and parts of Florida.

One of the Spaniards' most important methods of labor control was the **encomienda**. *Encomiendas*, granted to influential Spaniards in New Mexico, gave

Encomienda

Encomienda In the Spanish colonies, the grant to a Spanish settler of a certain number of Indian subjects, who would pay him tribute in goods and labor.

these colonists the right to collect tribute from the native peoples living on a specific piece of land. It was not supposed to include forced labor, but often it did.

The *repartimiento* was another Spanish technique for exploiting Native American labor. This was a mandatory draft of Indian labor for public projects, such as building forts, bridges, and roads. Laws stated that native workers should be paid and limited the length of their service, but the Spanish sometimes compelled Indians to work on private estates. Spaniards also acquired laborers by ransoming captives that Indian groups seized from one another. This practice, called *rescate*, obliged rescued Indians to work for those who had paid their ransom.

Together these Spanish strategies for controlling Indian labor aroused considerable resentment on the part of native peoples. Spanish demands for labor and tribute remained constant, even when Indian populations declined from disease or crops failed in bad weather. Workers who resisted were punished. Resentments simmered until late in the seventeenth century, when native anger burst forth in rebellion.

THE WEB OF TRADE

Europeans eager to trade with Indians had to prove their friendship by offering gifts and military aid as well as trading goods. French traders in Canada brought gifts and prepared feasts for their native partners, obliging the Indians to offer the furs that the French wanted. One seventeenth-century observer described the French governor giving the Hurons barrels of hatchets and arrowheads, in part "to waft their canoes gently homewards, [in] part to draw them to us next year." The Indians also got iron tools, kettles, cloth, beads, and—eventually—guns.

Trading with Europeans would gradually destroy the Indians' way of life. Contact with traders exposed Indians to deadly European diseases. The Huron population declined by half in just six years between 1634 and 1640. Indians trading with the Dutch in New Netherlands in the 1650s insisted "their population had been melted down" by smallpox.

Trade also undermined self-sufficiency. Before the French arrived, for instance, the Micmacs in easternmost Canada supported themselves mainly by fishing. After becoming partners of the French around 1610, they trapped beaver year round, relying on the French and New England Indians for food. After they had trapped virtually all the beavers on their lands, they were abandoned by the French, who turned instead to the Hurons. The once prosperous Micmacs barely survived.

Other groups would suffer a similar fate. "The Cloaths we wear, we cannot make ourselves," a Carolina Cherokee used to woolen garments observed in 1753. "We cannot make our Guns. . . . Every necessary Thing in Life we must have from the white People."

Before European contact, most Indian bands living north of the Rio Grande made war to seek revenge for violent acts committed against their own people. But after the Europeans arrived, Indians began to fight each other for economic advantage, and the hostilities became far more deadly. Rivalries among French, English, and Dutch traders led to conflicts among their Indian partners. The **Beaver Wars**, a long struggle between the Hurons and the Iroquois, began in the 1640s.

Because the French already traded with the Hurons, Dutch merchants in the Hudson River Valley seeking to break into the fur trade turned to the *Iroquois League*. Composed of five separate Indian nations—the Mohawks, Oneidas, Onondagas, Cayugas, and Senecas—it functioned as a religious organization to preserve peace among the five nations and strengthen them in their conflicts with other Indian peoples. The Iroquois agreed to supply the Dutch with furs in return for trade goods.

WHO WERE the first slaves in North America and what economic role did they play in early America colonies?

Repartimiento In the Spanish colonies, the assignment of Indian workers to labor on public works projects.

Rescate Procedure by which Spanish colonists would pay ransom to free Indians captured by rival natives.

Beaver Wars Series of bloody conflicts, occurring between 1640s and 1680s, during which the Iroquois fought the French for control of the fur trade in the east and the Great Lakes region.

By the 1630s, the Hurons and Iroquois had killed nearly all the beavers on their own lands and began to look elsewhere for furs. The Hurons traded corn for furs with Indians living north of the Great Lakes. The Iroquois began to raid Huron trading parties and then to attack Huron villages.

The Iroquois triumphed in the resulting conflict largely because the Dutch readily supplied them with guns while the French did not arm the Hurons. In the end, the Hurons were destroyed. A French traveler reported seeing no Hurons in "districts which, not ten years ago, I reckoned to contain eight or ten thousand men."

The cycle of warfare did not end with the destruction of the Hurons. The Iroquois went on to challenge Indian nations near the Great Lakes and in the Ohio Valley. Seeking iron kettles more durable than earthenware pots, cloth that was lighter and more colorful than animal skins, and guns that were deadlier than bows and arrows, Indians changed their lives in ways that suited their own needs as much as those of European traders.

DISPLACING NATIVE AMERICANS IN THE ENGLISH COLONIES

Trading colonies relied on Indian partners to supply them with furs and so maintained friendly relations with them out of self-interest. The European population of the trading colonies also stayed fairly low. Even after the devastation of disease, Indians outnumbered Europeans in New France and New Netherlands. As late as 1650, there were just 657 French people in Canada (compared to perhaps ten thousand Hurons) and only three thousand Europeans in New Netherlands. The English, in contrast, came mainly to settle. By 1650 there were more than fifty thousand Europeans and two thousand Africans in England's North American colonies.

The influx of settlers into the English colonies, as always, exposed native peoples to European diseases. So swift was the decline in native populations—and so rapid the influx of Europeans—that in coastal Massachusetts and eastern Virginia, colonists outnumbered Indians by 1650.

Largely because of the colonists' desire for land, violence between Europeans and Indians occurred with greater regularity in the English colonies than in New France or New Netherlands. Colonists thrilled at the sight of what they saw as vast unoccupied territory. One New England settler declared that the natives "do but run over the grass, as do also the foxes and wild beasts" and that therefore the "spacious and void" land was free for the taking.

The settlers misunderstood how Indians used their territory. Eastern Algonquian peoples cleared areas for villages and planting fields, which native women farmed until the soil grew less fertile. Then they moved to a new location, allowing the former village site to return to forest. In ten to twenty years, they or their descendants might return to that site to clear and farm it again. Indians often built villages near the seacoast or rivers so they could fish and use reeds and grasses for weaving. In the winter, village communities broke up into small bands to hunt in the forest for deer and other animals.

Thus what the colonists considered "vacant" lands were either being used for nonfarming activities or recovering from human occupation in order to be farmed in years to come. Settlers who built towns on abandoned native village sites deprived the Indians of these future planting fields. Competition from the rapidly increasing settlers threatened Indian survival.

Disputes between Europeans and Indians frequently arose from misunderstandings about land ownership and property rights. Indian villages claimed collective sovereignty over a certain territory to be used for farming, fishing, hunting,

QUICK REVIEW

Native Americans and English Settlers

- Influx of settlers exposed native peoples to disease.
- Settlers' desire for land led to violence between settlers and Indians.
- By 1650 settlers outnumbered Indians in some areas.

and gathering. For Europeans, ownership conferred on an individual the exclusive right to use or sell a piece of land.

When Indians transferred land to settlers, the settlers assumed that they had obtained complete rights to the land, whereas the Indians assumed that they had given the settlers not the land itself but only the right to use it, and that no Indian inhabitants would have to leave. It was the English understanding that ultimately prevailed, enforced in the settlers' courts under the settlers' laws.

Settlers' agricultural practices also strained relations with the Indians. Cutting down forests destroyed Indian hunting lands. When colonists dammed rivers, they disrupted Indian fishing. When they surrounded fields with log fences and stone walls, they made trespassers of natives who crossed them. Yet the colonists felt free to let their cattle and pigs loose to graze in the woods and meadows, where they could wander into unfenced Indian cornfields and damage the crops.

The settlers gradually displaced Indian inhabitants, acquiring their lands in various ways. Some colonial leaders, such as Roger Williams in Rhode Island and William Penn of Pennsylvania, insisted on buying it. But sometimes settlers bought collectively owned land from individual Indians who had no right to sell it. Indians frequently misunderstood the terms of sale recorded in English. Even Indian groups who had willingly sold land grew resentful as colonists approached them for more. Finally, native peoples could be forced to sell land to settle debts they had run up with English creditors.

Increasingly, colonists simply settled on Indian lands without permission and appealed to colonial governments for help when the Indians objected. Land speculators amplified this kind of unrest as they sought to acquire land as cheaply as possible and sell it for as much as they could.

Finally, the settlers often seized Indian lands in the aftermath of war, as befell, among others, the Pequots in Connecticut in 1637, and in Carolina the Tuscaroras in 1713 and the Yamasees in 1715. Sometimes colonial leaders contrived for some Indian groups to help them displace others. During the Pequot War, Narragansetts had aided Connecticut settlers' efforts to oust the Pequots. Carolina colonists enlisted the help of the Yamasees against the Tuscaroras and then turned to the Cherokees to help them against the Yamasees.

The English viewed the Indians, as they had the Irish, as savages with whom it would be better not to mix. Colonists built communities on lands bought or taken from natives and then discouraged them from living there. In New France and New Spain, Europeans and Indians mingled more freely and even intermarried, but in the English colonies, separation prevailed.

BRINGING CHRISTIANITY TO NATIVE PEOPLES

In early colonial North America, the three major New World empires—those of Spain, France, and England—competed for Indians' souls as well as their lands and riches.

Catholic missionaries—mainly Franciscan priests—were the driving force behind Spain's efforts to assert control over its colonies of New Mexico and Florida. Spain's bases in Florida helped protect Spanish ships bearing treasure from the mines of Mexico and Peru and discouraged the southward spread of English settlement. New Mexico similarly served as a buffer between the silver mines of northern Mexico and roaming Plains Indians. Neither colony attracted many settlers, however, because neither offered much opportunity for wealth. When Franciscan missionaries proposed to move into New Mexico and Florida in order to convert their inhabitants to Christianity, Spanish officials agreed and even provided financial support. (See Map 3–1.)

This Jesuit missionary, wearing his distinctive Catholic vestments, is baptizing an Indian in New France. French Jesuits proved to be more tolerant than most European missionaries in allowing Indian converts to retain at least some of their own customs.

Courtesy of Library of Congress.

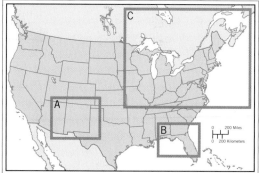

MAP 3–1

Spanish and French Missions in Seventeenth-Century North America   Spanish Franciscans in New Mexico (A) and Florida (B) and French Jesuits in New France (C) devoted considerable effort to converting native peoples to Catholic Christianity.

BASED ON this series of maps, what geographic rationale might have been behind Spanish and French decisions to convert native peoples to Catholic Christianity?

The priests wore their finest vestments and displayed religious paintings and statues, trying to impress the Indians with European goods and Catholic ceremonies. They gave away bells, knives, cloth, and food. According to one Franciscan in New Mexico, these gifts brought Indians to the missions "like fish to the fish hook." The natives believed that accepting these gifts obliged them to listen to the priests' Christian message and help them build houses and churches.

(handwritten note: ? How did diseases influence the conversion of NA's?)

(handwritten note: ? How are the conversion tactics of French/English/Spanish different? same? ⊛ mestizos)

WHERE TO LEARN MORE

Ste. Marie among the Hurons, near Midland, Ontario, Canada
www.saintemarieamongthehurons.on.ca

King Phillip's War Conflict in New England (1675–1676) between Wampanoags, Narragansetts, and other Indian peoples against English settlers; sparked by English encroachments on native lands.

Bacon's Rebellion Violent conflict in Virginia (1675–1676), beginning with settler attacks on Indians but culminating in a rebellion led by Nathaniel Bacon against Virginia's government.

Pueblo Revolt Rebellion in 1680 of Pueblo Indians in New Mexico against their Spanish overlords, sparked by religious conflict and excessive Spanish demands for tribute.

After brief religious instruction, the missionaries convinced many Indians to accept baptism into the Catholic Church and with it the promise of salvation and a heavenly afterlife. Such conversions often followed epidemics that devastated native villages but spared the Spanish, leading many Indians to wonder if the Christian God might indeed be more powerful than their own gods. In New Mexico, the Spanish offered Pueblo converts protection against Apache raids and access to Franciscan storehouses in times of famine.

Many Indians did not understand that baptism committed them to abandoning native beliefs and adopting Spanish food, clothing, and work routines. Priests in New Mexico, objecting to the ease with which Pueblo marriages could be dissolved, tried to enforce lifelong unions. Punishments for violating the new code were severe and in rare cases led to their victims' deaths.

By the mid-seventeenth century, Spanish missionaries claimed to have baptized tens of thousands of Indians. But many converts blended Christianity with native religion, adding Jesus, Mary, and the Catholic saints to the list of Indian gods and accepting missionaries as counterparts to native priests. Many converts were *mestizos*—people of mixed Indian and Spanish descent—who often practiced native rituals in secret. Some groups, such as the Zuni and Hopi peoples, rejected Christianity altogether. In the end, the spread of Christianity in the Spanish borderlands was not as complete as the Franciscans claimed.

French priests in Canada also tried to convert Indians to Catholicism. Like the Franciscans, they tried to impress potential converts with religious rituals and material objects. Priests amazed Indians with clocks, magnets, and their ability to predict eclipses and to read and write. "All this serves to gain their affections, and to render them more docile when we introduce the admirable and incomprehensible mysteries of our Faith," explained one priest.

French missionaries also resorted to economic pressure, convincing merchants to sell guns only to converted Indians and to offer them other trade goods at a discount. The Jesuits were generally more tolerant than the Franciscans of native ways. "One must be careful before condemning a thousand things among their customs," warned one priest, because to do so would "greatly offend minds brought up and nourished in another world."

The Protestant English were less successful at attracting Native American converts. Puritans frowned on the rituals and religious objects that drew Indian converts to Catholicism. And with its emphasis on the direct study of scripture, Protestantism required that potential converts learn to read.

Beginning in the 1650s, Puritan ministers in New England, such as John Eliot, established several praying towns, communities where Indians lived apart from settlers to learn Protestant Christianity and English ways. By 1674 about 2,300 Indians resided in these towns. Although individual ministers were interested in missionary work, efforts at conversion in the Anglican southern colonies enjoyed little success. English settlers preferred to isolate Indians rather than convert them.

AFTER THE FIRST HUNDRED YEARS: CONFLICT AND WAR

After nearly a century of European settlement, violence between colonists and Indians erupted in all three North American empires, in **King Philip's War** in New England, **Bacon's Rebellion** in Virginia, the **Pueblo Revolt** in New Mexico, and the resumption of the Beaver Wars in New France.

King Philip's War, which broke out in 1675, was sparked by the growing frustration of the Wampanoags—the Indians who had befriended the Pilgrims more than half a century before—with the land-hungry settlers whose towns now surrounded them. Massasoit's younger son, Metacom—called King Philip by the

(handwritten note at bottom: ⊛ Bacon's R. ⊛ Metacom)

English—led the Wampanoags and struggled to preserve their independence. He had little reason to trust the colonists. His older brother had died mysteriously while being questioned by colonial officials about rumors of an Indian conspiracy. Philip himself had been accused of plotting against the settlers and then forced to sign a treaty submitting to English authority.

In the spring of 1675, a colonial court found three Wampanoags guilty of murdering a Christian Indian who had warned the English of Wampanoag preparations for war. The court sentenced the men to be hanged. The Wampanoags decided to strike back against the English. Only "a small part of the dominion of my ancestors remains," declared Philip. "I am determined not to live until I have no country."

At least a thousand colonists and perhaps three thousand Indians died in King Philip's War. One out of every sixteen male colonists of military age was killed, making this the deadliest conflict in American history in terms of the proportion of casualties to total population. (See American Views: "Mary Rowlandson among the Indians.") The Indians succeeded in forcing back the line of settlement but lost what remained of their independence in New England. Philip died in an ambush in August 1676, and the war ended soon afterwards. The victorious English sold many native survivors, including Philip's wife and young son, into slavery in the West Indies. Philip's head, impaled on a stake, was left for decades on the outskirts of Plymouth as a grisly warning of the price to be paid for resisting colonial expansion.

A bloody conflict erupted in Virginia that had a similarly devastating effect on that colony's native population. Frustrated by shrinking economic opportunities in eastern Virginia, many settlers moved to Virginia's western frontier. In the summer of 1675, a group of frontier settlers attacked the Susquehannocks in order to seize their lands. The Indians struck back, prompting Nathaniel Bacon, a young, wealthy planter who had only recently arrived in Virginia, to lead the settlers in a violent campaign against all Indians, even those at peace with the colonial government. Governor William Berkeley ordered Bacon and his men to stop their attacks. They defied him and marched on Jamestown, turning a war between settlers and Indians into a rebellion of settlers against the colonial authorities.

The rebels believed that Berkeley and the colonial government represented the interests of established tobacco planters. Desperate because of the low price of tobacco, the rebels demanded lower taxes and easier access to land. They also wanted help exterminating the Indians. Rebels captured and burned the colonial capital at Jamestown, forcing Berkeley to flee. They burned Indian villages and massacred the inhabitants. Trying to appease the rebels, the House of Burgesses passed measures allowing them to seize native lands and legalizing the enslavement of Indians.

By the time troops arrived from England to put down the rebellion, Bacon had died of a fever and most of his men had drifted home. Berkeley hanged twenty-three rebels, but the real victims of the rebellion were Virginia's Indians. The remnants of the once-powerful Powhatans lost their remaining lands and either moved west or lived in poverty on the edges of English settlement. Hatred of Indians became a permanent feature of frontier life in Virginia.

In 1680 the Pueblo Revolt erupted against Spain's colony of New Mexico. Nearly twenty thousand Pueblo Indians in New Mexico had grown restless under the harsh rule of only 2,500 Spaniards. During a prolonged drought that began in the 1660s, many people starved. The Apaches, who had once traded with the Pueblos for corn, now raided their storehouses instead, and Spanish soldiers could not stop them.

3–4

Edward Randolph Describes King Philip's War (1865)

QUICK REVIEW

King Philip's War

♦ King Philip's War broke out in 1675.

♦ Conflict between Wampanoags and settlers led to war.

♦ Thousands of settlers and Indians died in the fighting.

WHERE TO LEARN MORE

Taos Pueblo, Taos, New Mexico

www.cr.nps.gov/worldheritage/taos.htm

• AMERICAN VIEWS •

MARY ROWLANDSON AMONG THE INDIANS

I *n February 1676, in the midst of King Philip's War, Indian warriors attacked the town of Lancaster, Massachusetts. They killed many inhabitants and took 23 colonists captive, including Mary Rowlandson and three of her children. Rowlandson spent the next three months traveling with various groups of Nipmucs, Narragansetts, and Wampanoags. She watched her youngest daughter die in her arms and worried about her other two children, from whom she was frequently separated. Rowlandson survived her captivity by adapting to the Indians' way of life until she was ransomed and rejoined her family. In 1682, she published an account of her captivity in which she explored the meaning of her experience. The narrative was so popular that three editions were printed in the first year.*

HOW DID Rowlandson describe the Indians? How did she characterize her encounter with King Philip? How did Rowlandson accommodate herself to the Indians' way of life? How did she employ her skills to fit in? How did her gender affect her captivity? How did Rowlandson's Puritan faith shape her narrative?

We travelled on till night; and in the morning, we must go over the River to Philip's crew. When I was in the Cannoo, I could not but be amazed at the numerous crew of Pagans that were on the Bank on the other side. When I came ashore, they gathered all about me, I sitting alone in the midst: I observed they asked one another questions, and laughed, and rejoyced over their Gains and Victories. Then my heart began to fail: and I fell a weeping which was the first time to my remembrance, that I wept before them. Although I had met with so much Affliction, and my heart was many times ready to break, yet could I not shed one tear in their sight: but rather had been all this while

in a maze, and like one astonished: but now I may say as, Psal. 137.1 *By the rivers of Babylon, there we sat down: yea, we wept when we remembered Zion.* There one of them asked me, why I wept, I could hardly tell what to say: yet I answered, they would kill me: No, said he, none will hurt you. Then came one of them and gave me two spoon-fulls of Meal to comfort me. . . . Then I went to see King Philip, he bade me come in and sit down, and asked me whether I would smoke (a usual Complement now adayes amongst Saints and Sinners) but this no way suited me. For though I had formerly used Tobacco, yet I had left it ever since I was first taken, *It seems to be a bait, the devil lays to make men loose their precious time. . . .*

During my abode in this place, Philip spake to me to make a shirt for his boy, which I did, for which he gave me a shilling: I offered the money to my master, but he bade me keep it: and with it I bought a piece of Horse flesh. Afterwards he asked me to make a Cap for his boy, for which he invited me to Dinner. I went, and he gave me a Pancake, about as big as two fingers; it was made of parched wheat, beaten, and fryed in Bears grease, but I thought I never tasted pleasanter meat in my life. There was a Squaw who spake to me to make a shirt for her *Sannup* [husband], for which she gave me a piece of Bear. Another asked me to knit a pair of Stockins, for which she gave me a quart of Pease. . . . Hearing that my son was come to this place, I went to see him, and found him lying flat upon the ground: I asked him how he could sleep so? He answered me, *That he was not asleep, but at Prayer,* and lay so, that they might not observe what he was doing. I pray God he may remember these things now he is returned in safety.

Source: Neal Salisbury, ed., *The Sovereignty and Goodness of God. Together with the Faithfulness of His Promises Displayed. . . .* (Boston, 1997), pp. 82–83.

The spark that ignited the revolt, however, was an act of religious persecution. Spanish officials unwisely chose this troubled time to stamp out Pueblo religion. In 1675, the governor arrested forty-seven native religious leaders on charges of sorcery. The court ordered most of them to be publicly whipped and released but sentenced four of them to death.

Spanish soldiers marched into Pueblo villages and destroyed kivas, the underground chambers that Indians used for religious ceremonies. Led by Popé, one of the freed leaders, the outraged Pueblos organized a network of rebels. By the summer of 1680, Popé commanded an enormous force drawn from twenty Pueblo villages. On August 10, the rebels attacked the Spanish settlements. Popé urged them to "break up and burn the images of the holy Christ, the Virgin Mary and the other saints, the crosses, and everything pertaining to Christianity." Within a few weeks, the rebels had destroyed or damaged every Spanish building and killed more than four hundred Spaniards, including twenty-one of the colony's thirty-three missionaries. By October, all Spaniards had fled New Mexico.

They did not return for thirteen years. By then, internal rivalries had split the victorious Pueblo coalition. Even so, the Spanish understood the folly of pushing the Indians too far. Officials reduced demands for tribute, and the Franciscans eased their attacks on Pueblo religion.

In the last phase of the Beaver Wars, what began as a struggle between the Iroquois and western native peoples for control of the fur trade blossomed into a larger conflict as it was absorbed into the imperial rivalry between England and France.

Looking for new trading partners, the French turned in the 1680s to the Ottawas, Wyandots, and other Indian peoples living near the Great Lakes. But the Iroquois had begun to raid these same peoples for furs and captives, much as they had attacked the Hurons in the first phase of the Beaver Wars in the 1640s. They exchanged the furs with their English allies. The Iroquois objected to French traders' attempt to "have all the Bevers" for themselves.

The French attacked the Iroquois to prevent them and their English allies from extending their influence in the west. In June 1687, a combined force of French and Christian Indian soldiers invaded the lands of the Senecas, the westernmost of the five nations of the Iroquois League. The Iroquois retaliated by besieging a French garrison at Niagara, where nearly two hundred soldiers starved to death, and killing hundreds of colonists in attacks on French villages along the St. Lawrence River.

In 1689, France and England went to war in Europe, and the struggle between them and their Indian allies for control of the fur trade in North America became part of a larger imperial contest between the two countries. The European powers made peace in 1697, but calm did not immediately return to the Great Lakes region.

The conflict was devastating for the Iroquois. Perhaps a quarter of their population died from disease and warfare by 1689. The devastation encouraged Iroquois diplomats to find a way to extricate themselves from future English-French conflicts. In 1701, a pair of treaties, negotiated separately with Albany and Montreal, recognized Iroquois neutrality and, at least for a few decades, prevented either the English or the French from dominating the western lands.

English settlers fought with Wampanoags, Powhatans, and Susquehannocks for control of land, and the losers were the outnumbered Indians. In 1680 a Pueblo revolt drove the Spanish from New Mexico for thirteen years. The Spanish were only able to re-establish control by abolishing the *encomienda system* and relaxing their strictures against Pueblo religious practices. French soldiers battled with the Iroquois over control of the fur trade until both sides agreed to an uneasy truce. In each case, nearly a century of contact culminated in a struggle that revealed how difficult, if not impossible, it was to reconcile European and native interests.

QUICK REVIEW

France, Britain, and the Iroquois
- France attacked the Iroquois to prevent them from extending their influence.
- France and England went to war in 1689.
- War spilled over into North America devastating Iroquois.

This ball-headed war club, carved of maple wood, is thought to have been owned by King Philip, who led a confederation of Wampanoags and other New England Indians in a war against the colonists in 1675–1676. It is inlaid on both sides with pieces of white and purple wampum, which supposedly represented the number of English and Indian enemies killed.

King Philip's War Club. Courtesy of Fruitlands Museums, Harvard, MA.

[handwritten: Section 3: pg 68-75.]

AFRICANS AND EUROPEANS

Many more Africans than Europeans came to the New World during the colonial period. Virtually all of them arrived as slaves; thus the history of African experience in America is inseparable from the history of slavery and the slave trade.

LABOR NEEDS AND THE TURN TO SLAVERY

Europeans in the New World thrilled to find that land was abundant and quite cheap by European standards. They were perplexed, however, by the unexpectedly high cost of labor. In Europe, the reverse had been true. There land was expensive but labor cheap because competition for jobs among large numbers of workers pushed wages down.

Colonial workers commanded high wages because there were so few of them compared to the supply of land waiting to be developed. Moreover, few settlers wanted to work for others when they could get farms of their own. The scarcity and high cost of labor led some colonial employers to turn to enslaved Africans as a solution.

Europeans had owned slaves (both white and black) long before the beginning of American colonization. But by 1500 slavery had all but disappeared in northern Europe. It persisted longer in southern Europe and the Middle East. Because neither Christians nor Muslims would hold as slaves members of their own faiths, Arab traders turned to sub-Saharan Africa to find slaves who did not belong to either religion. Eventually the Arabic word for slave—*abd*—became a synonym for "black man." By the fifteenth century, a durable link between slave status and black skin had been forged in European minds.

3–12
Alexander Falconbridge, The African Slave Trade (1788)

When Spanish and Portuguese adventurers needed workers to develop newly colonized Atlantic islands and New World lands, they turned to slavery. Masters exercised complete control over slaves and paid them no wages. English colonists later adopted slavery in America even though it was unknown as a system of labor at home.

It was Indians, however, not Africans, whom the Europeans first forced into slavery in the Americas. Spaniards held native slaves in all their New World colonies and English colonists condemned Indian enemies captured in wartime to slavery. In early Carolina, English traders encouraged Indians "to make War amongst themselves to get Slaves" whom the traders could buy and then resell to West Indian and local planters.

Native American slaves, however, could not fill the settlers' labor needs. Disease and harsh working conditions reduced their numbers. Enslaved Indian men refused to perform agricultural labor, which they considered women's work. Because they knew the land better than the colonists, Indians could easily escape and make their way back to their own people. By 1700 the Indian slave trade had given way to a much larger traffic in Africans.

The Spanish and Portuguese first brought Africans to the Americas to supplement the dwindling numbers of Indian slaves toiling in silver mines and on sugar plantations. English colonists adopted slavery more slowly. West Indian planters were the first to do so on a large scale in the 1640s, following the Portuguese example in using black slaves to grow sugar.

Black slaves first arrived in Virginia in 1619 when a Dutch trader sold "20. and odd Negroes" in Jamestown, but they did not form a significant portion of the colony's population until the end of the century. For decades, tobacco planters saw no reason to switch from white indentured servants to slaves. Servants were cheap, available, and familiar; slaves were expensive, difficult to obtain, and exotic.

QUICK REVIEW

The Demand for Labor

- Indians first forced into slavery in the Americas.
- By 1700 Indian slave trade replaced by slaves from Africa.
- Overtime slaves replaced servants on tobacco plantations.

[handwritten margin notes:]
(?) which group of people did the English/Spanish 1st attempt to enslave?
(?) why were the NA
not good/effective slaves?
(?) In which year where the first slaves sold in VA?

Beginning in the 1680s, planters in the Chesapeake colonies of Virginia and Maryland began to shift from servants to slaves. White indentured servants became harder to find. Fewer young English men and women chose to emigrate as servants after 1660 because an improving economy in England provided jobs for them at home. And Virginia's white population tripled between 1650 and 1700, rapidly increasing the competition for a shrinking supply of laborers. Chesapeake planters also faced competition from newer colonies.

As white servants grew scarcer, African slaves became more available, largely due to changes in the slave trade. After 1698, England's Royal African Company lost its monopoly rights and many English merchants—and New Englanders—entered the fiercely competitive trade.

Chesapeake planters eventually came to prefer slaves to servants. Although more expensive than servants, slaves were a better long-term investment. Buying both men and women gave planters a self-reproducing labor force. Runaway black slaves were more easily recaptured than escaped servants, who blended into the white population. And unlike indentured servants, slaves were slaves for life and would not someday compete as planters with their former masters.

Chesapeake planters' view of white servants as possessions, whose labor could be bought and sold like any other commodity, eased the gradual transition in the 1680s and 1690s to the much harsher system of slavery. In Carolina, slaves had arrived right from the start, brought in the 1670s by colony founders accustomed to slavery in Barbados. By 1720, one-third of Virginia's settlers—and nearly three-quarters of South Carolina's—were black people.

Slavery grew rapidly in the South because it answered the labor needs of planters engaged in the commercial production of tobacco and rice. When James Oglethorpe founded Georgia in 1732, however, he intended to keep slavery out. Oglethorpe's idea was to send English debtors to Georgia to produce exotic goods like silk and wine. But when only rice turned a profit in Georgia, its founders reluctantly legalized slavery. By 1770, slaves made up nearly half of the colony's settlers.

In the northern colonies, slaves were too expensive for farmers who mainly produced food for their families, not export crops. The relatively few northern slaves generally worked as domestic servants, craftsmen, and day laborers.

Race relations in the mainland colonies were less rigid in the seventeenth century than they would later become. In the few Chesapeake households that had slaves, white and black people lived and worked in close contact. Black slaves and white servants cooperated during Bacon's Rebellion. In some areas, free black people—often slaves who had bought their own freedom—prospered in an atmosphere of racial tolerance that would be unthinkable by the eighteenth century.

The career of an ambitious black Virginian named Anthony Johnson, for example, resembled that of many white settlers—a remarkable achievement given that he arrived in the colony as a slave in 1621. Once free, Johnson married and raised a family. By 1651, he owned a large plantation, and later he even bought a slave. Johnson belonged to the first or what one historian has called the "charter" generation of American slaves. These people mainly came from African port towns or via the West Indies or New Netherlands. Familiar with European ways and languages, they bargained with their masters in ways their descendants would not be able to replicate, and they often gained their freedom.

But Johnson's descendants, and the generations of slaves who came afterwards, encountered harsher conditions. After 1700, slavery became the dominant labor system in the Chesapeake. Tobacco planters feared that free black people might encourage slaves to escape. In 1699, Virginia's assembly passed a law requiring newly freed black people to leave the colony.

QUICK REVIEW

Growth of Slavery

- Slavery grew rapidly in the South.
- The use of slaves made economic sense on tobacco and rice plantations.
- Northern slaves worked as servants, craftsmen, and day laborers.

FROM THEN TO NOW
The Legacy of Slavery

As the twenty-first century begins, Americans continue to grapple with the social, economic, and political consequences of the nation's past involvement in the enslavement of Africans. Slavery's roots extend deeply into American history, reaching back before nationhood itself. White colonists, facing a New World labor shortage in the seventeenth century, chose to fill their need for workers by purchasing slaves from Africa. Seeking to produce as much tobacco, rice, or sugar as they could for as little cost as possible, they left a painful legacy that has shaped America's history for centuries.

By the early eighteenth century, slavery was a fixture in every colony, and white colonists had come to associate slave status with black skin. The Revolution, with its rhetoric of freedom, challenged slavery but did not end it. It took another, far bloodier, war in the following century to accomplish that end. But the constitutional amendments outlawing slavery and guaranteeing black people's civil rights that passed after the Civil War—important milestones though they were—still could not eradicate the racism that had become deeply ingrained in American life.

Even today, well over a century after the Civil War ended, problems persist. Many black Americans have joined the middle class, but many others continue to suffer from discrimination and poverty. Black Americans' average incomes lag behind those of white people, fewer black people attend college, more of them live in impoverished neighborhoods in decaying urban centers. Black victims occasionally become targets of hate crimes merely because of the color of their skin. To a considerable extent, these economic and social dislocations, and the racial attitudes that help to shape them, can be traced to the lingering effects of slavery.

Recent public and private efforts to address the condition of African Americans have sought to highlight that longstanding connection. In 1997, for instance, President Bill Clinton appointed a commission to study the persistent problem of race in America. That he chose an historian, John Hope Franklin, to head the group suggested that Clinton recognized the link between America's past involvement with slavery and the nation's current racial divisions. But when some of his supporters subsequently urged Clinton to issue a formal apology for slavery, he refused to take what would have been a highly controversial step.

The reluctance of political leaders to take on such a sensitive issue may explain the recent search for private remedies. Among the most prominent of these efforts was a federal lawsuit filed in March 2002 against the Aetna Insurance Company, the FleetBoston Financial Corporation, and the CSX Corporation. A group of black plaintiffs charged that these companies profited from slavery in the past, and ought to make restitution. In the 1850s the Aetna Insurance Company, for example, made money insuring the lives of slaves. Deandria Farmer-Paellmann, the lead plaintiff in the lawsuit and a descendant of slaves, discovered the connection as she researched the slave reparations issue for a law-school class. These companies, she suggested, "should be held responsible, and later on down the road there will be more companies."

Whether these suits will be any more successful than the push for a presidential apology remains to be seen. How reparations, if granted, would be used to ameliorate the condition of black Americans is also unclear. This lawsuit joins a host of earlier strategies, including constitutional amendments and civil rights legislation, in seeking to reverse the legacy of slavery and to make equality and justice a reality for all Americans. Even in the first decade of the twenty-first century, the nation is still contending with the consequences of decisions made by some of the earliest colonists almost four hundred years ago.

slave codes.

The condition of black people swiftly deteriorated. Laws defined slavery as lifelong and hereditary according to the condition of the mother and identified slave status with black skin. Other measures deprived black persons, slave or free, of basic civil rights. They could not testify in court against white people, hold property, congregate in public places, or travel without permission. Interracial marriages, never common, were now prohibited as "shameful Matches."

Colonists resorted to these slave codes—which reduced human beings to the status of property—largely because of fears generated by a rising black population. In 1720, a South Carolina planter predicted that slaves would soon rise up against their masters because black people were "too numerous in proportion to the White Men there." The changing composition of the slave labor force also created tensions.

Unlike the charter generation, slaves who came later usually came from the African interior. Planters commented on the strange appearance and behavior of these slaves, but the colonists' uneasiness scarcely compared to the Africans' harrowing experience.

THE SHOCK OF ENSLAVEMENT

European traders relied on other Africans to capture slaves for them, tapping into a preexisting African slave trade and helping to expand it. Europeans built forts and trading posts on the West African coast and bought slaves from African traders (see Map 3–2). Attracted by European cloth, iron, liquor, guns, and other goods, West Africans fought increasingly among themselves to secure captives and began kidnapping individuals from the interior.

People of all social ranks ended up on the slave ships. Some had been slaves in Africa; others had been village leaders. Even members of African royal families ended up in shackles as slavery reduced all Africans, regardless of their social origins, to the same degraded status.

Once captured, slaves marched in chains to the coast, to be confined in cages called "barracoons" until there were enough to fill a ship. Captains examined them to ensure their fitness and branded them like cattle with a hot iron. The slaves then boarded canoes to be ferried to the ships.

 MAP EXPLORATION
To explore an interactive version of this map, go to
http://www.prenhall.com/goldfield2/map3.2

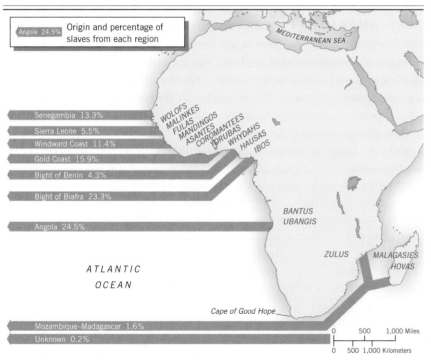

MAP 3–2

African Origins of North American Slaves, 1690–1807   Nearly all slaves in English North America were West Africans. Most had been captured or purchased by African slave traders, who then sold them to European merchants.

WHY MIGHT the Bight of Biafra and Angola together have made up nearly 50 percent of all slave trading out of West Africa?

Source: After Philip Curtin, *The Atlantic Slave Trade: A Census* (1969), tab. 45, p. 157.

⊕ Middle Passage.

As this nineteenth-century engraving indicates, slaves were often subjected to humiliating physical inspections so that potential buyers could be convinced of their good health and strength.

Courtesy of Library of Congress.

⊕ Creoles

Slaves suffered through a horrendous six- to eight-week-long ocean voyage known as the **Middle Passage**. Captains wedged men below decks into spaces about 6 feet long, 16 inches wide, and 30 inches high. Women and children were packed even tighter. They occasionally came up on deck for fresh air, but spent most of the time below decks, where the air grew foul from the vomit, blood, and excrement in which the terrified victims lay. Sailors sometimes heard a "howling melancholy noise" coming from below. Some slaves tried to commit suicide by jumping overboard or starving themselves. Between 5 and 20 percent of the slaves perished from disease, but captains had usually packed the ships tightly enough to make a profit selling the rest.

Survivors of the dreadful voyage endured the fear and humiliation of sale. Sometimes buyers rushed aboard ship in a scramble to choose slaves. Ship captains also sold slaves at public auctions, where eager purchasers poked them, looking for signs of disease. The terrified Africans often thought they were about to be eaten.

AFRICAN-AMERICAN FAMILIES AND COMMUNITIES

Most Africans brought to the New World went to New Spain, Brazil, or the West Indies. Black communities developed slowly in English America. In the northern colonies, most slaves lived alone or in pairs with their master's family. Only in the cities, where slaves were more numerous, could they have regular contact with other black people. In the South, until the eighteenth century, slaves were dispersed among a much larger white population. Slave numbers grew after 1700, but much of the increase consisted of African immigrants. These people retained African ethnic identities, which delayed their developing a sense of community.

By about 1750, more slaves in the southern colonies were *creoles* (American-born) than African natives. Creoles lived longer than African immigrants, and creole women usually bore twice as many children as African-born mothers. The mainland slave population began to grow by natural increase.

Creole slaves grew up without personal memories of Africa, so African ethnic differences seemed less important to them. Most creoles knew some English and spoke dialects they had created by mixing English and African words and speech patterns. The ability to communicate helped them develop a new identity as African Americans that mingled aspects of their African heritage and a common experience of slavery.

Kinship ties, crucial to West Africans' sense of identity, remained important to American slaves. But slave families were fragile units, subject to the whims of masters who could break up families by sale at any time, and who could take slave women as sexual partners at will. Even so, slaves managed to form families that preserved and modified African traditions.

Households headed by mothers reappeared in America. Slave fathers often belonged to different masters than their wives and children and had to live apart from their families. Some slave husbands, like West African men, took more than

Middle Passage The voyage between West Africa and the New World slave colonies.

one wife (a practice masters allowed because it led to more slave children). Slave parents gave their children African names, often secretly adding them to the "official" names given by masters.

Carolina slaves followed West African practice by building their houses of "tabby," a mixture of lime and seashells, and constructing houses on a circular plan. Potters and basketmakers used African designs in their work. Slaves raised African food plants (millet, yams, sesame seeds) in their gardens. They also made music, performed dances, and told folk tales derived from African models.

Traces of African religion also endured in America. Faith in magic and fortune tellers and the belief that relatives remained members of kin communities even after death, which made funerals extremely important, reflected slaves' West African background. During most of the colonial period Christianity offered little competition to these African religious practices. Few masters were interested in converting their slaves, and most slaves did not adopt Christianity until after the Revolution.

Labor, however, consumed most of a slave's waking hours. On tobacco plantations, slaves toiled in gangs supervised by overseers. Rice planters allowed their workers more flexibility, permitting them free time after they finished assigned tasks. On large plantations, masters selected slaves to be trained as shoemakers, weavers, or tailors. Only a few slave women—nurses, cooks—avoided the drudgery of field work. And after a day in the fields, slave women had to take care of their families, doing the cooking, child care, washing, and housework.

The growth of slave family and community ties made it much more difficult for slaves to risk escape or contemplate rebellion. The master could use his power to break up families as a tool to ensure compliant behavior. In effect, every slave child was his hostage.

Community life offered further opportunities to preserve elements of African heritage. Traces of African religious practices endured in America. Magical charms and amulets have been found buried in slave quarters, indicating that certain spiritual ceremonies may have been conducted out of sight of white masters. Slave conjurors told fortunes, concocted herbal potions, and placed curses on their clients' enemies. Reflecting their West African background, slaves placed great emphasis on funerals, in the belief that relatives remained members of kin communities even after death. Funerals were sometimes divided into two distinct ceremonies. First, the deceased received a somber burial, often with beads or other ceremonial objects placed in the grave; some weeks later, slaves played music and danced at livelier funeral rites.

Christianity offered little competition to African religious practices during most of the colonial period. Few masters showed much interest in converting their slaves. Evangelical ministers, who began to preach to slave audiences around the middle of the eighteenth century, did gain some converts, but the widespread adoption of Christianity by slaves did not occur until after the Revolution.

African influences shaped aspects of slaves' recreational activity and material life. Slave musicians used African-style instruments, including drums and banjos, to accompany traditional songs and dances. In parts of South Carolina, slaves enjoyed *papaw*, an African game with dice. Storytellers entertained audiences with folk tales that may have had African roots. Where slaves were allowed to build their own houses, they often incorporated African elements into the designs, for instance, by using mud walls and roofs thatched with palmetto leaves. Their gardens frequently contained African foods such as millet, yams, peppers, and sesame seeds along with European and Native American crops.

Family and community ties gave a sense of belonging and dignity to people whose masters treated them as outcasts. Working and living together, slaves preserved

QUICK REVIEW

Slave Society
- Traces of African culture remained in slave society.
- Labor consumed most of slave's time.
- Growth of slave families and communities inhibited escape and rebellion.

(?) Name some ways in which AA sustained their African heritage.

at least some elements of African culture despite the harrowing conditions of their forced migration. Out of their African past and their American experience, they created new identities as African Americans as they coped with the oppressiveness of slavery.

RESISTANCE AND REBELLION

Slaves on ships anchored off the Guinea Coast waiting to leave for America sometimes mutinied but rarely succeeded. The powerful desire for freedom and the spirit of resistance remained strong among Africans and their descendants in America.

Thousands of slaves ran away from masters. Deciding where to go posed a problem as slavery was legal in every colony. Some runaways went to Florida, where Spanish officials promised them freedom. Others tried to survive on their own in the woods or join the Indians. But South Carolina planters paid Indians to catch escaped slaves, causing distrust between the two peoples. Running away also carried the high emotional cost of separation from loved ones as well as physical danger. Many slaves chose other ways to resist their bondage.

Landon Carter of Virginia, who complained that his slaves "seem to be quite dead hearted and either cannot or will not work," was the target of another form of resistance. Slaves worked slowly, broke tools, and pretended to be ill in order to conserve strength and exert some control over their working lives. When provoked, they also took more direct action, damaging crops, stealing goods, and setting fire to their masters' barns, houses, and fields. Some occasionally tried to poison whites.

South Carolinians and coastal Virginians, who lived in regions where black people outnumbered white people, had a particular dread of slave revolt. No slave rebellion succeeded in the British colonies, however. In Charleston, South Carolina, rumors of a planned uprising in 1740 led to the torture and execution of fifty

WHERE TO LEARN MORE

Carter's Grove Slave Quarter, near Williamsburg, Virginia
www.williamsburg.com/plant/carter.html

This eighteenth-century painting from South Carolina records the preservation of certain African traditions in American slave communities. The dance may be Yoruba in origin, while the stringed instrument and drum were probably modeled on African instruments.

Colonial Williamsburg Foundation, Abby Aldrich Rockefeller Folk Art Center, Williamsburg, VA.

(handwritten note) name 3 ways in which slaves resisted their inferior status.

black suspects. The following year, thirty-five accused rebels (including four white people) were executed in New York City.

Two slave revolts did occur in the colonial period and instilled lasting fear in white colonists. In 1712 in New York City, about twenty slaves set a building on fire and killed nine white men who came to put it out. The revolt was quickly suppressed. The court sentenced twenty-four alleged rebels to death: Thirteen were hanged, three burned at the stake, one starved to death, and one was broken on the wheel. Six committed suicide before execution.

The **Stono Rebellion**, colonial America's largest slave uprising, occurred in South Carolina in 1739. About twenty slaves—including several recently arrived Angolans—broke into a store and armed themselves with stolen guns. As the rebels marched southward along the Stono River, their ranks grew to perhaps a hundred. Heading for freedom in Spanish Florida, they attacked white settlements along the way. White troops (with Indian help) defeated the rebels within a week, but tensions remained high for months. The death toll, in the end, was about two dozen white people and perhaps twice as many black rebels.

In the wake of the Stono Rebellion, South Carolina's assembly passed a law requiring stricter supervision of slave activities. Other measures encouraged more white immigration to offset the colony's black majority. But the colony continued to consider slavery indispensable to economic survival and would not end it.

EUROPEAN LABORERS IN NORTH AMERICA

Slavery was one of several responses to the scarcity of labor in the New World. It took hold mainly in areas where the profits from growing export crops such as sugar, rice, and tobacco offset the high purchase price of slaves and where a warm climate permitted year-round work. Elsewhere, Europeans found other means to acquire and manage laborers.

A SPECTRUM OF CONTROL

Most colonial laborers were, in some measure, unfree. One-half to two-thirds of all white emigrants to the English colonies arrived as indentured servants. Servants were most common in the Chesapeake, and to a lesser extent in Pennsylvania, where they produced export crops valuable enough to enable their masters, to feed, clothe, and shelter them—and still make a profit.

Slaves gradually replaced white indentured servants in Chesapeake tobacco fields. By the middle of the eighteenth century, white servitude was in decline as a dominant labor system throughout the colonies.

Eighteenth-century Chesapeake planters availed themselves of another unfree labor source: transported English convicts, serious criminals who might otherwise have been executed. Between 1718 and 1775, nearly fifty thousand convicts were sent to the colonies, 80 percent of whom ended up in the Chesapeake. Labor-hungry planters eagerly bought them for seven-year terms at relatively low prices and exploited them ruthlessly.

The **redemptioner** system brought many German families to the colonies in the eighteenth century. Instead of negotiating contracts for service before leaving Europe, as indentured servants did, redemptioners promised to redeem, or pay, the costs of passage on arrival in America. They often paid part of the fare themselves before sailing. If they could not raise the rest soon after landing, the ship captain who brought them sold them into servitude. The length of their service depended on how much they still owed. Most Germans went to Pennsylvania,

2-12
James Oglethorpe: The Stono Rebellion (1739)

WHAT FACTORS

motivated European immigrants to make the long journey to North America during the seventeenth and eighteenth centuries?

Stono Rebellion Uprising in 1739 of South Carolina slaves against whites; inspired in part by Spanish officials' promise of freedom for American slaves who escaped to Florida.

Redemptioner Similar to an indentured servant, except that a redemptioner signed a labor contract in America rather than in Europe.

W WHERE TO LEARN MORE

Ephrata Cloister,
Ephrata, Pennsylvania
www.cob-net.org/cloister.htm

where they hoped to find friends or relatives willing to help them pay off their debt quickly.

Purchasing slaves, servants, or convicts did not make sense for everyone. Colonists who owned undeveloped land faced many tasks—cutting trees, clearing fields, building fences and barns—that brought no immediate profit. These landowners, many of whom lived in Pennsylvania, New Jersey, and New York, rented undeveloped tracts to propertyless families. Both tenants and landlords benefited from this arrangement. Tenants enjoyed greater independence than servants and could save toward the purchase of their own farms. The landlord secured the labor necessary to transform his property into a working farm, which increased the land's value. He also received an annual rent payment, usually a portion of the tenant's crop, and eventually profited from selling the land—often to the tenant family that had rented it.

Merchants eager to develop New England's fisheries devised other means to fill their labor needs. Because it was fairly easy to get a farm, few New Englanders cared to take on the difficult and risky job of fishing. Moreover, few could afford the necessary equipment. New England fish merchants advanced credit to coastal villagers so they could outfit their own boats and become fishermen. To pay off the debt, the fishermen were legally bound to bring their catch to the merchant, who then sold it to Europe and the West Indies.

In the northern colonies, the cost of servants or slaves exceeded whatever small profit could be made on farms that produced no export crops and could not be worked during cold winter months. So northern farmers turned to the cheapest and most dependable workers they could find—their children.

Children as young as 5 or 6 years old began with simple tasks and moved on to more complex work as they grew older. By the time they were in their late teens, girls knew how to run households and boys knew how to farm. Fathers used their ownership of property to prolong the time their sons worked for them. Young men in New England could not marry until they could support a wife and family. Often sons did not actually own any land until their fathers died and left it to them in their wills.

Thus New England's labor shortage produced strong ties of dependency between generations. Fathers kept their sons working for them as long as possible; sons accepted this arrangement as a way to become independent farmers, eventually employing their own children in the same way.

Property owners in all the English colonies found different ways to control laborers. But where property owners saw problems—high wages (often twice what workers in England received) and abundant land (which deterred colonists from working for others when they could have their own farms)—others saw opportunities. For tens of thousands of Europeans, the chance to own or rent a farm or to find steady employment made North America an irresistible magnet, promising a prosperity that was beyond their reach at home.

NEW EUROPEAN IMMIGRANTS

European immigrants flooded into America in the seventeenth and eighteenth centuries. By 1773, the tremendous outflow of Britons—Protestant Scots-Irish, Scots, and Irish Catholics—to America sparked debate in England over whether emigration should be prohibited lest the British Isles be left empty. Continental Europe contributed another stream of emigrants, mostly from the German states. Perhaps 100,000 Protestants left the Rhine Valley, fleeing war, economic hardship, and religious persecution. French Protestants (known as Huguenots) began emigrating after 1685, when their faith was made illegal in France. Swiss Protestants likewise fled religious persecution. Even a few Poles, Greeks, Italians, and Jews reached the colonies in the eighteenth century.

Streams of emigrants flowed to places where land was cheap and labor most in demand (see Map 3–3). Few went to New England, where descendants of the first settlers already occupied the best land. They also avoided areas where slavery predominated—the Chesapeake tidewater and lowland South Carolina—in favor of the foothills of the Appalachian Mountains from western Pennsylvania to the Carolinas.

Not all emigrants realized their dreams of becoming independent landowners. The scarcity of labor in the colonies led as easily to the exploitation of white workers as of slaves and Indians. Even so, for many people facing bleak prospects in Europe, the chance that emigration might bring prosperity was too tempting to ignore.

CONCLUSION

By the middle of the eighteenth century, America offered a strikingly diverse mosaic of peoples and communities. Along the St. Lawrence River, lay Kahnawake, a village of Mohawks and Abenakis who had adopted Catholicism and French ways under Jesuit instruction. In Andover, Massachusetts, New Englanders tilled fields that their Puritan grandparents had cleared. German immigrants who had forsaken the world in search of spiritual perfection populated the isolated Pennsylvania settlement of Ephrata. The hundred or so slaves on Robert Carter's Virginia plantation at Nomini Hall gathered on Sunday evenings to nurture ties of community with songs and dances, while the master cultivated his very different sense of community with neighboring planters. Near St. Augustine, Florida, runaway slaves farmed and gathered shellfish under the protection of Spanish soldiers. Far to the west, the Spanish, *mestizo*, and Pueblo residents of Santa Fe warily reestablished ties broken during the Pueblo Revolt.

In these and many other communities, peoples from three continents adapted to one another and to American conditions. Indians struggled with the consequences of disease, trade, religious conversion, settlement, and warfare resulting from European immigration. Africans exchanged traditional ethnic connections for a new identity as African Americans. English settlers became landowners in unprecedented numbers and adopted new ways to control laborers, re-inventing slavery, unknown in England for centuries. No European settlement in America fully reproduced Old World patterns, and no native village fully preserved the precontact Indian way of life.

MAP EXPLORATION
To explore an interactive version of this map, go to
http://www.prenhall.com/goldfield2/map3.3

MAP 3–3

Ethnic Distribution of Settler Population in British Mainland Colonies, c. 1755   Settlers of different ethnic backgrounds tended to concentrate in certain areas. Only New Englanders were predominantly English, while Africans dominated in the Chesapeake tidewater and South Carolina. German, Scottish, and Scots-Irish immigrants often settled in the backcountry.

DO YOU think colonists from different ethnic backgrounds tended to settle in areas geographically similar to those from which they came?

SUMMARY

Indians and Europeans Although by 1750 European colonists and African slaves together outnumbered Indians north of the Rio Grande, Native Americans continued to dominate much of the continent. More than any other European colonists, the Spanish sought direct control over Indians. Using the practices of *encomienda, repartimiento,* and *rescate,* Spanish colonists were able to control Indians in use for labor. The English caused much displacement of Indian tribes through their constant expansion of land needs. Through the spread of disease and other means, they managed to push the Indians farther and farther away from prime land once considered theirs. After nearly a century of European settlement, violence between colonists and Indians erupted in all three North American empires. A series of wars and revolts began a period of decades of hostilities between Europeans and Indians.

Africans and Europeans Though many more Africans than Europeans came to the New World during the colonial period, virtually all of them arrived as slaves. The Spanish and the Portuguese first brought Africans to the Americas to supplement the dwindling numbers of Indian slaves. Then, beginning in the 1680s, planters in the Chesapeake colonies began to shift from servants to slaves. Slavery grew most rapidly in the south because of the type of labor needed. European traders relied on other Africans to capture slaves for them. Slaves suffered through a six- to eight-week-long ocean voyage known as the Middle Passage. By about 1750, more slaves in the southern colonies were American-born than African natives.

European Laborers in North America Most colonial laborers were, in some measure, unfree. More than one-half of all white emigrants to the English colonies arrived as indentured servants. And, Chesapeake planters tapped another unfree labor source: transported English convicts. Purchasing slaves, servants, and convicts, however, did not make sense for everyone. Northern farmers turned to the cheapest and most dependable workers they could find, their children.

REVIEW QUESTIONS

1. Why did English colonists experience more frequent, and more violent, conflicts with the Indians than the settlers of New France?

2. Why were Catholic missionaries more successful than Protestants in converting Indians to Christianity in early America?

3. When did Chesapeake planters switch from servants to slaves? Why did they make this change?

4. By about 1750, more slaves in the mainland British colonies were creoles (American-born) than African-born. What effects did this have on the formation of African-American communities in America?

5. Many European immigrants came to America in the eighteenth century, but they tended to settle only in certain colonial regions. What regions did they favor and why?

KEY TERMS

Bacon's Rebellion (p. 64)
Beaver Wars (p. 60)
Encomienda (p. 59)
King Philip's War (p. 64)

Middle Passage (p. 72)
Pueblo Revolt (p. 64)
Redemptioner (p. 75)
Repartimiento (p. 60)

Rescate (p. 60)
Stono Rebellion (p. 75)

WHERE TO LEARN MORE

Ste. Marie Among the Hurons, near Midland, Ontario, Canada. This site contains a reconstructed Jesuit mission from the seventeenth century. There is a museum with information about seventeenth-century France as well as life among the Huron Indians. Further information may be found at: **www.saintemarieamongthehurons.on.ca**

Taos Pueblo, Taos, New Mexico. Still a residence for Pueblo Indians, portions of this multi-storied pueblo date from the fifteenth century. This was the site from which Popé directed the beginnings of the Pueblo Revolt in 1680. Pictures and other information are available at: **www.cr.nps.gov/worldheritage/taos.htm**

Ephrata Cloister, Ephrata, Pennsylvania. Founded by German immigrants in the eighteenth century, the Ephrata community attracted religious pietists. The site now contains a museum, buildings that reflect medieval German architectural styles, and a collection of decorative art objects. The website **www.cob-net.org/cloister.htm** includes a biography of Ephrata's founder, Johann Conrad Beissel.

Carter's Grove Slave Quarter, near Williamsburg, Virginia. Site includes reconstructed eighteenth-century slave quarters on original site where slave cabins once stood. Costumed African-American interpreters show visitors around and tell stories about actual slaves who lived on the plantation. Information about the house and plantation can be found at: **www.williamsburg.com/plant/carter.html** Pictures of the plantation may also be seen at: **www.wise.virginia.edu**

 For additional study resources for this chapter, go to:
www.prenhall.com/goldfield/chapter3

*Mr. Lawrence, Be pleased to send me
a genteel sute of Cloaths made of superfine
broad Cloth handsomely chosen . . .*

CITY HALL AND GREAT DOCK.

New Amsterdam, 17th century. City Hall and Great Dock
in the late 17th century.

4

CONVERGENCE AND CONFLICT
1660s–1763

IN WHAT ways was trade regulated
between Britain and the colonies?

HOW DID prominent colonists go about
developing America's intellectual life?

WHEN DID the "Great Awakening"
reach the colonies and what effect
did it have there?

HOW DID the "Glorious Revolution" affect the colonists?

WHAT GEOGRAPHIC area
made up the "backcountry"
and who settled there?

HOW DID the French
and Indian War affect the colonists?

Virginia

26th April 1763

Mr. Lawrence

> *Be pleased to send me a genteel sute of Cloaths made of superfine broad Cloth handsomely chosen; I shou[l]d have Inclosed [for] you my measure but in a general way they are so badly taken here that I am convinced it wou[l]d be of very little service; I wou[l]d have you therefore take measure of a Gentleman who wears well made Cloaths of the following size—to wit—Six feet high & proportionably made; if any thing rather Slender than thick for a Person of that highth with pretty long arms & thighs—You will take care to make the Breeches longer than those you sent me last, & I wou[l]d have you keep the measure of the Cloaths you now make by you and if any alteration is required, in my next [letter] it shall be pointed out. Mr Cary will pay your Bill—& I am Sir Yr Very H[um]ble Serv[an]t . . .*

> *—George Washington*

W.W. Abbot and Dorothy Twohig, eds., *The Papers of George Washington*, Colonial Series, vol. 7 (Charlottesville, 1990).

IMAGE KEY
for pages 80–81

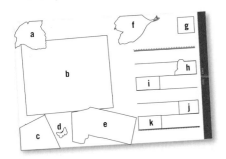

a. A brown patterned neckcloth.

b. New Amsterdam City Hall and Great Dock in the late 17th century.

c. A small pile of light muscovado sugar.

d. A mounted moth.

e. A half-loom width of oyster silk damask, 18th century.

f. Dried tobacco leaves.

g. A luxury merchant ship.

h. Portrait of Ben Franklin by Robert Feke.

i. George Whitefield extends his hands over kneeling worshippers while wearing black ministerial robes in a 1770 painting by John Wollaston.

j. A hand-colored woodcut of a settlers' log cabin in the Blue Ridge Mountains (Appalachians).

k. "The Death of General Wolfe" by American painter Benjamin West. Distraught soldiers huddle around the dying General James Wolfe at the Battle of Quebec.

GEORGE WASHINGTON, along with a few other privileged Virginians, had traveled to Williamsburg for a visit that mixed politics, business, and pleasure. These men had come to the capital to represent their respective counties in the House of Burgesses. When not engaged in government business, they attended to private affairs. They arranged to ship tobacco from their plantations to England, to pay debts, or to seek credit. Washington was surely not the only one to write to his London tailor and order fashionable clothing. He and his fellow burgesses donned their best coats and breeches to attend evening dinner parties and theater performances.

April 1763 marked the fourth time Washington had gone to Williamsburg to take his seat in the legislature. Just 31 years old in 1763, he had recently married Martha Custis, a wealthy widow, and inherited his older brother's plantation at Mount Vernon. He had served his king during the Seven Years' War; now he was eager to exchange his military uniform for the "genteel" broadcloth suits appropriate to his new station. With land and wealth to support his ambitions, he wanted to live, look, and behave like an English country gentleman, not merely like a Virginia planter.

But Washington could not be sure what an English gentleman wore. He had never been to England and trusted neither his own judgment nor Williamsburg tailors to know how a proper English gentleman should dress. So, while he instructed Mr. Lawrence about measurements and fabric quality, he had to trust his tailor to make him clothing as suitable for the drawing rooms of London as for the parlors of Williamsburg.

Throughout British America, colonists who had achieved wealth and power tried, like Washington, to imitate the English gentry. Prosperity and the demand of a growing population for English products tied the colonies ever more tightly into a trade network centered on the imperial metropolis, London. The flow of goods and information between England and America fueled the desires of Washington and other successful colonists for acceptance as transatlantic members of the English elite. No longer a collection of rough outposts clinging to the Atlantic seaboard, British America was growing in size and sophistication.

These developments in Britain's American colonies brought them to the attention of European statesmen, who increasingly factored North America into their calculations. Parliament devised legislation that would channel tobacco and other colonial goods into England and away from its European competitors. Spain and France viewed the economic growth and expansion of British North America as a threat to their own possessions, and they responded by augmenting their territorial claims. With expansion came conflict and four imperial wars, which themselves became powerful engines of change in the New World.

Economic Development and Imperial Trade in the British Colonies

The greatest assets that Great Britain could call on in its competition with other European nations were a dynamic economy and a sophisticated financial system that put commerce at the service of the state. In the century after 1690, England became the most advanced economic power in Europe.

England's leaders came to see colonies as indispensable to the nation's economic welfare. Colonies supplied raw materials unavailable in the mother country, and settlers provided a healthy market for English manufactures. As the eighteenth century progressed, colonial economies grew in tandem with England's. Parliament knitted the colonies into an empire with commercial legislation, while British merchants traded with and extended credit to growing numbers of colonial merchants and planters.

The Regulation of Trade

England, the Netherlands, and France competed vigorously in transatlantic trade. Between 1651 and 1733, Parliament passed laws that regulated trade to ensure that more wealth flowed into England's treasury than out of it (see the overview table "British Imperial Trade Regulations, 1651–1733" p. 84). This governmental intervention in the economy for the purpose of increasing national wealth—called **mercantilism**—aimed to draw the colonies into a mutually beneficial relationship with England.

Parliament enacted four types of mercantilist regulations. The first aimed at ending Dutch dominance in England's overseas trade. Beginning with the *Navigation Act of 1651*, all trade in the empire had to be conducted in English or colonial ships, with crews that were at least half Englishmen or colonists. The act stimulated rapid growth in both England's merchant marine and New England's shipping industry. Shipbuilding and earnings from what was called the "carrying trade" soon became the most profitable sector of New England's economy.

The second type of legislation channeled certain colonial goods, called **"enumerated products,"** through England or another English colony. These raw materials initially included tobacco, sugar, indigo, and cotton; other products, such as rice, were added later. European goods also had to pass through England before they could be shipped to the colonies. When these goods entered English ports, they were taxed, which made them more expensive and encouraged colonists to buy English-made items.

With the third and fourth sorts of regulation Parliament subsidized certain goods, including linen, gunpowder, and silks, to allow manufacturers to undersell European competitors in the colonies. Other laws protected English manufacturers

IN WHAT ways was trade regulated between Britain and the colonies?

QUICK REVIEW

British Trade Policy
- All trade in empire to be conducted in English or on colonial ships.
- Colonial trade to be channelled through England or another English colony.
- Subsidization of English goods offered for sale in the colonies.
- Colonists prohibited from large-scale manufacture of certain products.

Mercantilism   Economic system whereby the government intervenes in the economy for the purpose of increasing national wealth.

Enumerated products   Items produced in the colonies and enumerated in acts of Parliament that could be legally shipped from the colony of origin only to specified locations.

OVERVIEW

BRITISH IMPERIAL TRADE REGULATIONS, 1651–1733

Name of Act	Key Features
Navigation Act of 1651	• Aimed to eliminate Dutch competition in overseas trade • Required most goods to be carried in English or colonial ships • Required crews to be at least half English
Navigation Act of 1660	• Required all colonial trade to be carried in English ships • Required master and three-quarters of crew to be English • Created list of enumerated goods, such as tobacco and sugar, that could be shipped only to England or another English colony
Staple Act of 1663	• Required products from Europe, Asia, and Africa to be landed in England before being shipped to the colonies
Plantation Duty Act of 1673	• Attempted to reduce smuggling • Required captains of colonial ships to post bond that they would deliver enumerated goods to England or pay the "plantation duty" that would be owed in England
Navigation Act of 1696	• Plugged loopholes in earlier laws • Created vice-admiralty courts in colonies to enforce trade regulations
Woolens Act of 1699	• Forbade export of woolen cloth made in the colonies, to prevent competition with English producers
Hat Act of 1732	• Prohibited export of colonial-made hats
Molasses Act of 1733	• Placed high tax on French West Indian and other foreign molasses imported into colonies to encourage importation of British West Indian molasses

from colonial competition by prohibiting colonists from manufacturing wool, felt hats, and iron on a large scale.

The colonies prospered under mercantilist legislation. Between 1650 and 1770, the colonial economy grew twice as fast as England's did. Because the trade laws allowed colonial merchants to operate on equal terms with English traders, they could take full advantage of commercial opportunities within the empire.

THE COLONIAL EXPORT TRADE AND THE SPIRIT OF ENTERPRISE

By the mid-eighteenth century, the Atlantic had become a busy thoroughfare of international commerce (see Map 4–1). Between 1700 and 1770, the number of British merchant ships nearly tripled, from 3,300 to 9,400. At the heart of Anglo-American trade lay the highly profitable commerce in staple crops, most of which were produced by slave labor.

West Indian sugar was the most important colonial product. By the late 1760s, the value of sugar and sugar by-product exports reached almost £4 million per year—nearly 50 percent more than the total value of exports from all the other British American colonies combined. Many West Indian planters joined with the English merchants who marketed their sugar to lobby Parliament for favorable treatment. The "sugar interest" convinced Parliament in 1733 to pass the Molasses Act, which taxed sugar products from foreign sources, especially the French West Indies. Parliament removed sugar from the list of enumerated items in 1739, allowing merchants to ship it directly from the islands to southern Europe.

MAP EXPLORATION

To explore an interactive version of this map, go to **http://www.prenhall.com/goldfield2/map4.1**

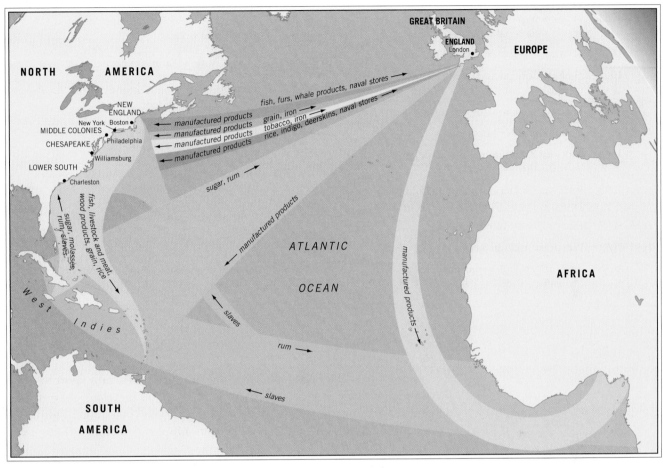

MAP 4–1

Anglo-American Transatlantic Commerce   By the eighteenth century, Great Britain and its colonies were enmeshed in a complex web of trade. Britain exchanged manufactured goods for colonial raw materials, while Africa provided the enslaved laborers who produced the most valuable colonial crops.

ACCORDING TO this map, how did trading between Great Britain and its colonies benefit Great Britain? How did it benefit the colonies? Why was Africa's role so crucial to virtually every aspect of trading between Great Britain and its colonies?

Tobacco from the Chesapeake colonies was the second most valuable staple crop. Exports worth about £750,000 arrived each year in England during the late 1760s. Nearly 90 percent of the crop was later reexported to continental Europe. But persistent low prices led many tobacco planters, after 1750, to sow some of their land with wheat.

Exports of rice and indigo helped make South Carolina planters some of the richest mainland colonists. Most of the rice went to England and the West Indies. Parliament subsidized indigo production as well as colonial production of naval stores—such as tar, pitch, and turpentine—to reduce England's dependence on Swedish suppliers for materials essential to its navy. The export of these items made up a small but important part of the North and South Carolina economies.

Wheat exports from the Middle Colonies boomed after 1750, when a combination of poor harvests and warfare in Europe created strong overseas demand. Ships traveling from Philadelphia or New York to English ports also carried a variety of

CHRONOLOGY

1651–1733	Parliament passes series of Navigation Acts to regulate imperial trade.
1660	Charles II becomes king of England.
1662	Halfway Covenant adopted by Massachusetts clergy.
1685	James II becomes king of England.
1686–1689	Dominion of New England.
1688	Glorious Revolution in England; James II loses the throne.
1689	William and Mary become English monarchs; Leisler's Rebellion begins in New York.
1689–1697	King William's War in America.
1691–1692	Witchcraft trials in Salem, Massachusetts.
1698	First French settlements near mouth of Mississippi River.
1701	Iroquois adopt policy of neutrality toward France and Britain.
1702–1713	Queen Anne's War in America.
1718	Establishment of San Antonio, Texas; New Orleans founded.
1734–1735	Jonathan Edwards leads religious revival in Northampton, Massachusetts.
1739	Great Awakening begins in Middle Colonies with George Whitefield's arrival.
1744–1748	King George's War in America.
1754–1763	Seven Years' War in America.
1760s	Spanish begin establishing missions in California.

goods, including unrefined iron, potash (used in making soap and glass), salted meats, and wood products.

New England had no staple crop and produced little for export to Great Britain except whale products, such as oil. The region's merchants nevertheless developed a thriving transatlantic trade, eventually dominating shipping within the empire. By 1770, New England's earnings from shipping fees, freight charges, and insurance exceeded the total value of its exports.

New England merchants also strengthened trade links to the West Indies. By the mid-eighteenth century, more than half of all New England exports went to the islands: salted meat for planters' dinners, salted fish for slaves, wood for sugar barrels and other equipment. Merchants accepted molasses and other sugar by-products in payment, bringing them back to New England to be distilled into cheap rum. Enterprising traders then carried rum to Africa to exchange for slaves. Because New Englanders trafficked in slaves and provisioned the West Indies, their commercial economy depended on the institution of slavery, even though few slaves lived in the region.

THE IMPORT TRADE AND TIES OF CREDIT

By the late 1760s, the colonists imported goods worth nearly £4 million each year, almost all of which came from Great Britain. Most imports consisted of manufactured goods, which could not be produced in America. Some of these goods—ironware, sugar, hats—were made of materials that had come from the colonies in the first place.

In terms of value, colonists in fact imported more goods than they exported. Earnings from shipping fees, as well as payments from the British government for colonial military expenses, made up most of the difference between imports and exports. The colonial economy may have run an annual deficit of £40,000 by the late 1760s, but that was only about 1 percent of a transatlantic trade worth over £4 million a year.

Great tobacco planters like Washington virtually lived on the easy credit that British merchants provided. These merchants marketed the planters' tobacco and supplied them with English goods, charging the costs of purchase and transportation against the profits they expected the next year's crop to bring.

Gradually, planters sank into debt. A Virginian noted that no planter would have dared run up a debt of £1,000 in the 1740s, but in the 1760s "Ten times that sum is . . . spoke of with Indifference." When tobacco prices dropped or an international crisis made overseas trading risky, creditors called in the debts owed to them. At such times, colonial debtors realized how much they (like Indians involved in European trade) depended on goods and credit supplied by distant merchants.

BECOMING MORE LIKE ENGLAND

By 1770, Philadelphia's population had reached 30,000, New York's 25,000, Boston's 16,000, and Charleston's 12,000. Baltimore was rapidly developing as the best harbor on Chesapeake Bay. Only about 5 percent of all mainland colonists lived in cities, but the influence of urban centers far out-weighed their size.

An English visitor declared in 1759 that Philadelphia "must certainly be the object of every one's wonder and admiration." Less than eighty years old, it already boasted three thousand houses, impressive public buildings, "handsomely built" streets, two libraries, eight or ten churches, and a college (chartered as the College of Philadelphia in 1755, now the University of Pennsylvania). This same visitor judged Boston to be a "most flourishing" place with "much the air of some of our best country towns in England."

All colonial cities (like England's major ones) were seaports. Indeed, in their bustle and cosmopolitan atmosphere, colonial cities resembled English provincial cities more than they did the villages and farms of the American countryside. Cities provided all sorts of amenities, including inns, taverns, coffeehouses, theaters, and social clubs. Their populations were much more diverse in ethnic origin and religion.

Perhaps two out of three adult white males living in cities worked at a craft. Many of them—shipbuilders, ropemakers, sailmakers—labored at trades directly related to overseas commerce. Others produced pottery, furniture, paper, glassware, iron tools, and various household items. Talented colonists such as the Boston silversmith Paul Revere and the Philadelphia furniture maker John Folwell fashioned goods that would have been prized possessions in any English gentleman's home.

Colonial manufacturing took place in workshops often attached to artisans' houses. Artisans managed a work force consisting of their wives and children, along with apprentices, usually teenage boys, who contracted to work for a master for four to seven years in order to learn the craft. Like indentured servants, they worked for food, clothing, shelter, and a small payment at the end of their service. Once an apprentice finished his training, he became a journeyman, working for a master but now earning wages and saving until he could afford to set up his own shop.

Many artisans flourished in colonial cities. Adino Paddock moved from the countryside to Boston in 1736 to learn how to make the light carriages known as chaises. By 1758, he had his own shop, and as his business prospered, Bostonians elected him to important local offices. As a gesture of public spirit; Paddock arranged for the transplanting of elm trees on Boston Common, to beautify the city where he had made his fortune, which by 1775 amounted to more than £3,000.

Craftwork also offered economic opportunities to city women that were generally unavailable to rural women. Mary

John Singleton Copley's portrait of the silversmith Paul Revere, painted about 1769, depicts one of Boston's most prominent artisans. As colonists grew wealthier, some commissioned portraits for their homes to serve as emblems of their rising social aspirations. Even so, Copley despaired that America would ever provide a suitable market for his artistic talents and he eventually moved to England.

Paul Revere, c. 1768–70. Copley, John Singleton, U.S., 1738–1815. Oil on canvas, 35 1/2 × 28 1/2 in. (88.9 × 72.3 cm). Gift of Joseph W., William B., and Edward H. R. Revere. Courtesy, Museum of Fine Arts, Boston.

Wallace and Clementia Ferguson stitched fashionable hats and dresses for New York customers. Nonetheless, even in cities, women's options were limited. Many employed women were widows striving to maintain a family business until sons grew old enough to take over.

Workers at less skilled crafts often earned only a bare living, and ordinary laborers faced seasonal unemployment. The gap between rich and poor widened during the eighteenth century. In 1687, the richest 10 percent of Boston residents owned 46 percent of the taxable property in the town; by 1771, the top tenth held 63 percent of taxable wealth. Similar changes occurred in Philadelphia, South Carolina, and the Chesapeake, wherever colonists engaged heavily in commerce. Over time, it became extremely difficult for newcomers to enter the ranks of the elite.

Most cities built workhouses and other shelters for people who could not take care of themselves. Towns collected funds for poor relief in greater amounts than ever before. Even so, poverty had not yet become an entrenched problem. Temporary downturns in the economy were more often than not the result of dislocations caused by war.

Even in the worst of times, no more than one out of ten white colonists (mainly city dwellers) depended on public assistance. As much as one-third of England's population regularly received relief, and the numbers swelled during hard times. As long as land was available—even if one had to move to the edges of settlement to get it—colonists could at least eke out a bare subsistence, and many did much better.

The growth of colonial cities mirrored British urban development. The widening gap between rich and poor convinced many colonists that their society had at last matured from its crude beginnings. Eighteenth-century Britons on both sides of the Atlantic believed that societies ought to be organized hierarchically, with people arranged in ranks from rich to poor according to their abilities and God's design. The more America resembled Britain, many colonists assumed, the more stable and prosperous it would be.

HOW DID prominent colonists go about developing America's intellectual life?

THE TRANSFORMATION OF CULTURE

Despite the convergence of English and colonial society, many influential settlers worried that America remained culturally inferior to Great Britain. Just as Washington trusted a London tailor, not a Virginian, to make him a fashionable suit, other colonial gentlemen tended to see American architecture, fashion, manners, and intellectual life as poor imitations of British models. Some colonial gentlemen even reshaped their religious beliefs to reflect European notions that God played only an indirect role in human affairs.

Most colonists, however, had little interest in copying the manners of the English elite, and very few altered their spiritual beliefs to fit European patterns. Indeed, religion flourished in eighteenth-century America and, when a tremendous revival swept through the colonies beginning in the 1730s, it occupied center stage in American life.

GOODS AND HOUSES

Eighteenth-century Americans imported more manufactures from England with every passing year. In the less secure economic climate of the seventeenth century, colonists had limited their purchases of goods, investing instead in land to pass on to their children. But by the eighteenth century, prosperous colonists felt secure enough to buy goods to make their lives more comfortable.

Benjamin Franklin described such changes in his own household. Accustomed to eating his breakfast of bread and milk with a pewter spoon from an earthenware bowl, he found it one morning "in a China Bowl with a Spoon of Silver" that had cost "the enormous Sum of three and twenty Shillings." His wife, Deborah, justified the purchase by declaring "that she thought her Husband deserved a Silver Spoon & China Bowl as well as any of his Neighbors." Many colonists likewise acquired such goods to advertise their refined style of life.

By the 1760s, nearly every item that George Washington ordered from his London agent could have been purchased in Philadelphia, but Washington and many other colonists wanted the latest English styles. One visitor to Maryland declared that he was "almost inclined to believe that a new fashion is adopted earlier by the polished and affluent American than by many opulent persons" in London.

Prosperous colonists built grand houses where they lived in greater comfort than ever before. In the seventeenth century, Virginia's governor lived in a four-room dwelling. His eighteenth-century counterpart, however, resided in Williamsburg in the Governor's Palace, an elegant two-storied mansion designed after British architectural styles. Washington extensively remodeled Mount Vernon, adding a second story and extra wings. In the northern colonies, merchants built the most impressive houses, often following architectural pattern books imported from England.

These houses were different in design from the homes of less affluent colonists. Most settlers cooked, ate, and slept in the same chamber. But the owners of great houses could devote rooms to specialized uses. Cooking and other domestic work took place in back or in separate outbuildings. Private bedrooms were located upstairs. The most distinctive feature of these grand homes was the parlor, an elaborately decorated room used for receiving guests. Prosperous colonists built such homes to emulate the English gentry in their country estates and London townhouses.

SHAPING MINDS AND MANNERS

Colonists knew that the manners of English gentlefolk set them apart from ordinary people. Many Americans imported "courtesy books," which contained the rules of polite behavior. The young George Washington studied such books carefully. At age 13, he copied 110 rules from *Youth's Behaviour, or Decency in Conversation Among Men*, including such advice as "In the Presence of Others Sing not to yourself with a humming Noise, nor Drum with your Fingers or Feet" and "In Company of those of Higher Quality than yourself Speak not till you are ask'd a Question then Stand upright put of[f] your Hat and Answer in few words."

In Charleston, South Carolina, dozens of girls' boarding schools advertised instruction in "the different branches of Polite Education." Female pupils studied reading, writing, and arithmetic but also learned French, music, dancing, and fancy needlework. This curriculum prepared them for married lives as mistresses of great houses, mothers of future gentlemen and ladies, and hostesses of grand entertainments. Invitations to balls, musical performances, and tea parties circulated among well-bred neighbors. Such occasions excluded ordinary settlers and reinforced elite colonists' sense of themselves as a separate—and better—class of people.

Prominent colonists, intent on developing America's intellectual life, began to participate in a transatlantic world of ideas. Literacy rates among white colonists were quite high by eighteenth-century standards. In New England, where settlers placed great emphasis on Bible study, about 70 percent of men and 45 percent of women

During the eighteenth century, quantities of imported English manufactures began to appear in many colonial houses. This elegant mahogany clothespress, made in England in the 1740s, may have graced the Boston home of Charles Apthorp, once called "the greatest and most noble merchant" in America.

Clothespress, 1730–1740. England, London, Mahogany, glass. H 98 in. (249 cm); W 45-3/4 in. (116 cm). Gift of Albert Sack. Courtesy, Museum of Fine Arts, Boston.

WHERE TO LEARN MORE

Colonial Williamsburg, Williamsburg, Virginia

www.colonialwilliamsburg.com/history/ index.cfm

WHERE TO LEARN MORE

★ Mount Vernon, Virginia
www.mountvernon.org

3–8
Manners and Etiquette in the Eighteenth Century

Age of Enlightenment Major intellectual movement occurring in Western Europe in the late seventeenth and early eighteenth centuries.

▪▪▪▪▪▪▪▪▪▪▪▪▪▪▪

WHEN DID the "Great Awakening" reach the colonies and what effect did it have there?

▪▪▪▪▪▪▪▪▪▪▪▪▪▪▪

could read and write. Farther south, literacy rates were lower, but still higher than in England, where only a third of all men and even fewer women could read and write.

Elite colonists, however, were more consumers of British and European ideas than producers of an American intellectual tradition. They imported thousands of books, subscribed to British journals, and established libraries in Philadelphia, Charleston, and New York where borrowing privileges could be purchased for a modest fee. Students at Harvard in Cambridge (founded in 1636) modeled their college newspaper on an English periodical, *The Spectator*. In Virginia, William Byrd—the son of an Indian trader who had risen to the rank of gentleman—composed verse in the style of contemporary English poets, and Thomas Jefferson copied out passages from the English novel *Tristram Shandy*. Benjamin Franklin honed his writing skills by rewriting essays from *The Spectator* and comparing his versions to the originals.

Educated colonists were especially interested in the new ideas that characterized what has been called the **Age of Enlightenment**. A group of European thinkers drew inspiration from recent advances in science—such as the English scientist Isaac Newton's explanation of the laws of gravity—that suggested that the universe operated according to natural laws that human reason could discover. They also drew on the work of the English philosopher John Locke, who maintained that God did not dictate human knowledge but rather gave us the power to acquire knowledge through experience and understanding. The hallmark of Enlightenment thought was a belief in the power of human reason to improve the human condition.

Enlightenment thinkers rejected earlier ideas about God's unknowable will and continued intervention in human and natural events. They instead assigned God a less active role as the creator of the universe, who had set the world running according to predictable laws, and then let nature—and human beings—shape events.

Colonial intellectuals sought membership in a growing international community of scholars. A few of them—the Reverend Cotton Mather of Massachusetts, William Byrd, Benjamin Franklin—gained election to the Royal Society of London, the most prestigious learned society in the empire. Most of their scholarly contributions were unimpressive, but Benjamin Franklin achieved genuine intellectual prominence. His experiments with a kite proved that lightning was electricity and gained him an international reputation. Franklin also invented the lightning rod (which prevented fires in wooden buildings by channeling the electrical charge of a lightning bolt into the ground), bifocal spectacles, the iron "Franklin stove" (in which wood burned more efficiently than in fireplaces), and the glass harmonica.

Very few prosperous and educated colonists could afford such intellectual pursuits. Only after retiring from business at age 42 could Franklin purchase the equipment for his electrical discoveries and begin his scientific work, devoting the "leisure during the rest of my life for philosophical studies and amusements." Most colonists remained ignorant of scientific advances and Enlightenment ideas. They had little leisure to devote to literature and polite conversation.

COLONIAL RELIGION AND THE GREAT AWAKENING

Church steeples dominated the skylines of colonial cities. Often the largest and finest buildings in town, they bore witness to the thriving—and diverse—condition of religion in America.

In all New England colonies except Rhode Island, the Puritan (or Congregationalist) faith was the established religion. The many Congregational churches in the region, headed by ministers trained at Harvard College and Yale (founded

1701), served the majority of the colonists and received financial support from their taxes. Ministers and believers adapted in important ways to changing social and religious conditions.

The principal adaptation consisted of a move away from strict requirements for church membership. New England's founders had required prospective members to give convincing evidence that they had experienced a spiritual conversion. Only members could receive communion and have their children baptized. By the 1660s, however, fewer colonists sought admission under such strict standards, which left them and their unbaptized children outside the church. In 1662 the clergy adopted the **Halfway Covenant**, which allowed adults who had been baptized (because their parents were church members), but who had not themselves experienced conversion, to have their own children baptized. By the 1680s, some ministers made church admission even easier, requiring members only to demonstrate knowledge of the Christian faith and to live godly lives.

The Congregational Church also had to accept a measure of religious toleration in New England. In 1691, Massachusetts received a royal charter granting "liberty of Conscience" to all Protestants, bringing the colony into line with England's religious policy. Anglicans and Baptists eventually won exemptions from paying taxes to support the Congregational Church. At the same time, some Congregationalist preachers began emphasizing personal piety and good works in their sermons, ideas usually associated with Anglicanism.

In the South, the established Church of England consolidated its authority in the early eighteenth century but never succeeded in exerting effective control over spiritual life. Parishes often lacked trained clergy, and those who did emigrate encountered unexpected obstacles.

Anglican clergymen in the southern colonies served parishes that were vast and sparsely settled. One South Carolina parish, for example, contained 10,400 square miles—and only seven hundred white residents. Aware that the planters' taxes paid their salaries, many ministers found it easiest simply to preach and behave in ways that offered the least offense. In frontier regions, dissenting religious groups, such as Presbyterians, Quakers, and Baptists, gained followers among people neglected by the Anglican establishment.

No established church dominated in the Middle Colonies of New York, New Jersey, and Pennsylvania. The region's ethnically diverse population and William Penn's policy of religious toleration guaranteed that a multitude of groups would compete for followers. By the mid-eighteenth century, the region had more congregations per capita than even New England.

Groups such as the Quakers and the Mennonites, who did not believe in having specially trained ministers, easily formed new congregations in response to local demand. Lutheran and German Reformed churches, however, required European-educated clergy, who were always scarce. So pious laymen held worship services in their homes. When more Lutheran and Reformed clergy arrived in the 1740s and 1750s, they sometimes discovered that laymen balked at relinquishing control of the churches. Because so many other religious alternatives were available, these ministers had to compete for their parishioners' allegiance.

Bewildering spiritual diversity, relentless religious competition, and a comparatively weak Anglican Church all distinguished the colonies from England. Yet in one important way, religious developments during the middle third of the eighteenth century drew the colonies closer to England. A transatlantic religious revival, the **Great Awakening**, originated in Scotland and England, and first touched the Middle Colonies in the 1730s.

> **QUICK REVIEW**
>
> **Church: Regional Variations**
> - New England: Congregational Church dominated.
> - South: Church of England dominated.
> - Middle colonies: no dominant church.

Halfway Covenant   Plan adopted in 1662 by New England clergy to deal with the problem of declining church membership, allowing children of baptized parents to be baptized whether or not their parents had experienced conversion.

Great Awakening   Tremendous religious revival in colonial America striking first in the Middle Colonies and New England in the 1740s and then spreading to the southern colonies.

George Whitefield (who, contemporaries noted, was cross-eyed) enjoyed a remarkable career as a powerful preacher on both sides of the Atlantic. This portrait shows him preaching indoors to a rapt audience. During his tour of the colonies, Whitefield reportedly had a similar effect on crowds of thousands who gathered outdoors to hear his sermons.

John Wollaston, "George Whitefield" ca. 1770. By courtesy of the National Portrait Gallery, London.

By 1730, Presbyterians in Pennsylvania had split into factions. One group was led by an immigrant Scottish evangelist, William Tennent Sr., and his four sons. In the 1730s, Tennent set up the Log College in Neshaminy, Pennsylvania, to train his sons and other young men to be evangelical ministers. His challenge to the Presbyterian establishment gained momentum in late 1739, when one of the most charismatic evangelists of the century, George Whitefield, arrived in the colonies from England.

Whitefield, an Anglican priest, had experienced an intense religious conversion while he was still a university student. Famous in Britain as a preacher of great emotional intensity, he embarked on a tour of the colonies. In Pennsylvania and New Jersey, Whitefield's powerful preaching on the experience of conversion lent support to the Presbyterian faction led by the Tennents and sparked local revivals. Whitefield then moved on to New England, where some communities had already experienced small, local awakenings.

Whitefield exhorted his audiences to examine their souls for evidence of the "indwelling of Christ" that would indicate that they were saved. He criticized most ministers for emphasizing good works and "head-knowledge" instead of the emotional side of religion.

Whitefield's sermons scarcely resembled the colonists' structured church services. His sermons were highly dramatic performances. He preached outdoors to thousands of strangers, jostling in crowds that often outnumbered the populations of several villages put together.

In the wake of Whitefield's visits, Benjamin Franklin noted, "it seem'd as if all the World were growing Religious." Revivals and mass conversions often followed his appearances, to the happy astonishment of local clergy. But their approval evaporated when disputes between individuals converted in the revivals—called **"New Lights"**—and those who were not ("Old Lights") split churches. "Formerly the People could bear with each other in Charity when they differ'd in Opinion," lamented one colonist, "but they now break Fellowship and Communion with one another on that Account."

The Awakening came late to the southern colonies, but it was there, in the 1760s, that it produced perhaps its greatest controversy. Many southern converts became Baptists, combining their religious criticism of the Anglicans with a condemnation of the wealthy planters' way of life. Planters, in turn, viewed Baptists as dangerous people who could not "meet a man upon the road, but they must ram a text of Scripture down his throat." Most of all, they hated the Baptists for their willingness to preach to slaves.

The Great Awakening had a lasting impact on colonial society, forging new links between Great Britain and the colonies. Evangelical ministers on both sides of the Atlantic exchanged correspondence. Periodicals such as *The Christian History* informed British and American subscribers of advances in true religion throughout the empire.

In the colonies, the Awakening led to the founding of new colleges. Middle Colony evangelicals founded the College of New Jersey (now Princeton University) in 1746. In the 1760s, New England Baptists established the College of Rhode Island (now Brown University). An evangelical wing of the Dutch Reformed Church founded Queens College (now Rutgers University) in 1766.

New Lights   People who experienced conversion during the revivals of the Great Awakening.

Everywhere, the New Light challenge to established ministers and churches undermined habits of deference to authority. Revivalists urged colonists to think for themselves in choosing which church to join and which minister to follow, not just conform to what the rest of the community did. As their churches fractured, Americans—particularly New Englanders—faced more choices than ever before in their religious lives.

The exercise of religious choice also influenced political behavior. Voters took note of whether candidates for office were New or Old Lights and cast their ballots for men on their own side. Tactics first used to mobilize religious groups—organizing committees, writing petitions and letters—proved useful for political activities as well.

THE COLONIAL POLITICAL WORLD

The political legacy of the Great Awakening—particularly the emphasis on individual choice and resistance to authority—corresponded to developments in the colonial political world. For most of the seventeenth century, ties within the empire developed from trade rather than governance. But as America grew in wealth and population, king and Parliament sought to manage colonial affairs more directly than ever before.

HOW DID the "Glorious Revolution" affect the colonists?

THE DOMINION OF NEW ENGLAND AND THE LIMITS OF BRITISH CONTROL

When Charles II became king in 1660, he initially showed little interest in the colonies except as sources of land and government offices with which he could reward his supporters. With the passage of mercantile regulations governing colonial trade, for example, Parliament required customs officers to administer the imperial trading system and thus created a certain number of jobs.

Charles's brother James, the duke of York, envisioned a more tightly controlled empire. He encouraged Charles to appoint military officers, with strong ties of loyalty to him, as royal governors in America. In 1675, James convinced Charles to create the *Lords of Trade*, a committee of the Privy Council (the group of nobles who served as royal advisers), to oversee colonial affairs.

When James became king in 1685, the whole character of the empire abruptly changed. James set out to reorganize it along the lines of Spain's empire, combining the colonies into three or four large provinces. He appointed powerful governors to carry out policies that he himself would formulate.

James began in the north, creating the **Dominion of New England** out of eight previously separate colonies stretching from Maine (then part of Massachusetts) to New Jersey. He chose Sir Edmund Andros, a former army officer, to govern the vast region with an appointive council but no elective assembly. Andros moved to Boston and antagonized New Englanders by rigidly enforcing the Navigation Acts, limiting towns to just one annual meeting, remodeling the law courts, challenging property titles, and levying taxes without the colonists' consent. He even compelled Boston Puritans to share a meetinghouse with Anglicans.

Events in England ultimately sealed the fate of the Dominion. For years, English Protestants had worried about James's absolutist governing style and his conversion to Catholicism. Their fears increased in 1688 when the queen bore a son to carry on a Catholic line of succession. Parliament's leaders invited James's Protestant daughter, Mary, and her husband, William of Orange, the Stadtholder of the Netherlands, to take over the throne. In November 1688, William landed in

Dominion of New England James II's failed plan of 1686 to combine eight northern colonies into a single large province, to be governed by a royal appointee with no elective assembly.

England and gained the support of most of the English army. In December, James fled to France, ending a bloodless coup known as the **Glorious Revolution**.

Bostonians overthrew Andros the following April, even before they knew for sure that William was king. In 1691, Massachusetts received a new charter. Massachusetts now included within its borders what had formerly been Plymouth Colony as well as Maine. Its colonists no longer elected their governor, who would instead be appointed by the English monarch. Voters no longer had to be church members, and religious toleration was extended to all Protestants.

The new charter ended exclusive Puritan control in Massachusetts but also restored political stability. During the three years between Andros's overthrow and the arrival of a royal governor in 1692, the colony lacked a legally established government. In this atmosphere of uncertainty, a local outbreak of accusations of witchcraft in Salem grew to unprecedented proportions. In the winter of 1691–1692, when several young girls of Salem experienced fits and other strange behavior, hundreds of settlers were accused of witchcraft, and nineteen were hanged. Salem's crisis gathered momentum because the courts, which would normally have intervened to settle matters, were unable to function.

The impact of the Glorious Revolution in other colonies likewise reflected distinctive local conditions. In New York, Jacob Leisler, a rich merchant and militia captain, gained power and ruled in dictatorial fashion. Too slow in relinquishing command to the newly arrived royal governor in 1691, Leisler was arrested for treason and executed. In Maryland, Protestants used the occasion of William and Mary's accession to challenge the Catholic proprietorship. The Calvert family lost its governing powers but retained rights to vast quantities of land. The Anglican Church became the established faith, and Catholics were barred from public office.

The colonists' support of the Glorious Revolution largely reflected powerful anti-Catholic sentiment. William's firm Protestantism reassured them. But the Glorious Revolution in England and the demise of the Dominion had long-lasting effects that shaped political life in England and America for years to come.

THE LEGACY OF THE GLORIOUS REVOLUTION

In England, the Glorious Revolution signaled a return to political stability after years of upheaval. In 1689, Parliament passed the Bill of Rights, which justified James's ouster and bound future monarchs to abide by the rule of law. They could not suspend parliamentary laws, collect taxes or engage in foreign wars without Parliament's consent, or maintain a standing army in peacetime. Parliamentary elections and meetings would follow a regular schedule without royal interference. In sum, Parliament claimed to be the crown's equal partner in governing England.

Colonists believed that their successful resistance to Andros confirmed that their membership in the empire was founded on voluntary allegiance and not forced submission to the mother country. Observing the similarity between Parliament and the colonial assemblies, they concluded that their own legislatures had a critical role in governance and in the protection of their rights. Parliament, however, claimed full authority over the colonies and did not recognize their assemblies as its equal.

William and his immediate successors lacked James's compulsion to control the colonies. In 1696, William replaced the Lords of Trade with the *Board of Trade*, which gathered information from the colonies and recommended policy changes but itself had no executive role. William also approved the *Navigation Act of 1696*, which closed loopholes in earlier laws and created vice-admiralty courts in the colonies similar to those of England. Admiralty judges settled maritime disputes and smuggling cases without using juries.

QUICK REVIEW

Glorious Revolution
- 1688: James II forced from throne in bloodless coup.
- Massachusetts receives new charter.
- Broad support for Glorious Revolution throughout colonies.

Glorious Revolution   Bloodless revolt that occurred in England in 1688 when parliamentary leaders invited William of Orange, a Protestant, to assume the English throne.

The mild imperial rule of the early eighteenth century, later called the era of "salutary neglect," allowed the colonies to grow in wealth, population, and self-government. It also encouraged colonial self-confidence, leading colonists to assume equality with the English as members of the empire.

DIVERGING POLITICS IN THE COLONIES AND GREAT BRITAIN

English people on both sides of the Atlantic believed that politics ought to reflect social organization. They often compared the state to a family. Just as fathers headed families, adult men led societies. In particular, adult male property holders, who enjoyed economic independence, claimed the right to vote and hold office. Women (who generally could not own property), propertyless men, and slaves had no political role because they, like children, were subordinate to the authority of others, which rendered them incapable of exercising freedom of choice.

English people believed that rulers ought to govern with the same fairness and benevolence that fathers presumably exercised within their families. When George II became king in 1727, he reassured Parliament of his "constant care" to "secure to All My subjects, the full Enjoyment of their religious and civil Rights." In return for protection, the people owed their rulers the same obedience that children accorded their parents. The House of Commons responded to George II's assurance of goodwill in 1727 with its own promise of "Duty, Zeal and Affection to Your Majesty's Person and Government." (See "American Views: Boston Celebrates a New King")

Eighteenth-century people also believed that government should reflect society's hierarchical organization. In England, the crown represented the interests of the royal family. Parliament represented society's two main divisions: the aristocracy in the *House of Lords* and the common people in the *House of Commons*. Americans shared the view that government should mirror social hierarchies but found it much more difficult to put the idea into practice.

American social and political structure never fully mirrored that of England. One of the most obvious differences was that America lacked an aristocracy. In England, the members of this tiny privileged minority were easily recognizable by their great wealth, prestigious family lines, leisured lives, and official titles of nobility. British America had elites but no aristocracy.

In both England and America, land ownership was the prerequisite for political participation. By the mid-eighteenth century, only one-tenth of all English heads of households owned all the country's land, and thus only a tiny portion of men could vote. In America, however, a large majority of white male farmers owned the land they tilled. In most colonies, 50 to 75 percent of white men were eligible to vote.

In England, electoral districts for Parliament often reflected their status in past centuries. Dunwich retained its right to elect a parliamentary representative long after the city itself had washed into the North Sea. Meanwhile, rapidly growing cities, such as Manchester, lacked any representative. Most of the English accepted the idea of **virtual representation**, which held that representatives served the interests of the nation as a whole, not just the locality from which they came. They assumed that since the colonists held interests in common with English people at home, they were virtually represented in Parliament—just like Manchester's residents.

Since the founding of their colonies, however, Americans had experienced **actual representation** and believed that elected representatives should be directly responsive to local interests. They were accustomed to instructing their legisla-

Virtual representation The notion that parliamentary members represented the interests of the nation as a whole, not those of the particular district that elected them.

Actual representation The practice whereby elected representatives normally reside in their districts and are directly responsive to local interests.

·AMERICAN VIEWS·

BOSTON CELEBRATES A NEW KING (AUGUST 1727)

The first colonial newspaper, the Boston News-Letter, *appeared in that city in 1704. By the 1720s, Bostonians could choose from three newspapers, and New York and Philadelphia each had one. Published weekly, these papers mainly reported on English and European affairs and often reprinted essays by English political writers. They carried little local news, though colonists could learn of this by word of mouth. But when extraordinary events occurred, such as the accession of a new British monarch, colonial newspapers reported on the local response. The following extract describes Bostonians' reaction to the accession of George II.*

HOW DID Bostonians commemorate the new king's accession? What does this reveal about their attitudes toward George II and British government in general? Who was invited to the "splendid Entertainment," and what does this reveal about the structure of Boston society?

On Wednesday Morning by order of His Honour William Dummer, Esq., our Lieut. Governour & Commander in chief[,] three Regiments of the Militia and five Troops of horse were under arms in the great street before the State-house, making a very fine appearance. The number of Spectators exceeded the Men in Arms, covering the houses on every side. As soon as the Herauld had said his Amen to God Save the King, the loud and joyful Huzza's of so great a multitude rent the skies, the Regiments made a tripple discharge, the Castle Forts & Ships fir'd their cannon; and a splendid Entertainment follow'd for the Lieut. Governour and his Majesty's Council, Officers, Justices, and the Rev[eren]d Ministers present; with suitable provisions for the Regiments and Troops. The bells rung all the day, and in the Evening the Rejoycing was continued with Fireworks and Bonfires, and the whole Town illuminated in an extraordinary manner, the Windows of each story of the Houses in the principal streets having three or four rows of candles in them. The streets were fill'd all the Evening with the Gentry of both Sexes, who appear'd with much decency and gravity, and with gayety and chearfulness. At nine of the clock a welcome rain, after a time of much heat and drought, put an end to the Ceremony. . . . We pray God, by whom Kings reign, that the royal smiles of His Majesty King George the Second, and the happy influences of his wise and just Government, may ever be falling on all his Majesty's Dominions, and on this loyal and dutiful Province in particular.

Source: *New England Weekly Journal* (August 21, 1727).

tors about how to vote on important issues. Colonial representatives, unlike members of Parliament, resided in their districts. The Americans' experience with actual representation made them extremely skeptical of Parliament's claims to virtual representation.

The most direct political confrontations between England and the colonies focused on the role of colonial governors. In every colony except Connecticut and Rhode Island, either the king or proprietors appointed the governors. Their interests thus lay with their English patrons and not the colonies. Governors exercised greater powers over the colonial assemblies than the king (after the Glorious Revolution) did over Parliament. Governors could veto laws enacted by the assemblies and initiate legislation in consultation with councilors whom they appointed. They could delay legislative sessions, dissolve the assemblies at will, and nominate and dismiss colonial judges as they wished.

Several conditions hampered governors' efforts to exercise their legal authority. Many arrived with detailed instructions on how to govern, which limited their ability to negotiate with colonists over sensitive issues. Governors controlled few offices or other prizes with which to buy the allegiance of their opponents.

They struggled to dominate assemblies that grew in size as the colonial population expanded. And in several colonies, including Massachusetts and New York, governors relied on the assemblies to appropriate the money for their salaries—a financial dependence that restrained even the most autocratic executive.

In response to the perceived threat of powerful governors, colonial assemblies asserted themselves as never before. They sent agents (including such prominent figures as Benjamin Franklin) to England to lobby on behalf of colonial interests. Local factions fought for election to the increasingly important legislature, leading to some of the most contentious politics in the British Empire.

Decades of struggles with governors led colonists to exalt the assemblies' role as the guarantors of their liberties. Most colonists, however, believed that as long as Parliament treated the Americans as partners in empire and refrained from ruling by coercion, colonists could celebrate British government as "the most perfect combination of human powers in society . . . for the preservation of liberty and the production of happiness."

Expanding Empires

During the first half of the eighteenth century, England, Spain, and France all enlarged their North American holdings. England's empire continued to expand as a result of the unrelenting growth of its colonial population. Spain and France still relied on missionaries, soldiers, and traders to stake their claims to American territory. In the eighteenth century as in the seventeenth, English settlement generally displaced native peoples. Newly established Spanish and French colonies, however, contained small numbers of Europeans amid much larger populations of Indians. Over time, these empires came into closer contact with one another, intensifying the competition for land, trade, resources, and Indian allies.

WHAT GEOGRAPHIC area made up the "backcountry" and who settled there?

British Colonists in the Backcountry

Black and white settlers in the mainland colonies numbered 265,000 in 1700; by 1770, they had increased to 2.3 million. Benjamin Franklin predicted in 1750 that if the colonial population continued to grow at this rate, within two hundred years "the greatest Number of Englishmen will be on this Side" of the Atlantic Ocean.

Much of this growth stemmed from natural increase. White families, particularly in the northern colonies, often had between five and ten children, most of whom survived to produce many more offspring. When 80-year-old Judith Coffin, the matriarch of an unusually large Massachusetts family, died in 1705, she had a total of 177 children and grandchildren. By the mid-eighteenth century, even the slave population began to reproduce itself, although more slowly than the white population.

Immigration also boosted the population. Thousands of Scots-Irish and German settlers—and many involuntary African immigrants—increased the population of the Lower South at nearly twice the rate of New England, which attracted few immigrants (and therefore remained the most thoroughly English of all colonial regions). By 1770, Pennsylvania had 240,000 settlers—ten times the number it had in 1710. Indeed, extensive German immigration worried Pennsylvania leaders. Like Benjamin Franklin, they feared that the newcomers would "never adopt our Language or Customs" and would soon "be so numerous as to Germanize us."

Most of the coast from Maine to Georgia was settled by 1760, forcing many immigrants and descendants of earlier settlers to move inland. The most dramatic

Painted at about the time Franklin retired from his printing business, this portrait depicts the one-time craftsman as an aspiring gentleman.

Robert Feke (1707–1752), Portrait of Benjamin Franklin (1706 - 1790), c. 1746. Oil on canvas, 127 x 02 cm. Courtesy of the Harvard University Portrait Collection. Bequest of Dr. John Collins Warren, 1856.

WHERE TO LEARN MORE

Berkeley and Westover Plantations,
Charles City, Virginia
www.jamesriverplantations.org

expansion occurred in the foothills and valleys of the Appalachian Mountains from Pennsylvania to Georgia, a region known as the backcountry. Between 1730 and 1770, nearly a quarter of a million German, Scots-Irish, and English colonists entered the backcountry. They mainly raised crops and livestock for subsistence on small, isolated farms. Community life developed slowly, in part because backcountry settlers often moved frequently. In addition, a surplus of men among the first settlers delayed the formation of families.

Contemporary observers derided the crudeness of frontier life. William Byrd, a wealthy planter from Virginia's Tidewater, scornfully described one backcountry house as a "castle containing of one dirty room with a dragging door to it that will neither open or shut." Charles Woodmason, an English-born Anglican missionary, was appalled by the sight of western Carolina settlers who "Live in Logg Cabbins like Hogs." Genteel observers offered what they considered the most damaging insult by referring to such settlers as "white Indians."

Yet many coastal planters—including William Byrd and George Washington—acquired vast tracts of western land with the intent to sell it to these "crude" settlers. During the 1740s and 1750s, scores of Virginia planters, northern merchants, and London investors formed companies whose purpose was to profit from this kind of land speculation. Their interests collided with those of settlers—squatters—who occupied the land without acquiring legal title in the hope that their labor in clearing farms would establish their property rights.

Backcountry settlers often complained that rich eastern planters, who dominated the colonial legislatures, ignored western demands for adequate representation. Many argued that the crudeness of frontier life was only temporary. Perhaps the best measure of their desire to resemble eastern planters was the spread of slaveholding. In one western Virginia county in 1750, only one-fifth of the household heads owned slaves. Just nineteen years later, more than half of them did.

Colonists who moved to the backcountry often displaced native groups. Indians moving to avoid friction with whites, however, frequently encroached on lands claimed by other tribes—particularly those of the Iroquois Confederacy—leading to conflict among native peoples.

Even where English settlers had not yet appeared, English and Scottish traders could often be found, aggressively pursuing trade with the Indians. Spanish and French observers feared this commercial expansion even more than the movement of settlers. Knowing that the Indians viewed trade as a counterpart to military alliance, the Spanish and French expanded their own territorial claims and tried to strengthen relations with Indian peoples.

THE SPANISH IN TEXAS AND CALIFORNIA

Spanish Florida had become the target of English raiders from South Carolina. Years of religious persecution and forced labor under Spanish rule encouraged Florida's Indians to oppose the Spanish, but the natives also liked English trade goods and guns. Spain held on to coastal bases at St. Augustine, San Marcos de Apalachee, and Pensacola, but by the mid-eighteenth century, control of Florida's interior effectively passed to Indian bands allied with the English.

In 1700, Franciscan priests in New Mexico, fearful of sparking another native revolt, eased their labor demands and avoided outright religious persecution, allowing the Pueblos to retain many of their customs and religious practices. New Mexican officials worried about news brought by Apache hunters that Frenchmen who might contest Spanish control had been seen on the plains.

To create a buffer zone around their existing colonies, the Spanish moved into Texas and California. Franciscan priests established several missions in east Texas be-

WHERE TO LEARN MORE

Mission Parkway,
San Antonio, Texas
http://hotx.com/missions/

tween 1690 and 1720. San Antonio, founded in 1718, served as a way station between the Rio Grande and east Texas missions; its fortified chapel, San Antonio de Valero, later became famous as the Alamo. The Spanish advance into Texas, however, met with resistance from the French (who also had outposts on the Gulf Coast) and from the Caddos and other Indians armed with French guns. With only 1,800 settlers there as late as 1742, Spain exerted a weak hold on Texas.

Largely through the efforts of two men—José de Gálvez, a royal official, and Junípero Serra, a Franciscan priest—the Spanish constructed a string of forts and missions in California from San Diego north to San Francisco between 1769 and 1776. They initially encountered little opposition from California's Indians, who lived in small, scattered villages and lacked experience with organized warfare. With no European rivals nearby to compete with them, the Spanish erected an extensive mission system designed to convert and educate Indians and set them to work. Thousands of native laborers farmed irrigated fields and tended horses, sheep, and cattle.

The Spanish worked the Indians hard and maintained them in overcrowded, unsanitary dwellings. Native women suffered from sexual exploitation by Spanish soldiers. Epidemics of European diseases reduced the Indian population from 300,000 in 1769 to about 200,000 fifty years later. Signs of native resistance met with quick and cruel punishment—including whipping, burning, and execution—so that the Indians would not (as one official later wrote) "come to know their power" over the vastly outnumbered Spanish. (As late as 1790, California had only 990 Spanish residents.) Despite the gruesome consequences, Indians staged several revolts during the eighteenth century, but Spanish soldiers usually suppressed them quickly.

Spain's empire grew, even as it weakened, during the eighteenth century. From the beginning, Spain's vision of empire had rested not on extensive settlement but on expansive territorial claims backed up by soldiers and missionaries who subjugated native peoples in order to control their labor for Spanish profit. After 1700, however, the Spanish simply could not compete with the vigorous commercial empires of France and England.

THE FRENCH ALONG THE MISSISSIPPI AND IN LOUISIANA

French expansion followed major waterways—the St. Lawrence River, the Great Lakes, the Mississippi—into the heart of North America. Explorers reached the Mississippi Valley in the 1670s. Within twenty years, French outposts appeared along the Gulf Coast. New Orleans, the capital and main port of French Louisiana, was founded in 1718. Soon forts, trading posts, and villages sprang up in the continent's interior—a chain of way stations between Canada and the Gulf of Mexico. Defying official regulators, French colonists settled in six villages along the Mississippi in a place they called the *Pays des Illinois*.

The first Illinois settlers were independent fur traders (*coureurs de bois*, or "woods runners") unwilling to return to Canada after the French government tried to prohibit their direct trade with Indians. Many found Christian Indian wives and began farming the rich lands along the river. The settlers and other Canadian emigrants, using the labor of their families and of black and Indian slaves, produced profitable surpluses of wheat, corn, and livestock to feed the growing population of New Orleans and the lower Mississippi Valley.

French Louisiana contained a diverse population of Indian peoples, French soldiers and settlers, German immigrants, and African slaves who, by the 1730s,

This panel of an eighteenth-century painting by an unknown Mexican artist is representative of a genre of portraits illustrating the categories Spanish colonists developed to designate the offspring of various kinds of mixed marriage. This one, labeled "Español, con India, Mestizo," depicts a Spanish father, an Indian mother, and their mestizo child. The scarcity of European women made mixed marriage common in Spanish colonies. Such unions were exceedingly rare in the English colonies, where cultural preferences and the relative abundance of European women discouraged intermarriage.

Schalkwijlk, Art Resource, N.Y.

WHERE TO LEARN MORE

Ste. Genevieve Historic District,
Ste. Genevieve, Missouri
www.stegenevieve.com/histsite.htm

3–3
Early French Explorations of
the Mississippi River (1673)

outnumbered European colonists. Louisiana's economy depended mainly on the combined efforts of Indians, settlers, and slaves, who farmed, herded, fished, and traded deerskins. Due to the lack of profits, however, substantial European emigration to Louisiana essentially ceased after the 1720s.

But the French approach to empire—in Louisiana as in Canada—had always depended more on Indian alliances than on settlement. Louisiana's principal allies, the Choctaws, and other Indians offered trade and military assistance in return for guns, trade goods, French help in fighting English raiders seeking Indian slaves, and occasional French mediation of Indian disputes.

French expansion along the Mississippi Valley drove a wedge between Florida and Spain's other mainland colonies; it also blocked the westward movement of English settlers. But France's enlarged empire was only as strong as the Indian alliances on which it rested. The fear of losing Indian favor preoccupied officials because France's empire in America consisted of two disconnected pieces: New France, centered in the St. Lawrence Valley and the Great Lakes basin, and Louisiana, stretching from New Orleans to the *Pays de Illinois.* Between them lay one thousand miles of wilderness through which only one thoroughfare passed— the Ohio River. For decades, communication between the two parts of France's North American empire posed no problem because Indians in the Ohio Valley allowed the French free passage through their lands. If that policy ended, however, France's New World empire would be dangerously divided.

A CENTURY OF WARFARE

From the time of the Glorious Revolution, English foreign policy aimed at limiting the expansion of French influence. This resulted in a series of four wars, which increasingly involved their American colonies as well as Spain and its colonies. The conclusion of the final conflict signaled a dramatic shift in North American history (see the overview table "The Colonial Wars, 1689–1763").

■ ■ ■ ■ ■ ■ ■
HOW DID the French and
Indian War affect the colonists?
■ ■ ■ ■ ■ ■ ■

IMPERIAL CONFLICT AND THE ESTABLISHMENT OF AN AMERICAN BALANCE OF POWER, 1689–1738

When he became king of England in 1688, the Dutch Protestant William of Orange was already fighting the War of the League of Augsburg against France's Catholic king, Louis XIV. William brought England into the conflict. The war lasted until 1697 and ended—as most eighteenth-century European wars did—in a negotiated peace that reestablished the balance of power. Little territory changed hands, either in this war or in the War of the Spanish Succession (1702–1713), which followed it.

In America, these two wars—known to British colonists as **King William's War** and **Queen Anne's War**, after the monarchs on the throne at the time—ended with equal indecisiveness. New France's Indian allies attacked New England's northern frontier with devastating success. New Englanders struck back at the exposed settlements of Acadia, which ultimately entered the British Empire as Nova Scotia, and tried unsuccessfully to seize Quebec. Neither war caused more than marginal changes for the colonies in North America. Both had profound effects, however, on the English state and on the Iroquois League.

All European states of the eighteenth century financed their wars by borrowing. But the English were the first to realize that wartime debts did not necessarily have to be repaid during the following peace. The government instead created a funded debt. Having borrowed heavily from large joint-stock corporations, the government agreed to use tax revenues to pay interest on those loans but not to pay off the loans themselves. The corporations agreed because the interest payments amounted to a steady form of income that over the long run could

King William's War   The first Anglo-French conflict in North America (1689–1697), the American phase of Europe's War of the League of Augsburg.

Queen Anne's War   American phase (1702–1713) of Europe's War of the Spanish Succession.

OVERVIEW

THE COLONIAL WARS, 1689–1763

Name in the Colonies	European Name and Dates	Dates in America	Results for Britain
King William's War	War of the League of Augsburg, 1688–1697	1689–1697	• Reestablished balance of power between England and France
Queen Anne's War	War of Spanish Succession, 1702–1714	1702–1713	• Britain acquired Nova Scotia
King George's War	War of Austrian Succession, 1739–1748	1744–1748	• Britain returned Louisbourg to France • British settlers began moving westward • Weakening of Iroquois neutrality
French and Indian War	Seven Years' War, 1756–1763	1754–1763	• Britain acquired Canada and all French territory east of Mississippi • Britain gained Florida from Spain

amount to more than the original loans. In this way, England became the first European country to harness its national economy efficiently to military ends.

As the debt grew larger, more taxes were necessary to pay interest on it and for a powerful navy and a standing army. When the treasury created a larger and more efficient bureaucracy to collect taxes, many Englishmen's anxiety emerged as a strain of thought known as **Country**, or "**Real Whig**," **ideology**, which stressed the threats that a standing army and a powerful state posed to personal liberty. It also emphasized the dangers of taxation to property rights and the need for property holders to retain their right to consent to taxation. Real Whig politicians publicized their fears but could not stop the growth of the state. In every successive war, the claims of national interest and patriotism—and the prospect of profit for parties rich enough to lend money to the government—overrode the objections of those who feared the expansion of state power.

In America, the first two imperial wars transformed the role of the Iroquois League. By 1700, the League had suffered such horrendous losses—perhaps a quarter of the population had died from causes related to King William's War—that its leaders created the **Grand Settlement of 1701**, a policy of neutrality with regard to the French and British Empires. Their goal was to refrain from alliances with either European power and instead maneuver between them. The Iroquois's strategic location between New France and the English colonies allowed them to serve as a geographical and diplomatic buffer between the two. This neutralist policy ensured that for nearly fifty years neither England nor France could gain ascendancy in North America.

Iroquois neutrality offered benefits to the Europeans as well as the Indians. To smooth relations with the English, the Iroquois sold them land formerly occupied by Delawares and Susquehannocks. This simultaneously helped satisfy the colonists' land hunger and enrich the Iroquois League. Meanwhile, a neutral Iroquois League claiming control over the Ohio Valley and blocking English access across the Appalachian Mountains helped the French protect the strategic corridor of the Ohio and Mississippi Valleys that linked Canada and Louisiana.

If the English ever established a permanent presence on this strategic corridor, however, the Iroquois would cease to be of use to the French. The Iroquois remained reasonably effective at keeping the British out of the Ohio Valley until the late 1740s. The next European war, however, altered these circumstances.

Country (Real Whig) ideology Strain of thought (focusing on the threat to personal liberty and the taxation of property holders) first appearing in England in the late seventeenth century in response to the growth of governmental power and a national debt.

Grand Settlement of 1701 Separate peace treaties negotiated by Iroquois diplomats at Montreal and Albany that marked the beginning of Iroquois neutrality in conflicts between the French and the British in North America.

This, the earliest known portrait of George Washington, was painted by Charles Wilson Peale in 1772. It depicts him in his military uniform from the French and Indian War. Military service helped to strengthen Washington's ties with the British Empire.

Washington|Custis/Lee Collection, Washington and Lee University, Lexington, VA.

King George's War The third Anglo-French war in North America (1744–1748), part of the European conflict known as the War of the Austrian Succession.

Treaty of Lancaster Negotiation in 1744 whereby Iroquois chiefs sold Virginia land speculators the right to trade at the Forks of the Ohio.

KING GEORGE'S WAR SHIFTS THE BALANCE, 1739–1754

The third confrontation between Britain and France in Europe, the *War of the Austrian Succession* (**King George's War** to the British colonists) began as a small war between Britain and Spain in 1739. Its immediate cause was British attempts to poach on trade to Spain's Caribbean colonies. But in 1744, France joined in the war against Britain and conflict erupted in North America.

New Englanders tried once again to attack Canada. This time, their target was the great fortress of Louisbourg on Cape Breton Island, a naval base that dominated the Gulf of St. Lawrence. An expedition from Massachusetts and Connecticut, supported by a squadron of Royal Navy warships, captured Louisbourg in 1745 and cut Canada off from French reinforcement and resupply. English forces should now have been able to conquer New France.

Instead, politically influential merchants in Albany, New York, continued to trade with the enemy via Lake Champlain, enabling Canada to hold out until the end of the war. When the peace treaty was signed in 1748, Britain, which had fared badly in the European fighting, returned Louisbourg to France. This diplomatic adjustment, routine by European standards, shocked New Englanders. New York's illegal trade with the enemy, unremarkable by previous colonial standards, appalled British administrators.

Even before the war's end, aggressive English traders from Pennsylvania began moving west to buy furs from Indians who had once traded with the French. The movements of these traders, along with the appearance of Virginians in the Ohio Valley after 1748, gravely concerned the French.

In 1749, the governor general of New France set out to assert direct control over the region by building a set of forts from Lake Erie to the Forks of the Ohio. This signaled the end of France's commitment to Iroquois neutrality. The chiefs of the Iroquois League now found themselves trapped between empires edging closer to confrontation in the Ohio Valley.

The appearance of English traders in the valley offering goods on better terms than the French or the Iroquois had ever provided also undermined Iroquois dominance. The Ohio Valley Indians increasingly ignored Iroquois claims of control and pursued their own independent course.

One spur to their disaffection from the Iroquois was the 1744 **Treaty of Lancaster**, by which Iroquois chiefs had sold a group of Virginia land speculators rights to trade at the Forks of the Ohio. The Virginians assumed that these trading rights included the right to acquire land for eventual sale to settlers. The Ohio Valley Indians found this intolerable, as did the French. When in 1754 the government of Virginia sent out a small body of soldiers under Lieutenant Colonel George Washington to protect Virginia's claims to the Forks of the Ohio, the French struck decisively to stop them.

THE FRENCH AND INDIAN WAR, 1754–1760: A DECISIVE VICTORY

In April 1754, French soldiers overwhelmed a group of Virginians who had been building a small fort at the Forks of the Ohio. They then erected a much larger fort of their own on the spot, Fort Duquesne. The French intended to follow up by similarly ousting Washington's weak, untrained troops, who had encamped further up the Monongahela River. However, at the end of May, Washington's men killed or captured all but one of the members of a small French reconnaissance party. The French decided to teach the Virginians a lesson. On July 3, they attacked Washington at his encampment, Fort Necessity. The next day, with a quarter of his troops killed or wounded, Washington surrendered.

British imperial officials worried that the Iroquois might ally with the French. Britain ordered New York's governor to convene an intercolonial meeting in Albany—known as the *Albany Congress*—to discuss matters with the Iroquois. Several prominent colonists, including Governor William Shirley of Massachusetts and Benjamin

Franklin, took advantage of the occasion to put forward the **Albany Plan of Union**, which called for an intercolonial union to coordinate colonial defense, levy taxes, and regulate Indian affairs. But the colonies, too suspicious of one another to see their common interests, rejected the Albany Plan.

Meanwhile, the French expulsion of the Virginians left the Indians of the region, Delawares and Shawnees, with no choice but to ally with the French in what came to be called the **French and Indian War**. Soon French and Indian attacks fell like hammer blows on backcountry settlements from Pennsylvania to the Carolinas. Iroquois neutrality no longer mattered. Europeans were at last contending directly for control of the Ohio Country.

The French and Indian War blazed in America for two years before it erupted as a fourth Anglo-French war in Europe in 1756. Known in Europe as the *Seven Years' War* (1756–1763), it involved fighting in the Caribbean, Africa, India, and the Philippine Islands as well as in Europe and North America. It was unlike any other eighteenth-century conflict not only in its immense scope and expense but also in its decisive outcome.

During the first phase of the war, the French enjoyed a string of successes as they followed what had been a proven strategy in previous conflicts, guerrilla war. Relying on Indian allies and Canadian soldiers, the French raided English frontier settlements, killing and capturing hundreds of civilians and forcing tens of thousands more to flee. Then they attacked fortified outposts whenever the opportunity appeared. This style of warfare allowed the Canadians' Indian allies—who came from all over the Northeast and the upper Midwest—to act independently in choosing targets and tactics.

In 1755, Britain dispatched troops to attack Fort Duquesne. Major General Edward Braddock marched to within ten miles of Fort Duquesne, only to have his 1,450-man force surrounded and destroyed by Indians and Canadian militiamen. Braddock's defeat set the tone for virtually every military engagement of the next three years and opened a period of demoralization and internal conflict in the British colonies.

Britain responded by sending a new commander in chief, Lord Loudoun, to set colonial military affairs on a professional footing. He insisted on managing every aspect of the war effort, not only directing the campaigns but also dictating the amount of support, in men and money, that each colony would provide. The colonists grew increasingly stubborn in response to Loudoun's high-handed style. Colonial soldiers objected to Loudoun's command and colonial assemblies refused to cooperate.

Britain's aim had been to "rationalize" the war by making it conform to European professional military standards. This approach to warfare required soldiers to advance in formation in the face of massed musket fire without breaking rank. Such iron discipline was enforced—as in the British army—by savage punishments, including hundreds of lashes at the whipping post. Few colonial volunteers met professional standards, and few colonists thought them necessary. British officers assumed that colonial soldiers were simply lazy cowards. Colonial volunteers, appalled to see men lashed "till the blood came out at the knee" of their breeches, saw British officers as brutal task-masters. They resisted all efforts to impose such discipline on their own units, even to the point of desertion and mutiny.

In 1756, the marquis de Montcalm, a strong proponent of European professional standards of military conduct, assumed command of French forces. In his first battle, the successful siege of Fort Oswego, New York, Montcalm was horrified by the behavior of his Indian allies, which included killing wounded prisoners, taking personal captives, and collecting scalps as trophies. He came to regard the Indians—so essential to the defense of New France—as mere savages.

Following his next victory, the capture of Fort William Henry, New York, Montcalm conformed to European practice by allowing the defeated garrison to go home in return for the promise not to fight again. Montcalm's Indian allies—a thousand or more strong—were not to take prisoners, trophies, or plunder.

WHERE TO LEARN MORE

Johnson Hall, Johnstown, New York
www.johnstown.com/city/johnson.html

 3–9
"The Storm Arising in the West," George Washington Delivers a Warning to the French (1753)

Albany Plan of Union   Plan put forward in 1754 calling for an intercolonial union to manage defense and Indian affairs. The plan was rejected by participants at the Albany Congress.

French and Indian War   The last of the Anglo-French colonial wars (1754–1763) and the first in which fighting began in North America. The war ended with France's defeat.

The tragic result came to be known as the Massacre of Fort William Henry. Feeling betrayed by their French allies, the Indians took captives and trophies anyway, killing as many as 185 defenders and taking about 300 captive. Ironically, Montcalm's efforts to limit the war's violence alienated his Indian allies and helped the British army and its colonial auxiliaries to win an unlimited victory.

At the same time that the Europeanization of the war was weakening the French, the British moderated their policies and reached accommodation with the colonists. William Pitt, who as secretary of state directed the British war effort from late 1757 through 1761, realized that friction between the colonists and the commander in chief arose from the colonists' sense that they were bearing all the financial burdens of the war without having any say in how the war was fought. Pitt's ingenious solutions were to promise reimbursements to the colonies in proportion to their contribution to the war effort, to deemphasize the power of the commander in chief, and to replace the arrogant Loudoun with a less objectionable officer.

Pitt's money and measures restored colonial morale. He sent thousands of British soldiers to America to fight alongside tens of thousands of colonial troops. The Anglo-American forces operated more successfully, seizing Louisbourg again in 1758. Once more, Canada experienced crippling shortages of supplies, weapons, and trade goods. British emissaries persuaded the Delawares and Shawnees to abandon their French alliance, and late in 1758, an Anglo-American force again marched on Fort Duquesne. In command of its lead battalion was Colonel George Washington. The French defenders, abandoned by their native allies and confronted by overwhelming force, blew up the fort and retreated to the Great Lakes.

From this point on, the Anglo-Americans suffered no setbacks and the French won no victories. Montcalm, forced back to Quebec, decided to risk everything in a European-style, open-field battle against a British force led by General James Wolfe. At the Battle of Quebec (September 13, 1759), Montcalm lost the gamble—and his life (as did the victorious General Wolfe).

What finally decided the outcome of the war in America was the Battle of Quiberon Bay in France (November 20, 1759), which cost the French navy its ability to operate on the Atlantic, preventing it from carrying reinforcements and supplies to Canada. The Iroquois decision to enter the war on the side of the Anglo-Americans tipped the balance irrevocably against the French. The last ragged, hungry defenders of Canada, surrounded at Montreal by a vastly superior Anglo-American-Iroquoian force, surrendered on September 8, 1760.

THE TRIUMPH OF THE BRITISH EMPIRE, 1763

The war pitting Britain against France and Spain (which had entered the fighting as a French ally in 1762) concluded with an uninterrupted series of British victories. In the Caribbean, every valuable sugar island the French owned came under British control. Britain's capture of the Philippine capital of Manila on October 5 literally carried British power around the world.

Hostilities ended formally on February 10, 1763, with the conclusion of the **Treaty of Paris**. France regained its West Indian sugar islands—its most valuable colonial possessions—but lost the rest of its North American empire. France ceded to Britain all its claims to lands east of the Mississippi River (except the city of New Orleans) and compensated Spain for the losses it had sustained as an ally by handing over all claims to the Trans-Mississippi West and the port of New Orleans (see Map 4–2). Britain returned Cuba and the Philippines to Spain and in compensation received Florida. Now Great Britain owned everything east of the Mississippi, from the Gulf of Mexico to Hudson's Bay. With France and Spain both humbled and on the verge of financial collapse, Britain seemed pre-eminent in Europe and ready to dominate in the New World. Never before had Americans felt more pride in being British.

Treaty of Paris The formal end to British hostilities against France and Spain in February 1763.

MAP EXPLORATION

To explore an interactive version of this map, go to **http://www.prenhall.com/goldfield2/map4.2**

Legend:
- French claims
- Under French control
- British
- Disputed between Britain and France
- Spanish

1750

1763

MAP 4–2

European Empires in North America, 1750–1763   Great Britain's victory in the French and Indian War transformed the map of North America. France lost its mainland colonies, England claimed all lands east of the Mississippi, and Spain gained nominal control over the Trans-Mississippi West.

USING THIS map and Map 4–1, explain why Great Britain's victory in the French and Indian War was so crucial to its continued dominance of the Western world.

CONCLUSION

The George Washington who ordered a suit in 1763 was not a revolutionary; on the contrary, he was a man who longed to be part of the elite of the great British Empire. For Washington, as for virtually all other colonial leaders, 1763 was a moment of great promise and patriotic devotion to the British Empire. It was a time to rejoice in the fundamental British identity and liberty and rights that seemed to ensure that life in the colonies would be better and more prosperous than ever.

SUMMARY

Economic Development and Imperial Trade in the British Colonies England, the Netherlands, and France competed vigorously in transatlantic trade. Between 1651 and 1733, Parliament passed laws that regulated trade to ensure that more wealth flowed into England's treasury than out of it. By the late 1760s, the colonists imported goods worth nearly £4 million each year, almost all of which came from Great Britain. Nearly two out of every three adult white males living in cities worked at a craft that directly related to overseas commerce. The growth of colonial cities mirrored British urban development, and many colonists assumed the more America resembled Britain, the more prosperous it would be.

The Transformation of Culture Despite the many similarities, many colonists worried that America remained culturally inferior to Britain. Eighteenth-century Americans imported more manufactures from England with every passing year. Many Americans imported "courtesy books," which contained the rules of polite behavior. Educated colonists were especially interested in the new ideas that characterized the Age of Enlightenment. Church steeples dominated the skylines of colonial cities. In all New England colonies except Rhode Island the Puritan faith was the established religion. And it was religion that drew the colonies closer to England through the Great Awakening.

The Colonial Political World During the mid-seventeenth century England began to realize they had limited control over the governance and politics of the colonies in New England. The Dominion of New England and the Lords of Trade were among several failed attempts to gain control. English people on both sides of the Atlantic believed that politics ought to reflect social organization. Differing opinions, however, on virtual representation versus actual representation caused greater disagreement. Indeed, the most direct political confrontations between England and the colonies focused on the role of colonial governors. And, in response to the perceived threat of powerful governors, colonial assemblies asserted themselves as never before.

Expanding Empires During the first half of the eighteenth century, England, Spain, and France all enlarged their North American holdings. The growth in populations was a result of natural increase as well as immigration. Most of the coast from Maine to Georgia was settled by 1760. Colonists who moved to the backcountry often displaced native groups. Spain's empire grew into Texas and California while the French expansion tended to follow major waterways like the Mississippi.

A Century of Warfare The English policy aimed at limiting the expansion of French influence resulted in four wars (King William's War, Queen Anne's War, King George's War, and the French and Indian War) between 1689 and 1763. The conclusion of the final war (the French and Indian War) signaled a dramatic shift in North American history as England would now claim all lands east of the Mississippi, Spain would nominally control the Trans-Mississippi West, and France would lose all of its mainland colonies.

REVIEW QUESTIONS

1. Why did George Washington prefer to order a suit from London rather than trust a Virginia tailor to make him one? How does this attitude reflect elite colonists attitudes about American society and culture in the eighteenth century?

2. How did economic ties between Britain and the colonies grow closer in the century after 1660?

3. What was the Great Awakening, and what impact did it have? How did it affect different groups in colonial society?

4. How were colonial and British political ideas and practices similar? How were they different?

5. Why did England, Spain, and France renew their competition for North America in the eighteenth century?

6. What role did warfare play in North America in the eighteenth century? What role did the Iroquois play?

KEY TERMS

Actual representation   (p. 96)
Age of Enlightenment   (p. 90)
Albany Plan of Union   (p. 103)
Country (Real Whig) ideology
(p. 101)
Dominion of New England   (p. 93)
Enumerated products   (p. 83)

French and Indian War   (p. 103)
Glorious Revolution   (p. 94)
Grand Settlement of 1701   (p. 101)
Great Awakening   (p. 91)
Halfway Covenant   (p. 91)
King George's War   (p. 102)
King William's War   (p. 100)

Mercantilism   (p. 83)
New Lights   (p. 92)
Queen Anne's War   (p. 100)
Treaty of Lancaster   (p. 102)
Treaty of Paris   (p. 104)
Virtual representation   (p. 96)

WHERE TO LEARN MORE

Mission Parkway, San Antonio, Texas. Three Spanish missions (Mission Nuestra Señora de la Purisima Concepción, Mission San Francisco de la Espada, Mission San Juan Capistrano) founded in the early eighteenth century are located along this road. Their architecture indicates that they were intended to be fortifications as well as churches. The website **http://hotx.com/missions/** has links to each mission, offering pictures, descriptions, and historical background.

Ste. Genevieve Historic District, Ste. Genevieve, Missouri. This restored site of an early eighteenth-century French settlement in the pays des Illinois contains many historic buildings open for tours. A general description of the site is at the website **http://rosecity.net/rhr/stegenevieve.html**. Descriptions and pictures of historic houses can be found at: **http://www.stegenevieve.com/histsite.htm**

Colonial Williamsburg, Williamsburg, Virginia. A reconstruction of the capital of eighteenth-century Virginia, this site covers 173 acres and contains many restored and rebuilt structures, including houses, churches, the House of Burgesses, and the Governor's Palace. Many educational and cultural programs are available. Historical interpreters, dressed in period costume, provide information about eighteenth-century Chesapeake life. The website **www.colonialwilliamsburg.com/history/index.cfm** has a variety of links that include biographical information on eighteenth-century residents of Williamsburg, aspects of colonial life, and material culture. The link to "Electronic Field Trips" has information on how to arrange for an interactive television program and special Internet activities.

Mount Vernon, Virginia. Site of George Washington's much refurbished home. There is also a reconstructed gristmill and barn, as well as various outbuildings. Exhibits include information on Washington's agricultural experiments. The website **www.mountvernon.org** offers virtual tours of the house and grounds, as well as information on "George Washington, Pioneer Farmer."

Johnson Hall, Johnstown, New York. Eighteenth-century home of William Johnson, who served as Superintendent of Indian Affairs and directed much of Britain's diplomacy with the Iroquois. Biographical information and pictures can be found at the website: **www.johnstown.com/city/johnson.html**

Berkeley and Westover Plantations, Charles City, Virginia. These two eighteenth-century James River plantations suggest the elegance of elite planters' lives. The house and grounds at Berkeley are open to the public, the grounds only at Westover, the home of William Byrd. Pictures, descriptions of the sites, and background on their owners can be found at **www.jamesriverplantations.org**, which has links to each plantation.

 For additional study resources for this chapter, go to:
www.prenhall.com/goldfield/chapter4

My dear Jack, All the Provinces [are]
arming and Training in the same Manner,
for they are all determined to die or be Free . . .

A NEW METHOD OF MACARONY MAKING AS PRACTISED AT BOSTON

Tarring and Feathering, 1773.
A New Method of Macarony Making,
as Practiced at Boston. American edition
of an English mezzotint satire, 1774,
on the treatment given to John Malcom,
an unpopular customs official.

5

IMPERIAL BREAKDOWN
1763–1774

HOW DID Great Britain deal with its growing empire at the conclusion of the French and Indian War?

HOW DID conflicts such as the Cherokee War and Pontiac's Rebellion affect relations between Native Americans and colonists?

WHAT EFFECT did the Sugar and Stamp Acts have on colonists' views of Great Britain?

WHO WERE the Regulators, and what were the Regulator movements?

WHO MADE up the first Continental Congress, and what was its purpose?

IMAGE KEY
for pages 108–109

a. Green tea and dried tea leaves.

b. Flank and breast feathers.

c. TARRING & FEATHERING, 1773. A New Method of Macarony Making, as Practiced at Boston. American edition of an English mezzotint satire, 1774, on the treatment given to John Malcom, an unpopular customs official.

d. A "No Stamp Act" teapot.

e. Three Imrie/Risley by Wilson 1750s 77mm diorama figures, Rogers' Ranger with two soldiers, French and Indian War, on diorama base.

f. Powder horn with intricate scrimshaw to commemorate Grant Expedition in the Cherokee War.

g. American colonials force feed hot tea to an English tax collector after tarring and feathering the agent under a Liberty Tree in colonial Boston.

h. The first Continental Congress is held in Carpenter's Hall, Philadelphia, to define American rights and organize a plan of resistance to the Coercive Acts imposed by the British Parliament as punishment for the Boston Tea Party.

Philadelphia,
January 1774

My Dear Jack,

 Your Uncle wrote the 27 Dec. by Capt. Ayres who brought the Tea. His ship came within four miles of this City on Sunday the 26th where she was stopped, not being suffered to come any farther. . . . The inhabitants sent a Supply of fresh provisions & a Pilot on board [who put them on course for England]. I believe they were glad they came off so well, for at Boston they threw it all into the River, and it would have gone near to have shared the same fate here, but the Capt. had more prudence than to endeavour to force a landing by which means he prevented a great deal of Mischief & Confusion, for they were all determined to oppose it. They think now that the India Company will get the Act which imposes a duty of 3d per pound repealed and then send more over.

Kensington,
September 19, 1774

Dear Jack,

 The Congress [The First Continental Congress] are now Setting here & have been a fortnight but nothing Transpires. All is kept a profound Secret. There was a [false] report the other day of the Town of Boston being Bombarded by the Men of War lying off the Town . . .which Occasioned a general consternation along the Continent, and in some parts of the Country they Armed and Marched to the Number of 15,000 & more were getting ready. . . . In Short the Provinces are determined one and all to stand by each other. What the Consequences will be we don't know. To be sure thy [they] may send Men of War and destroy the Towns on the sea shore but its Impossible to take the Country, and the damage they do in destroying the Towns will fall on the English in the end.

Kensington
Nov 1, 1774

My Dear Jack,

 Our Congress are broke up and are come to a great Spirited Resolves . . . together with a petition to his Majestie. . . . It is to be published and they have bound themselves to abide by those resolves . . . and if Necessitated to repel force with force. All Importation ceases after the first of December next.

April 28, 1775

Dear Jackey,

 The Provinces are all Arming themselves, and the men are almost all for inlisting as fast as they take them so am afraid we shall have Troublesome times. I heartily wish the Authors of all this Mischief may be brought to Justice.

Kensington
June 28, 1775

My Dear Jack,

All the Provinces [are] arming and Training in the same Manner, for they are all determined to die or be Free. It is not the low Idle Fellows that fight only for pay but Men of great property are Common Soldiers who say they are fighting for themselves and Posterity. . . . The People are getting in Manufactures of different sorts, particularly Salt Peter and Gunpowder. The Smiths are almost all turnd Gunsmiths and cannot work fast enough. God knows how it will end but I fear it will be very bad on both sides, and if your drivalish minestry and parliament dont make some concessions and Repeal the Acts, England will lose America for as I said before they are determined to be free.

—Eliza Farmar

Pennsylvania Magazine of History and Biography, vol. 40 (1916): 199–207

ELIZA FARMAR and her family had recently moved to Kensington, a suburb of Philadelphia, when she wrote these letters, and her ties to relatives in England remained strong. Jack, the recipient of these letters, was her nephew and a clerk in the London office of the East India Company, whose shipment of tea precipitated the Boston Tea Party. Although she hoped that he might come to America, she minced no words in emphasizing the determination of Americans to resist British measures that appeared to infringe upon their freedoms. These letters accordingly chronicle a psychological counterpart to her move to Kensington. She began both journeys as an English subject; she ended them as an American citizen. Her initial reports of political developments, though sympathetic to the colonial point of view, were fairly objective, but by the eve of the Revolution she had disowned the British government by referring to "your minestry and parliament" as "drivalish," a slip of the pen that covered ineffective and devilish.

Like most colonists, she started out proud to be a British subject and part of Britain's powerful empire. Americans had fought the king's enemies as well as their own in a series of imperial wars and had gloried in British successes. But they had also developed a sense of their identity as Americans. Largely governing themselves through their own legislatures, they believed that they enjoyed all the rights of British subjects anywhere.

But after the French and Indian War, British authorities faced a burdensome debt and vastly increased territory to administer. In response, they attempted to change how they governed the colonies and, for the first time, imposed direct taxes on the colonists. Most Americans opposed these measures as violations of their rights, although they disagreed over how far to carry their resistance.

IMPERIAL REORGANIZATION

At the close of the French and Indian War, British officials adopted a new and ultimately disastrous course in dealing with America. Lacking experience, they panicked at the magnitude of the problems confronting them, and led by a young and somewhat naive monarch (George III, who ascended to the English throne in 1760), they tried to fix a relationship between England and the colonies that most Americans would have said was not broken. They did this by adopting measures that worked mostly to the disadvantage of the colonies. As one contemporary critic observed, "A great Empire and little minds go ill together."

HOW DID Great Britain deal with its growing empire at the conclusion of the French and Indian War?

BRITISH PROBLEMS

Britain's empire in 1763 was indeed a great one, and the problems its rulers faced were correspondingly large. Its territories in North America stretched from Hudson's Bay in the north to the Caribbean Sea in the south and from the Atlantic Ocean west to the Mississippi River. French territory on the North American mainland had been reduced to two tiny islands in the Gulf of St. Lawrence. But France would be eager for revenge, and French inhabitants in the recently acquired territories might prove disloyal.

Spain was less powerful militarily than France but a more significant presence on the North American mainland. In the territorial settlement at the end of the French and Indian War, it surrendered East and West Florida to Britain but got back its possessions in Cuba and the Philippines and acquired Louisiana from France. Shocked by their inability to defend Cuba and the Philippines, Spanish officials stepped up the pace of reforms that they had begun making earlier in the century. They appointed new officials—who were generally Spaniards rather than colonials—to ensure better tax collection. Spain also expelled the Jesuit order from its dominions because Jesuit priests were too independent of royal control to suit Spanish officials. Spain further strengthened its military forces in much of the empire and began to settle in California and Louisiana.

Protecting and controlling the old and new territories in North America as inexpensively as possible presented British officials with difficult questions. How should they administer the new territories? How should they deal with Indians likely to resist further encroachments on their lands? And perhaps most vexing, how could they rein in the seemingly out-of-control colonists in the old territories?

Permitting most of the new areas to have their own assemblies appeared inadvisable and, indeed, for quite some time British authorities had wanted to roll back the power of the old colonial assemblies. Britain had needed the cooperation of the assemblies during the years of war with France, but now, with France vanquished, imperial officials felt they could crack down on the local governments. Some British statesmen, however, realized that with France gone from the continent, Americans would be less dependent on Britain for protection and therefore more inclined to resist unpopular restrictions.

Resentment against American conduct during the war colored British thinking. Some of the colonies failed to enlist their quota of recruits, and for this the British blamed the local assemblies. Worse yet, some Americans continued to smuggle goods to and from the enemy in the French West Indies during the war. Smuggling was so common in New England that it cost Britain more to operate the customs service in America than it collected in duties.

England emerged from the war with what was then an immense national debt of approximately £130 million. Interest payments alone accounted for half the government's annual expenditures after the war. Alarmed by the unprecedented debt, many Britons concluded that Americans should bear more of the financial burden of running the empire. The colonists certainly appeared prosperous to British soldiers who had served in America. Compared to the English, who paid on average perhaps a third of their income in taxes, many Americans normally rendered no more than 5 percent.

DEALING WITH THE NEW TERRITORIES

In 1763, the British government took several important steps to deal with the new territories, protect the old colonies, and maintain peace with the Indians. One was to keep a substantial body of troops stationed in America even in peacetime. Another, accomplished in the **Proclamation of 1763**, was to temporarily forbid white settlement west of the Appalachian Mountains. The purpose of the

Proclamation of 1763   Royal proclamation setting the boundary known as the Proclamation Line.

MAP EXPLORATION

To explore an interactive version of this map, go to
http://www.prenhall.com/goldfield2/map5.1

MAP 5–1
Colonial Settlement and the Proclamation Line of 1763   This map depicts the regions claimed and settled by the major groups competing for territory in eastern North America. With the Proclamation Line of 1763, positioned along the crest of the Appalachian Mountains, the British government tried to stop the westward migration of settlers under its jurisdiction and thereby limit conflict with the Indians. The result, however, was frustration and anger on the part of land-hungry settlers.

WHY DO you suppose the Proclamation Line of 1763 was positioned along the crest of the Appalachian Mountains?

Proclamation Line restricting white settlement was presumably twofold: to keep white settlers and Indians apart, preventing fighting between them, and to keep the colonists closer to the coast where they would be easier to control (see Map 5–1).

Neither the Proclamation Line nor the stationing of troops in America was particularly wise. The Proclamation Line provoked resentment because it threatened to deprive settlers and speculators in the rapidly developing colonies of the land they coveted, and it was often ignored. As for the troops, the British government further provoked American resentment with passage of **Quartering Acts** that required colonial assemblies to provide barracks and certain supplies for the troops.

Proclamation Line   Boundary, decreed as part of the Proclamation of 1763, that limited British settlements to the eastern side of the Appalachian Mountains.

Quartering Acts   Acts of Parliament requiring colonial legislatures to provide supplies and quarters for the troops stationed in America.

The presence of troops in peacetime alarmed Americans. Imbued with a traditionally English distrust of standing armies, they wondered whether the soldiers were there to coerce rather than to protect them. Given their wariness, Americans would doubtless have objected to the troops and the taxes necessary to support them even if the troops had done an exemplary job of protecting the frontiers. But conflicts with Indians cast doubt on their ability to do even that.

Indian Affairs

From a Native American standpoint, the problems Britain confronted in America were nothing compared to their own troubles in dealing with the British. Colonial settlers and livestock were displacing Indians from their ancient lands. Free-flowing rum and rampant cheating among traders were making the fur and deerskin trades increasingly violent. Regulation of the Indian traders by the colonists was uncoordinated and generally ineffective.

The British victory over the French and the westward expansion of British territory undermined the Indians' traditional strategies and alignments. British officials no longer found Native-American neutrality or military help as important as they once had. Increasingly superfluous as allies and unable to play the European powers off against each other, Native Americans lost much of their former ability to protect themselves by any means short of military resistance. The British took advantage of this increasing vulnerability: Traders exploited the Indians, and settlers encroached on their lands.

Two major Indian wars—one breaking out in the late 1750s during the closing years of the French and Indian War and the other erupting in its aftermath in the early 1760s—challenged British policy toward Native Americans. The first conflict, the **Cherokee War**, took place in the southern Appalachian highlands and resulted in a treaty in 1761 in which the Cherokees agreed to surrender land in the Carolinas and Virginia to the colonists. The second major conflict, **Pontiac's Rebellion**, represented a united effort to resist the British and revitalize Indian cultures. The spiritual catalyst for this movement was a Delaware leader named Neolin, also known as the Delaware Prophet, who began urging Native Americans to reject European goods and ways. The Pontiac Rebellion itself, named for an Ottawa chief who was one of its principal leaders, began when at least eight major groups joined in attacking British forces and American settlers from the Great Lakes to Virginia in 1763. Pontiac's Rebellion raged until 1766. The British eventually forced the Indians to give up portions of their territory in return for compensation and guarantees that traditional hunting grounds in the Ohio Valley would remain theirs.

At one point during the war, a British commander used germ warfare against the Indians, sending them blankets that smallpox victims had used. Settlers in Paxton township (near modern Harrisburg, Pennsylvania) were equally unrestrained. Angered by the Pennsylvania Assembly's lack of aggressive action against the Indians, the settlers lashed out at convenient targets, massacring their peaceful neighbors, the Conestogas. Facing arrest and trial for this outrage, the so-called *Paxton Boys* marched toward Philadelphia, threatening the Pennsylvania Assembly. Benjamin Franklin convinced them to disperse. Despite the government's efforts, the Paxton Boys were never effectively prosecuted.

Pontiac's Rebellion and the Cherokee War were costly for both sides, claiming the lives of hundreds of Indians and white settlers. Hoping to prevent such outbreaks, British officials began experimenting with centralized control of Indian affairs during the 1760s. Following the recommendations of the Albany Congress in 1754 (see Chapter 4), they had already created two districts,

HOW DID conflicts such as the Cherokee War and Pontiac's Rebellion affect relations between Native Americans and colonists?

W   **WHERE TO LEARN MORE**

★ Fort Michilimackinac National Historic Landmark, Mackinaw City, Michigan
www.mackinacparks.com/ michilimackinainach/html

4–2
Declaration of the Injured Frontier Inhabitants [of Pennsylvania] (1764)

Cherokee War   Conflict (1759–1761) on the southern frontier between the Cherokee Indians and colonists from Virginia southward.

Pontiac's Rebellion   Indian uprising (1763–1766) led by Pontiac of the Ottawas and Neolin of the Delawares.

CHRONOLOGY

1759–1761	Cherokee War.
1760	George III becomes king.
1761–1762	Writs of Assistance case in Massachusetts.
1763	Peace of Paris ends French and Indian War. Spanish accelerate imperial reforms. British troops remain in America. Proclamation Line of 1763 limits western expansion of colonial settlement. Pontiac's Rebellion begins. Paxton Boys murder peaceful Indians. Virginia Court decides Parson's Cause.
1764	Sugar Act passed. Currency Act passed.
1765	Quartering Act passed. Stamp Act passed. Stamp Act Congress meets in New York.
1766	Stamp Act repealed; Declaratory Act passed. New York Assembly refuses to comply with the Quartering Act.
1767	Townshend duties imposed. Regulator movements in North and South Carolina.
1770	Boston Massacre. Tea duty retained, other Townshend duties repealed.
1771	North Carolina Regulator movement defeated.
1772	*Gaspee* burned. Committees of Correspondence formed.
1773	Boston Tea Party.
1774	Coercive Acts passed. Quebec Act passed. First Continental Congress meets and agrees to boycott British imports.

northern and southern, for the administration of Indian affairs, each with its own superintendent. The Proclamation of 1763, and the line it established restricting further white settlement, gave these superintendents increased responsibility for protecting the Indians against the encroachments of settlers. But they faced daunting obstacles in their efforts to mediate between Indians and colonists and in 1768 Britain returned supervision of the Indian traders to the individual colonies.

CURBING THE ASSEMBLIES

As an episode in Virginia known as the **Parson's Cause** illustrates, British authorities took advantage of opportunities to curb the American legislatures as early as the 1750s. Anglican ministers in Virginia drew tax-supported salaries computed in pounds of tobacco. As a result, when a drought in the mid-1750s caused a sharp rise in tobacco prices, they expected a windfall. The Virginia House of Burgesses, however, restricted their payment to 2 pennies a pound, below the market value of the tobacco that backed their salaries. Lobbying by the clergy convinced the king to disallow the Two Penny Act, and some Virginia clergymen sued for the unpaid portion of their salaries.

In the most famous of these cases, the Virginia government was defended by Patrick Henry, a previously obscure young lawyer who looked like "a Presbyterian clergyman, used to haranguing the people." Henry gained instant notoriety when he declared that a king who vetoed beneficial acts became a tyrant and thereby forfeited "all right to his subjects' obedience." Given Henry's eloquence, the jury found in favor of the suing minister but awarded him only one penny in damages. This pittance reflected the hostility many Virginians of all denominations felt toward the pretensions of the Anglican clergy.

British authorities also sought to restrict the power of colonial legislatures to issue legal tender currency, paper notes that could be used to settle debts. These notes frequently depreciated to only a fraction of their face value in British money. Not surprisingly, British merchants who had to accept them felt cheated and complained.

Parson's Cause Series of developments (1758–1763) that began when the Virginia legislature modified the salaries of Anglican clergymen, who complained to the crown and sued to recover damages. British authorities responded by imposing additional restrictions on the legislature. Virginians, who saw this as a threat, reacted by strongly reasserting local autonomy.

Parliament had responded in 1751 by forbidding further issues of legal tender paper money in New England. In the **Currency Act** of 1764, Parliament extended this restriction to the rest of the colonies, prohibiting all of them from printing their own legal tender paper money. Because the new restrictions came when most colonies were in an economic recession, Americans considered this step an especially burdensome attempt to curtail the assemblies' powers. To deprive them of their paper money was, in the words of one American, "downright Robbery." Worse, however, was yet to come.

THE SUGAR AND STAMP ACTS

In 1764, the British Parliament, under Prime Minister George Grenville, passed the American Revenue Act, commonly known as the **Sugar Act**. The main purpose of this act, as stated in its preamble, was "for improving the revenue of this kingdom." To generate funds, the Sugar Act and its accompanying legislation combined new and revised duties on colonial imports with strict provisions for collecting those duties. To prevent trade with other countries the Sugar Act legislation also lengthened the list of enumerated products—goods that could be sent only to England or within the empire—and required that ships carry elaborate new documents certifying the legality of their cargoes. A ship's captain could have his entire cargo seized if any of the complicated documents were out of order.

To enforce these cumbersome regulations, the British government continued to use the Royal Navy to seize smugglers' ships, a practice begun during the French and Indian War. It also ordered colonial customs collectors to discharge their duties personally, rather than through the use of easily bribed deputies. Responsibility for trying violations would (three years later) eventually rest in vice-admiralty courts in Boston, Philadelphia, and Charleston, which normally operated without a jury and were more likely to enforce trade restrictions.

In the spring of 1765, Parliament enacted another tax on Americans, the **Stamp Act**. This required that all valid legal documents, as well as newspapers, playing cards, and various other papers, bear a government-issued stamp for which there was a charge. The Sugar Act, though intended to raise revenue, appeared to fall within Britain's accepted authority to regulate commerce; the Stamp Act, by contrast, was the first internal tax (as opposed to an external trade duty) that Parliament had imposed on the colonies. Grenville, a lawyer, realized that it raised a constitutional issue: Did Parliament have the right to impose direct taxes on Americans when Americans had no elected representatives in Parliament? Following the principle of virtual representation—that members of Parliament served the interests of the nation as a whole, not just the locality from which they came—Grenville maintained that it did. Americans, he would find, vigorously disagreed. Nor were they without at least some support in Parliament. Colonel Isaac Barré, a member who had served in the colonies, spoke out against the Stamp Act. In one speech he referred to Americans as "Sons of Liberty," a label Americans soon would adopt for themselves.

AMERICAN REACTIONS

The measures Britain took to solve its financial and administrative problems first puzzled, then shocked, and eventually outraged Americans. The colonists had emerged from the French and Indian War believing that they had done their fair share and more toward making Great Britain ruler of the greatest empire in the world, and they expected to be respected for their efforts. They were certain that as British-Americans they shared in the glory and enjoyed all the rights of Englishmen in England. The new restrictions and taxes accordingly hit them like a slap in the face.

Currency Act   Law passed by Parliament in 1764 to prevent the colonies from issuing legal tender paper money.

Sugar Act   Law passed in 1764 to raise revenue in the American colonies. It lowered the duty from 6 pence to 3 pence per gallon on foreign molasses imported into the colonies and increased the restrictions on colonial commerce.

Stamp Act   Law passed by Parliament in 1765 to raise revenue in America by requiring taxed, stamped paper for legal documents, publications, and playing cards.

WHAT EFFECT did the Sugar and Stamp Acts have on colonists' views of Great Britain?

CONSTITUTIONAL ISSUES

To Americans, it was self-evident that the British measures were unfair. It was difficult to contend, however, that the British authorities had no right to impose them. Then as now, the **British Constitution** was not a single written document. It consisted, rather, of the accumulated body of English law and custom, including acts of Parliament. How, then, could the colonists claim that an act of Parliament was unconstitutional?

Constitutional conflict surfaced early in Massachusetts over the issue of **writs of assistance**. These general search warrants, which gave customs officials in America the power to inspect virtually any building suspected of holding smuggled goods, had to be formally renewed at the accession of a new monarch. When George III became king in 1760, Massachusetts merchants—perhaps out of a fondness for smuggling as well as for liberty—sought to block the reissuance of the writs. Their attorney, James Otis Jr., arguing before the Massachusetts superior court, called the writs "instruments of slavery." Parliament, he maintained, lacked the authority to empower colonial courts to issue them. Otis lost, but "then and there," a future president of the United States, John Adams, would later write, "the child independence was born."

TAXATION AND THE POLITICAL CULTURE

The constitutional issue that most strained the bond between the colonies and the empire was taxation. British measures on other issues annoyed and disturbed Americans, but it was outrage over taxation—the most fundamental issue—that would be the midwife of American independence. Because Parliament had customarily refrained from taxing them, Americans assumed that it could not. To deprive them of the right to be taxed only by their own elected representatives was to deny them one of the most basic rights of Englishmen. If taxes were imposed "without our having a legal Representation where they are laid," one American asked, "are we not reduced from the Character of free Subjects to the miserable State of tributary Slaves?"

American views on taxation and the role of government reflected the influence of country ideology. As mentioned in Chapter 4, this opposition political philosophy emerged in England in the late seventeenth and early eighteenth centuries. Country ideology held that government power, no matter how necessary or to whom entrusted, is inherently aggressive and expansive. According to the English political philosopher John Locke, rulers have the authority to enforce law "only for the public good." When government exceeds this proper function, the people have the right to change it. But only in the last resort does this right justify revolution.

Country ideology stressed that in the English system of government, it was the duty of Parliament, in particular the House of Commons (which represented the people as a whole), to check the executive power of the Crown. The House of Commons' control of taxation enabled it to curb tyrannical rulers. When the Crown did its job properly, the Commons appropriated the necessary funds; when rulers infringed on the liberty of the people, the Commons restrained them by withholding taxes.

Such important responsibilities required that the people's representatives be men of sufficient property and judgment to make independent decisions. A representative should be "virtuous" (meaning public-spirited), and avoid political partisanship. A representative of the appropriate social status who exhibited the proper behavior, many assumed, was more qualified to understand and manage public affairs than his constituents and should accordingly be followed. But if he did not measure up, the people should be able to vote him out.

QUICK REVIEW

British Taxation
- Taxation was the fundamental issue between Britain and the colonies.
- Americans assumed that Parliament could not tax them.
- American views on taxation reflected country ideology.

British Constitution   The principles, procedures, and precedents that governed the operation of the British government.

Writs of assistance   Documents issued by a court of law that gave British officials in America the power to search for smuggled goods whenever they wished.

Country ideology appealed to Americans for a number of reasons. In part, colonists were drawn to it as they were to other English fashions. The works of Alexander Pope, the most widely read English poet of the eighteenth century and a proponent of a version of country ideology, appeared in many colonial libraries. So also did the works of two readable and prolific country ideology publicists, John Trenchard and Thomas Gordon, who collaborated in writing *Cato's Letters* (1720–1724) and the *Independent Whig* (1721). More important, country ideology's suspicion of those in power suited American politics on the local level, where rivalries and factionalism fostered distrust between those with and without power. And it emboldened the many Americans who feared they had no voice in the decisions of the government in London. Finally, with its insistence on the important political role of the propertied elite, country ideology appealed to America's local gentry. These ideas have had an enduring influence on American politics, surfacing even today in the suspicion of Washington and "big government," and they helped inspire the American Revolution.

PROTESTING THE TAXES

Given this ideological background, the initial American response to the Sugar Act was surprisingly mild. This was because not every colonist was equally affected by it. The speaker of the legislature in one southern colony commented that it was "much divided" over the effects of the act and would probably not petition against it. In New England, in contrast, the Sugar Act threatened to cut into the profits of the lucrative smuggling trade with the French West Indies. As a result, people there and in other northern colonies were quicker to recognize the act's implications. The legislative body that imposed it—Parliament—and whose constituents in England stood to gain from it, was not accountable to the people on whom it was imposed, the colonists. As one alarmed colonist noted, if his fellow Americans submitted to any tax imposed by Parliament, they were dumb and docile donkeys.

The size of the burden was less important than the principle involved. To Americans steeped in country ideology, direct taxation by London threatened to undercut the elected representatives' power of the purse and thereby remove the traditional first line of defense against a tyrannical executive. Eventually all the assemblies passed resolutions flatly maintaining that any parliamentary tax on America, including the Sugar Act, was unconstitutional. By the end of 1764, New York merchants had joined the artisans and merchants of Boston in a **nonimportation movement**, an organized boycott of British manufactured goods.

Unlike the Sugar Act, the Stamp Act had an equal impact throughout the colonies, and the response to it was swift and vociferous. Newspapers and pamphlets were filled with denunciations of the supposedly unconstitutional measure, and in taverns everywhere outraged patrons roundly condemned it. "The minds of the freeholders," wrote one observer, "were inflamed . . . by many a hearty damn of the Stamp Act over bottles, bowls and glasses." Parliament, Americans were convinced, did not represent them. The colonial legislatures were also quick to condemn the new measure. Virginia's lower house was the first to act, approving Patrick Henry's strong resolutions against the Stamp Act.

Shared outrage at the Stamp Act inspired the colonies to join in unified political action. The **Sons of Liberty**, a collection of loosely organized protest groups, put pressure on stamp distributors and British authorities. In August 1765, a Boston crowd led by shoemaker Ebenezer MacIntosh demolished property belonging to a revenue agent, and another mob sacked Lieutenant Governor Thomas Hutchinson's house. Later demonstrations organized by the Sons of Liberty in other cities were kept more peaceful with tighter discipline.

QUICK REVIEW

Resistance

◆ Response to the Sugar Act divided.

◆ 1764: New York and Boston merchants launch nonimportation movement.

◆ Response to Stamp Act overwhelming and intense.

Nonimportation movement A tactical means of putting economic pressure on Britain by refusing to buy its exports to the colonies.

Sons of Liberty Secret organizations in the colonies formed to oppose the Stamp Act.

Members of the Sons of Liberty included people from all ranks of society. The leaders, however, among them Christopher Gadsden, came mostly from the middle and upper classes. Often pushed by more radical common people, some of them doubtless joined in the hope of protecting their own positions and interests. Indeed, in Charleston, slaves alarmed their masters and other white people when they paraded through the streets crying, "Liberty!"

Movement leaders were also concerned that disorderly behavior could discredit the American cause. Even the fiery Samuel Adams, one of the leading organizers of the protest in Boston, would later claim, "I am no friend to *Riots*." Still, he added, "when the People are oppressed," they will be "discontented, and they are not to be blamed."

Partly as a result of the growing unrest, leaders throughout the colonies determined to meet and agree on a unified response to Britain. As Gadsden observed at the time, "There ought to be no New England men, no New Yorker, etc. known on the Continent, but all of us Americans." Nine colonies eventually sent delegates to the **Stamp Act Congress**, which met in New York City in October 1765. A humorist in the South Carolina legislature, who had opposed sending anyone, observed that the gathering would produce a most unpalatable combination: New England would throw in fish and onions; the middle provinces, flax seed and flour; Virginia and Maryland, tobacco; North Carolina, pitch, turpentine, and tar; South Carolina, indigo and rice—and Georgia would sprinkle the whole with sawdust. "Such an absurd jumble will you make if you attempt to form [a] union among such discordant materials as the thirteen British provinces," he concluded. A quick-witted member of the assembly shot back that he would not choose his colleague for a cook but that the congress would prepare a dish fit for any king.

It did indeed. The congress adopted the **Declaration of Rights and Grievances**, which denied Parliament's right to tax the colonies, and petitioned unsuccessfully both king and Parliament to repeal the Stamp and Sugar acts. As protests spread, the stamp distributors got the message and resigned, "for the welfare of the people." In some areas, Americans went about their business as usual without using stamped paper. In other places, they avoided activities that required taxed items. They also stepped up the boycott of British goods that had begun in response to the Sugar Act. British merchants, hurt by this economic pressure, petitioned Parliament for repeal of the Stamp Act, and a new ministry obliged them by rescinding it in March 1766.

THE AFTERMATH OF THE STAMP ACT CRISIS

At this point, Americans were in no mood to accept any tax imposed by Parliament, and they misunderstood the **Declaratory Act** that accompanied the repeal of the Stamp Act. Intended to make Parliament's retreat more acceptable to its members, this act stated that Parliament had the right to "legislate for the colonies in all cases whatsoever." Americans assumed the Declaratory Act was a mere face-saving gesture. Unfortunately, it was more than that. As one colonist later observed, it created a "platform for the Invincible Reasoning from the Mouths of four and twenty pounders [cannons]."

A STRAINED RELATIONSHIP

The aftermath of the Stamp Crisis was growing strain between Parliament and the colonies. Most members of Parliament continued to believe that they represented everyone in the empire and that they could therefore tax people in the colonies as well as in England. Americans believed just as strongly that "in taxing ourselves and making Laws for our own internal government . . . we can by no means allow

---

Stamp Act Congress   October 1765 meeting of delegates sent by nine colonies, that adopted the Declaration of Rights and Grievances and petitioned against the Stamp Act.

Declaration of Rights and Grievances Asserts that the Stamp Act and other taxes imposed on the colonists without their consent were unconstitutional.

WHO WERE the Regulators, and what were the Regulator movements?

4–4
"Letters From a Farmer in Pennsylvania" (1767)

Declaratory Act   Law passed in 1766 to accompany repeal of the Stamp Act that stated that Parliament had the authority to legislate for the colonies "in all cases whatsoever."

A satirical British engraving from 1766 showing English politicians burying the Stamp Act, "born 1765 died 1766." The warehouses in the background symbolize the revival of trade with America.

The Granger Collection, N.Y.

our Provincial legislatures to be subordinate to any legislative power on earth."

An exchange between British merchants and their American correspondents in the wake of the Stamp Act's repeal illustrates how far apart Englishmen and Americans had become. The British merchants lectured the Americans, enjoining them "to express filial duty and gratitude to your parent country." To which one Virginia planter tartly replied, "We rarely see anything from your side of the water free from the authoritative style of a master to a schoolboy." This, he observed, was more than "a little ridiculous."

Events likewise testified to continuing tensions between the two sides. When British authorities required Massachusetts to compensate those who had suffered damage in the Stamp Act rioting, the legislature complied but pardoned the rioters. In 1767, an irritated Parliament then passed an act suspending the New York legislature because it had not complied with the Quartering Act of 1765. The New York legislature finally obeyed before the suspending act went into effect, and it remained in business.

REGULATOR MOVEMENTS

Growing strain was also evident on the local level with the emergence in 1766 of vigilante groups calling themselves **Regulators** in response to official corruption in North Carolina and lawlessness in South Carolina. North Carolina's western farmers were oppressed by high taxes, court costs, and debt resulting from the limited supply of money in circulation after the Currency Act. In South Carolina, outlaws roamed the back country stealing livestock and raiding isolated houses. In neither colony did representation in the assemblies reflect the growing backcountry population and its pressing needs. As a result, the Regulators did by extralegal action what they couldn't do through legal channels—in North Carolina they closed courts and intimidated tax officials and in South Carolina they pursued outlaws and whipped people suspected of harboring them.

The activities of the Regulators brought them into conflict with the local elites in North and South Carolina, which were slow in redressing regulator grievances. British officials made matters worse by doing the opposite of what was required. Instead of encouraging the assemblies to increase their western representation, they tried to limit their power by forbidding them to increase their size. As for the shortage of currency, they callously dismissed "any possible local inconvenience" that might result.

Thanks to such help from London, as well as their own mistakes, a crisis confronted local authorities by 1767. In South Carolina, the assembly belatedly reapportioned itself, giving the backcountry some representation, and established courts for the area. But in North Carolina, peace returned only after fighting between the local militia and the Regulators killed twenty-nine men and wounded more than 150 on both sides. The rise of the Regulators demonstrated that while American leaders had to understand and respond to local conditions, British authorities remained inflexible.

QUICK REVIEW

Vigilante Justice

◆ 1766: Regulators form in response to corruption and lawlessness in North Carolina and South Carolina.

◆ Regulators conflict with local elites.

◆ Response to Regulators demonstrated inflexibility of British government.

Regulators Vigilante groups active in the 1760s and 1770s in the western parts of North and South Carolina. The South Carolina Regulators attempted to rid the area of outlaws; the North Carolina Regulators were more concerned with high taxes and court costs.

THE TOWNSHEND CRISIS

Affter an unsuccessful attempt by the British to introduce a new collection of taxes, the Townshend duties, in 1767, a relatively quiet period followed until Britain made yet another attempt to enforce compliance with the one duty still on the books, the duty on tea.

WHERE TO LEARN MORE **W**

Charleston, South Carolina
www.cr.nps.gov/nr/travel/charleston

TOWNSHEND'S PLAN

Charles Townshend became the leading figure in Britain's government in 1767. The **Townshend Duty Act** was based on Townshend's mistaken assumption that the colonists were willing to accept new duties or external taxes, but no direct, or internal, taxes like the Stamp Tax. The duties covered a number of items the colonists regularly imported—tea, paper, paint, lead, and glass. To make sure that the duties were collected, British authorities added a new board of customs commissioners for America and located its headquarters in Boston, the presumed home of many smugglers. To the alarm of the Americans, the new customs officials were far more diligent than their predecessors, going after wealthy Boston merchants like John Hancock, perhaps because he was so openly contemptuous of them. The officials seized Hancock's appropriately named vessel *Liberty* and accused him of smuggling. Hancock may indeed have violated the acts of trade at times, but in this case the accusations were apparently false. The incident sparked a riot in Boston during which a crowd on the waterfront roughed up members of the customs service. British authorities responded in 1768 by sending troops to Boston and maintaining them there for the next year and a half.

Townshend Duty Act Act of Parliament, passed in 1767, imposing duties on colonial tea, lead, paint, paper, and glass.

AMERICAN BOYCOTT

The Townshend duties, like the stamp tax, provoked resistance throughout the colonies. Rejecting the argument that duties were somehow different from taxes, John Dickinson, a wealthy lawyer who wrote under the pen name "A Farmer in Pennsylvania," asserted that a tax was a tax, whatever its form.

There was no equivalent to the Stamp Act Congress in response to the Townshend Act because British officials (acting through the colonial governors) barred the assemblies from sending delegates to such a meeting. Even so, Americans gradually organized an effective nonimportation movement. Many Americans signed subscription lists binding them, with the other signers, to buy only goods made in the colonies and nothing made in Great Britain. Handbills, like one urging "the Sons and Daughters of *LIBERTY*" to shun a particular Boston merchant, brought pressure to bear on uncooperative importers. To avoid imported English textiles, American women spun more thread and wove more cloth at home. Wearing homespun became a moral virtue, a sign of self-reliance, personal independence, and the rejection of "corrupting" English luxuries.

The nonimportation movement forged a sense of common purpose among all who participated in it—men and women, southern planters and northern artisans alike—giving them the sense of belonging to a larger community of fellow Americans (see American Views, "Social Status and the Enforcement of the Nonimportation Movement." p. 122). Although it was at this point more an imagined community than a political community, it was real enough and large enough to reduce imports from Britain by 40 percent after only one year.

By 1770, Britain was prepared to concede that the Townshend duties had been counterproductive because they interfered with

The Boston Massacre, March 5, 1770, in an engraving by Paul Revere. Copied from an earlier print, Revere's widely circulated version shows—somewhat inaccurately—well organized soldiers firing on helpless civilians; the names of the dead, including Crispus Attucks, appear below.

Courtesy of Library of Congress.

• AMERICAN VIEWS •

SOCIAL STATUS AND THE ENFORCEMENT OF THE NONIMPORTATION MOVEMENT

A few Americans openly opposed the nonimportation movement called in response to the Townshend Duty Act crisis of the late 1760s. The aristocratic William Henry Drayton of South Carolina objected to the composition of the committee that enforced nonimportation in his region. The committee included artisans and shopkeepers, men who, Drayton claimed, should have no role in public affairs. Their education prepared them only "to cut up a beast in the market to the best advantage, to cobble an old shoe in the neatest manner, or to build a necessary house [outhouse]," not to make public policy. As the following document makes clear, deference had its limits, and the committeemen emphatically disagreed with him. Drayton later actively supported the Continental Association's ban on importing British goods in 1775. "The people" wanted it, he explained, and "it was our duty, to satisfy our constituents; as we were only servants of the public [at large]."

WHO MAKES policy in the United States today? What qualifications do you think they should have? How do your answers to these questions differ from Drayton's and the "Mechanicks"? How would you explain Drayton's later switch?

The Mechanicks of the General Committee to William Henry Drayton

The gracious Giver of all good things, has been pleased to bestow a certain principle on mankind, which properly may be called common sense: But, though every man hath a natural right to a determined portion of this ineffable ray of the Divinity, yet, to the misfortune of society, many persons fall short of this most necessary gift of God; the want of which cannot be compensated by all the learning of the schools.

The Mechanicks pretend to nothing more, than having a claim from nature, to their share in this inestimable favour, in common with Emperors and Kings, and, were it safe to carry the comparison still higher, they would say with William-Henry Drayton himself; who, in his great condescention, has been pleased to allow us a place amongst human beings; But whether it might have happened from an ill construction of his sensory, or his upper works being damaged by some rough treatment of the person who conducted his birth, we know not; however so it is, that, to us, he seems highly defective in this point, whatever exalted notions he may entertain of his own abilities.

By attending to the dictates of common sense, the Mechanicks have been able to distinguish between RIGHT and WRONG; in doing which indeed no great merit is claimed, because every man's own feelings will direct him thereto, unless he obstinately, or from a pertinacious opinion of his own superior knowledge, shuts his eyes, and stoickally submits to all the illegal encroachments that may be made on his property, by an ill-designing and badly-informed ministry.

British trade. When Parliament eventually repealed most of the Townshend articles, it left the duty on tea. This symbolic equivalent of the Declaratory Act served to assert Parliament's continuing right to tax the colonies.

THE BOSTON MASSACRE

Ironically, on the same day that the proposal to rescind most of the Townshend duties was introduced to Parliament—March 5, 1770—British troops fired on American civilians in Boston. This incident, which came to be known as the **Boston Massacre**, resulted from months of increasing friction between townspeople and the British troops stationed in the city. The townspeople complained that the soldiers insulted them, leered at women, and competed for scarce jobs. Samuel Adams recounted these real and imagined misdeeds in a column called "A Journal of the Times" that he circulated to other American cities. The hostility was so great, complained a British officer, that "twenty" soldiers could be "knocked down in the Streets"

Boston Massacre After months of increasing friction between townspeople and the British troops stationed in the city, on March 5, 1770, British troops fired on American civilians in Boston.

Mr. Drayton may value himself as much as he pleases, on his having had a liberal education bestowed on him, tho' the good fruits thereof have not hitherto been conspicuous either in his public or private life: He ought however to know, that this is not so absolutely necessary to these, who move in the low sphere of mechanical employments. But still, though he pretends to view them with so contemptuous and oblique an eye, these men hope, that they are in some degree useful to society, without presuming to make any comparisons between themselves and him, except with regard to love for their country; for he has amply shewn, that an attachment of this sort is not one of his ruling passions. Nor does he appear in the least to have regarded the peace and good order of that community of which he is a member; otherwise he would not wilfully, and without any cause, have knocked his head against ninety-nine out of every hundred of the people, not only in this province, but of all North-America, not one of whom bore him any malice, nor yet do, though they may entertain what opinions they please, with respect to his want of patriotism, from his having proved a Felo de se [murderer of himself] in this point.

After an avowal of principles, incompatible with the essential rights of freemen under the English constitution, surely, no parish in this province, will ever think it prudent, to trust their interests in such hands, for the time to come? Besides, who can say he ever shewed any capacity for business, when he was honoured with a seat in the House of Assembly? . . .

Mr. Drayton may be assured, that so far from being ashamed of our trades, we are in the highest degree thankful to our friends, who put us in the way of being instructed in them; and that we bless God for giving us strength and judgment to pursue them, in order to maintain our families, with a decency suitable to their stations in life. Every man is not so lucky as to have a fortune ready provided to his hand, either by his own or his wife's parents, as has been his lot; nor ought it to be so with all men; and Providence accordingly hath wisely ordained otherwise, by appointing the greatest part of mankind, to provide for their support by manual labour; and we will be bold to say, that such are the most useful people in a community. . . .

We are, Yours, &c.
MECHANICKS of the COMMITTEE.
October 3d, 1769.

Source: South Carolina Gazette, October 5, 1769; reprinted in The Letters of Freeman, etc.: Essays on the Nonimportation Movement in South Carolina by William Henry Drayton, ed. Robert M. Weir (1977), University of South Carolina Press, pp. 111–114.

and nothing be heard of it, but if a soldier merely kicked a resident, "the Town is immediately in an Alarm."

The Boston Massacre occurred when angry and frightened British soldiers fired on a crowd that was pelting them with sticks and stones. Five men died, including Crispus Attucks—"that half Indian, half negro and altogether rowdy," as someone once called him—who has since become the most celebrated casualty of the incident. To preserve order, the troops withdrew from the city, but the damage had been done.

THE "QUIET PERIOD"

In the so-called Quiet Period that followed, no general grievance united all Americans. But in almost every colony, issues continued to simmer. Local circumstances produced the most spectacular confrontation in Rhode Island. The crew of a British revenue schooner, the *Gaspee*, had been patrolling Narragansett Bay, seizing smugglers and, it was said, stealing livestock and cutting down farmers' fruit

4–6
The Boston "Massacre" or Victims of Circumstance? (1770)

QUICK REVIEW

The *Gaspee* Incident
- Gaspee on patrol in Narragansett Bay.
- Ran aground while chasing American ships.
- Local merchants shot the captain and burned the ship.

"The Bostonian's Paying the Excise-Man or Tarring & Feathering."** This print, published in London in 1774, satirizes American resistance to British tax measures. Men representing a broad range of social classes pour tea down the throat of a tax collector while the Boston Tea Party takes place in the background.

© Christie's Images, Inc.

Committees of correspondence
Committees formed in the colonies to keep Americans informed about British measures that would affect them.

Tea Act of 1773 Act of Parliament that permitted the East India Company to sell through agents in America without paying the duty customarily collected in Britain, thus reducing the retail price.

Boston Tea Party Incident that occurred on December 16, 1773, in which Bostonians, disguised as Indians, destroyed £9,000 worth of tea belonging to the British East India Company in order to prevent payment of the duty on it.

Coercive Acts Legislation passed by Parliament in 1774; included the Boston Port Act, the Massachusetts Government Act, the Administration of Justice Act, and the Quartering Act of 1774.

trees for firewood. Thus when the *Gaspee* ran aground while chasing some American ships, Rhode Islanders got even. Led by John Brown, a local merchant, they boarded the vessel, shot its captain in the buttocks, putting him and his crew ashore, and burned the ship. The British government offered a reward for information about the incident but learned nothing. The British attempt to stamp out smuggling in the colonies was so heavy-handed that it offended the innocent more than it frightened the guilty.

Such incidents, and in particular the British threat to send Americans to England for trial, led American leaders to resolve to keep one another informed about British actions. Twelve colonies established **committees of correspondence** for this purpose, and Boston soon became the scene of a showdown between imperial authority and colonial resistance.

THE BOSTON TEA PARTY

During the Quiet Period, Americans drank smuggled (and therefore untaxed) Dutch tea. Partly as a result, the British East India Company, which had the exclusive right to distribute tea in the British Empire, nearly went bankrupt. Lord North, the prime minister, tried to rescue it with the **Tea Act of 1773**. This act permitted the company to ship tea from its warehouses in Britain without paying the duty normally collected there. The idea was to make its tea more competitive in price with the Dutch product and thereby induce Americans to buy it and simultaneously pay the old Townshend duty.

The colonists' response surprised British officials. What outraged most Americans was the attempt to trick them into paying the tax on tea. Thousands decided not to touch the stuff. Newspapers discussed its dangers to the body as well as to the body politic and offered recipes for substitutes. Many women rejected the tea and put pressure on others to do likewise, while schoolboys collected and burned tea leaves.

Thomas Hutchinson, who had been lieutenant governor of Massachusetts during the Stamp Act riots, was now the colony's royal governor. In most other cities, threats from the Sons of Liberty had convinced the captains of the tea ships to return to England without landing their cargo. Hutchinson, however, was determined to have the tea landed in Boston, and he barred the tea ships there from leaving. As a result, violence once again erupted in the city.

When the Sons of Liberty realized they could not force the ships to leave, they decided on dramatic action. On December 16, 1773, Samuel Adams reportedly told a large gathering at Old South Meeting House that it "could do nothing more to preserve the liberties of America." This remark was apparently a prearranged signal for what came to be known as the **Boston Tea Party**. War whoops immediately answered him from the street outside, and a well-organized band of men disguised as Indians raced aboard the tea ship *Dartmouth*, broke open 342 chests of tea, and heaved the contents in the harbor.

THE INTOLERABLE ACTS

The destruction of property in the Boston Tea Party shocked many Americans. British officials reacted even more strongly. The response in Parliament was to pass a series of repressive measures known as the **Coercive Acts**. The first of these, effective June 1, 1774, was the Boston Port Act, which closed the port of Boston to all incoming and outgoing traffic until the East India Company and the crown received payment for the dumped tea and its duties. The Administration of Justice Act, which followed, declared that an official who killed a colonist while performing his duties could be tried in England (where he would almost certainly receive sympathetic treatment) rather than in Massachusetts. The third measure, the Massachusetts Government Act, drastically modified that colony's charter of

1691, providing that the Crown would appoint members to the governor's council and limiting the number of town meetings that could be held without the governor's prior approval. A new Quartering Act declared that the troops under the governor's command could be lodged in virtually any uninhabited building.

On the same day that Parliament enacted these measures, it also passed the **Quebec Act**, which enlarged the boundaries of Quebec south to the Ohio River, provided for trial of civil cases without a jury, and recognized the Catholic Church, giving it the privileges it had enjoyed under the French. The colonists labeled the Quebec and Coercive Acts together as the **Intolerable Acts**.

Quebec Act   Law passed by Parliament in 1774 that provided an appointed government for Canada, enlarged the boundaries of Quebec, and confirmed the privileges of the Catholic Church.

Intolerable Acts   American term for the Coercive Acts and the Quebec Act.

THE ROAD TO REVOLUTION

Americans considered the Intolerable Acts so threatening that they organized the **First Continental Congress** to respond to them. Congress renewed and took measures to enforce the nonimportation movement. These measures further divided those who supported British authorities and those who opposed them.

WHO MADE up the first Continental Congress, and what was its purpose?

AMERICAN RESPONSE TO THE INTOLERABLE ACTS

Americans found the territorial, administrative, and religious provisions of the Quebec Act deeply disturbing. By giving Canada jurisdiction over lands north of the Ohio River that were claimed by Virginia, Connecticut, and Massachusetts, the Quebec Act deprived settlers of their hoped-for homesteads and speculators of their hoped-for profits, angering both. The religious provisions of the Quebec Act were ominous reminders of an attempt by Anglican clergymen during the 1760s to have a bishop appointed for America.

The Quebec Act accordingly "gave a General Alarm to all Protestants," whose ministers throughout the continent warned their congregations that they might be "bound by Popish chains."

The Boston Port Act arbitrarily punished innocent and guilty Bostonians alike. The Administration of Justice Act—which some with vivid imaginations dubbed the "Murder Act"—seemed to declare an open season on colonists, allowing crown officials to kill them without fear of punishment. The Massachusetts Government Act raised the more realistic fear that no colonial charter was safe. A Parliament that had stripped the Massachusetts legislature of an important power might equally decide to abolish the lower houses of all the colonies.

Nightmarish scenarios filled the colonial newspapers. One clergyman observed that the terms of the Coercive Acts were such that if someone were to "make water" on the door of the royal customs house, an entire colonial city "might be laid in Ashes." He undoubtedly knew that he exaggerated, but his words embodied real fear and anger. Trying to make an example of Boston, British authorities had taken steps that united Americans as nothing had ever done before (see the overview table "New Restraints and Burdens on Americans, 1759–1774" p. 126).

WHERE TO LEARN MORE

Philadelphia, Pennsylvania
www.ushistory.org/tour/index.html
Boston, Massachusetts
www.thefreedomtrail.org/virtual_tour.html

THE FIRST CONTINENTAL CONGRESS

Leaders in most colonies wanted to organize a coordinated response and called for another meeting like the Stamp Act Congress. The colonies accordingly agreed to send delegates to a meeting in Philadelphia that came to be called the First Continental Congress, and in the end, all the colonies except Georgia were represented.

The First Continental Congress met at Carpenter's Hall in Philadelphia from September 5 to October 26, 1774, with fifty-five delegates present at one time or another. All were leading figures in their home colonies, but only a few

First Continental Congress   Meeting of delegates from most of the colonies held in 1774 in response to the Coercive Acts. The Congress endorsed the Suffolk Resolves, adopted the Declaration of Rights and Grievances, and agreed to establish the Continental Association.

OVERVIEW

NEW RESTRAINTS AND BURDENS ON AMERICANS, 1759–1774

	Restraints on Legislative Action	Restraints on Territorial Expansion	Restraints on Colonial Trade	Imposition of New Taxes
1759	Royal instructions restrict the ability of the Virginia assembly to pass timely legislation.			
1762			Writs of assistance issued.	
1763		Proclamation Line keeps white settlement east of the Appalachians.	Peacetime use of the navy and new customs officials to enforce Navigation Acts.	
1764	Currency Act limits the colonial legislatures' ability to issue paper money.		Vice-admiralty courts strengthened for Sugar Act.	Sugar Act imposes taxes for revenue (modified 1766).
1765				Quartering Act requires assemblies to provide facilities for royal troops. Stamp Act imposes internal taxes on legal documents, newspapers, and other items (repealed 1766).
1767	Royal instructions limit the size of colonial assemblies.		Vice-admiralty courts strengthened for Townshend duties. American Customs Service established in Boston.	Townshend duties imposed on some imported goods in order to pay colonial officials. (All but tax on tea repealed, 1770.)
1773				Tea Act reduces duty and prompts Boston Tea Party.
1774 (Intolerable Acts)	Massachusetts Government Act limits town meetings, changes legislature, and violates Massachusetts charter.	Quebec Act enlarges Quebec at expense of colonies with claims in the Ohio River Valley.	Boston Port Act closes harbor until East India Company's tea is paid for.	Quartering Act of 1774 declares that troops could be lodged in virtually any uninhabited building in Boston.

knew members from elsewhere. Each colony had one vote, irrespective of the size of its delegation. Those who favored strong measures—like Samuel Adams and his cousin John, Patrick Henry, and Christopher Gadsden—prevailed. They persuaded most of their colleagues to endorse the **Suffolk Resolves**, which had been passed at a meeting held in Suffolk County (the site of Boston). These strongly worded resolves denounced the Coercive Acts as unconstitutional, advised the people to arm, and called for general economic sanctions against Britain. Learning of them, one British official told an American, "If these Resolves of your people are to be depended on, they have declared War against us."

THE CONTINENTAL ASSOCIATION

The Congress created the **Continental Association** to organize and enforce sanctions against the British. As a first step, the Association pledged Americans to cut off imports from Britain after December 1, 1774. If the dispute with Britain was not resolved by September 1775, the Association called for barring most exports to Britain and the West Indies. All who violated the terms of the association were to be considered "enemies of American liberty" and ostracized.

Congress also issued a declaration of rights and grievances summarizing its position. The declaration condemned most of the steps taken by British authorities since 1763 but "cheerfully" consented to trade regulations for the good of the whole empire. The Congress sent addresses to the people of America, to the inhabitants of Great Britain, and to the king. The address to the king asked him to use his "royal authority and interposition" to protect his loyal subjects in America.

The proceedings of the First Continental Congress revealed division as well as agreement among its delegates. All of the delegates believed that the Coercive Acts were unconstitutional, but they differed over how to resist them. Only a minority was prepared to take up arms against Britain. Most representatives tried to protect the interests of their own colonies. Some South Carolina delegates, in an early example of the sectional stubbornness that would culminate nearly a century later in the U.S. Civil War, threatened to walk out of the meeting unless the nonexportation agreement omitted rice, most of which went to northern Europe by way of Britain. To placate the Carolinians, northerners agreed to the exemption. But Gadsden was disgusted, feeling that these actions betrayed the spirit of united purpose that Patrick Henry had spoken of so stirringly earlier in the Congress: "The distinctions between Virginians, Pennsylvanians, New Yorkers and New Englanders are no more. I am not a Virginian, but an American."

POLITICAL DIVISIONS

In the wake of the First Continental Congress, Americans were forced to take sides for and against the Continental Association. But even such well-known radicals as Adams and Gadsden were far from advocating independence for the colonies. Throughout the pre-Revolutionary period, most colonists hoped and expected that imperial authorities would change their policy toward America. English history, Americans believed, was full of instances in which the resolute opposition of a free people forced oppressive ministries and tyrannical kings to back down. They were confident that it could happen again.

Samuel Adams, the leader of the Boston radicals. In this famous picture, thought to be commissioned by John Hancock, Adams points to legal documents guaranteeing American rights.

Samuel Adams, about 1772, John Singleton Copley, American, 1738–1815, Oil on canvas, 125.73x100.33 cm (49 1/2 x 39 1/2 in.), Deposited by the City of Boston, L-R 30.76c.

QUICK REVIEW

Congressional Response to the Coercive Acts

- All agreed that Acts were unconstitutional.
- A minority prepared to go to war with Britain.
- Most delegates thought of the interests of their own colony first.

Suffolk Resolves Militant resolves adopted in 1774 in response to the Coercive Acts by representatives from the towns in Suffolk County, Massachusetts, including Boston.

Continental Association Agreement, adopted by the First Continental Congress in 1774 in response to the Coercive Acts, to cut off trade with Britain until the objectionable measures were repealed.

Whigs The name used by advocates of colonial resistance to British measures during the 1760s and 1770s.

Tories A derisive term applied to Loyalists in America who supported the king and Parliament just before and during the American Revolution.

What Americans were divided over was the extent of Parliament's authority over them and the degree to which they could legitimately challenge its power. As British officials failed, with the passing of time, to accommodate American views of their rights, Americans began in increasing numbers to challenge London's control over them. The experience of James Wilson, a Pennsylvania lawyer, illustrates this shift. In *Considerations on the Nature and Extent of the Legislative Authority of the British Parliament* (published in 1774), Wilson writes that he set out to find a reasonable dividing line between those areas in which Parliament had legitimate authority over the colonies and those in which it did not. But the more he thought, the more he became convinced "that such a line does not exist" and that there can be "no medium between acknowledging and denying that power in all cases." Wilson therefore concluded that Parliament had no authority at all over the colonies.

During 1774 and early 1775, as the British-American confrontation grew more heated, lively debates raged in newspapers and pamphlets, and the colonists became increasingly polarized. In the last months before the outbreak of the American Revolution, the advocates of colonial rights began to call themselves **Whigs** and condemned their opponents as **Tories**. These traditional English party labels dated from the late seventeenth century, when the Tories had supported the accession of the Catholic King James II, and the Whigs had opposed it. By calling themselves Whigs and their opponents Tories (loyalist was a more accurate label), the advocates of colonial rights cast themselves as champions of liberty and their enemies as defenders of religious intolerance and royal absolutism.

CONCLUSION

All Americans, Whigs and loyalists alike, had considered themselves good British subjects. But Americans were a more diverse and more democratic people than the English. A considerably larger percentage of them could participate in government, and for all practical purposes, had been governing themselves for a long time.

British officials recognized the different character of American society and feared it might lead Americans to reject British controls. But the steps they took to prevent this from happening had the opposite effect.

From Britain's perspective, the measures it took in the wake of the French and Indian War were a reasonable response to its administrative and financial problems in the colonies. Taken one by one from the colonists' perspective, however, they were a rain of blows that finally impelled them to rebel. No wonder that Americans, whose political ideology had already made them wary of governmental power, believed that they were the victims of a conspiracy in London to deprive them of their liberty. That Parliament should be a party to this presumed conspiracy particularly shocked and offended them.

Yet Americans probably should not have been surprised at Parliament's role. Indeed, both Parliament and the colonial assemblies were doing what similar bodies throughout Europe were also doing at roughly the same time—asserting their powers and defending their liberties against encroachments from above and below.

The attempts to protect their accustomed autonomy first brought the colonial assemblies into conflict with Parliament. Asserting their rights led the individual colonies to cooperate more among themselves. This in turn led to increasingly widespread resistance, then to rebellion, and finally to revolution. Moving imperceptibly from one stage to the next, Americans grew conscious of their common interests and their differences from the English. They became aware, as Benjamin Franklin would later write, of the need to break "through the bounds, in which a dependent people had been accustomed to think, and act" so that they might "properly comprehend the character they had assumed."

Summary

Imperial Reorganization At the close of the French and Indian War, British officials adopted a new and ultimately disastrous course in dealing with America. In 1763, the British government took several steps to deal with the new territories, protect the old colonies, and maintain peace with the Indians. Among these steps were the Proclamation of 1763 and the Quartering Acts. Relations with Native Americans were also on the minds of British leaders, as they dealt with both the Cherokee War and Pontiac's Rebellion within a span of three years. Finally, the culmination of the reorganization efforts saw the Sugar Act and Stamp Act passed by Parliament in an effort to collect more taxes from the colonists.

American Reactions The measures Britain took to solve its financial and administrative problems first puzzled, then shocked, and eventually outraged Americans. The constitutional issue that most strained the bond between the colonies and the empire was taxation. With their country ideology, colonists reacted quickly. Shared outrage at the Stamp Act inspired the colonies to join in unified political action. The Sons of Liberty, a collection of protest groups, put pressure on British authorities. Leaders throughout the colonies met and collectively adopted the Declaration of Rights and Grievances, which denied Parliament's right to tax the colonies.

The Aftermath of the Stamp Act Crisis The aftermath of the Stamp Crisis was growing strain between Parliament and the colonies. Growing strain was also evident on the local level with the emergence in 1766 of vigilante groups calling themselves Regulators in response to official corruption in North Carolina and lawlessness in South Carolina.

The Townshend Crisis The Townshend duties, like the stamp tax, provoked resistance throughout the colonies. And, by 1770, Britain was ready to concede that they had been counterproductive. However, in March 1770 British troops fired on American civilians in Boston. This incident, known as the Boston Massacre, resulted from months of increased friction between townspeople and British troops stationed in the city. During the so-called Quiet Period following the Boston Massacre, Americans drank smuggled Dutch tea. When British officials tried to correct this, colonists responded with the Boston Tea Party, during which they heaved 342 chests of tea into the Boston Harbor.

The Road to Revolution Americans found the territorial, religious and constitutional aspects of the Intolerable Acts disturbing. Leaders in most colonies wanted to organize a coordinated response. They agreed to meet in Philadelphia in what was to be called the First Continental Congress. They agreed to endorse the Suffolk Resolves, which strongly denounced the Coercive Acts as unconstitutional. In the wake of the Congress, Americans were forced to take sides for and against the Continental Association. During 1774, as the British-American confrontation grew more heated, the colonies became increasingly polarized.

REVIEW QUESTIONS

1. What do Eliza Farmar's letters tell us about the crisis over dutied tea in 1773 and 1774? What makes her increasingly sympathetic to the colonial position?

2. How did the British victory in the French and Indian War affect the relations between Native Americans and white settlers? Between British authorities and Americans?

3. How did the expectations of American and British authorities differ in 1763? Why were new policies offensive to Americans?

4. How was stationing British troops in America related to British taxation of the colonists? Why did the colonists object to taxation by Parliament?

5. How did Americans oppose the new measures? Who participated in the various forms of resistance? How effective were the different kinds of resistance?

6. What led to the meeting of the First Continental Congress? What did the Congress achieve?

KEY TERMS

Boston Massacre   (p. 122)
Boston Tea Party   (p. 124)
British Constitution   (p. 117)
Cherokee War   (p. 114)
Coercive Acts   (p. 125)
Committees of correspondence
(p. 124)
Continental Association   (p. 127)
Currency Act   (p. 116)
Declaration of Rights and Grievances
(p. 119)

Declaratory Act   (p. 119)
First Continental Congress   (p. 125)
Intolerable Acts   (p. 125)
Nonimportation movement   (p. 118)
Parson's Cause   (p. 115)
Pontiac's Rebellion   (p. 114)
Proclamation Line   (p. 113)
Proclamation of 1763   (p. 112)
Quartering Acts   (p. 113)
Quebec Act   (p. 125)
Regulators   (p. 120)

Sons of Liberty   (p. 118)
Stamp Act   (p. 116)
Stamp Act Congress   (p. 119)
Sugar Act   (p. 116)
Suffolk Resolves   (p. 127)
Tea Act of 1773   (p. 124)
Tories   (p. 128)
Townshend Duty Act   (p. 121)
Whigs   (p. 128)
Writs of assistance   (p. 117)

WHERE TO LEARN MORE

Charleston, South Carolina. Many buildings date from the eighteenth century. Officials stored tea in one of them—the Exchange—to prevent a local version of the Boston Tea Party. The website for Historic Charleston, **http://www.cr.nps.gov/nr/travel/charleston**, provides a map, a list of buildings, and information about them.

Philadelphia, Pennsylvania. Numerous buildings and sites date from the eighteenth century. Independence National Historical Park, between Second and Sixth streets on Walnut and Chestnut streets, contains Carpenter's Hall, where the First Continental Congress met, and the Pennsylvania State House (now known as Independence Hall), where the Declaration of Independence was adopted. Philadelphia's Historic Mile, **http://www.ushistory.org/tour/index.html**, provides a virtual tour of the great landmarks of the city, including Independence Hall.

Boston, Massachusetts. Many important buildings and sites in this area date from the seventeenth and eighteenth centuries. They include Faneuil Hall (Dock Square), where many public meetings took place prior to the Revolution, and the Old State House (Washington and State streets), which overlooks the site of the Boston Massacre. The Freedom Trail, **http://www.thefreedomtrail.org/virtual_tour.html**, provides a well illustrated virtual tour of the historic sites.

 Fort Michilimackinac National Historic Landmark, Mackinaw City, Michigan. Near the south end of the Mackinac Bridge, the present structure is a modern restoration of the fort as it was when Pontiac's Rebellion took a heavy toll of its garrison. The Mackinac State Historic Parks website, **http://www.mackinacparks.com/michilimackinac/html**, provides a brief description and photographs of the reconstructed colonial village and fort.

For additional study resources for this chapter, go to:
www.prenhall.com/goldfield/chapter5

These are the times that try men's souls . . .

UNITE OR DIE

NC

NJ

V

NY

M

P

NE

The surrender of Lord Cornwallis at Yorktown on October 19, 1781, led to the British decision to withdraw from the war. Cornwallis, who claimed to be ill, absented himself from the ceremony and is not in the picture. Washington, who is astride the horse under the American flag, designated General Benjamin Lincoln (on the white horse in the center) as the one to accept the submission of a subordinate British officer. John Trumbull, who painted *The Battle of Bunker Hill* and some three hundred other scenes from the Revolutionary War, finished this painting while he was in London about fifteen years after the events depicted. A large copy of the work now hangs in the rotunda of the United States Capitol in Washington, D.C. Source: *Surrender of Lord Cornwallis at Yorktown,* by John Trumbull (American, 1756-1843). Oil on canvas, 20 7/8 × 30 5/8 in.

6

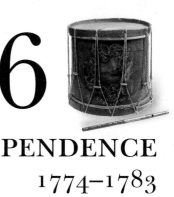

THE WAR FOR INDEPENDENCE
1774–1783

WHAT DEVELOPMENTS
led to mounting tensions
between the colonies and Britain?

WHAT WAS the mood of the colonists
leading up to the Declaration of Independence?

WHAT WERE some
of the key differences between
the British and American forces?

WHAT WERE the major
turning points of the war?

WHAT WERE the terms
of the Peace of Paris?

WHAT WERE
the social effects of the war?

IMAGE KEY
for pages 132–133

a. An 18th-century powder horn decorated with a map.

b. Engraving printed by Benjamin Franklin in 1754 urging the colonies to unite.

c. The 1783 Treaty of Paris that ended the American Revolution and recognized the independence of the United States.

d. Drum belonging to William Diamond (Lexington Historical Society) and fife said to have been played at the Lexington fight early in the morning of April 19, 1775.

e. The Declaration of Independence.

f. A portion of a print depicting the capture of Major John André, the British agent who acted as go-between for the British authorities and Benedict Arnold.

g. A portion of an engraving depicting John Paul Jones stopping an American sailor who was attempting to lower the ship's flag as a sign of surrender.

h. Benjamin West's painting of the American commissioners who negotiated the Peace of Paris.

i. A painting by a French army officer showing the diversity of American soldiers.

Headquarters, Valley Forge
January 14, 1778

I barely hinted to you my dearest Father my desire to augment the Continental Forces from an untried Source. . . . I would solicit you to cede me a number of your able bodied men Slaves, instead of leaving me a fortune. I would bring about a twofold good, first I would advance those who are unjustly deprived of the Rights of Mankind to a State which would be a proper Gradation between abject Slavery and perfect Liberty and besides I would reinforce the Defenders of Liberty with a number of gallant Soldiers. . . . If I could obtain authority for the purpose I would have a Corps of such men trained, uniformly clad, equip'd and ready in every respect to act at the opening of the next Campaign.

February 2, 1778

My dear Father,

The more I reflect upon the difficulties and delays which are likely to attend the completing our Continental Regiments, the more anxiously is my mind bent upon the Scheme which I lately communicated to you. . . . I was aware of having that monster popular Prejudice open-mouthed against me . . . [and] of being obliged to combat the arguments and perhaps the intrigues of interested persons. But zeal for the public Service and an ardent desire to assert the rights of humanity determined me to engage in this arduous business. . . .

You seem to think my dear Father, that men reconciled by long habit to the miseries of their Condition would prefer their ignominious bonds to the untasted Sweets of Liberty, especially when offer'd upon the terms which I propose. I confess indeed the minds of this unhappy species must be debased by a Servitude from which they can hope for no Relief but Death and that every motive to action but Fear must be also nearly extinguished in them. But do you think they are so perfectly moulded to their State as to be insensible that a better exists? Will the galling comparison between themselves and their masters leave them unenlightened in this respect? Can their Self-Love be so totally annihilated as not frequently to induce ardent wishes for a change? . . . I am tempted to believe that this trampled people have so much human left in them, as to be capable of aspiring to the rights of men by noble exertions, if some friend to mankind would point the Road, and give them prospect of Success.

I have long deplored the wretched State of these men and considered in their history, the bloody wars excited in Africa to furnish America with Slaves. The Groans of despairing multitudes toiling for the Luxuries of Merciless Tyrants. I have had the pleasure of conversing with you sometimes upon the means of restoring them to their rights. When can it be better done than when their enfranchisement may be made conducive to the Public Good.

—John Laurens

Henry Laurens Papers, vol 12, pp. 305, 309-392

JOHN LAURENS wrote these letters to his father, Henry, at one low point of the American Revolution, when victory seemed remote. The letters reveal much about the war and the aspirations and limitations of the Revolutionary generation. Henry, a wealthy slaveholder from South Carolina, was president of the Continental Congress; his son John was an aide to General Washington while the Continental Army wintered at Valley Forge.

John, then 23 years old, had been born in South Carolina but educated for the most part in Geneva and London, where he had been exposed to the progressive currents of the Enlightenment. Among these were compassion for the oppressed and the conviction that slavery should be abolished. The war for independence was a cause that appealed deeply to him. American republicanism combined a New Whig distrust of central authority with a belief in a government rooted in a virtuous citizenry. Clinging to this ideology, Americans at first expected to defeat the British Army with a citizens' militia, but they learned that they needed a professional fighting force of their own. With vital French assistance, the new American army triumphed, but the Continental Army was often critically short of soldiers.

Laurens sought to fill this need by enlisting slaves in the Army. This would also provide blacks with a stepping stone to freedom. However, he failed to convince legislatures in the Deep South to enroll black troops in exchange for their freedom.

His idealistic quest for social justice ended in South Carolina, where he died in one of the last skirmishes of the war.

The Outbreak of War and the Declaration of Independence, 1774–1776

After the Boston Tea Party, both the British and the Americans knew that they were approaching a crisis. A British officer in Massachusetts commented in late 1774 that "it is thought by every body here" that British forces would soon have "to take the field." "The people in general are very enraged," he explained, and some would "defend what they call their Liberties," to the death. Many Americans also expected a military confrontation but continued to hope that the king would not "reason with us only by the roar of his Cannon."

Mounting Tensions

In May 1774, General Thomas Gage, the commander in chief of the British army in America, replaced Thomas Hutchinson as governor of Massachusetts. After Gage dissolved the Massachusetts legislature, the General Court, it defied him by assembling anyway. Calling itself the Provincial Congress, the legislature in October 1774 appointed an emergency executive body, the **Committee of Safety**, headed by John Hancock, which began stockpiling weapons and organizing militia volunteers. Some localities had already provided for the formation of special companies of **Minute Men**, who were to be ready at "a minute's warning in Case of an alarm."

Enforcing the Continental Association's boycott of British goods, local committees sometimes assaulted suspected loyalists and destroyed their property. The increasingly polarized atmosphere, combined with the drift toward military confrontation, drove a growing wedge between American loyalists and the patriot anti-British American Whigs.

WHAT DEVELOPMENTS led to mounting tensions between the colonies and Britain?

Committee of Safety Any of the extralegal committees that directed the revolutionary movement and carried on the functions of government at the local level in the period between the breakdown of royal authority and the establishment of regular governments.

Minute Men Special companies of militia formed in Massachusetts and elsewhere beginning in late 1744.

This dramatic engraving of the first battle of the American Revolution at Lexington, Massachusetts, on April 19, 1775, is not the photographic work of an eyewitness to events but a close approximation to it. Ralph Earl, a painter, and Amos Doolittle, an engraver, walked over the battlefields at Lexington and Concord a few days after the engagement, interviewed spectators and participants, and collaborated in producing four large engravings that depict the events with considerable accuracy. This scene from the first plate shows British troops firing on the American militia at Lexington.

Battle of Lexington, April 19th 1775." OH: 13 3/4" OW: 19". Courtesy , Winterthur Museum"

4–8
Address of the Inhabitants of Anson County to Governor Martin (1774)

Conciliatory Proposition Plan whereby Parliament would "forbear" taxation of Americans in colonies whose assemblies imposed taxes considered satisfactory by the British government.

Battles of Lexington and Concord
The first two battles of the American Revolution which resulted in a total of 273 British soldiers dead, wounded, and missing and nearly one hundred Americans dead, wounded, and missing.

THE LOYALISTS' DILEMMA

Loyalists and Whigs began to part company in earnest during the fall and winter of 1774–1775 as the threat of war mounted. Most loyalists were farmers, officeholders and professionals, and many were recent immigrants to the colonies, who felt more secure under the protection of the Crown than with more established Americans. Including those who did not actually fight, the loyalists numbered close to half a million men and women—some 20 percent of the colonies' free population.

BRITISH COERCION AND CONCILIATION

The British parliamentary elections in the fall of 1774 strengthened Prime Minister Lord North's hand and enabled Parliament to prohibit the New England (and later other) colonies from trading outside the British Empire or sending their ships to the North Atlantic fishing grounds. Meanwhile, in a gesture of appeasement, Parliament endorsed Lord North's **Conciliatory Proposition** pledging not to tax the colonies if they would voluntarily contribute to the defense of the empire. Had it specified a maximum colonial contribution and had it been offered ten years earlier, the colonists might have found the Conciliatory Proposition acceptable. Now it was too late. North's government, in any case, had already sent orders to General Gage to take decisive action against the Massachusetts rebels. These orders triggered the first clash between British and American forces.

THE BATTLES OF LEXINGTON AND CONCORD

Gage received his orders on April 14, 1775. On the night of April 18, he assembled seven hundred men on the Boston Common and marched them toward the little towns of Lexington and Concord, some 20 miles away (see Map 6–1). Their mission was to arrest rebel leaders Samuel Adams and John Hancock (then staying in Lexington) and to destroy the military supplies the Committee of Safety had assembled at Concord. Patriots in Boston got wind of the troop movements and sent out riders—one of them the silversmith Paul Revere—to warn their fellows. Adams and Hancock escaped.

When the British soldiers reached Lexington at dawn, they found about seventy armed militiamen drawn up in formation on the village green. Their precise intentions are not clear. Outnumbered ten to one, they probably did not plan to begin a fight. More likely, they were there in a show of defiance.

Months of mounting tension exploded on the Lexington green. A British major ordered the militia to disperse. They were starting to obey when a shot cracked through the dawn stillness. No one now knows who fired. The British responded with a volley that killed or wounded eighteen Americans.

The British troops pressed on to Concord and burned what few supplies the Americans had not been able to hide. When their rear guard came under patriot fire at Concord's North Bridge, the British panicked. As they retreated to Boston, patriot Minute Men and other militia harried them from both sides of the road. By the time the column reached safety, 273 British soldiers were either dead, wounded, or missing. The four thousand Americans who had shot at them along the way suffered nearly one hundred dead, wounded, and missing. (See Overview p. 101 for summaries of this and other battles.)

The speed with which distant colonies heard about the outbreak of fighting at the **Battles of Lexington and Concord** suggests both the importance Americans attached to it and the extraordinary efforts patriots made to spread word of it.

MAP EXPLORATION

To explore an interactive version of this map, go to
http://www.prenhall.com/goldfield2/map6.1

MAP 6–1
The Battles of Lexington and Concord   This map shows the area around Boston, Massachusetts, where in April 1775 British and American forces fought the first military engagements of the Revolution.

WAS BRITAIN'S early strategy against the colonists effective?

Everywhere, news of Lexington and Concord spurred Whigs into action. The shots fired that April morning would, in the words of the nineteenth-century Concord philosopher and poet Ralph Waldo Emerson, be "heard round the world." They signaled the start of the American Revolution.

THE SECOND CONTINENTAL CONGRESS, 1775–1776

By the time the Second Continental Congress convened in Philadelphia on May 10, 1775, it had a war on its hands. Assuming leadership of the rebellion, Congress in the succeeding months became, in effect, a national government. It called for the patchwork of local forces to be organized into the Continental Army, authorized the formation of a navy, established a post office, and authorized the printing of paper continental dollars to meet its expenses. Denying Parliament's claim to govern the colonies but not yet ready to declare themselves independent, the delegates sought to preserve their ties to Britain by expressing loyalty to the crown. In the **Olive Branch Petition**, addressed to George III on July 5, they asked the king to protect his American subjects from the military actions ordered by Parliament. The following day, Congress approved the Declaration of the Causes and Necessity of Taking Up Arms, asserting the resolve of American patriots "to die freemen, rather than to live slaves."

COMMANDER IN CHIEF GEORGE WASHINGTON

To take command of the patriot forces around Boston—the newly named Continental Army—Congress turned to George Washington. John Adams, a Whig leader from Massachusetts, selected the Virginian. Realizing that this would help transform a local quarrel in New England into a continental conflict, Adams also expected Washington's leadership to help attract recruits from Virginia, which was then the most populous colony.

WHERE TO LEARN MORE

Minute Man National Historic Park
Lexington and Concord,
Massachusetts

Olive Branch Petition   Petition adopted by the Second Continental Congress as a last effort toward peace that avowed America's loyalty to George III and requested that he protect them from further aggressions.

Washington was the ideal person for the job. Some of his contemporaries had quicker minds and broader educations; Washington, however, was blessed with good judgment, a profound understanding of both the uses and the limitations of power, and a quiet air of authority. In short, he had the gift of command. He soon also realized that the fate of the patriot cause depended on the survival of the army. The troops revered him. In a crisis, wrote a man who served under him, "his likeness was worth more . . . than the British would have given for his person"—presumably a great deal.

EARLY FIGHTING

General Gage, finding himself besieged in Boston after the fighting at Lexington and Concord, decided to seize and fortify territory south of Boston, where his cannons could command the harbor. But the Americans seized high ground first, entrenching themselves on Breeds Hill north of town. On June 17, 1775, Gage sent 2,200 well-trained soldiers to drive the 1,700 patriot men and boys from their new position. The British succeeded, but at great cost. In three assaults, they suffered more than a thousand casualties. The Americans, who retreated when they ran short of gunpowder, lost just under four hundred dead or wounded. One glum British officer observed afterward that another such victory "would have ruined us." Misnamed for another hill nearby, this encounter has gone down in history as the Battle of Bunker Hill (see Map 6–2).

During the winter of 1775–1776, the Americans dragged some sixty cannons 300 miles through snow and over mountains from Fort Ticonderoga to Boston, mounting them overlooking Boston harbor, and putting the British in an indefensible position. The British then evacuated Boston and moved their troops to Halifax, Nova Scotia. New England was for the moment secure for the patriots. Initial fighting in the South also went well for the patriots, who defeated loyalist forces, who included slaves who had been promised their freedom if they fought for the Loyalist cause, at Great Bridge, near Norfolk, and Moore's Creek Bridge in North Carolina. In June 1776, patriot forces also repulsed a large British expedition sent to capture Charleston, South Carolina.

In contrast, an attempt to win Canada to the patriot side met with disaster. Two American armies attacked in late 1775. One quickly captured Montreal. The other, under Benedict Arnold, approached Quebec through the Maine wilderness in the face of great hardships. Linking up outside heavily fortified Quebec, the American commanders attacked the city on December 31. The assault, followed by the Siege of Quebec, failed. Canada remained a British province.

INDEPENDENCE

The stunning American successes in New England and the South in late 1775 and early 1776 bolstered the patriots' confidence.

This portrait of George Washington appears in multiple versions depicting the victorious general against different backgrounds, including the battles of Princeton and Yorktown. The painter, Charles Willson Peale, served under Washington at Princeton, and the French commander at Yorktown, the Count de Rochambeau, took an appropriate version home with him in 1783.

Peale, Charles Willson (1741–1827). (after): George Washington after the battle of Princeton, January 3, 1777. 1779. Oil on canvas, 234.5x155 cm. Inv.:MV 4560. Photo: Gerard Blot. Chateaux de Versailles et de Trianon, Versailles, France. Reunion des Musees Nationaux/Art Resource, NY

MAP 6–2
Early Fighting, 1775–1776   As this map clearly reveals, even the earliest fighting occurred in widely scattered areas, thereby complicating Britain's efforts to subdue the Americans.

WHAT WAS BRITAIN'S early strategy against the colonists?

In August 1775, King George III rejected Congress's Olive Branch Petition. Instead, he issued a proclamation declaring the colonies in rebellion and denying them his protection. In December, Parliament barred all exports from the American colonies. These aggressive actions, especially the king's, persuaded many colonists to abandon their loyalty to the crown. More and more, Whigs began to think seriously of declaring full independence from Britain.

CHRONOLOGY

1775	**April 19:** Battles of Lexington and Concord.
	May 10: Second Continental Congress meets.
	June 17: Battle of Bunker Hill.
	December 31: American attack on Quebec.
1776	**January 9:** Thomas Paine's *Common Sense*.
	July 4: Declaration of Independence.
	September 15: British take New York City.
	December 26: Battle of Trenton.
1777	**January 3:** Battle of Princeton.
	September 11: Battle of Brandywine Creek.
	October 17: American victory at Saratoga.
	Runaway inflation begins.
	Continental Army winters at Valley Forge.
1778	**February 6:** France and the United States sign an alliance.
	June 17: Congress refuses to negotiate with British peace commissioners.

	July 4: George Rogers Clark captures British post in the Mississippi Valley.
	December 29: British capture Savannah.
1779	**June 21:** Spain declares war on Britain.
	Americans devastate the Iroquois country.
	September 23: John Paul Jones captures the British ship *Serapis*.
1780	**May 12:** Fall of Charleston, South Carolina.
	October 7: Americans win Battle of Kings Mountain.
	Nathanael Greene takes command in the South.
1781	**January 17:** Americans defeat British at Battle of Cowpens.
	March 15: Battle of Guilford Court House.
	October 19: Cornwallis surrenders at Yorktown.
1783	**March 15:** Washington quells the Newburgh "Conspiracy."
	September 3: Peace of Paris signed.
	November 21: British begin evacuating New York.

5–4
A freelance writer urges his readers to use common sense (1776)

QUICK REVIEW

Common Sense

- Published by Tom Paine in January 1776.
- Denounced King George and made the case for independence.
- Sold more than 100,000 copies.

WHERE TO LEARN MORE

Independence National Historic Park, Philadelphia, Pennsylvania

At this critical moment, a ne'er-do-well Englishman, recently arrived on American soil, gave the cause of independence a powerful boost. Thomas Paine was by trade a corsetmaker—and a twice-fired tax collector. Also a man of radical ideas that he expressed forcefully in the everyday English of ordinary people, he became a powerful polemicist for the American cause. In his pamphlet *Common Sense*, published in Philadelphia in January 1776, Paine denounced King George and made the case for independence. He ridiculed the absurdity of "supposing a continent to be perpetually governed by an island," and described the king as "the Royal Brute" whose tyranny should be thrown off. Simple common sense, Paine concluded, dictated that " 'TIS TIME TO PART."

Common Sense, which promptly sold more than 100,000 copies throughout the colonies, helped predispose Americans toward independence. Tactical considerations also led patriot leaders toward a formal separation from Great Britain. Such a move would make it easier for America to gain desperately needed aid from foreign countries, especially from England's ancient enemy, France. Declaring independence would also give the local political elites leading the resistance to British rule a solid legal basis for their newly claimed authority.

On June 7, 1776, Virginian Richard Henry Lee introduced in Congress a resolution stating that the united colonies "are, and of right ought to be, free and independent States." Postponing a vote on the issue. Congress appointed a committee to draw up a declaration of independence. The committee turned to a young Virginian named Thomas Jefferson to compose the first draft. "You can write ten times better than I," John Adams supposedly told Jefferson. When the committee presented the document to Congress and it became clear that the majority favored independence, the Pennsylvania and South Carolina delegations switched sides in favor of it, and the New York delegation decided to abstain. Thus when Congress voted on the resolution for independence on July 2, 1776, it was approved unanimously by all voting delegations. After further tinkering with the wording, Congress officially approved the **Declaration of Independence** on July 4, 1776.

Congress intended the declaration to be a justification for America's secession from the British Empire. Jefferson later maintained that he did not write any more than what everyone was thinking. The political theory that lies behind the declaration is known as the **contract theory of government**. Developed by the late seventeenth-century English philosopher John Locke and others, the contract theory maintains that legitimate government rests on an agreement between the people and their rulers. The people are bound to obey their rulers only so long as the rulers offer them protection. Jefferson's prose, however, transformed what might have been a bland statement into one of history's great assertions of human rights.

The Declaration of Independence consists of a magnificently stated opening assumption, two premises, and a powerful conclusion. The opening assumption is that all men are created equal, that they therefore have equal rights, and that they can neither give up these rights nor allow them to be taken away. The first premise—that people establish governments to protect their fundamental rights to life, liberty, and property—is a restatement of contract theory. (With a wonderful flourish reflecting the Enlightenment's optimism about human potential, Jefferson changed "property" to "the pursuit of happiness.") The second premise is a long list of charges meant to justify the Americans' rejection of their hitherto legitimate ruler. Then follows the dramatic conclusion: Americans can rightfully overthrow King George's rule and replace it with something more satisfactory.

Historians have spilled oceans of ink debating Jefferson's use of the expression "all men." Almost certainly he was thinking in the abstract and meant "humanity in general." In practice, of course, many people were excluded from full participation in eighteenth-century American society. Women, propertyless white men, and free black men had no formal political rights and limited legal rights, and slaves enjoyed no rights at all. (Although himself a slaveowner, Jefferson was deeply troubled by American slavery. He had wanted to include a denunciation of the slave trade among the charges against George III in the Declaration of Independence, but Congress took it out, believing that to blame the king for this inhumane business would appear hypocritical.) But if the words "all men are created equal" had limited practical meaning in 1776, they have ever since confronted Americans with a moral challenge.

Thomas Jefferson. Mather Brown, an American artist living in England, painted this picture of Jefferson for John Adams while the two men were in London on diplomatic missions in 1786. A companion portrait of Adams that Jefferson ordered for himself also survives. Brown's sensitive portrait of a thoughtful Jefferson is the earliest known likeness of him.

Courtesy of Library of Congress

Declaration of Independence
The document by which the Second Continental Congress announced and justified its decision to renounce the colonies' allegiance to the British government.

Contract theory of government
The belief that government is established by human beings to protect certain rights—such as life, liberty, and property—that are theirs by natural, divinely sanctioned law and that when government protects these rights, people are obligated to obey it.

REPUBLICANISM

Americans reacted to news of the Declaration of Independence with mixed emotions. There was rejoicing as orators read the declaration to great crowds. But even many who favored independence worried how Americans would govern themselves. Most Whigs, animated by the political ideology known as **republicanism**, thought a republican government was best suited to American society.

Republicanism held that self-government—either directly by the citizens of a country or indirectly by their elected representatives—provided a more reliable foundation for the good society and individual freedom than rule by kings. Thus drawing on contract theory, as in the Declaration of Independence, republicanism called for government by consent of the governed. Drawing on country ideology, it was suspicious of excessively centralized government and insistent on the need for virtuous, public-spirited citizenry. Republicanism therefore helped give the American Revolution a moral dimension.

But other than a state that was not ruled by a hereditary king, what was a republic? Americans had at hand a recent example of a republic in the English Civil War of the mid-seventeenth century, in which English Puritans had for a time replaced the monarchy with a republican "Commonwealth," dedicated to advancing the "common weal," or common good. Some New Englanders, spiritual descendants of the Puritans, considered the Commonwealth to have been a noble experiment and regarded the American Revolution as another chance to establish a republic of the godly. "When the mere Politician weighs the Danger or Safety of his Country," warned one clergyman, "he computes them in Proportion to its Fortresses, Arms, Money, Provisions, Numbers of Fighting Men, and its Enemies." But, the clergyman continued, the "Christian Patriot" calculates them "by its Numbers of Sinful or praying People, and its Degrees of Holiness or Vice." Such language recalled the Great Awakening; it reached beyond the upper classes who had been directing resistance to the British and mobilized ordinary people for what their ministers repeatedly assured them was a just war against sin and despotism.

THE COMBATANTS

Republican theory mistrusted professional armies as the instruments of tyrants. A free people, republicans insisted, relied for defense on their own patriotism. When individual or community rights were in danger, free men should grab their muskets from over the fireplace, assemble as the local militia, take care of the problem, and go home. (See, American Views, "A British Woman Observes an American Militia Exercise in 1775." p. 146) But militiamen, as one American general observed, had trouble coping with "the shocking scenes of war" because they were not "steeled by habit or fortified by military pride." In real battles, they often proved unreliable. Americans therefore faced a hard choice: develop a professional army or lose the war. In the end, they did what they had to do. While state militias continued to offer support, it was the disciplined forces of the **Continental Army** that won the crucial battles.

PROFESSIONAL SOLDIERS

Washington tightened things up in the new Continental Army. Eventually, he prevailed on Congress to adopt stricter regulations and to require enlistments for three years or the duration of the war. Although he used militia effectively,

---

QUICK REVIEW

Republicanism
- Self-government: the best foundation for society and individual freedom.
- Called for consent of the governed.
- Suspicious of excessively centralized government.

Republicanism A complex, changing body of ideas, values, and assumptions, closely related to country ideology, that influenced American political behavior during the eighteenth and nineteenth centuries.

WHAT WERE some of the key differences between the British and American forces?

Continental Army The regular or professional army authorized by the Second Continental Congress and commanded by General George Washington during the Revolutionary War.

This print, *Ye Foil'd, Ye Baffled Brittons*, shows the capture of Major John André, the British agent who acted as the go-between for British authorities and the American General Benedict Arnold, who planned to turn over the American fortress at West Point to them. The three militiamen who captured André, who was later hanged as a spy, reportedly refused a bribe for his release. The strange facial expressions of all the participants were probably the artist's crude attempt to indicate surprise.

Mezzotint, 1780 – 1800. Size: 73 x 8 in., W. 93 x 4 in. Courtesy, Winterthur Museum

his consistent aim was to turn the Continental Army into a disciplined force that could defeat the British in the large engagements of massed troops characteristic of eighteenth-century European warfare. Guerrilla fighters shooting from behind trees like "savages" had their place in the American war effort, but they could never win a decisive, formal battle. And only such a "civilized" victory would impress the other European powers and establish the legitimacy of the United States.

Many soldiers of fortune, as well as a few idealists, offered their services to American representatives in Europe. France's 19-year-old Marquis de Lafayette was one of the youngest, wealthiest, and most idealistic. Two Poles, Tadeusz Kosciuszko, an engineer, and Kazimierz Pulaski, a cavalry commander mortally wounded at the Battle of Savannah in 1779, also rendered good service. Most useful of all, probably, was Baron von Steuben. His title was new, but he had genuine experience in the Prussian army, continental Europe's best. He knew how to get along with American soldiers by explaining the reasons for his orders. He became the Continental Army's drillmaster, and thanks partly to him, Washington's troops increasingly came to resemble their disciplined European counterparts.

The British troops—and the nearly thirty thousand German mercenaries (Americans called them "Hessians") whom the British government also employed—offered Americans the clearest model of a professional army. Most enlisted men did come from the lower classes and from economically depressed areas, but many also had skills. Most British troops carried the "Brown Bess" musket. With bayonet attached, it was almost 6 feet long and weighed over 16 pounds. In battle, soldiers usually stood close together in lines three deep. They were expected to withstand bombardment without flinching, fire on command in volleys, charge with

QUICK REVIEW

Soldiers for Liberty
- France: Marquis de Lafayette
- Poland: Tadeusz Kosciuszko and Kazimierz Pulaski
- Prussia: Baron von Steuben

the bayonet, and use their heavy musket stock (the wooden end) to crush the skulls of any wounded enemy they strode over.

Military life was tough. On the march, seasoned troops carrying 60-pound packs normally covered about 15 miles a day but could go 30 miles in a "forced" march. In all weather conditions, the British wore heavy woolen uniforms dyed bright red for visibility on smoke-filled battlefields (hence their nickname "red-coats"). They were frequently undernourished, however, and many more died of disease than of injury in battle. Medical care was, by modern standards, primitive: Treatments for illness included bleeding and purging (induced vomiting and diarrhea). Serious arm or leg wounds usually meant amputation, without antiseptics or anesthetics, and often proved fatal.

Severe discipline held soldiers in line. Striking an officer or deserting could bring death; lesser offenses usually incurred a beating. Several hundred lashes, "well laid on" with the notorious cat-o'-ninetails (a whip with multiple cords, each ending in a nasty little knot or a metal ball), were not uncommon.

Soldiers amused themselves with gambling (despite regulations against it) and drinking. Perhaps two-thirds of the Redcoats were illiterate, and they all suffered from loneliness and boredom. Camaraderie and a legendary loyalty to their regiments sustained them.

After the winter of 1777–1778, conditions in the Continental Army came to resemble those of the British army. Like British regulars, American recruits tended to be low on the social scale. The chances for talented enlisted men to win an officer's commission were greater in the Continental Army than the British army. And despite their ragged uniforms, they carried themselves like soldiers. Indeed, Continental soldiers frequently had little more than "their ragged shirt flaps to cover their nakedness," and more than once their bare marching feet left bloody tracks in the snow.

Both British and American authorities had trouble supplying their troops. Both sides suffered from bureaucratic inefficiencies, but the fundamental problems of each were different. The British had plenty of hard-coin money with a stable value, which many American merchants and farmers were happy to take in payment for supplies. But the British had to rely mostly on supplies shipped to them from the British Isles. The Continental Army, in contrast, had to pay for supplies in paper money, both Continental dollars and state-issued currency, whose value sank steadily as the war progressed.

Feeling themselves outcasts from an uncaring society, the professional soldiers of the Continental Army developed a community of their own. The soldiers were "as strict a band of brotherhood as Masons," one later wrote, and their spirit kept them together in the face of misery. Attempts at mutiny in Washington's camp were few and largely unsuccessful.

Occasionally, American officers let their disgruntlement get out of hand. The most notorious such case was that of Benedict Arnold, a general who compiled a distinguished record during the first three years of the war but then came to feel himself shabbily treated by Congress and his superiors. Seeking better rewards for his abilities, he offered to surrender the strategic fort at West Point (which he commanded) to the enemy; before he could act, however, his plot was discovered, and he fled to the British, serving with them until the end of the war. Among Americans, his name became a synonym for traitor.

What was perhaps the most serious expression of army discontent—one that threatened the future of republican institutions and civilian government in the United States—occurred near Newburgh, New York, in March 1783, after the fighting was over. During the war, Congress had promised officers a pension of half pay for life (the custom in Great Britain), but now many veterans demanded in-

QUICK REVIEW

Military Life

◆ Soldiers suffered from disease and lack of food.

◆ Discipline was severe.

◆ Soldiers of the Continental Army developed a community of their own.

stead full pay for six years. When Congress failed to grant real assurances that *any* pay would be forthcoming, hotheaded young officers called a meeting that could have led to an armed uprising and military coup. General Washington, in a dramatic speech, subtly warned the men of all that they might lose by insubordination. A military coup would "open the flood Gates of Civil discord" and "deluge" the nation in blood; loyalty now, he said, would be "one more distinguished proof" of their patriotism. With the fate of the Revolution and the honor of the army hanging apparently in the balance, the movement collapsed. The officers and politicians behind the "conspiracy" were only bluffing, using the threat of a discontented army to frighten the states into granting Congress the power (which it then lacked) to levy taxes so it would have the funds to pay the army.

WOMEN IN THE CONTENDING ARMIES

Women accompanied many units on both sides, as was common in eighteenth-century warfare. A few were prostitutes. Most were the married or common-law consorts of ordinary soldiers. These women "camp followers" cooked and washed for the troops, occasionally helped load artillery, and provided most of the nursing care. A certain number in a company were subject to military orders and were authorized to draw rations and pay. The role of these women found its way into American folklore in the legend of Molly Pitcher (perhaps Mary Ludwig Hays, the wife of a Continental artillery sergeant), who heroically carried water to gunners to cool them and their overheated guns at the Battle of Monmouth Court House in 1778.

AFRICAN-AMERICAN AND NATIVE-AMERICAN PARTICIPATION IN THE WAR

On June 30, 1779, the British commander in chief, Sir Henry Clinton, promised to allow slaves who fled from rebel owners to join the royal troops to "follow . . . any Occupation" they wished. Hedged as this promise of freedom was, news of it spread quickly among the slave communities, and late in the war enough black people flocked to the British army in South Carolina and Georgia to make feeding and housing them a serious problem. The British shared the racial prejudices of many Americans, however, and despite their efforts to recruit African Americans, they were reluctant to arm them. Instead, the British put most of the ex-slaves to work as agricultural or construction workers (many of the free and enslaved black people accompanying American troops were similarly employed). A few relatively well equipped black British dragoons (mounted troops), however, saw some combat in South Carolina, much to the horror of local Whigs.

Approximately 5,000 African Americans fought against the British and for American independence, hundreds of them in the Continental Army. Many were freemen from Massachusetts and Rhode Island. Several free black men served among the defenders at Bunker Hill, and at least one distinguished himself sufficiently for his commander to commend him as "an experienced officer as well as an excellent soldier." But the idea of arming African Americans was not well received in the South.

John Laurens, who hoped to raise black troops in South Carolina as a prelude to the general abolition of slavery, was the only member of George Washington's staff to be killed in battle. This commemorative portrait by Charles Willson Peale bears the Latin inscription "sweet and proper it is to die for one's country."

Independence National Historic Park

• AMERICAN VIEWS •

A British Woman Observes
an American Militia Exercise in 1775

The following description of North Carolinians preparing for war in 1775 comes from the travel journal of Janet Schaw, a Scotswoman visiting her brother Robert in America. Robert Schaw, although he was appointed a colonel in the North Carolina militia, disapproved of the American cause and eventually refused to take the oath of allegiance to the new state government. His wife, by contrast, according to Janet Schaw, was "so rooted an American, that she detests every thing that is European." Early in June 1775 Janet Schaw saw the militia train outside of Wilmington under their commander Robert Howe, who later became a major general in the Continental Army. She returned to Scotland in late 1775.

WHAT DOES this passage suggest about Janet Schaw's own views of the American cause? How accurately do you think it reflects the effectiveness of militia forces? What does it suggest about the relationship between patriots and loyalists?

We came down in the morning in time for the review, which the heat made as terrible to the spectators as to the soldiers, or what you please to call them. They had certainly fainted under it, had not the constant draughts of grog supported them. Their exercise was that of bush-fighting, but it appeared so confused and so perfectly different from any thing I ever saw, I cannot say whether they performed it well or not; but this I know that they were heated with rum till capable of committing the most shocking outrages. We stood in the balcony of Doctor Cobham's [a future loyalist] house and they were reviewed on a field mostly covered with what are called here scrubby oaks which are only a little better than brushwood. They at last however assembled on the plain field, and I must really laugh while I recollect their figures: 2000 men in their shirts and trousers, preceded by a very ill beat-drum and a fiddler, who was also in his shirt with a long sword and a cue at his hair, who played with all his might. They made indeed a most unmartial appearance. But the worst figure there can shoot from behind a bush and kill even a General Wolfe.

Before the review was over, I hear a cry of tar and feather. I was ready to faint at the idea of this dreadful operation. I would have gladly quitted the balcony, but was so much afraid the Victim was one of my friends, that I was not able to move; and he indeed proved to be one, tho' in a humble station. For it was Mr. Neilson's [a loyalist] poor English groom. You can hardly conceive what I felt when I saw him dragged forward, poor devil, frighted out of his wits. However at the request of some of the officers, who had been Neilson's friends, his punishment was changed into that of mounting on a table and begging pardon for having smiled at the regt. He was then drummed and fiddled out of the town, with a strict prohibition of ever being seen in it again.

Source: [Janet Schaw], *Journal of a Lady of Quality; Being the Narrative of a Journey from Scotland to the West Indies, North Carolina, and Portugal, in the Years 1774 to 1776*, ed. Evangeline Walker Andrews in Collaboration with Charles McLean Andrews (1923). Yale University Press.

Many Indians also favored the British. To Native Americans, the key issue of the American Revolution, as well as in most disputes with white settlers, was about their land. Many Indian peoples, including the Cherokees, decided that it was in their interest to back the British. Their aid mainly took the form of attacks on white frontier settlements. Usually they did not tell the British in advance what they were planning to do. Thus in one notorious incident, an Indian attack in the Hudson River Valley resulted in the mistaken scalping of Jane McCrae, the fiancé of a British officer. Whig propagandists exploited this tragedy to the fullest. Because they could not control the Indians, the British regarded their native allies as a liability as well as an asset and seldom made unrestricted use of them. Other Native Americans, such as the Oneidas and the Tuscaroras, however, joined the Americans.

THE WAR IN THE NORTH, 1776–1777

The Revolutionary War can be divided into three phases. In the first, from the outbreak of fighting in 1775 to 1778, most of the important battles took place in New England, New York, New Jersey, and Pennsylvania. During these years, the Americans faced the British alone. But in 1778, France entered the war on the American side, opening the second phase of the war. Fighting in the second phase would rage from 1778 to 1781 mainly in the South, at sea, and on the western frontier. The third phase of the war, from late 1781 to 1783, saw little actual fighting. With American victory assured, attention shifted to the diplomatic maneuvering leading up to the Treaty of Paris (1783), which ended the war and recognized American independence.

THE BRITISH ARMY HESITATES

During the first phase of the war, the British concentrated on subduing New England, the hotbed of what they saw as "rebellious principles." Replacing General Gage, the government appointed Sir William Howe as commander in chief of British forces and his brother, Richard Howe, as admiral of the naval forces in North American waters. New York City had been the headquarters of the British army during the late colonial period, and the Howes decided to make it their base of operations. In August 1776, the Howes landed troops on Long Island, and in the Battle of Brooklyn Heights they quickly drove the American forces deployed there from Brooklyn Heights and back to Manhattan Island (see Map 6–3, p. 148).

In the ensuing weeks, British forces overwhelmed Washington's forces, driving them out of Manhattan and then, moving north, clearing them from the area around the city at the Battle of White Plains. But the Howes were hesitant to deal a crushing blow, and the Americans were able to retreat across New Jersey into Pennsylvania. The American cause seemed lost, however; Congress fled from Philadelphia to Baltimore, and the Continental Army almost melted away.

On Christmas night, Washington led his forces back across the icy Delaware from Pennsylvania and, in the Battle of Trenton, launched an unorthodox surprise attack on a garrison of Hessian mercenaries at Trenton, New Jersey, on the morning of December 26. Still in the midst of their Christmas celebrations, the Hessians quickly surrendered. A week later, in the Battle of Princeton, Washington overwhelmed a British force at Princeton, New Jersey. Thereafter, Washington withdrew to winter quarters in Morristown, New Jersey, and the Howes made no further effort to pursue him. Both sides suspended operations until the spring.

The victories at Trenton and Princeton boosted morale and saved the American cause. But why did the Howes not annihilate the Continental Army while they had the chance? Clearly, they wanted to regain loyal subjects, not alienate them. But if they had inflicted a crushing defeat on the Americans, they would have risked making them permanent enemies of British rule. By the time it later became apparent that this cautious strategy was not working and the Howes were replaced with more aggressive commanders, the British had lost their best chance to win the war.

THE YEAR OF THE HANGMAN

Contemporaries called 1777 the Year of the Hangman because the triple sevens suggested a row of gallows. Living up to its ominous name, it was indeed a crucial year for the American cause.

WHAT WERE the major turning points in the war?

QUICK REVIEW

Victories at Trenton and Princeton

- 1776: a series of defeats devastated the Continental Army.
- Christmas night 1776: Washington crosses the Delaware and launches a surprise attack.
- Victories at Trenton and Princeton revive the American cause.

MAP 6–3

The War in the North, 1776–1777   Most of the fighting between the British and Americans during the first part of the war occurred in the North, partly because British authorities assumed that the New England colonies were the most rebellious.

HOW WAS the scope of the early fighting a detriment to the British?

The British began the year by mounting a major effort to end the rebellion. Their strategy was to send a force south from Canada down the Hudson River to link up with the Howes in New York City, separate New England from the rest of the states, and then crush the rebellion in that most recalcitrant region. Unfortunately, there was no effort to coordinate strategy between the forces advancing from Canada and the forces under the command of the Howes in New York. Thus in the end, poorly planned, poorly executed, and unsupported from the South, the campaign ended in disaster for the British.

Some five thousand Redcoats and three thousand German mercenaries assembled in Canada during the winter of 1776–1777 under the command of the jaunty, high-living, and popular "Gentleman Johnny" Burgoyne. The army finally set off in June with 1,500 horses hauling its heavy artillery and ponderous supply train. Crossing Lake Champlain, Burgoyne's army on July 5 recaptured Fort Ticonderoga, but success eluded him after that.

Trouble began as the troops started moving overland through the woods at the southern end of the lake. Forced to clear away huge trees in its path felled by American axmen, the army crawled along at only two or three miles a day. Promised reinforcements never arrived, and a Whig militia force wiped out a force of eight hundred men that Burgoyne had sent into Vermont to round up badly needed horses. By October 1777, Burgoyne's army was down to less than six thousand men and was facing disaster. A force of nearly three thousand Continentals and nine thousand militia, commanded by General Horatio Gates, had now assembled to confront the British. Unable to break through the American lines, Burgoyne surrendered to Gates following the Battle of Saratoga on October 17, 1777. A stunning reversal for the British, Burgoyne's defeat would help convince the French to join the fighting on the American side.

While Burgoyne was meeting disaster, William Howe, rather than moving north to support him, was making plans to destroy Washington's army and capture Philadelphia. In July 1777, Howe's troops sailed from New York to Chesapeake Bay and from there marched on Philadelphia from the south. They met Washington's army on the banks of Brandywine Creek, near the Pennsylvania-Delaware border. The Americans put up a good fight before giving way with a loss of 1,200 killed or captured (twice as many as the British).

Howe occupied Philadelphia, and his men settled down in comfortable winter quarters. Congress fled to York, Pennsylvania, and the Continental Army established its own winter camp outside Philadelphia, at **Valley Forge**. Here Washington was joined by his wife, Martha, in a small stone farmhouse, surrounded by the log huts that his men built for themselves. The Continental Army's miserable winter at Valley Forge has become legendary in American history. Suffering from cold, disease, and starvation, as many as 2,500 soldiers died. Yet the troops managed to transform themselves into a disciplined professional army by drilling endlessly under the watchful eye of General von Steuben, and with the coming of spring, American prospects improved dramatically.

THE WAR WIDENS, 1778–1781

Foreign intervention would transform the American Revolution into a virtual world war, engaging British forces in heavy fighting not only in North America but also in the West Indies and India. In the end, had it not been for French assistance, the American side probably would not have won the clear-cut victory it did.

THE UNITED STATES GAINS AN ALLY

Since late 1776, Benjamin Franklin and a team of American diplomats had been in Paris negotiating French support for the patriot cause. In the winter of 1777–1778, aware that a Franco-American alliance was close, Parliament belatedly tried to end the rebellion by granting the former colonies full autonomy,

WHERE TO LEARN MORE

Saratoga National Historic Park, New York

WHERE TO LEARN MORE

Valley Forge National Historic Park, Valley Forge, Pennsylvania

Valley Forge Area of Pennsylvania approximately 20 miles northwest of Philadelphia where General George Washington's Continental troops were quartered from December 1777 to June 1778 while British forces occupied Philadelphia during the Revolutionary War.

WHAT WERE the consequences of the American alliance with France?

including the exclusive right to tax themselves, in return for a resumption of allegiance to the Crown. But France and the United States concluded an alliance on February 6, 1778, and news of it reached America before the British commission arrived. Seeing independence within reach, Congress refused to negotiate.

The agreements the United States signed with France included both a commercial treaty and a military alliance. Both sides promised to fight together until Britain recognized the independence of the United States, and France pledged not to seek the return of lands in North America. In turn, France persuaded Spain to declare war on Britain in June 1779. The Spanish fleet augmented the naval power of the countries arrayed against Great Britain.

Meanwhile, Catherine the Great of Russia suggested that European powers form a League of Armed Neutrality to protect their trade with the United States and other warring countries against British interference. Denmark and Sweden soon joined; Austria, the Netherlands, Portugal, Prussia, and Sicily eventually followed. Britain, however, quickly went to war with Holland, ostensibly over another issue (to avoid war with the League), but really to cut off Dutch trade with the United States.

Great Britain thus found itself nearly completely isolated and even, briefly, threatened with invasion. Accordingly, as early in the spring of 1778, the British replaced the Howes with a tough new commander, Sir Henry Clinton, instructing him to detach some of his troops to attack the French West Indies. Knowing he now faced a serious French threat, Clinton began consolidating his forces. He evacuated Philadelphia and pulled his troops slowly back across New Jersey to New York.

On June 28, 1778, Washington caught up with the British and engaged them at the Battle of Monmouth Court House. The day was hot and the battle hard-fought. For a while, it looked as if the now well-trained Americans might win, but a mix-up in orders cost Washington the victory. This inconclusive battle proved to be the last major engagement in the North for the rest of the war. Clinton withdrew to New York, and Continental troops occupied the hills along the Hudson Valley north of the city. The war shifted to other fronts.

FIGHTING ON THE FRONTIER AND AT SEA

Native Americans called Kentucky "a dark and bloody ground," a designation that took on added meaning when Indians began raiding the territory in 1777 on British instructions. The nerve center for coordinating these attacks was the British post of Detroit, and the Americans accordingly made plans to capture it. After two unsuccessful expeditions, a third, under Virginian George Rogers Clark (see Map 6–4), captured three key British settlements in the Mississippi Valley (Kaskaskia, Cahokia, and Vincennes) in July 1778. These successes may have strengthened American claims to the West at the end of the war.

Blood also ran on the Pennsylvania and upstate New York frontiers with British and Indian raids on settlers in Pennsylvania's Wyoming Valley and New York's Cherry Valley. Both raids became the stuff of legends and stimulated equally savage reprisals against the Iroquois, destroying forty-one Indian villages in the New York Finger Lakes region.

Anglo-American clashes at sea had begun in 1775, shortly after the Battles of Lexington and Concord and continued until the end of the war as Americans struggled to break the British navy's blockade. Great Britain was the preeminent sea power of the age, and the United States never came close to matching it, in either the number or the size of its ships. But Congress did its best to challenge the British at sea, and the Americans engaged in what was essentially a guerrilla naval war. Their naval flag, appropriately, pictured a rattlesnake and bore the motto "Don't Tread on Me."

MAP EXPLORATION

To explore an interactive version of this map, go to **http://www.prenhall.com/goldfield2/map6.4**

MAP 6–4
The War on the Frontier, 1778–1779   Significant battles in the Mississippi Valley and the frontiers of the seaboard states added to the ferocity of the fighting and strengthened some American claims to western lands.

WERE THE BRITISH at more of a disadvantage the farther from the coast they fought?

The country's first naval hero, Scottish-born John Paul Jones, was primarily a hit-and-run raider. In the colonies by chance when the war broke out, this adventurer offered his services to Congress. Benjamin Franklin helped Jones secure an old French merchant ship, which he outfitted for war and renamed the *Bon Homme Richard.* After capturing seventeen enemy vessels, he encountered the formidable H.M.S. *Serapis* in the North Sea on September 23, 1779. Completely outgunned, Jones brought the *Bon Homme Richard* close enough to make his small arms fire more effective. Asked by the British if he was surrendering, Jones gave the legendary reply, "I have not yet begun to fight." More than four hours later, the *Serapis* surrendered. Jones's crew took possession of the British vessel and left the crippled *Bon Homme Richard* to sink.

Congress and the individual states supplemented America's naval forces by commissioning individual sea captains to outfit their merchant vessels with guns and act as privateers. Some two thousand American privateers captured more than six hundred British ships and forced the British navy to spread itself thin doing convoy duty.

THE LAND WAR MOVES SOUTH

During the first three years of the war, the British had made little effort to mobilize what they believed to be considerable loyalist strength in the South. In 1778, however, facing a threat from France and with their forces in the North concentrated and inactive, they gave southern loyalists a key role in a new strategy for subduing the rebellion. The British southern strategy began to unfold in November 1778, when General Clinton dispatched 3,500 troops to take control of Georgia (see Map 6–5). Meeting only light resistance, they quickly seized Savannah and Augusta. Indeed, enough inhabitants seemed happy to have the British back that the old colonial government was restored under civilian control. After their initial success, however, the British did suffer some serious setbacks. The Spanish entered the war and seized British outposts on the Mississippi and Mobile rivers. And in February 1779, at the Battle of Kettle Creek, South Carolina's Whig militia decimated a loyalist militia contingent.

But the Americans could not beat the British army. In late September and early October 1779, a combined force of 5,500 American and French troops, supported by French warships, unsuccessfully attacked Savannah. The way was now open for the British to attack Charleston, the military key to the Lower South. In December 1779, Clinton sailed through storm-battered seas from New York to the Carolina coast with about nine thousand troops. In the Battle of Charleston, he encircled the city, trapping the patriot forces inside. On May 12, 1780, more than five thousand Continentals and militia laid down their arms—the worst American defeat of the war and the largest single loss of United States troops to a foreign army until the surrender of American forces in the Philippines to Japan in 1942.

The British were now poised to sweep all the South before them. So complete did the British success seem that Clinton tried to force the American troops whom he had taken prisoner to resume their duties as British subjects and join the loyalist militia. Thinking that matters were now well in hand, Clinton sailed back to New York, leaving the southern troops under the command of Lord Cornwallis.

Clinton's confidence that the South had returned securely to the loyalist camp was premature. Atrocities like Colonel Banastre Tarleton's slaughter of 350 Virginia Continentals who had already offered to surrender inflamed anti-British feelings. And Clinton's decision to force former rebels into the loyalist militia backfired, infuriating real loyalists—who saw their enemies getting off lightly—as well as Whigs. Atrocities and reprisals mounted on both sides.

AMERICAN COUNTERATTACKS

In 1780, after a complete rout of General Horatio Gates's forces near Camden, South Carolina, American morale revived when "over mountain men" (militia) from Virginia, western North and South Carolina, and what is today eastern Tennessee

This engraving, published in London in 1779, shows an apocryphal incident during the battle in which John Paul Jones's ship *Bon Homme Richard* defeated the British *Serapis*. During the fighting, Jones supposedly shot an American sailor who attempted to lower the ship's flag as a sign of surrender; actually Jones only knocked him down with a pistol. Legend (and the artist) may have confused this incident with another earlier one—while Jones was still a Scotsman (note the bonnet)—in which Jones did kill a mutineer.

"Paul Jones Shooting a Sailor." Color engraving from the Olds Collection #366, no negative number. Collection of the New York Historical Society

WHERE TO LEARN MORE

★ Kings Mountain National Military Park and Cowpens National Battlefield, South Carolina

MAP EXPLORATION
To explore an interactive version of this map, go to
http://www.prenhall.com/goldfield2/map6.5

MAP 6–5

The War in the South, 1778–1781   During the latter part of the war, most of the major engagements occurred in the South. British forces won most of the early ones but could not control the immense territory involved and eventually surrendered at Yorktown.

WHY DID the war moved southward as it progressed?

OVERVIEW

IMPORTANT BATTLES OF THE REVOLUTIONARY WAR

	Battle	Date	Outcome
Early Fighting	Lexington and Concord, Massachusetts	Apr. 19, 1775	Contested
	Fort Ticonderoga, New York	May 10, 1775	American victory
	Breeds Hill ("Bunker Hill"), Boston, Massachusetts	June 17, 1775	Contested
	Great Bridge, Virginia	Dec. 9, 1775	American victory
	Quebec, Canada	Dec. 31, 1775	British repulse American assault
	Moore's Creek Bridge, North Carolina	Feb. 27, 1776	American victory
The War in the North	Brooklyn Heights, New York	Aug. 27, 1776	British victory
	White Plains, New York	Oct. 28, 1776	British victory
	Trenton, New Jersey	Dec. 26, 1776	American victory
	Princeton, New Jersey	Jan. 3, 1777	American victory
	Brandywine Creek, Pennsylvania	Sept. 11, 1777	British victory (opened way for British to take Philadelphia)
	Saratoga, New York	Sept. 19 and Oct. 17, 1777	American victory (helped persuade France to form an alliance with United States)
	Monmouth Court House, New Jersey	June 28, 1778	Contested
The War on the Frontier	Wyoming Valley, Pennsylvania	June and July 1778	British victory
	Kaskaskia and Cahokia, Illinois; Vincennes, Indiana	July 4, 1778– Feb. 23, 1779	American victories strengthen claims to Mississippi Valley
	Cherry Valley, New York	Nov. 11, 1778	British victory
The War in the South	Savannah, Georgia	Dec. 29, 1778	British victory (took control of Georgia)
	Kettle Greek, Georgia	Feb. 14, 1779	American victory
	Savannah, Georgia	Sept. 3– Oct. 28, 1779	British victory opened way for British to take Charleston
	Charleston, South Carolina	Feb. 11– May 12, 1780	British victory
	Camden, South Carolina	Aug. 16, 1780	British victory
	Kings Mountain, South Carolina	Oct. 7, 1780	American victory
	Cowpens, South Carolina	Jan. 17, 1781	American victory
	Guilford Court House, North Carolina	Mar. 15, 1781	Contested
	Yorktown, Virginia	Aug. 30– Oct. 19, 1781	American victory (persuaded Britain to end the war)

inflicted a defeat on the British at Kings Mountain, South Carolina, and Nathanael Greene replaced the discredited Gates, bringing competent leadership to the Continentals in the South. The resourceful Greene realized he would need an unorthodox strategy to defeat Cornwallis's larger army of seasoned professional troops. He divided his forces, keeping roughly half with him in northeastern South Carolina and sending the other half westward under General Daniel Morgan. At the Battle of Cowpens on January 17, 1781, Morgan cleverly posted his least reliable troops, the militia, in the front line, telling them to run after firing two volleys. When Tarleton attacked, the militia fired and withdrew. Thinking that the American ranks had broken, the Redcoats charged—straight into devastating fire from Morgan's Continentals. Tarleton escaped, but his reputation for invincibility had been destroyed.

Cornwallis now badly needed a battlefield victory. Burning his army's excess baggage, he set off in hot pursuit of Greene and Morgan, who had rejoined forces. The Continentals had the advantage of knowing the country, which was laced with rain-swollen rivers. Finally, on February 13, 1781, Greene's tired men crossed the Dan River into Virginia, and Cornwallis gave up the chase, marching his equally exhausted Redcoats southward. To his surprise, Cornwallis now found himself pursued—though cautiously, to be sure—by Greene. On March 15, the opposing forces met at Guilford Court House (near present-day Greensboro, North Carolina) in one of the war's bloodiest battles.

By the late summer of 1781, British fortunes were waning in the Lower South. The Redcoats held only the larger towns and the immediately surrounding countryside. With their superior staying power, they won most major engagements, but these victories brought them no lasting gain. As General Greene observed of the Americans, "We fight, get beat, and rise and fight again." Patriot guerrilla forces, led by such colorful figures as "Swamp Fox" Francis Marion, disrupted British communications between their Charleston headquarters and outlying garrisons. The loyalist militias that the British had hoped would pacify the countryside proved unequal to the task. Although Greene never defeated the Redcoats outright, his campaign was a strategic success. The British could not hold what they had taken; the Americans had time on their side. Frustrated, Cornwallis decided to conquer Virginia to cut off Greene's supplies and marched north to Yorktown, Virginia, during the summer of 1781.

The final military showdown of the war was at hand at Yorktown. By now, five thousand French soldiers were in America ready to fight alongside the Continentals, and a large French fleet in the West Indies had orders to support an attack on the British in North America. Faking preparations for an assault on British-occupied New York, the Continentals (commanded by Washington) and the French headed for the Chesapeake. Cornwallis and his six thousand Redcoats soon found themselves besieged behind their fortifications at Yorktown by 8,800 Americans and 7,800 French. A French naval victory gave the allies temporary command of the waters around Yorktown. Cornwallis had nowhere to go, and Clinton—still in New York—could not reinforce him quickly enough. On October 19, 1781, the British army surrendered.

WHERE TO LEARN MORE W

Yorktown Battlefield, Colonial National Historical Park, Yorktown, Virginia

THE AMERICAN VICTORY, 1782–1783

The British surrender at Yorktown marked the end of major fighting in North America, though skirmishes continued for another year. But the majority in Parliament now felt that enough men and money had been wasted trying to keep the Americans within the empire. In March 1782, the king accepted Lord North's resignation and appointed Lord Rockingham as prime minister, with a mandate to make peace.

WHAT WERE the terms of the Peace of Paris?

THE PEACE OF PARIS

The peace negotiations, which took place in Paris, were lengthy. The Americans demanded independence, handsome territorial concessions—Franklin, the senior American negotiator, asked for all of Canada—and access to the rich, British-controlled fishing grounds in the North Atlantic. The new British prime minister, Lord Shelburne (Rockingham had died in 1782), was inclined to be conciliatory, hoping to help British merchants recover their lost colonial trade.

The American negotiators, Franklin, John Adams, and John Jay, masterfully threaded their way among the conflicting interests of the Americans, British, French, and Spanish. With good reason, they feared that the French and Spanish would strike a bargain with the British at the expense of the United States. As a result, the Americans disregarded Congress's instructions to avoid making peace unilaterally. Instead, they secretly worked out their own arrangements with the British that would meet Shelburne's objective of restoring Anglo-American commercial ties. On November 30, 1782, the negotiators signed a preliminary Anglo-American treaty of peace. Its terms were embodied in the final **Peace of Paris**, signed by all the belligerents on September 3, 1783.

The Peace of Paris gave the United States nearly everything it sought except Canada (which was never really a serious issue). Great Britain acknowledged that the United States was "free, sovereign and independent." The northern boundary of the new nation extended west from the St. Croix River (which separated Maine from Nova Scotia) past the Great Lakes to what were thought to be the headwaters of the Mississippi River (see Map 6–6). The Mississippi itself—down to just north of New Orleans—formed the western border. Spain acquired the provinces of East and West Florida from Britain. This territory included a substantial chunk of present-day Louisiana, Mississippi, Alabama, and Georgia. The treaty did not, however, provide the United States with access to the Gulf of Mexico, which would be a source of diplomatic friction for years.

Several provisions of the treaty addressed important economic issues. Adams, on behalf of his fellow New Englanders, insisted on a provision granting American fishermen access to the waters off eastern Canada. The treaty also required that British forces, on quitting American soil, were to leave behind all American-owned property, including slaves. Another provision declared existing debts between citizens of Britain and the United States still valid, giving British merchants hope of collecting on their American accounts. Congress was to "recommend" that the states restore rights and property taken from loyalists during the war. Nothing was said about the slave trade, which Jay had hoped to ban.

THE COMPONENTS OF SUCCESS

The War for Independence was over. In December 1783, the last British transports put to sea with troops evacuated from New York. Despite the provisions of the peace treaty and the objections of Southern planters, about three thousand African Americans went with them. Washington's Continental Army had already disbanded in the summer of 1783 (but not, as we have seen, before a dispute over pay came close to provoking a military coup). The American commander said an emotional farewell to his officers at New York City's Fraunces Tavern, resigned his commission to Congress, and like the legendary citizen-soldier Cincinnatus, who after defending the ancient Roman Republic gave up his power and went back to plowing his land, went home to Mount Vernon.

Washington's leadership was only one of the reasons why the Americans won the Revolutionary War. French assistance played a crucial role. Some historians even

Peace of Paris Treaties signed in 1783 by Great Britain, the United States, France, Spain, and the Netherlands that ended the Revolutionary War.

MAP EXPLORATION

To explore an interactive version of this map, go to **http://www.prenhall.com/goldfield2/map6.6**

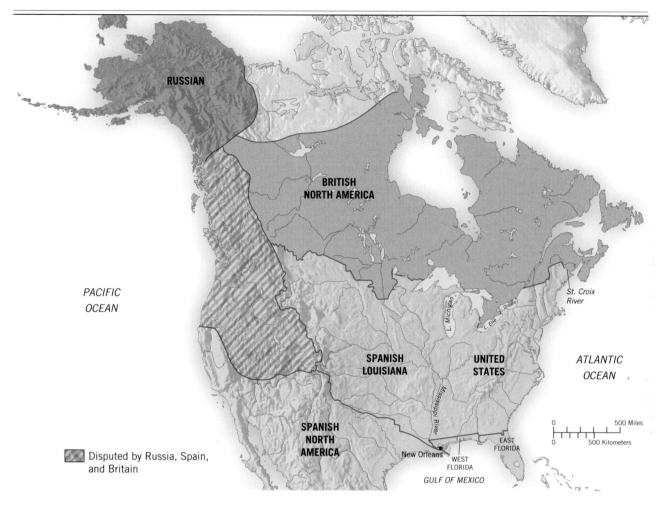

MAP 6–6

North America after the Peace of Paris, 1783   The results of the American Revolution redrew the map of North America, confining Britain to Canada and giving the United States most of the area east of the Mississippi River, though Spain controlled its mouth for most of the next twenty years.

WHAT EFFECT did the Peace of Paris have on the future of the United States?

contend that without the massive infusion of French men and money in 1781, the Revolution would have failed. The British also contributed heavily to their own downfall. Their fatal mistakes included bureaucratic inefficiency, hesitant command, and, worst of all, overconfidence.

Yet it took 175,000 to 200,000 soldiers—Continentals and militia troops—to prevent Great Britain from recovering the colonies. Of these, some seven thousand died in battle for their "country and for its just cause." Those who served in the Continental Army, probably more than half of all who fought, served the longest and saw the most action. Their casualty rate—30 to 40 percent—may have been the highest of any war in which the United States has been engaged.

War and Society, 1775–1783

WHAT WERE the social
effects of the war?

Regular combatants were not the only ones to suffer during the struggle for independence. Eight years of warfare also produced profound dislocations throughout American society. Military service wrenched families apart, and everyone endured economic disruptions. As a forge of nationhood, the Revolution tested all Americans, whatever their standing as citizens.

THE WOMEN'S WAR

Everywhere women had to see their husbands, sons, brothers, and fiancés go off to fight and die. Like Mary Silliman in Connecticut, they waited, trying to stay calm until they knew "what tidings God" had for them. At first, with spirits still running high, Mary's letters to her husband, Selleck, reveal an affectionate light-heartedness. Later the couple's letters grew less playful. Then her husband was captured. The daily round of domestic duties helped to keep her going, but his extended absence increased her burdens and enlarged her responsibilities. Such circumstances elevated women's domestic status. Women also assumed new public roles during the conflict. Some nursed the wounded. More wove cloth for uniforms. The Ladies' Association of Philadelphia was established in 1780 to demonstrate women's patriotism and raise money to buy shirts for the army. Similar associations formed in other states.

Despite their increasing private responsibilities and new public activities, it did not occur to most women to encroach very far on traditional male prerogatives. When John Adam's wife, Abigail, urged him and the Second Continental Congress to "Remember the Ladies," she was not expecting equal political rights. What she wanted, rather, was some legal protections for women and recognition of their value and need for autonomy in the domestic sphere.

Republican ideology, responding to the changing status of women, assigned them a role that was at once exalted and subordinate. It was their job to nurture wise, virtuous, and public-spirited men. It would be this view of women that would prevail in the post-Revolutionary era.

EFFECT OF THE WAR ON AFRICAN AMERICANS AND NATIVE AMERICANS

In the Northern states, where slavery was already economically marginal and where black men were welcome as volunteers in the Continental Army, the Revolutionary War helped bring an end to slavery, although it remained legal there for some time (see Chapter 7). In the South, however, slavery was integral to the economy, and white planters viewed it as crucial to their postwar recovery, so the war ultimately strengthened the institution, especially in the Carolinas and Georgia. Of the African Americans who left with the British at the end of the war, many, both slave and free, went to the West Indies. Others settled in Canada, and some eventually went back to Africa, where Britain established the colony of Sierra Leone for them.

Survivors among the approximately thirteen thousand Native Americans who fought for the British did not have the option of leaving with them at the end of the war. How many died during the war is not known, but certainly many did. Their families and their communities also paid a high price. The Americans repeatedly invaded the Cherokees' homeland in the southern Appalachian Mountains and ravaged the Iroquois country in western New York.

FROM THEN TO NOW
The American Revolution and the Teaching of American History

In October 1994, TV viewers saw politically conservative talk show host Rush Limbaugh hold up a history book and begin ripping out pages. "Here's Paul Revere. He's gone," he exclaimed, and out went a page. "Here's George Washington. . . . He's gone. . . ." More pages bit the dust. "This is what we're doing to American history with this stupid new book, folks." The volume that prompted his outburst was the National History Standards—"the standards from hell" according to conservative critics. In response to such outbursts, Gary Nash, a leading author of the standards and an expert in early American history, repeatedly went on television to defend them, appearing in one twenty-four hour period on ABC, NBC, and PBS.

The furor arose out of a bipartisan attempt to improve education in the nation's schools. In 1989, President George H. W. Bush and the nation's governors announced that it was time "to establish clear national performance goals, goals that will make us internationally competitive . . . in the twenty-first century." The plan called for knowledgeable professionals to establish voluntary guidelines governing what schools should expect students to know about several core subjects, including history. The development of the history standards, which involved thousands of historians and history teachers, took more than two and a half years.

The heated reaction to the standards caught many by surprise, but it probably should not have. History, Nash has pointed out, is "unceasingly controversial because it provides so much of the substance for the way a society defines itself." This is certainly true of the history of the American Revolution—the focus of much of the ire of the standard's critics—because it is from the Revolution that the founding propositions of the nation emerged.

The authors of the standards wanted students to learn the results of recent research that has given voice to African Americans, Native Americans, women, and ordinary people and documented their active role in history. But critics complained that including this material would unduly diminish coverage of prominent figures like Revere and Washington. They also worried that calling attention, say, to African American life under slavery or to such incidents as the Paxton Boys' assault on their Indian neighbors would darken the narrative of American history.

How should one tell the story of the United States? A state legislature once resolved that school textbooks should emphasize "the history of hearts and souls inspired by wonderful American principles and traditions." Those who wrote the National History Standards believed that the "governing narrative" should be "the struggle to fulfill the American ideals of liberty, equal justice, and equality" as "various groups [sought] to elbow their way under the canopy of the nation's founding promises."

Compromise eventually quieted the controversy. After the Senate rejected the history standards, blue-ribbon panels of experts reviewed them, recommended some changes, and predicted that the revised version would make an important contribution toward "developing a responsible and productive citizenry." And indeed, teachers and school administrators throughout the country now regularly consult the revised standards to help them design an appropriate history curriculum.

But such controversies—or "memory wars"—have long been, and doubtless will remain, a recurring part of American history as competing segments of society seek to sanction their aspirations and achievement with differing versions of the common past.

With the peace treaty of 1783, Britain surrendered its territory east of the Mississippi, shocking and infuriating the Native Americans living there. They had not surrendered, and none of them had been at the negotiations in Paris. With the Americans now claiming their country by conquest, the Revolutionary War was a disaster for most Native Americans.

American soldiers at Yorktown in 1781 as drawn by a young officer in the French army, Jean-Baptiste-Antoine de Verger. The African American on the left is an infantryman of the First Rhode Island Regiment; the next, a musketeer; the third, with the fringed jacket, a rifleman. The man on the right is a Continental artilleryman, holding a lighted match used to fire cannons.

Anne S.K. Brown Military Collection, John Hay Library, Brown University

THE PRICE OF VICTORY

The British and American armies both needed enormous quantities of supplies. This heavy demand disrupted the normal distribution of goods and drove up real prices seven- or eightfold. The widespread use of depreciating paper money by the American side amplified this rise in prices and triggered severe inflation. By March 1780, Congress was forced to admit officially that the continental dollar was worthless. (The popular expression "not worth a continental" suggests that the public had long since agreed.)

Necessity, not folly, drove Congress and the states to rely on the printing press. Rather than alienate citizens by immediately raising taxes to pay for the war, the states printed paper money supposedly redeemable by future tax revenues. Because the quantity of this paper money rose faster than the supply of goods and services, prices skyrocketed and the value of the money plunged. Savvy people tried to spend money before its value could drop further, whereas those who had salable commodities like grain tended to hoard them in the hope that the price would go even higher. The rampant inflation was demoralizing and divisive. Lucky speculators and unscrupulous profiteers grew rich while ordinary and patriotic people suffered. These conditions sparked more than thirty protest demonstrations. As usual, war and its deprivations brought out both the best and the worst in human nature.

The successful outcome of the war and the stable peace that followed suggest that most Americans somehow managed to cope. But during the last years of the conflict, their economic and psychological reserves ran low. The total real wealth of private individuals declined by an average of 0.5 percent annually from 1774 to 1805, even with the returning prosperity of the 1790s. Such statistics suggest the true economic cost of the War for Independence. And the atrocities committed on both sides—the burning, plundering, and murdering by regular troops, militias, and civilians acting on their own—provide nearly as accurate an indicator of the conflict's psychological cost.

CONCLUSION

Despite the devastation and divisiveness of the war, many people in Europe and the United States were convinced that it represented something momentous. The *Annual Register,* an influential British magazine reflecting respectable opinion, commented accurately in 1783 that the American Revolution . . . "has already overturned those favourite systems of policy and commerce, both in the old and in the new world, which the wisdom of the ages, and the power of the greatest nations, had in vain endeavored to render permanent; and it seems to have laid the seeds of still greater revolutions in the history and mutual relations of mankind."

Americans, indeed, had fired a shot heard round the world. Thanks in part to its heavy investment in the American Revolution, France suffered a grave financial crisis in the late 1780s. This in turn ushered in the political crisis that culminated in the French Revolution of 1789.

Once prosperous but distant provinces of a far-flung empire, the North American states had become an independent confederation, a grand experiment in republicanism whose fate mattered to enlightened men and women throughout the Western world. In his written farewell to the rank and file of his troops at the end of October 1783, Washington maintained that "the enlarged prospects of happiness, opened by the confirmation of our independence and sovereignty, almost exceed the power of description." He urged those who had fought with him to maintain their "strong attachments to the union" and "prove themselves not less virtuous and useful as citizens, than they have been persevering and victorious as soldiers." The work of securing the promise of the American Revolution, Washington knew, would now shift from the battlefield to the political arena.

SUMMARY

The Outbreak of War and the Declaration of Independence, 1774–1776   After the Boston Tea Party, both the British and the Americans knew they were heading for a crisis. In a gesture of appeasement, Parliament endorsed the Conciliatory Proposition, pledging not to tax the colonies if they would contribute to the defense of the empire. But, it was too late. General Gage received orders to march to Lexington and Concord to arrest rebels. What ensued were to be the first battles of the Revolutionary War. On July 4, 1776, Congress officially approved the Declaration of Independence.

The Combatants   The American forces were composed of a regular Continental Army and militiamen. British soldiers were, for the most part, better trained and organized. For both, military life was tough. And, often only severe discipline would hold soldiers in line. Women accompanied many units on both sides. Approximately 5,000 African Americans fought against the British and for American independence. Many Indians, however, decided it was in their best interest to join British forces in the war.

The War in the North, 1776–1777   During the first phase of the war, the British concentrated on subduing New England. As fighting moved down into New York and New Jersey, Washington won two key battles at Trenton and Princeton. The colonials continued on with a win at the Battle of Saratoga, only to suffer a costly defeat at Brandywine Creek. In the winter of 1777, a large number of colonial fighters camped at Valley Forge. Here, the hard winter and disease set in, but constant training improved their battle-reddiness by spring.

The War Widens, 1778–1781   Foreign intervention was to transform the American Revolution into a virtual world war. France allied with America and, Spain with France. Russia, Denmark, Sweden, Austria, the Netherlands, Portugal, Prussia, and Sicily joined a league to protect their trade with the combatants. The expansion of the war prompted the British to attack the southern states in the hope of gaining additional loyalist support. This strategy failed and in the last major battle of the war at Yorktown, Virginia, on October 19, 1781, the British army surrendered.

The American Victory, 1782–1783   The American victory accelerated peace talks, and the Peace of Paris was signed in 1783. Several provisions of the treaty addressed important economic issues such as access to fishing waters in Canada. The War for Independence was over, and British troops began their evacuation of America.

The War and Society, 1775–1783   The war had a great effect on many different aspects of American society. Women everywhere lost husbands, sons, and fathers. Women, also assumed new public roles and increased responsibilities at home. In the Northern states, the war helped bring an end to slavery. In the South, however, slavery was integral to the economy. The successful outcome of the war and the stable peace that followed suggest that most Americans somehow managed to cope with the new world in which they found themselves.

REVIEW QUESTIONS

1. Who were the loyalists and how many of them were there? Why did British and American attempts in 1775 to avert war fail?

2. What actions did the Second Continental Congress take in 1775 and 1776? Why did it choose George Washington to command its army? Why was he a good choice?

3. Why did Congress declare independence in July 1776? How did Americans justify their claim to independence?

4. What was republicanism, and why was the enthusiasm that it inspired insufficient to win the war?

5. Why did the British not crush the Americans immediately? Why did France decide to enter the war as an ally of the United States?

6. Why did the United States ultimately win? What were the immediate results of the American victory?

KEY TERMS

Committee of Safety   (p. 135)
Conciliatory Proposition   (p. 136)
Continental Army   (p. 142)
Contract theory of government
   (p. 141)

Battles of Lexington and Concord   (p. 137)

Declaration of Independence
   (p. 141)
Minute Men   (p. 135)
Olive Branch Petition   (p. 137)
Peace of Paris   (p. 156)

Republicanism   (p. 142)
Valley Forge   (p. 149)

WHERE TO LEARN MORE

Gnadenhutten Monument and Shoenbrunn Village near New Philadelphia, Ohio. Reconstructed buildings mark a Moravian Indian settlement whose inhabitants were massacred by American in 1782. The website for the museum and park, **http://www. geocities.com/tusc_hat/gnaden.html**, gives a brief history of the village and Revolutionary War massacre.

Independence National Historical Park, Philadelphia, Pennsylvania. Independence Hall, where Congress adopted the Declaration of Independence, is the most historic building in Philadelphia. The informative website can be accessed through Links to the Past: National Park Service Cultural Resources' comprehensive listing of historic sites in the National Park system, **http://www.cr.nps.gov**

Kings Mountain National Military Park and Cowpens National Battlefield, South Carolina. Situated approximately 20 miles apart, these were the sites of two battles in October 1780 and January 1781 that turned the tide of the war in the South. Both have museums and exhibits. The official site is accessible through Links to the Past: National Park Service Cultural Resources, **http://www.cr.nps.gov** But see also Battles of the American Revolutionary War, **http://www.ilt.columbia. edu/k12/history/aha/battles.html**, for a brief description of the battles and their contexts.

Minute Man National Historical Park, Lexington and Concord, Massachusetts. There are visitors' centers at both Lexington and Concord with explanatory displays. Visitors may also follow the self-guided Battle Road Automobile Tour. The official website is accessible through Links to the Past: National Park Service Cultural Resources, **http://www.cr.nps.gov**

Saratoga National Historical Park, New York. The park preserves and commemorates the American victory that led to French entry into the war. There is a museum with artifacts from the battlefield. Both the explanatory displays and the topography of the area make this an especially illuminating site. The official website is accessible through Links to the Past: National Park Service Cultural Resources, **http://www.cr.nps.gov**

Valley Forge National Historical Park, Valley Forge, Pennsylvania. Reconstructed huts convey a sense of life in the Continental Army camp at Valley Forge during the hard winter of 1777–1778. The official website is accessible through Links to the Past: National Park Service Cultural Resources, **http://www.cr.nps.gov**

Yorktown Battlefield, Colonial National Historical Park, Yorktown, Virginia. The park commemorates the great American victory here. Innovative exhibits enable visitors to follow the course of the war from a multicultural perspective. The official website is accessible through Links to the Past: National Park Service Cultural Resources, **http://www.cr.nps.gov**

 For additional study resources for this chapter, go to:
www.prenhall.com/goldfield/chapter6

The Rattlesnake as a National Symbol

WHAT OTHER characteristics of snakes in general, and rattlesnakes in particular, might have appealed to Revolutionary Era Americans in choosing a national symbol?

One of the tasks facing the Revolutionary generation was to create symbols around which to rally. There was no official flag, no anthem, no Uncle Sam. Benjamin Franklin made perhaps the earliest attempt to create a visual symbol for the prospective nation when he drew "Join, Or Die" to accompany his 1754 Plan of Union. He pictured the colonies as a snake cut into pieces. Why a snake? In mythology, snakes can reattach themselves. Twenty years later, Paul Revere used the snake for the masthead of the revolutionary newspaper, the *Massachusetts Spy*. Once war began, military units adopted the snake as their battle flag. The most famous of these is the Gadsden flag. Christopher Gadsden was a delegate to the Second Continental Congress from South Carolina who played a leading role in creating the U.S. Navy and in appointing Esek Hopkins of Rhode Island as its first commander. He gave the Gadsden flag to Hopkins for his personal standard.

In 1775, pleased with the popular adoption of the snake as a national symbol, Benjamin Franklin noted, that:

> As if anxious to prevent all pretentions of quarrelling with her, the weapons with which nature has furnished her, she conceals in the roof of her mouth, so that, to those who are unacquainted with her, she appears to be a most defenceless animal; and even when those weapons are shewn and extended for her defence, they appear weak and contemptible; but their wounds however small, are decisive and fatal: — Conscious of this, she never wounds till she has generously given notice, even to her enemy, and cautioned him against the danger of treading on her.—Was I wrong, Sir, in thinking this a strong picture of the temper and conduct of America?

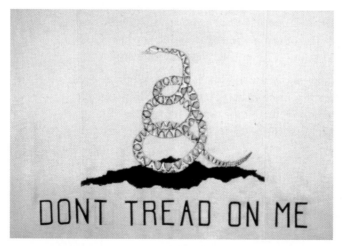

◀ The Gadsden flag, used initially by the U.S. Navy. By 1775 the lines indicating the divisions among the colonies have disappeared. The snake has become the rattlesnake, a reptile unique to North America, and one with a highly poisonous venom. "Don't Tread On Me" captured the revolutionaries' insistence that they fought only to defend their liberties.

Corbis / Bettmann

When rotated, Franklin's snake described the North American coastline: He omitted Georgia, only recently founded and inhabited largely by convicts freed from British prisons.

Revere's snake has reattached itself, although the lines where the divisions had been are still visible. Franklin only pictured twelve colonies, but Revere added "G" for Georgia. Further, Revere's snake confronts the British lion. The united serpent is far larger than the lion, something which anticipated Thomas Paine's argument in *Common Sense* that it made no sense for an island to rule a continent.

▲
When rotated, Franklin's snake imitated the North American coastline; he omitted Georgia, which was newly found and inhabited largely by convicts freed from British prisons.

North Wind Picture Archives

Here individuals of all nations are melted into a new race of men, whose labours and posterity will one day cause great changes in the world.

Congress voting on the issue of independence.

7

THE FIRST REPUBLIC
1776–1789

WHAT WERE

the Articles of Confederation?

WHAT WERE the weaknesses

of the United States after the Revolution?

WHAT WAS the

Constitutional Convention?

WHAT WAS the struggle

over ratification between

the Federalists and Antifederalists?

1789

1776

Springfield
Jan. 26, 1787

Sir,

The unhappy time is come in which we have been obliged to shed blood. Shays, who was at the head of about twelve hundred men, marched yesterday afternoon about four o'Clock, towards the public buildings in battle array. He marched his men in an open column by platoons. I sent several times [through aides] to him to know what he was after, or what he wanted. His reply was he wanted barracks, and barracks he would have and stores. The answer returned was he must purchase them dear if he had them. He still proceeded on his march until he approached within two hundred and fifty yards of the arsenal. He then made a halt. I immediately sent Major Lyman, one of my aides, and Capt. Buffington to inform him not to march his troops any nearer to Arsenal on his peril, as I was stationed here by order of your Excellency and the Secretary at War, for the defence of the public property, in case he did I should surely fire on him and his men. [After rebuffing Lyman and Buffington.] Shays immediately put his troops in motion, and marched on rapidly near one hundred yards. I then ordered Major Stephens, who commanded the Artillery to fire upon them. He accordingly did. The two first shott he endeavored to overshoot them, in hopes they would have taken warning without firing among them, but it had no effect on them. Major Stevens then directed his shott thro' the center of his column. The fourth or fifth shot put their whole column into the utmost confusion. Shays made an attempt to display [spread out] the column, but in vain. We had one howitz which was loaded with grape shot, which when fired, gave them great uneasiness. Had I been disposed to destroy them, I might have charged upon their rear and flanks with my Infantry and the two field pieces, and could have killed the greater part of his whole army within twenty five minutes. There was not a single musket fired on either side. I found three men dead on the spol, and one wounded, who is since dead. . . .

I am, Sir, with great respect, Your Excellency's most

Obedient lible Servt
—W. Shepard

General Shepard to Governor Bowdoin, Jan. 26, 1787, in *American Historical Review,* Vol 2: July 1897, p. 694.

IMAGE KEY
for pages 166–167

a. Articles of Confederation.
b. Congress voting Independence
c. Phyllis Wheatley
d. The first Stars and Stripes, 1777.
e. Georgia $4 banknote, 1777, issued "for the support of the Continental Troops and other Expences of Government."
f. The encounter on 26 January 1787 between Shay's rebels and government troops before the arsenal at Springfield, Massachusetts.
g. Constitutional Convention at Philadelphia, 1787.
h. The pillars of the "federal edifice" represented by the American colonies in a 1788 cartoon supporting the United States Constitution.

WILLIAM SHEPARD, the commander of the Hampshire County militia, informed Massachusets Governor James Bowdoin that the armed insurgents led by Daniel Shays had been routed in their attempt to seize the federal arsenal at Springfield. Shays was a hitherto obscure Revolutionary war captain. Like many of his fellow farmers in western Massachusetts, Shays faced hard times in the 1780s. Falling farm prices, a shortage of money, heavy taxes, and mounting debts produced an economic crisis that threatened many farmers with imprisonment for debt and the loss of their farms. Faced with an unresponsive state legislature, angry farmers protested and shut down the county courts. By 1786 Shays had emerged as one of their key leaders, and the ragtag army of farmers that he marched against the Springfield arsenal now aimed to overthrow the state government.

State leaders and eastern merchants were horrified. Liberty for them was equated with the right of the individual to pursue wealth and amass property. By contrast, the struggling farmers and artisans defined the liberty won in the Revolution more in terms of the right of communities to defend their interests against moneyed and aristocratic elites.

Driven out of Massachusetts when his army collapsed in 1787, Shays again became an obscure figure. Still, the movement that bears his name dramatized the fragile nature and conflicting values of America's first republic under the Articles of Confederation. Providing for little more than a loose union of the states, the Articles were ratified in 1781. The years that followed were marked by a running debate over the meaning of liberty and the extent of power to be entrusted to a national government. Americans favoring a stronger, more centralized government cited Shays's Rebellion as an example of the chaos that could destroy the republic unless fundamental changes were made. Those changes came with the writing and ratification of the Constitution of the United States in 1788.

THE NEW ORDER OF REPUBLICANISM

As royal authority collapsed during the Revolution, various provincial congresses and committees assumed power in each of the former colonies. The Continental Congress, seeking to build support for the war effort, was concerned that these new institutions should have a firm legal and popular foundation. In May 1776, the Congress called on the colonies to form new state governments "under the authority of the people."

This call reflected the political philosophy of republicanism that animated the Revolution (see Chapter 6). To Americans, republicanism meant that legitimate political authority derives from the people. The people are sovereign and should elect the officials who govern them; those officials should represent the people's interests. Another key aspect of republicanism was the revolutionary idea that the people could define and limit governmental power through written constitutions.

DEFINING THE PEOPLE

When news of the peace treaty with Britain reached New Bern, North Carolina, in June 1783, the citizens held a grand celebration. As reported by Francisco de Miranda, a visiting Spanish officer, "There was a barbecue [a roast pig] and a barrel of rum, from which the leading officials and citizens of the region promiscuously drank with the meanest and lowest kind of people, holding hands and drinking from the same cup."

For Miranda, this boisterous mingling of all citizens as seeming equals confirmed the republican belief that the people were sovereign. But republicanism also taught that political rights should be limited to property owners, as informed political judgment required economic self-sufficiency. This precept restricted political participation to propertied white men. Virtually everyone else—propertyless white men, servants legally bound to others, women, slaves, most free black people, and Native Americans—was denied political rights during the Revolutionary era. (See American Views: "A French Observer Describes a New Society." p. 170)

Some 60 to 85 percent of adult white men owned property and could participate in politics—a far higher proportion than elsewhere in the world of the eighteenth century. The greatest concentration of the remaining 25 percent or so shut

WHAT WERE the Articles of Confederation?

QUICK REVIEW

Property, Race, Gender, and Citizenship

◆ Republicans limited political rights to white male property owners.

◆ 60 to 80 percent of adult white men owned property.

◆ Revolution did not challenge exclusion of women from politics.

• AMERICAN VIEWS •

A FRENCH OBSERVER DESCRIBES A NEW SOCIETY

In 1782, J. Hector St. John Crèvecoeur, a Frenchman who had lived and traveled in British North America, published his impressions of America. The following selection from his Letters from an American Farmer *captures the optimism and sense of newness that he found. More so than any other literary work, the* Letters *stamped the new American republic, especially in the minds of Europeans, as the home of the world's freest and most equal people.*

WHAT IS Crèvecoeur's image of America? Do you believe it was overly optimistic? Why does Crèvecoeur emphasize the absence of titles and great disparities of wealth? What was so new about America to Crèvecoeur? Why did Crèvecoeur ignore African slaves and Native Americans in his definition of the American?

I wish I could be acquainted with the feelings and thoughts which must agitate the heart and present themselves to the mind of an enlightened Englishman when he first lands on this continent. . . . He is arrived on a new continent; a modern society offers itself to his contemplation, different from what he had hitherto seen. It is not composed, as in Europe, of great lords who possess everything and of a herd of people who have nothing. Here are no aristocratical families, no courts, no kings, no bishops, no ecclesiastical dominion, no invisible power giving to a few a very visible one, no great manufactures employing thousands, no great refinements of luxury. The rich and the poor are not so far removed from each other as they are in Europe. Some few towns excepted, we are all tillers of the earth, from Nova Scotia to West Florida. We are a people of cultivators scattered over an immense territory, communicating with each other by means of good roads and navigable rivers, united by the silken bands of mild government, all respecting the laws without dreading their power, because they are equitable. We are all animated with the spirit of an industry which is unfettered and unrestrained, because each person works for himself. . . . A pleasing uniformity of decent competence appears throughout our habitations. The meanest of our log-houses is a dry and comfortable habitation. Lawyer and merchant are the fairest titles our towns afford; that of a farmer is the only appellation of the rural inhabitants of our country. It must take some time ere he can reconcile himself to our dictionary, which is but short in words of dignity and names of honour. . . . We have no princes for whom we toil, starve, and bleed; we are the most perfect society now existing in the world. Here man is free as he ought to be, nor is this pleasing equality so transitory as many others are: Many ages will not see the shores of our great lakes replenished with inland nations, nor the unknown bounds of North America entirely peopled. . . .

The next wish of this traveller will be to know whence came all these people. They are a mixture of English, Scotch, Irish, French, Dutch, Germans, and Swedes. From this promiscuous breed, that race now called Americans have arisen. . . .

What, then, is the American, this new man? He is either an European or the descendant of an European; hence that strange mixture of blood, which you will find in no other country. . . . He is an American, who, leaving behind him all his ancient prejudices and manners, receives new ones from the new mode of life he has embraced, the new government he obeys, and the new rank he holds. He becomes an American by being received in the broad lap of our Alma Mater. Here individuals of all nations are melted into a new race of men, whose labours and posterity will one day cause great changes in the world.

Source: J. Hector St. John Crèvecoeur, *Letters from an American Farmer and Sketches of Eighteenth-Century America,* ed. Albert E. Stone (1986), pp. 66–70.

out of the political process were unskilled laborers and mariners living in port cities. In Philadelphia, for example, half the population of taxable adult men and women in the 1780s reported no taxable property. The city's working poor still included indentured servants, bound by contract to give personal service for a fixed time, as well as the walking poor—vagrants and transients.

The Revolution did little to change the traditional patriarchal assumption that politics and public life should be the exclusive domain of men. Women, according to republican beliefs, were dependent under the control of their husbands and fathers. Under common law (the customary, largely unwritten law that Americans had inherited from Britain), women surrendered their property rights at marriage. Legally and economically, husbands had complete control over their wives. As a result, argued Theophilus Parsons of Massachusetts in 1778, women were, as a matter of course, "so situated as to have no wills of their own."

To be sure, some women saw in the political and social enthusiasm of the Revolution an opportunity to protest the most oppressive features of their subordination. "I won't have it thought that because we are the weaker sex as to bodily strength we are capable of nothing more than domestic concerns," wrote Eliza Wilkinson of South Carolina. Men, she lamented, "won't even allow us liberty of thought and that is all I want." But most women accepted the view that their proper place was in the home with their families. Only the New Jersey constitution of 1776 defined **suffrage**—the right to vote—in gender-free terms, extending it to all propertied adults "worth fifty pounds," until 1807, when the state legislature changed its constitution.

The Revolution had a more immediate impact on the lives of many African Americans. Revolutionary principles of liberty and equality and evangelical notions of human fellowship convinced many white people for the first time to challenge black slavery. In 1784, Virginia Methodists condemned slavery as "contrary to the Golden Law of God on which hang all the Laws and Prophets, and the unalienable Rights of Mankind, as well as every Principle of Revolution." Black people seized opportunities for freedom that emerged from some whites' rejection of slavery, the disruptions of the war, and the needs of both sides for military manpower. As the number of free black people increased from a few thousand at mid-century to 100,000 by 1800, African-American communities and cultures also expanded and developed.

Upwards of fifty thousand slaves, or one in ten of those in bondage, gained their freedom as a result of the war. One route was through military service, which generally carried a promise of freedom. When the British began raising black troops, the Americans followed suit. All of the states except Georgia and South Carolina recruited black regiments. Some five thousand black men served in the Continental armies, and they, like their counterparts in British units, were mostly slaves. Most slaves who gained freedom during the war, however, were those who fled their owners and made their way to the port cities of the North.

By making slave property generally less secure, the Revolution encouraged many masters to free their slaves. Once freed, black people tried to break all the bonds of their former servitude. As the number of free black people increased, those still enslaved grew bolder in their efforts to gain freedom. "Henny," warned a Maryland slaveowner in 1783, "will try to pass for a free woman as several have lately been set free in this neighbourhood."

If slavery experienced some strain in the South during the Revolution, in the North, where slaves were only a small percentage of the population, it crumbled.

With the exception of New Jersey, where women meeting the property qualifications were eligible to vote, the state constitutions of the Revolutionary era prohibited women from voting.

Howard Pyle, Corbis / Bettmann

5–9
Rights of Women in an Independent Republic

QUICK REVIEW

African Americans and the Revolution

- Revolutionary principles sparked some to challenge slavery.
- More than 50,000 slaves gained freedom as result of the war.
- By 1800 free black population reached 100,000.

Suffrage The right to vote in a political election.

CHRONOLOGY

1776	States begin writing the first constitutions.	1785	Land Ordinance of 1785. States begin to issue more paper money. Treaty of Fort McIntosh.
1777	Articles of Confederation proposed.		
1781	Articles ratified.	1786	Shays's Rebellion breaks out. Jay-Gardoqui Treaty defeated. Annapolis Convention.
1783	Americans celebrate independence and the peace treaty with Britain.		
1784	Onset of the postwar depression. Spain closes the Mississippi. Separatist plots in the West. Treaty of Fort Stanwix.	1787	Constitutional Convention at Philadelphia. Northwest Ordinance.
		1788	Constitution ratified and goes into effect. Publication of *The Federalist*.

Phillis Wheatley was an acclaimed African-American poet. Kidnapped into slavery as a child in Africa, she was a domestic slave to the Wheatley family of Boston when her first poems were published in 1773.

Scipio Moorhead; Corbis / Bettmann

Most northern states ended slavery between 1777 and 1784. New York followed in 1799 and New Jersey in 1804. Although a majority of white Northerners now agreed that slavery was incompatible with the Revolution's commitment to **natural rights** (the inherent human rights to life and liberty), they refused to sanction an immediate emancipation. The laws ending slavery in most of the northern states called only for the children of slaves to be freed, and only when they reached adulthood.

Although black men were allowed to vote, most were too poor to meet the property qualifications. They faced discrimination in jobs and housing, were barred from juries, and were denied a fair share of funds for schools. With the help of the small class of property holders among them, they began establishing their own churches and self-help associations.

The impact of the Revolution on Native Americans was almost entirely negative (see Chapter 6). Most stayed neutral during the war or fought for the British. Just as the Americans sought to shake off British control, so the Indians—especially the western tribes and most of the Iroquois Confederation—sought to free themselves from American dominance. Thus British defeat deprived the Indians of a valuable ally and exposed them to the wrath of the victorious patriots. "The minds of these people appear as much agitated as those of the unhappy Loyalists," observed a British officer late in the war of the pro-British southern Indians; "they have very seriously proposed to abandon their country and accompany us [in an evacuation], having made all the world their enemies by their attachment to us."

The state governments and the Confederation Congress treated Indian lands after the Revolution as a prize of war to be distributed to white settlers. Even the few tribes that had furnished troops for the American cause lost control over most of their homelands. White Americans did not consider Native Americans to be part of their republican society. With the exception of Massachusetts, the states denied voting and legal rights to the Indians.

THE STATE CONSTITUTIONS

Natural rights   Political philosophy that maintains that individuals have an inherent right, found in nature and preceding any government or written law, to life and liberty.

"Oppose everything that leans to aristocracy, of power in the hands of the rich and chief men exercised to the oppression of the poor." So the voters of Mecklenburg County, North Carolina, instructed their delegates to the state's constitutional convention in 1776.

New state constitutions, ten of which were in place by 1777, were written documents, a striking departure from the English practice of treating a constitution as a collection of customary rights and practices that had evolved over time. In the American view, a constitution was a codification of the powers of government and the rights of citizenship that functioned as a fundamental law to which all public authority was held accountable. Annual elections were now the norm for governors, who were also made subject to *impeachment*—charges of misconduct, resolved at a public trial—and limited in the number of terms they could serve. Most important, for it struck at what patriots felt was the main source of executive domination and corruption, governors lost control over patronage, the power to appoint executive and judicial officials.

As the new constitutions curbed the power of governors, they increased that of the legislatures, making them the focal point of government. Colonial assemblies had been in the forefront of popular opposition to British authority; and the state legislatures that succeeded them were now seen as the most trustworthy defenders of individual liberty. The new constitutions expanded the power of the legislatures to appoint officials and to oversee military and financial matters. To make the legislatures more expressive of the popular will, the new constitutions included provisions that lowered property requirements for voting and officeholding, mandated annual elections, increased the number of seats in the legislatures, and made representation more proportional to the geographical distribution of population. Upper houses, whose members were previously appointed by the colonial governors, were made independent of the executive and opened to popular election.

Americans knew that legislatures, too, could act tyrannically. So in a final check on arbitrary power, each state constitution eventually included some form of a **bill of rights** that set explicit limits on the power of government to interfere in the lives of citizens. The Virginia Declaration of Rights, written by the planter George Mason and adopted in June 1776, set the precedent for this notable republican feature. By 1784, the constitutions of all thirteen states had provisions guaranteeing religious liberty, freedom of the press, and a citizen's right to such fair legal practices as trial by jury.

The new constitutions weakened but did not always sever the traditional tie between church and state. Many Americans held, as the Massachusetts Constitution of 1780 put it, that "the happiness of a people, and the good order and preservation of civil government, essentially depend upon piety, religion, and morality." Many states, notably in New England, levied taxes for the support of religion. The states of New England also continued to maintain Congregationalism as the state-supported religion while allowing dissenting Baptists and Methodists access to funds from the compulsory religious taxes.

The Mid-Atlantic states lacked the religious uniformity of New England. The region had several prominent denominations—Quaker, Episcopalian, Presbyterian, Dutch Reformed, and Lutheran—and this pluralism checked legislative efforts to impose religious taxes or designate any denomination as the established church. In the South, where many Anglican (or Episcopalian) clergymen had been Tories, the Anglican Church lost its former established status.

Although in general the executive lost power and the legislative gained power under the new state constitutions, the actual structure of each state government reflected the outcome of political struggles between radical and conservative republicans. The radicals wanted to open government to all male citizens. The conservatives, though they agreed that government had to be derived from the people, feared "mob rule" and wanted to limit government to an educated elite of substantial property holders. Most conservatives, like Jeremy Belknap of New

Bill of Rights A written summary of inalienable rights and liberties.

Hampshire, thought that the people had to be "taught . . . that they are not able to govern themselves."

In South Carolina, where conservative planters gained the upper hand, the constitution mandated property qualifications that barred 90 percent of the state's white males from holding elective public office. In contrast, Pennsylvania's Scots-Irish farmers and Philadelphia artisans took charge and gave the vote to all free males who paid taxes and eliminated property qualifications for officeholding. In addition, the constitution concentrated power in a unicameral (single-house) legislature, eliminating both the office of governor and the more elite upper legislative house. The constitution's framers also required legislators to stand for election annually and barred them from serving more than four years out of seven.

The constitutions of the other states, although not as bold in their democratic reforms as Pennsylvania's, typically enhanced the political influence of ordinary citizens more than the constitution of South Carolina did. Unlike the colonial assemblies, the new bicameral (two-house) legislatures included many artisans and small farmers. This growing political equality was accompanied by demands that those in government be more responsive to the people. Summing up the prevailing American view, William Hooper of North Carolina wrote in 1776, "Rulers must be conceived as the creatures of the people, made for their use, accountable to them, and subject to removal as soon as they act inconsistent with the purposes for which they were formed."

THE ARTICLES OF CONFEDERATION

Once the Continental Congress decided on independence in 1776, it needed to create a legal basis for a permanent union of the states. According to the key provision of the **Articles of Confederation** that Congress submitted to the states in November 1777, "Each State retains its sovereignty, freedom and independence, and every power, jurisdiction and right, which is not by this confederation expressly delegated to the United States, in Congress assembled." The effect was to create a loose confederation of autonomous states.

The powers the Articles of Confederation delegated to the central government were extremely limited. There were no provisions for a national judiciary or a separate executive branch of government. The Articles made Congress the sole instrument of national authority but restricted it with constitutional safeguards that kept it from theatening the interests of the states. Each state had one vote in Congress, making each politically equal regardless of size or population. State legislatures were to choose congressional delegations in annual elections, and delegates could serve only three years out of six. Delegates were to follow the instructions of their state legislatures and could be recalled at any time. Important measures, such as those dealing with finances or war and peace, required approval from a majority of nine states. Amendments to the Articles of Confederation, including the levying of national taxes, required the unanimous consent of the states.

Congress had authority primarily in the areas of foreign policy and national defense. It could declare war, make peace, conduct foreign affairs, negotiate with Native Americans, and settle disputes between states. But it had no authority to raise troops or impose taxes. It could only ask the states to supply troops and money.

The central principle behind the Articles was the fear of oppressive, centralized power. Edward Rutledge, a delegate from South Carolina to the Continental Congress, argued that the new Confederation Congress was vested "with no more Power than is absolutely necessary." Residents of West Springfield, Massachusetts, in instructions to their congressional representatives in 1778 resolved: "It is *freedom*, & not a choice of the *forms of servitude* for which we contend."

Articles of Confederation   Written document setting up the loose confederation of states that comprised the first national government of the United States.

Most states quickly ratified the Articles of Confederation, but because they needed the approval of all thirteen states, it was not until Maryland ratified the articles in 1781 that they officially took effect. What caused the delay was the demand of some states to give Congress a power not included in the Articles submitted for ratification in 1777.

The issue here concerned the unsettled lands in the West between the Appalachian Mountains and the Mississippi River. Some states claimed these lands by virtue of their colonial charter rights. The so-called landless states—those with no claim to the West—insisted that it be set aside as a reserve of public land. Land speculators, many of them leading politicians, who had purchased huge tracts of land from the Indians before the Revolution, sided with the landless states. They expected Congress would be more likely to honor their land titles than the individual states.

The British threat to the Chesapeake area in early 1781 finally broke the impasse. Though retaining control of Kentucky, Virginia gave up its claim in the West to a vast area extending north of the Ohio River. In turn, Maryland, now desperate for military aid from Congress, agreed to ratify the Articles.

QUICK REVIEW

Powers of the Central Government Under the Articles of Confederation
◆ No national judiciary.
◆ No separate executive branch.
◆ Congress sole national authority.
◆ No Congressional authority to raise troops or impose taxes.

PROBLEMS AT HOME

Neither prosperity nor political stability accompanied the return of peace in 1783. The national government struggled to avoid bankruptcy, and in 1784, an economic depression struck the country. As fiscal problems deepened, creditor and debtor groups clashed angrily in state legislatures. The only solid accomplishment of the Confederation Congress during this troubled period was to formulate an orderly and democratic plan for the settlement of the West.

WHAT WERE the weaknesses of the United States after the Revolution?

THE FISCAL CRISIS

The Continental Congress and the states incurred heavy debts to finance the Revolutionary War. Unable to impose and collect sufficient taxes to cover the debts and without reserves of gold or silver, they had to borrow funds and issue certificates or bonds pledging repayment. Congress had the largest responsibility for war debts. To do so it printed close to $250 million in paper notes backed only by its good faith. By the end of the war in 1781, these Continental dollars were nearly worthless, and the national debt stood at $11 million. As Congress issued new securities to settle claims by soldiers and civilians, this sum rose to $28 million in just a few years.

Congress never did put its tottering finances on a sound footing. Its fiscal problems ultimately discredited the Articles of Confederation to the **nationalists**, a loose bloc of congressmen, army officers, and public creditors who wanted to strengthen the Confederation at the expense of the states. The nationalists first began to organize in the dark days of 1780 and 1781 when inflation was rampant, the army was going unpaid, Congress had ceased paying interest on the public debt, and the war effort itself seemed in danger of collapsing. Galvanized by this crisis, the nationalists rallied behind Robert Morris, a Philadelphia merchant appointed as superintendent of finance for the Confederation government.

Morris sought to enhance national authority through a bold program of financial and political reform. He began by securing a charter from Congress in 1781 for the Bank of North America, the nation's first commercial bank. Morris wanted it to serve as a national institution, and he used it to hold government funds, make loans to the government, and issue bank notes—paper money that could be used to settle debts and pay taxes owed to the United States.

Nationalists Group of leaders in the 1780s who spearheaded the drive to replace the Articles of Confederation with a stronger central government.

Issued in 1777, this Georgia four-dollar banknote was an example of the type of paper money used to finance the Revolutionary War.

The Granger Collection, New York

QUICK REVIEW

Debt and the Balance of Trade

- Britain sought to keep America weak and dependent.
- Trade imbalance soared in the 1780s.
- Collapse of credit bubble in 1784 led to depression.

Morris temporarily stabilized the nation's finances. Nonetheless, he was blocked in his efforts to gain the taxing power needed to restore the shattered credit of the Confederation government.

Morris's central nationalist objective was to create a "bond of union" by having Congress assume payment of the entire national debt. Once paid back, the people who had financed the war would identify their economic self-interest with the effective exercise of power by the national government.

To achieve this political goal, Morris had to gain for Congress what it had always lacked: the power to tax. In 1781, he proposed a national impost, or tariff, of 5 percent on imported goods. Because this was a national tax, it required an amendment to the Articles of Confederation and the consent of all thirteen states. Rhode Island—critically dependent on its own import duties to finance its war debt—was the only state to reject it. When a revised impost plan was considered two years later, New York blocked its passage. These failures doomed Morris's financial reforms. He left office in 1784.

The failure of the impost tax was one of many setbacks that put the nationalists temporarily on the defensive. With the conclusion of peace in 1783, confidence in state government returned. The states continued to balk at paying Congress and denied it even limited authority to regulate foreign commerce. Most ominously for the nationalist cause, the states began to assume responsibility for part of the national debt. By 1786, New Jersey, Pennsylvania, Maryland, and New York had absorbed one-third of the debt by issuing state bonds to their citizens in exchange for national securities. As Morris had warned in 1781, such a policy entailed "a principle of disunion . . . which must be ruinous."

Without the power to tax, Congress was a hostage to the sovereignty of the individual states with no real authority over the nation's economic affairs. When the economy plunged into a severe depression in 1784, it could only look on helplessly.

ECONOMIC DEPRESSION

During the Revolutionary War, Britain closed its markets to American goods. After the war, the British continued this policy, hoping to keep the United States weak and dependent. In the summer of 1783, they excluded Americans from the lucrative trade with the British West Indies that before the Revolution had been the colonists' primary source for the credits they needed to offset their imports from Britain.

Meanwhile, British merchants were happy to satisfy America's pent-up demand for consumer goods. A flood of cheap British imports inundated the American market, and coastal merchants sold them to inland traders and shopkeepers by extending easy credit terms. In turn, these local businessmen sold the goods to farmers and artisans in the interior. Ultimately, however, the British merchants required payment in hard currency, gold and silver coins. By now, America's only source of hard currency was foreign loans obtained by Congress and what money the French army had spent during the war. This was soon exhausted as America's trade deficit with Britain—the excess of imports over exports—ballooned in the early 1780s to £5 million.

The result was an immense bubble of credit that finally burst in 1784, triggering a depression that would linger for most of the rest of the decade. As merchants began to press debtors for immediate payment, prices collapsed (they fell more than 25 percent between 1784 and 1786), and debtors were unable to pay.

Small farmers everywhere had trouble paying their taxes. In 1786, James Swan of Massachusetts wrote of farmers in his state: "There is no family that does not want some money for some purposes, and the little which the farmer carries home from market, must be applied to other uses, besides paying off the [tax] collector's bills." Rural shopkeepers often could not move goods unless they agreed to barter them for farm produce. Western Massachusetts storeowner Abigail Dwight reported in 1785 that "most of these People sell on credit for To-Morrow at large—for very little Cash stirring this way—to be pay'd for in old Horses—cows some Boards—cabbages—turnips—Potatoes etc."

Wages fell 25 percent between 1785 and 1789, and workers began to organize. They called for tariffs on British imports and for legislative measures to promote American manufacturers. Farmers faced a wave of lawsuits for the collection of debts and the dread possibility of losing their land. "To be tenants to landlords, we know not who," protested the farmers of Conway, Massachusetts, "and pay rent for lands, purchased with our money, and converted from howling wilderness, into fruitful fields, by the sweat of our brows, seems . . . truly shocking."

With insufficient money in circulation to raise prices and reverse the downturn, the depression fed on itself. Congress was powerless to raise cash and was unable to pay off its old debts, including what it owed to the Revolutionary soldiers. Many state governments made things worse by imposing heavy taxes payable in the paper money they had issued during the Revolution. The result was further to reduce the amount of money in circulation, forcing prices still lower.

No longer protected under the old Navigation Acts as British vessels, American ships were now barred from most ports in the British Empire. Cargoes from the West Indies to New England fell off sharply, and the market for whale oil and fish, two of New England's major exports, dried up.

The economy of the Mid-Atlantic region was stronger, but even there the loss of the provisioning trade to the British West Indies in grains, livestock, and dairy products cut into the income of merchants and farmers and forced layoffs among artisans who serviced the shipping trade.

In the Southern states, British policies compounded the problem of recovering from the physical damage and social disruptions of the war. Some 10 percent of the region's slaves had fled, and production levels on plantations fell. Chesapeake planters needed a full decade to restore tobacco production to its prewar levels. And a collapse in tobacco prices in 1785 left most of them in the same chronic state of indebtedness that had plagued them on the eve of the Revolution. Rice production in the Carolina lowcountry was similarly slow to recover, despite the debts planters piled up to purchase additional slaves and repair their war-damaged plantations and dikes. Burdened by new British duties on American rice, planters saw rice exports fall by 50 percent. Small farmers in the pine barrens of North Carolina likewise had to adjust to the loss of their formerly protected British market for naval stores—tar, pitch, and turpentine.

By the late 1780s, an economic upturn was under way in the Mid-Atlantic states. Food exports to continental Europe were on the rise, and American merchants were developing new trading ties with India and China. Commercial treaties with the Dutch, Swedes, and Prussians also opened up markets that had been closed to the colonists. Nonetheless, a full recovery had to await the 1790s.

A stagnant economy and burdensome debt combined with a growing population (there were 50 percent more Americans in 1787 than there had been in 1775) to reduce living standards. With more losers than winners, economic conflict dominated the politics of the Confederation period.

WHERE TO LEARN MORE

South Street Seaport Museum,
New York City, New York

THE ECONOMIC POLICIES OF THE STATES

Britain was an obvious target of popular anger over the economic depression. Merchants poorly positioned to adjust to the postwar dislocations of trade led a campaign to retaliate with duties on British ships and special taxes on their goods.

Artisans and workers, especially in the North, pushed for tariffs on British goods to encourage domestic manufacturing and protect jobs and wages.

Shippers evaded high tariffs by bringing their cargoes in through states with no tariffs or less restrictive ones. States without ports, like New Jersey and North Carolina, complained of economic discrimination. When they purchased foreign goods from a neighboring shipping state, they were forced to pay part of the tariff cost, but all the revenue from the tariff accrued only to the importing state. James Madison neatly summarized the plight of these states: "New Jersey, placed between Philadelphia and New York, was likened to a cask tapped at both ends; And North Carolina, between Virginia and South Carolina, to a patient bleeding at both Arms."

Tariff policies also undermined efforts to confer on Congress the power to regulate commerce. The agrarian states of the South had different interests from the states of the North. With the exception of Virginia, they favored free trade policies that encouraged British imports. Southern planters took advantage of the low rates charged by British ships for transporting their crops to Europe, putting pressure on northern shippers to reduce their rates.

The bitterest divisions, however, were between debtors and creditors within states. As the value of debt securities dropped during the Revolutionary War, speculators bought them up for a fraction of their face value and then put pressure on the states to raise taxes and repay the debts in full in hard currency. Wealthy landowners and merchants likewise supported higher taxes and the rapid repayment of debts in hard currency. Arrayed against these creditor groups by the mid-1780s was a broad coalition of debtors comprised of middling farmers, small shopkeepers, artisans, laborers, and people who had overextended themselves speculating in Western land. The debtors wanted the states to issue paper money that they could use instead of hard money—gold and silver—to pay their debts. The paper money would have an inflationary effect, raising wages and the prices of farm commodities and reducing the value of debts contracted in hard currency.

This was the economic context in which **Shays's Rebellion** exploded in the fall of 1786. Farm foreclosures and imprisonments for failure to pay debts increased sharply in western Massachusetts. Farmers petitioned the state legislators for economic relief. They demanded legislation that would temporarily prohibit creditors from seizing farms and processing suits for debt. When the creditor and seaboard interests in the legislature refused to pass any relief measures, some two thousand farmers took up arms against the state government. They shut down the courts and hence the legal machinery for collecting debts in three counties in western Massachusetts. When they marched on the state arsenal in Springfield, alarmed state officials raised troops to crush the uprising.

Outside of western Massachusetts, discontented debtors generally were successful in changing the monetary policy of their states. In 1785 and 1786, seven states enacted laws for new paper money issues. In most cases, combined with laws that prevented or delayed creditors from seizing property from debtors to satisfy debts, the currency issues helped keep a lid on popular discontent.

Rhode Island was an exception to this pattern of fiscal responsibility. A rural party that gained control of the Rhode Island legislature in 1786 pushed through

The clash between Shays's rebels and government troops at the Springfield arsenal marked the violent climax of the agrarian protests of the 1780s.

The Granger Collection, New York

6–7
Divergent Reactions to Shays's Rebellion

Shays's Rebellion   An armed movement of debt-ridden farmers in western Massachusetts in the winter of 1786–1787. The rebellion created a crisis atmosphere.

a currency law that flooded the state with paper money that could be used to pay all debts. Creditors who balked at accepting the new money at face value were subject to heavy penalties. Shocked, they went into hiding or left the state entirely, and merchants denounced the law as outright fraud.

The actions of the debtor party in Rhode Island alarmed conservatives everywhere. Now they were convinced that state legislatures dominated by farmers and artisans were dangerous. One South Carolina conservative declared that he could see nothing but an "open and outrageous . . . violation of every principle of justice" in paper money and debt relief laws. Conservatives, creditors, and nationalists alike now spoke of a democratic tyranny that would have to be checked if the republic were to survive and protect its property holders.

CONGRESS AND THE WEST

The Treaty of Paris and the surrender of charter claims by the states gave Congress control of a magnificent expanse of land between the Appalachian Mountains and the Mississippi River. Congress set forth a series of effective provisions for the settlement and governance of this first American West and its eventual absorption into the Union.

Asserting for the national government the right to formulate Indian policy, Congress negotiated a series of treaties with the Indians beginning in 1784 for the abandonment of their land claims in the West. By threatening to use military force, congressional commissioners in 1784 coerced the Iroquois Confederation of New York to cede half of its territory to the United States in the Treaty of Fort Stanwix. Similar tactics in 1785 resulted in the Treaty of Fort McIntosh in which the northwestern tribes ceded much of their land in Ohio. In opposition to states intent on grabbing Indian lands for themselves, Congress resolved in 1787 that its treaties were binding on all the states. Anxious for revenue, Congress insisted on payment from squatters who had filtered into the West before provisions for the land sales.

WHERE TO LEARN MORE

Northern Indiana Center for History, South Bend, Indiana

The most pressing political challenge was to secure the loyalty of the West to the new and fragile Union. To satisfy the demands of settlers for self-government, Congress resolved as early as 1779 that new states would be carved out of the western domain with all the rights of the original states. In the Ordinance of 1784, Thomas Jefferson proposed to create ten districts or territories, each of which could apply for admission as a state when its population equaled that of the free inhabitants in the least populous of the existing states. Jefferson also proposed that settlers be permitted to choose their own officials, and he called for the prohibition of slavery in the West after 1800. Shorn of its no-slavery features, the ordinance passed Congress but was never put into practice.

If it couldn't regulate land sales and pass on clear titles, Congress would, in effect, have surrendered its claim to govern. Congress had to act on national land policy, warned a western Pennsylvanian, or else "lose the only opportunity they ever will have of extending their power and influence over this new region." One way or another, settlers were going to get their land, but a pell-mell process of private acquisitions in widely scattered settlements threatened to touch off costly Indian wars, deprive the national government of vitally needed revenue, and encourage separatist movements.

Congress responded with the **Land Ordinance of 1785**. The crucial feature of this seminal legislation was its stipulation that public lands be surveyed in a rectangular grid pattern before being offered for sale (see Map 7-1). By requiring that land first be plotted into townships of thirty-six uniform sections of 640 acres each, the ordinance adopted the New England system of land settlement, an approach that promoted compact settlements and produced undisputed land titles.

Congress offered the plots of 640 acres at the then hefty sum of no less than $640, or $1 per acre, payable in hard currency or its equivalent. The goal here was

Land Ordinance of 1785   Act passed by Congress under the Articles of Confederation that created the grid system of surveys by which all subsequent public land was made available for sale.

MAP EXPLORATION

To explore an interactive version of this map, go to **http://www.prenhall.com/goldfield2/map7.1**

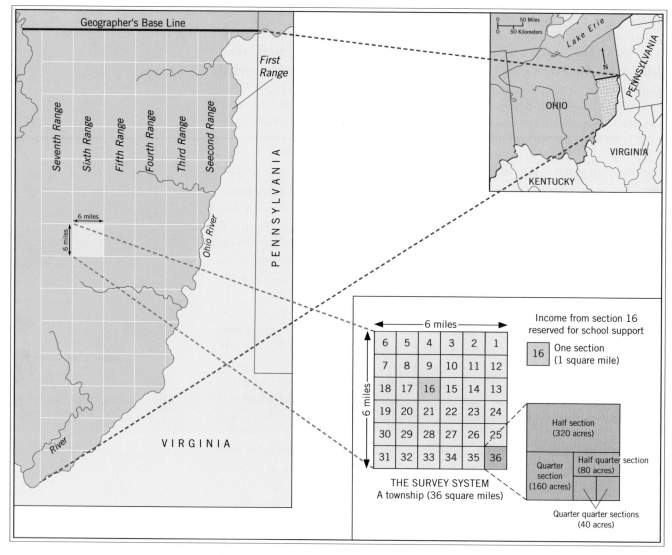

MAP 7–1

Land Ordinance of 1785 The precise uniformity of the surveying system initiated in the Land Ordinance of 1785 created a rectangular grid pattern that was the model for all future land surveyed in the public domain.

WHAT WAS the significance of the surveying system initiated in the Land Ordinance of 1785?

to keep out the shiftless poor and reserve the West for enterprising and presumably law-abiding farm families who could afford the entry cost. Congress also set aside the income from the sale of the sixteenth section in each township for the support of public schools. Support for education, as a congressional report of 1783 put it, would help provide for "security against the increase of feeble, disorderly and dispersed settlements in those remote and extended territories [and] against the depravity of manners which they have a tendency to produce."

Before any land sales occurred under the Ordinance of 1785, impatient settlers continued to push north of the Ohio River and claim homesteads as squatters. They clashed both with local Indian tribes and the troops sent by Congress to evict them. Impatient itself with the slow process of surveying, Congress sold off a million and a half acres to a group of New England speculators organized as the Ohio Company. The speculators bought the land with greatly depreciated loan office certificates that had been issued to Revolutionary War veterans, and their cost per acre averaged less than 10 cents in hard money. They now pressed their allies in Congress to establish a governmental structure for the West that would protect their investment by bringing the unruly elements in the West under control. The **Northwest Ordinance of 1787**, the most significant legislative act of the Confederation Congress, filled this need, creating a political structure for the territories and a phased process for achieving statehood that neatly blended public and private interests.

According to the ordinance, controls on a new territory were to be strictest in the early stage of settlement, when Congress would appoint a territorial government consisting of a governor, a secretary, and three judges. When a territory reached a population of five thousand adult males, those with 50 acres of land or more could elect a legislature. The actions of the legislature, however, were subject to an absolute veto by the governor. Once a territory had a population of sixty thousand, the settlers could draft a constitution and apply for statehood "on an equal footing with the original states in all respects whatsoever."

The Northwest Ordinance of 1787 stipulated that only three to five states were to be formed out of the Northwest. This was because the admission of new states would weaken the original thirteen states' control over Congress. Although less democratic in many respects than Jefferson's plan in mandating a period of outside control by Congress, the 1787 ordinance did provide greater protection for property rights as well as a bill of rights guaranteeing individual freedoms. Most significant, it prohibited slavery.

Southern congressmen agreed to the slavery ban in part because they feared that planters in the new states would compete with them in the production of slave-produced staples such as tobacco. More important, however, they expected slavery to be permitted in the region south of the Ohio River that was still under the administrative authority of Virginia, North Carolina, and Georgia in the 1780s. Indeed, slavery was allowed in this region when the **Southwest Ordinance of 1790** brought it under national control, a decision that would have grave consequences in the future sectionalization of the United States.

Although the Northwest Ordinance applied only to the national domain north of the Ohio River, it provided the organizational blueprint by which all future territory was brought into the Union. It went into effect immediately and set the original Union on a course of dynamic expansion through the addition of new states.

DIPLOMATIC WEAKNESSES

In the international arena of the 1780s, the United States was a weak and often ridiculed nation. Under the Articles of Confederation, Congress had the authority to negotiate foreign treaties but no economic or military power to enforce their terms. Unable to regulate commerce or set tariffs, it had no leverage with which to pry open the restricted trading empires of France, Spain, and most important, Britain.

France and the United States remained on friendly terms. The United States even had a favorable trade balance with France, selling more there than it bought. Both Britain and Spain, however, sought to block American expansion into the trans-Appalachian West. And a dispute with Spain over the West produced the most

QUICK REVIEW

Slavery and New States
- Northwest Ordinance of 1787 establishes political structure for new territories.
- Northwest Ordinance prohibited slavery in the Northwest.
- Southwest Ordinance of 1790 allowed slavery in the region south of the Ohio River.

Northwest Ordinance of 1787
Legislation that prohibited slavery in the Northwest Territories and provided the model for the incorporation of future territories into the union as co-equal states.

Southwest Ordinance of 1790
Legislation passed by Congress that set up a government with no prohibition on slavery in U.S. territory south of the Ohio River.

WHAT WAS the Constitutional Convention?

serious diplomatic crisis of the period, one that spilled over into domestic politics, increasing tensions between northern and southern states and jeopardizing the country's chances of survival.

IMPASSE WITH BRITAIN

Key among those issues that poisoned Anglo-American relations in the 1780s were provisions in the peace treaty of 1783 that concerned prewar American debts to the British and the treatment of Loyalists by the patriots. To justify its own violations of the treaty, Britain claimed that America had failed to satisfy those provisions. The result was a diplomatic deadlock that hurt American interests in the West and in foreign trade.

The peace treaty called for the payment of all prewar debts at their "full value in sterling money"—that is, in hard currency. Many tobacco planters in the Chesapeake region of Virginia and Maryland had outstanding debts to British creditors. During the Revolution, the British army had carried off and freed many of the region's slaves without compensating the planters. Still angry, the planters were in no mood to repay their debts and agreed only to pay the face value of their debts to their state treasuries in state or Continental paper money, which was practically worthless.

During the Revolution, all the states had passed anti-Loyalist legislation. Many state governments had seized Loyalists' lands and goods, selling them to raise revenue for the war effort. Upwards of 100,000 Loyalists fled to Canada and England, and their property losses ran into millions of dollars. The peace treaty pledged Congress to "recommend" to the states that they stop persecuting Loyalists and restore Loyalist property, but wartime animosities remained high. Despite the pleadings of John Jay, the secretary for foreign affairs in the Confederation government, the states were slow to rescind their punitive legislation or allow the recovery of confiscated property.

Unpaid debts and the continued failure of the states to make restitution to the Loyalists gave the British a convenient pretext to hold on to the forts in the West that they had promised to give up in the Treaty of Paris. Refusal to abandon the forts, from Lake Champlain in upstate New York and westward along the Great Lakes was part of a strategy to keep the United States weak, divided, and small. The continued British presence in the region shut Americans out of the fur trade with the Indians, insulted the sovereignty of the United States, and threatened the security of its northern frontier. In 1784, exasperated New Yorkers warned Congress that unless the British were forced to leave, New York would "be compelled to consider herself as left to pursue her own Councils, destitute of the Protection of the United States." Spurred on by Canadian officials, the British also encouraged secessionist movements in the Northwest and sought out Indian allies to fight for a possible buffer state south of the Great Lakes that would keep Americans hemmed in along the Atlantic seaboard.

In Vermont, politicians led by brothers Ethan, Ira, and Levi Allen offered the British a treaty of friendship in exchange for recognition of Vermont's independence and trading privileges within the British Empire. The British declined for fear of unduly antagonizing the United States. In 1791, Vermont joined the Union as the fourteenth state.

American officials viewed Britain's retaliatory trade policies as the gravest threat to American security and prosperity. John Adams, the American minister to London, sought in vain to counter Britain's anti-American economic policies. "I may reason till I die to no purpose," Adams reported to Jay in June 1785, and he complained that he was treated as a complete "cypher."

Adams soon concluded that the British would never lift their trading and shipping restrictions until forced to do so by a uniform American system of discriminatory duties on British goods. However a uniform policy was impossible to achieve under the Articles of Confederation.

THE FIRST REPUBLIC 1776–1789   CHAPTER 7   183

SPAIN AND THE MISSISSIPPI RIVER

At the close of the Revolutionary War, Spain reimposed barriers on American commerce within its empire. Spain also refused to recognize the southern and western boundaries of the United States as specified in the treaty with Britain in 1783, holding out instead for a more northerly border. And of greatest consequence, it denied the claim of the United States to free navigation of the entire length of the Mississippi River. Only with access to the Mississippi and the commercial right of deposit at New Orleans—that is, the right to transfer cargoes to oceangoing vessels—could the region's farmers, then mostly in what would become Tennessee and Kentucky, profitably reach national and international markets.

In the wake of the Revolution, the settlers of Kentucky, which was still part of Virginia, and Tennessee, which was still part of North Carolina, flirted with the idea of secession. Spain sought to trade on the divided loyalties of American speculators and frontier settlers to its advantage, employing some of them as spies and informers. Spain likewise sought to exploit divisions among Indian groups.

Spain stepped up pressure on the West in the summer of 1784 when it closed the Mississippi River within Spanish territory to American trade. Hoping now to benefit from American weakness, Spain also opened negotiations for a long-term settlement with the United States. The Spanish negotiator, Don Diego de Gardoqui, offered John Jay, negotiating for the Americans, a deal that cleverly played the interests of the North against those of the South and West. In exchange for an American agreement to surrender claims to navigate the Mississippi for thirty years, Gardoqui proposed to grant the United States significant trading concessions in the Spanish Empire that would benefit the financially pressed merchants of the north-eastern states. Jay reluctantly accepted the offer.

When Jay released the terms of the proposed treaty with Spain in 1786, Congress erupted in angry debate. Southerners, who had taken the lead in the settlement of the West, accused Jay of selling out their interests. The treaty threatened the agrarian alliance they hoped to forge with the West, and increased the odds that the West would break from the East and go its own way. Vowing that they would not surrender the West, southern congressmen united to defeat ratification of the treaty.

The regional antagonisms exposed by the Jay-Gardoqui talks heightened the alarm over the future of the republic provoked by Shays's Rebellion earlier in 1786. The Union had never appeared more fragile or Congress under the Articles of Confederation so powerless to resolve its differences. As the sense of crisis deepened in 1786, the nationalists, led by Alexander Hamilton of New York and James Madison of Virginia, grew in influence and numbers.

This portrait, sketched in about 1790 by John Trumbull, is the only known likeness of Alexander McGillivray, a Creek leader who effectively played off Spanish and American interests in the Southeast to gain a measure of independence for the Creeks in the 1780s.

Charles Allen Munn Collection, Fordham University Library, Bronx, N.Y.

TOWARD A NEW UNION

In June 1786, a worried John Jay wrote to George Washington that he was "uneasy and apprehensive; more so than during the war. Then we had a fixed object. . . . The case is now altered; we are going and doing wrong, and therefore I look forward to evils and calamities, but without being able to guess at the instrument, nature, or measure of them." Other nationalists fully shared

WHAT WAS the struggle over ratification between the Federalists and Antifederalists?

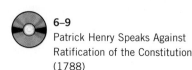

6–9
Patrick Henry Speaks Against Ratification of the Constitution (1788)

Annapolis Convention   Conference of state delegates at Annapolis, Maryland, that issued a call in September 1786 for a convention to meet at Philadelphia to consider fundamental changes.

Constitutional Convention
Convention that met in Philadelphia in 1787 and drafted the Constitution of the United States.

Constitution of the United States
The written document providing for a new central government of the United States.

Virginia Plan   Proposal calling for a national legislature in which the states would be represented according to population.

Jay's pessimism. Everywhere they saw unsolved problems and portents of disaster: unpaid debts, social unrest, squabbling states, sectional hostilities, the uncertain status of the West, blocked channels of trade, foreign intrigues, and a paralyzing lack of centralized authority.

In September 1786, delegates from several states met at the **Annapolis Convention**, in Annapolis, Maryland, seeking to devise a uniform system of commercial regulation for the country. While there, a group of nationalist leaders called on all the states to send delegates to a convention at Philadelphia "to devise such further provisions as shall appear to them necessary to render the constitution of the Federal Government adequate to the exigencies of the Union." The leaders who met at the **Constitutional Convention** in Philadelphia forged an entirely new framework of governance, the **Constitution of the United States**, that called for a federal republic with a powerful and effective national government. In 1788, after a close struggle in state ratifying conventions, the Constitution was adopted.

THE ROAD TO PHILADELPHIA

The timing of the call for the Philadelphia Convention could not have been better. During the fall and winter of 1786, the agrarian protests unleashed by Shays's Rebellion in Massachusetts spilled over into other states. Coupled with talk of a dismemberment of the Union in the wake of the Jay-Gardoqui negotiations, the agrarian unrest strengthened the case of the nationalists for more centralized authority.

All the states except Rhode Island sent delegates to Philadelphia. The fifty-five men who attended the convention were chiefly lawyers by training or profession, most of them had served in the Confederation Congress, and more than one-third had fought in the Revolution. The delegates were members of an intellectual and political elite and were far wealthier than the average American. Most had investments in land and the public securities of the United States. At least nineteen owned slaves. Their greatest asset as a working body was their common commitment to a nationalist solution to the crisis of confidence they saw gripping the republic. Strong supporters of the Articles of Confederation mostly refused to attend, perhaps because, as Patrick Henry of Virginia remarked, they "smelt a rat."

THE CONVENTION AT WORK

Congress authorized only a revision of the Articles of Confederation. Almost from the start, however, the delegates at the Philadelphia Convention set about replacing the Articles altogether. Their first action was to elect George Washington unanimously as the convention's presiding officer, gaining credibility for their deliberations from his prestige. The most ardent nationalists then immediately seized the initiative by presenting the **Virginia Plan**. Drafted by James Madison, this plan replaced the Confederation Congress with a truly national government organized like most state governments, with a bicameral legislature, an executive, and a judiciary.

Two features of the Virginia Plan stood out. First, it granted the national Congress power to legislate "in all cases in which the separate states are incompetent" and to nullify any state laws that in its judgment were contrary to the "articles of Union." Second, it made representation in both houses of Congress proportional to population. This meant that the most populous states would have more votes in Congress than the less populous states, giving them effective control of the government. In short, Madison sought to all but eliminate the independent authority of the states while also forcing the smaller states to defer to the more populous ones in national affairs.

Delegates from the small states countered with the **New Jersey Plan**, introduced on June 15 by William Paterson. This plan kept intact the basic structure of the Confederation Congress—one state, one vote—but otherwise amended the Articles by giving the national government the explicit power to tax and to regulate domestic and foreign commerce. In addition, it gave acts of Congress precedence over state legislation.

The New Jersey Plan was quickly voted down, and the convention remained deadlocked for another month. The issue was finally resolved on July 16 with the so-called **Great Compromise**. Based on a proposal by Roger Sherman of Connecticut, the compromise split the differences between the small and large states. Small states were given equal footing with large states in the Senate, or upper house, where each would have two votes. In the lower house, the House of Representatives, the number of seats was made proportional to population, giving larger states the advantage. The Great Compromise also settled a sectional dispute over representation between the free (or about to be free) states and slave states. The southern states wanted slaves counted for apportioning representation in the House but excluded from direct tax assessments. The northern states wanted slaves counted for tax assessments but excluded for apportioning representation. The Great Compromise settled on an expedient, if morally troubling, formula: Free residents were to be counted precisely; to that count would be added three-fifths "of all other persons," excluding Indians not taxed. Thus the slave states gained additional political representation while the states in the North received assurances that the owners of nonvoting slaves would have to bear part of the cost of any direct taxes levied by the new government.

Next the convention debated the specific powers to be delegated to the new government. It was at this point that the sectional cleavage between North and South came to a head. As Madison had warned in late June, "the great division of interests" in the United States would arise from the effect of states "having or not having slaves."

The sectional clash first erupted over the power of Congress to regulate commerce. To prevent a northern majority from passing navigation acts favoring northern shippers, delegates from the Lower South demanded that a two-thirds majority be required to enact trade legislation. Suddenly, the central plank in the nationalists' program—the unified power to force trading concessions from Britain—was endangered. A frustrated Madison urged his fellow southerners to remember that "as we are laying the foundation of a great empire, we ought to take a permanent view of the subject."

In the end, Madison had his way; the delegates agreed that enacting trade legislation would require only a simple majority. In return, however, southerners exacted concessions on the slavery issue. The convention abandoned a proposal to ban the foreign slave trade. Instead, antislavery New Englanders reached a compromise with the delegates from the Lower South: Congress would be barred from acting against the slave trade for twenty years. In addition, bowing to the fears of planters that Congress could use its taxing power to undermine slavery, the convention denied Congress the right to tax exports from any state. And to alleviate

Washington presides over the Constitutional Convention.

Will Brown; Print and Picture Collection, the Free Library of Philadelphia

New Jersey Plan   Proposal of the New Jersey delegation for a strengthened national government in which all states would have an equal representation in a unicameral legislature.

Great Compromise   Plan proposed at the 1787 Constitutional Convention for creating a national bicameral legislature in which all states would be equally represented in the Senate and proportionally represented in the House.

southern concerns that slaves might escape to freedom in the North, the new Constitution included an explicit provision calling on any state to return "persons held to Service or Labour" in another.

After settling the slavery question in late August, the convention had one last significant hurdle to clear: the question of the national executive. But in early September, the delegates moved quickly to fashion a chief executive office with broad discretionary powers. The prerogatives of the president included the rank of commander in chief of the armed forces, the authority to conduct foreign affairs and negotiate treaties, the right to appoint diplomatic and judicial officers, and the power to veto congressional legislation. The president's term of office was set at four years, with no limits on how often an individual could be reelected. Nearly everyone expected Washington to be the first president.

The delegates envisioned a forceful, energetic, and independent executive insulated from the whims of an uninformed public and the intrigues of the legislature. They rejected both popular election and election by Congress. The solution they hit upon was the convoluted system of an "electoral college." Each state was left free to determine how it would choose presidential electors equal to the number of its representatives and senators. These electors would then cast votes to select a president. If no candidate received a majority of the electoral votes, the election would be turned over to the House of Representatives, where each state would have one vote.

After a style committee polished the wording in the final draft of the Constitution, thirty-nine of the forty-two delegates still in attendance signed the document on September 17. The Preamble, which originally began with a list of the states, was reworded at the last minute to begin simply: "We the people of the United States, in order to form a more perfect Union . . . ." This subtle change had significant implications. By identifying the people, and not a collection of states, as the source of authority, it emphasized the national vision of the framers and their desire to create a government quite different from a confederation of states.

OVERVIEW OF THE CONSTITUTION

The central government outlined in the Constitution was to have far more powers than those entrusted to Congress under the Articles of Confederation (see the overview table "The Articles of Confederation and the Constitution Compared"). The Constitution's provision for a strong, single-person executive had no precedent in the Articles. Nor did the provision for a Supreme Court. The Constitution vested this Court, as well as the lower courts that Congress was empowered to establish, with the judicial power of the United States. In addition, the Constitution specifically delegated to Congress the powers to tax, borrow and coin money, regulate commerce, and raise armed forces that the Confederation government had lacked.

Most of the economic powers of Congress came at the expense of the states, which were prohibited from passing tariffs, issuing money, or—in an obvious reference to the debtor relief legislation in the 1780s—enacting any law that infringed on the contractual rights of creditors to collect money from debtors. Also included was a clause stipulating that the Constitution and all national legislation and treaties were to be "the supreme law of the land," in effect giving the central government the power to declare state laws unconstitutional.

The Constitution's underlying political philosophy was that, in Madison's wonderful phrase, "ambition must be made to counter ambition." Madison and

OVERVIEW

THE ARTICLES OF CONFEDERATION AND THE CONSTITUTION COMPARED

	Articles	Constitution
Sovereign power of the central government	No power to tax or raise armies	Power granted on taxes and armed forces
Source of power	Individual states	Shared through federalism between states and the national government
Representation in Congress	Equal representation of states in a unicameral Congress	A bicameral legislature with equal representation of the states in the Senate and proportional representation in the House
Amendment process	Unanimous consent of the states	Consent of three-fourths of the states
Executive	None provided for	Office of the president
National judiciary	None provided for	Established the Supreme Court

the other members of the national elite who met at Philadelphia were convinced that self-interest motivated political behavior. Accepting interest group politics as inevitable and seeking to prevent a tyrannical majority from forming at the national level, the architects of the Constitution designed a central government in which competing blocs of power counterbalanced one another.

The Constitution placed both internal and external restraints on the powers of the central government. The division of the government into executive, legislative, and judicial branches, each with ways to limit the powers of the others, created an internal system of checks and balances. For example, the Senate's authority to approve or reject presidential appointments and to ratify or reject treaties curbed the powers of the executive. The president commanded the armed forces, but only Congress could declare war. The president could veto congressional legislation, but Congress could override that veto with a two-thirds vote. To pass in the first place, legislation had to be approved by both the House of Representatives, which, with its membership proportional to population, represented the interests of the people at large, and the Senate, which represented the interests of the states. As an ultimate check against executive abuse of power, Congress could impeach, convict, and remove a president from office for "Treason, bribary, or other high crimes and misdemeanors."

Although the Constitution did not explicitly grant it, the Supreme Court soon claimed the right to invalidate acts of Congress and the president that it found to be unconstitutional. This power of **judicial review** provided another check against legislative and executive authority. To guard against an arbitrary federal judiciary, the Constitution empowered Congress to determine the size of the Supreme Court and to indict and remove federal judges appointed by the president.

The external restraints on the central government were to be found in the nature of its relationship to the state governments. This relationship was based on

Judicial review A power implied in the Constitution that gives federal courts the right to review and determine the constitutionality of acts passed by Congress and state legislatures.

federalism, the division of power between local and central authorities. By listing specific powers for Congress, the Constitution implied that all other powers were to be retained by the states. Thus while strengthening the national government, the Constitution did not obliterate the sovereign rights of the states, leaving them free to curb the potential power of the national government in the ambiguous areas between national and state sovereignty.

This ambiguity in the federalism of the Constitution was both its greatest strength and its greatest weakness. It allowed both nationalists and advocates of states' rights to support the Constitution. But the issue of slavery, left unresolved in the gray area between state and national sovereignty, would continue to fester, sparking sectional conflict over the extent of national sovereignty that would plunge the republic into civil war three-quarters of a century later.

THE STRUGGLE OVER RATIFICATION

The Philadelphia delegates knew that they had exceeded their instructions by proposing an entirely new government, not an amended version of the Articles. Also aware that the Articles' requirement of unanimous consent by the state legislatures to any amendment would result in certain defeat, the delegates boldly bypassed both Congress and the state legislatures.

The last article of the Constitution stipulated that it would go into effect when it had been ratified by at least nine of the states acting through specially elected popular conventions. Influenced by the nationalist sentiments of many of its members, one-third of whom had attended the Philadelphia Convention, and perhaps weary of its own impotence, Congress accepted this drastic and not clearly legal procedure, submitting the Constitution to the states in late September 1787.

The publication of the text of the Constitution touched off a great political debate. Those who favored the Constitution now referred to themselves as **Federalists**, a term that helped deflect charges that they favored an excessive centralization of political authority. By default, the opponents of the Constitution were known as **Antifederalists**, a negative-sounding label that obscured their support of the state-centered sovereignty that most Americans associated with federalism. Initially outmaneuvered in this way, the Antifederalists never did mount an effective campaign to counter the Federalists' output of pamphlets, speeches, and newspaper editorials (see the overview table "Federalists versus the Antifederalists").

The Antifederalists did attract some men of wealth and social standing. Three of them—Elbridge Gerry of Massachusetts and George Mason and Edmund Randolph of Virginia—had been delegates at Philadelphia. But most Antifederalists were backcountry farmers, men with mud on their boots who lived far from centers of communication and market outlets for their produce. They argued that a large republic, such as the one framed by the Constitution, would inevitably become tyrannical because it was too distant and removed from the interests of common citizen-farmers.

The Antifederalists attacked the Constitution as a danger to the individual liberties and local independence they believed the Revolution had been fought to safeguard, but they lacked the social connections, access to newspapers, and self-confidence of the more cosmopolitan and better-educated Federalists. The Federalists could also more easily mobilize their supporters, who were concentrated in the port cities and commercial farming areas along the coast.

The Federalists skillfully built on the momentum for change that had developed out of the crisis atmosphere of 1786. They successfully portrayed the Con-

Federalism   The sharing of powers between the national government and the states.

Federalists   Supporters of the Constitution who favored its ratification.

Antifederalists   Opponents of the Constitution in the debate over its ratification.

OVERVIEW

FEDERALISTS VERSUS THE ANTIFEDERALISTS

	Federalists	Antifederalists
Position on the Constitution	Favored the Constitution	Opposed the Constitution
Position on the Articles of Confederation	Felt the Articles had to be abandoned	Felt the Articles needed only to be amended
Position on the power of the states	Sought to curb the power of the states with a new central government	Felt the power of the states should be paramount
Position on the need for a bill of rights	Initially saw no need for a bill of rights in the Constitution	Saw the absence of a bill of rights in the proposed Constitution as a threat to individual liberties
Position on the optimum size of the republic	Believed a large republic could best safeguard personal freedoms	Believed only a small republic formed on common interests could protect individual rights
Source of support	Commercial farmers, merchants, shippers, artisans, holders of the national debt	State-centered politicians, most backcountry farmers

stitution as the best opportunity to erect a governing structure capable of preserving and extending the gains of the Revolution.

Conservatives shaken by Shays's Rebellion lined up behind the Constitution. So too did groups like creditors, merchants, manufacturers, urban artisans, and commercial farmers. A stronger national government, they believed, would promote economic development by protecting the home market from British imports, enlarging foreign markets for American exports, promoting a stable and uniform currency, and raising revenues to pay off the Revolutionary War debt.

In the early stages, the Federalists scored a string of easy victories. Delaware ratified the Constitution on December 7, 1787, and within a month, so too had Pennsylvania, New Jersey, Georgia, and Connecticut. Except for Pennsylvania, these were small, sparsely populated states that stood to benefit economically or militarily from a stronger central government. The Constitution carried in the larger state of Pennsylvania because of the Federalists' strength in the commercial center of Philadelphia.

The Federalists faced their toughest challenge in the large states that had generally been more successful in going it alone during the 1780s. One of the most telling arguments of the Antifederalists in these and other states was the absence of a bill of rights in the Constitution. The framers had felt it unnecessary to include such an explicit protection of individual rights in a document intended to specify the powers of a national government and had barely discussed the issue. Responding to this challenge, the Federalists promised to recommend amending the Constitution with a bill of rights once it was ratified. By doing so, they split the ranks of the Antifederalists in Massachusetts. After the Federalists

Although physically frail, James Madison, shown here in a portrait made in about 1815, was a formidable thinker whose essays in *The Federalist* endure as a lasting contribution to political theory.

The Granger Collection, New York

gained the support of two venerable heroes of the Revolution, John Hancock and Sam Adams, the Massachusetts convention approved the Constitution by a close vote in February 1788.

The major hurdles remaining for the Federalists were Virginia, the most populous state, and the strategically located New York. Technically, the Constitution could have gone into effect without them once Maryland, South Carolina, and New Hampshire had ratified it, bringing the total number of states to ratify to the required nine. But without Virginia and New York, the new Union would have been weak and the Federalist victory far from assured.

As in Massachusetts, the Federalists were helped in these two crucial states by their promise of a bill of rights. And for the New York campaign, Madison, Jay, and Hamilton wrote an eloquent series of eighty-five essays known collectively as *The Federalist* to allay fears that the Constitution would so consolidate national power as to menace individual liberties. In the two most original and brilliant essays in *The Federalist*, essays 10 and 51, Madison turned traditional republican doctrine on its head. A large, diverse republic like the one envisaged by the Constitution, he reasoned, not a small and homogeneous one, offered the best hope for safeguarding the rights of all citizens. This was because a large republic would include a multitude of contending interest groups, making it difficult for any combination of them to coalesce into a tyrannical majority that could oppose minority rights. With this argument Madison had developed a political rationale by which Americans could have both an empire and personal freedom.

New York ratified on June 25, and Virginia followed the next day. North Carolina and Rhode Island did not ratify until after the new government was functioning. North Carolina joined the Union in 1789 once Congress submitted the amendments that comprised the Bill of Rights. The obstinate Rhode Islanders stayed out until 1790, when Congress forced them in with a threat of commercial reprisal.

CONCLUSION

Between 1776 and 1780, Americans developed a unique system of constitutionalism. They proclaimed the supremacy of constitutions over ordinary legislation; detailed the powers of government in a written document; provided protection for individual freedoms in bills of rights; and fashioned a process for framing governments through the election of delegates to a special constitutional convention and the popular ratification of the work of that convention. In all of these areas, Americans were pioneers in demonstrating how common citizens could create their own governments.

The curbs on centralized power that characterized the state constitutions also applied to what amounted to the first national constitution, the Articles of Confederation. Indeed, the inability of the Confederation Congress to exercise effective power in the areas of taxation and foreign trade was a crippling flaw that thoroughly discredited the Articles in the eyes of the nationalist-minded leaders who had emerged during the Revolution. These leaders overthrew the Articles at the Constitutional Convention in 1787 and engineered a peaceful revolution in securing the ratification of the Constitution. Their victory in creating a new central government with real national powers was built on the foundation of constitutional concepts and mechanisms that Americans had laid down in their states.

The new Constitution did rest on the consent of the governed, and it endured because it could be amended to reflect shifts in popular will and to widen the circle of Americans granted the rights of political citizenship.

Accepting as a given that self-interest drove political action, the framers of the Constitution designed the new national government to turn ambition against itself. They created rival centers of power that forced selfish factions to compete in a constant struggle to form a workable majority. The Constitution thus set the stage for an entirely new kind of national politics.

SUMMARY

The New Order of Republicanism As royal authority collapsed during the Revolution, various provincial congresses and committees assumed power in each of the former colonies. In May 1776, the Congress called on the colonies to form new state governments. Although the role of women was redefined during the Revolution, little changed the traditional patriarchal assumption that politics and public life should be the exclusive domain of men. Ten new state constitutions were in place by 1777. New constitutions curbed the power of governors and increased that of the legislatures, and each state eventually adopted some form of a bill of rights. Also in 1777, Congress submitted to the states the Articles of Confederation.

Problems at Home 1783 and 1784 were marked by instability, near bankruptcy, and an economic depression, much of which was caused by the heavy burden of paying back debts from the war. Bittersweet divisions formed between debtors and creditors within the states. In 1784 Congress negotiated a series of treaties with the Indians for lands west of the Appalachian Mountains and east of the Mississippi River. A series of land ordinances were passed down from Congress between 1784 and 1790, expanding developed regions into the Midwest.

Diplomatic Weaknesses In the international arena of the 1780s, the United States was a weak and often ridiculed nation. While France and the United States remained on favorable terms, Britain and Spain tried to block American expansion into the West. At the close of the Revolutionary War, Spain reimposed barriers on American commerce with its empire. And, Spain stepped up the pressure on the West in the summer of 1784 when it closed the Mississippi River within Spanish territory to American trade. As the sense of crisis deepened in 1786, the nationalists grew in influence and numbers.

Toward a New Union In September 1786, delegates from several states met at the Annapolis Convention, seeking to devise a uniform system of commercial regulation for the country. While there, another meeting was called in Philadelphia to devise provisions necessary to render the constitution of the government adequate. This second meeting was the Constitutional Convention. Members of the Constitutional Convention proposed the Virginia Plan and the New Jersey Plan, each dealing with representation matters. What came out of both of these plans was the Great Compromise. The convention went on to deal with such issues as slavery and a national executive. Ratification was slow as Federalists and Antifederalists were in direct opposition, but state by state, ratification finally came.

REVIEW QUESTIONS

1. How would you assess the decision made by Shepard and Shays that resulted in the clash at the Springfield arsenal?

2. How would you define republicanism? Do you think Americans still believe in the basic tenets of republicanism?

3. What was so unprecedented about the new state constitutions? What new ideas of government did they use?

4. What were the problems of the economy in the 1780s? Could economic recovery have been achieved under the Articles of Confederation? Why or why not?

5. Were the diplomatic weaknesses of the United States under the Articles as serious as its internal problems? What were the sources of those weaknesses, and how did they threaten national unity?

6. What sorts of men drafted the Constitution in 1787, and how representative were they of all Americans? How widespread was popular backing of the Constitution, and why was it ratified?

7. What explains the differences between the Federalists and Antifederalists? Did they share the same vision of what they wanted America to become?

KEY TERMS

Annapolis Convention   (p. 184)
Antifederalists   (p. 188)
Articles of Confederation   (p. 174)
Bill of rights   (p. 173)
Constitutional Convention (p. 184)
Constitution of the United States (p. 184)

Federalism   (p. 188)
Federalists   (p. 188)
Great Compromise   (p. 185)
Judicial review   (p. 187)
Land Ordinance of 1785   (p. 179)
Nationalists   (p. 175)
Natural rights   (p. 172)
New Jersey Plan   (p. 185)

Northwest Ordinance of 1787 (p. 181)
Shays's Rebellion   (p. 178)
Southwest Ordinance of 1790 (p. 181)
Suffrage   (p. 171)
Virginia Plan   (p. 184)

WHERE TO LEARN MORE

South Street Seaport Museum, New York City, New York. Maritime commerce was the lifeblood of the postrevolutionary economy. The artifacts and the exhibits here offer a fine introduction to the seafaring world of the port city that became the nation's first capital in the new federal Union. See **www.southstseaport.org** for more on the impact of trade on the development of New York and information on preservation projects underway in the city.

Independence National Historical Park, Philadelphia, Pennsylvania. Walks and guided tours through this historic district enable one to grasp much of the physical setting in which the delegates to the Constitutional Convention met. The website **www.nps.gov/inde/home.htm** includes a virtual tour of many of the collections at the park, a portrait gallery of leading figures in the Revolution, and a look at the archaeological projects underway in the park.

Northern Indiana Center for History, South Bend, Indiana. The permanent exhibition on the St. Joseph River valley of northern Indiana and southern Michigan explains the material world of this region and how it changed as first Europeans and then Americans mingled and clashed with the Native American population. At **www.centerforhistory.org/** one can learn more about the center and the variety of programs that it offers.

 For additional study resources for this chapter, go to:
www.prenhall.com/goldfield/chapter7

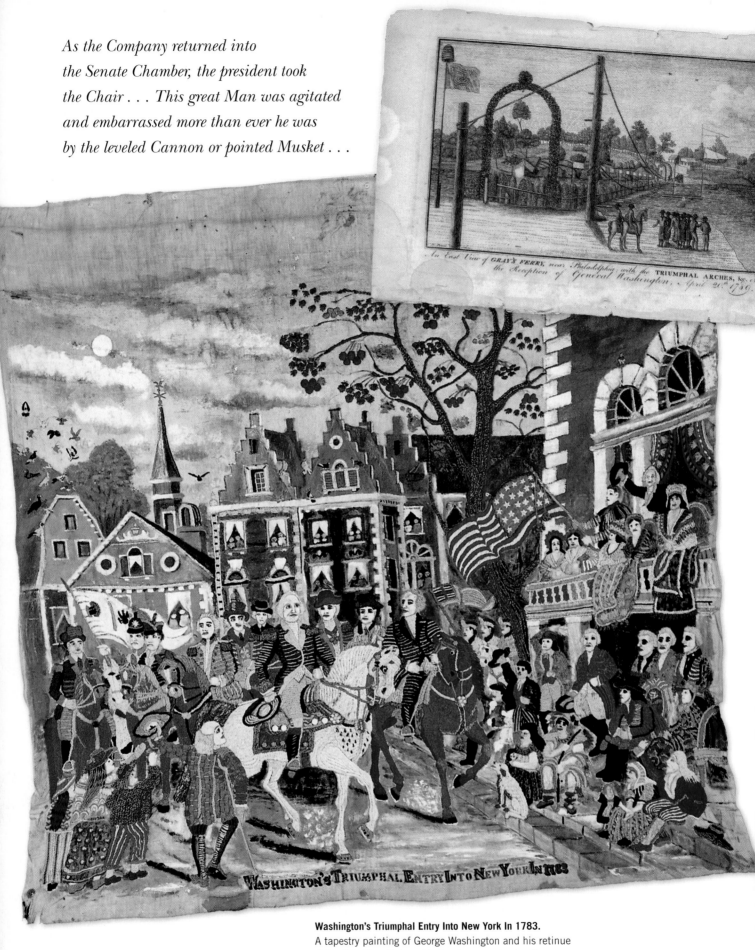

As the Company returned into the Senate Chamber, the president took the Chair . . . This great Man was agitated and embarrassed more than ever he was by the leveled Cannon or pointed Musket . . .

An East View of GRAY'S FERRY, near Philadelphia, with the TRIUMPHAL ARCHES, &c. the Reception of General Washington, April 20th 1789.

WASHINGTON'S TRIUMPHAL ENTRY INTO NEW YORK IN 1783.

Washington's Triumphal Entry Into New York In 1783.
A tapestry painting of George Washington and his retinue riding into New York amid cheering crowds standing on the street and on the balconies.

8

A NEW REPUBLIC AND THE RISE OF PARTIES

1789–1800

WHAT WERE the differences among the four major regions in the U.S. in 1789?

WHAT IS the Bill of Rights?

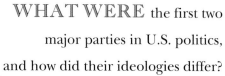

WHAT REACTION/ OPPOSITION was there to Hamilton's financial policies?

WHAT WERE the first two major parties in U.S. politics, and how did their ideologies differ?

WHY WAS Adams defeated in the election of 1800?

IMAGE KEY
for pages 194–195

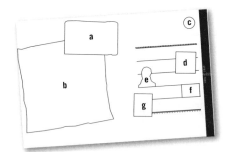

a. Manhattan end of the Brooklyn Ferry, c. 1790.

b. Washington's Triumphal Entry Into New York In [1783, 1789]. A tapestry, of George Washington and his retinue riding into New York amid cheering crowds standing on a street and balconies.

c. American political button from the 18th century.

d. The twelve amendments submitted by the Congress of the United States in 1790 to safeguard the rights of individuals from the interference of the federal government. Ten of these articles were adopted in 1791 as the Bill of Rights - the first ten amendments of the US Constitution. This document bears the signature of John Adams, then vice president of the United States.

e. American politician Alexander Hamilton (1757 - 1804), after service as *aide de camp* to George Washington during the War of Independence, wrote the majority of the federalist papers in support of acceptance of the constitution. Painting by John Trumbull (1756-1843).

f. Congressional Pugilists: American cartoon engraving, 1798, on the fight in Congress between Roger Griswold (weilding cane) the Matthew Lyon, the most notable victim of the Sedition Act of 1798.

g. John Adams wears a brown suit with a high folded collar over a white cravat in a framed painting by John Trumbull.

> *April 30, 1789*
> *New York City*
>
> *This is the great important day. Goddess of Etiquette assist me while I describe it. . . . The President was conducted out of the middle window into the Gallery [of Federal Hall] and the Oath administered by the Chancellor [Robert R. Livingston, Chancellor of New York]. Notice that the Business was done, was communicated to the Croud by Proclamation. . . . who gave three Cheers. . . . As the Company returned into the Senate Chamber, the president took the Chair, and the Senate and representatives their Seats. He rose & all arose also and [he] addressed them [in his inaugural address]. This great Man was agitated and embarrassed more than ever he was by the levelled Cannon or pointed Musket. He trembled and, several times could scarce make out to read, tho it must be supposed he had often read it before. He put part of the fingers of his left hand, into the side, of what I think the Taylors call the fall, of his Breeches. Changing the paper into his left hand, after some time, he then did the same with some of the fingers of his right hand. When he came to the Words all the World, he made a flourish with his right hand, which left rather an ungainly impression. . . . He was dressed in deep brown, with Metal buttons, with an Eagle on them, White Stockings a Bag and Sword—from the Hall there was a grand. Procession to St. Pauls Church where prayers were said by the Bishop. The Procession was well conducted and without accident, as far as I have heard. The Militias were all under Arms. [They] lined the Street near the Church, made a good figure and behaved well. The Senate returned to their Chamber after Service, formed & took up the Address. . . . In the Evening there were grand fire Works. . . . and after this the People went to bed.*
>
> *[William Maclay]*

Kenneth R. Bowling and Helen E. Veit, eds., *The Diary of William Maclay and Other Notes on Senate Debates*, March 4, 1789–March 3, 1791 (Baltimore: The Johns Hopkins University Press, 1988), pp. 11–13.

SENATOR WILLIAM MACLAY of Pennsylvania wrote this account of the inauguration of George Washington as the first president of the United States at Federal Hall in New York City on April 30, 1789. Born in Pennsylvania in 1737 he was selected by the Pennsylvania legislature in September 1788 as one of the state's first two U.S. senators. The Constitution had created the framework for a national government, but pressing problems demanded the fleshing out of that framework. The government urgently needed revenue to begin paying off the immense debt incurred during the Revolution. It also had to address unstable conditions in the West. Ultimately, the key to solving these and other problems was to establish the new republic's legitimacy. Washington and his supporters had to inspire popular backing for the government's right to exercise authority even though most Americans feared centralized authority.

The realities of governing would soon shatter the nonpartisan ideal that had prevailed when the Constitution was ratified. By the end of Washington's first term, two political parties had begun to form. The Federalist party (the name came from that used by the original backers of the Constitution), which included Washington and his successor John Adams, favored a strong central government. The opposition party, the Jeffersonian Republicans, which senator Macby came to support, took shape as a result of differences over financial policy and the American response to the French Revolution. Led by Thomas Jefferson, the Republicans distrusted excessive central power.

The Federalists, who governed through 1800, showed a doubting world ruled by kings and queens that the American experiment in republican government could work. But as inheritors of a political tradition that equated parties with factions—temporary coalitions of selfish private interests—the Federalists doubted the loyalty of the Republicans. When the Federalists under President Adams attempted to suppress the Republicans, the stage was set for the critical election of 1800. Jefferson's victory in that election ended both Federalist rule and the republic's first major internal crisis.

WASHINGTON'S AMERICA

Who were the Americans whom Washington was called on to lead? There is no easy answer. In 1789, as now, Americans identified and grouped themselves according to many factors, including race, sex, class, ethnicity, religion, and degree of personal freedom. Variations in climate and soil further divided them into regions and sections. The resulting hodge-podge sorely tested the assumption that a single national government could govern Americans as a whole.

WHAT WERE the differences among the four major regions in the U.S. in 1789?

THE UNIFORMITY OF NEW ENGLAND

The national census of 1790 counted nearly 4 million Americans, one in four of whom lived in New England. It alone of the nation's formative regions had largely shut itself off from outsiders. New England's poor soils and long, cold winters made it an impractical place to cultivate cash crops like the tobacco and rice of the South. As a result, New England farmers had little need of imported white indentured servants or black slaves. Puritan values and a harsh environment thus combined to make New England the most religiously and ethnically uniform region in the United States. Most of the people living there were descended from English immigrants who had arrived in the seventeenth century. Small pockets of Quakers, Baptists, and Catholics had gained the legal right of worship by the 1720s, but Congregationalism remained the official, state-supported religion in Connecticut and Massachusetts. Black people and Indians together barely constituted 3 percent of New England's population. The few remaining Indians lived on reservations of inferior land, which they usually left only to find work as servants or day laborers.

New Englanders found slavery incompatible with the natural rights philosophy that had emerged during the Revolution and abolished it in the 1780s. Slavery had, in any case, always been marginal in its economy. Women outnumbered men in parts of New England in 1789. This pattern—not found in other parts of the country—was the result of the pressure of an expanding population and the practice of dividing family farms among male heirs that left young men to migrate west in search of cheap, arable land. Thus by 1789, women formed a slight majority in Connecticut, Massachusetts, and Rhode Island. Yet despite their superior numbers, women in New England, as elsewhere, remained subordinate to men. Republican ideology, emphasizing the need of women to be intellectually prepared to raise virtuous, public-spirited children, led reformers in New England to seek equal access for

QUICK REVIEW

New Englanders
- Most of population were descendants of seventeenth-century English immigrants.
- Congregationalism deemed official religion in Connecticut and Massachusetts.
- Women outnumbered men in some parts of the region.
- Slavery abolished in 1780s.

This painting of a young woman reading—*General Schumacker's Daughter,* by Jacob Maentel—reflects women's increasing access to education in the early years of the nation. Nearly four hundred female academies and seminaries were established between 1790 and 1830.

Jacob Maentel (American, 1778 – 1863). "General Schumacker's Daughter," c. 1812, pen and watercolor, sight size: 365 x 240 (14 7/16 x 9 1/2). © Board of Trustees, National Gallery of Art, Washington. Gift of Edgar William and Bernice Chrysler Garbisch

women to education. In 1789, Massachusetts became the first state to allocate funds specifically for girls' elementary education. Liberalized divorce laws in New England also allowed a woman to seek legal separation from an abusive or unfaithful spouse.

In other respects, politics in New England remained rooted in the Puritan past. Age, property, and reputation determined one's standing in a culture that valued a clearly defined social order. The moral code that governed town life promoted curbs on individual behavior for the benefit of the community as a whole. With their notions of collective liberty, New Englanders subscribed to a version of republicanism that favored strong government, setting themselves apart from most other Americans, who embraced a more individualistic idea of liberty and a republicanism suspicious of government power.

MID-ATLANTIC PLURALISM

The states of the Mid-Atlantic region—New York, New Jersey, and Pennsylvania—were the most diverse in the nation. People of English descent comprised somewhat less than 40 percent of the population. Other major ethnic groups included the Dutch and Scots-Irish in New York and Germans and Scots-Irish in New Jersey and Pennsylvania. With ethnic diversity came religious diversity. In contrast to Puritan New England, the Middle Colonies had offered freedom of worship to attract settlers. In addition, economic opportunities for newcomers were much greater than in New England. The soil was better, the climate was milder, and market outlets for agricultural products were more abundant. These conditions made the mid-Atlantic region the nation's first breadbasket.

The demand for labor had also been met by importing African slaves. But despite its considerable strength in the port cities and adjacent rural areas, slavery was never an economically vital institution in most of the mid-Atlantic region. The region's major cash crop, wheat, required seasonal labor, which did not warrant tying up capital in slaves.

Consequently, Pennsylvania in 1780, New York in 1799, and New Jersey in 1804 each passed laws of gradual emancipation. These laws did not free adult slaves but provided that children born of a slave mother were to be freed at ages ranging between 18 and 28. Nevertheless, African Americans had to confront enduring white racism. The comments of one white New Yorker suggest what they were up against. "We may sincerely advocate the freedom of black men," he wrote, "and yet assert their moral and physical inferiority."

The diversity of the Mid-Atlantic region created a complex political environment. Some mid-Atlantic groups, including mercantile and financial leaders and commercial farmers, favored a strong central government to foster economic development and maintain traditional authority. Others, coming principally from the middle and lower classes, wanted to keep government weak so as to foster a republican equality that would promote individual freedom.

THE SLAVE SOUTH AND ITS BACKCOUNTRY

In the South—the region from Maryland and Delaware to Georgia—climate and soil conditions favored the production of cash staples for world markets. Cultivating these crops required backbreaking labor and Southern planters relied on the coerced labor of African slaves, whose numbers made the South the most populous region in the country. Just under 40 percent of all Southerners were slaves, but their concentration varied within each region.

The free black population in the South had grown rapidly during the 1780s. Thousands of slaves fled behind British lines to win their freedom, and patriots freed others as a reward for enlisting in their forces. The Revolutionary values of liberty and equality also led many slave owners to question the morality of slavery. Legislatures in the Upper South passed laws making it financially easier than before for masters to manumit (free) their slaves. In Virginia alone, ten thousand slaves were manumitted in the 1780s. Slavery, however, remained the foundation of the southern economy. As a result, no southern state embarked on a general program of emancipation, and slavery survived the turbulence of the Revolutionary era.

Economic conditions in the South, where the raw poverty of the backcountry offset the great wealth of the lowcountry, stamped the region's politics and culture. Tidewater planters were predominantly Anglican and of English descent. Piedmont farmers were more likely to be Scots-Irish Presbyterians and Baptists. More evangelical in their religion, and with simpler habits and tastes, the backcountry Baptists denounced the lowcountry planters for their luxury and arrogance.

Planters understood liberty to mean the power of white males, unchecked by any outside authority, to rule over others. The only acknowledged check on this power was the planter's sense of duty, his obligation to adhere to an idealized code of conduct befitting a gentleman and a man of honor. Backcountry farmers also jealously guarded their liberties.

THE GROWING WEST

Between the Appalachian Mountains and the Mississippi River stretched the most rapidly growing region of the new nation, the West. During the 1780s, the white population of the West exploded from less than 10,000 to 200,000. The region's Native-American population was, in contrast, about 150,000.

Although Indians and white settlers struck many friendships and mutually advantageous ties, their relations were more generally marked by tension and sporadic violence. For example, when James Boone, the eldest son of the fabled Daniel Boone, who had blazed the first trail for white settlers into Kentucky, was captured, tortured, and killed by a band of Indians, a group of white settlers sought vengeance. They lured some Mingo Indians into their camp, got them drunk, and then killed and scalped them. According to one account, they strung up a pregnant Mingo woman, "sliced open her belly with a tomahawk, and impaled her unborn child on a stake." Indians had every reason to oppose the white intrusion, and they strongly resisted white claims on their lands.

Most white migrants in Kentucky and Tennessee were the young, rural poor from the seaboard slave states. The West offered them the opportunity to claim their own farms and gain economic independence free from the dominance of planters and the economic competition of slave labor. But planters also saw the West as a land of opportunity, speculating in vast tracts of western land.

Life in the Western settlements was harsh and often cruel. Mortality was high, especially among infants. Travelers from the East described settlers living in crudely built log cabins with squalid, filthy interiors infested with fleas and lice. Many were *squatters*, occupying land in the hopes of someday gaining title to it. Easterners also found an appallingly casual acceptance of violence in the West. Men commonly settled disputes in knife-slashing, eye-gouging brawls.

In Kentucky, squatters, aligned with a small class of middling landowners, spearheaded the movement for political separation from Virginia that gained

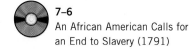

7–6
An African American Calls for an End to Slavery (1791)

MAP EXPLORATION

To explore an interactive version of this map, go to **http://www.prenhall.com/goldfield2/map8.1**

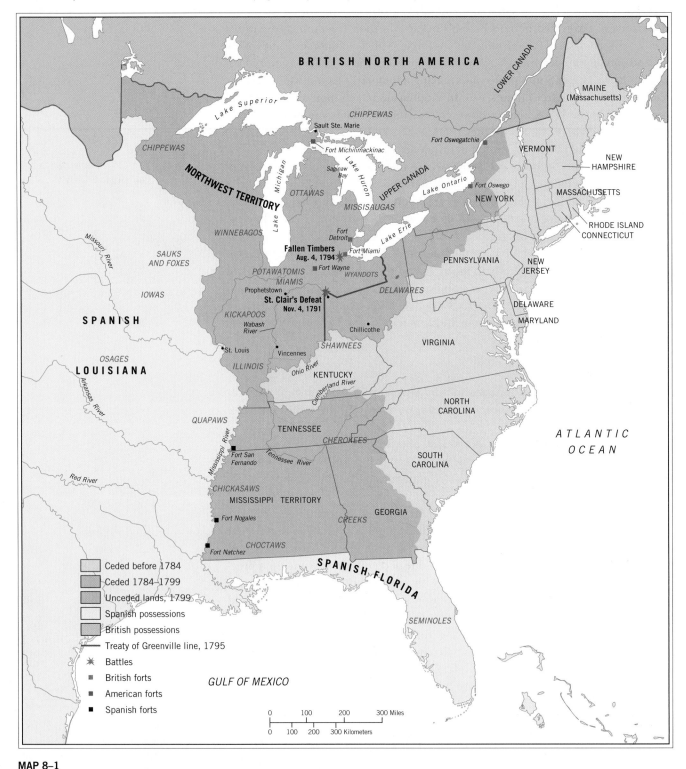

MAP 8–1

Indian Land Cessions, 1784–1800   The persistent pressure of white settlers and the military forces of the new national government forced Native Americans to cede huge tracts of their western lands.

WHICH INDIAN peoples were most directly affected by westward expansion?

CHRONOLOGY

1789	Inauguration of Washington. Congress establishes the first federal departments. French Revolution begins.
1790	Hamilton submits the first of his financial reports to Congress.
1791	Bill of Rights ratified. Congress charters the Bank of the United States.
1792	St. Clair's defeat along the Wabash. Re-election of Washington.
1793	France goes to war against Britain, Spain, and Holland. Genêt Mission. Washington issues Proclamation of Neutrality.
1794	Ohio is opened with the victory of General Anthony Wayne at the Battle of Fallen Timbers. Suppression of the Whiskey Rebellion in western Pennsylvania.

1795	Jay's Treaty with Britain ratified. Treaty of Greenville with Ohio Indians.
1796	Pinckney's Treaty with Spain ratified. Washington's Farewell Address. John Adams elected president.
1797	Beginning of the Quasi-War with France.
1798	XYZ Affair. Alien and Sedition Acts. Provisional army and direct tax. Virginia and Kentucky Resolutions.
1799	Fries's Rebellion in Pennsylvania.
1800	Franco-American Accord. Thomas Jefferson elected president.

statehood for the territory in 1792. But despite the statehood movement, the ultimate political allegiance of the West was uncertain in 1790. Westerners wanted the freedom to control their own affairs and outlets for their crops. Apparently, they were willing to strike a deal with any outside power including the British and the Spanish offering to meet these needs.

FORGING A NEW GOVERNMENT

The Congress that assembled in New York from 1789 to 1791 faced a challenge scarcely less daunting than that of the Constitutional Convention of 1787. It had to give form and substance to the framework of the new national government outlined in the Constitution. Executive departments had to be established, a federal judiciary organized, sources of revenue found, terms of international trade and foreign policy worked out, and a commitment to add a bill of rights to the Constitution honored.

Staunch supporters of the new government had easily carried the first national elections in 1788 and enjoyed large majorities in both houses of Congress. These people brought superb administrative talents to the task of governing. Many, however, were clumsy politicians and unsympathetic to the egalitarian sensibilities of the electorate. By 1792, they faced growing political opposition.

"MR. PRESIDENT" AND THE BILL OF RIGHTS

The first problem for Washington and Congress was to decide just how the chief executive of the new republic should be addressed. In a debate that tied up Congress for a month, the more democratically inclined members of the House argued that a title like "His Highness" smacked of a longing for monarchical rule; Adams and the others grudgingly agreed to accept "Mr. President." Whatever his title, Washington was intent on surrounding the presidency in a halo of respectability and he set down guidelines for presidential etiquette. He established strict rules for his interactions with the public. He met with visitors twice a week for an hour

WHAT IS the Bill of Rights?

WHERE TO LEARN MORE

Federal Hall National Memorial,
New York, New York
www.nps.gov/Feha

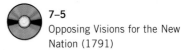

7–5
Opposing Visions for the New Nation (1791)

and bowed with republican deference to the people but refused to shake hands. He traveled outside New York in a luxurious coach pulled by six horses, and at all times he carried himself with stern reserve.

Meanwhile Congress got down to business. James Madison, now a representative from Virginia, early emerged as the most forceful leader in the House. To allay the fears of Antifederalists that the Constitution granted too much power to the national government, the Federalists had promised to consider amendments that protected both individual rights and liberties and the rights of states. But Madison, concerned not to have the new government immediately hobbled by concessions to states, astutely kept the focus of the amendments on personal liberties. He submitted nineteen amendments, and Congress soon settled on twelve. Ten of these amendments, known collectively as the **Bill of Rights**, were ratified by the states and became part of the Constitution as of December 15, 1791.

The Bill of Rights has been one of the most enduring legacies of the first Congress. The first eight amendments are concerned mostly with individual rights. They guarantee religious freedom, freedom of expression, and the safeguarding of individuals and their property against arbitrary legal proceedings. Only three amendments speak of state interests. Citing the necessity of a "well regulated militia" for "the security of a free State," the Second Amendment guarantees "the right of the people to keep and bear Arms." The Ninth and Tenth Amendments stipulate that the powers not granted to the national government in the Constitution are retained by the people and the states.

The Bill of Rights broadened the government's base of popular support. Once Congress submitted the amendments to the states for ratification, North Carolina (1789) and Rhode Island (1790) overcame their lingering objections and joined the Union. The Bill of Rights also assured Americans that the central government would not try to impose on them a uniform national culture.

DEPARTMENTS AND COURTS

In the summer of 1789, Congress authorized the first executive departments: the State Department for foreign affairs, the Treasury for finances, and the War Department for the nation's defense. These departments already existed under the Articles of Confederation, and the only debate about them concerned the extent of presidential control over the officials who would head them. The Constitution was silent on whether or not the president could dismiss an official without the Senate's consent. Congress decided that the president could do so, setting an important precedent that bolstered presidential power. Department heads would now be closely bound to the president. As a group, they would evolve into the *cabinet*, the president's chief advisory body.

Greater controversy attended the creation of the federal judiciary. The Constitution called for "one Supreme Court" but left it up to Congress to authorize lower federal courts. The framers were deliberately vague about the federal judiciary because Antifederalists and proponents of states' rights did not want national courts enforcing a uniform judicial system.

The **Judiciary Act of 1789** represented an artful compromise that balanced the concerns of the Antifederalists and states' rights advocates with the concerns of nationalists who strongly opposed leaving matters of national law up to state courts. It created a hierarchical national judiciary based on thirteen federal district courts, one for each state. Appeals from these courts were to be heard in one of three circuit courts, and the Supreme Court was to have the final say in contested cases. In a major concession to the Antifederalists, however, the act limited jurisdiction in federal courts to legal issues stemming from the Constitution and the

Bill of Rights   A written summary of inalienable rights and liberties.

Judiciary Act of 1789   Act of Congress that implemented the judiciary clause of the Constitution by establishing the Supreme Court and a system of lower federal courts.

laws and treaties of the national government. The distinctive legal systems and customs of the states remained intact. State courts would continue to hear and rule on the vast majority of civil and criminal cases.

REVENUE AND TRADE

The government's most pressing need was for revenue, and Madison acted to put the finances of the new federal government on a firm footing. Nearly everyone agreed that the government's chief source of income should be a tariff on imported goods and tonnage duties (fees based on cargo capacity) on ships entering American ports. The United States imported most of its manufactured goods, as well as many raw materials, and foreign-owned ships accounted for nearly half of entering tonnage.

The **Tariff Act of 1789** levied a duty of 5 percent on most imported goods but imposed tariffs as high as 50 percent on items such as steel, salt, cloth, and tobacco. The debate on the Tariff Act provoked some sectional sparring. In general, manufacturers, who were concentrated in the North, wanted high tariffs for protection against foreign competition. In contrast, farmers and southern planters wanted low tariffs to keep down the cost of the manufactured goods they purchased.

Madison originally hoped to use tonnage duties not only to raise revenue but also to strike at foreign nations like Great Britain that had not signed a commercial treaty with the United States. The duties Madison would impose on British ships entering American ports were in effect a declaration of economic warfare against Britain, and they failed to pass Congress, defeated by an unlikely coalition of sectional interests. Southerners voted against them because they feared their result would be to give New England merchants a monopoly on the carrying trade and raise the cost of shipping tobacco to Europe. Northern merchants, presumably the beneficiaries of the duties, also opposed them, leery of disrupting their profitable trade with Britain, especially with the economic slump of the 1780s abating. The **Tonnage Act of 1789**, as finally passed, treated all foreign ships equally.

HAMILTON AND THE PUBLIC CREDIT

The Treasury was the largest and most important new department. To its head, Alexander Hamilton of New York, fell the task of bringing order out of the nation's ramshackle finances. The basic problem was the huge debt left over from the Revolution. With interest going unpaid, the debt was growing, and by 1789, it had reached $52 million.

More than any other individual, Hamilton imparted energy and purpose to the Washington administration. Coming from humble beginnings, he was ambitious, egotistical, and overbearing. When he spoke of the people, he usually did so with a sneer. But he also had a brilliant financial mind and a sweeping vision of national greatness. He was convinced that the economic self-interests of the wealthy and well-born offered the only sound foundation for the success of the new government.

At the request of Congress, Hamilton prepared a series of four reports on the nation's finances and economic condition. In the first, issued in January 1790, Hamilton proposed a bold plan to address the Revolutionary War debt. The federal government, he maintained, should fund the national debt at full face value. To do this, he proposed exchanging the old debt, including accrued interest, for new government bonds bearing interest at about 4 percent. In addition, Hamilton maintained that the federal government should assume the remaining war debt of the state governments. The intent of this plan was to give the nation's creditors an economic stake in the stability of the new nation.

WHERE TO LEARN MORE **W**

Hamilton Grange National Memorial, New York, New York
www.npd/gov/hagr/

Tariff Act of 1789   Apart from a few selected industries, this first tariff passed by Congress was intended to raise revenue and not protect American manufacturers from foreign competition.

Tonnage Act of 1789   Duty levied on the tonnage of incoming ships to U.S. ports; tax was higher on foreign-owned ships to favor American shippers.

In his second report, Hamilton called for an excise tax (a tax on the production, sale, or consumption of a commodity) on distilled whiskey produced within the United States to raise additional revenue for interest payments on the national debt and establish the government's authority to levy internal taxes on its citizens.

The third report recommended the chartering of a national bank, the Bank of the United States. Hamilton patterned his proposed bank after the Bank of England and intended it to meet a variety of needs. Jointly owned by the federal government and private investors, it would serve as the fiscal (financial) and depository agent of the government and make loans to businesses. Through a provision that permitted up to three-fourths of the value of bank stock to be purchased with government bonds, the bank would create a market for public securities and hence raise their value. Most important, the bank would provide the nation with a stable currency.

Hamilton's final report, issued in December 1791, recommended government actions to promote industry. Looking, as always, to the British model of economic development, he argued that the United States would never become a great power as long as it imported most of its manufactured goods. Hamilton advocated aid in the form of protective tariffs (high tariffs meant to make imported goods more expensive than domestic goods) for such industries as iron, steel, and shoemaking—which had already begun to establish themselves—and direct subsidies to assist with start-up costs for other industries. He believed that such "patronage," as he called it, would ultimately foster interregional economic dependence.

REACTION AND OPPOSITION

The breadth and boldness of Hamilton's program invited opposition. About half of the members of Congress owned some of the nation's debt, and nearly all of them agreed with Hamilton that it should be paid off. Some opponents, however, were concerned that Hamilton's plan was unfair. Hard times had forced most of the original holders of the debt—by and large, ordinary citizens—to sell their certificates to speculators at a fraction of their face value. Others objected on republican grounds that Hamilton had no intention of actually eliminating the government's debt. He envisioned instead a permanent debt, with the government making regular interest payments as they came due. The debt, in the form of government securities, would serve as a vital prop for the support of moneyed groups.

Opposition to Hamilton's proposal to have the federal government assume state debts reflected sectional differences. With the exception of South Carolina, the southern states had already paid back a good share of their war debts. Thus Hamilton's plan stood to benefit the northern states disproportionately.

A compromise was reached in July 1790. Southerners agreed to accept funding in its original form because, as Hamilton correctly noted, it would be impractical, if not impossible, to distinguish between the original and current holders of the national debt. Assumption passed after Hamilton cut a deal with Virginians James Madison and Thomas Jefferson. In exchange for southern support of assumption, Hamilton agreed to line up northern votes for locating the nation's permanent capital on the banks of the Potomac River, where it would be surrounded by the slave states of Maryland and Virginia.

The bank bill passed Congress on a vote that divided on sectional lines. Madison objected that the Constitution did not explicitly authorize Congress to charter a bank or any other corporation. Washington sought the cabinet's opinion, provoking the first great debate over how the Constitution should be interpreted. Thomas Jefferson, the secretary of state, sided with Madison and for the first time

QUICK REVIEW

Hamilton's Reports
- Plan to address Revolutionary War debt.
- Call for an excise tax on distilled whiskey.
- Proposal to charter a national bank.
- Recommendation for government to promote industry.

openly clashed with Hamilton. Taking a strict constructionist position, he argued that all powers the Constitution had not expressly delegated to the national government were reserved to the states under the Tenth amendment. Hamilton, in a brilliant rejoinder, argued that Article 1, Section 8 of the Constitution, which declares that Congress has the right "to make all laws which shall be necessary and proper" to exercise its powers and those of the federal government, gives Congress implicit authority beyond its explicitly enumerated powers. With this broad constructionist position, he won Washington to his side.

With Washington's signature on the bill, Hamilton's bank was chartered for twenty years and a hefty 25 percent tax on distilled liquor was also passed. Little, however, of Hamilton's plan to promote manufacturing survived.

THE EMERGENCE OF PARTIES

By the end of Washington's first term, Americans were dividing into two camps. On one side stood those who still called themselves **Federalists**. These were the supporters of Hamilton's program—speculators, creditors, merchants, manufacturers, and commercial farmers. They were the Americans most fully integrated into the market economy and were concentrated in the North. In both economic and cultural terms, the Federalists were drawn from the more privileged segments of society.

Jefferson and Madison shrewdly gave the name *Republican* to the party that formed in opposition to the Federalists, thus identifying it with individual liberties and the heritage of the Revolution. The Republicans accused Hamilton and the Federalists of attempting to impose a British system of economic privilege and social exploitation. The Republicans were committed to an agrarian America in which power remained in the hands of farmers and planters.

In 1792, parties were still in a formative stage. Washington remained aloof from the political infighting and was still seen as a great unifier. Unopposed, he was reelected in 1792. However, a series of crises in his second term deepened and broadened the incipient party divisions. By 1796, rival parties were contesting the presidency and vying for the support of an increasingly politically organized electorate. (See the overview table on the two parties. p. 207)

THE FRENCH REVOLUTION

The French Revolution began in 1789, and in its early phase, most Americans applauded it. By 1792, however, the Revolution had turned violent and radical. Its supporters confiscated the property of aristocrats and the church, slaughtered suspected enemies, and executed the king, Louis XVI.

These excesses touched off a bitter debate in America. Federalists drew back in horror, arguing in the Federalist *Gazette of the United States* that "The American Revolution, it ought to be repeated, was not accomplished as the French has been, by massacres, assassinations, or proscriptions." For the Republicans, the French remained the standard-bearers of the cause of liberty for common people everywhere. Jefferson admitted that the French Revolution was tarnished by the loss of innocent lives but was convinced that its cause was just.

When the new French ambassador Edmond Genêt arrived in the United States in April 1793—just as the debate in America over the French Revolution was heating up—Franco-American relations reached a turning point. Genêt, it soon became clear, hoped to embroil the United States in the French war against the British. He commissioned American privateers to attack British shipping

WHAT WERE the first two major parties in U.S. politics, and how did their ideologies differ?

Federalists Supporters of the Constitution who favored its ratification.

Republican (Jeffersonian) party
Party headed by Thomas Jefferson that formed in opposition to the financial and diplomatic policies of the Federalist party; favored limiting the powers of the national government and placing the interests of farmers over those of financial and commercial groups.

FROM THEN TO NOW
Hamilton's Legacy and the National Debt

The debate over the national debt that figured so prominently in the rise of party politics in the 1790s has continued to echo throughout American history. The tripling of the debt in the 1980s, combined with a recession that hit during the presidency of George Bush, sharpened these debates and made the debt a major issue in the election of 1992.

Well into the twentieth century, a Jeffersonian bias against a large public debt dominated the fiscal policy of the federal government. Until 1930, government revenues usually exceeded expenditures, and the surplus was used to reduce the debt. Even so, except for a brief time in the mid-1830s during Andrew Jackson's presidency, the debt was never actually extinguished. This was because economic depressions periodically reduced government income, and wars periodically forced huge increases in expenditures, keeping the government perpetually in debt.

By 1860, the national debt was smaller than it had been when Alexander Hamilton took office as the first secretary of the treasury. To pay for the unprecedented expenses of the Civil War, however, the government borrowed funds, and by 1866, the debt had skyrocketed. The government then committed itself to lowering the debt, and, by the 1890s, when a depression ended twenty-eight consecutive years of budget surplus, it had declined by two-thirds. World War I began a similar cycle—a runup of the debt followed by a gradual reduction—until the onset of the Great Depression of the 1930s began a dramatic change in government policy toward the debt.

Under President Franklin Roosevelt's New Deal, the federal government responded to the length and severity of the depression with new relief programs that drove up outlays while revenues plunged. In what was highly unusual for peacetime, budget deficits piled up, and the national debt rose. It was the cost of World War II, however, that sent the debt soaring. By 1946 it stood at $271 billion, more than the entire economic output of the country. This time, after the war, the creation of surpluses to reduce the debt did not top the government agenda. On the contrary, the onset of the Cold War began an extended period of massive defense spending. At the same time, the government built on the New Deal with new spending on domestic welfare.

Many economists argue that the government's deficit spending since World War II has kept the economy healthy and helped to avert a new depression. In any case the size of the debt relative to the economy as a whole has declined since World War II—even after the runup of the 1980s—because the economy has grown faster than the debt.

Why, then, were the debt and federal deficits such potent political issues in 1992? One reason was surely that the country was just then emerging from a recession. All aspects of the economy were under intense scrutiny, as voters fearful for their jobs struggled with their own debt loads. Renewed economic growth and budgetary restraint allayed those fears by the late 1990s, when the budget was in surplus and the government was paying down some of the national debt. In the presidency of George W. Bush, however, another economic recession and the costs associated with the war on terrorism quickly converted projections of federal budgetary surpluses for the first decade of the twenty-first century into warnings of a new series of deficits. Whether this will revive concerns about the national debt that Jeffersonians first voiced in the 1790s remains to be seen.

and tried to enlist an army of frontiersmen to attack Spanish possessions in Louisiana and Florida.

The president feared that Genêt would stampede Americans into the European war, with disastrous results for the nation's finances. The bulk of America's foreign trade was with the British, and tariff duties on British imports were the main source of revenue to pay for Hamilton's assumption and funding programs. Hamilton urged Washington to declare American neutrality in the European war, maintaining that the president could commit the nation to neutrality on his own authority when Congress, as was then the case, was not in session. Jefferson, although he too wanted to avoid war, disputed Washington's power to act on his

OVERVIEW

FEDERALIST PARTY VERSUS REPUBLICAN PARTY

Federalists	Republicans
Favored strong central government	Wanted to limit the role of the national government
Supported Hamilton's economic program	Opposed Hamilton's economic program
Opposed the French Revolution	Generally supported the French Revolution
Supported Jay's Treaty and closer ties to Britain	Opposed Jay's Treaty and favored closer ties to France
In response to the threat of war with France, proposed and passed the Direct Tax of 1798, the Alien and Sedition Acts, and legislation to enlarge the size of the army	Opposed the Alien and Sedition Acts and the enlarged army as threats to individual liberties
Drew strongest support from New England; lost support in the mid-Atlantic region after 1798	Drew strongest support from the South and West

own, maintaining that the war-making powers of Congress reserved for it alone the right to issue a declaration of neutrality.

Washington accepted Hamilton's argument on his authority to declare neutrality and issued a proclamation on April 22, 1793, stating that the United States would be "friendly and impartial toward the belligerent powers."

After Genêt's visit, American politics became more open and aggressive. Pro-French enthusiasm lived on in a host of grass-roots political organizations known as the Democratic-Republican societies. As their name suggests, these societies reflected a belief that democracy and republicanism were one and the same. This was a new concept in American politics. As a letter writer to the Newark *Gazette* put it:

> It must be the mechanics and farmers, or the poorer class of people
> (as they are generally called), that must support the freedom which
> they and their fathers purchased with their blood—the nobility will
> never do it—they will be always striving to get the reins of government
> into their own hands, and then they can ride the people at pleasure.

The Democratic-Republican societies attacked the Washington administration for failing to assist France, and they expressed the popular feeling that Hamilton's program favored the rich over the poor. For the first time, Washington himself was personally assailed in the press.

SECURING THE FRONTIER

Control of the West remained an elusive goal throughout Washington's first term. Indian resistance in the Northwest Territory prevented whites from pushing north of the Ohio River. The powerful Miami Confederacy routed two ill-trained American armies in 1790 and 1791 and inflicted the worst defeat an American army ever suffered in frontier fighting.

By 1793, many western settlers felt abandoned by the national government. They believed that the government had broken a promise to protect them against Indians and foreigners. Much of the popularity of the Democratic-Republican societies in the West fed off these frustrations. Westerners also demanded free and open navigation on the Mississippi River.

WHERE TO LEARN MORE

Cincinnati Historical Society,
Cincinnati, Ohio
www.cincynusam.org

 7–8
George Washington, Farewell
Address (1796)

This painting by an officer on General Wayne's staff shows Little Turtle, a Miami chief, speaking through an interpreter to General Wayne (with one hand behind his back) during the negotiations that led to the Treaty of Greenville.

Painting; P & S – 1914.0001; "The Treaty of Fort Greenville, Ohio." 1795. Artist unknown. Member of Gen. Anthony Wayne's Staff

Treaty of Greenville   Treaty of 1795 in which Native Americans in the Old Northwest were forced to cede most of the present state of Ohio to the United States.

Whiskey Rebellion   Armed uprising in 1794 by farmers in western Pennsylvania who attempted to prevent the collection of the excise tax on whiskey.

Jay's Treaty   Treaty with Britain negotiated in 1794 in which the United States made major concessions to avert a war over the British seizure of American ships.

The Federalists, on the other hand, wanted submission to national authority from both the Indians and the western settlers. The War Department was reorganized, and it sent into the Ohio region a force built around veterans from the regular (or professional) army under General Anthony Wayne, a savvy, battle-hardened war hero.

On August 4, 1794, at the Battle of Fallen Timbers, near present-day Toledo, Wayne's army dealt a decisive blow to the Ohio Indians. In the **Treaty of Greenville**, signed in August 1795, twelve tribes ceded most of the present state of Ohio to the U.S. government in return for an annual payment of $9,500. The Ohio country was now open to white settlement. (See American View: "Little Turtle Defends the Miami Lands.)

THE WHISKEY REBELLION

Within a few months of Wayne's victory at Fallen Timbers, another American army was on the move. The target this time was the so-called whiskey rebels of western Pennsylvania, who were openly resisting Hamilton's excise tax on whiskey. Hamilton was determined to enforce the tax and assert the supremacy of national laws. Although resistance to the tax was widespread, he singled out the Pennsylvania rebels. Washington was convinced that the Democratic-Republican societies of western Pennsylvania were behind the defiance of federal authority there and welcomed the opportunity to chastise these organizations, which he identified with the dangerous doctrines of the French Revolution.

Washington called on the governors of the mid-Atlantic states to supply militia forces to crush the **Whiskey Rebellion**. The 13,000-man army that assembled at Harrisburg and marched into western Pennsylvania in October 1794 was larger than any Washington had commanded during the Revolution. But the rebellion, as Jefferson sardonically noted, "could never be found." The army met no resistance and expended considerable effort rounding up twenty prisoners. Still, the Federalists had made their point: When its authority was openly challenged, this national government was prepared to use military force to compel obedience.

The Whiskey Rebellion starkly revealed the conflicting visions of local liberty and national order that divided Americans of the early republic. The non-English majority on the Pennsylvania frontier—Irish, Scots-Irish, German, and Welsh—justified resistance to the whiskey tax with the same republican ideology that had fueled the American Revolution. In putting down the Pennsylvania rebels, Washington and Hamilton acted on behalf of more English and cosmopolitan groups in the East who valued central power as a check on any local resistance movement that might begin unraveling the still fragile republic.

TREATIES WITH BRITAIN AND SPAIN

Washington's government had the resources to suppress Indians and frontier dissidents but lacked sufficient armed might to push Spain and especially Britain out of the West. Meanwhile, on the high seas, the British began seizing American ships in an effort to prevent them from trading with the French. Desperate to avert a war, Washington sent John Jay, the chief justice of the United States, to London to negotiate an accord.

From the American point of view, the resulting agreement, known as **Jay's Treaty**, was flawed but acceptable. Jay had to abandon the right of the United

· AMERICAN VIEWS ·

LITTLE TURTLE DEFENDS THE MIAMI LANDS

The climax of what had become a thirty-year war between Native Americans and white settlers to control the Ohio country came in 1794 with the American victory at the Battle of Fallen Timbers. The most successful Indian leader in the conflict was the Miami war chief Mishikinakwa, or Little Turtle as he was known by white people. The following is from one of his speeches during the peace negotiations with the victorious Americans at Greenville, Ohio, in July, 1795.

WHAT WAS Little Turtle's stance during the negotiations? How did Little Turtle justify the land claims of the Miamis? How would this differ from the way in which whites staked their claim to the land? How did Little Turtle explain his leadership of the Miamis and how did this differ from white notions of leadership? What might account for the divisions among the Indians that were cited by Little Turtle?

"General Wayne: I hope you will pay attention to what I now say to you. I wish to inform you where your younger brothers, the Miamies, live, and, also, the Pottawatamies of St. Joseph's together with the Wabash Indians. You have pointed out to us the boundary line between the Indians and the United States, but I now take the liberty to inform you, that the line cuts off from the Indians a large portion of country, which has been enjoyed by my forefathers (from) time immemorial, without molestation or dispute. The print of my ancestors' houses are every where to be seen in this portion. . . . It is well known by all my brothers present, that my forefathers kindled the first fire at Detroit; from thence, he extended his lines to the head waters of Scioto; from thence; down the Ohio, to the mouth of the Wabash; and from thence to Chicago, on Lake Michigan. . . . I have now informed you of the boundaries of the Miami nation, where the Great Spirit placed my forefathers a long time ago, and charged him not to sell or part with his lands, but to preserve them for his posterity. This charge has been handed down to me. . . . I was much surprised to find that my other brothers differed so much from me on this subject for their conduct would lead one to suppose, that the Great Spirit, and their forefathers, had not given them the same charge that was give[n] to me but, on the contrary, had directed them to sell their lands to any white man who wore a hat, as soon as he should ask it of them. Now, elder brother, your younger brothers, the Miamis, have pointed out to you their country, and also to our brothers present. When I hear your remarks and proposals on this subject [of Miami lands], I will be ready to give you an answer; I came with an expectation of hearing you say good things, but I have not heard what I have expected."

Source: "Documents, Legislative and Executive, of the Congress of the United States, From the First Session of the First to the Third Session of the Thirteenth Congress, Inclusive: commencing March 3, 1789, and ending March 8, 1815 Vol. IV (Washington: Gales and Seaton, 1832), pp. 570–571.

States to continue trading with France without British harassment. He also had to grant Britain "most favored nation" status, giving up the American right to discriminate against British shipping and merchandise. And he had to reconfirm the American commitment that pre-Revolutionary debts owed by Americans to the British would be repaid in full. In return for these major concessions, Britain pledged to compensate American merchants for the ships and cargoes it had seized in 1793 and 1794, to abandon the six forts it still held in the American Northwest, and to grant the United States limited trading rights in India and the British West Indies. Signed in November 1794, Jay's Treaty caused an uproar in the United States when its terms became known in March 1795. Southerners saw in it another sellout of their interests. The Senate ratified the treaty in June 1795, but only because Washington backed it.

Jay's Treaty helped convince Spain to adopt a more conciliatory attitude toward the United States. In the **Treaty of San Lorenzo** (also known as **Pinckney's Treaty**) of 1795, Spain accepted the American position on the 31st parallel as the northern boundary of Spanish Florida and granted American farmers the right of free transit through the port of New Orleans.

THE FIRST PARTISAN ELECTION

Two terms in office were more than enough for Washington. The partisan politics that emerged during his second term—and its expression in an increasingly partisan press—disgusted him. He announced his decision to retire from public life in his Farewell Address of September 1796, less than two months before the presidential election. He intentionally delayed the announcement to minimize the time the Republicans would have to prepare for the campaign. Washington devoted most of his address to a denunciation of partisanship. He invoked the republican ideal of disinterested, independent statesmanship as the only sure and virtuous guide for the nation. He warned against any permanent foreign alliances and cautioned that the Union itself would be endangered if parties continued to be characterized "by geographical discriminations—*Northern* and *Southern, Atlantic* and *Western.*"

Confirming Washington's fears, the election of 1796 was the first openly partisan election in American history. John Adams was the Federalist candidate and Thomas Jefferson the Republican candidate. Each was selected at a party caucus, a meeting of party leaders.

Adams won despite Alexander Hamilton's interference, which inadvertently almost threw the election to Jefferson. Now a private citizen in New York, Hamilton wanted to be the power behind the throne in any new Federalist administration. Uncomfortable with Adams, he connived to have Thomas Pinckney of South Carolina, the other Federalist running with Adams, win the election. The Constitution did not originally call for electors to cast separate ballots for president and vice president. The Constitution was written with absolutely no thought of organized partisan competition for the presidency. Taking advantage of this weakness, Hamilton convinced some of the South Carolina electors to drop Adams from their ballots. He expected that with the solid support of the New England electors for both Adams and Pinckney, Pinkney would be elected president and Adams vice president. But the scheme backfired. When New Englanders learned of it, they refused to vote for Pinckney. As a result, Adams came in first with seventy-one votes, but Jefferson came in second with sixty-eight. Thanks to Hamilton, Adams entered office with his chief rival as vice president and a politically divided administration. Adams received all the northern electoral votes, with the exception of Pennsylvania's. Jefferson was the overwhelming favorite in the South.

THE LAST FEDERALIST ADMINISTRATION

The Adams administration got off to a rocky start from which it never recovered. Adams had been a lawyer before the Revolution; he was a veteran of both Continental Congresses, had been a diplomat in Europe for a decade, and had served as Washington's vice president for eight years. But despite this extraordinarily rich background in public affairs, he was politically naive. Scrupulously honest but quick to take offense, he lacked the politician's touch for inspiring per-

---

QUICK REVIEW

Party Politics
- Washington's Farewell Address denounced partisanship.
- Candidates in presidential election of 1796: John Adams (Federalist), Thomas Jefferson (Republican).
- Adams won despite Hamilton's interference.

Treaty of San Lorenzo (Pickney's Treaty) Treaty with Spain in 1795 in which Spain recognized the 31st parallel as the boundary between the United States and Spanish Florida.

WHY WAS Adams defeated in the election of 1800?

sonal loyalty and crafting compromises based on a realistic recognition of mutual self-interest. But putting the interests of the country before those of his party, he almost single-handedly prevented a nearly certain war with France and a possible civil war at home. The price he paid was a badly split Federalist party that refused to unite behind him when he sought reelection in 1800.

THE FRENCH CRISIS AND THE XYZ AFFAIR

An aggressive coalition known as the Directory gained control of revolutionary France in 1795 and denounced the Jay treaty as evidence of an Anglo-American alliance against France. The French annulled the commercial treaty of 1778 with the United States; ordered the seizure of American ships carrying goods to the British; and declared that any American sailors found on British ships, including those forcibly pressed into service, would be summarily executed.

In the fall of 1797, Adams sent three commissioners to Paris in an effort to avoid war. The French treated the three with contempt. Having just conquered the Netherlands and detached Spain from its British alliance, France was in no mood to compromise. Through three intermediaries—identified by Adams only as X, Y, and Z when he informed Congress of the negotiations—the French foreign minister demanded a large bribe to initiate talks and an American loan of $12 million.

In April 1798, the Senate published a full account of the insulting behavior of the French in what came to be called the **XYZ Affair**. The public was indignant, and war fever swept the country. By the fall of 1798, American ships were waging an undeclared war against the French in Caribbean waters, a conflict that came to be known as the **Quasi-War**. The Federalists, who had always warned against the French, enjoyed greater popularity than they ever had or ever would again. Congress acted to upgrade the navy and the army dramatically and adopted Washington's suggestion that Hamilton be appointed second in command. To pay for both the expanded army and the naval rearmament, the Federalists pushed through the Direct Tax of 1798, a levy on the value of land, slaves, and dwellings.

CRISIS AT HOME

The thought of Hamilton in charge of a huge army convinced many Republicans that their worst nightmares were about to materialize. The Federalists then passed four laws in the summer of 1798, known collectively as the **Alien and Sedition Acts**, that confirmed the Republicans' fears. The most dangerous of the four acts in the minds of Republicans was the **Sedition Act**, a measure that made it a federal crime to engage in any combination or conspiracy against the government or to utter or print anything "false, scandalous and malicious" against the government. Federalist judges were blatantly partisan in their enforcement of the Sedition Act. Twenty-five individuals, mostly Republican editors, were indicted under the act, and ten were convicted.

Facing a Congress and a Supreme Court dominated by the Federalists, Jefferson and Madison turned to the safely Republican legislatures of Kentucky and Virginia for resolution that attacked the constitutionality of the Alien and Sedition Acts, and they produced the first significant articulation of the southern stand on **states' rights**. The resolutions—adopted in the fall of 1798—proposed a compact theory of

With the horrors of the French Revolution forming a backdrop, this cartoon depicts France as a five-headed monster demanding a bribe from the three Americans sent by Adams. The Federalists hoped that such anti-French sentiments would lead to an open war.

The Granger Collection, New York

WHERE TO LEARN MORE

Adams National Historic Site, Quincy, Massachusetts
www.nps.gov/adam

XYZ Affair Diplomatic incident in 1798 in which Americans were outraged by the demand of the French for a bribe as a condition for negotiating with American diplomats.

Quasi-War Undeclared naval war of 1797 to 1800 between the United States and France.

Alien and Sedition Acts Collective name given to four acts passed by Congress in 1798 that curtailed freedom of speech and the liberty of foreigners resident in the United States.

States' rights Favoring the rights of individual states over rights claimed by the national government.

Short and pudgy, Adams had little of Hamilton's physical presence as a natural leader, but he had a first-rate mind and the political courage to place the nation's needs above those of his Federalist party when he peacefully ended the Quasi-War with France.

John Trumbull; White House Historical Association (White House Collection). (25)

Nullification A constitutional doctrine holding that a state has a legal right to declare a national law null and void within its borders.

Franco-American Accord of 1800 Settlement reached with France that brought an end to the Quasi-War and released the United Sates from its 1778 alliance with France.

the Constitution. They asserted that the states had delegated specific powers to the national government for their common benefit. It followed that the states reserved the right to rule whether the national government had unconstitutionally assumed power not granted to it. If a state decided that the national government had exceeded its powers, it could "interpose" its authority to shield its citizens from a tyrannical law. In a second set of resolutions, the Kentucky legislature introduced the doctrine of **nullification**, the right of a state to render null and void a national law it deemed unconstitutional.

Jefferson and Madison hoped that these resolutions would rally voters to the Republican party as the defender of threatened American liberties, yet not a single additional state seconded them. In the end, what aroused popular rage against the Federalists was not legislation directed against aliens and subversives but the high cost of Federalist taxes.

The Direct Tax of 1798 fell on all owners of land, dwellings, or slaves and provoked widespread resentment. Enforcing it required an army of bureaucrats—more than five hundred for the state of Pennsylvania alone. In February 1799, in the heavily German southeastern counties of Pennsylvania, a group of men led by an auctioneer named John Fries released tax evaders from prison in Bethlehem. President Adams responded to Fries's Rebellion with a show of force, but the fiercest resistance the soldiers he sent to Pennsylvania encountered was from irate farm wives, who doused them with hot water. The Federalists had now lost much of their support in Pennsylvania.

THE END OF THE FEDERALISTS

The events in Pennsylvania reflected an air of menace that gripped the country as the campaign of 1800 approached. The army was chasing private citizens whose only crime in the eyes of many was that they were honoring their Revolutionary heritage by resisting hateful taxes. Federal soldiers also roughed up Republican voters at polling places. Southern Republicans talked in private of the possible need to resist Federalist tyranny by force and, failing in that, to secede from the Union. Hamilton and his backers, known as the High Federalists, saw in the Kentucky and Virginia resolutions "a regular conspiracy to overturn the government."

No one did more to defuse this charged atmosphere than President Adams. The Federalists depended for their popular support on the expectation of a war with France, which as late as 1798 had swept them to victory in the congressional elections. Still, Adams refrained from asking for a declaration of war. Adams recognized that war with France could trigger a civil war at home. Hamilton and the High Federalists, he feared, would use war as an excuse to crush the Republican opposition in Virginia. Fearful of Hamilton's intentions and unwilling to run the risk of militarizing the government, Adams broke with his party and decided to reopen negotiations with France in February 1799.

The **Franco-American Accord of 1800** that resulted from Adams's initiative released the United States from its 1778 alliance with France and in return the United States surrendered all claims against the French for damages done to American shipping. The prospect of peace with France deprived the Hamilton Federalists of their trump card in the election. The Republicans could no longer be branded as the traitorous friends of an enemy state. The enlarged army, with no foe to fight, became a political embarrassment, and the Federalists dismantled it. Although rumors of possible violence continued to circulate, the Republicans grew increasingly confident that they could peacefully gain control of the government.

The Federalists, hampered by party disunity, could not counter the Republicans' aggressive organizational tactics. They found it distasteful to appeal to common people. Wherever the Republicans organized, they attacked the Federalists as monarchists plotting to undo the gains of the Revolution. The Federalists responded with emotional appeals that depicted Jefferson as a godless revolutionary whose election would usher in a reign of terror. "The effect," intoned the Reverend William Linn, "would be to destroy religion, introduce immorality, and loosen all bonds of society."

Attacks like Linn's reflected the fears of Calvinist preachers that a tide of disbelief was about to submerge Christianity in the United States. **Deism**, an Enlightenment religious philosophy popular among the leaders of the Revolutionary era, was making inroads among common citizens as well. Deists viewed God as a kind of master clockmaker who created the laws by which the universe runs but otherwise leaves it alone. They rejected revelation for reason, maintaining that the workings of nature alone reveal God's design. These developments convinced Calvinist ministers, nearly all of them Federalists, that the atheism of the French Revolution was infecting American republicanism.

The Republicans won the election by mobilizing voters through strong party organizations. Voter turnout in 1800 was twice what it had been in the early 1790s, and most of the new voters were Republicans. The Direct Tax of 1798 cost the Federalists the support of commercial farmers in the Mid-Atlantic states. Artisans in port cities had already switched to the Republicans in protest over Jay's Treaty, which they feared left them exposed to a flood of cheap British imports. Adams carried New England and had a smattering of support elsewhere. With New York added to their solid base in the South and the backcountry, the Jeffersonians gained an electoral majority (see Map 8–2).

Party unity among Republican electors was so strong that Jefferson and Burr each received seventy-three electoral votes. Consequently the election was thrown into the House of Representatives, which, until the newly elected Congress was seated, was still dominated by Federalists. Hoping to deny Jefferson the presidency, the Federalists in the House backed Burr. The result was a deadlock that persisted into the early months of 1801 when the Federalists yielded. Informed through intermediaries that Jefferson would not dismantle Hamilton's fiscal system, enough Federalists cast blank ballots to give Jefferson the majority he needed for election. The Twelfth Amendment to the Constitution, ratified in 1804, prevented a similar impasse from arising again by requiring electors to cast separate ballots for president and vice president.

CONCLUSION

In 1789, the American republic was little more than an experiment in self-government. The Federalists provided a firm foundation for that experiment. Hamilton's financial program, neutrality in the wars of the French Revolution, and the diplomatic settlement with Britain in Jay's Treaty bequeathed the young nation a decade of peace and prosperity.

Federalist policies, however, provoked strong opposition rooted in conflicting economic interests and contrasting regional views over the meaning of liberty and government in the new republic. The Federalist coalition split during Washington's

 MAP EXPLORATION
To explore an interactive version of this map, go to
http://www.prenhall.com/goldfield2/map8.2

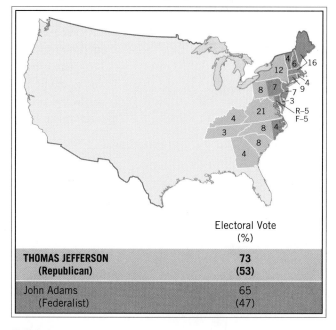

	Electoral Vote (%)
THOMAS JEFFERSON (Republican)	**73** **(53)**
John Adams (Federalist)	65 (47)

MAP 8–2
The Election of 1800   The sharp erosion of Federalist strength in New York and Pennsylvania after 1798 swung the election of 1800 to the Republicans.

WHAT DOES this map show you about the interests of Jeffersonian Republicans versus those of the Federalists? Based on geographic regions, which party was more likely to represent farmers?

QUICK REVIEW

Presidential Election of 1800

- Federalists could not overcome party disunity.
- Federalists attacked as disbelievers in Christianity.
- Strong party organization won election for Republicans Jefferson and Burr.

Deism   Religious orientation that rejects divine revelation and holds that the workings of nature alone reveal God's design for the universe.

second term when Southern planters joined urban artisans and backcountry Scots-Irish farmers in opposing Jay's Treaty and the commercially oriented program of the Federalists. When Quaker and German farmers in the Mid-Atlantic states defected from the Federalists over the tax legislation of 1798, three of the four regions in Washington's America now lined up behind the Republicans in the belief that measures such as expansion of the army and passage of the Alien and Sedition Acts threatened individual liberty and regional autonomy.

The openly partisan politics of the 1790s surprised the country's founders, who equated parties with the evils of factionalism. They had not foreseen that parties would forge a necessary link between the rulers and the ruled and create a mechanism by which group values and regional interests could be given a political voice. To the credit of the Federalists, they relinquished control of the national government peacefully. The importance of this precedent can scarcely be exaggerated. It marked the first time in modern political history that a party in power handed over the government to its opposition.

Party formation climaxed in the election of 1800, when the Republicans ended the Federalists' rule. The Republicans won by embracing the popular demand for a more egalitarian social and political order.

It now remained to be seen what the Republicans would do with their newfound power.

SUMMARY

Washington's America The national census of 1790 counted nearly four million Americans, one in four of whom lived in New England. New Englanders found slavery incompatible with the natural rights philosophy that had emerged during the Revolution and abolished it in the 1780s. In other respects, though, politics in New England remained rooted in the Puritan past. The states in the Mid-Atlantic region were the most diverse in the nation, which created a complex political environment. In the South climate and soil conditions favored the production of cash staples for world markets and the use of slavery. And, between the Appalachian Mountains and the Mississippi River stretched the most rapidly growing region of the new nation, the West. Life in the West was harsh and often cruel, and Westerners were willing to strike a deal with almost any outside power to meet their needs.

Forging a New Government The Congress that assembled in New York from 1789 to 1791 faced a challenge scarcely less daunting than that of the Constitutional Convention of 1787. Led by Madison, the Congress submitted twelve amendments to the Constitution to the states of which ten were ratified. These ten are known as the Bill of Rights. Congress was also busy working out the cabinet and the court system.

The Emergence of Parties Two parties formed by the end of Washington's first term: the Federalists and the Republicans. In 1792, still in their formative stages, the parties re-elected an unopposed Washington. Control of the West remained an elusive goal throughout Washington's presidency. Among the distractions were wars with the Indians (the Battle of Fallen Timbers) and a Whiskey Rebellion in western Pennsylvania. The first partisan election was the election of 1796, with a divided nation electing Adams over Jefferson.

The Last Federalist Administration The Adams administration got off to a rocky start from which it never recovered. His administration dealt with the XYZ Affair, the Quasi-War with France, the Alien and Sedition Acts, and Fries's Rebellion. With Adams's many failed policies and the turmoil surrounding his presidency, the election of 1800 saw Jefferson narrowly elected president and the end of the Federalist party.

REVIEW QUESTIONS

1. What role did the "people" play in Washington's inauguration in 1789? What was the purpose of the grand procession, and why were the militia present?

2. What was distinctive about the four regions of the United States in 1790? What were the common values and goals that brought white Americans together?

3. How were the major problems confronting the Washington administration resolved?

4. How did the Federalists and the Republicans differ over the meaning of liberty and the power of the national government?

5. Why did Jefferson call his election of 1800 the "revolution of 1800"?

KEY TERMS

Alien and Sedition Acts   (p. 211)
Bill of Rights   (p. 202)
Deism   (p. 213)
Federalists   (p. 205)
Franco-American Accord of 1800   (p. 212)

Jay's Treaty   (p. 208)
Judiciary Act of 1789   (p. 202)
Nullification   (p. 212)
Quasi-War   (p. 211)
Republican (Jeffersonian)   (p. 205)
States' rights   (p. 211)

Tariff Act of 1789   (p. 203)
Tonnage Act of 1789   (p. 203)
Treaty of Greeenville   (p. 208)
Treaty of San Lorenzo   (p. 210)
Whiskey Rebellion   (p. 208)
XYZ Affair   (p. 211)

WHERE TO LEARN MORE

Cincinnati Historical Society, Cincinnati, Ohio. Collections include written and visual materials on the history of the Old Northwest Territory. Visit its website **www.cincymuseum.org/** for information on its programs and the accessibility of its printed and audiovisual collections.

Federal Hall National Memorial, New York, New York. This museum and historic site holds artifacts relating to President Washington's inauguration. Its website **www.nps.gov/feha/** includes a printable travel guide to various sites in Manhattan administered by the National Parks Service.

Hamilton Grange National Memorial, New York, New York. The home of Alexander Hamilton contains materials on his life. A brief history of the home and Hamilton's life can be found at its website: **www.nps/gov/hagr/**

Adams National Historic Site, Quincy, Massachusetts. This site preserves buildings and manuscripts associated with four generations of the Adams family. See its website **www.nps.gov/adam/** for information on guided tours and the various homes that are part of the site.

 For additional study resources for this chapter, go to:
www.prenhall.com/goldfield/chapter8

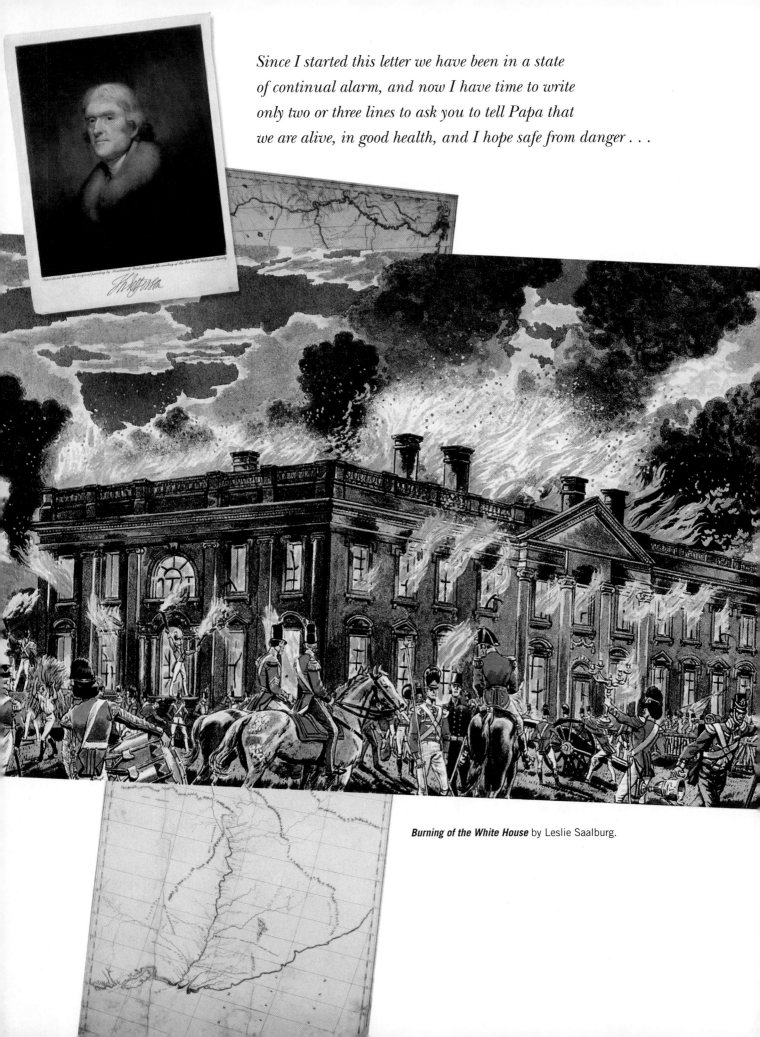

Since I started this letter we have been in a state of continual alarm, and now I have time to write only two or three lines to ask you to tell Papa that we are alive, in good health, and I hope safe from danger . . .

Burning of the White House by Leslie Saalburg.

9

THE TRIUMPH AND COLLAPSE OF JEFFERSONIAN REPUBLICANISM
1800–1824

WHAT DID Thomas Jefferson achieve as President?

WHAT CHALLENGES did James Madison face as president?

WHAT WERE the consequences of the War of 1812?

HOW DID nationalism increase during the Era of Good Feelings?

WHAT WAS the Missouri Compromise?

Riversdale,
30 August 1814

My dear Sister,

    Since I started this letter [on Aug. 9] we have been in a state of continual alarm, and now I have time to write only two or three lines to ask you to tell Papa that we are alive, in good health, and I hope safe from danger. I am sure that you have heard the news of the battle of Bladensburg where the English defeated the American troops with Madison 'not at their head, but at their rear.'

    From there they went to Washington where they burned the Capitol, the President's House, all the public offices, etc. During the battle I saw several cannonballs with my own eyes, and I will write all the details to your husband. At the moment the English ships are at Alexandria which is also in their possession.

    I don't know how all this will end, but I fear very badly for us. It is probable that it will also bring about a dissolution of the union of the states, and in that case, farewell to the public debt. You know I have predicted this outcome for a long time. Wouldn't it be wise to send your husband here without delay, in order to plan with me the best course to pursue for Papa's interests as well as yours?

    This letter will go, I think, by a Dutch ship. If I have time with the confusion we are in, I will write again in a few days, perhaps by the same vessel. At present my house is full of people every day and at night my bedroom is full of rifles, pistols, sabers, etc. Many thanks to your husband for the information in his letter of 27 April, and tell him that I invested all his money in the May loan [of the U.S. Treasury]. Please give many greetings to my dear Father and to Charles [her brother]. Embrace your children for me and believe me.

    Your affectionate sister,

    —Rosalie E. Calvert

Margaret Law Callcott, ed., *Mistress of Riversdale: The Plantation Letters of Rosalie Steir Calvert, 1795–1821* (Baltimore: The Johns Hopkins University Press, 1991), pp. 271–272.

IMAGE KEY
for pages 216–217

a. Thomas Jefferson.
b. "Burning of the White House" by Leslie Saalburg.
c. Map of the Great Lakes.
d. An antique wooden compass with a leather pouch used on the expedition of Meriwether Lewis and William Clark.
e. Portrait of Thomas Jefferson.
f. Portrait of James Madison.
g. War of 1812, Battle of Lake Erie.
h. James Monroe and Robert R. Livingstone completing negotiations with Comte Talleyrand for the Louisiana Purchase.

ROSALIE CALVERT, from her plantation home in Maryland, wrote to her sister about the British attack on Washington, D.C. in August 1814, the low point of the American cause in the War of 1812.

    The Calverts lived at Riversdale and managed three plantations worked by slave labor. Rosalie's wealth and elite social standing deepened her political conservatism. In her eyes, Jefferson and his followers were demagogues who catered to the poor and threatened to infect America with the political radicalism of the French Revolution. She blamed the War of 1812 on ill-conceived Republican policies and feared that the war would unleash massive unrest within the United States.

    Her fears were overblown. The United States weathered the War of 1812 and the Calverts were spared any property damage at their Riversdale estate. Rosalie, however, survived the war by only six years. The strain of having nine children and suffering one miscarriage in twenty-one years of marriage may have contributed to her death at the age of 43 from congestive heart failure.

Despite her denunciations of the Republicans, Jefferson and his Republican successors, James Madison and James Monroe, promoted the growth and independence of the United States. Expansionist policies to the south and west more than doubled the size of the republic and fueled the westward spread of slavery. The war against Britain from 1812 to 1815, if less than a military triumph, freed Americans to look inward for economic development.

At the height of Republican success during the Era of Good Feelings just after the War of 1812, the Federalist party collapsed. Without an organized opposition to enforce party discipline among themselves, the Republicans followed the Federalists into political oblivion. A financial panic and a battle over slavery in Missouri shattered Republican unity. By the mid-1820s, a new party system was emerging.

JEFFERSON'S PRESIDENCY

Thomas Jefferson believed that a true revolution had occurred in 1800, a peaceful overthrow of the Federalist party and its hated principles of government consolidation and military force. In his eyes, the defeat of the monarchical Federalists reconfirmed the true political legacy of the Revolution by restoring the Republican majority to its rightful control of the government.

Unlike the Hamiltonian Federalists, whose commercial vision of America accepted social and economic inequalities as inevitable, the Jeffersonians wanted a predominantly agrarian republic based on widespread economic equality for white yeomen families to counter any threat posed by the privileged few to the people's liberties. Jefferson's first administration was a solid success. A unified Republican party reduced the size and scope of the federal government, allowed the Alien and Sedition Acts to lapse, and celebrated the Louisiana Purchase. His second term, however, was a bitter disappointment, marked by the failure of his unpopular embargo on American foreign trade. As a result, Jefferson left his successor, James Madison, a divided party, a temporarily revived Federalism, and an unresolved crisis in foreign affairs.

REFORM AT HOME

Jefferson set the style and tone of his administration from the beginning. He was the first president to be inaugurated in Washington, D.C., and his inauguration was as unpretentious as the raw and primitive capital city itself. He walked from his lodgings to the Capitol building to be sworn in. His dress was neat but shorn of gentlemanly refinements such as a wig. After giving notice that an unadorned style of republican egalitarianism would now replace the aristocratic formalities of the Federalists, Jefferson emphasized in his inaugural address the overwhelming commitment of Americans to the "republican form" of government and affirmed his own support of civil liberties as an American principle.

A poor public speaker, Jefferson sent written messages to Congress to avoid having to read them in person. This change from Federalist policy both eliminated the impression of a monarch addressing his subjects and played to Jefferson's formidable skills as a writer. He replaced the stiff formalism and aristocratic etiquette of receptions for presidential visitors with more relaxed weekly meetings around a circular table at which fine food and wine were nevertheless served.

The cornerstone of Republican domestic policy was retrenchment, a return to the frugal, simple federal establishment the Jeffersonians believed was the original intent

WHAT DID Thomas Jefferson achieve as president?

WHERE TO LEARN MORE

Monticello,
Charlottesville, Virginia
www.monticello.org/

Dolley Madison, the engaging young wife of James Madison, Jefferson's secretary of state, served as the unofficial social hostess in the White House during the administration of Jefferson, a widower.

The Granger Collection, New York

QUICK REVIEW

Judiciary Act of 1801

◆ Enlarged the judiciary and packed it with Adams' appointees.

◆ Repealed by Republican Congress.

◆ Conflict came to head in case of Marbury v. Madison (1803).

Marbury v. Madison Supreme Court decision of 1803 that created the precedent of judicial review by ruling as unconstitutional part of the Judiciary Act of 1789.

of the Constitution. The Republicans began with fiscal policy. Jefferson's secretary of the treasury was Albert Gallatin, who convinced Jefferson that the Bank of the United States was essential for financial stability and yet succeeded in reducing the national debt from $83 million in 1800 to $57 million by 1809. Gallatin's conservative fiscal policies shrank both the spending and taxes of the national government. The Republicans eliminated all internal taxes, including the despised tax on whiskey. Slashes in the military budget enabled government expenditures to stay below the level of 1800. The cuts in military spending combined with soaring revenues from customs collections left Gallatin with a surplus in the budget that he could devote to debt repayment.

Jeffersonian reform targeted the political character, as well as the size, of the national government. He moved to break the Federalist stranglehold on federal offices and appoint officials with sound Republican principles, replacing those deemed guilty of misusing their offices for political gain. By the time Jefferson left the presidency in 1809, Republicans held nearly all the appointive offices.

Jefferson moved most aggressively against the Federalists in the judiciary. Just days before they relinquished power, the Federalists enraged the Jeffersonians by passing the Judiciary Act of 1801, legislation that both enlarged the judiciary and packed it with more Federalists appointed by Adams, the outgoing president.

The Republicans fought back. Now dominant in Congress, they quickly repealed the Judiciary Act of 1801. Frustrated Federalists now turned to John Marshall, a staunch Federalist-appointed chief justice of the United States by President Adams in 1801, in the hope that he would rule that Congress had acted unconstitutionally in removing the recently appointed federal judges. Marshall moved carefully, aware that the Republicans contended that Congress and the president had at least a coequal right with the Supreme Court to decide constitutional questions.

The issue came to a head in the case of *Marbury v. Madison* (1803), which centered on Secretary of State James Madison's refusal to deliver a commission to William Marbury, one of Adam's "midnight appointments." Marshall held that although Marbury had a legal right to his commission, the Court had no jurisdiction in the case. The Court ruled that the section of the Judiciary Act of 1789 granting it the power to order the delivery of Marbury's commission was unconstitutional because it conferred on the Court a power not specified in Article 3 of the Constitution on cases of original jurisdiction. Marshall created the precedent of judicial review, the power of the Supreme Court to rule on the constitutionality of federal law. This doctrine was of pivotal importance for the future of the Court. Marshall had brilliantly turned a threatening situation into a success for the judiciary.

THE LOUISIANA PURCHASE

In foreign affairs, fortune smiled on Jefferson during his first term. The European war that had almost sucked in the United States in the 1790s subsided. Jefferson, despite his distaste for a strong navy, ordered a show of force in the Mediterranean to punish the Barbary pirates who were preying on American shipping.

For years, the North African states of Morocco, Algeria, Tunis, and Tripoli had demanded cash tribute from foreigners as the price for allowing trade in the Mediterranean. Jefferson stopped the payments in 1801, and when the attacks on American shipping resumed, he retaliated by sending warships to the Mediterranean. The tribute system continued until 1815, but on much more favorable terms for the United States.

The Anglo-French peace was a mixed blessing for the United States. Although it removed any immediate threat of war, the return of peace also enabled Spain and France to reclaim their colonial trade in the Western Hemisphere. The new military ruler of France, Napoleon Bonaparte, in a secret treaty with Spain in 1800, reacquired for France the Louisiana Territory, a vast, vaguely defined area stretching between the Mississippi River and the Rocky Mountains. Sketchy, unconfirmed reports of the treaty in the spring of 1801 alarmed Jefferson. France, for its part, was a formidable opponent whose control of the Mississippi Valley, combined with the British presence in Canada, threatened to hem in the United States. Jefferson was prepared to reverse the traditional foreign policy of his party and opened exploratory talks with the British on an Anglo-American alliance to drive the French out of Louisiana. He also strengthened American forces in the Mississippi Valley and secured congressional approval for an exploring expedition through upper Louisiana led by Meriwether Lewis and William Clark. This was initially intended to be more of a military than a scientific mission.

Jefferson then sought to acquire New Orleans and control the mouth of the Mississippi River, outlet to world markets. He persuaded Congress to pass resolutions threatening an attack on New Orleans (see Map 9–1).

8–8
Sacagawea Interprets for Lewis and Clark (1804)

MAP EXPLORATION

To explore an interactive version of this map, go to **http://www.prenhall.com/goldfield2/map9.1**

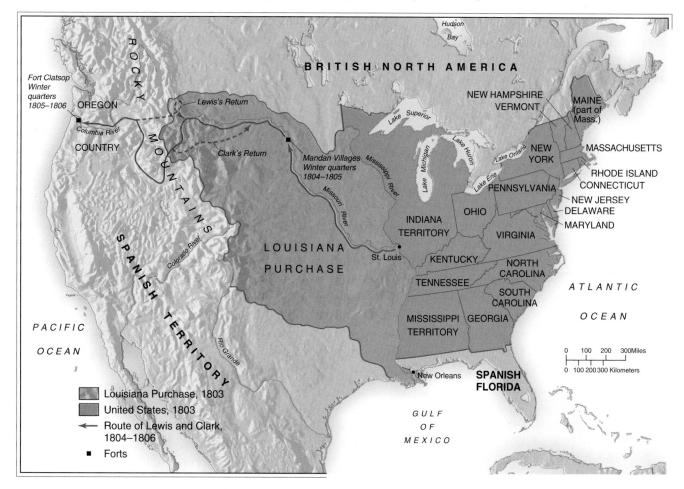

MAP 9–1

The Louisiana Purchase and the Lewis and Clark Expedition   The vast expanse of the Louisiana Purchase was virtually unknown territory to Americans before the Lewis and Clark expedition gathered a mass of scientific information about it.

BASED ON this map, how did the Louisiana Purchase impact United States trade and trade routes?

CHRONOLOGY

1801	Thomas Jefferson is inaugurated, the first Republican president. John Marshall becomes chief justice.
1802	Congress repeals the Judiciary Act of 1801.
1803	*Marbury* v. *Madison* sets the precedent of judicial review by the Supreme Court. Louisiana Purchase.
1804	Vice President Aaron Burr kills Alexander Hamilton in a duel. Judges John Pickering and Samuel Chase impeached by Republicans. Jefferson is reelected.
1806	Britain and France issue orders restricting neutral shipping. Betrayal of the Burr conspiracy.
1807	*Chesapeake* affair. Congress passes the Embargo Act.
1808	Congress prohibits the African slave trade. James Madison elected president.
1809	Repeal of the Embargo Act. Passage of the Nonintercourse Act.
1810	Macon's Bill No. 2 reopens trade with Britain and France. United States annexes part of West Florida. Georgia state law invalidated by the Supreme Court in *Fletcher* v. *Peck*.
1811	Battle of Tippecanoe and defeat of the Indian confederation. Charter of the Bank of the United States expires.
1812	Congress declares war on Britain. American loss of Detroit. Madison reelected.

1813	Perry's victory at Battle of Put-in-Bay. Battle of the Thames and death of Tecumseh.
1814	Jackson crushes the Creeks at the Battle of Horseshoe Bend. British burn Washington, D.C., and attack Baltimore. Macdonough's naval victory on Lake Champlain turns back a British invasion. Hartford Convention meets. Treaty of Ghent signed.
1815	Jackson routs British at the Battle of New Orleans.
1816	Congress charters the Second Bank of the United States and passes a protective tariff. James Monroe elected president.
1817	Rush-Bagot Treaty demilitarizes the Great Lakes.
1818	Anglo-American Accords on trade and boundaries. Jackson's border campaign in Spanish East Florida.
1819	Trans-Continental Treaty between United States and Spain. Beginning of the Missouri controversy. Financial panic sends economy into a depression. *Dartmouth College* v. *Woodward* upholds the charter rights of corporations. *McCulloch* v. *Maryland* upholds constitutionality of the Bank of the United States.
1820	Missouri Compromise on slavery in the Louisiana Purchase. Monroe reelected.
1823	Monroe Doctrine proclaims Western Hemisphere closed to further European colonization.
1825	John Quincy Adams elected president by the House of Representatives.

8–6
A Matter of Honor or
Vengeance? (1804)

Meanwhile, Napoleon had envisioned the rich sugar island of St. Domingue (today divided between Haiti and the Dominican Republic) as the jewel of his new empire and he intended to use the Louisiana Territory as a granary to supply the island. But he failed to recover St. Domingue from the slaves on the island, led by Touissant L'Ouverture, who had captured it in a bloody and successful bid for independence. Without firm French control of St. Domingue, Louisiana was of little use to Napoleon and a renewed war against Britain was looming. To Jefferson's surprise, Napoleon sold Louisiana to the United States for $15 million (the cost to the United States was about 3 1/2 cents per acre). Jefferson, the strict constructionist, now turned pragmatist. Despite the lack of any specific authorization in the Constitution for the acquisition of foreign territory, he accepted Napoleon's deal and doubled the size of the United States with the *Louisiana Purchase.* Jefferson was willing, as the Federalists had been when they were in power, to stretch the Constitution to support his definition of the national good. Ironically, it was now the Federalists, fearful of a further decline in their political power, who relied on a narrow reading of the Constitution.

FLORIDA AND WESTERN SCHEMES

The magnificent prize of Louisiana did not satisfy Republican territorial ambitions. Still to be gained were river outlets on the Gulf Coast essential for the development of plantation agriculture in Alabama and Mississippi. The boundaries of the Louisiana Purchase were so vague that Jefferson felt justified in claiming Spanish-held Texas and the Gulf Coast eastward from New Orleans to Mobile Bay, including the Spanish province of West Florida. This provoked the first challenge to his leadership of the party.

Once it was clear that Spain did not want to sell West Florida to the United States, Jefferson covertly accepted Napoleon's offer to act as a middleman in the acquisition. Former Republican stalwarts in Congress staged a party revolt against the president's devious tactics.

Jefferson's failed bid for West Florida emboldened Westerners to demand that Americans seize the territory by force. In 1805 and 1806, Aaron Burr, Jefferson's first vice president, apparently became entangled in an attempt at just such a land grab. Republicans had been suspicious of Burr since his dalliance with the Federalists in their bid to make him president rather than Jefferson in 1800. A minority of die-hard Federalists, fearing that incorporation of the vast territory of the Louisiana Purchase into the United States would reduce New England's power, backed Burr in the New York gubernatorial race of 1804. Burr lost, largely because Hamilton denounced his character. The enmity between the two men reached a tragic climax in July 1804, when Burr killed Hamilton in a duel. Facing murder charges, Burr fled to the West and lined up followers for a separatist plot.

The Burr conspiracy remains mysterious. Burr may have been thinking of carving out a separate western confederacy in the lower Mississippi Valley. Whatever he had in mind, he blundered in relying on General James Wilkinson as a coconspirator. Wilkinson, the military governor of the Louisiana Territory and also a double agent for Spain, betrayed Burr. Jefferson made extraordinary efforts to secure a conviction, but Burr was acquitted when the government failed to prove its case for treason in 1807.

EMBARGO AND A CRIPPLED PRESIDENCY

Concern about a possible war against Britain in 1807 soon quieted the uproar over Burr's trial. After Britain and France resumed their war in 1803, the United States became enmeshed in the same thicket of neutral rights, blockades, ship seizures, and impressment of American sailors that had almost dragged the country into war in the 1790s. Caught in the middle, but eager to supply both sides, was the American merchant marine, the world's largest carrier of neutral goods. American merchants and shippers had taken full advantage of the magnificent opportunities opened up by the European war. The flush years from 1793 to 1807 witnessed a tripling of American ship tonnage, and the value of exports soared five times over. American merchants dominated trade not only between Britain and the United States but also between the European continent and the French and Spanish colonies in the West Indies.

The ***Chesapeake*** **Incident** in June 1807 nearly triggered an Anglo-American war. When the commander of the U.S. frigate *Chesapeake* refused to submit to a British search in coastal waters off Norfolk, the British ship *Leopard* opened fire, and three Americans were killed. Jefferson resisted the popular outcry for revenge. Instead, he barred American ports to British warships and called for monetary compensation and an end to impressment, not only because the country was woefully unprepared for war but also because he passionately believed that

***Chesapeake* Incident**   Attack in 1807 by the British ship *Leopard* on the American ship *Chesapeake* in American territorial waters.

The caption on this 1807 illustration of a deserted pier in Portland, Maine—"And the grass literally grew upon the wharves."—reflects the hardship Jefferson's embargo caused as it choked off the American export trade.

North Wind Picture Archives

Embargo Act of 1807   Act passed by Congress in 1807 prohibiting American ships from leaving for any foreign port.

WHAT CHALLENGES

did James Madison face as president?

W   WHERE TO LEARN MORE

★ Montpelier, Montpelier Station, Virginia
www.montpelier.org

international law should resolve disputes between nations. In a last burst of the idealism that had animated the republicanism of the Revolution, Jefferson resorted to a trade embargo as a substitute for war. The **Embargo Act of 1807** prohibited American ships from clearing port to any nation until Britain and France repealed their trading restrictions on neutral shippers.

The basic premise of the embargo, that Europe was completely dependent on American-supplied foodstuffs and raw materials, was not so much wrong as unrealistic. The embargo did hurt Europe, but the people who first felt the pain were British textile workers and slaves in the colonies, hardly those who wielded the levers of power. Meanwhile, the American export trade and its profits dried up, and nearly all economic groups suffered. Especially hard hit were New England shippers and merchants, who accused the Republicans of near-criminal irresponsibility for forcing a depression on the country. Jefferson responded with a series of enforcement acts that consolidated executive powers far beyond what the Federalists themselves had been able to achieve while in power. As the embargo tightened and the 1808 election approached, Federalism revived. The Federalist Charles C. Pinckney of South Carolina tripled his electoral vote over that of 1804, but Secretary of State Madison carried the South and the West, the heartland of Republican support. Before Madison took office, the Republicans abandoned Jefferson's embargo in 1809, replacing it with the **Nonintercourse Act**, a measure that prohibited American trade only with Britain and France.

MADISON AND THE COMING OF WAR

Frail-looking and short, Madison struck most contemporaries as an indecisive and weaker version of Jefferson. Yet in intellectual toughness and resourcefulness he was at least Jefferson's equal. He failed because of an inherited foreign policy that was partly of his own making as Jefferson's secretary of state. The Republicans' idealistic stand on neutral rights was ultimately untenable unless backed up by military and political force. Madison concluded as much when he decided on war against Britain in the spring of 1812. Thus did the Republicans push for a war they were eager to fight but unprepared to wage.

THE FAILURE OF ECONOMIC SANCTIONS

Early in his administration, Madison became convinced that the impasse in Anglo-American relations was about to be broken. Britain benefited from the Nonintercourse Act at the expense of France. Once at sea, American ships were kept away from France and steered to England by the strong British navy. Perhaps in recognition of this unintended consequence of the new American policy, the British began to relax their restrictions on neutral shipping, known as the Orders in Council, in favor of U.S. commerce. At the same time, the British minister in Washington, David Erskine, reached an agreement with Madison that called for completely rescinding the Orders in Council as they applied to the United States. Unfortunately, Erskine had exceeded his instructions, and the Madison-Erskine agreement was later disavowed in London. Although Madison reimposed sanctions on Britain in August, he was left looking the fool.

Congress stepped in with its own policy in 1810. Macon's Bill No. 2 threw open American trade to everyone but stipulated that if either France or England lifted its restrictions, the president would resume trading sanctions against the other. Madison now looked even more foolish when he accepted Napoleon's duplicitous promises in 1810 to withdraw his decrees against American shipping on the condition that if Britain did not follow suit, Madison would force the British to respect American rights. French seizures of American ships continued, and by the time Napoleon's duplicity became clear, he had already succeeded in worsening Anglo-American tensions to the point that in November 1810, Madison reimposed nonintercourse against Britain, putting the two nations on a collision course.

THE FRONTIER AND INDIAN RESISTANCE

Mounting frustrations in the South and West also pushed Madison toward a war against Britain. Farm prices, including those for the southern staples of cotton and tobacco, plunged when Jefferson's embargo shut off exports and stayed low after the embargo was lifted. Blame for the persistent agricultural depression focused on the British and their stranglehold on overseas trade after 1808.

Western settlers also accused the British of inciting Indian resistance. After the *Chesapeake* incident, the British did seek alliances with Indians in the Old Northwest, reviving the strategy of using them as a buffer against any American move on Canada. It was the unceasing demand of Americans for ever more Indian land, however, not any British incitements, that triggered the **pan-Indian resistance movement** that so frightened western settlers on the eve of the War of 1812.

In the Treaty of Greenville (1795), the American government had promised that any future acquisitions of Indian land would have to be approved by all native peoples in the region. Nonetheless, government agents continued their former tactics of playing one group against another and of dividing groups from within. By such means, William Henry Harrison, the governor of the Indiana Territory, procured most of southern Indiana in the *Treaty of Vincennes* of 1804. Two extraordinary leaders, the Shawnee chief Tecumseh and his brother, the Prophet Tenskwatawa, channeled Indian outrage over this treaty into a movement to unify tribes throughout the West for a stand against the white invaders. As preached by Tecumseh and the Prophet, Indian land could be saved and self-respect regained only through racial solidarity and a spiritual rebirth. With the assistance of Tecumseh, Tenskwatawa established the Prophet's Town in 1808, at the confluence of the Wabash and Tippecanoe Rivers in north-central Indiana, as headquarters of an intertribal confederation. As he tried to explain to the worried Governor Harrison, his goals were peaceful. He admonished his followers, "[Do] not take up the tomahawk, . . . do not meddle with any thing that does not belong to you, but mind your own business, and cultivate the ground, that your women and your children have enough to live on."

That ground, of course, was the very reason the Indians could not live in peace and dignity. The white settlers wanted it and would do anything to get it. In November 1811, Harrison marched an army to Prophet's Town and provoked the *Battle of Tippecanoe.* While Tecumseh was absent on a recruiting mission among the southern tribes, impetuous young braves attacked Harrison's army. Harrison's victory came at a high cost, for Tecumseh now joined forces with the British.

While Harrison's aggressiveness was converting fears of a British-Indian alliance into a self-fulfilling prophecy, expansionist-minded Southerners struck at Britain through Spain, now its ally against Napoleon. With the covert support of President Madison, American adventurers staged a bloodless revolt in Spanish West Florida between Louisiana and the Pearl River. Hatred of Native Americans, expansionist pressures, the lingering agricultural depression, and impatience with the administration's policy of economic coercion all pointed in the same direction— a war against Britain coupled with an American takeover of British Canada and Spanish Florida. This was the rallying cry of the **War Hawks**, the forty or so prowar congressmen swept into office in 1810. Generally younger men from the South and

The Prophet Tenkswatawa was the spiritual leader of the pan-Indian movement that sought to revitalize native culture and block the spread of white settlement in the Old Northwest.

Courtesy of Library of Congress

QUICK REVIEW

Treaties and Resistance
- Treaty of Greenville (1795) promised all further acquisitions of Indian land would be approved by all native peoples in the region.
- Treaty of Vincennes (1804) procured most of southern Indiana in violation of Treaty of Greenville.
- Indian tribes throughout West unified for stand against settlers.

WHERE TO LEARN MORE

Tippecanoe Battlefield Museum, Battle Ground, Indiana
www.tcha.mus.in.us/battlefield.htm

Pan-Indian resistance movement Movement calling for the political and cultural unification of Indian tribes in the late eighteenth and early nineteenth centuries.

War Hawks Members of Congress, predominantly from the South and West, who aggressively pushed for a war against Britain after their election in 1810.

West, the War Hawks were led by Henry Clay of Kentucky. Along with other outspoken nationalists such as John C. Calhoun of South Carolina, Clay played a key role in building congressional support for Madison's growing aggressiveness on the British issue.

DECISION FOR WAR

In July 1811, deceived by Napoleon and dismissed by the British as the head of a second-rate power, Madison had run out of diplomatic options and was losing control of his party. When Congress met in November, Madison tried to lay the groundwork for war. But the Republican-controlled Congress balked at strengthening the military or raising taxes to pay for a war that seemed ever more likely, citing their party's traditional view of high taxes and a strong military as the tools of despots. Madison secretly asked Congress on April 1 for a sixty-day embargo, a move designed to give American merchant ships time to return safely to their home ports. On June 1, he sent a war message to Congress in which he laid out the stark alternative of submission or resistance to the British control of American commerce. For Madison and most other Republicans, the impending conflict was a second war for independence. Free and open access to world markets was certainly at stake, but so was national pride. The arrogant British policy of impressment was a humiliating affront to American honor and headed the list of grievances in Madison's war message.

A divided Congress declared war on Britain. Support for the war was strongest in regions like the South and the West, whose economies had been damaged the most by the British blockades and control of Atlantic commerce. The votes that carried the war declaration came from northern Republicans, who saw the impending struggle as a defense of America's experiment in self-government. Nine-tenths of the congressional Republicans voted for war, but not a single Federalist did so. For the Federalists, the real enemy was France, which had actually seized more American ships than the British. (See American Views: "Federalist Antiwar Resolutions.") The Federalists' anger increased when they learned that the British had been prepared to revoke for one year the Orders in Council against the United States. A poor harvest and the ongoing economic pressure exerted by Madison had finally caused hard times in England and produced a policy reversal intended to placate the Americans. This concession, however, did not address impressment or monetary compensation, and news of it reached America too late to avert a war.

THE WAR OF 1812

The Republicans led the nation into a war it was unprepared to fight (see Map 9–2, p. 228). The bungled American invasions verged on tragicomedy, and for much of the war, Britain was preoccupied with Napoleon in Europe. When free to concentrate on the American sideshow in 1814, the British failed to secure naval control of the Great Lakes, their minimal strategic objective. By the fall of 1814, both sides were eager for an end to the military stalemate.

Internal dissent endangered the Union almost as much as the British. The war exacerbated Federalist disenchantment with southern dominance of national affairs. A minority of Federalists, convinced that New England could never regain its rightful place in shaping national policy, prepared to lead a secession movement. Although blocked by party moderates at the Hartford Convention in 1814, the secessionists tarred Federalism with the brush of treason. Consequently, the Republicans, the party that brought the country to the brink of a military disaster, emerged from the war more powerful than ever.

QUICK REVIEW

Prelude to War

◆ Republican-controlled Congress balked at strengthening military.

◆ Divided Congress declared war.

◆ Support for war strongest in the South and West.

WHAT WERE the consequences of the war of 1812?

• AMERICAN VIEWS •

FEDERALIST ANTIWAR RESOLUTIONS

s the policies of the Madison administration in the spring of 1812 increasingly pointed toward war against Great Britain, New England Federalists protested. Passed at a meeting in Providence, Rhode Island, on April 7, 1812, the following resolutions make the Federalist case against a war against Britain and reveal the depths of the party divisions over foreign policy.

WHY DID the Federalists accuse the Republicans of anti-British bias? What did the Federalists argue would be the results of a war against Britain? Why did the Federalists depict France as a greater threat to American freedoms than Britain?

Voted and Resolved unanimously.

That, in our opinion, the peace, prosperity and happiness of these United States, are in great jeopardy, inasmuch as, we have the strongest reasons to believe, the general government have determined to make war on Great-Britain. . . .

We are further confirmed in our apprehensions . . . by the evident partiality [the Republicans] have for a long time manifested towards one of the belligerents; and their deep-rooted enmity towards the other. The decrees of both nations equally violate our neutral rights; but France by her Berlin Decree, was the first aggressor; and still persists in capturing and burning our vessels on the high seas; and in robbing, imprisoning, and insulting our citizens; yet all these atrocities have been either palliated, or excused; while every effort has been made to excite the prejudices and animosities of our people against Great Britain. British vessels are excluded from our harbors; and our citizens are forbidden to import goods of the growth and manufacture of Britain and her dependencies; at the same time that French privateers are suffered to refit in American ports; and French goods are received, and protected, by our government. . . . All this, too, is done, when our trade to France, is of little value; and that to England, and her dependence is, of more importance to the United States, than with all the world besides.

Resolved, That . . . believing as we most sincerely do, that a war with England, at this time, is neither necessary, nor expedient, we deem it a duty which we owe to our families, and to our country, to use our utmost efforts to avert so great a calamity; and . . . we are of opinion that this expression ought to be given in the approaching elections. If we choose Democratic [Republican] State Rulers, we choose war; if we choose Federal State Rulers, we choose peace. . . .

But should we, forgetful of our duties, elect democratic rulers, and thereby let loose this wild spirit of war, what calamities, and horrors must spread themselves over those devoted States! All the taxes proposed must fall upon us; our foreign and coasting commerce be cut off; our fisheries be destroyed; our agriculture neglected. . . . The destruction of our navigation would interrupt, and we fear, ruin our numerous, and flourishing manufactories; for, when the enemies['] ships cover our coasts, we can neither obtain the necessary materials, nor export the manufactured goods.

But these evils are only the beginning of sorrows. When war arrives, what will give protections to our harbours and maritime towns? [The enemy] will . . . make a war of frequent, and sudden descent on our long, and defenceless sea-coast. Ships manned, and now moored on the other side of the Atlantic Ocean, can, in forty days, be riding on the waters of our bay and river. What could then save our sea-port towns, together with all the vessels in our harbours from conflagration, pillage, and military exaction?

Dreadful are these consequences of war: but more dreadful will await us. A war with England will bring us into alliance with France. This alliance would make the last page of our history as a nation. All the horrors of war might be endured; but who can endure to become a Slave?—If we are allied to that putrid pestilence of tyranny; our laws, freedom, independence, national name and glory, are blotted out from the memory of man—If Bonaparte sends to this country, ships, and French soldiers, and French generals, we shall soon be like Holland, and Italy, and Switzerland, and every other country where this scourge of nations has been permitted to set his foot.

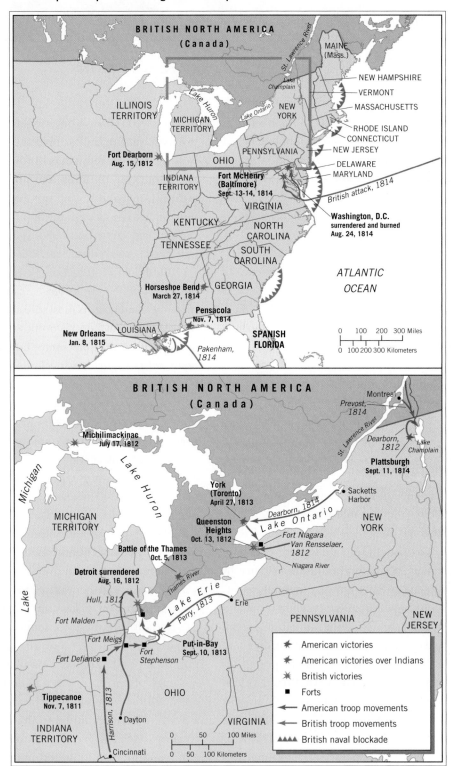

MAP 9–2

The War of 1812   Most of the battles of the War of 1812 were fought along the Canadian-American border, where American armies repeatedly tried to invade Canada. Despite the effectiveness of the British naval blockade, the American navy was successful in denying the British strategic control of the Great Lakes. Andrew Jackson's smashing victory at the Battle of New Orleans convinced Americans that they had won the war.

WHY WAS the successful British naval blockade not enough to secure a victory in the War of 1812?

SETBACKS IN CANADA

The outbreak of the **War of 1812** unleashed deep emotions that often divided along religious lines, with Federalists Congregationalists (mostly) opposing the war and the Baptists and Methodists favoring the war as "just, necessary, and indispensable." Fiercely loyal to Madison, who had championed religious freedom in Virginia, these Methodists and Baptists harbored old grudges against the established churches of both Britain and New England for suppressing their religious rights.

Madison hoped to channel this Christian, anti-British patriotism into the conquest of Canada. Assuming the Canadians would welcome the U.S. Army with open arms Madison expected American militia troops to overpower the small British force of five thousand soldiers that was initially stationed in Canada. By seizing Canada, Madison also hoped to weaken Britain's navy and undercut its navigation system by cutting off American foodstuffs and provisions from the British West Indies.

Madison's strategic vision was clear, but its execution was pathetic. Three offensives against Canada in 1812 were embarrassing failures. In the first, in July, General William Hull surrendered to a smaller British-Indian force.

The loss of Detroit and the abandonment of Fort Dearborn (present-day Chicago) exposed western settlements to the full fury of frontier warfare. Americans in the Indiana Territory fled outlying areas for the safety of forts in the interior. By the end of the year, the British controlled half of the Old Northwest.

Farther east, the Americans botched two offensives in 1812. In October, an American thrust across the Niagara River was defeated when a New York state militia refused to cross the river to join the regular army troops on the Canadian side. This left the isolated forces under General Stephen Van Rensselaer an easy prey for the British at the Battle of Queenston Heights. Then the long-delayed third offensive aimed at Montreal, the center of British operations in Canada, ended in a bloodless fiasco.

All the Republicans had to show for the first year of the war were morale-boosting but otherwise insignificant naval victories. The small American navy acquitted itself superbly in individual ship-to-ship combat.

Military setbacks and antiwar feelings in much of the Northeast hurt the Republicans in the election of 1812. Madison won only narrowly. The now familiar regional pattern in voting repeated itself with Madison sweeping the electoral vote of the South and West. He ran poorly in the Northeast and won only because his party held on to Pennsylvania.

WESTERN VICTORIES AND BRITISH OFFENSIVES

American forces fared better in 1813. In September, the navy won a major engagement on Lake Erie that opened up a supply line in the western theater. Commodore Oliver Hazard Perry attacked the British fleet in the **Battle of Put-in-Bay**, on the southwestern shore of the lake, and forced the surrender of all six British ships.

With the loss of Lake Erie, the British were forced to abandon Detroit. Demonstrating bold leadership and relying on battle-tested western militias, General William Henry Harrison won a decisive victory on the banks of the Thames River in Ontario. Tecumseh, the most visionary of the Indian warriors, was killed, and the backbone of the Indian resistance broken. The Old Northwest was again safe for American settlement.

A coalition of European powers forced Napoleon to abdicate in April 1814, thus freeing Britain to focus on the American war. British strategy in 1814 called

WHERE TO LEARN MORE

Perry's Victory and International Peace Memorial, Put-in-Bay, Ohio
www.nps.gov/pevi/

War of 1812   War fought between the United States and Britain from June 1812 to January 1815 largely over British restrictions on American shipping.

Battle of Put-in-Bay   American naval victory on Lake Erie in September 1813 in the War of 1812 that denied the British strategic control over the Great Lakes.

WHERE TO LEARN MORE

Fort McHenry National
Monument, Baltimore, Maryland
www.nps.gov/fomc/archeology/
overview.html

Treaty of Ghent Treaty signed in December 1814 between the United States and Britain that ended the War of 1812.

Battle of New Orleans Decisive American War of 1812 victory over British troops in January 1815 that ended any British hopes of gaining control of the lower Mississippi River Valley.

for two major offensives, an invasion south from Montreal down Lake Champlain in upstate New York and an attack on Louisiana aimed at seizing New Orleans with a task force out of Jamaica. The overall objective was nothing less than a reversal of America's post-1783 expansion.

The British attacks could hardly have come at a worse time for the Madison administration. The Treasury was nearly bankrupt. Against the wishes of Treasury Secretary Gallatin, Congress had refused to preserve the Bank of the United States when its charter expired in 1811. Lacking both a centralized means of directing wartime finances and any significant increase in taxes, the Treasury was forced to rely on makeshift loans. As the country's finances tottered toward collapse, political dissent in New England was reaching a climax. There was even talk of secession.

The darkest hour came in August 1814. A British amphibious force occupied and torched Washington, D.C. in retaliation for an American raid on York (now Toronto), the capital of Upper Canada. The defense of Washington was slipshod at best. Baltimore's defenses held, stirring Francis Scott Key, a young lawyer who viewed the bombardment from a British prisoner-of-war ship, to write "The Star Spangled Banner." Fittingly in this strange war, the future national anthem was set to the tune of a British drinking song.

The Chesapeake campaign was designed to divert American attention from the major offensive General George Prevost was leading down the shores of Lake Champlain. Prevost commanded the largest and best-equipped army the British had yet assembled, but he was forced to turn back when Commodore Thomas Macdonough defeated a British fleet on September 11 at the Battle of Plattsburgh. The British were now ready for peace, but one of their trump cards had yet to be played—the southern offensive against New Orleans.

THE TREATY OF GHENT AND THE BATTLE OF NEW ORLEANS

Although the British signed the **Treaty of Ghent** in December 1814, they were not irrevocably committed to the as yet nonratified peace settlement. The showdown between British and American forces at the **Battle of New Orleans** in January 1815 had immense strategic significance for the United States. The hero of New Orleans, in song and legend, was Andrew Jackson. A planter-politician from Tennessee, Jackson rose to prominence during the war as a ferocious Indian fighter. As a general in the Tennessee militia, Jackson crushed Indian resistance in the Old Southwest at the Battle of Horseshoe Bend in March 1814 and forced the vanquished Creeks to cede two-thirds of their territory to the United States. After his Indian conquests, Jackson was promoted to general in the regular army and given command of the defense of the Gulf Coast. In November 1814, he seized Pensacola in Spanish Florida and then hurried to defend New Orleans. The overconfident British frontally attacked Jackson's lines on January 8, 1815. The result was a massacre. More than two thousand British soldiers were killed or wounded while American casualties totaled twenty-one.

Strategically, Jackson's smashing victory at New Orleans ended any possibility of a British sphere of influence in Louisiana.

Creek war leader Red Eagle surrenders to Andrew Jackson after the Battle of Horseshoe Bend in 1814.

© Corbis

Politically, it was a deathblow to Federalism. As Americans were rejoicing with revived nationalism over the Treaty of Ghent and Jackson's routing of the British, the Federalists now seemed to be parochial sulkers who put regional interests above the national good.

THE ERA OF GOOD FEELINGS

In 1817, on the occasion of a presidential visit by James Monroe, a Boston newspaper proclaimed the **Era of Good Feelings**, an expression that nicely captured the spirit of political harmony and sectional unity that washed over the republic in the immediate postwar years. National pride surged with the humbling of the British at New Orleans, the demise of the Federalists lessened political tensions, and the economy boomed. The Republicans had been vindicated, and for a short time they enjoyed de facto status as the only governing party.

In 1819, however, an economic depression and a bitter controversy over slavery shattered the harmony, and the Republicans divided on sectional and economic issues.

ECONOMIC NATIONALISM

The War of 1812 had taught the Republicans to appreciate old Federalist doctrines on centralized national power. For Henry Clay and John Calhoun, leaders of a new generation of young nationalist Republicans, the first order of business was creating a new national bank. Introduced by Calhoun, the Bank bill passed Congress in 1816. Modeled after Hamilton's original Bank and also headquartered in Philadelphia, the **Second Bank of the United States** was capitalized at $35 million, making it by far the nation's largest bank. Its size and official status as the depository and dispenser of the government's funds, gave the Bank tremendous power over the economy.

After moving to repair the fiscal damage of the war, the Republicans then acted to protect what the war had fostered. In 1815 and again in 1816, the British inundated the American market with cheap imports to strangle American industry in its infancy. Responding to this challenge to the nation's economic independence, the Republicans passed the Tariff of 1816, the first protective tariff in American history. The act levied duties of 20 to 25 percent on manufactured goods that could be produced in the United States.

Revenue from the tariff and $1.5 million from the Bank of the United States were earmarked for internal improvements (roads and canals). The push for federal subsidies for transportation projects came from the War Department and the West. In early 1817, an internal improvements bill passed Congress. Despite the soaring rhetoric of John Calhoun, the bill's sponsor, seeking to "bind the republic together with a perfect system of roads and canals," President Madison remained unmoved. Though in agreement with the bill's objectives, he was convinced that the Constitution did not permit federal financing of primarily local projects. He vetoed the bill just before he left office.

Congressional passage of Calhoun's internal improvements bill marked the pinnacle of the Republicans' economic nationalism. Frightened by the sectional disunity of the war years, Republicans jettisoned many of the ideological trappings of Jefferson's original agrarian party. Their program was a call for economic, and therefore political, unity. Such unity was to be achieved through a generous program of national subsidies consisting of tariffs for manufacturers in the Northeast and transportation funds for planters and farmers in the South and West.

HOW DID nationalism increase during the Era of Good Feelings?

Era of Good Feelings   The period from 1817 to 1823 in which the disappearance of the Federalists enabled the Republicans to govern in a spirit of seemingly nonpartisan harmony.

Second Bank of the United States   A national bank chartered by Congress in 1816 with extensive regulatory powers over currency and credit.

OVERVIEW

TERRITORIAL EXPANSION UNDER THE REPUBLICANS

Benchmark	Year	Land Area of United States and Its Territories (square miles)
Republicans gain power	1801	864,746
Louisiana Purchase	1803	1,681,828
Trans-Continental Treaty	1819	1,749,462

Support for this program was strongest in the Mid-Atlantic and Western states, the regions that stood to gain the most economically. Opposition centered in the Southeast and took on an increasingly hard edge in the South as the Supreme Court outlined an ever more nationalist interpretation of the Constitution.

JUDICIAL NATIONALISM

Under Chief Justice John Marshall, the Supreme Court had long supported the nationalist perspective that Republicans began to champion after its war. A Virginia Federalist whose nationalism was forged during his service in the Revolutionary War, Marshall dominated the Court throughout his tenure (1801–1835) by his forceful personality and the logical power of his nationalist convictions. The defining principles of Marshall's jurisprudence were the authority of the Supreme Court in all matters of constitutional interpretation and the sanctity of contractual property rights. In *Fletcher v. Peck* (1810), the Court overturned a Georgia law by ruling that it violated the prohibition in the federal Constitution against any state "impairing the obligation of contracts."

In *Dartmouth College v. Woodward* (1819), the Court ruled that Dartmouth's original royal charter of 1769 was a contract protected by the Constitution. The ruling prohibited states from interfering with the rights and privileges they had bestowed on private corporations.

In *McCulloch v. Maryland* (1819), a unanimous Court, in language similar to but even more sweeping than that used by Alexander Hamilton in the 1790s, upheld the constitutional authority of Congress to charter a national bank and thereby regulate the nation's currency and finances. As long as the end was legitimate "within the scope of the Constitution," Congress had full power to use any means not expressly forbidden by the Constitution to achieve that end. Here was the boldest statement to date of the loose or "implied powers" interpretation of the Constitution.

TOWARD A CONTINENTAL EMPIRE

Marshall's legal nationalism paralleled the diplomatic nationalism of John Quincy Adams, secretary of state from 1817 to 1825. A former Federalist and the son of the second president, Adams broke with the Federalist party over its refusal to support an expansionist policy. Adams made few friends as a negotiator but he was an effective diplomat, using whatever tactics were necessary to realize his vision of an America that stretched from the Atlantic to the Pacific.

Adams shrewdly exploited the British desire for friendly and profitable relations after the War of 1812. The **Rush-Bagot Agreement** of 1817 signaled the new pattern of Anglo-American cooperation. The agreement strictly limited naval armaments on the Great Lakes, thus effectively demilitarizing the border. The

Fletcher v. Peck Supreme Court decision of 1810 that overturned a state law by ruling that it violated a legal contract.

Dartmouth College v. Woodward Supreme Court decision of 1819 that prohibited states from interfering with the privileges granted to a private corporation.

Rush-Bagot Agreement Treaty of 1817 between the United States and Britain that effectively demilitarized the Great Lakes by sharply limiting the number of ships each power could station on them.

Anglo-American Accords of the following year resolved a number of issues left hanging after the war. Of great importance to New England, the British once again recognized American fishing rights off Labrador and Newfoundland. The boundary of the Louisiana Territory abutting Canada was set at the 49th parallel.

Having secured the northern flank of the United States, Adams was now free to deal with the South and West. Adams wanted all of Florida and an undisputed American window on the Pacific. The adversary here was Spain. In March 1818, Jackson led his troops across the border into Spanish Florida in an attempt to stop Indian raids in the Alabama-Georgia frontier. He destroyed the encampments of the Seminole Indians, seized two Spanish forts, and executed two British subjects. Despite later protestations to the contrary, Jackson had probably exceeded his orders. He might well have been censured by the Monroe administration had Adams not taken the offensive by lecturing Spain that Jackson was acting in the defense of American interests and warning that he might be unleashed again.

Spain yielded to the American threat in the **Trans-Continental Treaty of 1819** (see Map 9–3 on page 234). The United States annexed East Florida, and Spain recognized the prior American seizures of West Florida in 1810 and 1813. Adams secured an American hold on the Pacific Coast by drawing a boundary between the Louisiana Purchase and the Spanish Southwest.

Adams's success in the Spanish negotiations turned on the British refusal to threaten war or assist Spain in the wake of Jackson's highhanded actions in Florida. Spanish possessions and the lives of two British subjects were worth little when weighed against the economic advantages of retaining close trading ties with the United States. Moreover, Britain had a vested interest in the Latin American market opened by the loss of Spain's monopoly.

Adams was confident that within a generation, the United States would acquire California, Texas, and perhaps Cuba as well. He wanted to maintain the maximum freedom of action for future U.S. policy and avoid any impression that America was beholden to Britain. Thus originated the most famous diplomatic statement in early American history, the **Monroe Doctrine**. In his annual message to Congress in December 1823, Monroe declared that the Americas "are henceforth not to be considered as subjects for future colonization by any European power." In turn, Monroe pledged that the United States would not interfere in the internal affairs of European states.

THE BREAKDOWN OF UNITY

For all the intensity with which he pursued his continental vision, John Quincy Adams worried in early 1819 that "the greatest danger of this union was in the overgrown extent of its territory, combining with the slavery question." His words were prophetic. A sectional crisis flared up in 1819 over slavery and its expansion when the territory of Missouri sought admission to the Union as a slave state. Simultaneously, a financial panic ended postwar prosperity and crystallized regional discontent over banking and tariff policies. Party unity cracked under these pressures, and each region backed its own presidential candidate in the wide-open election of 1824.

THE PANIC OF 1819

From 1815 to 1818, Americans enjoyed a wave of postwar prosperity. European markets were starved for American goods after a generation of war and trade restrictions, and farmers and planters met that demand by expanding production and bringing new land into cultivation. Before the bubble burst, cotton prices doubled to 30 cents a pound, real estate values became wildly inflated, and the money Westerners owed the federal government for the purchase of public lands rose to $21 million, an amount greater than the value of all western farm goods.

Anglo-American Accords Series of agreements reached in the British-American Conventions of 1818 that fixed the western boundary between the United States and Canada, allowed for joint occupation of Oregon, and restored American fishing rights.

Trans-Continental Treaty of 1819 Treaty between the United States and Spain in which Spain ceded Florida to the United States, surrendered all claims to the Pacific Northwest, and agreed to a boundary between the Louisiana Purchase territory and the Spanish Southwest.

Monroe Doctrine In December 1823, Monroe declared to Congress that the Americas "are henceforth not to be considered as subjects for future colonization by any European power."

WHAT WAS the Missouri Compromise?

MAP EXPLORATION

To explore an interactive version of this map, go to **http://www.prenhall.com/goldfield2/map9.3**

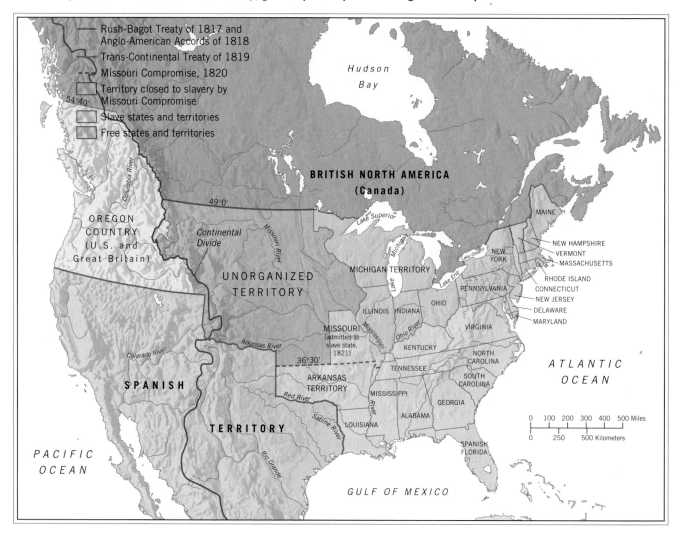

MAP 9–3

The Missouri Compromise of 1820 and Territorial Treaties with Britain and Spain, 1818–1819 Treaties with Britain and Spain in 1818 and 1819 clarified and expanded the nation's boundaries. Britain accepted the 49th parallel as the boundary between Canada and the United States in the Trans-Mississippi West to the Oregon Country; Spain ceded Florida to the United States and agreed to a boundary stretching to the Pacific between the Louisiana Purchase territory and Spanish possessions in the Southwest. Sectional disputes over slavery led to the drawing of the Missouri Compromise line of 1820 that prohibited slavery in the Louisiana Territory north of 36°30′.

HOW DID the treaties with Spain and Britain of 1818 and 1819 and the Missouri Compromise of 1820 geographically change the United States?

European markets for American cotton and food supplies returned to normal by late 1818. In January 1819, cotton prices sank in England, and the Panic of 1819 was on. The fall in cotton prices triggered a credit contraction that soon engulfed the overextended American economy. A sudden shift in policy by the Bank of the United States virtually guaranteed that the economic downturn would settle into a depression as the Bank stopped all loans, called in all debts, and refused to honor drafts drawn on its branches in the South and West. Hardest hit by these policies were farmers and businessmen in the West, who had mortgaged their economic futures. Bankruptcies mushroomed as creditors forced the liquidation of farms and real estate.

In addition to resenting the hard times brought on by low cotton prices, Southerners saw an ominous pattern of unchecked and unconstitutional federal power emerging in the form of high tariffs, the judicial nationalism of the Supreme Court, and Northern efforts to interfere with slavery in Missouri. If Northerners, they asked, could stretch the Constitution to incorporate a bank or impose a protective tariff, what could prevent them from emancipating the slaves?

THE MISSOURI COMPROMISE

Until 1819, slavery had not been a major divisive issue in American politics. The Northwest Ordinance of 1787, which banned slavery in federal territories north of the Ohio River, and the Southwest Ordinance of 1790, which permitted slavery south of the Ohio, represented a compromise that had allowed slavery in areas where climate and soil conditions favored slave-based agriculture. What was unforeseen in the 1780s, however, was the explosive demand for slave-produced cotton generated by the English textile industry in the early nineteenth century. By 1819, Kentucky, Tennessee, Louisiana, Mississippi, and Alabama had all been added to the Union as slave states. Florida was expected to be another slave state, and even Missouri, a portion of the Louisiana Purchase, had fallen under the political control of slaveholders.

The Missouri issue increased long-simmering Northern resentment with the spread of slavery and the Southern dominance of national affairs under the Virginia presidents. In February 1819, James Tallmadge, a Republican congressman from New York, introduced an amendment in the House mandating a ban on future slave importations and a program of gradual emancipation as preconditions for the admission of Missouri as a state. Missourians, as well as Southerners in general, rejected the Tallmadge Amendment as completely unacceptable, arguing that any attempt by Congress to set conditions for statehood was unconstitutional. Without a two-party system in which each of the parties had to compromise to protect its intersectional interests, voting followed sectional lines. The Northern-controlled House passed the amendment, but it was repeatedly blocked in the Senate, where there were eleven free and eleven slave states.

The stalemate persisted into the next session of Congress. Finally, Speaker of the House Henry Clay engineered a compromise in March 1820. Congress put no restrictions on slavery in Missouri, and the admission of Missouri as a slave state was balanced by admitting Maine (formerly part of Massachusetts) as a free state. In return for their concession on Missouri, northern congressmen obtained a prohibition on slavery in the remainder of the Louisiana Purchase north of the 36°30′ parallel, the southern boundary of Missouri (see Map 9–3 on page 234).

The compromise almost unraveled when Missouri submitted a constitution the next November that required the state legislature to bar the entry of free black people. This mandate violated the guarantee in the U.S. Constitution that "the citizens of each State shall be entitled to all privileges and immunities of citizens in the several States." The nearly universal acceptance of white Americans of second-class citizenship for free black Americans permitted Clay to dodge the issue. Missouri's constitution was accepted with the proviso that it "shall never be construed" to discriminate against citizens in other states. In short, with meaningless words that begged the issue of Missouri's defiance of the federal Constitution, the **Missouri Compromise** was salvaged. At the cost of ignoring the claims of free black people

9–5
Thomas Jefferson Reacts to the "Missouri Question" (1820)

QUICK REVIEW

Tallmadge Amendment

◆ Tallmadge Amendment (1819): ban on future slave importations and imposition of program of gradual emancipation as condition of Missouri statehood.

◆ Passed by the House but rejected by the Senate.

◆ Voting broke down on regional lines.

Missouri Compromise Sectional compromise in Congress in 1820 that admitted Missouri to the Union as a slave state and Maine as a free state and prohibited slavery in the northern Louisiana Purchase territory.

FROM THEN TO NOW
The Lewis and Clark Expedition in Their World and Ours

In its day the Lewis and Clark expedition was as daring a venture as space exploration is today. The expedition, which began in 1803, ended in 1806, and lasted 863 days, brought Americans their first knowledge of the vast territory they had secured in the Louisiana Purchase. Traveling more than seven thousand miles by foot, boat, and horseback from St. Louis to the Pacific Coast and back, the explorers compiled a detailed record of their experiences and observations. In these journals they have bequeathed to us a vivid picture of the natural environment of the trans-Mississippi West before white settlement.

The West described by Lewis and Clark was a land of change, diversity, and abundance. The Missouri River that their party of forty-five followed to the north and west up to central Montana was wild and unpredictable. Its currents were ceaselessly eroding its banks, forming and displacing sandbars, and cutting new channels as they deposited soil eroded from the Rocky Mountains onto its immense floodplain. Today, a series of dams has tamed the river, controlling floods, generating electricity, and diverting water for irrigation. But the dams have had unforeseen consequences. The fertile sediments the Missouri once deposited on its floodplain, replenishing the soil in the farm states of the midwest, now flow into the Gulf of Mexico. As Midwesterners learned in the summer of 1993, the levees and retaining walls that confine the river can sometimes result in floods far more disastrous than ever occurred under natural conditions.

Lewis and Clark passed through regions of incredible biological diversity and abundance. They catalogued 122 animals and 178 plants that were new to American science. Traveling through present-day South Dakota in September, 1804, Lewis observed "Vast herds of Buffaloe deer elk and Antilopes . . . feeding in every direction as far as the eye of the observer could reach." Upon seeing the salmon in the Columbia River in 1805, Clark wrote that their numbers were "almost inconceivable."

Before the end of the nineteenth century, the great herds of grazing animals in the West and the carnivores that stalked them had nearly been wiped out by government-sponsored extermination programs. The industrialization of the Pacific Northwest in the twentieth century reduced the natural habitat essential for the spawning and rearing of salmon, and their numbers fell sharply. Even more striking, most of the vast prairie landscape that Lewis and Clark crossed from the Mississippi Valley to the Rocky Mountains has disappeared, replaced by uniform fields of row-to-row crops. The prairie grasslands were once the largest ecosystem in North America, a patchwork of native grasses and herbs that supported a wide diversity of habitats.

Lewis and Clark were hardly romantic sentimentalists. Their West was dangerous and threatening, and their supplies included the latest in scientific equipment. They fully shared American notions of progress, and they carefully noted locations that were favorably situated for settlement. Still, the West they saw often left them with a sense of awe. For Lewis, the White Cliffs of the Missouri River in Montana were a spectacle "of visionary enchantment." He described the Great Falls of the Missouri as "the grandest sight I ever beheld."

The journals of Lewis and Clark provide a baseline from which to gauge how much the West has changed, putting Americans in a better position to preserve what is left and even restore some of what has been lost.

In commemoration of their epic expedition, President George W. Bush designated 2003 through 2006 as the Lewis and Clark Bicentennial. Beginning at Monticello in January 2003, a series of bicentennial events will highlight key dates and stages in the expedition and allow the public to gain a sense of how their journey unfolded. For information on these events, access the website listed in Web Resources.

for equal treatment as citizens, the Union survived its first great sectional crisis over slavery.

The Missouri crisis made white Southerners realize that they were now a distinct political minority within the Union. More rapid population growth in the North had reduced Southern representation in the House to just over 40 percent. Of greater concern was the crystallization in Congress of a Northern majority arraigned against the expansion of slavery.

THE ELECTION OF 1824

The election of 1820 made Monroe, like both his Republican predecessors, a two-term president. Voters had no choice in 1820, and without two-party competition, no outlets existed for expressing popular dissatisfaction with the Republicans. Instead, the Republicans split into factions as they began jockeying almost immediately for the election of 1824 (see Map 9–4).

The politics of personality dominated Monroe's second administration. Monroe had no obvious successor, and five candidates competed to replace him. All of them (Secretary of War Calhoun, Secretary of the Treasury William Crawford, Secretary of State John Quincy Adams, Henry Clay and Andrew Jackson) were nominal Republicans, and three were members of his cabinet.

None of the candidates ran on a platform, but Crawford was identified with states' rights and Clay and Adams with centralized government. Clay in particular was associated with the national bank, protective tariffs, and federally funded internal improvements, a package of federal subsidies he called the **American System**. Jackson took no stand on any of the issues.

Jackson's noncommittal stance turned out to be a great asset. It helped him project the image of a military hero fresh from the people who was unsullied by any connection with Washington politicians, whom the public associated with hard times and sectional controversies. He was the highest vote getter (43 percent of the popular vote), but none of the four candidates had a majority in the electoral college.

As in 1800, the election was thrown into the House of Representatives. Anxious to undercut Jackson, his chief rival in the West, Clay used his influence as speaker of the House to line up support for Adams, a fellow advocate of a strong centralized government.

Adams won the election, and he immediately named Clay as his secretary of state, the office traditionally viewed as a stepping-stone to the presidency. Jackson and his followers were outraged. They smelled a "corrupt bargain" in which Clay had bargained away the presidency to the highest bidder. Vowing revenge, they began building a new party that would usher in a more democratic era of mass-based politics.

CONCLUSION

In 1800, the Republicans were an untested party whose coming to power frightened many Federalists into predicting the end of the Union and constitutional government. The Federalists were correct in sensing that their days of power had passed, but they underestimated the ideological flexibility the Republicans would reveal once in office and the imaginative ways in which Jefferson and his successors would wield executive power to expand the size of the original Union. Far from being anarchists and demagogues, the Republicans were shrewd empire builders astute enough to add to their base of political support in the South and West. They also paved the way for the nation to evolve as a democratic republic rather than the more aristocratic republic preferred by the Federalists.

American System The program of government subsidies favored by Henry Clay and his followers to promote American economic growth and protect domestic manufacturers from foreign competition.

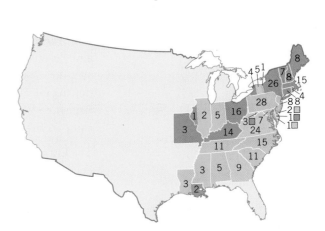

	Electoral Vote (%)	Popular Vote (%)
Andrew Jackson (Republican)	99 (38)	153,544 (43)
JOHN QUINCY ADAMS (Republican)	**84 (32)**	**108,740 (31)**
William H. Crawford (Republican)	41 (16)	46,618 (13)
Henry Clay (Republican)	37 (14)	47,136 (13)

MAP 9–4
The Election of 1824 The regional appeal of each of the four presidential candidates in the election of 1824 prevented any candidate from receiving a majority of the electoral vote. Consequently, and as set forth in the Constitution, the House of Representatives now had to choose the president from the three leading candidates. Its choice was John Quincy Adams.

WHAT DOES this map suggest about the political climate in the United States in 1824?

By the mid-1820s, with no Federalist threat to enforce party discipline, the Republicans lost their organizational strength. Embracing economic nationalism after the war made the party's original focus on states' rights all but meaningless. But the party left as its most enduring legacy the foundations of a continental empire.

SUMMARY

Jefferson's Presidency Thomas Jefferson believed that a true revolution had occurred in 1800, a peaceful overthrow of the Federalist party. Unlike Federalists, Jeffersonian Republicans wanted an agrarian republic based on widespread economic equality for white yeomen farmers. The cornerstone of his Republican policy was retrenchment, a return to the frugal, simple federal establishment. His foreign policy successes included the Louisiana Purchase; however, his Embargo Act of 1807 crippled his presidency in its final year.

Madison and the Coming of War Early in his administration, Madison became convinced that the impasse in Anglo-American relations was about to be broken. Mounting frustrations in the South and West also pushed Madison toward a war against Britain. On the eve of war Madison had to deal with the pan-Indian resistance movement and the Battle of Tippecanoe. And, as war with Britain seemed imminent, the war cries of the War Hawks pushed the nation ever closer to the brink.

The War of 1812 In 1812, Republicans in a divided Congress led the nation into a war it was unprepared to fight. Internal dissent endangered the Union almost as much as the British. Early losses to the British in Canada were embarrassing defeats for Madison; however, later battles saw U.S. victories despite a successful British naval blockade. The final and decisive battle (the Battle of New Orleans) came in 1815 as Andrew Jackson led the United States to victory in the war.

The Era of Good Feelings In 1817 a Boston newspaper proclaimed the Era of Good Feelings, a spirit of political harmony in the postwar years. Henry Clay and John Calhoun, having learned to appreciate old Federalist doctrines on centralized national power, created the Second Bank of the United States. And, after moving to repair the fiscal damage of the War of 1812, Republicans then acted to protect what the war had fostered through tariffs. Nationalism also took hold in the form of judicial nationalism in several landmark Supreme Court rulings. Finally, diplomatic nationalism paved the way for expanding the United States through treaties with Britain and Spain.

The Breakdown of Unity In 1819, an economic depression and a bitter controversy over slavery shattered the harmony, and Republicans divided on sectional and economic issues. Sinking prices for American products overseas led to the Panic of 1819. Soon the economic panic led Southerners to worry about the North's emancipation powers. The slavery controversy was partly quelled by the Missouri Compromise. And, in 1824, John Quincy Adams became president in an election that effectively ended the unity in the Republican party.

REVIEW QUESTIONS

1. What changes did the Republicans bring to the federal government? How did their policies differ from those of their Federalist predecessors?

2. Why did the United States go to war against Britain? Could this war have been avoided?

3. Why was the war widely viewed as a great American victory despite several defeats? How did the war lead to increased diplomatic cooperation between the United States and Britain?

4. Why did nationalism increase in the Era of Good Feelings? Why did Republican party unity collapse after 1819?

KEY TERMS

American System (p. 237)
Anglo-American Accords (p. 233)
Chesapeake **Incident** (p. 223)
Dartmouth College v. *Woodward*
(p. 232)
Embargo Act of 1807 (p. 224)
Era of Good Feelings (p. 231)
Fletcher v. *Peck* (p. 232)

Ghent, Treaty of (p. 230)
Marbury v. *Madison* (p. 220)
Missouri Compromise (p. 235)
Monroe Doctrine (p. 233)
New Orleans, Battle of (p. 230)
Pan-Indian resistance movement
(p. 225)
Put-in-Bay, Battle of (p. 229)

Rush-Bagot Agreement (p. 232)
Second Bank of the United States
(p. 231)
Trans Continental Treaty of 1819
(p. 233)
War Hawks (p. 225)
War of 1812 (p. 229)

WHERE TO LEARN MORE

☐ **Monticello, Charlottesville, Virginia.** The architecturally unique home of Thomas Jefferson and the headquarters for his plantation serves as a museum that provides insights into Jefferson's varied interests. Information on educational programs and upcoming events at Monticello, as well as the new Jefferson Library in Charlottesville, can be found at: **www.monticello.org/**

☐ **Montpelier, Montpelier Station, Virginia.** The museum here was the home of James Madison, and it includes material on his life as a politician and planter. Its website at **www.montpelier.org/** provides information on tours and programs and a look at the archeological findings at Montpelier.

☐ **Tippecanoe Battlefield Museum, Battle Ground, Indiana.** This museum includes artifacts from the Indian and white settlement of Indiana and visual materials on the Battle of Tippecanoe of 1811. The museum's website at **www.tcha.mus.in.us/battlefield.htm** includes an account of the battle and its aftermath.

☐ **Perry's Victory and International Peace Memorial, Put-in-Bay, Ohio.** At the site of Perry's decisive victory on Lake Erie in 1813 now stands a museum that depicts the role of the Old Northwest in the War of 1812. For a printable travel guide and information on the new visitor center, see: **www.nps.gov/pevi/**

☐ **Fort McHenry National Monument, Baltimore, Maryland.** This historic site preserves the fort that was the focal point of the British attack on Baltimore and contains a museum with materials on the battle and the writing of "The Star-Spangled Banner." For the military history of the fort and the archeological work at the site, see: **www.nps.gov/fomc/archeology/overview.html**

 For additional study resources for this chapter, go to:
www.prenhall.com/goldfield/chapter9

I blush for my country when I see such things, and I often tremble with apprehension that our Constitution will not long withstand the current which threatens to overwhelm it . . .

Andrew Jackson speaking to a crowd after his election. Politics in the olden time—General Jackson, President-elect, on his way to Washington.

10

THE JACKSONIAN ERA
1824–1845

WHAT MADE Andrew Jackson so popular among ordinary Americans?

HOW WERE free black people and women disenfranchised in the 1820s and 1830s?

WHAT SOCIAL, political, and economic events led to the creation of the Whig party?

HOW DID the Whigs come to dominate American politics?

WHAT DID the Whigs achieve while in power?

Newport, New Hampshire
September, 1828

Wherever a person may chance to be in company, he will hear nothing but politicks discussed. In the ballroom, or at the dinner table, in the Stage-coach & in the tavern; even the social chitchat of the tea table must yield up to the everlasting subject.

How many friendships are broken up! With what rancor the political war is carried on between the editorial corps! To what meanness[.] vulgarity & abuse is that champion of liberty, in proper hands, the press prostituted! With what lies and scandal does the columns of almost every political paper abound! I blush for my country when I see such things, & I often tremble with apprehension that our Constitution will not long withstand the current which threatens to overwhelm it. Our government is so based that an honest difference between American citizens must always exist. But the rancorous ex-citement which now threatens our civil liberties and a dissolution of this Union does not emanate from an honest difference of opinion, but from a de-termination of an unholy league to trample down an Administration, be it ever so pure, & be its acts ever so just. It must not be. There is a kind Provi-dence that overlooks the destinies of this Nation and will not suffer it to be overthrown by a party of aspiring office seekers & political demagogues.

—*Benjamin B. French*

Donald B. Cole and John J. McDonough, eds., *Witness to the Young Republic: A Yankee's Jour-nal*, 1828–1870 (Hanover, N. H.: University Press of New England, 1989), pp. 15–16.

IMAGE KEY

for pages 240–241

a. $5 note of the Second Bank of the United States.

b. Andrew Jackson speaking to a crowd after his election.

c. Cherokee Indian newspaper.

d. An old, antique Bible bound in leather with a gold cross on the front cover.

e. General Andrew Jackson portrait by Thomas Sully.

f. Americans endure poverty and unemployment by drinking, begging, and rioting in the streets of a city during the 1837 Specie Panic.

g. A banner for William Henry Harrison and John Tyler features political slogans of the Log Cabin campaign above the date of the rally.

BENJAMIN BROWN FRENCH, a young editor and county clerk in Newport, New Hampshire, penned these words in his journal in September 1828. Like most other Americans, he was amazed by the intense partisanship stirred up in the presidential election of 1828 between Andrew Jackson and John Quincy Adams. Whether mea-sured by the vulgar personal attacks launched by a partisan press, the amount of whiskey and beef consumed at political barbecues, or the huge increase in voter turnout, this election marked the entrance of ordinary Americans onto the political stage.

The partisanship that French found so disturbing in 1828 quickly became the basis of his livelihood. After joining the Democrats in 1831, he held a variety of ap-pointive jobs in Washington, first as a Democratic and then, after breaking with the Democrats in the 1850s over slavery, in Republican administrations until his death in 1870.

What had made possible French's career was the democratization of American politics. The number and potential power of the voters expanded, and party success depended on reaching and organizing this enlarged electorate. Men like French, working for the party, could help them do this. The "Jacksonian Democrats," named for their leader Andrew Jackson, were the first party to learn this fundamental lesson. They won a landslide victory in 1828 and held national power through the 1830s. The Jacksonians promised to protect farmers and workers from the monied elite.

The Whig party, formed in opposition to the Jacksonians in the mid 1830s offered an ordered vision of American progress and liberty, anchored in the use of governmental power to expand economic opportunities and promote morality. Their capture of the presidency in 1840s heralded a new party system based on massive voter turnouts and two-party competition in every state.

However, the Whigs's newly elected president, William Henry Harrison, died shortly after entering office, and Vice President John Tyler, his successor, blocked their economic program. Spurned by the Whigs as a traitor, Tyler then reopened the explosive question of slavery and territorial expansion by pushing to annex Texas, where slavery was legal.

The Democrats regained power in 1844 by exploiting the Texas issue, but debates over the expansion of slavery became embedded in the political system, and the mass-based parties' ability to tap and unleash popular emotions now became their greatest weakness. Party leaders lost control of the slavery issue. The seeds of the Civil War were being sown.

THE EGALITARIAN IMPULSE

Political democracy, defined as the majority rule of white males, was far from complete in early-nineteenth-century America. Legal barriers prevented the full expression of majority sentiments. Property requirements for voting and officeholding, the prevalence of appointed over elected offices, and the overrepresentation of older and wealthier regions in state legislatures came under increasing attack after 1800 and were all but eliminated by the 1820s.

As politics opened to mass participation, popular styles of religious leadership and worship erupted in a broad reaction against the formalism and elitism of the dominant Protestant churches. The same egalitarian impulse drove these twin democratic revolutions, and both movements represented an empowerment of the common man. (Women would have to wait longer.)

HOW WERE free black people and women disenfranchised in the 1820s and 1830s?

THE EXTENSION OF WHITE MALE DEMOCRACY

In 1816, Congress voted itself a hefty pay raise, which seemed prudent and justified. The public thought otherwise. The citizens of Saratoga, New York, resolved that Congress was guilty of "wanton extravagance" and "a daring and profligate trespass against . . .the *morals* of the *Republic*."

So sharp was the reaction against the Salary Act of 1816 that 70 percent of the members of Congress were turned out of office at the next election. Congress quickly repealed the salary increase, but not before John C. Calhoun spoke for many in Congress when he plaintively asked, "Are we bound in all cases to do what is popular?" The answer was apparently yes. As Richard M. Johnson of Kentucky noted, "The presumption is, that the people are always right." The uproar over the Salary Act marked a turning point in the transition from the deferential politics of the Federalist-Republican period to the egalitarianism of the Jacksonian era. The public would no longer passively accept decisions handed down by local elites or established national figures.

Individual states, not the federal government, defined who could vote. Six states—Indiana, Mississippi, Illinois, Alabama, Missouri, and Maine—entered the Union between 1816 and 1821, and none of them required white male voters to own property. Constitutional conventions in Connecticut in 1818 and Massachusetts and New York in 1821 eliminated longstanding property requirements for voting. By the end of the 1820s, universal white male suffrage was the norm everywhere except Rhode Island, Virginia, and Louisiana.

Representation in most state legislatures was made more equal by giving more seats to newer, rapidly growing regions in the backcountry. States removed

QUICK REVIEW

Salary Act of 1816
- Congress voted itself pay raise.
- Outraged public rejects 70 percent of incumbents at next election.
- Conflict represents turn toward the politics of Jacksonian era.

or reduced property qualifications for officeholding. The selection of local officials and, in many cases, judges was taken out of the hands of governors and executive councils and given to the voters in popular elections. With the end of oral or "stand-up" voting, the act of casting a ballot became more private and freer from the intimidation of influential neighbors. Written ballots were the norm by the 1820s. Most significant for national politics, voters acquired the power to choose presidential electors. In 1800, only two states had provided for a statewide popular vote in presidential elections; by 1832 only South Carolina still clung to the practice of having the state legislature choose the electors.

Several currents swelled the movement for democratic reform. Limiting voting rights to those who owned landed property seemed increasingly elitist when economic changes were producing new classes—workers, clerks, and small tradesmen—whose livelihoods were not tied directly to the land. Propertyless laborers in Richmond argued in an 1829 petition that "virtue [and] intelligence are not among the products of the soil. Attachment to property, often a sordid sentiment, is not to be confounded with the sacred flame of patriotism."

Of greatest importance, however, was the incessant demand that all white men be treated equally. Seth Luther, an advocate for workers' rights, insisted that "we wish nothing, but those equal rights, which were designed for us all." This demand for equality was the logical extension of the ideology of the American Revolution. Only the will of the majority could be the measure of a republican government.

As political opportunities expanded for white males, they shrank for women and free black people. New Jersey's constitution of 1776 was exceptional in also granting the suffrage to single women and widows who owned property. By the early 1800s, race and gender began to replace wealth and status as the basis for defining the limits of political participation. Thus when New Jersey's new constitution in 1807 broadened suffrage by requiring only a simple taxpaying qualification to vote, it specifically denied the ballot to women and free black men. None of the ten states that entered the Union from 1821 to 1861 allowed black suffrage. African Americans protested in vain. "Foreigners and aliens to the government and laws," complained New York blacks in 1837, "strangers to our institutions, are permitted to flock to this land and in a few years are endowed with all the privileges of citizens; but we *native* born Americans . . .are most of us shut out." By the 1850s, black males could vote only in certain New England states.

Advocates of greater democratization explicitly argued that only white males had the rational intelligence and love of liberty necessary to be entrusted with political rights. Women were too weak and emotional, black people too lazy and lascivious. The white egalitarians simultaneously erected new distinctions based on race and sex that were supposedly natural and hence immutable. Thus personal liberties were now to be guarded by all white men, whose equality ultimately rested on assumptions of their shared political superiority over women and nonwhites.

THE POPULAR RELIGIOUS REVOLT

In a blaze of fervor known as the **Second Great Awakening**, evangelical sects led by the Methodists and Baptists radically transformed the religious landscape between 1800 and 1840. A more popularly rooted Christianity moved outward and downward as it spread across frontier areas and converted marginalized and common folk. By 1850, one in three Americans was a regular churchgoer, a dramatic increase since 1800.

The Baptists and Methodists were the largest religious denominations by the 1820s. The key to their success was their ability to give a religious expression

Second Great Awakening   Series of religious revivals in the first half of the nineteenth century characterized by great emotionalism in large public meetings.

to the same popular impulse behind democratic reform. Especially in the back-country of the South and West, where the first revivals occurred, itinerant preachers reshaped religion to fit the needs and values of ordinary Americans.

Evangelical Christianity emphasized personal, heartfelt experience that would produce a spiritual rebirth. Preaching became a form of theater in which scenes of damnation and salvation were acted out by both preacher and audience. "The scene that then presented itself to my mind was indescribable," recalled James Finley of the camp meeting at Cane Ridge, Kentucky, in 1801. "At one time I saw at least five hundred swept down in a moment, as if a battery of a thousand guns had been opened upon them, and then immediately followed shrieks and shouts that rent the very heavens."

Salvation no longer passively depended on an implacable God as taught by the Calvinist doctrine of individual predestination. Ordinary people could now actively choose salvation, and this possibility was exhilarating. "Why, then, I can be saved!" exclaimed Jesse Lee upon hearing a Methodist preacher in Massachusetts. "I have been taught that only a part of the race could be saved, but if this man's singing be true, all may be saved." Evangelical churches bound the faithful into tightly knit communities that expressed and enforced local values and standards of conduct. Their hymns borrowed melodies from popular music and were accompanied by fiddles and other folk instruments.

The revivals converted about twice as many women as men. Church membership offered them, as the wife of a Connecticut minister explained, a welcome release from "being treated like beasts of burden [and] drudges of domineering masters." In the first flush of evangelical excitement, female itinerant preachers spread the gospel up and down the East Coast. Other women organized their own institutions within denominations still formally controlled by men. Women activists founded and largely directed hundreds of church-affiliated charitable societies and missionary associations.

Evangelicalism also empowered black Americans. Baptists and Methodists welcomed slaves at their revivals, encouraged preaching by blacks, and, above all else, advocated secular and spiritual equality. Many of the early Baptist and Methodist preachers directly challenged slavery. In converting to Methodism, one slave stated that "from the sermon I heard, I felt that God had made all men free and equal, and that I ought not be a slave."

But for all its liberating appeal to women and African Americans, evangelicalism was eventually limited by race and gender in much the same way as the democratic reform movement. Denied positions of authority in white-dominated churches and resentful of white opposition to integrated worship, free black Northerners founded their own independent churches. Southern evangelical attacks on slavery were replaced by a full-blown religious defense of it. Just as southern Protestant ministers rested their proslavery case on the biblical sanctioning of human bondage, they also used the Old Testament patriarchs to shore up the position of fathers as the unquestioned authority figures in their households, the masters of slaves, women, and children. Many popular religious sects in the North also used a particular reading of the Bible in the same way.

In religion as well as politics, white men still held the power in Jacksonian America. Still, the Second Great Awakening removed a major intellectual barrier to political democracy. Traditional Protestant theology—whether Calvinist, Anglican, or Lutheran—viewed the mass of humanity as sinners predestined to damnation. In rejecting this theology, ordinary Americans made a fundamental breakthrough in intellectual thought. "Salvation open to all" powerfully reinforced the legitimacy of "one man, one vote."

This 1845 painting captures the heroic, forceful side of Andrew Jackson that made him so appealing to many voters.

Thomas Sully, *General Andrew Jackson*, 1845. Oil on canvas. In the Collection of The Corcoran Gallery of Art, Washington, D.C. Gift of William Wilson Corcoran

Democratic party   Political party formed in the 1820s under the leadership of Andrew Jackson; favored states' rights and a limited role for the federal government.

Albany Regency   The tightly disciplined state political machine built by Martin Van Buren in New York.

THE RISE OF THE JACKSONIANS

At the core of the Jacksonian appeal was the same rejection of established authority that was the hallmark of the secular and religious populists. By tapping into the hopes and fears of ordinary Americans the Jacksonians built the first mass-based party in American history.

In Andrew Jackson the new **Democratic party** that formed between 1824 and 1828 had the perfect candidate for the increasingly democratic temperament of the 1820s. Born of Scots-Irish ancestry on the Carolina frontier in 1767, Jackson was a self-made product of the southern backcountry. Lacking any formal education, family connections, or inherited wealth to ease his way, he relied on his own wits and raw courage to carve out a career as a frontier lawyer and planter in Tennessee. He won fame as the military savior of the republic with his victory at the Battle of New Orleans. Conqueror of the British, the Spanish, and the Indians, all of whom had blocked frontier expansion, he achieved incredible popularity in his native South. His strengths and prejudices were those most valued by the restless, mobile Americans to whom he became a folk hero.

Jackson lost the election of 1824, but his defeat turned out to be a blessing in disguise. The wheeling and dealing in Congress that gave the presidency to John Quincy Adams enveloped that administration in a cloud of suspicion from the start. It also enhanced Jackson's appeal as the honest tribune of the people. His supporters now claimed that the people, as well as Jackson, had been swindled by the "corrupt bargain" between Adams and Clay.

The ill-fated Adams presidency virtually destroyed itself. Though the same age as Jackson, Adams seemed frozen in an eighteenth-century past in which gentlemanly statesmen were aloof from the people.

Adams revealed how out of touch he was when he delivered his first annual message to Congress in 1825. He presented a bold vision of an activist federal government promoting economic growth, social advancement, and scientific progress. The Jacksonians charged that an administration born in corruption now wanted to waste the people's money by promoting more corruption and greed. They also pounced on Adams's political gaffe of urging Americans not to "proclaim to the world that we are palsied by the will of our constituents." Besides being depicted as the tool of the Northeastern monied interests, Adams was attacked as an arrogant aristocrat contemptuous of the common man.

Little of Adams's program passed Congress, and his nationalist vision drove his opponents into the Jackson camp. Southern planters jumped onto the Jackson bandwagon out of fear that Adams might use federal power against slavery; more Westerners joined because Adams revived their suspicions of the East. The most important addition came from New York, where Martin Van Buren had built the **Albany Regency**, a tightly disciplined state political machine.

Van Buren was a new breed of politician. The son of a tavern keeper, he became a professional who made a business out of politics. The discipline and regularity of strict party organization gave him a winning edge in competition against his social betters. In battling against the system of family-centered wealth and prestige on which politics had previously been based, Van Buren redefined parties as indispensable instruments for the successful expression of the popular will against the dominance of elites.

CHRONOLOGY

1826	Disappearance of William Morgan.
1827	Emergence of the Anti-Masons, the first third party.
1828	Andrew Jackson elected president. John Calboun writes *The South Carolina Exposition and Protest.*
1830	Congress passes the Indian Removal Act.
1831	William Lloyd Garrison starts publication of *The Liberator.* Nat Turner leads a slave uprising in Virginia.
1832	Jackson vetoes bill for rechartering the Second Bank of the United States; Bank War begins. South Carolina nullifies the Tariffs of 1828 and 1832. Jackson reelected.
1833	Congress passes the Force Act and the Compromise Tariff. American Anti-Slavery Society established.
1834	Whig party begins to organize.
1836	Texas War of Independence and establishment of the Republic of Texas. Congress passes first gag rule on abolitionist petitions. Van Buren elected president.
1837	Panic of 1837 sets off a depression.
1840	Independent Treasury Act passes. William Henry Harrison elected as first Whig president.
1841	John Tyler succeeds to presidency on death of Harrison.
1842	United States and Britain sign the Webster-Ashburton Treaty.
1844	Polk elected president. Gag rule repealed.
1845	Texas admitted to the Union.

State leaders such as Van Buren organized the first national campaign that relied extensively on new techniques of mass mobilization. In rallying support for Jackson against Adams in 1828, they put together chains of party-subsidized newspapers and coordinated a frantic schedule of meetings and rallies. Grass-roots Jackson committees reached out to the voters by knocking on their doors, pressing party literature into their hands, dispensing mass-produced medals and buttons with a likeness of Jackson, and lavishly entertaining all who would give them a hearing.

The election of 1828 centered on personalities, not issues. This in itself was a victory for Jackson's campaign managers, who proved far more skillful in image making.

Jackson carried every state south and west of Pennsylvania in 1828 and polled 56 percent of the popular vote. Voter turnout shot up to 55 percent from the apathetic 25 percent of 1824. Adams ran well only in New England and in commercialized areas producing goods for outside markets. Aside from the South, where he was virtually untouchable, Jackson's appeal was strongest among ordinary Americans who valued their local independence and felt threatened by outside centers of power beyond their control. He rolled up heavy majorities from Scots-Irish farmers in the Baptist-Methodist evangelical belt of the backcountry and unskilled workers with an Irish Catholic background.

JACKSON'S PRESIDENCY

Once in office, Jackson tolerated no interference from his subordinates. At one time or another, his administration angered Southern planters, frightened Eastern bankers and commercial interests, and outraged New England reformers. Nonetheless, Jackson remained popular because he portrayed himself as the embodiment of the people's will.

WHAT MADE Andrew Jackson so popular among ordinary Americans?

WHERE TO LEARN MORE

★ The Hermitage,
Hermitage, Tennessee
www.thehermitage.com/

10–4
The " Commoner" Takes Office
(1828)

10–5
Andrew Jackson, First Annual
Message to Congress (1829)

Bank War   The political struggle
between President Andrew Jackson
and the supporters of the Second
Bank of the United States.

Nullification crisis   Sectional crisis
in the early 1830s in which a states'
rights party in South Carolina
attempted to nullify federal law.

Spoils system   The awarding of
government jobs to party loyalists.

The Jacksonians had no particular program in 1828. Two political struggles
that came to a head in 1832–1833—the **Bank War** and the **nullification crisis**—
stamped the Jacksonians with a lasting party identity. By destroying the Second
Bank of the United States and rejecting the attempt of South Carolina to nullify
(or annul) a national tariff, Jackson firmly established the Democrats as the enemy
of special privilege, the friend of the common man, and the defender of the Union.

THE JACKSONIAN APPEAL

Jackson's inauguration struck many conservatives as ushering in a vulgar new order
in national affairs. A vast crowd poured into Washington to applaud their hero.
They cheered loudly when Jackson took his oath of office and then rushed to the
White House for a postinauguration reception. Bowls of liquor-laced punch went
flying, and glass and china crashed to the floor as a seeming mob surged through
the White House. "But it was the People's day," reported one conservative on-
looker, "and the People's President and the People would rule. God grant that
one day or other, the People do not put down all rule and rulers."

Jackson proclaimed his task as one of restoring the federal government to
the ideal of Jeffersonian republicanism, in which farmers and artisans could
pursue their individual liberty free of any government intervention that favored
the rich and powerful. Jackson began his assault on special privilege by proclaiming a reform of the appointment process for federal officeholders. Accusing his predecessors, especially Adams, of having created a social elite of
self-serving bureaucrats, he vowed to make government service more responsive to the popular will. He insisted that federal jobs required no special expertise or training and proposed to rotate honest, hard-working citizens in and
out of the civil service.

In reality, Jackson removed only about one-fifth of the officeholders he inherited, and most of his appointees came from the same relatively high status
groups as the Adams people, but he opened the way for future presidents to move
more aggressively against incumbents by providing a democratic rationale for government service. Thus emerged the **spoils system**, in which the victorious party gave
government jobs to its supporters and removed the appointees of the defeated
party, tying party loyalty to the reward of a federal appointment.

When Jackson railed against economic privilege, he had in mind Henry
Clay's American System, which called for a protective tariff, a national bank, and
federal subsidies for internal improvements. Clay's goal was to bind Americans
together in an integrated national market. To the Democrats, Clay's system represented government favoritism at its worst, a set of costly benefits at the public's
expense for special-interest groups. In 1830, Jackson struck a blow for the Democratic conception of the limited federal role in economic development. He vetoed the Maysville Road Bill, which would have provided federal money for a road
to be built entirely within Kentucky. The bill was unconstitutional, he claimed,
because it benefited only the citizens of Kentucky and not the American people
as a whole. Moreover, since the Maysville project was within Clay's congressional
district, Jackson also embarrassed his most prominent political enemy.

Jackson's Maysville veto did not rule out congressional appropriations for
projects deemed beneficial to the general public. This pragmatic loophole allowed Democrats to pass more internal improvement projects during Jackson's presidency than during all of the previous administrations together.

Jackson's strongest base of support was in the West and South. By driving
Native Americans from these regions, he enhanced his appeal as the friend of the
common (white) man.

INDIAN REMOVAL

Some 125,000 Indians lived east of the Mississippi when Jackson became president. Five Indian confederations—the Cherokees, Creeks, Choctaws, Chickasaws, and Seminoles— controlled millions of acres of land in the Southeast that white farmers coveted for their own economic gain.

Pressure from the states to remove the Indians had been building since the end of the War of 1812. It was most intense in Georgia. In early 1825, Georgia authorities finalized a fraudulent treaty that ceded most of the Creek Indians' land to the state.

For the Cherokees, the *Trail of Tears* stretched 1,200 miles from the homeland in the East to what became the Indian Territory in Oklaoma.

The Granger Collection, New York

When Adams tried to obtain fairer terms for the Creeks in a new treaty, he was brazenly denounced in Georgia. Not willing to risk an armed confrontation between federal and state authorities, Adams backed down.

In 1828, Georgia moved against the Cherokees. By now a prosperous society of small farmers with their own written alphabet and schools for their children, the Cherokees wanted to avoid the fate of their Creek neighbors. In 1827, they adopted a constitution declaring themselves an independent nation with complete sovereignty over their land. The Georgia legislature reacted by placing the Cherokees directly under state law, annulling Cherokee laws and even their right to make laws, and legally defining the Cherokees as tenants on land belonging to the state of Georgia. By also prohibiting Indian testimony in cases against white people, the legislature stripped the Cherokees of any legal rights. They were now easy prey for white settlers, who scrambled onto Cherokee land after gold was discovered in northern Georgia in 1829. Alabama and Mississippi followed Georgia's lead in denying Indians legal rights.

The stage was set for what Jackson always considered the most important measure of his first administration, the **Indian Removal Act**. Jackson allowed state officials to override federal protection of Native Americans. In his first annual message, Jackson sided with state authorities in the South and advised the Indians "to emigrate beyond the Mississippi or submit to the laws of those States." This advice enabled Jackson to pose as the friend of the Indians, the wise father who would lead them out of harm's way and save them from rapacious white people. Congress acted on Jackson's recommendation in the Indian Removal Act of 1830. The act appropriated $500,000 for the negotiation of new treaties under which the Southern Indians would surrender their territory and be removed to land in the trans-Mississippi area (primarily present day Oklahoma). Although force was not authorized and Jackson stressed that removal should be voluntary, no federal protection was provided for Indians harassed into leaving by land-hungry settlers. Ultimately, Jackson did deploy the U.S. Army, but only to round up and push out Indians who refused to comply with the new removal treaties.

And so most of the Indians were forced out of the Eastern United States— the Choctaws in 1830, the Creeks and Chickasaws in 1832, and the Cherokees in

QUICK REVIEW

Georgia and the Cherokees

◆ Georgia stole land of Creek Indians in 1825.

◆ Georgia moved against Cherokees in 1828, stripping them of all legal rights.

◆ Stage was set for Indian Removal Act.

Indian Removal Act President Andrew Jackson's measure that allowed state officials to override federal protection of Native Americans.

1838 (see Map 10–1). The private groups who won the federal contracts for transporting and provisioning the Indians were a shady lot interested only in making a quick buck. Thousands of Indians, perhaps as many as one-fourth of those who started the trek, died on the way to Oklahoma, the victims of cold, hunger, disease, and the general callousness of whites they met along the way. "It is impossible to conceive the frightful sufferings that attend these forced migrations," noted a Frenchman who observed the Choctaw removal. It was indeed, as recalled in the collective memory of the Cherokees, a **Trail of Tears**.

Federal troops joined local militias in 1832 in suppressing the Sauk and Fox Indians of Illinois and Wisconsin in what was called **Black Hawk's War**. This affair ended in the slaughter of five hundred Indian men, women, and children by white troops and their Sioux allies. The Seminoles held out in the swamps of Florida for seven years between 1835 and 1842 in what became the longest Indian war in American history. Their resistance continued even after their leader, Osceola, was captured while negotiating under a flag of truce.

Aligned with conservatives concerned by Jackson's cavalier disregard of federal treaty obligations, eastern reformers and Protestant missionaries came with-

Trail of Tears　The forced march in 1838 of the Cherokee Indians from their homelands in Georgia to the Indian Territory in the West.

Black Hawk's War　Short 1832 war in which federal troops and Illinois militia units defeated the Sauk and Fox Indians led by Black Hawk.

 MAP EXPLORATION

To explore an interactive version of this map, go to
http://www.prenhall.com/goldfield2/map10.1

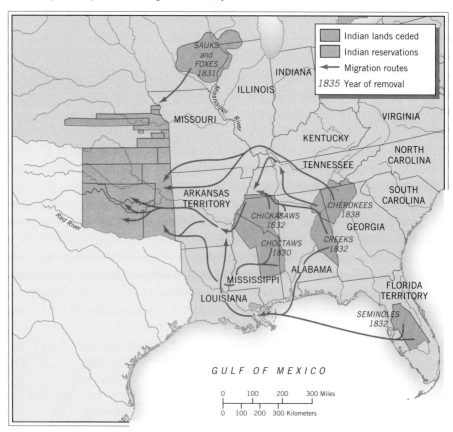

MAP 10–1

Indian Removals　The fixed policy of the Jackson administration and pressure from the states forced Native Americans in the 1830s to migrate from their Eastern homelands to a special Indian reserve west of the Mississippi River.

WHY DO you think the Indian reservations are located west of the Mississippi?

in three votes of defeating the removal bill in the House of Representatives. Jackson ignored their protests as well as the legal rulings of the Supreme Court. (*See* American Views: Memorial and Protest of the Cherokee Nation, 1836. p. 252) In *Cherokee Nation* v. *Georgia* (1831) and *Worcester* v. *Georgia* (1832), the Court ruled that Georgia had violated the U.S. Constitution in extending its jurisdiction over the Cherokees. Chief Justice Marshall defined Indian tribes as "dependent domestic nations subject only to the authority of the federal government. But Marshall was powerless to enforce his decisions without Jackson's cooperation. Jackson ignored the Supreme Court rulings and pushed Indian removal to its tragic conclusion.

THE NULLIFICATION CRISIS

Jackson's stand on Indian removal confirmed the impression of many of his followers that on issues of centralized power, Jackson could be trusted to take the states' rights position. The most sensitive issue involving the power of the national government concerned tariffs. States' rights forces in South Carolina directly challenged Jackson in the early 1830s over tariff policy. After the first protective tariff in 1816, rates increased further in 1824 and then jumped to 50 percent in 1828 in what was denounced as the "Tariff of Abóminations." Southerners were especially angry over the last tariff because it had been contrived by Northern Democrats to win additional Northern support for Jackson's presidential campaign. What fueled antitariff sentiment was not just the economic argument that high tariffs worsened the agricultural depression in the state. Protective tariffs were also denounced as an unconstitutional extension of national power over the states; many southern planters feared that it was only a prelude to forced emancipation.

South Carolina was the only state where African Americans made up the majority of the population. In the marshes and tidal flats south of Charleston, South Carolina, the lowcountry district of huge rice plantations, blacks outnumbered whites ten to one in the summer months. Nat Turner's Rebellion, a bloody slave uprising in Virginia in 1831, and earlier aborted rebellions in the 1820s (see Chapter 13) left fearful planters convinced that growing antislavery agitation in the North and in England was feeding slave unrest. Turner's revolt and renewed talk of emancipation would be "nothing to what we shall see," warned the South Carolina planter James Hamilton Jr., "if we do not stand manfully at the Safety Valve of Nullification."

Led by the lowcountry planters, the antitariff forces in South Carolina controlled state politics by 1832. They called themselves the nullifiers, a name derived from the constitutional theory developed by Calhoun in an anonymous tract of 1828 entitled *The South Carolina Exposition and Protest.* Calhoun argued that a state, acting through a popularly elected convention, had the sovereign power to declare an act of the national government null and inoperative. Once a state nullified a law, it was to remain unenforceable within that state's borders unless three-fourths of all the states approved a constitutional amendment delegating to the national government the power that was challenged. If such an amendment passed, the nullifying state had the right to leave the Union.

Calhoun, who had been elected Jackson's vice president in 1828, openly embraced nullification only after he had broken with the president. Jackson felt betrayed by Calhoun and vowed political revenge. With Calhoun's approval, a South Carolina convention in November 1832 nullified the tariffs of 1828 and 1832 and decreed that customs duties were not to be collected in South Carolina after February 1, 1833.

Calhoun always insisted that nullification was not secession. He defended his doctrine as a constitutional means of protecting minority rights within a Union

WHERE TO LEARN MORE

Rice Museum,
Georgetown, South Carolina
www.ricemuseum.com/

QUICK REVIEW

**Fear of Rebellion
and Northern Intentions**

◆ African Americans were majority of South Carolina's population.

◆ Rebellions convinced planters that anti-slavery movement was feeding slave unrest.

◆ Southerners feared that protective tariffs were a prelude to emancipation.

• AMERICAN VIEWS •

MEMORIAL AND PROTEST OF THE CHEROKEE NATION, 1836

O f the major tribes in the Southeast, the Cherokees fought longest and hardest against the Jacksonian policy of Indian removal. Led by their principal chief, John Ross, the son of a Scot and a mixed-blood Cherokee woman, they submitted the following protest to Congress against the fraudulent 1835 Treaty of New Echota forced on them by the state of Georgia. Although clearly opposed by an overwhelming majority of the Cherokees, this treaty provided the legal basis for the forced removal of the Cherokee people from Georgia to the Indian Territory.

ON WHAT legal grounds did the Cherokees base their protest? What pledges had been made to them by the U.S. government? What did the Cherokees mean when they said they had been "taught to think and feel as the American citizen"? If the Cherokees had become "civilized" by white standards, why did most whites still insist on their removal? Why would President Jackson have allowed white intruders to remain on land reserved by treaties for the Cherokees? Were the Cherokees justified in believing that they had been betrayed by the American government?

The undersigned representatives of the Cherokee nation, east of the river Mississippi, impelled by duty, would respectfully submit . . .the following statement of facts: It will be seen, from the numerous treaties between the Cherokee nation and the United States, that from the earliest existence of this government, the United States, in Congress assembled, received the Cherokees and their nation into favor and protection; and that the chiefs and warriors, for themselves and all parts of the Cherokee nation, acknowledged themselves and the said Cherokee nation to be under the protection of the United States of America, and of no other sovereign whatsoever: they also stipulated, that the said Cherokee nation will not hold any treaty with any foreign power, individual State, or with individu-

als of any State: that for, and in consideration of, valuable concessions made by the Cherokee nation, the United States solemnly guaranteed to said nation all their lands not ceded, and pledged the faith of the government, that "all white people who have intruded, or may hereafter intrude, on the lands reserved for the Cherokees, shall be removed by the United States, and proceeded against, according to the provisions of the act, passed 30th March, 1802," entitled "An act to regulate trade and intercourse with the Indian tribes, and to preserve peace on the frontiers." It would be useless to recapitulate the numerous provisions for the security and protection of the rights of the Cherokees, to be found in the various treaties between their nation and the United States. The Cherokees were happy and prosperous under a scrupulous observance of treaty stipulations by the government of the United States, and from the fostering hand extended over them, they made rapid advances in civilization, morals, and in the arts and sciences. Little did they anticipate, that when taught to think and feel as the American citizen, and to have with him a common interest, they were to be despoiled by their guardian, to become strangers and wanderers in the land of their fathers, forced to return to the savage life, and to seek a new home in the wilds of the far west, and that without their consent. An instrument purporting to be a treaty with the Cherokee people, has recently been made public by the President of the United States, that will have such an operation, if carried into effect. This instrument, the delegation aver before the civilized world, and in the presence of Almighty God, is fraudulent, false upon its face, made by unauthorized individuals, without the sanction, and against the wishes, of the great body of the Cherokee people. Upwards of fifteen thousand of those people have protested against it, solemnly declaring they will never acquiesce.

Source: U.S. Congress, *Executive Documents* (1836)

dominated by a tyrannical national majority. Jackson rejected such reasoning as the talk of a scheming disunionist and vowed to crush any attempt to block the enforcement of federal laws. He told a congressman from South Carolina that "if a single drop of blood shall be shed there in opposition to the laws of the United States, I will hang the first man I can lay my hand on engaged in such treasonable conduct, upon the first tree I can reach."

In January 1833, Jackson received full Congressional authorization in the Force Act to put down nullification by military force. Simultaneously, he worked to defuse nullification by supporting a new tariff that would cut duties by half within two years. Because Jackson's opponents in Congress did not want him to get political credit for brokering a compromise, they pushed through their own tariff measure. The Compromise Tariff of 1833 lowered duties to 20 percent but extended the reductions over a ten-year period. Up against this combination of the carrot and the stick, the nullifiers backed down.

Jackson's stand established the principle of national supremacy grounded in the will of the majority. Despite his victory, however, states' rights doctrines remained popular both in the South and among many Northern Democrats. Many Southerners, and especially slaveholders, agreed that the powers of the national government had to be strictly limited. By dramatically affirming his right to use force against a state in defense of the Union, Jackson drove many planters out of the Democratic party. In the shock waves set off by the nullification crisis, a new anti-Jackson coalition began to form in the South.

THE BANK WAR

What amounted to a war declared by Jackson against the Bank of the United States became the centerpiece of his presidency and a defining event for the shaping of the Democratic party. Like most Westerners, Jackson distrusted banks. As a result of the scarcity of gold and silver coins and the absence of any paper currency issued and regulated by the national government, money consisted primarily of notes issued as loans by private and state banks. These bank notes fluctuated in value in accordance with the reputation and credit worthiness of the issuing banks. In the credit-starved West, many banks were "wildcat" operations that made a quick profit by issuing notes without the gold or silver reserves to redeem them and then skipping town when they were on the verge of being found out. Even when issued by honest bankers, notes often could not be redeemed at face value because of market conditions. All of this struck many Americans, and especially farmers and workers, as inherently dishonest. They wanted to be paid in "real" money, gold or silver coin, and they viewed bankers suspiciously.

The largest and most powerful bank was the Bank of the United States, and citizens who were wiped out or forced to retrench drastically by the Panic of 1819 never forgave the Bank for saving itself at the expense of its debtors. Still, prosperous times had returned, and the Bank underwrote the economic expansion with its healthy credit reserves and stable banknotes.

Beginning with his first annual message, Jackson had been making noise about not rechartering the Bank. In the presidential campaign of 1832, Clay then forced Jackson's hand and convinced Bank president Nicholas Biddle to apply to Congress for a new charter. Clay reasoned that he had Jackson trapped. If Jackson went along with the new charter, Clay could take credit for the measure. If he vetoed it, Clay could attack Jackson as the enemy of a sound banking system.

Clay's clever strategy backfired. Jackson turned on Clay and the Bank with a vengeance. As he told his heir apparent, "The bank, Mr. Van Buren, is trying to kill me, *but I will kill it!*" On July 10, 1832, Jackson vetoed the rechartering bill for

This Democratic cartoon portrays Jackson as the champion of the people attacking the Bank of the United States, a many-headed monster whose tentacles of corruption spread throughout the states.

"General Jackson caricature slaying the many-headed monster," 1836. Courtesy of Collection of The New York Historical Society

QUICK REVIEW

Jackson and the Bank of the United States

- Jackson and most Westerners distrusted banks.
- Jackson talked about not rechartering the Bank of the United States.
- Struggle over future of Bank ended with victory for Jackson at expense of Democrats image.

the Bank in a message that appealed both to state bankers and to foes of all banks. He took a ringing "stand against all new grants of monopolies and exclusive privileges, against any prostitution of our Government to the advancement of the few at the expense of the many."

The business community and Eastern elites in general lashed out at Jackson's veto as the demagogic ravings of an economic fool. For Biddle, the veto message had "all the fury of a chained panther, biting the bars of his cage." But Jackson won the political battle, and he went to the people in the election of 1832 as their champion against the banking aristocracy. Although his support was no stronger than in 1828, he easily defeated Clay, the candidate of the short-lived National Republican party that had also backed Adams in 1828.

Having blocked the rechartering of the Bank when Congress failed to override his veto, Jackson then set out to destroy it. He claimed that the people had given him a mandate to do so by reelecting him in 1832. He finally found a secretary of the treasury (his first two choices refused) who agreed to sign the order removing federal deposits from the Bank in 1833. The government's monies were deposited in "pet banks," state banks controlled by loyal Democrats.

Jackson won the Bank War, but he left the impression that the Democrats had played fast and loose with the nation's credit system. In his second term, high commodity prices and abundant credit, both at home and abroad, propelled a buying frenzy of western lands. Prices soared, and inevitably the speculative bubble had to burst. Jackson was out of office when the Panic of 1837 hit; Van Buren, his successor, paid the political price for Jackson's economic policies.

VAN BUREN AND HARD TIMES

Like John Adams and James Madison, Martin Van Buren followed a forceful president who commanded a strong popular following. Where Jackson forged ahead regardless of consequences, Van Buren tended to hang back, carefully calculating all the political angles. Facing a sharp economic downturn, Van Buren appeared indecisive and unwilling to advance a bold program. When the rise of a radical abolitionist movement in the North revived sectional tensions over slavery, he awkwardly straddled the middle of the divisive issue. In the end, he undermined himself by failing to offer a compelling vision of just what he wanted his presidency to be.

THE PANIC OF 1837

Van Buren was barely settled into the White House when the nation was rocked by a financial panic. For over a decade, the economy had benefited from easy credit and the availability of Western territories opened up by Jackson's Indian removal policy. Government land sales ballooned from under 4 million acres in 1833 to 20 million acres by 1836. As in 1817 and 1818, Americans piled up debt. A banking crisis in 1837 painfully reintroduced economic reality.

Even as it expanded, the American economy had remained vulnerable to disruptions in the supply of foreign capital and the sale of agricultural exports. The key foreign nation was Britain, a major source of credit and demand for exports. In late 1836, the Bank of England tightened its credit policies. Concerned with the large outflow of specie to the United States, it raised interest rates and reduced the credit lines of British merchants heavily involved in the American trade. Consequently, the British demand for cotton fell and with it the price of cotton. Because cotton, as the leading export, was the main security for most loans is-

WHAT SOCIAL, political, and economic events led to the creation of the Whig party?

WHERE TO LEARN MORE

Martin Van Buren National Historic Site, Kinderhook, New York

www.nps.gov/mava/home.htm

sued by American banks and mercantile firms, its drop in value set off a chain reaction of contracting credit and falling prices. When panic-stricken investors rushed to the banks to redeem their notes in specie, the hard-pressed banks suspended specie payments.

The shock waves hit New Orleans in March 1837 and spread to the major New York banks by May. What began as a bank panic soon dragged down the entire economy. Bankruptcies multiplied, investment capital dried up, and business stagnated. State governments slashed their budgets and halted all construction projects. Nine states in the South and West defaulted (stopped making payments) on their bonds. Workers in the shoe, textile, mining, and construction industries suddenly found themselves without jobs. "Workmen thrown out of employ by the hundreds daily," nervously noted a wealthy merchant in New York City in May 1837. He half expected that "we shall have a revolution here."

After a brief recovery in 1838, another round of credit contraction drove the economy into a depression that did not bottom out until 1843. In the manufacturing and commercial centers of the Northeast, unemployment reached an unheard-of 20 percent. The persistence of depressed agricultural prices meant that farmers and planters who had incurred debts in the 1830s faced the constant threat of losing their land or their slaves. Many fled west to avoid their creditors.

THE INDEPENDENT TREASURY

Although the Democrats bore no direct responsibility for the economic downturn, their political opponents, now coalescing as the **Whig party**, pinned the blame on Jackson's destruction of the Bank of the United States. In their view, Jackson had then compounded his error by trying to force a hard-money policy on the state banks that had received federal deposits.

Jackson had taken his boldest step against paper money when he issued the **Specie Circular** of 1836, which stipulated that henceforth large blocks of public land could be bought only with specie. The Specie Circular likely contributed to the Panic of 1837 by requiring the transfer of specie to the West for land transactions just when Eastern banks were strapped for specie reserves to meet demands on their own bank notes. Bankers and speculators denounced Jackson for unwarranted government interference with the natural workings of the economy and blundering into a monetary disaster.

By dramatically politicizing the banking issue and removing federal monies from the national bank, the Democrats had in effect assumed the burden of protecting the people from the paper aristocrats in the banking and business community. Once they shifted treasury receipts to selected state banks, they had to try to regulate these banks. But even the "pet banks" joined in the general suspension of specie payments when the Panic of 1837 hit. Thus the banks favored by the Democrats proved themselves unworthy of the people's trust.

Van Buren reestablished the Democrats' tarnished image as the party of limited government when he came out for the **Independent Treasury System**. Under this plan, the government would dispense with banks entirely. The Treasury would conduct its business only in gold and silver coin and would store its specie in regional vaults or subtreasuries.

The Independent Treasury System passed Congress in 1840 and restored the ideological purity of the Democrats as the friends of honest money, but it prolonged the depression. Specie locked up in government vaults was unavailable for loans in the private banking system that could expand the credit needed to revive the economy. The end result was to reduce the money supply and put even more downward pressure on prices.

Whig party Political party, formed in the mid-1830s in opposition to the Jacksonian Democrats, that favored a strong role for the national government for promoting economic growth.

Specie Circular Proclamation issued by President Andrew Jackson in 1836 stipulating that only gold or silver could be used as payment for public land.

Independent Treasury System Fiscal arrangement first instituted by President Martin Van Buren in which the federal government kept its money in regional vaults and transacted its business in hard money.

Gag rule   A procedural device
whereby antislavery petitions were
automatically tabled in Congress
with no discussion.

HOW DID the Whigs come to
dominate American politics?

Second Party System   The national
two-party competition between
Democrats and Whigs from
the 1830s through the early 1850s.

UPROAR OVER SLAVERY

In 1831, the year that Nat Turner led a slave uprising in Virginia, William Lloyd Garrison of Boston inaugurated a radical new phase in Northern attacks on slavery with the publication of his abolitionist paper *The Liberator*. The abolitionists embraced the doctrine of *immediatism*, an immediate moral commitment to begin the work of emancipation. Inspired by the wave of religious revivals sweeping the North in the late 1820s, they called upon all Americans to recognize their Christian duty of ending a system of human bondage that deprived the enslaved of their God-given right to be free moral beings. (For more on the abolitionists, see Chapter 14.)

Most white Southerners ignored the abolitionists until 1835, the year that the abolitionists produced over a million pieces of antislavery literature, much of which was sent to the South through the U.S. mails. Alarmed whites vilified the abolitionists as fanatics intent on enticing the slaves to revolt. Abolitionist tracts were burned, and, with the open approval of Jackson, Southern postmasters violated federal law by censoring the mails to keep out antislavery materials.

Beginning in 1836 and continuing through Van Buren's presidency, hundreds of thousands of antislavery petitions, some of them with thousands of signatures, flooded into Congress. Most of them called for the abolition of slavery in the District of Columbia. Southern congressmen responded by demanding that free speech be repressed with the **gag rule**, a procedural device whereby antislavery petitions were automatically tabled with no discussion.

The gag rule first passed in 1836. With Van Buren's reluctant support, it became a Democratic party measure, and it identified the Democrats as a prosouthern party in the minds of many Northerners. Ironically, while Van Buren was attacked in the North as a lackey of the slave interests, he was damned in the South as a nonslaveholder from the North. His fate was to be cast as a vacillating president fully trusted by neither section.

THE RISE OF THE WHIG PARTY

The Bank War and Jackson's reaction to nullification shook loose pro-Bank Democrats and many Southern states' righters from the original Jacksonian coalition, and these groups joined the opposition to Jackson. By 1834, the anti-Jacksonians started to call themselves Whigs, a name associated with the eighteenth-century American and British opponents of monarchical tyranny.

By 1840, the Whigs had mastered the techniques of political organization and mobilization pioneered by the Democrats in the late 1820s. They ran William Henry Harrison, their own version of a military hero, and swept to victory. The **second party system** of intense national competition between Whigs and Democrats was now in place (see the overview table "The Second Party System"). It would dominate politics until the rise of the antislavery Republican party in the 1850s.

THE PARTY TAKING SHAPE

The Whig party was born in the congressional reaction to Jackson's Bank veto and his subsequent attacks on the national bank. Led by the unlikely trio of Henry Clay and Daniel Webster, nationalists from the West and New England, and John C. Calhoun, a states' righter from the South, the congressional opposition accused Jackson of demagogic appeals to the poor against the rich. What upset them was the way Jackson wielded his executive power like a bludgeon. Whereas all earlier presidents together had used the veto only ten times, Jackson did so a dozen times. He openly defied the Supreme Court and Congress. To his opponents, Jackson was threatening to undermine the constitutional system of checks and balances.

OVERVIEW
THE SECOND PARTY SYSTEM

	Democrats	Whigs
Ideology	Favor limited role of federal government in economic affairs and in matters of individual conscience: support territorial expansion	Favor government support for economic development and controls over individual morality; opposed to expansion
Voter support	Mainly subsistence farmers, unskilled workers, and Catholic immigrants	Mainly manufacturers, commercial farmers, skilled workers, and Northern evangelicals
Regional strength	South and West	New England and Upper Midwest

Local and state coalitions of the Whigs sent an anti-Jackson majority to the House of Representatives in 1835. The most powerful of these coalitions was in New York, where a third party, the **Anti-Masons**, joined the Whigs. The party had originated in western New York in the late 1820s as a grass-roots response to the sudden disappearance and presumed murder of William Morgan, an itinerant artisan who threatened to expose the secrets of the Order of Freemasons. An all-male order steeped in ritual and ceremony, the Masons united urban and small-town elites into a tightly knit brotherhood of personal contacts and mutual aid. Rumors spread that the Masons constituted a vast conspiracy that conferred special privileges and legal protection on its exclusive members. Farmers and townspeople flocked to the new Anti-Masonic party, seeking, in the words of an 1831 Anti-Masonic address, "equal rights and equal privileges among the freemen of the country."

Despite spreading into New England and the neighboring Mid-Atlantic states, the Anti-Masons were unable to sustain themselves as a separate party. Shrewd politicians, led by Thurlow Weed and William Seward of New York, took up the movement and absorbed most of it into the anti-Jackson coalition. They thus broadened the Whigs' mass base and added an egalitarian message to their appeal.

By 1836, the Whigs were strong enough to mount a serious challenge for the presidency. They ran three candidates—Webster of Massachusetts, William Henry Harrison of Ohio, and Hugh Lawson White of Tennessee—and some Whigs hoped that the regional popularity of these candidates would siphon off enough votes from Van Buren to throw the election into the House of Representatives. But Van Buren won an electoral majority by holding on to the populous Mid-Atlantic states and improving on Jackson's showing in New England. Still, the Whigs were encouraged by the results. Compared to Jackson, Van Buren did poorly in what had been the overwhelmingly Democratic South, which was now open to further Whig inroads.

WHIG PERSUASION

The Whigs, like the Democrats, based their mass appeal on the claim that they could best defend the republican liberties of the people. They attributed the threat to those liberties to the expansive powers of the presidency as wielded by Jackson and in the party organization that put Jackson and Van Buren into office. In 1836, the Whigs called for the election of "a president of the *nation*, not a president of party." Underlying this call was the persistent Whig belief that parties fostered and rewarded the selfish interests of the party faithful. The Whigs always insisted that Congress should be the locus of power in the federal system.

Anti-Masons Third party formed in 1827 in opposition to the presumed power and influence of the Masonic order.

This cotton banner used by the Whigs in the campaign of 1840 celebrated their ticket as the friends of common Americans who had been raised in a log cabin.

Smithsonian Institution / Office of Imaging, Printing, and Photographic Services

The Whigs were quicker than the Democrats to embrace economic change in the form of banks and manufacturing corporations. Most Whigs viewed governmental power as a positive force to promote economic development. They favored encouraging the spread of banking and paper money, chartering corporations, passing protective tariffs to support American manufacturers, and opening up new markets for farmers through government-subsidized transportation projects.

The Whigs drew heavily from commercial and planting interests in the South. They were also the party of bankers, manufacturers, small-town entrepreneurs, farmers prospering from the market outlets of canals and railroads, and skilled workers who valued a high tariff as protection from the competition of goods produced by cheap foreign labor. These Whig groups also tended to be native-born Protestants of New England or Yankee ancestry, particularly those caught up in the religious revivals of the 1820s and 1830s. The strongest Whig constituencies comprised an arc of Yankee settlement stretching from rural New England through central New York and around the southern shores of the Great Lakes.

Whigs believed in promoting social progress and harmony through an interventionist government. The Whigs favored such social reforms as prohibiting the consumption of alcohol; preserving the sanctity of the Protestant Sabbath through bans on business activities on Sundays; caring for orphans, the physically handicapped, and the mentally ill in state-run asylums and hospitals; and teaching virtuous behavior and basic knowledge through a centralized system of public education.

Much of the Whigs' reform impulse was directed against non-English and Catholic immigrants, those Americans whom the Whigs believed most needed to be taught the virtues of self-control and disciplined work habits. Not coincidentally, these groups—the Scots-Irish in the backcountry, the Reformed Dutch, and Irish and German Catholics—were the most loyal Democrats. They resented the aggressive moralism of the Whigs. These Democrats were typically subsistence farmers on the periphery of market change or unskilled workers who equated an activist government with special privileges for the economically and culturally powerful and identified with the Democrats' demand for keeping the government out of the economy and individual religious practices.

THE ELECTION OF 1840

Aside from the Independent Treasury Act and legislation establishing a ten-hour workday for federal employees, the Van Buren administration had no program to combat the Whig charge of helplessness in the face of economic adversity. The natural choice for the Whigs against Van Buren in 1840 was seemingly Henry Clay running on his American System to revive the economy with government aid. Yet the party dumped Clay for their version of a military hero popular with the people, William Henry Harrison of Ohio.

Harrison had run surprisingly well as one of the Whigs' regional candidates in 1836 and had revealed a common touch with the voters that the Whigs generally lacked. Unlike Clay, he was untainted by any association with the Bank of the United States, the Masonic Order, or slaveholding. As the victor at the Battle of Tippecanoe and a military hero in the War of 1812, he enabled Whigs to cast him in Jackson's former role as the honest, patriotic soldier worthy of the people's trust. In a decision that came back to haunt them the Whigs geographically balanced their ticket by selecting John Tyler, a planter from Virginia, as Harrison's running mate. Tyler was an advocate of states' rights and a former Democrat who had broken with Jackson over the Force Bill.

When a Democratic editor wisecracked that "Old Granny" Harrison (he was 67) was such a simpleton that he would like nothing better than to retire to a log cabin with a government pension and a barrel of hard cider, the Whigs created a Harrison who never was—a yeoman farmer of humble origins and homespun tastes whose rise to prominence was a democratic model of success for other Americans to follow. Thus Harrison, who was descended from the Virginia slaveholding aristocracy, became a Whig symbol of the common man. Indeed, the Whigs pinned the label of the dandified and elitist aristocrat on Van Buren whom they called "Martin Van Ruin."

The Whigs beat the Democrats at their own game of mass politics in 1840. They reversed the roles and symbolism of the Jackson-Adams election of 1828 and seized the high ground as the party of the people. In a further adaptation of earlier Democratic initiatives, Whig politics became a carnival in which voters were shamelessly wooed with food, drink, and music in huge rallies complete with live animals and gigantic buckskin balls that were triumphantly rolled from one rally to another.

The Whigs gained control of both Congress and the presidency in 1840. Harrison won 53 percent of the popular vote, and for the first time the Whigs carried the South (see Map 10–2). Voter turnout surged to an unprecedented 78 percent, a whopping increase over the average of 55 percent in the three preceding presidential elections (see Figure 10.1). As the new majority party, they finally had the opportunity, or so they thought, to implement their economic program.

THE WHIGS IN POWER

The Whigs expected that Clay would move quickly on Whig economic policies by marshaling his forces in Congress and trying to dominate a pliant Harrison. Harrison's death from pneumonia in April 1841, barely a month after his inauguration, ruined Clay's plans.

WHAT DID the Whigs achieve while in power?

HARRISON AND TYLER

As president, Harrison fumed that "I am bothered almost to death with visitors. I have not time to attend to my person, not even to change my shirt, much less to attend to the public business." He had pledged to follow the dictates of party leaders in Congress and defer to the judgment of his cabinet. Bowing to Clay's demands, he agreed to call Congress into special session to act on Whig party measures. Thus his death was a real blow to Whig hopes of establishing the credibility of their party as an effective agent for positive change.

The first vice president to succeed on the death of a president, Tyler was cut from quite different cloth than Harrison. This stiff, unbending planter subscribed to a states' rights agrarian philosophy that put him at odds with the urban and commercial elements of the Whig party even in his home state of Virginia. Clay's economic nationalism struck him as a program of rank corruption that surrendered the constitutional rights of the South to power-hungry politicians and manufacturers in the North. Clay forged ahead with the party agenda—the repeal of the Independent Treasury System and its replacement by a new national bank, a protective tariff, and the distribution of the proceeds of the government's public land sales to the states as funds for internal improvements.

Tyler used the negative power of presidential vetoes to stymie the Whig program. He twice vetoed bills to reestablish a national bank. The second veto led to the resignation of the cabinet he had inherited from Harrison, save for Secretary of State Daniel Webster, who was in the midst of negotiations with

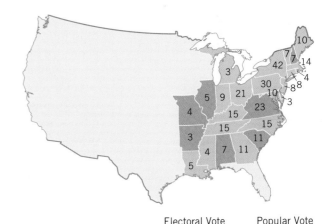

	Electoral Vote (%)	Popular Vote (%)
WILLIAM HENRY HARRISON (Whig)	**234 (80)**	**1,274,624 (53)**
Martin Van Buren (Democrat)	60 (20)	1,127,781 (47)

MAP 10–2
The Election of 1840 Building upon their strength in the commercializing North, the Whigs attracted enough rural voters in the South and West to win the election of 1840.

WHY WERE Southerners not unified in their support for a party in the election of 1840?

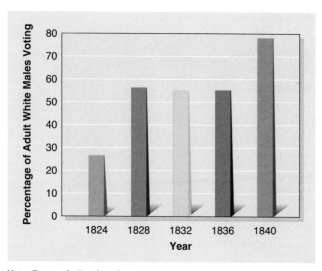

Voter Turnout in Presidential Elections, 1824–1840

The creation of mass-based political parties dramatically increased voter turnout in presidential elections. Voting surged in 1828 with the emergence of the Jacksonian Democratic party, and again in 1840 when the Whig party learned to appeal to the mass electorate.

Source: Richard P. McCormick, "New Perspectives on Jacksonian Politics" in *The Nature of Jacksonian America,* ed. Douglas T. Miller (1972), p. 103.

the British. Enraged congressional Whigs then expelled Tyler from the party.

A now desperate Clay sought to salvage what was left of his American System. He lined up Southern votes for the distribution of federal funds to the states by agreeing to a ceiling of 20 percent on tariff rates. Westerners were won over by Clay's support for the Preemption Act of 1841, a measure that allowed squatters—settlers on public land that had not yet been surveyed and put on the market—to purchase with noncompetitive bids up to 160 acres of land at the minimum government price of $1.25 per acre.

Clay's legislative wizardry got him nowhere. When the Whigs passed a higher tariff in 1842 with a provision for distribution, Tyler vetoed it and forced them to settle for a protective tariff with no distribution. In the end, Clay had no national bank, no funds for internal improvements, and only a slightly higher tariff. Although Clay's leadership of the Whigs was strengthened, Tyler had deprived that leadership of meaning by denying the Whigs the legislature fruits of their victory in 1840.

THE TEXAS ISSUE

In 1842, Webster wrapped up his negotiations with the British. The **Webster-Ashburton Treaty** of that year settled a long-standing dispute over the boundary between British Canada and Maine and parts of the Upper Midwest. An agreement was also reached to cooperate in suppressing the African slave trade. Webster now resigned from the cabinet to join his fellow Whigs, allowing Tyler to follow a prosouthern policy of expansion that he hoped would gain him the Democratic nomination for the presidency in 1844. His goal was the annexation of Texas.

Texas had been a slaveholding republic since 1836, when rebellious Americans, joined by some *tejanos* (Texans of Mexican descent), declared their independence from Mexico. Jackson extended diplomatic recognition before leaving office, but he refused the new nation's request to be annexed to the United States out of fear of provoking a war with Mexico. But he was also aware that the addition of Texas, a potentially huge area for the expansion of plantation slavery, would inflame sectional tensions and endanger Van Buren's chances in the upcoming presidential election. In private, however, he urged Texans to seize harbors on the Pacific Coast from Mexican control and thus make annexation more attractive to the commercial interests of the Northeast.

Party leaders sidestepped the Texas issue after 1836. Spurned by the Whigs and anxious to return to the Democrats, Tyler renewed the issue in 1843 to curry favor among Southern and Western Democrats. He replaced Webster as secretary of state with a proannexationist Virginian, Abel P. Upshur, and secretly opened negotiations with the Texans. After Upshur's death, Calhoun, his successor, completed the negotiations and dramatically politicized the slavery issue. Calhoun made public his correspondence with Richard Pakenham, the British minister in Washington. He accused the British of seeking to force emancipation on Texas to block American expansion and destroy slavery in the South. Calhoun concluded that the security and preservation of the Union demanded the annexation of Texas.

The Pakenham letter hit the Senate like a bombshell, and antislavery Northerners were now convinced that the annexation of Texas was a slaveholders' conspiracy to extend slavery and swell the political power of the South. In June 1844, the Senate rejected Calhoun's treaty of annexation by a two-to-one margin. Still, the issue was hardly dead.

Webster-Ashburton Treaty Treaty signed by the United States and Britain in 1842 that settled a boundary dispute between Maine and Canada.

THE ELECTION OF 1844

The Whig and Democratic National Conventions met in the spring of 1844. Both Clay, who had the Whig nomination locked up, and Van Buren, who was the strong favorite for the Democratic one, came out against immediate annexation. Clay's stand was consistent with Whig fears that territorial expansion would disrupt the party's plans for ordered economic development, but Van Buren's anti-Texas stand cost him his party's nomination. In a carefully devised strategy, Western and Southern Democrats united to deny him the necessary two-thirds vote of convention delegates. A deadlocked convention turned to James K. Polk of Tennessee, a confirmed expansionist who had received the blessing of Jackson, the party's patriarch.

To counter the charge that they were a prosouthern party, the Democrats ran in 1844 on a platform that linked Oregon to Texas as territorial objectives. Glowing reports from Protestant missionaries of the boundless fertility of Oregon's Willamette Valley triggered a migration by Midwestern farm families still reeling from the Panic of 1837. The report of a naval expedition sent to explore the Pacific aroused the interest of New England merchants in using Oregon for expanded trade with China.

Some six thousand Americans were in Oregon by the mid-1840s, and demands mounted, especially from Northern Democrats, that the United States abandon its 1818 agreement of joint occupation with the British and lay exclusive claim to Oregon far to the north of the area of American settlement. The Polk Democrats seemed to endorse them when they asserted an American claim "to the whole of the Territory of Oregon."

Polk's expansionist program united the Democrats and enabled them to campaign with much more enthusiasm than in 1840. Acquiring Texas and Oregon not only held out the economic hope of cheap, abundant land to debt-burdened farmers in the North and planters in the South but also played on the anti-British sentiments of many voters. In contrast, the Whig campaign was out of focus. Clay began to waver on the issue of annexation of Texas but he failed to stem the defection of proslavery southern Whigs to the Democrats and lost support among antislavery Whigs in the North. Clay lost to Polk by less than 2 percent of the popular vote.

Tyler claimed Polk's victory as a mandate for the immediate annexation of Texas. He knew that it would still be impossible to gain the two-thirds majority in the Senate necessary for the approval of a treaty. Thus he resorted to the constitutionally unprecedented expedient of a joint resolution in Congress inviting Texas to join the Union. By the narrow margin of twenty-seven to twenty-five, the Senate concurred with the House in favor of annexation. Tyler signed the joint resolution on March 1, 1845.

Although Tyler had failed to secure the Democratic nomination in 1844, he had gained Texas. He also had the satisfaction of getting revenge against the Whigs, the party that had disowned him. Texas, more than any other issue, defeated Clay and the Whigs in 1844.

CONCLUSION

The Jacksonian era ushered in a revolution in American political life. Politicians learned how to appeal to a mass electorate and to build disciplined parties that channeled popular desires into distinctive party positions. Voter participation in national elections tripled, and Democrats and Whigs competed on nearly equal terms in every region.

Politics did not fully enter the mainstream of American life until the rise of the second party system of Democrats and Whigs. The election of 1824 revived interest in presidential politics, and Jackson's forceful style of leadership highlighted the presidency as the focal point of American politics. Voters in favor of government aid for economic development and a social order based on Protestant moral controls turned to the Whigs' program of economic and moral activism. Conversely, those who saw an activist government as a threat to their economic and cultural equality turned to the Democrats.

The national issues around which the Democrats and Whigs organized and battled down to 1844 were primarily economic. Slavery in the form of the Texas question replaced the economy as the decisive issue in the election of 1844. Once this shift occurred and party appeals began to focus on the place of slavery in American society, an escalating politics of sectionalization was set into motion.

SUMMARY

The Egalitarian Impulse As politics opened to mass participation in the early nineteenth century, popular styles of religious leadership and worship erupted in broad reaction against the dominant Protestant churches. The Second Great Awakening further transformed the religious landscape between 1800 and 1840. In politics, longstanding property requirements for voting were dropped by many states, and the rise of Jacksonian Democrats resulted in the election and reelection of Andrew Jackson as president.

Jackson's Presidency Once in office, Jackson tolerated no interference from his subordinates. His dealings in such crises as the Bank War and the nullification movement further showed his intolerance for interference in any form. And, in his dealings with the Native Americans, as shown through the Indian Removal Act, the Trail of Tears, and Black Hawk's War, Jackson further illustrated his unwillingness to compromise.

Van Buren and Hard Times Where Jackson forged ahead regardless of consequences, Martin Van Buren tended to hang back, carefully calculating all of the political angles. Early in his presidency he was forced to deal with the economic Panic of 1837. Following this crisis, Van Buren reestablished the Democrats tarnished image as the party of limited government when he came out for the Independent Treasury System. His support, though reluctant, of the gag rule in 1836 may have been the beginning of the end for his presidency as he was beaten handedly in electoral votes by William Henry Harrison in the election of 1840.

The Rise of the Whig Party The Whig party was born in the congressional reaction to Jackson's Bank veto and his subsequent attacks on the national bank. By 1836, the Whigs were strong enough to mount a serious challenge for the presidency. The Whigs, like the Democrats, based their mass appeal on the claim that they could best defend the republican liberties of the people. Whigs believed in promoting social progress and harmony through an interventionist government. By 1840, Whigs had mastered the techniques of political organization and mobilization, and in 1840 they gained control of both Congress and the presidency.

The Whigs in Power William Henry Harrison's death was a real blow to Whig hopes of establishing the credibility of their party as an effective agent for positive change. John Tyler, the first vice president to succeed on the death of a president, was cut from a different cloth than Harrison. Tyler used the negative power of presidential vetoes to stymie the Whig program. Enraged congressional Whigs then expelled Tyler from the party. In the 1844 election, the Whigs ran Henry Clay as their candidate, losing in a close race to James K. Polk.

REVIEW QUESTIONS

1. What role did race and gender play in the democratic movements of the nineteenth century?

2. How did Jackson redefine the role of the president?

3. Why did American politics change between 1824 and 1840?

4. In terms of ideology and voter appeal, how did the Democrats and Whigs differ? How did each party represent a distinctive response to economic and social change?

KEY TERMS

Albany Regency (p. 246)
Anti-Masons (p. 257)
Bank War (p. 248)
Black Hawk's War (p. 250)
Democratic Party (p. 246)
Gag rule (p. 256)

Independent Treasury System (p. 255)
Indian Removal Act (p. 249)
Jacksonian Democrats (p. 295)
Nullification crisis (p. 248)
Second Great Awakening (p. 244)

Second party system (p. 256)
Specie Circular (p. 255)
Spoils system (p. 248)
Trail of Tears (p. 250)
Webster-Ashburton Treaty (p. 260)
Whig party (p. 255)

WHERE TO LEARN MORE

Rice Museum, Georgetown, South Carolina. Rice planters were the leaders of the nullification movement, and the interpretive materials here on the history of rice cultivation help one understand how slave labor was employed to produce their great wealth. Maps to the museum and news of special events can be found at: **www.ricemuseum.com/**

The Hermitage, Hermitage, Tennessee. This site, the plantation home of Andrew Jackson, includes a museum with artifacts of Jackson's life. Its website **www.thehermitage.com/** lists events and programs and examines the archeological projects undertaken at the Hermitage.

Martin Van Buren National Historic Site, Kinderhook, New York. The site preserves Lindenwald, Van Buren's home after he left the presidency and includes a library with materials on Van Buren and his political era. Its recently expanded website **www.nps.gov/mava/home.htm** discusses the history of Lindenwald and includes a virtual tour of its art collection.

 For additional study resources for this chapter, go to: **www.prenhall.com/goldfield/chapter10**

. . . whatever accidents or misfortunes might attend my flight nothing could be worse than what threatened my stay.

A Slave auction in Virginia. 1861.

NEGROES FOR SALE.

Will be sold at public auction, at Spring Hill, in the County of Hempstead, on a credit of twelve months, on Friday the 28th day of this present month, 15 young and valuable Slaves, consisting of 9 superior Men & Boys, between 12 and 27 years of age, one woman about 43 years who is a good washer and cook, one woman about twenty-seven, and one very likely young woman with three children.

Also at the same time, and on the same terms, three Mules, about forty head of Cattle, plantation tools, one waggon, and a first rate Gin stand, manufactured by Pratt &Co.

Bond with two or more approved securities will be required. Sale to commence at 10 o'clock.

E. E. Hundley,
W. Robinson,
H. M. W. binson.

ring Hill, Jan. &c, 1842.

11

SLAVERY AND THE OLD SOUTH
1800–1860

HOW DID the increasing demand for cotton make slavery highly profitable in the Lower South?

WHAT CAUSED the decline of slavery after 1800 in the Upper South?

WHAT WERE the living and working conditions of most slaves?

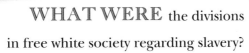

WHAT WERE the divisions in free white society regarding slavery?

WHAT WERE Southern defenses of slavery?

Had Mrs. Wheeler condemned me to the severest corporal punishment, or exposed me to be sold in the public slave market in Wilmington [N.C.] I should probably have resigned myself with apparent composure to her cruel behests. But when she sought to force me into a compulsory union with a man whom I could only hate and despise it seemed that rebellion would be a virtue, that duty to myself and my God actually required it, and that whatever accidents or misfortunes might attend my flight nothing could be worse than what threatened my stay.

Marriage like many other blessings I considered to be especially designed for the free, and something that all the victims of slavery should avoid as tending essentially to perpetuate that system. Hence to all overtures of that kind from whatever quarter they might come I had invariably turned a deaf ear. I had spurned domestic ties not because my heart was hard, but because it was my unalterable resolution never to entail slavery on any human being. And now when I had voluntarily renounced the society of those I might have learned to love should I be compelled to accept one, whose person, and speech, and manner could not fail to be ever regarded by me with loathing and disgust. Then to be driven in to the fields beneath the eye and lash of the brutal overseer, and those miserable huts, with their promiscuous crowds of dirty, obscene and degraded objects, for my home I could not, I would not bear it.

—Hannah Crafts

Henry Louis Gates, J., ed., *The Bondwoman's Narrative* (New York: Warner Books, 2002), pp. 206–207.

IMAGE KEY
for pages 264–265

a. A chain used to tie together gangs of slaves.

b. "The Shadow" Plantation of Louisiana.

c. "Slavery and the Old South, 1800–1860." A Slave auction in Virginia, 1861. English engraving.

d. A whip of coiled rope with a wooden handle; used on slaves.

e. An advertisement promoting the auction of eight black slaves together with miscellaneous inanimate property belonging to a North Carolina gentleman.

f. Fluffy white, mature cotton bolls on the stem of a plant.

g. African American slave / farm workers carry sacks of cotton on their heads while leaving a South Carolina plantation field. "Returning from the Cotton Fields in South Carolina," ca. 1860.

h. A runaway slave is depicted on the frontispiece of the Anti Slavery Record of 1837.

i. A slave collar with an attached tag from the slave market in Richmond, Virginia.

j. Colonel and Mrs. James A. Whiteside, son Charles, and servants by James Cameron. A wealthy colonial family and two servants sit on a posh veranda with a checkered floor overlooking an expansive rugged landscape.

k. Pro slavery cartoon, 1841.

HANNAH CRAFTS was the name adopted by an African-American woman after escaping from slavery in the late 1850s. This passage is from *The Bondwoman's Narrative*, the only known novel written by a female black slave. Crafts was probably a house slave of John Hill Wheeler of North Carolina who fled North in the spring of 1857, and merged into the black middle class of southern New Jersey. As a fugitive slave in the North, Crafts risked recapture at any time prior to the outbreak of the Civil War. Her decision not to publish her autobiographical slave narrative might well have been based on the fear that it would reveal her whereabouts to an owner intent on reclaiming her. Among other details the novels reveals the brutal living conditions that field slaves had to endure.

Knowing that masters frequently violated the sanctity of slave marriages and could keep any resulting children as slaves, she believed that all slaves should remain celibate: "Marriage can only be filled with profit, and honor, and advantage by the free." Triggering her decision to flee was Mrs. Wheeler's demand that she "marry" the field hand Bill—that is, submit to being raped by a man she despised and to living in the squalor of the slave quarter.

Only the system of slavery that Crafts described with revulsion makes it possible to speak of the antebellum South as a single region despite its geographical and cultural diversity. Black slavery created a bond among white Southerners and cast them in a common mold.

Slavery was also the source of the South's immense agricultural wealth, and the means by which white people controlled a large black minority. Slavery also frightened white Southerners with a vision of what might happen to them should they not protect their own personal liberties, including, paradoxically, the liberty to enslave African Americans. Because slavery was so embedded in Southern life and customs, white leadership reacted to mounting attacks on slavery after 1830 with an ever more defiant defense of the institution, which reinforced a growing sense among white Southerners that their values divided them from their fellow citizens in the Union.

The South of 1860 was much larger and more diverse than it had been in 1800, but it was also more uniformly committed to a single cash crop, cotton. King cotton provided the economic basis for Southern sectionalism. During its reign, however, regional differences emerged between the Lower South, where the linkage between cotton and slavery was strong, and the Upper South, where slavery was relatively less important and the economy more diversified.

THE LOWER SOUTH

South and west of South Carolina in 1800 stretched some of the best cotton land in the world. A long growing season, adequate rainfall, navigable rivers, and untapped fertility gave the Lower South—consisting in 1850 of South Carolina, Georgia, Florida, Alabama, Mississippi, Louisiana, and Texas—incomparable natural advantages for growing cotton. Ambitious white Southerners exploited these advantages by extending slavery after 1800 to the newer cotton lands that opened up in the Lower South. Cotton production and slavery thus went hand in hand.

COTTON AND SLAVES

Once the cotton gin removed the technical barrier to its commercial production, upland, or short-staple, cotton could be planted far inland, and small farmers could grow it profitably because it required no additional costs for machinery. As a result, after the 1790s, the production of short-staple cotton boomed. Moreover, like the South's other cash crops, upland cotton required fairly continuous tending throughout most of the year. Once the harvest was in—a time when Northern agricultural workers were laid off—the slaves cleared land, cut wood, and made repairs. The long workyear maximized the return on capital invested in slave labor.

The cultivation of cotton left plenty of time for slaves to grow food. The major grain in the Southern diet was corn, which needed little attention while cotton was being harvested and could be planted earlier or later than cotton during the long growing season. Surplus corn could be fed to hogs and converted into pork. Because almost all cotton farms and plantations also raised corn and hogs, the South virtually fed itself.

From its original base in South Carolina and Georgia, the cotton kingdom moved into the Old Southwest and then into Texas and Arkansas. As wasteful agricultural practices exhausted new lands, planters moved to the next cotton frontier farther west. Cotton output exploded from 73,000 bales (each bale weighed close to 500 pounds) in 1800 to over 2 million bales by midcentury, thanks to the fertility of virgin land and technological changes, such as improved seed varieties and steam-powered cotton gins. Slave labor accounted for more than 90 percent of cotton production.

Plantations, large productive units specializing in a cash crop and employing at least twenty slaves, were the leading economic institution in the Lower South. Planters were the most prestigious social group, and, though less than 5 percent of white families were in the planter class, they controlled more than 40 percent of the slaves, cotton output, and total agricultural wealth. Most had inherited

HOW DID the increasing demand for cotton make slavery highly profitable in the Lower South?

WHERE TO LEARN MORE

Cottonlandia Museum, Greenwood, Mississippi
www.gcgv.com/CL.html

13–1
State v. Boon (1801)

or married into their wealth, but they could stay at the top of the South's class structure only by continuing to profit from slave labor.

Planters had the best land. The ownership of twenty or more slaves enabled planters to use gangs to do both routine and specialized agricultural work. This **gang system**, a cruder version of the division of labor that was being introduced in Northern factories, permitted a regimented pace of work that would have been impossible to impose on free agricultural workers. Teams of field hands, made up of women as well as men, had to work at a steady pace or else feel the lash. They were supervised by white overseers and black drivers, slaves selected for their management skills and agricultural knowledge.

"During two days' sail on the Alabama River from Mobile to Montgomery," noted a traveler in 1860, "I did not see so many houses standing together in any one spot as could be dignified with the appellation of village." The plantation districts of the Lower South stifled the growth of towns and the economic enterprise they fostered. Planters, as well as ordinary farmers, strove to be self-sufficient. The most significant economic exchange—exporting cotton—took place in international markets and was handled by specialized commission merchants in Charleston, Mobile, and New Orleans. The Lower South had amassed great wealth, but most outsiders saw no signs of progress there.

THE PROFITS OF SLAVERY

The average rate of return on capital invested in a slave was about 10 percent a year, a rate that at least equaled what was available in alternative investments in the South or the North. The newer regions of the cotton kingdom in the Lower South, with the most productive land and the greatest commitment to plantation agriculture, consistently led the nation in per capita income.

The profitability of slavery ultimately rested on the enormous demand for cotton outside the South. This demand grew at about 5 percent a year in the first half of the nineteenth century. Demand was so strong that prices held steady at around 10 cents a pound in the 1850s even as Southern production of cotton doubled. Textile mills in Britain were always the largest market, but demand in continental Europe and the United States grew even faster after 1840.

Prices for a male field hand rose from $250 in 1815 to $900 by 1860. The steady appreciation of prices meant that owners could sell some of their slaves and realize a profit over and above what they had already earned from the slaves' labor. Slave women of childbearing age were therefore valued nearly as much as male field hands. More than 800,000 slaves were moved between regions in the South from 1790 to 1860, and professional slave traders transported at least 60 percent of them. Drawing on lines of credit from banks, the traders paid cash for slaves, most of whom they bought from plantations in the Upper South. By selling these slaves in regional markets where demand had driven up the price, they turned a tidy profit. About half of all slave sales separated family members. Slave children born in the Upper South after 1820 stood a one-in-three chance of being sold during their lifetime.

As long as slaves employed in growing cash staples returned 10 percent a year, slave owners had little economic incentive to shift their capital resources into manufacturing or urban development. The South had one-third of the nation's population in 1860 but produced by value only 10 percent of the nation's manufacturing output. Fewer than one in ten Southerners lived in a city, compared to more than one in three Northeasterners and one in seven Midwesterners.

The Lower South had the smallest urban population and the fewest factories. Planters here were not opposed to economic innovations, but they feared social changes that might undermine the stability of slavery. Urbanization and industrialization both entailed such risks.

Gang system The organization and supervision of slave field hands into working teams on Southern plantations.

CHRONOLOGY

1790s	Large-scale conversions of slaves to Christianity begin.	**1831–1832**	Virginia legislature debates and rejects gradual emancipation.
1793	Eli Whitney patents the cotton gin.	**1832**	Thomas R. Dew publishes the first full-scale defense of slavery.
1800	Gabriel Prosser leads a rebellion in Richmond, Virginia.		
1808	Congress prohibits the African slave trade.	**1837–1845**	Slavery issue divides Presbyterians, Methodists, and Baptists into separate sectional churches.
1811	Slaves rebel in Louisiana.		
1816–1819	First cotton boom in the South.	**1845**	Florida and Texas, the last two slave states, are admitted to the Union.
1822	Denmark Vesey's Conspiracy fails in Charleston, South Carolina.	**1850s**	Cotton production doubles.
1831	Nat Turner leads a rebellion in Southampton County, Virginia.	**1857**	Hinton R. Helper publishes *The Impending Crisis of the South*.

An editorial in the New Orleans *Crescent* charged that slaves in the city were "demoralized to a deplorable extent, all owing to the indiscriminate license and indulgence extended them by masters, mistresses, and guardians, and to the practice of *forging passes*, which has now become a regular business in New Orleans." Urban slaves, though scarcely free, enjoyed a degree of personal and economic independence that blurred the line between freedom and servitude.

Urban slaves were artisans, semi-skilled laborers, and domestics, and unlike their rural counterparts, they usually lived apart from their owners. They had much more freedom than field hands to move around and interact with white people and other black people. If they had a marketable skill, such as carpentry or tailoring, they could hire out their labor and retain some wages for themselves after reimbursing their owners. In short, the direct authority of the slave owner was less clear-cut in the town than in the country.

From 1820 to 1860 slaves decreased from 22 percent to 10 percent of the urban population. This decline reflected both doubts about the stability of slavery in an urban setting and the large profits that slave labor earned for slave owners in the rural cotton economy.

The ambivalence of planters toward urban slavery also characterized their attitudes toward industrialization itself. Many planters considered free workers potential abolitionists.

But the use of slaves as factory operatives threatened slave discipline because an efficient level of production required special incentives. "Whenever a slave is made a mechanic, he is more than half freed," complained James Hammond, a South Carolina planter. Elaborating on Hammond's fears, a Virginian noted of slaves that he had hired out for industrial work: "They were worked hard, and had too much liberty, and were acquiring bad habits. They earned money by overwork, and spent it for whisky, and got a habit of roaming about and *taking care of themselves*; because, when they were not at work in the furnace, nobody looked out for them."

The anxieties of planters over industrialization and their refusal to shift capital from plantation agriculture to finance it ensured that manufacturing played only a minor economic role in the Lower South. Planters did invest in railroads and factories, but their holdings remained concentrated in land and slaves. They augmented their income by renting slaves to manufacturers and railroad contractors but were quick to recall these slaves to work on the plantations when needed.

QUICK REVIEW

Urban Slavery
- 1820–1860: slaves decreased from 22 percent to 10 percent of urban population.
- Planters had a general ambivalence toward indusrialization.
- Many planters saw factory work as a threat to slave discipline.

THE UPPER SOUTH

WHAT CAUSED the decline of slavery after 1800 in the Upper South?

WHERE TO LEARN MORE

Appalachian Museum of Berea College, Berea, Kentucky
www.museum.appstate.edu/exhibits/ exhibits.shtml

Climate and geography distinguished the Upper South from the Lower South. The eight slave states of the Upper South lay north of the best growing zones for cotton. The northernmost of these states—Delaware, Maryland, Kentucky, and Missouri—bordered on free states and were known as the Border South. The four states south of them—Virginia, North Carolina, Tennessee, and Arkansas—constituted a middle zone. Slavery was entrenched in all these states, but it was less dominant than in the cotton South.

The key difference from which others followed was the suitability of the Lower South for growing cotton with gangs of slave labor. For the most part, the Upper South lacked the fertile soil and long growing season necessary for the commercial production of cotton, rice, or sugar (see Map 11–2). Consequently, the demand for slaves was less than in the Lower South. Percentages of slave ownership and of slaves in the overall population were roughly half those in the cotton South.

While the Lower South was undergoing a cotton boom after the War of 1812, the Upper South was mired in a long economic slump from which it did not emerge until the 1850s. The improved economy of the Upper South in the late antebellum period increasingly relied on free labor, a development that many cotton planters feared would splinter Southern unity in defense of slavery.

A PERIOD OF ECONOMIC ADJUSTMENT

Upper South land values fell as farmers dumped their property and headed west. "Emigration is here raging with all the strength of fanaticism," wrote a Virginian in 1837, "and nothing else can be talked of but selling estates, at a great sacrifice, and '*packing off*' for the '*far west*.'"

Agricultural reform emerged in the 1830s as one proposed solution to the economic crisis. Its leading advocate was Edmund Ruffin, a Virginia planter who tirelessly promoted the use of marl (shell deposits) to neutralize the overly acidic and worn-out soils of the Upper South. He also called for deeper plowing, systematic rotation of crops, and upgrading the breeding stock for animal husbandry.

Ruffin's efforts, and reform programs pushed in agricultural societies and fairs, met with some success but only a minority of farmers ever embraced reform. These were generally the well-educated planters who read the agricultural press and could afford to change their farming practices. The landscape of Ruffin's beloved Virginia Tidewater still provoked travelers to remark, as one did in the early 1850s, "I've heard 'em say out West that old Virginny was the mother of statesmen—reckon she must be about done, eh? This 'ere's about the *barrenest* look for a mother ever I see."

MAP EXPLORATION

To explore an interactive version of this map, go to
http://www.prenhall.com/goldfield2/map11.1

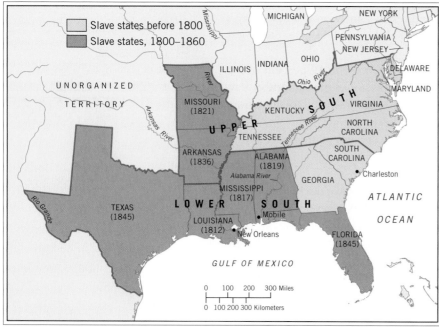

MAP 11–1

The Spread of Slavery: New Slave States Entering the Union, 1800–1850   Seven slave states entered the Union after 1800 as cotton production shifted westward.

WHY WAS cotton production especially suited to slave labor?

Although soil exhaustion and wasteful farming persisted, agriculture in the Upper South had revived by the 1850s. A rebound in the tobacco market accounted for part of this revival, but the growing profitability of general farming was responsible for most of it.

Particularly in the Border South, farmers and planters lessened their dependence on slave labor or on a single cash crop and practiced a thrifty, efficient agriculture geared to producing grain and livestock for urban markets. Western Maryland and the Shenandoah Valley and northern sections of Virginia grew wheat, and in the former tobacco districts of the Virginia and North Carolina Tidewater, wheat, corn, and garden vegetables became major cash crops.

Expanding urban markets and a network of internal improvements facilitated this transition to general farming. Although not far advanced by Northern standards, urbanization and industrialization in the Upper South were considerably greater than in the Lower South. By 1860, the Upper South accounted for three-fourths of the South's manufacturing capital and output and nearly all of its heavy industry. Canals and railroads linked cities and countryside in a denser transportation grid than in the Lower South.

The Upper South at midcentury was gradually becoming less tied to plantation agriculture and slave labor. The rural majority increasingly prospered by growing foodstuffs for city dwellers and factory workers. The labor market for railroad construction

African American field hands return from a South Carolina cotton field in the 1860s. The economy of the prewar South was based on the production of cotton by a large enslaved labor force.

Collection of The New York Historical Society, negative number 47843

MAP EXPLORATION

To explore an interactive version of this map, go to
http://www.prenhall.com/goldfield2/map11.2

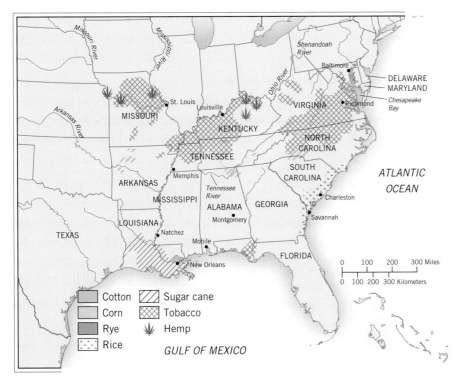

MAP 11–2

Cotton and Other Crops in the South, 1860   Most of the Upper South was outside the cotton belt where the demand for slave labor was greatest.

and manufacturing work was strong enough to attract Northern immigrants and help reduce the loss of the native-born population that had migrated to other states.

The economic adjustment in the Upper South converted the labor surplus of the 1820s into a labor scarcity by the 1850s. "It is a fact," noted Edmund Ruffin in 1859, "that labor is greatly deficient in all Virginia, and especially in the rich western counties, which, for want of labor, scarcely yet yield in the proportion of one tenth of their capacity." Like many planters in the cotton states, Ruffin feared that free labor was about to replace scarce and expensive slave labor in Virginia and much of the Upper South.

THE DECLINE OF SLAVERY

Slavery was clearly growing weaker in the Upper South by the 1850s. The decline was most evident along the northern tier of the Upper South. By 1860, slaves in the Border South had dropped to 2 percent of the population in Delaware, 13 percent in Maryland, 19 percent in Kentucky, and 10 percent in Missouri. In Virginia from 1830 to 1860, slaves fell from 39 to 31 percent of the population.

Elsewhere in the Upper South, slavery was more or less holding its own by the 1850s. Only in Arkansas, whose alluvial lands along the Mississippi River offered a new frontier for plantation agriculture, was slavery growing rapidly. Still, slaves made up only 25 percent of the population of Arkansas in 1860 and were confined mainly to the southeastern corner of the state.

In every decade after 1820, the internal slave trade drained off about 10 percent of the slaves in the Upper South, virtually the entire natural increase. The sale of surplus slaves was a windfall for planters whose slaves had become an economic burden. This same windfall gave planters the capital to embark on agricultural reform and shift out of tobacco production. Investment capital in the Upper South was not flowing into slave property but into economic diversification that expanded urban manufacturing. Both of these structural changes increasingly put slavery at a competitive disadvantage against free labor.

The wheat, small grains, and fodder crops that replaced tobacco in much of the Upper South did not require the nearly continuous attention of a work force. As planters abandoned tobacco, they kept fewer slaves and relied on seasonal and cheap agricultural workers to meet peak labor demand.

Cheapness and flexibility were also what urban manufacturers wanted in their labor supply—workers who could be hired and fired at a moment's notice. Immigrant workers displaced slaves in most of the factories in the Border South. By 1860, slaves made up just 1 percent of the population in St. Louis and Baltimore, the South's major industrial cities.

After 1830, there were still plantation districts with large concentrations of slaves, and slave owners retained enough political power to defeat all challenges to their property interests. Nevertheless, the gradual turn to free labor was unmistakable. Agitation for emancipation had begun in the cities of the Border South. As Alfred Iveson, a Georgia planter, noted with alarm in 1860: "Those border States can get along without slavery. Their soil and climate are appropriate to white labor; they can live and flourish without African slavery; but the cotton States cannot."

SLAVE LIFE AND CULTURE

Nearly 4 million slaves lived in the South by 1860, more than a fivefold increase since the ratification of the Constitution. Although some slaves were smuggled in after the African slave trade was banned in 1808, an excess of births over deaths accounted for nearly all of this population increase.

Almost all Southern slaves were thus native-born by the mid-nineteenth century. They were not Africans but African Americans, and they shared the com-

WHAT WERE the living and working conditions of most slaves?

mon fate of bondage. In their family life and religious beliefs, slaves found the strength to sustain themselves under nearly intolerable circumstances.

WORK ROUTINES AND LIVING CONDITIONS

Each southern state had its own **slave codes**, laws defining the status of slaves and the rights of masters; the codes gave slave owners near-absolute power over their human property.

"The right of personal liberty in the slave is utterly inconsistent with the idea of slavery," wrote Thomas R. R. Cobb of Georgia in a legal treatise on slavery. Slaves could not own property, make contracts, possess guns or alcohol, legally marry (except in Louisiana), leave plantations without the owner's written permission, or testify against their masters or any other white person in a court of law. Many states also prohibited teaching a slave to read or write. The murder of a slave by a master was illegal, but in practice the law and community standards looked the other way if a disobedient slave was killed while being disciplined.

Whippings were the most common authorized punishment for slaves' infractions of plantation rules: twenty lashes on the bare back for leaving a plantation without a pass, one hundred lashes for writing a pass for another slave, and so on. Striking a master, committing arson, or conspiring to rebel were punishable by death.

The owner, as expressed in the Alabama Slave Code of 1852, had "the right to the time, labor and services of the slave." Most masters recognized that it was good business sense to feed, clothe, and house their slaves well enough to ensure productive labor and to encourage a family life that would enable the slave population to reproduce itself. However, planters rarely provided more than the bare necessities. The slaves lived mainly on rations of cornmeal, salt pork, vegetables they grew on small garden plots, and occasional catches of game and fish. This diet was often insufficient in vitamins and nutrients. As a result, diseases such as beriberi and pellagra were common. Slaves also faced frequent outbreaks of dysentery and cholera. According to one study, the life expectancy for slaves at birth was twenty-one to twenty-two years, roughly half that for whites.

Planters furnished slaves with two sets of coarse clothing, one for summer and one for winter. Their housing, typically a 15-by-15-foot one-room cabin for five or six occupants, provided little more than basic shelter against the elements. "They were built of logs," a traveler noted of slave cabins in South Carolina, "with no windows— no opening at all, except the doorway, with a chimney of sticks and mud; with no trees about them, no porches, or shades, of any kind. Except for the chimney . . . I should have conjectured that it had been built for a powder-house, or perhaps an ice-house—never for an animal to sleep in." Large planters placed these cabins in a row, an arrangement that projected precision and undifferentiated order.

The diet and housing of most slaves may have been no worse than that of the poorest whites in both the North and the South, but their workload was undoubtedly heavier. Just over half of the slave population at midcentury was concentrated on plantation units with twenty or more slaves, and most of these slaves worked as field hands in gang labor. Overseers freely admitted that they relied on whippings to make slaves work in these gangs.

The fear of the whip on a bare back set the work pace. At daybreak, recalled Solomon Northrup of his enslavement on a Louisiana plantation, "the fears and labors of another day begin; and until its close there is no such thing as rest. [The slave] fears he will be caught lagging through the day; he fears to approach the gin-house with his basket-load of cotton at night; he fears, when he lies down, that he will over-sleep himself in the morning."

Some 15 to 20 percent of plantation slaves were house servants or skilled artisans who had lighter and less regimented workloads than field hands. Some

WHERE TO LEARN MORE

The Anacostia Museum Center for African-American History, Washington, D.C.
www.si.edu/anacostia/

Slave codes   A series of laws passed mainly in the Southern colonies in the late seventeenth and early eighteenth centuries to define the status of slaves and codify the denial of basic civil rights to them.

planters used the prospect of transfer to these relatively privileged positions as an incentive to field hands to work harder. Extra rations, time off on weekends, passes to visit a spouse on a nearby plantation, and the right to have a garden plot were among the other incentives planters used to keep labor productivity high.

Nearly three-fourths of the slaves worked on plantations and medium-sized farms. Most of the remainder—those in units with fewer than ten slaves—worked on small farms in close contact with the master's family. Slave couples in small holdings were more likely to live on separate farms, and the owners of only a few slaves were more vulnerable than planters to market downturns that could force them to sell their slaves and thus further divide families.

Ten percent of slaves were not attached to the land. Instead, they labored at jobs that most white workers shunned. Every Southern industry—but most particularly extractive industries like mining and lumbering—relied heavily on slaves. The Tredegar Iron Works in Richmond, the largest iron foundry in the South, used slaves as its main work force after 1847, partly to curb strikes by its white workers. Racial tensions often flared in Southern industry. When the races worked together, skilled white laborers typically insisted on being placed in supervisory positions over the slaves.

Compared to plantation slaves, industrial slaves had more independence off the job and greater opportunities to earn money of their own. By undertaking extra factory work, known as "overwork," industrial slaves could earn $50 or more a month, money that could be used to buy goods for their families or, in rare cases, to purchase their freedom.

FAMILIES AND RELIGION

The core institution of slave life was the family. Despite all the obstacles arrayed against them, many slave marriages produced enduring commitments and a supportive moral code for family members. Most slave unions remained intact until death or, more likely, the sale of a spouse ended the partnership. Close to one-third of slave marriages were broken up by sales or forced removals. A slave bitterly recalled that "the separation of slaves in this way is little thought of. A few masters regard their union as sacred, but where one does, a hundred care nothing about it."

Both parents were present in about two-thirds of slave families, the same ratio as in contemporary peasant families in Western Europe. Most slave fathers struggled to help feed their families by hunting and fishing, and they risked beating and death to defend their wives from sexual abuse by the overseer or master. Besides their field labor, slave mothers had all the burdens of pregnancy, caring for children, laundering, and preparing meals. After escaping from slavery, Sojourner Truth told how she placed her babies in a basket hanging from a tree while she worked in the field and had older children care for them.

No anguish under slavery was more heartrending than that of a mother whose child was sold away from her. "Oh, my heart was too full!" recalled Charity Bowery on being told that her boy Richard was sold. "[My mistress] had sent me away on an errand, because she didn't want to be troubled with our cries. I hadn't any chance to see my poor boy. I shall never see my poor boy. I shall never see him again in this world. My heart felt as if it was under a great load."

Most parents could only teach their children the skills of survival in a world in which white people had a legal monopoly on violence. The most valuable of these skills was the art of hiding one's true feelings from white people and telling them what they wanted to hear. As a perceptive traveler noted: "When therefore a white man approaches [the slaves] with inquiries concerning their condition, they are at once put upon their guard, and either make indefinite and vague replies, or directly contradict their real sentiments."

QUICK REVIEW

Slave Families

- Both parents present in two-thirds of slave family.
- Most slave fathers did extra work and risked punishment to support and defend their families.
- Parents concentrated on teaching children survival skills.

Extensive kinship ties provided a support network for the vulnerable slave family. These networks included both blood relatives and other significant people. Children were taught to address elders as "Aunt" and "Uncle" and fellow slaves as "sister" and "brother." If separated from a parent, a child could turn to relatives or the larger slave community for care and assistance.

The ancestors of nineteenth-century slaves brought no common religion with them when they were taken to the New World. However, beliefs common to a variety of African religions survived. In keeping with African traditions, the religion of the slaves fused the natural and spiritual worlds, accepted the power of ghosts over the living, and relied on an expressive form of worship in which the participants shouted and swayed in rhythm with the beat of drums and other instruments. Associated with reverence for ancestors, dance was sacred in Africa. Spirituals, the religious songs of the slaves, were sung in a dance known in America as the "ring shout." Moving counterclockwise and stamping their feet to establish a beat for the music, slaves blended dance and song in a religious ceremony that helped them endure oppression and sustain their self-confidence.

By most estimates, no more than 20 percent of the slaves ever converted to Christianity. Those who did convert found in Christianity a message of deliverance rooted in the liberation of Moses's people from bondage in Egypt. The Jesus of the New Testament spoke to them as a compassionate God who had shared their burden of suffering so that all peoples could hope to find the Promised Land of love and justice. By blending biblical imagery into their spirituals, the slaves expressed their yearning for freedom: "Didn't my Lord deliver Daniel/Then why not every man?"

The initial exposure of slaves to Christianity usually came from evangelical revivalists. The evangelical message of universal spiritual equality confirmed the slaves' sense of personal worth. Less formal in both their doctrines and organization than the Presbyterians and Episcopalians, the evangelical sects allowed the slaves more leeway to choose their own preachers and engage in the physical activism and the call-and-response pattern that characterized slave religion. Perhaps because they baptized by total immersion, which evoked the purifying power of water so common in African religions, the Baptists gained the most slave converts.

Most planters favored Christianity among their slaves only if they could control it. Worried that abolitionist propaganda might attract the slaves to Christianity as a religion of secular liberation, some planters invited white ministers to their plantations to preach a gospel of passivity and obedience centered on Paul's call for servants to "obey in all things your Masters."

Slaves often feigned acceptance of the religious wishes of their masters at the special slave chapels on some plantations or in the segregated galleries of white churches on Sunday mornings. But in the evening, out of sight of the master or overseer, they held their own services in the woods and listened to their own preachers. As much as they could, the slaves hid their religious life from white people. Many slaves experienced religion as a rebirth that gave them the inner strength to endure their bondage. As one of them recalled, "I was born a slave and lived through some hard times. If it had not been for *my God*, I don't know what I would have done."

RESISTANCE

Open resistance to slavery was futile. The fate of Richard, Charity Bowery's boy who was sold away from her, typified that of the openly defiant slave. He resisted the efforts of his new owner in Alabama to break his will. When the owner threatened to shoot him if he did not consent to being whipped, Richard replied, "Shoot away, I won't come to be flogged." The master shot and killed him.

Especially on large plantations, slave nursemaids cared for the young children in the white planter's family.

From the Collection of the Louisiana State Museum

QUICK REVIEW

Religion and Slavery

◆ A variety of African religions survived in America.

◆ No more than 20 percent of slaves converted to Christianity.

◆ Most planters favored Christianity among slaves only if the planters had control.

After fleeing from slavery in Maryland in 1849, Harriet "Moses" Tubman, standing on left, risked reenslavement by returning to the South on several occasions to assist other slaves in escaping. She is photographed here with some of those she helped free.

Smith College, Sophia Smith Collection, Northampton, MA

13–3
Nat Turner, Confession (1831)

Gabriel Prosser's Rebellion Slave revolt that failed when Gabriel Prosser, a slave preacher and blacksmith, organized a thousand slaves for an attack on Richmond, Virginia, in 1800.

Denmark Vesey's Conspiracy The most carefully devised slave revolt in which rebels planned to seize control of Charleston in 1822 and escape to freedom in Haiti, a free black republic, but they were betrayed by other slaves, and seventy-five conspirators were executed.

Nat Turner's Rebellion Uprising of slaves in Southampton County, Virginia, in the summer of 1831 led by Nat Turner that resulted in the death of fifty-five white people.

Underground Railroad Support system set up by antislavery groups in the Upper South and the North to assist fugitive slaves in escaping the South.

Although the odds of succeeding were infinitesimal, four major uprisings occurred in the nineteenth century. The first, **Gabriel Prosser's Rebellion** in 1800, involved about fifty armed slaves around Richmond. State authorities executed Prosser and twenty-five of his followers before the rebellion got under way.

A decade later, in what seems to have been a spontaneous bid for freedom, several hundred slaves in the river parishes (counties) above New Orleans marched on the city. Poorly armed, they were no match for the U.S. Army troops and militiamen who stopped them. More than sixty slaves died, and the heads of the leading rebels were posted on poles along the Mississippi River to warn others of the fate that awaited rebellious slaves.

The most carefully planned slave revolt, **Denmark Vesey's Conspiracy**, like Prosser's, failed before it got started. Vesey, a literate carpenter and lay preacher in Charleston who had purchased his freedom with the money he had won in a lottery, planned the revolt in the summer of 1822. Vesey assigned teams of rebels specific targets, such as the municipal guardhouse and arsenal. Once Charleston was secured, the rebels apparently planned to flee to Haiti. The plot collapsed when two domestic servants betrayed it. White authorities hanged thirty-five conspirators, including Vesey, and banished thirty-seven others. After destroying the African Methodist Episcopal Church where Vesey had preached, they also passed the Negro Seamen's Act, which mandated the imprisonment of black sailors while their ships were berthed in Charleston.

Nat Turner's Rebellion in Southampton County, Virginia, did erupt before it could be suppressed. Turner was a literate field hand driven by prophetic visions of black vengeance against white oppressors, who led a small band of followers on a murderous rampage in late August 1831. The first white man to be killed was Joseph Travis, Turner's owner. In the next two days, sixty other white people were also killed. An enraged posse, aided by slaves, captured or killed most of Turner's party. Turner hid for two months before being apprehended. He and more than thirty other slaves were executed, and panicky white people killed more than a hundred other slaves.

Slaves well understood that the odds against a successful rebellion were insurmountable. They could see who had all the guns. White people were also more numerous. Mounted patrols of whites were part of the police apparatus of slavery, and their surveillance limited organized rebellion by slaves to small, local affairs that were quickly suppressed.

Nor could many slaves escape to freedom. The **Underground Railroad**, a secret network of stations and safe houses organized by Quakers and other antislavery whites and blacks, provided some assistance. However, out of more than 3 million slaves in the 1850s, only about a thousand a year permanently escaped. (See American Views: "A Letter from an Escaped Slave to His Former Master." p. 278)

The few who made it to the North did so by running at night and hiding during the day. The most ingenious resorted to clever stratagems. Henry "Box" Brown arranged to have himself shipped in a box from Richmond to Philadelphia. Ellen Craft, a light-skinned slave who could pass as white, disguised herself as a male slaveholder accompanied by his dark-skinned servant (her husband, William).

OVERVIEW

STRUCTURE OF FREE SOCIETY IN THE SOUTH, C. 1860

Group	Size	Characteristics
Large planters	Less than 1 percent of white families	Owned fifty or more slaves and plantations in excess of one thousand acres; the wealthiest class in America
Planters	About 3 percent of white families	Owned twenty to forty-nine slaves and plantations in excess of one hundred acres; controlled bulk of Southern wealth and provided most of the political leaders
Small slaveholders	About 20 percent of white families	Owned fewer than twenty slaves, and most often less than five; primarily farmers, though some were part of a small middle class in towns and cities
Nonslaveholding whites	About 75 percent of white families	Most were yeomen farmers who owned their own land and stressed production for family use; one in five owned neither slaves nor land and squatted on least desirable land where they planted some corn and grazed some livestock; in cities they worked as artisans or, more typically, day laborers
Free black people	About 3 percent of all free families	Concentrated in the Upper South; hemmed in by legal and social restrictions; most were tenants or farm laborers; about one-third lived in cities and were generally limited to lowest paying jobs

What could have been a fatal flaw in their plan as they traveled from Savannah to Philadelphia—their inability to write and hence sign their names or document their assumed identities—was overcome by having Ellen pose as a sickly, rheumatic master whose right hand had to be kept bandaged.

Running away was common, but most runaways fled no farther than to nearby swamps and woods. Most voluntarily returned or were tracked down by bloodhounds within a week.

Slaves resisted complete domination by their masters in less overt ways. They mocked white people in folktales like those about Brer Rabbit, for example, in which weak but wily animals cunningly outsmart their stronger enemies. Slave owners routinely complained of slaves malingering at work, abusing farm animals, losing tools, stealing food, and committing arson. These subversive acts of protest never challenged the system of slavery itself, but they did help slaves maintain a sense of dignity and self-respect.

FREE SOCIETY

Southern cities, though small by Northern standards, provided jobs for a growing class of free workers who increasingly clashed with planters over the use of slave labor. These same cities, notably in the Upper South, were also home to the nation's largest concentration of free blacks. Though restricted in their freedom, these blacks competed with white workers for jobs. Pressure was mounting on

WHAT WERE the divisions in free white society regarding slavery?

• AMERICAN VIEWS •

A LETTER FROM AN ESCAPED SLAVE TO HIS FORMER MASTER

In 1859, Jackson Whitney was one of six thousand fugitive slaves living in Canada beyond the reach of the Fugitive Slave Act of 1850. Like most fugitives, he was male, and he had been forced to leave his family behind in Kentucky. His letter gives us information about slavery that only a slave could provide.

WHAT IS the tone of Whitney's letter?

- How did he express his joy at being a free man?

- Why did Whitney feel that Riley, his former owner, had betrayed him?

- What did Whitney mean by the phrase "a slave talking to 'massa'"? How did he indicate that he had been hiding his true feelings as a slave?

- How did Whitney contrast his religious beliefs and those of Riley? How did he expect Riley to be punished?

- What pained Whitney about his freedom in Canada, and what did he ask of Riley?

March 18, 1859

Mr. Wm. Riley, Springfield, Ky.—Sir:

I take this opportunity to dictate a few lines to you, supposing you might be curious to know my whereabouts. I am happy to inform you that I am in Canada, in good health, and have been here several days. Perhaps, by this time, you have concluded that robbing a woman of her husband, and children of their father does not pay, at least in your case; and I thought, while lying in jail by your direction, that if you had no remorse or conscience that would make you feel for a poor, broken-hearted man, and his worse-than-murdered wife and child, . . . and could not by any entreaty or permission be induced to do as you promised you would, which was to let me go with my family for $800—but contended for $1,000, when you had promised to take the same you gave for me (which was $660,) at the time you bought me, and let me go with my dear wife and children! but instead would render me miserable, and lie to me, and to your neighbors . . . and when you was at Louisville trying to sell me! then I thought it was

them by the 1850s to leave the South or be enslaved. Overriding racism bonded most white people together to defend the prerogatives of white supremacy.

THE SLAVEHOLDING MINORITY

The white-columned plantation estate approached from a stately avenue of shade trees and framed by luxuriant gardens remains the most popular image of the slave South. In fact, only the wealthiest planters could live in such splendor, and they comprised less than 1 percent of Southern white families in 1860. Yet displayed in their homes and grounds, their wealth and status were so imposing that they created an idealized image of grace and grandeur that has obscured the cruder realities of the slave regime.

Families of the planter class—defined as those who held a minimum of twenty slaves—constituted only around 3 percent of all Southern families in 1860. Most planters lived in drab log cabins. "The planter's home is generally a rude ungainly structure, made of logs, rough hewn from the forest; rail fences and rickety gates guard its enclosures," complained a speaker to the Alabama horticultural society in 1851. "We murder our soil with wasteful culture because there is plenty of fresh land West—and we live in tents and huts when we might live in rural palaces."

Most planters were acquisitive and restless. The sheer drive and penny-pinching materialism of these planters on the make impressed Tyrone Power, an

W **WHERE TO LEARN MORE**

Jarrell Plantation, Juliette, Georgia
www.mylink.net/~jarrell/

time for me to make my feet feel for Canada, and let your conscience feel in your pocket.—Now you cannot say but that I did all that was honorable and right while I was with you, although I was a slave. I pretended all the time that I thought you, or some one else had a better right to me than I had to myself, which you know is rather hard thinking.

—You know, too, that you proved a traitor to me in the time of need, and when in the most bitter distress that the human soul is capable of experiencing; and could you have carried out your purposes there would have been no relief. But I rejoice to say that an unseen, kind spirit appeared for the oppressed, and bade me take up my bed and walk—the result of which is that I am victorious and you are defeated. I am comfortably situated in Canada, working for George Harris [another fugitive slave from Kentucky who had bought a farm in Canada]. . . .

There is only one thing to prevent me being entirely happy here, and that is the want of my dear wife and children, and you to see us enjoying ourselves together here. I wish you could realize the contrast between Freedom and slavery; but it is not likely that we shall ever meet again on this earth.

But if you want to go to the next world and meet a God of love, mercy, and justice, in peace; who says, "Inasmuch as you did it to the least of them my little ones, you did it unto me"—making the professions that you do, pretending to be a follower of Christ, and tormenting me and my little ones as you have done—[you] had better repair the breaches you have made among us in this world, by sending my wife and children to me; thus preparing to meet your God in peace; for, if God don't punish you for inflicting such distress on the poorest of His poor, then there is no use of having any God, or talking about one. . . .

I hope you will consider candidly, and see if the case does not justify every word I have said, and ten times as much. You must not consider that it is a slave talking to 'massa' now, but one as free as yourself.

I subscribe myself one of the abused of America, but one of the justified and honored of Canada.

Jackson Whitney

Source: John W. Blassingame, ed., *Slave Testimony: Two Centuries of Letters, Speeches, Interviews, and Autobiographies* (Louisiana State University Press, 1977).

Irish actor who visited the South in the 1830s. The slaveholders he saw carving plantations out of the wilderness were "hardy, indefatigable, and enterprising to a degree; despising and condemning luxury and refinement, courting labour, and even making a pride of the privations which they, without any necessity, continue to endure with their families."

Besides raising her own children, the plantation mistress managed the household staff, oversaw the cooking and cleaning, gardened, dispensed medicine and clothing to the slaves, and often assisted in their religious instruction. When guests or relatives came for an extended visit, the wife had to make all the special arrangements that this entailed. On the occasions when the master was called off on a business or political trip, she kept the plantation accounts. In many respects, she worked harder than her husband.

Planter wives often complained in their journals and letters of their social isolation from other white women and the physical and mental toil of managing slaves. Still, they only rarely questioned the institution of slavery. Their deepest anger stemmed from their humiliation by husbands who kept slave mistresses or sexually abused slave women. "Sometimes white mistresses will surmise that there is an intimacy between a slave woman & the master," recalled a former slave, "and perhaps she will make a great fuss & have her whipped, & perhaps there will be no peace until she is sold."

QUICK REVIEW

Plantation Mistresses

- Mistresses ran the household staff.
- Mistresses were responsible for arrangements for visitors.
- Planter's wives found the management of slaves a burden.

Generally younger than the planters, small slaveholders were a diverse lot. About 10 percent were women, and another 20 percent or so were merchants, businessmen, artisans, and urban professionals. Most were farmers trying to acquire enough land and slaves to enter the ranks of planters.

Small slaveholders enjoyed scant economic security. A deadly outbreak of disease among their slaves or a single bad crop could destroy their credit and force them to sell their slaves to clear their debts. Owners of fewer than ten slaves stood a fifty-fifty chance within a decade of dropping out of the slaveholding class. In any given area suitable for plantations, small holders were gradually pushed out as planters bought up land to raise livestock or more crops.

Especially in the Lower South, owning slaves was a necessary precondition for upward mobility, but it was hardly a sufficient one. As a Baptist opponent of slavery put it, "Without slaves a man's children stand but poor chance to marry in reputation." Aside from conferring status, owning a few slaves could relieve a white household of much hard domestic labor. "I wish to God every head of a family in the United States had one [slave] to take the drudgery and menial service off his family," proclaimed Andrew Johnson of Tennessee in the U.S. Senate.

THE WHITE MAJORITY

Three-fourths of Southern white families owned no slaves in 1860. Nonslaveholders predominated wherever the soil and climate were not suitable for plantation agriculture. Most of them were yeoman farmers who worked their own land with family labor.

These farmers were quick to move when times were bad and their land was used up, but once settled in an area, they formed intensely localized societies. The community extended 5 to 10 miles around the nearest country store or county courthouse. Networks of kin and friends provided labor services when needed, fellowship in evangelical churches, and staple goods that an individual farm could not produce. The yeomanry aimed to be self-sufficient and limited market involvement to the sale of livestock and an occasional cotton crop that could bring in needed cash.

Yeoman farmers prized their independence. They tried to avoid debt and wanted to limit government authority. Rather than risk financial ruin by buying slaves on credit to grow cotton, they grew food crops and depended on their sons and, when needed, their wives and daughters to work the fields. Far longer than most Northern farmers, they continued to make their own clothes, shoes, soap, and other consumer items.

In areas where there were both small farms and scattered plantations, the interests of the yeomen and the planters were often complementary. Planters provided local markets for the surplus grain and livestock of nonslaveholders and, for a small fee, access to grist mills and gins for grinding corn and cleaning cotton. They lent small sums to poorer neighbors in emergencies or to pay taxes. The yeomen staffed the slave patrols and became overseers on the plantations. Both groups sought to protect property rights from outside interference and to maintain a system of racial control in which white liberties rested on black degradation.

When yeomen and planters did clash, it was usually over economic issues. Large slaveholders needing better credit and marketing facilities gravitated toward the Whig party, which called for banks and internal improvements. Nonslaveholding farmers, especially in the Lower South, tended to be Democrats who opposed banks and state-funded economic projects. But as long as planters deferred to the egalitarian sensibilities of the yeomen by courting them at election time and promising to safeguard their liberties, the planters were able to maintain broad support for slavery across class lines.

Around 15 percent of rural white families owned neither land nor slaves. These were the so-called poor whites, stigmatized by both abolitionists and planters as lazy and shiftless. The abolitionists considered them a kind of underclass who proved that slavery so degraded the dignity of labor that it led people to shun work and lapse into wretched poverty. Planters habitually complained that poor whites demoralized the slaves by showing that a person could survive without steady labor.

A yeoman farmstead in New Braumfels, Texas. The yeomanry strove for self-sufficiency by growing food crops and grazing livestock.

Daughters of the Republic of Texas Library. Yanaguana Society Collection

Most landless white people were resourceful and enterprising enough to squat on a few acres of land, put up crude cabins for shelter, plant some corn, and graze livestock in the surrounding woods. Although poor by most standards, they were also defiantly self-reliant.

Nonslaveholders were a growing majority in Southern cities, and their numbers were growing fastest among the working classes. These urban workers shared no agricultural interests or ties with the planters. Nor were most of them, especially in the unskilled ranks, southern-born. Northerners and immigrants dominated the urban work force.

Free workers, especially Irish and German immigrants, increasingly replaced slaves in urban labor markets. These white workers bitterly resented competition from black slaves, and their demands to exclude slaves from the urban workplace reinforced planters' belief that cities bred abolitionism.

FREE BLACK PEOPLE

A few Southern black people—6 percent of the total in 1860—were "free persons of color" and constituted 3 percent of the free population in the South. White intimidation and special legal provisions known as **black codes** (found throughout the North as well) denied them nearly all the rights of citizenship. Because of the legal presumption in the South that all black people were slaves, they had to carry freedom papers, official certificates of their freedom. Many occupations, especially those involved in the communication of ideas, such as the printing trades, were closed to them.

Every slave state forbade the entry of free black people, and every municipality had its own rules and regulations that forced them to live as an inferior caste. In Charleston, for example, a free black person could not smoke a cigar or carry a cane in public. White people had the right of way, and a free black person who bumped into a white person on the street was likely to be flogged.

More than four-fifths of the Southern free black population lived in the Upper South. Most of them were the offspring of slaves freed by private manumissions between 1780 and 1800 when a slump in tobacco markets and the Revolutionary War creed of natural rights had loosened slavery in the Chesapeake region.

Black codes   Laws passed by states and municipalities denying many rights of citizenship to free black people before the Civil War.

Barbering was one of the skilled trades open to black men during the antebellum years. Several wealthy African Americans began their careers as barbers.

The Granger Collection, New York

As in the North, legal barriers and white prejudice generally confined free black people to the poorest paying and most menial work. In rural areas, most were farm laborers or tenants. The best economic opportunities came in the cities, where some found factory jobs and positions in the skilled trades. The percentage of black people in the skilled trades was generally higher in the South than in the North. Talented artisans, such as Thomas Day, widely recognized as the finest cabinet-maker in North Carolina, could command a premium in wages from white employers.

Cities offered free black people not only jobs but also enough social space to found their own churches and mutual-aid associations. Especially after 1840, urban African-American churches proliferated to become the center of black community life. These churches sponsored Sunday schools and day schools that were about the only means of education open to black people. Despite white opposition to black schools, the demand for schooling persisted. A "good education," declared a black schoolmaster in Baltimore, "is the *sine qua non* as regards the elevation of our people."

Less than 2 percent of the black people in the Lower South were free in 1860. Most of them descended from black emigrants who fled the revolutionary unrest in Haiti in the 1790s. Able to secure a solid economic footing, they left their descendants wealthier than any other free black people in the United States. Free black people in the Lower South were more likely than those in the Upper South to have a marketable skill, and two-thirds of them lived in cities.

A light skin also enhanced the social standing of free black people among color-conscious whites in the Lower South. Nearly 70 percent of free black people in 1860 were mulattoes, and from their ranks came nearly all of the very small number of black planters. A mulatto elite emerged in Charleston, Mobile, and New Orleans that carefully distanced itself from most black people, slave or free. In New Orleans, where the tradition of racially mixed unions dated back to French and Spanish rule, mulattoes put on lavish "octoroon balls" attended by free women of color and white men. Even here, however, the mulatto elite remained suspended between black and white worlds that never fully accepted them.

Despite the tendency toward a three-tiered racial hierarchy in the port cities of the Lower South, white people still insisted on making a racial dichotomy between white and black the overriding social division in the South. As the racial defense of slavery intensified in the 1850s, more calls were made for laws to banish or enslave free black people.

Despised and feared by white people as a subversive element in a slave society, free black Southerners were daily reminded that their freedom rested on the whims of the white majority. As white attitudes turned uglier in the late antebellum period, that freedom was less secure than ever.

THE PROSLAVERY ARGUMENT

WHAT WERE Southern
defenses of slavery?

In the early nineteenth century, most Southern whites would have called slavery a necessary evil, an unfortunate legacy from earlier generations that was needed to maintain racial peace. The 1830s marked a turning point. After the twin shocks of Nat Turner's Rebellion and the onset of the abolitionist crusade, white mobs emerged to stifle any open criticism of slavery in the Lower South. White Southerners also began to develop a defense of slavery. By the 1850s, politicians, intellectuals, and evangelical ministers were arguing that it was a positive good, an institution ordained by God as the foundation of southern prosperity, white democracy, and Christian instruction for heathen Africans. Slavery, they insisted, was a mild, paternalistic, and even caring institution.

Evangelical Protestantism dominated Southern religious expression by the 1830s, and its ministers took the lead in combating abolitionist charges that slavery was a moral and religious abomination. Most of the Southern churches had always supported slavery. This support grew more pronounced and articulate once the abolitionists stepped up their attacks on slavery in the mid-1830s. Through a selective reading of the Bible, the proslavery ideologues found abundant evidence to proclaim slavery fully in accord with God's moral dictates.

As this cartoon reflects, a staple of proslavery propaganda was to contrast the allegedly contented and healthy lot of slaves with that of starving factory workers exploited by the system of wage labor.

Courtesy of Library of Congress

Southern evangelicals also turned to the Bible to support their argument that patriarchal authority—the unquestioned power of the father—was the basis of all Christian communities. Slavery thus became a matter of family governance, a domestic institution in which Christian masters of slaves accepted responsibility for caring for their workers in sickness and old age. Slavery was part of God's plan to Christianize an inferior race and teach its people how to produce raw materials that benefited the world's masses.

The growing commitment of Southern evangelicals to slavery clashed with the antislavery position and the generally more liberal theology of Northern evangelicals. In 1837, the Presbyterians split along sectional lines because of differences over slavery. In 1844, and as a direct result of the slavery issue, the Methodist Episcopal Church, the nation's largest, divided into Northern and Southern churches. The Baptists did the same a year later. These religious schisms foreshadowed the sectionalized political divisions of the 1850s; they also severed one of the main emotional bonds between white Northerners and Southerners.

The religious defense of slavery was central to the slaveholding ethic of paternalism that developed after 1830. By the 1850s, planters commonly described slaves as members of an extended family who were treated better than free workers in the North. Led by Charles Colcock Jones, a minister and planter in the Georgia lowcountry, a group of evangelical masters founded religious missions to the slaves and sought reforms, such as legal measures that would prevent the separation of slave families. Such efforts to reform slavery failed largely because most masters would accept no limits on their power to control and work their slaves as they saw fit.

More common than the biblical defense of slavery was the racial argument that black people were unfit for freedom among white people. The racial defense alleged that black people were naturally lazy and inherently inferior to white people. If freed, so went the argument, they would turn to crime and sexually assault white women.

Slavery as a necessary means of racial control was a central theme in Thomas R. Dew's *Review of the Debates in the Virginia Legislature of 1831 and 1832*, the first major justification of slavery by a Southerner. Concerned by the efforts of nonslaveholders in Virginia to enact a program of gradual emancipation, Dew, a tidewater planter tried to unite white people behind slavery by stressing the issue of race.

The racial argument resonated powerfully among white people. The attitude of a Tennessee farmer, as recorded by a northern traveler in the 1850s, was typical: "He said he'd always wished there hadn't been any niggers here . . . , but he wouldn't like to have them free." Most white Southerners could see no middle ground between slavery and the presumed social chaos of emancipation.

 13–7
George Fitzhugh, "The Blessings of Slavery" (1857)

FROM THEN TO NOW
The Economic Legacy of Slavery

The South today enjoys one of the highest rates of economic growth in the nation and plays host to business conglomerates, bank mergers, and Olympic games. Yet as late as the 1930s, the South was so impoverished that it was labeled the nation's number-one economic problem. The key to this remarkable transformation was the way in which the South finally overcame the economic legacy of slavery.

Because slavery persisted in the South and was abolished in the North, the Northern and Southern economies developed separately before the Civil War. The key difference was the markedly lower level of Southern investment in manufacturing and transportation compared to the levels in the North. Slaveowners had invested two-thirds of their wealth in slaves and were reluctant to promote changes that would diversify their economy along northern lines through the introduction of manufacturing based on low-wage labor. On the contrary, they had every incentive to keep wages high to protect the value of their investment in human labor.

The end of slavery reversed the basic dynamic shaping the southern economy. Planters now had to derive their wealth primarily from their land, not their slaves. As a result, they encouraged low-wage policies that transformed many former slaves and poor white farmers into impoverished tenant farmers and sharecroppers. When cotton prices began a steady decline in the 1870s, Southern investors turned to manufacturing in an effort to generate economic growth, but the abundance of cheap agricultural labor kept industrial wage rates well below the national level. Consequently, the South attracted little in the way of outside labor. And with investment opportunities more attractive elsewhere, it attracted little capital for modernizing its factories. Education in the South likewise remained behind, because the white southern elite was leery of reforms that would increase workers' skills and encourage them to leave the region in search of better wages. Thus, although southern industry grew, it remained labor-intensive and failed to keep pace with the region's rising population. By the 1930s, when the Great Depression hit, the South was mired in poverty and backwardness.

Sweeping new federal policies initiated in the wake of the Depression began fundamentally to change the Southern economy, raising wages and bringing them more in line with the national average. Farm subsidies encouraged planters to take land out of production, forcing poor tenants and sharecroppers to leave the land and migrate out of the region. Abundant, well-paying jobs in Northern factories during World War II accelerated the outflow of the South's low-skill workers. Meanwhile, federal money poured into the South for new defense plants and war-related projects.

By the 1950s, the formerly insulated, low-wage southern economy had turned the corner. Southern politicians dropped the region's corporate taxes to the lowest in the nation and became adept at attracting new sources of capital and large federal subsidies. After initially opposing the black-led civil rights revolution of the 1950s and 1960s, most of the white business elite backed the formal end of racial segregation in an attempt to improve the South's image. Today, well over a century after slavery had placed it on a separate path of economic development, the Southern economy has lost nearly all traces of its distinctiveness and can boast of being in the forefront of national economic trends.

Despite its apparent success in forging white solidarity, the racial argument could be turned on its head and used to weaken slavery. Most white Northerners were about as racist as their Southern counterparts, but they were increasingly willing to end slavery on the grounds that the stronger white race should help black people improve themselves as free persons. Some white Southerners challenged the economic prerogatives of slaveholders. Why, for example, should any white people, as members of the master race, be forced into economic competition against skilled slave artisans? Why should not all nonagricultural jobs be legally reserved for white people? Doctrines of black inferiority could not prevent white unity from cracking when the economic interests of nonslaveholders clashed with those of planters.

CONCLUSION

The spread of plantation agriculture across the Lower South after 1830 deepened the involvement of white Southerners in cotton and slavery. At the same time, an abolitionist movement in the North morally attacked slavery and demanded that it be abolished. As Southern interests became more enmeshed in an institution that outsiders condemned, religious and intellectual leaders portrayed slavery as a Christian institution and a positive good necessary for white democracy and harmonious race relations. Proslavery ideologues stridently described the South as separate from and superior to the rest of the nation.

The proslavery argument depicted a nearly ideal society blessed by class and racial harmony. In reality, social conditions in the slave South were far more contradictory and conflict ridden. Slaves were not content in their bondage. They dreamed of freedom and sustained that dream through their own forms of Christianity and the support of family and kin. Relations between masters and their slaves were antagonistic, not affectionate, and wherever the system of control slackened, slaves resisted their owners. The publication in 1857 of Hinton Rowan Helper's *Impending Crisis of the South*, a scathing indictment by a white North Carolinian of how slavery stunted economic opportunities for average white people, vividly showed that not all were convinced by the proslavery argument.

Planters were not fooled by the public rhetoric of white unity. They knew that slavery was increasingly confined to the Lower South, and that elsewhere in the South white support for it was gradually eroding. They feared the double-edged challenge to their privileged positions from outside interference with slavery and internal white disloyalty. By the 1850s, many of them were concluding that the only way to resolve their dilemma was to make the South a separate nation.

SUMMARY

The Lower South Cotton was king in the Lower South and provided an economic basis for Southern sectionalism. The Lower South had incomparable natural advantages for growing cotton and short-staple cotton expanded westward after the invention of the cotton gin. The plantation system, relying on the labor of slaves, provided cotton to the world's textile mills. While cotton was economically profitable, the Lower South lagged behind in industrialization and urbanization. Slavery was not confined to agriculture; slaves lived in cities and towns with a few more freedoms, including the ability to earn wages.

The Upper South Climate and geography distinguished the Upper South from the Lower South; the eight slave states lay north of the best growing zones for cotton. The Upper South emerged from an economic slump in the 1850s with diversified agriculture, urbanization, and an expansion of manufacturing and trade. The region served as a slave exporter to the Lower South and had an economic stake in slavery although the institution was not as widespread in the Upper South or as profitable.

Slave Life and Culture By the mid-nineteenth century Southern slaves were native-born; their number had increased more than five times. African-American slaves had shaped a culture of their own to deal with the humiliations and difficulties of their lives; in their family life and religious beliefs they found the strength to sustain themselves with hope. In addition to day to day resistance, slave uprisings occurred; the only real opportunity for escape was the Underground Railroad, but only a relatively small number were able to permanently escape northward or to Canada.

Free Society While the planter society of the South was numerically small, their influence was extensive. The majority of Southern white people owned no slaves; they were farmers who worked their own land with family labor. This group sometimes clashed with the planters; however, all white southerners sought to maintain their status through degradation and intimidation. A small number of free blacks lived precariously between slave and white society, their freedoms growing less secure as the 1800s progressed.

The Proslavery Argument By the 1830s, slavery was under attack, and Southerners countered by defending slavery as a positive good and used Biblical examples to support their arguments. Some Protestant churches split between Northern and Southern branches foreshadowing the sectional political divisions that were to come. Even Southern white people opposed to slavery feared emancipation; they could see no middle ground between slavery and freedom.

REVIEW QUESTIONS

1. Why did cotton production expand in the South? How was this expansion linked to slavery and westward movement?

2. How was the Upper South different from the Lower South? What role did slavery play in each region after 1815?

3. How would you characterize the life of a plantation slave?

4. How did most nonslaveholding white Southerners live?

5. How did white Southerners defend slavery and reconcile it with Christianity?

KEY TERMS

Black codes (p. 281)
Denmark Vesey's Conspiracy
(p. 276)

Gabriel Prosser's Rebellion (p. 276)
Gang system (p. 268)
Nat Turner's Rebellion (p. 276)

Slave codes (p. 273)
Underground Railroad (p. 276)

WHERE TO LEARN MORE

○ **The Anacostia Museum Center for African-American History.** This museum of the Smithsonian Institution explores American history and cultures from an African-American perspective. Go to **www.si.edu/anacostia/** for information on its exhibits and a calendar of events.

○ **Appalachian Museum of Berea College, Berea, Kentucky.** This museum is an excellent source for understanding the lifestyles and material culture of the nonslaveholding farmers in the Appalachian highlands. For an overview of its exhibits, see: **www.museum.appstate.edu/exhibits/exhibits.shtml**

Cottonlandia Museum, Greenwood, Mississippi. The library and museum depict the history of cotton in the Mississippi Delta. Special collections include some Native-American artifacts. Information on its displays can be found at: **www.gcvg.com/CL.html**

Jarrell Plantation, Juliette, Georgia. This state historic site consists of a fifteen-building farm complex that conveys a good sense of the physical dimensions of a nineteenth-century Georgia plantation. For a visual tour of the plantation, go to: **www.mylink.net/~jarrell/**

Meadow Farm Museum, Richmond, Virginia. The archives and museum are especially strong on Southern farm life in the mid-nineteenth century. A description of the museum is at: **www.co.henrico.va.us/rec/kmfarm.html**

 For additional study resources for this chapter, go to:
www.prenhall.com/goldfield/chapter11

*Our duties originate, not from difference of sex,
but from the diversity of the relations of life,
the various gifts and talents committed to our care,
and the different eras in which we live.*

An abolitionist freeing a slave from his shackles: A colored woodcut, c. 1840, from an American anti-slavery almanac.

12

THE MARKET REVOLUTION
AND SOCIAL REFORM
1815–1850

WHAT MARKED the increasing industrialization in the U.S. economy between 1815 and 1850?

HOW AND why did inequalities increase among the rich, the middle class, and the working classes?

WHAT ROLE did women play in the reform movement that followed the War of 1812?

WHY DID the abolitionist agitation and sentiment in the North grow?

1850

1815

East Boylston, Mass.
10th mo. 2d, 1837.

Dear Friend: . . .

The investigation of the rights of the slave has led me to a better under-standing of my own. I have found the Anti-Slavery cause to be the high school of morals in our land—the school in which human rights *are more fully inves-tigated, and better understood and taught, than in any other. Here a great fun-damental principle is uplifted and illuminated, and from this central light, rays innumerable stream all around. Human beings have* rights, *because they are* moral *beings: the rights of* all *men grow out of their moral nature; and as all men have the same moral nature, they have essentially the same rights. These rights may be wrested from the slave, but they cannot be alienated; his title to himself is as perfect* now, *as is that of Lyman. Beecher [a prominent minis-ter]: it is stamped on his moral being, and is, like it, imperishable. Now if rights are founded on the nature of our moral being, then the* mere circumstance of sex *does not give to man higher rights and responsibilities, than to woman. To suppose that it does, would be to deny the self-evident truth, that the "physical constitution is the mere instrument of the moral nature." To suppose that it does, would be to break up utterly the relations, of the two natures, and to re-verse their functions, exalting the animal nature into a monarch, and hum-bling the moral into a slave; making the former a proprietor, and the latter its property. When human beings are regarded as* moral *beings, sex, instead of being enthroned upon the summit, . . . sinks into insignificance and nothing-ness. My doctrine then is, that whatever it is morally right for man to do, it is morally right for woman to do. Our duties originate, not from difference of sex, but from the diversity of our relations in life, the various gifts and talents com-mitted to our care, and the different eras in which we live.*

—Angelina Emily Grimké

Aileen S. Kraditor, ed., *Up from the Pedestal: Selected Writings in the History of American Feminism* (New York: Quadrangle, 1968), pp. 62–63.

IMAGE KEY
for pages 288–289

a. A map of western New York State in 1811 including the proposed Erie Canal route, the Finger Lakes, Lake Ontario, and Lake Erie.

b. An abolitionist freeing a slave from his shackles: colored woodcut, c. 1840, from an American anti-slavery almanac.

c. Pages from an American Pictorial Primer, c. 1845.

d. The original cotton gin of inventor Eli Whitney, stuffed with cotton.

e. Pawtucket Bridge and Falls, watercolor and ink on paper, 15 × 19 1/2.

f. Six females model American Victorian fashion in Godey 's *Lady 's Book for April, 1867.* Colored, painted lithograph.

g. American feminists include clockwise from top: Lucretia Mott, Elizabeth Cady Stanton, Mary A. Livermore, Lydia Maria Child, Susan B. Anthony, Grace Greenwood and in center is Anna E. Dickinson.

h. Frederick Douglass (1817?–1895). Oil on canvas, c1844, attr. to E. Hammond.

ANGELINA GRIMKÉ wrote the above as part of a public letter to Catherine Beecher, a pioneer in women's education and the daughter of the evangelical preach-er Lyman Beecher mentioned in the letter. In 1837, on an abolitionist lecture tour in New England, Angelina had become the first American woman to defy the social taboo against women speaking in public to a mixed audience of men and women. Catherine Beecher was among her many critics, and Angelina publicly responded to her attacks.

Born in 1805 to a wealthy slaveholding family in Charleston, Angelina nonetheless rejected slavery and joined the abolitionist movement in 1835. As she made clear in her letter to Beecher, her commitment to women's rights flowed out of her exposure to abolitionism.

Soon after her marriage in 1838 to the abolitionist Theodore Weld, Angelina com-piled much of the firsthand documentation on slavery for his *American Slavery As It Is,* a popular antislavery tract that appeared in 1839. Her marriage also coincided with her withdrawal from public life for a dozen years. Although she worked for the emancipation of the slaves during the Civil War, she spoke only rarely in public.

Although Angelina's commitment to radical reform was hardly typical of antebellum American women, her social activism speaks to the radicalizing potential of the reform impulse that swept over the nation after the War of 1812.

This reform impulse was strongest in the North, where traditional social and economic relations were undergoing wrenching changes as a market revolution accelerated the spread of cities, factories, and commercialized farms. Urbanization also brought new production patterns and increasingly separated one's home from one's place of work. New middle and working classes evolved in response to such changes. The North was also the area where the emotional fires of evangelical revivals burned the hottest.

The religious message of the Second Great Awakening that began in the early 1800s provided a framework for responding to the changes that accompanied the market revolution. Through Christian activism, individuals could strive toward moral perfectibility. Social evils, and the sinful consequences of economic and social changes, could be cleansed if good Christians helped others find the path of righteousness.

The first wave of reform after the War of 1812 focused on individual behavior, targeting drinking, gambling, sexual misconduct, and Sabbath-breaking. A second phase of reform turned to institutional solutions for crime, poverty, and social delinquency. The third phase of the reform cycle rejected the social beliefs and practices that prescribed fixed and subordinate positions to certain Americans based on race and sex. This radical phase culminated in the abolitionist and women's right's movements.

INDUSTRIAL CHANGE AND URBANIZATION

In 1820, four in five of the free labor force worked in agriculture, and manufacturing played a minor role in economic activity. Over the next three decades, however, the United States joined England as a world leader in industrialization. By 1850, manufacturing accounted for one-third of total commodity output, and nonfarm employment had more than doubled to 45 percent of the labor force.

The most direct cause of this surge in manufacturing was the increasing consumption within the United States of the goods the country was producing. The **transportation revolution** dramatically reduced transportation costs and shipping times, opened up new markets for farmers and manufacturers alike, and provided an ongoing incentive for expanding production (see Table 12.1). As agricultural and manufactured goods were exchanged more efficiently, a growing home market stimulated the development of American manufacturing.

TABLE 12.1
Impact of the Transportation Revolution on Traveling Time

Route	1800	1830	1860
New York to Philadelphia	2 days	1 day	Less than 1 day
New York to Charleston	More than 1 week	5 days	2 days
New York to Chicago	6 weeks	3 weeks	2 days
New York to New Orleans	4 weeks	2 weeks	6 days

WHAT MARKED the increasing industrialization in the U.S. economy between 1815 and 1850?

WHERE TO LEARN MORE **W**

Baltimore Center for Urban Archaeology, Baltimore, Maryland

Transportation revolution   Dramatic improvements in transportation that stimulated economic growth after 1815 by expanding the range of travel and reducing the time and cost of moving goods and people.

WHERE TO LEARN MORE

Erie Canal Museum,
Syracuse, New York
www.eriecanalmuseum.org/

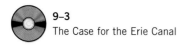

9–3
The Case for the Erie Canal

THE TRANSPORTATION REVOLUTION

In 1815 the cost of moving goods by land transportation was prohibitively high. It cost as much to haul heavy goods by horse-drawn wagons 30 miles into the interior as to ship them 3,000 miles across the Atlantic Ocean. Water transportation was much cheaper, but it was limited to the coast or navigable rivers. Only farmers located near a city or a river could grow surplus crops for sale in an outside market. Western farm surpluses followed the southerly flow of the Ohio and Mississippi river systems to market outlets in New Orleans.

Steamboats provided the first transportation breakthrough. In 1807, Robert Fulton demonstrated their commercial practicality when he sent the *Clermont* 150 miles up the Hudson River from New York City to Albany. By the 1820s, steamboats had reduced the cost and the time of up-river shipments by 90 percent. More and more farmers could now export corn, pork, and other regional foodstuffs.

Western trade did not start to flow eastward until the completion of the Erie Canal in 1825, the first and most successful of the artificial waterways designed to link eastern seaboard cities with Western markets (see Map 12–1). Funded by the New York legislature, the Erie Canal stretched 364 miles from Albany to Buffalo. Its construction by Irish immigrants was the greatest engineering feat of its era. The Erie canal reduced the cost of sending freight from Buffalo to New York City by more than 90 percent, and by the 1840s, it was pulling in more Western trade than was being sent to New Orleans on the Mississippi River.

Before the Panic of 1837 abruptly ended the canal boom, three broad networks of canals had been built. One set linked seaboard cities on the Atlantic with their agricultural hinterlands, another connected the Mid-Atlantic states with the Ohio River Valley, and a third funneled western grain to ports on the Great Lakes.

Railroads were the most important link in the transportation improvements that spurred economic development in Jacksonian America. Moving at 15 to 20 miles per hour—four times as fast as a canal boat and twice the speed of a stagecoach—the railroads of the 1830s were a radically new technology that overturned traditional notions of time and space. "I cannot describe the strange sensation produced on seeing the train of cars come up. And when I started in them . . . it seemed like a dream," exclaimed Christopher Columbus Baldwin of Massachusetts when he saw his first railroad car in 1835.

In 1825, the same year the Erie Canal was completed, the world's first general-purpose railroad, the Stockton and Darlington, opened in England. The construction of the first American railroads began in the late 1820s, and they all pushed outward from seaboard cities eager to connect to the Western market. The Baltimore and Ohio, crossed the Appalachians and connected Baltimore with Wheeling, Virginia, on the Ohio River. The Boston and Worcester linked New England and the eastern terminus of the Erie Canal at Albany. By 1840, U.S. rails had become the most dynamic booster of interregional trade. Whereas the canal network stopped expanding after 1840, the railroads tripled their mileage in the 1840s. By 1849, trunk lines from Atlantic Coast cities had reached the Great Lakes and the Ohio Valley and were about to enter the Mississippi Valley.

The rail network in place by midcentury was already altering the North-South sectional balance. Western trade was most shipped to the East, and Northern-born settlers, manufactured goods, and cultural values increasingly unified the free states east of the Mississippi into a common economic and cultural unit. The Northeast and the Old Northwest were becoming just the North. No direct rail connection linked the North and the South.

Both national and state government promoted the transportation revolution. High construction costs and the uncertainty of profits made private investors

QUICK REVIEW

Railroads

◆ Most important link in Jacksonian transportation revolution.

◆ 1825: first general-purpose railroad opened in England.

◆ By mid-century, railroads were a vital part of American economy.

MAP EXPLORATION

To explore an interactive version of this map, go to **http://www.prenhall.com/goldfield2/map12.1**

MAP 12–1

The Transportation Revolution   By 1830, a network of roads, canals, and navigable rivers was spurring economic growth in the first phase of the transportation revolution. By 1850, railroads, the key development in the second phase of the transportation revolution, were opening up additional areas to commercial activity.

WHICH CITIES probably benefited the most from the new transportation infrastructure and why?

CHRONOLOGY

1790	Samuel Slater opens the first permanent cotton mill in Rhode Island.
1793	Eli Whitney patents the first cotton gin.
1807	Robert Fulton's steamboat, the *Clermont*, makes its pioneering voyage up the Hudson River.
1814	The Boston Associates opens its Waltham mill, the first textile factory to mechanize all phases of production.
1817	Construction on the Erie Canal begins. American Colonization Society is founded.
1819–1823	Economic depression.
1824	In *Gibbons* v. *Ogden*, the Supreme Court strikes down a state monopoly over steamboat navigation.
1825	Erie Canal is completed.
1826	American Temperance Society launches its crusade.
1828	The Baltimore and the Ohio, the most important of the early railroads, is chartered.
1829	David Walker publishes *Appeal to the Colored Citizens of the World*.
1830	Joseph Smith founds the Church of Jesus Christ of Latter-day Saints.
1830–1831	Evangelical revivals are held in northern cities.
1831	William Lloyd Garrison begins publishing *The Liberator*.
1833	Slaves in the British Empire are emancipated. American Anti-Slavery Society is organized.

1834	New York Female Reform Society is founded. Female workers at the Lowell Mills stage their first strike.
1836	Congress passes gag rule.
1837	Horace Mann begins campaign for school reform in Massachusetts. Antiabolitionist mob kills Elijah P. Lovejoy. In *Charles River Bridge* v. *Warren Bridge*, the Supreme Court encourages economic competition by ruling that presumed rights of monopolistic privileges could not be used to block new economic enterprises.
1839–1843	Economic depression.
1840	Abolitionists split into Garrisonian and anti-Garrisonian societies. Political abolitionists launch the Liberty party.
1841	Brook Farm is established.
1842	Massachusetts Supreme Court in *Commonwealth* v. *Hunt* strengthens the legal right of workers to organize trade unions.
1845	Potato famine in Ireland sets off a mass migration of Irish to the United States.
1846–1848	Mormons migrate to the West.
1847	John Humphrey Noyes establishes the Oneida Community.
1848	Seneca Falls Convention outlines a program for women's rights.

Gibbons v. *Ogden* Supreme Court decision of 1824 involving coastal commerce that overturned a steamboat monopoly granted by the state of New York on the grounds that only Congress had the authority to regulate interstate commerce.

leery of risking their capital in long-term transportation projects. State legislatures furnished some 70 percent of the funding for canals and about half of all railroad capital. By the 1830s, the states were also making it easier for private businesses, and especially those in transportation, to receive the legal privileges of incorporation, which included the protection of limited liability—that is, the limiting of an investor's liability to one's direct financial stake in the company—and the power of eminent domain—the legal right to purchase land for rights-of-way. The federal government provided engineers for railroad surveys, lowered tariff duties on iron used in rail construction, and subsidized the railroads in the form of public land. Two decisions of the Supreme Court helped open up the economy to competition. In *Gibbons* v. *Ogden* (1824), the Court overturned a New York law that had given Aaron Ogden a monopoly on steamboat service between New York and New Jersey. Thomas Gibbons, Ogden's competitor, had a federal license for the coastal trade. The right to compete under the national license, the Court ruled, took legal precedence over Ogden's monopoly. The decision affirmed the supremacy of the national government to regulate interstate commerce.

A new Court, presided over by Roger B. Taney, who became chief justice when John Marshall died in 1835, struck a bolder blow against monopoly in the case of *Charles River Bridge* v. *Warren Bridge* in 1837. Taney ruled that the older Charles River Bridge Company had not received a monopoly from Massachusetts to collect tolls across the Charles River. Any uncertainties in the charter rights of corporations, reasoned Taney, should be resolved in favor of the broader community interests that free and open competition would serve.

Charles River Bridge v. *Warren Bridge*
Supreme Court decision of 1837 that promised economic competition by ruling that the broader rights of the community took precedence over any presumed right of monopoly granted in a corporate charter.

CITIES AND IMMIGRANTS

At midcentury, more than one in seven Americans was a city dweller, and the nation had ten cities whose population exceeded fifty thousand. The transportation revolution triggered this surge in urban growth. The cities that prospered were those with access to the expanding network of cheap transport on steamboats, canals, and railroads. This network opened up the rural interior for the purchase of farm commodities by city merchants and the sale of finished goods by urban importers and manufacturers. A huge influx of immigrants after the mid-1840s and advances in steam engines provided the cheap labor and power that made cities manufacturing centers.

America's largest cities in the early nineteenth century were its Atlantic ports: New York, Philadelphia, Baltimore, and Boston. These seaports all benefited from the transportation revolution, but only New York experienced phenomenal growth. By 1810, it had become the largest American city, and its population exceeded 800,000 by the 1850s. One-third of the nation's exports and more than three-fifths of its imports passed through New York between 1820 and 1860. No wonder poet Walt Whitman trumpeted this metropolis as "the great place of the Western Continent, the heart, the brain, the focus, the main spring, the pinnacle, the extremity, the no more beyond of the new world."

New York's harbor gave oceangoing ships direct, protected access to Manhattan Island, and from there the Hudson River provided a navigable highway flowing 150 miles north to Albany, deep in the state's agricultural interior. No other port was so ideally situated for trade. New York City merchants established the Black Ball Line in 1817, the first line of packet ships that ran on a regular schedule for moving cargoes, passengers, and mail across the Atlantic. The city's merchants also convinced the state legislature to finance the Erie Canal, which guaranteed the ongoing commercial preeminence of the port of New York.

New York City also benefited from the swelling flow of finished goods shipped out of New York for sale in the West. Western families with access to the Erie Canal became increasingly specialized economically. New markets encouraged them to concentrate on cash crops, and profits were spent on finished goods. The rise in the disposable income of farmers generated a demand for the consumer goods that the Erie Canal brought in. These goods came out of New York, but most were not manufactured in the city. Nonetheless, the jobs created by handling these goods and the profits derived from supplying the western market solidified the city's position as the nation's most dynamic economic center.

New Yorkers plowed the profits of this commerce into local real estate and into financial institutions such as the New York Stock Exchange, founded in 1817. The city's banks brought together the capital that made New York the country's chief financial center. Agents for the city's mercantile and financial interests used this capital to offer advantageous terms to capture much of the Southern trade and dominate commerce with South America.

Commercial rivals in other port cities launched their own canal and railroad ventures to penetrate the West, but none developed a hinterland as rich or extensive as New York's. Still, Boston, Baltimore, and Philadelphia at midcentury remained the nation's largest cities behind New York.

As they grew, the Atlantic ports pioneered new forms of city transportation. Omnibuses (horse-drawn coaches carrying up to twenty passengers) and steam ferries were in common use by the 1820s. The first commuter railroad, the Boston and Worcester, began service in 1838. Horse-drawn street railway lines in the 1850s moved at speeds of about 6 miles an hour, over-coming some of the limitations of the "walking cities" of the early nineteenth century. Cities began to spread outward as cheaper, faster ways of traveling to work became available.

The first slums also appeared. Small, flimsy wooden structures, often crammed into a back alley, housed the working poor in cramped, fetid conditions. Back-yard privies, supplemented by chamber pots, were the standard means of disposing of human wastes. These outhouses overflowed in heavy rain and often contaminated private wells, the source of drinking water. Garbage and animal wastes accumulated on streets, scavenged by roving packs of hogs.

A densely packed population in a poorly drained, garbage-strewn setting made cities unhealthy. Mortality rates were much higher than in rural areas, and the death rate in New York City was double that of London. Stagnant pools of water bred mosquitoes that carried yellow fever, and contaminated water supplies produced frequent epidemics of cholera and typhus. But the cities continued to grow.

The fastest-growing cities were in the interior. Their share of the urban population quadrupled from 1800 to 1840. Pittsburgh, at the head of the Ohio River, was the first Western city to develop a manufacturing sector to complement its exchange function. With access to the extensive coalfields of western Pennsylvania, Pittsburgh had a cheap fuel that provided the high heat needed to manufacture iron and glass. It emerged as America's best-known and most polluted manufacturing city. "It is surrounded," noted the French traveler Michel Chevalier in the 1830s, "with a dense, black smoke which, bursting forth in volumes from the foundries, forges, glass-houses, and the chimneys of all the factories and houses, falls in flakes of soot upon the dwellings and persons of the inhabitants. It is, therefore, the dirtiest town in the United States."

Cincinnati, downstream on the Ohio, soon became famous for its hogs. "Porkopolis," as it was called, was the West's first meatpacking center. Industries in animal by-products, such as soap, candles, shoes, and boots, gave the city a diversified manufacturing base that kept it in the forefront of Western urban growth.

By the 1840s, St. Louis and the Great Lakes ports of Buffalo, Cleveland, Detroit, Milwaukee, and Chicago were the dynamic centers of Western urbanization. St. Louis, just below the merger of the Missouri and the Mississippi Rivers, serviced American trade with the trans-Mississippi West. The city was also the eastern end of the Santa Fe Trail, a corridor of Anglo-Mexican trade that stretched across the southern plains to Santa Fe, New Mexico. St. Louis tripled in population in the 1830s, and by midcentury, it was developing rail connections that linked it to the Great Lakes cities.

The Great Lakes served as an extension of the Erie Canal, and cities on the lakes where incoming and outgoing goods had to be unloaded for transshipment benefited enormously. They soon evolved into regional economic centers serving the surrounding agricultural communities. They also promoted themselves into major rail hubs and thus reaped the economic advantages of being at the juncture of both water and rail transport.

The combined populations of Cleveland, Detroit, Milwaukee, and Chicago increased twenty-five-fold between 1830 and 1850. The only other cities experiencing such phenomenal rates of growth were the new industrial towns. The densest cluster of these was in rural New England along the fall line of rivers, where the rapidly falling water provided cheap power to drive the industrial machinery

QUICK REVIEW

Midwestern City

- America's fastest growing cities in interior.
- Pittsburgh became center of iron and glass manufacturing.
- St. Louis, Buffalo, Cleveland, Detroit, Milwaukee, and Chicago were centers of Western urbanization.

of factories and machine shops. Each town was tied to a transportation network that brought in raw cotton for the textile mills from the mercantile centers of Boston and Providence and shipped out the finished goods.

Lowell, Massachusetts, was America's first large-scale, planned manufacturing city. Founded in 1822 by Boston businessmen, Lowell was built around the falls of the Merrimack River. Within a decade, rural fields had been transformed into a city of eighteen thousand people. Lowell's success became a model for others to follow, and by 1840, New England led the North in both urbanization and industrialization.

A surge of immigrants swelled the size of the cities after the 1830s. At midcentury, most of the population in New York was foreign-born, and in all the port cities of the Northeast, immigrants dominated the manufacturing work force. Most of these immigrants were Irish and Germans who settled in the Northeast.

In the 1840s, economic and political upheavals in Europe spurred mass migration, mostly to America. Catholic peasants of Ireland, dominated by their Protestant English landlords, eked out a subsistence as tenants on tiny plots of land. A potato blight wiped out the crop in 1845 and 1846, and in the next five years about 1 million Irish died of malnutrition and disease. Another 1.5 million fled, many to America.

Without marketable skills, the Irish had to take the worst and lowest paying jobs: ragpickers, porters, day laborers, and unskilled factory hands. Wives and daughters became laundresses and maids for the urban middle class. Packed into dark cellars, unventilated attics, and rank tenements, they suffered from high mortality rates.

German immigrants came to America to escape poor harvests and political turmoil. Far more Germans than Irish had the capital to purchase land in the West and the skills to join the ranks of small businesspeople in the cities. They were also more likely than the Irish to have entered the country through Baltimore or New Orleans, Southern ports engaged in the tobacco and cotton trade with continental Europe. From there they fanned out into the Mississippi and Ohio Valleys. With the Irish, they made up over half of the population of St. Louis by the 1850s and were close to a majority in the other large cities of the Midwest and Northeast. With their diversified skills, the Germans found ample economic opportunities in the fast-growing cities and a setting in which to build neighborhoods of German-speaking shops, churches, schools, and benevolent societies.

About four in five of the 4.2 million immigrants from all nations who arrived from 1840 to 1860 settled in the New England and Mid-Atlantic states. Their sheer numbers transformed the size and ethnic composition of the working class, especially in the cities of the Northeast. And their cheap labor provided the final ingredient in the expansion of industrialization that began after the War of 1812.

THE INDUSTRIAL REVOLUTION

The Northeast led America's industrial revolution. In 1815, this region had the largest cities, the most developed capital markets, the readiest access to the technological skills of artisans, and the greatest supply of available labor. For the next thirty years, the United States had the most rapidly developing industrial economy in the world.

The household and the small workshop were the sites of manufacturing in Jefferson's America. Wider markets for household manufactures began to develop in the late eighteenth century with the coming of the **putting-out system**. Local merchants furnished ("put out") raw materials to rural households and paid at a piece rate for the labor that converted those raw materials into manufactured products. The supplying merchant then marketed and sold these goods.

As revealed in this portrait of the blacksmith Pat Lyon, the self-image of the artisans was closely related to the pride and dignity they derived from their craft work.

Pat Lyon at the Forge, 1826–27, John Neagle, American, 1796-1865, Oil on canvas, 238.12x172.72 cm (93 3/4x68 in), Museum of Fine Arts, Boston, Henry H. and Zoe Oliver Sherman Fund, 1975.806©2003 Museum of Fine Arts, Boston

Putting-out system System of manufacturing in which merchants furnished households with raw materials for processing by family members.

FROM THEN TO NOW
Immigration: An Ambivalent Welcome

Americans have long extended an ambivalent welcome to newcomers. In the mid-nineteenth century, employment posters often read "Irish Need Not Apply," and today stepped-up border patrols seek to keep out Mexican and other Latin American immigrants. Yet America is a nation settled and built by immigrants whose founding ideals promise equality and opportunity to all. And for much of its history it has offered asylum for the world's oppressed.

In the early years of the republic, Federalists worried that immigrants from Europe might be contaminated by the radical ideas of the French revolution and sought to make it harder for them to become naturalized citizens. The nation's first naturalization law in the 1790s also barred black immigrants from citizenship. The first sustained attack against newcomers, however, emerged as a result of the surge in immigration during the 1840s and 1850s. It was directed by established immigrant groups—the descendants of settlers from Britain and northwestern Europe—at unfamiliar newcomers, particularly the Irish.

Nativist arguments of that time have found an echo in all subsequent immigration debates. The Irish, it was claimed, would take jobs away from American workers and lower their wages. Taxpayers would have to foot the bill for the strains the newcomers imposed on schools, hospitals, and other civic services. The ignorant immigrants would corrupt the political process. Nativists especially feared religious contamination, claiming that the Catholicism of the Irish was alien to the Protestant values held to be indispensable to the preservation of American liberties. So many Irish arrived so quickly that many nativists were convinced of a Papal plot to undermine American freedom. "The bloody hand of the Pope," one wrote, "has stretched itself forth to our destruction."

Eventually the Irish and Germans merged into the economic and political fabric of American life. But in the late nineteenth century a massive new immigrant surge dominated by people from Southern and Eastern Europe seeking economic opportunity and fleeing religious oppression transformed American society and renewed nativist fears. This time, race replaced religion as the basis for drawing invidious comparisons between established residents and the newcomers. Pseudo-scientific theories relegated Jews, Slavs, and Mediterranean peoples, together with Africans, to an inferior status below people of Northern European and especially Anglo-Saxon descent. The newcomers, it was claimed, were unfit for democratic government and would endanger American civilization. Strict anti-immigrant legislation in the 1920s sharply curtailed immigration from outside the Western Hemisphere, banning Asians entirely and setting quotas based on national origin for others.

Recent concerns about immigration result from the unforeseen consequences of a 1965 reform in immigration law that abolished quotas. Since then, immigration has risen sharply, and the national origin of the immigrants has diverged from previous patterns. By the 1980s, Europeans constituted but 10 percent of the newcomers. The bulk of the remainder came from Asia (40 percent) and Mexico, Central America, and the Caribbean. Once again, anti-immigrant voices worry that alien newcomers are threatening the cohesiveness of the nation's institutions and values. But, once again as well, a more inclusive vision of American identity and ideals seems likely to prevail as the newcomers establish themselves. As Abraham Lincoln expressed it, "There was no exclusively American race entitled to claim liberty by heredity. What held the nation together was an idea of equality that every newcomer could claim and defend by free choice."

In the cities and larger towns, most manufacturing was done by artisans, skilled craftsmen who were also known as mechanics. Working in their own shops and with their own tools, they produced small batches of finished goods. Close to half of the population in the seaport cities, artisans and their families fed, clothed, and housed the urban population. Each artisan had a skill that set him above common laborers. These skills came from hands-on experience and craft traditions that were handed down from one generation to the next.

The "mysteries of the craft" were taught by master craftsmen to the journeymen and apprentices who lived with them and worked in their shops.

Journeymen had learned the skills of their craft but lacked the capital to open their own shops. Before establishing their own businesses, they saved their earnings and honed their skills while working for a wage under a master. Apprentices were adolescent boys sent by their fathers to live with and obey a master craftsman in return for being taught a trade. By the terms of the contract, known as an indenture, the master also provided for the apprentice's schooling and moral upbringing. An apprentice could expect to be promoted to journeyman in his late teens and begin advancement toward his competency, a secure income from an independent trade that would support a family.

Shown here working at power looms under the supervision of a male overseer, young single women comprised the bulk of the labor force in the first textile factories of New England.

Corbis

Artisans controlled entry into their trades and the process of production from start to finish. They set their own work rules and were their own bosses. "The Mechanics are a class [of] men," proudly wrote "Peter Single" in the *Mechanic's Free Press* of Philadelphia, "who compose that proportion of the population of our country, on whom depends its present and future welfare; from them emanates her glory, her greatness and her power."

The factory system of production that undercut both household and artisanal manufacturing could produce goods far more quickly and cheaply per worker than artisans or rural households. Factories subdivided the specialized skills of the artisan into a series of semiskilled tasks. Factories also put workers under systematic controls, and in the final stage of industrialization, they boosted workers' productivity through the use of power-driven machinery.

Britain pioneered the technological advances that drove early industrialization. The secrets of this technology, especially the designs for the machines that mechanized textile production, were closely guarded by the British government. Despite attempts to prohibit the emigration of artisans who knew how this machinery worked, some British mechanics got to the United States. Samuel Slater was one of them, and he took over the operation of a fledging mill in Providence, Rhode Island. With his knowledge of how to build water-powered spinning machinery, Slater made the mill the nation's first permanent cotton factory.

Slater's factory, and those modeled after it, manufactured yarn that was put out to rural housewives to be woven into cloth. The first factory to mechanize the operations of spinning and weaving and turn out finished cloth was incorporated in Waltham, Massachusetts in 1813 by the Boston Associates, a group of wealthy merchants. The Waltham factory was heavily capitalized, relied on the latest technology, and recruited its work force from rural farm families.

The first real spurt of factory building came with the closing off of British imports during the Embargo and the War of 1812. Hundreds of new cotton and woolen mills were established from 1808 to 1815. But the great test of American manufacturing came after 1815 when peace with Britain brought a flood of cheap British manufactured goods. If factories were to continue to grow, American manufacturers had to reach more consumers in their home market and overcome the British advantage of lower labor costs.

Industrial labor was more expensive in America than in England, where the high cost of land forced the peasantry into the cities to find work. In contrast, land was cheap and plentiful in the United States, and Americans preferred the independence of farm work to the dependence of factory labor. Consequently, the first mill workers were predominantly children. The owners set up the father on a plot of company-owned land, provided piecework for the mother, and put the children to work in the mills.

But this so-called Rhode Island system of family employment was inadequate for the larger, more mechanized factories that were built in New England after the War of 1812. These mill owners recruited single, adolescent daughters of farmers from across New England as their laborers in the **Waltham system**.

Throughout the 1820s and 1830s, most mill hands in New England were young farm daughters. Factory wages (a little over a dollar per week after deductions for room and board) were more than these young women could earn doing piecework in the home or as domestics. The wages also brought a liberating degree of financial independence. "When they felt the jingle of silver in their pockets," recalled Harriet Hanson Robinson of her fellow workers at Lowell in the 1830s, "there for the first time, their heads became erect and they walked as if on air."

Based on what they had heard of conditions in British factories, most Americans associated mill towns with morally depraved, impoverished workers. To overcome these fears New England manufacturers set up paternalistic moral controls. Single female workers had to live in boardinghouses owned by the company. Curfews were imposed, visitors were screened, and church attendance was mandatory.

The mill women still worked six days a week from dawn to dusk for low wages. The operatives tended clattering, fast-moving machinery in a work environment kept humid to minimize the snapping of threads in the machines. In 1834 and 1836, the female hands at Lowell "turned out" to protest wage reductions in demonstrations that were the largest strikes in American history up to that time.

After the economic downturn of the late 1830s, conditions in the mills got worse. By the mid-1840s, however, the Irish, desperate for work, sent their children into the mills at an earlier age than Yankee farm families had. These workers did not leave after two or three years of building up a small dowry for marriage, as many New Englanders did. By the early 1850s more than half of the textile operatives in New England were Irish women.

The rise in immigration after the 1820s was crucial for urban manufacturing. By drawing on this cheap pool of immigrant labor, manufacturers could increase production while driving down the cost. Urban manufacturing became labor-intensive, depending more heavily on workers than on investment in machines and other capital. New York and Philadelphia, followed by Boston in the 1840s, thus built up a diversified manufacturing sector in consumer goods.

Except in New England textile factories and the smaller factories and shops in the seaboard cities, native-born males were the largest group of early manufacturing workers. As late as 1840, women, including those working at home, made up about half of the manufacturing work force and one-quarter of the factory hands. Regardless of their sex, few of these workers brought skills to their jobs. Economic necessity forced them to accept low wages and harsh working conditions. The sheer increase in their numbers, as opposed to productivity gains from technological innovations, accounted by 1850 for two-thirds of the gains in manufacturing output.

After 1815 American manufacturers began to close the technological gap with Britain by drawing on the skills of American mechanics. Mechanics experimented with and improved designs and patented inventions that had new industrial applications.

The most famous early American invention was the cotton gin. Eli Whitney, a Massachusetts Yankee, built the first prototype in 1793 while working as a tutor

QUICK REVIEW

Mill Work

- In the 1820s and 1830s most New England mill hands were young farm daughters.
- Most Americans associated mill towns with moral depravity.
- Mill workers workerd six-day weeks for low wages.

W WHERE TO LEARN MORE

★ Hanford Mills Museum, East Meredith, New York
www.hanfordmills.org/

Waltham system During the industrialization of the early nineteenth century, the recruitment of unmarried young women for employment in factories.

on a Georgia plantation. By cheaply and mechanically removing the seeds from cotton fibers, the cotton gin spurred the cultivation of cotton across the South.

Whitney also pushed the idea of basing production on interchangeable parts. After receiving a federal contract to manufacture muskets, he designed new milling machines and turret lathes that transformed the technology of machine tool production. The federal arsenal at Harpers Ferry, Virginia, developed machine tools that could manufacture standardized, interchangeable parts. The new techniques were first applied in 1815 to the manufacture of wooden clocks and by the 1840s to sewing machines, farm machinery, and watch parts. The **American system of manufacturing**—low-cost, standardized mass production, built around interchangeable parts stamped out by machines—was America's unique contribution to the industrial revolution.

The 1840s registered the highest rate of expansion in the manufacturing sector of the economy in the nineteenth century. The adoption of the stationary steam engine in urban manufacturing fueled much of this expansion.

In the 1840s, high-pressure steam engines enabled power-driven industry to locate in the port cities of the Northeast and the booming cities on the Great Lakes. The West became the center of the farm machinery industry, and the region produced 20 percent of the nation's manufacturing output by the 1850s.

Steam power was beginning to transform the American landscape by the mid-nineteenth century. However, most of the change evident in the countryside by 1850 was the product of preindustrial technologies and the aftermath of impounding water for factory use.

About one-fifth of the original forest cover in the United States east of the Mississippi was gone by 1850. Most of this loss resulted from agricultural use. Wood that was not needed for farmhouses, fences, and fuel found a ready market in the cities and factories, where it was both the primary energy source and the basic building material.

As the land was being cleared and carved into private farms, the lakes and streams became dumping grounds for agricultural and industrial wastes. By 1840, the woolens industry alone was discarding some 18,000 tons of grease into rivers and streams.

To provide their mills with a steady, reliable source of water, one that would not be affected by the whims of nature, the Boston Associates constructed a series of dams and canals that extended to the headwaters of the Merrimack River in northern New Hampshire. Inevitably, the ecology of the region changed. Farmers protested when their fields and pastures were submerged, but lawyers for the Boston Associates argued that water, like any other natural resource, should be treated as a commodity that could contribute to economic progress. Increasingly, the law treated nature as an economic resource to be engineered, bought, and sold.

American system of manufacturing
A technique of production pioneered in the United States in the first half of the nineteenth century that relied on precision manufacturing with the use of interchangeable parts.

GROWING INEQUALITY AND NEW CLASSES

As the economy expanded after 1815 and the industrial revolution began to take hold, per capita income doubled in the first half of the century. Living standards for most Americans improved. Houses, for those who could afford them, became larger, better furnished, and heated. Food was more plentiful and varied, and factory-made consumer goods made domestic life easier and more comfortable.

There was a price to be paid, however, for the benefits of economic growth. Half of the adult white males were now propertyless. Wealth had become more concentrated, and extremes of wealth and poverty eroded the Jeffersonian ideal of a republic of independent proprietors who valued liberty because they were economically free.

HOW AND why did inequalities increase between the rich, the middle class, and the working classes?

MAP EXPLORATION

To explore an interactive version of this map, go to **http://www.prenhall.com/goldfield2/map12.2a**

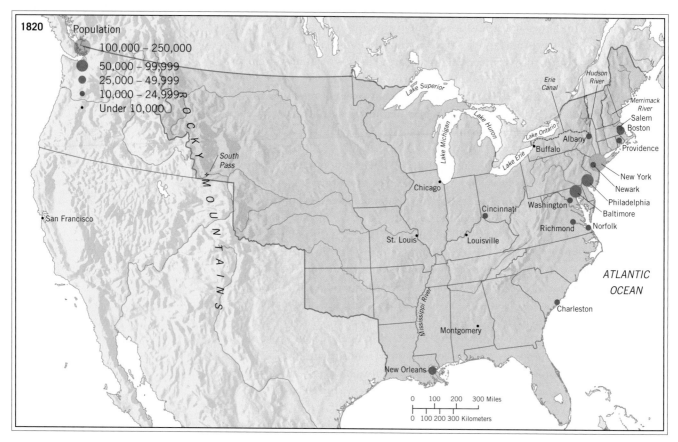

MAP 12–2A

The Growth of Cities, 1820–1860   In 1820, most cities were clustered along the Atlantic seaboard. By 1860 (map 12-B), new transportation outlets—canals and railroads—had fostered the rapid growth of cities in the interior, especially at trading locations with access to navigable rivers or to the Great Lakes. Much of this growth occurred in the 1850s.

Data Source: *Statistical Abstract of the United States.*

WHY WAS the growth of cities the slowest in the South?

The gap between the rich and the poor widened considerably in the early phases of industrialization. In 1800, the richest 10 percent of Americans owned 40 to 50 percent of the national wealth. By the 1850s, that share was about 70 percent. The most glaring discrepancies in wealth appeared in the large cities. In all American cities by the 1840s, the top 10 percent of the population owned over 80 percent of urban wealth.

Most of the urban rich at midcentury had been born wealthy, the offspring of old-money families who had married and invested wisely. They belonged to exclusive clubs, attended lavish balls and dinners, were waited on by a retinue of servants in their mansions, and recoiled from what they considered the "mob government" ushered in by the Jacksonian Democrats.

The faster pace of economic growth also created opportunities for an expanding new middle class. This class grew as the number of nonmanual jobs increased. Most of these jobs were in Northern cities and bustling market towns, where the need was greatest for office and store clerks, managerial personnel,

MAP EXPLORATION

To explore an interactive version of this map, go to **http://www.prenhall.com/goldfield2/map12.2b**

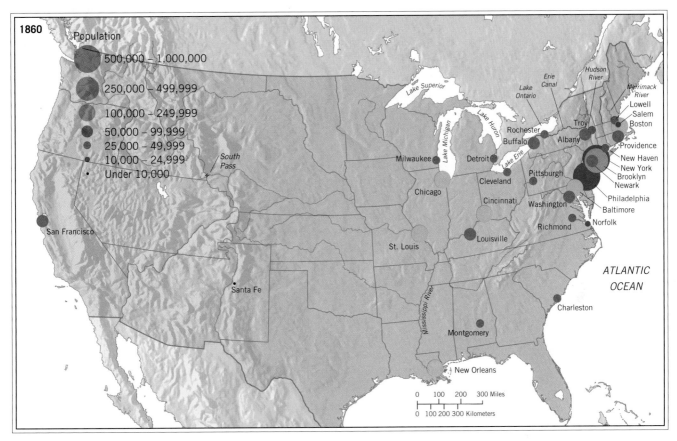

MAP 12–2B

sales agents, and independent retailers. The result by midcentury was a new middle class superimposed on the older one of independent farmers, artisans, shopkeepers, and professionals.

The apparent separation of work and home constituted the first step in an evolving sense of class consciousness. As the market revolution advanced, the workplace increasingly became a specialized location of production or selling. Middle-class fathers left for their jobs in the morning, while mothers governed households that were primarily residential units.

Homes became places of material comfort for the rising middle class. Growing quantities of consumer goods—pianos, carpets, draperies, mirrors, oil lamps, and ornate furniture—filled their homes. Stoves replaced open fireplaces as the main source of heat, and plumbing eliminated outdoor privies.

Having servants, the single largest field of employment in the cities, became a status symbol. Shunned as degrading by most native-born white women, these low-paying jobs were filled by African-American and young immigrant (especially Irish) women. Work had not left the middle-class home; instead, it was disguised as the "domestic duties" of middle-class wives who supervised servants.

Besides seeking guidance from etiquette books on proper manners, the middle class also tried to shape its behavior by the tenets of evangelical religion. Revivals swept Northern cities in the late 1820s. Charles G. Finney led the most dramatic and successful ones in the cities along the Erie Canal in upstate New York. Finney preached that salvation was available to those who willed it.

QUICK REVIEW

Class Consciousness

◆ Separation of home and work first step in evolving class consciousness.

◆ Home a place of material comfort for rising middle class.

◆ Having servants a sign of status.

◆ Middle class shaped by evangelical religion.

He also stressed that economic and moral success depended on the virtues of sobriety, self-restraint, and hard work. Aggressiveness and ambition were not necessarily sinful as long as businessmen led moral lives and helped others do the same. This message reassured the urban middle class, for it confirmed and sanctified their pursuit of economic self-interest. It also provided them with a religious inspiration for attempting to exert moral control over their communities and employees. **Temperance**—the prohibition of alcoholic beverages—was the greatest of the evangelically inspired reforms, and abstinence from alcohol became the most telling evidence of middle-class respectability.

In a reversal of traditional Calvinist doctrine, the evangelical ministers of the Northern middle class enshrined women as the moral superiors of men. Held to be uniquely pure and pious, women were now responsible for converting their homes into loving, prayerful centers of domesticity. "There is a ministry that is older and deeper and more potent than ours," wrote a liberal Presbyterian clergyman; "it is the ministry that presides over the crib and impresses the first gospel influence on the infant soul."

This sanctified notion of motherhood reflected and reinforced shifting patterns of family life. Families became smaller as the birthrate fell by 25 percent in the first half of the nineteenth century. The decline was greatest in the urban middle class after 1820. Children were no longer an economic asset as they had been as workers on a family farm. Middle-class couples limited the size of their families, and women stopped having children at a younger age.

Beginning in the 1820s, ministers and female writers elevated the family role of middle-class women into a **cult of domesticity**. This idealized conception of womanhood insisted that the biological differences of God's natural order determined separate social roles for men and women. Characterized as strong, aggressive, and ambitious, men naturally belonged in the competitive world of business and politics. Women's providential task was to preserve religion and morality in the home and family. Only they possessed the moral purity necessary for rearing virtuous children and preserving the home as a refuge from the outside world.

Parents could now devote more care and resources to child rearing. Middle-class children lived at home longer than children had in the past and received more schooling than working-class children.

Unlike the wealthy, whose riches were inherited, members of the middle class believed that their property was the product of hard work and self-denial. They also saw themselves as the industrious Americans whose moral fortitude and discipline enabled them to escape the clutches of poverty, the fate of those who were presumed to be lazy and undisciplined.

The economic changes that produced a new middle class also transformed the working class. In preindustrial America, the working class was predominantly native-born and of artisan origins. By midcentury, most urban workers were immigrants or the children of immigrants and had never been artisans in a skilled craft.

Job skills, sex, race, and ethnicity all divided workers after 1840. Master craftsmen were the most highly skilled and best-paid members of the labor force. Industrialization splintered the unity of the old artisan class. Ambitious master craftsmen with access to capital ignored craft traditions to rise into the ranks of small businessmen and manufacturers. They expanded output and drove down the cost of production by contracting out work at piece wages and hiring the cheapest workers they could find. The result was to transform the apprentice system into a system of exploited child labor.

By the 1830s, most journeymen were becoming a class of permanent wage earners with little prospect of opening their own shops. They denounced the new industrial relations as a "system of mental and physical slavery." To protect their liberties from what they considered a new aristocracy of manufacturers, they organized

Temperance Reform movement originating in the 1820s that sought to eliminate the consumption of alcohol.

Cult of domesticity The belief that women, by virtue of their sex, should stay home as the moral guardians of family life.

workingmen's political parties in the 1830s. At the top of these parties' list of reforms were free public education, the abolition of imprisonment for debt, and a ten-hour workday. But the depression of 1839–1843 forced mechanics to concentrate on their economic survival, and the Democrats siphoned off many of their political leaders.

Journeymen also turned to trade union activity in the 1820s and 1830s to gain better wages, shorter hours, and enhanced job security. Locals from various trades formed the National Trades Union, the first national union, in 1834. The new labor movement launched more than 150 strikes in the mid-1830s.

Although the Panic of 1837 decimated union membership, the early labor movement achieved two notable victories. First, by the late 1830s, it had forced employers to accept the ten-hour day as the standard for most skilled workers. Second, in a landmark decision handed down in 1842, the Massachusetts Supreme Court ruled in *Commonwealth* v. *Hunt* that a trade union was not necessarily subject to laws against criminal conspiracies and that a strike could be used to force employers to hire only union members.

The unions were the defenders of artisanal rights and virtues, and they ignored workers whose jobs had never had craft status. As massive immigration merged with industrialization after 1840, this basic division between workers widened. On one side was the male, Protestant, and native-born class of skilled artisans. On the other side was the working-class majority of factory laborers and the unskilled. These workers were predominantly immigrants and women who worked for a wage as domestic or factory hands. On average, they earned less than $500 a year, about half what skilled workers earned. Their financial survival rested on a family economy in which all members contributed whatever they could earn.

Increasingly fearing these workers as a threat to their job security and Protestant values, American-born artisans joined **nativist organizations** in the 1840s, which sought to curb mass immigration from Europe and limit the political rights of Catholic immigrants. Ethnic workers viewed temperance as business-class meddling in their lives, while successful native-born workers tended to embrace the evangelical, middle-class ideology of temperance and self-help. The greatest unity achieved by labor was the nearly universal insistence of white workers that black workers be confined to the most menial jobs.

Gender also divided workers. Working-class men shared the dominant ideology of female dependence. They measured their own status as husbands by their ability to keep their wives and daughters from having to work. Male workers also argued that their wages would be higher if women were barred from the work force. A report of the National Trades Union in 1836 cited women's "ruinous competition to male labor." It insisted that a woman's "efforts to sustain herself and family are actually the same as tying a stone around the neck of her natural protector, Man, and destroying him with the weight she has brought to his assistance."

With these views, male workers helped lock wage-earning women into the lowest-paying and most exploited jobs. Of the 25,000 women in 1860 working in manufacturing in New York City, two-thirds were in the clothing trades. Many were seamstresses working at home fifteen to eighteen hours a day for starvation wages of less than $100 a year. Over half of them were the sole breadwinners in their households.

"If we do not come forth in our defence, what will become of us?" asked Sarah Monroe of New York City in the midst of a strike by seamstresses in 1831. Women tried to organize as workers, but the male labor movement refused to lend much support. The men tried to channel the discontent of women workers into "proper female behavior" and generally restricted their assistance to pushing for legislation that would limit the hours worked by women and children, a stand that enhanced their male image as protectors of the family.

QUICK REVIEW

Unions

- In the late 1830s and early 1840s unions won important victories.
- Union concentrated on artisanal rights and virtues.
- American-born artisans increasingly saw immigrants as a threat to job security.

Nativist organizations Joined by American-born artisans in the 1840s which sought to curb mass immigration from Europe and limit the political rights of Catholic immigrants.

WHAT ROLE did women play in the reform movement that followed the War of 1812?

REFORM AND MORAL ORDER

The rapidity and extent of the social and economic changes that accompanied the market revolution were disorienting, even frightening, to many Americans, particularly religious leaders and wealthy businessmen in the East. Alarmed by what they perceived as a breakdown in moral authority, they sought to impose moral discipline on Americans.

These Eastern elites, with the indispensable support of their wives and daughters, created a network of voluntary church-affiliated reform organizations known collectively as the **benevolent empire**. Revivals in the 1820s and 1830s then broadened the base of reform to include the newly evangelicalized middle class in Northern cities and towns.

THE BENEVOLENT EMPIRE

For the Reverend Lyman Beecher, the American condition in 1814 presented "a scene of destitution and wretchedness." He believed that only religion, as preached by "pious, intelligent, enterprising ministers through the nation," could provide the order that would preserve the Union and place it under "the moral government of God."

Evangelical businessmen in the seaboard cities backed Beecher's call to restore moral order. Worried by the increasing number of urban poor, wealthy merchants financed a network of reform associations that grew to include the American Board of Commissioners for Foreign Missions (1810), the American Bible Society (1816), the American Sunday School Union (1824), the American Tract Society (1825), and the American Home Missionary Society (1826).

The reform societies built on the Second Great Awakening's techniques of organization and communication. The Christian reformers sent out speakers on regular schedules along prescribed routes. They developed organizations that maintained a constant pressure for reform. National and local boards of directors supervised the work of salaried managers, who inspired volunteers to combat sin among the unconverted.

When steam presses and stereotype plates halved the cost of printing and dramatically increased its speed, the American Bible Society was the first to exploit this revolution in the print media. By 1830 religious presses were churning out more than 1 million Bibles and 6 million tracts a year. These publications were mass distributed by traveling agents and heavily promoted in national advertising campaigns. As the *Christian Herald* editorialized in 1823, "Preaching of the gospel is a Divine institution—'printing' is no less so. . . . The PULPIT AND THE PRESS are inseparably connected."

A host of local societies were more concerned with stamping out individual vices. Their purpose, as summed up by a Massachusetts group, the Andover South Parish Society for the Reformation of Morals, was "to discountenance [discourage] immorality, particularly Sabbath-breaking, intemperance, and profanity, and to promote industry, order, piety, and good morals." These goals linked social and moral discipline in a way that appealed both to pious churchgoers concerned about godlessness and profit-oriented businessmen eager to curb their workers' unruly behavior.

With volunteers drawn largely from the teenage daughters of evangelical businessmen, Sunday interdenominational schools combined elementary education with the teaching of the Bible and Christian principles. The American Sunday School Union was both a coordinating agency for local efforts and a publishing house for books and periodicals. By 1832, nearly 10 percent of all American children aged 5 to 14 were attending one of eight thousand Sunday schools.

Benevolent empire Network of reform associations affiliated with Protestant churches in the early nineteenth century dedicated to the restoration of moral order.

The boldest expression of the drive to enhance Christian power was the **Sabbatarian movement**. In 1828, evangelicals led by Lyman Beecher formed the General Union for Promoting the Observance of the Christian Sabbath whose immediate goal was the repeal of a law passed by Congress in 1810 directing post offices to deliver mail on Sunday. This law symbolized to Christian reformers the moral degeneracy into which the republic had fallen. Its broader mission was to enforce local statutes that shut down business and leisure activities on Sundays. The Sabbatarians considered such statutes no less "necessary to the welfare of the state" than "laws against murder and polygamy." To their opponents, such statutes were "repugnant to the rights of private property and irreconcilable with the free exercise of civil liberty."

In 1829, insisting on the separation of church and state, the Democratic Congress upheld the postal law of 1810. Businessmen, workingmen, Southern evangelicals, and religious conservatives in New England all felt that the Sabbath purists had gone too far.

The General Union disbanded in 1832, but it left an important legacy for future reform movements. On the one hand, it developed techniques that converted the reform impulse into direct political action. In raising funds, training speakers, holding rallies, disseminating literature, lobbying for local Sunday regulations, and coordinating a petition to Congress, the Sabbatarians created an organizational model for other reformers to follow in mobilizing public opinion and influencing politicians. On the other hand, the failure of the Sabbatarians revealed that heavy-handed attempts to force the "unconverted" to follow Christian standards of conduct were self-defeating. A new approach was needed that encouraged individuals to reform themselves without coercive controls. It soon emerged in the temperance movement.

THE TEMPERANCE MOVEMENT

Temperance—the drive against the consumption of alcohol—had the greatest immediate impact on the most people of any reform movement. Its success rested on what Lyman Beecher called "a new moral power." Dismayed by popular resistance to the coercive moralism of the first wave of Christian reform, evangelicals like the Reverend John Chester concluded in 1821 that "you cannot coerce a free people that are jealous to fastidiousness of their rights." Therefore, reform had to rest on persuasion, and it had to begin with the voluntary decision of individuals to free themselves from sin. For these evangelicals, the self-control to renounce alcohol became the key to creating a harmonious Christian society of self-regulating citizens.

In 1826, evangelicals founded the American Temperance Society in Boston and took control of the movement. They were inspired by Beecher's *Six Sermons on Temperance*, a stirring call for voluntary associations dedicated to the belief that "the daily use of ardent spirits, in any form, or in any degree" was a sin. They now sought a radical change in American attitudes toward alcohol and its role in social life.

American consumption of alcohol reached an all-time high by 1830 of 7.1 gallons of pure alcohol per year for every American aged 14 and over (about three times present-day levels). Alcoholic beverages were plentiful and cheaper than tea or coffee. Alcohol was used to pay both common laborers and the itinerant preachers on the early Methodist circuit. Masters and journeymen shared a drink as a customary way of taking a break from work. No wedding, funeral, or meeting of friends was complete without alcohol.

For the temperance crusade to succeed, the reformers had to finance a massive propaganda campaign and link it to an organization that could energize

11–2
Lyman Beecher, Six Sermons on Intemperance (1828)

Sabbatarian movement Reform organization founded in 1828 by Congregationalist and Presbyterian ministers that lobbied for an end to the delivery of mail on Sundays and other Sabbath violations.

thousands of people. They built such a mass movement by merging temperance into the network of churches and lay volunteers that the benevolent empire had developed and by adopting the techniques of revivals to win new converts.

Evangelical reformers denounced intemperance as the greatest sin of the land. Alcohol represented all that was wrong in America—crime, poverty, insanity, broken families, boisterous politicking, Sabbath-breaking.

This message was thundered from the pulpit and the public lectern. It was also broadcast in millions of tracts printed on the latest high-speed presses. As in the revivals, temperance rallies combined emotionally charged sermons with large, tearful prayer meetings to evoke guilt among sinners, who would then take the pledge of abstinence.

Within a decade, the American Temperance Society had more than five thousand local chapters and statewide affiliates. A million members had pledged abstinence by 1833. New England and New York alone claimed 72 percent of all temperance societies in the mid-1830s. Most of the converts came from the upper and middle classes. Businessmen welcomed temperance as a model of self-discipline in their efforts to regiment factory work. Young, upwardly mobile professionals and petty entrepreneurs learned in temperance how to be thrifty, self-controlled, and more respectable and creditworthy. Many of them presumably agreed with the *Temperance Recorder* that "the enterprise of this country is so great, and competition so eager in every branch of business . . . , that profit can only result from . . . *temperance.*"

Women were indispensable to the temperance movement. As the moral protectors of the family, they pressured their husbands to take the teetotaler's pledge and stick by it, raised sons to shun alcohol, and banished liquor from their homes. By the 1840s, temperance and middle-class domesticity had become synonymous.

Temperance made its first significant inroads among the working classes during the economic depression of 1839–1843. Joining together in what they called Washington Temperance Societies, small businessmen and artisans, many of them reformed drunkards, carried temperance into working-class districts. The Washingtonians gained a considerable following by insisting that workers could survive the depression only if they stopped drinking and adopted the temperance ethic of frugality and self-help. Their wives organized auxiliary societies and pledged to enforce sobriety and economic restraint at home.

By 1845, per capita consumption of alcohol had fallen to less than two gallons. In 1851, Maine passed the first statewide prohibition law. Other northern states followed suit, but antitemperance coalitions soon overturned most of these laws outside New England. Nonetheless, alcohol consumption remained at the low level set in the 1840s.

WOMEN'S ROLES IN REFORM

The first phase of women's reform activities represented an extension of the Cult of Domesticity. Assumptions about their unique moral qualities encouraged women to assume the role of "social mother" inspired by the revivalist call of the 1820s they founded maternal associations, sponsored revivals, visited the poor, established Sunday Schools, and distributed Bibles and religious tracts. These reformers widened the public role of women, but their efforts also reinforced cultural stereotypes of women as nurturing helpmates who deferred to males.

A second phase in the reform efforts by women developed in the 1830s. Unlike their benevolent counterparts, the reformers now began to challenge male prerogatives and move beyond moral suasion. The crusade against prostitution exemplified the new militancy. Women seized leadership of the movement in 1834 with the founding of the New York Female Moral Reform Society. In the pages of

OVERVIEW

THE REFORM IMPULSE

Type	Objects of Reform	Means	Example	Origin
Moral reform	Individual failings such as drinking, sexual misconduct, Sabbath-breaking	Mass distribution of literature, speaker tours, lobbying	American Temperance Society	1810s–1820s
Institutional reform	Crime, poverty, delinquency	Penitentiaries, asylums, almshouses, state-supported schools	Massachusetts Board of Education	1830s
Utopian societies	Selfish materialism of society	New, highly structured communities	Shakers	1820s
Abolition	Slavery	Petition and mailing campaigns	American Anti-Slavery Society	1830s
Women's rights	Legal subordination of women	Lobbying, petition campaigns	Seneca Falls Convention	1840s

their journal, *Advocate for Moral Reform*, members identified male greed and licentiousness as the causes for the fallen state of women. Identified, too, were the male patrons of the city's brothels. The society blamed businessmen for the low wages that forced some women to resort to prostitution and denounced lustful men for engaging in "a regular crusade against [our] sex."

In 1839, this attack on the sexual double standard became a national movement with the establishment of the American Female Moral Reform Society. With 555 affiliates throughout the evangelical heartland of the North, female activists mounted a lobbying campaign that reached out to a mass audience for signatures. By the 1840s, such unprecedented political involvement enabled women to secure the first state laws criminalizing seduction and adultery.

Other women's groups developed a more radical critique of American society and its male leadership. The Boston Seamen's Aid Society, founded in 1833 by Sarah Josepha Hale, a widow with five children, soon rejected the benevolent tradition of distinguishing between the "respectable" and the "unworthy" poor. Hale discovered that her efforts to guide poor women toward self-sufficiency flew in the face of the low wages and substandard housing that trapped her clients in poverty. She concluded in 1838 that "it is hardly possible for the hopeless poor to avoid being vicious." Hale attacked male employers for exploiting the poor. "Combinations of selfish men are formed to beat down the price of female labor," she wrote in her 1836 annual report, "and then they call the diminished rate the market price."

The temperance crusade brought women out of their homes and into the streets to pray in front of taverns filled with drunken men.

Getty Images Inc. – Hulton Archive Photo

BACKLASH AGAINST BENEVOLENCE

Some of the benevolent empire's harshest critics came out of the populist revivals of the early 1800s. They considered the Christian reformers' program a conspiracy of orthodox Calvinists to impose social and moral control on behalf of a religious and economic elite. The goal of the "orthodox party," warned the Universalist *Christian Intelligencer*, was the power of "governing the nation."

These criticisms revealed a profound mistrust of the emerging market society. In contrast to the evangelical reformers, drawn from the well-educated business and middle classes who were benefiting from economic change, most evangelical members of the grass-roots sects and followers of the itinerant preachers were unschooled, poor, and hurt by market fluctuations that they could not control. Often they were farmers forced by debt to move west or artisans and tradesmen displaced by new forms of factory production and new commercial outlets. Socially uprooted and economically stranded, they found a sense of community in their local churches and resisted control by wealthier, better-educated outsiders. Above all, they clung to beliefs that shored up the threatened authority of the father over his household.

With the elevation of women to the status of moral guardians of the family and agents of benevolent reform outside the household, middle-class evangelicalism in the Northeast was becoming feminized. This new social role for women was especially threatening—indeed, galling—for men who were the causalities of the more competitive economy. Raised on farms where the father had been the unquestioned lawgiver and provider, these men attacked feminized evangelicalism for undermining their paternal authority. They found in Scripture an affirmation of patriarchal power for any man, no matter how poor.

The **Church of Jesus Christ of Latter-day Saints** (also known as the **Mormon Church**) represented the most enduring religious backlash of economically struggling men against the aggressive efforts of reforming middle-class evangelicals. Joseph Smith, who established the church in upstate New York in 1830, came from a New England farm family uprooted and impoverished by market speculations gone sour. He and his followers were alienated, not only from the new market economy but also from what they saw as the religious and social anarchy around them.

Based on Smith's divine revelations as set forth in *The Book of Mormon* (1830), their new faith offered converts to Mormonism both a sanctuary as a biblical people and a release from social and religious uncertainties. Mormonism assigned complete spiritual and secular authority to men. Only through subordination and obedience to their husbands could women hope to gain salvation.

To be a Mormon was to join a large extended family that was part of a shared enterprise. Men bonded their labor in a communal economy to benefit all the faithful. Driven by a strong sense of social obligation, the Mormons forged the most successful alternative vision in antebellum America to the individualistic Protestant republic of the benevolent reformers. (For the Mormons' role in the westward movement, see Chapter 13.)

Church of Jesus Christ of Latter-day Saints (Mormon Church) Church founded in 1830 by Joseph Smith and based on the revelations in a sacred book he called the Book of Mormon.

INSTITUTIONS AND SOCIAL IMPROVEMENT

Although evangelical Protestantism was its main-spring, antebellum reform also had its roots in the European Enlightenment. Enlightenment thinkers, like the evangelicals inspired by religious optimism, had unbounded faith in social improvement.

Studies published in the 1820s that documented increasing urban poverty, crime, and teenage delinquency created a sense of urgency for many reformers.

Guided by the Enlightenment belief that environmental conditions shaped human character, reformers created a new system of public schooling in the North. They also prodded state legislatures to fund penitentiaries for criminals, asylums for the mentally ill, reformatories for the delinquent, and almshouses for the poor.

As reformers were implementing new institutional techniques for shaping individual character after 1820, a host of utopian communities also tapped into an impulse for human betterment. They typically rejected either private property or families based on monogamous marriage and offered a communitarian life designed to help a person reach perfection. Most of these communities were short-lived.

SCHOOL REFORM

Before the 1820s, schooling in America was an informal, haphazard affair that nonetheless met the basic needs for reading, writing, and arithmetic skills of an overwhelmingly rural population. Private tutors and academies for the wealthy, a few charitable schools for the urban poor, and rural one-room schoolhouses open for a few months a year comprised formal education at the primary level.

The first political demands for free tax-supported schools originated with the Workingmen's movement in Eastern cities in the 1820s. Decrying what the Philadelphia Working Men's Committee in 1830 described as "a monopoly of talent, which consigns the multitude to comparative ignorance, and secures the balance of knowledge on the side of the rich and the rulers," workers called for free public schooling. In pushing for what they called "equal republican education," they were also seeking to guarantee that all citizens, no matter how poor, could achieve meaningful liberty and equality. Wealthier property holders, however, refused to be taxed to pay for the education of working-class children.

The breakthrough in school reform came in New England. Increasing economic inequality, growing numbers of Irish Catholic immigrants, and the emergence of a mass democracy based on nearly universal white male suffrage convinced reformers of the need for state-supported schools.

In 1837, the Massachusetts legislature established the nation's first state board of education. The head of the board for the next twelve years was Horace Mann, a former Whig politician and temperance advocate who now tirelessly championed educational reform. Mann demanded that the state government assume centralized control over Massachusetts schools. All schools should have the same standards of compulsory attendance, strict discipline, common textbooks, professionally trained teachers, and graded, competitive classes of age-segregated students.

Once this system was in place, Mann promised, poverty would no longer threaten social disruption because the ignorant would have the knowledge to acquire property and wealth. Trained in self-control and punctuality, youths would be able to take advantage of economic opportunities and become intelligent voters concerned with the rights of property.

Democrats in the Massachusetts legislature denounced Mann's program as "a system of centralization and of monopoly of power in a few hands, contrary in every respect, to the true spirit of our democratical institutions." The laboring poor, who depended on the wages their children could earn, resisted compulsory attendance laws and a longer school year. Farmers fought to maintain local control over schooling and to block the higher taxes needed for a more comprehensive and professionalized system. The Catholic Church protested the attempts of the reformers to indoctrinate students in the moral strictures of middle-class Protestantism. Catholics began building their own parochial schools.

Mann and his allies prevailed in most of the industrializing states with strong support from the professional and business constituencies of the Whig party.

16   ECLECTIC FIRST READER.

LESSON XI.

Boys at Play.

Can you fly a kite? See how the boy flies his kite. He holds the string fast, and the wind blows it up.

Now it is high in the air, and looks like a bird. When the wind blows hard, you must hold fast, or your kite will get away.

Boys love to run and play.

But they must not be rude. Good boys do not play in a rude way, but take care not to hurt any one.

Moral Lessons such as this one for boys at play filled the page of the McGuffey's readers.

Richard Nowitz Photography

In the concern etched in her face, this photograph captures the compassion that Dorothea Dix brought to her crusade for mental health reforms.

Courtesy of Library of Congress

School reform appealed to the growing Northern urban middle class. Schools would instill the moral and economic discipline that the middle class deemed essential for a progressive and ordered society. Teaching morality and national pride was central to the educational curriculum, and from the popular McGuffey Readers students learned that "God gives a great deal of money to some persons, in order that they may assist those [who] are poor."

Out of the Northern middle class also came the young female teachers who increasingly staffed elementary schools. Presumed by their nature to be more nurturing than men, women now had an entry into teaching, the first profession open to them. Besides, women could also be paid far less than men; school boards assumed that they would accept low wages while waiting to be married.

By 1850 just over 50 percent of the white children between 5 and 19 years of age in the United States were enrolled in school—the highest percentage in the world at the time, although the slave states, especially in the Lower South, lagged behind the rest of the nation in public education.

PRISONS, WORKHOUSES, AND ASYLUMS

Up to this time, Americans had depended on voluntary efforts to cope with crime, poverty, and social deviance. Reformers now turned to public authorities to establish a host of new institutions—penitentiaries, workhouses, mental hospitals, orphanages, and reformatories—to deal with social problems.

Eighteenth-century Americans never thought of rehabilitating criminals, but the institutional reformers of the Jacksonian era believed that criminals, the poor, and other deviants, could be morally redeemed. In the properly ordered environment of new institutions, discipline and moral character would be instilled in those who lacked the self-control to resist the corrupting vices and temptations that pervaded society.

As two French observers noted in the early 1830s, "The penitentiary system . . . to them seems the remedy for all the evils of society." Unlike earlier prisons, the penitentiaries were huge, imposing structures that isolated the prisoners from each other and the outside world. No longer were criminals to be brutally punished or thrown together under inhumane conditions that perpetuated a cycle of moral depravity. Now, cut off from all corrupting influences, forced to learn that hard work teaches moral discipline, and uplifted by religious literature, criminals would be guided toward becoming law-abiding, productive citizens.

The same philosophy of reform provided the rationale for asylums to house the poor and the insane. The number of transient poor and the size of urban slums increased as commercial capitalism uprooted farmers from the land and undercut the security of craft trades. Believing that the poor, much like criminals, had only themselves to blame, public officials and their evangelical allies prescribed a therapeutic regimen of discipline and physical labor to cure the poor of their moral defects. The structured setting for that regimen was the workhouse.

The custodians of the workhouses banished drinking, gambling, and idleness. Inmates lived in a tightly scheduled daily routine built around manual labor. Once purged of their laziness and filled with self-esteem as the result of work discipline, the poor would be released to become useful members of society.

Public insane asylums offered a similar order for the mentally ill. Reformers believed that too many choices in a highly mobile, materialistic, and competitive society drove some people insane. By 1860, twenty-eight states had established mental hospitals. These facilities set rigid rules and work assignments to teach patients how to order their lives.

While the reformers did provide social deviants with cleaner and safer living conditions, their penitentiaries and asylums succeeded more in classifying and segregating their inmates than in reforming them. Submission to routine turned out not to be the best builder of character. Witnessing the rigorous control of every movement of the isolated prisoners at the Eastern State Penitentiary in Philadelphia, English novelist Charles Dickens declared "this slow and daily tampering with the mysteries of the brain to be immeasurably worse than any torture of the body."

Penitentiaries, reformatories, and workhouses failed to eliminate or noticeably check poverty, crime, and vice. By midcentury, reformers were defining deviants and dependents as permanent misfits who suffered from ingrained character defects. Stripped of their earlier optimism, the asylums became little more than holding pens for the outcasts of society.

UTOPIAN ALTERNATIVES

Unlike the reformers, who aimed to improve the existing order by guiding individuals to greater self-discipline, the utopians sought perfection by withdrawing from society. A radically new social order, not an improved old one, was their goal.

Though following different religious and secular philosophies of communitarian living, all the utopians wanted to fashion a more rational and personally satisfying alternative to the competitive materialism of antebellum America. Nearly all the communities sought to transform the organization and rewards of work, thus challenging the prevailing dogmas about private property.

The most successful utopian communities were religious sects whose reordering of both sexual and economic relations departed most sharply from middle-class norms. The **Shakers**, at their height in the 1830s, attracted some six thousand followers. Named for the convulsive dancing that was part of their religious ceremonies, the Shakers traced their origins to the teachings of Ann Lee ("Mother Ann"). An illiterate factory laborer in mid-eighteenth-century England, Lee had a revelation in 1770 that the Second Coming of Christ was to be fulfilled in her own womanly form, the embodiment of the female side of God. Fired by another vision in 1774, Lee led eight of her followers to America, where, after her death in 1784, her disciples established the first Shaker community in New Lebanon, New York.

Organized around a doctrine of celibate **communism**, Shaker communities held all property in common. The sexes worked and lived apart from each other. Dancing during religious worship brought men and women together and provided an emotional release from enforced sexual denial. As an early Shaker leader explained, "There is evidently no labor which so fully absorbs all the faculties of soul and body, as real spiritual devotion and energetic exercise in sacred worship." In worldly as well as spiritual terms, women enjoyed an equality in Shaker life that the outside world denied them. For this reason, twice as many women as men joined the Shakers.

The Shakers gradually dwindled. Their rule of celibacy meant, of course, that they could propagate themselves only by recruiting new members and few new converts joined the movement after 1850. The Shakers today are best remembered for the beautiful simplicity of the furniture they made in their workshops.

John Humphrey Noyes established the **Oneida Community** in upstate New York in 1847. He attracted over two hundred followers with his perfectionist vision of plural marriage, community nurseries, group discipline, and common ownership of property. Charged with adultery, Noyes fled to Canada in 1879, but the Oneida Community, reorganized in 1881 as a joint-stock company in the United

WHERE TO LEARN MORE

Shaker Museum at South Union, Kentucky www.shakermuseum.com/

Shakers The followers of Mother Ann Lee, who preached a religion of strict celibacy and communal living.

Communism A social structure based on the common ownership of property.

Oneida Community Utopian community established in upstate New York in 1848 by John Humphrey Noyes and his followers.

WHERE TO LEARN MORE

★ Historic New Harmony,
New Harmony, Indiana
www.newharmony.org/

States and committed thereafter to conventional sexual mores, survived into the twentieth century.

Secular utopians aspired to perfect social relations through the rational design of planned communities. Bitter critics of the social evils of industrialization, they tried to construct models for a social order free from poverty, unemployment, and inequality. They envisioned cooperative communities that balanced agricultural and industrial pursuits in a mixed economy that recycled earnings to the laborers who actually produced the wealth.

Despite their high expectations, nearly all the planned communities ran into financial difficulties and collapsed. The pattern was set by the first of the controversial socialist experiments, **New Harmony** in Indiana, the brainchild of the wealthy, Scottish industrialist and philanthropist Robert Owen who was a proponent of utopian **socialism**. But within two years of its founding in 1825, New Harmony fell victim to inadequate financing and internal bickering.

Brook Farm established in 1841 in West Roxbury, Massachusetts (today part of Boston), was a showcase for the transcendentalist philosophy of Ralph Waldo Emerson. A former Unitarian minister in Boston, Emerson taught that intuition and emotion could grasp a truer ("transcendent") reality than the senses alone could. Boston intellectuals saw Brook Farm as a refuge from the pressures and coarseness of commercial society, a place where they could realize the Emersonian ideal of spontaneous creativity. Although disbanded after six years as an economic failure, Brook Farm inspired intellectuals such as Nathaniel Hawthorne. His writings and those of others influenced by **transcendentalism** flowed into the great renaissance of American literature in the mid-nineteenth century.

In an 1837 address at Harvard, Emerson had called for a national literature devoted to the democratic possibilities of American life. "The literature of the poor, the feelings of the child, the philosophy of the street, the meaning of household life, are the topics of the time," he proclaimed. Writers soon responded to Emerson's call.

Walt Whitman, whose *Leaves of Grass* (1855) foreshadowed modern poetry in its use of free verse, shared Emerson's faith in the possibilities of individual fulfillment, and his poems celebrated the democratic variety of the American people. Henry David Thoreau, Emerson's friend and neighbor, embodied the transcendentalist fascination with nature and self-discovery by living in relative isolation for sixteen months at Walden Pond, near Concord, Massachusetts. His *Walden, or Life in the Woods* (1854) became an American classic. "I went to the woods," he wrote, "because I wished to . . . confront only the essential facts of life, and see if I could not learn what it had to teach, and not, when I came to die, discover that I had not lived."

Novelists Nathaniel Hawthorne and Herman Melville focused on the existence of evil and the human need for community. In *The Scarlet Letter* (1850) and *The House of the Seven Gables* (1851), Hawthorne probed themes of egoism and pride to reveal the underside of the human soul. Melville's *Moby Dick* (1851) depicted the consequences of a competitive individualism unchecked by a social conscience.

Much of the appeal of the utopian communities flowed from the same concern about the splintering and selfishness of antebellum society that animated Hawthorne and Melville. The works of these novelists have endured, but the utopian experiments quickly collapsed. Promising economic security and social harmony to buttress a threatened sense of community, the utopians failed to lure all but a few Americans from the acquisitiveness and competitive demands of the larger society.

New Harmony   Short-lived utopian community established in Indiana in 1825, based on the socialist ideas of Robert Owen, a wealthy Scottish manufacturer.

Socialism   Political and economic theory advocating that land, natural resources, and the chief industries should be owned by the community as a whole.

Brook Farm   A utopian community and experimental farm established in 1841 near Boston.

Transcendentalism   A philosophical and literary movement centered on an idealistic belief in the divinity of individuals and nature.

OVERVIEW

TYPES OF ANTISLAVERY REFORM

Type	Definition	Example
Gradualist	Accepts notions of black inferiority and attempts to end slavery gradually by purchasing the freedom of slaves and colonizing them in Africa	American Colonization Society
Immediatist	Calls for immediate steps to end slavery and denounces slavery and racial prejudice as moral sins	Abolitionists
Political antislavery	Recognizes slavery in states where it exists but insists on keeping slavery out of the territories	Free-Soilers

ABOLITIONISM AND WOMEN'S RIGHTS

Abolitionism emerged from the same religious impulse that energized reform throughout the North. Like other reformers, the abolitionists came predominantly from evangelical, middle-class families, particularly those of New England stock. What distinguished the abolitionists was their insistence that slavery was *the* great national sin, mocking American ideals of liberty and Christian morality.

Under the early leadership of William Lloyd Garrison, the abolitionists attacked slaveholders and those whose moral apathy helped support slavery. After provoking a storm of protest in both North and South, the abolitionist movement split in 1840. Crucial in this division was Garrison's support of women's rights. Most abolitionists broke with him and founded their own antislavery organization. Female abolitionists organized a separate women's rights movement.

REJECTING COLONIZATION

In the early nineteenth century, when slavery was expanding westward, almost all white Americans regardless of class or region were convinced that emancipation would lead to a race war or the debasement of their superior status through racial interbreeding. This paralyzing fear, rooted in racism, long shielded slavery from sustained attack.

In 1817, antislavery reformers from the North and South founded the **American Colonization Society**. Slaveholding politicians from the Upper South, notably Henry Clay, James Madison, and President James Monroe, were its leading organizers. Gradual emancipation followed by the removal of black people from America to Africa was the only solution that white reformers could imagine for ridding the nation of slavery and avoiding a racial bloodbath. Their goal was to make America all free and all white.

The American Colonization Society had no chance of success. No form of emancipation could appeal to slave owners who could profit from the demand for their slaves in the Lower South. Black people already free accounted for nearly all of those the society transported to its West African colony, Liberia. At the height of its popularity in the 1820s, the society sent only fourteen hundred colonists to Africa. During that same decade, the American slave population increased by 700,000.

WHY DID abolitionist agitation and sentiment in the North grow?

American Colonization Society
Organization, founded in 1817 by antislavery reformers, that called for gradual emancipation and the removal of freed blacks to Africa.

Free African Americans bitterly attacked the colonizers' assumption that free black people were unfit to live as free citizens in America. Most free African Americans were native-born, and they considered themselves Americans with every right to enjoy the blessings of republican liberty. As a black petition in 1817 stated, banishment from America "would not only be cruel, but in direct violation of the principles, which have been the boast of this republic."

Organizing through their own churches in northern cities, free African Americans founded some fifty abolitionist societies, offered refuge to fugitive slaves, and launched the first African-American newspaper in 1827, *Freedom's Journal.* David Walker, a free black man who had moved from North Carolina to Massachusetts, published his ***Appeal to the Colored Citizens of the World*** in 1829. Rejecting colonization, Walker insisted that "America is more our country, than it is the whites'—we have enriched it with our *blood and tears*," and he warned white Americans that "wo, wo, will be to you if we have to obtain our freedom by fighting."

As if in response to his call for revolutionary resistance by the enslaved, Nat Turner's Rebellion exploded in the summer of 1831 (see Chapter 11). Both alarmed and inspired by the increased tempo of black militancy, a small group of antislavery white people abandoned all illusions about colonization and embarked on a radically new approach for eradicating slavery.

ABOLITIONISM

The leading figure in early abolitionism was William Lloyd Garrison, a Massachusetts printer, who became coeditor of an antislavery newspaper in Baltimore in 1829. Before the year was out, Garrison was convicted of criminal libel for his editorials against a Massachusetts merchant engaged in the domestic slave trade and spent seven weeks in jail. Garrison emerged with an unquenchable hatred for slavery. Returning to Boston, he launched his own antislavery newspaper, *The Liberator*, in 1831. A year later, he was instrumental in founding the New England Anti-Slavery Society.

As militant as the free African Americans who comprised the bulk of the early subscribers to *The Liberator*, Garrison thundered, "If we would not see our land deluged in blood, we must instantly burst asunder the shackles of the slaves." He committed abolitionism to the twin goals of immediatism—an immediate moral commitment to end slavery—and racial equality. Only by striving toward these goals, he insisted, could white America ever hope to end slavery without massive violence.

The demand of the abolitionists for the legal equality of black people was as unsettling to public opinion as their call for immediate, uncompensated emancipation. Discriminatory laws, aptly described by abolitionist Lydia Maria Child as "this legalized contempt of color," restricted the political and civil liberties of free African Americans in every state. (See American Views: "Appeal of a Female Abolitionist." pp. 318–319) Denied the vote outside New England, segregated in all public facilities, prohibited from moving into several western states, and excluded from most jobs save menial labor, free black people everywhere were walled off as an inferior caste unfit for equality.

Garrison was uncompromising in denouncing slavery and advocating black rights. But without the organizational and financial resources of a national society, the message of the early Garrisonians rarely extended beyond free black communities in the North. The success of British abolitionists in 1833 when gradual, compensated emancipation was enacted for Britain's West Indian colonies, inspired white and black abolitionists to gather at Philadelphia in December 1833 and form the **American Anti-Slavery Society**.

Appeal to the Colored Citizens of the World   Written by David Walker, a published insistence that "America is more our country, than it is the whites'—we have enriched it with our *blood and tears.*"

American Anti-Slavery Society   The first national organization of abolitionists, founded in 1833.

Arthur and Lewis Tappan, two wealthy merchants from New York City, provided financial backing, and Theodore Dwight Weld, a young evangelical minister, fused abolitionism with the moral passion of religious revivalism. Weld brought abolitionism to the West in 1834 with the revivals he preached at Lane Theological Seminary in Cincinnati. The "Lane rebels," students gathered by Weld, fanned out as itinerant agents to seek converts for abolitionism throughout the Yankee districts of the rural North. Weld's *American Slavery as It Is: Testimony of a Thousand Witnesses*, a massively documented indictment of slavery, became a bestseller in 1839. Abolitionist women, notably Angelina Grimké, Weld's wife and the daughter of a South Carolina planter, contributed much of the research.

Revivalistic exhortations were just one technique the abolitionists exploited to mobilize public opinion against slavery. They spread their message through rallies, paid lecturers, children's games and toys, and the printed word. Drawing on the experience of reformers in Bible and tract societies, the abolitionists harnessed steam printing to the cause of moral suasion. They distributed millions of antislavery tracts, and by the late 1830s, abolitionist sayings appeared on posters, emblems, song sheets, and even candy wrappers.

To change public opinion, the abolitionists described slavery in terms of moral and physical degradation. By 1840, nearly 200,000 Northerners belonged to the American Anti-Slavery Society. Most whites, however, remained unmoved, and some violently opposed the abolitionists.

In the mid-1830s antiabolitionist mobs in the North disrupted antislavery meetings, beat and stoned speakers, destroyed printing presses, burned the homes of the wealthy benefactors of the movement, and vandalized free black neighborhoods in a wave of terror that drove black people from several northern cities. Elijah P. Lovejoy, an abolitionist editor in Illinois, was killed by a mob in 1837. The mobs' fury expressed the anxieties of semiskilled and common laborers who thought they might lose their jobs if freed slaves moved North.

In the South, the hostility to abolitionism took the form of burning and censoring antislavery literature, offering rewards for the capture of leading abolitionists to stand trial for inciting slave revolts, and tightening up slave codes and the surveillance of free black people. Meanwhile, Democrats in Congress passed a gag rule that automatically tabled antislavery petitions.

In 1838, Garrison helped found the New England Non-Resistant Society, dedicated to the belief that a complete moral regeneration, based on renouncing force in all human relationships, was necessary if America were ever to live up to its Christian and republican ideals. The Garrisonian nonresistants rejected all coercive authority, whether expressed in human bondage, clerical support of slavery, male dominance in the patriarchical family, the racial oppression of black people, or the police power of government. The logic of their stand as Christian **anarchists** drove them to denounce all formal political activities and even the legitimacy of the Union, based as it was on a pact with slaveholders.

Garrison's support for the growing demand of antislavery women to be treated as equals in the movement split the American Anti-Slavery Society in 1840. In turn, the opposition of most male abolitionists to the public activities of their female counterparts provoked a militant faction of these women into founding their own movement to achieve equality in American society.

THE WOMEN'S RIGHTS MOVEMENT

Feminism grew out of abolitionism because of the parallels many women drew between the exploited lives of the slaves and their own subordinate status in Northern society. Considered biologically inferior to men, women were denied the vote,

Mobs of angry men often broke up meetings organized by women to vote. Shown here is a male escort offering protection to Lucretia Mott and another suffragette at one such meeting.

Corbis

anarchists Persons who believe that all government interferes with individual liberty and should be abolished by whatever means necessary.

• AMERICAN VIEWS •

APPEAL OF A FEMALE ABOLITIONIST

ydia Maria Child's Appeal, published in Boston in 1833, was a landmark in abolitionist literature for both its thorough attack on slavery and its refutation of racism. The condemnation of racial prejudice directly challenged the deep beliefs and assumptions of nearly all white Americans, in the North and the South. Racism and slavery, as Child shows in this excerpt from her Appeal, fed off one another in the national curse of slavery.

HOW DOES Child argue that Northern white people must bear some responsibility for perpetuating slavery? What arguments does Child make against racial discrimination in Northern society? What did Child mean when she wrote that "the Americans are peculiarly responsible for the example they give"? Do you agree with her? How does Child deal with the charge that the abolitionists threatened the preservation of the Union?

While we bestow our earnest disapprobation on the system of slavery, let us not flatter ourselves that we are in reality any better than our brethren of the South.

Thanks to our soil and climate, and the early exhortions of the Quakers, the form of slavery does not exist among us; but the very spirit of the hateful and mischievous thing is here in all its strength. . . . Our prejudice against colored people is even more inveterate than it is at the South. The planter is often attached to his negroes, and lavishes caresses and kind words upon them, as he would on a favorite hound: but our cold-hearted, ignoble prejudice admits of no exception—no intermission.

The Southerners have long continued habit, apparent interest and dreaded danger, to palliate the wrong they do; but we stand without excuse. . . . If the free States wished to cherish the system of slavery forever, they could not take a more direct course than they now do. Those who are kind and liberal on all other subjects, unite with the selfish and the proud in their unrelenting efforts to keep the colored population in the lowest state of degradation; and the influence they unconsciously exert over children early infuses into their innocent minds the same strong feelings of contempt. . . .

The state of public feeling not only makes it difficult for the Africans to obtain information, but it pre-

11–3
Sojourner Truth, Address to the Woman's Rights Convention, Akron, Ohio (1851)

deprived of property or control of any wages after marriage, and barred from most occupations and advanced education. "In striving to cut [the slave's] irons off, we found most surely that *we* were manacled *ourselves*," argued Abby Kelley, a Quaker abolitionist.

Antislavery women now demanded an equal voice in the abolitionist movement. Despite strong opposition from male abolitionists, Garrison helped Abby Kelley win a seat on the business committee of the American Anti-Slavery Society at its convention in 1840. The anti-Garrisonians walked out of the convention and formed a separate organization in 1840, the American and Foreign Anti-Slavery Society.

The "woman question" also disrupted the 1840 World Anti-Slavery Convention in London. The refusal of the convention to seat the American female delegates was the final indignity that transformed the discontent of women into a self-conscious movement for women's equality. Two of the excluded delegates, Lucretia Mott and Elizabeth Cady Stanton, vowed to build an organization to "speak out for *oppressed* women."

Their work went slowly. Early feminists were dependent on the abolitionists for most of their followers. Many women sympathetic to the feminist movement vents them from making profitable use of what knowledge they have. A colored man, however intelligent, is not allowed to pursue any business more lucrative than that of a barber, a shoe-black, or waiter. These, and all other employments, are truly respectable, whenever the duties connected with them are faithfully performed; but it is unjust that a man should, on account of his complexion, be prevented from performing more elevated uses in society. Every citizen ought to have a fair chance to try his fortune in any line of business, which he thinks he has ability to transact. Why should not colored men be employed in the manufactories of various kinds? If their ignorance is an objection, let them be enlightened, as speedily as possible. If their moral character is not sufficiently pure, remove the pressure of public scorn, and thus supply them with motives for being respectable. All this can be done. It merely requires an earnest wish to overcome a prejudice, which . . . is in fact opposed to the spirit of our religion, and contrary to the instinctive good feelings of our nature. . . . When the majority heartily desire a change, it is effected, be the difficulties what they may. The Americans are peculiarly responsible for the example they give; for in no other country does the unchecked voice of the people constitute the whole of government. . . .

The strongest and best reason that can be given for our supineness on the subject of slavery, is the fear of dissolving the Union. The Constitution of the United States demands our highest reverence. . . . But we must not forget that the Constitution provides for any change that may be required for the general good. The great machine is constructed with a safety valve, by which any rapidly increasing evil may be expelled whenever the people desire it.

If the Southern politicians are determined to make a Siamese question of this also—if they insist that the Union shall not exist without slavery—it can only be said that they join two things, which have no affinity with each other, and which cannot permanently exist together.—They chain the living and vigorous to the diseased and dying; and the former will assuredly perish in the infected neighborhood.

The universal introduction of free labor is the surest way to consolidate the Union, and enable us to live together in harmony and peace. If a history is ever written entitled. "The Decay and Dissolution of the North American Republic," its author will distinctly trace our downfall to the existence of slavery among us.

Source: Lydia Maria Child. *An Appeal in Favor of That Class of Americans Called Africans* (originally published 1833), ed. Carolyn L. Karcher (University of Massachusetts Press, 1996).

---

held back lest they be shunned in their communities. A minister's wife in Portsmouth, New Hampshire, spoke for many of these women when she wrote to a feminist friend, "There are but few here who think of women as anything more than slave or a plaything, and they think I am different from most women."

In 1848, Stanton and Mott were finally able to call the first national convention ever devoted to women's rights at Seneca Falls, in upstate New York. The **Seneca Falls Convention** issued the **Declaration of Sentiments**, a call for full female equality. It identified male patriarchy as the source of women's oppression and demanded the vote for women as a sacred and inalienable right of republican citizenship.

The Seneca Falls agenda defined the goals of the women's movement for the rest of the century. The call for the vote met the stiffest opposition. The feminists' few successes before the Civil War came in economic rights. By 1860, fourteen states had granted women greater control over their property and wages—most significantly under New York's Married Women's Property Act of 1860. Largely the result of the intense lobbying of Susan B. Anthony, the act established women's legal right to their own wage income and to sue fathers and husbands who tried to deprive them of their wages.

WHERE TO LEARN MORE

Women's Rights Historical Park, Seneca Falls, New York
www.nps.gov/wori/wrnhp.htm

Seneca Falls Convention   The first convention for women's equality in legal rights, held in upstate New York in 1848.

Declaration of Sentiments   The resolutions passed at the Seneca Falls Convention in 1848 calling for full female equality, including the right to vote.

The feminist movement did not attract broad support. Most women found in the doctrine of separate spheres a reassuring feminine identity that they could express either at home or in benevolent and reform societies. Within the reform movement as a whole, women's rights were always of minor concern.

POLITICAL ANTISLAVERY

Most abolitionists who had broken with Garrison in 1840 believed that emancipation could best be achieved by moving abolitionism into the mainstream of American politics. Political abolitionism had its roots in the petition campaign of the late 1830s. Congressional efforts to suppress the discussion of slavery backfired when John Quincy Adams, the former president who had become a Massachusetts congressman, resorted to an unending series of parliamentary ploys to get around the gag rule. Adams became a champion of the constitutional right to petition Congress for redress of grievances. White Northerners who had shown no interest in abolitionism as a moral crusade for black people now began to take a stand against slavery when the issue involved the civil liberties of whites and the political power of the South. By the hundreds of thousands, they signed abolitionist petitions in 1837 and 1838 to protest the gag rule and block the admission of Texas as a slave state.

In 1840, anti-Garrison abolitionists formed the **Liberty party** and elected several antislavery congressmen in antislavery districts dominated by evangelical New Englanders. The Liberty party condemned racial discrimination in the North, as well as slavery in the South, and won the support of most black abolitionists.

Frederick Douglass was the black abolitionists' most dynamic spokesman. After escaping from slavery in 1838, Douglass became a spellbinding lecturer for abolitionism and in 1845 published his classic autobiography, *Narrative of the Life of Frederick Douglass, an American Slave.* Dissatisfied with Garrison's Christian pacifism and his stand against political action, Douglass broke with Garrison in 1847 and founded a black abolitionist newspaper, *The North Star.* The break became irreparable in 1851 when Douglass publicly denied the Garrisonian position that the Constitution was a proslavery document. If properly interpreted, Douglass insisted, "the Constitution is a *glorious liberty document,*" and he called for a political war against slavery.

That war had started in the 1840s with the Liberty party, which kept slavery in the limelight of national politics. Led by Joshua R. Giddings, a small but vocal bloc of antislavery politicians began to popularize the frightening concept of "the Slave Power"—a vast conspiracy of planters and their Northern lackeys who had seized control of the federal government and was plotting to spread slavery and subvert any free institutions that opposed it. As proof, they cited the gag rule shutting off debate on slavery and the campaign of the Tyler administration to annex slaveholding Texas. The Michigan Liberty party in 1843 claimed that slavery was "not only a monstrous legalized system of wickedness . . . but an overwhelming political monopoly . . . which has thus tyrannically subverted the constitutional liberties of more than 12,000,000 of nominal American freemen." The Liberty party blamed the depression of 1839–1843 on the "withering and impoverishing effect of slavery on the free States." Planters, it was charged, had reneged on their debts to Northern creditors and manipulated federal policies on banking and tariffs to the advantage of the South.

The specter of the Slave Power made white liberties and not black bondage central to Northern concerns about slavery. White people who had earlier been apathetic now began to view slavery as a threat to their rights of free speech and self-improvement through free labor untainted by the degrading competition of slave labor.

The image of the Slave Power predisposed many Northerners to see the expansionist program of the incoming Polk administration as part of a Southern plot

WHERE TO LEARN MORE

Oberlin College Library, Oberlin, Ohio
www.oberlin.edu/library/

Liberty party The first antislavery political party, formed in 1840.

to secure more territory for slaveholders at the expense of Northern farmers. Northern fears that free labor would be shut out of the new territories won in the Mexican War provided the rallying cry for the Free-Soil Party of 1848 that foreshadowed the more powerful Republican Party of the late 1850s.

CONCLUSION

After 1815, transportation improvements, technological innovations, and expanding markets drove the economy toward industrialization. Wealth inequality increased, old classes were reshaped, and new ones formed. These changes were most evident in the Northeast, where capital, labor, and growing urban markets spurred the acceleration of manufacturing. The reform impulse that both reflected and shaped these changes was also strongest in the Northeast.

The new evangelical Protestantism promised that human perfectibility was possible if individuals strove to free themselves from sin. Influenced by this promise, the Northern middle class embraced reform causes that sought to improve human character. Temperance established sobriety as the cultural standard for respectable male behavior. Middle-class reform also emphasized institutional solutions for what were now defined as the social problems of ignorance, crime, and poverty.

The most radical reform movements focused on women's equality and the elimination of slavery. The women's rights movement emerged out of women's involvement in reform, especially in abolitionism. Feminism and abolitionism triggered a backlash from the conservative majority. That prevented women from gaining legal and political equality, and convinced most abolitionists that they had to switch from moral agitation to political persuasion. Political abolitionists found that the most effective approach was their charge that a Slave Power conspiracy threatened the freedoms of white Northerners.

After escaping to freedom in 1838, Frederick Douglass became a commanding figure in the abolitionist movement. His speeches denouncing slavery were fiery and eloquent.

Frederick Douglass (1817?–1895). Oil on canvas, c. 1844, attr. to E. Hammond. The Granger Collection

SUMMARY

Industrial Change and Urbanization In the 1800s the United States experienced a transportation and manufacturing revolution; this accelerated the spread of cities, factories, and commercial farming. Urbanization brought new work patterns as manufacturing moved from the home to factories. The Northeast experienced the greatest growth; swelling the size of all cities were immigrants, most coming from Ireland and Germany. The new middle class was the product of the changes in employment opportunities; the new working classes contained native-born artisans competing for jobs with immigrants and women.

Reform and Moral Order The changes to society that accompanied this market revolution frightened religious leaders and businessmen in the East. The benevolent empire responded with a host of societies targeted at individual vices, especially the consumption of alcohol. Women played a significant role in these reform movements, not always with the approval of males who saw their authority being undermined.

Institutions and Social Improvement Based in the Enlightenment belief that people and society could be improved, the reformers implemented new institutions to shape individual character. Free, tax-supported public education was one of their most lasting achievements; prisons and asylums for the mentally ill were also targeted. Utopian reformers sought self-improvement by withdrawing into communitarian societies; the intellectuals who were drawn to Brook Farm had a lasting impact, as these transcendentalists were the catalyst for the nineteenth-century renaissance of American literature.

Abolitionism and Women's Rights Abolitionism emerged from the same religious impulse that energized reform throughout the North. Believing slavery was the great national sin, abolitionists attacked the institution and all its supporters. After provoking a storm of protests in the North and the South, the abolitionist movement divided, with women expanding their efforts into a women's rights movement. Abolitionists moved their cause into the political mainstream and focused attention on what they called the growing "Slave Power" threatening the nation.

REVIEW QUESTIONS

1. Why were improvements in transportation essential to the growth of the economy after 1815?

2. What is an industrial revolution? Why did manufacturing surge in the United States from 1815 to 1850?

3. What drew women into reform?

4. Why was abolitionism the most radical reform of all?

5. Why was Angelina Grimké's journey from social privilege to social activism so exceptional?

KEY TERMS

American Anti-Slavery Society (p. 316)
American Colonization Society (p. 315)
American system of manufacturing (p. 301)
Anarchists (p. 317)
Appeal to the Colored Citizens of the World (p. 316)
Benevolent empire (p. 306)
Brook Farm (p. 314)

Charles River Bridge v. *Warren Bridge* (p. 295)
Church of Jesus Christ of Latter-day Saints (Mormon Church) (p. 310)
Communism (p. 313)
Cult of domesticity (p. 304)
Declaration of Sentiments (p. 319)
Gibbons v. *Ogden* (p. 294)
Liberty party (p. 320)
Nativist organizations (p. 305)
New Harmony (p. 314)

Oneida Community (p. 313)
Putting-out system (p. 297)
Sabbatarian movement (p. 307)
Seneca Falls Convention (p. 319)
Shakers (p. 313)
Socialism (p. 314)
Temperance (p. 304)
Transcendentalism (p. 314)
Transportation revolution (p. 291)
Waltham system (p. 300)

WHERE TO LEARN MORE

Baltimore Center for Urban Archaeology, Baltimore, Maryland. Operated by Baltimore City Life Museum, the center has a large collection of artifacts depicting urban life in the eighteenth and nineteenth centuries and a working archaeological library.

Hanford Mills Museum, East Meredith, New York. This museum preserves and interprets water-powered machinery and explains the role played by local mills in the community life of the nineteenth century. For a map and links to events, workshops, and education programs, visit: **www.hanfordmills.org/**

Slater Hill Historic Site, Pawtucket, Rhode Island. The Sylvanus Brown House of 1758, the Slaren Mill of 1793, and the Wilkinson Mill of 1810 are on the site. An extensive library and holdings provide insight into the social and economic world of the early industrial revolution. Information on hours, collections, and exhibits can be found at: **www.artcom.com/museums/vs/sz/02862-06.htm**

Erie Canal Museum, Syracuse, New York. The museum houses extensive collections on the building and maintenance of the Erie Canal, and its photo holdings visually record much of the history of the canal. In addition to information on exhibits, tours, and school programs, its website, **www.eriecanalmuseum.org/**, includes pictures of a replica of an Erie Canal line boat.

Historic New Harmony, New Harmony, Indians. The tours and museum holdings at this preserved site offer a glimpse into the communal living that Robert Owen tried to promote in his utopian plan. For a brief history of New Harmony and links to special events and programs at the site, go to: **www.newharmony.org/**

Oberlin College Library, Oberlin, Ohio. Oberlin was a hotbed of reform agitation, and the tracts, broadsides, photographs, and other memorabilia here are especially rich on the activities of white evangelicals and black abolitionists. For an introduction to the library and its holdings, visit: **www.oberlin.edu/library/**

Shaker Museum at South Union, Kentucky. The exhibits, artifacts, and archives are a superb source for understanding the history and material culture of the Shakers and other radical sects. Its website, **www.shakermuseum.com/**, includes a brief history of the Shakers, photographs of restored buildings, and an overview of the museum's holdings.

Women's Rights Historical Park, Seneca Falls, New York. The park provides an interpretive overview of the first women's rights convention and includes among its historical sites the restored home of Elizabeth Cady Stanton. Go to **www.nps.gov/wori/wrnhp.htm** for links to the museum's summer calendar of events and information on programs.

 For additional study resources for this chapter, go to:
www.prenhall.com/goldfield/chapter12

*They immigrate constantly, hardly no one
to prevent them, and take possession of
the location that best suits them without either
asking leave or going through any formality
other than that of building their homes.*

Albert Bierstadt (1830–1902), *"The Oregon Trail"* **(oil on canvas).**
Private Collection/Bridgeman Art Library International Ltd., New York

13

THE WAY WEST
1815–1850

HOW DID economic
and demographic pressures
in the East spur Western migration?

HOW DID Westward expansion
affect the life of Plains Indians?

HOW WAS the United States
able to annex Texas from Mexico?

WHICH PEOPLES
lived in the Southwest?

"On an occasion when I had interrogated a Sioux chief, on the upper Missouri, about their Government—their punishments and tortures of prisoners, for which I had freely condemned them for the cruelty of the practice, he took occasion, when I had got through, to ask me some questions relative to modes in the civilized *world, which, with his comments upon them, were nearly as follows: and struck me, as I think they must every one, with great force.*

He . . . told me he had often heard that white people hung their criminals by the neck, and choked them to death like dogs, and those their own people to which I answered, "yes." He then told me he had learned that they shut each other up in prisons, where they keep them a great part of their lives because they can't pay money. *I replied in the affirmative to this, which occasioned great surprise and excessive laughter, even among the women. . . . He said . . . that he had been along the Frontier, and a good deal amongst the white people, and he had seen them whip their little children—a thing that is very cruel—he had heard also, from several white* medicine-men, *that the Great Spirit of the white people was the child of a white woman, and that he was at the last put to death by the white people! This seemed to be a thing that he had not been able to comprehend, and he concluded by saying, "the Indians, Great Spirit got no mother—the Indians no kill him, he never die." He put me a chapter of other questions as to the trespasses of the white people on their lands—their continual corruption of the morals of their women—and digging open the Indians graves to get their bones, &c. To all of which I was compelled to reply in the affirmative, and quite glad to close my note-book, and quietly to escape from the throng that had collected around me, and saying (though to myself and silently), that these and an hundred other vices belong to the civilized world, and are practiced upon (but certainly, in no instance, reciprocated by) the "cruel and relentless savage."*

—*George Catlin*

Virgil J. Vogel, ed., *A Documentary History of the American Indian* (New York: Harper and Row, 1972), pp. 138–139.

IMAGE KEY
for pages 324–325

a. A tanned buffalo skin.

b. A long wooden pipe of the Mandan tribe drawn by Swiss artist Karl Bodmer.

c. Albert Bierstadt (1830–1902), "The Oregon Trail" (oil on canvas).

d. Cactus with thick green stem with thick glossy spines and a large pinkish coloured flower near the top of the plant.

e. A scale model of a Native American Plains Indian tepee, with an accompanying figure of a man for perspective.

f. John Gast (Active 1870'S). "American Progress", c. 1872. Depicts the diaphanously clad America floating over a variety of American people and animals heading westward. The emblematic figure carries a school book and a telegraph wire.

g. George Catlin, "Commanche Village Life," 1834.

h. Nathaniel Currier, "General Winfield Scott at the Siege of Vera Cruz, March 1847."

i. Alfred Jacob Miller, "The Interior of Fort Laramie," 1858–60.

GEORGE CATLIN, one of the great illustrators of the West of the American Indians, recorded these words in the 1830s when he traveled over the trans-Mississippi West painting and sketching, in his words, "the looks and customs of the vanishing races of native man in America." Unlike most white people of his generation, he approached Indian cultures with respect, and he realized that native peoples had a valid critique of white America. Born in 1796, he was raised among memories of Indians and their warfare. After briefly practicing law, he turned to painting as a career in the 1820s, and was so taken with the grace and dignity of Indians that he set out to record Indian history and customs before their way of life was engulfed by a surging tide of white settlement.

Some 300,000 Americans traveled the Oregon Trail in the 1840s and 1850s in a trek that eventually made the United States a nation that spanned the continent. They were part of a tide of white migration that eventually saw more than fifty thousand Americans a year migrate west of the Appalachians after the War of 1812.

In the 1840s, the edge of settlement pushed into the Louisiana Purchase territory and across a huge area of plains, desert, mountains, and ocean coast that had seen few American settlers before then.

The broad expanse of the trans-Mississippi region (stretching from the Mississippi Valley to the Pacific Coast) became a meeting ground of people from diverse cultures as Anglo-Americans came into contact and conflict with the Indians of the Plains and the Mexicans of the Southwest. Convinced of their own superiority, Anglo-Americans asserted a God-given right to spread across the continent and impose their notions of liberty and democracy on peoples whose land they coveted. In the process, they defeated and subjugated those who stood in their way.

Manifest Destiny, the label for this presumed providential right, provided a justification for the expansionist Democratic administration of James K. Polk that came to power in 1845. The most dramatic result of these policies was the Mexican War of 1846–1848, which made California and the present-day Southwest part of the American continental empire.

THE AGRICULTURAL FRONTIER

The U.S. population ballooned from 5.3 million in 1800 to more than 23 million by 1850. Four-fifths of this extraordinary gain was from natural increase—the surplus of births over deaths. As the population expanded, it shifted westward. Fewer than one in ten Americans lived west of the Appalachians in 1800; by 1850, about half did (see Map 13–1 p.328).

Through purchase and conquest, the land area of the United States more than tripled in the first half of the nineteenth century. Here was space where Americans could raise the large families of a rural society in which, on average, six to eight children survived to adolescence.

Declining soil fertility and rising population pressure in the rural East propelled these migrations. A common desire for greater economic opportunity, however, resulted in two distinct western societies by the 1840s. North of the Ohio River, in the Old Northwest, free labor and family farms defined the social order. South of the Ohio was the Old Southwest, a society dominated by slave labor and the plantation.

THE CROWDED EAST

Looking back at his rural youth, Omar H. Morse recalled, "My Parents were in very limited circumstances financially yet blessed with a large family of children which is a poor man's capital though capital of this kind is not considered very available in case of financial Depression." Born in 1824 in the upstate New York village of Hastings, Morse had no prospect of inheriting land from his father and was tired of taking orders as a farm hand for temporary wages. He moved in the 1840s to Wisconsin, but he lost three farms and eventually settled in Minnesota, where he worked at odd jobs and built houses. Heading west did not guarantee economic success, but it was the best option open to land-starved easterners who dreamed of leaving a productive farm to their children.

By the early nineteenth century, land was scarce in the East, especially in New England. Most New England communities no longer had enough arable land to satisfy all the young men who wanted their own farms. Even recently opened areas such as Vermont felt the pressure of rural overpopulation.

Land was more productive and expensive farther south, in the Mid-Atlantic states. Keyed to the major export crop of wheat, agriculture was more commercialized

HOW DID economic and demographic pressures in the East spur western migration?

Manifest Destiny Doctrine, first expressed in 1845, that the expansion of white Americans across the continent was inevitable and ordained by God.

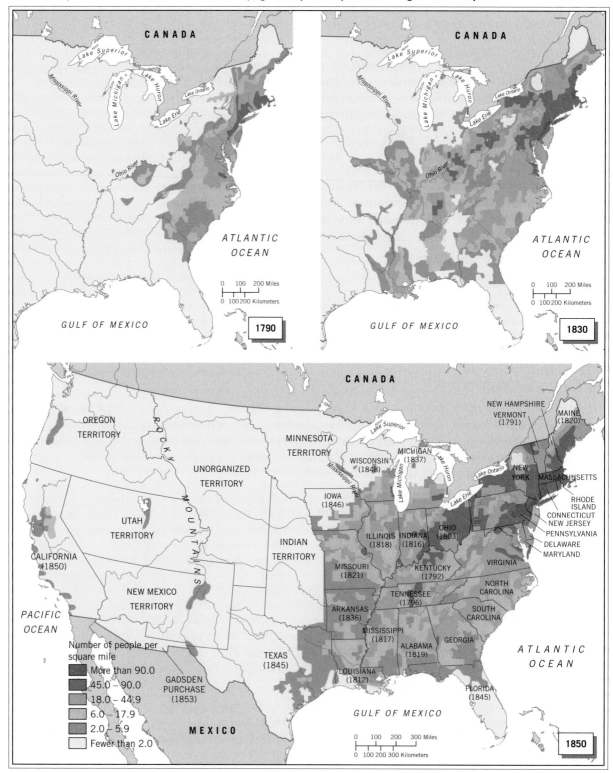

MAP 13–1

The Westward Shift of the United States Population, 1790–1850 With a speed that was unimaginable in 1790, the United States quickly became a continental nation that stretched from the Atlantic to the Pacific by 1850. Particularly dramatic was the population growth in what became the Midwest.

WHAT CHANGES occurred between 1830 and 1850 to encourage the settlement of territories in the West?

than in New England, and economic inequality was thus higher. One-third to one-half of the young men in the commercialized agricultural districts of New Jersey and Pennsylvania were landless by the end of the eighteenth century. These men and their families, many of whom were recently arrived Scots-Irish and German immigrants, led the western migration from Pennsylvania.

The pressure to move west was greatest in the slave states along the eastern seaboard. Although population density here was just two-thirds of that in New England, landholdings were more concentrated and the soil more exhausted than in the Northeast. Tenants who wanted their own land and small farmers tired of competing against slave labor were forced west across the mountains. They were joined by the sons of planters. Despite marriages arranged to keep land within the wealthy families, there was no longer enough good land left to carve out plantations for all the younger sons.

By the early 1800s, the young and the poor in the rural East had every incentive to head west, where fertile land was abundant, accessible, and, at $2 to $3 per acre, far cheaper than in the East. Land was the basis of wealth and social standing, and its ownership separated the independent from the dependent, the rooted from the rootless. "Those who labor in the earth," Jefferson wrote in 1785, "are the chosen people of God . . . whose breasts He has made his peculiar deposit for substantial and genuine virtue."

The western settler, observed a traveler on the Missouri frontier in the 1820s, wanted "to be a freeholder, to have plenty of rich land, and to be able to settle his children around him." Public policy and private aspirations merged in the belief that access to land was the key to preserving American freedom.

When Jefferson took office in 1801, the minimum price for public land was $2 per acre, and a block of 320 acres had to be purchased at one time. By the 1830s, the price was down to $1.25 per acre, and the minimum purchase was only 80 acres. Congress also protected squatters, who had settled on public land before it was surveyed, from being outbid by speculators at a land sale. The Preemption Act of 1841 guaranteed the right to purchase up to 160 acres at the minimum price of $1.25 when the public auction was held.

WHERE TO LEARN MORE

Living History Farms,
Des Moines, Iowa
www.lhf.org/

THE OLD NORTHWEST

The number of Americans who settled in the heartland of the Old Northwest—Ohio, Indiana, and Illinois—rose tenfold from 1810 to 1840. Ohio had already entered the Union in 1803; Indiana joined in 1816, Illinois in 1818. The end of the War of 1812 and the abandonment by the British of their former Indian allies opened up the region to a flood of migrants.

Two streams of migrants, one predominantly northern and the other southern, met in the lower Midwest and viewed each other as strangers. Lucy Maynard, a New Englander living in south-central Illinois, noted that her neighbors were "principally from Indiana and Kentucky, some from Virginia, all friendly but very different from our people in their manners and language and every other way."

The Old Northwest was less a melting pot in which regional cultures merged than a mosaic of settlements in which the different values and folkways of regional cultures from throughout the East took root and expanded. Belts of migration generally ran along a line from east to west as settlers sought out soil types and ecological conditions similar to those they had left behind. Thus a transplanted Yankee culture from New England and upstate New York spread over the upper Midwest—northern Ohio, Indiana, and Illinois, as well

WHERE TO LEARN MORE

Conner Prairie,
Noblesville, Indiana
www.connerprairie.org

Cyrus McCormick pioneered the development of horse-drawn mechanical reapers. Shown here demonstrating his reaper to potential customers, McCormick helped revolutionize American agriculture with labor-saving machinery that made possible far larger harvests of grain crops.

The Old Print Shop

Claims clubs Groups of local settlers on the nineteenth-century frontier who banded together to prevent the price of their land claims from being bid up by outsiders at public land auctions.

as Michigan and Wisconsin. These westerners were Whiggish in their politics, tended to be antislavery, and valued a communal sense of responsibility that regulated moral behavior and promoted self-improvement. The highland Southerners who settled the lower Midwest—southern Ohio, Indiana, and Illinois, as well as Kentucky—were Democrats: They fiercely distrusted any centralized authority, political or moral, and considered Yankees intolerant do-gooders. Holding the balance of cultural and political power were the migrants from Pennsylvania and New Jersey, who were accustomed to ethnic diversity and the politics of competing economic groups. They settled principally in central Ohio, Indiana, and Illinois. By emphasizing economic growth and downplaying the cultural politics that pitted Yankees against Southerners, they built a consensus around community development.

It took about ten years of backbreaking labor to create an 80-acre farm in heavily wooded sections. Wives and daughters helped tend the field crops, milked cows and churned butter, and produced the homespun cloth that, along with their dairy goods, found a market in the first country stores on the frontier. Charlotte Webb Jacobs, from the Sugar Creek community on the Illinois prairie, proudly recalled, "I made everything that we wore; I even made my towels and table cloths, sheets and everything in the clothing line."

Communities pooled their efforts for such tasks as raising a cabin. Groups of settlers also acted as a cooperative unit at public land auctions. Members of local **claims clubs** physically intimidated speculators who refused to step aside until local settlers had acquired the land they wanted.

Surplus goods were sold to newcomers moving into the area or bartered with local storekeepers for essentials such as salt, sugar, and metalwares. This initial economy, however, soon gave way to a more commercially oriented agriculture when steamboats, canals, and railroads opened up vast new markets (see Chapter 11).

The first large market was in the South, down the corridor of the Ohio and Mississippi Rivers, and the major staples were corn and hogs. By the 1830s, the Erie Canal and its feeder waterways in the upper Midwest began to reorient much of the western farm trade to the Northeast.

Wheat production skyrocketed when settlers overcame their initial reluctance to farming in a treeless terrain and moved into the prairies of Indiana and Illinois in the 1840s. New plows—a cast-iron one patented by Jethro Wood in 1819 and a steel version developed by John Deere in 1837—helped break the thick prairie sod. The plows were followed in the 1840s by horse-drawn mechanical harvesters equipped with a self-rake reaper that enabled family farmers to harvest vastly more wheat. Using traditional harvesting methods, a scythe

CHRONOLOGY

1803–1806	Lewis and Clark travel up the Missouri River in search of a water route to the Pacific.
1816	Settlers surge into the trans-Appalachian region.
1821	Mexico gains its independence from Spain. Santa Fe Trail opens. Stephen F. Austin establishes the first American colony in Texas.
1824	Rocky Mountain Fur Company begins the rendezvous system.
1830	Congress creates the Indian Territory.
1834	Protestant missions are established in Oregon. Santa Anna seizes power in Mexico.
1836	Texas wins its independence from Mexico.

1837	Smallpox epidemic hits the Plains Indians.
1842	First large parties of migrants set out on the Oregon Trail.
1845	United States annexes Texas. Democrats embrace Manifest Destiny.
1846	Mexican War breaks out. United States and Britain reach an agreement on Oregon.
1847	Mormons begin settlement of Utah.
1848	Oregon Territory is organized. Treaty of Guadalupe Hidalgo ends the Mexican War.
1851	Fort Laramie Treaty with the Plains Indians is signed.

with a cradle frame, an experienced worker could cut no more than 2 acres a day. With the new machinery the same worker could harvest 12 acres a day. Once railroads provided direct access to eastern markets, the Midwest became the nation's breadbasket.

The commercialization of agriculture in the West also contributed to the growth of eastern manufacturing. Western farms supplied eastern manufacturers with inexpensive raw materials for processing into finished goods. Western corn and wheat not only supplied eastern workers with cheap food but also forced noncompetitive eastern farmers either to move west or to work in factories in eastern cities. In turn, the West itself became an ever-growing market for eastern factory goods. For example, nearly half of the nation's iron production in the 1830s was fashioned into farm implements. At midcentury, the Old Northwest had become part of a larger Midwest whose economy was increasingly integrated with that of the Northeast. Settlers continued to pour into the region, and three additional states—Michigan (1837), Iowa (1846), and Wisconsin (1848)—joined the Union.

The combination of favorable farm prices and steadily decreasing transportation costs generated a rise in disposable income that was spent on outside goods or invested in internal economic development. Manufacturing cities grew out of towns that were favorably situated by water or rail transport. The West north of the Ohio was now economically specialized and socially diverse.

QUICK REVIEW

Commercialization of Agriculture

- New technology spurred production.
- Commercialization of agriculture contributed to growth of eastern manufacturing.
- West became a market for eastern factory goods.

THE OLD SOUTHWEST

"The *Alabama Feaver* rages here with great violence and has *carried off* vast numbers of our Citizens," wrote a North Carolina planter in 1817 about the westward migration from his state. "I am apprehensive, if it continues to spread as it has done, it will almost depopulate the country." By 1850, more than 600,000 white settlers from Maryland, Virginia, and the Carolinas lived in slave states to the south and west, and many of them had brought their slaves with them. Indeed, from 1790 to 1860, more than 800,000 slaves were moved from the South Atlantic region

OVERVIEW

WESTWARD EXPANSION AND THE GROWTH OF THE UNION, 1815–1850

New Free States	New Slave States	Territories (1850)
Indiana, 1816	Mississippi, 1817	Minnesota
Illinois, 1818	Alabama, 1819	Oregon
Maine, 1820	Missouri, 1821	New Mexico
Michigan, 1837	Arkansas, 1836	Utah
Iowa, 1846	Florida, 1845	
Wisconsin, 1848	Texas, 1845	
California, 1850		

into the Old Southwest. Soaring cotton prices after the War of 1812 and the smashing of Indian confederations during the war, which opened new lands to white settlement, propelled the first surge of migration into western Tennessee and the Black Belt, a crescent-shaped band of rich, black loamy soil arcing westward from Georgia through central Alabama and Mississippi.

Migration surged anew in the 1830s when cotton prices were again high and the Chickasaws and Choctaws had been forced out of the incredibly fertile Delta country between the Yazoo and Mississippi Rivers (see Chapter 10). In less than thirty years, six new slave states—Mississippi (1817), Alabama (1819), Missouri (1821), Arkansas (1836), Florida (1845), and Texas (1845)—joined the Union (see the overview table "Westward Expansion and the Growth of the Union, 1815–1850").

The southwestern frontier attracted both slaveholding planters and small independent farmers. The planters, though a minority, had the capital or the credit to acquire the best lands and the slave labor to make those lands productive. These slaveholders were responding both to the need for fresh land and to the extraordinary demand for short-staple cotton. As one North Carolina planter put it, Alabama would be a "garden of plenty" compared to the "old-fields and empty corn-houses" of his native state.

Short-staple cotton could be grown anywhere with a minimum of 210 consecutive frost-free days. Eli Whitney's gin, which eliminated the problem of removing the sticky, green seeds from the fiber, was fifty times faster than hand separation. Meanwhile, the mechanization of the British textile industry had created a seemingly unquenchable demand for raw cotton. With new fertile land and a slave labor force, the South increased its share of world cotton production from 9 percent in 1800 to 68 percent in 1850.

More typical settlers on the southern frontier were small independent yeomen farmers, who generally owned no slaves. Many of them shared the belief of the yeoman farmer Gideon Linecum "in the pleasure of frequent change of country."

The yeomanry moved onto the frontier in two waves. The first consisted of stockmen-hunters, a restless, transient group who spread from the pine barrens in the Carolina backcountry to the coastal plain of eastern Texas. They prized unfettered independence and measured their wealth in the livestock left to roam and fatten on the sweet grasses of uncleared forests. They were quick to move on when farmers, the second wave, started to clear the land for crops.

Like the stock herders, the yeoman farmers valued self-sufficiency and the leisure to hunt and fish. They practiced a diversified agriculture aimed at feeding their families. Corn and pork were the mainstays of their diet, and both could readily be produced as long as there was room for the open-range herding of swine and growing patches of corn and small grains. The yeoman's chief source of labor was his immediate family.

Measured by per capita income, and as a direct result of the profits from slave-produced cotton on virgin soils, the Old Southwest was a wealthier society than the Old Northwest in 1850. The settlement of the Old Southwest was also more significant for national economic development. More than any other commodity, cotton paid for American imports and underpinned national credit.

The Southwest Ordinance, enacted by Congress in 1790, opened all territories south of the Ohio River to slavery. Slaves, land, and cotton were the keys to wealth on the southern frontier, and agricultural profits were continually plowed back into these assets. In contrast, prosperous farmers in the Old Northwest were much more likely to invest their earnings in promotional schemes designed to attract settlers whose presence would raise land values and increase business for local entrepreneurs. As early as the 1840s, rural communities in the Old Northwest were supporting bustling towns that offered jobs in trade and manufacturing on a scale far surpassing anything in the slave West. By the 1850s, the Midwest was almost as urbanized as the Northeast had been in 1830, and nearly half the labor force no longer worked on farms.

The Old Southwest remained overwhelmingly agricultural. Once the land was settled, the children of the first generation of slaveholders and yeomen moved west to the next frontier. Relatively few newcomers took their place. By the 1850s, Kentucky, Tennessee, Alabama, and Mississippi were all losing more migrants than they were gaining.

THE FRONTIER OF THE PLAINS INDIANS

Few white Americans had ventured west of the Mississippi by 1840. What scanty knowledge there was of this huge inland expanse was the result of government-sponsored expeditions. Reports of explorations led by Zebulon Pike in 1806 and Stephen Long in 1819 dismissed much of the area as the Great American Desert, an arid, treeless landscape with little agricultural potential.

Beyond Texas and the boundary line drawn by the Trans-Continental Treaty of 1819 lay the northern possessions of Mexico, where horse-mounted Indian tribes dominated by the Sioux were a formidable power. Before the 1840s, only fur trappers and traders, who worked with and not against the powerful Sioux, had pushed across the Great Plains and into the Rockies. The 1840s brought a sudden change, a large migration westward that radically altered the ecology of the Great Plains. Farm families trapped in an agricultural depression and enticed by Oregon's bounty turned the trails blazed by the fur traders into ruts on the **Oregon Trail**, the route that led to the first large settlement of Americans on the Pacific Coast.

TRIBAL LANDS

At least 350,000 Native Americans lived in the plains and mountains of the Trans-Mississippi West in 1840. The point where the prairies of the Midwest gave way to the higher, drier plains marked a rough division between predominantly agricultural

HOW DID westward expansion affect the life of Plains Indians?

Oregon Trail   Overland trail of more than two thousand miles that carried American settlers from the Midwest to new settlements in Oregon, California, and Utah.

WHERE TO LEARN MORE

★ Indian Museum of North America, Crazy Horse, South Dakota
www.crazyhorse.org/museum.shtml

tribes to the east and nomadic, hunting tribes to the west. The Kansas, Osages, and Omahas in what is now Kansas and Iowa and the Arikaras, Mandans, and Hidatsas along the upper Missouri River grew corn, beans, and squash and lived in semipermanent villages, much as woodland Indians had in the East. On the open plains were hunting and raiding peoples, such as the western Sioux, Crows, Cheyennes, and Arapahos.

In the 1830s, the U.S. government set aside a broad stretch of country between the Platte River to the north and the Red River to the south (most of present-day Oklahoma and eastern Kansas) exclusively for tribes resettled from the East under the Indian Removal Act of 1830 and for village-living groups native to the area. Many government officials envisioned this territory as a permanent sanctuary that would separate Indians from whites and allow them to live in peace on allotments of land granted as compensation for the territory they had ceded to the federal government. However, the pressure exerted on native peoples in the Mississippi Valley both from raiding parties of Plains Indians and the incessant demands of white farmers and speculators for more land was rendering a stable Indian-white boundary meaningless.

On the eve of Indian removal in the East, the defeat of the Sauks and Foxes in what white Americans called Black Hawk's War of 1832 opened Iowa to white settlement and forced tribes to cede land. In 1838, Congress created the Territory of Iowa, which encompassed all the land between the Mississippi and Missouri Rivers north of the state of Missouri. The Indians were now on the verge of being pushed completely out of Iowa. Throughout the upper Mississippi Valley in the 1830s, other groups suffered a similar fate.

Farming peoples whose villages straddled the woodlands to the east and the open plains to the west were caught in a vise between the loss of their land to advancing white settlers and the seizure of their horses and agricultural provisions by Indian raiders from the plains. The Pawnees were among the hardest hit.

By the 1830s, the Pawnees were primarily an agricultural people who embarked on seasonal hunts for game in the Platte River Valley. In 1833, they signed a treaty with the U.S. government, agreeing to withdraw from south of the Platte in return for subsidies and military protection from the hostile Indians on the plains. Once they moved north of the Platte, the Pawnees were attacked by Sioux who seized control of the prime hunting grounds. Sioux raiders seeking provisions and horses also harassed Pawnee agricultural villages. When the desperate Pawnees filtered back south of the Platte, they were constantly harassed by white settlers. In vain Pawnee leaders cited the provisions of the treaty that promised them protection from the Sioux. Forced back north of the Platte by the U.S. government, the Pawnees were eventually driven out of their Nebraska homeland by the Sioux.

The Sioux were more than able to hold their own against white Americans in the first half of the nineteenth century. In the eighteenth century, the western Sioux, armed with guns they had acquired from the French, dominated the prairies east of the Missouri.

The Sioux learned to use the horse from the Plains Indians. Horses made buffalo hunting vastly more productive, they made it easier to transport bulky possessions, and they made possible an aggressive, highly mobile form of warfare. The Sioux were the most successful of all the tribes in melding two facets of white culture, the gun and the horse, into an Indian culture of warrior-hunters.

Although the Sioux frequently fought other tribes, casualties from these encounters were light. The Sioux and other Plains Indians fought not to kill the greatest number of the enemy but rather to dominate hunting grounds and to win individual honor by "counting coup" (touching a live foe). When an Army officer in 1819 urged the Sioux to make peace with the Chippewas, Little Crow, a Santee Sioux, explained why war was preferable: "Why, then, should we give up such an extensive country to save the life of a man or two annually?"

When the United States acquired title to the Great Plains in the Louisiana Purchase of 1803, the western Sioux economy was based on hunting buffalo on horse in summer and trapping beaver in winter. In spring, great trading fairs were held in which the western Sioux exchanged their buffalo robes and beaver pelts for goods acquired by the Santee Sioux from European traders.

As the supply of beaver dwindled and the demand for buffalo hides from American and European traders increased in the early 1800s, the Sioux extended their buffalo hunts. Sioux war parties pushed aside or subjugated weaker tribes to the south and west of the Missouri River basin.

Epidemic diseases brought to the plains by white traders helped Sioux expansion. The nomadic Sioux were less susceptible to these epidemics than the more sedentary village peoples. The Sioux were also one of the first tribes to be vaccinated against smallpox by doctors sent by the Bureau of Indian Affairs in the early 1830s. A major smallpox epidemic in 1837 probably halved the region's Indian population. Sioux losses were relatively light and, unlike the other tribes, their population grew.

Some 25,000 strong by 1850, the western Sioux had increased in power and numbers since they first encountered American officials during the Lewis and Clark Expedition in 1804 and 1805. Even then, Jefferson had cautioned Lewis to cultivate good relations with the Sioux "because of their immense power." "These are the vilest miscreants of the savage race," wrote Lewis and Clark of the Sioux, "and must ever remain the pirates of the Missouri, until such measures are pursued by our government as will make them feel a dependence on its will for their supply of merchandise."

Americans could vilify the Sioux, but they could not force them into dependence in the first half of the nineteenth century.

THE FUR TRADERS

"Curiosity, a love of wild adventure, and perhaps also a hope of profit—for times *are* hard, and my best coat has a sort of sheepish hang-dog hesitation to encounter fashionable folk—combined to make me look upon the project with an eye of favour." These were the motives that induced Warren A. Ferris, a New York civil engineer, to join the American Fur Company in 1829 at the age of 19 and go west as a fur trapper and mountain man. During their golden age in the 1820s and 1830s, the trappers blazed the trails that far greater numbers of white settlers would follow in the 1840s.

Until the early 1820s, the Hudson's Bay Company, a well-capitalized British concern, dominated the trans-Mississippi fur trade. A breakthrough for American interests came in 1824 when two St. Louis businessmen, William Henry Ashley and Andrew Henry of the Rocky Mountain Fur Company, developed the rendezvous system, which, in keeping with Indian traditions of periodic intertribal meetings, brought together trappers, Indians, and traders in a grand annual fair at a designated site in the high mountain country of Wyoming. White trappers and Indians exchanged the animal skins they had gathered in the seasonal hunt for the guns, traps, tobacco, whiskey, textiles, and other trading goods that agents of the fur companies in St. Louis brought to the fair.

The trappers' closest relations were with Indians, and about 40 percent of the trappers married Indian women, unions that often linked them economically and diplomatically to their bride's tribe. Living conditions in the wilderness

Shown here is a Lakota shirt, c. 1850, that was specially woven for those Sioux warriors who had distinguished themselves in battle. The blue and yellow dyes symbolize sky and earth, and the strands of human hair represent the acts of bravery performed in defense of the Lakota people.

Shirt, about 1860s, unknown Sioux artist Deer skin, hair, quills, feathers, paint, 1947.235. Denver Art Museum Collection, Native Arts Acquisitions Funds. ©Photo by Denver Art Museum. All Rights Reserved

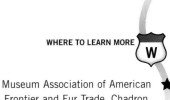

WHERE TO LEARN MORE **W**

Museum Association of American Frontier and Fur Trade, Chadron, Nebraska
www.stepintohistory. com/states/NE/Fur_Trade.htm

MAP EXPLORATION

To explore an interactive version of this map, go to
http://www.prenhall.com/goldfield2/map13.2

MAP 13–2

Western Overland Trails The great overland trails to the West began at the Missouri River. The Oregon Trail crossed South Pass in Wyoming and then branched off to Oregon, California, or Utah. The Santa Fe Trail carried American goods and traders to the Mexican Southwest.

WHAT ROLE did geography play in determining overland trails?

 12–3
Across the Plains With
Catherine Sager Pringle in 1844

were primitive, even brutal. Mortality rates among trappers ran as high as 80 percent a year. Death could result from an accidental gunshot wound, an encounter with a grizzly, or an Indian arrow. "Peg-Leg" Smith became a legend for amputating his own leg after it was shattered by a bullet.

For all its dangers, the life of a trapper appealed to unattached young men like Warren Ferris fleeing the confinements, as well as the comforts, of white civilization. "Fancy to yourself," Ferris asked readers of his published journals, "three thousand horses of every variety of size and colour, with trappings almost as varied as their appearance . . . ridden by a thousand souls . . . their persons fantastically ornamented. . . . Listen to the rattle of numberless lodgepoles [trailed] by pack-horses. . . . Yonder see a hundred horsemen pursuing a herd of antelopes." He was describing the color, bustle, and motion at the start of a hunt with the Salish Indians of Montana in the 1830s, played out on "a beautiful level prairie, with dark blue snow-capped mountains in the distance for the *locale*."

Such spectacles were increasingly rare after 1840, the year of the last mountain men's rendezvous on the Green River in Wyoming. The most exploitive phase of the fur trade in the 1830s had ravaged the fur-bearing animals and accelerated the spread of smallpox among the tribes. Whiskey, the most profitable item among the white man's trading goods, had corrupted countless Indians and undermined the vitality of tribal cultures.

The main trading corridor of the fur trade—up the lower Missouri to the North Platte and across the plains to the South Pass, a wide plateau crossing the Continental Divide, and into the Wyoming basin—became the main overland route to the West that migrating farm families followed in the 1840s. The mountain men had removed the mystery of western geography, and in so doing they hastened the end of the frontier conditions that had made their unique way of life possible.

THE OREGON TRAIL

The ruts are still there. One can follow them to the horizon in the Platte River Valley of Nebraska and the dry tablelands of Wyoming, Idaho, and Nevada. They were put there by the wheels of wagons hauled by oxen on a jolting 2,000-mile journey across plains, mountains, and deserts from Missouri to Oregon, Utah, and California (see Map 13–2). Some 150,000 Americans made this overland trek in the heyday of the Oregon Trail in the 1840s and early 1850s. Most of them walked alongside their wagons. They covered up to 15 miles a day on a trip that lasted close to six months.

Under an agreement reached in 1818, the Oregon Country was still jointly administered by the United States and Great Britain. Furs—whether beaver pelts or the skins of the Pacific sea otter—had attracted a few American trappers and merchants, but the British-controlled Hudson's Bay Company dominated the region. Protestant missionaries established the first permanent white settlements in the 1830s. Under the leadership of Jason Lee, they set up their missions in the fertile Willamette Valley, south of the Columbia River.

The missionaries repeatedly failed to convert the Indians to Christianity. Unlike the trappers, the missionaries sought to change the entire structure of Indian life and beliefs. With their numbers already thinned by the diseases brought in by the trappers, Oregon tribes such as the Cayuses refused to abandon their traditional culture based on hunting and fishing and become farm laborers for whites. During a measles epidemic in 1847, the Cayuses killed two of the most prominent missionaries, Marcus and Narcissa Whitman. In retaliation, white Americans, who now numbered more than five thousand, virtually exterminated the Cayuses.

The first large party of overlanders on the Oregon Trail left Independence, Missouri, in 1842 for the Willamette Valley. Independence and St. Joseph in Missouri and, by the 1850s, Council Bluffs in Iowa competed to capture the lucrative trade of outfitting the migrants. Merchants profited from supplying, usually at inflated prices, wagons, mules, oxen, guns, ammunition, and staples like flour, bacon, and sugar.

Most overlanders were young farm families from the Midwest, who restlessly searched for the perfect farm that would keep them out of debt. Medorum Crawford said of one family that made the journey to Oregon with him in 1842 and then quickly left for California: "They had practically lived in the wagon for more than twenty years, only remaining in one locality long enough to make a crop, which they had done in every State and Territory in the Mississippi Valley."

Usually the male head of a household made the decision to move. Besides their usual work of minding the children and cooking and cleaning, women would now have to help drive wagons and tend livestock. Still, many women were also optimistic about the journey. "Ho—for California—at last we are on the way," exclaimed Helen Carpenter in 1857, "and with good luck may some day reach the 'promised land.' " A study of 159 women's trail diaries indicates that about one-third of the women strongly favored the move. Margaret Frink, for example, recalled that she "never had occasion to regret the prolonged hardships of the toilsome journey."

In the 1840s, some five thousand of the ninety thousand men, women, and children who set out on the Oregon Trail died along the way. Few died from Indian attacks. Indians killed only 115 migrants in the 1840s, and trigger-happy white migrants provoked most clashes. Disease, especially cholera, was the great killer. Second to disease were accidents, especially drownings when drivers tried to force overloaded wagons across swollen rivers.

Cooperation among families was the key to a successful overland crossing. The men often drew up a formal, written constitution at the start of the trip spelling out the assignments and work responsibilities of each wagon. The wagon train had to leave late enough in the spring to get good grass in Nebraska for the oxen and mules. A wagon train that departed too early risked getting bogged down in spring mud; one that left late risked the danger in the Pacific coastal ranges of being trapped in the mountain snows.

Before "Oregon fever" had run its course, the flow of white settlers across the continent radically changed the economy and ecology of the Great Plains. Pressure mounted on plants and animals, reducing the land's ability to support all the Native-American tribes accustomed to living off it. Far from being separated from white people by a permanent line of division, the Plains Indians now stood astride the main path of white migration to the Pacific.

In response, officials in the Bureau of Indian Affairs organized a great gathering of the tribes in 1851 to push through the Fort Laramie Treaty, the first U.S. government attempt to draw boundaries within which to contain the Plains Indians. In exchange for accepting limitations on their movement and for the loss of

WHERE TO LEARN MORE

Scotts Bluff National Monument, Gering, Nebraska
www.nps.gov/scbl/

In trunks such as this, women transported their fine pieces of china to the West on the Oregon trail.

Courtesy of the Lane County Historical Museum

game, the tribes were to receive annual compensation of $50,000 a year for fifty years (later reduced by the U.S. Senate to ten years). When American negotiators tried to restrict Sioux hunting to north of the Platte, the Sioux demanded and received treaty rights to lands south of the Platte as well. "These lands once belonged to the Kiowas and the Crows," argued a western Sioux, "but we whipped those nations out of them, and in this we did what the white men do when they want the lands of the Indians." The Americans conceded the point.

The Fort Laramie Treaty represented a standoff between the Sioux and the U.S. government, the two great powers on the Plains. If neither yielded its claims to the region, war was inevitable.

THE MEXICAN BORDERLANDS

WHICH PEOPLES lived in the Southwest?

By the mid-1840s, parties of emigrant Americans were beginning to branch off the main Oregon Trail on their way to Utah and California. These areas were then part of the northern borderlands of Mexico. Mostly a semiarid and thinly populated land of high plateaus, dry basins, and desert bisected north to south by mountain ranges, the borderlands had been part of the Spanish empire in North America. Mexico inherited this territory when it won independence from Spain in 1821. Mexico's hold on this region was always weak. It lost Texas in 1837, and in the next decade, the American penetration of Utah and California set the stage for the American seizure of most of the rest in the Mexican War.

THE PEOPLES OF THE SOUTHWEST

Imperial Spain had divided the population of the Southwest into four main groupings: Indians, full-blooded Native Americans who retained their own languages and customs; *mestizos*, those of racially mixed ancestry, usually Spanish and Indian; *criollos*, American-born whites of Spanish ancestry; and Spaniards.

By far the smallest group were the Spaniards. Despite their small numbers, the Spanish, along with the *criollos*, monopolized economic and political power. This wealthy elite controlled the labor of the *mestizos* in the predominantly ranching economy of the borderlands.

The largest single group in the borderlands were the Indians, about half the population in the 1820s. Most had not come under direct Spanish or Mexican control. Those who had were part of the mission system. This instrument of Spanish imperial policy forced Indians to live in a fixed area, to convert to Catholicism, and to work as agricultural laborers.

Spanish missions, most of them established by the Franciscan order, aimed both to Christianize and to "civilize" the Indians. Mission Indians were forced to abandon their native economies and culture and accept a European definition of civilization that demanded that they live in settled agricultural communities and work under the tight supervision of the friars. Spanish soldiers and royal officials, who lived in military garrisons known as *presidios*, accompanied the friars.

The largest concentration of Indians—some 300,000 when the Spanish friars arrived in the 1760s—was in California. The Paiutes in the Owens Valley perfected an intricate system for irrigating wild grasses, but only the Yumans along the Colorado River in southeastern California practiced full-scale agriculture. The Spanish marveled at their lush fields of wheat, maize, beans, tobacco, and melons. The Yumans also had an elaborate religion based on an oral tradition of dream songs. (Dream songs remain a distinctive feature of Native American culture.)

The major farming Indians east of California were the Pueblo peoples of Arizona and New Mexico. Formally a part of the Spanish mission system, they had incorporated the Catholic God and Catholic rituals into their own polytheistic religion, which stressed the harmony of all living things with the forces of nature. They continued to worship in their underground sanctuaries known as *kivas*.

Once the Pueblos made their peace with the Spaniards after their great revolt in 1680 (see Chapter 3), their major enemies were the nomadic tribes that lived by hunting and raiding. These tribes outnumbered the Pueblos four to one and controlled most of the Southwest until the 1850s. Horses enabled them to gain the means of ranging far and wide for the economic resources that sustained their transformation into societies of mounted warriors.

Other tribes in the Mexican borderlands included the Navajos, the Apaches, the Comanches, and the Kiowas. The Comanches, a branch of the mountain Shoshonis who moved to the plains when horses became available, were the most feared of the nomadic peoples. They took to the horse as few other people ever had. They were utterly fearless, confident, and masterful horsemen. Their stature as mounted warriors reached mythic proportions. For food and clothing, they relied on the immense buffalo herds of the southern plains. For guns, horses, and other trading goods, they lived off their predatory raids. When the Santa Fe Trail opened in the early 1820s, their shrewdness as traders gave them a new source of firearms that strengthened their raiding prowess.

The three focal points of white settlement in the northern borderlands of Mexico—Texas, New Mexico, and Alta California (as distinguished from Lower, or Baja, California)—were never linked by an effective network of communications or transportation. Travel was limited to tortuous journeys along Indian and Spanish trails that barely indented the dry and largely barren landscape. Each of these settlements was an isolated offshoot of Hispanic culture with a semiautonomous economy based on ranching and a mostly illegal trade with French, British, and American merchants that brought in a trickle of needed goods.

Mexico's most pressing problem in the 1820s was protecting its northern states from the Comanches. To serve as a buffer against the Comanches, the Mexican government in 1821 invited Americans into Texas, opening the way to the eventual American takeover of the territory.

THE AMERICANIZATION OF TEXAS

The Mexicans faced the same problems governing Texas that the Spanish had. Sparsely populated and economically struggling, Mexican Texas shared a border with the United States along the Sabine River in Louisiana and the Red River in the Arkansas Territory. As one Mexican official noted with alarm: "If we do not take the present opportunity to people Texas, day by day the strength of the United States will grow until it will annex Texas, Coahuila, Saltillo, and Nuevo León like the Goths, Visigoths, and the other tribes that assailed the Roman Empire." However, attempts to promote immigration into Texas from other parts of Mexico failed. Reasoning that the Americans were going to come in any event, and anxious to build up the population of Texas against Indian attacks, the Mexican government encouraged Americans to settle in Texas by offering huge grants of land in return for promises to accept Mexican citizenship, convert to Catholicism, and obey the authorities in Mexico City.

The first American *empresario*—the recipient of a large grant in return for a promise to bring in settlers—was Stephen F. Austin, who founded the first American colony in Texas. The Austin grant encompassed 18,000 square miles. The *empresarios* stood to grow wealthy by leasing out land, selling parcels to settlers,

WHERE TO LEARN MORE Ⓦ

Indian Pueblo Cultural Center, Albuquerque, New Mexico **www.indianpueblo.org/**

Empresarios Agents who received a land grant from the Spanish or Mexican government in return for organizing settlements.

MAP EXPLORATION

To explore an interactive version of this map, go to
http://www.prenhall.com/goldfield2/map13.3

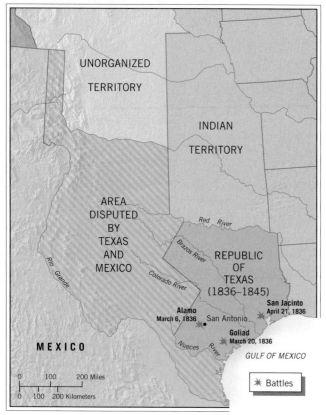

MAP 13–3

Texas and Mexico after the Texas Revolt   The Battle of San Jacinto was the decisive American victory that gained the independence of Texas, but the border dispute between Texas and Mexico would not be resolved until the Mexican War a decade later.

HOW WAS the border dispute between Texas and Mexico resolved, and how did its resolution affect each geographically?

Tejanos   Persons of Spanish or Mexican descent born in Texas.

Alamo   Franciscan mission at San Antonio, Texas, that was the site in 1836 of a siege and massacre of Texans by Mexican troops.

and organizing the rest into large-scale farms that produced cotton with slave labor in the bottomlands of the Sabine, Colorado, and Brazos Rivers. For the Americans who followed in their wake, Texas offered the chance to acquire good land that was so cheap it was almost free. As early as 1830, eastern and south central Texas were becoming an extension of the plantation economy of the Gulf coastal plain. More than 25,000 white settlers, with around a thousand slaves, had poured into the region.

Many settlers simply ignored Mexican laws, especially the Emancipation Proclamation of 1829 that forbade slavery in the Republic of Mexico. In 1830, the Mexican government levied the first taxes on the Americans, prohibited the further importation of slaves, and closed the international border to additional immigration (See American Views: "A Mexican View of the Texans in 1828"). Still, another ten thousand Americans spilled in during the early 1830s, and they continued to bring in slaves.

Unlike the *empresarios,* many of whom became Catholic and married into elite **Tejano** families, these newcomers lived apart from Mexicans and rejected Mexican citizenship. Cultural tensions escalated. Most of these new arrivals sneered at the Mexicans as a mongrelized race of black people, Indians, and Spaniards and resented having to submit to their rule. As Protestants, Americans considered Catholicism a despotic, superstitious religion and ignored legal requirements that they accept the Catholic faith.

When General Santa Anna, elected president of Mexico in 1833, overturned the liberal Mexican constitution of 1824, his dictatorial centralist rule ended any hope that Texas might become an autonomous state within a federated Mexico. Skirmishing between Mexican troops and rebellious Texans began in the fall of 1835.

At first, the Anglo-Tejano leadership sought to overthrow Santa Anna, restore the constitution of 1824, and win separate statehood for Texas within a liberal Mexican republic. When Santa Anna raised a large army to crush the uprising, he radicalized the rebellion and pushed it to declare complete independence on March 2, 1836. Four days later, a Mexican army of four thousand annihilated the 187 defenders of the **Alamo**, an abandoned mission in San Antonio. A few weeks later at Goliad, another three hundred Texans were killed after they had agreed to surrender (see Map 13–3).

"Remember the Alamo!" and "Remember Goliad!" were powerful rallying cries for the beleaguered Texans. Volunteers from the American South rushed to the aid of the main Texan army, commanded by Sam Houston. A product of the Tennessee frontier and a close friend of Andrew Jackson's, Houston's victory in April 1836 at the Battle of San Jacinto established the independence of Texas. Captured while trying to flee, Santa Anna signed a treaty in May 1836, recognizing Texas as an independent republic with a boundary on the south and west at the Rio Grande. However, the Nueces River to the north of the Rio Grande had been the administrative border of Texas under Mexican rule. The Mexican Congress rejected the treaty, and the boundary remained in dispute.

• AMERICAN VIEWS •

A MEXICAN VIEW OF THE TEXANS IN 1828

By the late 1820s, Mexico was reassessing its policy of encouraging American immigration to Texas. The Mexican government appointed a commission in 1827 whose real purpose was to recommend policies that would strengthen Mexico's hold on Texas. The following excerpt is from a journal kept by Jose Maria Sánchez, member of the boundary commission.

WHY WAS the Mexican government so ineffective in maintaining control over Texas? What was the appeal of Texas for Americans? How did most of them enter Texas and take up land? Why did Sánchez have such a low opinion of the Americans in the Austin colony? What did he think of Stephen Austin? Why did the Mexicans fear that they would lose Texas?

The Americans from the north have taken possession of practically all the eastern part of Texas, in most cases without the permission of the authorities. They immigrate constantly, finding no one to prevent them, and take possession of the *sitio* [location] that best suits them without either asking leave or going through any formality other than that of building their homes. Thus the majority of inhabitants in the Department are North Americans, the Mexican population being reduced to only Bejar, Nacogdoches, and La Bahía del Espiritu Santo, wretched settlements that between them do not number three thousand inhabitants, and the new village of Guadalupe Victoria that has scarcely more than seventy settlers. The government of the state with its seat at Saltillo, that should watch over the preservation of its most precious and interesting department, taking measures to prevent its being stolen by foreign hands, is the one that knows the least not only about actual conditions, but even about its territory. . . . Repeated and urgent appeals have been made to the Supreme Gov-

ernment of the Federation regarding the imminent danger in which this interesting Department is of becoming the prize of the ambitious North Americans, but never has it taken any measures that may be called conclusive. . . .

[Sánchez goes on to describe the village of Austin and the American colony founded by Stephen Austin.]

Its population is nearly two hundred persons, of which only ten are Mexicans, for the balance are all Americans from the North with an occasional European. Two wretched little stores supply the inhabitants of the colony: one sells only whiskey, rum, sugar, and coffee; the other rice, flour, lard and cheap cloth. . . . The Americans from the North, at least the great part of those I have seen, eat only salted meat, bread made by themselves out of corn meal, coffee, and home-made cheese. To these the greater part of those who live in the village add strong liquor, for they are in general, in my opinion, lazy people of vicious character. Some of them cultivate their small farms by planting corn; but this task they usually entrust to their negro slaves, whom they treat with considerable harshness. Beyond the village in an immense stretch of land formed by rolling hills are scattered the families brought by Stephen Austin, which today number more than two thousand persons. The diplomatic policy of this empresario evident in all his actions, has, as one may say, lulled the authorities into a sense of security, while he works diligently for his own ends. In my judgment, the spark that will start the conflagration that will deprive us to Texas, will start from this colony. All because the government does not take vigorous measures to prevent it. Perhaps it does not realize the value of what it is about to lose.

Source: José Maria Sánchez, excerpted from. "A Trip to Texas in 1828," trans, Carlos E. Castaneda from *Southwestern Historical Quarterly*, 29 Copyright © 1926. Reprinted courtesy of Texas State Historical Association, Austin Texas. All rights Reserved.

In part because Mexico refused to recognize the Texas Republic, Anglos feared Tejanos as a subversive element. Pressure mounted on them to leave, especially after Santa Anna launched a major counterattack in 1842, capturing San Antonio. Those who stayed lost much of their land and economic power as Anglos used their knowledge of American legal codes or just plain chicanery to reduce the Tejanos to second-class citizens.

More difficult to subordinate were the Comanches. By the early 1840s, Texans and Comanches were in a state of nearly permanent war. Only the force of the federal army after the Civil War ended the Comanches' long reign as the effective rulers of the high, dry plains of northern and western Texas.

THE PUSH INTO CALIFORNIA AND THE SOUTHWEST

Mexican rule in California was always weak. The Sonoran desert and the resistance of the Yuman Indians in southeastern California cut off Mexico from any direct land contact with Alta California. Only irregular communications were maintained over a long sea route. For *Californios*, Californians of Spanish descent, Mexico was literally *la otra banda,* "the other shore." In trying to strengthen its hold on this remote and thinly populated region, the Mexican government relied on a program of economic development. The centerpiece of the Mexican program was the secularization of the missions, opening up the landholdings of the Catholic Church to private ownership and releasing the mission Indians from paternalistic bondage. Small allotments of land were set aside for the Indians, but most returned to their homelands. Those who remained became a source of cheap labor for the *rancheros* who carved up the mission lands into huge cattle ranches. Thus by the 1830s, California entered its *rancho* era. The main beneficiaries of this process, however, were not Mexican authorities but the American traders who responded to the economic opportunities presented by the privatization of the California economy.

New England merchants shipped out hides and tallow, a trade fed by the immense cattle resources of the rancheros, for processing into shoes and candles. Ships from New England and New York sailed around Cape Horn to California ports, where they unloaded trading goods. Servicing this trade in California was a resident colony of American agents, some three hundred strong by the mid-1840s.

Whereas Yankees dominated the American colonies in coastal California, it was mostly Midwestern farm families who filtered into the inner valleys of California from the Oregon Trail in the 1830s and 1840s. About one in ten of the overland parties ended up in the fertile Sacramento River Valley. Nearly a thousand Americans had arrived by 1846.

California belonged to Mexico in name only by the early 1840s. The program of economic development had strengthened California's ties to the outside world at the expense of Mexico. American merchants and California rancheros ran the economy, and both groups had joined separatist movements against Mexican rule.

Except for Utah, the American push into the interior of the Mexican Southwest followed the California pattern of trade preceding settlement. When Mexico liberalized the formerly restrictive trading policies of Spain, American merchants opened up the 900-mile-long **Santa Fe Trail** from Independence, Missouri, to Santa Fe, New Mexico. Starved for mercantile goods, the New Mexicans were a small but highly profitable market. They paid for their American imports with gold, silver, and furs.

Brent's Old Fort on the Arkansas River at the point where the Santa Fe Trail turned to the southwest and Taos, enabled the Brent brothers from Missouri to control a flourishing and almost monopolistic trade with Indians, trappers, caravans on the Santa Fe Trail, and the large landowners and merchants of New Mexico.

Californios Californians of Spanish descent.

Santa Fe Trail The 900-mile trail opened by American merchants for trading purposes following Mexico's liberalization of the formerly restrictive trading policies of Spain.

This trade pulled New Mexico into the cultural and economic orbit of the United States and undermined what little sovereign power Mexico held in the region.

Ties of blood and common economic interests linked a small group of American businessmen with an influential faction of the local elite. After thwarting an 1841 Texan attempt to occupy Santa Fe, the leaders of New Mexico increasingly looked to the United States to protect their local autonomy. They quickly decided to cooperate with the American army of invasion when the Mexican War got under way. Over the opposition of the clergy and ranchers still loyal to Mexico, this group was instrumental in the American takeover of New Mexico.

At the extreme northern and inner reaches of the Mexican borderlands lay Utah. Dominated by an intermountain depression called the Great Basin, Utah was home to the Bannocks, Utes, Navajos, Hopis, and small bands of other Indians. Mexico had largely ignored this remote region. Its isolation made Utah appealing to the leaders of the Mormons, the Church of Jesus Christ of Latter-day Saints.

Founded by Joseph Smith in upstate New York in the 1820s, Mormonism grew rapidly within a communitarian framework that stressed hard work and economic cooperation under the leadership of patriarchal leaders. Harassed out of New York, Ohio, and Missouri, the Mormons thought they had found a permanent home by the late 1830s in Nauvoo, Illinois, but the murder of Joseph Smith and his brother by a mob in 1844 convinced the beleaguered Mormons that they had to leave the settled East. Under the leadership of Brigham Young, they established a new community in 1847 at the Great Salt Lake on the western slopes of the Wasatch Mountains. Ten thousand Mormons joined them.

The Mormons' intense communitarianism was ideally suited to dispensing land and organizing an irrigation system that coordinated water rights with the amount of land under production. To their dismay, however, they learned in 1848 that the United States had acquired Utah, along with the rest of the northern borderlands of Mexico, as a result of the Mexican War. (For more on the Mormons, see Chapter 14.)

POLITICS, EXPANSION, AND WAR

In 1844, James K. Polk, the new Democratic president, fully shared the expansionist vision of his party. The greatest prize in his eyes was California. Although silent in public on California for fear of further antagonizing the Mexicans, who had never accepted the loss of Texas, Polk made the acquisition of California the cornerstone of his foreign policy. When he was stymied in his efforts to purchase California and New Mexico, he tried to force concessions from the Mexican government by ordering American troops to the mouth of the Rio Grande, far within the territory claimed by Mexico. When the virtually inevitable clash of arms occurred in late April 1846, war broke out between the United States and Mexico.

Victory resulted in the **Mexican Cession of 1848**, which added half a million square miles to the United States. Polk's administration also finalized the acquisition of Texas and reached a compromise with the British on the Oregon Territory that recognized American sovereignty in the Pacific Northwest up to the 49th parallel. The United States was now a nation that spanned a continent.

MANIFEST DESTINY

With a phrase that soon entered the nation's vocabulary, John L. O'Sullivan, editor and Democratic politician, proclaimed in 1845 America's "manifest destiny to overspread and to possess the whole of the continent which Providence has given us for the development of the great experiment of Liberty and federated self-government entrusted to us." Central to Manifest Destiny was the assumption that

WHERE TO LEARN MORE W

Fort Union National Monument, Watrous, New Mexico
www.nps.gov/foun/

HOW WAS the United States able to annex Texas from Mexico?

Mexican Cession of 1848 The addition of half a million square miles to the United States as a result of victory in the 1846 war between the United States and Mexico.

12–4
John L. O'Sullivan, "The Great Nation of Futurity" (1845)

white Americans were a special people, a view that dated back to the Puritans' belief that God had appointed them to establish a New Israel cleansed of the corruption of the Old World. Evangelical revivals in the early nineteenth century then added an aggressive sense of urgency to America's presumed mission to spread the benefits of Christian civilization. Protestant missionaries, as in Oregon, were often in the vanguard of American expansion.

What distinguished Manifest Destiny was its explicitly racial component. Caucasian Anglo-Saxon Americans, as the descendants of ancient Germanic tribes that purportedly brought the seeds of free institutions to England, were now said to be the foremost race in the world. This superior racial pedigree gave white Americans the natural right as a chosen people to expand westward, carrying the blessings of democracy and progress.

Advocates of Manifest Destiny were not warmongers calling for conquest. Still, the doctrine was undeniably a self-serving justification for what other peoples would see as territorial aggrandizement. Manifest Destiny and popular stereotypes lumped Indians and Mexicans together as inferior peoples. An emigrant guide of 1845 spoke of the Mexican Californians as "scarcely a visible grade in the scale of intelligence, above the barbarous tribes by whom they are surrounded." For Waddy Thompson, an American minister to Mexico in the early 1840s, the Mexicans in general were "lazy, ignorant, and, of course, vicious and dishonest." This alleged Mexican inferiority was attributed to racial intermixture with the Indians, who, it was said, were hopelessly unfit for civilization.

Manifest Destiny was closely associated with the Democratic party. For Democrats, expansionism would counterbalance the debilitating effects of industrialization and urbanization. As good Jeffersonians, they stressed the need for more land to realize the ideal of a democratic republic rooted in the virtues and rough equality of independent farmers. For their working-class Irish constituency, the Democrats touted the broad expanses of the West as the surest means to escape the misery of wage slavery.

Manifest Destiny captured the popular imagination when the country was still mired in a depression after the Panic of 1837. The way out of the depression, according to many Democrats, was to revive the export trade. Thomas Hart Benton, a Democratic senator from Missouri, promoted American trade with India and China, to be secured by American possession of the harbors on the Pacific Coast.

THE MEXICAN WAR

Once in office, Polk was willing to compromise on Oregon because he dreaded the possibility of a two-front war against both the Mexicans and the British.

In the spring of 1846, after Polk had abrogated the agreement on the joint occupation of Oregon, the British agreed to a boundary at the 49th parallel if they were allowed to retain Vancouver Island in Puget Sound. The Senate quickly approved the offer in June 1846. British-American trade continued to flourish, Mexico lost a potential ally, and most important, Polk could now concentrate on the Mexican War that had erupted a month earlier.

Polk refused to budge on the American claim (inherited from the Texans, when the United States annexed Texas in 1845) that the Rio Grande was the border between Texas and Mexico. The Mexicans insisted that the Nueces River, 100 miles to the north of the Rio Grande, was the border, as it had been when Texas was part of Mexico. A boundary on the Rio Grande would more than double the size of Texas.

Polk sent 3,500 troops under General Zachary Taylor to the Nueces River in the summer of 1845. Polk also stepped up his efforts to acquire California, instructing Thomas Larkin, the American consul in Monterey, California, to inform the *Californios* and Americans that the United States would support them if they revolted against

12–5
Thomas Corwin, Against the Mexican War (1847)

FROM THEN TO NOW
Manifest Destiny and American Foreign Policy

From the birth of the nation in 1776 to the U.S. led NATO air strikes on Yugoslavia in 1999, a sense of mission has often imbued American foreign policy. Manifest Destiny was one expression of that sense of mission.

Thomas Paine, in *Common Sense,* declared that America had the "power to begin the world over again." The shining force of the American republic's free government, Paine believed, would redeem those suffering under despotic monarchies. According to the lofty rhetoric of Manifest Destiny, America would fulfill this divinely ordained mission by absorbing all the people of North America—at least those deemed capable of self-government—into the republic.

Manifest Destiny helped inspire the American surge to the Pacific and justify the Mexican War. But the war also provoked a contrary fear: Was the United States guilty of an imperial conquest that threatened liberty rather than promoting it? When expansionists pushed for the acquisition of all of Mexico, opponents objected. Mexicans, they claimed, were unfit to join Anglo-Saxon Americans in assuming the responsibilties of self-rule. At the same time, to subject Mexico to colonial rule would deny it the democratic liberty that Manifest Destiny promised. Consequently, the All Mexico movement soon collapsed.

After cresting in the 1840s, Manifest Destiny lost its appeal. Expansionists in the late nineteenth century invoked Manifest Destiny to justify America's acquisition of an overseas empire following the Spanish-American War, but the new empire didn't really fit that model. The advocates of Manifest Destiny had envisioned neighboring peoples in North America voluntarily joining the Republic. According to critics, the new empire, on the contrary, rested on the once-despised imperialist doctrines of Old World Europe. For former President Grover Cleveland, the annexation of the Hawaiian Islands in 1898 was "a perversion of our national mission," a signal that the nation was prepared to "abandon old landmarks and . . . follow the lights of monarchical hazards."

Cleveland and the other anti-imperialists lost the turn-of-the-century debate over whether the nation should acquire dependent possessions abroad. Still, by insisting, with Thomas Paine, that America's true mission must be to serve as the "model republic" for others to follow, they established the theme that characterized at least the public face of American diplomacy in the twentieth century. President Woodrow Wilson, for example, justified American intervention in World War I as a moral crusade to save democracy in Europe, and he sought in vain to bring the United States into a new international body—the League of Nations—designed to curb aggressive nations and prevent future wars. Wilsonian idealism infused the foreign policy of President Franklin D. Roosevelt during World War II and inspired the formation of the United Nations. Throughout the Cold War, America identified itself as the protector of democratic freedoms from the threat of international communism. In the post–Cold War world, both Presidents George H. W. Bush and Bill Clinton have cited the need to uphold human rights as grounds for U.S. military intervention abroad.

Critics have charged that the mantle of human rights cloaks the pursuit of less noble U.S. interests in other nations. Whether or not this critique is valid, it is clear that as the twenty-first century dawns, any interventionist foreign policy must present itself in the idealistic terms of a special American mission if it is to have public support.

In this late 1872 evocation of the spirit of Manifest Destiny, Indians retreat westward as white settlers, guided by a diaphanously clad America, spread the benefits of American civilization.

© Christie's Images, Inc.

Mexican rule. Polk also secretly ordered the U.S. Pacific naval squadron to seize California ports if war broke out with Mexico. Polk's final effort at peaceful expansion was to send John L. Slidell to Mexico City to offer $30 million to purchase California and New Mexico and to secure the Rio Grande boundary.

When Polk learned that the Mexican government had refused to receive Slidell, he set out to draw Mexico into a war that would result in the American acquisition of California. In early 1846, Taylor blockaded the mouth of the Rio Grande (an aggressive act even if the river had been an international boundary) and built a fort on the northern bank across from the Mexican town of Matamoros. The Mexicans attacked and were repulsed on April 24 (see Map 13–4).

Even before the news reached Washington, Polk had decided on war. Informed of the clash between Mexican and American troops in early May (it took ten days for the news to reach Washington), he sent a redrafted war message to Congress on May 9 asserting that Mexico "has invaded our territory, and shed American blood on American soil." Congress declared war on May 13, 1846.

The Mexicans fought bravely, but they lacked the leadership, modern artillery, and naval capacity to check the American advances. An army sent west under Colonel Stephen W. Kearny occupied New Mexico. The conquest was relatively bloodless because most of the local elite cooperated with the American authorities. Sporadic resistance was largely confined to poorer Mexicans and the Pueblo Indians, who feared that their land would be confiscated. The largest uprising, one that was ruthlessly suppressed, was the **Taos Revolt** in January 1847, led by Jesús Trujillo and Tomasito, a Pueblo chieftain. A sympathetic observer described the rebels as "those who defend to the last their country and their homes."

Kearny's army then moved to Tucson and eventually linked up in southern California with pro-American rebels and U.S. forces sent ashore by the Pacific squadron. Despite the loss of its northern provinces, Mexico refused to concede defeat. Taylor established a secure defensive line in northeastern Mexico with a victory at Monterrey in September 1846 and repulsed a Mexican counterattack at Buena Vista in February 1847. Polk then directed General Winfield Scott to invade central Mexico. Following an amphibious assault on Vera Cruz in March 1847, Scott captured Mexico City in September.

Peace talks finally got under way and concluded in the Treaty of Guadalupe Hidalgo, signed on February 2, 1848. Mexico surrendered its claim to Texas north of the Rio Grande and ceded Alta California and New Mexico (including present-day Arizona, Utah, and Nevada). The United States paid $15 million, assumed over $3 million in claims of American citizens against Mexico, and agreed to grant U.S. citizenship to Mexicans resident in its new territories.

Polk had gained his strategic goals, but the cost was thirteen thousand American lives (most from diseases such as measles and dysentery), fifty thousand Mexican lives, and the poisoning of Mexican-American relations for generations. The war also, as will be seen in Chapter 14, heightened sectional tensions over slavery and weakened the political structure that was vital to preserving the Union.

Taos Revolt Uprising of Pueblo Indians in New Mexico that broke out in January 1847 over the imposition of American rule during the Mexican War; the revolt was crushed within a few weeks.

CONCLUSION

Population pressure on overworked farms in the East impelled much of the westward migration, but by the 1840s, expansion had seemingly acquired a momentum all its own, one that increasingly rejected the claims of other peoples to the land.

Far from being a process of peaceful, evolutionary, and democratic change, as was once thought, expansion involved the spread of slavery, violent confrontations, and

MAP EXPLORATION

To explore an interactive version of this map, go to **http://www.prenhall.com/goldfield2/map13.4**

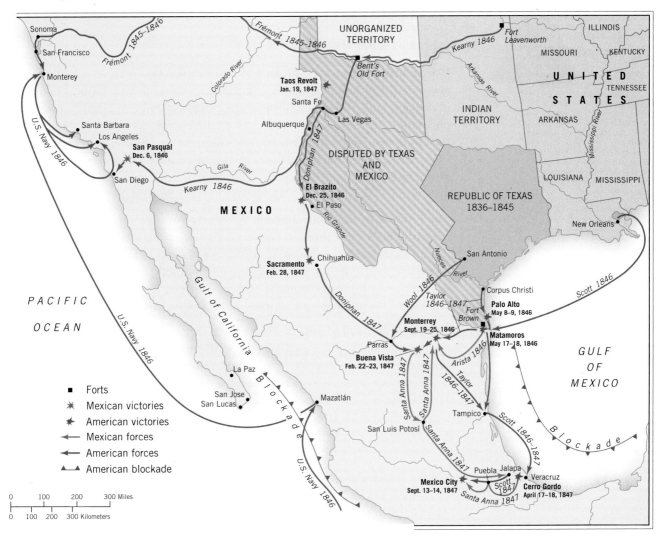

MAP 13–4

The Mexican War   Victories under General Zachary Taylor in northern Mexico secured the Rio Grande as the boundary between Texas and Mexico. Colonel Stephen Kearny's expedition won control of New Mexico, and reinforcements from Kearny assured the success of American troops landed by the Pacific Squadron in gaining Alta California for the United States. The success of General Winfield Scott's amphibious invasion at Vera Cruz and his occupation of Mexico City brought the war to an end.

WHY DID the United States feel the need to employ naval blockades to the east and west of Mexico?

the uprooting and displacement of native peoples. By 1850, the earlier notion of reserving the trans-Mississippi West as a permanent Indian country had been abandoned. The Sioux and Comanches were still feared by whites, but their final subjugation was not far off. The derogatory stereotypes of Mexican Americans that were a staple of both popular thought and expansionist ideology showed clearly that American control after the Mexican War would relegate Spanish-speaking people to second-class status.

However misleading and false much of it was, the rhetoric of Manifest Destiny did highlight a central truth. A broad, popular base existed for expanding across the continent. As the Mexican War made clear, the United States was now unquestionably the dominant power in North America. The only serious threat to its dominance in the near future would come from inside, not outside, its continental domain.

SUMMARY

The Agricultural Frontier The American population boomed in the 1800s; by 1850 about half of all Americans lived west of the Appalachian Mountains. The amount of available land, the economic opportunities associated with land ownership, and population pressure in the East propelled these migrants westward. New states in the Northwest joined the Union; while culturally tied to the Northeast, this area experienced migration from all sections of the country. Wheat was the major crop grown by Northern and Midwestern farmers; in the expanding Old Southwest it was cotton as slaveholding planters and independent farmers moved westward.

The Frontier of the Plains Indians Knowledge of the Trans-Mississippi West in the early 1800s was scanty and incorrect. The Great Plains were dominated by native tribes, especially the Sioux in the north and Comanche in the south. The first Americans to venture into the West were the mountain men in the 1820s, followed by farm family pioneers from the Midwest trekking toward the Oregon Country and California on the overland trails in the 1840s.

The Mexican Borderlands Northern Mexico's borderlands were semiarid and thinly populated by diverse ethnic groups, the majority Native American. Mexico's hold on the region was weak; in the 1820s Americans, at the invitation of the Mexican government, began settling Texas. The eventual clash between the settlers and Mexico resulted in warfare and independence for Texas. Mexico's grip on California and New Mexico was weakened by the appearance of American traders who were soon followed by settlers. In Mexican-held Utah, the Mormons, led by Brigham Young, found a home free from the threat of persecution.

Politics, Expansion, and War President Polk's expansionist vision included adding California, Texas, New Mexico, and the Oregon Country to the United States. Americans believed in their Manifest Destiny to possess the continent; this philosophy was not welcomed by those occupants already living in the West. Conflict over the southern border of Texas provided an excuse for declaring war; the Mexican War was a one-sided conflict, and the American victory resulted in California and the present day Southwest being added to the United States.

REVIEW QUESTIONS

1. Why did Americans move westward? How did slavery affect how the new settlements developed?

2. How did migration transform the West of the Plains Indians after 1830?

3. Who lived in the Mexican borderlands of the Southwest? Why was it difficult for Mexican authorities to control the region?

4. What did Americans mean by Manifest Destiny?

5. Who was responsible for the outbreak of the Mexican War? Were Mexicans the victims of American aggression?

KEY TERMS

Alamo   (p. 340)
Californios   (p. 342)
Claims clubs   (p. 330)
Empresarios   (p. 339)

Manifest Destiny   (p. 327)
Mexican Cession of 1848   (p. 343)
Oregon Trail   (p. 333)
Santa Fe Trail   (p. 342)

Taos Revolt   (p. 346)
Tejanos   (p. 340)

WHERE TO LEARN MORE

Indian Pueblo Cultural Center, Albuquerque, New Mexico. This center provides an excellent orientation to the culture, crafts, and community life of the Pueblo and Southwestern Indians. It also includes much material on archaeological findings. Visit **www.indianpueblo.org/** for a calendar of events and an introduction to the history of the nineteen pueblos.

Museum Association of American Frontier and Fur Trade, Chadron, Nebraska. The library in the museum holds archives, maps, and some photographs dealing with the western fur trade. In addition to an event calendar, its website **www.stepintohistory.com/states/NE/Fur_Trade.htm** provides links to other museums and preservation sites.

Indian Museum of North America, Crazy Horse, South Dakota. This is one of the best sources for learning of the culture of the Teton Sioux and other American and Canadian tribes on the Great Plains. Holdings include outstanding examples of Indian art and artifacts. For information on exhibits, educational and cultural programs, and special collections of Native American art, go to: **www.crazyhorse.org/ museum.shtml**

Living History Farms, Des Moines, Iowa. This site includes several working farms, operated as they were at different points in the nineteenth century, as well as a mid-twentieth-century farm. A vintage town with a general store, church, and other buildings has also been re-created. Its website **www.lhf.org/** lists events and provides a look at four farm sites.

Scotts Bluff National Monument, Gering, Nebraska. Scotts Bluff was a prominent landmark on the Oregon Trail, and the museum exhibits here have interpretive material on the trail and the western phase of expansion. Go to **www.nps.gov/scbl/** to print a park travel guide and to access a website devoted to the frontier photographer and artist William Henry Jackson.

Conner Prairie, Noblesville, Indiana. The museum and historic area re-create a sense of life on the Indiana frontier during the period of the Old Northwest. **www.connerprairie.org**

Fort Union National Monument, Watrous, New Mexico. Fort Union was a nineteenth-century military post, and the holdings and exhibits in the museum relate to frontier military life and the Santa Fe Trail. For a printable travel guide and a history of the park that includes bibliographical aides, go to: **www.nps.gov/foun/**

 For additional study resources for this chapter, go to:
www.prenhall.com/goldfield/chapter13

*This horror, this nightmare abomination!
Can it be in my country! It lies like lead on
my heart, it shadows my life with sorrow . . .*

The slave Eliza is attacked by vicious dogs while crossing with her baby the ice floes of a frozen river in a poster advertising an 1881 theatrical production of *Uncle Tom's Cabin.*

14

THE POLITICS OF SECTIONALISM
1846–1861

WHY DID the issue of slavery
in the territories cause so much controversy?

WHAT WERE the causes
and consequences of political
realignment in the 1850s?

WHY WAS Lincoln elected in 1860?

WHY COULD the political system
not fix the secession crisis?

1846 ‖ 1861

IMAGE KEY
for pages 350–351

a. Dredd Scott and his family. ca. 1857.

b. The slave Eliza is attacked by vicious dogs while crossing ice floes of a frozen river with her baby in a poster advertising a production of Uncle Toms Cabin.

c. John Brown portrait photo (1800–1859).

d. An old fashioned black stovepipe hat with a narrow brim like the one worn by Abe Lincoln.

e. A poster for "*Uncle Tom's Cabin*" with an illustration of a slave woman standing in the doorway of a log cabin where children play and a man approaches with a hoe over his shoulder. Copy describes various editions of the book available for sale.

f. A thoughtful Henry Clay addresses attentive senators on the floor of the US Senate in 1850. Spectators sit in the balcony encircling the ornate domed ceiling while listening to the speech below.

g. President Abraham Lincoln, Washington D.C., April 10, 1865.

h. Inside the Armory at Harper's Ferry, Virginia, where John Brown and his men were trapped by the fire of the U.S. Marines under the command of Colonel Robert E Lee, 18 October 1859 in a contemporary colored engraving.

i. Gold ore and gravel in a shallow pan.

December 16, 1852

My Dear Madam,

So you want to know what sort of woman I am! Well, if this is any object, you shall have statistics free of charge. To begin, then, I am a little bit of a woman—somewhat more than forty, about as thin and dry as a pinch of snuff— never very much to look at in my best days and looking like a used up article now.

I was married when I was twenty-five years old to a man rich in Greek and Hebrew and Latin and Arabic, and alas, rich in nothing else. . . . But then I was abundantly furnished with wealth of another sort. I had two little curly headed twin daughters to begin with and my stock in this line has gradually increased, till I have been the mother of seven children, the most beautiful and the most loved of whom lies buried near my Cincinnati residence. It was at his dying bed and at his grave that I learned what a poor slave mother may feel when her child is torn away from her. In those depths of sorrow which seemed to me immeasurable, it was my only prayer to God that such anguish might not be suffered in vain. There were circumstances about his death of such peculiar bitterness, of what seemed al- most cruel suffering that I felt that I could never be consoled for it unless this crushing of my own heart might enable me to work out some great good to others.

I allude to this here because I have often felt that much that is in that book had its root in the awful scenes and bitter sorrow of that summer. It has left now, I trust, no trace on my mind except a deep compassion for the sor- rowful, especially for mothers who are separated from their children. . . .

This horror, this nightmare abomination! Can it be in my country! It lies like lead on my heart, it shadows my life with sorrow; the more so that I feel, as for my own brothers, for the South, and am pained by every horror I am obliged to write, as one who is forced by some awful oath to disclose in court some family disgrace. . . .

Yours affectionately,
—H. B. Stowe

Harriet Beecher Stowe to Eliza Cabot Follen, December 16, 1852; From Jeanne Boydston, Mary Kelley, Anne Margolis, *The Limit of Sisterhood* (Chapel Hill: University of North Carolina Press, 1988) 178–180.

HARRIET BEECHER STOWE, while writing to poet and fellow abolitionist Eliza Cabot Follen, in the year that *Uncle Tom's Cabin* became an international bestseller, re- vealed how being a wife and a mother influenced her perception of slavery and inspired her writing. The deep piety and self-effacement expressed in the letter, as well as her transparent grief over the loss of her son, typified mid-nineteenth-century corre- spondence between women. Her beloved son had died of cholera in 1849; that wrench- ing event, coupled with the passage of the Fugitive Slave Act a year later, galvanized Stowe to pour her grief and indignation into a novel about plantation slavery.

Stowe personalized slavery in a way that made white Northerners see it as an institution that oppressed black people, destroyed families, and debased Christian masters. The book changed people's moral perceptions about slavery.

Stowe's father, Lyman Beecher, was a prominent evangelical reformer. He believed that personal and societal salvation were closely connected, a principle that is apparent in Harriet's letter.

Stowe's personal journey transformed awareness into a moral crusade for the millions who read her book, the political became personal. Yet, the anguish she expressed in her writing and the outrage it generated among her readers were hardly prefigured when a Congressman from Pennsylvania stepped forward in 1846 with a modest proposal that not only placed slavery front and center as a national issue, but would also shake the Union to its very core.

Slavery was not a new political issue, but after 1846, the clashes between Northern and Southern congressmen over slavery became more frequent and more difficult to resolve. In the coming years, several developments—including white Southerners' growing consciousness of themselves as a minority, the mixture of political issues with religious questions, and the rise of the Republican party—would aggravate sectional antagonism. But the flash point that first brought slavery to the fore was the issue of slavery in the territories acquired from Mexico.

SLAVERY IN THE TERRITORIES

Whatever its boundaries over the years, the West symbolized the hopes and dreams of white Americans. It was the region of fresh starts, of possibilities. For white Southerners, to exclude slavery from the Western territories was to exclude them from pursuing their vision of the American dream. Northern politicians, on the other hand, argued that exclusion preserved equality—the equality of all white men and women to live and work without competition from slave labor or rule by despotic slaveholders. From the late 1840s until 1861, four proposals dominated the debate:

- Outright exclusion

- Extension of the Missouri Compromise line to the Pacific

- Popular sovereignty—allowing the residents of a territory to decide the issue

- Protection of the property of slaveholders (meaning their right to own slaves) even if few lived in the territory

The first major debate on these proposals occurred during the early days of the Mexican War and culminated with the Compromise of 1850.

THE WILMOT PROVISO

In August 1846, David Wilmot, a Pennsylvania Democrat, offered an amendment to an appropriations bill for the Mexican War called the **Wilmot Proviso**, which stipulated that "as an express and fundamental condition to the acquisition of any territory from the Republic of Mexico . . . neither slavery nor involuntary servitude shall ever exist in any part of said territory." This language deliberately reflected Thomas Jefferson's Northwest Ordinance of 1787, which had prohibited slavery in the Old Northwest. Wilmot had, he explained, no "morbid sympathy for the slave" but by linking the exclusion of slavery to freedom for white people, he hoped to generate support across the North and even some areas of the Upper South regardless of party.

Linking freedom for white people to the exclusion of slaves infuriated Southerners by implying that the mere proximity of slavery degraded white

WHY DID the issue of slavery in the territories cause so much controversy?

Wilmot Proviso The amendment offered by Pennsylvania Democrat David Wilmot in 1846 which stipulated that "as an express and fundamental condition to the acquisition of any territory from the Republic of Mexico . . . neither slavery nor involuntary servitude shall ever exist in any part of said territory."

people and that Southerners were a degraded people, unfit to join other Americans in the territories. Georgia's Whig senator, Robert Toombs, issued a warning that reflected the feelings of many Southerners. "I do not hesitate to avow before this House and the Country, that if, by your legislation, you seek to drive us from territories of California and New Mexico, purchased by the common blood and treasure of the whole people . . . , thereby attempting to fix a national degradation upon half the states of this Confederacy, *I am for disunion.*" An Ohio congressman responded, "We [the North] will establish a cordon of free states that will surround you; and then we will light up the fires of liberty on every side until they melt your present chains and render all your people free."

This disagreement was reflected in Congress, where Northern congressmen, now a majority in the House of Representatives, passed more than fifty versions of the proviso between 1846 and 1850. In the Senate, where each state had equal representation, the proviso was consistently rejected.

The proviso debate sowed distrust and suspicion between Northerners and Southerners. Congress had divided along sectional lines before, but seldom had divisions become so personal. The leaders of both the Democratic and Whig parties, disturbed that the issue of slavery in the territories could so monopolize Congress and poison sectional relations, sought to defuse the issue as the presidential election of 1848 approached.

THE ELECTION OF 1848

Both Democrats and Whigs wanted to avoid identification with either side of the Wilmot Proviso controversy, and they selected their presidential candidates accordingly. The Democrats nominated Michigan senator Lewis Cass, a veteran party stalwart whose public career stretched back to the War of 1812. Cass understood the destructive potential of the slavery issue and suggested that territorial residents, not Congress, should decide slavery's fate. This solution, **popular sovereignty**, had a do-it-yourself charm: Keep the politicians out of it and let the people decide. Cass was deliberately ambiguous, however, on *when* the people should decide. If residents could decide only when applying for statehood, slavery would be legal up to that point. The ambiguity aroused more fears than it allayed.

The Whigs were silent on the slavery issue. Reverting to their winning 1840 formula of nominating a war hero, they selected General Zachary Taylor of Mexican War fame. Taylor belonged to no party and had never voted. He was also inarticulate to the point of unintended humor. If one had to guess his views, it may have been significant that he lived in Louisiana in the Lower South, owned a one-hundred-slave plantation, and he was related by marriage to Jefferson Davis, currently Mississippi's staunch proslavery senator.

Taylor's background disturbed many antislavery Northern Whigs. These *Conscience Whigs* along with remnants of the old Liberty party and a scattering of Northern Democrats bolted their parties and formed the *Free-Soil party.* Its slogan—"Free soil, free speech, free labor, free men"—was a catalog of white liberties that the South had allegedly violated. The Free-Soilers nominated former president Martin Van Buren, the old New Yorker, who had little hope of winning but might cause the election to be thrown into the House of Representatives. Van Buren ran strongly enough in eleven of the fifteen Northern states to deny the winning candidate in those states a majority of the votes cast, but he could not overcome Taylor's strength in the South. Taylor was elected, giving the nation its first president from the Lower South.

Popular sovereignty A solution to the slavery crisis suggested by Michigan senator Lewis Cass by which territorial residents, not Congress, would decide slavery's fate.

THE COMPROMISE OF 1850

Taylor had little time to savor his victory. Gold had been discovered in California in January 1848, and in little more than a year, eighty thousand people, most of them from the North, had rushed into the territory. These *Forty-Niners*, as they were called, included free black people as well as slaves brought into the gold fields by their Southern masters. Open hostility flared between white prospectors and their black competitors. The territory's residents drafted a state constitution that contained no provision for slavery, reflecting antiblack rather than antislavery sentiment. Keeping California white shielded residents against social and economic interaction with black people. "Free" in the context of territorial politics became a synonym for "whites only."

If Congress accepted the residents' request for statehood, California would enter the Union as a free state, tipping the balance between the fifteen free and fifteen slave states in the Senate. New Mexico (which then included most of present-day New Mexico, Arizona, part of Nevada, and Colorado) appeared poised to follow suit and enter the Union as the seventeenth free state. Southerners saw their political power slipping away.

When Congress confronted the issue of California statehood in December 1849, partisans on both sides began marshaling forces for what promised to be a long and bitter struggle. South Carolina senator John C. Calhoun understood that only a politically unified South could protect its interests.

No one, at first, knew where Taylor stood. Later it became apparent that he favored allowing California and the other territories acquired from Mexico to decide the slavery issue for themselves. Since California already easily exceeded the population threshold for statehood, Taylor proposed bypassing the territorial stage—and congressional involvement in it—and having California and New Mexico admitted as states directly. The result would be to bring both into the Union as free states. Taylor did not oppose slavery, but he abhorred the slavery issue because it threatened his vision of a continental empire. He was thus willing to forgo the extension of slavery into the territories. "Whatever dangers may threaten [the Union] I shall stand by it and maintain it in its integrity."

Southerners resisted Taylor's plan, and Congress deadlocked on the territorial issue. Henry Clay then stepped forward with his last great compromise. To break the impasse, Clay urged that Congress should take four steps:

- Admit California as a free state, as its residents clearly preferred
- Allow the residents of the New Mexico and Utah territories to decide the slavery issue for themselves too
- End the slave trade in the District of Columbia
- Pass a new fugitive slave law to enforce the constitutional provision stating that a person "held to Service or Labor in one state . . . escaping into another . . . shall be delivered upon Claim of the party to whom such Service or Labor may be due."

Clay's proposal provoked a historic Senate debate in February 1850, featuring America's three most prominent elder statesmen—Clay, Calhoun, and Daniel Webster, all of whom would be dead in the next two years. After a tumultuous six-month debate that lasted into the summer of 1850, the Senate rejected the compromise. President Taylor, who had vowed to veto any compromise, died unexpectedly of a stomach ailment after overindulging in cherries and milk in the hot sun at a July 4 celebration in Washington. Vice President Millard Fillmore, a pro-Clay New Yorker, assumed the presidency after Taylor's death. A back-room

WHAT WERE the causes and consequences of political realignment in the 1850s?

CHRONOLOGY

1846   Wilmot Proviso is submitted to Congress but is defeated.

1848   Gold is discovered in California.
Whig party candidate Zachary Taylor defeats Democrat Lewis Cass and Free-Soiler Martin Van Buren for the presidency.

1850   California applies for statehood.
President Taylor dies; Vice President Millard Fillmore succeeds him.
Compromise of 1850 is passed.

1851   Harriet Beecher Stowe publishes *Uncle Tom's Cabin.*

1852   Democrat Franklin Pierce is elected president in a landslide over Whig candidate Winfield Scott.
Whig party disintegrates.

1853   National Black Convention called in Rochester, New York, to demand repeal of the Fugitive Slave Act.

1854   Ostend Manifesto is issued.
Kansas-Nebraska Act repeals the Missouri Compromise.
Know-Nothing and Republican parties are formed.

1855   Civil war erupts in "Bleeding Kansas."
William Walker attempts a takeover of Nicaragua.

1856   "Sack of Lawrence" occurs in Kansas; John Brown makes a retaliatory raid at Pottawatomie Creek.
Democratic congressman Preston Brooks of South Carolina canes Massachusetts senator Charles Sumner in the U.S. Senate.

Democrat James Buchanan is elected president over Republican John C. Frémont and American (Know-Nothing) candidate Millard Fillmore.

1857   Supreme Court issues *Dred Scott* decision.
Kansas territorial legislature passes the proslavery Lecompton Constitution.
Panic of 1857 begins.

1858   Senatorial candidates Abraham Lincoln and Stephen A. Douglas hold series of debates in Illinois.

1859   John Brown's Raid fails at Harpers Ferry, Virginia.

1860   Constitutional Union party forms.
Democratic party divides into northern and southern factions.
Republican candidate Abraham Lincoln is elected president over Southern Democratic candidate John C. Breckinridge, Northern Democratic candidate Stephen A. Douglas, and Constitutional Unionist candidate John Bell.
South Carolina secedes from the Union.

1861   The rest of the Lower South secedes from the Union.
Crittenden Plan and Tyler's Washington peace conference fail.
Jefferson Davis assumes presidency of the Confederate States of America.
Lincoln is inaugurated.
Fort Sumter is bombarded; Civil War begins.
Several Upper South states secede.

14–4
A Dying Statesman Speaks Out Against the Compromise of 1850

Compromise of 1850   The four-step compromise which admitted California as a free state, allowed the residents of the New Mexico and Utah territories to decide the slavery issue for themselves, ended the slave trade in the District of Columbia, and passed a new fugitive slave law to enforce the constitutional provision stating that a slave escaping into a free state shall be delivered back to the owner.

Fugitive Slave Act   Law, part of the Compromise of 1850, that required the authorities in the North to assist Southern slave catchers and return runaway slaves to their owners.

man, quiet, at home with the cigar-and-brandy crowd, and effective with the deal, Fillmore let it be known that he favored Clay's package and would sign it if passed.

Although the Senate had rejected the compromise, Illinois senator Stephen A. Douglas kept it alive. A small man with a large head that made him mushroomlike in appearance, Douglas epitomized the promise of American life for men of his generation. He envisioned an urban, industrial West linked to the East by a vast railroad network eventually extending to the Pacific. Like Webster, Douglas feared for the Union if the compromise failed. Realizing that it would never pass as a package, he proposed to break it up into its components and hold a separate vote on each. With a handful of senators voting for all parts, and with different sectional blocs supporting one provision or another, Douglas engineered a majority for the compromise, and Fillmore signed it.

The **Compromise of 1850** (see Map 14–1) was not a compromise in the sense of opposing sides consenting to certain terms desired by the other. Southern leaders looked to the West and saw no slave territories awaiting statehood. They gained the **Fugitive Slave Act**, which reinforced their right to seize and return to bondage slaves who had fled to free territory, but it was slight consolation. Few slave owners from the Lower South would bear the expense and uncertainty of chasing an escaped slave into free territory. And the North's hostile reception to the law made Southerners doubt their commitment to the compromise.

MAP EXPLORATION

To explore an interactive version of this map, go to **http://www.prenhall.com/goldfield2/map14.1**

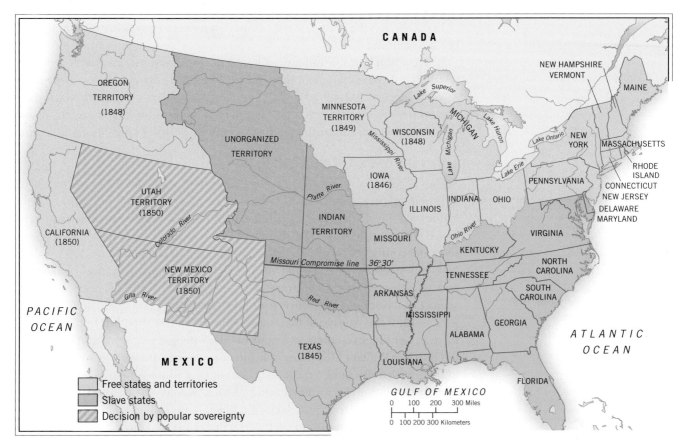

MAP 14–1
The Compromise of 1850   Given the unlikely prospect that any of the Western territories would opt for slavery, the compromise sealed the South's minority status in the Union.

WHAT WERE the results of the Compromise of 1850, and how did the country react to the news of the Compromise?

RESPONSE TO THE FUGITIVE SLAVE ACT

The effect of the Fugitive Slave Act on public opinion, however, was to polarize North and South even further. The strongest reaction to the act was in the black communities of the urban North. Previously, black abolitionists in the North had focused on freeing slaves in the South. The Fugitive Slave Act brought the danger of slavery much closer to home. Black Northerners formed associations to protect each other and repel—violently, if necessary—any attempt to capture and reenslave fellow black people. Boston's black leaders created the League of Freedom. Black Chicagoans organized the Liberty Association, with teams assigned to "patrol the city, spying for possible slave-hunters." Similar associations appeared in Cleveland and Cincinnati. Black leader Frederick Douglass, an escaped slave himself, explained the need for such organizations: "We must be prepared . . . to see the streets . . . running with blood . . . should this law be put into operation."

WHERE TO LEARN MORE

The Underground Railroad Freedom Center, Cincinnati, Ohio
www.undergroundrailroad.org

During the early 1850s, black people across the North gathered in conventions to demand the repeal of the Fugitive Slave Act. Frederick Douglass convened the National Black Convention in Rochester, New York, in July 1853, at which he established a national council of black leaders to address issues of political and civil rights. Although the council was short-lived, it reflected a growing militancy among black Northerners.

How much of this militancy filtered down to slaves in the South is difficult to say. Slaveholders noted an increase in black resistance during the early 1850s. A white Virginian observed in 1852 that "it is useless to disguise the fact, that a greater degree of insubordination has been manifested by the negro population within the last few months, than at any previous period in our history as a state."

UNCLE TOM'S CABIN

Sectional controversy over the Fugitive Slave Act was relatively modest compared to the firestorm abolitionist writer Harriet Beecher Stowe ignited with the publication of a novel about Southern slavery. *Uncle Tom's Cabin*, which first appeared in serial form in 1851, moved many white Northerners from the sidelines of the sectional conflict to more active participation.

Stowe was the daughter of Lyman Beecher, a prominent evangelical reformer, and an active opponent of slavery. What first drew Harriet Beecher Stowe to the subject of slavery was her concern about its impact on family life in the South. It was not until the passage of the Fugitive Slave Act that abolition became a major focus in her life. Even then, her views on black people remained ambivalent. She did not, like William Lloyd Garrison, advocate racial equality. She supported abolition, but she also believed America should be a white person's country, and favored repatriating the former slaves to Africa. Slavery was an abstract concept to most white Northerners. Stowe's challenge was to personalize it in a way that would make them see it as an institution that not just oppressed black people but also destroyed families and debased well-meaning Christian masters as well.

At the beginning of *Uncle Tom's Cabin*, a Kentucky slave owner is reluctantly forced by financial ruin to sell some of his slaves. Among them are the son of two mulatto slaves, George and Eliza Harris, and an older slave, Tom. Eliza escapes across the ice-choked Ohio River, clutching her son to her breast as slavecatchers and their bloodhounds pursue them. Tom submits to sale to a New Orleans master. When that master dies, Tom is sold to Simon Legree, a Vermonter who owns a plantation on the Red River in Louisiana. Legree is vicious and sadistic—the only major slaveholding character in the book whom Stowe portrays in this manner. Tom, a devout Christian, remains loyal and obedient until Legree asks him to whip another slave. When Tom refuses, Legree beats him to death.

Stowe offered not abstractions but characters who seemed real. She aimed to evoke strong emotions in the reader. The broken family, the denial of freedom, and the Christian martyr were emotional themes. The presence of mulattoes in the book testified to widespread interracial and extramarital sex, which Northerners, then in the midst of a religious revival, viewed as an abhorrent sin destructive to family life. And the depiction of Southern masters struggling unsuccessfully with their consciences focused public attention on how slavery subverted Christianity.

Uncle Tom's Cabin created a sensation in the United States and abroad. By the time of the Civil War, the book had sold an unprecedented 3 million copies in the United States and tens of thousands more in Europe. Stowe's book gave slavery a face. Black Northerners embraced *Uncle Tom's Cabin*. Frederick Douglass's National Black Convention resolved that the book was "a work plainly marked by the finger of God" on behalf of black people. Some black people hoped that the pop-

14–2
Harriet Beecher Stowe, from
Uncle Tom's Cabin (1852)

The Fugitive Slave Act threatened the freedom of escaped slaves living in the North, and even of free black Northerners. This notice, typical of warnings posted in northern cities, urged Boston's African American population to take precautions.

Courtesy of Library of Congress

ularity of *Uncle Tom's Cabin* would highlight the hypocrisy of white Northerners who were quick to perceive evil in the South but were often blind to discrimination against African Americans in the North. For Southerners, *Uncle Tom's Cabin* was a damnable lie, a political tract disguised as literature.

THE ELECTION OF 1852

While the nation read and reacted to *Uncle Tom's Cabin*, a presidential election campaign took place. The Compromise of 1850 had divided the Whigs deeply. The Democratic party entered the campaign more united. Despite reservations, both northern and southern wings of the party announced their support for the Compromise of 1850. Southern Democrats viewed the party's nominee, Franklin Pierce of New Hampshire, as safe on the slavery issue despite his New England heritage. Pierce satisfied Northerners as a nationalist devoted to the idea of Manifest Destiny. He belonged to *Young America*, a mostly Democratic group that advocated extending American influence into Central and South America and the Caribbean with an aggressive foreign policy. His service in the Mexican War and his good looks and charm won over doubters from both sections, winning him the election.

But Pierce's landslide victory could not obscure the deep fissures in the American party system. The Whigs were ultimately finished as a national party. And the Democrats, despite their electoral success, emerged frayed from the election. In the Lower South, conflicts within the party between supporters and opponents of the Compromise of 1850 had overshadowed the contests between Democrats and Whigs.

As Franklin Pierce took office in March 1853, it seemed that the only thing holding Democrats together was the thirst for political patronage. The low voter turnout in the 1852 election—Whig participation declined by 10 percent and Democratic participation by 17 percent, mostly in the Lower South—reflected public apathy and disgust at the prevailing party system. As the slavery issue confronted the nation with the most serious challenge it had faced since its inception, American voters were losing faith in their parties' ability to govern and in each other.

Harriet Beecher Stowe, the daughter of a prominent Northern evangelist, catapulted to international fame with the publication of *Uncle Tom's Cabin*. The novel helped raise the debate over slavery from a political to a moral level.

Southworth, Albert Sands (1811–1894), and Hawes, Josiah Johnson (1808–1901), Harriet Beecher Stowe. Daguerreotype, 4 1/2 × 3 1/2 in. The Metropolitan Museum of Art, Gift of I. N. Phelps Stokes, Edward S. Hawes, Ailce Mary Hawes, and Marion Augusta Hawes, 1937

POLITICAL REALIGNMENT

Franklin Pierce, only 48 when he took office, was one of the youngest presidents in American history. He hoped to duck the slavery issue by focusing on Young America's dreams of empire. Americans were still susceptible to nationalist fervor. For all their sectional, religious, ethnic, and racial differences, they shared a common language and political institutions. New technologies like the railroad and the telegraph were working to bind them together physically as well. As Florida senator Stephen R. Mallory claimed, "It is no more possible for this country to pause in its career, than for the free and untrammeled eagle to cease to soar." But President Pierce's attempts to forge national sentiment around an aggressive foreign policy failed. And his administration's inept handling of a new territorial controversy in Kansas forced him to confront the slavery debate.

No matter what policies a president pursued, Congress and the American people interpreted them in the light of their impact, real or potential, on slavery. The issue,

WHY WAS Lincoln elected in 1860?

said Missouri Senator Thomas Hart Benton, was like the plague of frogs that God had inflicted on the Egyptians to convince them to release the Hebrews from bondage. So it was with "this black question, forever on the table, on the nuptial couch, everywhere!"

Franklin Pierce lacked the skilled leadership the times demanded. Troubled by alcoholism, worried about his chronically ill wife, and grief-stricken over the death of three young sons, Pierce presided weakly over the nation and increasingly deferred to proslavery interests in his policies.

YOUNG AMERICA'S FOREIGN MISADVENTURES

Pierce's first missteps occurred in pursuit of Young America's foreign ambitions. The administration turned a greedy eye toward Spanish-ruled Cuba, just 90 miles off the coast of Florida. Southerners supported an aggressive Cuba policy, seeing the island as a possible new slave state. And nationalists saw great virtue in replacing what they perceived as a despotic colonial regime with a democratic government under the guidance of the United States.

In October 1854, three American diplomats met in Ostend, Belgium, to compose a document on Cuba called the *Ostend Manifesto* that claimed that the island belonged "naturally to the great family of states of which the Union is the Providential Nursery." The implication was that if Spain wouldn't sell, the United States could wrest control of Cuba. The Ostend Manifesto caused an uproar and embarrassed the Pierce administration when it became public. In the polite world of nineteenth-century diplomacy, it was a significant breach of etiquette. It also provoked a reaction in the United States, raising suspicions in the North that the South was willing to provoke a war with Spain to expand the number of slaveholding states. The Pierce administration also suffered from the greedy and ultimately unsuccessful exploits of self-styled "General" William Walker, who invaded Mexican-owned Baja California and later temporarily gained control of Nicaragua.

QUICK REVIEW

The Ostend Manifesto (1854)

- Pierce administration coveted Cuba.

- Manifesto claimed that Cuba naturally belonged in a family of states with United States.

- Public revelation of the manifesto produced criticism and embarrassment for administration.

STEPHEN DOUGLAS'S RAILROAD PROPOSAL

As Pierce was fumbling in foreign policy, Senator Stephen A. Douglas of Illinois was developing another national project that promised to draw the country together—the construction of a transcontinental railroad and the settling of the land it traversed. Douglas had in mind a transcontinental route extending westward from Chicago through the Nebraska Territory. Unfortunately for his plans, Indians already occupied this region, many of them on land the U.S. government had set aside as Indian Territory and barred to white settlement. Once again, and not for the last time, the federal government responded by reneging on earlier promises and forcing Indians to move. With the Indian "obstacle" removed, Douglas sought congressional approval to establish a government for the Nebraska Territory. As he predicted, the new bill did "raise a hell of a storm."

THE KANSAS-NEBRASKA ACT

Douglas's Kansas-Nebraska Bill split the Nebraska Territory into two territories, Kansas and Nebraska, with the implicit understanding that Kansas would become a slave state and Nebraska a free state. Consistent with Douglas's belief in popular sovereignty, it left the actual decision on slavery to the residents of the territories. But because it allowed Southerners to bring slaves into an area formerly closed to slavery, it repealed the Missouri Compromise.

Northerners of all parties were outraged, using language indicative of the way religious and conspiratorial imagery had infected political debate. Transforming it into a contest of good against evil, of liberty against oppression, they said it was "a gross violation of a sacred pledge," "a criminal betrayal of precious rights," and "part and parcel of an atrocious plot" to make a free territory a "dreary region of despotism, inhabited by masters and slaves." President Pierce, however, backed the bill, assuring the support of enough Northern Democrats to secure it a narrow margin of victory. The **Kansas-Nebraska Act** was law, but dissatisfaction with it continued to fester.

In August 1854, shortly after Congress adjourned, Douglas left Washington for his home in Chicago, to rest and mend political fences. He did not enjoy a pleasant journey home. "I could travel," he later recalled, ". . . by the light of my own effigy on every tree we passed." Arriving in Chicago, he addressed a large, hostile crowd outside his hotel balcony. As he departed, he lost his temper and blurted, "It is now Sunday morning. I'll go to church; you can go to hell."

Armed Missourians cross the border into Kansas to vote for a proslavery government in 1855.

The Newberry Library

"BLEEDING KANSAS"

Because of its fertile soil, favorable climate, and location adjacent to the slave state of Missouri, Kansas was the most likely of the new territories to support slavery. As a result, both Southerners and antislavery Northerners began an intensive drive to recruit settlers and establish a majority there.

After much legislative maneuvering by both sides, a sporadic civil war erupted in Kansas in November 1855 and reached a climax in the spring of 1856. Journalists dubbed the conflict **"Bleeding Kansas,"** for it was characterized by an unprecedented level of personal hatred and hostility including a proslavery attack on the town of Lawrence, which the Northern press inflated into the **"sack of Lawrence"** and a bloody retaliatory raid by antislavery agitator John Brown.

WHERE TO LEARN MORE **W**

Adair Cabin and John Brown Museum, John Brown Memorial Park, Osawatomie, Kansas **www.kshs.org/places/adair.htm**

KNOW-NOTHINGS AND REPUBLICANS: RELIGION AND POLITICS

The conflict in Kansas reflected deepening divisions throughout the nation that altered the political landscape and sharpened sectional conflict. From 1854 to 1856, Northerners moved into new political parties. Although the slavery issue was mainly responsible for party realignment in the North, other factors played a role as well. Nearly 3.5 million immigrants entered the United States between 1848 and 1860, the greatest influx in American history in proportion to the total population. Some of these newcomers, especially the Germans, were escaping failed democratic revolutions in Europe. They were predominantly middle-class Protestants who, along with fewer German Catholics and Jews, settled mostly in the cities, where they established shops and other businesses. More than 1 million of the immigrants, however, were poor Irish Roman Catholics fleeing their homeland to avoid starvation.

The Irish immigrants made their homes in Northern cities, at the time in the midst of Protestant revivals and reform. They also competed for jobs with native-born Protestant workers. Because the Irish would work for lower wages, the job competition bred animosity and sometimes violence. But it was their Roman Catholic religion that most concerned some urban Protestants. Democrats wooed the Irish newcomers. The champions of individual rights against intrusive government and meddling reformers, they supported the strict separation of church and state. Evangelical Protestants, especially those who were not Democrats, took a different view. As a Boston minister wrote during the debate on the Wilmot Proviso, "The great problem for the Christian world now to accomplish is to effect a closer union between religion and politics. . . . We must make men do good and be good."

Kansas-Nebraska Act Law passed in 1854 creating the Kansas and Nebraska Territories but leaving the question of slavery open to residents, thereby repealing the Missouri Compromise.

"Bleeding Kansas" Violence between pro- and antislavery forces in Kansas Territory after the passage of the Kansas-Nebraska Act in 1854.

"Sack of Lawrence" Vandalism and arson committed by a group of proslavery men in Lawrence, the free-state capital of Kansas Territory.

New parties emerged from this cauldron of religious, ethnic, and sectional strife. Anti-immigrant, anti-Catholic sentiment gave rise to the **Know-Nothing party**, which began as a secret organization in July 1854. Its name derived from the reply that members gave when asked about the party: "I know nothing." In addition to their biases against Catholics and foreigners, the Know-Nothings shared a fear that the slavery issue could destroy the Union. Know-Nothing candidates fared surprisingly well in local and congressional elections during the fall of 1854, carrying 63 percent of the statewide vote in Massachusetts and making strong showings in New York and Pennsylvania. In office, Know-Nothings achieved some notable reforms. In Massachusetts, where they pursued an agenda similar to that of the Whigs in earlier years, they secured administrative reforms and supported public health and public education programs.

The Know-Nothings' anti-Catholicism, however, overshadowed their reform agenda. Ethnic and religious bigotry were weak links to hold together a national party. Southern and Northern Know-Nothings fell to quarreling among themselves over slavery, despite their vow to avoid it, and the party split. Many Northern Know-Nothings soon found a congenial home in the new **Republican party**.

The Republican party formed in the summer of 1854 from a coalition of antislavery Conscience Whigs and Democrats disgusted with the Pierce administration's Kansas policy. The Republicans supported many of the same kinds of reforms as the Know-Nothings, and like them, the Republicans also supported strong state and national governments to promote those reforms. The overriding bond among Republicans was their opposition to the extension of slavery in the territories. Unlike the Know-Nothings, the Republicans confronted the slavery issue head on.

Reflecting its opposition to slavery, the Republican party was an anti-Southern sectional party. The overwhelming majority of its members were Northerners. Northern Whig merchants and entrepreneurs who joined the party were impatient with Southern obstruction in Congress of federal programs for economic development, such as a transcontinental railroad, harbor and river improvements, and high tariffs to protect American industries (located mostly in the North) from foreign competition. In a bid to keep slavery out of the territories, the Republicans favored limiting homesteads in the West to 160 acres. Not incidentally, populating the territories with white Northerners would ensure a western base for the new party.

Heightened sectional animosity laced with religious and ethnic prejudice fueled the emergence of new parties and the weakening of old political affiliations in the early 1850s and the Republican party was becoming an important political force in the North and, to Southerners, the embodiment of evil.

THE ELECTION OF 1856

The presidential election of 1856 proved one of the strangest in American history. The Know-Nothings and the Republicans faced a national electorate for the first time. The Democrats were deeply divided over the Kansas issue. Rejecting both Pierce and Douglas, they turned instead to a longtime insider, James Buchanan, whose major asset was that he had been absent from the country the previous three years as ambassador to Great Britain and was thus untainted by the Kansas controversy. The Republicans passed over their most likely candidate, the New York senator and former Whig William H. Seward. Instead, they followed a tried-and-true Whig precedent and nominated a military hero, John C. Frémont, a handsome, dark-haired soldier of medium height and medium intelligence. His wife, Jessie Benton, the daughter of Missouri senator Thomas Hart Benton, was his greatest asset. In effect, she ran the campaign and wisely

---

QUICK REVIEW

Republican Values

◆ Supporters of reform.

◆ Opposed to slavery.

◆ Anti-Southern sectional party.

Know-Nothing party Anti-immigrant party formed from the wreckage of the Whig Party and some disaffected Northern democrats in 1854.

Republican party Party that emerged in the 1850s in the aftermath of the bitter controversy over the Kansas-Nebraska Act, consisting of former Whigs, some Northern Democrats, and many Know-Nothings.

encouraged her husband to remain silent. The Know-Nothings nominated former president Millard Fillmore.

Openly reviling what they called the "Black Republican party," Southerners threatened disunion if Frémont won. Buchanan claimed to be the only national candidate on the ballot. Voters agreed, for Buchanan bested Frémont in the North and Fillmore in the South to win the presidency.

The overall result pleased Southerners, but the details left them uncomfortable. Buchanan won by carrying every southern state and the Lower North—Pennsylvania, New Jersey, Illinois, Indiana, and California. But Frémont, a political novice running on his party's first national ticket, carried eleven free states, and the rest he lost by scant margins to Buchanan. It was a remarkable showing for a two-year-old party. In the South and border states, Fillmore managed more than 40 percent of the vote and carried Maryland, despite bearing the standard of a fragmented party.

Buchanan, who brought more than a generation of political experience to the presidency, would need every bit and more. He had scarcely settled into office when two major crises confronted him: a Supreme Court decision that challenged the right of Congress to regulate slavery in the territories and renewed conflict over Kansas.

THE DRED SCOTT CASE

Dred Scott was a slave owned by an army surgeon based in Missouri. In the 1830s and early 1840s, he had traveled with his master to the state of Illinois and the Wisconsin Territory before returning to Missouri. In 1846, Scott sued his master's widow for freedom on the grounds that the laws of Illinois and the Wisconsin Territory barred slavery. After a series of appeals, the case reached the Supreme Court.

Chief Justice Roger Taney of Maryland, joined by five other justices of the nine-member Supreme Court (five of whom came from slave states), dismissed Scott's suit two days after Buchanan's inauguration in March 1857. Taney's opinion contained two bombshells. First, using dubious logic and failing to take into account the status of black people in several Northern states, he argued that black people were not citizens of the United States. Because Scott was not a citizen, he could not sue. In reaching this conclusion, Taney noted that the framers of the Constitution had never intended citizenship for slaves.

Second, Taney held that even if Scott had standing in court, his residence in the Wisconsin Territory did not make him a free man. This was because the Missouri Compromise, which was still in effect in the 1840s, was, in Taney's view, unconstitutional. The compromise, the chief justice explained, deprived citizens of their property (slaves) without the due process of law granted by the Fifth Amendment to the U.S. Constitution. In effect, Taney ruled that Congress could not bar slavery from the territories.

Black Americans reacted bitterly to the **Dred Scott decision**. Throughout the struggle of black abolitionists to free their compatriots in the South, they had appealed to the basic American ideals of freedom, liberty, and self-determination. Now Taney was saying that these ideals did not apply to black people. Throughout the urban North, black people held meetings to denounce the decision.

Dred Scott and his wife Harriet are portrayed here with their children as an average middle-class family, an image that fueled Northern opposition to the Supreme Court's 1857 decision that denied both Scott's freedom and his citizenship.

Courtesy of Library of Congress

Dred Scott Decision Supreme Court ruling, in a lawsuit brought by Dred Scott, a slave demanding his freedom based on his residence in a free state, that slaves could not be U.S. citizens and that Congress had no jurisdiction over slavery in the territories.

The decision also shocked Republicans. The right of Congress to ban slavery from the territories, which Taney had apparently voided, was one of the party's central tenets. Republicans responded by ignoring the implications of the decision for the territories while promising to abide by it so far as it affected Dred Scott himself. Once in office, Republicans vowed, they would seek a reversal. This position allowed them to attack the decision without appearing to defy the law.

The *Dred Scott* decision boosted Republican fortunes in the North even as it seemed to undercut the party. Fears of a southern Slave Power conspiracy, which some had dismissed as fanciful and politically motivated, now seemed justified.

THE LECOMPTON CONSTITUTION

Establishing a legitimate government in Kansas was the second major issue to bedevil the Buchanan administration. The president made a good start, sending Mississippi resident Robert Walker, a man of integrity, to Kansas as territorial governor to oversee the election of a constitutional convention in June 1857.

But free-staters, fearing that the slavery forces planned to stuff the ballot box with fraudulent votes, announced a boycott of the June election. As a result, proslavery forces dominated the constitutional convention, which was held in Lecompton. And Walker, although a slaveholder, let it be known that he thought Kansas would never be a slave state and thereby put himself at odds with proslavery residents.

Walker convinced the free-staters to vote in October to elect a new territorial legislature. The returns gave the proslavery forces a narrow victory, but Walker discovered irregularities. Undeterred, the proslavery forces drafted a proslavery constitution at the constitutional convention in Lecompton. Buchanan, who had promised Southerners a proslavery government in Kansas, dismissed Walker before he could rule on the **Lecompton Constitution** and submitted the constitution to the Senate for approval even though it clearly sidestepped the popular sovereignty requirement of the Kansas-Nebraska Act.

As with the Kansas-Nebraska Act, many Northerners were outraged by the Lecompton Constitution. The proslavery Kansans behind the constitution had a record of fraud. Northern Democrats, among them Stephen A. Douglas, killed the constitution in Congress. Douglas knew that the *Dred Scott* decision and Buchanan's support of the Lecompton Constitution would help the Republicans and hurt him and his fellow Northern Democrats in the 1858 congressional elections.

The **Panic of 1857**, a severe economic recession that lingered into 1858, also worked to the advantage of the Republicans. The Democratic administration did nothing as unemployment rose, starvation stalked the streets of Northern cities, and homeless women and children begged for food and shelter.

The panic had scarcely touched the South. Cotton seemed indeed to be king. The financial crisis in the North reinforced the Southern belief that Northern society was corrupt and greedy. The Republicans' proposed legislative remedies, in their view, would enrich the North and beggar the South.

Such were the issues confronting Douglas as he returned home to Illinois in the summer of 1858 to begin his reelection campaign.

THE LINCOLN-DOUGLAS DEBATES

Douglas faced a forceful opponent. The Republicans had nominated Abraham Lincoln, a 49-year-old lawyer and former Whig congressman. The Kentucky-born Lincoln had risen from modest circumstances to become a prosperous lawyer in the Illinois state capital of Springfield. His marriage to wealthy and well-connected Mary Todd helped both his law practice and his pocketbook. Strongly opposed to

WHERE TO LEARN MORE

★ Constitution Hall,
Lecompton, Kansas
www.kshs.org/places/constit.htm

Lecompton Constitution   Proslavery draft written in 1857 by Kansas territorial delegates elected under questionable circumstances; it was rejected by two governors, supported by President Buchanan, and decisively defeated by Congress.

Panic of 1857   Banking crisis that caused a credit crunch in the North; it was less severe in the South, where high cotton prices spurred a quick recovery.

the extension of slavery into the territories, Lincoln had developed a reputation as an excellent stump speaker with a homespun sense of humor, a quick wit, and a self-deprecating style that fit well with the small-town residents and farmers who composed the majority of the Illinois electorate.

But substance counted more than style with Illinois voters. Most of them opposed the extension of slavery into the territories, not out of concern for the slaves, but to keep the territories free for white people. Little known beyond the Springfield area, Lincoln also had to find a way to gain greater exposure. So in July 1858, he challenged Douglas to a series of debates across the state.

The **Lincoln-Douglas debates** were defining events in American politics that put the differences between Lincoln and Douglas, Republicans and Democrats, and North and South into sharp focus. In the debates, Lincoln asked Douglas to reconcile popular sovereignty, which Douglas had long championed, with the *Dred Scott* decision, which seemed to outlaw it by prohibiting a territorial legislature from excluding slavery before statehood. Douglas replied with what became known as the *Freeport Doctrine.* Slavery, he argued, could exist in a territory only if residents passed a law to protect it. Without such a law, no slaveholders would move in, and the territory would be free. Thus if residents did nothing, there could be no slavery in the territory.

For Douglas, slavery was not a moral issue. What mattered was what white people wanted. For Lincoln and many Republicans, slavery *was* a moral issue. As such, it was independent of what the residents of a territory wanted. In the final Lincoln-Douglas debate, Lincoln turned to his rival and explained, "The real issue in this controversy . . . is the sentiment on the part of one class that looks upon the institution of slavery *as a wrong,* and of another class that *does not* look upon it as a wrong. . . ."

Lincoln tempered his moralism with practical politics. He took care to distance himself from abolitionists, asserting that he abided by the Constitution and did not seek to interfere where slavery existed. Privately, however, he prayed for its demise. Nor did he agree, publicly at least, with abolitionist calls for racial equality. At the Springfield debate, he echoed the wishes of most white Illinoisans when he declared, "What I would most desire would be the separation of the white and black races." The Republican party was antislavery, but it did not advocate racial equality. Lincoln lost the senatorial contest but won national respect and recognition.

Despite Lincoln's defeat in Illinois, the Republicans made a strong showing in the 1858 congressional elections across the North. The increased Republican presence and the sharpening sectional divisions among Democrats portended a bitter debate over slavery in the new Congress. *Northern* and *Southern* took on meanings that expressed a great deal more than geography.

14–9
Abraham Lincoln, "A House Divided" (1858)

Lincoln-Douglas Debates Series of debates in the 1858 Illinois senatorial campaign during which Douglas and Lincoln staked out their differing opinions on the issue of slavery.

THE ROAD TO DISUNION

The unsatisfying Compromise of 1850, the various misadventures in the Caribbean and Central America, the controversies over Kansas and the Dred Scott case, and abolitionist John Brown's failed attempt to spark a slave revolt in 1859 drove a wedge between the North and South.

The presidential election campaign of 1860 began before the uproar over Brown's raid had subsided. In the course of that contest, one of the last nationally unifying institutions, the Democratic party, broke apart. The election of Abraham Lincoln, an avowedly sectional candidate, as president in 1860 triggered a crisis that defied peaceful resolution.

WHY COULD the political system not fix the secession crisis?

OVERVIEW

SOUTH AND NORTH COMPARED IN 1860

	South	North
Population	Biracial: 35 percent African American	Overwhelmingly white: less than 2 percent African American
Economy	Growing though relatively undiversified; 84 percent of work force in agriculture	Developing through industrialization and urbanization; 40 percent of work force in agriculture
Labor	Heavily dependent on slave labor, especially in Lower South	Free wage labor
Factories	15 percent of national total	85 percent of national total; concentrated in the Northeast
Railroads	Approximately 10,000 miles of track; primarily shorter lines, with fewer links to trunk lines	Approximately 20,000 miles of track; more effectively linked in trunk lines connecting east and west
Literacy	17 percent illiteracy rate for free population	6 percent illiteracy rate

Although the crisis spiraled into a civil war, this outcome did not signal the triumph of sectionalism over nationalism. Ironically, in defending their stands, both sides appealed to time-honored nationalist and democratic sentiments.

NORTH-SOUTH DIFFERENCES

Behind the ideological divide that separated North and South lay real and growing social and economic differences (see the overview table "South and North Compared in 1860"). As the North became increasingly urban and industrial, the South remained primarily rural and agricultural. The demand for farm machinery in the North reflected growing demand for manufactured products in general. The need of citydwellers for ready-to-wear shoes and clothing, household iron products, processed foods, homes, workplaces, and public amenities boosted industrial production in the North. In contrast, in the South, the slower rate of urbanization, the lower proportion of immigrants, and the region's labor-intensive agriculture kept industrial development modest.

More subtle distinctions in culture and values between North and South became evident as well by midcentury. Southerners tended to be more violent than Northerners. Southern values stressed courtesy, honor, and courage. Southerners were more inclined to military service than Northerners. The South had a high illiteracy rate, nearly three times greater than the North—eight times greater if black Southerners are included.

Evangelical Protestantism attracted increasing numbers in both North and South, but its character differed in the two regions. The Methodist Church divided along sectional lines over slavery in 1844, and the Baptists split the following year. The Presbyterians splintered in 1837 over mainly doctrinal issues, but the rupture became complete in 1861. In the North, evangelical Protestants viewed social reform as a prerequisite for the Second Coming of Christ. As a result, they were in the forefront of most reform movements. Just as Southern politics stressed individual rights, Southern religion emphasized individual salvation over social reform and defended slavery. Northern churches hunted sinners outside their congregations (and often found them in Southerners) and sermonized on political issues; Southern churches confined their preaching to their members and their message to the Gospel.

Slavery accounted for many of the differences between the North and the South. Investment in land and slaves limited investment in manufacturing. The availability of a large slave labor force reduced the need for farm machinery and limited the demand for manufactured products. Slavery contributed to the South's martial tradition and its lukewarm attitude toward public education. Fully 95 percent of the nation's black population lived in the South in 1860, 90 percent of them slaves.

The South's defense of slavery and the North's attack on it fostered an array of stereotypes that exaggerated the real differences between the sections. Like all stereotypes, these reduced individuals to dehumanized categories. They encouraged the people of each section to view those of the other less as fellow Americans than as aliens in their midst.

Ironically, although slavery increasingly defined the character of the South in the 1850s, a growing majority of white Southerners did not own slaves. Slavery nonetheless implicated nonslaveholders in ways that assured their support for it. By satisfying the demand for labor on large plantations, it relieved many rural white people from serving as farm hands and enabled them to work their own land. Slaveholders also recruited nonslaveholders to suppress slave violence or rebellion. Finally, regardless of a white man's social or economic status, he shared an important feature with the largest slaveholder: As long as racial slavery existed, the color of his skin made him a member of a privileged class that could never be enslaved.

While white Southerners were more united on slavery than on other issues, their defense of slavery presented them with a major dilemma: It left them vulnerable to moral condemnation because in the end, slavery was morally indefensible.

JOHN BROWN'S RAID

Ever intent on igniting a revolution among the slaves, abolitionist John Brown proposed in 1859 to attack and capture the federal arsenal at Harpers Ferry, Virginia, a small town near the Maryland border. The assault, Brown imagined, would spark a slave uprising in the area, eventually spreading to the rest of the state. With funds from his New England friends, he equipped a few dozen men and hired an English army officer to train them. When Brown outlined his scheme to Frederick Douglass, the noted black abolitionist warned him against it. But his white New England friends were less cautious, and a group of six prominent abolitionists (the "*Secret Six*") gave Brown additional funds for his project. On the night of October 16, 1859, Brown and twenty-two followers captured the federal arsenal at Harpers Ferry and waited for the slaves to rally to his banner. Meanwhile, the townspeople alerted outside authorities. The Virginia militia and a detachment of United States Marines under the command of Colonel Robert E. Lee arrived and put a quick end to **John Brown's Raid**. They wounded Brown and killed or captured most of his force.

Brown had launched the ill-conceived operation without provisions and at a site from which escape was impossible. Although the primary goal of the attack

WHERE TO LEARN MORE

Harpers Ferry National Historical Park, West Virginia
www.nps.gov/hafe

John Brown's Raid   New England abolitionist John Brown's ill-fated attempt to free Virginia's slaves with a raid on the federal arsenal at Harper's Ferry, Virginia, in 1859.

THE PRISONER BROWN AND HIS BOSTON COUNSEL, MR. HOYT,—DRAWN BY PORTE CRAYON.—[SEE PAGE 729.]

John Brown, wounded during his raid on the federal arsenal at Harpers Ferry, lies on a cot during his trial for murder and treason in Charlestown, Virginia, in 1859.

The Granger Collection, New York

had been to inspire a slave insurrection, no one had bothered to inform the local slaves. Was Brown crazy? As the *Boston Post* editorialized after the raid, "John Brown may be a lunatic, [but if so] then one-fourth of the people of Massachusetts are madmen."

The raid, though foolish and unsuccessful, played on Southerners' worst fears of slave rebellion, adding a new dimension: Here was an attack engineered not from within the South but from the North. Some white Southerners may have dismissed the ability or even the desire of slaves to mount revolts on their own, but they less easily dismissed the potential impact of outside white agitators.

The state of Virginia tried Brown on the charge of treason to the state, and the jury sentenced him to hang. Throughout his brief imprisonment and trial, Brown maintained a quiet dignity that impressed even his jailers. The governor of Virginia spoke admirably of him as "a man of clear head, of courage, fortitude, and simple ingenuousness." Some Northerners compared Brown's execution with the death of a religious martyr. Abolitionist William Lloyd Garrison asked readers of *The Liberator* to "let the day of [Brown's] execution . . . be the occasion of such a public moral demonstration against the bloody and merciless slave system as the land has never witnessed." When the state of Virginia hanged Brown, church bells tolled across the North. Thoreau compared Brown with Jesus and called the abolitionist "an angel of light." Emerson observed that Brown would "make the gallows glorious like the cross." Condemning Brown's deed, these Northerners nevertheless embraced the cause.

The outpouring of Northern grief over Brown's death convinced white Southerners that the threat to their security was not over. John Brown's Raid significantly changed Southern public opinion. It was one thing to condemn slavery in the territories but another to attack it violently where it was long established. Southerners now saw in the Republican party the embodiment of John Brown's ideals and actions. So in their view, the election of a Republican president would be a death sentence for the South.

The impact of this shifting sentiment was immediately apparent in Congress when it reconvened three days after Virginia hanged Brown. Debate quickly turned tense and ugly. South Carolina senator James H. Hammond captured the mood well, remarking of his colleagues on the Senate floor that "the only persons who do not have a revolver and a knife are those who have two revolvers."

THE ELECTION OF 1860

An atmosphere of mutual sectional distrust and animosity characterized the campaign for the presidential election of 1860. The Democrats disintegrated into two sectional factions united respectively behind Stephen A. Douglas and John C. Breckinridge. Former Whigs from the upper South who could not support Southern Democrat Breckinridge and Northern Whigs who had not defected to the Republicans or to Douglas formed the **Constitutional Union** party and nominated

Constitutional Union Party
National party formed in 1860, mainly by former Whigs, that emphasized allegiance to the Union and strict enforcement of all national legislation.

John Bell of Tennessee for president. Sensing victory, the Republicans convened in Chicago. If they could hold the states won by Frémont in 1856, add Minnesota (a new Republican-leaning state), and win Pennsylvania and one of three other Lower North states—Illinois, Indiana, or New Jersey—their candidate would win. These calculations dictated a platform and a candidate who could appeal to the four Lower North swing states where antislavery sentiment was not so strong. Along with the issue of slavery in the territories, the Republicans' now embraced a tariff plank calling for the protection of American industry.

In selecting an appropriate presidential nominee, the Republicans faced a dilemma. Senator William H. Seward came to Chicago as the leading Republican candidate, but his immoderate condemnation of Southerners and slavery made moderate northern voters wary of him. Reservations about Seward benefited Abraham Lincoln. A year after his losing 1858 Senate campaign, he had embarked on a speaking tour of the East at the invitation of influential newspaper editor Horace Greeley. Lincoln's lieutenants at the convention stressed their candidate's moderation and morality, distancing him from both the abolitionists and Seward. When Seward faltered, Lincoln rose and won the Republican nomination.

The presidential campaign of 1860 actually comprised two campaigns. In the South, the contest was between Breckinridge and Bell; in the North, it was Lincoln against Douglas. Lincoln did not even appear on the ballot in most southern states.

Lincoln's strategy was to say practically nothing. He spent the entire campaign in Springfield, Illinois. When he did speak, it was to a reporter or friends but not in a public forum. He discounted Southern threats of disunion if he were to become president.

States in those days held gubernatorial elections on different days, even in different months, from the national presidential election. When, in mid-October, Republicans had swept the statehouses in two crucial states, Pennsylvania and Indiana, Douglas made an extraordinary decision, but one consistent with his ardent nationalism. He abandoned his campaign and headed south at great personal peril to urge Southerners to remain in the Union now that Lincoln's election was inevitable.

Lincoln became the nation's sixteenth president with 40 percent of the popular vote (see Map 14–2). He took most Northern states by significant margins and won all the region's electoral votes except three in New Jersey. This gave him a substantial majority of 180 electoral votes.

SECESSION BEGINS

The events following Lincoln's election demonstrated how wildly mistaken were those who dismissed Southern threats of secession. Four days after Lincoln's victory, the South Carolina legislature called on the state's citizens to elect delegates to a convention to consider secession. Meeting on December 20, the delegates voted unanimously to leave the Union. By February 1, six other states—Mississippi, Florida, Alabama, Georgia, Louisiana, and Texas—had all held similar conventions and decided to leave the Union. Representatives from the seven

WHERE TO LEARN MORE   W

"A House Divided," mounted by the Chicago Historical Society, Chicago, Illinois
www.chicagohs.org

MAP EXPLORATION

To explore an interactive version of this map, go to
http://www.prenhall.com/goldfield2/map14.2

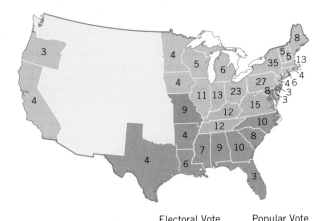

	Electoral Vote (%)	Popular Vote (%)
ABRAHAM LINCOLN (Republican)	**180** **(59)**	**1,865,593** **(40)**
John C. Breckinridge (Southern Democrat)	72 (24)	848,356 (18)
John Bell (Constitutional Union)	39 (13)	592,906 (13)
Stephen A. Douglas (Northern Democrat)	12 (4)	1,382,713 (29)

MAP 14–2
The Election of 1860   The election returns from 1860 vividly illustrate the geography of sectionalism.

BASED ON the geographic sectionalism shown in this map, what issues were important to voters in the election of 1860?

FROM THEN TO NOW
Religion and Politics

When evangelical Protestantism first emerged in the late eighteenth century, its adherents advocated the separation of church and state. By the 1850s, however, the social landscape of America had changed. A wave of immigrants, many of them Roman Catholic, threatened Protestant dominance. Growing cities and rapid technological and economic change strained the traditional moral and social order. Alarmed by these changes, evangelicals entered the political arena. Their convictions, as we saw in Chapter 12, helped drive the antebellum reform movement.

The give and take of politics, however, posed a challenge to the evangelical belief in an absolute truth grounded in the Bible. Eventually the two great evangelical crusades of the 1850s—anti-Catholicism and abolitionism—were subsumed within the Republican Party. And after the Civil War, the Republican Party gradually lost its radical fervor.

By the twentieth century, the evangelical movement had begun to turn away from politics and revert to its traditional focus on saving souls. In 1950, Jerry Falwell, an emerging evangelical leader, declared himself "a soul-winner and a separatist," meaning he wanted little involvement with society at large, much less with politics. But then came the upheavals of the 1960s and 1970s that challenged traditional morality and authority, including the Supreme Court's decision in *Roe v. Wade* to legalize abortion. In addition, the Internal Revenue Service began questioning the tax-exempt status of various religious groups. Once again, a changing social landscape compelled evangelicals to enter the political arena, this time to defend themselves against what they perceived to be an encroaching government. Organizations emerged to mobilize evangelical voters, including Jerry Falwell's Moral Majority in the late 1970s and Pat Robertson's Christian Coalition in 1989.

In the 1850s the Northeast was the center of evangelical politics. Now evangelical political organizations speak with a mostly Southern accent. In the 1850s opposition to slavery was the focus of evangelical politics. Now it is opposition to abortion and other social issues that have risen to prominence with the end of the Cold War and the nation's growing prosperity. Evangelical activists have once again found a home in the Republican Party. The Democrats, they believe, are too permissive and too committed to abortion rights, just as nineteenth century Democrats had been committed to the defense of slavery.

And again, as in the 1850s, evangelical involvement has heated political discourse with the language of righteousness. In 1992, Randall Terry, founder of Operation Rescue, a militant antiabortion organization, wrote in his newsletter that "to vote for Bill Clinton is to sin against God." In a similar if more flowery declaration, a New England evangelical journal proclaimed the 1856 presidential contest a choice between "the bloodstained ticket of the Democratic party, responsible for the murder of your brothers and mine on the plains of Kansas," and a Republican ticket designated by "the God of peace and purity as the one that shall smile upon you."

Most Americans today, as in the 1850s, recoil from the overt intrusion of religion into politics, and groups like the Christian Coalition have had only limited success in electing their favored candidates. Despite these disappointments, they have been as wary of compromise as their nineteenth-century predecessors. As one evangelical leader explained in 1999: "I would rather go to bed with a clear conscience after losing."

But if evangelical political organizations cannot gain control of Congress and the presidency, it is unlikely that their social agenda—which, in addition to antiabortion legislation, includes prayer in school, the posting of the Ten Commandments in public places, and laws restricting the rights of homosexuals—will be enacted. Today, some evangelical strategists call for a "popular front" approach, allying themselves with candidates not openly associated with the evangelical agenda. Abolitionists in the 1850s faced the same quandary between ideological purity and political pragmatism. Their support of Abraham Lincoln in 1860 reflected a bow toward pragmatism, a course that ultimately proved successful for their cause, but not without a bloody civil war.

seceding states met to form a separate country, the **Confederate States of America**. On February 18, Jefferson Davis was sworn in as its president.

Secessionists mounted an effective propaganda campaign, deftly using the press to convince voters to elect their delegates to the state conventions. Framing the issue as a personal challenge to every southern citizen, they argued that it would be cowardly to remain in the Union, a submission to despotism and enslavement. Southerners, they maintained, were the true heirs to the spirit of 1776. Lincoln and the Republicans were like King George III and the British—they meant to deny Southerners the right to life, liberty, and the pursuit of happiness. Unionists, in response, could only offer voters a wait-and-see strategy.

PRESIDENTIAL INACTION

Because Lincoln would not take office until March 4, 1861, it was the Buchanan administration that had to cope with the secession crisis during the critical months of December and January. The president's failure to work out a solution with Congress as secession fever swept the Lower South further undermined Unionist forces in the seceding states.

Thereafter, Buchanan's administration quickly fell apart. As the Lower South states left the Union, their representatives and senators left Washington, and with them went Buchanan's closest advisers and key cabinet officials. Commenting on the emotionally charged atmosphere in the Senate as prominent Southerners gave their farewells and departed, one observer wrote, "There was everywhere a feeling of suspense, as if, visibly, the pillars of the temple were being withdrawn and the great Government structure was tottering." Buchanan, a lame duck, bereft of friends and advisers, did little more than condemn secession. He hoped that waiting might bring an isolated Lower South to its senses and give efforts to mediate the sectional rift a chance to succeed.

PEACE PROPOSALS

Kentucky senator John J. Crittenden in January 1861 and later ex-President John Tyler in February proposed similar packages of constitutional amendments designed to solve the sectional crisis. The central feature of the *Crittenden Plan* was the extension of the Missouri Compromise line through the territories all the way to the state of California. The plan was of marginal interest to the South, however, because it was unlikely to result in any new slave states. Neither plan got anywhere in Congress.

LINCOLN'S VIEWS ON SECESSION

President-elect Lincoln monitored the secession of the Lower South states and the attempts to reach a compromise from his home in Springfield. Although he said nothing publicly, he made it known that he did not favor compromises such as those proposed by Crittenden and Tyler. Lincoln counted on Unionist sentiment to keep the Upper South from seceding. Like Buchanan, he felt that the longer the Lower South states remained isolated, the more likely they would be to return to the fold. For a while, events seemed to bear him out. In North Carolina, the *Wilmington Herald* responded to South Carolina's secession by asking readers, "Will you suffer yourself to be spit upon in this way? Are you *submissionists* to the

> ### QUICK REVIEW
>
> **Buchanan and Secession**
> - Buchanan had to deal with secession crisis in the months between Lincoln's election and inauguration.
> - Buchanan failed to work with Congress to find a solution.
> - Buchanan hoped waiting would bring the South to its senses.

Confederate States of America
Nation proclaimed in Montgomery, Alabama, in February 1861, after the seven states of the Lower South seceded from the United States.

OVERVIEW

THE EMERGING SECTIONAL CRISIS

Event	Year	Effect
Wilmot Proviso	1846	Congressman David Wilmot's proposal to ban slavery from territories acquired from Mexico touched off a bitter sectional dispute in Congress.
Compromise of 1850	1850	Law admitted California as a free state, granted the population of Utah and New Mexico Territories the right to decide on slavery, and established a new and stronger Fugitive Slave Act, all of which "solved" the territorial issue raised by the Wilmot Proviso but satisfied neither North nor South and planted the seeds of future conflict.
Election of 1852	1852	Results confirmed demise of the Whig party, initiating a period of political realignment.
Kansas-Nebraska Act	1854	Law created the Kansas and Nebraska Territories and repealed the Missouri Compromise of 1820 by leaving the question of slavery to the territories' residents. Its passage enraged many Northerners, prompting some to form the new Republican party.
"Bleeding Kansas"	1855–1856	Sometimes violent conflict between pro- and antislavery forces in Kansas further polarized the sectional debate.
Election of 1856	1856	Presidency was won by Democrat James Buchanan of Pennsylvania, but a surprisingly strong showing by the recently formed Republican party in the North set the stage for the 1860 election.
Dred Scott Case	1857	The Supreme Court ruling that slaves were not citizens and that Congress had no authority to ban slavery from the territories boosted Republican prospects in the North.
Lecompton Constitution	1857	Proslavery document, framed by a fraudulently elected convention in Kansas and supported by President Buchanan, further convinced Northerners that the South was subverting their rights.
John Brown's Raid	1859	Unsuccessful attempt to free the South's slaves, this attack on a federal arsenal in Harpers Ferry, Virginia, increased sectional tension.
Election of 1860	1860	Republican Abraham Lincoln won a four-way race for the presidency. The last major national party, the Democrats, disintegrated. Lower South states seceded.
Fort Sumter	1861	Confederate forces attacked the fort in April 1861, Lincoln called for troops, and several Upper South states seceded. The Civil War was underway.

dictation of South Carolina . . .?" One by one, Upper South states registered their support for the Union. A closer look, however, reveals that there were limits to the Upper South's Unionism. Most voters in the region went to the polls assuming that Congress would eventually reach a compromise based on Crittenden's or Tyler's proposals, or some other remedy. Leaders in the Upper South saw themselves as peacemakers, but it was unlikely that the Upper South would ever abide the use of federal force against its Southern neighbors.

Lincoln believed that the slavery issue had to come to a crisis before the nation could solve it. Although he said in public that he would never interfere with slavery in the slave states, the deep moral revulsion he felt toward the institution left him more ambivalent in private. As he confided to a colleague in 1860, "The tug has to come, and better now, than any time hereafter." (See American Views: "Lincoln on Slavery, p. 374.")

FORT SUMTER: THE TUG COMES

In his inaugural address on March 4, 1861, Abraham Lincoln denounced secession and vowed to uphold federal law but tempered his firmness with a conciliatory conclusion. Addressing Southerners specifically, he assured them, "We are not enemies but friends. . . . Though passion may have strained, it must not break our bonds of affection. The mystic chords of memory, stretching from every battlefield, and patriot grave, to every living heart and hearthstone, all over this broad land, will yet swell the chorus of the Union, when again touched, as surely they will be, by the better angels of our nature."

Southerners wanted concessions, not conciliation, however. The new president said nothing about slavery in the territories, nothing about constitutional amendments proposed by Crittenden and Tyler, and nothing about the release of federal property in the South to the Confederacy. Even some Northerners hoping for an olive branch were disappointed.

One day after Lincoln's inauguration, Major Robert Anderson (like Lincoln, a native Kentuckian), the commander of **Fort Sumter** in Charleston harbor, informed the administration that he had only four to six weeks' worth of provisions left. Sumter was one of three Southern forts still under federal control. Anderson assumed that Lincoln would understand the hopeless military situation and order him to evacuate Fort Sumter.

News of Anderson's plight changed the mood in the North. The Slave Power, some said, was holding him and his men hostage. Frustration grew over Lincoln's silence and inaction. The Confederacy's bold resolve seemed to contrast sharply with the federal government's confusion and inertia. By the end of March, nearly a month after Anderson had informed Lincoln of the situation at Fort Sumter, the president finally made an effort to provision Major Anderson.

The president still hoped to avoid a confrontation. He did not send the troops that Anderson had requested. Instead he ordered unarmed boats to proceed to the fort, deliver the provisions, and leave. Only if the Confederates fired on them were they to force their way into the fort with the help of armed reinforcements.

President Davis wanted to take Sumter before the provisions arrived to avoid fighting Anderson and the reinforcements at the same time. He also realized that the outbreak of fighting could compel the Upper South to join the Confederacy, but his impatience to force the issue placed the Confederacy in the position of firing, unprovoked, on the American flag.

On April 10, Davis ordered Beauregard to demand the immediate evacuation of Fort Sumter. Anderson did not yield, and before dawn on April 12, 1861, the first Confederate shell whistled down on the fort. After more than a day of shelling, during which more than five thousand artillery rounds struck Fort Sumter, Anderson surrendered. Remarkably, neither side suffered any casualties, a deceptive beginning to an exceptionally bloody war.

QUICK REVIEW

From Inauguration to War

◆ Lincoln struck conciliatory tone in inaugural address.

◆ South wanted concessions, not conciliation.

◆ Crisis over Fort Sumter sparks the war.

WHERE TO LEARN MORE

Fort Sumter National Monument, Charleston, South Carolina
www.nps.gov/fosu

Fort Sumter A Fort Located in Charleston, South Carolina, where President Lincoln attempted to provision federal troops in 1861, triggering a hostile response from on-shore Confederate forces, opening the Civil War.

• AMERICAN VIEWS •

LINCOLN ON SLAVERY

fter the 1860 election, Northern and Southern leaders sought out President-elect Abraham Lincoln for his views on slavery. Yet, Lincoln had spoken often on the institution before the election. His speech two years earlier, excerpted here, offered an unequivocal statement of Lincoln's moral and philosophical opposition to slavery. It implied that the contradiction between American ideals and slavery could not be brokered, compromised, or ignored.

HOW DO Lincoln's actions from his election in November 1860 to the firing on Fort Sumter in April 1861 reflect the principles in his Springfield address? The two letters, one to fellow Illinois Republican Lyman Trumbull and the other to Virginia Democrat John A. Gilmer, indicate Lincoln's opposition to the extension of slavery into the territories. Are they consistent with the views expressed in Springfield two years earlier? Do you think the letters both say essentially the same thing?

Speech of Hon. Abraham Lincoln

Springfield, Illinois, June 17, 1858

We are now far into the fifth year since policy was initiated with the avowed object and confident promise of putting an end to slavery agitation. Under the operation of that policy, that agitation has not only not ceased, but has constantly augmented. In my opinion, it will not cease until a crisis shall have been reached and passed. "A house divided against itself cannot stand." I believe this government cannot endure permanently half slave and half free. I do not expect the Union to be dissolved; I do not expect the house to fall; but I do expect it will cease to be divided. It will become all one thing, or the other. . . . So I say in relation to the principle that all men are created equal, let it be as nearly reached as we can. If we cannot give free-

dom to every creature, let us do nothing that will impose slavery upon any other creature. . . . I leave you, hoping that the lamp of liberty will burn in your bosoms until there shall no longer be a doubt that all men are created free and equal.

Springfield, Ills. Dec. 10, 1860
Hon. L. Trumbull

My dear Sir: Let there be no compromise on the question of extending slavery. If there be, all our labor is lost, and ere long, must be done again. The dangerous ground—that into which some of our friends have a hankering to run—is Pop[ular] Sov[ereignty]. Have none of it. Stand firm. The tug has to come, & better now, than any time hereafter. Yours as ever,

A. Lincoln

Springfield, Ill. Dec. 15, 1860
Hon. John A. Gilmer:

My dear Sir: . . . I have no thought of recommending the abolition of slavery in the District of Columbia, nor the slave trade among the slave states . . . and if I were to make such recommendation, it is quite clear Congress would not follow it. As to the use of patronage in the slave states, where there are few or no Republicans, I do not expect to inquire for the politics of the appointee, or whether he does or not own slaves. . . . In one word, I never have been, am not now, and probably never shall be, in a mood of harassing the people, either North or South. On the territorial question, I am inflexible. . . . On that, there is a difference between you and us; and it is the only substantial difference. You think slavery is right and ought to be extended; we think it is wrong and ought to be restricted. For this, neither has any just occasion to be angry with the other.

Your obt. Servt.
A. Lincoln

Source: John G. Nicolay and John Hay, eds., *Works of Abraham Lincoln,* vol. 6 (New York, Century Co., 1905).

When the verdict of Fort Sumter reached President Lincoln, he called on the Southern states still in the Union to send troops to put down the rebellion. Refusing to make war on South Carolina, the Upper South states of Virginia, North Carolina, Tennessee, and Arkansas seceded, and the Confederacy expanded to eleven states.

CONCLUSION

When David Wilmot had submitted his amendment to ban slavery from the territories gained from Mexico, he could not have foreseen that the debate he unleashed would end in civil war just fifteen years later (see the overview table "The Emerging Sectional Crisis," p. 372). By the 1850s the slavery issue had become weighted with so much moral and political freight that it defied easy resolution. Northerners and Southerners eventually interpreted any incident or piece of legislation as an attempt by one side to gain moral and political advantage at the other's expense.

By 1861, the national political parties that had muted sectional animosities were gone, and so were national church organizations and fraternal associations. The ideals that had inspired the American Revolution remained in place, especially the importance of securing individual liberty against encroachment by government. But with each side interpreting them differently, these ideals served more to divide than to unite.

Ironically, as Americans in both sections talked of freedom and self-determination, the black men and women in their midst had little of either. Lincoln went to war to preserve the Union, Davis, to defend a new nation. Slavery was the spark that ignited the conflict, but white Americans seemed more comfortable embracing abstract ideals than real people. Northerners and Southerners would confront this irony during the bloodiest war in American history—but they would not resolve it.

SUMMARY

Slavery in the Territories As Americans expanded westward and new territories were added, the nation's attention became focused on the expansion of slavery. Clashes between the North and the South became more frequent and shrill; the existing political parties seemed unable to resolve the issue. The admission of California triggered a new crisis; the resulting Compromise of 1850 and Fugitive Slave Act left both sides unhappy. The publication of *Uncle Tom's Cabin* brought the evils of slavery to ordinary Americans and galvanized opposition to slavery in the North. The presidential election of 1852 revealed an increasingly divided nation.

Political Realignment By the 1850s, all policies were interpreted in the light of their impact on slavery. Expansionist plans involving Cuba, the building of a transcontinental railroad, and organization of the Kansas and Nebraska Territories were all tied to either expanding or limited slavery. Political parties in the North realigned over slavery and immigration with a new party, the Republican party, emerging in 1854. The *Dred Scott* case and Lecompton Constitution caused bitter reactions; the Lincoln-Douglas debates put the divisions and moral issue of slavery in sharp focus.

The Road to Disunion   Ideological, economic, and social differences separated North and South. The South saw itself as increasingly victimized by the North; the raid of John Brown and its aftermath convinced Southerners their security in the Union was in jeopardy. The election of a Republican president would be a death sentence in Southern eyes; extremists believed it would give them the justification to secede. The election of Abraham Lincoln, the Republican candidate in 1860, was the signal for secession and formation of a separate nation. Lincoln initially took no action against the South, but when Fort Sumter was fired upon, Lincoln responded.

REVIEW QUESTIONS

1. Why was Harriet Beecher Stowe's *Uncle Tom's Cabin* such a great success?

2. If you were a Democratic representative to the U.S. Congress in 1854, would you have supported or opposed the Kansas-Nebraska Bill? Why?

3. How did evangelical religion affect the sectional conflict between North and South?

4. Between the time he was elected president in November and his inauguration in March, how might Abraham Lincoln have resolved the sectional crisis?

5. Could Northerners and Southerners both have been correct in their positions?

KEY TERMS

"Bleeding Kansas"   (p. 361)
Compromise of 1850   (p. 356)
Confederate States of America (p. 371)
Constitutional Union Party   (p. 368)
Dred Scott **decision**   (p. 363)

Fort Sumter   (p. 373)
Fugitive Slave Act   (p. 356)
John Brown's Raid   (p. 367)
Kansas-Nebraska Act   (p. 361)
Know-Nothing party   (p. 362)
Lecompton Constitution   (p. 364)

Lincoln-Douglas Debates   (p. 365)
Panic of 1857   (p. 364)
Popular sovereignty   (p. 354)
Republican party   (p. 362)
Sack of Lawrence   (p. 361)
Wilmot Proviso   (p. 353)

WHERE TO LEARN MORE

The Underground Railroad Freedom Center, Cincinnati, Ohio. The Center provides information on the northern response to the Fugitive Slave Act. It also sponsors a traveling exhibition, "Free at Last: A History of the Abolition of Slavery in America." **www.undergroundrailroad.org**

Harpers Ferry National Historical Park, West Virginia. Exhibits interpret John Brown's Raid and re-create some of the atmosphere and structures of the 1850s village and the federal arsenal. **www.nps.gov/hafe**

Fort Sumter National Monument, Charleston, South Carolina. This historic site interprets the bombardment of the fort and the events that immediately preceded the Civil War. **www.nps.org/fosu**

For additional study resources for this chapter, go to:
www.prenhall.com/goldfield/chapter14

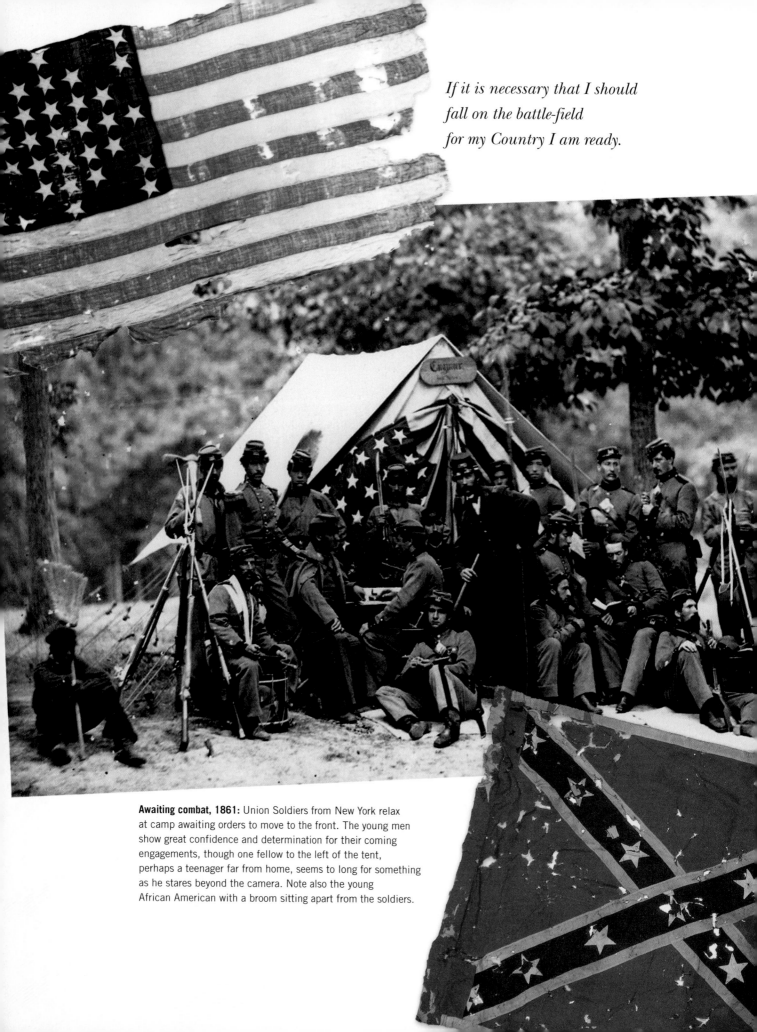

If it is necessary that I should fall on the battle-field for my Country I am ready.

Awaiting combat, 1861: Union Soldiers from New York relax at camp awaiting orders to move to the front. The young men show great confidence and determination for their coming engagements, though one fellow to the left of the tent, perhaps a teenager far from home, seems to long for something as he stares beyond the camera. Note also the young African American with a broom sitting apart from the soldiers.

15

BATTLE CRIES AND FREEDOM SONGS
THE CIVIL WAR 1861–1865

WHAT WERE the resource advantages
of the North at the outcome of the war?

WHAT WERE the Confederate
and Union military strategies?

WHAT WAS the Emancipation Proclamation?

WHAT IMPACT did the war
have on Northern political,
economic, and social life?

HOW DID military reversals affect
Confederate political and economic life
and civilian morale?

WHAT DID the Civil War
and it's outcome mean
for the nation and its citizens?

IMAGE KEY

for pages 378–379

a. Federal flag that flew over Ft. Sumter.

b. Photo of engineers of the 8th New York State Militia in front of a tent, 1861.

c. Battle flag of the Second Battalion Hilliard's Alabama Legion. This flag was pierced 83 times during the charge up Snod Grass Hill, at Chickamauga, Georgia.

d. Gray cap of a Confederate solider from the American Civil War.

e. Blue Union soldier hat with a bugle emblem embroidered on the front.

f. Robert E. Lee (1807–1870). Commander in chief of the Confederate armies during the Civil War.

g. American President Abraham Lincoln presents the Emancipation Proclamation to grateful black slaves and white peasants in a political cartoon about education, freedom, and equality.

h. Nurse Ann Bell tending to wounded soldier in a Union hospital.

i. Southern women incite their men to rebellion and war. The same women participate in bread riots during the hardships of war in two undated illustrations entitled "Sowing and Reaping."

j. President Abraham Lincoln, Washington D.C., April 10, 1865.

July 14, 1861
Camp Clark, Washington, DC

My very dear Sarah:

The indications are very strong that we shall move in a few days— perhaps tomorrow. And lest I should not be able to write you again I feel impelled to write a few lines that may fall under your eye when I am no more. Our movement may be one of a few days' duration and be full of pleasure. And it may be one of severe conflict and death to me. "Not my will but thine o God be done." If it is necessary that I should fall on the battle-field for my Country I am ready. I have no misgivings about, or lack of confidence in the cause in which I am engaged, and my courage does not halt or falter. I know how American Civilization now leans upon the triumph of the government and how great a debt we owe to those who went before us through the blood and suffering of the Revolution. And I am willing—perfectly willing—to lay down all my joys in this life, to help maintain this government, and to pay that debt. But my dear wife, when I know that with my own joys I lay down nearly all of yours, and replace them in this life with cares and sorrows, when after having eaten for long years the bitter fruit of orphanage myself, I must offer it as the only sustenance to my dear little children, is it weak or dishonorable that while the banner of my purpose floats calmly and proudly in the breeze, underneath, my unbounded love for you my darling wife and children should struggle in fierce though useless contest with my love of country? . . .

Sarah, my love for you is deathless, it seems to bind me with mighty cables that nothing but omnipotence can break; and yet my love of Country comes over me like a strong wind and bears me irresistibly with all those chains to the battle-field.

The memories of the blissful moments I have enjoyed with you come crowding over me, and I feel most deeply grateful to God and you, that I have enjoyed them for so long. And how hard it is for me to give them up and burn to ashes and hopes and future years, when, God willing, we might still have lived and loved together, and see our boys grown up to honorable manhood around us. . . . If I do not [return], my dear Sarah, never forget how much I loved you, nor that when my last breath escapes me on the battle-field, it will whisper your name.

Forgive my many faults, and the many pains I have caused you. How thoughtless, how foolish I have sometimes been! . . .

But, O Sarah, if the dead can come back to this earth and flit unseen around those they love, I shall be with you, in the gladdest days and the darkest nights . . . always, always, and if there be a soft breeze upon your cheek, it shall be my breath[;] as the cool air fans your throbbing temple, it shall be my spirit passing by. Sarah do not mourn me dead; think I am gone and wait for thee, for we shall meet again . . .

—Sullivan

Sullivan Ballou to Sarah Ballou, July 14, 1861. Geoffrey C. Ward, et al., *The Civil War: An Illustrated History* (New York: Alfred A. Knopf, 1990), 82–83.

SULLIVAN BALLOU'S letter to his wife on the eve of the First Battle of Bull Run typified the sentiments of the civilian armies raised by both North and South: a clear purpose of the importance of their mission, a sense of foreboding, an acknowledgment of the guiding hand of God, and words of love for family. He wrote this letter from his camp. A few days later, on July 21, Ballou was killed at the First Battle of Bull Run.

The Civil War preserved the Union, abolished slavery, and killed at least 620,000 soldiers—more than in all other wars the country fought, from the Revolution to the Korean conflict, combined. Union and freedom came at a dear price, we are still paying off its legacy.

When the war began, few Northerners linked the preservation of the Union with the abolition of slavery, but by 1863, Union and freedom had become inseparable Federal objectives. The Confederacy fought for independence and the preservation of slavery. The Confederate objectives dictated a defensive military strategy; the Union objectives dictated an offensive strategy.

At the end of the war's first year, the Confederacy's strong position east of the Appalachians belied its numerical and economic inferiority. By the end of 1862, however, Union officers had begun to expose Southern military shortcomings, and within a year, the trans-Mississippi portion of the Confederacy capitulated as dissent and despair mounted on the home front. Victory at Gettysburg, Sherman's demoralizing march through Georgia, and the relentless assaults of Ulysses S. Grant overwhelmed Confederate resistance and civilian hope.

Black Southerners seized the initiative in the war against slavery, especially after the Emancipation Proclamation, eventually joining Union forces in combat against their former masters. Soon, another war to secure the fruits of freedom would begin.

MOBILIZATION, NORTH AND SOUTH

Neither side was prepared for a major war. The Confederacy lacked a national army and navy. Each Southern state had a militia, but by the 1850s, these companies had become more social clubs than fighting units. The Union had a regular army of only sixteen thousand men, most of whom were stationed west of the Mississippi River.

Each government augmented these meager military reserves with thousands of new recruits and developed a bureaucracy to mount a war effort. At the same time, the administrations of Presidents Lincoln and Davis secured the loyalty of their civilian populations and devised military strategies for a war of indeterminate duration. How North and South went about these tasks reflected both the different objectives of the two sides and the distinctive personalities of their leaders, Abraham Lincoln and Jefferson Davis.

WHAT WERE the resource advantages of the North at the onset of the war?

WAR FEVER

The day after Major Robert Anderson surrendered Fort Sumter, President Lincoln moved to enlarge his small army by mobilizing state militias for ninety days. Despite the defection of Virginia, Arkansas, North Carolina, and Tennessee and about one-third of the officer corps in the regular army, Lincoln seemed likely to meet his target of 75,000 troops. Both North and South believed that the war would end quickly. William T. Sherman, however, who would become one of the Union's few great commanders, wrote in April 1861, "I think it is to be a long war—very long—much longer than any politician thinks."

CHRONOLOGY

1861 April:	Confederates fire on Fort Sumter; Civil War Begins.
July:	First Battle of Bull Run.
1862 February:	Forts Henry and Donelson fall to Union Forces.
March:	Peninsula Campaign Begins. Battle of Glorieta Pass, New Mexico.
April:	Battle of Shiloh. New Orleans falls to Federal Forces.
May:	Union captures Corinth, Mississippi.
July:	Seven Days' Battles end. Congress passes the Confiscation Act.
August:	Second Battle of Bull Run.
September:	Battle of Antietam.
December:	Battle of Fredericksburg.
1863 January:	Emancipation Proclamation takes effect.
May:	Battle of Chancellorsville; Stonewall Jackson is mortally wounded.
July:	Battle of Gettysburg. Vicksburg falls to Union Forces.

	New York Draft Riot occurs Black Troops of the 54th Massachusetts Volunteer Infantry Regiment assault Fort Wagner outside Charleston.
September:	Battle of Chickamauga.
November:	Battle of Chattanooga.
1864 May:	Battle of the Wilderness.
June:	Battle of Cold Harbor.
September:	Sherman captures Atlanta.
November:	President Lincoln is reelected. Sherman begins his march to the sea.
1865 January:	Congress passes Thirteenth Amendment to the Constitution, outlawing slavery (ratified December 1865).
February:	Charleston surrenders.
March:	Confederate Congress authorizes enlistment of black soldiers.
April:	Federal troops enter Richmond. Lee surrenders to Grant at Appomattox Court House. Lincoln is assassinated.

15–2
The "Cornerstone" Speech
(1861)

Northerners closed ranks behind the president after the Confederacy's attack on Fort Sumter. Leading Democrat Stephen A. Douglas said. "There can be no neutrals in this war *only patriots—or traitors.*" American flags flew everywhere. The *New York Daily Tribune,* an abolitionist paper, made the objective of this patriotic fervor clear: "We mean to conquer [the Southern people]—not merely to defeat, but to conquer, to SUBJUGATE them . . . They must find poverty at their firesides, and see privation in the anxious eyes of mothers and rags of children."

Southerners were equally eager to support their new nation. Enlistment rallies, wild send-offs at train stations, and auctions and balls to raise money for the troops were staged throughout the Confederacy during the war's early months. As in the North, war fever fired hatred of the enemy. A Louisiana plantation overseer wrote:

My prayer Sincerely to God is that Every Black Republican . . .
that is opposed to negro slavery . . . shal be trubled with pestilences
& calamitys of all kinds . . . and O God I pray the to Direct a bullet
or a bayonet to pirce the art of every northern Soldier that invades
southern Soil.

Volunteers on both sides filled the quotas of both armies. Most soldiers were motivated by patriotism, a desire to defend their homes and loved ones, and a craving for glory and adventure. The initial enthusiasm, however, wore off quickly. After four months of war, a young Confederate soldier admitted, "I have seen quite enough of a Soldier's life to satisfy me that it is not what it is cracked up to be."

The South in particular faced a contradiction between its ideology and the demands of full-scale war. Southern leaders had been fighting for decades to defend states' rights against national authority. Now they had to forge the states of the Confederacy into a nation. By early spring 1862, the Confederate government was compelled to order the first general draft in U.S. history, but the law allowed one white man on any plantation with more than twenty slaves to be excused from service to assure the security and productivity of large plantations. It led some Southerners to conclude that the struggle had become "a rich man's war but a poor man's fight."

The initial enthusiasm also faded in the North. In March 1863, Congress passed a draft law that allowed a draftee to hire a substitute. This aroused resentment among working-class Northerners, but the North was less dependent on conscription than the South.

The armies of both sides included men from all walks of life. An undetermined number of women, typically disguised as men, also served in both armies. They joined for the same reasons as men: adventure, patriotism, and glory.

THE NORTH'S ADVANTAGE IN RESOURCES

The resources of the North—including its population, industrial and agricultural capacity, and transportation network—greatly exceeded those of the South (see Figure 15–1). The 2.1 million men who fought for the Union represented roughly half the men of military age in the North. The 900,000 men who fought for the Confederacy, in contrast, represented 90 percent of its eligible population. Nearly 200,000 black men, most of them ex-slaves from the South, also took up arms for the Union.

The Union's greater numbers left the South vulnerable to a war of attrition. At the beginning of the war, the North controlled 90 percent of the nation's industrial capacity and had dozens of facilities for producing the tools to make war material. The South had no such factories and only one munitions plant, the Tredegar Iron Works in Richmond. The North's railroad system was more than twice the size of the South's.

Thanks to the North's abundance of resources, no soldier in any previous army had ever been outfitted as well as the blue-uniformed Union trooper. The official color of the Confederate uniform was gray, but most Southern soldiers did not wear distinguishable uniforms, especially toward the end of the war. They also often lacked proper shoes or any footwear at all. Still, the South never lost a battle because of insufficient supplies or inadequate weaponry. New foundries and manufacturing enterprises kept the Confederate armies equipped with the supplies they needed to keep fighting.

Unstable finances proved more of a handicap to the Confederacy than low industrial capacity. The Confederate economy—and its treasury—depended heavily on cotton exports, but a Union naval blockade and the ability of textile manufacturers in Europe to find new sources of supply restricted this crucial source of revenue. Because Southerners resisted taxation, the government sold interest-bearing bonds to raise money, but as Confederate fortunes declined, so did bond sales. The Confederacy financed more than 60 percent of the $1.5 billion it spent on the war with printing-press money, and inflation spiraled out of control.

FIGURE 15–1

A Comparison of the Union and Confederate Control of Key Resources at the Outset of the Civil War.

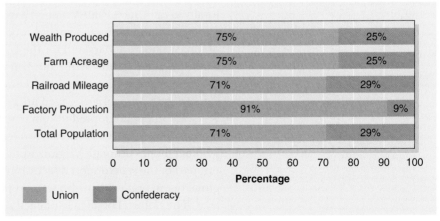

	Union	Confederacy
Wealth Produced	75%	25%
Farm Acreage	75%	25%
Railroad Mileage	71%	29%
Factory Production	91%	9%
Total Population	71%	29%

Percentage (0–100)

■ Union ■ Confederacy

The Federal government was more successful than the Confederate government at developing innovative ways to meet the great cost of the war. Its interest-bearing bonds and treasury notes accounted for 66 percent of the $4 billion that the Union raised to wage the war. Like the Confederacy, the federal government issued paper money—derisively called "greenbacks"—that was not backed by gold or silver and it also levied the country's first income tax, which citizens could pay in greenbacks, a move that bolstered the value and credibility of the paper currency. Ruinous inflation was thereby averted in the North.

LEADERS, GOVERNMENTS, AND STRATEGIES

Leadership ability, like resources, played an important role in the war. Confederate president Jefferson Davis had to build a government from scratch during the war. Abraham Lincoln at least had the benefit of an established government, a standing army, healthy financial resources, and diplomatic relations with the nations of Europe.

Although Davis's career qualified him for the task of running the Confederacy, colleagues found him aloof. He was inclined to equate compromise with weakness and interpreted any opposition as a personal attack.

Southerners viewed themselves as the genuine heirs of the American Revolution and the true defenders of the United States Constitution. If the South were to establish itself as a separate country, however, Southerners had to develop a distinctive idea based on Southern life. Slavery was distinctively Southern, but most white Southerners did not own slaves. Southerners had forcefully advanced the ideology of states' rights during the 1840s and 1850s, but the primacy of state sovereignty over central authority was too a weak foundation on which to build a national consciousness. Although Southerners sought to protect their home and families, Davis found it difficult to build a loyal base of support.

Northerners also needed a convincing reason to fight. Lincoln and other Northern leaders secured support by convincing their compatriots of the importance of preserving the Union. The president viewed the conflict in global terms, its results affecting the hopes for democratic government around the world.

Lincoln handled disagreement better than Davis did. He defused tense situations with folksy humor, and his simple eloquence captured the imagination of ordinary people. Lincoln viewed himself as a man of the people and was not aloof, like Davis. But even if Jefferson Davis had been a more effective leader than Lincoln, it is unlikely that he could have overcome the odds against him. The key to Southern independence lay with its forces on the battlefield.

The secession of Virginia, Arkansas, North Carolina, and Tennessee left four border slave states—Maryland, Delaware, Kentucky, and Missouri—hanging in the balance. Maryland's strategic location north of Washington, D.C., rendered its loyalty to the Union vital. Although a majority of its citizens opposed secession, pro-Southern sentiment was strong. Lincoln therefore sent federal troops in a show of force that saved Maryland for the Union. Delaware, although nominally a slave state remained staunchly for the Union. Missourians settled their indecision in fighting that culminated with a Union victory in March 1862 although pro-Confederate Missourians waged an unsuccessful guerrilla war over the next two years. Kentucky attempted to remain neutral but became a battleground in September 1861, when Confederate forces invaded the state and Union forces moved to expel them. Although Virginia went with the Confederacy, counties in the western part of the state opposed secession and became the separate state of West Virginia, the nation's thirty-fifth state in June 1863.

The political objectives of each side largely determined its military strategy. Southerners wanted independence; Northerners fought to preserve the Union.

15–4
Why They Fought (1861)

The North's goal required conquest. The Confederacy had only to fight a defensive battle in its own territory until growing Northern opposition to the war or a decisive Northern military mistake convinced the Union to give up.

But the South's strategy had two weaknesses. First, it demanded more patience than the South had shown in impulsively attacking Fort Sumter. Second, Southern resources might give out before Northern public opinion demanded peace. The question was what would break first: Northern support for the war or Southern ability to wage it?

THE EARLY WAR, 1861–1862

The North's offensive strategy dictated the course of the war for the first two years. In the West, the Federal army's objectives were to hold Missouri, Kentucky, and Tennessee for the Union, to control the Mississippi River, and eventually to detach the area west of the Appalachians from the rest of the Confederacy. In the East, Union forces sought to capture Richmond, the Confederate capital. The U.S. Navy blockaded the Confederate coast and pushed into inland waterways to capture Southern ports. The Confederates defended strategic locations throughout their territory or abandoned them when prudence required. By the end of 1862, the result remained in the balance.

WHAT WERE the Confederate and Union military strategies?

FIRST BULL RUN

By July 1861, when the border states appeared more secure for the Union, President Lincoln ordered Union general Irvin McDowell to take Richmond (see Map 15–1 p. 386). Confronting McDowell 20 miles southwest of Washington at Manassas was a Confederate army under General P. G. T. Beauregard. McDowell and Beauregard's armies clashed on July 21 at the First Battle of Bull Run (known to the Confederacy as the First Battle of Manassas). The Union forces seemed on the verge of winning, but Beauregard's forces repulsed the assault. At the height of the battle, General Barnard Bee of South Carolina in exasperation called out to Colonel Thomas J. Jackson for assistance, shouting, "There stands Jackson—like a damned stone wall!" Somehow the rebuke became a shorthand for courage and steadfastness. Jackson's men henceforth called him "Stonewall."

Bull Run boosted Southerners' confidence and destroyed the widespread belief in the North that the war would be over quickly.

QUICK REVIEW

The First Battle of Bull Run
- July 21, 1861: Beauregard (Confederacy) and McDowell (Union) meet at Manassas.
- Confederate troops repulse a strong Union attack.
- Colonel Thomas J. Jackson earns his nickname "Stonewall."

THE WAR IN THE WEST

While Federal forces retreated in Virginia, they advanced in the West. Two Confederate forts, Fort Henry on the Tennessee River and Fort Donelson on the Cumberland River, guarded the strategic waterways that linked Tennessee and Kentucky to the Mississippi Valley. The forts also defended Nashville, the Tennessee state capital (see Map 15–2 p. 387). In February 1862, Union general Ulysses S. Grant coordinated a land and river campaign against the forts that caught the Southerners unprepared and outflanked. By February 16, both forts had fallen. The Union victory drove a wedge into Southern territory and closed the Confederacy's quickest path to the West from Virginia and the Carolinas. The Confederacy never recovered the strategic advantage in the West.

Grant next moved his main army south to prepare for an assault on the key Mississippi River port and rail center of Vicksburg. After blunting a surprise Confederate attack at Shiloh Church, Grant pushed the Southerners back to Corinth, Mississippi. Another important Federal success came when Admiral

MAP EXPLORATION

To explore an interactive version of this map, go to
http://www.prenhall.com/goldfield2/map15.1

MAP 15–1

From First Bull Run to Antietam: The War in the East, 1861–1862 The early stages of the war demonstrated the strategies of both Confederate and Union forces. Federal troops stormed into Virginia hoping to capture Richmond and bring a quick end to the war. Through a combination of poor generalship and Confederate tenacity, they failed. Confederate troops hoped to defend their territory, prolong the war, and eventually win their independence as Northern patience evaporated. They proved successful initially, but, with the abandonment of the defensive strategy and the invasion of Maryland in the fall of 1862, the Confederates suffered a political and morale setback at Antietam.

WHY DID the South abandon its defensive strategy in the fall of 1862?

David G. Farragut captured New Orleans in April 1862. Two hundred miles of the Mississippi River, the nation's most vital commercial waterway, were now open to Union traffic. After Memphis fell to Union forces in June, Vicksburg remained the only major river town still in Confederate hands. The fall of New Orleans and Memphis underscored a major problem with the Confederates' defensive strategy: Their military reserves were stretched too thin to defend their vast territory.

REASSESSING THE WAR: THE HUMAN TOLL

More American soldiers were lost at Shiloh than in all of the nation's wars combined up to that time. Each side suffered more than ten thousand casualties. By the time the smoke had cleared, the soldiers' initial bravado was replaced by the realization that death or capture was a likely outcome and that heroism, courage, and piety did not guarantee survival. A hunger for peace replaced the thirst for battle.

Kate Cumming, the nurse at the Confederate hospital in Corinth, wrote of soldiers brought from the battle "mutilated in every imaginable way." Piercing the air were the screams of men undergoing amputations, often with little or no anesthetic. Some pleaded with physicians to kill them and end their misery. Others bore the pain stoically and entrusted last words and letters to nurses, dying with the word "Mother" on their lips.

Women on both sides cared for the wounded and sick. In the North, members of the U.S. Sanitary Commission, a voluntary organization formed in 1861 and staffed mainly by women, attempted to upgrade hospital and medical care. But in the months after Shiloh and with the resumption of fighting in the East, the extent of casualties often overwhelmed the volunteers. And the bloodiest fighting lay ahead.

Even if a soldier escaped death on the battlefield and survived a hospital stay, he often died from disease. Roughly twice as many men died from disease than on the battlefield during the Civil War. Typhoid, appropriately known as camp fever, claimed the most lives.

Many soldiers turned to religion for consolation. Camp prayer meetings and revivals increased after Shiloh. Soldiers often gathered to sing hymns before retiring for the night. Stories circulated of a Bible that stopped a bullet. But veterans knew that a deck of cards did just as well, and neither Bibles nor cards offered protection against artillery.

Soldiers responded in various ways to constant danger and fear. Some talked or yelled loudly. (The Confederate rebel yell probably relieved some of the tension of battle as well as frightened the enemy.) Others shook uncontrollably. A few soldiers could not wake up in the morning without being doused with cold water. Soldiers suffered from strained relations between officers and enlisted men, heavy chores, incessant drills and boredom. Women camp followers

MAP EXPLORATION

To explore an interactive version of this map, go to
http://www.prenhall.com/goldfield2/map15.2

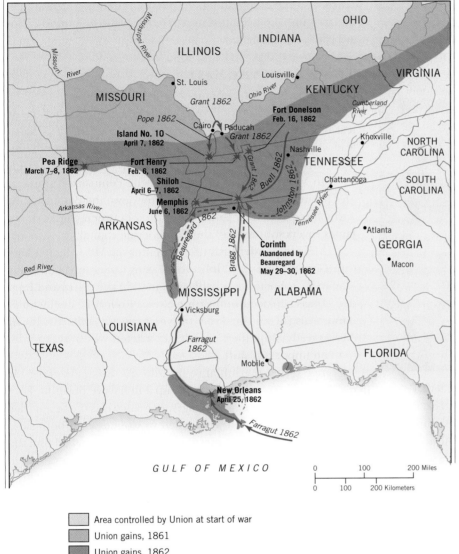

MAP 15–2

The War in the West, 1861–1862   Because of the early Union emphasis on capturing Richmond, the war in the West seemed less important to Northerners. But, from a strategic standpoint, the victories at Forts Henry and Donelson, which drove a wedge into southern territory and closed the Confederacy's quickest path to the West from Virginia and the Carolinas, and the capture of New Orleans and its Mississippi River port, were crucial and set the stage for greater Federal success in the West in 1863.

BASED ON this map, what was the Union's overall strategy in these campaigns?

A career army officer who resigned his commission to serve his state and new country, Confederate General Robert E. Lee's quiet courage and sense of duty inspired his men.

Corbis/Bettman

cooked, did laundry, and provided sexual services for a price. Venereal disease was rampant.

By 1862, the war's carnage and brutality had dispelled any lingering notions of war as a chivalrous enterprise. The reluctance of some commanders to pursue retreating armies or to initiate campaigns resulted in part from their recognition of how awful the war really was.

THE WAR IN THE EAST

With Grant and Farragut squeezing the Confederacy in the West, Lincoln ordered a new offensive against Richmond. After the defeat at Bull Run, he had appointed General George B. McClellan to lead what was now called the Army of the Potomac. A superb organizer, McClellan would prove overly cautious on the field of battle.

In March 1862, at the outset of the Peninsula Campaign, McClellan moved his 112,000-man army down the Potomac River and Chesapeake Bay to the peninsula between the York and James Rivers southeast of the Confederate capital.

Moving ponderously up the peninsula, McClellan clashed with General Joseph E. Johnston's army at Seven Pines in late May 1862. Johnston was badly wounded in the clash, and President Davis replaced him with General Robert E. Lee, who renamed his forces the Army of Northern Virginia. Under his daring leadership, the Confederacy's defensive strategy underwent an important shift.

Lee seized the initiative on June 25, 1862, attacking McClellan's right flank. The nervous McClellan took up a defensive position. For a week, the armies sparred in a series of fierce engagements known as the Seven Days' Battles. More than thirty thousand men were killed or wounded on both sides. Although McClellan prevailed in these contests, the carnage so shocked him that he withdrew down the peninsula and away from Richmond. The exasperated Lincoln, replaced McClellan with John Pope.

Although Lee had lost one-fourth of his eighty thousand-man army, he remained convinced of the wisdom of his offensive-defensive strategy. Better coordination between his staff and field commanders, he believed, would have reduced his casualties and inflicted greater damage on the enemy.

Lee went to work to vindicate these tactics. After a series of inconclusive skirmishes, Union and Confederate armies gathered once more near Manassas Junction. The Second Battle of Bull Run was another disaster for the Union. Lee's generalship completely befuddled Pope and again saved Richmond. Lee and the Army of Northern Virginia were developing a reputation for invincibility.

TURNING POINTS, 1862–1863

WHAT WAS the
Emancipation Proclamation?

The Confederate victories in the East masked the delicate condition of Southern fortunes. The longer the Confederacy held off Union offensives, the greater the likelihood of securing the South's independence. But the longer the war continued, the higher the probability that the Confederacy's shortcomings in men and resources would erode its ability to keep fighting. The Union was also choking the South's commercial link to Europe to which Davis looked for diplomatic recognition as well as trade.

But the most important arena of the war remained the battlefield. Having stymied the Union war machine, Lee contemplated a thrust into Northern territory to stoke Northerners' hostility to the war. President Lincoln also harbored a bold plan. During the spring and summer of 1862, he had concluded that emancipation of the Confederacy's slaves was essential for preserving the Union, but Lincoln was reluctant to take this step before the Union's fortunes on the battlefield improved. As the fall of 1862 approached, both Union and Confederate governments prepared for the most significant conflicts of the war to date.

THE NAVAL WAR AND THE DIPLOMATIC WAR

The Union's naval strategy was to blockade the Southern coast and capture its key seaports and river towns. The intention was to prevent supplies from reaching the Confederacy and cash crops from leaving. Destroying the South's ability to carry on trade would also prevent the Confederacy from raising money to purchase goods to wage war.

With more than 3,000 miles of Confederate coastline to cover, the Union blockade was weak at first. As time passed and the number of ships in the Union navy grew, the blockade tightened. The skyrocketing prices of Southern staples on world markets by 1862 attested to the effectiveness of the Union strategy.

The Confederate naval strategy was to break the blockade and defend the South's rivers and seaports. Confederate blockade runners and privateers attacked Union merchant ships and disrupted Federal operations. Historians disagree about the effectiveness of the Union naval blockade, but any restriction to the flow of trade hurt the Southern cause.

Southerners, remembering the crucial role that French assistance had played in the American Revolution, thought that the recognition of their independence by overseas governments would legitimize their cause in the eyes of the world. Britain had no great love of the United States. If the country divided, it would pose less of a threat to British interests. The aristocratic pretensions of some Southerners also appealed to their British counterparts. British foreign policy, however, had been antislavery for half a century, and the slavery issue turned many Britons against the South. The Union cause had support in high ruling circles, especially the Royal Family, as well as from middle-class and working-class Britons.

Emperor Napoleon III of France, who had imperial designs on Mexico, favored the Confederacy. A restored Union, he thought, would pose a greater threat to his ambitions than a divided one. But Napoleon would not intervene in the Confederate cause without British support. He did, however, invade Mexico in 1863 and install Archduke Maximillian of Austria as emperor. This Mexican empire was short-lived. American pressure and foreign policy reverses in Europe forced the French to withdraw their troops in 1867. Insurgents led by Benito Juarez then captured and executed Maximillian and restored the Mexican republic.

The Russians were probably the staunchest supporters of the Union abroad. Tsar Alexander II saw the United States as a counterweight to British power.

Southerners were convinced that they could use cotton as a diplomatic bargaining chip. "You dare not to make war on cotton. . . . Cotton is King" declared South Carolina senator James H. Hammond in 1858. But King Cotton was no more successful at coercing the British—who had large cotton reserves and an alternate source of supply in Egypt—into granting recognition to the Confederacy than it was at stopping the North from going to war against the South.

Great Britain and France, however, did declare themselves neutral and allowed their merchants to sell arms and supplies to both sides. This policy benefited the Confederacy, with its limited arsenal, but the Confederacy's hopes for

QUICK REVIEW

The War at Sea
- Union naval blockade strengthened over time.
- Confederate ships had limited success running the blockade.
- Restriction of trade hurt the Southern cause.

diplomatic recognition depended on its ability to win its independence on the battlefield. After Lee's victories in Virginia in the spring of 1862 and his subsequent decision to invade the North, British intervention in the war grew more likely.

ANTIETAM

Lee was convinced that the South could not sustain a prolonged conflict. If possible his army had to destroy Union forces quickly. He established camp at Frederick, Maryland in September 1862, scattering his army at various sites, convinced that McClellan and the Army of the Potomac would not attack him.

At this point, luck intervened for the North when a Union corporal found a copy of Lee's orders for the disposition of his army. But, "Little Mac" still moved so cautiously that Lee had time to retreat to defensive positions at Sharpsburg, Maryland, along Antietam Creek. There Lee's army of 50,000 men came to blows with McClellan's army of 75,000.

The Battle of Antietam saw the bloodiest single day of fighting in American history. About 2,100 Union soldiers and 2,700 Confederates died on the battlefield, and another 18,500, equally divided, were wounded. McClellan squandered his numerical superiority with timid attacks. The armies fought to a tactical draw, but the battle was a strategic defeat for the Confederacy.

Antietam marked a major turning point in the war. It kept Lee from directly threatening Northern industry and financial institutions. It prompted Britain and France to abandon plans to grant recognition to the Confederacy. And it provided Lincoln with the victory he needed to announce the abolition of slavery.

EMANCIPATION

President Lincoln despised slavery, but he had always maintained that preserving the Union was his primary war goal. Lincoln realized that he had to stress union to keep the Northern public united in support of the war, but from the war's outset, pressure grew to declare emancipation.

Lincoln said in his inaugural address that he had "no purpose, directly or indirectly, to interfere with the institution of slavery in the states where it exists." But pressure from Northern civilians, Union soldiers, and Congress for some form of emancipation mounted in the spring of 1862. In response, the Republican Congress prohibited slavery in the territories and abolished slavery in the District of Columbia. The act emancipating the district's slaves called for compensating slave owners and colonizing the freed slaves in black republics such as Haiti and Liberia. Then in July 1862, the **Confiscation Act** ordered the seizure of land from disloyal Southerners and the emancipation of their slaves.

Although support for emancipation had grown, it was still not favored by a majority in the North, especially not in the border states. But freeing the slaves would gain support for the Union cause abroad and it would weaken the Confederacy's ability to wage war by removing a crucial source of labor.

By mid-1862, Lincoln had resolved to act on his moral convictions and proclaim emancipation. Taking the advice of Secretary of State Seward, however, he decided to wait for a battlefield victory so that the measure would not appear an act of desperation. Antietam gave the president his opening, and on September 22, 1862, he announced his intention to issue the **Emancipation Proclamation**, to take effect January 1, 1863, in all states still in rebellion. The proclamation exempted slaves in the border states loyal to the Union and in areas under Federal occupation.

Southerners reacted with outrage, while Northerners generally approved. But the Emancipation Proclamation represented far more than its qualified words and phrases expressed. "A mighty *act*," Massachusetts governor John Andrew called it.

WHERE TO LEARN MORE

Antietam National Battlefield, Sharpsburg, Maryland
www.nps.gov/anti/

Confiscation Act   Second confiscation law passed by Congress, ordering the seizure of land from disloyal Southerners and the emancipation of their slaves.

Emancipation Proclamation   Decree announced by President Abraham Lincoln in September 1862 and formally issued on January 1, 1863, freeing slaves in all Confederate states still in rebellion.

• AMERICAN VIEWS •

A SOLDIER PROMOTES THE UNION CAUSE

Soldiers wrote their thoughts down in diaries, in letters to their families, and, as in the case here of D. Beardsley, from Tompkins County, New York, to newspapers. Morale faltered in both the civilian and military ranks on both sides during the Civil War as this excerpt indicates. At the same time, Beardsley is buoyed by the sense of mission brought about by Abraham Lincoln's Emancipation Proclamation, which took effect one month before this letter.

DEMOCRATIC SOCIETIES have to balance civil liberties with the necessity of carrying on a war. What does this soldier think about where the balance ought to occur? The writer refers to "desertion" in the ranks. Why was there a morale problem in the Union armies in February 1863? How does this soldier hope the Emancipation Proclamation will affect the war effort in the North?

I having the honor of being a volunteer from old Tompkins County, and also fighting under the same banner and for the same principles that Washington did— still holding to my priviledges [sic] as a citizen of the United States, I think it will not be out of place for me to speak a few words through your columns, to the good people of my native county. . . .

If our Government would have no rebellion, she must pluck the tares of rebellion from the heart of the nation; and if we would have this rebellion crushed, we must cease to have traitors in power. Let that class in the Northern States, who would kiss the red hand of treason for a momentary peace, remember that the hand will be no less red by the kiss, or the blow no less sure by the pause; and I would humbly beg the people of the North, in the name of a soldier for the Union, that they will, in this dark and trying hour of our country's history, give us their undivided support, first, by stripping all power from the traitors at home, and then by their repentant prayers for our success in battles. . . . A few have deserted, and may God have mercy upon them. Let them go, their *blood* is altogether too poor to enrich the soil of worn out Virginia. We want the blood of patriots to make it bring forth the fruits of freedom. . . . We hope that in future the people and the army will become more pure, and work with a nobler purpose of heart. The first step toward this reformation has already been taken. We begin to see that all men have rights, whether white or black, and we hope that when the smoke of battle shall have cleared away, that the bright sun of peace will shine upon a truly free people.

Source: D. Beardsley, "Co. K, 137th Reg't, N.Y. Vols" that appeared in the *Ithaca Journal*, March 3, 1863; dated February 16, 1863 and written from Acquia Landing, Virginia.

Lincoln and the Union war effort were now tied to the cause of freedom. The war had became a holy war of deliverance. Freedom and Union entwined in the public consciousness of the North. Emancipation also unified the Republican party and strengthened the president's hand in conducting the war. (See American Views: "A Soldier Promotes the Union Cause.")

As word of the Emancipation Proclamation raced through the slave grapevine, slaves rejoiced that their long-awaited day of jubilee had arrived. Southern masters fought to deter their slaves by punishing the families of black men who fled to Union lines and employing slavecatchers to reclaim runaways. But, slaveholders could not stem the tide of slaves fleeing toward the Union lines and freedom. The 1862 Confiscation Act included slaves with other Confederate property as the "contraband" of war and subject to confiscation, a term Union general Benjamin Butler had applied to escaped slaves as early as May 1861. As they helped the Union cause, contrabands also sought to help fellow slaves "steal" their freedom. The former slaves who arrived at Federal

Even before the Emancipation Proclamation, slaves throughout the South "stole" their freedom. After the Proclamation, the trickle of black slaves abandoning their masters became a flood, as they sought freedom behind Union lines.

Theo Kaufman, "On to Liberty," 1887, oil on canvas, 36″ × 56″. The Metropolitan Museum of Art, Gift of Erving and Joyce Wolf, 1982. (1982, 443.3) Photograph © 1982 The Metropolitan Museum of Art

WHERE TO LEARN MORE

Gettysburg National Military Park, Gettysburg, Pennsylvania
www.nps.gov/gett/

camps after emancipation often encountered poor conditions but relished their freedom nonetheless. After 1863, ex-slaves served in increasing numbers in the Union army.

More than 80 percent of the roughly 180,000 black soldiers and 20,000 black sailors who fought for the Union were slaves and free black men from the South. For the typical black Southerner who joined the army, the passage from bondage to freedom came quickly. Making his escape from his master, he perhaps "stole" his family as well. He typically experienced his first days of freedom behind Union lines, where he may have learned to read and write. Finally, he put on the Federal uniform, experiencing as one Southern black volunteer commented, "the biggest thing that ever happened in my life."

Although black troops fought as ably as their white comrades, they received lower pay than white soldiers and performed the most menial duties in camp. Abolitionists and black leaders in the North pressured President Lincoln for more equitable treatment of African-American recruits. When Frederick Douglass complained to Lincoln about the lower pay that black troops received, the president defended the practice. Despite discrimination, black soldiers fought valiantly at Port Hudson, Louisiana; near Charleston; and, late in the war, at the siege of Petersburg, Virginia. The most celebrated black encounter with Confederate troops occurred in July 1863 during a futile assault by the 54th Massachusetts Regiment on Fort Wagner outside Charleston. The Northern press, previously lukewarm toward black troops, heaped praise on the effort.

FROM FREDERICKSBURG TO GETTYSBURG

In late 1862, after Antietam, the president replaced Mc-Clellan with General Ambrose E. Burnside. Moving swiftly against Lee's dispersed army in northern Virginia, Burnside reached the Rappahannock River opposite Fredericksburg in November 1862 (see Map 15–3). On December 13, the Union forces launched a foolish frontal assault that the Confederates repelled, inflicting heavy Federal casualties. Burnside was relieved of his command, and Major General Joseph Hooker was installed in his place.

Hooker was as incompetent as Burnside. Between May 1 and May 4, Lee's army delivered a series of crushing attacks on Hooker's forces at Chancellorsville. Out-numbered two to one, Lee had pulled off another stunning victory but he had lost some thirteen thousand men and Stonewall Jackson. Nervous Confederate sentries mistakenly shot and wounded him as he returned from a reconnoitering mission, and he died a few days later. Jackson had helped Lee win some of the Confederacy's most stunning victories. Lee recognized the tragedy of Jackson's loss for himself and his country.

Chancellorsville thrust Lincoln into another bout of despair. "My God!" he exclaimed in agony, "What will the country say! What will the country say!" Meanwhile, Lee headed north once again.

President Lincoln sent the Union Army of the Potomac after Lee. But General Hooker dallied, and Lincoln replaced him with George Gordon Meade who set out after the Confederate army, which was encamped at Cashtown, Pennsylvania, 45 miles from Harrisburg. That the greatest battle of the war erupted at nearby Gettysburg was pure chance (see Map 15–4 on p. 394). During the first day of battle, July 1, the Confederates forced Union forces back from the town to a new position on Cemetery Hill. On the second day, they took several key locations along Cemetery Ridge before Federal forces pushed them back to the previous day's positions. On July 3, Lee made a fateful error. Believing that the center of Meade's line was weak, he ordered an all-out assault against it by General George Pickett. Meade was prepared for Lee's assault. As the Confederate infantry marched out with battle colors flying, the Union artillery and Federal riflemen tore apart the charging Southerners and half of Pickett's thirteen thousand-man division lay dead or wounded.

After the battle, Lee explained, "I believed my men were invincible." Meade allowed Lee to withdraw to Virginia. Gettysburg was the bloodiest battle of the war. The Union suffered 23,000 casualties; the Confederacy, 28,000.

VICKSBURG, CHATTANOOGA, AND THE WEST

On July 4, one day after Pickett's charge at Gettysburg, Vicksburg, the last major Confederate strong-hold on the Mississippi, surrendered to Ulysses S. Grant. Grant is often perceived, incorrectly, as a general who ground out victories through superior numbers, with little finesse or concern for his troops' safety. But in his

 # MAP EXPLORATION
To explore an interactive version of this map, go to
http://www.prenhall.com/goldfield2/map15.3

MAP 15–3

From Fredericksburg to Gettysburg: The War in the East, December 1862–July 1863 By all logic, the increasingly outgunned and outfinanced Confederacy should have been showing signs of faltering by 1863. But bungling by Union generals at Fredericksburg and Chancellorsville sustained Southern fortunes and encouraged Robert E. Lee to attempt another Northern invasion.

HOW WAS Robert E. Lee able to press on, outgunned and outfinanced, into 1863 and beyond?

MAP 15–4

The Battle of Gettysburg, July 1–3, 1863   In a war that lasted four years, it is difficult to point to the decisive battle, but clearly the outcome during those hot July days at Gettysburg set the tone for the rest of the war. The result was unclear until the final day of battle and, even then, it might have gone either way. Winning by a whisker was enough to propel Union armies to a string of victories over the next year, and throw Confederate forces back on their defenses among an increasingly despairing population. Gettysburg marked the last major Southern invasion of the North.

WHY WAS the Battle of Gettysburg so crucial?

campaigns in the West, he used his forces creatively, swiftly, and with a minimum loss of life.

Grant had devised a brilliant plan to take Vicksburg that called for rapid maneuvering and expert coordination (see Map 15–5). Grant had his twenty thousand Union troops ferried across the Mississippi from the Louisiana side south of Vicksburg. Then they moved northeastward, captured the Mississippi state capital at Jackson, and turned west toward Vicksburg. On May 22, 1863, Grant settled down in front of the city and cut it off completely. Their situation hopeless, General John Pemberton and his thirty thousand–man garrison surrendered on July 4.

As Grant was besieging Vicksburg in June 1863, Union general William S. Rosecrans advanced on Confederate general Braxton Bragg, whose army held Chattanooga, a "doorway" on the railroad that linked Richmond to the Lower South. The capture of the city would complete the uncoupling of the West from the eastern Confederacy.

At Rosecrans's approach, Bragg abandoned Chattanooga and took up positions at nearby Chickamauga Creek. When the two armies clashed at Chickamauga on September 19, Bragg pushed Rosecrans back and bottled up Rosecrans in Chattanooga much as Grant had confined Pemberton at Vicksburg. Suddenly, the Union's strategy for the conquest of the western Confederacy seemed in jeopardy.

The Confederate position on the heights overlooking Chattanooga appeared impregnable. But Union generals Grant, Sherman, and Hooker broke the siege and forced Bragg's army to retreat into Georgia. The Union now dominated most of the West and faced an open road to the East.

The Confederacy's reverses at Vicksburg and Chattanooga mirrored its misfortunes beyond the Mississippi River. Texas was critical to Confederate fortunes, both as a source of supply for the East and as a base for the conquest of the Far West, but it was far from secure. Texas suffered from internal dissent and violence on its borders. For a time, it maintained commercial contact with the rest of the Confederacy through Matamoros, Mexico. But by 1864, with the Union in control of the Mississippi, Texas had lost its strategic importance. The Confederacy's transcontinental aspirations died early in the war. In March 1862, a Confederate army seeking to conquer the Southwest was overwhelmed by Union forces at the Battle of Glorieta Pass in New Mexico. The Southwest from New Mexico to California would remain firmly in Union hands.

Native American tribes in the Trans-Mississippi West spent much of the Civil War battling Federal troops for territory and resources. Three regiments of Cherokee Indians, however, fought for the South at the Battle of Pea Ridge in 1862. The Union won the battle and with it control of Missouri and northern Arkansas. Most battles between pro-Union and pro-Southern Native Americans occurred in the Indian Territory (now Oklahoma).

MAP 15–5

Vicksburg and Chattanooga: The War in the West, 1863 Devising a brilliant strategy, Union General Ulysses S. Grant took the last major Mississippi River stronghold from Confederate hands on July 4, 1863, dealing a significant economic and morale blow to southern forces. Coupled with the defeat at Gettysburg a day earlier, the fall of Vicksburg portended a bitter finale to hopes for Southern independence. Grant completed his domination of the West by joining forces with several Union generals to capture Chattanooga and push Confederate forces into Georgia, setting the stage for the capture of that key Southern state by the Federals in 1864.

BASED ON this map, how was Grant able to take the last major Mississippi stronghold from Confederate hands?

FROM THEN TO NOW
Gettysburg

Each year more than 1.8 million visitors track across Pennsylvania's rolling hills to retrace the steps of the competing armies as they fought the Battle of Gettysburg in July 1863. The fascination has become big business at the Gettysburg National Military Park, where tourists spend more than $40 million annually on items ranging from Pickett's Charge T-shirts to ersatz battlefield relics. For a nation not ordinarily fixated on the past, the devotion to this battle—to which a majority of Americans have no ancestral connections—is extraordinary. What accounts for it?

The Civil War was a defining event in American history, and the Battle of Gettysburg was the defining moment of the Civil War, a guidepost on the American journey. The battle has thus become a metaphor for the national ideals the war brought into focus symbolizing them in an enduring form for subsequent generations of Americans and serving as a reminder of the work still to be done to translate those ideals into reality for all. The battle also emerged as a symbol of national reconciliation after the fratricidal conflict of the war.

For generations of white Southerners after the Civil War, Gettysburg was the place where the young men of a doomed cause displayed incomparable courage against long odds. "For every Southern boy fourteen years old," William Faulkner wrote, "not once but whenever he wants it, there is the instant when it's still not yet two o'clock"—the hour of Pickett's charge—"on that July afternoon in 1863."

But today most Americans, North and South, see Gettysburg not as a missed opportunity, but thanks to President Lincoln's famous address dedicating the battlefield cemetery, as a place that gives meaning to the sacrifices of both sides. Consecrating the battlefield to a renewal of the nation's founding ideals, Lincoln asked his listeners to

> highly resolve that these dead shall not have died in vain—that this nation, under God, shall have a new birth of freedom—and that government of the people, by the people, for the people, shall not perish from the earth.

In the years after the war, veterans from both sides came to the battlefield seeking reconciliation, posing together for pictures and shaking hands. Tourists strike similar poses today.

African Americans, however, have not by and large shared the national fascination with Gettysburg and make up less than three percent of the visitors to the battlefield. "When you're black," African-American historian Allan B. Ballard explained, "the great battlefield holds mixed messages." Although the National Park Service, which oversees the site, has put up an exhibit on the role of African-American troops in the Civil War, black visitors remain ambivalent about the place. Aware of the long and continuing struggle they would face to secure true equality in American society after the Civil War, they see irony in Lincoln's call for "a new birth of freedom." Yet, if, as Ballard notes, "we are still fighting our civil wars," at Gettysburg at least, it is possible for Americans today to see and learn how their freedoms were paid for in blood and to reflect, in Lincoln's words, on the "unfinished work which they who fought here have thus far so nobly advanced."

These Union and Confederate dead at Gettysburg represent the cost of the war, the price of freedom. President Lincoln transformed the battleground from a killing field to a noble symbol of sacrifice for American ideals. Gettysburg continues to occupy a special place in our nation's history and in the memory of its citizens.

Corbis/Bettman

WAR TRANSFORMS THE NORTH

Union successes by 1863 profoundly affected both sides. For the North, hopes of victory and reunion increased. The Federal government expanded its bureaucracy to wage war efficiently, and a Republican-dominated Congress broadened Federal power. The Lincoln administration successfully weathered dissent thanks to the president's political skill, the desire of the Republicans to remain in power, and the Union's improving military fortunes. Boosted by Federal economic legislation and wartime demand, the Northern economy boomed. Women entered the work force in growing numbers, but labor unrest and class and racial tensions suggested that prosperity had a price.

WARTIME LEGISLATION AND POLITICS

Before the Civil War, the Federal government rarely affected citizens' lives directly. But mobilizing for war required a strong central government. With the departure of the South from the Union, Republicans dominated all branches of the Federal administration. This left them in a position to test the constitutional limits of federal authority.

President Lincoln began almost immediately to use executive authority to suppress opposition to the war effort in the North. Within the first few weeks of the conflict, he ordered the seizure of telegrams to intercept seditious messages to the South. He also suspended the writ of habeas corpus, the constitutional requirement that protects a defendant against illegal imprisonment. Suspending it allowed authorities to hold suspects indefinitely and was permitted by the Constitution "when in cases of Rebellion or Invasion the public Safety" require it.

Executive sanctions fell particularly hard on the Democratic party. "Disloyalty" was difficult to define in the midst of war. Though many Democrats opposed secession and supported the Union, they challenged the president on the conduct of the war, on emancipation, and on Lincoln's coolness toward peace initiatives. A few had ties with Confederate agents. Republicans called these dissenters "**Copper-heads**," after the poisonous snake.

Despite the suspension of habeas corpus, Lincoln compiled a fairly good record for upholding basic American civil liberties. The administration made no attempt to control the news or subvert the electoral process. In the off-year election in 1862, Republicans retained control of Congress but lost several seats to Democrats. In the presidential election of 1864, Lincoln won reelection in a hard-fought contest.

While fellow Republicans sometimes chastised the president for violating civil liberties, mismanaging military assignments, or moving too slowly on emancipation, they rarely threatened to disrupt the party. Lincoln also found support from Republican governors and state governments.

But dissent in the Republican party did affect national policy. **Radical Republicans** hounded Lincoln, establishing the Joint Committee on the Conduct of the War to examine and monitor military policy. They also pressed Lincoln for quicker action on emancipation, but they supported the president on most crucial matters.

Lincoln likewise supported his party on an array of initiatives in Congress. Turning to the settlement of the West, they passed the **Homestead Act** in May 1862, which granted 160 acres of land free to any settler in the territories who agreed to improve the land within five years of the grant. The act was a boon for railroad companies.

Other legislation to boost the nation's economy and the fortunes of individual manufacturers and farmers included the **Land Grant College Act** of 1862, a protective tariff that same year, and the National Banking Act of 1863. The Land Grant Act awarded the proceeds from the sale of public lands to the states for the establishment of colleges offering instruction in "agriculture and mechanical arts." The tariff legislation protected Northern industry from foreign competition while raising revenue for the Union. The National Banking Act of 1863 replaced the bank notes of individual states, which were often backed by flimsy reserves and subject to wild fluctuations in value, with a uniform national currency and brought order to a chaotic monetary system.

However, the expansion of government into some quarters, such as the draft laws, was not welcomed.

CONSCRIPTION AND THE DRAFT RIOTS

Congress passed the first national conscription law in 1863. Almost immediately, evasion, obstruction, and weak enforcement threatened to undermine it. As military authorities began arresting draft dodgers and deserters, secret societies formed to harbor draftees and instruct them on evasion. Conflicts between citizens and federal officials over the draft sometimes erupted in violence. The worst draft riot occurred in New York City in July 1863, when a mostly Irish mob protesting conscription burned the federal marshal's headquarters. Racial and class antagonisms quickly joined antidraft anger as the mob went on a rampage through the city's streets, fighting police, plundering houses of the wealthy, and crying, "Down with the rich!" Racial antagonisms contributed to the violence. The mob lynched two black men and burned the Colored Orphan Asylum. More than one hundred lives were lost in the riot, which was finally quelled by army units fresh from Gettysburg, and the draft resumed a month later.

THE NORTHERN ECONOMY

"The North," one historian has said, "was fighting the South with one hand and getting rich with the other behind its back." After an initial downturn during the uncertain months preceding the war, the Northern economy picked up quickly. High tariffs and massive federal spending soon made up for the loss of Southern markets and the closing of the Mississippi River. Profits skyrocketed for some businesses like the railroads. New industries boomed, and new inventions increased manufacturing efficiency as in the sewing machine industry, which was first commercialized in the 1850s. Technological advances greatly increased the output of the North's garment factories.

Despite the loss of manpower to the demands of industry and the military, the productivity of Northern agriculture grew during the war. As machines replaced men on the farm, the manufacturers of farm machinery became wealthy. Crop failures in Europe dramatically increased the demand for American grain.

Working people should have benefited from wartime prosperity, with men off to war, immigration down, and labor in short supply. Although wages increased, prices rose more. Declining real wages led to exploitation, especially of women in garment factories. The trade union movement, which suffered a serious setback in the depression of 1857, revived. Local unions of shoemakers, carpenters, and miners emerged in 1862 across the North, and so did a few national organizations. By 1865, more than 200,000 Northern workers belonged to a labor union.

Employers struck back at union organizing by hiring strikebreakers, usually black workers. Labor conflicts between striking white workers and black strikebreakers sparked riots in New York City and Cincinnati. The racial antagonism accounted in part for workers' opposition to Lincoln's Emancipation Proclamation and for the continued strength of the Democratic party in Northern cities.

The promise of enormous profits bred greed and corruption as well as exploitation. Illicit trade between North and South was inevitable when cotton could be bought at 20 cents a pound in New Orleans and sold for $1.90 a pound at Boston. Profiteers not only defied the government to trade with the enemy but also sometimes swindled the government outright, supplying defective clothing to soldiers at inflated prices.

Some Northerners viewed the spending spree uneasily. They were disturbed to see older men flaunting their wealth while young men were dying on the battlefield. "The lavish profusion in which the old southern cotton aristocracy used to indulge," wrote an indignant reporter for the *New York World*, "is completely eclipsed by the dash, parade, and magnificence of the new northern shoddy aristocracy. . . ." Exploited workers likewise resented the "shoddy aristocracy."

Comments like these hinted at the deep social and ethical problems that were emerging in Northern society and would become more pronounced in the decades after the Civil War. For the time being, the benefits of economic development for the Union cause outweighed its negative consequences. The thriving Northern economy fed, clothed, and armed the Union's soldiers and kept most civilians employed providing Northern women with unprecedented opportunities.

NORTHERN WOMEN AND THE WAR

More than 100,000 Northern women took jobs in factories, sewing rooms, and arsenals during the Civil War. They often performed tasks previously reserved for men, but at lower pay.

Women also served the war effort directly in another profession previously dominated by men—nursing. Physicians and officers, however, although they tolerated women nurses as nurturing morale boosters, thought little of their ability to provide medical care. Women sometimes challenged this condescending view, braving dismissal to confront the medical-military establishment head-on. Clara Barton, among the most notable nurses of the war, treated soldiers on the battlefield at great peril and to the consternation of officers.

But the war also left tens of thousands of women widowed and devastated. In a society that assumed that men supported women, the death of a husband could be a financial and psychological disaster. Many women were left to survive on meager pensions.

The new economic opportunities the war created for women left Northern society more open to a broader view of women's roles. One indication of this change was the admission of women to eight previously all-male state universities after the war. Like the class and racial tensions that surfaced in Northern cities, the shifting role of women during the Civil War hinted at the promises and problems of postwar life. The changing scale and nature of the American economy, the expanded role of government, and the shift in class, racial, and gender relations are all trends that signaled what historians call the "modernization" of American society.

Nurse Ann Bell tends a fallen Union soldier. Although medical practices were primitive and many young men died from poorly treated wounds or disease, the U.S. Sanitary Commission attempted to improve care in Union hospitals during the war. The war helped open nursing as a respectable occupation for women.

Corbis/Bettman

THE CONFEDERACY DISINTEGRATES

HOW DID military reversals affect Confederate political and economic life and civilian morale?

A s battlefield losses mounted, the Confederacy disintegrated. Defeat dissolves the bonds that hold a small society like the Confederacy together and exposes the large and small divisions within it. After 1863, defeat infected Confederate politics, ruined the Southern economy, and eventually invaded the hearts and minds of the Southern people. The South pinned its waning hopes on its defensive military strategy. If it could prolong the conflict a little longer, perhaps a war-weary North would replace Lincoln and the Republicans in the 1864 elections with Democrats inclined to make peace.

SOUTHERN POLITICS

Dissent plagued Southern politics. Residents of western Virginia declared themselves for the Union and formed the new state of West Virginia. Counties in north Alabama, in German-speaking districts in Texas, and throughout the mountains of Tennessee and North Carolina contemplated similar action.

As the war turned against the Confederacy, Southerners increasingly turned against each other. States' rights, a major principle of the seceding states, proved an obstacle to the Davis administration's efforts to exert central authority. The governors of Georgia and North Carolina hoarded munitions, soldiers, supplies, food, and money. Even cooperative governors refused to allow state agents to collect taxes for the Confederacy.

Unlike Abraham Lincoln, Jefferson Davis could not appeal to party loyalty to control dissent because the Confederacy had no parties. Davis's frigid personality, his insistence on attending to minute details, and his inability to accept even constructive criticism gracefully worsened political tensions within the Confederacy.

Parts of the South began clamoring for peace during the fateful summer of 1863. In North Carolina, Jonathan Worth heard calls for the overthrow of the Davis administration and a separate peace with the North. "Every man [I] met," he concluded "was for reconstruction on the basis of the old [U.S.] constitution." By November 1864, the Confederacy suffered as much from internal disaffection as from the attacks of Union armies.

Davis and other Confederate leaders might have averted some of these problems had they succeeded in building a strong sense of Confederate nationalism. Despite several strategies to do so—identifying the Confederacy's fight for independence with the American Revolution of 1776, for example, and casting the Confederacy as a bastion of freedom standing up to Lincoln's despotic abuse of executive authority, they failed. The diaries of Southern soldiers seldom reveal devotion to the Confederacy. In a devout society convinced it was fighting a holy war, some Southerners sought some moral failing to account for their mounting losses. Some identified slavery as the culprit.

WHERE TO LEARN MORE

Museum of the Confederacy, Richmond, Virginia **www.moc.org**

THE SOUTHERN ECONOMY

The South lost, according to one historian, "not because the government failed to mobilize the South's resources" but "because there was virtually nothing left to mobilize." By 1863, the Confederacy was having a difficult time feeding itself. Destruction of farms and growing Union control of waterways and rail lines restricted the distribution of food. Speculators made shortages worse. People ate rats and mules to supplement their meager diets. More than one-quarter of Alabama's population was receiving public welfare by the end of the war. "Deaths from starvation have absolutely occurred," a Confederate official in the state informed President Davis in 1864.

he surrendered on April 9. Grant allowed Lee's men to go home unmolested and to take with them horses or mules "to put in a crop." Grant reported feeling "sad and depressed" at "the downfall of a foe who had fought so long and valiantly."

The fleeing Davis met Joseph E. Johnston at Greensboro, North Carolina, hoping to convince him to continue fighting, but Johnston surrendered to Sherman near Durham, North Carolina, on April 26. On May 10, Union cavalry captured Davis and his companions and within two weeks the Civil War came to an end.

Washington greeted the Confederate surrender at Appomattox with raucous rejoicing. On April 11, President Lincoln spoke briefly of his plans to reconstruct the South with the help of persons loyal to the Union, including recently freed slaves. At least one listener found the speech disappointing. Sometime actor and full-time Confederate patriot John Wilkes Booth muttered to a friend in the throng, "That means nigger citizenship. Now, by God . . . That is the last speech he will ever make."

On the evening of April 14, Good Friday, the president went to Ford's Theater in Washington to view a comedy, *Our American Cousin*. During the performance, Booth shot the president, wounding him mortally, then jumped from Lincoln's box to the stage shouting "Sic semper tyrannis" ("Thus ever to tyrants") and fled the theater. Union troops tracked him down to a barn in northern Virginia and killed him.

Southerners reacted to Lincoln's assassination with mixed emotions. Many saw in the death of the man they had regarded as their bitterest enemy for four years some slight hope of relief for the South's otherwise bleak prospects. But General Johnston and others like him understood Lincoln's influence with the radical elements in the Republican party who were pressing for harsh terms against the South. The president's death, Johnston wrote, was "the greatest possible calamity to the South."

WHERE TO LEARN MORE

Ford's Theatre National Historical Site, Washington, D.C.
www.nps.gov/foth/index2.htm

CONCLUSION

Just before the war, William Sherman had warned a friend from Virginia, "You people of the South don't know what you are doing. This country will be drenched in blood. . . ." He was right. More than 365,000 Union soldiers died during the war, 110,000 in battle, and more than 256,000 Confederate soldiers, 94,000 of them in battle. Total casualties on both sides, including wounded, were more than 1 million. Compounding the suffering of the individuals behind these gruesome statistics was the incalculable suffering—in terms of grief, fatherless children, women who never married, families never made whole—of the people close to them.

The war devastated the South. The region lost one-fourth of its white male population between the ages of 20 and 40, two-fifths of its livestock, and half its farm machinery. Union armies destroyed many of the South's railroads and shattered its industry. Between 1860 and 1870, the wealth of the South declined by 60 percent, and its share of the nation's total wealth dropped from more than 30 percent to 12 percent. The wealth of the North, in contrast, increased by half in the same period.

For black Southerners, emancipation was the war's most significant achievement. The issue that dominated the prewar sectional debate had vanished.

The Civil War stimulated other significant changes. It taught the effectiveness of centralized management, new financial techniques, and the coordination

OVERVIEW

MAJOR BATTLES OF THE CIVIL WAR, 1861–1865

Battle or Campaign	Date	Outcome and Consequences
First Bull Run	July 21, 1861	Confederate victory; destroyed the widespread belief in the North that the war would end quickly, fueled Confederate sense of superiority.
Forts Henry and Donelson	Feb. 6–16, 1862	Union victory; gave the North control of strategic river systems in the western Confederacy and closed an important link between the eastern and western Confederacy.
Shiloh Church	Apr. 6–7, 1862	Union victory; high casualties transformed attitudes about the war on both sides.
Seven Days' Battles	June 25–July 1, 1862	Standoff; halted Union General McClellan's advance on Richmond in the Peninsula Campaign.
Second Bull Run	Aug. 29–30, 1862	Confederate victory; reinforced Confederate general Robert E. Lee's reputation for invincibility.
Antietam	Sept. 17, 1862	Standoff; halted Lee's advance into the North, eliminated Confederacy's chance for diplomatic recognition, encouraged Lincoln to issue the Emancipation Proclamation.
Fredericksburg	Dec. 13, 1862	Confederate victory; revived morale of Lee's army.
Chancellorsville	May 2–6, 1863	Confederate victory; Confederate General Stonewall Jackson killed, encouraged Lee to again invade North.
Gettysburg	July 1–3, 1863	Union victory; halted Confederate advance in the North, major psychological blow to Confederacy.
Vicksburg	Nov. 1862–July 1863	Union victory; closed the key Confederate port on the Mississippi, also dealt a severe blow to Confederate cause.
Chattanooga	Aug.–Nov. 1863	Union victory; solidified Union dominance in the West.
Wilderness and Cold Harbor	May and June 1864	Both Confederate victories inflicted huge losses on Grant's army, turned public opinion against Grant but failed to force him to withdraw.
Atlanta	May–September 1864	Union victory; Confederacy lost key rail depot and industrial center
Sherman's March	November 1864–March 1865	Nearly unopposed, Sherman's army cut a path of destruction through Georgia and South Carolina, breaking Southern morale.
Battles of Franklin and Nashville	November and December 1864	Union victories in Tennessee; effectively destroyed Army of Tennessee.
Siege of Petersburg	June 1864–April 1865	Long stalemate ended in Union victory; led to fall of Richmond and surrender of Lee's army at Appomattox Court House.

of production, marketing, and distribution. Entrepreneurs would apply these lessons to create the expanding corporations of the postwar American economy. By opening new opportunities to women in fields such as nursing and teaching, the war also helped lay the foundation for the woman suffrage movement of the 1870s and 1880s.

The war was not responsible for every postwar change in American society, and it left many features of American life intact. For example, the war did not soften class antagonisms. Capitalism, not labor, triumphed during the war and industrialists and entrepreneurs not working people, most benefited from its bonanza. Lincoln brutally suppressed strikes at defense plants and threw labor leaders into military prisons.

The war to end slavery did change some American racial attitudes, especially in the North. When Lincoln broadened the war's objectives to include the abolition of slavery, he connected the success of the Union to freedom for the slave. By the end of the war, perhaps a majority of Northerners supported granting freedmen the right to vote and to equal protection under the law, even if they believed (as many did) that black people were inferior to white people. The courage of black troops and the efforts of African American leaders to link the causes of reunion and freedom were influential in bringing about this shift.

Most white Southerners did not experience a similar enlightenment. They greeted the end of slavery with fear, anger, and regret. The freed slaves were living reminders of the South's defeat and the end of a way of life grounded in white supremacy.

If the Civil War resolved the sectional dispute of the 1850s by ending slavery and denying the right of the Southern states to secede, it created two new equally troubling problems: how to reunite South and North and how to deal with the legacy of slavery.

In November 1863, President Lincoln was asked to say a few words at the dedication of the federal cemetery at Gettysburg. There, surrounded by fresh graves, Lincoln bound the cause of the Union to that of the country's founders: "Fourscore and seven years ago our fathers brought forth upon this continent a new nation, conceived in liberty and dedicated to the proposition that all men are created equal. Now we are engaged in a great civil war, testing whether that nation, or any nation so conceived and so dedicated can long endure." A Union victory, Lincoln hoped, would not only honor the past but also call forth a new nation, cleansed of its sins, to inspire oppressed peoples around the world. He called on the nation to resolve "that the nation shall, under God, have a new birth of freedom; and that government of the people, by the people, for the people, shall not perish from the earth." The two-minute Gettysburg Address captured what Union supporters were fighting and connected their sacrifices to the noble causes of freedom and democratic government. That would be both the hope and the challenge of the peace that followed a hard war.

Summary

Mobilization, North and South In the initial rush of enthusiasm, both the North and South believed the Civil War would be short. While neither side was well prepared, the North's resources for fighting a lengthy conflict greatly exceeded the South's. The North also had the leadership of Abraham Lincoln who eloquently articulated the goal of preserving the Union. The Confederacy's tactic was to wage a defensive war and wear down Northern public opinion; sufficient patience and resources would be necessary for success.

The Early War, 1861–1862 The North's offensive strategy dictated the course of the war for the first two years. The first battle of the war at Bull Run was a Confederate victory, but as Union forces retreated in the East, they had made some advances in the West under General Ulysses S. Grant. The carnage in 1862 at Shiloh blunted the initial enthusiasm of both sides with the realization that much bloody fighting lay ahead. A new Union offensive in Virginia aimed at the Confederate capital Richmond was halted by Robert E. Lee's generalship. By the end of 1862, the outcome of the war remained in the balance.

Turning Points, 1862–1863 Could the South overcome its human and economic shortcomings by victory on the battlefield? Would the Confederacy gain a valuable ally in Great Britain or France? Diplomatic recognition never came; Lee was defeated at Antietam as he attempted a Northern invasion. Lincoln used this victory to issue the Emancipation Proclamation making the war to save the Union also a war free the slaves. Confederate defeats at Gettysburg and Vicksburg in July 1863 marked key turning points; Union forces were becoming dominate in the East and the West.

War Transforms the North Such a large-scale war called for a strong and active central government. Constitutional limitations were tested; new economic measures were passed; racial and ethnic tensions erupted in the New York draft riots. The thriving Northern economy fed, clothed, and armed the Union's soldiers and kept most civilians employed and well fed.

The Confederacy Disintegrates Battlefield losses increased discontent over the unequal sharing of hardships including the draft, food shortages, and inflation, but support for Lee and the Confederate army remained high. After 1864, President Davis could not keep the Confederacy from fracturing; with food scarce and money worthless, many, especially the South's women, wanted the war to end.

The Union Prevails, 1864–1865 Lincoln's appointment of General Grant as commander of all Union armies meant that relentless pressure would now be on Lee and the Southern armies. After Union victories in Virginia, the capture of Atlanta, and Sherman's "march to the sea," the capture of the Confederate capital Richmond would result in Lee's surrender at Appomattox. The Union wave of victories had brought the reelection of Lincoln and the passage of the Thirteenth Amendment; joy over the war's end was tempered by the assassination of President Lincoln by a Southern sympathizer.

REVIEW QUESTIONS

1. How did the Union and the Confederacy compare in terms of resources, leadership, and military strategies? How did these factors affect the course of the war?

2. Why were the battles of Antietam and Gettysburg turning points in the war?

3. How did the Emancipation Proclamation affect the Union and Confederate causes?

4. What roles did women play in the North and in the South during the Civil War?

5. What changes resulted from the Civil War?

6. Why did Sullivan Ballou fight?

KEY TERMS

Confiscation Act   (p. 390)

Copper-heads   (p. 397)

Emancipation Proclamation   (p. 390)

Homestead Act   (p. 397)

Land Grant College Act   (p. 397)

Radical Republicans   (p. 397)

Thirteenth Amendment   (p. 405)

WHERE TO LEARN MORE

 Museum of the Confederacy, Richmond, Virginia. This museum has rotating exhibits on various aspects of the confederate effort during the Civil War, both on the home front and on the battlefield. The Confederate White House, which is open to the public, is next door to the museum. **www.moc.org**

Gettysburg National Military Park, Gettysburg, Pennsylvania. An excellent and balanced interpretation awaits the visitor at this national park. **www.nps.gov/gett/**

Antietam National Battlefield, Sharpsburg, Maryland. Also an excellent and balanced interpretation at this battlefield site. **www.nps.gov/anti/**

Ford's Theater National Historic Site, Washington, D.C. The place where John Wilkes Booth assassinated President Abraham Lincoln not only depicts those events, including artifacts from the assassination, but also presents period plays. **www.nps.gov/foth/index2.htm**

Appomattox Court House, Appomattox, Virginia. What historian Bruce Catton termed "a stillness at Appomattox" can be felt at the McLean house in this south-central Virginia town. The house is much as it was when Confederate General Robert E. Lee surrendered his forces to Union General Ulysses s. Grant on April 9, 1865. An almost reverential solitude covers the house and the well-maintained grounds today. **www.nps.org/apco/**

 For additional study resources for this chapter, go to:
www.prenhall.com/goldfield/chapter15

The Civil War

WHAT DID the photographer include that is missing from the illustrations? What did the illustrators include that is missing from the photograph? What did war look like to the civilian who saw only the illustrations? To the civilian who saw only the photograph? To the civilian who saw both?

Two new media drastically altered the ways in which people on the home front experienced war. One was photography. Mathew B. Brady and other pioneering photographers took thousands of pictures of battlefield scenes, which were then shown in weekly exhibits. For a small fee, the spectator could see photographs of battles fought just days before. The images themselves are of very good quality and quite large. The major drawback was technical. The photographer had to expose his glass plate to the light for a full minute, any movement during that time, created a blur. So, Brady's and other photographic images captured the look of the battlefield after the fighting was over.

The other new medium was the illustrated magazine. *Harper's Illustrated Weekly,* only a few years old at the outbreak of the war, was the biggest with a circulation running into the hundreds of thousands. Its illustrators drew battles as they were happening capturing the charges and the hand-to-hand fighting that the photographer could not. Below is a stereopticon photograph of a *Harper's* artist at Gettysburg, taken for the Brady Company. Viewers looked through a special device which fused the two images. As you examine the images included in this essay, consider these questions.
▼

Courtesy of Library of Congress

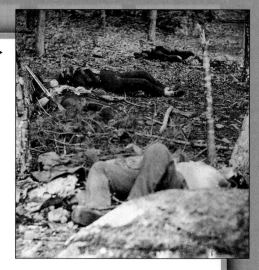

"Dead at Gettysburg," a photograph taken for the Brady Company. The dead included ▶ both Union soldiers and a Confederate. For the vast majority of those paying admission to see this and other images, this was the first time they witnessed the carnage of battle.

Courtesy of Library of Congress

◀ "The Battle of Gettysburg—Longstreet's Attack Upon Our Left Center—Blue Ridge In the Distance" appeared in *Harper's Weekly* for July 22, 1863. Note the use of "our" to describe the position of the Union troops. Note too that the viewer is positioned behind the Union lines.

American Antiquary Society

"The Harvest of ▶ Death—Gettysburg, July 4, 1863" appeared in *Harper's Weekly* for July 22, 1863. It shows only Union dead along with dead horses and overturned wagons.

American Antiquary Society

THE HARVEST OF DEATH—GETTYSBURG, JULY 4, 1863.—[PHOTOGRAPHED BY A. GARDNER, WASHINGTON.]

413

The war passed from words to stones which the white children began to hurl at the colored. Several colored children were hurt and, as they had not resented the rock throwing . . . , the white children became more aggressive and abusive.

Mississippi Freedman School, 1866. Noon at the primary school for Freedmen at Vicksburg, Mississippi.

16

RECONSTRUCTION
1865–1877

WHY DID Southerner's remember
the Civil War as a Lost Cause?

WHAT WERE
African-American
aspirations in 1865?

HOW DID Presidential Reconstruction
differ from Congressional Reconstruction?

WHAT ROLE did the Ku Klux Klan
play in Counter-Reconstruction?

WHAT WERE the effects
of the Civil Rights Act of 1875
and the Compromise of 1877?

WHY AND HOW did Reconstruction end,
and what were its failed promises?

Marianna, Florida 1866

The white academy opened about the same time the church opened the school for the Negro children. As the colored children had to pass the academy to reach the church it was easy for the white children to annoy them with taunts and jeers. The war passed from words to stones which the white children began to hurl at the colored. Several colored children were hurt and, as they had not resented the rock-throwing in kind because they were timid about going that far, the white children became more aggressive and abusive.

One morning the colored children armed themselves with stones and determined to fight their way past the academy to their school. [They] approached the academy in formation whereas in the past they had been going in pairs or small groups. When they reached hailing distance, a half dozen white boys rushed out and hurled their missiles. Instead of scampering away, the colored children not only stood their ground and hurled their missiles but maintained a solemn silence. The white children, seeing there was no backing down as they expected, came rushing out of the academy and charged the colored children.

During some fifteen minutes it was a real tug of war. In the close fighting the colored children got the advantage gradually and began to shove the white children back. As they pressed the advantage the white children broke away and ran for the academy. The colored fighters did not follow them but made it hot for the laggards until they also took to their heels. There were many bruises on both sides, but it taught the white youngsters to leave the colored ones alone thereafter.

—*T. Thomas Fortune,*
Norfolk Journal and Guide

T. Thomas Fortune, "Norfolk Journal and Guide," August 20, 1927, reprinted in Dorothy Sterling, ed., *The Trouble They Seen: Black People Tell the Story of Reconstruction* (Garden City, NY: Doubleday & Co., 1976): 22–24.

IMAGE KEY
for pages 414–415

a. A young African American boy with new clothes and a book provided by the Freedman Bureau.

b. Rocks and stones like those used to hurl at former slaves.

c. Noon at the primary school for Freedmen at Vicksburg, Mississippi: colored engraving, 1866.

d. Two members of the Ku Klux Clan holding guns and wearing hoods and long robes, pictured in Harper's Weekly.

e. Pages from the New England Primers; primers such as this one were used to educate former slaves.

f. A dead Confederate soldier lies prostrate beneath his rifle in an earthen trench on the battlefield at Petersburg, Virginia during the Civil War, April 3, 1865.

g. Freedmen (freed black slaves) vote in 1867.

h. Three white men decry the Reconstruction Acts of Congress as "usurpations and unconstitutional, revolutionary, and void" while clasping hands above the fallen body of a black man.

i. African American worshippers during a tumultuous church service on New Years Eve. Sketch by Joseph Becker.

T. THOMAS FORTUNE, a New York newspaper editor, recalled this battle between black and white schoolchildren sixty years earlier, at the beginning of the Reconstruction era. In the scheme of things, it did not amount to much. However, for ten-year-old Thomas, born a slave in Marianna, the incident encapsulated the dilemma of Reconstruction. In the journey from slavery to freedom, education was an important element of full citizenship for African Americans. The eagerness with which black children (and adults) flooded schools was matched by the hostility of the white community who resented any pretense of equality that education implied.

Reconstruction was not merely a series of white aggressions against African-American aspirations, followed by black retreats. The violence and disorder that punctuated Southern society after the Civil War was due in part to the refusal of black people to relinquish their dreams of equal citizenship, including the right to a decent education.

Young Thomas did not back down, though by 1878 he felt that the journey from slavery to freedom would always be incomplete in the South. Together with his young bride, Carrie Smiley of Jacksonville, Florida, Thomas left for New York City, where he obtained a job as a printer for the *New York Sun*. He died there in 1928. New York's gain was the South's loss, a process repeated many times over after the Civil War as talented young black men and women left the region of their birth and their ancestors. It was a double tragedy for the South: losing people who could have rebuilt a shattered region, and missing the opportunity to create a society based on racial equality.

The position of African Americans in American society and how to reform the Former Confederate states were the two great issues of the Reconstruction era. Americans disagreed about both of them. The formation of a national consensus on freedom and reunification began with the demands and hopes of three broad groups: the Republican party, the more than 4 million former slaves, and white Southerners.

Between 1865 and 1867, under President Andrew Johnson's Reconstruction plan, white Southerners pretty much had their way with the former slaves and with their own state governments. Congressional action between 1867 and 1870 attempted to balance black rights and home rule, with mixed results. After 1870, white Southerners regained control, denying black Southerners their political gains while Republicans in Washington lost interest in policing their former enemies.

WHITE SOUTHERNERS AND THE GHOSTS OF THE CONFEDERACY, 1865

Confederate soldiers—generals and troops alike—returned to devastated homes they could scarcely recognize. Their cause lost and their society reviled, white Southerners lived through the summer and fall of 1865 surrounded by ghosts—the ghosts of lost loved ones, joyful times, bountiful harvests, self-assurance, and slavery. Defeat shook the basic tenets of their religious beliefs. But many other white Southerners refused to accept their defeat as a divine judgment. Instead, they insisted, God had spared the South for a greater purpose. Robert E. Lee became the patron saint of this cause, his poignant nobility a contrast to the crassness of the Yankee warlords. Some white Southerners would not allow the memory of the bloody struggle to die, transforming it into the **Lost Cause**, a symbol of courage against great odds. The Old South was transformed into a stainless civilization, worth fighting and dying for, and the Civil War became not a savage conflict, but a romantic and chivalrous contest.

Fifteen years after the war, Mark Twain traveled the length of the East Coast. After visiting a gentlemen's club in Boston, he recalled that the conversation had covered a variety of topics, none of which included the Civil War. Northerners had relegated that conflict to history books and moved on. In the South, on the other hand, defeat and destruction demanded rationalization and remembrance.

Most white Southerners approached the great issues of freedom and reunification with unyielding views. They saw African Americans as adversaries whose attempts at self-improvement were a direct challenge to white people's beliefs in their own racial superiority. They also saw outside assistance to black Southerners as another invasion.

WHY DID Southerners remember the Civil War as a Lost Cause?

Lost Cause   The phrase many white Southerners applied to their Civil War defeat. They viewed the war as a noble cause but only a temporary setback in the South's ultimate vindication.

More than Freedom: African-American Aspirations in 1865

WHAT WERE African American aspirations in 1865?

I f black people could have peered into the minds of white Southerners, they would have been stunned. The former slaves did not initially even dream of social equality; far less did they plot the kind of vengeful murder and mayhem white people feared. They did harbor two potentially contradictory aspirations. The first was to be left alone, free of white supervision. The second was land, voting and civil rights, and education. To secure these, they needed the intervention and support of the white power structure.

The first step Congress took beyond emancipation was to establish the Bureau of Refugees, Freedmen, and Abandoned Lands in March 1865. Congress envisioned the **Freedmen's Bureau**, as it came to be called, as a multipurpose agency to provide social, educational, and economic services, advice, and protection to former slaves and destitute whites. The Bureau marked the federal government's first foray into social welfare legislation. Congress also authorized the bureau to rent confiscated and abandoned farmland to freedmen in 40-acre plots with an option to buy. This auspicious beginning to realizing African-American aspirations belied the great disappointments that lay ahead.

EDUCATION

The greatest success of the Freedmen's Bureau was in education. The bureau coordinated more than fifty northern philanthropic and religious groups, which in turn established three thousand freedmen's schools in the South serving 150,000 men, women, and children.

Initially, single young women from the Northeast comprised much of the teaching force. One of them, a 26-year-old Quaker named Martha Schofield, came to Aiken, South Carolina, from rural Pennsylvania in 1865. The school she founded has been part of Aiken's public school system since 1953.

By the time Schofield opened her own school in 1871, black teachers outnumbered white teachers in the "colored" schools. Support for them came from black churches, especially the African Methodist Episcopal (AME) Church. The former slaves crowded into basements, shacks, and churches to attend school. At the end of the Civil War, only about 10 percent of black Southerners were literate, compared with more than 70 percent of the white Southerners. Within a decade, the freedmen's schools had reduced illiteracy among the former slaves to below 70 percent.

Some black Southerners went on to one of the thirteen colleges established by the American Missionary Association and black and white churches. Between 1860 and 1880 more than one thousand black Southerners earned college degrees at institutions still serving students today such as Howard University in Washington, D.C., Fisk University in Nashville, and Biddle Institute (now Johnson C. Smith University) in Charlotte.

Pursuing freedom of the mind involved challenges beyond those of learning to read and write. Many white Southerners condemned efforts at "Negro improvement." They viewed the time spent on education as wasted, forcing the former slaves to catch their lessons in bits and pieces between work, often by candlelight or on Sundays. After the Freedmen's Bureau folded in 1872, education for black Southerners became more haphazard.

WHERE TO LEARN MORE

Penn Center Historic District, St. Helena Island, South Carolina
www.penncenter.com

Freedmen's Bureau Agency established by Congress in March 1865 to provide social, educational, and economic services, advice, and protection to former slaves and destitute whites; lasted seven years.

The engraving shows Southerners decorating the graves of rebel soldiers at Hollywood Memorial Cemetery in Virginia, 1867. Northerners and Southerners alike honored their war dead. But in the South, the practice of commemorating fallen soldiers became an important element in maintaining the myth of the Lost Cause that colored white Southerners' view of the war.

The Granger Collection, New York

"FORTY ACRES AND A MULE"

Although education was important to the freed slaves in their quest for civic equality, land ownership offered them the promise of economic independence.

Even before the war's end, rumors circulated through black communities in the South that the government would provide each black family with 40 acres and a mule. These rumors were fueled by General William T. Sherman's **Field Order No. 15** in January 1865, which set aside a vast swath of abandoned land along the South Atlantic coast from the Charleston area to northern Florida for grants of up to 40 acres. The Freedmen's Bureau likewise raised expectations when it was initially authorized to rent 40-acre plots of confiscated or abandoned land to freedmen.

By June 1865, about forty thousand former slaves had settled on "Sherman land" along the southeastern coast. In 1866, Congress passed the **Southern Homestead Act**, giving black people preferential access to public lands in five southern states. By the late 1870s, more than fourteen thousand African-American families had taken advantage of a program to finance land purchases with state-funded, long-term, low-interest loans.

Land ownership did not ensure financial success. Most black-owned farms were small and on marginal land. Black farmers also had trouble obtaining credit to purchase or expand their holdings. A lifetime of field work left some freedmen without the managerial skills to operate a farm.

The vast majority of former slaves, especially those in the Lower South, never fulfilled their dreams of land ownership. Rumors to the contrary, the federal government never intended to implement a land redistribution program in the South. General Sherman viewed his field order as a temporary measure to support freedmen for the remainder of the war. President Andrew Johnson nullified the order in September 1865, returning confiscated lands to their former owners. Even Republican supporters of black land ownership questioned the constitutionality of seizing privately owned real estate. They envisioned former slaves assuming the status of free laborers, not necessarily of independent landowners.

For most officials of the Freedmen's Bureau, who shared these views, reviving the southern economy was a higher priority than helping former slaves acquire farms. They wanted both to get the crop in the field and start the South on the road to a free labor system. They thus encouraged freedmen to work for their former masters under contract and postpone their quest for land.

At first, agents of the Freedmen's Bureau supervised labor contracts between former slaves and masters. But after 1867, bureau surveillance declined. Agents assumed that both black laborers and white landowners had become accustomed to the mutual obligations of contracts. The bureau, however, underestimated the power of white landowners to coerce favorable terms or to ignore those they did not like.

MIGRATION TO CITIES

While some black Southerners asserted their rights as workers on southern farms, others affirmed their freedom by moving to towns and cities. Even before the war, the city had offered slaves and free black people a measure of freedom unknown in the rural South. After the war, African Americans moved to cities to find families, seek work, escape the tedium and supervision of farm life, or simply test their right to move about. Between 1860 and 1870, the official African American population in every major Southern city rose significantly.

WHERE TO LEARN MORE

Hampton University Museum, Hampton, Virginia
www.hamptonu.edu/museum

Field Order No. 15 Order by General William T. Sherman in January 1865 to set aside abandoned land along the southern Atlantic coast for forty-acre grants to freedmen, rescinded by President Andrew Johnson later that year.

Southern Homestead Act Largely unsuccessful law passed in 1866 that gave black people preferential access to public lands in five southern states.

Milk sampling at Hampton Institute. Hampton, which opened in Virginia in 1868, was one of the first of several schools established with the help of Northern philanthropic and missionary societies to allow freedmen to pursue a college education. Hampton stressed agricultural and vocational training. The military uniforms were typical for male students, black and white, at agricultural and mechanical schools.

Courtesy of Hampton University Archives

Once in the city, freedmen had to find a home and a job. They usually settled for the cheapest accommodations in low-lying areas or on the outskirts of town where building codes did not apply. Rather than developing one large ghetto, as in many Northern cities, black Southerners lived in several concentrations in and around cities.

Sometimes armed with a letter of reference from their former masters, black people went door to door to seek employment. Many found work serving white families—as guards, laundresses, maids—for very low wages. Both skilled and unskilled laborers found work rebuilding war-torn cities like Atlanta. Most rural black Southerners, however, arrived in cities untrained in the kinds of skills sought in an urban work force and so worked as unskilled laborers. In both Atlanta and Nashville, black people comprised more than 75 percent of the unskilled work force in 1870.

FAITH AND FREEDOM

Religious faith framed and inspired the efforts of African Americans to test their freedom on the farm and in the city. White Southerners used religion to transform the Lost Cause from a shattering defeat to a premonition of a greater destiny. Black Southerners, in contrast, saw emancipation in biblical terms as the beginning of an exodus from bondage to the Promised Land.

Some black churches in the postwar South originated in the slavery era, but most split from white-dominated congregations after the war. The church became a primary focus of African-American life. It gave black people the opportunity to hone skills in self-government and administration that white-dominated society denied them. Within the supportive confines of the congregation, they could assume leadership positions, render important decisions, deal with financial matters, and engage in politics. The church also operated as an educational institution.

The church spawned other organizations that served the black community over the next century. Burial societies, Masonic lodges, temperance groups, trade unions, and drama clubs originated in churches. By the 1870s, African Americans in Memphis had more than two hundred such organizations.

African Americans took great pride in their churches, which became visible measures of their progress. In Charleston, the first building erected after the war was a black church. Black people donated a greater proportion of their earnings to their churches than white people did. The church and the congregation were a cohesive force in black communities. They supported families under stress from discrimination and poverty. Most black churches looked inward to strengthen their members against the harsh realities of postbellum Southern society. Few ministers dared to engage in or even support protest activities. Some, especially those in the Colored Methodist Episcopal Church, counseled congregants to abide by the rules of second-class citizenship and to trust in God's will to right the wrongs of racism.

Northern-based denominations, however, notably the AME Church, were more aggressive advocates of black rights. AME ministers stressed the responsibility of individual black people to realize God's will of racial equality. Henry McNeal Turner, probably the most influential AME minister of his day, helped expand the denomination into the South from its small primarily northern base at the end of the Civil War. His church elevated him to bishop in 1880.

Turner's career and the efforts of former slaves in the classroom, on the farm, in cities, and in the churches reflect the enthusiasm and expectations with which black Southerners greeted freedom. But the majority of white Southerners were unwilling to see those expectations fulfilled. For this reason, African Americans could not secure the fruits of their emancipation without the support and

The black church was the center of African American life in the postwar urban South. Most black churches formed after the Civil War, but some, such as the first African Baptist Church in Richmond, shown here in an 1874 engraving, traced their origins to before 1861.

The Granger Collection, New York

CHRONOLOGY

1863	Lincoln proposes his Ten Percent Plan.
1864	Congress proposes the Wade Davis Bill.
1865	Sherman issues Field Order No. 15. Freedmen's Bureau is established. Andrew Johnson succeeds to the presidency, unveils his Reconstruction plan. Massachusetts desegregates all public facilities. Black people in several Southern cities organize Union Leagues. Former Confederate states begin to pass black codes.
1866	Congress passes Southern Homestead Act, Civil Rights Act of 1866. Ku Klux Klan is founded. Fourteenth Amendment to the Constitution is passed (ratified in 1868). President Johnson goes on a speaking tour.
1867	Congress passes Military Reconstruction Acts, Tenure of Office Act.
1868	President Johnson is impeached and tried in the Senate for defying the Tenure of Office Act. Republican Ulysses S. Grant is elected president.
1869	Fifteenth Amendment passed (ratified 1870).
1870	Congress passes Enforcement Act. Republican regimes topple in North Carolina and Georgia.

1871	Congress passes Ku Klux Klan Act.
1872	Freedmen's Bureau closes down. Liberal Republicans emerge as a separate party. Ulysses S. Grant is reelected.
1873	Severe depression begins. Colfax Massacre occurs. U.S. Supreme Court's decision in the *Slaughter-house* cases weakens the intent of the Fourteenth Amendment. Texas falls to the Democrats in the fall elections.
1874	White Leaguers attempt a coup against the Republican government of New Orleans. Democrats win off year elections across the South amid widespread fraud and violence.
1875	Congress passes Civil Rights Act of 1875.
1876	Supreme Court's decision in *United States* v. *Cruikshank* nullifies Enforcement Act of 1870. Outcome of the presidential election between Republican Rutherford B. Hayes and Democrat Samuel J. Tilden is contested.
1877	Compromise of 1877 makes Hayes president and ends Reconstruction.

protection of the federal government, and the issue of freedom was therefore inextricably linked to that of the rejoining of the Confederacy to the Union, as expressed in federal Reconstruction policy.

FEDERAL RECONSTRUCTION, 1865–1870

W hen the Civil War ended in 1865, no acceptable blueprint existed for reconstituting the Union. In 1863, Lincoln proposed to readmit a seceding state if 10 percent of its prewar voters took an oath of loyalty to the Union and it prohibited slavery in a new state constitution. But this Ten Percent Plan did not require states to grant equal civil and political rights to former slaves, and many Republicans in Congress thought it was not stringent enough. In 1864, a group of them responded with the Wade-Davis Bill, which required a *majority* of a state's prewar voters to pledge their loyalty to the Union and demanded guarantees of black equality before the law. The bill was passed, but Lincoln kept it from becoming law by refusing to sign it (an action known as a pocket veto).

The controversy over these plans reflected two obstacles to Reconstruction that would continue to plague the ruling Republicans after the war. First, neither the Constitution nor legal precedent offered any guidance on whether the president or Congress should take the lead on Reconstruction policy. Second, there was no agreement on what that policy should be.

HOW DID Presidential Reconstruction differ from Congressional Reconstruction?

16–2
Carl Schurz, Report on the Condition of the South (1865)

President Andrew Johnson, some conservative Republicans, and most Democrats believed that because the Constitution made no mention of secession, the Southern states never left the Union, so there was no need for a formal process to readmit them. Moderate and radical Republicans disagreed, arguing that the defeated states had forfeited their rights. Moderates and radicals parted company, however, on the conditions necessary for readmission to the Union. No group held a majority in Congress, and legislators sometimes changed their positions (see the overview table "Contrasting Views of Reconstruction").

PRESIDENTIAL RECONSTRUCTION, 1865–1867

When the Civil War ended in April 1865, Congress was not in session and would not reconvene until December. Thus the responsibility for developing a Reconstruction policy initially fell on Andrew Johnson, who succeeded to the presidency upon Lincoln's assassination. Johnson seemed well suited to the difficult task. Johnson was the only Southern senator to remain in the U.S. Senate after secession. This defiant Unionism won him popular acclaim in the North and credibility among Republican leaders.

Most Northerners and many Republicans approved Johnson's Reconstruction plan when he unveiled it in May 1865. Johnson extended pardons and restored property rights, except in slaves, to Southerners who swore an oath of allegiance to the Union and the Constitution. The plan had nothing to say about the voting rights and civil rights of former slaves.

Northern Democrats applauded the plan's silence on these issues and its promise of a quick restoration of the Southern states to the Union. They expected the Southern states to favor their party and expand its political power. White Southerners, however, were not so favorably impressed, and their response turned Northern public opinion against the president. On the two great issues of freedom and reunion, white Southerners quickly demonstrated their eagerness to reverse the results of the Civil War. Although most states accepted President Johnson's modest requirements, several objected to one or more provisions. Mississippi and Texas refused to ratify the Thirteenth Amendment, which abolished slavery. South Carolina declined to nullify its secession ordinance. No Southern state authorized black voting. When Johnson ordered special congressional elections in the South in the fall of 1865, the all-white electorate returned many prominent Confederate leaders to office.

In late 1865, the newly elected Southern state legislatures revised their antebellum slave codes. The updated and renamed **black codes** allowed local officials to arrest black people who could not document employment and residence, or who were "disorderly," and sentence them to forced labor on farms or road construction crews. The codes also restricted black people to certain occupations, barred them from jury duty, and forbade them to possess firearms. (see American Views: "Mississippi's 1865 Black Codes"). President Johnson did not seem perturbed about this turn of events.

The Republican-dominated Congress reconvened in December 1865 in a belligerent mood. A consensus formed among radical Republicans, who comprised nearly half of the party's strength in Congress, that to gain readmission, a state would have to extend suffrage to black citizens, protect freedmen's civil rights, and have its white citizens officially acknowledge these rights. Some radicals also supported the redistribution of land to former slaves, but few pressed for social equality.

Thaddeus Stevens of Pennsylvania led the radical forces in the House of Representatives, while abolitionist veteran Charles Sumner of Massachusetts rallied radicals in the Senate. Stevens dreamed of a South populated by white and black yeoman farmers. With no large plantations and few landless farmers, the

Black codes   Laws passed by states and municipalities denying many rights of citizenship to free blacks after the Civil War.

• AMERICAN VIEWS •

MISSISSIPPI'S 1865 BLACK CODES

White Southerners feared emancipation would produce a labor crisis; freedmen, they expected, would either refuse to work or strike hard bargains with their former masters. White Southerners also recoiled from having to treat former slaves as social equals. Thus, beginning in late 1865, several Southern states, including Mississippi, enacted laws to control black labor, mobility, and social status. Northerners saw the codes as a bold move to deny the result of the war and its consequences.

HOW DID the black codes fit into President Andrew Johnson's Reconstruction program? Some Northerners charged that the black codes were a backdoor attempt at reestablishing slavery. Do you agree?

From an Act to Confer Civil Rights on Freedmen, and for other Purposes

Section 1. All freedmen, free negroes and mulattoes may sue and be sued, implead and be impleaded, in all the courts of law and equity of this State, and may acquire personal property, and choose in action, by descent or purchase, and may dispose of the same in the same manner and to the same extent that white persons may: Provided, That the provisions of this section shall

not be so construed as to allow any freedman, free negro or mulatto to rent or lease any lands or tenements except in incorporated cities or towns, in which places the corporate authorities shall control the same.

From an Act to Amend the Vagrant Laws of the State

Section 2. All freedmen, free negroes and mulattoes in this State, over the age of eighteen years, found on the second Monday in January, 1866, or thereafter, with no lawful employment or business, or found unlawful assembling themselves together, either in the day or night time, and all white persons assembling themselves with freedmen, Free negroes or mulattoes, or usually associating with freedmen, free negroes or mulattoes, on terms of equality, or living in adultery or fornication with a freed woman, freed negro or mulatto, shall be deemed vagrants, and on conviction thereof shall be fined in a sum not exceeding, in the case of a freedman, free negro or mulatto, fifty dollars, and a white man two hundred dollars, and imprisonment at the discretion of the court, the free negro not exceeding ten days, and the white man not exceeding six months.

Source: "Laws in Relation to Freedmen," 39 Congress, 2 Session, Senate Executive Document 6, Freedmen's Affairs, 182–86.

South would become an ideal republic, a boon to the rest of the nation instead of a burden. Few shared his vision, and when he died in 1868, a reporter noted that "no man was oftener outvoted."

Charles Sumner was among the foremost abolitionist politicians before the Civil War. His combative nature won him few friends, even within his own party. As fierce as Stevens was in the promotion of black civil and political rights after the war, he also believed that the Reconstruction era offered a "golden moment" to remake the South into an egalitarian region. Sumner died in 1874 as his dream was fading.

But the radicals could not unite behind a program, and it fell to their moderate colleagues to take the first steps toward a Congressional Reconstruction plan. The moderates shared the radicals' desire to protect the former slaves' civil and voting rights, but they would not support land redistribution schemes or punitive measures against prominent Confederates. The Civil Rights Act of 1866 was a direct response to the black codes. The act specified the civil rights to which all U.S. citizens were entitled. In creating a category of national citizenship with rights that superseded state laws restricting them, the act changed federal–state relations (and in the process overturned the *Dred Scott* decision). President Johnson

QUICK REVIEW

Thaddeus Stevens
- Stevens of Pennsylvania led the radical forces in the House of Representatives.
- Stevens envisioned a South with no large plantations and few landless farmers.
- Stevens found few supporters for his ideas.

OVERVIEW

CONTRASTING VIEWS OF RECONSTRUCTION: PRESIDENT AND CONGRESS

Politician or Group	Policy on Former Slaves	Policy on Readmission of Former Confederate States
President Johnson	Opposed to black suffrage Silent on protection of black civil rights Opposed to land redistribution	Maintained that rebellious states were already readmitted Granted pardons and restoration of property to all who swore allegiance to the United States
Radical Republicans	Favored black suffrage Favored protection of black civil rights Favored land redistribution	Favored treating rebellious states as territories and establishing military districts* Favored limiting franchise to black people and loyal white people
Moderate Republicans	Favored black suffrage Favored protection of civil rights Opposed land redistribution	Favored some restrictions on white suffrage* Favored requiring states to meet various requirements before being readmitted* Split on military rule

* True of most but not all members of the group.

vetoed the act, but it became law when Congress mustered a two-thirds majority to override his veto, the first time in American history that Congress passed major legislation over a president's veto.

Andrew Johnson's position reflected both his view of government and his racial attitudes. The Republican president remained a Democrat in spirit. Like most Democrats, he favored a balance between federal and state power. He also shared with many of his white Southern neighbors a belief in black inferiority.

To keep freedmen's rights safe from presidential vetoes, state legislatures, and federal courts, the Republican-dominated Congress moved to incorporate some of the provisions of the 1866 Civil Rights Act into the Constitution with an amendment. The **Fourteenth Amendment**, which Congress passed in June 1866, addressed the issues of civil and voting rights. It guaranteed every citizen equality before the law. The two key sections of the amendment prohibited states from violating the civil rights of their citizens, thus outlawing the black codes, and gave states the choice of enfranchising black people or losing representation in Congress.

The amendment disappointed advocates of woman suffrage, because for the first time the word *male* in the Constitution was used to define who could vote. Susan B. Anthony, who had campaigned for the abolition of slavery before the war and helped mount a petition drive that collected 400,000 signatures for the Thirteenth Amendment, formed the American Equal Rights Association in 1866 with her colleagues to push for woman suffrage at the state level.

The amendment had little immediate impact on the South. Although enforcement of black codes diminished, white violence against blacks increased. In the 1870s, several decisions by the U.S. Supreme Court would weaken the amendment's provisions. Eventually, however, the Fourteenth Amendment would play a major role in securing the civil rights of African Americans when the issue reemerged in the 1950s.

President Johnson seemed to encourage white intransigence by openly denouncing the Fourteenth Amendment. The president's diatribes against the Republican Congress won him followers in those Northern states with a reservoir of opposition

Fourteenth Amendment Passed by Congress in 1866, guaranteed every citizen equality before the law by prohibiting states from violating the civil rights of their citizens, thus outlawing the black codes.

to black suffrage. But the tone and manner of his campaign offended many as undignified. In the November elections, Republicans managed better than two-thirds majorities in both the House and Senate, sufficient to override presidential vetoes. Radical Republicans, joined by moderate colleagues buoyed by the election results and revolted by the president's and the South's intransigence, seized the initiative.

CONGRESSIONAL RECONSTRUCTION, 1867–1870

The radicals' first salvo in their attempt to take control over Reconstruction occurred with the passage over President Johnson's veto of the Military Reconstruction Acts. The measures, passed in March 1867, inaugurated a period known as **Congressional Reconstruction** or Radical Reconstruction. They generally divided the ex-Confederate states into five military districts (see Map 16–1) and provided for elections to a state constitutional convention guaranteeing universal manhood suffrage.

The Reconstruction Acts fulfilled the radicals' three major objectives. First, they secured the freedmen's right to vote. Second, they made it likely that Southern states would be run by Republican regimes that would enforce the new constitutions, protect former slaves' rights, and maintain the Republican majority in Congress. Finally, the acts set standards for readmission that required the South to accept the consequences of defeat: the preeminence of the federal government and the end of involuntary servitude.

To limit presidential interference with their policies, Republicans passed the Tenure of Office Act, prohibiting the president from removing certain officeholders without the Senate's consent. Johnson, angered at what he believed was an unconstitutional attack on presidential authority, deliberately violated the act in February 1868. He fired Secretary of War Edwin M. Stanton, a leading radical. The House responded to this defiance of congressional authority by approving, for the first time in American history, articles of impeachment against the president. The Senate voted thirty-five to nineteen to convict, one vote short of the two-thirds necessary to remove Johnson. The outcome weakened the radicals' clout in Congress and eased the way for moderate Republican Ulysses S. Grant to gain the party's nomination for president in 1868.

The Republicans viewed the 1868 presidential election as a referendum on Congressional Reconstruction. Grant won the election, but his margin of victory was uncomfortably narrow.

The Republicans retained a strong majority in both houses of Congress and managed to pass another major piece of Reconstruction legislation, the **Fifteenth Amendment**, in February 1869. In response to growing concerns about voter fraud and violence against freedmen, the amendment guaranteed the right of American men to vote, regardless of race. Although the amendment provided a loophole allowing states to impose restrictions on the right to vote based on literacy requirements or property qualifications, it was nonetheless a milestone. It made the right to vote perhaps the most distinguishing characteristic of American citizenship.

The Fifteenth Amendment allowed states to keep the franchise a male prerogative. Susan B. Anthony now broke with her abolitionist colleagues and opposed the amendment. Fellow abolitionist and woman suffragist Elizabeth Cady Stanton warned

MAP EXPLORATION
To explore an interactive version of this map, go to
http://www.prenhall.com/goldfield2/map16.1

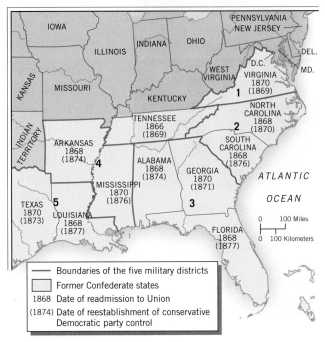

MAP 16–1

Congressional Reconstruction, 1865–1877   When Congress wrested control of Reconstruction policy from President Andrew Johnson, it divided the South into the five military districts depicted here. The commanding generals for each district held the authority both to hold elections and decide who could vote.

WHAT DID each of the former Confederate states have to do to be eligible for readmission to the Union?

QUICK REVIEW

The Tenure of Office Act and Johnson's Impeachment

♦ Act prohibited the president from removing certain officeholders without the Senate's consent.

♦ Johnson deliberately violated the act in February 1868.

♦ Johnson escaped impeachment by one vote.

Congressional Reconstruction   Name given to the period 1867–1870 when the Republican-dominated Congress controlled Reconstruction era policy.

Fifteenth Amendment   Passed by Congress in 1869, guaranteed the right of American men to vote, regardless of race.

Casting a ballot. Black voters in Richmond vote on a state constitutional conventions in 1867. A key objective of Congressional Reconstruction was to secure the voting rights of freedman.

The Granger Collection, New York

WHERE TO LEARN MORE

★ Beauvoir, Biloxi, Mississippi
www.beauvoir.org

Scalawags Southern whites, mainly small landowning farmers and well-off merchants and planters, who supported the Southern Republican party during Reconstruction.

Carpetbaggers Northern transplants to the South, many of whom were Union soldiers who stayed in the South after the war.

Union Leagues Republican party organizations in Northern cities that became an important organizing device among freedmen in Southern cities after 1865.

that "if you do not wish the lower orders of Chinese, African, Germans and Irish, with their low ideas of womanhood to make laws for you and your daughters . . . awake to the danger . . . and demand that woman, too, shall be represented in the government!" Such ethnic and racial animosity created a major rift in the nascent women's movement. Women who supported the amendment formed the New England Woman Suffrage Association, challenging Anthony's American Equal Rights Association.

SOUTHERN REPUBLICAN GOVERNMENTS, 1867–1870

Away from Washington, the first order of business was to draft state constitutions. The documents embodied progressive principles new to the former Confederacy. They mandated the election of numerous local and state offices. Self-perpetuating local elites could no longer appoint themselves or cronies to powerful positions. The constitutions committed Southern states, many for the first time, to public education. Lawmakers enacted a variety of reforms, including social welfare, penal reform, legislative reapportionment, and universal manhood suffrage.

The Republican regimes that gained control in Southern states promoted vigorous state government and the protection of civil and voting rights. Three diverse Republican constituencies supported these governments. One consisted of white natives, most of them yeomen farmers, who resided mainly in the upland regions of the South and long ignored by lowland planters and merchants in state government. The conflict had left many of them devastated. They struggled to keep their land and hoped for an easing of credit and for debt-stay laws to help them escape foreclosure. They wanted public schools for their children and good roads to get their crops to market. Collectively, these native white Southerners were called **scalawags**, a derogatory term derived from the name of the district of Scalloway, on Scotland's Shetland Islands, known for its scraggly livestock. The term was first applied in western New York before the Civil War to an idle person and then to a mischievous one. Although their opponents may have perceived them as a unified group, scalawags in fact held a variety of views.

Northern transplants, or **carpetbaggers**, as their opponents called them, constituted a second group of Southern Republicans. The term also had antebellum origins, referring to a suspicious stranger. Cartoonists depicted carpetbaggers as shoddily dressed and poorly groomed men, their worldly possessions in a ratty cloth satchel, slinking into a town and swindling the locals before departing with their ill-gotten gains. The reality was far different from the caricature. Many were Union soldiers who simply enjoyed the climate and perhaps married a local woman. Most were drawn by economic opportunity. Land was cheap and the price of cotton high. Some also hoped to aid the freedmen.

Carpetbaggers never comprised more than 2 percent of any state's population. Most white Southerners viewed them as an alien presence, instruments of a hated occupying force. They provoked resentment because they seemed to prosper while most Southerners struggled in poverty.

African Americans constituted the Republican party's largest Southern constituency. In three states—South Carolina, Mississippi, and Louisiana—they also formed the majority of eligible voters. They viewed the franchise as the key to civic equality and economic opportunity and demanded an active role in party and government affairs. In February 1865, black people in Norfolk, Virginia, gathered to demand a say in the new government that Union supporters were forming in that portion of the state. In April, they created the Colored Monitor Union club, modeled after Republican party organizations in northern cities, called **Union Leagues**. They demanded "the right of *universal* suffrage" for "*all* loyal men, without distinction of color." Despite white threats, black people thronged to Union League meetings in 1867, even forging interracial alliances in states such as North Carolina and Alabama. Focusing on political education and recruitment, the leagues successfully mobilized black voters.

Black Southerners were not content just to vote; they also demanded political office. The number of Southern black congressmen in the U.S. House of Representatives increased from two in 1869 to seven in 1873, and more than six hundred African Americans, most of them former slaves from plantation counties, were elected to Southern state legislatures between 1867 and 1877.

White fears that black officeholders would enact vengeful legislation proved unfounded. African Americans generally did not promote race-specific legislation. Rather, they supported measures such as debt relief and state funding for education that benefited all poor and working-class people. Like all politicians, however, black officials in Southern cities sought to enact measures beneficial to their constituents.

Republicans gained support by expanding the role of state government to a degree unprecedented in the South. Southern Republican administrations appealed to hard-pressed upland whites by prohibiting foreclosure and passing stay laws that allowed farm owners extra time to repay debts. They undertook building programs that benefited both blacks and whites, erecting hospitals, schools, and orphanages. Stepping further into social policy than most Northern states at the time, Republican governments in the South expanded women's property rights, enacted legislation against child abuse, and required child support from fathers of mulatto children. In South Carolina, the Republican government provided medical care for the poor; in Alabama, it provided free legal aid for needy defendants.

Despite these impressive policies, southern Republicans were unable to hold their diverse constituency together. The high costs of their activist policies further undermined the Republicans by forcing them to raise state taxes. Small property holders, already reeling from declining staple prices, found the taxes especially burdensome, despite liberal stay laws. Revenues nonetheless could not keep pace with expenditures. The expenditures and the liberal use of patronage sometimes resulted in waste and corruption.

COUNTER-RECONSTRUCTION, 1870–1874

Republicans might have survived battles over patronage, differences over policy, and the resentment provoked by extravagant expenditures and high taxes; but they could not overcome racism. Racism killed Republican rule in the South because it deepened divisions within the party, encouraged white violence, and eroded support in the North. Southern Democrats discovered that they could use race baiting and racial violence to create racial solidarity among white people that overrode their economic and class differences. Unity translated into election victories.

Northerners responded to the persistent violence in the South not with outrage but with a growing sense of tedium. Racism became respectable. Noted intellectuals and journalists espoused "scientific" theories that claimed to demonstrate the natural superiority of white people over black people. These theories influenced the Liberal Republicans, followers of a new political movement that splintered the Republican party, further weakening its will to pursue Reconstruction policy.

By 1874, Americans were concerned with an array of domestic problems that overshadowed Reconstruction. With the rest of the nation thus distracted and weary, white Southerners reclaimed control of the South.

THE USES OF VIOLENCE

Racial violence preceded Republican rule. As African Americans moved about, attempted to vote, haggled over labor contracts, and carried arms as part of occupying Union forces, they tested the patience of white Southerners.

WHAT ROLE did the Ku Klux Klan play in Counter-Reconstruction?

16–8
Albion W. Tourgee, Letter on Ku Klux Klan Activities (1870)

The Klan directed violence at African Americans primarily for political activity. Here, a black man, John Campbell, vainly begs for mercy in Moore County, North Carolina, in August 1871.

The Granger Collection, New York

Ku Klux Klan   Perhaps the most prominent of the vigilante groups that terrorized black people in the South during Reconstruction era, founded by Confederate veterans in 1866.

Cities, where black and white people competed for jobs and where black political influence was most visible, became flashpoints for interracial violence.

White paramilitary groups flourished in the South during the Reconstruction era and were responsible for much of the violence directed against African Americans. Probably the best known of these groups was the **Ku Klux Klan**. Founded in Tennessee by six Confederate veterans in 1866, the Klan was initially a social club that soon assumed a political purpose. Klan night riders in ghostlike disguises intimidated black communities. The Klan directed much of its violence toward subverting the electoral process. One historian has estimated that roughly 10 percent of all black delegates to the 1867 state constitutional conventions in the South became victims of political violence during the next decade. The most serious example of political violence occurred in Colfax, Louisiana, in 1873 when a white Democratic mob attempted to wrest control of local government from Republicans. For three weeks, black defenders held the town against the white onslaught. When the white mob finally broke through, they massacred the remaining black people, including those who had surrendered and laid down their weapons.

Racial violence and the combative reaction it provoked both among black people and Republican administrations energized white voters. Democrats regained power in North Carolina during the election of 1870, and that same year, the Republican regime in Georgia fell as well.

The federal government responded with a variety of legislation. One example was the Fifteenth Amendment, ratified in 1869, which guaranteed the right to vote. Another was the Enforcement Act of 1870, which enabled the federal government to appoint supervisors in states that failed to protect citizens' voting rights. A more sweeping measure was the Ku Klux Klan Act of 1871, which permitted federal authorities, with military assistance, if necessary, to arrest and prosecute members of groups that denied a citizen's civil rights if state authorities failed to do so and established a new precedent in federal–state relations.

THE FAILURE OF NORTHERN WILL

The success of political violence after 1871 reflected less the inadequacy of congressional legislation than the failure of will on the part of Northern Republicans to follow through on commitments to Southern Republican administrations. The commitment to voting rights for black Southerners, widespread among Republicans in 1865 and affirmed in the Fifteenth Amendment passed in 1869, faded as well. American politics in the 1870s seemed increasingly corrupt and irresponsible. Scandal abounded. Democratic boss William M. Tweed and his associates transformed Tammany Hall, a Democratic club, into a full-fledged political machine that robbed New York City of an astounding $100 million. Federal officials allowed private individuals to manipulate the stock market for spectacular gains. Several members of Congress and President Grant's vice president exchanged government favors for railroad stock.

Racism gained an aura of scientific respectability in the late nineteenth century. Science was held in high esteem at the time, helping assure public acceptance of the putatively scientific views of the racial theorists. According to those views, some peoples are inherently inferior to others, a natural state of affairs that no government interference can change.

Concerns about the quality of the electorate, also tinged with racism, reflected the rising stakes of public office in post–Civil War America. The urban industrial economy boomed in the five years after the war. Engineers flung railroads across the continent. Steam propelled factories to unprecedented levels of productivity and ships to new speed records. Discoveries of rich natural resources such as oil and iron presaged a new age of industrial might. Republicans promoted and benefited from the boom, and it influenced their priorities. Railroad, mining, and lumber lobbyists crowded Washington and state capitals begging for financial subsidies and favorable legislation. In an era before conflict-of-interest laws, leading Republicans sat on the boards of railroads, land development companies, and industrial corporations. While the federal government denied land to the freedmen, it doled out millions of acres to corporations.

Not all Republicans approved the party's promotion of economic development. Some questioned the prudence of government intervention in the "natural" operation of the nation's economy. The emerging scandals of the Grant administration led to calls for reform. Republican governments, North and South, were condemned for their lavish spending and high taxes. The time had come to restore good government.

LIBERAL REPUBLICANS AND THE ELECTION OF 1872

Liberal Republicans put forward an array of suggestions to improve government and save the Republican party. They advocated civil service reform to reduce reliance on patronage and the abuses that accompanied office seeking. To limit government and reduce artificial economic stimuli, the reformers called for tariff reduction and an end to federal land grants to railroads. For the South, they recommended a general amnesty for white people and a return to "local self-government" by men of "property and enterprise."

When the Liberals failed to convince other Republicans to adopt their program, they broke with the party. Taking advantage of this split, the Democrats forged an alliance with the Liberals. Together, the Democrats and Liberals nominated journalist Horace Greeley to challenge Ulysses S. Grant for the presidency in the election of 1872. Grant won resoundingly, helped by high turnout among black voters in the South. The election suggested that the excesses of the Grant administration had not yet exceeded public tolerance and that the Republican experiment in the South retained some public support. But within a year, an economic depression, continued violence in the South, and the persistent corruption of the Grant administration would turn public opinion against the Republicans. With this shift, support for Reconstruction and black rights would also fade.

REDEMPTION, 1874–1877

For Southern Democrats, the Republican victory in 1872 underscored the importance of turning out larger numbers of white voters and restricting the black vote. They accomplished these goals over the next four years with a surge in political violence. Preoccupied with corruption and economic crisis and increasingly indifferent, if not hostile, to African-American aspirations, most Americans looked the other way. The elections of 1876—on the local, state, and national levels—affirmed the triumph of white Southerners. Reconstruction did not end; it was overthrown. Southern Democrats called their victory "Redemption," and this interpretation of the Reconstruction era would affect race relations for nearly a century.

WHAT WERE the effects of the Civil Rights Act of 1875 and the Compromise of 1877?

THE DEMOCRATS' VIOLENT RESURGENCE

The violence between 1874 and 1876 differed in several respects from earlier attempts to restore white government by force. Attackers operated more openly and more closely identified themselves with the Democratic party. Mounted, gray-clad ex-Confederate soldiers flanked Democratic candidates at campaign rallies and "visited" black neighborhoods afterward to discourage black people from voting. With black people intimidated and white people already prepared to vote, election days were typically quiet.

Democrats swept to victory across the South in the 1874 elections. "A perfect reign of terror" redeemed Alabama for the Democrats. In Louisiana, a group of elite Democrats in New Orleans organized a military organization known as the *White League* in 1874 to challenge the state's Republican government. In September 1874, more than eight thousand White Leaguers staged a coup to overthrow the Republican government of New Orleans.

THE WEAK FEDERAL RESPONSE

Unrest like that in Louisiana also plagued Mississippi and South Carolina. When South Carolina governor Daniel H. Chamberlain could no longer contain the violence in his state in 1876, he asked the president for help. Although President Grant acknowledged the gravity of Chamberlain's situation, the president would only offer the governor the lame hope that South Carolinians would exercise "better judgment and cooperation" and assist the governor in bringing offenders to justice "without aid from the federal Government."

Congress responded to the violence with the Civil Rights Act of 1875. Introduced by Charles Sumner, the bill finally passed in a watered-down version after Sumner's death. The act prohibited discrimination against black people in public accommodations such as theaters, parks, and trains and guaranteed freedmen's rights to serve on juries. It had no provision for voting rights, which Congress presumed the Fifteenth Amendment protected. The only way to enforce the law was for individuals to bring grievances related to it before federal courts in the South.

When black people tested the law by trying to make free use of public accommodations, they were almost always turned away. In 1883, the U.S. Supreme Court overturned the act declaring that only the states, not Congress, could redress "a private wrong, or a crime of the individual."

THE ELECTION OF 1876 AND THE COMPROMISE OF 1877

Reconstruction officially ended with the presidential election of 1876 in which Democrat Samuel J. Tilden ran against Republican Rutherford B. Hayes. When the ballots were counted, it appeared that Tilden, a conservative New Yorker respectable enough for Northern voters and Democratic enough for white Southerners, had won. But despite a majority in the popular vote, disputed returns in three Southern states left him with 184 of the 185 electoral votes needed to win. The three states—Florida, South Carolina, and Louisiana—were the last in the South still to have Republican adminstrations.

Both camps maneuvered intensively in the months following the election to claim the disputed votes. Congress appointed a fifteen-member commission to settle the issue. Eventually the so-called **Compromise of 1877** installed Hayes in the White House and gave Democrats control of all state governments in the South.

Southern Democrats emerged the major winners of the Compromise of 1877. President Hayes and his successors into the next century left the South alone. In practical terms, the Compromise of 1877 signaled the revocation of civil rights and voting rights for black Southerners. The Fourteenth and Fifteenth Amendments would be dead letters in the South until well into the twentieth century. On the two great issues confronting the nation at the end of the Civil War, reunion and freedom, the white South had won. It reentered the Union largely on its own terms with the freedom to pursue a racial agenda consistent with its political, economic, and social interests.

THE MEMORY OF RECONSTRUCTION

Southern Democrats used the memory of Reconstruction to help maintain themselves in power. As white Southerners elevated Civil War heroes into saints, and battles into holy struggles, Reconstruction became the Redemption. Whenever Southern

---

QUICK REVIEW

Civil Rights Act of 1875

◆ Introduced by Charles Sumner, the bill passed in a watered-down version.

◆ Prohibited discrimination in public accommodations.

◆ Overturned by the U.S. Supreme Court in 1883.

Compromise of 1877 The Congressional settling of the 1876 election which installed Republican Rutherford B. Hayes in the White House and gave Democrats control of all state governments in the South.

Democrats felt threatened over the next century, they reminded their white constituents of the "horrors of Reconstruction," the menace of black rule, and the cruelty of Yankee occupiers. The Southern view of Reconstruction permeated textbooks, films, and standard accounts of the period. By the early 1900s, professional historians at the nation's finest institutions concurred in this view, and most Americans believed that the policies of Reconstruction had been misguided and had brought great suffering to the white South. This view allowed the South to maintain its system of racial segregation and exclusion without interference from the federal government.

Not all memories of Reconstruction conformed to this thesis. In 1913, John R. Lynch, a former black Republican congressman from Mississippi, published *The Facts of Reconstruction* to "present the other side." But most Americans ignored his book. Two decades later, W.E.B. Du Bois's *Black Reconstruction* (1935) met a similar fate.

The national historical consensus grew out of a growing national reconciliation concerning the war, a mutual agreement that it was time to move on. Lost in all the good will was the tacit agreement among both Southern and Northern whites that the South was free to work out its own resolution to race relations.

There is much to be said in favor of sectional reconciliation as opposed to persistent animosity. There are enough examples in the world today of antagonists in the same country never forgetting or never forgiving their bloody histories. Ideally, Americans could have had *both* healing and justice, but instead, they settled for the former. Frederick Douglass worried about what the peace that followed the Civil War would mean for race relations: "If war among the whites brought peace and liberty to the blacks, what will peace among the whites bring?" But white Americans seemed intent on shaking hands and getting on with their lives.

THE FAILED PROMISE OF RECONSTRUCTION

Most black people and white people in 1877 would have agreed on one point: Reconstruction had failed. If the demise of Reconstruction elicited a sigh of relief from most white Americans, black Americans greeted it with frustration. Their dreams of land ownership faded as a new labor system relegated them to a lowly position in Southern agriculture. Redemption reversed their economic and political gains and deprived them of most of the civil rights they had enjoyed under Congressional Reconstruction.

The former slaves were certainly better off in 1877 than in 1865. They were free, however limited their freedom. Some owned land; some held jobs in cities. But by 1877, the "golden moment"—an unprecedented opportunity for the nation to live up to its ideals by extending equal rights to all its citizens, black and white alike—had passed.

SHARECROPPING

When they lost political power, black Southerners also lost economic independence. As the Freedmen's Bureau retreated from supervising farm labor contracts and opportunities for black people to possess their own land dried up, the bargaining power of black farm laborers decreased, and the power of white landlords increased.

The upshot was that by the late 1870s, most former slaves in the rural South had been drawn into a subservient position in a new labor system called **sharecropping**. The premise of this system was relatively simple: The landlord furnished the sharecroppers a house, a plot of land to work, seed, some farm animals and farm implements and advanced them credit at a store the landlord typically owned. In exchange, the sharecroppers promised the landlord a share of their crop, usually one-half. The croppers kept the proceeds from the sale of the other half to pay off their debts at the store and save or spend as they and their families saw fit. In theory, a sharecropper could save enough to secure economic independence.

WHY AND how did Reconstruction end, and what were its failed promises?

WHERE TO LEARN MORE

Levi Jordan Plantation, Brazoria County, Texas
www.webarchaeology.com

16–12
A Sharecrop Contract (1882)

Sharecropping Labor system that evolved during and after Reconstruction whereby landowners furnished laborers with a house, farm animals, and tools and advanced credit in exchange for a share of the laborers' crop.

As this Thomas Nast cartoon makes clear, the paramilitary violence against black Southerners in the early 1870s threatened not only the voting rights of freedmen, but also their dreams of education, prosperity, and family life as well. In this context, the slogan, "The Union As It Was" is highly ironic.

Courtesy of Library of Congress

Slaughterhouse cases Group of cases resulting in one sweeping decision by the U.S. Supreme Court in 1873 that contradicted the intent of the Fourteenth Amendment by decreeing that most citizenship rights remained under state, not federal, control.

United States v. *Cruikshank* Supreme Court ruling of 1876 that overturned the convictions of some of those responsible for the Colfax Massacre, ruling that the Enforcement Act applied only to violations of black rights by states, not individuals.

With landlords holding the accounts at the store, black sharecroppers found that the proceeds from their share of the crop never left them very far ahead. In exchange for extending credit to sharecroppers, store owners felt justified in requiring collateral. But sharecroppers had no assets other than the cotton they grew. So Southern states passed crop lien laws, which gave the store owner the right to the next year's crop in exchange for this year's credit. The sharecropper sank deeper into dependence.

Sharecropping represented a significant step down from tenancy. Tenants owned their own draft animals, farm implements, and seed. Once they negotiated with a land owner for a fixed rent, they kept whatever profits they earned. Eventually, they could hope to purchase some land and move into the landlord class themselves.

Historians have often depicted the sharecropping system as a compromise between white landlord and black laborer. But compromise implies a give-and-take between relatively equal negotiators. As Northern and federal support for Reconstruction waned after 1870 and Southern Democrats regained political control, white power over black labor increased. Black people had no recourse to federal and state authorities or, increasingly, to the polls as a white reign of terror stripped them of their political rights.

The only difference between Northern and Southern employers' outlook on labor was that Southerners exercised more control over their workers. What had been a triangular debate—among white Northerners, white Southerners, and freedmen—had become a lopsided discourse divided along racial rather than sectional lines.

MODEST GAINS AND FUTURE VICTORIES

Black Southerners experienced some advances in the decade after the Civil War, but these owed little to Reconstruction. Black families functioned as economic and psychological buffers against unemployment and prejudice. Black churches played crucial roles in their communities. Self-help and labor organizations offered mutual friendship and financial assistance. All of these institutions had existed in the slavery era, although on a smaller scale. And some of them, such as black labor groups, schools, and social welfare associations, endured because comparable white institutions excluded black people. Black people also scored some modest economic successes during the Reconstruction era, mainly from their own pluck.

The Fourteenth and Fifteenth Amendments to the Constitution are among the few bright spots in Reconstruction's otherwise dismal legacy. The Fourteenth Amendment guaranteed former slaves equality before the law; the Fifteenth Amendment protected their right to vote. Both amendments elevated the federal government over the states by protecting freedmen from state attempts to deny them their rights. But the benefits of these two landmark amendments did not accrue to African Americans until well into the twentieth century. In the *Slaughterhouse cases* (1873), the Supreme Court contradicted the intent of the Fourteenth Amendment by decreeing that most citizenship rights remained under state, not federal, control. In *United States v. Cruikshank* (1876), the Court overturned the convictions of some of those responsible for the Colfax Massacre, ruling that the Enforcement Act applied only to violations of black rights by states, not individuals. Within the next two decades, the Supreme Court would uphold the legality of racial segregation and black disfranchisement, in effect declaring that the Fourteenth and Fifteenth Amendments did not apply to African Americans. The Civil War had killed secession forever, but states' rights enjoyed a remarkable revival.

As historian John Hope Franklin accurately concluded, Reconstruction "had no significant or permanent effect on the status of the black in American life. . . . [Black people] made no meaningful steps toward economic independence or even stability."

FROM THEN TO NOW
African-American Voting Rights in the South

Right from the end of the Civil War, white Southerners resisted African-American voting rights. Black people, with equal determination, used the franchise to assert their equal right to participate in the political process. Black voting rights proved so contentious that Congress sought to secure them with the Fourteenth and Fifteenth Amendments to the U.S. Constitution. But U.S. Supreme Court decisions in *United States* v. *Cruikshank* (1876) and in the *Civil Rights Cases* (1883) undermined federal authority to protect the rights of freedmen, including voting rights. A combination of violence, intimidation, and legislation effectively disfranchised black Southerners by the early twentieth century.

During the 1960s, Congress passed legislation designed to override state prohibitions and earlier court decisions limiting African-American voting rights. The key measure, the 1965 Voting Rights Act, not only guaranteed black Southerners (and later, other minorities) the right to register and vote but protected them from procedural subterfuges, many of which dated from the first Reconstruction era; that would dilute their votes. These protections proved necessary because of the extreme racial polarization of Southern elections: White people rarely voted for black candidates.

To ensure African-American candidates an opportunity to win elections, the federal government after 1965 insisted that states and localities establish procedures to increase the likelihood of such a result. As part of this process, the federal government also monitored state redistricting for Congressional elections, which occurs every decade in response to population shifts recorded in the national census.

By the early 1990s, states were being directed to draw districts with majority-black voting populations to ensure African-American representation in the Congress and state legislatures. The federal government cited the South's history of racial discrimination and racially polarized voting to justify these districts. But white Southerners challenged such claims.

In 1993, the U.S. Supreme Court issued a decision in a North Carolina redistricting case, *Shaw* v. *Reno*, that struck down a majority-black Congressional district in that state. Subsequent decisions in other southern districts produced similar rulings. The general principle followed by the Court has been that if race is a key justification for drawing these districts, then they violate the Fourteenth Amendment, which, according to the Court majority, demands color-blind electoral procedures. But, as the late Supreme Court Justice William Brennan noted, "to read the Fourteenth Amendment to state an abstract principle of color-blindness is itself to be blind to history." The framers of the Reconstruction Amendments had the protection of the rights of the freedmen (including and especially voting rights) in mind when they wrote those measures. One voting rights expert has charged that the Court rulings have ushered in a "Second Redemption."

CONCLUSION

Formerly enslaved black Southerners had entered freedom with many hopes, among the most prominent of which was to be let alone. White Southerners, after four bloody years of unwanted attention from the federal government, also longed to be left alone. But they did not include their ex-slaves as equal partners in their vision of solitude. Northerners, too, began to seek escape from the issues and consequences of the war, eventually abandoning their commitment to secure civil and voting rights for black Southerners.

White Southerners robbed blacks of their gains and sought to reduce them again to servitude and dependence, if not to slavery. But in the process, the majority of white people lost as well. Yeoman farmers missed an opportunity to break cleanly from the Old South and establish a more equitable society. Instead, they allowed the old elites to regain power and gradually ignore their needs. They preserved the social benefit of a white skin at the cost of almost everything else. Many lost their farms and sank into tenancy, leasing land from others. Fewer had a voice in state legislatures or Congress. A new South, rid of slavery and sectional antagonism, had indeed emerged, redeemed, regenerated, and disenthralled. But the old South lingered on in the new like Spanish moss on live oaks.

As Federal troops left the South to be redeployed restraining striking workers in the North and suppressing Native Americans on the Great Plains, an era of possibility for American society ended and a new era began. "The southern question is dead," a Charleston newspaper proclaimed in 1877. "The question of labor and capital, work and wages" had moved to the forefront. The chance to redeem the sacrifice of a bloody civil war with a society that fulfilled the promise of the Declaration of Independence and the Constitution for all citizens slipped away. It would take a new generation of African Americans a long century later to revive it.

SUMMARY

White Southerners and the Ghosts of the Confederacy, 1865. While some white Southerners saw the destruction of the Confederacy as punishment, others came to view the war as the "Lost Cause" and would not allow the memory of the Civil War to die. The myth of the Lost Cause was a need to rationalize and justify the devastation and loss of life; the Reconstruction era became the Redemption and forged community in a time of uncertainty about the future. In this mythology, African Americans were cast in the role of adversaries who challenged whites' belief of their own racial superiority.

More than Freedom: African-American Aspirations in 1865 Former slaves wanted to be free of white supervision; they also desired land, voting and civil rights, and education. At the end of the Civil War, African Americans had reason to hope their dreams might be achieved through such actions as the establishment of the Freedmen's Bureau. The vast majority of former slaves was never able to realize their dreams of independent land ownership and continued to work as farm laborers; others migrated to cities. Their religious faith inspired them; they saw their emancipation in biblical terms and the church became the primary focus of the African-American community.

Federal Reconstruction, 1865–1870 The federal government had two great challenges following the Civil War; supporting the freedom of former slaves and rejoining the Confederacy to the Union. No blueprint for Reconstruction existed; the Constitution was silent on the issue and there was no agreement on policy. Presidential Reconstruction and Congressional Reconstruction brought mixed results. The Civil Rights Act and the Fourteenth and Fifteenth Amendments were key legislative acts during this period; however, by 1870, white Southerners were gradually regaining control of their states and using violence and intimidation to erode gains made by African Americans.

Counter-Reconstruction, 1870–1874 While most of the nation was distracted by political scandals and a serious economic depression, white Southerners regained control of the South. Racial violence through groups like the Ku Klux Klan subverted the electoral process; the success of political violence reflected the erosion of Northern support for Congressional Reconstruction.

Redemption, 1874–1877 After more than fifteen years of Reconstruction, Republicans lost interest in policing their former enemies. By 1877 the Redeemers had triumphed, and all the former Confederate states had returned to the Union in the Compromise of 1877 following the disputed 1876 presidential election. Southern states now had all of their rights and many of their leaders restored to pre-Civil War conditions. Freed slaves remained in mostly subservient positions with few of the rights and privileges enjoyed by other Americans.

The Failed Promise of Reconstruction The tacit agreement between Southern and Northern whites was that the South was now free to work out its own resolution to race relations. The price of sectional reconciliation was that the dream that former slaves held of economic independence and equality would not materialize.

The Fourteenth and Fifteenth Amendments were bright spots in the legacy of Reconstruction; the overwhelming majority of African Americans had become landless agricultural workers, eking out a meager income that merchants and landlords often snatched to cover debts. For most, Reconstruction was a failed promise.

REVIEW QUESTIONS

1. Do you think white Southerners should have supported black people's aspirations for civil rights, land, and suffrage? How differently would things had turned out if they had?

2. Is it fair to blame Reconstruction's failures on Southern Republicans? Explain your response.

3. What gains did black people achieve during Reconstruction, despite its overall failure?

4. In T. Thomas Fortune's recollection of a boyhood incident, why was it important for him and his friends to fight back?

KEY TERMS

Black codes   (p. 422)
Carpetbaggers   (p. 426)
Compromise of 1877   (p. 430)
Congressional Reconstruction   (p. 425)
Field Order No. 15   (p. 419)
Fifteenth Amendment   (p. 425)

Fourteenth Amendment   (p. 424)
Freedmen's Bureau   (p. 418)
Ku Klux Klan   (p. 428)
Lost Cause   (p. 417)
Scalawags   (p. 426)
Sharecropping   (p. 431)

Slaughterhouse **cases**   (p. 432)
Southern Homestead Act   (p. 419)
Union Leagues   (p. 427)
United States **v.** *Cruikshank*   (p. 432)

WHERE TO LEARN MORE

🛡 **Penn Center Historic District, St. Helena Island, South Carolina.** The Penn School was a sea-island experiment in the education of free black people established by northern missionaries Laura Towne and Ellen Murray in 1862 that they operated until their deaths in the early 1900s. The Penn School became Penn Community Services in 1948, serving as an educational institution, health clinic, and a social service agency. **www.penncenter.com**

🛡 **Hampton University Museum, Hampton, Virginia.** Hampton University was founded by the Freedmen's Bureau in 1868 to provide "practical" training in the agricultural and mechanical fields for former slaves. In addition to a history of the institution, the museum includes one of the oldest collections of African art in the United States. **www.hamptonu.edu/museum**

🛡 **Beauvoir, Biloxi, Mississippi.** The exhibits at Beauvoir, the home of Jefferson Davis, evoke the importance of the Lost Cause for the white survivors of the Confederacy. Especially interesting is the Jefferson Davis Soldiers Home on the premises and the Confederate Veterans Cemetery. Davis spent his retirement in Beauvoir. **www.beauvoir.org**

🛡 **Levi Jordan Plantation, Brazoria County, Texas.** This site provides an excellent depiction and interpretation of the lives of sharecroppers and tenants during and immediately after the Reconstruction era. The site is especially valuable for demonstrating the transition from slavery to sharecropping. **www.webarchaeology.com**

 For additional study resources for this chapter, go to:
   www.prenhall.com/goldfield/chapter16

The colored woman of to-day
occupies a unique position in this country . . .

Teaching a laboratory class at the Tuskegee Institute, c. 1900.

17

A NEW SOUTH
PROGRESS AND SOCIAL TRADITION
1877–1900

WHAT CHANGED in the New South between 1870 and 1900, and what stayed the same?

WHAT WERE the origins and nature of Southern Populism?

WHAT WERE women's roles in the New South?

HOW DID segregation and disenfranchisement change race relations in the South?

Ida B. Wells

Black Heritage USA 25

1900

1877

The colored woman of to-day occupies . . . a unique position in this country. . . . She is confronted by both a woman question and a race problem. . . . While the women of the white race can with calm assurance enter upon the work they feel by nature appointed to do [including reform efforts both inside and outside the home], while their men give loyal support and appreciative countenance to [these] efforts, recognizing in most avenues of usefulness the propriety and the need of woman's distinctive co-operation, the colored woman too often finds herself hampered and shamed by a less liberal sentiment . . . on the part of those for whose opinion she cares most. . . .

You do not find the colored woman selling her birthright for a mess of pottage. . . . It is largely our women in the South to-day who keep the black men solid in the Republican party. The black woman can never forget—however lukewarm the party may to-day appear—that it was a Republican president who struck the manacles from her own wrists and gave the possibilities of manhood to her helpless little ones; and to her mind a Democratic Negro is a traitor and a time-server.

To be a woman in a . . . [new] age carries with it a privilege and an opportunity never implied before. But to be a woman of the Negro race in America, and to be able to grasp the deep significance of the possibilities of the crisis, is to have a heritage, it seems to me, unique in the ages. In the first place, the race is young and full of the elasticity and hopefulness of youth. All its achievements are before it. . . . Everything to this race is new and strange and inspiring. There is a quickening of its pulses and a glowing of its self-consciousness. Aha, I can rival that! I can aspire to that! I can honor my name and vindicate my race! Something like this, it strikes me, is the enthusiasm which stirs the genius of young Africa in America; and the memory of past oppression and the fact of present attempted repression only serve to gather momentum for its irrepressible power. . . . What a responsibility then to have the sole management of the primal lights and shadows! Such is the colored woman's office. She must stamp weal or woe on the coming history of this people. May she see her opportunity and vindicate her high prerogative.

Anna J. Cooper,
—A Voice from the South, 1892

Anna Julia Cooper, *A Voice from the South* (Xenia, OH: The Aldine Printing House, 1892): 134–135, 138–140, 142–145. The book may be accessed from the Internet: **http://docsouth.unc.edu/church/cooper/cooper.html**

IMAGE KEY

for pages 436–437

a. Texas and Pacific Railway and its maps showing the connections.

b. Students and a teacher work in a laboratory at the Tuskegee Institute in Alabama., c. 1900.

c. An ad for Juliet chewing tobacco.

d. Thread on a large spool.

e. E. A. Overstreet and members of the class of 1900 of the Georgia State Independent College.

f. Women spin yarn and tend children on the porch of a log cabin in North Carolina in 1907.

g. A woman in a hoop skirt grips gently the handle of an old fashioned water pump next to an antebellum house in Natchez, Mississippi.

h. Ida B. Wells (1862–1931) pictured on a United States postage stamp from 1989.

ANNA J. COOPER undertook an incredible journey that took her from slavery at her birth in Raleigh, North Carolina, in 1858 to a doctoral degree at the Sorbonne in Paris, France, and to a prominent career as an educator. She was a firm believer in the role women, especially black women, should play in striking down both white supremacy and male domination. In 1892, Cooper published *A Voice from the South,* excerpted here. The book appeared when the first African-American generation raised in freedom had generated a relatively prosperous, educated middle-class intent on challenging the limits of race in the New South. This assertiveness alarmed white Southerners who responded with a campaign of violent repression.

Despite these threats, Cooper's tone reflects the optimism of the New South and an enthusiasm for the expanding public role of women. Though Cooper overestimated white women's freedom of choice outside the home, she believed that black men, unlike their white counterparts, held black women back. She also suggests that black men share the blame for the white assault on their political rights. Her solution for racial advancement was to increase the public profile of black women. But, traditional views of Southern whites on race and gender rendered that solution untenable.

Cooper lived to see the dawn of a new racial and gender era in the South and in America, but that journey took many years and many lives. She died at the age of 106 in 1964.

Solid South   The one-party (Democratic) political system that dominated the South from the 1890s to the 1950s.

THE NEWNESS OF THE NEW SOUTH

Southerners of both races and genders shared Anna J. Cooper's optimism in the decades after Reconstruction. They did what other Americans were doing between 1877 and 1900—they built railroads and factories and moved to towns and cities, only on a smaller scale and with more modest results. The factories did not dramatically alter the South's rural economy, and the towns and cities did not make it an urban region. The changes, nonetheless, brought political and social turmoil, emboldening black people, like Cooper, to assert their rights, encouraging women to work outside the home and pursue public careers, and frightening some white men.

By 1900, however, Southern white leaders had used the banner of white supremacy to stifle dissent. They removed African Americans from political life and constricted their social and economic role.

The New South's "newness" was thus to be found primarily in its economy, not in its social relations, though the two were complementary. After Reconstruction, new industries absorbed tens of thousands of first-time industrial workers from impoverished rural areas. Southern cities grew faster than those in any other region of the country. Railroad construction linked these cities to one another and to the rest of the country, giving them increased commercial prominence. Cities extended their influence into the countryside with newspapers, consumer products, and new values. But this urban influence had limits. It did not bring electricity, telephones, public health services, or public schools to the rural South. It did not greatly broaden the rural economy with new jobs. And it left the countryside without the daily contact with the outside world that fostered a broader perspective.

The Democratic party dominated Southern politics after 1877. Democrats purged most black people and some white people from the electoral process and suppressed challenges to their leadership. The result was the emergence by 1900 of the **Solid South**, a period of white Democratic party rule that lasted into the 1950s.

Although most Southern women remained at home or on the farm, some enjoyed new options after 1877. Middle-class women in the cities, both white and black, became increasingly active in civic work and reform. They organized clubs, preserved and promoted the memories

WHAT CHANGED in the New South between 1870 and 1900, and what stayed the same?

The pride of accomplishment is evident in this photograph of the Georgia State College class of 1900. By this time, black institutions of higher education in the South were turning out ambitious and talented graduates who faced an increasingly grim future in their native region.

Shivery Family Photograph Collection, Photographs and Prints Division, Schomburg Center of Research in Black Culture, The New York Public Library, Astor, Lenox, and Tilden Foundations of war, lobbied for various causes, and assumed regional leadership on important issues. Many young white women from impoverished rural areas found work in textile mills, in city factories, or as servants. These new options challenged prevailing views about the role of women but ultimately did not change them.

The status of black Southerners changed significantly between 1877 and 1900. The members of the first generation born after Emancipation sought more than just freedom. They also expected self-respect and the right to work, vote, go to school, and travel freely. White Southerners responded with the equivalent of a second Civil War—and they won. By 1900, black Southerners where more isolated from white Southerners and had less political power than at any time since 1865. Despite these setbacks, they built, especially in the cities, a rich community life and spawned a vibrant middle class.

AN INDUSTRIAL AND URBAN SOUTH

Since the 1850s, public speakers calling for economic reform in the South had been rousing audiences with the tale of the burial of a southern compatriot whose headstone, clothes, and coffin, as well as the grave-diggers' tools all came from the North. The speakers urged their listeners to found industries, build railroads, and grow great cities so that the South could make its own goods and no one in the future would have to suffer the indignity of journeying to the next world accompanied by Yankee artifacts.

Certainly, Southerners manufactured little in 1877, less than 10 percent of the national total. By 1900, however, they boasted a growing iron and steel industry, textile mills that rivaled those of New England, a world-dominant tobacco industry, a timber-processing industry that helped make the South a leading furniture-manufacturing center, and prominent regional enterprises, including Coca-Cola.

Birmingham, barely a scratch in the forest in 1870, exemplified one aspect of what was new about the New South. By 1889, Birmingham was preparing to challenge Pittsburgh, the nation's preeminent steelmaking city.

The Southern textile industry also expanded during the 1880s. Several factors drew local investors into textile enterprises, including low farm income. The entrepreneurs located their mills mostly in rural areas, not in cities. The center of the industry was in the Carolina Piedmont, a region with good railroads, plentiful labor, and cheap energy. By 1900, the South had surpassed New England to become the nation's foremost textile-manufacturing center.

Virginia was the dominant tobacco producer, and its main product was chewing tobacco. The discovery of bright-leaf tobacco, a strain suitable for smoking in the form of cigarettes, changed Americans' tobacco habits. In 1884, James B. Duke installed the first cigarette-making machine in his Durham, North Carolina, plant. By 1900, Duke's American Tobacco Company controlled 80 percent of all tobacco manufacturing in the United States.

Atlanta pharmacist Dr. John Pemberton developed a soft drink—a mixture of oils, caffeine, coca leaves, and cola nuts—in his backyard in an effort to find a good-tasting cure for headaches. He called it Coca-Cola. Pemberton, short of cash, sold the rights to it to another Atlantan, Asa Candler, in 1889. Candler improved the taste and marketed the product heavily. By the mid-1890s, Coca-Cola enjoyed a national market.

Southern track mileage doubled between 1880 and 1890, with the greatest increases in Texas and Georgia. By 1890, nine out of ten Southerners lived in a county with a railroad running through it. In 1886, the Southern railroads agreed to conform to a national standard for track width, linking the region into a national transportation network and ensuring access for Southern products to the booming markets of the Northeast.

QUICK REVIEW

Southern Women: 1877–1900

◆ Most Southern women remained at home or on the farm.

◆ Middle-class women increasingly active in civic work and reform.

◆ Young white women found work in mills, factories, and as servants.

WHERE TO LEARN MORE

★ Levine Museum of the New South, Charlotte, North Carolina **www.museumofthenewsouth.org**

The railroads connected formerly isolated small Southern farmers to national and international markets and gave them access to new products, from fertilizers to fashions.

The railroad also opened new areas of the South to settlement and economic development. In 1892, according to one guidebook, Florida was "in the main inaccessible to the ordinary tourist, and unopened to the average settler." By 1912, there were tourist hotels as far south as Key West. Railroads also opened the Appalachian Mountains to timber and coal-mining interests.

The railroad increased the prominence of interior cities at the expense of older cities along the southern Atlantic and Gulf Coasts. Antebellum ports such as New Orleans, Charleston, and Savannah declined as commerce rode the rails more than the water. Cities such as Dallas, Atlanta, Nashville, and Charlotte, astride great railroad trunk lines, emerged to lead Southern urban growth. Five major rail lines converged on Atlanta by the 1870s. As early as 1866, it had become "the radiating point for Northern and Western trade coming Southward, and . . . the gate through which passes Southern trade and travel going northward." When the Texas and Pacific Railway linked Dallas to Eastern markets in 1872, it was a small town of three thousand people. Eight years later, its population had grown to more than ten thousand, and within thirty years it had become the South's twelfth largest city. By 1920, New Orleans and Norfolk were the only coastal ports still among the ten most populous southern cities.

A town on a rail line that invested in a cotton press and a cottonseed oil mill would become a marketing hub for the surrounding countryside within a day's wagon ride away. Local merchants would stock the latest fashions from New York, canned foods, and current issues of popular magazines such as *Atlantic* or *Harper's*. The number of towns with fewer than five thousand people doubled between 1870 and 1880 and had doubled again by 1900.

By the 1890s, textile mills were a common sight in towns throughout the South. The mills provided employment for impoverished rural families, especially women and children.

T.E. Armistead Collection, University of South Alabama Archives

QUICK REVIEW

Railroads and the South
- Connected small Southern farmers to national and international markets.
- Opened new areas in the South to settlement and development.
- Increased the importance of interior cities at the expense of older cities.

THE LIMITS OF INDUSTRIAL AND URBAN GROWTH

Rapid as it was, urban and industrial growth in the South barely kept pace with that of the booming North (see Chapter 18). Between 1860 and 1900, the South's share of the nation's manufacturing increased only marginally from 10.3 percent to 10.5 percent, and its share of the nation's capital declined slightly from 11.5 percent to 11 percent. About the same percentage of people worked in manufacturing in the Southern states east of the Mississippi in 1900 as in 1850. Between 1860 and 1880, the per capita income of the South declined from 72 percent of the national average to 51 percent and by 1920 had recovered to only 62 percent (see Figure 17–1).

Southern industrial workers earned roughly half the national average manufacturing wage during the late nineteenth century. Business leaders promoted the advantages of this cheap labor to Northern investors. In 1904, a Memphis businessman boasted that his city "can save the northern manufacturer . . . who employs 400 hands, $50,000 a year on his labor bill."

Despite their attractiveness to industrialists, low wages undermined the Southern economy in several ways. Poorly paid workers didn't buy much, lim-

CHRONOLOGY

1872	Texas and Pacific Railway connects Dallas to Eastern markets.
1880	First Southern local of the Women's Christian Temperance Union is formed in Atlanta.
1881	Booker T. Washington establishes Tuskegee Institute.
1882	Agricultural Wheel is formed in Arkansas.
1883	Laura Haygood founds the home mission movement in Atlanta.
1884	James B. Duke automates his cigarette factory.
1886	Dr. John Pemberton creates Coca-Cola.
	Southern railroads conform to national track gauge standards.
1887	Charles W. Macune expands the Southern Farmer's Alliance from its Texas base to the rest of the South.
1888	The Southern Farmers' Alliance initiates a successful boycott of jute manufacturers.
1890	Mississippi becomes the first state to restrict black suffrage with literacy tests.

1892	The Populist party forms.
1894	United Daughters of the Confederacy is founded. Populist and Republican fusion candidates win control of North Carolina.
1895	Booker T. Washington delivers his "Atlanta Compromise" address.
1896	Populists endorse the Democratic presidential candidate and fade as a national force.
	In *Plessy* v. *Ferguson*, the Supreme Court permits segregation by law.
1898	North Carolina Mutual Life Insurance is founded. Democrats regain control of North Carolina.
1903	W.E.B. Du Bois publishes *The Souls of Black Folk.*
1905	James B. Duke forms the Southern Power Company. Thomas Dixon publishes *The Clansman.*
1906	Bloody race riots break out in Atlanta.
1907	Pittsburgh-based U.S. Steel takes over Birmingham's largest steel producer.

FIGURE 17–1

Per Capita Income in the South as a Percentage of the U.S. Average, 1860–1920
This graph illustrates the devastating effect of the Civil War on the Southern economy. Southerners began a slow recovery during the 1880s that accelerated after 1900. But even as late as 1920, per capita income in the South was still lower relative to the country as a whole than it had been before the Civil War.

Data Source: *Richard A. Easterlin, "Regional Economic Trends, 1840–1950," in* American Economic History. *ed. Seymour E. Harris (1961).*

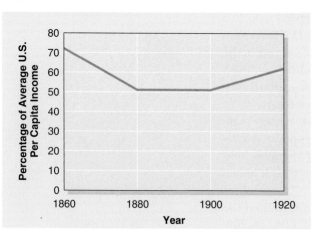

iting the market for Southern manufactured goods. They kept tax revenue low, restricting the states' ability to fund services like public education. Birmingham, Alabama, probably spent more on public education than any other Southern city, but the skilled workers in its steel mills tended to leave as soon as they could for higher-wage opportunities in Northern cities like Pittsburgh and Cleveland. Investment in education lagged in the South. Per-pupil expenditure in the region was at least 50 percent below that of the rest of the nation in 1900.

Low wages kept immigrants—and the skills and energy they brought with them—out of the South. With steady work available at higher wages north of the Mason-Dixon line, only a scattering of Italian farm laborers, Chinese railroad workers, and Jewish peddlers ventured below it. Between 1860 and 1900—during one of the greatest waves of immigration the United States has yet experienced— the foreign-born population of the South actually declined from about 10 percent to less than 2 percent.

Why didn't the South benefit more from the rapid expansion of the national economy in the last three decades of the nineteenth century? The simple answer is that the Civil War had wiped out the South's capital resources. Northern goods flowed into the South, but Northern capital, technology, and people did not. Northern-based national banks emerged in the wake of the Civil War to fund Northern economic expansion. The South, in contrast, had few banks, and those lacked sufficient capital reserves to fuel an equivalent expansion there.

Northern banks imposed higher interest rates and shorter terms on loans to Southerners than on loans to their northern customers. When Southern rail lines failed during a depression in the 1870s, Northern financiers purchased the companies at bargain prices. By the 1890s, Northern firms owned the five major rail lines serving the South.

With limited access to other sources of capital, the South's textile industry depended on thousands of small investors in towns and cities. These investors avoided risk, shunned innovation, and remained small-scale.

The lumber industry, the South's largest, typified the shortcomings of Southern economic development in the late nineteenth century. It required little capital, relied on unskilled labor, and processed its raw materials on site. After clear-cutting—felling all the trees—in one region, sawmills moved quickly to the next stand of timber, leaving behind a bare landscape, rusting machinery, and a work force no better off than before.

Birmingham's iron and steel industry also suffered from financial weakness. Mill owners relied on cheap black labor rather than investing in expensive technology. Another problem was the limited market for steel in the mostly agricultural South. Pittsburgh-based U.S. Steel took over Birmingham's largest steel producer in 1907. Thereafter, pricing policies favoring Pittsburgh plants limited Birmingham's growth.

The tobacco industry, however, avoided the problems that plagued other Southern enterprises. James B. Duke's American Tobacco Company was so immensely profitable that he became, in effect, his own bank. With more than enough capital to install the latest technology in his plants, Duke bought out his competitors. He then diversified into electric power generation and endowed what became Duke University.

Southern industry fit into a narrow niche of late-nineteenth-century American industrialization. With an unskilled and uneducated work force, poor access to capital and technology, and a weak consumer base, the South processed raw agricultural products, and produced cheap textiles, cheap lumber products, and cheap cigarettes. "Made in the South" became synonymous with bottom-of-the-line goods.

In the South most textile mills were typically located in the countryside, often in mill villages, where employers could easily recruit families and keep them isolated from the distractions and employment alternatives of the cities. The timber industry similarly remained a rural-based enterprise. Tobacco manufacturing helped Durham and Winston, North Carolina, grow, but they remained small compared to Northern industrial cities. Duke moved his corporate headquarters to New York to be near that city's financial, advertising, and communications services.

FARMS TO CITIES: IMPACT ON SOUTHERNERS

If industrialization in the South was limited compared to the North, it nonetheless had an enormous impact on Southern society. In the southern Piedmont, for example, failed farmers moved to textile villages to earn a living. Entire families secured employment and often a house in exchange for their labor. Widows and single young men also moved to the mills, usually the only option outside farm work in the South. Nearly one-third of the textile mill labor force by 1900 consisted of children under the age of 14 and women. They worked twelve hours a day, six days a week, although some firms allowed a half-day off on Saturday.

Southern urban growth, which also paled in comparison with that of the North, had a similarly disproportionate impact on Southern society. One observer noted the changes in a North Carolina town between 1880 and 1890. The town in 1880 presented a sorry aspect: rutted roads, a shanty for a school, a few forlorn churches, and perhaps three families of prominence. Twenty years later, another

WHERE TO LEARN MORE

Sloss Furnaces National Historical Landmark, Birmingham, Alabama
www.slossfurnaces.com

QUICK REVIEW

Southern Industry

- Textile industry depended on thousands of small investors.
- Lumber industry typified the shortcomings of Southern industry.
- Tobacco industry avoided problems that plagued other Southern enterprises.

MAP EXPLORATION

To explore an interactive version of this map, go to **http://www.prenhall.com/goldfield2/map17.1a**

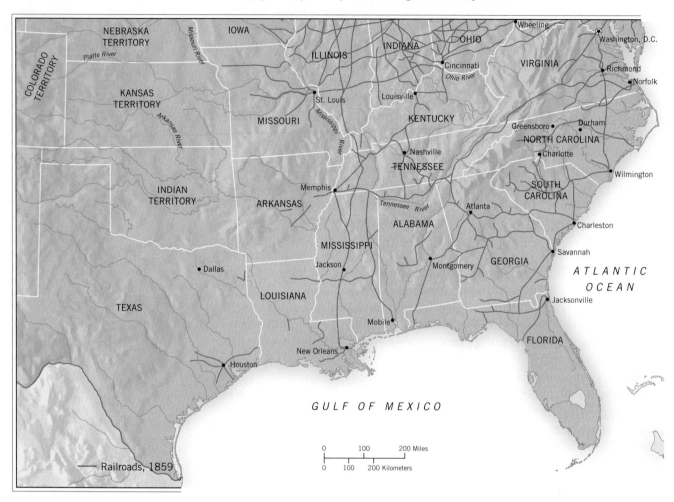

MAP 17–1A

Railroads in the South, 1859 and 1899 A postwar railroad construction boom promoted commercial agriculture and industry in the South. Unlike the railroads of the prewar South, uniform gauges and connections to major trunk lines in the North linked Southerners to the rest of the nation. Northern interests, however, owned the major southern railroads in 1899, and most of the products flowing northward were raw materials to be processed by northern industry or shipped elsewhere by northern merchants.

railroad, bustling commerce, and textile mills had produced a new scene: paved streets, two public schools—one for blacks, one for whites—and a cosmopolitan frame of mind among its residents. "The men have a wider range of activities and the women have more clothes." In another twenty years, the observer predicted, it will be "very like hundreds of towns in the Middle West."

By 1900, a town in the New South would boast a business district and more elegant residences than before. Its influence would extend into the countryside. Farm families visited nearby towns and cities more often. A South Carolina writer related in 1900 that "Country people who . . . went to town annually or semiannually, can now go quickly, safely, pleasantly, and cheaply several times a day." Many never returned to the farm. "Cheap coal, cheap lights, convenient water supply offer inducements; society and amusements draw the young; the chance to speculate, to make a sudden rise in fortunes, to get in the swim attracts others."

MAP EXPLORATION

To explore an interactive version of this map, go to **http://www.prenhall.com/goldfield2/map17.1b**

MAP 17–1B

WHAT EFFECT did railroads have on the Southern workforce?

The urban South drew the region's talented and ambitious young people. White men like William Henry Belk moved to cities to open shops or take jobs as bank clerks, bookkeepers, merchants, and salesmen. White women worked as retail clerks, telephone operators, and office personnel. Black women filled the growing demand for laundresses and domestic servants. And black men also found prospects better in towns than on the farm, despite a narrow and uncertain range of occupations available to them.

To some Southerners, urbanization and the emphasis on wealth, new technology, and display represented a second Yankee conquest. Ministers warned against traffic with the urban devil, whose temptations could overcome even the most devout individual. Evangelist Sam Jones, a reformed alcoholic, chose Atlanta for his largest revivals in the 1890s, challenging its residents to keep the Sabbath holy, reject alcohol, and obey the Golden Rule.

White Southerners in town and country, who not long ago had lived similar lives, grew distant. White farmers and their families had fallen on hard times. The market that lured them into commercial agriculture threatened to take away their independence. They faced the loss of their land and livelihood. Their way of life was no longer the standard for the South. New South spokesmen promoted cities and industries and ordered farmers to get on board the train of progress before it left the station without them.

THE SOUTHERN AGRARIAN REVOLT

WHAT WERE the origins and nature of Southern Populism?

Even more than before the Civil War, cotton dominated Southern agriculture between 1877 and 1900. And the economics of cotton brought despair to cotton farmers. Rice and tobacco production increased, and Louisiana and Arkansas overtook South Carolina in rice production. Steady demand, however, allowed rice and tobacco growers to maintain a decent standard of living. Cotton was another matter. The size of the cotton crop continued to set annual records after 1877. The railroad opened new areas for cultivation in Mississippi and eastern Texas. But the price of cotton fell while the price of fertilizers, agricultural tools, food, and most other necessities went up. As a result, the more cotton the farmers grew, the less money they made.

Before the Civil War, the South fed itself. After the war, with railroads providing direct access to major cotton-marketing centers, the South became an importer of food. As a common lament went in 1890, "Five-cent cotton, forty-cent meat, how in the world can a poor man eat?"

COTTON AND CREDIT

The solution to this agrarian dilemma seemed simple: Grow less cotton. But in a cash-poor economy, credit ruled. Food crops generated less income per acre than cotton, even in the worst years. Local merchants, themselves bound in a web of credit to merchants in larger cities, accepted cotton as collateral. "No cotton, no credit" became a standard refrain throughout the South after 1877.

Trapped in debt by low cotton prices and high interest rates, small landowning farmers lost their land in record numbers. Less than one-third of white farmers in the South were tenants or sharecroppers just after the Civil War. By the 1890s, nearly half were.

Some areas did diversify. Good rail connections in Georgia, for example, made peach farming profitable for some farmers. Cattle ranching spread in Texas. But few crops or animals had the geographical range of cotton. Soil type, rainfall, animal parasites, and frost made alternatives unfeasible for many farmers. Cotton required no machinery or irrigation system. James Barrett, a farmer outside Augusta, Georgia, said of his experiment with diversification in 1900: "I have diversified, and I have not made any money by diversification. . . . I grow green peas and everything I know of. I have raised horses, cows, and hogs, and I have diversified it for the last three years and have not been able to make a dollar."

SOUTHERN FARMERS ORGANIZE, 1877–1892

As their circumstances deteriorated, farmers lobbied for debt-stay laws and formed organizations to widen the circle of their community to include other farmers sharing their plight. They wanted to make the market fairer, to lower interest rates and ease credit, to regulate railroad freight rates, and to keep the prices of necessities in check.

These goals required legislation. But presidential administrations between 1877 and 1900, Republican or Democrat, did not favor debt relief or extensive regulation of business. And the Redeemer Democrats who gained control of the Southern state governments after Reconstruction represented large landowners and merchants, not poor farmers.

To strengthen their authority and suppress dissent, the Redeemer Democrats portrayed themselves as having saved the South from the rule of black people and Republicans. Insurgent farmers who challenged this leadership risked being branded as disloyal.

The Democrats nonetheless faced some opposition. In some states, like North Carolina, the Republicans retained support in mountain areas and among black voters. In addition, disaffected white farmers mounted independent political campaigns against the Redeemers in several states in the late 1870s and early 1880s to demand currency reform and the easing of credit. But the Democrats, in firm control of the election machinery throughout the South, turned back these challenges. Although Independents at one point succeeded in gaining control of the Virginia legislature, their few other victories were confined to the local level. Hard-pressed farmers began to organize on a broader scale.

By 1875, nearly 250,000 Southern landowners had joined the National Grange of the Patrons of Husbandry, more popularly known as the **Grange** (see Chapter 22). The leaders of the Grange, however, were large landowners. Their interests were not the same as the small farmers who made up the organization's rank and file. The Grange leadership in the South, for example, favored fence laws, limited government assistance, controls on farm labor, and other policies that hurt small farmers. The rank-and-file members, in contrast, pushed a more radical agenda including establishing community stores, cotton gins, and warehouses to bypass the prevailing credit system.

The Grange failed to stem the reverses of small Southern farmers. In 1882 a group of farmers in Arkansas formed an organization called the **Agricultural Wheel** that had attracted more than 500,000 Southern farmers by 1887. Wheelers tried to purchase farm equipment directly from manufacturers, avoiding merchant middlemen. Unlike the Grange, they called for an array of federal programs to ease the credit and cash burdens of farmers, including a graduated income tax and the printing and distribution of more paper money.

The most potent agricultural reform organization, the **Southern Farmers' Alliance**, originated in Texas in the late 1870s. Alliance-sponsored farmers' cooperatives provided their members with discounts on supplies and credit. Members also benefited from marketing their cotton crops collectively. Although it endorsed some candidates for office, the Alliance was not a political party and did not challenge Democratic domination of the South.

The Alliance was still very much a Texas organization in 1887 when Charles W. Macune, a Wisconsin native, became its driving force. Macune sent a corps of speakers to create a network of Southern cooperatives. Within two years, the Alliance had spread throughout the South and into the North and West. By 1890, it claimed more than a million members. Almost all were small farmers who owned their own land. The success of the Alliance reflected both the desperate struggle of these small farmers to keep their land and the failure of other organizations to help them.

The Alliance operated like a religious denomination. Its leaders preached a message of salvation through cooperation to as many as twenty thousand people at huge revival-like rallies. Qualifications for membership included a belief in the divinity of Christ and the literal truth of the Bible. Alliance speakers, many of them rural ministers, often held meetings in churches, combining biblical nostrums with economic policy. They urged members to visit "the homes where lacerated hearts are bleeding, to assuage the suffering of a brother or a sister, bury the dead, care for the widows and educate the orphans." The Alliance lobbied state legislatures to fund rural public schools. To increase the sense of community, the Alliance sponsored picnics, baseball games, and concerts.

Grange   The National Grange of the Patrons of Husbandry, a national organization of farm owners formed after the Civil War.

Agricultural Wheel   One of several farmer organizations that emerged in the South during the 1880s. It sought federal legislation to deal with credit and currency issues.

Southern Farmer's Alliance   The largest of several organizations that formed in the post-Reconstruction South to advance the interests of beleaguered small farmers.

The faces of this white sharecropper family in North Carolina reflect the harshness of farm life in the late nineteenth- and early twentieth-century South, a period when thousands of Southerners, white and black alike, slipped from land ownership to sharecropping.

Courtesy of the North Carolina Division of Archives and History

Colored Farmer's Alliance   An organization of Southern black farmers formed in Texas in 1886 in response to the Southern Farmer's Alliance, which did not accept black people as members.

Subtreasury plan   A program promoted by the Southern Farmer's Alliance in response to low cotton prices and tight credit. Farmers would store their crop in a warehouse until prices rose, in the meantime borrowing up to 80 percent of the value of the stored crops from the government at a low interest rate.

The Alliance imposed strict morality on its members, prohibiting drinking, gambling, and sexual misconduct. Alliance leaders criticized many Baptist, Methodist, and Presbyterian ministers for straying from the traditional emphasis on individual salvation and for defending a status quo that benefited large planters and towns. Cyrus Thompson, North Carolina Alliance president and a prominent Methodist, declared in 1889 that "the church today stands where it has always stood, on the side of human slavery."

Some Alliance members left their churches for new religious groups. Holiness movement disciples advocated simple dress, avoided coffee and pork, and swore off all worldly amusements. The members of the Church of God, which formed in the mountains of Tennessee and North Carolina in 1886, similarly sought to cleanse themselves of secular evils. The new churches promoted a vision of an egalitarian South. They accepted women on an equal basis and occasionally black people as well. As many as a third of Holiness preachers were women.

Women also found an active role as officers and speakers in the Alliance. As a Texas woman declared, "The Alliance has come to redeem woman from her enslaved condition. She is admitted into the organization as the equal of her brother, and the ostracism which has impeded her intellectual progress in the past is not met with."

However, the Alliance did not accept black members. Black farmers formed the first **Colored Farmers' Alliance** in Texas in 1886, which had fewer landowners and more tenants and sharecroppers in its ranks than the white organization. It concerned itself with issues relevant to this constituency, such as higher wages for cotton pickers. In 1891, the Colored Alliance attempted a regionwide strike over farm wages but was unable to enforce it in the worsening Southern economy.

The white Alliance had better results with a protest over price fixing. To protect cotton shipped to market, farmers wrapped it in a burlaplike material called jute. In 1888, jute manufacturers combined to raise the price from 7 cents to as much as 14 cents a yard. The Alliance initiated a jute boycott throughout the South, telling farmers to use cotton bagging as an alternative. The protest worked, forcing the chastened jute manufacturers to offer farmers their product at a mere 5 cents per yard.

This success encouraged Macune to propose his **subtreasury plan**. Alliance members were to store their crops in a subtreasury (a warehouse), keeping their cotton off the market until the price rose. In the meantime, the government would loan the farmers up to 80 percent of the value of the stored crops at a low interest rate of 2 percent per year. This arrangement would free farmers from merchants' high interest rates and crop liens.

Macune urged Alliance members to endorse political candidates who supported the subtreasury scheme. Many Democratic candidates for state legislatures throughout the South did endorse it and were elected with Alliance backing in 1890. Once in office, however, they failed to deliver.

The failure of the subtreasury plan combined with a steep drop in cotton prices after 1890 undermined the Alliance. Its cooperatives collapsed as crop liens cut down small landowners as though with scythes. A Georgia Allianceman wrote in 1891 that "Hundreds of farmers will be turned adrift, and thousands of acres of our best land allowed to grow up in weeds through lack of necessary capital to work them." Alliance membership declined by two-thirds in Georgia that year. Desperate Alliance leaders merged their organization with a new national political party in 1892, the People's or **Populist party**. Populists appropriated the Alliance program and challenged Democrats in the South and Republicans in the West. The merger reflected desperation more than calculation.

SOUTHERN POPULISTS

Northern farmers, like their Southern counterparts, faced growing financial pressure in the 1880s that by the early 1890s had led them too to join the Alliance. Just as Southern farmers had turned to the Democratic party to redress their grievances, Northern farmers turned to the dominant party in the Northern farming states—the Republican party—to redress theirs. Like the Democrats, the Republicans failed to respond. Beginning in Kansas in 1890, disillusioned farmers formed the People's party, soon called the Populist party.

The Populists supported a wide range of reforms, many adopted from the Alliance, including the direct election of United States senators by popular vote rather than by state legislatures, an income tax, woman suffrage, government ownership of railroads, and various proposals to ease credit. In the South, they challenged the Democratic party, sometimes courting the votes of Republicans, including black voters.

Southern Populists were ambivalent about African Americans. On the one hand, black people constituted a potential voting bloc the Populists could ill afford to ignore. On the other hand, appealing to blacks would expose Populists to demagogic attacks from Democrats for undermining white supremacy, frightening away potential white backers. The *Baton Rouge Daily Advocate*, for example, informed its readers in 1892 that the Populist party was "the most dangerous and insidious foe of white supremacy."

Despite the risks, in Texas, black Populist John B. Rayner, the "silver-tongued orator of the colored race," spoke to racially mixed audiences around the state. The Texas Populist platform called for "equal justice and protection under the law to all citizens without reference to race, color or nationality." In Georgia, Populist leader Tom Watson supported a biracial party organization and counseled white people to accept black people as partners in their common crusade. "You are kept apart," Watson told black and white Georgians, "that you may be separately fleeced of your earnings. You are made to hate each other because upon that hatred is rested the keystone of the arch of financial despotism which enslaves you both."

Despite Rayner's and Watson's efforts, most black people remained loyal to the Republican party for its role in abolishing slavery and for the few patronage crumbs the party still threw their way. Black people also suspected Populists' motives. The party appealed mainly to small, landowning farmers, not, as most black Southerners were, propertyless tenants and sharecroppers. And even the Texas Populists opposed black officeholding and jury service.

The Populists finished a distant third in the 1892 presidential election. In the South, their only significant inroads were in the state legislatures of Texas, Alabama, and Georgia. Even in these states, widespread voter fraud among Democrats undermined Populist strength.

Despite a deepening economic depression, the Populists had only a few additional successes in the South after 1892. Adopting a fusion strategy, the Populists ran candidates on a combined ticket with Republicans in North Carolina. The fusion candidates captured the governorship and state legislature.

Higher cotton prices and returning prosperity in the late 1890s, however, undermined Populist support in North Carolina, as in the rest of the South. In 1896,

17–9
The Omaha Platform of the Populist Party (1892)

QUICK REVIEW

Political Affiliation of African Americans

◆ Some populists made appeals to African Americans.

◆ Most African Americans remained loyal to the Republican party.

◆ Many blacks were suspicious of the populists' motives.

Populist party   A major third party of the 1890s formed on the basis of the Southern Farmer's Alliance and other reform organizations.

the Populists assisted in their own nationwide demise by merging with the Democrats for the presidential election of 1896. In 1898, Democrats surged back into office in North Carolina on the strength of a virulent white supremacy campaign and promptly undid the work of the fusionists.

WOMEN IN THE NEW SOUTH

Just as farm women found their voices in the Alliance movement of the 1880s, a growing group of middle-class white and black urban women entered the public realm and engaged in policy issues. In the late-nineteenth-century North, women became increasingly active in reform movements, including woman suffrage, labor legislation, social welfare, and city planning. Building on their antebellum activist traditions, Northern women, sometimes acting in concert with men, sought to improve the status of women in society.

Southern women had a meager reform tradition to build on. The war also left them ambivalent about independence. With male family members dead or incapacitated, some determined never again to depend on men. Others, responding to the stress of running a farm or business, would have preferred less independence.

Southern men had been shaken by defeat. They had lost the war and placed their families in peril. Many responded with alcoholism and violence. To regain their self-esteem, they recast the war as a noble crusade and imagined Southern white women as paragons of virtue and purity who required men to defend them. Even small changes in traditional gender roles would threaten this image. Southern women never mounted an extensive reform campaign like their sisters in the North.

Urban middle-class Southern women found opportunities to broaden their social role and enter the public sphere in the two decades after 1880 when servants, stores, and schools freed them of many of the productive functions—like making clothing, cooking, and child care—that burdened their sisters in the country and kept them tied to the home.

CHURCH WORK AND PRESERVING MEMORIES

Southern women waded warily into the public arena. The movement to found home mission societies, for example, was led by single white women in the Methodist church to promote industrial education among the poor and help working-class women become self-sufficient. Laura Haygood, an Atlantan who had served as a missionary in China, founded a home mission in Atlanta when she returned in 1883. Lily Hammond, another Atlantan, extended the mission concept when she opened settlement houses in black and white city neighborhoods in Atlanta in the 1890s. Settlement houses, pioneered in New York in the 1880s, promoted middle-class values in poor neighborhoods and provided them with a permanent source of services. In the South, they were supported by the Methodist church and known as *Wesley Houses*, after John Wesley, the founder of Methodism.

Religion also prompted Southern white women to join the **Women's Christian Temperance Union (WCTU)**. The first Southern local formed in Lucy Haygood's church in Atlanta in 1880. WCTU members visited schools to educate children about the evils of alcohol, addressed prisoners, and blanketed men's meetings with literature. As a result, they became familiar with the South's abysmal school system and its archaic criminal justice system. They thus began advocating education and prison reform as well as legislation against alcohol.

By the 1890s, many WCTU members realized that they couldn't achieve their goals unless women had the vote. Rebecca Latimer Felton, an Atlanta suffragist and

Women's Christian Temperance Union (WCTU) Women's organization whose members visited schools to educate children about the evils of alcohol, addressed prisoners, and blanketed men's meetings with literature.

WCTU member, reflected the frustration of her generation of Southern women in an address to working women in 1892:

> But some will say—you women might be quiet—you can't vote, you can't do anything! Exactly so—we have kept quiet for nearly a hundred years hoping to see relief come to the women of this country—and it hasn't come. How long must our children be slain? If a mad dog should come into my yard, and attempt to bite my child or myself—would you think me out of my place, if I killed him with a dull meat axe? . . . [You] would call that woman a brave woman . . . and yet are we to sit by while drink ruins our homes?

WCTU rhetoric implied a veiled attack on men. Felton, for example, often referred to men who drank as "beasts." When the WCTU held its national convention in Atlanta in 1890, local Baptist and Methodist ministers launched a bitter attack against the organization, claiming that it drew women into activities contrary to the Scriptures and that its endorsement of woman suffrage subverted traditional family values.

Few women, however, had such radical objectives in mind. Rebecca Felton and her husband Dr. William H. Felton, a physician and minister, eked out a modest living teaching school and working a small farm during the Civil War and its aftermath. Four of their five children died. Seeing Southern families worse off than her own, Felton threw herself into a variety of reform activities, ranging from woman suffrage to campaigns against drinking, smoking, and Coca-Cola. She fought for child-care facilities, sex education, and compulsory school attendance and pushed for the admission of women to the University of Georgia. But she had no qualms about the **lynching** of black men—executing them without trial—"a thousand times a week if necessary" to preserve the purity of white women. In 1922, she became the first woman member of the U.S. Senate.

The dedication of Southern women to commemorating the memory of the Confederate cause also suggested the conservative nature of middle-class women's reform in the New South. Ladies' Memorial Associations formed after the war to ensure the proper burial of Confederate soldiers and suitable markings for their graves. These activities reinforced white solidarity and constructed a common heritage for all white Southerners regardless of class or location. A new organization, the United Daughters of the Confederacy (UDC), appeared in 1894 to preserve Southern history and honor its heroes.

The Confederate battle flag on this parade float reflects its emerging status as an icon of the Lost Cause in the late nineteenth century.

Courtsy of Library of Congress

WOMEN'S CLUBS

A broader spectrum of Southern middle-class women joined women's clubs than joined church-sponsored organizations or memorial associations. By 1890, some clubs and their members had begun to discuss political issues such as child labor reform, educational improvement, and prison reform. The Lone Star (Texas) Federation scrutinized public hospitals, almshouses, and orphanages at the turn of the century. Its president asserted, "The Lone Star Federation stands for the highest and truest type of womanhood—that which lends her voice as well as her hand." Southern women's club members sought out their sisters in the North. As Georgia's federated club president, Mrs. A. O. Granger, wrote in 1906, "Women of intellectual keenness in the South could not be left out of the awakening of the women of the whole country to a realization of the responsibility which they properly had in the condition of their fellow-women and of the children."

The activities of black women's clubs paralleled those of white women's clubs. Only rarely, however—as at some meetings of the Young Women's Christian Association (YWCA) or occasional meetings in support of prohibition—did black and white club members interact.

Lynching   Execution, usually by a mob, without trial.

Most white clubwomen were unwilling to sacrifice their own reform agenda to the cause of racial reconciliation. Some women suffragists in the South argued that the combined vote of white men and women would further white interests.

The primary interest of most Southern white women's clubs was the plight of young white working-class and farm women. Single and adrift in the city, many worked for low wages, and some slipped into prostitution. The clubs sought to help them make the transition from rural to urban life or to improve their lives on the farm. To this end, they focused on child labor reform and on upgrading public education.

SETTLING THE RACE ISSUE

HOW DID segregation and disenfranchisement change race relations in the South?

To counter black aspirations, white leaders enlisted the support of young white men. African Americans resisted the resulting efforts to deprive them of their remaining freedoms. Though some left the South, many more built new lives and communities within the restricted framework white Southerners allowed them.

THE FLUIDITY OF SOUTHERN RACE RELATIONS, 1877–1890

Race relations remained remarkably fluid in the South between the end of Reconstruction and the early 1890s. Despite the departure of Federal troops and the end of Republican rule, many black people continued to vote and hold office. Some Democrats even courted the black electorate.

In 1885, T. McCants Stewart, a black newspaperman from New York, traveled to his native South Carolina expecting a rough reception once his train headed south from Washington, D.C. To his surprise, the conductor allowed him to remain in his seat while white riders sat on baggage or stood. He provoked little reaction among white passengers when he entered the dining car. Some of them struck up a conversation with him. Stewart, who admitted he had begun his journey with "a chip on my shoulder . . . [daring] any man to knock it off," now observed that "the whites of the South are really less afraid to [have] contact with colored people than the whites of the North." In Columbia, South Carolina, Stewart found that he could move about with no restrictions. "I can ride in first-class cars. . . . I can go into saloons and get refreshments even as in New York. I can stop in and drink a glass of soda and be more politely waited upon than in some parts of New England."

To be sure, black people faced discrimination in employment and voting and random retaliation for perceived violations of racial barriers. But those barriers were by no means fixed.

THE WHITE BACKLASH

The black generation that came of age in this environment demanded full participation in American society. As the young black editor of Nashville's *Fisk Herald* proclaimed in 1889, "We are not the Negro from whom the chains of slavery fell a quarter of a century ago. . . . We are now qualified, and being the equal of whites, should be treated as such." Charles Price, an educator from North Carolina, admonished colleagues in 1890, "If we do not possess the manhood and patriotism to stand up in the defense of . . . constitutional rights and protest long, loud and unitedly against their continual infringements, we are unworthy of heritage as American citizens and deserve to have fastened on us the wrongs of which many are disposed to complain."

Many young white Southerners, raised on the myth of the Lost Cause, were continually reminded of the heroism and sacrifice of their fathers during the Civil War. For many, conditions were worse than their families had enjoyed before the war, and they resented the changed status of black people. David Schenck, a Greensboro,

North Carolina, businessman wrote in 1890 that "the breach between the races widens as the young free negroes grow up and intrude themselves on white society and nothing prevents the white people of the South from annihilating the negro race but the military power of the United States Government." Using the Darwinian language popular among educated white people at the time, Schenck concluded, "I pity the Negro, but the struggle is for the survival of the fittest race."

The South's deteriorating rural economy and the volatile politics of the late 1880s and early 1890s exacerbated the growing tensions between assertive black people and threatened white people. In the cities, black and white people came in close contact, competing for jobs and jostling each other for seats on streetcars and trains. Racist rhetoric and violence against black people accelerated in the 1890s.

Lynching became a public spectacle, a ritual designed to reinforce white supremacy. Note the matter-of-fact satisfaction of the spectators to this gruesome murder of a black man.

Courtesy Library of Congress

LYNCH LAW

In 1892, three prominent black men, Tom Moss, Calvin McDowell, and William Stewart, opened a grocery on the south side of Memphis, an area with a large African-American population. The People's Grocery prospered while a white-owned store across the street struggled. The proprietor of the white-owned store, W. H. Barrett, secured an indictment against Moss, McDowell, and Stewart for maintaining a public nuisance. Outraged black community leaders called a protest meeting at the grocery during which two people made threats against Barrett. Barrett learned of the threats, notified the police, and warned the gathering at the People's Grocery that white people planned to attack and destroy the store. Nine sheriff's deputies, all white, approached the store to arrest the men who had threatened Barrett. Fearing Barrett's threatened white assault, the people in the grocery fired on the deputies, unaware who they were, and wounded three. When the deputies identified themselves, thirty black people surrendered, including Moss, McDowell, and Stewart, and were imprisoned. Four days later, deputies removed the three owners from jail, took them to a deserted area, and shot them dead.

The men at the People's Grocery had violated two of the unspoken rules that white Southerners imposed on black Southerners to maintain racial barriers: They had prospered, and they had forcefully challenged white authority. White mobs lynched nearly two thousand black Southerners between 1882 and 1903. Most lynchers were working-class white people with rural roots who were struggling in the depressed economy of the 1890s and enraged at the fluidity of urban race relations.

The substitution of lynch law for a court of law seemed a cheap price to pay for white solidarity at a time when political and economic pressures threatened entrenched white leaders. In 1893, Atlanta's Methodist bishop, Atticus G. Haygood, typically a spokesman for racial moderation, objected to the torture some white lynchers inflicted on their victims but added, "Unless assaults by Negroes on white women and little girls come to an end, there will most probably be still further displays of vengeance that will shock the world."

Haygood's comments reflect the most common justification for lynching—the presumed threat posed by black men to the sexual virtue of white women. Sexual "crimes" could include remarks, glances, and gestures. Yet only 25 percent of the

QUICK REVIEW

Lynch Law

♦ 1882–1903: nearly 2,000 black Southerners lynched.

♦ Lynching justified by alleged threat of black male sexuality to white female virtue.

♦ Ida B. Wells took the lead in campaigning against lynchings.

Ida B. Wells, an outspoken critic of lynching, fled to Chigago following the People's Grocery lynchings in Memphis in 1892 and became a national civil-rights leader

The Granger Collection, New York

Segregation   A system of racial control that separated the races, initially by custom but increasingly by law during and after Reconstruction.

DisFranchisement   The use of legal means to bar individuals or groups from voting.

Plessy v. Ferguson   Supreme Court decision holding that Louisiana's railroad segregation law did not violate the Constitution as long as the railroads or the state provided equal accommodations.

lynchings that took place in the thirty years after 1890 had some alleged sexual connection. Certainly, the men of the People's Grocery had committed no sex crime.

Ida B. Wells, who owned a black newspaper in Memphis, used her columns to publicize the People's Grocery lynchings. The great casualty of the lynchings, she noted, was her faith that education, wealth, and upright living guaranteed black people the equality and justice they had long sought. The reverse was true. The more black people succeeded, the greater was their threat to white people. She investigated other lynchings, countering the claim that they were the result of assaults on white women. When she suggested that, on the contrary, perhaps some white women were attracted to black men, she enraged the white citizens of Memphis, who destroyed her press and office. Exiled to Chicago, Wells devoted herself to the struggle for racial justice.

SEGREGATION BY LAW

Southern white lawmakers sought to cement white solidarity and ensure black subservience in the 1890s by instituting **segregation** by law and the **disfranchisement** of black voters. Racial segregation restricting black Americans to separate and rarely equal public facilities had prevailed nationwide before the Civil War. After 1870, the custom spread rapidly in southern cities. In Richmond by the early 1870s, segregation laws required black people registering to vote to enter through separate doors, and registrars to count their ballots separately. The city's prisons and hospitals were segregated. So too were its horse-drawn railways, its schools, and most of its restaurants, hotels, and theaters.

During the same period, many Northern cities and states, often in response to protests by African Americans, were ending segregation. Massachusetts, for example, passed the nation's first public accommodations law in May 1865, desegregating all public facilities. Cities such as New York, Cleveland, and Cincinnati desegregated their streetcars. Chicago, Cleveland, Milwaukee, and the entire state of Michigan desegregated their public school systems. Roughly 95 percent of the nation's black population, however, lived in the South. In reality, integration in the North consequently required white people to give up very little to black people. And as African-American aspirations increased in the South during the 1890s as their political power waned, they became more vulnerable to segregation by law at the state level. At the same time, migration to cities, industrial development, and technologies such as railroads and elevators increased the opportunities for racial contact and muddled the rules of racial interaction.

White passengers objected to black passengers' implied assertion of economic and social equality when they sat with them in dining cars and first-class compartments. Black Southerners, in contrast, viewed equal access to railroad facilities as a sign of respectability and acceptance. When Southern state legislatures required railroads to provide segregated facilities, black people protested.

In 1890, Homer Plessy, a Louisiana black man, refused to leave the first-class car of a railroad traveling through the state. Arrested, he filed suit, arguing that his payment of the first-class fare entitled him to sit in the same first-class accommodations as white passengers. He claimed that under his right of citizenship guaranteed by the Fourteenth Amendment, neither the state of Louisiana nor the railroad could discriminate against him on the basis of color. The Constitution, he claimed, was colorblind.

The U.S. Supreme Court ruled on the case, *Plessy v. Ferguson*, in 1896. In a seven-to-one decision, the Court held that Louisiana's railroad segregation law did not violate the Constitution as long as the railroads or the state provided equal accommodations. The decision left unclear what "equal" meant. In the Court's view, "Legislation is powerless to eradicate racial instincts," meaning that segregation of the races was natural and transcended constitutional considerations. The only justice to vote

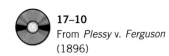

17–10
From *Plessy* v. *Ferguson*
(1896)

against the decision was John Marshall Harlan, a Kentuckian and former slave owner. In a stinging dissent, he predicted that the decision would result in an all-out assault on black rights. "The destinies of the two races . . . are indissolubly linked together," Harlan declared, "and the interests of both require that the common government of all shall not permit the seeds of race hate to be planted under the sanction of law."

Both Northern and Southern states enacted new segregation laws in the wake of *Plessy* v. *Ferguson*. In practice, the separate facilities for black people these laws required, if provided at all, were rarely equal. By 1900, segregation by law extended to public conveyances, theaters, hotels, restaurants, parks, and schools.

The segregation statutes came to be known collectively as **Jim Crow laws**, after the blackface stage persona of Thomas Rice, a white Northern minstrel show performer in the 1820s. Reflecting white stereo-types of African Americans, Rice caricatured "Jim Crow" as a foolish, elderly, lame slave who spoke in an exaggerated dialect.

Economic segregation followed social segregation. Before the Civil War, black men had dominated crafts such as carpentry and masonry. By the 1890s, white men were replacing them in these trades and excluding them from new trades such as plumbing and electrical work. Trade unions, composed primarily of craftworkers, began systematically to exclude African Americans. Confined increasingly to low or unskilled positions in railroad construction, the timber industry, and agriculture, black workers underwent *deskilling*—a decline in work force expertise—after 1890. With lower incomes from unskilled labor, they faced reduced opportunities for better housing and education.

WHERE TO LEARN MORE

Atlanta History Center,
Atlanta, Georgia
**www.atlhist.org/exhibitions/html/
metropolitan_frontiers.htm**

DISFRANCHISEMENT

Following the political instability of the late 1880s and the 1890s, white leaders determined to disfranchise black people altogether, thereby reinforcing white solidarity and eliminating the need to consider black interests. Obstacles loomed—the Fifteenth Amendment, which guaranteed freedmen the right to vote, and a Republican-dominated Congress—but with a national consensus emerging in support of white supremacy, they proved easy to circumvent.

Support for disfranchisement was especially strong among large landowners in the South's plantation districts, where heavy concentrations of black people threatened their political domination. Urban leaders, especially after the turmoil of the 1890s, looked on disfranchisement as a way to stabilize politics and make elections more predictable.

Democrats enacted a variety of measures to attain their objectives without violating the letter of the Fifteenth Amendment. States enacted **poll taxes**, requiring citizens to pay to vote. They adopted the secret ballot, which confused and intimidated illiterate black voters accustomed to using ballots with colors to identify parties. States set literacy and educational qualifications for voting or required prospective registrants to "interpret" a section of the state constitution. To avoid disfranchising poor, illiterate white voters with these measures, states enacted **grandfather clauses** granting the vote automatically to anyone whose grandfather could have voted prior to 1867 (the year Congressional Reconstruction began). The grandfathers of most black men in the 1890s had been slaves, ineligible to vote.

Tennessee was the first state to pass disfranchising legislation. A year later, Mississippi amended its constitution to require voters to pass a literacy test and prove they "understood" the state constitution. When a journalist asked an Alabama lawmaker if Jesus Christ could pass his state's "understanding" test, the legislator replied, "That would depend entirely on which way he was going to vote."

Alarmed by the Populist uprising, Democratic leaders also used disfranchisement to gut dissenting parties. During the 1880s, minority parties in the

Jim Crow laws Segregation laws that became widespread in the South during the 1890s.

Poll taxes Taxes imposed on voters as a requirement for voting.

Grandfather clause Rule that required potential voters to demonstrate that their grandfathers had been eligible to vote; used in some Southern states after 1890 to limit the black electorate.

South consistently polled an average of 40 percent of the statewide vote; by the mid-1890s, that figure had diminished to 30 percent, despite the Populist insurgency. Turnout dropped even more dramatically. In Mississippi, for example, voter turnout in gubernatorial races during the 1880s averaged 51 percent; during the 1890s, it was 21 percent. Black turnout in Mississippi, which averaged 39 percent in the 1880s, plummeted to near zero in the 1890s. Overall turnout, which averaged 64 percent during the 1880s, fell to only 30 percent by 1910.

When 160 South Carolina delegates gathered to amend the state constitution in 1895, the six black delegates among them mounted a passionate but futile defense of their right to vote. Black delegate W.J. Whipper noted the irony of white people clamoring for supremacy when they already held the vast majority of the state's elected offices. Robert Smalls, the state's leading black politician, urged delegates not to turn their backs on the state's black population. Such pleas fell on deaf ears. (See American Views: "Robert Smalls Argues against Disfranchisement.")

A NATIONAL CONSENSUS ON RACE

How could the South get away with it? How could Southerners openly segregate, disfranchise, and lynch African Americans without a national outcry? Apparently, most Americans in the 1890s believed that black people were inferior to white people and deserved to be treated as second-class citizens. Contemporary depictions of black people show scarcely human stereotypes: black men with bulbous lips and bulging eyes, fat black women wearing turbans and smiling vacuously, and black children contentedly eating watermelon or romping with jungle animals. These images appeared on cereal boxes, in advertisements, in children's books, in newspaper cartoons, and as lawn ornaments. The widely read book *The Clansman* by Thomas Dixon, a North Carolinian living in New York City and an ardent white supremacist, glorified the rise of the Ku Klux Klan. D. W. Griffith transformed *The Clansman* into an immensely popular film under the title *Birth of a Nation*.

So-called scientific racism purported to establish white superiority and black inferiority on biological grounds. Northern-born professional historians reinterpreted the Civil War and Reconstruction in the white South's favor. Historian William A. Dunning, the generation's leading authority on Reconstruction, wrote in 1901 that the North's "views as to the political capacity of the blacks had been irrational." The progressive journal *Outlook* hailed disfranchisement because it made it "impossible in the future for ignorant, shiftless, and corrupt negroes to misrepresent their race in political action." Harvard's Charles Francis Adams Jr. chided colleagues who disregarded the "fundamental, scientific facts" he claimed demonstrated black inferiority. The *New York Times*, summarizing this national consensus in 1903, noted that "practically the whole country" supported the "southern solution" to the race issue, since "there was no other possible settlement."

Congress and the courts upheld discriminatory legislation. As a delegate at the Alabama disfranchisement convention of 1901 noted, "The race problem is no longer confined to the States of the South, [and] we have the sympathy instead of the hostility of the North."

By the mid-1890s, Republicans were so entrenched in the North and West that they did not need Southern votes to win presidential elections

Racial stereotypes permeated American popular culture by the turn of the twentieth century. Images like this advertisement for Pullman railroad cars, which depicts a deferential black porter attending to white passengers, reinforced racist beliefs that black people belonged in servile roles. Immersed in such images, white people assumed they depicted the natural order of things.

Cincinnati, Hamilton & Dayton Railroad Advertisement, lithographic poster, 1894, Strobridge Lithographic Company, from the Bella C. Landauer Collection, negative number 51391. Collection of the New York Historical Society

• AMERICAN VIEWS •

ROBERT SMALLS ARGUES AGAINST DISFRANCHISEMENT

orn in Beaufort, South Carolina, in 1839, Robert Smalls served as a slave pilot in Charleston Harbor. In 1862, he emancipated himself, with his family and friends, when he delivered a Confederate steamer to a Union blockading fleet. He entered politics in 1864 as a delegate from his state to the Republican National Convention. He helped write South Carolina's Reconstruction constitution, which guaranteed the right of former slaves to vote and hold office. Smalls won election to the state legislature in 1869, and the U.S. House of Representatives in 1875. With opportunities for African Americans to hold public office declining following Reconstruction, Smalls was appointed collector of the Port of Beaufort, a federal post he occupied until his death in 1915. In the speech excerpted here—delivered to the South Carolina Constitutional Convention of 1895—he assails the state's plan to disfranchise black voters.

FROM THE white perspective, what is Smalls's most telling argument against the disfranchisement and the planned strategies to implement it? How does Smalls depict the black citizens of South Carolina? Why were white political leaders unmoved by Small's plea?

Mr. President, this convention has been called for no other purpose than the disfranchisement of the negro. . . .

The negroes are paying taxes in the south on $263,000,000 worth of property. In South Carolina, according to the census, the negroes pay tax on $12,500,000 worth of property. That was in 1890. You voted down without discussion . . . a proposition for a simple property and education qualification [for voting]. What do you want? . . . In behalf of the 600,000 negroes in the State and the 132,000 negro voters all that I demand is that a fair and honest election law be passed. We care not what the qualifications imposed are, all that we ask is that they be fair and honest, and honorable, and with these provisos we will stand or fall by it. You have 102,000 white men over 21 years of age, 13,000 of these cannot read nor write. You dare not disfranchise them, and you know that the man who proposes it will never be elected to another office in the State of South Carolina. . . . Fifty-eight thousand negroes cannot read nor write. This leaves a majority of 14,000 white men who can read and write over the same class of negroes in this State. We are willing to accept a scheme that provides that no man who cannot read nor write can vote, if you dare pass it. How can you expect an ordinary man to "understand and explain" any section of the Constitution, to correspond to the interpretation put upon it by the manager of election, when by a very recent decision of the supreme court, composed of the most learned men in State, two of them put one construction upon a section, and the other justice put an entirely different construction upon it. To embody such a provision in the election law would be to mean that every white man would interpret it aright and every negro would interpret it wrong. . . . Some morning you may wake up to find that the bone and sinew of your country is gone. The negro is needed in the cotton fields and in the low country rice fields, and if you impose too hard conditions upon the negro in this State there will be nothing else for him to do but to leave. What then will you do about your phosphate works? No one but a negro can work them; the mines that pay the interest on your State debt. I tell you the negro is the bone and sinew of your country and you cannot do without him. I do not believe you want to get rid of the negro, else why did you impose a high tax on immigration agents who might come here to get him to leave?

Now, Mr. President we should not talk one thing and mean another. We should not deceive ourselves. Let us make a Constitution that is fair, honest and just. Let us make a Constitution for all the people, one we will be proud of and our children will receive with delight.

Source: The Columbia State, October 27, 1895.

or to control Congress. Besides, business-oriented Republicans found common ground with conservative Southern Democrats on fiscal policy and foreign affairs.

Although no Northern states threatened to deny black citizens the right to vote, they did increase segregation. The booming industries of the North generally did not hire black workers. Antidiscrimination laws on the books since the Civil War went unenforced. In 1904, 1906, and 1908, race riots erupted in Springfield, Ohio, Greensburg, Indiana, and Springfield, Illinois, matching similar disturbances in Wilmington, North Carolina, and Atlanta, Georgia.

RESPONSE OF THE BLACK COMMUNITY

African Americans organized more than a dozen boycotts of streetcar systems in the urban South between 1896 and 1908 in an effort to desegregate them, but not one succeeded. The Afro-American Council, formed in 1890 to protest the deteriorating conditions of black life, accomplished little and disbanded in 1908. W. E. B. Du Bois organized an annual Conference on Negro Problems at Atlanta University beginning in 1896, but it produced no effective plan of action.

A few black people chose to leave the South. Henry McNeal Turner of Georgia, an African Methodist Episcopal (AME) bishop, promoted migration to Liberia, but only a few hundred made the trip in the late 1870s, Turner not included, and most of those returned disappointed. Most black people who moved in the 1890s stayed within the South.

More commonly, black people withdrew to develop their own rich community life. Particularly in the cities of the South, they could live relatively free of white surveillance and even white contact. In 1890, fully 70 percent of black city dwellers lived in the South; and between 1860 and 1900, the proportion of black people in the cities of the South rose from one in six to more than one in three.

By the 1880s, a new black middle class had emerged in the South. Urban-based, professional, business-oriented, and serving a primarily black clientele, its members fashioned an interconnected web of churches, fraternal and self-help organizations, families, and businesses. Black Baptists, AME, and AME Zion churches led reform efforts in the black community, seeking to eliminate drinking, prostitution, and other vices in black neighborhoods.

African-American fraternal and self-help groups, led by middle-class black people, functioned as surrogate welfare organizations for the poor. Some groups, such as the Colored Masons and the Colored Odd Fellows, paralleled white organizations. Black membership rates usually exceeded those in the white community. More than 50 percent of Nashville's black men, for example, belonged to various fraternal associations in the city. Fraternal orders also served as the seedbed for such business ventures as the North Carolina Mutual Life Insurance Company, founded in Durham in 1898. Within two decades, North Carolina Mutual became the largest black-owned business in the nation and helped transform Durham into the "capital of the black middle class." Most Southern cities boasted active black business districts by the 1890s.

Nashville's J. C. Napier typified the activism of the African-American urban middle class in the New South era. He belonged to two of the city's prominent black churches, was active in Republican politics, played an important role in several temperance and fraternal societies, served as president of the local black YMCA chapter, and as an attorney helped his fellow African Americans with numerous legal matters.

The African-American middle class worked especially hard to improve black education. Black students in cities had only makeshift facilities; those in the countryside had almost no facilities. To improve these conditions, black middle-class leaders solicited educational funds from Northern philanthropic organizations.

Black women played an increasingly active and prominent role in African-American communities after 1877, especially in cities. Ida B. Wells moved to Memphis from Mississippi in 1884. In 1886, she attended a lecture at an interracial Knights of Labor meeting and witnessed a religious revival conducted by the nation's leading evangelist, Dwight Moody. The following year, Wells began her journalism career and soon purchased a one-third interest in a local black newspaper.

Black women's clubs supported day-care facilities for working mothers and settlement houses in poor black neighborhoods modeled after those in northern cities. Atlanta's Neighborhood Union, founded by Lugenia Burns Hope in 1908, provided playgrounds and a health center and secured a grant from a New York foundation to improve black education in the city. Black women's clubs also established homes for single black working women to protect them from sexual exploitation, and they worked for woman suffrage "to reckon with men who place no value on her [black woman's] virtue," as Nannie H. Burroughs of the National Association of Colored Women argued at the turn of the century.

Anna J. Cooper, a Nashville clubwoman, wrote in 1892 that to be a member of this generation was "to have a heritage unique in the ages." Assertive black women did not arouse the same degree of white antagonism as assertive black men. They could operate in a broader public arena than men and speak out more forcefully.

After disfranchisement, middle-class black women assumed an even more pivotal role in the black community. They often used their relations with prominent white women and organizations such as the WCTU and the YWCA to press for public commitments to improve the health and education of African Americans. Absent political pressure from black men, as well as the danger of African-American males asserting themselves in the tense racial climate after 1890, black women became critical spokespersons for their race.

The extension of black club work into rural areas of the South, where the majority of the African-American population lived, to educate families about hygiene, nutrition, and child care, anticipated similar efforts among white women after 1900. But unlike their white counterparts, these middle-class black women worked with limited resources in a context of simmering racial hostility and political and economic impotence. In response, they nurtured a self-help strategy to improve the conditions of the people they sought to help. One of the most prominent African-American leaders of the late nineteenth and early twentieth centuries, Booker T. Washington, adopted a similar approach to racial uplift.

Born a slave in Virginia in 1856, Washington and his family worked in the salt and coal mines of West Virginia after the Civil War. Ambitious and flushed with the postwar enthusiasm for advancement that gripped freedmen, he worked his way through Hampton Normal and Agricultural Institute, the premier black educational institution in the South at that time. In 1881, he founded the Tuskegee Institute for black students in rural Alabama. By learning industrial skills, Washington maintained, black people could secure self-respect and economic independence. Tuskegee emphasized vocational training over the liberal arts.

At an Atlanta exposition in 1895, Washington argued that African Americans should accommodate themselves to segregation and disfranchisement until they could prove their economic worth to American society. In exchange, white people should help provide black people with the education and job training they would need to gain their independence. This position was known as the **Atlanta Compromise**. Despite his conciliatory public stance, Washington secretly helped finance legal challenges to segregation and disfranchisement. But increasingly, black people were shut out of the kinds of jobs for which Washington hoped to train them. Facing a depressed rural economy and growing racial violence, they had little prospect of advancement.

17–11
W.E.B. Du Bois, from "Of Mr. Booker T. Washington and Others"

Atlanta Compromise Booker T. Washington's policy accepting segregation and disenfranchisement for African Americans in exchange for white assistance in education and job training.

FROM THEN TO NOW
The Confederate Battle Flag

Memories of the Civil War and Reconstruction formed a crucial part of southern civic and religious culture from the late nineteenth century onward. Southerners perceived themselves and the rest of the nation through the lens of the heroic Lost Cause and the alleged abuses of Reconstruction, and the symbols associated with those events took on the status of icons. During the 1890s, the memory industry that white political and religious leaders had promoted since the end of the war became institutionalized. Organizations such as the United Daughters of the Confederacy and the Sons of Confederate Veterans strove to educate a new generation of white Southerners on the meanings of the sacrifices of the war generation, bolstering the imposition of white supremacy through racial segregation and disfranchisement.

The Confederate battle flag emerged from this process as an icon of the Lost Cause and a symbol of white supremacy. Alabama, for example, redesigned its state flag in the 1890s to resemble more closely the battle flag. Its red St. Andrews cross on a white background symbolized the blood spilled in defense of the Southern homeland and the supremacy of the white race.

Still, the Confederate battle flag itself was displayed mostly at veterans' reunions and only rarely at other public occasions—until the late 1940s, that is, when civil rights for African Americans emerged as a national issue for the first time since the Reconstruction era. In 1948, Mississippians waved the flag at Ole Miss football games for the first time. In 1956, as the civil rights struggle in the South gained momentum, the state of Georgia incorporated the battle flag into its state flag. And, in 1962, as sit-ins and Freedom Riders spread throughout the South, officials in South Carolina—claiming to be commemorating the Civil War centennial—hoisted the battle flag above the State House in Columbia.

Long after the centennial celebration concluded, the battle flag continued to fly in Columbia. This official display became a focus of heated controversy. Proponents argued that the battle flag represents heritage, not hate. Opponents denounced it as a symbol of white supremacy. In the mid-1990s, South Carolina's Republican Governor David Beasley, seeking to defuse the issue, proposed removing the flag from atop the Capitol and installing it at a nearby history museum. The resulting firestorm of protest from some of the Governor's white constituents forced him to reverse himself, however, and contributed to his defeat in his bid for reelection.

The flag controversy erupted again in 1999, when South Carolina's state Democratic Party chairman urged voters to return a Democratic legislature that would, once and for all, remove the flag from the State Capitol. The angry response from both Republicans and some Democrats forced the new Democratic governor to quickly distance himself from the proposal. Then, in July 1999, the National Association for the Advancement of Colored People (NAACP) announced a national boycott of South Carolina, beginning in January 2000. Facing the loss of convention and tourist revenues, business groups pleaded with lawmakers to lower the flag, which they did in July 2000. But the flag's new home, near a monument on the Capitol grounds, is even more visible to the public, prompting the continuation of the NAACP boycott.

In 2001, Mississippians voted overwhelmingly to keep their state flag which includes the battle flag. That same year, an interracial group of Georgia legislators agreed to remove the battle flag from the state banner; the new design includes the Confederate emblem, but only as part of a ribbon that includes all of the flags that have flown over Georgia through its history. Legislators did not submit the new design to a referendum, though in 2003, Georgia's recently-elected Republican Governor Sonny Perdue reversed that decision.

When people in other parts of the country sometimes remark that white Southerners are still fighting the Civil War, it is controversies like the one over the battle flag that they have in mind. But the controversy is less about the past than it is about the way we use history to shape our understanding of the society we live in and our vision of its future. At issue is not just history, but whose history. In that sense the flag controversy, as much as it picks at wounds more than a century old, can at least generate positive dialogue. Even so, in the interests of reconciliation, it may be time for Southerners to follow Robert E. Lee's final order to his men and "Furl the flag, boys."

Another prominent African-American leader, W. E. B. Du Bois, challenged Washington's acceptance of black social inequality. Du Bois, the first African American to earn a doctorate at Harvard, promoted self-help, education, and black pride. A gifted teacher and writer, he taught at Atlanta University and wrote eighteen books on black life in America. Du Bois was a cofounder, in 1910, of the **National Association for the Advancement of Colored People (NAACP)**, an interracial organization dedicated to restoring African-American political and social rights.

Despite their differences, which reflected their divergent backgrounds, Washington and Du Bois agreed on many issues. Both believed that black success in the South required some white assistance. As Du Bois wrote in *The Souls of Black Folk*, "Any movement for the elevation of the Southern Negro needs the cooperation, the sympathy, and the support of the best white people in order to succeed." But "the best white people" did not care to elevate black Southerners. In 1906, after a bloody race riot in Atlanta, Du Bois left the South, a decision millions of black Southerners would make over the next two decades.

As long as it provided the raw materials for the North's new urban industrial economy and maintained the peace, the South could count on the rest of the country not to interfere in its solution to race relations. Indeed, to the extent that most white Americans concerned themselves with race, they agreed with the Southern solution.

National Association for the Advancement of Colored People (NAACP)   Interracial organization co-founded by W. E. B. DuBois in 1910 dedicated to restoring African-American political and social rights.

CONCLUSION

In many respects, the South was more like the rest of the nation in 1900 than at any other time since 1860. Young men and women migrated to Southern cities to pursue opportunities unavailable to their parents. Advances in the production and marketing of cigarettes and soft drinks would soon make Southern entrepreneurs and their products household names. Southerners ordered fashions from Sears, Roebuck catalogs and enjoyed electric lights, electric trolleys, and indoor plumbing as much as other urban Americans.

Americans idealized a mythical South of rural grace and hospitality, a land of moonlight and magnolias, offering it as a counterpoint to the crowded, immigrant-infested, factory-fouled, money-grubbing North. Northern journalists offered admiring portraits of southern heroes like Robert E. Lee, of whom one declared in 1906, "the nation has a hero to place beside her greatest."

White Southerners cultivated national reconciliation but remained fiercely dedicated to preserving the peculiarities of their region: a one-party political system, disfranchisement, and segregation by law. The region's urban and industrial growth, impressive from the vantage of 1865, paled before that of the North. The South remained a colonial economy characterized more by deep rural poverty than urban prosperity.

Middle-class white people in the urban South enjoyed the benefits of a national economy and a secure social position. Middle-class women enjoyed increased influence in the public realm, but not to the extent of their Northern sisters. And the institutionalization of white supremacy gave even poor white farmers and factory workers a place in the social hierarchy a rung or two above the bottom.

For black people, the New South proved a crueler ruse than Reconstruction. No one now stepped forward to support their cause and stem the erosion of their economic independence, political freedom, and civil rights. They built communities and worked as best they could to challenge restrictions on their freedom.

The New South was thus both American and Southern. It shared with the rest of the country a period of rapid urban and industrial growth. But the legacy of war and slavery still lay heavily on the South, manifesting itself in rural poverty, segregation, and black disfranchisement.

Booker T. Washington counseled acquiescence to segregation, maintaining that black people could ultimately gain the acceptance of white society through self-improvement and hard work.

The Granger Collection, New York

SUMMARY

The Newness of the New South The "newness" of the New South was to be found primarily in its economic shift toward industrialization and urbanization rather than its social relations. Urban and rural white leaders had used the banner of white supremacy to constrict African-American social and economic roles; the Solid South, a white Democratic voting bloc emerged. Industry from textiles to steel dotted the Southern landscape, young men and women migrated to cities, and railroads connected the growing urban centers. Economically, the South remained behind the booming North; a weak agricultural economy, high birthrate, and low wages were some of the undermining factors.

The Southern Agrarian Revolt More than even before the Civil War, cotton dominated Southern agriculture; the price of cotton was low, and the prices of fertilizer, tools and necessities rose. Curtailing production to raise prices was not an option; the credit-based economy of the South was dependent upon cotton. Black and white sharecroppers and tenant farmers fought back by organizing, scoring limited successes; it took higher cotton prices and returning prosperity in the late 1890s to bring relief to farmers.

Women in the New South White women in the South were cast in the roles of paragons of virtue and purity who needed men to defend them. With these limitations, middle-class women entered the public arena slowly. Women's involvement in church organizations, temperance, and as protectors of Southern history allowed them involvement without challenging the class and racial inequalities of the New South, while women's club activities addressed their self-improvement and allowed them to help other women.

Settling the Race Issue The generation of black people who had come of age by the 1890s demanded full participation; white Southerners raised on the myth of the Lost Cause resented the changed status of black people. Economic and political violence worsened the tensions, and violence, including lynchings, accelerated. Segregation and disfranchisement laws were passed; the U.S. Supreme Court condoned separate accommodations in the case *Plessy* v. *Ferguson*. The majority of white Americans, North and South, ascribed to the notion of black inferiority; no national debate resulted in response to the new restrictions. African Americans responded by creating their own community life within these new confines. Booker T. Washington and W.E.B. DuBois differed on the approaches black people should take to accommodate and improve themselves.

REVIEW QUESTIONS

1. How did the activism of white middle-class women affect the politics of the South in the late 1880s and early 1890s?

2. How did the assertiveness of young urban black people affect the politics of the South in the late 1880s and early 1890s?

3. Why did white people believe that segregation and disenfranchisement were reforms?

4. How did black Southerners respond to decreasing economic and political opportunities in the New South?

5. Why was Anna J. Cooper optimistic for African-American women in the South?

KEY TERMS

Agricultural Wheel   (p. 447)
Atlanta Compromise   (p. 459)
Colored Farmer's Alliance   (p. 448)
DisFranchisement   (p. 454)
Grandfather clause   (p. 455)
Grange   (p. 447)
Jim Crow laws   (p. 455)

Lynching   (p. 451)
National Association for the Advancement of Colored people (NAACP)   (p. 461)
Plessy v. *Ferguson*   (p. 454)
Poll taxes   (p. 455)
Populist party   (p. 449)

Segregation   (p. 454)
Solid South   (p. 439)
Southern Farmers' Alliance   (p. 447)
Subtreasuray Plan   (p. 448)
Women's Christian Temperance Union (WCTU)   (p. 450)

WHERE TO LEARN MORE

🏛 **Levine Museum of the New South, Charlotte, North Carolina.** The museum has exhibits on various New South themes and a permanent exhibit on the history of Charlotte and the Carolina Piedmont. **www.museumofthenewsouth.org**

🏛 **Atlanta History Center, Atlanta, Georgia.** The major exhibit, "Metropolitan Frontiers, 1835–2000," includes a strong segment on the New South era, including the development of separate black and white economies in Atlanta. The Herndon home, also on the grounds of the center, has an exhibit on black upper-class life in Atlanta from 1880 to 1930. **www.atlhist.org/exhibitions/html/metropolitan_frontiers.htm**

🏛 **Sloss Furnaces National Historical Landmark, Birmingham, Alabama.** The site recalls the time when Birmingham challenged Pittsburgh as the nation's primary steel-producing center. **www.slossfurnaces.com**

 For additional study resources for this chapter, go to:
www.prenhall.com/goldfield/chapter17

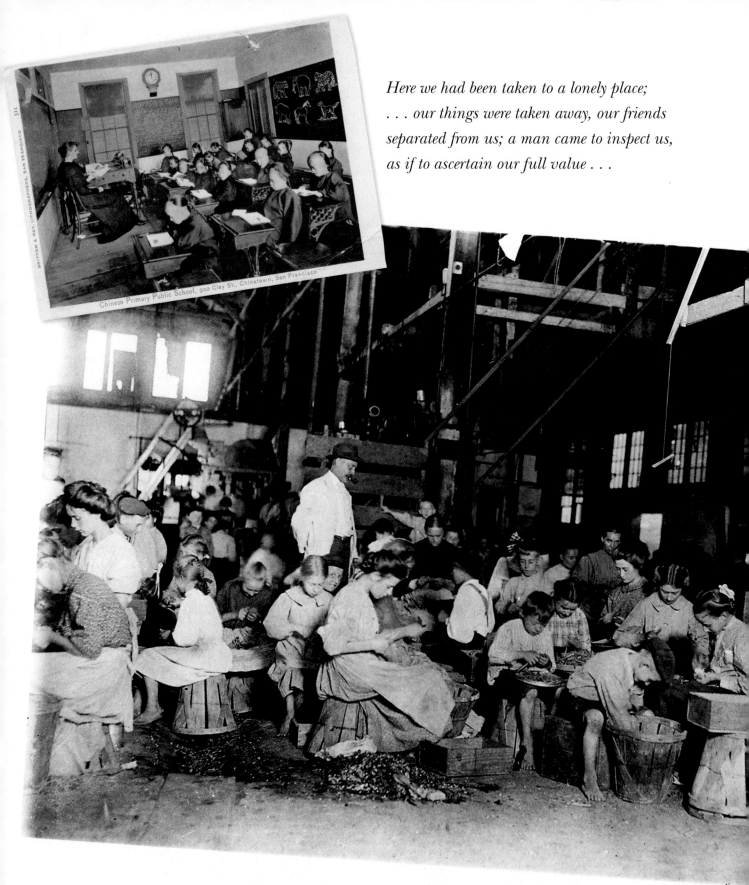

Chinese Primary Public School, 920 Clay St., Chinatown, San Francisco

Here we had been taken to a lonely place;
. . . our things were taken away, our friends
separated from us; a man came to inspect us,
as if to ascertain our full value . . .

Noted urban photographer Lewis Hines captures the cramped working conditions
and child labor in this late nineteenth-century canning factory. Women and children
provided a cheap and efficient work force for labor-intensive industries.

18

INDUSTRY, IMMIGRANTS, AND CITIES
1870–1900

WHAT CHANGES did the American workforce experience in the late nineteenth century?

WHAT IMPACT did new immigration have on cities in the North?

WHO MADE up the new middle class?

ATLANTIC CITY, N.J. Easter Sunday on the Boardwalk.

We were homeless, houseless, and friendless in a strange place. We had hardly money enough to last us through the voyage for which we had hoped and waited for three long years. We had suffered much that the reunion we longed for might come about; we had prepared ourselves to suffer more in order to bring it about, and had parted with those we loved, with places that were dear to us in spite of what we passed through in them, never again to see them, as we were convinced—all for the same dear end. With strong hopes and high spirits that hid the sad parting, we had started on our long journey. And now we were checked so unexpectedly but surely . . . When my mother had recovered enough to speak, she began to argue with the gendarme, telling him our story and begging him to be kind. The children were frightened and all but I cried. I was only wondering what would happen. . . .

Here we had been taken to a lonely place; . . . our things were taken away, our friends separated from us; a man came to inspect us, as if to ascertain our full value; strange-looking people driving us about like dumb animals, helpless and unresisting; children we could not see crying in a way that suggested terrible things; ourselves driven into a little room where a great kettle was boiling on a little stove; our clothes taken off, our bodies rubbed with a slippery substance that might be any bad thing; a shower of warm water let down on us without warning. . . . We are forced to pick out our clothes from among all the others, with the steam blinding us; we choke, cough, entreat the women to give us time; they persist, "Quick! Quick!—or you'll miss the train!"—Oh, so we really won't be murdered! They are only making us ready for the continuing of our journey, cleaning us of all suspicions of dangerous sickness. Thank God! . . .

Oh, what solemn thoughts I had! How deeply I felt the greatness, the power of the scene! The immeasurable distance from horizon; . . . the absence of any object besides the one ship; . . . I was conscious only of sea and sky and something I did not understand. And as I listened to its solemn voice, I felt as if I had found a friend, and knew that I loved the ocean.

—Mary Antin

Mary Antin, *The Promised Land* (Boston: Houghton Mifflin Company, 1912), Chapter VIII.

IMAGE KEY
for pages 464–465

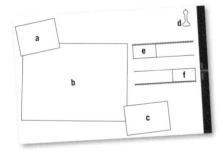

a. A classroom at work in the Chinese Public Primary School in Chinatown, San Francisco, with a Caucasian teacher.

b. A crowd of children at work in a 19th century canning factory. The children sit on overturned baskets while poring over their work under the gaze of an adult male supervisor in their midst.

c. Fashionable people crowded the Boardwalk in Atlantic City each Easter Sunday in the early 20th Century to see and be seen.

d. A replica of the first light bulb.

e. The Sixth Maryland militia in Baltimore fires into a hostile crowd of laborers chucking rocks during the Great Railroad Strike of 1877.

f. A family rides in a historic Ford Model T automobile.

MARY ANTIN, a thirteen-year old Jewish girl from Russia, describes her family's journey in 1884 from the persecution of Jews in tsarist Russia to the ship that sailed from Hamburg, Germany, that would take her to join her father in Boston.

Millions of European and Asian immigrants made similar journeys across the Atlantic and the Pacific, fraught with danger, heartbreak, fear and the sundering of family ties. So powerful was the promise of American life that the immigrant willingly risked these obstacles to come to the United States. Mary's letter to her uncle, was both a way of recounting her family's exodus and of maintaining contact with a world and a family she had left behind.

For Mary, America did indeed prove to be *The Promised Land*, as she entitled a memoir, published in 1912. After attending Barnard College in New York City, she wrote on immigrant issues, lectured widely, and worked for Theodore Roosevelt's Progressive Party. Her life shows how a teenage girl moved from a medieval life in tsarist Russia to a career as a writer in the United States.

Mary and her family were part of a major demographic and economic transformation in the United States between 1870 and 1900. Rapid industrial development changed the nature of the work force and the workplace. Large factories staffed by semiskilled laborers displaced the skilled artisans and small shops that had dominated American industry before 1870. Industrial development also accelerated urbanization. Between the Civil War and 1900, the proportion of the nation's population living in cities increased from 20 to 40 percent.

New opportunities opened as old opportunities disappeared. Vast new wealth was created, but poverty increased. New technologies eased life for some but left others untouched. The great dilemma of early-twentieth-century America was to reconcile these contradictions and provide a decent life for all.

Few locations encapsulated this dilemma better than Philadelphia during the Centennial Exposition of 1876, marking the nation's hundredth birthday. Its millions of visitors witnessed the ingenuity of the world's newest industrial power. Thomas Edison explained his new automatic telegraph, and Alexander Graham Bell demonstrated his telephone to the wonder of onlookers. A giant Corliss steam engine loomed over the entrance to Machinery Hall, dwarfing the other exhibits and providing them with power. "Yes," a visitor concluded, "it is in these things of iron and steel that the national genius most freely speaks."

For many Americans, however, the fanfare of the exposition rang hollow. The country was in the midst of a depression. Thousands were out of work, and others had lost their savings in bank failures and sour investments. With the typical daily wage a dollar, most Philadelphians could not afford the exposition's 50-cent admission price. They celebrated instead at "Centennial City," a ragtag collection of cheap bars, seedy hotels, small restaurants, and sideshows hurriedly constructed of wood and tin across the street from the imposing exposition.

This small area of Philadelphia reflected the promise and failure of the **Gilded Age**. The term is taken from the title of a novel by Mark Twain that satirizes the materialistic excesses of his day. It reflects the period's shallow worship of wealth—and its veneer of respectability and prosperity covering deep economic and social divisions.

Gilded Age Term applied to late-nineteenth-century America that refers to the shallow display and worship of wealth characteristic of that period.

New Industry

Between 1870 and 1900, the United States transformed itself from an agricultural nation—a nation of farmers, merchants, and artisans—into the world's foremost industrial power, producing more than one-third of the world's manufactured goods. By the early twentieth century, factory workers made up one-fourth of the work force, and agricultural workers had dropped from a half to less than a third (see Figure 18.1). A factory with a few dozen employees would have been judged fair-sized in 1870. By the early twentieth century, many industries employed thousands of workers in a single plant. Some industries—petroleum, steel, and meatpacking, for example—had been unknown before the Civil War.

Although the size of the industrial work force increased dramatically, the number of firms in a given industry shrank. Mergers, changes in corporate management and the organization of the work force, and a compliant government left a few companies in control of vast segments of the American economy. Workers, reformers, and eventually government challenged this concentration of economic power.

WHAT CHANGES did the American workforce experience in the late nineteenth century, and what was the reaction of organized labor?

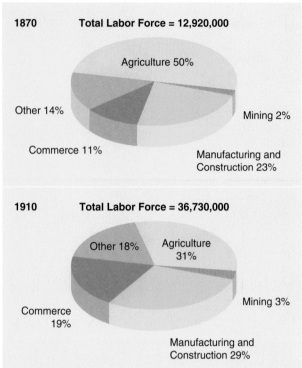

Figure 18–1 Changes in the American Labor Force, 1870–1910

The transformation of the American economy in the late nineteenth century changed the nature and type of work. By 1910 the United States was an urban, industrial nation with a matching work force that toiled in factories and for commercial establishments (including railroads), and less frequently on farms.

WHERE TO LEARN MORE

Edison National Historic Site, West Orange, New Jersey
www.nps.gov/edis

INVENTING TECHNOLOGY: THE ELECTRIC AGE

Technology transformed factory work and increased the scale of production. Steam engines and, later, electricity, freed manufacturers from dependence on water power. Factories could now be built anywhere accessible to the transportation system and a concentration of labor. Managers could substitute machines for workers, skewing the balance of power in the workplace toward employers. Technology also transformed city life. By the early twentieth century, electric lights, appliances, ready-made clothing, and store-bought food eased middle-class life. Electric trolleys whisked clerks, salespeople, bureaucrats, and bankers to new urban and suburban subdivisions. Electric street-lights lit up city streets at night. Movies entertained the masses. As the historian and novelist Henry Adams put it, "In the essentials of life . . . the boy of 1854 stood nearer [to] the year one than to the year 1900."

For much of the nineteenth century, the United States was dependent on the industrial nations of Europe for technological innovation. American engineers often went to England and Germany for training, and industries and railroads benefited from Europeans inventions.

In the late nineteenth century, the United States changed from a technological borrower to a technological innovator. By 1910, a million patents had been issued in the United States, 900,000 of them after 1870. Nothing represented this shift better than Thomas A. Edison's electric light bulb and electric generating system, which transformed electricity into a new and versatile form of industrial energy. Until the late nineteenth century, advances in scientific theory usually followed technological innovation. Techniques for making steel, for example, developed before scientific theories explained how they worked. Textile machinery and railroad technology developed similarly. In contrast, a theoretical understanding of electricity preceded its practical use as a source of energy. Scientists had been experimenting with electricity for half a century before Edison unveiled his light bulb in 1879. Edison's research laboratory at Menlo Park, New Jersey, also established a model for corporate-sponsored research and development that would rapidly increase the pace of technological innovation.

In 1876, Edison established his research laboratory at Menlo Park and turned his attention to the electric light. Scientists had already discovered that passing an electric current through a filament in a vacuum produced light. They had not yet found a filament, however, that could last for more than a few minutes. Edison tried a variety of materials, from grass to hair from a colleague's beard, before succeeding with charred sewing thread. In 1879, he produced a bulb that burned for an astounding forty-five hours. Then he devised a circuit that provided an even flow of current through the filament. After thrilling a crowd with the spectacle of five hundred lights ablaze on New Year's Eve in 1879, Edison went on to build a power station in New York City to serve businesses and homes by 1882. The electric age had begun.

Edison's initial success touched off a wave of research and development in Germany, Austria, Great Britain, France, and the United States. Whoever could light the world cheaply and efficiently held the key to an enormous fortune. Ultimately the prize fell not to Edison but to Elihu Thomson, a high school chemistry teacher in Philadelphia. Leaving teaching to devote himself to research full time, Thomson founded his own company and in 1883 moved to Connecticut. Thomson

CHRONOLOGY

1869   The Knights of Labor is founded in Philadelphia.

1870   John D. Rockefeller forms the Standard Oil Company.
        Congress passes the Naturalization Act barring Asians from citizenship.

1876   The Centennial Exposition opens in Philadelphia.

1877   The Great Uprising railroad strike, the first nationwide work stoppage in the United States, provokes violent clashes between workers and federal troops.

1879   Thomas Edison unveils the electric light bulb.

1880   Founding of the League of American Wheelmen in 1880 helps establish bicycling as one of urban American's favorite recreational activities.

1881   Assassination of Russian Tsar Alexander II begins a series of pogroms that triggers a wave of Russian Jewish immigration to the United States.

1882   Congress passes the Chinese Exclusion Act.
        First country club in the United States founded in Brookline, Massachusetts.

1883   National League merges with the American Association and opens baseball to working-class fans.

1886   The Neighborhood Guild, the nation's first settlement house, opens in New York City.
        Riot in Chicago's Haymarket Square breaks the Knights of Labor.
        American Federation of Labor is formed.

1887   Anti-Catholic American Protective Association is formed.

1888   Wanamaker's department store introduces a "bargain room," and competitors follow suit.

1889   Jane Addams opens Hull House, the nation's most celebrated settlement house, in Chicago.

1890   Jacob A. Riis publishes *How the Other Half Lives*.

1891   African-American Chicago physician Daniel Hale Williams establishes Provident Hospital, the nation's first interracially staffed hospital.

1892   General Electric opens the first corporate research and development division in the United States.
        Strike at Andrew Carnegie's Homestead steel works fails.

1894   Pullman Sleeping Car Company strike fails.
        Immigration Restriction League is formed.

1895   American-born Chinese in California form the Native Sons of the Golden State to counter nativism.

1897   George C. Tilyou opens Steeplechase Park on Coney Island in Brooklyn, New York.

1898   Congress passes the Erdman Act to provide for voluntary mediation of railroad labor disputes.

purchased Edison's General Electric Company in 1892 and established the country's first corporate research and development division. By 1914, General Electric was producing 85 percent of the world's light bulbs.

Other major American companies now established research and development laboratories. Standard Oil, U.S. Rubber, the chemical giant Du Pont, and the photographic company Kodak all became world leaders in their respective industries because of innovations their laboratories developed.

A humorous view of Thomas Edison's laboratories in Menlo Park, New Jersey, around 1880. There was no joking, however, about the potential of Edison's incandescent bulb and his other practical adaptations of electricity for everyday use. Electricity would soon transform life for millions of people. Edison's methods set the precedent for corporate research and development that would accelerate the pace of new discoveries with practical applications.

National Park Service, Edison National Historic Site

The modernization of industry that made the United States the world's foremost industrial nation after 1900 reflected organizational as well as technological innovation. As industries applied new technology and expanded their markets within and beyond national borders, their work forces expanded and their need for capital expenditures mounted. Coping with these changes required significant changes in corporate management.

THE CORPORATION AND ITS IMPACT

A corporation is an association of individuals with legal rights and liabilities separate from those of its members. This form of business organization had existed since colonial times but became a significant factor in the American economy with the growth of railroad companies in the 1850s. A key feature of a corporation is the separation of ownership from management. A corporation can raise capital by selling stock—ownership shares—to shareholders who may have no direct role in running it. The shareholders benefit from dividends drawn on the profits and, if the corporation thrives, from the rising value of its stock.

The corporation had two major advantages over other forms of business organization that made it attractive to investors. First, unlike a partnership, which can dissolve when a partner dies, a corporation can outlive its founders. This organizational stability permits long-term planning. Second, corporations enjoy limited liability. That means officials and shareholders are not personally liable for a corporation's debts. If it goes bankrupt, they stand to lose only what they have invested in it.

As large corporations emerged in major American industries, they had a ripple effect throughout the economy. Large corporations needed huge supplies of capital. They turned to the banks to help meet those needs, and the banks grew in response. The corporations stimulated technological change as they looked for ways to speed production, improve products, and lower costs. As they grew, they generated jobs throughout the economy.

By the early twentieth century, control of the workplace was shifting from well-paid, skilled artisans to managers, and semiskilled and unskilled workers were replacing skilled artisans. These new workers, often foreign-born, performed repetitive tasks for low wages.

Because the large industrial corporations usually located factories in cities, they stimulated urban growth. Large industrial districts sprawled along urban rivers and near urban rail lines, attracting thousands of workers. There were exceptions. Southern textile manufacturers tended to locate plants in villages and small towns and on the outskirts of larger cities. A few Northern entrepreneurs also constructed industrial communities outside major cities to save on land costs and ensure control over labor. Nonetheless, by 1900, fully 90 percent of all manufacturing occurred in cities.

Two organizational strategies—vertical integration and horizontal integration—helped successful corporations reduce competition and gain dominance in their industries. **Vertical integration** involved the consolidation of all functions related to a particular industry, from the extraction and transport of raw materials to the manufacture of products to finished-product distribution and sales. Geographical dispersal went hand in hand with vertical integration. Different functions—a factory and its source of raw materials, for example—were likely to be in different places, a development made possible by advances in communication like the telephone. The multiplication of functions also prompted the growth of corporate bureaucracy.

A good example of vertical integration occurred in the meatpacking industry under the influence of Gustavus Swift. Swift, a Boston native who moved to Chicago

Vertical integration The consolidation of numerous production functions, from the extraction of the raw materials to the distribution and marketing of the finished products, under the direction of one firm.

in 1875, realized that refrigerated railway cars would make it possible to ship butchered meat from Western ranges to Eastern markets, eliminating the need to transport live cattle. When he invented a refrigerated car, however, he could not sell it to the major railroads. They feared losing the heavy investment they had already made in cattle cars and pens. Swift had the cars built himself and convinced a Canadian railroad with only a small stake in cattle shipping to haul them to Eastern markets. He established packing houses in Omaha and Kansas City, near the largest cattle markets; built refrigerated warehouses at key distribution points to store beef for transport or sale; and hired a sales force to convince Eastern butchers of the quality of his product. He now controlled the production, transportation, and distribution of his product, the essence of vertical integration. By 1881, he was shipping $200,000 worth of beef a week. Competitors soon followed his example.

Horizontal integration involved the merger of competitors in the same industry. John D. Rockefeller's Standard Oil Company pioneered horizontal integration in the 1880s. Born in western New York State, the son of a traveling patent medicine salesman, Rockefeller moved to Ohio at the age of 14 in 1853. He began investing in Cleveland oil refineries by his mid-twenties and formed Standard Oil in 1870. Using a variety of tactics—including threats, deceit, and price wars—Rockefeller rapidly acquired most of his competitors. Supported by investment bankers like J.P. Morgan, Standard Oil controlled 90 percent of the nation's oil refining by 1890. Acquiring oil fields and pipelines as well as refineries, Standard Oil achieved both vertical and horizontal integration. Rockefeller's dominant position allowed him to impose order and predictability in what had been an often chaotic industry, ensuring a continuous flow of profits. He closed inefficient refineries, opened new ones, and kept his operations up-to-date with the latest technologies.

Other entrepreneurs achieved similar dominance in other major industries and amassed similarly enormous personal fortunes. James B. Duke, who automated cigarette manufacturing, gained control of most of the tobacco industry. Andrew Carnegie consolidated much of the U.S. steel industry within his Carnegie Steel Company (later U.S. Steel). By 1900, Carnegie's company was producing one-quarter of the country's steel.

The giant corporations threatened to restrict opportunities for small entrepreneurs like the shopkeepers, farmers, and artisans who abounded at midcentury. In the words of one historian, the corporations "seemed to signal the end of an open, promising America and the beginning of a closed, unhappier society." Impersonal and governed by the profit margin, the modern corporation challenged the ideal of the self-made man and the belief that success and advancement would reward hard work.

Tabloid newspapers reinforced distrust of the corporations with exposés of the sharp business practices of corporate barons like Rockefeller and Carnegie and accounts of the sumptuous lifestyles of the corporate elite. Public concern notwithstanding, however, the giant corporations helped increase the efficiency of the American economy, raise the national standard of living, and transform the United States into a major world power. Corporate expansion generated jobs that attracted rural migrants and immigrants by the millions from Europe and Asia to American cities.

THE CHANGING NATURE OF WORK

The corporations provided abundant jobs, but they firmly controlled working conditions. A Pennsylvania coal miner spoke for many of his fellows in the 1890s when he remarked: "The working people of this country . . . find monopolies as strong as government itself. They find capital as rigid as absolute monarchy. They find their so-called independence a myth."

WHERE TO LEARN MORE

Senator John Heinz Pittsburgh Regional History Center, Pittsburgh, Pennsylvania
www.pghhistory.org

Horizontal integration   The merger of competitors in the same industry.

The deskilling process accelerated in the 1890s in response to new technologies, new workers, and workplace reorganization. By 1906, according to a U.S. Department of Labor report, industrial labor had been reduced to minute, low-skilled operations, making skilled artisans obsolete.

On the other hand, the birth of whole new industries—steel, automobiles, electrical equipment, cigarettes, food canning, and machine tools—created a huge demand for workers. Innovations in existing industries, like railroads, similarly spurred job growth. The number of people working for U.S. railroads increased from eighty thousand to more than 1 million between 1860 and 1910.

With massive waves of immigrants arriving from Europe and Asia between 1880 and 1920 (joined after 1910 by migrants from the American South), the supply of unskilled workers seemed limitless. The new workers, however, shared little of the wealth generated by industrial expansion and enjoyed few of the gadgets and products generated by the new manufacturing. The eastern European immigrants who comprised three-quarters of U.S. Steel's work force during the first decade of the twentieth century received less than $12.50 a week, significantly less than the $15.00 a week a federal government survey in 1910 said an urban family needed to subsist.

Nor did large corporations put profits into improved working conditions. In 1881, on-the-job accidents maimed or killed thirty thousand railroad workers. At a U.S. Steel plant in Pittsburgh, injuries or death claimed one out of every four workers between 1907 and 1910. In Chicago's meat plants, workers grew careless from fatigue and long-term exposure to the extreme temperatures of the workplace. Meat cutters working rapidly with sharp knives often sliced fingers off their numb hands. Upton Sinclair wrote in his novel *The Jungle* (1906), a chronicle of the killing floors of meatpacking plants in Chicago, "It was to be counted as a wonder that there were not more men slaughtered than cattle."

Factory workers typically worked ten hours a day, six days a week in the 1880s. Steel workers put in twelve hours a day. Because the mills operated around the clock, once every two weeks, when the workers changed shifts, one group took a "long turn" and stayed on the job for twenty-four hours.

Long hours affected family life. By Sunday, most factory workers were too tired to do more than sit around home. During the week, they had time only to eat and sleep. As one machinist testified before a U.S. Senate investigative committee in 1883:

> They were pretty well played out when they come home, and the first thing they think of is having something to eat and sitting down, and resting, and then of striking a bed. Of course when a man is dragged out in that way he is naturally cranky, and he makes all around him cranky . . . and staring starvation in the face makes him feel sad, and the head of the house being sad, of course the whole family are the same, so the house looks like a dull prison.

Workers lived as close to the factory as possible to reduce the time spent going to and from work and to save transportation expenses. The environment around many factories, however, was almost as unwholesome as the conditions inside. A visitor to Pittsburgh in 1884 noticed "a drab twilight" hanging over the areas around the steel mills, where "gas-lights, which are left burning at mid-day, shine out of the murkiness with a dull, reddish glare." Industrial wastes fouled streams and rivers around many plants.

In some industries, like the "needle," or garment, trade, operations remained small-scale. But salaries and working conditions in these industries were, if anything, worse than in the big factories. The garment industry was dominated by small manufacturers who contracted to assemble clothing for retailers from cloth provided by textile manufacturers. The manufacturers squeezed workers into small, cramped, poorly ventilated **sweatshops**. The workers pieced together garments on the manufacturer's sewing machines. A government investigator in Chicago in the 1890s described one sweatshop in a three-room tenement where the workers—a family of eight—both lived and worked: "The father, mother, two daughters, and a cousin work together making trousers at seventy-five cents a dozen pairs. . . . They work seven days a week. . . . Their destitution is very great."

Sweatshops   Small, poorly ventilated shops or apartments crammed with workers, often family members, who pieced together garments.

CHILD LABOR

Child labor was common in the garment trade and other industries. Shocked reformers in the 1890s told of the devastating effect of factory labor on children's lives. The legs of a 7-year-old girl were paralyzed and deformed because she toiled "day after day with little legs crossed, pulling out bastings from garments."

In the gritty coal mines of Pennsylvania, breaker boys, youths who stood on ladders to pluck waste matter from coal tumbling down long chutes, breathed harmful coal dust all day. Girls under sixteen made up half the work force in the

Noted urban photographer Lewis Hine captures the cramped working conditions and chid labor in this late nineteenth-century canning factory. Women and children provided a cheap and efficient work force for labor-intensive industries.

George Eastman House

silk mills of Scranton and Wilkes-Barre, Pennsylvania. Girls with missing fingers from mill accidents were a common sight in those towns.

By 1900, Pennsylvania and a few other states had passed legislation regulating child labor, but enforcement of these laws was lax. Parents desperate for income often lied about their children's age, and authorities were often sympathetic toward mill or mine owners, who paid taxes and provided other civic benefits.

WORKING WOMEN

The head of the Massachusetts Bureau of Labor Statistics observed in 1882, "A family of workers can always live well, but the man with a family of small children to support, unless his wife works also, has a small chance of living properly." Between 1870 and 1920, the number of women and children in the work force more than doubled.

Middle-class reformers worried about the impact on family life and on the women themselves. Employers paid them less than they paid men. A U.S. Department of Labor commissioner asserted that women worked only for "dress or pleasure." In one St. Louis factory in 1896, women received $4 a week for work for which men were paid $16 a week. An Iowa shoe saleswoman complained in 1886, "I don't get the salary the men clerks do, although this day I am 600 sales ahead! Call this justice? But I have to grin and bear it, because I am so unfortunate as to be a woman."

In 1900, fully 85 percent of wage-earning women were unmarried and under the age of 25. They supported siblings and contributed to their parents' income. A typical female factory worker earned $6 a week in 1900. On this wage, a married woman might help pull her family up to subsistence level. For a single woman on her own, however, it allowed little more, in writer O. Henry's words, "than marshmallows and tea."

Some working-class women turned to prostitution. The income from prostitution could exceed factory work by four or five times. "So is it any wonder," asked the Chicago Vice Commission in 1894, "that a tempted girl who receives only six dollars per week working with her hands sells her body for twenty-five dollars per week . . . ?" As much as 10 percent of New York City's female working-age population worked in the sex business in the 1890s. During depression years, the percentage was probably higher.

Victorian America condemned anyone guilty of even the most trivial moral transgression to social ostracism and treated the prostitute as a social outcast. Even those who urged understanding for women who violated convention faced exclusion. Kate Chopin, a New Orleans novelist, caused a tremendous uproar in the 1890s with stories that took a compassionate view of women involved in adultery, alcoholism, and divorce. Booksellers boycotted Theodore Dreiser's 1900 novel *Sister Carrie*, whose title character lived with a succession of men, one of them married.

Over time, more work options opened to women, but low wages and poor working conditions persisted. Women entered the needle trades after widespread introduction of the sewing machine in the 1870s. Factories gradually replaced sweatshops in the garment industry after 1900, but working conditions improved little.

The introduction of the typewriter transformed clerical office work, dominated by men until the 1870s, into a female preserve. Women were alleged to have the greater dexterity and tolerance for repetition that the new technology required. But they earned only half the salary of the men they replaced. Middle-class parents saw office work as clean and honorable compared with factory or

QUICK REVIEW

Working Women in 1900

◆ 85 percent of wage-earning women unmarried and under 25.

◆ Typical female factory worker earned $6 per week.

◆ Some working-class women turned to prostitution.

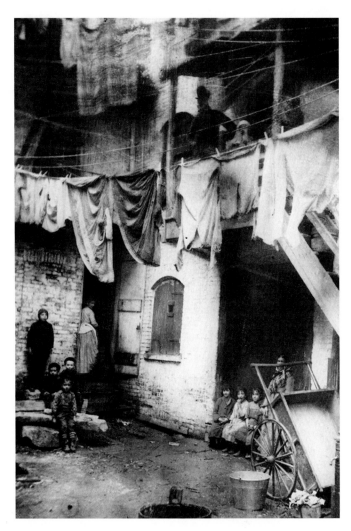

The new industrial age created great wealth and abject poverty, and the city became the stage upon which these hard economic lessons played out. Here, a "modest" Fifth Avenue mansion in turn-of-the-century new York City; further downtown, Jacob Riis found this tenement courtyard.

Getty Images Inc. Hutton Archive Photos

Photograph by Jacob A. Riis, The Jacob A. Riis Collection, Museum of the City of New York

sales work. Consequently, clerical positions drew growing numbers of native-born women into the urban work force after 1890. A top-paid office worker in the 1890s earned as much as $900 a year. Teaching, another acceptable occupation for middle-class women, typically paid only $500 a year.

By the turn of the century, women were gaining increased access to higher education. Coeducational colleges were rare, but by 1900 there were many women-only institutions. By 1910, women comprised 40 percent of all American college students, compared to 20 percent in 1870. Despite these gains, many professions—including those of physician and attorney—remained closed to women. Men still accounted for more than 95 percent of all doctors in 1900. Women also were rarely permitted to pursue doctoral degrees.

Women college graduates mostly found employment in such "nurturing" professions as nursing, teaching, and library work. Between 1900 and 1910, the number of trained women nurses increased sevenfold. In response to the growing problems of urban society, a relatively new occupation, social work, opened to women. Reflecting new theories on the nurturing role of women, school boards after 1900 turned exclusively to female teachers for the elementary grades.

Despite these gains, women's work remained segregated. Some reforms meant to improve working conditions for women reinforced this state of affairs. Protective legislation restricted women to "clean" occupations and limited their ability to compete with men in other jobs. As an economist explained in 1901,

QUICK REVIEW

Stereotypes

- Most Americans believed that a woman's proper role was to care for her home and her family.
- Stereotypes reinforced notion that working women were promiscuous.
- Sexual harassment at work was rarely punished.

"The wage bargaining power of men is weakened by the competition of women and children, hence a law restricting the hours of women and children may also be looked upon as a law to protect men in their bargaining power."

Women also confronted negative stereotypes. Most Americans in 1900 believed a woman's proper role was to care for home and family. The system of "treating" on dates reinforced stories about loose sales-girls, flirtatious secretaries, and easy factory workers. Newspapers and magazines published exposés of working girls descending into prostitution. These images encouraged sexual harassment at work, which was rarely punished.

Working women faced a difficult dilemma. To justify their desire for education and training, they had to argue that it would enhance their roles as wives and mothers. To gain improved wages and working conditions, they increasingly supported protective legislation that restricted their opportunities in the workplace.

RESPONSES TO POVERTY AND WEALTH

While industrial magnates flaunted their fabulous wealth, working men and women led hard lives on meager salaries and in crowded dwellings. In his exposé of poverty in New York, *How the Other Half Lives* (1890), Danish-born urban reformer Jacob Riis wrote that "the half that is on top cares little for the struggles, and less for the fate of those who are underneath so long as it is able to hold them there and keep its own seat." (See American Views: "Tenement Life" p. 477)

The industrial economy strained working-class family life. Workplace accidents and deaths left many families with only one parent. Infant mortality among the working poor in New York was nearly twice the citywide norm in 1900. Epidemic diseases, especially typhoid, an illness spread by impure water, devastated crowded working-class districts.

Inadequate housing was the most visible badge of poverty. Crammed into four- to six-story buildings on tiny lots, **tenement** apartments in urban slums were notorious for their lack of ventilation and light.

Authorities did nothing to enforce laws prohibiting overcrowding for fear of leaving people homeless. The population density of New York's tenement district in 1894 was 986.4 people per acre, the highest in the world at the time. (Today, the densest areas of American cities rarely exceed 400 people per acre, and only Calcutta, India, and Lagos, Nigeria, approach the crowding of turn-of-the-century New York; today Manhattan has 84 residents per acre).

The settlement house movement, which originated in England, sought to moderate the effects of poverty through neighborhood reconstruction. New York's Neighborhood Guild, established in 1886, was the first settlement house in the country; Chicago's **Hull House**, founded in 1889 by Jane Addams, a young Rockford (Illinois) College graduate, became the most famous.

The settlement house provided the working poor with facilities and education to help them improve their environment and, eventually, to escape it. By 1900, there were more than one hundred settlement houses throughout the country.

At Hull House, a rambling old residence in a working-class immigrant neighborhood, Italian immigrants and their families came to settle legal disputes and formed the Young Citizens' Club to discuss municipal issues. Addams renovated an adjacent saloon and transformed it into a gym. She began a day nursery as well. When workers at a nearby knitting factory went on strike, Addams arbitrated the conflict.

Settlement house gyms like the one Addams built for Hull-House provided them with much-needed recreational space. So too did the athletic fields and playgrounds built adjacent to public schools after 1900.

Tenements Four- to six-story residential dwellings, once common in New York, built on tiny lots without regard to providing ventilation or light.

Hull House Chicago settlement house that became part of a broader neighborhood revitalization project led by Jane Addams.

• AMERICAN VIEWS •

TENEMENT LIFE

I n 1890, the Danish immigrant Jacob A. Riis published How the Other Half Lives, an exposé of conditions among immigrants in New York City's Lower East Side. Riis's gruesome depictions, complete with vivid photographs, shocked readers and provided an impetus for housing reform in New York and other cities. His scientific tone, devoid of sensationalism, rendered the scenes that much more dramatic. For a nation that valued family life and the sanctity of childhood, Riis's accounts of how the environment, inside and outside the tenement, destroyed young lives provided moving testimony that for some, and perhaps many immigrants, the "promise" had been taken out of the Promised Land.

WHAT IS Jacob Riis's attitude toward the tenement dwellers? Considering the destitute character of the family Riis describes, what sort of assistance do you think they receive? Why do you suppose the authorities were reluctant to enforce sanitary, capacity, and building regulations in these neighborhoods?

Look into any of these houses, everywhere the same piles of rags, of malodorous bones and musty paper all of which the sanitary police flatter themselves they have banished. . . . Here is a "parlor" and two pitch-dark coops called bedrooms. Truly, the bed is all there is room for. The family teakettle is on the stove, doing duty for the time being as a wash-boiler. By night it will have returned to its proper use again, a practical illustration of how poverty . . . makes both ends meet. One, two, three beds are there, if the old boxes and heaps of foul straw can be called by that name; a broken stove with crazy pipe from which the smoke leaks at every joint, a table of rough boards propped up on boxes, piles of rubbish in the corner. The closeness and smell are appalling. . . .

Well do I recollect the visit of a health inspector to one of these tenements on a July day when the thermometer outside was climbing high in the nineties; but inside, in that awful room, with half a dozen persons washing, cooking, and sorting rags, lay the dying baby alongside the stove, where the doctor's thermometer ran up to 115 degrees! Perishing for the want of a breath of fresh air in this city of untold charities! . . .

A message came one day last spring summoning me to a Mott Street tenement in which lay a child dying from some unknown disease. With the "charity doctor" I found the patient on the top floor, stretched upon two chairs in a dreadfully stifling room. She was gasping in the agony of peritonitis [abdominal infection] that had already written its death-sentence on her wan and pinched face. The whole family, father, mother, and four ragged children, sat around looking on with the stony resignation of helpless despair that had long since given up the fight against fate as useless. A glance around the wretched room left no doubt as to the cause of the children's condition. "Improper nourishment," said the doctor, which translated to suit the place, meant starvation. The father's hands were crippled from lead poisoning. He had not been able to work for a year. A contagious disease of the eyes, too long neglected, had made the mother and one of the boys nearly blind. The children cried with hunger. . . . For months the family had subsisted on two dollars a week from the priest, and a few loaves and a piece of corned beef which the sisters sent them on Saturday. The doctor gave direction for the treatment of the child, knowing that it was possible only to alleviate its sufferings until death should end them, and left some money for food for the rest. An hour later, when I returned, I found them feeding the dying child with ginger ale, bought for two cents a bottle at the pedlar's cart down the street. A pitying neighbor had proposed it as the one thing she could think of as likely to make the child forget its misery.

According to the **Gospel of Wealth**, a theory popular among industrialists, intellectuals, and some politicians, any intervention on behalf of the poor was of doubtful benefit. Hard work and perseverance, in this view, led to wealth. Poverty, by implication, resulted from the flawed character of the poor. Steel tycoon Andrew Carnegie sought to soften this doctrine by stressing the responsibility of the affluent to set an example for the working class and to return some of their wealth to the communities in which they lived. Carnegie accordingly endowed libraries, cultural institutions, and schools throughout the country. Beneficial as they might be, however, these philanthropic efforts scarcely addressed the causes of poverty, and few industrialists followed Carnegie's example.

Social Darwinism, a flawed attempt to apply Charles Darwin's theory of biological evolution to human society, emerged as a more common justification than the Gospel of Wealth for the growing gap between rich and poor. According to social Darwinism, the human race evolves only through competition. The fit survive, the weak perish, and humanity moves forward. Wealth reflects fitness; poverty, weakness. For governments or private agencies to interfere with this natural process is futile. Thus Columbia University president Nicholas Murray Butler, claiming that "nature's cure for most social and political diseases is better than man's," warned against charity for the poor in 1900. Standard Oil's John D. Rockefeller concurred, asserting that the survival of the fittest is "the working out of a law of nature and a law of God."

WORKERS ORGANIZE

The growing power of industrial corporations and the declining power of workers generated social tensions reminiscent of the sectional crisis that triggered the Civil War. Two prolonged depressions, one beginning in 1873 and the other in 1893—threw as many as 2 million laborers out of work. Skilled workers, their security undermined by deskilling and their hopes of becoming managers or starting their own businesses disappearing, saw the nation "drifting," as a carpenter put it in 1870, "to that condition of society where a few were rich, and the many very poor."

Beginning after the depression of 1873 and continuing through World War I, workers fought their loss of independence to industrial capital by organizing and striking (see the overview table "Workers Organize" p. 479). The first episode in this conflict was the railroad strike of 1877, sometimes referred to as the **Great Uprising**. When Baltimore & Ohio Railroad workers struck in July to protest another series of pay cuts, President Rutherford B. Hayes dispatched federal troops to protect the line's property. The use of federal troops infuriated railroad workers throughout the East and Midwest, and they stopped work as well. Violence erupted in Pittsburgh when the state militia opened fire on strikers and their families, killing twenty-five, including a woman and three children. As news of the violence spread, so did the strike, as far as Galveston, Texas, and San Francisco. Over the next two weeks, police and federal troops continued to clash with strikers. By the time this first nationwide work stoppage in American history ended, more than one hundred had been killed. The wage cuts remained.

The **Knights of Labor**, a union of craft workers founded in Philadelphia in 1869, grew dramatically after the Great Uprising under the leadership of Terence V. Powderly. The Knights saw "an inevitable . . . conflict between the wage system of labor and [the] republican system of government." Remarkably inclusive for its time, the Knights welcomed black workers and women to its ranks. Victories in several small railroad strikes in 1884 and 1885 boosted its membership to nearly one million workers by 1886.

In that year, the Knights led a movement for an eight-hour workday. Ignoring the advice of the national leadership to avoid strikes, local chapters staged more than 1,500 strikes involving more than 340,000 workers. Workers also organized boycotts against manufacturers and ran candidates for local elections. Social

Gospel of Wealth Thesis that hard work and perseverance lead to wealth, implying that poverty is a character flaw.

Social Darwinism The application of Charles Darwin's theory of biological evolution to society, holding that the fittest and wealthiest survive, the weak and the poor perish, and government action is unable to alter this "natural" process.

Great Uprising Unsuccessful railroad strike of 1877 to protest wage cuts and the use of federal troops against strikers; the first nationwide work stoppage in American history.

Knights of Labor Labor union founded in 1869 that included skilled and unskilled workers irrespective of race or gender.

OVERVIEW

WORKERS ORGANIZE

Organization	History	Strategies
Knights of Labor	Founded in 1869; open to all workers; declined after 1886	Disapproved of strikes; supported a broad array of labor reforms, including cooperatives; favored political involvement
American Federation of Labor	Founded in 1886; open to craft-workers only, and organized by craft; hostile to black workers and women; became the major U.S. labor organization after 1880s	Opposed political involvement; supported a limited number of labor reforms; approved of strikes
Industrial Workers of the World	Founded in 1905; consisted mainly of semiskilled and unskilled immigrant workers; represented a small portion of the work force; disappeared after World War I	Highly political; supported socialist programs; approved of strikes and even violence to achieve ends

reformer Henry George made a strong, though losing, effort in the New York City mayoral race, and labor candidates won several local offices in Chicago.

Employers convinced the courts to order strikers back to work and used local authorities to arrest strikers for trespassing or obstructing traffic. In early May 1886, police killed four unarmed workers during a skirmish with strikers in Chicago. A bomb exploded at a meeting to protest the slayings in the city's Haymarket Square, killing seven policemen and four strikers and wounding one hundred. Eight strike leaders were tried for the deaths, and despite a lack of evidence linking them to the bomb, four were executed.

The Haymarket Square incident and a series of disastrous walkouts that followed it weakened the Knights of Labor. By 1890, it had shrunk to less than 100,000 members. Thereafter, the **American Federation of Labor (AFL)**, formed in 1886, became the major organizing body for skilled workers.

The AFL, led by British immigrant Samuel Gompers, emphasized **collective bargaining**—negotiations between management and union representatives—to secure workplace concessions. The AFL also discouraged political activism among its members. With this business unionism, the AFL proved more effective than the Knights of Labor at meeting the needs of skilled workers, but it left out the growing numbers of unskilled workers, black workers, and women to whom the Knights had given a glimmer of hope.

The AFL organized skilled workers by craft and focused on a few basic workplace issues important to each craft. The result was greater cohesion and discipline. In 1889 and 1890, more than 60 percent of AFL-sponsored strikes were successful. A series of work stoppages in the building trades between 1888 and 1891, for example, won an eight-hour day and a national agreement with builders.

In 1892, Andrew Carnegie dealt the steelworkers' union a major setback in the Homestead strike. Carnegie's manager, Henry Clay Frick, announced that he would negotiate only with workers individually at Homestead and not renew the union's collective bargaining contract. Frick locked the union workers

18–5
Address by George Engel, Condemned Haymarket Anarchist (1886)

American Federation of Labor (AFL)
Union formed in 1886 that organized skilled workers along craft lines and emphasized a few workplace issues rather than a broad social program.

Collective bargaining
Representatives of a union negotiating with management on behalf of all members.

out of the plant and hired three hundred armed guards to protect the nonunion ("scab") workers he planned to hire in their place. Union workers, with the help of their families and unskilled workers, seized control of Homestead's roads and utilities. In a bloody confrontation, they drove back Frick's forces. Nine strikers and seven guards died. But Pennsylvania's governor called out the state militia to open the plant and protect the nonunion workers. After four months, the union capitulated. With the defeat of the union, skilled steelworkers lost their power on the shop floor. Eventually, mechanization cost them their jobs.

In 1894, workers suffered another setback in the Pullman strike, against George Pullman's Palace Sleeping Car Company. When the company cut wages for workers at its plant in the "model" suburb it built outside Chicago without a corresponding cut in the rent it charged workers for their company-owned housing, the workers appealed for support to the American Railway Union (ARU), led by Eugene V. Debs. The membership of the ARU, an independent union not affiliated with the AFL, had swelled to more than 150,000 workers after it won a strike earlier in 1894 against the Great Northern Railroad. Debs ordered a boycott of any trains with Pullman cars. The railroads fired workers who refused to handle trains with Pullman cars. Debs called for all ARU members to walk off the job, crippling rail travel nationwide. When Debs refused to honor a federal court injunction against the strike, President Cleveland, at the railroads' request, ordered federal troops to enforce it. Debs was arrested, and the strike and the union were broken.

These setbacks and the depression that began in 1893 left workers and their unions facing an uncertain future. But, growing public opposition to the use of troops, the high-handed tactics of industrialists, and the rising concerns of Americans about the power of big business sustained the unions. Workers would call more than 22,000 strikes over the next decade, the majority of them union-sponsored. Still, no more than 7 percent of the American work force was organized by 1900.

NEW IMMIGRANTS

The late-nineteenth-century was a period of unprecedented worldwide population movements. The United States was not the only New World destination for the migrants of this period. Many also found their way to Brazil, Argentina, and Canada.

The scale of overseas migration to the United States after 1870 dwarfed all that preceded it. Between 1870 and 1910, the country received more than 20 million immigrants. Before the Civil War, most immigrants came from northern Europe. Most of the new immigrants, in contrast, came from southern and eastern Europe. Swelling their ranks were migrants from Mexico and Asia, as well as internal migrants moving from the countryside to American cities (see Map 18–1).

By that time, the industrial work force was charging. As the large factories installed labor- and time-saving machinery, unskilled foreign-born labor flooded onto the shop floor. For many reasons, not least of which were the adjustments required for life in a new country, labor radicalism was not a high priority for many of the newcomers. Immigrants transformed not only the workplace, but the cities where they settled and the nation itself. In the process, they changed themselves.

OLD WORLD BACKGROUNDS

A growing rural population combined with unequal land distribution to create economic distress in late-nineteenth-century Europe. More and more people found themselves working ever-smaller plots as laborers rather than owners. In Poland, laborers accounted for 80 percent of the agricultural population in the

QUICK REVIEW

Pullman Strike

◆ 1894 strike against Pullman's Palace Sleeping Car Company.

◆ Pullman workers sought solidarity with Eugene Debs' American Railway Union.

◆ President Cleveland ordered federal troops to enforce injunction against strike.

WHAT IMPACT did new immigration and migration have on cities in the North?

MAP EXPLORATION

To explore an interactive version of this map, go to **http://www.prenhall.com/goldfield2/map18.1**

Number of Immigrants

From Asia	700,000
Main groups	
Chinese	370,000
Japanese	275,000
From Canada	2,200,000
From Europe	30,000,000
Main groups	
Germans	5,000,000
Irish	4,500,000
Italians	4,500,000
Poles	2,600,000
English	2,600,000
Jews	2,000,000
From Latin America	900,000

MAP 18–1

Patterns of Immigration, 1820–1914   The migration to the United States was part of a worldwide transfer of population that accelerated with the industrial revolution and the accompanying improvements in transportation.

WHAT FORCES propelled so many people to emigrate from European countries?

1860s. Similar conditions prevailed in the Mezzogiorno region of southern Italy, home of three out of four Italian emigrants to America.

For Russian Jews, religious persecution compounded economic hardship. In tsarist Russia, Jews could not own real estate and were barred from work in farming, teaching, the civil service, and the law. Confined to designated cities, they struggled to support themselves. After the assassination of Tsar Alexander II in 1881, which some leaders falsely blamed on Jews, the government sanctioned a series of violent attacks on Jewish settlements known as **pogroms**. At the same time, the government forced Jews into fewer towns, deepening their poverty and making them easier targets for violence.

The late-nineteenth-century transportation technologies permitted people to leave Europe. Railroad construction boomed in Europe during the 1870s and 1880s, and steamship companies in several European countries built giant vessels to transport passengers quickly and safely across the Atlantic. The companies sent agents into Russia, Poland, Italy, and the Austro-Hungarian empire to solicit business.

Sometime during the 1880s, an agent from the Hamburg-American Line (HAPAG), a German steamship company, visited a village in the Russian Ukraine where the great grandparents of one of this book's authors lived. Shortly after his visit, they boarded a train to Austrian-occupied Poland and Hamburg. There they boarded a HAPAG steamer emblazoned with a large banner proclaiming "Willkommen" ("Welcome"). Just boarding that ship they felt they were entering the United States. Millions of others like them sailed on ocean liners from Germany, Italy, and Great Britain over the next thirty years.

WHERE TO LEARN MORE

★ Strawbery Banke,
Portsmouth,
New Hampshire
www.strawberybanke.org

Pogroms   Government-directed attacks against Jewish citizens, property, and villages in tsarist Russia beginning in the 1880s; a primary reason for Russian Jewish migration to the United States.

WHERE TO LEARN MORE

Japanese American National
Museum, Los Angeles, California
www.janm.org

19–12
Mary Antin, *The Promise Land*
(1912)

Chain migration Process common
to many immigrant groups whereby
one family member brings over
other family members, who in turn
bring other relatives and friends and
occasionally entire villages.

Chinese and Japanese immigrants also came to the United States in appreciable numbers for the first time during the late nineteenth century. Most Chinese immigrants came from Canton in South China and worked on railroads and in mines throughout the West and as farm laborers in California. Many eventually settled in cities such as San Francisco where they established residential enclaves referred to as Chinatowns. The first wave of Japanese immigrants came by way of Hawaii to work on farms in California, taking the place of Chinese workers who had moved to the cities.

Most migrants intended to stay only a year or two, long enough to earn money to buy land or, more likely, to enter a business back home and improve life for themselves and their families. Roughly half of all immigrants to the United States between 1880 and World War I returned to their country of origin. Some made several round trips. As Jews were unwelcome in the lands they left, no more than 10 percent of Jewish immigrants returned to Europe.

Most newcomers were young men. (Jews again were the exception: They tended to migrate permanently in families.) Immigrants easily found work in the large urban factories with their voracious demands for unskilled labor. Except for the Japanese, few immigrants came to work on farms after 1880.

By 1900, women began to equal men among all immigrant groups as young men who decided to stay sent for their families. The success of Francesco Barone, a Buffalo tavern owner, convinced eight thousand residents of his former village in Sicily to migrate to that city, many arriving on tickets Barone purchased, a process called **chain migration**.

Immigrants tended to live in neighborhoods among people from the same homeland and preserve key aspects of their Old World culture. For Italians from the Mezzogiorno, for example, the family was the basic institution for obtaining work and securing assistance in times of stress, death, or sickness.

The desire of the new immigrants to retain their cultural traditions led contemporary observers to doubt their ability to assimilate into American society. Even sympathetic observers, such as social workers, marveled at the utterly foreign character of immigrant districts. In 1900, Philadelphia social worker Emily Dinwiddie visited an Italian neighborhood and described "black-eyed children, rolling and tumbling together, the gaily colored dresses of the women and the crowds of street vendors, that give the neighborhood a wholly foreign appearance."

THE NEIGHBORHOOD

Rarely did a particular ethnic group comprise more than 50 percent of a neighborhood. Chinese were the exception, but even the borders of Chinatowns usually overlapped with other neighborhoods.

In smaller cities and in the urban South, where foreign-born populations were smaller, ethnic groups were more geographically dispersed, though occasionally they might inhabit the same neighborhood. In turn-of-the-century Memphis, for example, Irish, Italian, and Jewish immigrants lived cheek by jowl in a single immigrant district (called the "Pinch"), sharing schools and recreational space even as they led their singular institutional, religious, and family lives.

Immigrants maintained their cultural traditions through the establishment of religious and communal institutions. The church or synagogue became the focal point for immigrant neighborhood life. Much more than a place of worship, it was a school for transmitting Old World values and language to American-born children and a recreational facility and a gathering place for community leaders. Jewish associations called *landsmanshaften* arranged for burials, jobs, housing, and support for the sick, poor, and elderly.

Religious institutions played a less formal role among Chinese and Japanese neighborhoods. For them, the family functioned as the source of religious activity and communal organization. Chinatowns were organized in clans of people with the same surname. An umbrella organization called the Chinese Consolidated Benevolent Association emerged; it functioned like the Jewish *landsmanshaften*. Perhaps most important, the association shipped the bones of deceased members back to China for burial in ancestral cemeteries. A similar association, the Japanese Association of America, governed the Japanese community in the United States. This organization was sponsored by the Japanese government, which was sensitive to mistreatment of its citizens abroad and anxious that immigrants set a good example. The Japanese Association, unlike other ethnic organizations, actively encouraged assimilation and stressed the importance of Western dress and learning English.

Ethnic newspapers, theaters, and schools supplemented associational life for immigrants. The Jewish *Daily Forward*, first published in New York in 1897, reminded readers of the importance of keeping the Sabbath while admonishing them to adopt American customs.

THE JOB

All immigrants perceived the job as the way to independence and as a way out, either back to the Old World or into the larger American society. Immigrants typically received their first job with the help of a countryman. Italian, Chinese, Japanese, and Mexican newcomers worked with contractors who placed them in jobs. They exacted a fee, sometimes extortionate, for their services. Other immigrant groups, such as Poles and Russian Jews, often secured work through their ethnic associations or village or family connections. Family members sometimes exchanged jobs with one another.

The type of work available to immigrants depended on their skills, the local economy, and local discrimination. Mexican migrants to southern California, for example, concentrated in railroad construction, replacing Chinese laborers when the federal government excluded Chinese immigration after 1882. Mexicans built the interurban rail lines of Los Angeles in 1900 and established communities at their construction camps. Los Angeles businessmen barred Mexicans from other occupations. Similarly, Chinese immigrants were confined to work in laundries and restaurants within the boundaries of Los Angeles's Chinatown. The Japanese who came to Los Angeles around 1900 were forced into sectors of the economy native-born whites had either shunned or failed to exploit. The Japanese turned this discrimination to their benefit when they transformed the cultivation of market garden crops into a major agricultural enterprise. By 1904, Japanese farmers owned more than 50,000 acres in California. George Shima, who came to California from Japan in 1889 with a little capital, made himself the "Potato King" of the Sacramento Delta. By 1913, Shima owned 28,000 acres of farmland.

Stereotypes also channeled immigrants' work options, sometimes benefiting one group at the expense of another. Jewish textile entrepreneurs, for example, sometimes hired only Italians because they thought them less prone to unionization than Jewish workers. Pittsburgh steelmakers preferred Polish workers to the black workers who began arriving in northern cities in appreciable numbers after 1900. This began the decades-long tradition of handing down steel mill jobs through the generations in Polish families.

Jews, alone among European ethnic groups, found work almost exclusively with one another. Jews comprised three-quarters of the more than half-million workers in New York's City's garment industry in 1910. Jews were also heavily concentrated in the retail trade.

WHERE TO LEARN MORE

Pasa al Norte, El Paso, Texas
**www.utminers.utep.edu/panihm/
default.htm**

Like their native-born counterparts, few married immigrant women worked outside the home, but unlike the native-born, many Italian and Jewish women did piecework for the garment industry in their apartments. Unmarried Polish women often worked in factories or as domestic servants. Japanese women, married and single, worked with their families on farms. Until revolution in China in 1911 began to erode traditional gender roles, married Chinese immigrant women typically remained home.

The paramount goal for many immigrants was to work for themselves rather than someone else. Most new arrivals, however, had few skills and no resources beyond their wits with which to realize their dreams. Major banks at the time were unlikely to extend even a small business loan to a budding ethnic entrepreneur. Family members and small ethnic-based community banks provided the initial stake for most immigrant businesses. Many of these banks failed, but a few survived and prospered. For example, the Bank of Italy, established by Amadeo Pietro Giannini in San Francisco in 1904, eventually grew into the Bank of America, one of the nation's largest financial institutions today.

Immigrants could not fully control their own destinies in the United States any more than native-born Americans could. Hard work did not always ensure success. Almost all immigrants, however, faced the antiforeign prejudice of American **nativism**.

NATIVISM

Immigrants have not always received a warm reception. Ben Franklin groused about the "foreignness" of German immigrants during the colonial era. From the 1830s to 1860, nativist sentiment, directed mainly at Irish Catholic immigrants, expressed itself in occasional violence and job discrimination.

When immigration revived after the Civil War, so did antiforeign sentiment. But late-nineteenth-century nativism differed in two ways from its antebellum predecessor. First, the target was no longer Irish Catholics but the even more numerous Catholics and Jews of southern and eastern Europe, people whose language and usually darker complexions set them apart from the native-born majority. Second, late-nineteenth-century nativism maintained that there was a natural hierarchy of race. At the top, with the exception of the Irish, were northern European whites, especially those of Anglo-Saxon descent. Following below them were French, Slavs, Poles, Italians, Jews, Asians, and Africans. Social Darwinism, which justified the class hierarchy, reinforced scientific racism.

When the "inferior" races arrived in the United States in significant numbers after 1880, a prominent Columbia University professor wrote in 1887 that Hungarians and Italians were "of such a character as to endanger our civilization." Nine years later, the director of the U.S. census warned that eastern and southern Europeans were "beaten men from beaten races. They have none of the ideas and aptitudes which fit men to take up readily and easily the problem of self-care and self-government." The result of unfettered migration would be "race suicide."

In the mid-1870s, a Chicago newspaper described recently arrived Bohemian immigrants (from the present-day Czech Republic) as "depraved beasts, harpies, decayed physically and spiritually, mentally and morally, thievish and licentious." A decade later, with eastern Europeans still pouring into Chicago, another newspaper suggested: "Let us whip these slavic wolves back to the European dens from which they issue, or in some way exterminate them." The *New York Times* concluded that Americans "pretty well agreed" that these foreigners were "of a kind which we are better without." *Scientific American* warned immigrants to "assimilate" quickly or "share the fate of the native Indians" and face "a quiet but sure extermination."

Nativism   Favoring the interests and culture of native-born inhabitants over those of immigrants.

Such sentiments generated proposals to restrict foreign immigration. Chinese immigrants' different culture and their willingness to accept low wages in mining and railroad construction provoked resentment among native- and European-born workers. In 1870, the Republican-dominated Congress passed the Naturalization Act, which limited citizenship to "white persons and persons of African descent." The act was specifically intended to prevent Chinese from becoming citizens—a ban not lifted until 1943—but it affected other Asian groups also. The Chinese Exclusion Act of 1882 made the Chinese the only ethnic group in the world that could not emigrate freely to the United States. Anti-Asian violence raced through mining communities in the West for the next two years.

Labor competition also contributed to the rise of another anti-immigrant organization. A group of skilled workers and small businessmen formed the American Protective Association (APA) in 1887 and claimed half a million members a year later. The APA sought to limit Catholic civil rights in the United States to protect the jobs of Protestant workingmen.

The Immigration Restriction League (IRL), formed in 1894, proposed to require prospective immigrants to pass a literacy test that they presumed most southern and eastern Europeans would fail. The IRL vowed that its legislation would protect "the wages of our workingmen against the fatal competition of low-price labor."

The IRL ultimately failed to have its literacy requirement enacted. The return of prosperity and the growing preference of industrialists for immigrant labor put an end to calls for formal restrictions on immigration for the time being.

Immigrants and their communal associations fought attempts to impede free access of their countrymen to the United States. The Japanese government even hinted at violent retaliation if Congress ever enacted restrictive legislation similar to that imposed on the Chinese. But most immigrants believed that the more "American" they became, the less prejudice they would encounter.

In 1895, a group of American-born Chinese in California formed a communal association called the Native Sons of the Golden State (a deliberate response to a nativist organization that called itself the Native Sons of the Golden West). The association's constitution declared, "It is imperative that no members shall have sectional, clannish, Tong [a secret fraternal organization] or party prejudices against each other. . . . Whoever violates this provision shall be expelled." A guidebook written at the same time for immigrant Jews recommended that they "hold fast," calling that attitude "most necessary in America. Forget your past, your customs, and your ideals." Although it is doubtful whether most Jewish immigrants followed this advice whole, it nonetheless reflects the way the pressure to conform modified the cultures of all immigrant groups.

Assimilation connotes the loss of one culture in favor of another. The immigrant experience of the late nineteenth and early twentieth centuries might better be described as a process of adjustment between old ways and new, which resulted in entirely new cultural forms. The Japanese, for example, had not gone to Los Angeles to become truck farmers, but circumstances led them to that occupation. Sometimes economics and the availability of alternatives resulted in cultural modifications. In the old country, Portuguese held *festas* every Sunday honoring a patron saint. In New England towns, they confined the tradition to their churches instead of parading through the streets.

In a few cases, the New World offered greater opportunities to follow cultural traditions than the Old. Young women who migrated from Italy's Abruzzi region to Rochester, New York, found that it was easier to retain their Old World moral code and marry earlier in late-nineteenth-century Rochester, where young men outnumbered them significantly. In a similar way, Sicilians who migrated to lower

QUICK REVIEW

The Naturalization Act of 1870

◆ Limited citizenship to "white persons and persons of African descent."

◆ Act intended to bar Chinese from becoming citizens.

◆ Chinese Exclusion Act of 1882 made Chinese the only group that could not emigrate freely to the United States.

WHERE TO LEARN MORE

W

Angel Island State Park, San Francisco Bay, California
www.angelisland.org

African Americans gather for a religious service at night in the streets of New York City near the turn of the century.

Brown Brothers

⬡ **WHERE TO LEARN MORE**

★ Statue of Liberty National Monument and Ellis Island, New York, New York
www.nps.gov/stli

Great Migration The mass movement of African Americans from the rural South to the urban North.

Manhattan discovered that ready access to work and relatively high geographical mobility permitted them to live near and among their extended families much more easily than in Sicily.

Despite native-born whites' antagonism toward recent immigrants, the greatest racial divide in America remained that between black and white. New-comers viewed their "whiteness" as both a common bond with other European immigrant groups and a badge of acceptance into the larger society.

ROOTS OF THE GREAT MIGRATION

Nearly 90 percent of African Americans still lived in the South in 1900, most in rural areas. Between 1880 and 1900 black families began to move into the great industrial cities of the Northeast and Midwest. They were drawn by the same economic promise that attracted overseas migrants and were pushed by growing persecution in the South. They were also responding to the appeals of black Northerners. As a leading black newspaper, the *Chicago Defender* argued in the early 1900s, "To die from the bite of frost is far more glorious than at the hands of a mob. I beg you, my brother, to leave the benighted land." Job opportunities probably outweighed all other factors in motivating what became known as the **Great Migration.**

In most northern cities in 1900, black people typically worked as common laborers or domestic servants. They competed with immigrants for jobs, and in most cases they lost. Immigrants even claimed jobs that black workers had once dominated, like barbering and service work in hotels, restaurants, and transportation. Fannie Barrier Williams, a turn-of-the-century black activist in Chicago, complained that between 1895 and 1905, "the colored people of Chicago have lost . . . nearly every occupation of which they once had almost a monopoly."

Black women had particularly few options in the northern urban labor force. The retail and clerical jobs that attracted young working-class white women remained closed to black women. As one historian concluded, advertisers and corporate executives demanded "a pleasing physical appearance (or voice)—one that conformed to a native-born white American standard of female beauty [and served] as an important consideration in hiring office receptionists, secretaries, department store clerks, and telephone operators." Addie W. Hunter, who qualified for a civil service clerical position in Boston, could not find work to match her training. She concluded in 1916, "For the way things stand at present, it is useless to have the requirements. Color . . . will always be in the way."

Black migrants confronted similar frustrations in their quest for a place to live. They were restricted to segregated urban ghettos. In 1860, four out of every five black people in Detroit lived in a clearly defined district, for example. The black districts in Northern cities were more diverse than those of Southern cities. Migration brought rural Southerners, urban Southerners, and West Indians (especially in New York) together with the black Northerners already living there. People of all social classes lived in these districts.

The difficulties that black families faced to make ends meet paralleled in some ways those of immigrant working-class families. Restricted job options, however, limited the income of black families, even with black married women five times more likely to work than married white women. In black families, moreover, working teenage children were less likely to stay home and contribute their paychecks to the family income.

Popular culture reinforced the marginalization of African Americans, belittling black people and black characters with names like "Useless Peabody" and "Moses Abraham Highbrow." Immigrants frequented vaudeville and minstrel shows and absorbed the culture of racism from them. The new medium of film perpetuated the negative stereotypes.

An emerging middle-class leadership—including Robert Abbott, publisher of the *Chicago Defender*—sought to develop black businesses. But chronic lack of capital kept black businesses mostly small and confined to the ghetto. Black businesses failed at a high rate. Most black people worked outside the ghetto for white employers. Economic marginalization often attracted unsavory businesses to black neighborhoods. One recently arrived migrant from the South complained that in his Cleveland neighborhood, his family was surrounded by loafers, "gamblers [and] pocket pickers; I can not raise my children here like they should be. This is one of the worst places in principle you ever looked on in your life."

Other black institutions proved more lasting than black businesses. In Chicago in 1891, black physician Daniel Hale Williams established Provident Hospital, the nation's first interracially staffed hospital, with the financial help of wealthy white Chicagoans. Although it failed as an interracial experiment, the hospital thrived, providing an important training ground for black physicians and nurses.

The organization of black branches of the Young Men's and Young Women's Christian Association provided living accommodations, social facilities, and employment information for young black people. By 1910, black settlement houses modeled after white versions appeared in several cities.

NEW CITIES

Despite the hardships associated with urban life for both immigrants and black people, the American city continued to act, in the words of contemporary novelist Theodore Dreiser, as a "giant magnet." Immigration from abroad and migration from American farms to the cities resulted in an urban explosion during the late nineteenth century (see Map 18–2). The nation's population tripled between 1860 and 1920, but the urban population increased ninefold. Of the 1,700 cities listed in the 1900 census, only a handful—less than 2 percent—even existed in 1800.

In Europe, a few principal cities like Paris and Berlin absorbed most of the urban growth during this period. In the United States, in contrast, growth was more evenly distributed among many cities.

Despite the relative evenness of growth, a distinctive urban system had emerged by 1900, with New York and Chicago anchoring an urban-industrial core extending

WHO MADE up the new middle class?

MAP EXPLORATION

To explore an interactive version of this map, go to **http://www.prenhall.com/goldfield2/map18.2**

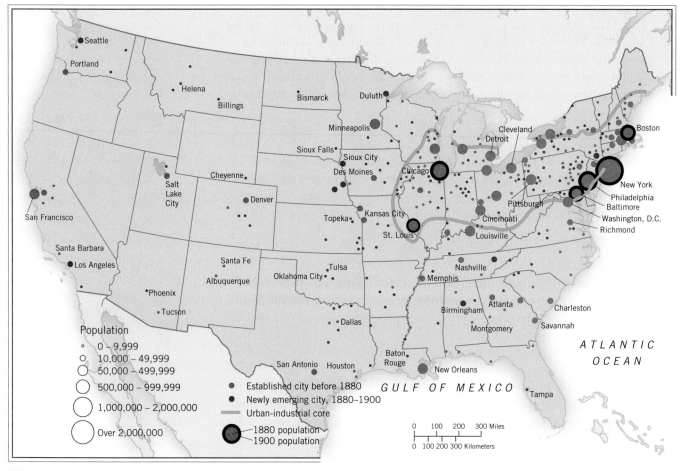

MAP 18–2

The Growth of America's Cities, 1880–1900   Several significant trends stand out on this map. First is the development of an urban-industrial core stretching from New England to the Midwest where the largest cities were located. And second is the emergence of relatively new cities in the South and West, reflecting the national dimensions of innovations in industry and transportation.

WHAT WERE the economic forces that contributed to the growth of some cities and the decline of others?

in a crescent from New England to the cities bordering the Great Lakes. This region included nine of the nation's ten largest cities in 1920. Western cities such as Denver, San Francisco, and Los Angeles emerged as dominant urban places in their respective regions but did not challenge the urban core for supremacy. Southern cities, limited in growth by low consumer demand, low wages, and weak capital formation, were drawn into the orbit of the urban core. Atlanta, an offspring of the railroad, prospered as the region's major way station for funneling wealth into the urban North. Dallas emerged as Atlanta's counterpart in the western South (see Chapter 19).

The crush of people and the emergence of new technologies expanded the city outward and upward as urban dwellers sorted themselves by social class and ethnic group. While the new infrastructure of water and sewer systems, bridges, and trolley tracks kept steel mills busy, it also fragmented the urban population by allowing settlements well beyond existing urban boundaries.

CENTERS AND SUBURBS

The centers of the country's great cities changed in scale and function in this era, achieving a prominence they would eventually lose in the twentieth century. Downtowns expanded up and out as tall buildings arose—monuments to business and finance—creating urban skylines. Residential neighborhoods were pushed out, leaving the center dominated by corporate headquarters and retail and entertainment districts.

Corporate heads administered their empires from downtown, even if their factories were located on the urban periphery or in other towns and cities. Banks and insurance companies clustered in financial centers like Atlanta's Five Points district to service the corporations. Department stores and shops clustered in retail districts in strategic locations along electric trolley lines. It was to these areas that urban residents usually referred when they talked about going "downtown." In the entertainment district, electric lights lit up theaters, dance halls, and restaurants into the night.

As retail and office uses crowded out residential dwellings from the city center, a new phenomenon emerged: the residential neighborhood. Advances in transportation technology, first the horse-drawn railway and, by the 1890s, the electric trolley, eased commuting for office workers. Some in the growing and increasingly affluent middle class left the crowded, polluted city altogether to live in new residential suburbs, leaving it to the growing ranks of working-class immigrants and African Americans.

The suburb emerged as the preferred residence for the urban middle class after 1870. The ideals that had promoted modest suburban growth earlier in the nineteenth century—privacy, aesthetics, and home ownership—became increasingly important for the growing numbers of middle-class families after 1880.

Consider the Russells of Short Hills, New Jersey. Short Hills lay 18 miles by railroad from New York City. William Russell, his wife, Ella Gibson Russell, and their six children moved there from Brooklyn in the late 1880s, seeking a "pleasant, cultured people whose society we could enjoy" and a cure for Russell's rheumatism. Russell owned and managed a small metal brokerage in New York and enjoyed gardening, reading, and socializing with his new neighbors. Ella Russell cared for the six children with the help of a servant and also belonged to several clubs and charities.

The design of the Russells's home reflected the principles Catherine Beecher and Harriet Beecher Stowe outlined in their suburban home Bible, *American Woman's Home* (1869). The new technology of central heating made it unnecessary to divide a house into many small rooms, each with its own fireplace or stove. Beecher and Stowe recommended that a home's ground floor have fewer but larger rooms to encourage the family to pursue their individual activities in a common space.

The entire Russell family was to be found enjoying the tennis, swimming, and skating facilities on the grounds of the Short Hills Athletic Club.

The emphasis on family togetherness also reflected the changing role of men in late-nineteenth-century society. Beecher and Stowe praised fathers who took active roles in child rearing and participated fully in the family's leisure activities. Women's roles also broadened, as Ella Russell's club work attested.

With the growth after 1890 of the electric trolley, elevated rail lines, and other relatively inexpensive forms of commuter travel, suburbs became accessible to a broader spectrum of the middle class. The social structure, architecture, and amenities of suburbs varied, depending on the rail service and distance from the city. The trolley and elevated railroads generated modest middle-class urban

WHERE TO LEARN MORE

Missouri Historical Society,
St. Louis, Missouri
www.mohistory.org

neighborhoods and suburbs, with densities decreasing and income increasing toward the ends of the lines. But for the working class—even skilled artisans—suburban living remained out of reach.

Residence, consumer habits, and leisure activities reflected growing social and class divisions. Yet, at the same time, the growing materialism of American society promised a common ground for its disparate ethnic, racial, and social groups.

THE NEW MIDDLE CLASS

From the colonial era, America's urban middle class had included professionals—physicians, lawyers, ministers, educators, editors—as well as merchants, shopkeepers, and skilled artisans (until they dropped from the middle class in the late nineteenth century). In the late nineteenth century, industrial technology and urban growth expanded the urban middle class to include salespeople, factory supervisors, managers, civil servants, technicians, and a broad range of "white-collar" office workers like insurance agents, bank tellers, and legal assistants. This newer middle class set national trends in residential patterns, consumption, and leisure.

The more affluent members of the new middle class repaired to new subdivisions within and outside the city limits. Simple row houses sheltered the growing numbers of clerks and civil servants who remained in the city. These dwellings contrasted sharply with the crowded one- or two-room apartments that confined the working class. Rents for these apartments ran as much as $3 a week at a time when few workers made more than $9 or $10.

The new middle class was a class of consumers. In earlier times, land had been a symbol of prestige. Now it was things. And the new industries obliged with a dazzling array of goods and technologies to make life easier and allow more time for family and leisure.

By 1910, the new middle class lived in all-electric homes, with indoor plumbing and appliances that eased food preparation. The modern city dweller worked by the clock, not by the sun. Eating patterns changed: cold, packaged cereals replaced hot meats at breakfast; fast lunches of Campbell's soup—"a meal in itself"—or canned stews weaned Americans from the heavy lunch. In Nashville Joel Cheek ground and blended coffee beans in his store for customers' convenience. He convinced the city's Maxwell House Hotel to serve his new concoction, and in 1907, when President Theodore Roosevelt visited the hotel and drained his cup, he declared that the coffee was "good to the very last drop." A slogan and Maxwell House coffee were born.

Advertisers now told Americans what they wanted; they created demand and developed loyalty for brand-name products. In early-twentieth-century New York, a six-story-high Heinz electric sign was a sensation, especially the 40-foot-long pickle at its top.

The middle class liked anything that saved time: trolleys, trains, electric razors, vacuum cleaners. By 1900, some 1.4 million telephones were in service, and many middle-class homes had one.

The middle class liked its news in an easy-to-read form. Urban tabloids multiplied after 1880, led by Joseph Pulitzer's *New York World* and William Randolph Hearst's *New York Journal*. The newspapers organized the news into topical sections, used bold headlines and graphics to catch the eye, ran human interest stories to capture the imagination, inaugurated sports pages to attract male readers, and offered advice columns for women.

As the visual crowded out the printed in advertising, newspapers, and magazines, these materials became more accessible to a wider urban audience. The tabloid press drew urban society together with new features such as the comic strip, and heartrending personal sagas drawn from real life. Immigrants received their initiation into the mainstream of American society through the tabloids.

Originating in the 1850s and 1860s with the construction of retail palaces such as Boston's Jordan Marsh, Philadelphia's Wanamaker & Brown, New York's Lord & Taylor, and Chicago's Marshall Field, the department store came to epitomize the bounty of the new industrial capitalism. The department store exuded limitless abundance with its extensive inventories, items for every budget, sumptuous surroundings, and efficient, trained personnel.

At first, most department store customers were middle-class married women. Industry churned out uniform, high-quality products in abundance, and middle-class salaries absorbed them. Department stores maintained consumers' interest with advertising campaigns arranged around holidays such as Easter and Christmas, the seasons, and the school calendar. Each event required new clothing and accessories, and the ready-made clothing industry changed fashions accordingly.

Soon the spectacle and merchandise of the department store attracted shoppers from all social strata, not just the middle class. "The principal cause of the stores' success," one shopper explained in 1892, "is the fact that their founders have understood the necessity of offering a new democracy whose needs and habits" are satisfied "in the cheapest possible way," providing "a taste for elegance and comfort unknown to previous generations." After 1890, department stores increasingly hired young immigrant women to cater to their growing foreign-born clientele. Mary Antin recalled how she and her teenage friends and sister would spend their Saturday nights in 1898 patrolling "a dazzlingly beautiful palace called a 'department store.'" It was there that Mary and her sister "exchanged our hateful home-made European costumes . . . for real American machine-made garments, and issued forth glorified in each other's eyes."

By 1900, department stores had added sporting goods and hardware sections and were attracting male as well as female customers from a wide social spectrum.

The expanding floor space devoted to sporting goods reflected the growth of leisure in urban society. And like other aspects of that society, leisure and recreation both separated and cut across social classes. As sports like football became important extracurricular activities at Harvard, Yale, and other elite universities, intercollegiate games became popular occasions for the upper class to congregate, renew school ties, and, not incidentally, discuss business. The first country club in the United States was founded in Brookline, Massachusetts, a Boston suburb, in 1882. Country clubs built golf courses for men and tennis courts primarily for women. The clubs offered a suburban retreat, away from the diverse middle- and working-class populations, where the elite could play in privacy.

Middle-class urban residents rode electric trolleys to suburban parks and bicycle and skating clubs. Both middle-class men and women participated in these sports, especially bicycling. New bikes cost at least $50, putting them beyond the reach of the working class.

Baseball was the leading spectator sport among the middle class. Baseball epitomized the nation's transition from a rural to an urban industrial society. Reflecting industrial society, baseball had clearly defined rules and was organized into leagues. Professional leagues were profit-making enterprises, and like other enterprises of the time, they frequently merged. Initially, most professional baseball games were played on weekday afternoons, making it hard for working-class

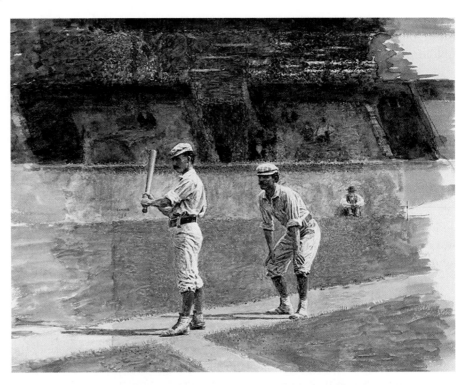

Thomas Eakins created this painting of baseball players practicing in 1875. Originating as a sport of urban gentlemen, baseball eventually broadened its appeal, drawing fans from all spectrums of city life.

Eakins, Thomas, *Baseball Players Practicing*, 1875. Watercolor; 10 7/8″ × 12 7/8″. Museum of Art, Rhode Island School of Design, Jesse Metcalf and Walter H. Kimball Funds. Photography by Cathy Carver

spectators to attend. After merging with the American Association (AA) in 1883, the National League adopted some of the AA's innovations to attract more fans, including beer sales, cheap admission, and, over the objections of Protestant churches, began playing Sunday games.

The tavern, or saloon, was the workingman's club. Typically an all-male preserve, the saloon provided drink, cheap food, and a place for workingmen to read a newspaper, socialize, and learn about job opportunities.

The amusement park, with its mechanical wonders, was another hallmark of the industrial city. Declining trolley fares made them accessible to the working class around 1900. Unlike taverns, they provided a place for working-class men and women to meet and date.

The most renowned of these parks was Brooklyn's Coney Island. In 1897, George C. Tilyou opened Steeplechase Park on Coney Island. He brought an invention by George Washington Ferris—a giant rotating vertical wheel equipped with swinging carriages—to the park from Chicago, and the Ferris Wheel quickly became a Coney Island signature. Together with such attractions as mechanical horses and 250,000 of Thomas Edison's light bulbs, Steeplechase dazzled patrons with its technological wonders. Steeplechase Park was quickly followed by Luna Park and Dreamland, and the Coney Island attractions became collectively known as "the poor man's paradise." One German immigrant opened a small café serving sausages that he named "frankfurters" after his native Frankfurt.

After 1900, the wonders of Coney Island began to lure people from all segments of an increasingly diverse city. Sightseers came from around the world. Notables such as Herman Melville, Mark Twain, and even Sigmund Freud (what did he think of Dreamland?) rubbed shoulders with factory workers, domestics, and department store clerks. Baseball was also becoming a national pastime as games attracted a disparate crowd of people who might have little in common but their devotion to the home team.

Increasing materialism had revealed great fissures in American urban society by 1900. Yet places like department stores, baseball parks, and amusement parks provided democratic spaces for some interaction. Newspapers and schools also indirectly offered diverse groups the opportunity to share similar experiences.

18–4
Richard K. Fox,
from *Coney Island Frolics*
(1883)

CONCLUSION

By 1900, the factory worker and the department store clerk were more representative of the new America than the farmer and small shopkeeper. Industry and technology had created thousands of new jobs, but they also eliminated the autonomy many workers had enjoyed and limited their opportunities to advance.

Immigrants thronged to the United States to realize their dreams of economic and religious freedom. They found both to varying degrees but also discovered a darker side to the promise of American life. The great cities thrilled newcomers with their possibilities and their abundance of goods and activities. But the cities also bore witness to the growing divisions in American society. As the new century dawned, the prospects for urban industrial America seemed limitless, yet the stark contrasts that had appeared so vividly inside and outside the Centennial Exposition persisted and deepened.

Labor unions, ethnic organizations, government legislation, and new urban institutions promised ways to remedy the worst abuses of the new urban, industrial economy.

SUMMARY

New Industry The Gilded Age of the late 1800s saw America transformed into the world's foremost industrial power. Technological and scientific advances, the modernization of industry, and the development of the modern corporation created changes in work life and urban living. The demand for workers drew immigrants to America and women and children into the work place. In the new urban landscape poverty abounded; the growing gap between rich and poor was seen as a result of Social Darwinism and survival of the fittest. Industrial tensions resulted in workers organizing into unions, and labor strikes, some violent, resulted as employers fought back to break the power of the unions.

New Immigrants The period saw a dramatic rise in immigration to the United States, as the number of people moving to America from northern and western Europe slackened, the numbers from southern and eastern Europe, Latin America, and Asia increased. Work, and the resulting independence it would bring, was the goal; immigrants maintained their religious and cultural traditions while some Americans attempted to restrict their numbers through legislation. African Americans moved into the industrial cities of the North and Midwest drawn by the same promise that attracted overseas immigrants.

New Cities Cities acted like giant magnets; an urban-industrial core extended from New England to the Great Lakes; the crush of people and the emergence of new technologies expanded the city outward and upward. Urban dwellers sorted themselves by social class and ethnic groups; residential neighborhoods, downtowns, and suburbs became fixtures of the modern city. The new middle class transformed America into a consumer society and leisure activities, spectator sports, and amusement parks became hallmarks of urban life.

REVIEW QUESTIONS

1. Could the benefits of industrialization have been achieved without its social costs? Explain your answer.

2. How did working-class women respond to the new economy? How did their participation and responses differ from those of working-class men?

3. Why is it said that immigrant groups adjusted to, rather than assimilated, American society?

4. Would individuals from other immigrant groups likely have expressed sentiments similar to those of Mary Antin about the adjustment to American life, or is Mary's reaction specific to her Jewish background?

KEY TERMS

American Federation of Labor (p. 479)
Chain migration (p. 482)
Collective bargaining (p. 479)
Gilded Age (p. 467)
Gospel of Wealth (p. 478)

Great Migration (p. 486)
Great Uprising (p. 478)
Horizontal integration (p. 471)
Hull House (p. 476)
Knights of Labor (p. 478)
Nativism (p. 484)

Pogroms (p. 481)
Social Darwinism (p. 478)
Sweatshops (p. 473)
Tenements (p. 476)
Vertical integration (p. 470)

WHERE TO LEARN MORE

Edison National Historic Site, West Orange, New Jersey. The site contains the Edison archives, including photographs, sound recordings, and industrial and scientific machinery. Its twenty historic structures dating from the 1880–1887 period include Edison's home and laboratory. **www.nps.gov/edis**

Japanese American National Museum, Los Angeles, California. Housed in a converted Buddhist temple, this museum includes artifacts and photographs of early Japanese immigration and settlement. The core exhibit is "Issei Pioneers: Japanese Immigration to Hawaii and the Mainland from 1885 to 1924." **www.janm.org**

Pasa al Norte. This museum, located in El Paso, Texas, serves as the Mexico-United States International Immigration History Center. Its exhibits focus on the importance of El Paso ("the Southwest Ellis Island") as a port-of-entry between the United States and Mexico from the late sixteenth century to the present. **utminers.utep.edu/panihm/default.htm**

Missouri Historical Society, St. Louis, Missouri. The Society displays a long-term exhibition accompanied by public programs called, "St. Louis in the Gilded Age," which focuses on the changes generated by industrialization and urban development in St. Louis from 1865 to 1900. **www.mohistory.org**

Senator John Heinz Pittsburgh Regional History Center, Pittsburgh, Pennsylvania. Through its long-term exhibition, "Points in Time: Building a Life in Western Pennsylvania, 1750–Today," the Center explores the growth of the Pittsburgh metropolitan area, especially its expansion during the great industrial boom at the turn of the twentieth century. **www.pghhistory.org**

Angel Island State Park, San Francisco Bay. Angel Island served as a detention center from 1910 to 1940 for Asian immigrants who were kept there for days, months, and, in some cases, years, while immigration officials attempted to ferret out illegal entries. Exhibits depict the era through pictures and artifacts. **www.angelisland.org**

Strawbery Banke, Portsmouth, New Hampshire. This museum includes an exhibit and audiovisual presentations on the adjustment of one immigrant family to American life: "Becoming Americans: The Shapiro Story, 1898–1929," presents the story of an immigrant Jewish family in the context of immigration to the small, coastal city of Portsmouth at the turn of the twentieth century. **www.strawberybanke.org**

Statue of Liberty National Monument and Ellis Island, New York, New York. More than 12 million immigrants were processed at Ellis Island between 1892 and 1954. The exhibits provide a fine overview of American immigration history during this period. There is an ongoing oral history program as well. **www.nps.gov/stli**

For additional study resources for this chapter, go to:
www.prenhall.com/goldfield/chapter18

The two locomotives then moved up until they touched each other, . . .and at one p.m., under an almost cloudless sky, and in the presence of about one thousand one hundred people, the completion of the greatest railroad on earth was announced.

This engraving, showing passengers shooting buffalo from a train crossing the plains, suggests the often casual approach Americans took toward the Western Environment. The destruction of the buffalo herds, for both profit and "sport," also destroyed the basis of the Plains Indians' economy and culture.

19

TRANSFORMING THE WEST
1865–1890

WHAT WAS the federal government's policy toward Indians in the late nineteenth century?

HOW DID Western railroads shape the West and affect the East?

WHAT BROUGHT the flood of migrants to the West in the late nineteenth century?

HOW WAS the environment transformed by Westward expansion?

After a pleasant ride of about six miles we attained a very high eleva-
tion, and, passing through a gorge of the mountains, we entered a level, cir-
cular valley, about three miles in diameter, surrounded on every side by
mountains. The track is on the eastern side of the plain, and at the point of
junction extends in nearly a southwest and northeast direction. Two lengths
of rails are left for today's work. . . . At a quarter to nine A.M. the whistle of
the C.P. [Central Pacific Railroad] is heard, and soon arrives, bringing a
number of passengers. . . . Two additional trains arrive from the East. At a
quarter to eleven the Chinese workmen commenced leveling the bed of the road
with picks and shovels, preparatory to placing the ties. . . . At a quarter past
eleven the Governor's train arrived. The engine was gayly decorated with little
flags and ribbons, the red, white, and blue. At 12 M. the rails were laid, and
the iron spikes driven. The last tie that was laid is 8 feet long, 8 inches wide,
and 6 inches thick. It is of California laurel, finely polished, and is orna-
mented with a silver escutcheon bearing the following inscription: "The last
tie laid on the Pacific Railroad, May 10th, 1869.". . .

The point of contact is 1,085 4/5 miles from Omaha, leaving 690
miles for the C.P. portion of the work. The engine Jupiter, of the C.P., and en-
gine 119, of the U.P.R.R. [Union Pacific Railroad] moved up within thirty
feet of each other. . . . Three cheers were given for the Government of the Unit-
ed States, for the railroad, for the President, for the Star Spangled Banner, for
the laborers, and for those who furnished the means respectively. The four
spikes—two gold and two silver—were furnished by Montana, Idaho, Cali-
fornia, and Nevada. They were about seven inches long, and a little larger
than the iron spike. Dr. Harkness, of Sacramento, on presenting to Governor
Stanford a spike of pure gold, delivered a short and appropriate speech. The
Hon. F.A. Tuttle, of Nevada, presented Dr. Durant with a spike of silver, say-
ing: 'To the iron of the East, and the gold of the West, Nevada adds her link
of silver to span the continent and wed the oceans'. . . . The two locomotives
then moved up until they touched each other, . . . and at one P.M., under an
almost cloudless sky, and in the presence of about one thousand one hundred
people, the completion of the greatest railroad on earth was announced.

Andrew J. Russell, "The Completion of the Pacific Railroad," *Frank Leslie's Illustrated Newspaper,* June 5, 1869.

WHERE TO LEARN MORE

Golden Spike National Historic
Site, near Promontory, Utah
www.nps./gov/gosp

IMAGE KEY

for pages 496–497

a. A feather fan carried by Yuchi
dancers. American Museum of
Natural History

b. Passengers and the train crew
shooting buffalo on the line of the
Kansas-Pacific Railroad: color line
engraving, 1871.

c. Confederate cavalry spurs from the
American Civil War.

d. An old fashioned steam locomotive
engine with an attached coal car.

e. Chief Wooly Head's Wife and Child.

f. A Chinese mine worker steadies a
water cannon in a shallow riverbed in
Idaho with a fellow laborer standing
nearby.

g. Thirty-three horse team harvester,
cutting, threshing and sacking wheat,
c. 1902.

ANDREW J. RUSSELL'S short journey on the morning of May 10, 1869, from Ogden to Promontory Summit, Utah, enabled him to document what he called "the completion of the greatest work of the age, by which this vast continent is spanned, from ocean to ocean, by the iron path of travel and commerce." The transcontinental railroad symbolized the classic American journey, a people and a nation moving westward.

Its construction also set a precedent for western development. The two railroads that met in a desolate sagebrush basin were huge corporate enterprises, not individual efforts, and corporations dominated-Western growth as much as they did Eastern industrialization. The federal government also played a crucial role. Congress had authorized the Union Pacific and Central Pacific to build the railroad link, given them the right-of-way for their tracks, and provided huge land grants and financial subsidies.

The railroads' dependence on capital investment, engineering knowledge, technological innovations, and labor skills also typified Western development. Their labor forces both reflected and reinforced the region's racial and ethnic diversity. European immigrants, Mexicans, Paiute Indians, both male and female, and especially Chinese, recruited in California and Asia, chiseled the tunnels through the mountains, built the bridges over the gulches, and laid the ties and rails across the plains. But Russell kept the Chinese out of the famous photographs he took at Promontory, an indication of the racism that marred so many Western achievements.

Laying track as quickly as possible to collect the subsidies awarded by the mile, the railroad corporations adopted callous and reckless construction tactics, resulting in waste, deaths (perhaps as many as a thousand Chinese), and environmental destruction—consequences that would also characterize other forms of economic development in the West. And as with most other American undertakings in the West, the construction provoked conflict with the Cheyenne, Sioux, and other tribes.

The most important feature of the railroad, however, was that traffic moved in both directions. The railroads not only helped move soldiers and settlers into the West, but they also moved western products to the growing markets in the East. Thus the railroad both integrated the West into the rest of the nation and made it a crucial part of the larger economic revolution that transformed America after the Civil War.

This photograph, taken by A.J. Russell, records the celebration at the joining of the Central Pacific and Union Pacific railroads on May 10, 1869, at Promontory Summit, Utah. Railroads transformed the American West, linking the region to outside markets, spurring rapid settlement, and threatening Indian survival.

Union Pacific Historical Collection

 17–3
Horace Greeley, An Overland Journey (1860)

SUBJUGATING NATIVE AMERICANS

The initial obstacle to exploiting the West was the people already living there, for despite Easterners' image of the West as an unsettled wilderness, Native Americans had long inhabited it and had developed a variety of economies and cultures. As white people pressed westward, they attempted to subjugate the Indians, displace them from their lands, and strip them of their culture. Conquest forced Indians onto desolate reservations, but efforts to destroy their beliefs and transform their way of life were less successful.

TRIBES AND CULTURES

Throughout the West, Indians had adapted to their environment. Each activity encouraged their sensitivity to the natural world, and each had social and political implications.

In the Northwest, abundant food from rich waters and dense forests gave rise to complex and stable Indian societies. During summer fishing runs, the Tillamooks, Chinooks, and other tribes caught salmon, which sustained them

WHAT WAS the federal government's policy toward Indians in the late nineteenth century?

WHERE TO LEARN MORE

National Museum of the American Indian, New York, New York
www.nmai.si.edu/index.asp

Chronology

1858	Gold is discovered in Colorado and Nevada.
1860	Gold is discovered in Idaho.
1862	Homestead Act is passed. Gold is discovered in Montana.
1864	Militia slaughters Cheyennes at Sand Creek, Colorado.
1867	Cattle drives make Abilene the first cow town.
1868	Fort Laramie Treaty is signed.
1869	First transcontinental railroad is completed.
1874	Gold is discovered in the Black Hills. Turkey Red wheat is introduced to Kansas. Barbed wire is patented.
1876	Indians devastate U.S. troops in the Battle of the Little Bighorn.
1879	"Exodusters" migrate to Kansas.
1885	Chinese massacred at Rock Springs, Wyoming.
1887	Dawes Act is passed.
1890	Government troops kill two hundred Sioux at Wounded Knee, South Dakota.
1892	Mining violence breaks out at Coeur d'Alene, Idaho.
1893	Western Federation of Miners is organized.

throughout the year. During the mild winters, they developed artistic handicrafts, elaborate social institutions, and a satisfying religious life.

The Cahuillas of the southern California desert survived only through their ability to extract food and medicines from desert plants. In the dry and barren Great Basin of Utah and Nevada, Shoshones and Paiutes ate grasshoppers and other insects to supplement their diet of rabbits, mice, and other small animals. Such harsh environments restricted the size, strength, and organizational complexity of societies.

In the Southwest, the Pueblos dwelled in permanent towns of adobe buildings and practiced intensive agriculture. Because tribal welfare depended on maintaining complex irrigation systems, the Zunis, Hopis, and other Pueblos emphasized community solidarity rather than individual ambition. Town living encouraged social stability and the development of effective governments, elaborate religious ceremonies, and creative arts.

The most numerous Indian groups in the West lived on the Great Plains. The largest of these tribes included the Lakotas or Sioux, who roamed from western Minnesota through the Dakotas; the Cheyennes and Arapahos, who controlled much of the central plains between the Platte and Arkansas Rivers; and the Comanches, predominant on the southern plains.

Despite their diversity, all tribes emphasized community welfare over individual interest. Their economies were based on subsistence rather than profit. They tried to live in harmony with nature to ward off sickness, injury, death, or misfortune. And they were absorbed with the need to establish proper relations with supernatural forces that linked human beings with all other living things. These connections also shaped Indians' attitude toward land, which they regarded—like air and water—as part of nature to be held and used communally.

Disdaining Native Americans and their religion, white people condemned them as "savages" to be converted or exterminated. Rejecting the concept of communal property, most white people demanded land for the exclusive use of ambitious individuals.

Perhaps no one expressed these cultural differences better than the great Sioux leader Sitting Bull. Referring to the forces of the spirit world, he declared:

> It is through this mysterious power that we too have our being and we therefore yield to our neighbors, even our animal neighbors, the same

QUICK REVIEW

Indians in the West

◆ Desert tribes had to contend with a harsh environment.

◆ The cultures of many Southwest tribes emphasized communal solidarity.

◆ The most numerous Indian groups in the West lived on the Great Plains.

right as ourselves, to inhabit this land. Yet, hear me, people. We have now to deal with another race. . . . Possession is a disease with them. These people have made many rules that the rich may break but the poor may not. . . . They claim this mother of ours, the earth, for their own and fence their neighbors away; they deface her with their buildings. . . . That nation is like a spring freshet that overruns its banks and destroys all who are in its path. We cannot dwell side by side.

FEDERAL INDIAN POLICY

The government had in the 1830s adopted the policy of separating white people and Indians. Eastern tribes were moved west of Missouri and resettled on land then scorned as "the Great American Desert," unsuitable for white habitation and development. This division collapsed in the 1840s when the United States acquired Texas, California, and Oregon. Mormons developed a trail through Indian country in 1847 and settled on Indian lands; gold and silver discoveries beginning in 1848 prompted miners to migrate across Indian lands. Rather than curbing white settler entry into Indian country, the government built forts along the overland trails and ordered the army to punish Indians who threatened travelers.

White migration devastated the Plains Indians. Livestock destroyed timber and pastures along streams in the semiarid region; trails eliminated buffalo from tribal hunting ranges. The Pawnees in particular suffered from the violation of their hunting grounds. One observer reported that "their trail could be followed by the dead bodies of those who starved to death." The Plains Indians also suffered from the white migrants' diseases for which Indians had no natural immunity. Cholera killed more than half of the Comanches and Kiowas, and most other tribes lost up to 40 percent of their population from the new diseases. Emigrants along the Platte River routes came across "villages of the dead."

Recognizing that the Great American Desert could support agriculture, white settlers pressed on the eastern edge of the plains and demanded the removal of the Indians. Simultaneously, railroad companies developed plans to lay tracks across the plains. The federal government decided to relocate the tribes to separate and specific reserves. In exchange for accepting such restrictions, the government would provide the tribes with annual payments of livestock, clothing, and other materials. To implement this policy, the government negotiated treaties, extinguishing Indian rights to millions of acres, and ordered the army to keep Indians on their assigned reservations.

The commissioner of Indian affairs aptly described the Indians' lot: "By alternate persuasion and force these tribes have been removed, step by step, from mountain to valley, and from river to plain, until they have been pushed halfway across the continent. They can go no further; on the ground they now occupy the crisis must be met, and their future determined."

WARFARE AND DISPOSSESSION

From the 1850s to the 1880s, warfare engulfed the advancing frontier. Invading Americans bore ultimate responsibility for these wars. Even the men who led the white military assault conceded as much. General Philip Sheridan, for example, declared of the Indians: "We took away their country and their means of support, broke up their mode of living, their habits of life, introduced disease and decay among them, and it was for this and against this that they made war. Could anyone expect less?"

> **QUICK REVIEW**
>
> **White Migration and the Plains Indians**
> - Livestock destroyed timber and pastures.
> - Buffalo were eliminated from tribal hunting grounds.
> - New diseases killed as much as 40 percent of some Indian groups.

One notorious example of white aggression occurred in 1864 at Sand Creek, Colorado. When gold was discovered on land only recently guaranteed to the Cheyennes and Arapahos, white settlers wanted to eliminate the Indian presence altogether. John Chivington, a Methodist minister, led a militia force to the Sand Creek camp of a band of Cheyennes under Black Kettle, an advocate of peace and accommodation. An American flag flew over the Indian camp. Under Chivington's orders to "kill and scalp all, big and little," the militia attacked Black Kettle's sleeping camp without warning. One white trader later described the helpless Indians: "They were scalped, their brains knocked out; the [white] men used their knives, ripped open women, clubbed little children, knocked them in the head with their guns, beat their brains out, mutilated their bodies in every sense of the word."

The **Sand Creek Massacre** appalled many Easterners. The Cheyennes, protested the commissioner of Indian affairs, were "butchered in cold blood by troops in the service of the United States." A congressional investigating committee denounced Chivington for "a foul and dastardly massacre which would have disgraced the veriest savage among those who were the victims of his cruelty." Westerners, however, justified the brutality as a means to secure their own opportunities. One Western newspaper demanded, "Kill all the Indians that can be killed. Complete extermination is our motto."

Other tribes were more formidable. None was more powerful than the Sioux, whose military skills had been honed in conflicts with other tribes. On the Bozeman Trail, in what the Lakotas called the Battle of One Hundred Slain, the Sioux wiped out an army detachment led by a captain who had boasted that he would destroy the Sioux nation. General William T. Sherman, who had marched through Georgia against Confederates, knew that the odds were different in the West. Fifty Plains Indians, he declared, could "checkmate" three thousand soldiers. General Philip Sheridan calculated that the army suffered proportionately greater losses fighting Indians than either the Union or the Confederacy had suffered in the Civil War.

Describing white actions as "uniformly unjust," a federal peace commission in 1868 negotiated the **Second Treaty of Fort Laramie**, in which the United States abandoned the Bozeman Trail and other routes and military posts on Sioux territory—one of the few times Indians forced the advancing whites to retreat. The United States also guaranteed the Sioux permanent ownership of the western half of South Dakota and the right to inhabit and hunt in the Powder River country in Wyoming and Montana, an area to be henceforth closed to all whites.

For several years, peace prevailed on the northern plains, but in 1872, the Northern Pacific Railroad began to build westward on a route that would violate Sioux territory. Rather than stopping the railroad, the government sent an army to protect the surveyors. Sherman regarded railroad expansion as the most important factor in defeating the Indians, for it would allow troops to travel as far in a day as they could march in weeks. Other technological developments, from the telegraph to rapid-fire weapons, also undercut the skills of the Indian warrior.

The white people's destruction of the buffalo also threatened Native Americans. From 1872 to 1874, white hunters killed 4 million buffalo. Railroad construction disrupted grazing areas, and hunters working for the railroads killed hordes of buffalo, both to feed construction crews and to prevent the animals from obstructing rail traffic. Hide hunters slaughtered even more of the beasts for their skins, leaving the bodies to rot. Reporters found vast areas covered with "decaying, putrid, stinking remains" of buffalo. Federal officials encouraged the buffalo's extermination because it would destroy the Indians' basis for survival.

The climactic provocation of the Sioux began in 1874 when Colonel George A. Custer led an invasion to survey the Black Hills for a military post and confirm

---

WHERE TO LEARN MORE

Fort Laramie National Historic Site, near Guernsey, Wyoming
www.nps.gov/fola/

Sand Creek Massacre The near annihilation in 1864 of Black Kettle's Cheyenne band by Colorado troops under Colonel John Chivington's orders to "kill and scalp all, big and little."

Second Treaty of Fort Laramie The treaty acknowledging U.S. defeat in the Great Sioux War in 1868 and supposedly guaranteeing the Sioux perpetual land and hunting rights in South Dakota, Wyoming, and Montana.

the presence of gold. Thousands of white miners then illegally poured onto Sioux land. The army insisted that the Sioux leave their Powder River hunting grounds. When the Sioux refused, the army attacked. The Oglala Sioux under Crazy Horse checked one prong of this offensive at the Battle of the Rosebud in June 1876 and then joined a larger body of Sioux under Sitting Bull and their Cheyenne and Arapaho allies to overwhelm a second American column, under Custer, at the **Battle of the Little Bighorn**.

But the Indians had to divide their forces to find fresh grass for their horses and to hunt for their own food. "We have been running up and down in this country, but they follow us from one place to another," lamented Sitting Bull about the Army's pursuit. He led his followers to Canada, but the other bands capitulated in the winter of 1876–1877. The conquest of the northern plains came through attrition and the inability of the traditional Indian economy to support resistance to the technologically and numerically superior white forces.

The defeat of the Sioux nearly completed the Indian Wars. Smaller tribes, among them the Kiowas, Modocs, and Utes, had been overrun earlier. In the Northwest, the Nez Percé had outwitted and outfought the larger forces of the U.S. Army over a 1,500-mile retreat toward Canada. The exhausted Nez Percé surrendered after being promised a return to their own land, but the government refused to honor that pledge too and imprisoned the tribe in Oklahoma, where more than a third perished within a few years.

In the Southwest, the Navajos and the Comanches were subdued as the Sioux had been—by persistent pursuit that prevented them from obtaining food. The last to abandon resistance were the Apaches, under Geronimo. In 1886, he and thirty-six followers, facing five thousand U.S. troops, finally surrendered. Geronimo and other Apaches were sent to a military prison in Florida; the tribes were herded onto reservations. The Oglala chief Red Cloud concluded of the white invasion: "They made us many promises, more than I can remember, but they never kept but one. They promised to take our land, and they took it."

LIFE ON THE RESERVATION: AMERICANIZATION

The next objective of government policy was to require Indians to adopt white peoples' ways. This goal did not involve assimilation but merely "Americanization," an expression of cultural conquest.

The government received aid from many Christian denominations, which had long proposed nonviolent methods of controlling Indians. Beginning in the 1860s, they gained influence in reaction to the military's brutality. Religious groups helped staff the reservations as agents, missionaries, or civilian employees. Reformers wanted to change Indian religious and family life, train Indian children in Protestant beliefs, and force Indians to accept private ownership and market capitalism.

Confined on reservations and dependent on government rations, Indians were a captive audience for white reformers. White administrators sought to destroy traditional Indian government by prohibiting tribal councils from meeting and imprisoning tribal leaders.

Protestant religious groups persuaded the Bureau of Indian Affairs to frame a criminal code prohibiting and penalizing tribal religious practices. Established in 1884, the code remained in effect until 1933. It was first invoked to ban the Sun Dance, the chief expression of Plains Indian religion. To enforce the ban, the government withheld rations and disrupted the religious ceremonies that transmitted traditional values. In 1890, the army even used machine guns to suppress the Ghost Dance religion, killing at least two hundred Sioux men, women, and children at **Wounded Knee**, South Dakota.

W WHERE TO LEARN MORE

★ Little Bighorn Battlefield National Monument. Crow Agency, Montana
www.nps.gov/libi/home.htm

17–7
Tragedy at Wounded Knee (1890)

Battle of the Little Bighorn Battle in which Colonel George A. Custer and the Seventh Cavalry were defeated by the Sioux and Cheyennes under Sitting Bull and Crazy Horse in Montana in 1876.

Wounded Knee Massacre The U.S. Army's brutal winter massacre in 1890 of at least two hundred Sioux men, women, and children as part of the government's assault on the tribe's Ghost Dance religion.

·AMERICAN VIEWS·

ZITKALA-SA'S VIEW OF AMERICANIZATION

itkala-Sa, or Red Bird, was an 8-year-old Sioux girl when she was taken from her South Dakota reservation in 1884 and placed in a Midwestern missionary school, where she encountered what she called the "iron routine" of the "civilizing machine." Here she recalls her first day at the school.

WHAT LESSONS were the missionaries trying to teach Zitkala-Sa? What lessons did Zitkala-Sa learn?

Soon we were being drawn rapidly away by the white man's horses. When I saw the lonely figure of my mother vanish in the distance, a sense of regret settled heavily upon me. . . . I no longer felt free to be myself, or to voice my own feelings. The tears trickled down my cheeks, and I buried my face in the folds of my blanket. Now the first step, parting me from my mother, was taken, and all my belated tears availed nothing. . . . Trembling with fear and distrust of the palefaces . . . I was as frightened and bewildered as the captured young of a wild creature. . . .

[At the missionary school,] the constant clash of harsh noises, with an undercurrent of many voices murmuring an unknown tongue, made a bedlam within which I was securely tied. And though my spirit tore itself in struggling for its lost freedom, all was useless. . . .

We were placed in a line of girls who were marching into the dining room. . . . A small bell was tapped, and each of the pupils drew a chair from under the table. Supposing this act meant they were to be seated, I pulled out mine and at once slipped into it from one side. But when I turned my head, I saw that I was the only one seated, and all the rest at our table remained standing. Just as I began to rise, looking shyly around to see how chairs were to be used, a second bell was sounded. All were seated at last, and I had to crawl back into my chair again. I heard a man's voice at one end of the hall, and I looked around to see him. But all others hung their heads over their plates. As I glanced at the long chain of tables, I caught the eyes of a pale-face woman upon me. Immediately I dropped my eyes, wondering why I was so keenly watched by the strange woman. The man ceased his mutterings, and then a third bell was tapped. Every one picked up his

knife and fork and began eating. I began crying instead, for by this time I was afraid to venture anything more.

But this eating by formula was not the hardest trial in that first day. Late in the morning, my friend Judewin gave me a terrible warning. Judewin knew a few words of English; and she had overhead the paleface woman talk about cutting our long, heavy hair. Our mothers had taught us that only unskilled warriors who were captured had their hair shingled by the enemy. Among our people, short hair was worn by mourners, and shingled hair by cowards!

. . . I remember being dragged out, though I resisted by kicking and scratching wildly. In spite of myself, I was carried downstairs and tied fast in a chair. I cried aloud, shaking my head all the while until I felt the cold blades of the scissors against my neck, and heard them gnaw off one of my thick braids. Then I lost my spirit. . . . My long hair was shingled like a coward's. In my anguish I moaned for my mother, but no one came to comfort me. Not a soul reasoned quietly with me, as my own mother used to do; for now I was only one of many little animals driven by a herder. . . .

I blamed the hard-working, well-meaning, ignorant [missionary] woman who was inculcating in our hearts her superstitious ideas. Though I was sullen in all my little troubles, as soon as I felt better I was . . . again actively testing the chains which tightly bound my individuality like a mummy for burial. . . .

Many specimens of civilized peoples visited the Indian school. The city folks with canes and eyeglasses, the countrymen with sunburnt cheeks and clumsy feet, forgot their relative social ranks in an ignorant curiosity. Both sorts of these Christian palefaces were alike astounded at seeing the children of savage warriors so docile and industrious. . . .

In this fashion many [whites] have passed idly through the Indian schools during the last decade, afterward to boast of their charity to the North American Indian. But few there are who have paused to question whether real life or long-lasting death lies beneath this semblance of civilization.

Source: Zitkala-Sa, "The School Days of an Indian Girl" (1900). Reprinted in *American Indian Stories* (Glorieta, NM: Rio Grande Press, 1976).

FROM THEN TO NOW
The Legacy of Indian Americanization

The assumptions, objectives, and failures of the Americanization policies of the nineteenth century continue to affect American Indians more than a century later. Although periodically modified (see Chapter 27), these policies long persisted, as did their consequences. In the 1970s official investigations reported that the continuing attempts of the Bureau of Indian Affairs to use education to force Indians into an Anglo-American mold "have been marked by near total failure, haunted by prejudice and ignorance."

Similarly, the economic problems on reservations in the nineteenth century foreshadowed conditions a century later. Today Indians rank at the bottom of almost all measures of economic well-being. Lack of economic opportunity leaves isolated reservations with unemployment rates averaging 40 percent. Off the reservation, discrimination, limited skills, and inadequate capital further restrict Indians' job prospects.

Indians also continue to suffer from poor health standards. They have the highest rates of infant mortality, pneumonia, hepatitis, tuberculosis, and suicide in the nation and a life expectancy twenty-five years less than the national average.

Indian culture, however, did not succumb to the pressure to Americanize. In the words of a Shoshone writer, "Indian history didn't end in the 1800s. Indian cultures . . . evolve, grow, and continually try to renew themselves."

In recent decades, Indian peoples have begun to reclaim their past and assert control over their future. Dramatic protests—most notably a confrontation in 1973 between Indian activists and the FBI at Wounded Knee, the site of the notorious 1890 massacre—have called attention to Indian grievances. But Indians have also moved effectively to regain control of the institutions that define their cultural identity. They have established community schools and tribal community colleges that provide a bilingual, bicultural education, seeking to preserve traditions while opening new opportunities. They have built tribal museums and visitor centers in order to shape the presentation of their histories and cultures. By the late 1990s there were more than 200 such institutions, from the Seneca-Iroquois Museum in upstate New York to the Makah Tribal Museum on the Olympic peninsula.

Indians have also secured legal recognition of their right to their cultural patrimony. The Native American Graves Protection and Repatriation Act of 1990 gives Indian communities the right to reclaim, or "repatriate," material artifacts and skeletal remains from museums and historical societies. The Native American Religious Freedom Act of 1978 affirmed their right to practice their traditional religions and have access to sacred sites. Indian dance—once suppressed by white authorities—has revived, and the powwow has become a national Indian institution and symbol of Indian identity.

With the help of historians and lawyers, Indians are also winning enforcement of long-ignored treaty provisions guaranteeing them land ownership and water, hunting, and fishing rights. Court decisions have recognized the right of tribes to permit gambling on their reservations, and some tribes have built profitable casinos, attracting economic development that creates new job opportunities for their people and permits them to stay on their land.

Indians still confront hostility and condescension reminiscent of attitudes a century ago. A white museum official, for example—seeking to prevent the repatriation of Pawnee artifacts—claimed recently that Indians do not have a real religion. But Indians have proved resilient in preserving their cultural heritage and keeping it vibrant for future generations.

The government and religious groups also used education to eliminate Indian values and traditions. They isolated Indian children from tribal influences at off-reservation boarding schools. Troops often seized Indian children for these schools, where they were confined until after adolescence. The schoolchildren were forced to speak English, attend Christian services, and profess white American values. (American Views: "Zitkala-Sa's View of Americanization.")

Finally, government agents taught Indian men how to farm and distributed agricultural implements; Indian women were taught household tasks. These tactics reduced the status of Indian women, whose traditional responsibility for agriculture had guaranteed them respect and authority. Nor could men farm successfully on reservation lands, which white settlers had already rejected as unproductive. White people, however, believed that the real obstacle to economic prosperity for the Indians was their rejection of private property. As one Bureau of Indian Affairs official declared, Indians must be taught to be more "mercenary and ambitious to obtain riches." Congress in 1887 passed the **Dawes Act**, which divided tribal lands among individual Indians. Western settlers and developers who had no interest in the Indians supported the law because it provided that reservation lands not allocated to individual Indians should be sold to white people. Under this "reform," the amount of land held by Indians declined by more than half by 1900.

White acquisition and exploitation of Indian land seemed to be the only constant in the nation's treatment of Native Americans. Assimilation itself failed because most Indians clung to their own values and rejected as selfish, dishonorable, and obsessively materialistic those favored by white people. But if it was not yet clear what place Native Americans would have in America, it was at least clear by 1900 that they would no longer stand in the way of Western development.

EXPLOITING THE MOUNTAINS: THE MINING BONANZA

Migrants to the American West exploited the region's natural resources in pursuit of wealth and success. Promoters, artists, and novelists developed images of the West as a land of adventure, opportunity, and freedom; pioneers as self-reliant individuals. All too often, however, reality differed from legend.

In the later nineteenth century, the West experienced several stages of economic development, but all of them transformed the environment, produced economic and social conflict, and integrated the region into the modern national economy. The first stage of development centered on mining, which attracted swarms of eager prospectors into the mountains and deserts in search of gold and silver. They founded vital communities, stimulated the railroad construction that brought further development, and contributed to the disorderly heritage of the frontier (see Map 19–1). But few gained the wealth they had expected.

RUSHES AND MINING CAMPS

The first important gold rush in the Rocky Mountains came in Colorado in 1859. More than 100,000 prospectors crowded into Denver and the nearby mining camps. Simultaneously, the discovery of the famous Comstock Lode in Nevada produced an eastward rush of miners from California. Some 17,000 claims were made around Virginia City, Nevada, the main mining camp. Strikes in the northern Rockies followed in the 1860s. Boise City and Lewiston in Idaho and Helena in Montana became major mining centers, and other camps prospered briefly before fading into ghost towns. Later, other minerals shaped frontier development: silver in Nevada, silver and lead in Colorado and Idaho, silver and in Arizona and Montana.

Mining camps were often isolated by both distance and terrain. They frequently consisted of only flimsy shanties, saloons, crude stores, dance halls, and brothels, all hastily built by entrepreneurs. Such towns reflected the speculative, exploitive, and transitory character of mining itself. And yet they did contribute to permanent settlement by encouraging agriculture, industry, and transportation in the surrounding areas.

Dawes Act   An 1887 law terminating tribal ownership of land and allotting some parcels of land to individual Indians with the remainder opened for white settlement.

HOW DID Western railroads shape the West and affect the East?

WHERE TO LEARN MORE

Bodie State Historic Park, Bodie, California
www.bodie.net/

MAP EXPLORATION

To explore an interactive version of this map, go to **http://www.prenhall.com/goldfield2/map19.1**

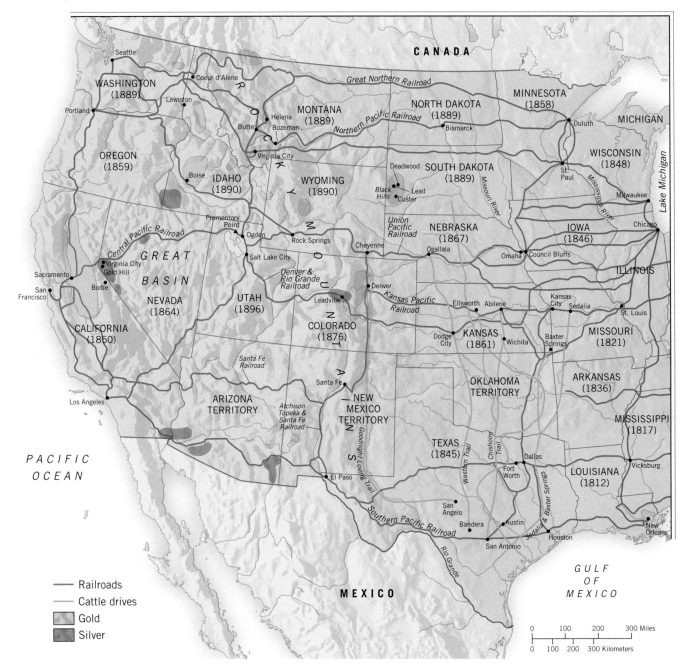

MAP 19–1
Economic Development of the West: Railroads, Mining, and Cattle, 1860–1900 The spread of the railroad network across the West promoted economic development by providing access to outside markets for its resources. The discovery of precious metals often attracted the railroads, but stockraisers had to open cattle trails to reach the railheads.

WHICH CITIES were most affected by the growth of railroads in the West?

The camps had an unusual social and economic structure. The population was overwhelmingly male. In 1860, for example, about 2,300 men and only thirty women resided in the Nevada mining camps of Virginia City and Gold Hill. Women found far fewer economic opportunities than men did on the mining frontier. Several opened hotels. Those with less capital worked as seamstresses and cooks and took in washing. The few married women often earned more than their husbands by boarding other miners willing to pay for the trappings of family life.

But the largest source of paid employment for women was prostitution. Mary Josephine Welch, an entrepreneurial Irish immigrant, settled in Helena in 1867 and soon established the Red Light Saloon, the first of many saloons, dance halls, and brothels that she owned and operated. Most women who engaged in such activities, however, were far less successful, and they entered brothels because they already suffered from economic hardship or a broken family. But prostitution usually only worsened their distress. By the 1890s, as men gained control of the vice trade, violence, suicide, alcoholism, disease, drug addiction, and poverty overcame most prostitutes. Public authorities showed little concern for the abuse and even murder of prostitutes, although they used "sporting women" to raise revenue by fining or taxing them. Protestant women in Denver and other cities established "rescue homes" to protect or rehabilitate prostitutes and dance hall girls from male vice and violence.

The gender imbalance in mining camps also made saloons prevalent among local businesses. An 1879 business census of Leadville, Colorado, reported 10 dry goods stores, 4 banks, and 4 churches, but 120 saloons, 19 beer halls, and 118 gambling houses. Saloons were social centers in towns where most miners lived in crowded and dirty tents and rooming houses. As Mark Twain wrote in *Roughing It* (1872), his account of Virginia City, "The cheapest and easiest way to become an influential man and be looked up to by the community at large, was to stand behind a bar, wear a cluster-diamond pin, and sell whiskey." One observer of the Montana camps reported that men, "unburdened by families, drink whenever they feel like it, whenever they have money to pay for it, and whenever there is nothing else to do. . . . Bad manners follow, profanity becomes a matter of course. . . . Excitability and nervousness brought on by rum help these tendencies along, and then to correct this state of things the pistol comes into play." Disputes over mining claims could become violent, adding to the disorder. The California mining town of Bodie experienced twenty-nine killings between 1877 and 1883. But such killings occurred only within a small group of males who were known as the Badmen of Bodie. Daily life for most people was safe.

Indeed, personal and criminal violence, which remains popularly associated with the West, was less pervasive than collective violence. White men often drove Mexicans and Chinese from their claims or refused to let them work in higher paid occupations in the mining camps. The Chinese had originally migrated to the California gold fields and thereafter spread to the new mining areas of the Rockies and the Great Basin, where they worked in mining when possible, operated laundries and restaurants, and held menial jobs like hauling water and chopping wood. In 1870, more than a quarter of Idaho's population and nearly 10 percent of Montana's was Chinese. Where they were numerous, the Chinese built their own communities and maintained their customs.

But racism and fear of economic competition sparked hostility and violence against the Chinese almost everywhere. The worst anti-Chinese violence occurred in Rock Springs, Wyoming, in 1885 when white miners killed twenty-eight unresisting Chinese miners and drove away all seven hundred residents from the local

QUICK REVIEW

Prostitution

♦ Largest source of paid employment for women in the West.

♦ Most women entered prostitution as a result of economic or familial hardship.

♦ Authorities showed little interest in welfare of prostitutes.

Chinatown. Although the members of the mob were well known, the grand jury, speaking for the white majority, found no cause for legal action: "Though we have examined a large number of witnesses, no one has been able to testify to a single criminal act committed by any known white person." There was community sanction for violence against racial minorities.

LABOR AND CAPITAL

New technology had dramatic consequences for both miners and the mining industry. Initially, mining was an individual enterprise in which miners used simple tools, such as picks and shovels, wash pans, and rockers, to work shallow surface deposits known as placers. More expensive operations were needed to reach the precious metal buried in the earth.

Hydraulic mining, for example, required massive capital investment to build reservoirs, ditches, and troughs to power high-pressure water cannons that would pulverize hillsides and uncover the mineral deposits. Still more expensive and complex was quartz, or lode, mining, sometimes called hard rock mining. Time, money, and technology were required to sink a shaft into the earth. Timber was needed for underground chambers and tunnels. Pumps were installed to remove underground water, and hoists were constructed to lower men and lift out rock. Stamp mills and smelters were built to treat the ore.

Such complex, expensive, and permanent operations necessarily came under corporate control. Often financed with Eastern or British capital, new corporations integrated the mining industry into the larger economy. Hard rock mining produced more complex ores than could be treated in remote mining towns, but with the new railroad network, they were shipped to smelting plants as far away as Kansas City and St. Louis and then to refineries in Eastern cities. Western ores thus became part of national and international business. The mining industry's increasing development of lower grade deposits led to greater capital investment and larger operations employing more workers and machinery.

But the new corporate mining had many disturbing effects. Hydraulic mining washed away hillsides, depositing debris in canyons and valleys to a depth of 100 feet or more, clogging rivers and causing floods, and burying thousands of acres of farmland. Such damage provoked an outcry and eventually led to government regulation.

Corporate mining also transformed prospectors into wage workers with restricted opportunities. Miners' status declined as new machinery like power drills reduced the need for skilled laborers and prompted employers to hire cheaper workers from eastern and southern Europe. Moreover, mining corporations did little to protect miners' health or safety. Miners died in cave-ins, explosions, and fires or from the great heat and poisonous gases in underground mines. Miners called the power hoists "man killers" because they frequently crushed and dismembered workers. In 1889, a Montana inspector of mines concluded that "death lurks even in the things which are designed as benefits."

To protect their interests, miners organized unions. These functioned as benevolent societies, using members' dues to pay benefits to injured miners or their survivors. Several unions established hospitals. Union halls offered an alternative to the saloons by serving as social and educational centers. The Miners' Union Library in Virginia City was the largest library in Nevada. Unions also promoted miners' interests on the job. They persuaded governments to adopt mine safety legislation and, beginning in the 1880s, to appoint mine inspectors. The chief role of these state officials was to answer the question posed by the Colorado mining inspector: "How far should an industry be permitted to advance its material welfare at the expense of human life?"

A Chinese mine worker steadies a water cannon in a shallow riverbed in Idaho with a fellow laborer standing nearby.

Chinese mining laborers, Idaho, 76-119.2/A, Idaho State Historical Society

But mining companies frequently controlled state power and used it to crush unions. Thus in 1892, in the Coeur d' Alene district of Idaho, mining companies locked out strikers and imported a private army, which battled miners in a bloody gunfight. Management next persuaded the governor and the president to send in the state militia and the U.S. Army. State officials then suppressed the strike and the union by confining all union members and their sympathizers in stockades. When mining companies in Utah, Colorado, and Montana pursued the same aggressive tactics, the local miners' unions in the West united for strength and self-protection. In 1893, they formed one of the nation's largest and most militant unions, the Western Federation of Miners.

As the law grew stronger and the owners adopted "legalized violence" as a repressive tool, miners turned to extralegal violence. In the Western mines, then, both management's tactics—blacklisting union members, locking out strikers, obtaining court injunctions against unions, and using soldiers against workers—and labor's response mirrored conditions in the industrial East. In sum, reflecting the industrialization of the national economy, Western mining had been transformed from a small-scale prospecting enterprise characterized by individual initiative and simple tools into a large-scale corporate business characterized by impersonal management, outside capital, advanced technology, and wage labor.

Exploiting the Grass: The Cattle Kingdom

The development of the range cattle industry reflected the needs of an emerging Eastern urban society, the economic possibilities of the grasslands of the Great Plains, the technology of the expanding railroad network, and the requirements of corporations and capital. It also brought "cow towns" and urban development to the West.

Cattle Drives and Cow Towns

The cattle industry originated in southern Texas, where the Spanish had introduced cattle in the eighteenth century. Developed by Mexican ranchers, "Texas longhorns" proved well adapted to the plains grasslands.

Following the Civil War, industrial expansion in the East and Midwest enlarged the urban market for food and increased the potential value of Texas steers. The extension of the railroad network into the West, moreover, opened the possibility of tapping that market. The key was to establish a shipping point on the railroads west of the settled farming regions, a step first taken in 1867 by Joseph McCoy, an Illinois cattle shipper. McCoy selected Abilene, Kansas, in his words "a very small, dead place, consisting of about one dozen log huts, low, small, rude affairs." But Abilene was also the Western railhead of the Kansas Pacific Railroad and was ringed by lush grasslands for cattle. McCoy bought 250 acres for a stockyard and imported lumber for stock pens, loading facilities, stables, and a hotel for cowhands. Texans opened the **Chisholm Trail** through Indian Territory to drive their cattle northward to Abilene. Within three years, a million and a half cattle arrived in Abilene, divided into herds of several thousand, each directed by a dozen cowhands on a "long drive" taking two to three months. With the arrival of the cattle trade, other entrepreneurs created a bustling town. As both railroads and settlement advanced westward, a series of other cow towns—Ellsworth, Wichita, Dodge City, Cheyenne—attracted the long drives, cattle herds, and urban development.

WHAT BROUGHT the flood of migrants to the West in the late nineteenth century?

WHERE TO LEARN MORE

National Cowboy Hall of Fame, Oklahoma City, Oklahoma
www.cowboyhalloffame.org/index2.html

Chisholm Trail The route followed by Texas cattle raisers driving their herds north to markets at Kansas railheads.

As with the mining camps, the cow towns' reputation for violence was exaggerated. They adopted gun control laws, prohibiting the carrying of handguns within city limits, and established police forces to maintain order. The towns taxed prostitutes and gamblers and charged high fees for liquor licenses. By collecting such "sin taxes," Wichita was able to forgo general business taxes, thereby increasing its appeal to prospective settlers.

Most cow towns, like Abilene, dwindled into small towns serving farm populations, but like mining camps, cow towns contributed to the growth of an urban frontier. Railroads often determined the location and growth of Western cities, providing access to markets for local products, transporting supplies and machinery for residents, and attracting capital for commercial and industrial development. The West, in fact, had become the most urban region in the nation by 1890, with two-thirds of its population living in communities of at least 2,500 people.

RISE AND FALL OF OPEN-RANGE RANCHING

Indian removal and the extension of the railroad network opened land for ranching in Kansas, Nebraska, Wyoming, Colorado, Montana, and the Dakotas. Cattle reaching Kansas were increasingly sold to stock these northern ranges rather than for shipment to the packing houses. Ranches soon spread across the Great Plains and into the Great Basin, the Southwest, and even eastern Oregon and Washington. Calves were cheap, and ranchers did not buy, but merely used, the grazing lands of the open range, which was public land. It sufficed to acquire title to the site for a ranch house and a water source because controlling access to water in semiarid lands gave effective control of the surrounding public domain "the same as though I owned it," as one rancher explained. Ranchers thus needed to invest only in horses, primitive corrals, and bunkhouses. Their labor costs were minimal: They paid cowboys in the spring to round up new calves for branding and in the fall to herd steers to market.

By the early 1880s, the high profits from this enterprise and an expanding market for beef attracted speculative capital and reshaped the industry. Eastern and European capital flooded the West, with British investors particularly prominent. British and American corporations acquired, expanded, and managed huge ranches.

Large companies soon dominated the industry, just as they had gained control of mining. Some large companies illegally began to enclose the open range, building fences to exclude newcomers and minimize labor costs by reducing the number of cowboys needed to control the cattle. One Wyoming newspaper complained that "some morning we will wake up to find that a corporation has run a wire fence about the boundary lines of Wyoming and all within the same have been notified to move." And a Coloradan wondered, "Will the government protect us if we poor unite and cut down their fences and let our stock have some of Uncle Sam's feed as well as them?"

The industry eventually collapsed in an economic and ecological disaster. Overgrazing replaced nutritious grasses with sagebrush, Russian thistle, and other plants that livestock found unpalatable. Ten times as much land was required to support a steer by the 1880s. Droughts in the mid-1880s further withered vegetation and enfeebled the animals. Millions of cattle starved or froze to death in terrible blizzards in 1886 and 1887.

The surviving ranchers reduced their operations, restricted the size of their herds, and tried to ensure adequate winter feed by growing hay. To decrease their dependence on natural vegetation even further, they introduced drought-resistant sorghum and new grasses; to reduce their dependence on rainfall, they drilled wells and installed windmills to pump water.

17–4
Joseph G. McCoy, Historic Sketches of the Cattle Trade of the West and Southwest (1874)

Employees of the Prairie Cattle Company at the ranch headquarters in Dry Cimarron, New Mexico, in 1888. This company, a British corporation, held 8,000 square miles of land.

The Denver Public Library, Western History Department

COWHANDS AND CAPITALISTS

Cowboys' work was hard, dirty, seasonal, tedious, sometimes dangerous, and poorly paid. Many early cowboys were white Southerners unwilling or unable to return home after the Civil War. Black cowhands made up perhaps 25 percent of the trail-herd outfits. Mexican cowboys developed most of the tools, techniques, and trappings that characterized the cattle industry: from boots, chaps, and the "western" saddle to roundups and roping. Black and Mexican cowboys were often relegated to the more lowly jobs, such as wrangler, a "dust-eater" who herded horses for others to use, but most were ordinary hands on ranch or trail. Except in the few all-black outfits, they were rarely ranch or trail bosses. As the industry expanded northward, more cowboys came from rural Kansas, Nebraska, and neighboring states.

Initially, in the frontier-ranching phase dominated by the long drive, cowboys were seasonal employees who worked closely with owners. They frequently expected to become independent stock raisers themselves and typically enjoyed the right to "maverick" cattle, or put their own brand on unmarked cattle. These informal rights provided opportunities to acquire property and move up the social ladder.

With the appearance of large, corporate enterprises, the traditional rights of cowboys disappeared. Employers now prohibited cowhands from running a brand of their own. One cowboy complained that these restrictions deprived a cowhand of his one way "to get on in the world." To increase labor efficiency, some companies prohibited their cowboys from drinking, gambling, and carrying guns.

Cowboy strikes broke out where corporate ranching was most advanced. The first such strike occurred in Texas in 1883 when the Panhandle Stock Association, representing large operators, prohibited ranch hands from owning their own cattle and imposed a standard wage. More than three hundred cowboys struck seven large ranches for higher wages—$50 rather than $30 per month—and the right to brand mavericks for themselves and to run small herds on the public domain. Ranchers evicted the cowboys, hired scabs, and brought in the Texas Rangers for assistance. The strikers were forced to leave the region.

Other strikes also failed because corporate ranches and their stock associations had the power and cowhands faced long odds in their efforts to organize. They were isolated across vast spaces and had little leverage in the industry. Members of the Northern New Mexico Cowboys Union, formed in 1886, recognized their weakness. After asking employers for "what we are worth after many years' experience," they conceded, "We are dependent on you."

The transformation of the Western cattle industry and its integration into a national economy dominated by corporations thus made the cherished image of cowboy independence and rugged individualism more myth than reality. One visitor to America in the late 1880s commented: "Out in the fabled West, the life of the 'free' cowboy is as much that of a slave as is the life of his Eastern brother, the Massachusetts mill-hand. And the slave-owner is in both cases the same—the capitalist."

OVERVIEW

GOVERNMENT LAND POLICY

Legislation	Result
Railroad land grants (1850–1871)	Granted 181 million acres to railroads to encourage construction and development
Homestead Act (1862)	Gave 80 million acres to settlers to encourage settlement
Morrill Act (1862)	Granted 11 million acres to states to sell to fund public agricultural colleges
Other grants	Granted 129 million acres to states to sell for other educational and related purposes
Dawes Act (1887)	Allotted some reservation lands to individual Indians to promote private property and weaken tribal values among Indians and offered remaining reservation lands for sale to white settlers (by 1906, some 75 million acres had been acquired by white people)
Various laws	Permitted direct sales of 100 million acres by the Land Office

EXPLOITING THE EARTH: HOMESTEADERS AND AGRICULTURAL EXPANSION

Even more than ranching and mining, agricultural growth boosted the Western economy and bound it tightly to national and world markets. In this process, the government played a significant role, as did the railroads, science and technology, Eastern and foreign capital, and the dreams and hard work of millions of rural settlers. The development of farming produced remarkable economic growth, but it left the dreams of many unfulfilled.

HOW WAS the environment transformed by Westward expansion?

SETTLING THE LAND

To stimulate agricultural settlement, Congress passed the most famous land law, the Homestead Act of 1862 (see the overview table "Government Land Policy"). The measure offered 160 acres of free land to anyone who would live on the plot and farm it for five years. The governor of Nebraska exclaimed, "What a blessing this wise and humane legislation will bring to many a poor but honest and industrious family."

However, prospective settlers found less land open to public entry than they expected. Federal land laws did not apply in much of California and the Southwest, where Spain and Mexico had previously transferred land to private owners, or in all of Texas. Elsewhere, the government had given away millions of acres to railroads, or authorized selling millions more for educational and other purposes.

Settlers in Kansas, Nebraska, Minnesota, and the Dakotas in the late 1860s and early 1870s often found most of the best land unavailable for homesteading and much of the rest remote from transportation facilities and markets. Forty percent of the land in Kansas, for example, was closed to homesteading, which prompted the editor of the *Kansas Farmer* to complain that "the settlement of the state is retarded by land monopolists, corporate and individual." Although 375,000 farms were claimed by 1890 through the Homestead Act—a success by any measure—most settlers had to purchase their land.

The Homestead Act also reflected traditional Eastern conceptions of the family farm, which were inappropriate in the West. Here larger-scale farming was

W WHERE TO LEARN MORE

★ American Historical Society of Germans from Russia Museum, Lincoln, Nebraska

necessary. And the law ignored the need for capital—for machinery, buildings, livestock, and fencing—that was required for successful farming on the Great Plains.

Other forces stimulated and promoted settlement. Newspaper editors trumpeted the prospects of their region. Land companies, eager to sell their speculative holdings, sent agents through the Midwest and Europe to encourage migration. Steamship companies, interested in selling transatlantic tickets, advertised the opportunities in the American West across Europe. The Scandinavian Immigration Society generated both publicity and settlers for Minnesota; the Hebrew Emigrant Aid Society established Jewish agricultural colonies in Kansas and North Dakota. The Mormons organized the Perpetual Emigrating Fund Company, which helped more than 100,000 European immigrants settle in Utah and Idaho. Their agricultural communities, relying on communal cooperation under church supervision, succeeded where individual efforts often failed in developing this region.

Most important, railroad advertising and promotional campaigns attracted people to the West. In 1882 alone, the Northern Pacific distributed more than 630,000 pieces of promotional literature in English, Swedish, Dutch, Danish, and Norwegian. "The glowing accounts of the golden west sent out by the R.R. companies," one pioneer later recalled, had convinced her that "they were doing a noble work to let poor people know there was such a grand haven they could reach." Only later did she realize that not only would the railroads profit from selling their huge land reserves to settlers, but also a successful agricultural economy would produce crops to be shipped East and a demand for manufactured goods to be shipped West on their lines. The railroads therefore advanced credit to prospective farmers, provided transportation assistance, and extended technical and agricultural advice.

Migrants poured into the West, occupying and farming more acres between 1870 and 1900 than Americans had in the previous 250 years. Farmers settled in every region. But most streamed into the Great Plains states, from the Dakotas to Texas. Much of Oklahoma was settled in virtually a single day in 1889 when the government opened up lands previously reserved for Indians. A reporter described the wild land rush that created Oklahoma City in hours and claimed 2 million acres of land by nightfall: "With a shout and a yell the swift riders shot out, then followed the light buggies or wagons and last the lumbering prairie schooners and freighters' wagons, with here and there even a man on a bicycle and many too on foot—above all a great cloud of dust hovering."

White migrants predominated in the mass migration, but African Americans initiated one of its most dramatic episodes, a millenarian folk movement they called the Exodus, which established several black communities in Kansas and Nebraska. Many settlers came from Europe, sometimes in a chain migration of entire villages, bringing with them not only their own attitudes toward the land but also special crops, skills, settlement patterns, and agricultural practices. By 1890, the foreign-born population of North Dakota exceeded 40 percent, and nonnatives made up much of the population in California and other Western states.

Migrants moved into the West in search of opportunity, which they sometimes seized at the expense of others already there. In the Southwest, Hispanics had long lived in village communities largely outside a commercial economy, farming small tracts of irrigated land and herding sheep on communal pastures. But as more Anglos, or white Americans, arrived, their political and economic influence undermined traditional Hispanic society. Congress restricted the original Hispanic land grants to only the villagers' home lots and irrigated fields, throwing open most of their common lands to newcomers. The notorious Santa Fe Ring, a group of lawyers and land speculators, seized millions of acres through fraud and legal chicanery.

QUICK REVIEW

Westward Migration

◆ The Homestead Act, promoters, and the railroad prompted migration.

◆ Migrants poured into the West between 1870 and 1900.

◆ Most migrants were whites, but African-American communities were established in Kansas and Nebraska.

Spanish Americans resisted these losses, in court or through violence. *Las Gorras Blancas* (the White Caps) staged night raids to cut fences erected by Anglo ranchers and farmers and to attack the property of railroads, the symbol of the encroaching new order. "Our purpose," they announced, "is to protect the rights of the people in general and especially those of the helpless classes." Such resistance, however, had little success.

As their landholdings shrank, Hispanic villagers could not maintain their pastoral economy. Many became seasonal wage laborers in the Anglo-dominated economy, sometimes working as stoop labor in the commercial sugar beet fields that emerged in the 1890s, sometimes working on the railroads or in the mines. Women also participated in this new labor market. Previously crucial to the subsistence village economy, they now sought wage labor as cooks and domestic servants in railroad towns and mining camps. Hispanics retained some cultural autonomy, but they had little influence over the larger processes of settlement and development.

HOME ON THE RANGE

Farmers and their families encountered many difficulties, especially on the Great Plains, where they had to adapt to a radically new environment. The scarcity of trees on the plains meant that there was little wood for housing, fuel, and fencing. Until they had reaped several harvests and could afford to import lumber, pioneer families lived in dark and dirty sod houses. One Nebraska homesteader recalled that her first sight of a sod house "sickened me."

For fuel, settlers often had to rely on buffalo or cattle "chips"—dried dung. One farmer reported in 1879 that "it was comical to see how gingerly our wives handled these chips at first. They commenced by picking them up between two sticks, or with a poker. Soon they used a rag, and then a corner of their apron. Finally, growing hardened, a wash after handling them was sufficient. And now? Now it is out of the bread, into the chips and back again—and not even a dust of the hands!"

The scarcity of water also complicated women's domestic labor. They often transported water over long distances, pulling barrels on "water sleds" or carrying pails on neck yokes. Where possible, they also helped dig wells by hand.

Some women farmed the land themselves. Single women could claim land under the Homestead Act, and in some areas, women claimants made up 18 percent of the total and succeeded more frequently than men in gaining final title. At times, married women operated the family farm while their husbands worked elsewhere to earn money. In the 1870s, one Dakota woman recounted the demands women faced: "I had lived on a homestead long enough to learn some fundamental things: that while a woman had more independence here than in any other part of the world, she was expected to contribute as much as a man—that people who fought the frontier had to be prepared to meet any emergency; that the person who wasn't willing to try anything once wasn't equipped to be a settler."

Women especially suffered from isolation and loneliness on the plains because they frequently had less contact with others than the farm men. One farm woman complained that "being cut off from everybody is almost too much for me." Luna Kellie recalled that from her Nebraska farm "there were no houses in sight and it seemed like the end of the world." To break the silence, to provide some music and color, many homesteading families kept canaries among their few belongings.

FARMING THE LAND

Pioneer settlers had to make daunting adjustments to develop the agricultural potential of their new land. Advances in science, technology, and industry made such adjustments possible. The changes would not only reshape the agricultural

Each of the four Chrisman sisters claimed a homestead and built a sodhouse near Goheen, Nebraska. Farming on the Great Plains was typically a family operation, with all members of the family having important tasks.

Corbis/Bettmann

economy but also bring their own great challenges to traditional rural values and expectations.

Fencing was an immediate problem on the treeless plains. Barbed wire, developed in the mid-1870s, solved the problem. By 1900, farmers were importing nearly 300 million pounds of barbed wire each year from Eastern and Midwestern factories.

The aridity of most of the West also posed difficulties. In California, Colorado, and a few other areas, settlers used streams fed by mountain snowpacks to irrigate land. Elsewhere, enterprising farmers developed variants of the "dry farming" practices that the Mormons had introduced in Utah, attempting to preserve and maximize the limited rainfall. Some farmers erected windmills to pump underground water. The scarce rainfall also encouraged farmers to specialize in a single cash crop for market. Many plains farmers turned from corn to wheat, especially the drought-resistant Turkey Red variety of hard winter wheat that German Mennonites had introduced into Kansas from Russia. Related technological advancements included grain elevators that would store grain for shipment and load it into rail cars mechanically and mills that used corrugated, chilled-iron rollers rather than millstones to process the new varieties of wheat.

In semiarid regions, farmers required special plows to break the tough sod, new harrows to prepare the soil for cultivation, grain drills to plant the crop, and harvesting and threshing machines to bring it in. Thanks to more and better machines, agricultural efficiency and productivity shot up. By the 1890s, machinery permitted the farmer to produce eighteen times more wheat than hand methods had.

These developments reflected both the expansion of agriculture and its increasing dependence on the larger society. The rail network provided essential transportation for crops; the nation's industrial sector produced necessary agricultural machinery. Banks and loan companies extended the credit and capital that allowed farmers to take advantage of mechanization and other new advances; and many other businesses graded, stored, processed, and sold their crops. In short, because of its market orientation, mechanization, and specialization, Western agriculture relied on other people or impersonal forces as it was incorporated into the national and international economy.

When conditions were favorable—good weather, good crops, and good prices—Western farmers prospered. Too often, however, they faced adversity. In the late 1880s, drought coincided with a slump in crop prices. Expanding production in Argentina, Canada, Australia, and Russia helped create a world surplus of grain that drove prices steadily downward. Prices for other farm commodities also declined.

Squeezed between high costs for credit, transportation, and manufactured goods and falling agricultural prices, Western farmers faced disaster. They responded by lashing back at their points of contact with the new system. They especially condemned the railroads. Luna Kellie complained, "The minute you crossed the Missouri River your fate both soul and body was in their hands. What you should eat and drink, what you should wear, everything was in their hands and they robbed us of all we produced except enough to keep body and soul together and many many times not that."

Farmers censured the grain elevators in the local buying centers that were often owned by Eastern corporations, including the railroads themselves. A Minnesota state investigation found systematic fraud by elevators, which collectively cost farmers a massive sum.

Farmers also denounced the many Eastern bankers and mortgage lenders who had provided the credit for them to acquire land, equipment, and machinery. With failing crops and falling prices, many Western farms were foreclosed.

Stunned and bitter, Western farmers concluded that their problems arose because they had been incorporated into the new system, an integrated economy directed by forces beyond their control. And it was a system that did not work well. "There is," one of them charged, "something radically wrong in our industrial system. There is a screw loose."

CONCLUSION

With determination, ingenuity, and hard work millions of people settled vast areas, made farms and ranches, built villages and cities, brought forth mineral wealth, and imposed their values on the land. These achievements were tempered by a shameful treatment of Indians and an often destructive exploitation of natural resources. But if most Westerners took pride in their accomplishments, and a few enjoyed wealth and power, many also grew discontented with the new conditions they encountered as the "Wild" West receded.

Railroad expansion, population movements, Eastern investment, corporate control, technological innovations, and government policies had incorporated the region fully into the larger society. Indians experienced this incorporation most thoroughly and most tragically, losing their lands, their traditions, and often their lives; the survivors were dependent on the decisions and actions of interlopers. Cowboys and miners also learned that the frontier merely marked the cutting edge of Eastern industrial society; neither could escape integration into the national economy by managerial decisions, transportation links, and market forces. Most settlers in the West were farmers, but they too learned that their distinctive environment did not insulate them from assimilation into larger productive, financial, and marketing structures.

SUMMARY

Subjugating Native Americans As white people pressed westward, the initial obstacle to exploiting the West was the people who already lived there. The native peoples used the land in their own way, had different concepts of progress and civilization, and had developed a variety of economies and cultures. From the 1850s to the 1880s, warfare engulfed the advancing frontier; railroad expansion, the destruction of the buffalo, and technological development undercut the ability of the Native Americans to resist. The conquest gradually forced Indians onto reservations, but efforts to "Americanize" the Indian way of life were less successful.

Exploiting the Mountains: The Mining Bonanza The first stage of the economic development of the West centered on mining as swarms of eager prospectors were attracted into the mountains and deserts in search of gold and silver.

The male-dominated saloon society of the mining camps generated violence and social conflicts. Mining was transformed from an individual effort into a corporate one; as minerals became more difficult to uncover, mining became technologically complex and expensive. Corporate mining permanently changed the landscape of the West through its environmental impact.

Exploiting the Grass: The Cattle Kingdom   The development of the range cattle industry opened a second stage in the exploitation of the West. It reflected the needs of the Eastern urban society for food and the ability of the expanding rail network to deliver it. The cattle kingdom spread from Texas into the Great Plains; after the era of the long drives, cattle ranching became an increasingly corporate endeavor. While the romantic image of the cowboy is one of a rugged individualist freed of societal constraints, the actual work was hard, dirty, seasonal, dangerous, and poorly paid.

Exploiting the Earth: Homesteaders and Agricultural Expansion   Even more than ranching and mining, agricultural growth boosted the West's economy and bound it to national and world markets. Government played a significant role in the expansion of farming, as did railroads, science and technology, Eastern capital, and hard work. The Homestead Act, along with land, railroad, and steamship companies, encouraged Western migration. Settlers encountered many difficulties: a radically new environment, the need for new farming techniques, weather conditions, loneliness, and isolation. These were combined with farmers being part of a global economic system; farmers reached the conclusion that something was terribly wrong with the system, and that bankers, grain elevator operators, and the railroads were to blame.

REVIEW QUESTIONS

1. Why was the completion of the first transcontinental railroad so celebrated?

2. What factors most influenced the subjugation of American Indians?

3. What were the major goals of federal Indian policy, and how did they change?

4. How did technological developments affect Indians, miners, and farmers in the West?

5. How did the federal government help transform the West?

KEY TERMS

Battle of the Little Bighorn   (p. 503)
Chisholm Trail   (p. 510)
Dawes Act   (p. 505)
Sand Creek Massacre   (p. 502)

Second Treaty of Fort Laramie (p. 502)
Wounded Knee Massacre (p. 503)

WHERE TO LEARN MORE

Bodie State Historic Park, Bodie, California. The largest authentic ghost town in the West, Bodie was an important mining center from the 1860s to the 1880s. About 170 buildings remain, including a museum with mining equipment and artifacts of everyday life. **www.bodie.net/**

Little Bighorn Battlefield National Monument, Crow Agency, Montana. The site of Custer's crushing defeat includes a monument to the Seventh Cavalry atop Last Stand Hill. A new authorized Indian Memorial will include sacred texts, artifacts, and pictographs of the Plains Indians. **www.nps.gov/libi/home.htm**

American Historical Society of Germans from Russia Museum, Lincoln, Nebraska. This unique museum, consisting of a complex of restored homes, exhibitions, and archives, preserves the history and culture of Germans who emigrated to Russia and then to the American Great Plains, where they contributed importantly to the development of a multicultural society and an agricultural economy.

National Museum of the American Indian, New York, New York. Part of the Smithsonian Institution, this museum has a collection of artifacts illustrative of more than ten thousand years of the Native American culture. **www.nmai.si.edu/index.asp**

National Cowboy Hall of Fame, Oklahoma City, Oklahoma. This large institution contains an outstanding collection of Western art, displays of cowboy and Indian artifacts, and both kitschy exhibitions of the mythic, Hollywood West and serious galleries depicting the often hard realities of the cattle industry. Its many public programs also successfully combine fun with learning. **www.cowboyhalloffame.org/index2.html**

Golden Spike National Historic Site, near Promontory, Utah. The completion of the transcontinental railroad here in 1869 is reenacted from May to October, using reproductions of the original locomotives. Visitors can drive the route of the railroad, now a National Backway Byway through abandoned mining and railroad towns, from Promontory to Nevada. Virtual tour, history, and tourist links on: **www.nps./gov/gosp**

Fort Laramie, National Historic Site, near Guernsey, Wyoming. A fur-trading post, stop on the Oregon Trail, site of treaty negotiations with the Plains Indians, and staging area for military campaigns, Fort Laramie is now a living history museum with many original buildings. For a virtual tour of the fort and information about visiting see: **www.nps.gov/fola/**

 For additional study resources for this chapter, go to: **www.prenhall.com/goldfield/chapter19**

Mythologizing the "Wild West"

WHAT ELEMENTS do the Remington sculptures, the Curtis photograph, and the "dime novel" illustrations have in common? What, to judge from these images, made the West "wild"? How much do you think these images match up with reality?

One artist, Frederic Remington, deserves much of the credit for creating the West of our imagination. In Montana in 1881 an "old-timer" told him that "there is no more West." Remington decided to "try to record some facts around me." He recorded them first in a series of illustrations, then in paintings, and then in sculpture. Another who determined to "record some facts" was Edward S. Curtis who produced the twenty volume collection, *The North American Indian,* between 1906 and 1930. Curtis persuaded Native American peoples to reenact traditional practices, such as hunting or war parties. Often there was a twenty to fifty year gap between the reenactment and the practice itself. In contrast to Remington and Curtis who sought to (re)capture the truth about the West, "dime novels" sought simply to provide thrills. The "Wild West" is still part of our imaginative landscape.

Edward S. Curtis, "On the Warpath — Atsina," from The North American Indian, v.04; Curtis notes: "These grim-visaged old warriors made a thrilling picture as they rode along, breaking out now and then into wild song of the chase or raid." The image recreates a raiding party. Note the headdress on the party's leader, fourth from left. The photograph was taken in 1908.

▼

▲

Frederick Remington, "The Cheyenne," a 1901 bronze statue, now at the Amon Carter Museum, Fort Worth, Texas. Remington loved to portray action; here a warrior is galloping on his pony into battle.

Frederick S. Remington, "The Cheyenne," 1901, cast 1904. Amon Carter Museum

http://memory.loc.gov/ammem/award98/ienhtml/curthome.html

▲

Frederick Remington, "The Rattlesnake," (1905) Bronze (Height 23 7/8 inches), now at Amon Carter Museum, Fort Worth, Texas. Note how the rattlesnake has reverted from national symbol to natural menace as the cowboy's horse rears up and threatens to throw its rider.

Frederick S. Remington, "The Rattlesnake," 1905. Amon Carter Museum

◀ **"Dime novels" purported to tell true tales of western adventure.** Jesse James was an historical figure, even if the stories in this "Log Cabin Library" edition bore no resemblance to his actual deeds. "The King of the Wild West" was a purely fictional creation.

From the Library of Congress's American Memory site
http://www.loc.gov/exhibits/treasures/tri015.html

*Dear Father, In the 5th, 8th, and 19th Wards . . .
the negroes were driven away from the polls,
beaten and wounded . . . No colored votes were
polled in those precincts after twelve o'clock.*

Presidential Campaign, 1988. Grover Cleveland and Allen G. Thurman
as the Democratic Party candidates for President and Vice President
on a lithograph campaign poster by Kurz & Allison, 1888.

20

POLITICS AND GOVERNMENT
1877–1900

HOW WERE the campaigns run in the late 1800s, and what role did partisan politics play?

HOW EFFECTIVE was the federal government in addressing the problems of America's industrializing economy?

WHAT WERE the main policy issues of the 1880s and the 1890s?

WHAT WAS the platform of the Populist Party?

IMAGE KEY

for pages 522–523

a. 1892 Benjamin Harrison presidential campaign poster sponsored by the Republican Club.

b. Susan B. Anthony medal. It was for the 1906 NY State Suffrage Association Convention, honoring Susan B Anthony in the year of her death.

c. Presidential Campaign, 1888. Grover Cleveland and Allen G. Thurman as the Democratic party candidates for President and Vice President on a lithograph campaign poster by Kurz & Allison, 1888.

d. Campaign buttons for William McKinley, 1896.

e. McKinley-Roosevelt campaign paraphernalia.

f. Benjamin Harrison 1888 Presidential campaign paraphernalia.

g. New Yorkers outside the Madison Square Garden during the Democratic National Convention of 1888, engraving from a contemporary American newspaper.

h. Coxey's Army with band passing a lumber yard.

i. Bosses of the Senate by Joseph Keppler. Giant corpulent (steel, copper, oil, sugar) trust figures loom over the deliberations of the US Senate in a 19th century political cartoon.

j. William Jennings Bryan (1860–1925)-Democratic Convention, 1896, in which he made the "Cross of Gold" speech.

k. Campaign button for William McKinley, 1896.

l. "Tilden and Hendricks have been elected" ribbon.

Cincinnati, Ohio
September 28, 1884

Dear Fanny,

Will has been appointed chief supervisor and so has to take means to prevent fraud at the election. He must appoint assistants for each ward.

—Horace

October 12, 1884

Dear Father,

Will has no time for anything but the election and his duties as chief supervisor. . . . I am afraid the election will be a stormy one & violence will not surprise me. I am one of a citizens' committee of the 18th ward and we propose to be on hand from 6 in the morning till the votes are counted at night.

—Horace

October 22, 1884

Dear Mother,

We had an exciting time election day. The Democrats tried to introduce their Southern methods into northern elections and succeeded in one or two wards, but in general the U.S. Deputy Marshals managed to keep the scoundrels quiet. The negroes in many precincts voted at the risk of their lives. I saw a man shot & killed about fifteen feet from me at our polling place. . . . He drew a pistol on a Deputy Marshal but the Deputy was too quick for him.

—Horace

October 22, 1884

Dear Father,

In the 5th, 8th, and 19th Wards the marshals were utterly useless and were soon overpowered. The police did nothing except to set on [incite] the crowd. . . . The negroes were driven away from the polls, beaten and wounded and exposed to as much abuse as they could have been south of Mason's and Dixon's line. No colored votes were polled in those precincts after twelve o'clock.

—Will

William H. Taft Papers, Manuscript Division, Library of Congress.

HORACE AND WILL TAFT kept their parents and sister Fanny informed of the 1884 congressional election in their hometown of Cincinnati. Alphonso, Louise, and Fanny Taft, all staunch Republicans, were desperate for such political news. Alphonso had served in President Ulysses S. Grant's cabinet and was now American minister to Austria. In Vienna, they eagerly awaited news of their party's success.

As the Taft brothers reported, Cincinnati voters had a difficult journey to the polls. Rabid partisans had staged competing torchlight parades, with thousands of uniformed marchers; orators had stirred the huge crowds for hours with patriotic, religious, and cultural bombast. And the election itself produced the violence Horace had expected. The Republican brothers condemned the Democrats for intimidating African Americans and others likely to vote Republican, "importing" Democratic voters from other states, and using the local police to frighten or arrest Republicans.

But the Democrats also complained. The U.S. marshals so praised by Horace had been appointed by Republican federal officials under Will's supervision, and many of those marshals were merely thugs, paid and armed by local Republicans to improve Republican election prospects. As Will conceded, they first "drove from the city the night before election" hundreds of Democrats they alleged might commit election fraud. On election day itself they sought to incite violence in the city's Irish wards to keep other Democratic voters from the polls, and they made mass arrests of others trying to vote, often claiming that they were Kentucky Democrats who had crossed the Ohio River to "colonize" Cincinnati's election. Some deputies fired point-blank into Democratic crowds. As Will admitted to his father about those deputies, "it is attended with risk to furnish revolvers to men who are close to or belong to the criminal class."

"The Democrats are so mad at not being able to perpetrate these frauds," Will concluded with unwitting irony, "that they are trying to get even by crying fraud at us."

Not all American elections in the late nineteenth century were as riotous as this Cincinnati contest, but it suggests much about American politics at the time. From the military-style campaign to the rough act of voting itself, elections were a masculine business—although women were intensely interested. Campaigns attracted mass participation but often avoided substantive issues. The two major political parties shaped campaigns and controlled elections, which were tumultuous if not always violent. Partisan divisions overlapped with ethnic, racial, and other social divisions, and suffrage was a contested issue. Partisanship often determined both the membership and the activities of government agencies, even those charged with maintaining order. Local concerns took precedence over national concerns.

While these features of late-nineteenth century politics endured, they shaped not only campaigns and elections but the form and role of government as well. William Howard Taft eventually became president of the United States. His success, he explained, stemmed from his father's reputation, his own loyalty to his party, and keeping his "plate the right side up when offices were falling."

The Structure and Style of Politics

Political parties dominated political life. They organized campaigns, controlled balloting, and held the unswerving loyalty of most of the electorate. While the major parties worked to maintain a sense of unity and tradition among their followers, third parties sought the support of those the major parties left unserved. Other Americans looked outside the electoral arena to fulfill their political goals.

HOW WERE campaigns run in the late 1800s, and what role did partisan politics play?

Campaigns and Elections

Campaign pageantry absorbed communities large and small. The town of Emporia, Kansas, once witnessed a campaign rally of twenty thousand people, several times its population. A parade of wagons stretched 5 miles, reported the proud local newspaper. "When the head of the procession was under the equator the tail was coming around the north pole."

The excitement of political contests prompted the wife of Chief Justice Morrison Waite to write longingly on election day, 1876, "I should want to vote all day." But women could not vote at all. Justice Waite himself had just a year earlier written the unanimous opinion of the Supreme Court (in *Minor* v. *Happersett*) that the Constitution did not confer suffrage on women.

But turnout among male voters was remarkably high, averaging nearly 80 percent in presidential elections between 1876 and 1900, a figure far greater than ever achieved thereafter. In many states, even immigrants not yet citizens were eligible to vote and flocked to the polls. African Americans voted regularly in the North and irregularly in the South before being disfranchised at the end of the century.

Political parties kept detailed records of voters, transported them to the polls, saw that they were registered where necessary, and sometimes even paid their poll taxes or naturalization fees to make them eligible. With legal regulations and public machinery for elections negligible, parties dominated the campaigns and elections. Election clerks and judges were not public officials but partisans chosen by the political parties. Until the 1890s, most states had no laws to ensure secrecy in voting, and ballots were printed by the parties. Because they had only the names of the candidates of the party issuing them and often varied in size and color, ballots revealed the voters' party allegiance.

Paid party workers known as peddlers or hawkers stationed themselves near the polls, each trying to force his party ticket on prospective voters. Fighting and intimidation were so commonplace at the polls that one state supreme court ruled in 1887 that they were "acceptable" features of elections.

As the court recognized, the open and partisan aspects of the electoral process did not necessarily lead to election fraud, however much they shaped the nature of political participation.

MAP EXPLORATION

To explore an interactive version of this map, go to
http://www.prenhall.com/goldfield2/map20.1

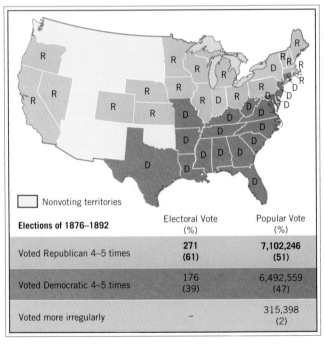

Elections of 1876–1892	Electoral Vote (%)	Popular Vote (%)
Voted Republican 4–5 times	271 (61)	7,102,246 (51)
Voted Democratic 4–5 times	176 (39)	6,492,559 (47)
Voted more irregularly	–	315,398 (2)

☐ Nonvoting territories

MAP 20–1

The Two-Party Stalemate of the Late Nineteenth Century   Strong parties, staunch loyalties, and an evenly divided electorate made for exciting politics but often stalemated government in the late nineteenth century. Most states voted consistently for one of the major parties, leaving the few swing states like New York and Indiana the scenes of fierce partisan battles.

WHAT WAS the geographical pattern of Republican versus Democratic voting during this time period?

PARTISAN POLITICS

Democrats and Republicans had virtually the same level of electoral support, so they worked hard to get out the vote (see Map 20–1). Rarely did either party control both the presidency and Congress at once. The party balance also gave great influence to New York, New Jersey, Ohio, and Indiana, whose evenly divided voters could swing an election either way. Both parties concentrated campaign funds and strategy on the swing states. Thus Republican presidential candidate James Garfield of Ohio commented during the election campaign in 1880: "Nothing is wanting except an immediate and liberal supply of money for campaign expenses to make Indiana certain. With a victory there, the rest is easy." Garfield carried Indiana by six thousand votes and the nation by nine thousand out of 9.2 million cast.

Interrelated regional, ethnic, religious, and local factors determined the party affiliations of most Americans. Economic issues generally did not decide party ties. Like religious belief and ethnic identity, partisan loyalty was largely a cultural trait passed from father to son, which helps explain the electoral stability of most communities.

Republicans were strongest in the North and Midwest, where they benefited from their party's role as the defender of the Union in the Civil War. The Republican party appealed primarily to old-stock Americans and other Protestants, including those of German and Scandinavian descent. African Americans, loyal to the party that had emancipated and enfranchised the slaves of the South, also supported the Grand Old Party, or GOP, where they could vote. Democrats were strongest in the South, where they stood as the defenders of the traditions of the region's white population. But Democrats also drew support in the urban Northeast, especially from Catholics and recent immigrants.

Each major party thus consisted of a complex coalition of groups with differing traditions and interests. One observer described the Democratic party in California as "a sort of Democratic happy family, like we see in the prairie-dog villages, where owls, rattlesnakes, prairie dogs, and lizards all live in the same hole."

Republicans identified their party with nationalism and national unity and attacked the Democrats as an "alliance between the embittered South and the slums of the Northern cities." They combined a "bloody shirt" appeal to the memories of the Civil War with campaigns for immigration restriction and cultural uniformity. Republican legislatures in several Eastern and Midwestern states in the 1880s and 1890s enacted laws regulating parochial schools, the use of foreign languages, and alcohol consumption.

Democrats portrayed themselves as the party of limited government and "personal liberties," a theme that appealed both to the racism of white Southerners and the resentment immigrants felt about the nativist meddling the Republicans favored. The Democrats' commitment to personal liberties had limits. They supported the disfranchisement of African Americans, the exclusion of Chinese immigrants, and the dispossession of American Indians from their lands. Nevertheless, their emphasis on traditional individualism and localism proved popular.

Both major parties had party machines, especially at the local level, led by powerful bosses like Democrat Richard Croker of New York or Republican George Cox of Cincinnati. These machines not only controlled city politics but also municipal government. Well-organized ward clubs mobilized working-class voters, who were rewarded by municipal jobs and baskets of food or coal doled out by the machine. Such assistance was often necessary given the lack of public welfare systems, but to buy votes the machine also sold favors. Public contracts and franchises were peddled to businesses whose high bids covered kickbacks to the machine.

Third parties organized around specific issues or groups. The **Prohibition party** championed the abolition of alcohol but also introduced many important reform ideas into American politics. Some farmers and workers formed larger but shorter lived third parties, charging that Republicans and Democrats had failed to respond to economic problems caused by industrialization or, worse still, had deliberately promoted powerful business interests at the expense of ordinary Americans. The **Greenback party** of the 1870s denounced "the infamous financial legislation which takes all from the many to enrich the few." Its policies of labor reform and currency inflation (to stimulate and democratize the economy) attracted supporters from Maine to Texas. The most significant third party was the **People's** or **Populist party** of the 1890s.

ASSOCIATIONAL POLITICS

Associations of like-minded citizens, operating outside the electoral arena, worked to achieve public policies beneficial to their members. Farmers organized the Patrons of Husbandry, known familiarly as the Grange (see Chapter 19). Its campaign for public regulation to control the rates charged by railroads and grain elevators helped convince Midwestern states to pass the so-called **Granger laws**. The Grange also sought reforms in the nation's financial system.

To the Grangers' dismay, industrialists also formed pressure groups. Organizations such as the American Iron and Steel Association and the American Protective Tariff League lobbied Congress for high tariff laws and made campaign

Prohibition party A venerable third party still in existence that has persistently campaigned for the abolition of alcohol but has also introduced many important reform ideas into American politics.

Greenback party A third party of the 1870s and 1880s that garnered temporary support by advocating currency inflation to expand the economy and assist debtors.

Populist party A major third party of the 1890s, formed on the basis of the Southern Farmers' Alliance and other organizations, mounting electoral challenges against Democrats in the South and the Republicans in the West.

Granger Laws State laws enacted in the Midwest in the 1870s that regulated rates charged by railroads, grain elevator operators, and other middlemen.

FROM THEN TO NOW
Political Parties

Few things in contemporary American politics present a sharper contrast to the nineteenth century than the role of political parties. In the late nineteenth century, parties dominated politics. They commanded the allegiance of Americans, controlled the selection of candidates, mobilized voters, shaped voting behavior, provided ballots, and ran elections. They also shaped public policies and, through patronage, staffed government positions. At the beginning of the twenty-first century, parties do virtually none of these things.

This transformation began at the end of the nineteenth century. Extreme partisanship prompted states to assert control over elections. The corruption attributed to party machines led gradually to such changes as nonpartisan municipal elections and increased public control over parties. Restrictions on campaign expenditures reduced the party hoopla that had made politics so exciting and voter turnout so high. The connection between parties and voters declined further as new voters unfamiliar with the passions and loyalties of the past joined the electorate.

The inability of the major parties to deal effectively with important national problems, so evident in the depression of the 1890s, prompted Americans to find other ways to influence public policy. Associational groups that had acted outside the partisan arena evolved into effective special-interest lobbying groups. Civil service reform, beginning with the Pendleton Act, steadily reduced party influence in government. So did the growing reliance in the twentieth century on independent regulatory commissions, rather than partisan legislative committees, to make and implement policies.

In recent decades, party decline has accelerated. The introduction and spread of primary elections have stripped parties of their control over nominations. Individual candidates have come increasingly to rely more on personal organizations than party apparatus to manage campaigns. Candidates often appeal for votes as individuals rather than as party members and communicate directly to voters through the mass media, relying less on the old door-to-door personal campaign requiring party workers. Television, in particular, with its focus on dramatic and personal sound bites, is better at promoting individual candidates than abstract entities like parties.

Campaign finance reform laws have reduced party control over the funding of campaigns. So too has the rise of political action committees (PACs) as an important source of support for candidates. PACs represent particular interests, not a collection of interests the way parties do. Candidates dependent on specific interests find it harder to make broader partisan appeals.

Polls show fewer and fewer Americans identifying with a particular party and indicate that partisanship has greatly declined as a factor in voting decisions. Americans increasingly regard parties as neither meaningful nor even useful, let alone essential to democratic government. Nearly half of the electorate favors making all elections nonpartisan or even abolishing parties. More and more people believe that interest groups better represent their political needs than parties. At the same time, fewer and fewer Americans bother to vote. Those who do are much more likely than before to split their ticket, voting for candidates of different parties for different offices. This often results in divided government—with the presidency controlled by one party and Congress by the other. The resulting stalemate increases public cynicism about parties.

Of course, parties endure and retain some importance. Election laws favor the two established parties and obstruct independent candidacies. Public funds subsidize party activities, and party coffers harvest unregulated "soft money" campaign contributions. Congress and state legislatures continue to rely on party divisions to organize their leadership and committee structures, and party discipline still influences the way legislators vote. But while such institutional factors guarantee the continued presence of a two-party system, the parties themselves no longer enjoy the influence they had in the nineteenth century.

CHRONOLOGY

1867 Patrons of Husbandry (the Grange) is founded.

1869 Massachusetts establishes the first state regulatory commission.

1873 Silver is demonetized in the "Crime of '73."

1874 Woman's Christian Temperance Union is organized.

1875 U.S. Supreme Court, in *Minor* v. *Happersett*, upholds denial of suffrage to women.

1876 Greenback party runs presidential candidate.

1877 Rutherford B. Hayes becomes president after disputed election.
Farmers' Alliance is founded.
Supreme Court, in *Munn* v. *Illinois*, upholds state regulatory authority over private property.

1878 Bland-Allison Act obliges the government to buy silver.

1880 James A. Garfield is elected president.

1881 Garfield is assassinated; Chester A. Arthur becomes president.

1883 Pendleton Civil Service Act is passed.

1884 Grover Cleveland is elected president.

1886 Supreme Court, in *Wabash* v. *Illinois*, rules that only the federal government, not the states, can regulate interstate commerce.

1887 Interstate Commerce Act is passed.

1888 Benjamin Harrison is elected president.

1890 Sherman Antitrust Act is passed.
McKinley Tariff Act is passed.
Sherman Silver Purchase Act is passed.
National American Woman Suffrage Association is organized.
Wyoming enters the Union as the first state with woman suffrage.

1892 People's party is organized.
Cleveland is elected to his second term as president.

1893 Depression begins.
Sherman Silver Purchase Act is repealed.

1894 Coxey's Army marches to Washington.
Pullman strike ends in violence.

1895 Supreme Court, in *Pollock* v. *Farmers' Loan and Trust Company*, invalidates the federal income tax.
Supreme Court, in *United States* v. *E. C. Knight Company*, limits the Sherman Antitrust law to commerce, excluding industrial monopolies.

1896 William Jennings Bryan is nominated for president by Democrats and Populists.
William McKinley is elected president.

1900 Currency Act puts U.S. currency on the gold standard.

---

contributions to friendly politicians of both parties. A small group of conservative reformers known derisively as **Mugwumps** (the term derives from the Algonquian word for *chief*) devoted most of their efforts to campaigning for honest and efficient government through civil service reform. They organized the National Civil Service Reform League to publicize their plans, lobby Congress and state legislatures, and endorse sympathetic candidates.

Women were also active in associational politics. Susan B. Anthony and others formed groups to lobby Congress and state legislatures for constitutional amendments extending the right to vote to women. The leading organizations merged in 1890 as the **National American Woman Suffrage Association**. Despite the opposition of male politicians of both major parties, suffragists had succeeded by the mid-1890s in gaining full woman suffrage in four western states—Wyoming, Colorado, Idaho, and Utah—and partial suffrage (the right to vote in school elections) in several other states, East and West.

With petition campaigns, demonstrations, and lobbying, women's social service organizations sought to remedy poverty and disease, improve education and recreation, and provide day nurseries for the children of workingwomen. The Illinois Woman's Alliance, organized in 1888 by suffragists, women assemblies of the Knights of Labor, and middle-class women's clubs, investigated the conditions of women and children in workshops and factories and campaigned for protective labor legislation and compulsory school attendance laws.

The Woman's Christian Temperance Union (WCTU) gained a massive membership campaigning for restrictive liquor laws. Under the leadership of Frances

WHERE TO LEARN MORE

Susan B. Anthony House National Historic Landmark, Rochester, New York
www.susanbanthonyhouse.org/main.html

Mugwumps Elitist and conservative reformers who favored sound money and limited government and opposed tariffs and the spoils system.

National American Woman Suffrage Association The organization, formed in 1890, that coordinated the ultimately successful campaign to achieve women's right to vote.

A meeting in 1880 of the National Woman Suffrage Association protested the exclusion of women from electoral politics. Susan B. Anthony noted with regret that "to all men woman suffrage is only a side issue."

The Granger Collection, New York

HOW EFFECTIVE was the federal government in addressing the problems of America's industrializing economy?

18–3
The Gilded Age (1880)

Willard, however, it inserted domestic issues into the political sphere with a campaign for social and economic reforms far beyond temperance. It particularly sought to strengthen and enforce laws against rape. Willard bitterly noted that twenty states fixed the age of consent at ten and that "in Massachusetts and Vermont it is a greater crime to steal a cow" than to rape a woman. The WCTU also pushed for improved health conditions and workplace and housing reforms.

THE LIMITS OF GOVERNMENT

Despite enthusiasm for politics and the activity of associations, government in the late nineteenth century was neither active nor productive by present standards. The receding government activism of the Civil War and Reconstruction years coincided with a resurgent belief in localism and laissez-faire policies. In addition, a Congress and presidency divided between the two major parties, a small and inefficient bureaucracy, and judicial restraints joined powerful private interests to limit the size and objectives of the federal government.

THE WEAK PRESIDENCY

The presidency was a weak and restricted institution. The impeachment of President Johnson at the outset of Reconstruction had undermined the office. Then President Grant subordinated it to the legislative branch by deferring to Congress on appointments and legislation. And the presidents between 1877 and 1897—Republicans Rutherford B. Hayes (1877–1881), James A. Garfield (1881), and Chester A. Arthur (1881–1885), Democrat Grover Cleveland (1885–1889 and 1893–1897), and Republican Benjamin Harrison (1889–1893)—were all conservatives who proposed few initiatives. The most aggressive of them, Cleveland, vetoed two-thirds of all the bills Congress passed, more than all his predecessors combined. Vetoing relief for drought-stricken Texas farmers, Cleveland stated, "though the people support the Government, the Government should not support the people."

The presidents of this era made little effort to reach out to the public or to exert legislative leadership. In 1885, Woodrow Wilson, at the time a professor of history and government, described "the business of the president" as "not much above routine" and concluded that the office might be made purely administrative, its occupant a sort of tenured civil servant. (Wilson took a different view when he became president himself in 1913.) Benjamin Harrison spent six hours a day dealing with office seekers, and Garfield lamented, "My day is frittered away by the personal seeking of people, when it ought to be given to the great problems which concern the whole country."

The presidency was also hampered by its limited control over bureaus and departments and by its small staff, which consisted of half a dozen secretaries, clerks, and telegraphers. As Cleveland complained, "If the President has any great policy in mind or on hand he has no one to help him work it out."

THE INEFFICIENT CONGRESS

Congress exercised authority over the federal budget, oversaw the cabinet, debated public issues, and controlled legislation. Its members, as one senator conceded, "tolerated no intrusion from the President or from anybody else."

But Congress was inefficient. Its chambers were chaotic, and members rarely paid attention to the business at hand. Instead they played cards, read newspapers, or sent a page to get fruit or tobacco from the vendors who lined the hallways of the capitol. The repeated shifts in party control of Congress also impeded effective action. So too did the loss of experienced legislators to rapid turnover. In some Congresses, most members were first-termers.

Procedural rules often kept Congress from acting. The most notorious rule required that a quorum be not only present but also voting. When the House was narrowly divided along party lines, the minority could block all business by refusing to answer when the roll was called.

But as a nationalizing economy required more national legislation, business before Congress grew relentlessly (see Figure 20–1). The expanding scale of congressional work prompted a gradual reform of procedures and the centralization of power in the speaker of the House and the leading committees. These changes did not, however, create a coherent program for government action.

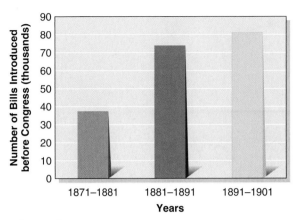

Figure 20–1 Increase in Congressional Business, 1871–1901
Industrialization, urbanization, and western expansion brought increased demands for government action, but the party stalemate, laissez-faire attitudes, and inefficient public institutions often blocked effective responses.

THE FEDERAL BUREAUCRACY AND THE SPOILS SYSTEM

The federal bureaucracy remained small and limited in the late nineteenth century. There were little more than fifty thousand government employees in 1871, and three-fourths of them were local postmasters scattered across the nation. Only six thousand, from President Grant to janitors, worked in Washington.

Most federal employees were selected under the so-called spoils system. Its basic principle was that victorious politicians awarded government jobs to party workers, with little regard for qualifications, and ousted the previous employees. Appointees then typically promised part of their salary and time to the political interests of their patron or party. The spoils system enabled party leaders to strengthen their organizations, reward loyal party service, and attract the political workers that parties needed to mobilize the electorate.

Critics charged that the system was riddled with corruption, abuse, and inefficiency. Rapid turnover bred instability; political favoritism bred incompetence. One secretary of the navy, appointed at the behest of Indiana's Republican machine, was said to have exclaimed during his first official inspection of a ship: "Why, the thing's hollow!" Certainly the spoils system was ineffective for filling positions that required special skills. More serious, the spoils system also absorbed the president and Congress in unproductive conflicts over patronage.

INCONSISTENT STATE GOVERNMENT

Considered closer and more responsible to the people, state governments had long exercised police power and regulatory authority. They collected taxes for education and public works, and they promoted private enterprise and public health. Still, they did little by today's standards. Few people thought it appropriate for government at any level to offer direct help to particular social groups, and state constitutions often restricted the scope of public authority.

But state governments gradually expanded their role in response to the stresses produced by industrialization. Following the lead of Massachusetts in

1869, a majority of states had by the turn of the century created commissions to investigate and regulate industry. One observer noted in 1887 that state governments enacted many laws and established numerous state agencies in "utter disregard of the *laissez-faire* principle." In Minnesota, for example, the state helped dairy farmers by establishing a dairy commission, prohibiting the manufacture or sale of margarine, creating a bureau of animal industry, and employing state veterinarians. Other laws regulated railroads, telegraphs, and dangerous occupations, prohibited racial discrimination in inns, and otherwise protected the public welfare.

Not all such agencies and laws were effective. Southern states especially lagged, and one Midwesterner complained that his legislature merely "meets in ignorance, sits in corruption, and dissolves in disgrace every two years." Still, the widening scope of state action represented a growing acceptance of public responsibility for social welfare and economic life.

PUBLIC POLICIES AND NATIONAL ELECTIONS

Several great issues dominated the national political arena in the late nineteenth century, including civil service reform, tariffs, and business and financial regulation. Rarely, however, did these issues clearly and consistently separate the major political parties. Instead they divided each party into factions along regional, interest, and economic lines. As a consequence, these leading issues often played only a small role in determining elections and were seldom resolved by government action.

CIVIL SERVICE REFORM

Reform of the spoils system emerged as a prominent issue during the Hayes administration. Reformers like the Mugwumps wanted a professional civil service based on merit and divorced from politics. They wanted officeholders to be selected on the basis of competitive written examinations and protected from removal on political grounds. They expected such a system to promote efficiency, economy, and honesty in government. But they also expected it to increase their own influence and minimize that of "mere politicians." As one Baltimore Mugwump said, civil service reform would replace ignorant and corrupt officeholders with "gentlemen . . . who need nothing and want nothing from government except the satisfaction of using their talents."

President Hayes favored civil service reform. He struck a blow for change when he fired Chester A. Arthur from his post as New York customs house collector after an investigation pronounced Arthur's patronage system to be "unsound in principle, dangerous in practice, . . . and calculated to encourage and perpetuate the official ignorance, inefficiency, and corruption . . ."

The weakness of the civil service reformers was dramatically underscored in 1880 when the Republicans, to improve their chances of carrying the crucial state of New York, nominated Arthur for vice president on a presidential slate headed by James A. Garfield of Ohio. They won, and Garfield immediately found himself enmeshed in the demands of the unreformed spoils system. He once complained to his wife, "I had hardly arrived before the door-bell began to ring and the old stream of office-seekers began to pour in. They had scented my coming and were lying in wait for me like vultures for a wounded bison. All day long it has been a

WHAT WERE the main public policy issues of the 1880s and 1890s?

WHERE TO LEARN MORE

★ Rutherford B. Hayes Presidential Center, Fremont, Ohio
www.rbhayes.org/

WHERE TO LEARN MORE

★ James A Garfield Home, Mentor, Ohio
www.nps.gov/jaga/index.htm

steeple chase, I fleeing and they pursuing." Within a few months of his inauguration in 1881, Garfield was assassinated by a disappointed and crazed office seeker, and Arthur became president.

Public dismay over this tragedy finally spurred changes in the spoils system. Arthur himself urged Congress to act, and in 1883, it passed the **Pendleton Civil Service Act**. This measure prohibited federal employees from soliciting or receiving political contributions from government workers and created the Civil Service Commission to administer competitive examinations to applicants for government jobs. A professional civil service free from partisan politics gradually emerged, strengthening the executive branch's ability to handle its increasing administrative responsibilities.

The new emphasis on merit and skill rather than party ties opened new opportunities to women. By the early 1890s, women held a third of the clerical positions in the executive departments in Washington. Their work in public life challenged the conventional belief that a woman's ability and personality limited her to the domestic sphere. Julia Henderson described her work as an examiner of accounts in the Interior Department in 1893 as "brain work of a character that requires a knowledge not only of the rulings of this Department, but also those of the Treasury, Second Auditor, Second Comptroller, and Revised Statutes; demanding the closest and most critical attention, together with a great deal of legal and business knowledge."

THE POLITICAL LIFE OF THE TARIFF

Tariffs on imported goods provided revenue for the federal government and protected American industry from European competition. They promoted industrial growth but often allowed favored industries to garner high profits. By the 1880s, separate tariffs covered more than four thousand items and generated more revenue than the government needed to carry on its limited operations.

Reflecting its commitment to industry, the Republican party vigorously championed protective tariffs. Party leaders also claimed that American labor benefited from tariff protection. "Reduce the tariff, and labor is the first to suffer," declared William McKinley of Ohio. Most Democrats, by contrast, favored tariff reduction. They argued that lower tariffs would encourage foreign trade and, by reducing the treasury surplus, minimize the temptation for the government to pursue activist policies. (See the overview table "Arguments in the Tariff Debates.")

Regardless of party position, congressmen of both parties voted for tariffs that would benefit their districts. California Democrats called for protective duties on wool and raisins, products produced in California; Massachusetts Republicans, to aid their state's shoe manufacturers, supported tariffs on shoes but opposed tariffs on leather. A Democratic senator from Indiana, elected on a campaign pledge to reduce tariffs, summed up the prevailing rule succinctly: "I am a protectionist for every interest which I am sent here by my constituents to protect."

In the 1884 campaign, Republican presidential candidate James G. Blaine maintained that prosperity and high employment depended on high duties. The Democrats' platform endorsed a lowered tariff, but their candidate, Grover Cleveland, generally ignored the issue, and both parties turned to scandalmongering. The Democrats exploited Blaine's image as a beneficiary of the spoils system. Republicans responded by exposing Cleveland as the father of an illegitimate child.

Cleveland continued to avoid the tariff issue for three years after his election, until the growing treasury surplus and rising popular pressure for tariff reduction prompted him to act. He devoted his entire 1887 annual message to attacking the "vicious, inequitable, and illogical" tariff, apparently making it the dominant issue

18–7
The Assassination of President Garfield (1889)

QUICK REVIEW

Tariffs and Politics

- Tariffs provided revenues and protected American industries from competition.

- Republicans were strong supporters of protective tariffs.

- Congressmen voted for tariffs that benefited their home districts.

Pendelton Civil Service Act   A law of 1883 that reformed the spoils system by prohibiting government workers from making political contributions and creating the Civil Service Commission to oversee their appointment on the basis of merit rather than politics.

OVERVIEW

ARGUMENTS IN THE TARIFF DEBATES

Area Affected	High-Tariff Advocates	Low-Tariff Advocates
Industry	Tariffs promote industrial growth.	Tariffs inflate corporate profits.
Employment	Tariffs stimulate job growth.	Tariffs restrict competition.
Wages and prices	Tariffs permit higher wages.	Tariffs increase consumer prices.
Government	Tariffs provide government revenue.	Tariffs violate the principle of laissez-faire and produce revenues that tempt the government to activism.
Trade	Tariffs protect the domestic market.	Tariffs restrict foreign trade.

WHERE TO LEARN MORE

President Benjamin Harrison's Home, Indianapolis, Indiana
www.presidentbenjaminharrison.org/

Interstate Commerce Act The 1887 law that expanded federal power over business by prohibiting pooling and discriminatory rates by railroads and establishing the first federal regulatory agency, the Interstate Commerce Commission.

Sherman Antitrust Act The first federal antitrust measure, passed in 1890; sought to promote economic competition by prohibiting business combinations in restraint of trade or commerce.

of his 1888 reelection campaign. However, Cleveland then proposed a Democratic platform that ignored his recent message and did not even use the word *tariff*. When the party convention adopted a tariff reduction plank, Cleveland named high-tariff advocates to manage his campaign. "What a predicament the party is placed in," lamented one Texas Democrat, with tariff reform "for its battle cry and with a known protectionist . . . as our chairman." Cleveland won slightly more popular votes than his Republican opponent, Benjamin Harrison of Indiana, but Harrison carried the electoral college, indicating the decisive importance of strategic campaigning, local issues, and large campaign funds rather than great national issues.

The triumphant Republicans raised tariffs to unprecedented levels with the McKinley Tariff Act of 1890. The law provoked a popular backlash that helped return the Democrats to power. Still, the Democrats made little effort to push tariff reform. The *Atlanta Constitution* mused about such tariff politics in a bit of doggerel:

It's funny 'bout this tariff—how they've lost it or forgot;
They were rushing it to Congress once; their collars were so hot;
They could hardly wait to fix it 'till we harvested a crop;
Was it such a burnin' question that they had to let it drop?

THE BEGINNINGS OF FEDERAL REGULATION

Popular pressure compelled Congress to take the first steps toward the regulation of business with the passage of the **Interstate Commerce Act** in 1887 and the **Sherman Antitrust Act** in 1890.

Farmers condemned the power of corporations over transportation facilities and their monopolization of industries affecting agriculture, from those that manufactured farm machinery to those that ran flour mills. Small business owners suffered from the destructive competition of corporations, workers were exploited by the corporations' control of the labor market, and consumers felt victimized by high prices. The result was a growing clamor to rein in the corporations.

The first target of this concern was the nation's railroads, the preeminent symbol of big business. Both farm groups and businesses complained of discriminatory shipping rates levied by railroads. Consumers condemned the railroads' use of pooling arrangements to suppress competition and raise rates. The resulting pressure was responsible for the Granger laws enacted in several Midwestern states in the 1870s to regulate railroad freight and storage rates.

In 1886, the Supreme Court ruled in *Wabash, St. Louis, and Pacific Railway Company* v. *Illinois* that only the federal government could regulate interstate commerce. This decision effectively ended state regulation of railroads but simultaneously increased popular pressure for congressional action. "Upon no public question are the people so nearly unanimous as upon the proposition that Congress should undertake in some way the regulation of interstate business," concluded a Senate committee. With the support of both major parties, Congress in 1887 passed the Interstate Commerce Act.

The act prohibited rebates, discriminatory rates, and pooling and established the Interstate Commerce Commission (ICC) to investigate and prosecute violations. The ICC was the first federal regulatory agency, but its powers were too limited to be effective. Senator Nelson Aldrich of Rhode Island, a leading spokesman for business interests, described the law as an "empty menace to great interests, made to answer the clamor of the ignorant." The railroads continued their objectionable practices. In its first fifteen years, only one court case was decided in favor of the ICC. Not surprisingly, then, popular dissatisfaction with the railroads continued into the twentieth century.

As with railroad regulation, the first antitrust laws—laws intended to break up or regulate corporate monopolies—were passed by states. Exposés of the monopolistic practices of such corporations as Standard Oil forced both major parties to endorse national antitrust legislation. In 1890, Congress enacted the Sherman Antitrust Act with only a single vote in opposition. Although it emphatically prohibited any combination in restraint of trade (any attempt to restrict competition), it was otherwise vaguely written and hence weak in its ability to prevent abuses. The courts further weakened it, and presidents of both parties made little effort to enforce it. Large corporations remained an ominous threat in the eyes of many Americans.

THE MONEY QUESTION

Persistent wrangling over questions of currency and coinage made monetary policy the most divisive political issue in the late nineteenth century. President Garfield hinted at the complexities of this subject when he wryly suggested that a member of Congress had been committed to an asylum after "he devoted himself almost exclusively to the study of the currency, became fully entangled with the theories of the subject, and became insane."

Creditors, especially bankers, as well as conservative economists and many business leaders favored limiting the money supply. They called this a **sound money** policy and insisted that it would ensure economic stability, maintain property values, and retain investor confidence. Farmers and other debtors feared this would depress already low crop prices, drive debtors further into debt, and restrict economic opportunities. They favored expanding the money supply to match the country's growing population and economy. They expected this inflationary policy to raise prices, stimulate the economy, reduce debt burdens, and increase opportunities.

The conservative leadership of both major parties supported the sound money policy, but their rank-and-file membership, especially in the West and the South, included many inflationists. As a result, the parties avoided confronting each other on the money issue.

The conflict between advocates of sound money and inflation centered on the use of paper money—"greenbacks"—and silver coinage. To meet its expenses during the Civil War, the federal government issued $450 million in greenbacks—paper money backed only by the credit of the United States, not by gold or silver, the traditional basis of currency. After the war, creditors demanded that these greenbacks be withdrawn from circulation. Debtors and other Americans caught

Sound money Misleading slogan that referred to a conservative policy of restricting the money supply and adhering to the gold standard.

up in a postwar depression favored retaining the greenbacks and even expanding their use.

In 1875 sound money advocates in Congress enacted a deflationary law that withdraw some greenbacks from circulation and required that the remainder be convertible into gold after 1878. Outraged inflationists organized the Greenback party. The Greenbackers polled more than a million votes in 1878 and elected fourteen members of Congress, nearly gaining the balance of power in the House. As the depression faded, however, so did interest in the greenback issue, and the party soon withered.

Inflationists then turned their attention to the silver issue, which would prove more enduring and disruptive. Historically, the United States had used both gold and silver as the basis of its currency, but in 1873, Congress passed a law "demonetizing" silver, making gold the only standard for American currency. Gold standard supporters hoped the law would promote international trade by aligning U.S. financial policy with that of Great Britain, which insisted on gold-based currency. But they also wanted to prevent new silver discoveries in the American West from expanding the money supply.

Indeed, silver production soon boomed, flooding the commercial market and dropping the value of the metal. Dismayed miners wanted the Treasury Department to purchase their surplus silver on the old terms and demanded a return to the bimetallic system. More important, the rural debtor groups seeking currency inflation joined in this demand. Many passionately denounced the "Crime of '73" as a conspiracy of Eastern bankers and foreign interests to control the money system to the detriment of ordinary Americans.

Eastern conservatives of both parties denounced silver; Southerners and Westerners demanded **free silver**, which meant unlimited silver coinage. By 1878, a bipartisan coalition succeeded in passing the Bland-Allison Act. This compromise measure required the government to buy at least $2 million of silver a month. However, the government never exceeded the minimum, and the law had little inflationary effect.

As hard times hit rural regions in the late 1880s, inflationists secured the passage of the Sherman Silver Purchase Act of 1890. The Treasury now had to buy more silver and pay for it with Treasury notes redeemable in either gold or silver, but this too produced little inflation because the government did not coin the silver it purchased, redeemed the notes only with gold, and, as Western silver production increased further, had to spend less and less to buy the stipulated amount of silver. Debtors of both parties remained convinced that the government favored the "classes rather than the masses." Gold standard advocates (again of both parties) were even less happy with the law and planned to repeal it at their first opportunity.

Free Silver Philosophy that the government should expand the money supply by purchasing and coining all the silver offered to it.

THE CRISIS OF THE 1890s

WHAT WAS the platform of the Populist party?

In the 1890s, a third-party political challenge generated by agricultural discontent disrupted traditional party politics. A devastating depression spawned social misery and labor violence. Changing public attitudes led to new demands on the government and a realignment of parties and voters.

AGRICULTURAL PROTEST

In the late 1880s, falling crop prices and rising debt overwhelmed many people already exhausted from overwork and alarmed by the new corporate order. "At the age of 52 years, after a long life of toil, economy, and self-denial, I find myself and family virtual paupers," lamented one Kansan. Their farm, rather than being "a house of refuge for our declining years, by a few turns of the monopolistic crank has been rendered valueless." To a large extent, the farmers' plight was the result of bad weather and an international overproduction of farm products. Looking for remedies, however, the farmers focused on the inequities of railroad discrimination, tariff favoritism, a restrictive financial system, and apparently indifferent political parties.

Angry farmers particularly singled out the systems of money and credit that worked so completely against agricultural interests. Government rules for national banks directed credit into the urbanized areas of the North and East at the expense of the rural South and West and prohibited banks from making loans on farm property and real estate. In the West, farmers borrowed money from mortgage companies to buy land and machinery. In hard times, mortgage foreclosures crushed the hopes of many farmers. In the South, the credit shortage interacted with the practices of cotton marketing and retail trade to create the sharecropping system, which trapped more and more farmers, black and white, in a vicious pattern of exploitation. The government's policies of monetary deflation worsened the debt burden for all farmers.

Farmers also protested railroad freight rates that were two or three times higher in the West and South than in the North and East. The near-monopolistic control of grain elevators and cotton brokerages left farmers feeling exploited. Protective tariff rates on agricultural machinery and other manufactured goods further raised their costs. The failure of the government to correct these inequities capped their anger.

In response, farmers turned to the **Farmers' Alliance**, the era's greatest popular movement of protest and reform. Originating in Texas, the Southern Farmers' Alliance spread throughout the South and across the Great Plains to the Pacific coast. By 1890, it had 1.2 million members. African-American farmers organized the Colored Farmers' Alliance. The Northwestern Farmers' Alliance spread westward and northward from Illinois to Nebraska and Minnesota. In combination, these groups constituted a massive grass-roots movement committed to an agenda of economic and ultimately political reform.

The Farmers' Alliance restricted its membership to men and women of the "producing class" and urged them to stand "against the encroachments of monopolies and in opposition to the growing corruption of wealth and power." The Alliance attempted to establish farmers' cooperatives to market crops and purchase supplies. It also developed ingenious proposals to remedy rural credit and currency problems. In the South, the Alliance pushed the subtreasury system, which called on the government to warehouse farmers' cotton and advance them credit based on its value (see Chapter 19). In the West, the Alliance proposed a system of federal loans to farmers using land as security. These proposals were immensely popular among farmers, but the major parties and Congress rejected them. The Alliance also took up earlier calls for free silver, government control of railroads, and banking reform, again to no avail. William A. Peffer, the influential editor of the Alliance newspaper the *Kansas Farmer*, declared that the "time has come for action. The people will not consent to wait longer. . . . The future is full of retribution for delinquents."

THE PEOPLE'S PARTY

In the West, discontented agrarians organized independent third parties, which eventually adopted the labels "People's" or "Populist." The founders of the Kansas People's Party, including members of the Farmers' Alliance, the Knights of Labor, the Grange, and the old Greenback party, launched a campaign marked by grim determination and fierce rhetoric. These people, women as well as men, were earnest organizers and powerful orators. One was *Kansas Farmer* editor Peffer. Others included "Sockless Jerry" Simpson, Annie Diggs, and Mary E. Lease. When hostile

Farmers' Alliance A broad mass movement in the rural South and West during the late nineteenth century, encompassing several organizations and demanding economic and political reforms.

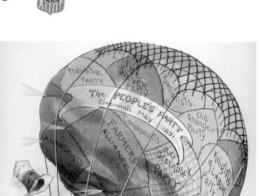

A PARTY OF PATCHES.
Grand Balloon Ascension—Cincinnati, May 20th, 1891.

Established interests ridiculed the Populists unmercifully. This hostile cartoon depicts the People's party as an odd assortment of radical dissidents committed to a "Platform of Lunacy."

Kansas City Historical Society

19–5
The People's Party Platform (1892)

Omaha Platform   The 1892 platform of the Populist party repudiating laissez-faire and demanding economic and political reforms to aid distressed farmers and workers.

business and political leaders attacked the Populist plans as socialistic, Lease retorted, "You may call me an anarchist, a socialist, or a communist. I care not, but I hold to the theory that if one man has not enough to eat three times a day and another has $25,000,000, that last man has something that belongs to the first." Lease spoke as clearly against the colonial status experienced by the South and West: "The great common people of this country are slaves, and monopoly is the master. The West and South are bound and prostrate before the manufacturing East."

The Populist parties gained control of the legislatures of Kansas and Nebraska and won congressional elections in Kansas, Nebraska, and Minnesota. Their victories contributed to a massive defeat of the GOP in the 1890 midterm elections after the passage of the McKinley Tariff and the Sherman Silver Purchase Act. Thereafter, Populists gained further victories throughout the West. In the mountain states, where their support came more from miners than farmers, they won governorships in Colorado and Montana. On the Pacific coast, angry farmers found allies among urban workers and the Populists elected a governor in Washington, congressmen in California, and legislators in both states.

In Oklahoma, the Populist party drew support from homesteaders and tenant farmers, in Arizona, from miners and railroad workers. In New Mexico, the Southern Alliance established itself among small ranchers who felt threatened by corporate ranchers and land companies. The fear of corporate expansion even united usually antagonistic Anglo New Mexicans and poor Hispanics. One Alliance paper wrote of the need to defend Hispanics from the "mighty land monopoly which is surely grinding their bones into flour that it may make its bread." In the 1890 election, Populists gained the balance of power in the New Mexico legislature.

In the South, the Alliance did not initially form third parties but instead swept "Alliance Democrats" into office, electing four governors, several dozen members of Congress, and a majority of legislators in eight states.

With their new political power, farmers enacted reform legislation in many Western states. New laws regulated banks and railroads and protected poor debtors by capping interest rates and restricting mortgage foreclosures. Others protected unions and mandated improved workplace conditions. Populists were also instrumental in winning woman suffrage in Colorado and Idaho, although the united opposition of Democrats and Republicans blocked their efforts to win it in other states. In the South, however, the Democratic party frustrated reform, and most Alliance Democrats abandoned their promise to support Alliance goals in favor of loyalty to their party and its traditional opposition to governmental activism.

Populists met in Omaha, Nebraska, on July 4, 1892, to organize a national party and nominated former Greenbacker James B. Weaver for president. The party platform, known as the **Omaha Platform**, rejected the *laissez-faire* policies of the old parties and declared: "We believe that the powers of government—in other words, of the people, should be expanded . . . to the end that oppression, injustice, and poverty shall eventually cease in the land." The platform demanded government ownership of the railroads and the telegraph and telephone systems; a national currency issued by the government rather than private banks; the sub-treasury system; free and unlimited silver coinage; a graduated income tax; and the redistribution to settlers of land held by railroads and speculative corporations. Accompanying resolutions endorsed the direct popular election of senators, the secret ballot, and other electoral reforms to make government more democratic and responsive to popular wishes. When the platform was adopted, "cheers and yells," one reporter wrote, "rose like a tornado from four thousand throats and raged without cessation for 34 minutes, during which women shrieked and wept, men embraced and kissed their neighbors . . . in the ecstasy of their delirium."

The Populists left Omaha to begin an energetic campaign. Southern Democrats, however, used violence and fraud to intimidate Populist voters and cheat Populist candidates out of office. Some local Populist leaders were murdered. One Democrat confessed that Alabama's Populist gubernatorial candidate "carried the state, but was swindled out of his victory . . . with unblushing trickery and corruption." Southern Democrats also appealed effectively to white supremacy, which undermined the Populist effort to build a biracial reform coalition.

Midwestern farmers unfamiliar with Alliance ideas and organization ignored Populist appeals and stood by their traditional political allegiances. So did most Eastern working-class voters, who learned little of the Populist program beyond its demand for inflation, which they feared would hurt them.

The Populists lost the election but got more than a million votes (one out of every twelve votes cast). Populist leaders began immediately working to expand their support, to the alarm of both Southern Democrats and Northern Republicans.

THE CHALLENGE OF THE DEPRESSION

A harsh and lengthy depression began in 1893, worsening conditions for farmers and most other Americans. Labor unrest and violence engulfed the nation, reflecting workers' distress but frightening more comfortable Americans. The failure of the major parties to respond to serious problems swelled popular discontent.

Although the Populists had not triumphed in 1892, the election nonetheless reflected the nation's spreading dissatisfaction. Voters decisively rejected President Harrison and the incumbent Republicans in Congress. Turning again to the other major party, they placed Grover Cleveland and the Democrats in control. But almost oblivious to the mounting demand for reform, Cleveland delivered an inaugural address championing the doctrine of laissez-faire and rejecting government action to solve social or economic problems.

The economy collapsed in the spring of 1893. Railroad overexpansion, a weak banking system, tight credit, and plunging agricultural prices all contributed to the disaster. A depression in Europe reduced American export markets and prompted British investors to sell their American investments for gold. Hundreds of banks closed, and thousands of businesses, including the nation's major railroads, went bankrupt. By winter, 20 percent of the labor force was unemployed, and the jobless scavenged for food in a country that had no public unemployment or welfare programs. "Never within memory," said one New York minister, "have so many people literally starved to death as in the past few months."

Most state governments offered little relief beyond encouraging private charity to the homeless. In Kansas, however, the Populist governor insisted that traditional laissez-faire policies were inadequate. (See American Views, "A Populist views American Government.") Cleveland disagreed. The functions of the government, he said in 1893, "do not include the support of the people."

Jacob Coxey, a Populist businessman from Ohio, proposed a government public works program for the unemployed to be financed with paper money. This plan would improve the nation's infrastructure, create jobs for the unemployed, and provide an inflationary stimulus to counteract the depression's deflationary effects. In short, Coxey was advocating positive government action to combat the depression.

Coxey organized a march of the unemployed to Washington as "a petition with boots on" to support his ideas. **Coxey's Army** of the unemployed, as the excited press

Coxey's Army   A protest march of unemployed workers, led by Populist businessman Jacob Coxey, demanding inflation and a public works program during the depression of the 1890s.

• AMERICAN VIEWS •

A POPULIST VIEWS AMERICAN GOVERNMENT

*n educator, merchant, and former editor, Loren-
zo D. Lewelling became an articulate champion
of the Populist party. Elected governor of Kansas
in 1892, he headed what was heralded as "The
First People's Party Government on Earth." The following passages from his inaugural address sketch out both Lewelling's
views of the 1890s and his "dream of the future."*

HOW DOES Lewelling's rhetoric reflect the deep divisions of the 1890s? What is Lewelling's view of the proper role of government? Why does Lewelling criticize the
government of the 1890s? What does Lewelling mean
by his statement that "the rich have no right to the property of the poor"?

The survival of the fittest is the government of brutes
and reptiles, and such philosophy must give place to a
government which recognizes human brotherhood. It
is the province of government to protect the weak, but
the government today is resolved into a struggle of the
masses with the classes for supremacy and bread, until
business, home, and personal integity are trembling in
the face of possible want in the family. Feed a tiger regularly and you tame and make him harmless, but hunger

makes tigers of men. If it be true that the poor have no
right to the property of the rich let it also be declared that
the rich have no right to the property of the poor.

It is the mission of Kansas to protect and advance
the moral and material interests of all its citizens. It is its
especial duty at the present time to protect the producer from the ravages of combined wealth. National legislation has for twenty years fostered and protected the
interests of the few, while it has left the South and West
to supply the products with which to feed and clothe the
world, and thus to become the servants of wealth.

The demand for free coinage has been refused. The
national banks have been permitted to withdraw their circulation, and thus the interests of the East and West have
been diverged until the passage of the McKinley bill culminated in their diversement. The purchasing power of
the dollar has become so great [that] corn, wheat, beef,
pork, and cotton have scarcely commanded a price equal
to the cost of production.

The instincts of patriotism have naturally rebelled
against these unwarranted encroachments of the power of
money. Sectional hatred has also been kept alive by the old
powers, the better to enable them to control the products

---

dubbed it, marched through the industrial towns of Ohio and Pennsylvania and into
Maryland, attracting attention and support. Other armies formed in Eastern cities from
Boston to Baltimore and set out for the capital. Some of the largest armies organized
in the Western cities of Denver, San Francisco, and Seattle. Three hundred men in
an army from Oakland elected as their commander Anna Smith, who promised to
"land my men on the steps of the Capitol at Washington." "I am a San Francisco
woman, a woman who has been brought up on this coast, and I'm not afraid of anything," Smith explained. "I have a woman's heart and a woman's sympathy, and these
lead me to do what I have done for these men, even though it may not be just what
a woman is expected to do."

Despite public sympathy for Coxey, the government acted to suppress him.
When he reached Washington with 600 marchers, police and soldiers arrested
him and his aides, beat sympathetic bystanders in a crowd of twenty thousand,
and herded the marchers into detention camps. Unlike the lobbyists for business
and finance, Coxey was not permitted to reach Congress to deliver his statement,
urging the government to assist "the poor and oppressed."

The depression also provoked labor turmoil. There were some 1,400 industrial strikes involving nearly 700,000 workers in 1894. One result was the government's violent suppression of the Pullman strike (see Chapter 18).

and make the producer contribute to the millionaire; and thus, while the producer labors in the field, the shop, and the factory, the millionaire usurps his earnings and rides in gilded carriages with liveried servants. . . .

The problem of today is how to make the State subservient to the individual, rather than to become his master. Government is a voluntary union for the common good. It guarantees to the individual life, liberty, and the pursuit of happiness. The government then must make it possible for the citizen to enjoy liberty and pursue happiness. If the government fails of these things, it fails in its mission. . . . If old men go to the poor-house and young men go to prison, something is wrong with the economic system of the government.

What is the State to him who toils, if labor is denied him and his children cry for bread? What is the State to the farmer who wearily drags himself from dawn till dark to meet the stern necessities of the mortgage on the farm? What is the State to him if it sanctions usury and other legal forms by which his home is destroyed and his innocent ones become a prey to the fiends who lurk in the shadow of civilization? What is the State to the business man, early grown gray, broken in health and spirit by successive failures; anxiety like a boding owl his constant companion by day and the disturber of his dreams by night? How is life to be sustained, how is liberty to be enjoyed, how is happiness to be pursued under such adverse conditions as the State permits if it does not sanction? Is the State powerless against these conditions?

This is the generation which has come to the rescue. Those in distress who cry out from the darkness shall not be heard in vain. Conscience is in the saddle. We have leaped the bloody chasm and entered a contest for the protection of home, humanity, and the dignity of labor.

The grandeur of civilization shall be emphasized by the dawn of a new era in which the people shall reign, and if found necessary they will "expand the powers of government to solve the enigmas of the times." The people are greater than the law or the statutes, and when a nation sets its heart on doing a great and good thing it can find a legal way to do it.

I have a dream of the future. I have the evolution of an abiding faith in human government, and in the beautiful vision of a coming time I behold the abolition of poverty. A time is foreshadowed when the withered hand of want shall not be outstretched for charity; when liberty, equality, and justice shall have permanent abiding places in the republic.

Source: *People's Party Paper* (Atlanta), January 20, 1893.

In a series of decisions in 1895, the Supreme Court strengthened the bonds between business and government. First, it upheld the use of a court-ordered injunction to break the Pullman strike. As a result, injunctions became a major weapon for courts and corporations against labor unions until Congress finally limited their use in 1932. In *United States* v. *E. C. Knight Company*, the Court gutted the Sherman Antitrust Act by ruling that manufacturing, as opposed to commerce, was beyond the reach of federal regulation. The Court thus allowed the American Sugar Refining Company, a trust controlling 90 percent of the nation's sugar, to retain its great power. Finally, the court invalidated an income tax that agrarian Democrats and Populists had maneuvered through Congress as an "assault upon capital." Not until 1913, and then only with an amendment to the Constitution, would it be possible to adopt an equitable system of taxation.

Cleveland's financial policies stirred further discontent. Cleveland blamed the economic collapse on the Sherman Silver Purchase Act, which he regarded as detrimental to business confidence and a threat to the nation's gold reserve. He persuaded Congress in 1893 to repeal the law but thereby enraged Southern and Western members of his own party, including William Jennings Bryan of Nebraska, who saw the silver issue in the context of a struggle between "the corporate interests of the United States, the moneyed interests, aggregated wealth

William Jennings Bryan (1860–1925) at the Democratic Convention, 1896, in which he made the "Cross of Gold" speech.

Culver Pictures, Inc.

and capital, imperious, arrogant, compassionless" and "an unnumbered throng . . . work-worn and dust-begrimed."

By 1894, the Treasury had begun borrowing money from Wall Street to bolster the gold reserve. These transactions benefited a syndicate of bankers headed by J. P. Morgan. It seemed to critics that an indifferent Cleveland was helping rich bankers profit from the nation's economic agony. "A set of vampires headed by a financial trust has control of our destiny," cried one rural newspaper.

THE BATTLE OF THE STANDARDS AND THE ELECTION OF 1896

These unpopular actions, coupled with the unrelenting depression, alienated workers and farmers from the Cleveland administration and the Democratic party. In the off-year elections of 1894, the Democrats suffered the greatest loss of congressional seats in American history. Populists increased their vote by 42 percent, making especially significant gains in the South, but the real beneficiaries of Cleveland's unpopularity were the Republicans, who gained solid control of Congress as well as state governments across the North and West. All three parties began to plan for the presidential election of 1896.

The silver issue came to overshadow all others. Populist Weaver declared the silver issue "the line upon which the battle should be fought. It is the line of least resistance and we should hurl our forces against it at every point." Both to undercut the Populists and to distance themselves and their party from the despised Cleveland, leading Democrats began using the silver issue to reorganize their party.

William McKinley, governor of Ohio and author of the McKinley Tariff Act of 1890, emerged as the leader of a crowd of hopeful Republican presidential candidates. His candidacy benefited particularly from the financial backing and political management of Marcus A. Hanna, a wealthy Ohio industrialist. Hanna thought McKinley's passion for high tariffs as the key to revived prosperity would appeal to workers as well as industry and business. Republicans nominated McKinley on the first ballot at their 1896 convention. Their platform called for high tariffs but also endorsed the gold standard, placating Eastern delegates but prompting several Western Silver Republicans to withdraw from the party.

The Democratic convention met shortly thereafter. With a fervor that conservatives likened to "scenes of the French Revolution," the Silver Democrats revolutionized their party. They adopted a platform that repudiated the Cleveland administration and its policies and endorsed free silver, the income tax, and tighter regulation of trusts and railroads. A magnificent speech supporting this platform by William Jennings Bryan helped convince the delegates to nominate him for president.

Holding their convention last, the Populists now faced a terrible dilemma. The Democratic nomination of Bryan on a silver platform undercut their hopes of attracting into their own ranks disappointed reformers from the major parties. Some Populists urged the party to endorse Bryan rather than split the silver vote and ensure the victory of McKinley and the gold standard. Others argued that fusing—joining with the Democrats—would cost the Populists their separate identity and subordinate their larger political principles to the issue of free silver. After anguished discussion, the Populists nominated Bryan.

The campaign was intense and dramatic, with each side demonizing the other. Eastern financial and business interests contributed millions of dollars to Hanna's campaign for McKinley. Standard Oil alone provided $250,000, about the same amount as the Democrats' total national expenses. Hanna used these funds to organize an unprecedented campaign. Republicans issued 250 million campaign documents, printed in a dozen languages. Many newspapers not only shaped their editorials but also distorted their news stories to Bryan's disadvantage.

The Democrats relied on Bryan's superb voice, oratorical virtuosity, and youthful energy. Bryan was the first presidential candidate to campaign systematically for election, speaking hundreds of times to millions of voters. McKinley stayed home in Canton, Ohio, where he conducted a "front porch" campaign. Explaining his refusal to campaign outside Canton, McKinley said, "I might just as well put up a trapeze . . . and compete with some professional athlete as go out speaking against Bryan." But Hanna brought groups of Republicans from all over the country to visit McKinley every day, and McKinley reiterated his simple promise to restore prosperity.

In the depression, that appeal proved enough. As the Democratic candidate, Bryan was ironically burdened with the legacy of the hated Cleveland administration. The intense campaign brought a record voter turnout. McKinley won decisively by capturing the East and Midwest as well as Oregon and California (see Map 20–2). Bryan carried the traditionally Democratic South and the mountain and plains states where Populists and silverites dominated. He failed to gain support in either the Granger states of the Midwest or the cities of the East. His silver campaign had little appeal to industrial workers. Hanna realized that Bryan was making a mistake in subordinating other popular grievances to silver: "He's talking silver all the time, and that's where we've got him."

The elections of 1894 and 1896 ended the close balance between the major parties. Cleveland's failures, coupled with an economic recovery in the wake of the election of 1896, gained the Republicans a reputation as the party of prosperity and industrial progress, firmly establishing them in power for years to come. By contrast, the Democratic party receded into an ineffectual sectional minority dominated by Southern conservatives, despite Bryan's liberal views. The People's party simply dissolved.

McKinley plunged into his presidency. Unlike his predecessors, he had a definite, if limited, program, consisting of tariff protection, sound money, and overseas expansion. He worked actively to see it through Congress and to shape public opinion, thereby helping establish the model of the modern presidency. He had promised prosperity, and it returned, although not because of the record high tariff his party enacted in 1897 or the Currency Act of 1900, which firmly established the gold standard. Prosperity returned instead because of reviving markets and a monetary inflation that resulted from the discovery of vast new deposits of gold in Alaska, Australia, and South Africa. The silverites had recognized that an expanding industrial economy required an expanding money supply. Ironically, the new inflation was greater than would have resulted from free silver. With the return of prosperity and the decline of social tensions, McKinley easily won reelection in 1900, defeating Bryan a second time.

MAP EXPLORATION

To explore an interactive version of this map, go to
http://www.prenhall.com/goldfield2/map20.2

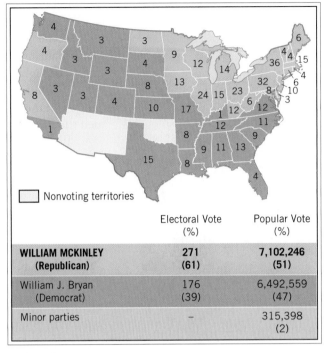

Nonvoting territories

	Electoral Vote (%)	Popular Vote (%)
WILLIAM MCKINLEY (Republican)	**271** **(61)**	**7,102,246** **(51)**
William J. Bryan (Democrat)	176 (39)	6,492,559 (47)
Minor parties	–	315,398 (2)

MAP 20–2
The Election of 1896   William Jennings Bryan carried most of the rural South and West, but his free silver campaign had little appeal to more urban and industrial regions, which swung strongly to Republican candidate William McKinley.

WAS THE election of 1896 closer than the electoral vote would suggest?

CONCLUSION

In late-nineteenth-century America, politics and government often seemed at cross-purposes. Closely balanced political parties commanded the zealous support of their constituents and wielded power and influence. The institutions of government, by contrast, were limited in size, scope, and responsibility. A weakened presidency and an inefficient Congress, hampered by

WHERE TO LEARN MORE

Fairview, Lincoln, Nebraska
www.bryanlgh.org/aboutus/ fairviewhistory.htm

a restrictive judiciary, were often unable to resolve the very issues that were so dramatically raised in the political arena. The issue that most reflected this impasse was civil service reform. The patronage system provided the lifeblood of politics but also disrupted government business.

The localism, laissez-faire, and other traditional principles that shaped both politics and government were becoming increasingly inappropriate for America's industrializing society. The national nature of the railroad network, for example, finally brought the federal government into the regulatory arena, however imperfectly, with the Interstate Commerce Act of 1887. Both the depression of the 1890s and the popular discontent underscored the need for change and discredited the limited government of the Cleveland administration.

By the end of the decade, the Republicans had emerged as the dominant party, ending the two-party stalemate of previous decades. Campaign hoopla in local communities had given way to information-based campaigns directed by and through national organizations. A new activist presidency was emerging, and the disruptive currency issue faded with the hard times that had brought it forth.

SUMMARY

The Structure and Style of Politics   Politics in the late nineteenth century expressed social values as they determined who held the reins of government. While the two major political parties dominated, third parties sought to activate those the Democrats and Republicans left unserved. Virtually all men participated in politics; the voter turnout of that era has never been equaled. Religious, ethnic, and regional factors determined party ties, but third parties, such as the Populists, emerged around issues. Women also participated in politics and some states now allowed full or partial suffrage.

The Limits of Government   Government in the late nineteenth century was neither active nor productive by present standards; localism and laissez-faire policies were resurgent. Congress and a presidency divided between the two political parties, a small and inefficient federal bureaucracy, and judicial restraints joined powerful private interests to limit the size and objectives of the federal government.

Public Policies and National Elections   The spoils system, the system for selecting and supervising federal employees, was finally reformed as a result of the assassination of President Garfield. The Pendleton Civil Service Act emphasized merit and skill; it also opened new opportunities for women. Americans heatedly debated the tariff policies; popular pressure compelled Congress to take the first steps toward the regulation of business; the most divisive political issue of the era was monetary policies with inflationists wanting more money, especially silver, in circulation.

The Crisis of the 1890s   Protests from Midwestern farmers over freight rates, tariffs, and the money supply resulted in popular movements of protest and reform. The Populists, a third party, funneled the discontent into politics; their emergence was but one of the many developments combining to produce a national political crises. A severe economic depression, labor unrest, and government inaction, along with the silver issue underscored the need for change. The presidential election of 1896 was an intense campaign with record voter turnout; with William McKinley's victory over William Jennings Bryan, the Republicans became established as the party of prosperity and individual progress.

REVIEW QUESTIONS

1. What social factors shaped the nature of elections in the late nineteenth century?

2. How and why did the role of government change during this period?

3. Why did so many third parties develop during this era?

4. How might the Omaha Platform have helped farmers?

5. Why did McKinley win in 1896? How did that election differ from earlier ones?

KEY TERMS

Coxey's Army (p. 539)
Farmers' Alliance (p. 537)
Free silver (p. 536)
Granger laws (p. 527)
Greenback Party (p. 527)

Interstate Commerce Act (p. 534)
Mugwumps (p. 529)
National American Woman Suffrage Association (p. 529)
Omaha Platform (p. 538)

Pendleton Civil Service Act (p. 533)
Populist Party (p. 527)
Prohibition Party (p. 527)
Sherman Antitrust Act (p. 534)
Sound money (p. 535)

WHERE TO LEARN MORE

Rest Cottage, Evanston, Illinois. Frances Willard's home, from which she directed the Woman's Christian Temperance Union, is carefully preserved as a museum. The Willard Memorial Library contains more memorabilia and papers of Willard and the WCTU. **www.wctu.org/house.html**

President Benjamin Harrison's Home, Indianapolis, Indiana. President Harrison's brick Italianate mansion, completed in 1875, has been completely restored with the family's furniture and keepsakes. The former third-floor ballroom serves as a museum with exhibits of many artifacts of the Harrisons' public and private lives. **www.presidentbenjaminharrison.org/**

Fairview, Lincoln, Nebraska. A National Historic Landmark, Fairview was the home of William Jennings Bryan, who described it as "the Monticello of the West." Faithfully restored to depict the Bryan family's life in the early 1900s, it includes a museum and interpretive center. **www.bryanlgh.org/aboutus/fairviewhistory.htm**

Susan B. Anthony House National Historic Landmark, Rochester, New York. This modest house was the home of the prominent suffragist and contains Anthony's original furnishings and personal photographs. **www.susanbanthonyhouse.org/main.html**

Rutherford B. Hayes Presidential Center, Fremont, Ohio. This complex contains President Hayes's home, office, and extensive grounds together with an excellent library and museum holding valuable collections of manuscripts, artifacts, and photographs illustrating his personal interests and political career. **www.rbhayes.org/**

James A. Garfield Home, Mentor, Ohio. Operated by the Western Reserve Historical Society as a museum, Garfield's home is the site of his successful 1880 front-porch campaign for president. **www.nps.gov/jaga/index.htm**

 For additional study resources for this chapter, go to:
www.prenhall.com/goldfield/chapter20

The women, trudging stoutly along under great difficulties, were able to complete their march only when troops of cavalry from Fort Meyers were rushed into Washington . . . No inauguration has ever produced such scenes . . .

THE JUNGLE

UPTON SINCLAIR

The great woman suffrage parade leaves Capitol Hill and heads for the White House, March 3, 1913. Dramatic tactics and careful organizing like those that marked this parade helped secure reform in the Progressive Era. The head of a suffrage parade at Washington D.C. oil over a photograph, 1913, (Granger Collection 4E 1028.04).

VOTES FOR WOMEN

21

THE PROGRESSIVE ERA
1900–1917

WHAT WAS the nature of progressivism?

WHAT ROLE did women play in Progressive Era movements?

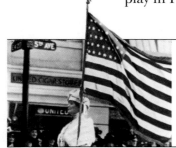

HOW DID electoral and municipal reforms improve voting and government during the Progressive Era?

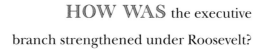

HOW WAS the executive branch strengthened under Roosevelt?

HOW DID Woodrow Wilson bring progressivism to its climax?

IMAGE KEY
for pages 546–547

a. "The Jungle" by Upton Sinclair cover featuring a factory.

b. Photo of Women's suffrage parade in D.C., 1913.

c. Dorothy Newell has Votes for Women written on her back.

d. Bull Moose party campaign paraphernalia.

e. Flanner House Baby Clinic, about 1918. The old Flanner house Building on Colton Street was soon abandoned for better quarters.

f. Illustration "A WOMAN'S WORK IS NEVER DONE".

g. Detail of photo of Women's suffrage parade in D.C., 1913.

h. American cartoon showing President Theodore Roosevelt slaying those trusts he considered 'bad' for the public interest while restraining those whose business practices he considered 'good' for the country.

i. Woodrow Wilson (1856–1924). Oil on canvas.

Five thousand women, marching in the woman suffrage pageant yesterday, practically fought their way foot by foot up Pennsylvania avenue, through a surging mass of humanity that completely defied the Washington police, swamped the marchers, and broke their procession into little companies. The women, trudging stoutly along under great difficulties, were able to complete their march only when troops of cavalry from Fort Myer were rushed into Washington to take charge of Pennsylvania avenue. No inauguration has ever produced such scenes, which in many instances amounted to little less than riots. . . .

The parade in itself, in spite of the delays, was a great success. . . . As a spectacle the pageant was entrancing. Beautiful women, posing in classic robes, passed in a bewildering array, presenting an irresistible appeal to the artistic, and completely captivating the hundred thousand spectators who struggled for a view along the entire route.

Miss Margaret Foley, bearing aloft a large "Votes for Women" flag, and Mrs. G. Farquhar, carrying an American flag, led the procession. . . . After the float reading, "We Demand an Amendment to the United States Constitution Enfranchising the Women of This Country," came a body of ushers clad in light blue capes. . . . Two large floats . . . represented the countries in which women are working for equal rights, followed by a large body of women on foot dressed in street clothes, who bore the banners and pennants of scores of suffrage associations throughout the world. . . . The Homemakers . . . were dressed in long purple robes over their street clothes. Following them came a float, "In Patriotic Service," . . . and Miss Lillian Wald, the walking leader of a large body of women who followed the float, dressed as trained nurses, with gray caps and coats.

Miss Margaret Gage and Maurice Cohen, wearing college gowns with mortar boards, represented "Education," which was followed by nearly 1,000 women of the college section. . . . A group of young girls in blue capes represented the wage-earners, followed by "A Labor Story," which depicted the crowded condition of tenements, with women and children bending over sewing machines, dirty and disheveled, in squalid quarters. . . . [Then followed] the women in the government section, all wearing light blue capes, . . . the business women, dressed in similar manner. . . . the teachers, . . . the social workers, . . . the white and pink costumed delegation of "writers," . . . club women and women clergy.

The greatest ovation was given to "General" Rosalie Jones, who led her little band of hikers from New York over rough roads and through snow and rain to march for the "cause." . . .

But there were hostile elements in the crowd through which the women marched. . . . Passing through two walls of antagonistic humanity, the marchers for the most part kept their temper. They suffered insult and closed their ears to jibes and jeers. Few faltered, although several of the older women were forced to drop out from time to time.

The pageant moved up Pennsylvania avenue with great difficulty and surrounded with some danger. Crowds surged into the streets, completely over-

whelming the police and stopping the pageant's progress. Mounted police charged into the crowds, but failed at times to drive them back, even with the free use of clubs. In more than an hour the pageant had moved only ten blocks.

Miss Inez Milholland, a New York society girl, mounted on her white horse and dressed as a herald, finally rode up beside a mounted policeman, and helped charge the crowd. Miss Milholland gesticulated and shouted at the crowd and rode her horse into it with good effect. . . .

When the surging multitude was driven back in one place it flowed back into the street at another. The pageant slowly moved along, sometimes not more than a dozen feet at a time. . . .

As a result of the unruly spirit of the biggest crowd that ever witnessed a parade on Pennsylvania avenue, or of the inactivity of the police, who seemed powerless to protect the marching suffragists, the Emergency Hospital last night was filled to overflowing. . . . While an automobile and ambulance and horse-drawn vehicle ran back and forth, with all the surgeons in the institution taking turns at riding on it, people who had fainted or been overcome by exhaustion, or crushed and trampled, were brought to the hospital.

Washington Post, March 4, 1913.

INEZ MILHOLLAND'S charge and the jumbled news accounts in the *Washington Post* convey the intensity of the woman suffrage parade on March 3, 1913. The women's difficult journey down Pennsylvania Avenue that day, illustrated critical features of life in the **Progressive Era**.

Important movements challenged traditional relationships and attitudes— here involving women's role in American life—and often met resistance. "Progressives" seeking reforms organized their supporters across lines of class, education, occupation, geography, gender, and, at times, race and ethnicity— as the variety of groups in the suffrage parade demonstrated. Rather than rely on traditional partisan politics, reformers adopted new political techniques, including lobbying and demonstrating, as nonpartisan pressure groups. Reform work begun at the local and state levels—where the suffrage movement had already met some success—inexorably moved to the national level as the federal government expanded its authority and became the focus of political interest. Finally, this suffrage demonstration revealed the diversity of the progressive movement, for the women marched, in part, against Woodrow Wilson, a fellow progressive.

Progressivism had no unifying organization, central leadership, or consensus on objectives. Instead, it represented the coalescing of different and even contradictory movements that sought changes in the nation's social, economic, and political life. But reformers did share certain convictions. They believed that to correct the disorders that industrialization and urbanization had produced required new ideas and methods. They rejected the ideology of individualism in favor of broader concepts of social responsibility, and they sought to achieve social order through organization and efficiency. Finally, most progressives believed that government itself, as the agent of public responsibility, should address social and economic problems.

The interaction among the reformers and the conflict with their opponents made the two decades before World War I a period of ferment and excitement. The progressives' achievements and failures profoundly shaped America.

Progressive Era   An era in the United States (roughly between 1900 and 1917) in which important movements challenged traditional relationships and attitudes.

WHAT WAS the nature
of progressivism?

WHERE TO LEARN MORE

★ National Museum of American
History, Smithsonian Institution,
Washington, D.C.

QUICK REVIEW

Triangle Shirtwaist Fire

◆ 1911: Fire kills 146 workers.

◆ Managers had locked the exits.

◆ The United States had the
highest rate of industrial
accidents in the world.

WHERE TO LEARN MORE

★ Lowell National Historic Park,
Lowell, Massachusetts
www.nps.gov/lowe/

THE FERMENT OF REFORM

The diversity of progressivism reflected the diverse impulses of reform. Clergy and professors provided new ideas to guide remedial action. Journalists exposed corporate excesses and government corruption and stirred public demand for reform. Business leaders sought to curtail disorder through efficiency and regulation, while industrial workers struggled to improve the horrible conditions in which they worked and lived. Women organized to protect their families and homes from new threats and even to push beyond such domestic issues. Nearly every movement for change encountered fierce opposition, while also helping America grapple with the problems of industrial society. (See the overview table "Major Progressive Organizations and Groups.")

THE CONTEXT OF REFORM: INDUSTRIAL AND URBAN TENSIONS

The origins of progressivism lay in the crises of the new urban-industrial order that emerged in the late nineteenth century. The severe depression and consequent mass suffering of the 1890s, the labor violence and industrial armies, the political challenges of Populism and an ineffective government shattered the complacency many middle-class Americans had felt about their nation and made them aware of social and economic inequities that rural and working-class families had long recognized.

By 1900, a returning prosperity had eased the threat of major social violence, but the underlying problems intensified. Big business, which had disrupted traditional economic relationships in the late nineteenth century, suddenly became bigger in a series of mergers between 1897 and 1903. Giant corporations threatened to squeeze opportunities for small firms and workers, dominate markets, and raise social tensions. They also inspired calls for public control.

Most workers still toiled nine to ten hours a day; steelworkers and textile employees usually worked twelve-hour shifts. Wages were minimal; an economist in 1905 calculated that 60 percent of all adult male breadwinners made less than a living wage. Family survival, then, often required women and children to work, often in the lowest paid, most exploited positions. Southern cotton mills employed children as young as 7; coal mines paid 12-year-old slate pickers 39 cents for a ten-hour day. Dangerous work environments and an absence of safety programs threatened not only workers' health but their lives as well. In 1911 a fire killed 146 workers, most of them young women, trapped inside the factory of the Triangle Shirtwaist Company in New York, because management had locked the exits. The fire chief found "skeletons bending over sewing machines." The United States had the highest rate of industrial accidents in the world. Half a million workers were injured and thirty thousand killed at work each year. These terrible conditions cried out for reform.

Other Americans saw additional social problems in the continuing flood of immigrants who were transforming America's cities. From 1900 to 1917, more than 14 million immigrants entered the United States, and most became urban dwellers. By 1910, immigrants and their children comprised more than 70 percent of the population of New York, Chicago, Buffalo, Milwaukee, and other cities. Most of the arrivals were so-called new immigrants from southern and eastern Europe, rather than the British, Irish, Germans, and Scandinavians who had arrived earlier. Crowding into urban slums, immigrants overwhelmed municipal sanitation, education, and fire protection services. One Russian described his new life as "all filth and sadness."

OVERVIEW

MAJOR PROGRESSIVE ORGANIZATIONS AND GROUPS

Group	Activity
Social Gospel movement	Urged churches and individuals to apply Christian ethics to social and economic problems
Muckrakers	Exposed business abuses, public corruption, and social evils through investigative journalism
Settlement House movement	Attempted through social work and public advocacy to improve living and working conditions in urban immigrant communities
National Consumers' League (1898)	Monitored businesses to ensure decent working conditions and safe consumer products
Women's Trade Union League (1903)	United workingwomen and their middle-class "allies" to promote unionization and social reform
National Child Labor Committee (1904)	Campaigned against child labor
Country Life movement	Attempted to modernize rural social and economic conditions according to urban-industrial standards
National American Woman Suffrage Association	Led the movement to give women the right to vote
Municipal reformers	Sought to change the activities and structure of urban government to promote efficiency and control
Conservationists	Favored efficient management and regulation of natural resources rather than uncontrolled development or preservation

Ethnic prejudices abounded. Woodrow Wilson, then president of Princeton University, declared in 1902: "The immigrant newcomers of recent years are men of the lowest class from the South of Italy, and men of the meaner sort out of Hungary and Poland, men out of the ranks where there was neither skill nor energy, nor any initiative or quick intelligence." Americans of the Old Stock often considered the predominantly Catholic and Jewish newcomers a threat to social stability and cultural identity and so demanded programs to reform either the urban environment or the immigrants themselves.

CHURCH AND CAMPUS

Many groups, drawing from different traditions and inspirations, responded to such economic and social issues. Reform-minded Protestant ministers created the **Social Gospel movement**, which sought to introduce religious ethics into industrial relations and appealed to churches to meet their social responsibilities. Washington Gladden, a Congregational minister in Columbus, Ohio, was shocked in 1884 by a bloody strike crushed by wealthy members of his own congregation. Gladden began a ministry to working-class neighborhoods that most churches ignored. He endorsed unions and workers' rights and proposed replacing a cruelly competitive wage system with profit sharing.

Social Gospel Movement Movement created by reform-minded Protestant ministers seeking to introduce religious ethics into industrial relations and appealing to churches to meet their social responsibilities.

CHRONOLOGY

1893–1898 Depression grips the nation.

1898 South Dakota adopts initiative and referendum.
National Consumers' League is organized.

1900 Robert La Follette is elected governor of Wisconsin.

1901 United States Steel Corporation is formed, the world's largest business at the time.
President William McKinley is assassinated; Theodore Roosevelt becomes president.
Socialist Party of America is organized.
Galveston, Texas, initiates the city commission plan.

1902 Antitrust suit is filed against Northern Securities Company.
Mississippi enacts the first direct primary law.
National Reclamation Act is passed.
Roosevelt intervenes in coal strike.

1903 Women's Trade Union League is organized.

1904 National Child Labor Committee is formed.
Roosevelt is elected president.

1905 Industrial Workers of the World is organized.

1906 Hepburn Act strengthens the Interstate Commerce Commission.

Meat Inspection Act extends government regulation. Pure Food and Drug Act is passed.

1908 *Muller* v. *Oregon* upholds maximum workday for women.
William Howard Taft is elected president.

1910 National Association for the Advancement of Colored People is organized.
Ballinger-Pinchot controversy erupts.

1912 Children's Bureau is established.
Progressive Party organizes and nominates Roosevelt.
Woodrow Wilson is elected president.

1913 Sixteenth and Seventeenth Amendments are ratified.
Underwood-Simmons Tariff Act establishes an income tax.
Federal Reserve Act creates the Federal Reserve System.

1914 Federal Trade Commission is established.
Harrison Act criminalizes narcotics.

1915 National Birth Control League is formed.

1916 Keating-Owen Act prohibits child labor.

1917 Congress enacts literacy test for immigrants.

1920 Nineteenth Amendment is ratified.

Social Gospeler Walter Rauschenbusch, a Baptist minister, argued in his book *Christianity and the Social Crisis* (1907) that Christians should support social reform to alleviate poverty, slums, and labor exploitation. He attacked low wages for transforming workers "into lean, sallow, hopeless, stupid, and vicious young people, simply to enable some group of stockholders to earn 10 percent."

The Social Gospel movement flowered mainly among certain Protestant denominations, especially Episcopalians, Congregationalists, and Methodists. It climaxed in 1908 in the formation of the Federal Council of Churches of Christ in America. The council, representing thirty-three religious groups, adopted a program that endorsed welfare and regulatory legislation to achieve social justice. By linking reform with religion (as "applied Christianity," in the words of Washington Gladden), the Social Gospel movement gave progressivism a powerful moral drive that affected much of American life.

The Social Gospel movement provided an ethical justification for government intervention to improve the social order. Scholars in the social sciences such as Lester Ward also called for social progress through rational planning and government intervention rather than through unrestrained and unpredictable competition. Economists rejected laissez-faire principles in favor of state action to accomplish social evolution. Industrialization, declared economist Richard T. Ely, "has brought to the front a vast number of social problems whose solution is impossible without the united efforts of church, state, and science."

MUCKRAKERS

Journalists also spread reform ideas by developing a new form of investigative reporting known as **muckraking**. Samuel S. McClure sent his reporters to uncover political and corporate corruption for *McClure's Magazine*. Sensational exposés sold magazines, and soon *Cosmopolitan, Everybody's*, and other journals began publishing investigations of business abuses, dangerous working conditions, and the miseries of slum life.

Muckraking articles aroused indignant public demands for reform. Lincoln Steffens detailed the corrupt links between "respectable" businessmen and crooked urban politicians in a series of articles called "The Shame of the Cities." Ida Tarbell revealed John D. Rockefeller's sordid construction of Standard Oil. Muckraking novels also appeared. *The Octopus* (1901) by Frank Norris dramatized the Southern Pacific Railroad's stranglehold on California's farmers, and *The Jungle* (1906) by Upton Sinclair exposed nauseating conditions in Chicago's meatpacking industry.

THE GOSPEL OF EFFICIENCY

Many progressive leaders believed that efficiency and expertise could control or resolve the disorder of industrial society. President Theodore Roosevelt (1901–1909) praised the "gospel of efficiency." Like many other progressives, he admired corporations' success in applying management techniques to guide economic growth. Drawing from science and technology as well as from the model of the corporation, many progressives attempted to manage or direct change efficiently. They used scientific methods to collect extensive data and relied on experts for analysis and recommendations. "Scientific management" seemed the key to eliminating waste and inefficiency in government, society, and industry. Rural reformers thought that "scientific agriculture" could bring prosperity to the impoverished Southern countryside; urban reformers believed that improvements in medical science and the professionalization of physicians through uniform licensing standards could eradicate the cities' wretched public health problems.

Industrialists were drawn to the ideas of Frederick Taylor, a proponent of scientific management. Taylor proposed to increase worker efficiency through imposed work routines, speedups, and mechanization. Workers, Taylor insisted, should "do what they are told promptly and without asking questions. . . . It is absolutely necessary for every man in our organization to become one of a train of gear wheels." By assigning workers simple and repetitive tasks on machines, Taylorization made their skills expendable and enabled managers to control the production, pace of work, and hiring and firing of personnel. When labor complained, one business leader declared that unions failed "to appreciate the progressivism of the age."

Sophisticated managers of big business combinations favored government regulations that could bring about safer and more stable conditions in society and the economy. Government regulations, they reasoned, could reassure potential consumers, open markets, mandate working conditions that smaller competitors could not provide, or impose systematic procedures that competitive pressures would otherwise undercut.

LABOR'S DEMAND FOR RIGHTS

Industrial workers with different objectives also hastened the ferment of reform. Workers resisted the new rules of efficiency experts and called for improved wages and working conditions and reduced work hours. They and their middle-class

Muckraking   Journalism exposing economic, social, and political evils, so named by Theodore Roosevelt for its "raking the muck" of American society.

sympathizers sought to achieve some of these goals through state intervention, demanding laws to compensate workers injured on the job, curb child labor, and regulate the employment of women. After the Triangle Shirtwaist fire, for example, urban politicians with working-class constituencies created the New York State Factory Commission and enacted dozens of laws dealing with fire hazards, machine safety, and wages and hours for women.

Workers also organized unions to improve their lot. The American Federation of Labor (AFL) claimed 4 million members by 1920, but it recruited mainly skilled workers, particularly native-born white males. New unions organized the factories and sweatshops where most immigrants and women worked. Despite strong employer resistance, the International Ladies Garment Workers Union (1900) and the Amalgamated Clothing Workers (1914) organized the garment trades, developed programs for social and economic reforms, and led their members—mostly young Jewish and Italian women—in spectacular strikes. The "Uprising of the 20,000," a 1909 strike in New York City, included months of massive rallies, determined picketing, and police repression. One observer marveled at the women strikers' "emotional endurance, fearlessness, and entire willingness to face danger and suffering."

A still more radical union tried to organize miners, lumberjacks, and Mexican and Japanese farm workers in the West, black dockworkers in the South, and immigrant factory hands in New England. Founded in 1905, the Industrial Workers of the World (IWW), whose members were known as "**Wobblies**," used sit-down strikes, sit-ins, and mass rallies, tactics adopted by other industrial unions in the 1930s and the civil rights movement in the 1960s. "Respectable people" considered the Wobblies violent revolutionaries, but most of the violence was committed against them.

EXPANDING THE WOMAN'S SPHERE

Women reformers and their organizations played a key role in progressivism. By the early twentieth century, more women than before were working outside the home—in the factories, mills, and sweatshops of the industrial economy and as clerks in stores and offices. In 1910, more than a fourth of all workers were women, increasing numbers of them married. Their importance in the work force and participation in unions and strikes challenged assumptions that woman's "natural" role was to be a submissive housewife.

Often founded for cultural purposes, women's clubs soon began adopting programs for social reform and gave their members a route to public influence. In 1914, an officer of the General Federation of Women's Clubs proudly declared that she could not find a cause for social reform that "has not received a helpful hand from the clubwomen."

Women also joined or created other organizations that pushed beyond the limits of traditional domesticity. By threatening healthy and happy homes, urban problems required that women become "social housekeepers" in the community. The National Congress of Mothers, organized in 1897, worried about crime and disease and championed kindergartens, foster-home programs, juvenile courts, and compulsory school attendance. Led by the crusading Florence Kelley, the National Consumers' League tried to protect both women wage earners and middle-class housewives by monitoring stores and factories to ensure decent working conditions and safe products. The Women's Trade Union League, or WTUL, united working women and their self-styled middle-class "allies" to unionize women workers and eliminate sweatshop conditions. Its greatest success came in the 1909 garment workers' strike when the allies—dubbed by one worker the "mink brigade"—assisted strikers with relief funds, bail money, food supplies, and public relations campaign.

Wobblies Popular name for the members of the Industrial Workers of the World (IWW).

Although most progressive women stressed women's special duties and responsibilities as social housekeepers, others began to demand women's equal rights. In 1914, for example, critics of New York's policy of dismissing women teachers who married formed a group called the Feminist Alliance and demanded "the removal of all social, political, economic and other discriminations which are based upon sex, and the award of all rights and duties in all fields on the basis of individual capacity alone."

TRANSATLANTIC INFLUENCES

A major source of America's progressive impulse lay outside its borders. European nations were grappling with many of the same problems that stemmed from industrialization and urbanization, and they provided guidance and possible solutions. As one American observer said in 1915. What "the men and women who call themselves progressive . . . propose to do is to bring the United States abreast of Germany and other European countries in the matter of remedial legislation." Progressive reformers soon learned that the political, economic, and social structures of America required modifying, adapting, or even abandoning these imported ideas, but their influence was obvious.

International influences were particularly strong in the Social Gospel movement, symbolized by William T. Stead, a British social evangelist, whose idea of a "Civic Church" (a partnership of churches and reformers) captured great attention in the United States.

Muckrakers not only exposed American problems but also looked for foreign solutions. *McClure's* sent Ray Stannard Baker to Europe in 1900 "to see why Germany is making such progress."

Institutional connections also linked progressives with European reformers. By 1912, American consumer activists, trade unionists, factory inspectors, and feminists participated in international conferences on labor legislation, child welfare, social insurance, and housing reform and returned home with new ideas and strategies. State governments organized commissions to analyze European policies and agencies for lessons that might be applicable in the United States.

WHAT ROLE did immigrants and women play in Progressive-Era movements?

SOCIALISM

The growing influence of socialist ideas also promoted the spirit of progressivism. Socialists never attracted a large following, even among workers, but their criticism of the industrial economy gained increasing attention in the early twentieth century. American socialists condemned social and economic inequities, criticized limited government, and demanded public ownership of railroads, utilities, and communications. They also campaigned for tax reforms, better housing, factory inspections, and recreational facilities for all. Muckrakers like Lincoln Steffens and Upton Sinclair were committed socialists, as were some Social Gospel ministers and labor leaders, but the most prominent socialist was Eugene Debs. In 1901, Debs helped organize the Socialist Party of America. In the next decade, the party won many local elections, especially in Wisconsin and New York, where it drew support from German and Russian immigrants, and in Oklahoma, among poor tenant farmers. Socialism was also promoted by newspapers and magazines, including the *Appeal to Reason* in Girard, Kansas, which had a circulation of 500,000 by 1906.

Striking garment workers and their supporters in the 1909 "Uprising" in New York City. Working women and their allies contributed to the growing pressure for improved working conditions.

Cornell University School of Industrial and Labor Relations.

21–3
Eugene V. Debs, "The Outlook for Socialism in the United States" (1900)

Most progressives considered socialist ideas too drastic. Nevertheless, socialists contributed to the reform ferment, by providing support for reform initiatives and by prompting progressives to push for changes to undercut increasingly attractive radical alternatives.

OPPONENTS OF REFORM

Not all Americans supported progressive reforms, and many people regarded as progressives on some issues opposed change in other areas. Social Gospeler Rauschenbusch, for instance, opposed expanding women's rights. More typically, opponents of reform held consistently traditional attitudes.

Social Gospelers themselves faced opposition. Particularly strong among evangelical denominations with rural roots, **Protestant fundamentalists** stressed personal salvation rather than social reform. "To attempt reform in the black depths of the great city," said one, "would be as useless as trying to purify the ocean by pouring into it a few gallons of spring water." The most famous evangelist was Billy Sunday, who scorned all reforms but prohibition and denounced labor unions, women's rights, and business regulation as interfering with traditional values. Declaring that the Christian mission was solely to save individual souls, he condemned the Social Gospel as "godless social service nonsense" and attacked its advocates as "infidels and atheists."

Business interests angered by exposés of corporate abuse and corruption attacked muckrakers. Major corporations like Standard Oil created public relations bureaus to improve their image and to identify business, not its critics, with the public interest. Advertising boycotts discouraged magazines from running critical stories, and credit restrictions forced some muckraking journals to suspend publication. By 1910, the heyday of muckraking was over.

Labor unions likewise encountered resistance. Led by the National Association of Manufacturers, business groups denounced unions as corrupt and radical, hired thugs to disrupt them, organized strikebreaking agencies, and used blacklists to eliminate union activists. The antiunion campaign peaked in Ludlow, Colorado, in 1914. John D. Rockefeller's Colorado Fuel and Iron Company used the state militia to shoot striking workers and their families. The courts aided employers by issuing injunctions against strikes and prohibited unions from using boycotts, one of their most effective weapons.

Progressives campaigning for government intervention and regulation also met stiff resistance. Many Americans objected to what they considered unwarranted interference in private economic matters. Their political representatives were called the "Old Guard," implying their opposition to political and economic change. The courts often supported these attitudes. In *Lochner v. New York* (1905), the Supreme Court overturned a maximum-hours law on the grounds that it deprived employers and employees of their "freedom of contract." Progressives constantly had to struggle with such opponents, and progressive achievements were limited by the persistence and influence of their adversaries.

QUICK REVIEW

Opponents of Reform
◆ Protestant fundamentalists.
◆ Business interests.
◆ Anti-union forces.

Protestant Fundamentalists
Religious conservatives who believe in the literal accuracy and divine inspiration of the Bible.

HOW DID the Progressives reform Society?

REFORMING SOCIETY

With their varied motives and objectives, progressives worked to transform society by improving living conditions, educational opportunities, family life, and social and industrial relations. They sought what they called "social justice," but their plans for social reform sometimes also smacked of social control—coercive efforts to impose uniform standards on a diverse population.

SETTLEMENT HOUSES AND URBAN REFORM

The spearheads for social reform were settlement houses, community centers in urban immigrant neighborhoods. Reformers created four hundred settlement houses, largely modeled after Hull House in Chicago, founded in 1889 by Jane Addams.

Most settlements were led and staffed primarily by middle-class young women. Settlement work did not immediately violate prescribed gender roles because it initially focused on the "woman's sphere": family, education, domestic skills, and cultural "uplift." Thus settlement workers organized kindergartens and nurseries; taught classes in English, cooking, and personal hygiene; held musical performances and poetry readings; and sponsored recreation.

However, settlement workers soon saw that the root problem for immigrants was widespread poverty that required more than changes in individual behavior. Unlike earlier reformers, they regarded many of the evils of poverty as products of the social environment rather than of moral weakness. Slum dwellers, Addams sadly noted, suffered from "poisonous sewage, contaminated water, infant mortality, adulterated food, smoke-laden air, juvenile crime, and unwholesome crowding." Thus settlement workers campaigned for stricter building codes to improve slums, better urban sanitation systems to enhance public health, public parks to revive the urban environment, and laws to protect women and children.

Lawrence Veiller played the leading role in the crusade for housing reform. His work at the University Settlement in New York City convinced him that "the improvement of the homes of the people was the starting point for everything." Veiller relied on settlement workers to help investigate housing conditions, prepare public exhibits depicting rampant disease in congested slums, and agitate for improvements. Based on their findings, Veiller drafted a new housing code limiting the size of tenements and requiring toilet facilities, ventilation, and fire protection. In 1901, the New York Tenement House Law became a model for other cities. To promote uniform building codes throughout the nation, the tireless Veiller founded the National Housing Association in 1910.

PROTECTIVE LEGISLATION FOR WOMEN AND CHILDREN

Settlement workers eventually concluded that only government power could achieve social justice and demanded that state and federal governments protect the weak and disadvantaged. As Veiller insisted, it was "unquestionably the duty of the state" to enforce justice in the face of "greed on the part of those who desire to secure for themselves an undue profit."

The maiming and killing of children in industrial accidents made it "inevitable," Addams said, "that efforts to secure a child labor law should be our first venture into the field of state legislation." The National Child Labor Committee, organized in 1904, led the campaign. Reformers met stiff resistance from manufacturers who used child labor, conservatives who opposed government action as an intrusion into family life, and some poor parents who needed their children's income. Child labor reformers documented the problem with extensive investigations and also benefited from the public outrage stirred by socialist John Spargo's muckraking book *The Bitter Cry of the Children* (1906). By 1914, every state but one had a minimum working age law. Effective regulation, however, required national action, for many state laws were weak or poorly enforced. (See American Views, Mother Jones and the Meaning of Child Labor in America.)

Social reformers also lobbied for laws regulating the wages, hours, and working conditions of women and succeeded in having states from New York to Oregon pass maximum-hours legislation. After the Supreme Court upheld such laws in *Muller*

21–6
Jane Addams, Twenty Years at Hull House (1910)

WHERE TO LEARN MORE

Hull House, Chicago, Illinois
**www.uic.edu/jaaddams/hull/
hull_house.html**

WHERE TO LEARN MORE

Lower East Side Tenement
Museum, New York City, New York
www.tenement.org/

OVERVIEW

MAJOR LAWS AND CONSTITUTIONAL AMENDMENTS OF THE PROGRESSIVE ERA

Legislation	Effect
New York Tenement House Law (1901)	Established a model housing code for safety and sanitation
Newlands Act (1902)	Provided for federal irrigation projects
Hepburn Act (1906)	Strengthened authority of the Interstate Commerce Commission
Pure Food and Drug Act (1906)	Regulated the production and sale of food and drug products
Meat Inspection Act (1906)	Authorized federal inspection of meat products
Sixteenth Amendment (1913)	Authorized a federal income tax
Seventeenth Amendment (1913)	Mandated the direct popular election of senators
Underwood-Simmons Tariff Act (1913)	Lowered tariff rates and levied the first regular federal income tax
Federal Reserve Act (1913)	Established the Federal Reserve System to supervise banking and provide a national currency
Federal Trade Commission Act (1914)	Established the FTC to oversee business activities
Harrison Act (1914)	Regulated the distribution and use of narcotics
Smith-Lever Act (1914)	Institutionalized the county agent system
Keating-Owen Act (1916)	Indirectly prohibited child labor
Eighteenth Amendment (1919)	Instituted prohibition
Nineteenth Amendment (1920)	Established woman suffrage

v. *Oregon* (1908), thirty-nine states enacted new or stronger laws on women's maximum hours between 1909 and 1917. Fewer states established minimum wages for women.

Protective legislation for women posed a troubling issue for reformers. In California, for example, middle-class clubwomen favored protective legislation on grounds of women's presumed weakness. More radical progressives, as in the socialist-led Women's Trade Union League of Los Angeles, supported legislation to help secure economic independence and equality in the labor market for women, increase the economic strength of the working class, and serve as a precedent for laws improving conditions for all workers.

Progressive Era lawmakers limited protective legislation to measures reflecting the belief that women needed paternalist protection, even by excluding them from certain occupations. Laws establishing a minimum wage for women, moreover, usually set a wage level below what state commissions reported as subsistence rates. Protective legislation thus assured women not economic independence but continued dependence on husbands or fathers.

Social justice reformers forged the beginnings of the welfare state, as many states began in 1910 to provide "mothers' pensions" to indigent widows with dependent children. Twenty-one states, led by Wisconsin in 1911, enacted workers' compensation programs.

Compared to social insurance programs in Western Europe, however, these were feeble responses to the social consequences of industrialization. Proposals for health insurance and old-age pension programs went nowhere. Business groups and other conservative interests curbed the movement toward state responsibility for social welfare.

RESHAPING PUBLIC EDUCATION

Concerns about child labor overlapped with increasing attention to public schools. In 1900, for example, women's clubs in North Carolina launched a program to improve school buildings, increase teachers' salaries, and broaden the curriculum. Claiming efficiency and expertise, school administrators also pushed for changes, both to upgrade their own profession and to expand their public influence. And some intellectuals predicted that schools themselves could promote social progress and reform. Philosopher John Dewey sketched his plans for such progressive education in *The School and Society* (1899).

Between 1880 and 1920, compulsory school attendance laws, kindergartens, age-graded elementary schools, professional training for teachers, vocational education, parent-teacher associations, and school nurses became standard elements in American education. School reformers believed in both the educational soundness of these measures and their importance for countering slum environments. As Jacob Riis contended, the kindergartner would "rediscover . . . the natural feelings that the tenement had smothered."

Public education in the South lagged behind the North. After 1900, per capita expenditures for education doubled, school terms were extended, and high schools spread across the region. But the South frittered away its limited resources on a segregated educational system that shortchanged both races. South Carolina spent twelve times as much per white pupil as per black pupil. Booker T. Washington complained in 1906 that the educational reforms meant "almost nothing so far as the Negro schools are concerned." As a Northern critic observed, "To devise a school system which shall save the whites and not the blacks is a task of such delicacy that a few surviving reactionaries are willing to let both perish together."

CHALLENGING GENDER RESTRICTIONS

Most progressives held fairly conservative, moralistic views about sexuality and gender roles. Margaret Sanger, however, radically challenged conventional ideas of the social role of women. A public health nurse and an IWW organizer, she soon made the struggle for reproductive rights her personal crusade. Sanger saw in New York's immigrant neighborhoods the plight of poor women worn out from repeated pregnancies or injured or dead from self-induced knitting-needle abortions. Despite federal and state laws against contraceptives, Sanger began promoting birth control as a way to avert such tragedies. In 1914, Sanger published a magazine, *Woman Rebel*, in which she argued that "a woman's body belongs to herself alone. It does not belong to the United States of America or any other government on the face of the earth." Prohibiting contraceptives meant "enforced motherhood," Sanger declared. "Women cannot be on an equal footing with men until they have full and complete control over their reproductive function."

> ### QUICK REVIEW
>
> **Public Education**
> - Concern about child labor overlapped with attention to public education.
> - Widespread reforms carried out between 1880 and 1920.
> - Public education in the South lagged behind the North.

Women and girls in an Alabama canning factory, 1911. On the right end is Marie Colbeck, 8 years old, who shucked 6 or 7 pots of oysters a day for about 30 or 35 cents at the Alabama Canning Factory. At the left is Johnnie Schraker, 8 years old, who earned 45 cents a day after shucking oysters for 3 years.

Courtesy National Archives, photo no. 102-LH-1986

· AMERICAN VIEWS ·

MOTHER JONES AND THE MEANING OF CHILD LABOR IN AMERICA

orn in Ireland in 1830, the legendary Mother Jones (Mary Harris Jones) became one of America's greatest social activists, protesting social and industrial conditions from the 1870s through the 1920s. Here she recounts an effort to end child labor, one of the most persistent progressive goals. Using the techniques of exposure and publicity characteristic of the period and employing patriotic symbols and references, Jones raised troubling questions about the concepts of social and economic opportunity that many Americans associated with national development and identity.

HOW DID Mother Jones direct public attention to child labor? How did she invoke the treasured American concept of opportunity to gain support for her goal? What did she argue was the relationship between child labor and the privileged status of other Americans? How successful was her crusade against child labor?

In the spring of 1903 I went to Kensington, Pennsylvania, where 75,000 textile workers were on strike. Of this number at least 10,000 were little children.

The workers were striking for more pay and shorter hours. Every day little children came into Union Headquarters, some with their hands off, some with the thumb missing, some with their fingers off at the knuckle. They were stooped little things, round shouldered and skinny. Many of them were not over ten years of age. . . .

We assembled a number of boys and girls one morning in Independence Park and from there we arranged to parade with banners to the court house where we would hold a meeting.

A great crowd gathered in the public square in front of the city hall. I put the little boys with their fingers off and hands crushed and maimed on a platform. I held up their mutilated hands and showed them to the crowd and made the statement that Philadelphia's mansions were built on the broken bones, the quivering hearts, and drooping heads of these children. . . .

I called upon the millionaire manufacturers to cease their moral murders, and I cried to the officials in the open windows opposite, "Some day the workers will take possession of your city hall, and when we do, no child will be sacrificed on the altar of profit."

Sanger's crusade infuriated those who regarded birth control as a threat to the family and morality. Indicted for distributing information about contraception, Sanger fled to Europe. Other women took up the cause, forming the National Birth Control League in 1915 to campaign for the repeal of laws restricting access to contraceptive information and devices.

REFORMING COUNTRY LIFE

Although most progressives focused on the city, others sought to reform rural life. They worked to improve rural health and sanitation, to replace inefficient one-room schools with modern consolidated ones under professional control, and to extend new roads and communication services into the countryside. To further these goals, President Theodore Roosevelt created the Country Life Commission in 1908.

Agricultural scientists, government officials, and many business interests also sought to promote efficient, scientific, and commercial agriculture. A key innovation was the county agent system: the U.S. Department of Agriculture and business groups placed an agent in each county to teach farmers new techniques and

The reporters quoted my statement that Philadelphia mansions were built on the broken bones and quivering hearts of children. The Philadelphia papers and the New York papers got into a squabble with each other over the question. The universities discussed it. Preachers began talking. That was what I wanted. Public attention on the subject of child labor.

The matter quieted down for a while and I concluded the people needed stirring up again. . . . I decided to go with the children to see President Roosevelt to ask him to have Congress pass a law prohibiting the exploitation of childhood. I thought that President Roosevelt might see these mill children and compare them with his own little ones who were spending the summer at the seashore at Oyster Bay. . . .

Everywhere we had meetings, showing up with living children, the horrors of child labor. . . . [In New Jersey] I called on the mayor of Princeton and asked for permission to speak opposite the campus of the University. I said I wanted to speak on higher education. The mayor gave me permission. A great crowd gathered, professors and students and the people; and I told them that the rich robbed these little children of any education of the lowest order that they might send their sons and daughters to places of higher education. . . . And I showed those professors children in our army who could scarcely read or write because they were working ten hours a day in the silk mills of Pennsylvania. . . .

[In New York] I told an immense crowd of the horrors of child labor in the mills around the anthracite region and . . . I showed them Gussie Rangnew, a little girl from whom all the childhood had gone. Her face was like an old woman's. Gussie packed stockings in a factory, eleven hours a day for a few cents a day. . . . "Fifty years ago there was a cry against slavery and men gave up their lives to stop the selling of black children on the block. Today the white child is sold for two dollars a week to the manufacturers."

. . . We marched down to Oyster Bay but the president refused to see us and he would not answer my letters. But our march had done its work. We had drawn the attention of the nation to the crime of child labor. And while the strike of the textile workers in Kensington was lost and the children driven back to work, not long afterward the Pennsylvania legislature passed a child labor law that sent thousands of children home from the mills, and kept thousands of others from entering the factory until they were fourteen years of age.

Source: The Autobiography of Mother Jones, 3rd ed. (Chicago: Kerr Publishing Company, 1977).

encourage changes in the rural social values that had spawned the Populist radicalism that most progressives decried. The Smith-Lever Act (1914) provided federal subsidies for county agents throughout the country. Its purpose, claimed Woodrow Wilson, was to produce "an efficient and contented population" in rural America.

Few farmers, however, welcomed these efforts. As one Illinois county agent said in 1915, "Farmers, as a whole, resent exceedingly those forces which are at work with missionary intent trying to uplift them." School consolidation meant the loss of community control of education; good roads would raise taxes and chiefly benefit urban business interests. Besides, most farmers believed that their problems stemmed not from rural life but from industrial society.

Even so, government agencies, agricultural colleges, and railroads and banks steadily tied farmers to urban markets. Telephones and rural free delivery of mail lessened countryside isolation but quickened the spread of city values. Improved roads and the coming of the automobile eliminated many rural villages and linked farm families directly with towns and cities. Consolidated schools wiped out the social center of rural neighborhoods and carried children out of their communities, many never to return.

SOCIAL CONTROL AND MORAL CRUSADES

The tendency toward social control evident in the movements to pass protective legislation and transform country life also marked other less attractive progressive efforts. These efforts, moreover, often meshed with the restrictive attitudes that conservative Americans held about race, religion, immigration, and morality. The result was widespread attempts to restrict certain groups and control behavior.

Many Americans wanted to limit immigration for racist reasons. Nativist agitation in California prompted the federal government to restrict Japanese immigration in 1907. Californians, including local progressives, also hoped to curtail the migration of Mexicans. A Stanford University researcher condemned Mexicans as an "undesirable class" compared to "the more progressive races."

Nationally, public debate focused on restricting the flow of new immigrants from southern and eastern Europe. Many backed their prejudice with a distorted interpretation of Darwinism, labeling the Slavic and Mediterranean peoples "inferior races." As early as 1894, nativists had organized the Immigration Restriction League, which favored a literacy test for admission, sure that it would "bear most heavily upon the Italians, Russians, Poles, Hungarians, Greeks, and Asiatics, and very lightly or not at all upon English-speaking immigrants or Germans, Scandinavians, and French." Congress enacted a literacy law in 1917.

Other nativists demanded the "Americanization" of immigrants already in the country. The Daughters of the American Revolution sought to inculcate loyalty, patriotism, and conservative values. Settlement workers and Social Gospelers also attempted to transfer their own values to the newcomers. The most prominent advocate of Americanization was a stereotypical progressive, Frances Kellor. She studied social work at the University of Chicago, worked in New York settlement houses, wrote a muckraking exposé of employment agencies that exploited women, and became director of the New York Bureau of Immigration. In 1915, she helped organize the National Americanization Committee and increasingly emphasized destroying immigrants' old-country ties and imposing an American culture.

Closely linked to progressives' worries about immigrants was their campaign for **prohibition**. Social workers saw liquor as a cause of crime, poverty, and family violence; employers blamed it for causing industrial accidents and inefficiency; Social Gospel ministers condemned the "spirit born of hell" because it impaired moral judgment and behavior. But also important was native-born Americans' fear of new immigrants. Many immigrants, in fact, viewed liquor and the neighborhood saloon as vital parts of daily life, and so prohibition became a focus of nativist hostilities, cultural conflict, and Americanization pressures.

Protestant fundamentalists also stoutly supported prohibition, working through the Anti-Saloon League, founded in 1893. Their nativism and antiurban bias surfaced in demands for prohibition to prevent the nation's cities from lapsing into "raging mania, disorder, and anarchy." With most urban Catholics and Jews opposing prohibition, the Anti-Saloon League justified imposing its reform on city populations against their will: "Our nation can only be saved by turning the pure stream of country sentiment . . . to flush out the cesspools of cities and so save civilization from pollution."

With these motivations, prohibitionists campaigned against the manufacture and sale of alcohol. Eventually, the Eighteenth Amendment made prohibition the law of the land by 1920.

Less controversial was the drive to control narcotics, then readily available, and prostitution. Fears that drug addiction was spreading, particularly among black people and immigrants, led Congress in 1914 to pass the Harrison Act, which

---

QUICK REVIEW

Opposition to Immigration

◆ Nativists in California wanted to restrict the entry of Japanese and Mexicans.

◆ The national debate focused on immigrants from southern and eastern Europe.

◆ Some nativists demanded the "Americanization" of immigrants.

Prohibition A ban on the production, sale, and consumption of liquor, achieved temporarily through state laws and the Eighteenth Amendment.

prohibited the distribution and use of narcotics except for medical purposes. The progressive attack on prostitution, which was seen as symptomatic of the exploitation and disorder that affected industrial cities, resulted in state and city attacks on "red light" districts and in the federal Mann Act of 1910, which banned the interstate transport of women "for immoral purposes."

California provided other examples of progressives' interest in social control and moral reform. The state assembly, prohibited gambling, cardplaying, and prizefighting, and Los Angeles banned premarital sex and introduced artistic censorship.

The Flanner House, a black settlement house in Indianapolis, provided the black community with many essential services, including health care. In addition to this baby clinic, pictured in 1918, it established a tuberculosis clinic at a time when the city's public hospitals refused to treat black citizens afflicted with the disease.

Indians Historical Society.

FOR WHITE PEOPLE ONLY?

Racism permeated the Progressive Era. In the South, progressivism was built on black disfranchisement and segregation. Like most white Southerners, progressives believed that racial control was necessary for social order. Governors Hoke Smith of Georgia and James Vardaman, "the White Chief," of Mississippi supported progressive reforms, but they also viciously attacked black rights. Their racist demagogy incited antiblack violence throughout the South. Antiblack race riots, like the riot produced in Atlanta by Smith's election in 1906, and lynching—defended on the floor of the U.S. Senate by a Southern progressive—were part of the system of racial control that made the era a terrible time for African Americans.

Even in the North, where relatively few black people lived, race relations deteriorated. A reporter in Pennsylvania found "this disposition to discriminate against Negroes has greatly increased within the past decade." Antiblack race riots exploded in New York in 1900 and in Springfield, Illinois—Lincoln's hometown—in 1908.

But African Americans also pursued progressive reforms. Even in the South, some black activists struggled to improve conditions. In Atlanta, for example, black women created progressive organizations and established settlement houses, kindergartens, and day-care centers. The women of the Neighborhood Union, organized in 1908, even challenged the discriminatory policies of Atlanta's board of education, demanding equal facilities and appropriations for the city's black schools. They had only limited success, but their efforts demonstrated a persisting commitment to reforming society.

In the North, African Americans more openly criticized discrimination. Ida Wells-Barnett, the crusading journalist who had fled the South for Chicago, became nationally prominent for her militant protests. She fought fiercely against racial injustices, especially school segregation, agitated for woman suffrage, and organized kindergartens and settlement houses for Chicago's black migrants.

Still more important was W.E.B. Du Bois, who campaigned tirelessly against all forms of racial discrimination. In 1905, Du Bois and other black activists met in Niagara Falls, Canada, to make plans to promote political and economic equality. In 1910, this **Niagara Movement** joined with a small group of white reformers, including Jane Addams, to organize the National Association for the Advancement of Colored People. The NAACP sought to overthrow segregation

Niagara Movement African-American group organized in 1905 to promote racial integration, civil and political rights, and equal access to economic opportunity.

and establish equal justice and educational opportunities. As its director of publicity and research, Du Bois launched the influential magazine *The Crisis* to shape public opinion. "Agitate," he counseled, "protest, reveal the truth, and refuse to be silenced." By 1918, the NAACP had 44,000 members in 165 branches.

REFORMING POLITICS AND GOVERNMENT

HOW DID electoral and municipal reforms improve voting and government during the Progressive Era?

P rogressives of all kinds clamored for the reform of politics and government, but their political activism was motivated by different concerns, and they sometimes pursued competing objectives. Many wanted to change procedures and institutions to promote greater democracy and responsibility. Others hoped to improve the efficiency of government, to eliminate corruption, or to increase their own influence. All justified their objectives as necessary to adapt the political system to the nation's new needs.

WOMAN SUFFRAGE

The woman suffrage movement had begun in the mid-nineteenth century, but suffragists had been frustrated by the prevailing belief that women's "proper sphere" was the home and the family. Woman suffrage, particularly when championed as a step toward women's equality, seemed to challenge the natural order of society, and it generated much opposition among traditionalist-minded men and women.

In the early twentieth century, under a new generation of leaders like Carrie Chapman Catt, suffragists adopted activist tactics, including parades, mass meetings, and "suffrage tours" by automobile. They also organized by political districts and attracted workingwomen and labor unions. By 1917, the National American Woman Suffrage Association had over 2 million members.

But some suffrage leaders shifted arguments to gain more support. Rather than insisting on the "justice" of woman suffrage or emphasizing equal rights, they spoke of the special moral and maternal instincts women could bring to politics if allowed to vote. The suffrage movement now appeared less a radical, disruptive force than a vehicle for extending traditional female benevolence and service to society. The new image of the movement increased public support by appealing to conventional views of women. Noted one Nebraska undergraduate, women students no longer feared "antagonizing the men or losing invitations to parties by being suffragists."

Gradually, the suffrage movement began to prevail. In 1910, Washington became the first state to approve woman suffrage since the mid-1890s, followed by California in 1911 and Arizona, Kansas, and Oregon in 1912. Suffragists also mounted national action, such as the dramatic inaugural parade in March 1913 described at the beginning of this chapter. By 1919, thirty-nine states had established full or partial woman suffrage, and Congress finally approved an amendment. Ratified by the states in 1920, the **Nineteenth Amendment** marked a critical advance in political democracy.

ELECTORAL REFORM

Other electoral reforms changed the election process and the meaning of political participation. The so-called **Australian ballot** adopted by most states during the 1890s provided for secret voting and replaced the individual party tickets with an official ballot listing all candidates and distributed by public officials. The Australian ballot led to quiet, orderly elections. One Cincinnati editor, who recalled

---

QUICK REVIEW

Votes for Women

◆ Woman suffrage movement began in the mid-nineteenth century.

◆ Early twentieth-century leaders adopted activist tactics.

◆ Nineteenth Amendment ratified in 1920.

Nineteenth Amendment
Constitutional revision that in 1920 established women citizens' right to vote.

Australian ballot Secret voting and the use of official ballots rather than party tickets.

the "howling mobs" and chaos at the polls in previous elections, declared: "The political bummer and thug has been relegated to the background . . . while good citizenship . . . has come to the front."

Public regulation of other parts of the electoral process previously controlled by parties soon followed. Beginning with Mississippi in 1902, nearly every state provided for direct primaries to remove nominations from the boss-ridden caucus and convention system. Many states also reformed campaign practices.

The decreasing ability of parties to mobilize voters was reflected in a steady decline in voter participation, from 79 percent in 1896 to 49 percent in 1920. As parties contracted, the influence of nonpartisan organizations and pressure groups grew, promoting narrower objectives. Thus the National Association of Manufacturers (1895) and the United States Chamber of Commerce (1912) lobbied for business interests; the National Farmers Union (1902), for commercial agriculture; the American Federation of Teachers (1916), for professional educators. The organized lobbying of special-interest groups would give them greater influence over government in the future and contribute to the declining popular belief in the value of voting or participation in politics.

Disfranchisement more obviously undermined American democracy. In the South, Democrats—progressive and conservative alike—eliminated not only black voters but also many poor white voters from the electorate through poll taxes, literacy tests, and other restrictions. Republicans in the North adopted educational or literacy tests in ten states, enacted strict registration laws, and gradually abolished the right of aliens to vote. These restrictions reflected both the progressives' anti-immigrant prejudices and their obsessions with social control and with purifying politics and "improving" the electorate. Such electoral reforms reduced the political power of ethnic and working-class Americans, often stripping them of their political rights and means of influence.

MUNICIPAL REFORM

Muckrakers had exposed crooked alliances between city bosses and business leaders that resulted in wasteful or inadequate municipal services. In some cities, urban reformers attempted to break these alliances and improve conditions for those suffering most from municipal misrule. For example, in Toledo, Ohio, Samuel "Golden Rule" Jones won enough working-class votes to be elected mayor four times despite the hostility of both major parties. Serving from 1897 to 1904, Jones opened public playgrounds and kindergartens, established the eight-hour day for city workers, and improved public services. Influenced by the Social Gospel, he also provided free lodging for the homeless and gave his own salary to the poor. Other reforming mayors also fought municipal corruption, limited the political influence of corporations, and championed public ownership of utilities.

More elitist progressives attempted to change the structure of urban government. Middle-class reformers worked to replace ward elections with citywide elections which required greater resources and therefore helped swell middle-class influence at the expense of working-class wards. So did nonpartisan elections, which reformers introduced to weaken party loyalties.

Urban reformers developed two other structural innovations: the city commission and the city manager. Both attempted to institutionalize efficient, businesslike government staffed by professional administrators. By 1920, hundreds of cities had adopted one of the new plans.

Business groups often promoted these reforms. In Des Moines, for example, the president of the Commercial Club declared that "the professional politician must be ousted and in his place capable businessmen chosen to conduct the

QUICK REVIEW

Municipal Reform
- Urban reformers sought to break alliances between city bosses and business leaders.
- Urban reformers developed the concept of the city commission and the city manager.
- Business groups often promoted these reforms.

affairs of the city." Again, then, reform in municipal government often shifted political power from ethnic and working-class voters, represented however imperfectly by partisan elections, to smaller groups with greater resources.

PROGRESSIVE STATE GOVERNMENT

Progressives also reshaped state government. Some tried to democratize the legislative process, regarding the legislature—the most important branch of state government in the nineteenth century—as ineffective and even corrupt, dominated by party bosses and corporate influences. The Missouri legislature reportedly "enacted such laws as the corporations paid for, and such others as were necessary to fool the people." Populists had first raised such charges in the 1890s and proposed novel solutions adopted by many states in the early twentieth century. The **initiative** enabled reformers themselves to propose legislation directly to the electorate, bypassing an unresponsive legislature; the **referendum** permitted voters to approve or reject legislative measures.

Other reforms also expanded the popular role in state government. The **Seventeenth Amendment**, ratified in 1913, provided for the election of U.S. senators directly by popular vote instead of by state legislatures. Beginning with Oregon in 1908, ten states adopted the **recall**, enabling voters to remove unsatisfactory public officials from office.

As state legislatures and party machines were curbed, dynamic governors like Robert La Follette pushed progressive programs into law. Elected in 1900, "Fighting Bob" La Follette turned Wisconsin into "the laboratory of democracy." "His words bite like coals of fire," wrote one observer. "He never wearies and he will not allow his audience to weary." Overcoming fierce opposition from "stalwart" Republicans, La Follette established direct primaries, railroad regulation, the first state income tax, workers' compensation, and other important measures before being elected to the U.S. Senate in 1906.

La Follette also stressed efficiency and expertise. The Legislative Reference Bureau that he created was staffed by university professors to advise on public policy. He used regulatory commissions to oversee railroads, banks, and other interests. Most states followed suit, and expert commissions became an important feature of state government, gradually gaining authority at the expense of local officials.

"Experts" were presumed to be disinterested and therefore committed to the general welfare. In practice, however, regulators were subject to pressures from competing interest groups, and some commissions became captives of the very industries they were supposed to control. This irony was matched by the contradiction between the expansion of democracy through the initiative and referendum and the increasing reliance on nonelected professional experts to set and implement public policy.

THEODORE ROOSEVELT AND THE PROGRESSIVE PRESIDENCY

When a crazed anarchist assassinated William McKinley in 1901, Theodore Roosevelt entered the White House, and the progressive movement gained its most prominent leader. The son of a wealthy New York family, Roosevelt had been a New York legislator, U.S. civil service commissioner, and assistant secretary of the navy. After his exploits in the Spanish-American War, he was elected governor of New York in 1898 and vice president in 1900. His public life was matched by an active private life in which he both

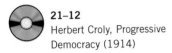

21-12
Herbert Croly, Progressive Democracy (1914)

Initiative Procedure by which citizens can introduce a subject for legislation, usually through a petition signed by a specific number of voters.

Referendum Submission of a law, proposed or already in effect, to a direct popular vote for approval or rejection.

Seventeenth Amendment Constitutional change that in 1913 established the direct popular election of U.S. senators.

Recall The process of removing an official from office by popular vote, usually after using petitions to call for such a vote.

HOW WAS the executive branch strengthened under Roosevelt?

wrote works of history and obsessively pursued what he called the "strenuous life": boxing, wrestling, hunting, rowing, even ranching and chasing rustlers in Dakota Territory. His own son observed that Roosevelt "always wanted to be the bride at every wedding and the corpse at every funeral."

Mark Twain fretted that "Mr. Roosevelt is the Tom Sawyer of the political world of the twentieth century; always showing off; always hunting for a chance to show off; in his frenzied imagination the Great Republic is a vast Barnum circus with him for a clown and the whole world for audience." But Roosevelt's flamboyance and ambitions made him the most popular politician of the time and enabled him to dramatize the issues of progressivism and to become the first modern president.

WHERE TO LEARN MORE

Sagamore Hill,
Oyster Bay, New York
www.nps.gov/sahi/

TR AND THE MODERN PRESIDENCY

Roosevelt believed that the president could do anything to meet national needs that the Constitution did not specifically prohibit. "Under this interpretation of executive power," he later recalled, "I did and caused to be done many things not previously done. . . . I did not usurp power, but I did greatly broaden the use of executive power." Indeed, the expansion of government power and its consolidation in the executive branch were among his most significant accomplishments.

Roosevelt spelled out his policy goals in more than four hundred messages to Congress, sent drafts of bills to Capitol Hill, and intervened to win passage of "his" measures. Some members of Congress resented such "executive arrogance" and "dictatorship." Roosevelt generally avoided direct challenges to the conservative Old Guard Republicans who controlled Congress, but his activities helped shift the balance of power within the national government.

Roosevelt also reorganized the executive branch. He believed in efficiency and expertise. To promote rational policymaking and public management, he staffed the expanding federal bureaucracy with able professionals. The president, complained one Republican, was "trying to concentrate all power in Washington . . . and to govern the people by commissions and bureaus."

Finally, Roosevelt exploited and skillfully handled the mass media, which made him a celebrity, "TR" or "Teddy." The publicity kept TR in the spotlight and enabled him to mold public opinion.

ROOSEVELT AND LABOR

One sign of TR's vigorous new approach to the presidency was his handling of a coal strike in 1902. Members of the United Mine Workers Union walked off their jobs, demanding higher wages, an eight-hour day, and recognition of their union. The mine owners closed the mines and waited for the union to collapse. But led by John Mitchell, the strikers held their ranks. Management's stubborn arrogance contrasted with the workers' orderly conduct and willingness to negotiate and hardened public opinion against the owners. TR's legal advisers told him that the government had no constitutional authority to intervene.

As public pressure mounted, however, Roosevelt decided to act. He invited both the owners and the union leaders to a White House conference and declared that the national interest made government action necessary. Mitchell agreed to negotiate. The owners, however, refused even to speak to the miners and demanded that Roosevelt use the army to break the union, as Cleveland had done in the Pullman strike in 1894.

Roosevelt was not a champion of labor. But furious with the owners' "arrogant stupidity" and "insulting" attitude toward the presidency, he announced that he would use the army to seize and operate the mines, not to crush the union. Questioned about the constitutionality of such an action, Roosevelt bellowed: "To hell with the Constitution when the people want coal." Reluctantly, the owners accepted the arbitration commission they had previously rejected. The commission gave the miners a 10 percent wage increase and a nine-hour day, but not union recognition, and permitted the owners to raise coal prices by 10 percent. Roosevelt described his intervention as simply giving both labor and management a "square deal." It also set important precedents for an active government role in labor disputes and a strong president acting as a steward of the public.

MANAGING NATURAL RESOURCES

Federal land policy had helped create farms and develop transportation, but it had also ceded to speculators and business interests much of the nation's forests, mineral deposits, waterpower sites, and grazing lands. A new generation believed in the **conservation** of natural resources through efficient and scientific management. Conservationists achieved early victories in the Forest Reserve Act (1891) and the Forest Management Act (1897), which authorized the federal government to withdraw timberlands from development and to regulate grazing, lumbering, and hydroelectric sites in the forests (see Map 21–1).

Roosevelt and his friend Gifford Pinchot made conservation a major focus of his presidency. Appointed in 1898 to head the new Division of Forestry (renamed the Forest Service in 1905), Pinchot brought rational management and regulation to resource development. With his advice, TR used presidential authority to triple the size of the forest reserves to 150 million acres, set aside another 80 million acres valuable for minerals and petroleum, and establish dozens of wildlife refuges. In 1908, Roosevelt held a White House conference of state and federal officials that led to the creation of the National Conservation Commission, forty-one state conservation commissions, and widespread public support for the conservation movement.

Some interests opposed conservation. Many Westerners resented having Easterners make key decisions about Western growth and saw conservation as a perpetuation of this colonial subservience. Many ranchers refused to pay federal grazing fees. Colorado arsonists set forest fires to protest the creation of forest reserves.

But Westerners were happy to take federal money for expensive irrigation projects that private capital would not undertake. They favored the 1902 National Reclamation Act, which established the **Bureau of Reclamation**. Its engineers were to construct dams, reservoirs, and irrigation canals, and the government was to sell the irrigated lands in tracts no larger than 160 acres. With massive dams and networks of irrigation canals, it reclaimed fertile valleys from the desert. Unfortunately, the bureau did not enforce the 160-acre limitation and thus helped create powerful corporate farms in the West.

CORPORATE REGULATION

Nothing symbolized Roosevelt's active presidency better than his popular reputation as a "trust buster." TR regarded the formation of large business combinations favorably, but he knew he could not ignore the public anxiety about corporate power. Business leaders and Old Guard conservatives opposed any government intervention in the large trusts, but Roosevelt knew better. "You have no conception of the revolt that would be caused if I did nothing," he said privately. TR proposed to "develop an orderly system, and such a system can only come through the gradually exercised right of efficient government control." Rather than invoking "the foolish antitrust law," he favored government regulation to prevent corporate abuses and defend the public interest. But he did sue some "bad trusts."

WHERE TO LEARN MORE

John Muir National Historic Site, Martinez, California
www.nps.gov/jomu/

Conservation The efficient management and use of natural resources, such as forests, grasslands, and rivers, as opposed to preservation or controlled exploitation.

Bureau of Reclamation Federal agency established in 1902 providing public funds for irrigation projects in arid regions.

MAP EXPLORATION

To explore an interactive version of this map, go to **http://www.prenhall.com/goldfield2/map21.1**

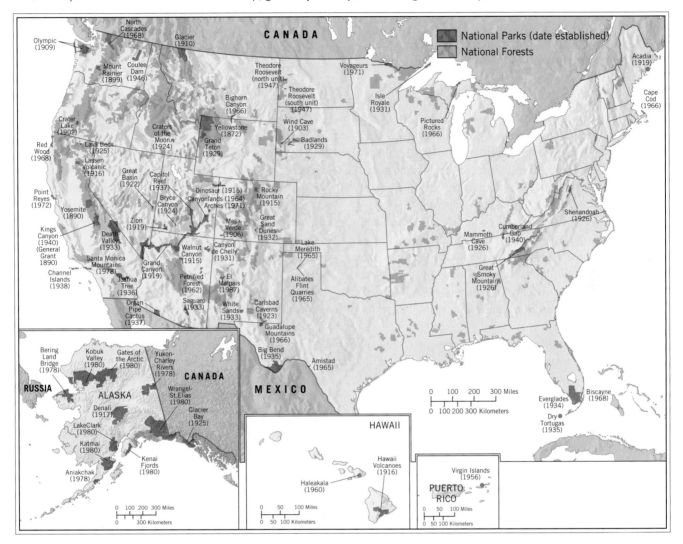

MAP 21–1

The Growth of National Forests and National Parks   Rapid exploitation of the West prompted demands to preserve its spectacular scenery and protect its remaining forests. In 1872 Yellowstone became the first National Park, and the National Forest system began in the 1890s. Conservation became increasingly important during the Progressive Era but often provoked Western hostility.

WHICH STATES have the most national forests and national parks?

In 1902, the Roosevelt administration filed its most famous antitrust suit, against the Northern Securities Company, a holding company organized by J.P. Morgan to control the railroad network of the Northwest. For TR, this suit was an assertion of government power that reassured a worried public and made corporate responsibility more likely. In 1904, the Supreme Court ordered the dissolution of the Northern Securities Company.

Elected president in his own right in 1904 over the colorless and conservative Democratic candidate Judge Alton B. Parker, Roosevelt responded to the growing popular demand for reform by pushing further toward a regulatory government.

CHAPTER 21

FROM THEN TO NOW
The Environmental Movement

Many of the issues that concern environmentalists today were first raised by the conservationists and preservationists of the Progressive Era. Conservationists favored the planned and regulated management of America's natural resources for the public benefit. Led by Theodore Roosevelt, they dominated the new agencies like the Forest Service that were responsible for federal lands. In contrast, preservationists—like John Muir, who founded the Sierra Club in 1892—sought to protect wilderness from any development whatsoever. Opposing both were those who championed the uncontrolled development of public lands.

Preservationists' reasons for protecting wilderness were primarily aesthetic—to preserve natural splendors intact for future generations. By the second half of the twentieth century, however, the disturbing consequences of technological change, rapid economic development, and spiraling population growth began to raise the stakes. Air pollution from smokestack industries and automobile exhaust damaged natural vegetation and caused respiratory diseases; water pollution from sewage and chemical waste spread disease; and oil spills fouled beaches and devastated marine habitats.

Public concern over these problems gave birth to the environmental movement, which drew on the legacy of both the conservation and preservation movements but had wider interests and broader support than either. Responding to the environmental movement's quickly growing strength, Congress in the 1970s passed laws to protect endangered species, reduce pollution, limit the use of pesticides, and control hazardous waste. The Environmental Protection Agency, created in 1970, subsequently became the largest federal regulatory agency.

Again, however, as during the Progressive Era, efforts to protect the environment encountered opposition from proponents of unrestricted development, especially in the West.

In the Sagebrush Rebellion in the late 1970s and 1980s, some Westerners condemned "outside" federal regulation and tried to seize control of public lands for private exploitation. One oil company dismissed catastrophic oil spills as merely "Mother Earth letting some oil come out."

Three Republican presidents from the West—Californians Richard Nixon and Ronald Reagan and Texan George H. W. Bush, all closely tied to oil and real estate interests—sought in varying degrees to curtail environmental policies, agencies, and budgets and to promote development. This repudiation of Theodore Roosevelt's conservationism reflected the shift of the party's base to the sunbelt. As one Nixon adviser said, when a pipeline across the Alaskan wilderness was approved, "Conservation is not in the Republican ethic."

Ronald Reagan in particular was convinced that environmental protection fundamentally conflicted with economic growth. The business executives and corporate lawyers he appointed to key federal positions rescinded or weakened environmental regulations.

Congress, the courts, and the public, however, resisted efforts to weaken environmental policy. "Green" groups proliferated, demanding greater attention to environmental issues; some, like Greenpeace, undertook direct action to protect the environment, and even Western communities organized to oppose strip-mining, nuclear power plants, and toxic waste dumping.

Despite fluctuations, public opinion and mainstream politics now appear to favor greater environmental protection. Debate is sure to continue over the cost and effectiveness of specific policies. But as ever more challenging ecological problems arise—like ozone depletion and global warming—Americans are increasingly inclined to stand with Theodore Roosevelt and John Muir in looking to the federal government for effective action to meet them.

He proposed legislation "to work out methods of controlling the big corporations without paralyzing the energies of the business community."

The Hepburn Act, passed in 1906, authorized the Interstate Commerce Commission to set maximum railroad rates and extended its jurisdiction. It was a weaker law than many progressives had wanted, but it marked the first time the federal government gained the power to set rules in a private enterprise.

In the same year, Congress passed the Pure Food and Drug Act and the Meat Inspection Act. In part, this legislation reflected public demand, but many business leaders also supported government regulation of food and drugs, convinced that it would expand their markets by certifying the quality of their products and drive their smaller competitors out of business. The meat and food and drug acts did thus extend government regulation over business to protect the public health and safety, but they also served some corporate purposes.

Despite the compromises and weaknesses in the three laws, TR contended that they marked "a noteworthy advance in the policy of securing federal supervision and control over corporations." In 1907 and 1908, he pushed for an eight-hour workday, stock market regulation, and inheritance and income taxes. Republican conservatives in Congress blocked such reforms. Old Guard Republicans thought Roosevelt had extended government powers dangerously, but in fact his accomplishments had been relatively modest. As La Follette noted, Roosevelt's "cannonading filled the air with noise and smoke, which confused and obscured the line of action, but, when the battle cloud drifted by and the quiet was restored, it was always a matter of surprise that so little had really been accomplished."

TAFT AND THE INSURGENTS

TR handpicked his successor as president: a loyal lieutenant, William Howard Taft. Member of a prominent Ohio political family, Taft had been a federal judge, governor-general of the Philippines, and TR's secretary of war. Later he would serve as chief justice of the United States. But Taft's election as president in 1908, over Democrat William Jennings Bryan in his third presidential campaign, led to a Republican political disaster.

Taft did preside over a more active and successful antitrust program than Roosevelt's. He supported the Mann-Elkins Act (1910), which extended the ICC's jurisdiction to telephone and telegraph companies. Taft set aside more public forest lands and oil reserves than Roosevelt had. He also supported a constitutional amendment authorizing an income tax, which went into effect in 1913 under the **Sixteenth Amendment**. One of the most important accomplishments of the Progressive Era, the income tax would provide the means for the government to expand its activities and responsibilities.

Nevertheless, Taft soon alienated progressives and floundered into a political morass. His problems were twofold. First, Midwestern reform Republicans, led by La Follette, clashed with more conservative Republicans led by Senator Nelson Aldrich of Rhode Island. Second, Taft was politically inept. He was unable to mediate between these two groups, and the party split apart.

Reformers wanted to restrict the power of the speaker of the House, "Uncle Joe" Cannon, a reactionary who blocked reform. After seeming to promise support,

Roosevelt enjoyed this cartoon illustrating his distinction between good trusts, retrained by government regulations for public welfare, and bad trusts. On those he put his foot down.

The Granger Collection, New York

WHERE TO LEARN MORE

William Howard Taft National Historic Site, Cincinnati, Ohio

Sixteenth Amendment
Constitutional revision that in 1913 authorized a federal income tax.

Taft backed down when conservatives threatened to defeat important legislation. The insurgents in Congress never forgave what they saw as Taft's betrayal. The tariff also alienated progressives from Taft. He had campaigned in 1908 for a lower tariff to curb inflation, and Midwestern Republicans favored tariff reduction to trim the power of big business. But when they introduced tariff reform legislation, the president failed to support them. Aldrich's Senate committee added 847 amendments, many of which raised tariff rates. Taft justified his inaction as avoiding presidential interference with congressional business, but progressives concluded that Taft had sided with the Old Guard.

That perception solidified when Taft stumbled into a controversy over conservation. When Pinchot challenged secretary of the interior Richard Ballinger's role in a questionable sale of public coal lands in Alaska to a J. P. Morgan syndicate, Taft upheld Ballinger and fired Pinchot. Progressives concluded that Taft had repudiated Roosevelt's conservation policies.

In 1911, reformers formed the National Progressive League to champion La Follette for the Republican nomination in 1912. They appealed to TR for support, but Roosevelt's own position was closer to Taft's than to what he called "the La Follette type of fool radicalism." But condemning Taft as "disloyal to our past friendship . . . [and] to every canon of ordinary decency," TR began to campaign for the Republican nomination himself. In thirteen state primaries, TR won 278 delegates to only 46 for Taft. But most states did not then have primaries; that allowed Taft to dominate the Republican convention and win renomination. Roosevelt's forces formed a third party—the Progressive party—and nominated the former president. The Republican split almost guaranteed victory for the Democratic nominee, Woodrow Wilson.

WOODROW WILSON AND PROGRESSIVE REFORM

Elected president in 1912 and 1916, Woodrow Wilson mediated among differing progressive views to achieve a strong reform program, enlarge the power of the executive branch, and make the White House the center of national politics.

HOW DID Woodrow Wilson bring progressivism to its climax?

THE ELECTION OF 1912

In Congress, Southern Democrats more consistently supported reform measures than Republicans did, and Democratic leader William Jennings Bryan surpassed Roosevelt as a persistent advocate of significant political and economic reform. As the Democrats pushed progressive remedies and the Republicans quarreled during Taft's administration, Democrats achieved major victories in the state and congressional elections of 1910. To improve the party's chances in 1912, Bryan announced he would step aside. The Democratic spotlight shifted to the governor of New Jersey, Woodrow Wilson.

Born in Virginia as the son and grandson of Presbyterian ministers, Wilson combined public eloquence with a cold personality; he balanced a self-righteousness that led to stubborn inflexibility with an intense ambition that permitted the most expedient compromises. Wilson first entered public life as a conservative. In 1910, while he was president of Princeton University, New Jersey's Democratic bosses selected him for governor to head off the progressives. But once in office, Wilson championed popular reforms and immediately began to campaign as a progressive for the party's 1912 presidential nomination.

Wilson's progressivism differed from that of Roosevelt. TR emphasized a strong government that would promote economic and social order. He defended big business as inevitable and healthy provided that government control ensured that it would benefit the entire nation. Roosevelt called this program the **New Nationalism**, reflecting his belief in a powerful state and a national interest. He also supported demands for social welfare, including workers' compensation and the abolition of child labor.

Wilson was horrified by Roosevelt's vision. His **New Freedom** program rejected what he called TR's "regulated monopoly." Wilson wanted "regulated competition," with the government's role limited to breaking up monopolies through antitrust action and preventing artificial barriers like tariffs from blocking free enterprise. Wilson opposed social welfare legislation as "paternalistic."

Unable to add progressive Democrats to the Republicans who followed him into the Progressive party, TR could not win despite his personal popularity. Other reform voters embraced the Socialist candidate, Eugene V. Debs, who captured 900,000 votes—6 percent of the total. Taft played little role in the campaign. "I might as well give up as far as being a candidate," he lamented. "There are so many people in the country who don't like me."

Wilson won an easy electoral college victory, though he received only 42 percent of the popular vote. Roosevelt came in second, Taft third. The Democrats also gained control of Congress, giving Wilson the opportunity to enact his New Freedom program.

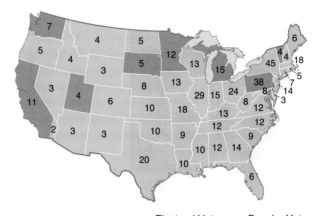

	Electoral Vote (%)	Popular Vote (%)
WOODROW WILSON (Democrat)	**435** **(82)**	**6,296,547** **(42)**
Theodore Roosevelt (Progressive)	88 (17)	4,118,571 (27)
William Taft (Republican)	8 (1)	3,486,720 (23)
Eugene Debs (Socialist)	–	900,672 (6)

MAP 21-2

The split within the Republican party enabled Woodrow Wilson to carry most states and became president even through he won only a minority of the popular vote

HOW IS it possible that Woodrow Wilson received 82 percent of the electoral vote but only 42 percent of the popular vote?

IMPLEMENTING THE NEW FREEDOM

Wilson built on Roosevelt's precedent to strengthen executive authority. He summoned Congress into special session in 1913 and delivered his message in person, the first president to do so since John Adams. Wilson proposed a full legislative program and worked forcefully to secure its approval. He held regular conferences with Democratic leaders and had a private telephone line installed between the Capitol and the White House to keep tabs on congressional actions. When necessary, he appealed to the public for support or doled out patronage and compromised with conservatives.

Wilson turned first to the traditional Democratic goal of reducing the high protective tariff. "The object of the tariff duties," Wilson announced, "must be effective competition." He forced through the **Underwood-Simmons Tariff Act** of 1913, the first substantial reduction in duties since before the Civil War. The act also levied the first income tax under the recently ratified Sixteenth Amendment.

Wilson next reformed the nation's banking and currency system, which was inadequate for a modernizing economy. He skillfully maneuvered a compromise measure through Congress, balancing the demands of agrarian progressives for government control with the bankers' desires for private control. The **Federal Reserve Act** of 1913 created twelve regional Federal Reserve banks that, although privately controlled, were to be supervised by the Federal Reserve Board, appointed by the president. The law also provided for a flexible national currency and improved access to credit. Serious problems remained, but the new system

New Nationalism   Theodore Roosevelt's 1912 program calling for a strong national government to foster, regulate, and protect business, industry, workers, and consumers.

New Freedom   Woodrow Wilson's 1912 program for limited government intervention in the economy to restore competition by curtailing the restrictive influences of trusts and protective tariffs, thereby providing opportunities for individual achievement.

Underwood-Simmons Tariff Act   The 1913 reform law that lowered tariff rates and levied the first regular federal income tax.

Federal Reserve Act   The 1913 law that revised banking and currency by extending limited government regulation through the creation of the Federal Reserve System.

U.S. President Woodrow Wilson sits
at his desk in an oil painting on canvas
by Edmund Charles Tarbell.

The Granger Collection, New York

promoted the progressive goals of order and efficiency and fulfilled Wilson's New Freedom principle of introducing limited government regulation while preserving private business control.

Wilson's third objective was new legislation to break up monopolies. To this end, he initially supported the Clayton antitrust bill, which prohibited unfair trade practices and restricted holding companies. But when business leaders and other progressives strenuously objected, Wilson reversed himself. Opting for continuous federal regulation rather than for the dissolution of trusts, Wilson endorsed the creation of the **Federal Trade Commission (FTC)** to oversee business activity and prevent illegal restrictions on competition.

The Federal Trade Commission Act of 1914 embraced the New Nationalism's emphasis on positive regulation. Wilson now accepted what he had earlier denounced as a partnership between trusts and the government that the trusts would dominate. Indeed, Wilson's conservative appointments to the FTC ensured that the agency would not seriously interfere with business.

Wilson now announced that no further reforms were necessary. He refused to support woman suffrage and helped kill legislation abolishing child labor and expanding credits to farmers. Race relations provided a flagrant instance of Wilson's indifference to social justice issues. Raised in the South, he believed in segregation and backed the Southern Democrats in his cabinet when they introduced formal segregation within the government itself. Government offices, shops, restrooms, and restaurants were all segregated; employees who complained were fired.

THE EXPANSION OF REFORM

Wilson had won in 1912 only because the Republicans had split. By 1916, Roosevelt had returned to the GOP, and Wilson realized that he had to attract some of TR's former followers. Wilson therefore promoted measures he had previously condemned as paternalistic. He now also recognized that some problems could be resolved only by positive federal action. "Old political formulas," he said, "do not fit the present."

In 1916, Wilson convinced Congress to pass the Federal Farm Loan Act, which provided farmers with federally financed, long-term agricultural credits. The Warehouse Act of 1916 improved short-term agricultural credit. The Highway Act of 1916 provided funds to construct and improve rural roads.

Wilson and the Democratic Congress also reached out to labor. Wilson signed the Keating-Owen Act prohibiting the interstate shipment of products made by child labor. In 1902, Wilson had denounced Roosevelt's intervention in the coal strike, but in 1916, he broke a labor-management impasse and averted a railroad strike by helping pass the Adamson Act establishing an eight-hour day for railway workers. Wilson pushed the Kern-McGillicuddy Act, which achieved the progressive goal of a workers' compensation system for federal employees.

Wilson also promoted activist government when he nominated Louis Brandeis to the Supreme Court. Known as the "people's lawyer," Brandeis had successfully defended protective labor legislation before the conservative judiciary. Brandeis was the first Jew nominated to the court, and anti-Semitism motivated some of his opponents. Wilson overcame a vicious campaign against Brandeis and secured his confirmation.

By these actions, Wilson brought progressivism to a culmination of sorts and consolidated reformers behind him for a second term. Less than a decade earlier, Wilson the private citizen had assailed government regulation and social legislation; by 1916, he had guided an unprecedented expansion of federal power.

Federal Trade Commission
Government agency established in 1914 to provide regulatory oversight of business activity.

Conclusion

Progressive reformers responded to the tensions of industrial and urban development by moving to change society and government. Programs and laws to protect women, children, and injured workers testified to their compassion; the creation of new agencies and political techniques indicated their interest in order and efficiency; campaigns to end corruption, whether perceived in urban political machines, corporate influence, drunkenness, or "inferior" immigrants, illustrated their self-assured vision of the public good.

Americans had come to accept that government action could resolve social and economic problems, and the role and power of government expanded accordingly. The emergence of an activist presidency, capable of developing programs, mobilizing public opinion, directing Congress, and taking forceful action, epitomized this key development.

Progressivism had its ironies and paradoxes. It called for democratic reforms—and did achieve woman suffrage, direct legislation, and popular election of senators—but helped disfranchise black Southerners and Northern immigrants. It advocated social justice but often enforced social control. It demanded responsive government but helped create bureaucracies largely removed from popular control. It endorsed the regulation of business in the public interest but forged regulatory laws and commissions that tended to aid business. Some of these seeming contradictions reflected the persistence of traditional attitudes and the necessity to accommodate conservative opponents; others revealed the progressives' own limitations in vision, concern, or nerve.

Summary

The Ferment of Reform Progressivism was a diverse movement; reformers responded to the tensions of industrialization and urbanization by developing programs to give women the right to vote, expose business abuses, end child labor, make government more efficient, manage natural resources and bring about social reform. The Social Gospel movement sought to introduce religious ethics into industrial relations; as businesses adopted Taylorization to improve workplace efficiency, workers resisted these new rules of efficiency. Opponents of reform held to traditional values and religious fundamentalism; businesses, angered by muckraking, used public relations as well as less desirable tactics to counter their critics.

Reforming Society Progressives worked to transform society by improving living conditions, educational opportunities, family life, and social and industrial relations. Settlement houses were the spearheads of social reform in urban immigrant neighborhoods; however, many reformers concluded it would take government intervention to end some of the abuses. Today's modern public school system emerged, and reformer Margaret Sanger crusaded for birth control. Nativists sought to limit immigration; the prohibition of alcohol was linked to social controls; the Eighteenth Amendment made prohibition the law of the land. The Niagara Movement sought to extend equal justice to African Americans; most Progressive reforms had not extended to them.

Reforming Politics and Government Progressives clamored for the reform of politics and the government; many wanted to change procedures and institutions to promote greater democracy; others hoped to improve the efforts of government and eliminate corruption. One of the most important achievements was woman suffrage; the Nineteenth Amendment gave women across America the right to vote. The secret ballot, initiative, referendum, recall, and direct election of senators were all introduced into the American political landscape during this period.

Theodore Roosevelt and the Progressive Presidency Progressive proponent Theodore Roosevelt entered the White House upon the assassination of President McKinley in 1901. He rejected the limited role of the Gilded Age presidents and believed it was the role of the president to meet any national needs not prohibited by the Constitution. Called the first "modern president," Roosevelt's flamboyance and ambitions made him the most popular president of the time and enabled him to take aggressive approaches toward a coal strike, conservation, "busting" trusts, and regulating business abuses. His administration marks the first time that the federal government gained the power to set rules in private enterprise.

Woodrow Wilson and Progressive Reform Progressivism was not limited to the Republican party; following Taft's administration Democrats pushed progressive remedies. President Woodrow Wilson, elected in 1912, introduced the New Freedom program; though he believed government's role should be more limited, he took steps to reduce the high protective tariff, create the Federal Reserve, break up monopolistic practices through the Federal Trade Commission, assist farmers, help workers and build highways. Wilson's "limited" view of Progressivism resulted in an unprecedented expansion of federal power.

REVIEW QUESTIONS

1. How and why did the presidency change during the Progressive Era?

2. How did the progressive concern for efficiency affect social reform efforts, public education, government, and rural life?

3. What factors, old and new, stimulated the reform movements of progressivism?

4. How did the changing role of women affect progressivism?

5. Why did the demand for woman suffrage provoke such determined support and such bitter opposition?

KEY TERMS

Australian ballot (p. 564)
Bureau of Reclamation (p. 568)
Conservation (p. 568)
Federal Reserve Act (p. 573)
Federal Trade Commission (p. 574)
Fundamentalists (p. 556)
Initiative (p. 566)
Muckraking (p. 553)

New Freedom (p. 573)
New Nationalism (p. 573)
Niagara Movement (p. 563)
Nineteenth Amendment (p. 564)
Progressive Era (p. 549)
Prohibition (p. 562)
Recall (p. 566)
Referendum (p. 566)

Seventeenth Amendment (p. 566)
Sixteenth Amendment (p. 571)
Social Gospel Movement (p. 551)
Underwood-Simmons Tariff Act (p. 573)
Wobblies (p. 554)

WHERE TO LEARN MORE

John Muir National Historic Site, Martinez, California. The architecture and furnishings of this seventeen-room house reflect the interests of John Muir, the writer and naturalist who founded the Sierra Club and led the preservationists in the Progressive Era. **www.nps.gov/jomu/**

National Museum of American History, Smithsonian Institution, Washington, D.C. A permanent exhibition, "Parlor to Politics: Women and Reform, 1890–1925," uses design, artifacts, and recent scholarship to vividly illustrate the changing role of women in the Progressive Era. It effectively emphasizes their work in settlement houses and their growing politicization and demonstrates the importance of the work of black women's organizations.

Hull House, Chicago, Illinois. This pioneering settlement house is now a museum on the campus of the University of Illinois, Chicago. **www.uic.edu/jaddams/hull/hull_house.html**

Lowell National Historic Park, Lowell, Massachusetts. "The Working People," a permanent exhibition, uses artifacts and photographs to chart the activities of immigrant workers at different times in the past, particularly during the Progressive Era. **www.nps.gov/lowe/**

Lower East Side Tenement Museum, New York City, New York. A six-story tenement building containing twenty-two apartments, this museum vividly illustrates the congested and unhealthy living conditions of urban immigrants from the 1870s to the early twentieth century. See **www.tenement.org/** for a virtual tour.

Sagamore Hill, Oyster Bay, New York. Theodore Roosevelt's home is now a National Historic Site and open to the public. **www.nps.gov/sahi/**

William Howard Taft National Historic Site, Cincinnati, Ohio. Taft was born in this house, the only national Taft memorial. An informative tour focuses on Taft's public and private life.

Staunton, Virginia. The birthplace and childhood home of Woodrow Wilson, restored with period furnishings, reveals many of the influences that shaped Wilson's career.

For additional study resources for this chapter, go to:
www.prenhall.com/goldfield/chapter21

*The effect will be to uplift the people,
gaining their permanent friendship and support
and greatly increasing our own commerce. . . .*

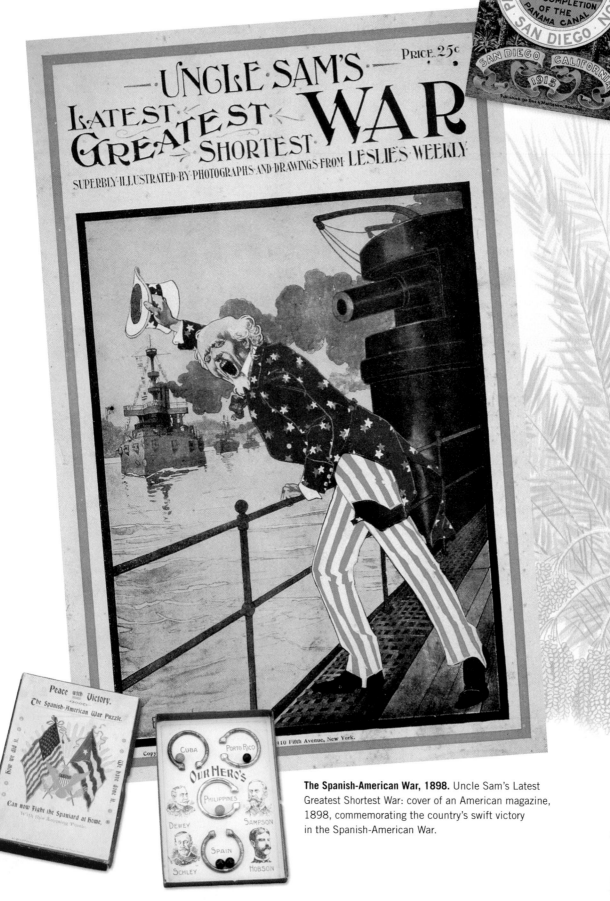

The Spanish-American War, 1898. Uncle Sam's Latest Greatest Shortest War: cover of an American magazine, 1898, commemorating the country's swift victory in the Spanish-American War.

22

CREATING AN EMPIRE
1865–1917

WHY DID the United States build an overeas empire?

HOW DID the United States move toward expanding its influence before the 1890s?

WHAT EVENTS led to the Spanish-American War?

WHAT WAS the nature of U.S. involvement in Asia?

WHAT WAS at stake for the United States in Puerto Rico, Cuba, and Panama?

Havana, Cuba
October 1901

When the Spanish-American war was declared the United States took a step forward, and assumed a position as protector of the interests of Cuba. It became responsible for the welfare of the people, politically, mentally, and morally. The mere fact of freeing the island from Spanish rule has not ended the care which this country should give. . . . The effect will be to uplift the people, gaining their permanent friendship and support and greatly increasing our own commerce. At present there are two million people requiring clothing and food, for but a small proportion of the necessaries of life are raised on the island. It is folly to grow food crops when sugar and tobacco produce such rich revenues in comparison. The United States should supply the Cubans with their breadstuffs, even wine, fruit, and vegetables, and should clothe the people. . . . The money received for their crops will be turned over in a great measure in buying supplies from the United States. . . .

Naturally the manufacturers of the United States should have precedence in furnishing machinery, locomotives, cars, and rails, materials for buildings and bridges, and the wide diversity of other supplies required, as well as fuel for their furnaces. With the present financial and commercial uncertainty at an end the people of the island will . . . come into the American market as customers for products of many kinds.

The meeting of the Constitutional Convention on November 5th will be an event in Cuban history of the greatest importance, and much will depend upon the action and outcome of this convention as to our future control of the island. . . . I considered it unwise to interfere, and I have made it a settled policy to permit the Cubans to manage every part of their constitution-making. This has been due to my desire to prevent any possible charge of crimination being brought against the United States in the direction of their constitutional affairs. . . .

There is no distrust of the United States on the part of the Cubans, and I know of no widespread antipathy to this country, its people, or its institutions. There are, of course, a handful of malcontents, as there must be in every country. . . .

I could not well conceive how the Cubans could be otherwise than grateful to the United States for its efforts in their behalf. The reconstruction of the island has proceeded rapidly from the first, and I think the transformation is without any superior in the history of modern times. The devastation of the long war had left the island in an unparalleled condition when the United States interfered, and in the brief time since the occupation of the island by American troops the island has been completely rehabilitated—agriculturally, commercially, financially, educationally, and governmentally. This improvement has been so rapid and so apparent that no Cuban could mistake it. To doubt in the face of these facts that their liberators were not still their faithful friends would be impossible.

Major-General Leonard Wood, "The Future of Cuba," *The Independent* 54 (January 23, 1902): 193–194; and Wood, "The Cuban Convention," *The Independent* 52 (November 1, 1900): 265–266.

IMAGE KEY
for pages 578–579

a. A colorful poster for the Panama-California Exhibition in San Diego.

b. Catalog Illustration of a Date Palm Tree ca. 1900.

c. Cover of an American magazine, 1898, commemorating the country's swift victory in the Spanish-American War.

d. Spanish American War puzzle.

e. Spanish American War game.

f. Grey And Red Battle Ship.

g. Uncle Sam rides a bicycle with globes of the western and eastern hemisphere for wheels while being watched by angry national leaders.

h. Charles Post, "Spanish Civil War."

i. Cartoon concerning the "Open Door Policy" 1899. "A Fair Field and No Favor. Uncle Sam: I'm out for commerce, not conquest."

j. Theodore Roosevelt on a steam shovel during the Panama Canal construction.

GENERAL LEONARD WOOD'S reports on Cuba, where he was military governor, captured the mixture of attitudes and motives that marked the United States's emergence as a world power. Plans for economic expansion, a belief in national mission, a sense of responsibility to help others, religious impulses and racist convictions—all combined in an uneasy mixture of self-interest and idealism that helped garner support for the new policies that the nation's leaders adopted, including American control over Cuba.

Wood himself had taken a symbolic journey in American expansionism. His earlier career had been with the troops on the American Southwestern frontier, but in 1898 he and Theodore Roosevelt formed the Rough Riders cavalry to participate in the Spanish-American War in Cuba. Upon Spain's surrender, Wood was appointed military governor of the island.

Wood's support for the war was reflected in his activities as a colonial administrator. Convinced of the superiority of American institutions, he favored their expansion. But expansion would also promote American interests. Thus while Wood brought improved sanitation, schools, and transportation to Cuba, he regarded Cubans as backward and incapable of self-government. He expected that American business interests would "naturally" benefit from his reorganization of Cuban life. Wood thus combined paternalistic or humanitarian reforms with attempts to incorporate Cuba into America's new commercial empire, fulfilling the traditional colonial role of providing raw materials and serving as a market for American products and capital.

His claim that he was not interfering with Cuba's constitutional convention was disingenuous, for he had already undertaken to limit those who could participate as voters or delegates and was devising means to restrict Cuba's autonomy. And despite his repeated insistence that the Cubans were "grateful" for the intervention of "their faithful friends," the Americans, Cubans, as well as Filipinos, Puerto Ricans, and others, rarely perceived American motives or American actions as positively as did Wood and other proponents of American expansion. Victory in the Spanish-American War had provided the United States with an empire, status as a world power, and opportunities and problems that would long shape American foreign policy.

THE ROOTS OF IMPERIALISM

The United States had a long-established tradition of expansion across the continent. Through purchase, negotiation, or conquest, the vast Louisiana Territory, Florida, Texas, New Mexico, California, and Oregon had become U.S. territory. Indeed, by the 1890s, Republican Senator Henry Cabot Lodge of Massachusetts boasted that Americans had "a record of conquest, colonization, and territorial expansion unequalled by any people in the nineteenth century." Lodge now urged the country to build an overseas empire, emulating the European model of **imperialism** based on the acquisition and exploitation of colonial possessions. Other Americans favored a less formal empire, in which U.S. interests and influence would be assured through extensive trade and investments rather than through military occupation. Still others advocated a cultural expansionism in which the nation exported its ideals and institutions.

IDEOLOGICAL ARGUMENTS

Scholars, authors, politicians, and religious leaders provided interlocking ideological arguments for the new imperialism (see the overview table "Rationales for Imperialism"). Some intellectuals, for example, invoked social Darwinism, maintaining that "the survival of the fittest" was "the law of nations as well as a law

WHY DID the United States build an overseas empire?

Imperialism The policy and practice of exploiting nations and peoples for the benefit of an imperial power either directly through military occupation and colonial rule or indirectly through economic domination of resources and markets.

OVERVIEW

RATIONALES FOR IMPERIALISM

Category	Beliefs
Racism and social Darwinism	Convictions that "Anglo-Saxons" were racially superior and should dominate other peoples, either to ensure national success, establish international stability, or benefit the "inferior" races by imposing American ideas and institutions on them.
Righteousness	The conviction that Christianity, and a supporting American culture, should be aggressively spread among the benighted peoples of other lands.
Mahanism	The conviction, following the ideas advanced by Alfred Thayer Mahan, that U.S. security required a strong navy and economic and territorial expansion.
Economics	A variety of arguments holding that American prosperity depended on acquiring access to foreign markets, raw materials, and investment opportunities.

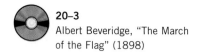

20–3
Albert Beveridge, "The March of the Flag" (1898)

of nature." As European nations expanded into Asia and Africa in the 1880s and 1890s, seeking colonies, markets, and raw materials, these advocates argued that the United States had to adopt similar policies to ensure national success.

Related to social Darwinism was a pervasive belief in the superiority of people of English, or Anglo-Saxon, descent. To many Americans, the industrial progress, military strength, and political development of England and the United States were proof of an Anglo-Saxon superiority that carried with it a responsibility to extend the blessings of their rule to less able people. As a popular expression put it, colonialism was the "white man's burden." The political scientist John W. Burgess argued that Anglo-Saxons "must have a colonial policy" and "righteously assume sovereignty" over "incompetent" or "barbaric races" in other lands.

American missionaries also promoted expansionist sentiment. Hoping to evangelize the world, American religious groups increased the number of Protestant foreign missions sixfold from 1870 to 1900. Missionaries publicized their activities throughout the United States, generating interest in foreign developments and support for what one writer called the "imperialism of righteousness." Abroad they pursued a religious transformation that often resembled a cultural conversion, for they promoted trade, developed business interests, and encouraged Westernization through technology and education as well as religion. Sometimes, as in the Hawaiian Islands, American missionaries even promoted annexation by the United States.

The Reverend J. H. Barrows in early 1898 lectured on the "Christian conquest of Asia," suggesting that American Christianity and commerce would cross the Pacific to fulfill "the manifest destiny of the Christian Republic." Missionaries also contributed to the imperial impulse by describing their work, as Barrows did, in terms of the "conquest" of "enemy" territory. Thus while missionaries were motivated by what they considered to be idealism and often brought real benefits to other lands, especially in education and health, religious sentiments reinforced the ideology of American expansion.

STRATEGIC CONCERNS

Other expansionists were motivated by strategic concerns, shaped by what seemed to be the forces of history and geography. Alfred Thayer Mahan, a naval officer and president of the Naval War College, emphasized the importance of a strong navy for national greatness in his book *The Influence of Sea Power upon History.* Mahan also proposed that the United States build a canal across the isthmus of Panama to link its coasts, acquire naval bases in the Caribbean and the Pacific to protect the canal, and annex Hawaii and other Pacific islands. The United States must "cast aside the policy of isolation which befitted her infancy," Mahan declared, and "begin to look outward."

Mahanism found a receptive audience. Vocal advocates of Mahan's program were a group of nationalistic Republicans, predominantly from the Northeast. They included politicians like Henry Cabot Lodge and Theodore Roosevelt, journalists like Whitelaw Reid of the *New York Tribune* and Albert Shaw of the *Review of Reviews*, and diplomats and lawyers like John Hay and Elihu Root.

Such men favored imperial expansion, as Shaw wrote, "for the sake of our destiny, our dignity, our influence, and our usefulness." One British observer concluded that Mahan's influence had transformed the American spirit, serving "as oil to the flame of 'colonial expansion' everywhere leaping into life." (See American Views, "An American Views the World.")

An American missionary and her Chinese converts study the Bible in Manchuria in 1903 under a U.S. flag. American missionaries wanted to spread the Gospel albroad but inevitably spread American influence as well.

Photograph reproduced with permission of Wider Church Ministries of the United Church of Christ by permission of the Houghton Library, Harward University

The large navy policy popular among imperialists began in 1881, when Congress established the Naval Advisory Board. An extensive program to replace the navy's obsolete wooden ships with modern cruisers and battleships was well under way by 1890 when the first volume of Mahan's book appeared. The United States soon possessed a formidable navy, which, in turn, demanded strategic bases and coaling stations. One writer indicated the circular nature of this development by noting in 1893 that Manifest Destiny now meant "the acquisition of such territory, far and near," that would secure "to our navy facilities desirable for the operations of a great naval power."

ECONOMIC DESIGNS

Nearly all Americans favored economic expansion through foreign trade. Such a policy promised national prosperity: larger markets for manufacturers and farmers, greater profits for merchants and bankers, more jobs for workers. Far fewer favored the acquisition of colonies that was characteristic of European imperialism. One diplomat declared in 1890 that the nation was more interested in the "annexation of trade" than in the annexation of territory.

As early as 1844, the United States had negotiated a trade treaty with China, and ten years later, a squadron under Commodore Matthew Perry had forced the Japanese to open their ports to American products. In the late nineteenth century, the dramatic expansion of the economy caused many Americans to favor more government action to open foreign markets to American exports. Alabama Senator John Morgan had the cotton and textiles produced in the New South in mind when he warned in 1882: "Our home market is not equal to the demands of our producing and manufacturing classes and to the capital which is seeking

Mahanism The ideas advanced by Alfred Thayer Mahan, stressing U.S. naval, economic, and territorial expansion.

AN IMPERIALIST VIEWS THE WORLD

*T*heodore Roosevelt, Henry Cabot Lodge, Alfred Thayer Mahan, and other influential imperialists frequently corresponded with one another. The following excerpts are from Roosevelt's private correspondence in 1897, while he was assistant secretary of the Navy and before the Spanish-American War began.

HOW DOES Roosevelt reflect the influence of Mahan? What is Roosevelt's view of war? How does he view European states and the independence of other nations in the Western Hemisphere?

I suppose that I need not tell you that as regards Hawaii I take your views absolutely, as indeed I do on foreign policy generally. If I had my way we would annex those islands tomorrow. If that is impossible I would establish a protectorate over them. I believe we should build the Nicaraguan canal at once, and in the meantime that we should build a dozen new battleships, half of them on the Pacific Coast; and these battleships should have a large coal capacity and a consequent increased radius of action. . . . I think President Cleveland's action [in rejecting the annexation of Hawaii] was a colossal crime, and we should be guilty of aiding him after the fact if we do not reverse what he did. I earnestly hope we can make the President [McKinley] look at things our way. Last Saturday night Lodge pressed his views upon him with all his strength.

I agree with all you say as to what will be the result if we fail to take Hawaii. It will show that we either have lost, or else wholly lack, the masterful instinct which alone can make a race great. I feel so deeply about it I hardly dare express myself in full. The terrible part is to see that it is the men of education who take the lead in trying to make us prove traitors to our race.

I fully realize the importance of the Pacific coast . . . But there are big problems in the West Indies also.

Until we definitely turn Spain out of those islands (and if I had my way that would be done tomorrow), we will always be menaced by trouble there. We should acquire the Danish Islands [in the West Indies], and by turning Spain out should serve notice that no strong European power, and especially not Germany, should be allowed to gain a foothold by supplanting some weak European power. I do not fear England; Canada is a hostage for her good behavior.

I wish we had a perfectly consistent foreign policy, and that this policy was that every European power should be driven out of America, and every foot of American soil, including the nearest islands in both the Pacific and the Atlantic, should be in the hands of independent American states, and so far as possible in the possession of the United States or under its protection.

To speak with a frankness which our timid friends would call brutal, I would regard a war with Spain from two standpoints: first, the advisability on the grounds both of humanity and self-interest of interfering on behalf of the Cubans, and of taking one more step toward the complete freeing of America from European dominion; second, the benefit done our people by giving them something to think of which isn't material gain, and especially the benefit done our military forces by trying both the Navy and the Army in actual practice. I should be very sorry not to see us make the experiment of trying to land, and therefore feed and clothe, an expeditionary force [on Cuba], if only for the sake of learning from our own blunders. I should hope that the force would have some fighting to do. It would be a great lesson, and we would profit much by it.

I wish there was a chance that the [U.S. battleship] Maine was going to be used against some foreign power; by preference Germany—but I am not particular, and I'd take even Spain if nothing better offered.

Source: Reprinted by permission of the publisher from *The Letters of Theodore Roosevelt* Volume I 1868–1898, selected and edited by Elting E. Morison, Cambridge: Harvard University Press.

employment. . . . We must either enlarge the field of our traffic, or stop the business of manufacturing just where it is." More ominous, a naval officer trying to open Korea to U.S. products declared in 1878, "We must *export* these products or *deport* the people who are creating them."

Exports, particularly of manufactured goods, which grew ninefold between 1865 and 1900, did increase greatly in the late nineteenth century. Still, periodic depressions fed these fears of overproduction, and the massive unemployment and social unrest that accompanied these economic crises also provided social and political arguments for economic relief through foreign trade.

In the depression of the 1890s, this interest in foreign trade became obsessive. More systematic government efforts to promote trade seemed necessary, a conclusion strengthened by new threats to existing American markets, including higher European tariffs. Moreover, Japan and the European imperial powers began to restrict commercial opportunities in the areas of China that they controlled.

First Steps

Before the mid-1890s, the government did not pursue a policy of *isolationism* from international affairs, for the nation maintained normal diplomatic and trade ties and at times vigorously intervened in Latin America and East Asia. But in general the government deferred to the initiative of private interests, reacted haphazardly to outside events, and did little to create a professional foreign service. In a few bold if inconsistent steps, however, the United States moved toward expanding its influence.

HOW DID the United States move toward expanding its global influence before the 1890s?

Seward and Blaine

Two secretaries of state, William H. Seward, secretary under Presidents Lincoln and Andrew Johnson (1861–1869), and James G. Blaine, secretary under Presidents Garfield and Harrison (1881, 1889–1892), laid the foundation for a larger and more aggressive American role in world affairs. Seward possessed an elaborate imperial vision, based on his understanding of commercial opportunities, strategic necessities, and national destiny. Seward purchased Alaska from Russia in 1867, approved the navy's occupation of the Midway Islands in the Pacific, pushed American trade on a reluctant Japan, and repeatedly tried to acquire Caribbean naval bases (see Map 22–1). But his policy of expansion, as one observer noted, "went somewhat too far and too fast for the public," and many of his plans fizzled. Congressional opposition frustrated his efforts to obtain Haiti and the Dominican Republic and to purchase the Danish West Indies; Colombia blocked his attempt to gain construction rights for a canal across the isthmus of Panama.

Blaine was an equally vigorous advocate of expansion. He worked to extend what he called America's "commercial empire" in the Pacific. And he sought to ensure U.S. sovereignty over any canal in Panama, insisting that it be "a purely American waterway to be treated as part of our own coastline." In an effort to induce the nations of Latin America to import manufactured products from the United States rather than Europe, Blaine proposed a conference among the nations of the Western Hemisphere in 1881. The First International American Conference finally met in 1889. There Blaine called for the establishment of a customs union to reduce trade barriers. He expected this union to strengthen U.S. control of hemispheric markets. The Latin America nations, however, wary of economic subordination to the colossus of the north, rejected Blaine's plan.

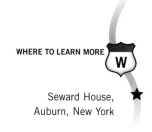

WHERE TO LEARN MORE W

Seward House,
Auburn, New York

WHERE TO LEARN MORE W

James G. Blaine House,
Augusta, Maine

MAP EXPLORATION

To explore an interactive version of this map, go to **http://www.prenhall.com/goldfield2/map22.1**

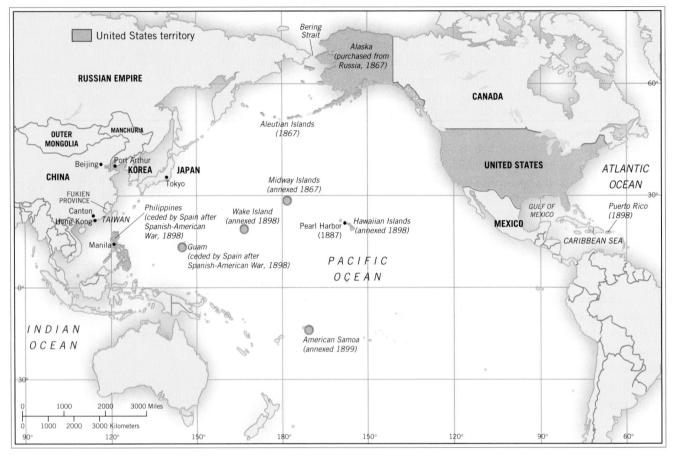

MAP 22–1

United States Expansion in the Pacific, 1867–1899   Pursuing visions of a commercial empire in the Pacific, the United States steadily expanded its territorial possessions as well as its influence there in the late nineteenth century.

WHAT DID the United States gain from its expansion in the Pacific?

HAWAII

Blaine regarded Hawaii as "indispensably" part of "the American system." As early as 1842, the United States had announced its opposition to European control of Hawaii, a key way station in the China trade where New England missionaries and whalers were active. Although the islands remained under native monarchs, American influence grew, particularly as other Americans arrived to establish sugar plantations and eventually dominate the economy.

Treaties in 1875 and 1887 integrated the islands into the American economy and gave the United States control over Pearl Harbor on the island of Oahu. In 1887, the United States rejected a proposal from Britain and France for a joint guarantee of Hawaii's independence and endorsed a new Hawaiian constitution that gave political power to wealthy white residents. The obvious next step was U.S. annexation, which Blaine endorsed in 1891.

American planters soon bid for annexation. The McKinley Tariff Act of 1890 effectively closed the U.S. market to Hawaiian sugar producers, facing them with economic ruin. At the same time, Queen Liliuokalani moved to restore native control of Hawaiian affairs. To ensure market access and protect their political authority, the American planters decided to seek annexation to the United States. In 1893, they overthrew the queen. John Stevens, the American minister, ordered U.S. Marines to help the rebels. He then declared an American protectorate over the new Hawaii government and wired Washington: "The Hawaiian pear is now fully ripe, and this is the golden hour for the United States to pluck it." A delegation from the new provisional government, containing no native Hawaiians, went to Washington to draft a treaty for annexation. President Harrison signed the pact but could not get Senate approval before the new Cleveland administration took office.

Cleveland immediately called for an investigation of the whole affair. Soon convinced that "the undoubted sentiment of the people is for the Queen, against the provisional Government, and against annexation," Cleveland apologized to the queen for the "flagrant wrong" done her by the "reprehensible conduct of the American minister and the unauthorized presence on land of a military force of the United States." But the American-dominated provisional government refused to step down, and Cleveland's rejection of annexation set off a noisy debate.

Many Republicans strongly supported annexation. One Eastern Republican manufacturer called for the annexation of Hawaii as the first step toward making the Pacific "an American ocean, dominated by American commercial enterprise for all time." On the West Coast, where California business interests had close ties with the islands, the commercial and strategic value of Hawaii seemed obvious. The *San Francisco Examiner* declared, "Hoist the Stars and Stripes. It is a case of manifest destiny." Reflecting racial imperialism, others argued that annexation would both fittingly reward the enterprising white residents of Hawaii and provide an opportunity to civilize native Hawaiians.

Democrats generally opposed annexation. They doubted, as Missouri Senator George Vest declared, whether the United States should desert its traditional principles and "venture upon the great colonial system of the European powers." The Hawaiian episode of 1893 thus foreshadowed the arguments over imperialism at the end of the century and emphasized the policy differences between Democrats and the increasingly expansionist Republicans.

CHILE AND VENEZUELA

American reactions to developments in other countries in the 1890s also reflected an increasingly assertive national policy and excitable public opinion. In 1891, American sailors on shore leave in Chile became involved in a drunken brawl that left two of them dead, seventeen injured, and dozens in jail. Encouraged by a combative navy, President Harrison threatened military retaliation against Chile, provoking an outburst of bellicose nationalism in the United States. Harrison relented only when Chile apologized and paid an indemnity.

A few years later, the United States again threatened war over a minor issue, but against a more formidable opponent. In 1895, President Cleveland intervened in a boundary dispute between Great Britain and Venezuela over British Guiana. Cleveland was motivated not only by the long-standing U.S. goal of challenging Britain for Latin American markets but also by ever more expansive notions of the **Monroe Doctrine** and the authority of the United States. Secretary of State Richard Olney sent Britain a blunt note (a "twenty-inch gun," Cleveland called it) demanding arbitration of the disputed territory and stoutly asserting American supremacy in the Western Hemisphere. Cleveland urged Congress to establish a commission to determine the boundary and enforce its decision by war if necessary. As war fever swept the United States, Britain agreed to arbitration, recognizing the limited nature of the issue that so convulsed Anglo-American relations.

WHERE TO LEARN MORE

Mission Houses,
Honolulu, Hawaii
www.missionhouses.org/

Monroe Doctrine Declaration by President James Monroe in 1823 that the Western Hemisphere was to be closed off to further European colonization and that the United States would not interfere in the internal affairs of European nations.

CHRONOLOGY

1861–1869	Seward serves as secretary of state.
1867	U.S. purchases Alaska from Russia.
1870	Annexation of the Dominican Republic is rejected.
1881	Naval Advisory Board is created.
1887	U.S. gains naval rights to Pearl Harbor.
1889	First Pan-American Conference is held.
1890	Alfred Thayer Mahan publishes *The Influence of Sea Power upon History*.
1893	Harrison signs but Cleveland rejects a treaty for the annexation of Hawaii.
1893–1897	Depression increases interest in economic expansion abroad.
1894–1895	Sino-Japanese War is fought.
1895	U.S. intervenes in Great Britain–Venezuelan boundary dispute. Cuban insurrection against Spain begins.
1896	William McKinley is elected president on an imperialist platform.
1898	Spanish-American War is fought. Hawaii is annexed. Anti-Imperialist League is organized. Treaty of Paris is signed.
1899–1902	Filipino-American War is fought.
1899	Open Door note is issued.
1901	Theodore Roosevelt becomes president.
1903	Platt Amendment restricts Cuban autonomy. Panama "revolution" is abetted by the United States.
1904	United States acquires the Panama Canal Zone. Roosevelt Corollary is announced.
1904–1905	Russo-Japanese War is fought.
1905	Treaty of Portsmouth ends the Russo-Japanese War through U.S. mediation.
1906–1909	United States occupies Cuba.
1907–1908	Gentlemen's Agreement restricts Japanese immigration.
1909	United States intervenes in Nicaragua.
1912–1933	United States occupies Nicaragua.
1914	Panama Canal opens.
1914–1917	United States intervenes in Mexico.
1915–1934	United States occupies Haiti.
1916–1924	United States occupies the Dominican Republic.
1917	Puerto Ricans are granted U.S. citizenship.
1917–1922	United States occupies Cuba.

The United States' assertion of hemispheric dominance angered Latin Americans, and their fears deepened when it decided arbitration terms with Britain without consulting Venezuela, which protested before bowing to American pressure. The further significance of the Venezuelan crisis, as Captain Mahan noted, lay in its "awakening of our countrymen to the fact that we must come out of our isolation . . . and take our share in the turmoil of the world."

THE SPANISH-AMERICAN WAR

WHAT EVENTS led to the Spanish-American War?

The forces pushing the United States toward imperialism and international power came to a head in the Spanish-American War. Cuba's quest for independence from the oppressive colonial control of Spain activated Americans' long-standing interest in the island. But few foresaw that the war that finally erupted in 1898 would dramatically change America's relationships with the rest of the world and give it a colonial empire.

THE CUBAN REVOLUTION

Cuba was the last major European colony in Latin America, with an economic potential that attracted American business interests and a strategic significance for any Central American canal. In the 1880s, Spanish control became increasingly harsh, and in 1895 the Cubans launched a revolt.

The rebellion was a classic guerrilla war in which the rebels controlled the countryside and the Spanish army the towns and cities. American economic interests were seriously affected, for both Cubans and Spaniards destroyed American property and disrupted American trade. But the brutality with which Spain attempted to suppress the revolt promoted American sympathy for the Cuban insurgents. Determined to cut the rebels off from their peasant supporters, the Spaniards herded most civilians into "reconcentration camps," where tens of thousands died of starvation and disease.

Americans' sympathy was further aroused by the sensationalist **yellow press**. To attract readers and boost advertising revenues, the popular press of the day adopted bold headlines, fevered editorials, and real or exaggerated stories of violence, sex, and corruption. A circulation war between William Randolph Hearst's *New York Journal* and Joseph Pulitzer's *New York World* helped stimulate interest in Cuban war. "Blood on the roadsides, blood on the fields, blood on the doorsteps, blood, blood, blood! The old, the young, the weak, the crippled—all are butchered without mercy," the *World* feverishly reported of Cuba. "Is there no nation wise enough, brave enough to aid this blood-smitten land?" The nation's religious press, partly because it reflected the prejudice many Protestants held against Catholic Spain, also advocated American intervention.

As the Cuban rebellion dragged on, more and more Americans advocated intervention to stop the carnage, protect U.S. investments, or uphold various principles. Expansionists like Roosevelt and Lodge clamored for intervention, but so did their opponents. Populists, for example, sympathized with a people seeking independence from colonial rule and petitioned Congress to support the crusade for Cuban freedom. In the election of 1896, both major parties endorsed Cuban independence.

GROWING TENSIONS

President William McKinley's administration soon focused on Cuba. McKinley's principal complaint was that chronic disorder in Cuba disrupted America's investments and agitated public opinion. Personally opposed to military intervention, McKinley first used diplomacy to press Spain to adopt reforms that would settle the rebellion. Following his instructions, the U.S. minister to Spain warned the Spanish government that if it did not quickly establish peace, the United States would take whatever steps it "should deem necessary to procure this result." In late 1897, Spain modified its brutal military tactics and offered limited autonomy to Cuba. But Cubans insisted on complete independence, which Spain refused to grant.

Relations between the United States and Spain deteriorated. On February 15, 1898, the U.S. battleship *Maine* blew up in Havana harbor, killing 260 men. The Spaniards were not responsible for the tragedy, which a modern naval inquiry has attributed to an internal accident. But many Americans agreed with Theodore Roosevelt, the assistant secretary of the navy, who called it "an act of dirty treachery on the part of the Spaniards" and told McKinley that only war was "compatible with our national honor."

Other pressures soon began to build on the president. Senator Lodge reported a consensus "that this situation must end. We cannot go on indefinitely with this strain, this suspense, and this uncertainty, this tottering upon the verge of war. It is killing to business." McKinley also feared that a moderate policy would endanger congressional candidates. Again Senator Lodge, although hesitant to suggest "war for political reasons," nevertheless advised McKinley, "If the war in Cuba drags on through the summer with nothing done, we shall go down in the greatest [election] defeat ever known."

QUICK REVIEW

The Press and Cuba

♦ Yellow press stimulated interest in Cuba.

♦ Newspapers emphasized violence, sex, and corruption.

♦ Much of America's religious press advocated American intervention.

Yellow press A deliberately sensational journalism of scandal and exposure designed to attract an urban mass audience and increase advertising revenues.

At the end of March 1898, McKinley sent Spain an ultimatum. He demanded an armistice in Cuba, an end to the reconcentration policy, and the acceptance of American arbitration, which implied Cuban independence. Desperately, Spain made concessions, abolishing reconcentration and declaring a unilateral armistice, but McKinley had already begun war preparations. He submitted a war message to Congress on April 11, asking for authority to use force against Spain "in the name of humanity, in the name of civilization, in behalf of endangered American interests." Congress declared war on Spain on April 25, 1898.

Most interventionists were not imperialists, and Congress added the **Teller Amendment** to the war resolution, disclaiming any intention of annexing Cuba and promising that Cubans would govern themselves. Congress also refused to approve either a canal bill or the annexation of Hawaii. Nevertheless, the Spanish-American War did turn the nation toward imperialism.

WAR AND EMPIRE

The decisive engagement of the war took place not in Cuba but in another Spanish colony, the Philippines, and it involved the favored tool of the expansionists, the new navy (see Map 22–2). Once war was declared, Commodore George Dewey led the U.S. Asiatic squadron into Manila Bay and destroyed the weaker Spanish fleet on May 1, 1898. The navy had long coveted Manila Bay as a strategic harbor, but other Americans, casting an eye on commercial opportunities in China, saw a greater significance in the victory. With Dewey's triumph, exulted one expansionist, "We are taking our proper rank among the nations of the world. We are after markets, the greatest markets now existing in the world." To expand this foothold in Asia, McKinley ordered troops to the Philippines, postponing the military expedition to Cuba itself.

Dewey's victory also precipitated the annexation of Hawaii, which had seemed hopeless only weeks before. Annexationists now pointed to the islands' strategic importance as steppingstones to Manila. "To maintain our flag in the Philippines, we must raise our flag in Hawaii," the *New York Sun* contended. McKinley himself privately declared, "We need Hawaii just as much and a good deal more than we did California. It is Manifest Destiny." In July, Congress approved annexation, a decision welcomed by Hawaii's white minority. Natives solemnly protested this step taken "without reference to the consent of the people of the Hawaiian Islands." Filipinos would soon face the same American imperial impulse.

Military victory also came swiftly in Cuba, once the U.S. Army finally landed in late June. Victory depended largely on Spanish ineptitude, for the American troops had to fight with antiquated weapons and wear wool uniforms in the sweltering tropics. They were issued rotting and poisoned food by a corrupt and inefficient War Department. More than five thousand Americans died of diseases and accidents brought on by such mismanagement; only 379 were killed in battle. State militias supplemented the small regular army, as did volunteer units, such as the famous Rough Riders, a cavalry unit of cowboys and eastern dandies assembled by Theodore Roosevelt.

U.S. naval power again proved decisive. In a lopsided battle on July 3, the obsolete Spanish squadron in Cuba was destroyed, isolating the Spanish army and guaranteeing its defeat. U.S. forces then seized the nearby Spanish colony of Puerto Rico without serious opposition. Humbled, Spain signed an armistice ending the war on August 12.

Americans were delighted with their military achievements, but the *Philadelphia Inquirer* cautioned, "With peace will come new responsibilities, which must be met. We have colonies to look after and develop."

W WHERE TO LEARN MORE

Funston Memorial Home, Iola, Kansas
http://skyways.lib.ks.us/museums/funston/

QUICK REVIEW

Dewey's Victory

◆ May 1, 1898: Dewey's squadron destroys Spanish fleet in Manila Bay.

◆ Expansionists saw victory as an opportunity for greater U.S. presence in the region.

◆ McKinley followed up Dewey's victory by sending troops to the Philippines.

Teller Amendment   A congressional resolution adopted in 1898 renouncing any American intention to annex Cuba.

MAP EXPLORATION

To explore an interactive version of this map, go to **http://www.prenhall.com/goldfield2/map22.2**

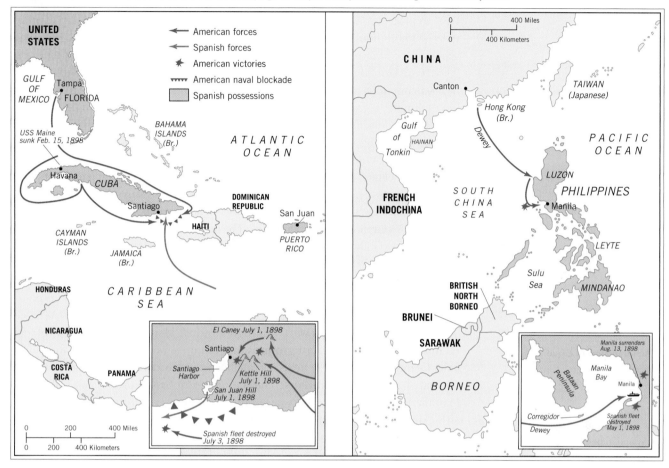

MAP 22–2

The Spanish-American War   The United States gained quick victories in both theaters of the Spanish-American War. Its naval power proved decisive, with Commodore Dewey destroying one enemy fleet in the Philippines and a second U.S. naval force cutting off the Spanish in Cuba.

WHY DID the United States want to control the Philippines?

THE TREATY OF PARIS

The armistice required Spain to accept Cuban independence, cede Puerto Rico and Guam (a Pacific island between Hawaii and the Philippines), and allow the Americans to occupy Manila pending the final disposition of the Philippines at a formal peace conference. The acquisition of Puerto Rico and Guam indicated the expansionist nature the conflict had assumed for the United States. So did the postponement of the Philippine issue. McKinley knew that delay would permit the advocates of expansion to build public support for annexation.

But he was motivated to acquire the Philippines primarily by a determination to use the islands to strengthen America's political and commercial position in East Asia. Moreover, he believed the Filipinos poorly suited to self-rule, and he feared that Germany or Japan might seize the Philippines if the United States did not. Meeting in Paris in December, American and Spanish negotiators settled the final terms for peace. Spain agreed—despite Filipino demands for independence—to cede the Philippines to the United States.

20–5
William McKinley, "Decision on the Philippines" (1900)

The decision to acquire the Philippines sparked a dramatic debate over the ratification of the Treaty of Paris. The *United States Investor* spoke for business leaders, for example, in demanding the Philippines as "a base of operations in the East" to protect American interests in China; other economic expansionists argued that the Philippines themselves had valuable resources and were a market for American goods or warned that "our commercial rivals in the Orient" would grab the islands if the United States did not. The *Presbyterian Banner* spoke for what it termed a nearly unanimous religious press in affirming "the desirability of America's retaining the Philippines as a duty in the interest of human freedom and Christian progress."

Opponents of the treaty included such prominent figures as the civil service reformer Carl Schurz, steel baron Andrew Carnegie, social reformer Jane Addams, labor leader Samuel Gompers, and author Mark Twain. Their organizational base was the Anti-Imperialist League, which campaigned against the treaty, distributing pamphlets, petitioning Congress, and holding rallies. League members' criticisms reflected a conviction that imperialism was a repudiation of America's moral and political traditions embodied in the Declaration of Independence. The acquisition of overseas colonies, they argued, conflicted with the nation's commitment to liberty and its claim to moral superiority. They regarded as loathsome and hypocritical the transformation of a war to free Cuba into a campaign for imperial conquest and subjugation. Some African Americans derided the rhetoric of Anglo-Saxon superiority that underlay imperialism and even organized the Black Man's Burden Association to promote Philippine independence.

But other arguments were less high-minded. Many anti-imperialists objected to expansion on the racist grounds that Filipinos were inferior and unassimilable. Gompers feared that cheap Asian labor would undercut the wages and living standards of American workers. The *San Francisco Call*, representing California-Hawaiian sugar interests, also wanted no competition from the Philippines.

Finally, on February 6, 1899, the Senate narrowly ratified the treaty. Then, by a single vote, the Republicans defeated a Democratic proposal for Philippine independence once a stable government had been established; the United States would keep the islands.

William Jennings Bryan attempted to make the election of 1900 a referendum on "the paramount issue" of imperialism, promising to free the Philippines if the Democrats won. But some of the most ardent anti-imperialists were conservatives who remained loyal to McKinley because they could not tolerate Bryan's economic policies. Republicans also played on the nationalist emotions evoked by the war, especially by nominating Theodore Roosevelt for vice president. "If you choose to vote for America, if you choose to vote for the flag for which we fought," Roosevelt said, "then you will vote to sustain the administration of President McKinley." Bryan lost again, as in 1896, and under Republican leadership, the United States became an imperial nation.

QUICK REVIEW

The Anti-Imperialist League

- Central to campaign against the Treaty of Paris (ratified 1899).

- League members saw treaty as a repudiation of American moral and political traditions.

- Many anti-imperialists objected to expansion on racist grounds.

IMPERIAL AMBITIONS: THE UNITED STATES AND EAST ASIA, 1899–1917

In 1899, as the United States occupied its new empire, Assistant Secretary of State John Bassett Moore observed that the nation had become "a world power. . . . Where formerly we had only commercial interests, we now have territorial and political interests as well." American policies to promote those expanded interests focused first on East Asia and Latin America, where the Spanish-American War had provided the United States with both opportunities and challenges. In Asia, the first issue concerned the fate of the Philippines, but looming beyond it were American ambitions in China, where other imperial nations had their own goals.

WHAT WAS the nature of
U.S. involvement in Asia?

THE FILIPINO-AMERICAN WAR

Filipino nationalists, like Cuban insurgents, were already fighting Spain for their independence before the sudden American intervention. The Filipino leader, Emilio Aguinaldo, welcomed Dewey's naval victory as the sign of a de facto alliance with the United States; he then issued a declaration of independence and proclaimed the Philippine Republic. But the Filipinos' optimism declined as American officials acted in an increasingly imperious manner toward them, first refusing to meet with the "savages," then insisting that Filipino forces withdraw from Manila or face "forcible action," and finally dismissing the claims of Aguinaldo and "his so-called government." When the Treaty of Paris provided for U.S. ownership rather than independence, Filipinos felt betrayed. Mounting tensions erupted in a battle between American and Filipino troops outside Manila on February 4, 1899, sparking a long and brutal war.

Ultimately, the United States used nearly four times as many soldiers to suppress the Filipinos as to defeat Spain in Cuba and, in a tragic irony, employed many of the same brutal methods for which it had condemned Spain. Americans often made little effort to distinguish between soldiers and noncombatants, viewing all Filipinos with racial antagonism. Before the military imposed censorship on war news, reporters confirmed U.S. atrocities; one wrote that "American troops have been relentless, have killed to exterminate men, women, and children, prisoners and captives, active insurgents and suspected people, from lads of 10 and up." A California newspaper defended such actions with remarkable candor: "Let us all be frank. WE DO NOT WANT THE FILIPINOS. WE DO WANT THE PHILIPPINES. . . . The more of them killed the better. It seems harsh. But they must yield before the superior race."

The overt racism of the war repelled African Americans. John Mitchell, a Virginia editor, condemned all the talk of "white man's burden" as deceptive rhetoric for brutal acts that could not be "defended either in moral or international law."

The Anti-Imperialist League revived, citing the war as proof of the corrosive influence of imperialism on the nation's morals and principles. Professors addressed antiwar rallies on college campuses. "Alas, what a fall," one University of Michigan professor told his audience. "Within the circuit of a single year to have declined from the moral leadership of mankind into the common brigandage of the robber nations of the world."

By 1902, however, the American military had largely suppressed the rebellion, and the United States had established a colonial government. Compared to the Americans' brutal war policies, U.S. colonial rule was relatively benign, though paternalistic. William Howard Taft, the first governor general, launched a program that brought the islands new schools and roads, a public health system, and an economy tied closely to both the United States and a small Filipino elite.

CHINA AND THE OPEN DOOR

America's determined involvement in the Philippines reflected its preoccupation with China. By the mid-1890s, other powers threatened prospects for American commercial expansion in China. Japan, after defeating China in 1895, annexed Taiwan and secured economic privileges in the mainland province of Fukien (Fujian); the major European powers then competed aggressively to claim other areas of China as their own **spheres of influence**. In Manchuria, Russia won control of Port Arthur (Lüshun) and the right to construct a railway. Germany secured a ninety-nine year lease on another Chinese port and mining and railroad privileges on the Shandong Peninsula. The British wrung special concessions in Kowloon, opposite Hong Kong, as well as a port facing the Russians in Manchuria. France gained a lease on ports and exclusive commercial privileges in southern China.

QUICK REVIEW

Filipino-American War
- Filipinos felt betrayed by Treaty of Paris.
- February 4, 1899: fighting between American and Filipino troops sparked war.
- 1902: U.S. colonial rule is established after a brutal war.

Spheres of Influence Regions dominated and controlled by an outside power.

These developments alarmed the American business community. It was confident that given an equal opportunity, the United States would prevail in international trade because of its efficient production and marketing systems. But the creation of exclusive spheres of influence would limit the opportunity to compete. In early 1898, business leaders organized the Committee on American Interests in China to lobby Washington to promote American trade in the shrinking Chinese market. The committee persuaded the nation's chambers of commerce to petition the McKinley administration to act. And the State Department soon reported that, given overproduction for the home market, "the United States has important interests at stake in the partition of commercial facilities in regions which are likely to offer developing markets for its goods. Nowhere is this consideration of more interest than in its relation to the Chinese Empire."

In 1899, Secretary of State John Hay asked the imperial powers to maintain an **Open Door** for the commercial and financial activities of all nations within their Chinese spheres of influence. Privately, Hay had already approved a plan to seize a Chinese port for the United States if necessary to join in the partition of China, but equal opportunity for trade and investment would serve American interests far better. It would avoid the expense of military occupation, avert further domestic criticism of U.S. imperialism, and guarantee a wider sphere for American business.

The other nations replied evasively, except for Russia, which rejected the Open Door concept. In 1900, an antiforeign Chinese nationalist movement known as the Boxers laid siege to the diplomatic quarters in Beijing. The defeat of the Boxer Rebellion by a multinational military force, to which the United States contributed troops, again raised the prospect of a division of China among colonial powers. Hay sent a second Open Door note, reaffirming "the principle of equal and impartial trade" and respect for China's territorial integrity.

The Open Door became a cardinal doctrine of American foreign policy in the twentieth century. The United States promoted an informal or economic empire, as opposed to the traditional territorial colonial empire that Americans preferred to identify with European powers. Henceforth, American economic interests expected the U.S. government to oppose any developments that threatened to close other nations' economies to American penetration and to advance "private enterprise" abroad.

RIVALRY WITH JAPAN AND RUSSIA

At the turn of the twentieth century, both the Japanese and the Russians were more deeply involved in East Asia than the United States was. They expressed little support for the Open Door, which they correctly saw as favoring American interests over their own. But in pursuing their ambitions in China, the two came into conflict with each other. Japan in 1904 attacked the Russian fleet at Port Arthur and defeated the Russians in Manchuria.

In this Russo-Japanese war, American sympathies lay with Japan, for the Russians were attempting to close Manchuria to foreign trade. President Theodore Roosevelt thus welcomed the Japanese attack in the belief that "Japan is playing our game." But he soon feared that an overwhelming Japanese victory could threaten American interests as much as Russian expansionism did, so he skillfully mediated an end to the war. In the Treaty of Portsmouth in 1905, Japan won control of Russia's sphere of influence in Manchuria, half the Russian island of Sakhalin, and recognition of its domination of Korea.

This treaty marked Japan's emergence as a great power, but ironically, it worsened relations with the United States. Anti-American riots broke out in Tokyo. The Japanese people blamed Roosevelt for obstructing further Japanese gains. Tensions were then aggravated by San Francisco's decision in 1906 to segregate

Open Door American policy of seeking equal trade and investment opportunities in foreign nations or regions.

Asian schoolchildren to avoid affecting the "youthful impressions" of white children. Japan regarded this as a racist insult, and Roosevelt worried that "the infernal fools in California" would provoke war. Finally he got the school order rescinded in exchange for his limiting Japanese immigration. Under the **Gentlemen's Agreement**, Japan agreed not to issue passports to workers coming to the United States, and the United States promised not to prohibit Japanese immigration overtly or completely.

To calm their mutual suspicions in East Asia, the United States and Japan adopted other agreements but failed to halt the deteriorating relationship. Increasingly, Japan began to exclude American trade from its territories in East Asia and to press for further control over China. Elihu Root, Roosevelt's secretary of state, insisted that the Open Door and American access be maintained but asserted also that the United States did not want to be "a protagonist in a controversy in China with Russia and Japan or with either of them." This paradox would plague American foreign policy in Asia for decades.

Gentlemen's Agreement A diplomatic agreement in 1907 between Japan and the United States curtailing but not abolishing Japanese immigration.

IMPERIAL POWER: THE UNITED STATES AND LATIN AMERICA, 1899–1917

In Latin America, where no major powers directly challenged American objectives, the United States was more successful in exercising imperial power (see Map 22–3). In the two decades after the Spanish-American War, the United States intervened militarily in Latin America no fewer than twenty times to promote its own strategic and economic interests. Policymakers believed that these goals required restricting the influence of European nations in the region, building an isthmian canal under American control, and establishing the order thought necessary for American trade and investments to expand. Intervention at times achieved these goals, but it often ignored the wishes and interests of Latin Americans, provoked resistance and disorder, and created lasting ill will.

WHAT WAS at stake for the United States in Puerto Rico, Cuba, and Panama?

U.S. RULE IN PUERTO RICO

Well before 1898, expansionists like James G. Blaine had advocated acquiring Puerto Rico because of its strategic location in the Caribbean. During the Spanish-American War, Roosevelt urged Washington, "Do not make peace until we get" Puerto Rico. Military invasion and the Treaty of Paris soon brought the island under American rule.

In 1900, the United States established a civil government, but it was under U.S. control, and popular participation was even less than under Spain. In the so-called *Insular Cases* (1901), the Supreme Court upheld Congress's authority to establish an inferior status for Puerto Rico, as an "unincorporated territory" without promise of statehood. Disappointed Puerto Ricans pressed to end this colonial status. In 1917, the United States granted citizenship and greater political rights to Puerto Ricans, but their island remained an unincorporated territory under an American governor appointed by the president.

Economic development also disappointed most islanders, for American investors quickly gained control of the best land and pursued large-scale sugar production for the U.S. market. By 1929, the new governor—ironically, Theodore Roosevelt Jr.—found that under the domination of American capital, "poverty was wide spread and hunger, almost to the verge of starvation, common." A subsequent investigation concluded that while "the influx of capital has increased the efficiency of production and promoted general economic development," the benefits had gone largely to Americans, not ordinary Puerto Ricans, whose conditions were "deplorable." Increasingly, they left their homes to seek work in the United States.

MAP EXPLORATION

To explore an interactive version of this map, go to **http://www.prenhall.com/goldfield2/map22.3**

MAP 22–3

The United States in the Caribbean For strategic and economic reasons, the United States repeatedly intervened in the Caribbean in the first three decades of the twentieth century. Such interventions protected the U.S. claim to dominance but often provoked great hostility among Latin Americans.

WHAT WERE the arguments for and against the repeated United States interventions in the Caribbean?

CUBA AS A U.S. PROTECTORATE

Despite the Teller Amendment, the Spanish-American War did not leave Cuba independent. McKinley opposed independence and a U.S. military government was established in the island. Only in 1900, when the Democrats made an issue of imperialism, did McKinley summon a Cuban convention to draft a constitution under the direction of the American military governor, General Leonard Wood. This constitution restricted suffrage on the basis of property and education, leaving few Cubans with the right to vote.

The United States made troop withdrawal contingent on Cuba's adding to its constitution the provisions of the **Platt Amendment**, which restricted Cuba's autonomy in diplomatic relations with other countries and in internal financial policies, required Cuba to lease naval bases to the United States, and, most important, authorized U.S. intervention to maintain order and preserve Cuban

Platt Amendment A stipulation the United States had inserted into the Cuban constitution in 1901 restricting Cuban autonomy and authorizing U.S. intervention and naval bases.

independence. As General Wood correctly observed, "There is, of course, little or no independence left Cuba under the Platt Amendment."

Cubans quickly learned that fact when the United States prevented Cuba from extending the same trade privileges to the British that U.S. merchants enjoyed. The Open Door would not apply in the Caribbean, which was to be an American sphere of influence. To preserve that influence, the United States sent troops into Cuba three times between 1906 and 1917 (Roosevelt admitted his recurrent itch to "wipe its people off the face of the earth"). The last occupation lasted six years.

During their occupations of Cuba, the Americans modernized its financial system, built roads and public schools, and developed a public health and sanitation program that eradicated the deadly disease of yellow fever. But most Cubans thought these material benefits did not compensate for their loss of political and economic independence.

THE PANAMA CANAL

The Spanish-American War intensified the long American interest in a canal through Central America to eliminate the lengthy and dangerous ocean route around South America. Its commercial value seemed obvious, but the war emphasized its strategic importance. McKinley declared that a canal was now "demanded by the annexation of the Hawaiian Islands and the prospective expansion of our influence and commerce in the Pacific."

Theodore Roosevelt moved quickly to implement McKinley's commitment to a canal after becoming president in 1901. His canal diplomacy helped establish the assertive presidency that has characterized U.S. foreign policy in the twentieth century.

Possible canal sites included Nicaragua and Panama, then part of Colombia. A canal through Panama would require an elaborate system of locks. But the French-owned Panama Canal Company had been unsuccessfully trying to build a canal in Panama and was now eager to sell its rights to the project before they expired in 1904.

In 1902, Congress directed Roosevelt to purchase the French company's claims for $40 million and build the canal in Panama if Colombia ceded a strip of land across the isthmus on reasonable terms. Otherwise, Roosevelt was to negotiate with Nicaragua for the alternate route. In 1903, Roosevelt pressed Colombia to sell a canal zone to the United States for $10 million and an annual payment of $250,000. Colombia, however, rejected the proposal, fearing the loss of its sovereignty in Panama and hoping for more money. After all, when the Panama Canal Company's rights expired, Colombia could then legitimately collect the $40 million so generously offered the company.

Roosevelt warned "those contemptible little creatures" in Colombia that they were "imperiling their own future." Instead of using direct force Roosevelt worked with Philippe Bunau-Varilla, a French official of the Panama Canal Company, to exploit long-smoldering Panamanian discontent with Colombia. Roosevelt's purpose was to get the canal zone, Bunau-Varilla's to get the American money. Roosevelt ordered U.S. naval forces to Panama; from New York, Bunau-Varilla coordinated a revolt against Colombian authority directed by officials of the Panama Railroad, owned by Bunau-Varilla's canal company. The bloodless "revolution" succeeded when U.S. forces prevented Colombian troops from landing in Panama, although the United States was bound by treaty to maintain Colombian sovereignty. Bunau-Varilla promptly signed a treaty accepting Roosevelt's original terms for a canal zone and making Panama a U.S. protectorate. Panamanians themselves denounced the treaty for surrendering sovereignty in the zone to the United States, which took formal control of the canal zone in 1904 and completed construction of the Panama Canal in 1914.

Many Americans were appalled by what the *Chicago American* called Roosevelt's "rough-riding assault upon another republic over the shattered wreckage of international law and diplomatic usage." But others, as *Public Opinion* reported, wanted a

20–6
Theodore Roosevelt, Third Annual Message to Congress (1903)

QUICK REVIEW

Acquisition of the Canal Zone
- Possible canal sites were located in Nicaragua and Panama (then part of Colombia).
- 1903: Colombia rejects Roosevelt's offer to purchase canal zone in Panama.
- 1903–1904: U.S. forces support Panamanian rebellion against Colombia and take control of canal zone.

"canal above all things" and were willing to overlook moral questions and approve the acquisition of the canal zone as simply "a business question." Roosevelt himself boasted, "I took the Canal Zone and let Congress debate," but his unnecessary and arrogant actions generated resentment among Latin Americans that rankled for decades.

THE ROOSEVELT COROLLARY

To protect the security of the canal, the United States increased its authority in the Caribbean. The objective was to establish conditions there that would both eliminate any pretext for European intervention and promote American control over trade and investment. "If we intend to say hands off to the powers of Europe," Roosevelt concluded, "then sooner or later we must keep order ourselves."

In his 1904 annual message to Congress, Roosevelt announced a new policy, the so-called **Roosevelt Corollary** to the Monroe Doctrine. "Chronic wrongdoing," he declared, would cause the United States to exercise "an international police power" in Latin America. The Monroe Doctrine had expressed American hostility to European intervention in Latin America; the Roosevelt Corollary attempted to justify U.S. intervention and authority in the region. Roosevelt invoked his corollary immediately, imposing American management of the debts and customs duties of the Dominican Republic in 1905. Financial insolvency was averted, popular revolution prevented, and possible European intervention forestalled.

Latin Americans vigorously resented the United States' unilateral claims to authority. By 1907, the so-called Drago Doctrine (named after Argentina's foreign minister) was incorporated into international law, prohibiting armed intervention to collect debts. Still, the United States would continue to invoke the Roosevelt Corollary to advance its interests in the hemisphere. As Secretary of State Elihu Root asserted, "The inevitable effect of our building the Canal must be to require us to police the surrounding premises." He then added, "In the nature of things, trade and control, and the obligation to keep order which go with them, must come our way."

DOLLAR DIPLOMACY

Roosevelt's successor as president, William Howard Taft, hoped to promote U.S. interests without such combative rhetoric and naked force. He described his plan as one of "substituting dollars for bullets"—using government action to encourage private American investments in Latin America to supplant European interests, promote development and stability, and gain profits for American bankers. Under this **dollar diplomacy**, American investments in the Caribbean increased dramatically during Taft's presidency from 1909 to 1913, and the State Department helped arrange for American bankers to establish financial control over Haiti and Honduras.

But Taft employed military force more frequently than Roosevelt had, with Nicaragua a major target. In 1909, Taft sent U.S. troops there to aid a revolution fomented by an American mining corporation and to seize the Nicaraguan customs houses. Under the new government, American bankers then gained control of Nicaragua's national bank, railroad, and customs service. To protect these arrangements, U.S. troops were again dispatched in 1912. To control popular opposition to the American client government, the marines remained in Nicaragua for two decades. Military power, not the social and economic improvement promised by dollar diplomacy, kept Nicaragua's minority government stable and subordinate to the United States.

Dollar diplomacy increased American power and influence in the Caribbean and tied underdeveloped countries to the United States economically and strategically, but this policy failed to improve conditions for most Latin Americans. U.S. officials remained primarily concerned with promoting American control and extracting American profits from the region, not with the well-being of its population. Not surprisingly, dollar diplomacy proved unpopular in Latin America.

Roosevelt Corollary   President Theodore Roosevelt's policy asserting U.S. authority to intervene in the affairs of Latin American nations; an expansion of the Monroe Doctrine.

Dollar diplomacy   The U.S. policy of using private investment in other nations to promote American diplomatic goals and business interests.

WILSONIAN INTERVENTIONS

Taking office in 1913, the Democrat Woodrow Wilson promised that the United States would "never again seek one additional foot of territory by conquest" but would instead work to promote "human rights, national integrity, and opportunity" in Latin America. Wilson also named as his secretary of state the Democratic symbol of anti-imperialism, William Jennings Bryan. Their generous intentions were apparent when Bryan signed a treaty with Colombia apologizing for Roosevelt's seizure of the Panama Canal Zone in 1903.

Nonetheless, Wilson believed that the United States had to expand its exports and investments abroad and that U.S. dominance of the Caribbean was strategically necessary. He also shared the racist belief that Latin Americans were inferior and needed paternalistic guidance from the United States, through military force if necessary. His self-righteousness and determination to transform other peoples' behavior led his policies to be dubbed "missionary diplomacy," but they also contained elements of Roosevelt's commitment to military force and Taft's reliance on economic power.

In 1915, Wilson ordered U.S. Marines to Haiti. The U.S. Navy selected a new Haitian president, but real authority rested with the American military, which controlled Haiti until 1934, protecting the small elite who cooperated with foreign interests and exploited their own people. As usual, American military rule improved the country's transportation, sanitation, and educational systems, but the forced-labor program that the U.S. adopted to build such public works provoked widespread resentment. In 1919, marines suppressed a revolt against American domination, killing more than three thousand Haitians.

Wilson also intervened elsewhere in the Caribbean. In 1916, when the Dominican Republic refused to cede control of its finances to U.S. bankers, Wilson ordered the marines to occupy the country. The marines ousted Dominican officials, installed a military government to rule "on behalf of the Dominican government," and ran the nation until 1924. In 1917, the United States intervened in Cuba, which remained under American control until 1922.

Wilson also involved himself in the internal affairs of Mexico. In 1913, General Victoriano Huerta seized control of the country from revolutionaries who had recently overthrown dictator Porfirio Diaz. Wilson was appalled by the violence of Huerta's power grab and was aware that opponents had organized to reestablish constitutional government.

Wilson hoped to bring the Constitutionalists to power and "to secure Mexico a better government under which all contracts and business and concessions will be safer than they have been." He authorized arms sales to their forces, led by Venustiano Carranza; pressured Britain and other nations to deprive Huerta of foreign support; and blockaded the Mexican port of Vera Cruz. In April 1914 Wilson exploited a minor incident to have the marines attack and occupy Vera Cruz. Even Carranza and the Constitutionalists denounced the American occupation as unwarranted aggression. By August, Carranza had toppled Huerta, and Wilson shifted his support to Francisco ("Pancho") Villa. But Carranza's growing popular support in Mexico and Wilson's preoccupation with World War I in Europe finally led the United States to grant de facto recognition to the Carranza government in October 1915.

Villa then began terrorizing New Mexico and Texas, hoping to provoke an American intervention that would undermine Carranza. In 1916, Wilson ordered troops under General John J. Pershing to pursue Villa into Mexico, leading Carranza to fear a permanent U.S. occupation of northern Mexico. Soon the American soldiers were fighting the Mexican army rather than Villa's bandits. On the brink of full-fledged war, Wilson finally ordered U.S. troops to withdraw in January 1917 and extended full recognition to the Carranza government. His aggressive tactics had not merely failed but had also embittered relations with Mexico.

CONCLUSION

By the time of Woodrow Wilson's presidency, the United States had been expanding its involvement in world affairs for half a century. Several themes had emerged from this activity: increasing American domination of the Caribbean, continuing interest in East Asia, the creation of an overseas empire, and the evolution of the United States into a major world power. Underlying these developments was an uneasy mixture of ideas and objectives. The American involvement in the world reflected a traditional, if often misguided, sense of national rectitude and mission. Generous humanitarian impulses vied with ugly racist prejudices as Americans sought both to help other peoples and to direct them toward U.S. concepts of religion, sanitation, capitalist development, and public institutions. American motives ranged from ensuring national security and competing with European colonial powers to the conviction that the United States had to expand its economic interests abroad. But if imperialism, both informal and at times colonial, brought Americans greater wealth and power, it also increased tensions in Asia and contributed to anti-American hostility and revolutionary ferment in Latin America. It also entangled the United States in the Great Power rivalries that would ultimately result in two world wars.

SUMMARY

The Roots of Imperialism The United States had a long tradition of expansion across the continent; now America embarked on building an overseas empire. Some Americans favored acquiring and exploiting colonies; others wanted an empire based on trade and investments; still others advocated the United States exporting its ideas and institutions. Social Darwinism, Protestant evangelism, and naval expansion were all rationales for America becoming a world power.

First Steps Despite the growing pro-imperialist arguments, America was generally passive toward foreign affairs until the end of the nineteenth century. The purchase of Alaska from Russia, the growing American commercial influence in Hawaii, and the assertion of hemispheric domination in Latin America demonstrated America's increasingly assertive national policy throughout the late 1800s.

The Spanish-American War The war originated in Cuba's quest for independence from Spain. Spain's brutality in suppressing the revolt prompted American sympathy; the sensationalist yellow press fanned the flames for war. The Spanish-American War made America an imperialist nation; the Battle of Manila Bay gave America a foothold in the Philippines; Hawaii was annexed as part of America's "Manifest Destiny"; and a short campaign in Cuba resulted in the defeat of Spanish troops there. The Treaty of Paris gave America Puerto Rico and Guam and set the stage for the acquisition of the Philippines; anti-imperialists questioned national goals and America's commitment to liberty and freedom.

Imperial Ambitions: The United States and East Asia, 1899–1917 The Filipino-American War resulted from the betrayed hope of the Filipino people for independence following the Treaty of Paris. A brutal war fought to put down rebellion resulted in America's establishing a colonial government in the Philippines. America's involvement in the Philippines reflected its interest in China; European nations and Japan claimed areas of influence in China, limiting America's options to develop trade. Involvement in China brought the United States into conflict with Japan and Russia; Japan's emergence as a great power saw growing discord between the two countries.

Imperial Power: The United States and Latin America, 1899–1917 Following the Spanish-American War, America often intervened in Latin America to promote its own strategic and economic interests; trade expanded and ill will increased. Puerto

Rico became unincorporated, Cuba, a U.S. protectorate, and land in Panama was acquired to build a canal; each was part in America's exercise of imperial power. President Theodore Roosevelt's Corollary to the Monroe Doctrine announced America's role as a policeman and debt collector; President Taft attempted dollar diplomacy; President Wilson intervened in the Caribbean, and his tactics in Mexico created lasting ill will.

REVIEW QUESTIONS

1. What were the roots of American imperialism in the late nineteenth century?

2. What factors shaped American foreign policy in the late nineteenth century?

3. Was the United States' emergence as an imperial power a break from a culmination of its earlier policies and national development?

4. What were the objectives and consequences of U.S. interventions in Latin America?

KEY TERMS

Dollar diplomacy   (p. 598)
Gentlemen's Agreement   (p. 595)
Imperialism   (p. 581)
Mahanism   (p. 583)

Monroe Doctrine   (p. 587)
Open Door   (p. 594)
Platt Amendment   (p. 596)
Roosevelt Corollary   (p. 598)

Spheres of Influence   (p. 593)
Teller Amendment   (p. 590)
Yellow press   (p. 589)

WHERE TO LEARN MORE

Mission Houses, Honolulu, Hawaii. Built between 1821 and 1841, these buildings were homes and shops of missionaries sent to Hawaii by the American Board of Commissioners for Foreign Missions. Their exhibits include furnishings and memorabilia of a group important in developing American ties with Hawaii. **www.missionhouses.org/**

Funston Memorial Home, Iola, Kansas. Operated as a museum by the Kansas State Historical Society, this is the boyhood home of General Frederick Funston, prominent in the Spanish-American War and the Filipino-American War. For a virtual tour, together with military information, political cartoons, Roosevelt correspondence, and Funston links, see **http://skyways.lib.ks.us/museums/funston/**

James G. Blaine House, Augusta, Maine. The Executive Mansion of Maine's governor since 1919, this house was formerly Blaine's home and still contains his study and furnishings from the time he served as secretary of state and U.S. senator.

Rough Riders Memorial and City Museum, Las Vegas, Nevada. Together with the nearby Castaneda Hotel, this site provides intriguing information on Roosevelt's volunteer cavalry, recruited primarily from the Southwest. **www.arco-iris.com/teddy/index.htm**

Seward House, Auburn, New York. The home of William H. Seward contains furniture and mementos from his career as secretary of state.

 For additional study resources for this chapter, go to:
www.prenhall.com/goldfield/chapter22

On the other hand, if there is little enthusiasm, the people everywhere are taking the war as a grim necessity, feeling that they have been forced into it by events beyond their control . . .

Female workers build a vehicle in an engineering shop in 1917.

23

AMERICA AND THE GREAT WAR
1914–1920

HOW WAS U.S. neutrality
during World War I undermined?

WHY DID the United States join
the conflict on the side of the Allies?

HOW DID the war effort
threaten civil liberties?

WHAT WERE the terms of the Treaty of Versailles?

WHAT WAS the post-war backlash?

I have been traveling for nearly three weeks through six Middle Western States, talking about the war, with all classes of people: farmers, labor leaders, newspaper editors, college professors, business men, and state officials. I have been trying to get at the bedrock sentiment of the people regarding it, and to set it down exactly as I find it.

Almost without exception, even among those who favor the war most vigorously, the people I have talked with have commented upon the lack of popular enthusiasm for the war. The more closely these people were connected with the farmers or the workingmen, the more sweeping and positive were their statements.

The attitude of the people is wholly different from what it was at the opening of our Spanish War in 1898. There are no heroic slogans, no boastfulness, no excitement, no glamour of war. There is still a great deal of haziness about the real issues and a great deal of doubt about how far America should go beyond mere defensive measures. One of the foremost political leaders of the West, himself an ardent supporter of the war, told me that if a secret ballot were taken as to whether American armies should be sent to France, the vote would be overwhelmingly against it. It is noteworthy, also, that the newspapers are full of a-b-c explanations of the reasons why we are at war and why we should go forward with it. . . . And finally, there are nowhere as yet any evidences of the passions and the hatred which war engenders. People do not hate Germans or Austrians or Turks; nor do they love the British.

On the other hand, if there is little enthusiasm, the people everywhere are taking the war as a grim necessity, feeling that they have been forced into it by events beyond their control, and they are going forward, more or less reluctantly, with the preparations; but they are really going forward. The draft was not popular; people wished it might have been done in some other way; and in some groups of population it was hated and feared, and yet, through all this country, there has been a wonderful and complete compliance with the law. In the same way the liberty loan is not popular. There is no popular rush to subscribe, and it has required an enormous amount of organization, advertising, and pressure to sell the bonds, and yet they are being sold and will be sold. . . . And there have been no signs of any popular rush to enlist, and men have been obtained only by dint of the most vigorous advertising and pressure. It is significant also that more than half of those registered in Chicago are demanding exemption.

The only real enthusiasm that I could find was in such campaigns as that of the Red Cross, the Y.M.C.A., and here and there in work for the American Ambulance in France. The work of women everywhere for the Red Cross is remarkably organized and well supported. . . . Of the value of these activities, no matter what happens, the people are convinced.

This is as nearly a true statement of the general situation as I can make. I have met a good many men who think that this state of the popular mind, this deliberate and passionless method of doing what is regarded as a disagreeable duty, is the best possible method of getting into the great war. . . .

IMAGE KEY
for pages 602–603

a. British Prime Minister Lloyd George, French Prime Minister George Clemenceau, and U.S. President Wilson in Versailles, Paris in 1919.

b. Women war workers working in an engineering shop, 1917.

c. The New York Times front page reports the sinking of the Lusitania in 1915.

d. British Biplane shot down

e. "Beat back the HUN:" American World War I Liberty Loan poster.

f. Women draft protesters demonstrate in front of New York's City Hall on June 16, 1917.

g. A policeman on horseback swings a truncheon at strikers on a Pittsburgh street.

On the other hand, I met a good many people, especially among the leaders of war organizations of various sorts, to whom the popular attitude is not only irritating but dangerous. They feel that the people are not fully awakened to the emergency, that they do not realize that the country is really at this moment at war, and that unless America meets with more enthusiasm and more speed the problems of raising money, producing food, and hurrying the training of men for armies in France the war may result in disaster.

Ray Stannard Baker, "West in Grim Business of War Without Passion," *St. Louis Post–Dispatch,* June 17, 1917.

RAY STANNARD BAKER, the famous journalist, thus described his journey across the Midwest in 1917, three years after World War I began in Europe and two months after the United States had declared war on Germany. The American people were reluctant participants, unconvinced that national interests were really involved.

But as Baker discovered, the nation's leaders were determined to whip up support for the war through "organization, advertising, and pressure." The goal would be not only to train soldiers but also to demonize Germany, mobilize the economy, and transform American social attitudes.

The Great War changed American life. Government authority increased sharply. Business, labor unions, farmers, ministers were all incorporated into the war effort. Women's organizational activities expanded dramatically; and often developed in unexpected ways. Journalists, too, put their skills to new and sometimes unfortunate uses; Baker, who had initially opposed the war, eventually went to Europe to file confidential reports for the State Department and then to control news at the Versailles Peace Conference.

Many of the changes in American life, from increased efficiency to Americanization, often reflected prewar progressivism, and the war years did promote some reforms. But the war also diverted reform energies into new channels, encouraged coercion impulses ("the passions and the hatred" which Baker found lacking in mid-1917 were soon widespread), and strengthened the conservative opposition to reform. The results were often reactionary and contributed to a postwar mood that curtailed further reform and helped defeat the peace treaty upon which so much had been gambled.

WAGING NEUTRALITY

With near unanimity, Americans supported neutrality when the Great War erupted in Europe in 1914. But American attitudes, decisions, and actions, both public and private, undercut neutrality, and the policies of governments in Berlin, London, and Washington drew the United States into the war.

HOW WAS U.S. neutrality during World War I undermined?

THE ORIGINS OF CONFLICT

Since the 1870s, the competing imperial ambitions of the great European powers had led to economic rivalries, military expansion, diplomatic maneuvering, and international tensions. In central Europe, the expansionist Germany of Kaiser Wilhelm II allied itself with the multinational Austro-Hungarian Empire. Confronting them, Great Britain and France formed alliances with Tsarist

Russia. Observing this precarious balance of power in May 1914, an American diplomat reported anxiously, "There is too much hatred, too many jealousies." He predicted "an awful cataclysm."

On June 28, a Serbian terrorist assassinated Archduke Franz Ferdinand, the heir to the Austro-Hungarian throne. With Germany's support, Austria declared war on Serbia on July 28. Russia then mobilized its army against Austria to aid Serbia, its Slavic client state. To assist Austria, Germany declared war on Russia and then on Russia's ally France. Hoping for a quick victory, Germany struck at France through neutral Belgium; in response, Britain declared war on Germany on August 4. Soon Turkey and Bulgaria joined Germany and Austria to form the **Central Powers**. The **Allies**—Britain, France, and Russia—were joined by Italy and Japan. Britain drew on its empire for resources, using troops from India, Canada, Australia, New Zealand, and South Africa. The war had become a global conflict, waged not only in Europe but also in Africa, the Middle East, and East Asia.

Mass slaughter enveloped Europe as huge armies battled to a stalemate. The British and French faced the Germans along a line of trenches stretching across France and Belgium from the English Channel to Switzerland. The British once suffered 300,000 casualties in an offensive that gained only a few square miles before being pushed back. Machine gunners went into shock at the carnage they inflicted. In the trenches, soldiers suffered in the cold and mud, surrounded by decaying bodies and human waste, enduring lice, rats, and nightmares, and dying from disease and exhaustion. The Great War, said one German soldier, had become "the grave of nations."

AMERICAN ATTITUDES

Few Americans had expected this calamity. As one North Carolina congressman said, "This dreadful conflict of the nations came to most of us as lightning out of a clear sky." Most people believed that the United States had no vital interest in the war and would not become involved. "Our isolated position and freedom from entangling alliances," noted the *Literary Digest*, "inspire our press with the cheering assurance that we are in no peril of being drawn into the European quarrel." President Wilson issued a proclamation of neutrality and urged Americans to be "neutral in fact as well as in name . . . impartial in thought as well as in action."

However, ethnic, cultural, and economic ties bound most Americans to the British and French. Politically, too, most Americans felt a greater affinity for the democratic Western Allies. And whereas Britain and the United States had enjoyed a rapprochement since 1895, Germany had repeatedly appeared as a potential rival.

Wilson himself admired Britain's culture and government and distrusted Germany's imperial ambitions. Like other influential Americans, Wilson believed that a German victory would threaten America's economic, political, and perhaps even strategic interests. "England is fighting our fight," he said privately. Secretary of State William Jennings Bryan was genuinely neutral, but most officials favored the Allies. Early in the war, Colonel Edward House, Wilson's closest adviser on foreign affairs, wrote: "I cannot see how there can be any serious trouble between England and America, with all of us feeling as we do."

British writers, artists, and lecturers depicted the Allies as fighting for civilization against a brutal Germany that mutilated nuns and babies, shaping America's view of the conflict. Britain also cut the only German cable to the United States and censored war news to suit itself. German propaganda directed at American opinion proved ineffectual.

Sympathy for the Allies, however, did not mean that Americans favored intervention. The British ambassador complained that it was "useless" to expect any

Central Powers Germany and its World War I allies in Austria, Turkey, and Bulgaria.

Allies In World War I, Britain, France, Russia, and other belligerent nations fighting against the Central Powers but not including the United States.

"practical" advantage from the Americans' sympathy, for they had no intention of joining the conflict. Wilson was determined to pursue peace as long as his view of national interests allowed.

THE ECONOMY OF WAR

International law permitted neutral nations to sell or ship war material to all belligerents, and with the economy mired in a recession when the war began, many Americans looked to war orders to spur economic recovery. But the British navy prevented trade with the Central Powers. Only the Allies could buy American goods. Their orders for steel, explosives, uniforms, wheat, and other products, however, pulled the country out of the recession. One journalist rejoiced that "war, for Europe, is meaning devastation and death; for America a bumper crop of new millionaires and a hectic hastening of prosperity revival."

President Woodrow Wilson reads his war message to Congress, April 2, 1917. He predicted "many months of fiery trial and sacrifice ahead of us."

Library of Congress

Other Americans worried that this one-sided war trade undermined genuine neutrality. Congress even considered embargoing munitions. But few Americans supported that idea. One financial journal declared of the Allied war trade: "We need it for the profits which it yields." The German ambassador noted that American industry was "actually delivering goods only to the enemies of Germany."

A second economic issue complicated matters. To finance their war purchases, the Allies borrowed from American bankers. Initially, Secretary of State Bryan persuaded Wilson to prohibit loans to the belligerents as "inconsistent with the true spirit of neutrality." But Wilson soon ended the ban. Secretary of the Treasury William McAdoo argued that it would be "disastrous" *not* to finance the Allies' purchases, on which "our prosperity is dependent." By April 1917, American loans to the Allies exceeded $2 billion, nearly one hundred times the amount lent to Germany. These financial ties, like the war trade they underwrote, linked the United States to the Allies and convinced Germany that American neutrality was only a formality.

THE DIPLOMACY OF NEUTRALITY

This same imbalance characterized American diplomacy. Wilson acquiesced in British violations of American neutral rights while sternly refusing to yield on German actions. Wilson argued that while British violations of international law cost Americans property, markets, and time, German violations cost lives. As the *Boston Globe* noted, the British were "a gang of thieves" and the Germans "a gang of murderers. On the whole, we prefer the thieves, but only as the lesser of two evils."

When the war began, the United States asked belligerents to respect the 1909 **Declaration of London** on neutral rights. Germany agreed to do so; the British refused. Instead, Britain instituted a blockade of Germany, mined the North Sea, and forced neutral ships into British ports to search their cargoes and confiscate material deemed useful to the German war effort. Wilson branded Britain's blockade illegal and unwarranted, but by October he had conceded many of America's neutral rights to avoid conflict with Britain.

Declaration of London Statement drafted by an international conference in 1909 to clarify international law and specify the rights of neutral nations.

CHRONOLOGY

1914	World War I begins in Europe. President Woodrow Wilson declares U.S. neutrality.
1915	Germany begins submarine warfare. *Lusitania* is sunk. Woman's Peace Party is organized.
1916	Gore-McLemore resolutions are defeated. *Sussex* Pledge is issued. Preparedness legislation is enacted. Woodrow Wilson is reelected president.
1917	Germany resumes unrestricted submarine warfare. The United States declares war on Germany. Selective Service Act establishes the military draft. Espionage Act is passed. Committee on Public Information, War Industries Board, Food Administration, and other mobilization agencies are established. American Expeditionary Force arrives in France. East St. Louis race riot erupts. Bolshevik Revolution occurs in Russia.
1918	Wilson announces his Fourteen Points. Sedition Act is passed. Eugene Debs is imprisoned. The United States intervenes militarily in Russia. Armistice ends World War I.
1919	Paris Peace Conference is held. Steel, coal, and other strikes occur. Red Scare breaks out. Prohibition amendment is adopted. Wilson suffers a massive stroke.
1920	Palmer Raids round up radicals. League of Nations is defeated in the U.S. Senate. Woman suffrage amendment is ratified. U.S. troops are withdrawn from Russia. Warren Harding is elected president.
1921	United States signs a separate peace treaty with Germany.

The British then prohibited food and other products that Germany had imported during peace-time, thereby interfering further with neutral shipping. One American official complained privately: "England is playing a . . . high game, violating international law every day." But when the Wilson administration finally protested, it undermined its own position by noting that "imperative necessity" might justify a violation of international law. In January 1915, Wilson yielded further by observing that "no very important questions of principle" were involved in the Anglo-American quarrels over ship seizures and that they could be resolved after the war.

This policy tied the United States to the British war effort and provoked a German response. Germany decided in February 1915 to use its submarines against Allied shipping in a war zone around the British Isles. Germany maintained that Britain's blockade and the acquiescence of neutral countries in British violations of international law made submarine warfare necessary.

Submarines could not readily follow traditional rules of naval warfare. Small and fragile, they depended on surprise attacks. They could not surface to identify themselves, as the rules mandated, without risking disaster from the deck guns of Britain's armed merchant ships, and they were too small to rescue victims of their sinkings. Yet Wilson refused to see the "imperative necessity" in German tactics that he found in British tactics, and he warned that he would hold Germany responsible for any loss of American lives or property.

In May 1915, a German submarine sank a British passenger liner, the *Lusitania*. It had been carrying arms, and the German embassy had warned Americans against traveling on the ship, but the loss of life—1,198 people, including 128 Americans—caused Americans to condemn Germany. "To speak of technicalities and the rules of war, in the face of such wholesale murder on the high seas, is a waste of time," trumpeted one magazine. Wilson saw he had to "carry out the double wish of our people, to maintain a firm front in respect of what we demand of Germany and yet do nothing that might by any possibility involve us in the war."

Wilson demanded that Germany abandon its submarine campaign. But his language was so harsh that Bryan resigned, warning that by requiring more of

QUICK REVIEW

Anglo-American Ties

- 1915: U.S. give tacit support to British naval blockade of Germany.
- May 1915: German submarine sinks the *Lusitahia*.
- Americans demanded a tough stand against Germany, but did not want to be drawn into the war.

Germany than of Britain, the president violated neutrality and threatened to draw the nation into war. Bryan proposed prohibiting Americans from traveling on belligerent ships. His proposal gained support in the South and West, and Senator Thomas Gore of Oklahoma and Representative Jeff McLemore of Texas introduced it in congressional resolutions in February 1916.

Wilson moved to defeat the Gore-McLemore resolutions, insisting that they impinged on presidential control of foreign policy and on America's neutral rights. In truth, the resolutions abandoned no vital national interest while offering to prevent another provocative incident. Moreover, neither law nor tradition gave Americans the right to travel safely on belligerent ships. Of the nation's "double wish," then, Wilson placed more priority on confronting what he saw as the German threat than on meeting the popular desire for peace.

In April 1916, a German submarine torpedoed the French ship *Sussex*, injuring four Americans. Wilson threatened to break diplomatic relations if Germany did not abandon unrestricted submarine warfare against all merchant vessels. This implied war. Germany promised not to sink merchant ships without warning but made its *Sussex* **Pledge** contingent on the United States' requiring Britain also to adhere to "the rules of international law universally recognized before the war." Wilson's diplomatic victory, then, was hollow. Peace for America would depend on the British adopting a course they rejected. As Wilson saw it, however, "any little German lieutenant can put us into the war at any time by some calculated outrage." Wilson's diplomacy had left the nation's future at the mercy of others.

THE BATTLE OVER PREPAREDNESS

The threat of war sparked a debate over military policy. Theodore Roosevelt and a handful of other politicians, mostly Northeastern Republicans convinced that Allied victory was in the national interest, had advocated what they called **preparedness**, a program to expand the armed forces and establish universal military training. Conservative business groups also joined the agitation, combining demands for preparedness with attacks on progressive reforms.

But most Americans opposed expensive military preparations. Leading feminists like Jane Addams, Charlotte Perkins Gilman, and Carrie Chapman Catt formed the Woman's Peace Party in 1915, and other organizations like the American League to Limit Armaments also campaigned against preparedness. William Jennings Bryan denounced the militarism of Roosevelt as a "philosophy [that] can rot a soul" and condemned preparedness as a program for turning the nation into "a vast armory with skull and cross-bones above the door."

Wilson also opposed preparedness initially, but he reversed his position when the submarine crisis with Germany intensified. In early 1916, an election year, he made a speaking tour to generate public support for expanding the armed forces. Congress soon passed the National Defense Act and the Naval Construction Act, increasing the strength of the army and authorizing a naval construction plan.

THE ELECTION OF 1916

Wilson's preparedness plans stripped the Republicans of one issue in 1916, and his renewed support of progressive reforms helped hold Bryan Democrats in line. The slogan "He Kept Us Out of War" appealed to the popular desire for peace, and the Democratic campaign became one long peace rally. Wilson disliked the peace emphasis but exploited its political appeal. He warned, "The certain prospect of the success of the Republican party is that we shall be drawn, in one form or another, into the embroilments of the European war."

Sussex **Pledge**   Germany's pledge during World War I not to sink merchant ships without warning, on the condition that Britain also observe recognized rules of international laws.

Preparedness   Military buildup in preparation for possible U.S. participation in World War I.

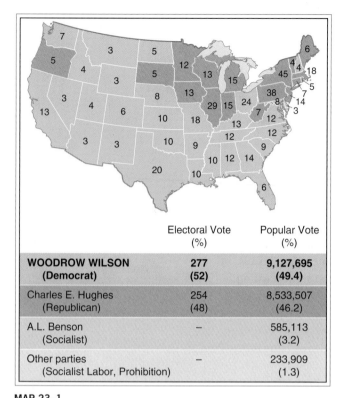

	Electoral Vote (%)	Popular Vote (%)
WOODROW WILSON (Democrat)	**277 (52)**	**9,127,695 (49.4)**
Charles E. Hughes (Republican)	254 (48)	8,533,507 (46.2)
A.L. Benson (Socialist)	–	585,113 (3.2)
Other parties (Socialist Labor, Prohibition)	–	233,909 (1.3)

MAP 23–1
The Election of 1916 Woodrow Wilson won reelection in 1916 despite a reunified Republican party by sweeping the South and West on campaign appeals to peace and progressive reform.

HOW WAS Woodrow Wilson able to win reelection in 1916 despite the reunification of the Republican party?

Self-determination The right of a people or a nation to decide on its own political allegiance or form of government without external influence.

The Republicans had hoped to regain the support of their progressive members after Roosevelt urged the Progressive party to follow him back into the GOP. But many joined the Democratic camp instead. The GOP nominated Charles Evans Hughes, a Supreme Court justice and former New York governor. The platform denounced Wilson's "shifty expedients" in foreign policy and promised "strict and honest neutrality." Unfortunately for Hughes, Roosevelt's attacks on Wilson for not pursuing a war policy persuaded many voters that the GOP was a war party. "If Hughes is defeated," wrote one observer, "he has Roosevelt to thank for it."

The election was the closest in decades (see Map 23–1). When California narrowly went for Wilson, it decided the contest. The desire for peace, all observers concluded, had determined the election.

DESCENT INTO WAR

Still, Wilson knew that war loomed, and he made a last effort to avert it. In January 1917, he sketched out the terms of what he called a "peace without victory." Anything else, he warned, would only lead to another war. The new world order should be based on national equality and **self-determination**, arms reductions, freedom of the seas, and an international organization to ensure peace. It was a distinctly American vision.

But both the Allies and the Central Powers had sacrificed too much to settle for anything short of outright victory. Germany wanted to annex territory in eastern Europe, Belgium, and France and to take over Belgian and French colonies in Africa; Austria sought Balkan territory. The Allies wanted to destroy German military and commercial power, weaken the Austro-Hungarian empire, take Germany's colonies in Africa, and supplant Turkish influence in the Middle East. One British leader denounced Wilson as "the quintessence of a prig" for suggesting that after three years of "this terrible effort," the two sides should accept American principles rather than their own national objectives.

Germany now moved to win the war by cutting the Allies off from U.S. supplies. On January 31, Germany unleashed its submarines in a broad war zone.

Wilson was now virtually committed to a war many Americans opposed. He broke diplomatic relations with Germany and asked Congress to arm American merchant vessels. When the Senate refused, Wilson invoked an antipiracy law of 1819 and armed the ships anyway. Although no American ships had yet been sunk, he also ordered the naval gun crews to shoot submarines on sight. Wilson's own secretary of the navy warned that these actions violated international law and were a step toward war. Huge rallies across America demanded peace.

Yet several developments soon shifted public opinion. On March 1, Wilson released an intercepted message from the German foreign minister, Arthur Zimmermann, to the German minister in Mexico. It proposed that in the event of war between the United States and Germany, Mexico should ally itself with Germany; in exchange, Mexico would recover its "lost territory in Texas, New Mexico, and Arizona." The Zimmermann note produced a wave of hostility toward Germany and increased support for intervention in the war, especially in the Southwest, which had opposed involvement. A revolution in Russia overthrew the tsarist regime and established a provisional government. Russia was now "a fit partner" for the United States, said Wilson. When submarines sank four American freighters in mid-March, anti-German feeling broadened.

On April 2, 1917, Wilson delivered his war message, declaring that neutrality was no longer possible, given Germany's submarine "warfare against mankind." To build support for joining a war that most people had long regarded with revulsion and as alien to American interests, Wilson set forth the nation's war goals as simple and noble. The United States would not fight for conquest or domination but for "the ultimate peace of the world and for the liberation of its peoples. . . . The world must be made safe for democracy."

After vigorous debate, the Senate passed the war resolution 82 to 6 and the House 373 to 50. On April 6, 1917, the United States officially entered the Great War, what Representative Claude Kitchin of North Carolina predicted would be "one vast drama of horrors and blood, one boundless stage upon which will play all the evil spirits of earth and hell."

WHERE TO LEARN MORE

National Infantry Museum, Fort Benning, Georgia
www.benningmwr.com/index.cfm

WAGING WAR IN AMERICA

Mobilizing for military intervention was a massive undertaking. "It is not an army that we must shape and train for war," announced President Wilson; "it is a Nation." The government reorganized the economy to emphasize centralized management, developed policies to control public opinion and suppress dissent, and transformed the role of government itself. Mobilization often built on progressives' moralism and sense of mission. In other respects, however, the war experience withered the spirits of reformers. In many different ways, people on the home front—like soldiers in Europe—would participate in the Great War; all would find their lives changed.

WHY DID the United States join the conflict on the side of the Allies?

MANAGING THE WAR ECONOMY

Federal and state governments developed a complex structure of agencies and controls for every sector of the economy (see the overview table "Major Government Wartime Agencies"). Supervised by the Council of National Defense, these agencies shifted resources to war-related enterprise, increased production of goods and services, and improved transportation and distribution.

The most important agency was the **War Industries Board (WIB).** Led by financier Bernard Baruch, the WIB exercised unprecedented powers over industry by setting prices, allocating scarce materials, and standardizing products and procedures to boost efficiency. Yet Baruch was not an industrial dictator; he aimed at business-government integration. The WIB promoted major business interests, helped suspend antitrust laws, and guaranteed huge corporate profits. So many business leaders became involved in the WIB that there was a popular outcry against business infiltration of the government, and one corporate executive admitted, "We are all making more money out of this war than the average human being ought to." Some progressives began to see the dangers, and business leaders the advantages, of government economic intervention.

Under William McAdoo, the Railroad Administration operated the nation's railroads as a unified system to move supplies and troops efficiently. Centralized management eliminated competition, permitted improvements in equipment, and brought great profits to the owners but higher prices to the general public.

Equally effective and far more popular was the Food Administration, headed by Herbert Hoover. Hoover persuaded millions of Americans to accept meatless and

War Industries Board (WIB) The federal agency that reorganized industry for maximum efficiency and productivity during World War I.

OVERVIEW

MAJOR GOVERNMENT WARTIME AGENCIES

Agency	Purpose
War Industries Board	Reorganized industry to maximize wartime production
Railroad Administration	Modernized and operated the nation's railroads
Food Administration	Increased agricultural production, supervised food distribution and farm labor
National War Labor Board	Resolved labor-management disputes, improved labor conditions, and recognized union rights as means to promote production and efficiency
Committee on Public Information	Managed propaganda to build public support for the war effort

wheatless days so that the Food Administration could feed military and foreign consumers. Half a million women went door to door to secure food conservation pledges from housewives. City residents planted victory gardens in parks and vacant lots.

Hoover also worked closely with agricultural processors and distributors. Farmers profited from the war, too. To encourage production, he established high prices for farm commodities, and agricultural income rose 30 percent. The Food Administration organized the Woman's Land Army to recruit women to work in the fields, providing sufficient farm labor despite the military draft. Most states formed units of the Boys' Working Reserve for agricultural labor. Agribusinesses in the Southwest persuaded the federal government to permit them to import Mexicans to work under government supervision and be housed in special camps.

In exchange for labor's cooperation, the National War Labor Board guaranteed the rights of unions to organize and bargain collectively. With such support, labor unions sharply increased their membership. The labor board also encouraged improved working conditions, higher wages, and shorter hours. These improvements limited labor disputes during the war, and Secretary of War Newton Baker praised labor as "more willing to keep in step than capital." But when unions like the Industrial Workers of the World did not keep in step, the government suppressed them.

These and other government regulatory agencies reinforced many longstanding trends in the American economy, from the consolidation of business to the commercialization of agriculture and the organization of labor. They also set a precedent for governmental activism that would prove valuable during the crises of the 1930s and 1940s.

WOMEN AND MINORITIES, NEW OPPORTUNITIES, OLD INEQUALITIES

The reorganization of the economy also had significant social consequences, especially for women and African Americans. In response to labor shortages, women took jobs previously closed to them. Besides farm work, they built airplanes, produced guns and ammunition, manufactured tents and cartridge belts, and worked in a wide variety of other heavy and light industries. "One of the lessons from the war," said one manufacturer, "has been to show that women can do exacting work."

QUICK REVIEW

National War Labor Board

- Federal and state governments created agencies to oversee the war-time economy.
- The National War Labor Board guaranteed the rights of unions to organize and bargain collectively.
- Labor unions sharply increased their membership under this protection.

Harriot Stanton Blatch, a suffragist active in the Food Administration, estimated that a million women had replaced men in industry, where "their drudgery is for the first time paid for."

Many working women simply shifted to other jobs where their existing skills earned better wages and benefits. The reshuffling of jobs among white women opened new vacancies for black women in domestic, clerical, and industrial employment. As black women replaced white women in the garment and textile industries, social reformers spoke of "a new day for the colored woman worker." But racial as well as gender segregation continued to mark employment, and wartime improvements were temporary.

The war helped middle-class women reformers achieve two long-sought objectives: woman suffrage and prohibition. Emphasizing the national cooperation needed to wage the war, one magazine noted that "arbitrarily to draw the line at voting, at a time when every man and woman must share in this effort, becomes an absurd anomaly." Even Woodrow Wilson finally endorsed the reform, terming it "vital to the winning of the war." Congress approved the suffrage amendment, which was ratified in 1920. Convinced that abstaining from alcohol would save grain and make workers and soldiers more efficient, Congress also passed the prohibition amendment, which was ratified in 1919.

The demand for industrial labor caused a huge migration of black people from the rural South, where they had had little opportunity, few rights, and no hope. Half a million African Americans moved north during the war, doubling and tripling the black population of Chicago, Detroit, and other industrial cities.

Unfortunately, fearful and resentful white people started race riots in Northern cities. In East St. Louis, Illinois, where thousands of black Southerners sought defense work, a white mob in July 1917 murdered at least thirty-nine black people. The *Literary Digest* noted, "Race-riots in East St. Louis afford a lurid background to our efforts to carry justice and idealism to Europe." And Wilson was told privately that the riot was "worse than anything the Germans did in Belgium."

FINANCING THE WAR

To finance the war, the government borrowed money and raised taxes. Business interests favored the first course, but Southern and Western progressives argued that taxation was more efficient and equitable and would minimize war profiteering. California Senator Hiram Johnson noted, "Our endeavours to impose heavy war profit taxes . . . have brought into sharp relief the skin-deep dollar patriotism of some of those who have been loudest in declamations on war and in their demands for blood." Nevertheless, the tax laws of 1917 and 1918 established a graduated tax structure with increased taxes on large incomes, corporate profits, and wealthy estates.

The government raised two-thirds of the war costs by borrowing. Most of the loans came from banks and wealthy investors, but the government also campaigned to sell **Liberty Bonds** to the general public. Celebrities went to schools, churches, and rallies to persuade Americans to buy bonds as their patriotic duty. "Every person who refuses to subscribe," Secretary of the Treasury McAdoo told a California audience, "is a friend of Germany."

CONQUERING MINDS

The government also tried to promote a war spirit among the American people by establishing propaganda agencies and enacting legislation to control social attitudes and behavior. This program drew from the restrictive side of progressivism

> **QUICK REVIEW**
>
> **Women and the War**
> ◆ The war opened jobs in industry for women.
> ◆ New job opportunities appeared for black women.
> ◆ Middle-class women reformers achieved two objectives: woman suffrage and prohibition.

Liberty Bonds　Interest-bearing certificates sold by the U.S. government to finance the American World War I effort.

Female workers stack bricks from wheel barrows at a brickyard under the supervision of a man in a suit.

National Archives and Records Administration

but also reflected the interests of more conservative forces. The Wilson administration adopted this program of social mobilization because many Americans opposed the war, including German Americans with ethnic ties to the Central Powers, Irish Catholics and Russian Jews who condemned the Allies for persecution and repression, Scandinavian immigrants averse to military service, pacifists, radicals who denounced the war as capitalist and imperialist, and many others.

To rally Americans behind the war effort, Wilson established the **Committee on Public Information (CPI)** under George Creel. Despite its title, the CPI sought to manipulate, not inform, public opinion. Creel described his goal as winning "the fight for the *minds* of men, for the 'conquest of their convictions.'" The CPI flooded the country with press releases, advertisements, cartoons, and canned editorials. It made newsreels and war movies to capture public attention. It hired artists to draw posters, professors to write pamphlets in twenty-three languages, and poets to compose war poems for children.

Other government agencies launched similar campaigns. The Woman's Committee of the Council of National Defense established the Department of Educational Propaganda and Patriotic Education. This agency worked to win over women who opposed the war.

Government propaganda had three themes: national unity, the loathsome character of the enemy, and the war as a grand crusade for liberty and democracy. Germans were depicted as brutal, even subhuman, rapists and murderers. The campaign suggested that any dissent was unpatriotic, if not treasonous, and dangerous to national survival. This emphasis on unreasoning conformity helped prompt hysterical attacks on German Americans, radicals, and pacifists.

SUPPRESSING DISSENT

The government also suppressed dissent, now officially branded disloyalty. For reasons of their own, private interests helped shape a reactionary repression that tarnished the nation's professed idealistic war goals.

Congress rushed to stifle antiwar sentiment. The **Espionage Act** provided heavy fines and up to twenty years in prison for obstructing the war effort, a vague phrase but one "omnipotently comprehensive," warned one Idaho senator who opposed the law. "No man can foresee what it might be in its consequences." In fact, the Espionage Act became a weapon to crush dissent and criticism. In 1918, Congress passed the still more sweeping **Sedition Act**. Based on state laws in the West designed to suppress labor radicals, the Sedition Act provided severe penalties for speaking or writing against the draft, bond sales, or war production or for criticizing government personnel or policies. Senator Hiram Johnson lamented: "It is war. But, good God, . . . when did it become war upon the American people?"

Postmaster General Albert Burleson banned antiwar or radical newspapers and magazines from the mail, suppressing literature so indiscriminately that one observer said he "didn't know socialism from rheumatism." The reactionary

Committee on Public Information (CPI) Government agency during World War I that sought to shape public opinion in support of the war effort through newspapers, pamphlets, speeches, films, and other media.

Espionage Act Law whose vague prohibition against obstructing the nation's war effort was used to crush dissent and criticism during World War I.

Sedition Act Broad law restricting criticism of America's involvement in World War I or its government, flag, military, taxes, or officials.

attorney general, Thomas Gregory, made little distinction between traitors and pacifists, war critics, and radicals. Eugene Debs was sentenced to ten years in prison for a "treasonous" speech in which he declared it "extremely dangerous to exercise the right of free speech in a country fighting to make democracy safe in the world." By war's end, a third of the Socialist party's national leadership was in prison, leaving the party in shambles.

Gregory also enlisted the help of private vigilantes, including several hundred thousand members of the reactionary American Protective League, which sought to purge radicals and reformers from the nation's economic and political life. They wiretapped telephones, intercepted private mail, burglarized union offices, broke up German-language newspapers, harassed immigrants, and staged mass raids, seizing thousands of people they claimed were not doing enough for the war effort.

State and local authorities established 184,000 investigating and enforcement agencies known as councils of defense or public safety committees. They encouraged Americans to spy on one another, required people to buy Liberty Bonds, and prohibited teaching German in schools or using the language in religious services and telephone conversations. When Oklahoma abolished German in its schools, a newspaper crowed: "German Deader than Latin Now." (See American Views, Mobilizing America for Liberty.") In Tulsa, a member of the county council of defense shot and killed someone for making allegedly pro-German remarks. The council declared its approval, and community leaders applauded the killer's patriotism.

"Beat Back the Hun," a poster to induce Americans to buy Liberty Bonds, demonizes the enemy in a raw, emotional appeal. Liberty bond drives raised the immense sum of $23 billion.

The Granger Collection, New York

Members of the business community exploited the hysteria to promote their own interests at the expense of farmers, workers, and reformers. As one Wisconsin farmer complained, businessmen "now under the guise of patriotism are trying to ram down the farmers' throats things they hardly dared before." On the Great Plains from Texas to North Dakota, the business target was the Nonpartisan League, a radical farm group demanding state control or ownership of banks, grain elevators, and flour mills. Although the League supported the war, oversubscribed bond drives, and had George Creel affirm its loyalty, conservatives depicted it as seditious to block its advocacy of political and economic reforms. Minnesota's public safety commission proposed a "firing squad working overtime" to deal with League members. Public officials and self-styled patriots broke up the League's meetings and whipped and jailed its leaders.

In the West, business interests targeted labor organizations, especially the Industrial Workers of the World. In Arizona, for example, the Phelps-Dodge Company armed and paid a vigilante mob to seize twelve hundred striking miners, many of them Wobblies and one-third of them Mexican Americans, and herd them into the desert without food or water. Federal investigators found that the company and its thugs had been inspired not by "considerations of patriotism" but by "ordinary strike-breaking motives." Corporate management was merely "raising the false cry of 'disloyalty' " to suppress workers' complaints.

Nonetheless, the government itself used the army to break loggers' support for the IWW in the Pacific Northwest, and it raided IWW halls across the country in September 1917. The conviction of nearly two hundred Wobblies on charges

◆ AMERICAN VIEWS ◆

MOBILIZING AMERICA FOR LIBERTY

The war years witnessed official and popular efforts to repress dissent and diversity. Much of this repression was aimed at America's immigrant groups and sought to create national unity through coercive Americanization that trampled on the rights and values that the nation claimed to be defending. The following is an official proclamation of Governor W.L. Harding of Iowa, issued May 23, 1918.

WHAT IS the rationale for the governor's proclamation? What do you think of his interpretation of the constitutional guarantees of individual rights? What other "inconvenience or sacrifice" might the proclamation impose on minorities? How might the proclamation incite vigilantism?

The official language of the United States and the State of Iowa is the English language. Freedom of speech is guaranteed by federal and State Constitutions, but this is not a guaranty of the right to use a language other than the language of this country—the English language. Both federal and State Constitutions also provide that "no laws shall be made respecting an establishment of religion or prohibiting the free exercise thereof." Each person is guaranteed freedom to worship God according to the dictates of his own conscience, but this guaranty does not protect him in the use of a foreign language when he can as well express his thought in English, nor entitle the person who cannot speak or understand the English language to employ a foreign language, when to do so tends in time of national peril, to create discord among neighbors and citizens, or to disturb the peace and quiet of the community.

Every person should appreciate and observe his duty to refrain from all acts or conversation which may excite suspicion or produce strife among the people, but in his relation to the public should so demean himself that every word and act will manifest his loyalty to his country and his solemn purpose to aid in achieving victory for our army and navy and the permanent peace of the world . . . .

The great aim and object of all should be unity of purpose and a solidarity of all the people under the flag for victory. This much we owe to ourselves, to posterity, to our country, and to the world.

Therefore, the following rules should obtain in Iowa during the war:

First. English should and must be the only medium of instruction in public, private, denominational, or other similar schools.

Second. Conversation in public places, on trains, and over the telephone should be in the English language.

Third. All public addresses should be in the English language.

Fourth. Let those who cannot speak or understand the English language conduct their religious worship in their homes.

This course carried out in the spirit of patriotism, though inconvenient to some, will not interfere with their guaranteed constitutional rights and will result in peace and tranquility at home and greatly strengthen the country in battle. The blessings of the United States are so great that any inconvenience or sacrifice should willingly be made for their perpetuity.

Therefore, by virtue of authority in me vested, I, W.L. Harding, Governor of the State of Iowa, commend the spirit of tolerance and urge that henceforth the within outlined rules be adhered to by all, that petty differences be avoided and forgotten, and that, united as one people with one purpose and one language, we fight shoulder to shoulder for the good of mankind.

Source: B.F. Shambaugh, ed., *Iowa and War* (Iowa City; State Historical Society of Iowa, 1919).

22–2
Boy Scouts of America from, "Boy Scouts Support the War Effort" (1917)

of sedition in three mass trials in Illinois, California, and Kansas crippled the nation's largest industrial union.

The government was primarily responsible for the war hysteria. It encouraged suspicion and conflict by its own inflammatory propaganda, repressive laws, and violation of basic civil rights, by supporting extremists who used the war for their own purposes, and by not opposing mob violence against German Americans.

WAGING WAR AND PEACE ABROAD

While mobilizing the home front, the Wilson administration undertook an impressive military effort to help the Allies defeat the Central Powers. Wilson also struggled to secure international acceptance for his plans for a just and permanent peace.

THE WAR TO END ALL WARS

When the United States entered the war, the Allied military position was dire. The losses from three years of trench warfare had sapped military strength and civilian morale. French soldiers mutinied after 120,000 casualties in five days; the German submarine campaign was devastating the British. On the eastern front, the Russian army collapsed, and the Russian government gradually disintegrated.

What the Allies needed, said French Marshal Joseph Joffre in April 1917, was simple: "We want men, men, men." In May, Congress passed the **Selective Service Act of 1917**, establishing conscription. More than 24 million men eventually registered for the draft, and nearly 3 million entered the army when their numbers were drawn in a national lottery. Almost two million more men volunteered, as did more than ten thousand women who served in the navy. Nearly one-fifth of America's soldiers were foreign-born (Europeans spoke of the "American Foreign Legion"); 367,000 were black people.

Civilians were transformed into soldiers in hastily organized training camps operated according to progressive principles. Prohibition prevailed in the camps; the poorly educated and largely working-class recruits were taught personal hygiene; worries about sin and inefficiency produced campaigns against venereal disease; and immigrants were taught English and American history. Some units were ethnically segregated: At Camp Gordon, Georgia, Italians and Slavs had separate units with their own officers. Racial segregation was more rigid. The navy assigned black sailors to menial positions, and the army used black soldiers primarily as gravediggers and laborers. But one black combat division was created, and four black regiments fought under French command. France decorated three of these units with its highest citations for valor.

The first American troops landed in France in June 1917. This American Expeditionary Force (AEF) was commanded by General John J. Pershing. Full-scale American intervention did not begin until the late spring of 1918 (see Map 23–2). The influx of American troops in June and July tipped the balance toward Allied victory. By July 18, the German chancellor later acknowledged, "even the most optimistic among us knew that all was lost."

In July, Wilson also agreed to commit fifteen thousand American troops to intervene in Russia. Russia's provisional government had collapsed when the **Bolsheviks**, or Communists, had seized power in November 1917. Under V.I. Lenin, the Bolsheviks had then signed an armistice with Germany in early 1918, which freed German troops for the summer offensive in France. The Allies' interventions were designed to reopen the eastern front and help overthrow the Bolshevik government. Lenin's call for the destruction of capitalism and imperialism alarmed the Allied leaders. One Wilson adviser urged the "eradication" of the Russian government. Soon American and British troops were fighting Russians in an effort to influence Russia's internal affairs. U.S. forces remained in Russia until 1920, but these military interventions failed.

On the western front, the Allies launched their own advance. In late September an American army over 1 million strong attacked German trenches in the Argonne Forest. Some soldiers had been drafted only in July and had spent

■ ■ ■ ■ ■ ■ ■ ■ ■ ■
HOW DID the war effort threaten civil liberties?
■ ■ ■ ■ ■ ■ ■ ■ ■ ■

WHERE TO LEARN MORE **W**

Fort George G. Meade Museum, Fort Meade, Maryland

22–5
Eugene Kennedy, A "Doughboy" Describes the Fighting Front (1918)

WHERE TO LEARN MORE **W**

General John J. Pershing Boyhood Home, Laclede, Missouri
www.mostateparks.com/ pershingsite.htm

Selective Service Act of 1917 The law establishing the military draft for World War I.

Bolshevik Member of the Communist movement in Russia that established the Soviet government after the 1917 Russian Revolution.

MAP EXPLORATION

To explore an interactive version of this map, go to **http://www.prenhall.com/goldfield2/map23.2**

MAP 23–2
The Western Front, 1918   After three years of trench warfare, the arrival of large numbers of American troops in 1918 enabled the Allies to launch an offensive that drove back the Germans and forced an armistice.

AT THE time of the armistice, how far back had the Germans been forced to retreat from their farthest advance?

W WHERE TO LEARN MORE

★ Sgt. Alvin C. York Homeplace and State Historic Site, Pall Mall, Tennessee
www.alvincyork.org

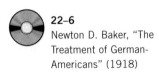

22–6
Newton D. Baker, "The Treatment of German-Americans" (1918)

more time traveling than training. One officer worried, "With their unfamiliarity with weapons, a gun was about as much use as a broom in their hands." Nevertheless, the Americans advanced steadily, despite attacks with poison gas and heavy artillery. Lieutenant Maury Maverick (later a Texas congressman) described the shelling: "We were simply in a big black spot with streaks of screaming red and yellow, with roaring giants in the sky tearing and whirling and roaring." An exploding shell terrified him: "There is a great swishing scream, a smash-bang, and it seems to tear everything loose from you. The intensity of it simply enters your heart and brain, and tears every nerve to pieces."

The battle for the Argonne raged for weeks. One German general reported that his exhausted soldiers faced Americans who "were fresh, eager for fighting, and brave." But he found their sheer numbers most impressive. Despite severe casualties, the AEF helped the British and French defeat the enemy. Soon thereafter, Germany asked for peace. On November 11, 1918, an armistice ended the Great War. More than 115,000 Americans were among the 8 million soldiers and 7 million civilians dead.

WHERE TO LEARN MORE

Wisconsin Veterans Museum,
Madison, Wisconsin

THE FOURTEEN POINTS

The armistice was only a step toward final peace. President Wilson had already enunciated American war objectives on January 8, 1918, in a speech outlining what became known as the Fourteen Points. In his 1917 war message, Wilson had advocated a more democratic world system, and this new speech spelled out how to achieve it. But Wilson also had a political purpose. The Bolsheviks had published the secret treaties the Allies had signed dividing up the economic and territorial spoils of war. Lenin called for an immediate peace based on the liberation of all colonies, self-determination for all peoples, and the rejection of annexations and punitive indemnities. Wilson's Fourteen Points reassured the American and Allied peoples that they were fighting for more than imperialist gains and offered an alternative to what he called Lenin's "crude formula" for peace.

Eight of Wilson's points proposed creating new nations, shifting old borders, or assuring self-determination for peoples previously subject to the Austrian, German, or Russian empires. The point about Russia called on all nations to evacuate Russian territory and permit Russia "an unhampered and unembarrassed opportunity for the independent determination of her own political development" under "institutions of her own choosing." Another five points invoked principles to guide international relations: freedom of the seas, open diplomacy instead of secret treaties, reduction of armaments, free trade, and the fair settlement of colonial claims. Wilson's fourteenth and most important point proposed a league of nations to carry out these ideals and ensure international stability.

Wilson and the German government had these principles in mind when negotiating the armistice. The Allies, however, had never explicitly accepted the Fourteen Points. While Wilson favored a settlement that would promote international stability and economic expansion, he recognized that the Allies sought "to get everything out of Germany that they can."

Convinced of the righteousness of his cause, Wilson decided to attend the peace conference in Paris himself. But Wilson weakened his position before he even set sail. First, he urged voters to support Democratic candidates in the November 1918 elections to indicate approval of his peace plans. But the electorate, responding primarily to domestic problems like inflation, gave the Republicans control of both houses of Congress. This meant that a treaty would have to be approved by Senate Republicans angry that Wilson had tried to use war and peace for partisan purposes. Second, Wilson refused to consult with Senate Republicans on plans for the peace conference and failed to name important Republicans to the Paris delegation. It would be Wilson's treaty, but Republicans would feel no responsibility to approve it.

THE PARIS PEACE CONFERENCE

The peace conference opened on January 18, 1919. Meeting at the Palace of Versailles, the delegations were dominated by the principal Allied leaders themselves: Wilson of the United States, David Lloyd George of Britain, Georges Clemenceau of France, and Vittorio Orlando of Italy. The Central Powers and Bolshevik Russia were excluded. Clemenceau remarked, "God gave us the Ten Commandments and we broke them. Mr. Wilson has given us the Fourteen Points. We shall see."

Wilson himself had broken two of the Fourteen Points before the conference began. He had acquiesced in Britain's rejection of freedom of the seas, and he had sent U.S. troops to intervene in Russia in violation of its right to self-determination.

QUICK REVIEW

Wilson's Fourteen Points
- Wilson articulated U.S. war aims in his Fourteen Points.
- The Allies did not explicitly support Wilson's program.
- Domestic political failures undermined Wilson's position at the Paris peace conference.

For months, the conference debated Wilson's other goals and the Allies' demands for compensation and security. Lloyd George later commented, with reference to the self-righteous Wilson and the assertive Clemenceau, "I think I did as well as might be expected, seated as I was between Jesus Christ and Napoleon Bonaparte." Under protest, Germany signed the **Treaty of Versailles** on June 28, 1919. Its terms were far more severe than Wilson had proposed or Germany had anticipated. Germany had to accept sole responsibility for starting the war; to pay huge reparations to the Allies; to give up land to France, Poland, Belgium, and Denmark; to cede its colonies; to limit its army and navy; and to promise not to manufacture or purchase armaments.

Wilson gained some acceptance of self-determination. As the German, Austro-Hungarian, Turkish, and Russian empires had collapsed at the end of the war, nationalist groups had proclaimed their independence. On one hand, the peace settlement formally recognized these new nation-states in Eastern Europe. On the other hand, France, Italy, Romania, and Japan all annexed territory regardless of the wishes of the inhabitants. Germans were placed under Polish control in Silesia and Czech control in Bohemia. Austrians were not allowed to merge with Germany. And the conference sanctioned colonialism by establishing a trusteeship system that enabled France, Britain, and Japan to take over German colonies and Turkish territory.

Moreover, the Allied leaders endorsed the changes in eastern Europe in part because the new states there were anti-Communist. Western leaders soon called these countries the *cordon sanitaire*, a barrier against Bolshevism. Indeed, the Allies at Versailles were preoccupied with Bolshevik Russia, which one of Wilson's aides called the "black cloud of the east, threatening to overwhelm and swallow up the world." The Allies hoped to isolate and weaken Bolshevik Russia. This hostility to Russia, like the punitive terms for Germany and the concessions to imperial interests, boded ill for a stable and just postwar order.

But Wilson hoped that the final section of the Versailles treaty would resolve the flaws of the agreement by establishing his great international organization to preserve peace: the **League of Nations**. The Covenant, or constitution, of the League was built into the treaty. Its crucial feature, Article Ten, bound the member nations to guarantee each other's independence, which was Wilson's concept of collective security. Sailing home, he mused: "Well, it is finished, and, as no one is satisfied, it makes me hope we have made a just peace; but it is all on the lap of the gods."

WAGING PEACE AT HOME

Wilson was determined to defeat opposition to the peace treaty. But many Americans were engaged in their own struggles with the new conditions of a nation suddenly at peace but riven by economic, social, and political conflict shaped by the war experience. Wilson's battle for the League of Nations would fail tragically. The other conflicts would rage until the election of 1920 restored a normalcy of sorts.

BATTLE OVER THE LEAGUE

Most Americans favored the Versailles treaty. A survey of fourteen hundred newspapers found fewer than two hundred opposed. Thirty-three governors and thirty-two state legislatures approved of the League of Nations. But when Wilson called for the Senate to accept "the moral leadership . . . and confidence of the world" by ratifying the treaty, he met resistance. Republican

Treaty of Versailles The treaty ending World War I and creating the League of Nations.

League of Nations International organization created by the Versailles Treaty after World War I to ensure world stability.

WHAT WERE the terms of the Treaty of Versailles?

opponents of the treaty raised serious questions. Nearly all Democrats favored the treaty, but they were a minority; some Republicans had to be converted for the treaty to be approved.

Progressive Republican senators, such as Robert La Follette and Hiram Johnson, led one group of opponents. Called the **Irreconcilables**, they opposed participation in the League of Nations, which they saw as designed to perpetuate the power of imperialist countries. Article Ten, they feared, would require the United States to help suppress rebellions in Ireland against British rule or to enforce disputed European borders. Most of the Irreconcilables gave priority to restoring civil liberties and progressive reform at home.

A larger group of opponents, the **Reservationists**, were led by Senator Henry Cabot Lodge, the chair of the Senate Foreign Relations Committee. They regarded Article Ten as eroding congressional authority to declare war. They also fretted that the League might interfere with domestic questions, such as immigration laws. Lodge held public hearings on the treaty to rouse and focus opposition. German Americans resented the war guilt clause; Italian and Polish Americans complained that the treaty did not satisfy the territorial ambitions of Italy and Poland; Irish Americans condemned the treaty's failure to give self-determination to Ireland. Many progressives also criticized the treaty's compromises on self-determination, reparations, and colonies.

When Lodge proposed reservations or amendments to the treaty, Wilson opened "a direct frontal attack" on his opponents. If they wanted war, he declared, he would "give them a belly full." In early September 1919, Wilson set out across the country to win popular support for the League. In three weeks, he traveled 8,000 miles and delivered thirty-seven speeches. He collapsed in Pueblo, Colorado. Confused and in tears, Wilson mumbled, "I seem to have gone to pieces." Taken back to Washington, Wilson on October 2 suffered a massive stroke that paralyzed his left side and left him psychologically unstable and temporarily blind. Wilson's physician and his wife, Edith Galt Wilson, kept the nature of his illness secret from the public, Congress, and even the vice president and cabinet. The administration was immobilized.

By February 1920, Wilson had partially recovered, but he remained suspicious and quarrelsome. He still refused to compromise to win Senate approval of the treaty. On March 19, 1920, the Senate killed the treaty.

ECONOMIC READJUSTMENT AND SOCIAL CONFLICT

The League was not the only casualty of the struggle to conclude the war. Grave problems shook the United States in 1919 and early 1920. An influenza epidemic had erupted in Europe in 1918 among the massed armies. It now hit the United States, killing perhaps 700,000 Americans, far more than had died in combat.

Meanwhile, the Wilson administration had no plans for an orderly reconversion of the wartime economy. The secretary of the Council of National Defense later reported, "the mobilization that had taken many months was succeeded by an instantaneous demobilization." The government canceled war contracts and dissolved the regulatory agencies. Noting that "the war spirit of cooperation and sacrifice" had disappeared with the Armistice, Bernard Baruch decided to "turn industry absolutely free" and abolished the War Industries Board as of January 1, 1919. Other agencies followed in such haste that turmoil engulfed the economy.

The army discharged 600,000 soldiers still in training camps; the navy brought AEF soldiers home from France. With no planning or assistance, troops were hustled

Irreconcilables   Group of U.S. senators adamantly opposed to ratification of the Treaty of Versailles after World War I.

Reservationists   Group of U.S. senators favoring approval of the Treaty of Versailles, after amending it to incorporate their reservations.

A policeman on horseback swings a truncheon at strikers on a Pittsburgh street.

Corbis/Bettman

back into civilian life. There they competed for scarce jobs with workers recently discharged from the war industries.

As unemployment mounted, the removal of wartime price controls brought runaway inflation. The cost of food, clothing, and other necessities more than doubled over prewar rates. The return of the soldiers caused a serious housing shortage, and rents skyrocketed. Farmers also suffered from economic readjustments. Net farm income declined by 65 percent between 1919 and 1921. Farmers who had borrowed money for machinery and land to expand production for the war effort were left impoverished and embittered.

Women also lost their wartime economic advances. Returning soldiers took away their jobs. Male trade unionists insisted that women go back to being housewives. One New York union maintained that "the same patriotism which induced women to enter industry during the war should induce them to vacate their positions after the war." At times, male workers struck to force employers to fire women. "During the war they called us heroines," one woman complained, "but they throw us on the scrapheap now." By 1920, women constituted a smaller proportion of the work force than they had in 1910.

The postwar adjustments also left African Americans disappointed. During the war, they had agreed with W. E. B. Du Bois to "forget our special grievances and close our ranks shoulder to shoulder with our own white fellow citizens." They had contributed to the fighting and home fronts. Now, housing shortages and job competition interacted with racism in 1919 to produce race riots in twenty-six towns and cities, resulting in at least 120 deaths. In Chicago, thirty-eight people were killed and more than five hundred injured in a five-day riot that began when white thugs stoned to death a black youth swimming too near "their" beach. White rioters then fired a machine gun from a truck hurtling through black neighborhoods. But black residents fought back, no longer willing, the *Chicago Defender* reported, "to move along the line of least resistance as did their sires." Racial conflict was part of a postwar battle between Americans hoping to preserve the new social relations fostered by the war effort and those wanting to restore prewar patterns of power and control.

Even more pervasive discontents roiled as America adjusted to the postwar world. More than 4 million angry workers launched a wave of 3,600 strikes in 1919. They were reacting not only to the soaring cost of living, which undermined the value of their wages, but also to employers' efforts to reassert their authority and destroy the legitimacy labor had won by its participation in the war effort. The abolition of government controls on industry enabled employers not only to raise prices but also to rescind their recognition of unions and reimpose objectionable working conditions. In response, strikers demanded higher wages, better conditions, and recognition of unions and the right of collective bargaining.

The greatest strike involved the American Federation of Labor's attempt to organize steelworkers, who endured dangerous conditions and twelve-hour shifts. When the steel companies refused to recognize the union or even discuss issues, 365,000 workers went out on strike in September 1919. Strikers in Pennsylvania pointed out that they had worked "cheerfully, without strikes or trouble of any kind" during the war to "make the world safe for democracy" and that they now sought "industrial democracy." Employers hired thugs to beat the strikers, used strikebreakers to take their jobs, and exploited ethnic and racial divisions among them. Management also portrayed the strikers as disruptive radicals influenced by Bolshevism. After four months, the strike failed.

Employers used the same tactic to defeat striking coal miners. Coal operators claimed that Russian Bolsheviks financed the strike to destroy the American economy. Attorney General Mitchell Palmer secured an injunction against the strike under the authority of wartime legislation. Since the government no longer controlled coal prices or enforced protective labor rules, miners complained bitterly that the war had ended for corporations but not for workers.

Two municipal strikes in 1919 also alarmed the public when their opponents depicted them as revolutionary attacks on the social order. In Seattle in February, the Central Labor Council called a general strike to support 35,000 shipyard workers striking for higher wages and shorter hours. When 60,000 more workers from 110 local unions also walked out, the city ground to a halt. Seattle's mayor, business leaders, and newspapers attacked the strikers as Bolsheviks and anarchists. Threatened with military intervention, the labor council called off the strike. In Boston, the police commissioner fired police officers for trying to organize a union to improve their inadequate pay. In response, the police went on strike. As in Seattle, Boston newspapers, politicians, and business leaders attributed the strike to Bolshevism. Governor Calvin Coolidge mobilized the National Guard and gained nationwide acclaim when he stated, "There is no right to strike against the public safety by anybody, anywhere, anytime." The police were all fired; many of their replacements were war veterans.

RED SCARE

The strikes contributed to an anti-Bolshevik hysteria that swept the country in 1919. This **Red Scare** reflected fears that the Bolshevik revolution in Russia might spread to the United States. Steeped in the antiradical propaganda of the war years, many Americans were appalled by Russian Bolshevism, described by the *Saturday Evening Post* as a "compound of slaughter, confiscation, anarchy, and universal disorder." Their alarm grew in 1919 when Russia established the Third International to foster revolution abroad, and a few American socialists formed the American Communist Party. But the Red Scare also reflected the willingness of antiunion employers, ambitious politicians, sensational journalists, zealous veterans, and racists to exploit the panic to advance their own purposes.

The Red Scare reached panic levels by mid-1919. Bombs mailed anonymously to several prominent people on May Day seemed proof enough that a Bolshevik conspiracy threatened America. The Justice Department, Congress, and patriotic organizations like the American Legion joined with business groups to suppress radicalism, real and imagined. The government continued to enforce the repressive laws against Wobblies, socialists, and other dissenters. Indeed, Wilson and Attorney General Palmer called for more stringent laws. State governments harassed and arrested hundreds.

Palmer created a new agency, headed by J. Edgar Hoover, to suppress radicals and impose conformity. Its war on radicalism became the chief focus of the

Red Scare Post-World War I public hysteria over Bolshevik influence in the United States directed against labor activism, radical dissenters, and some ethnic groups.

Justice Department. Hoover collected files on labor leaders and other "radical agitators" from Senator La Follette to Jane Addams, issued misleading reports on Communist influence in labor strikes and race riots, and contacted all major newspapers "to acquaint people like you with the real menace of evil-thinking, which is the foundation of the Red Movement." Indeed, the Justice Department itself promoted the Red Scare hysteria, which Palmer hoped would lead to his presidential nomination and Hoover hoped would enhance his own power and that of his bureau.

In November 1919, Palmer and Hoover began raiding groups suspected of subversion. A month later, they deported 249 alien radicals, including the anarchist Emma Goldman, to Russia. Rabid patriots endorsed such actions. One minister favored deporting radicals "in ships of stone with sails of lead, with the wrath of God for a breeze and with hell for their first port." In January 1920, Palmer and Hoover rounded up more than four thousand suspected radicals in thirty-three cities. Without warrants, they broke into union halls, club rooms, and private homes, assaulting and arresting everyone in sight. People were jailed without access to lawyers; some were beaten into signing false confessions. In Lynn, Massachusetts, thirty-nine people meeting to organize a bakery were arrested for holding a revolutionary caucus. The *Washington Post* clamored, "There is no time to waste on hairsplitting over infringement of liberty."

Other Americans began to recoil from the excesses and illegal acts. Assistant Secretary of Labor Louis Post stopped further deportations by demonstrating that most of the arrested were "working men of good character, who are not anarchists or revolutionists, nor politically or otherwise dangerous in any sense." When Palmer's predictions of a violent attempt to overthrow the government on May 1, 1920, came to naught, most Americans agreed with the *Rocky Mountain News*: "We can never get to work if we keep jumping sideways in fear of the bewhiskered Bolshevik." Even one conservative Republican concluded that "too much has been said about Bolshevism in America." But if the Red Scare faded in mid-1920, the hostility to immigrants, organized labor, and dissent it reflected endured.

THE ELECTION OF 1920

The Democratic coalition that Wilson had cobbled together on the issues of progressivism and peace came apart after the war. Workers resented the administration's hostility to the postwar strikes. Ethnic groups brutalized by the Americanization of the war years blamed Wilson for the war or condemned his peace settlement. Farmers grumbled about wartime price controls and postwar falling prices. Wartime taxes and the social and economic turmoil of 1919–1920 alienated the middle class. In the words of Kansas journalist William Allen White, Americans were "tired of issues, sick at heart of ideals, and weary of being noble." They yearned for what Republican presidential candidate Warren Harding of Ohio called "normalcy."

The Republican ticket in 1920 symbolized the reassurance of simpler times. Harding was a genial, Old Guard conservative. His running mate, Calvin Coolidge, governor of Massachusetts, owed his nomination to his handling of the Boston police strike.

Wilson called the election of 1920 "a great and solemn referendum" on the League of Nations, but the League was not a decisive issue in the campaign.

Harding defeated Democratic nominee James Cox, former governor of Ohio, in a landslide. "The Democrats are inconceivably unpopular," wrote Walter Lippmann, a prominent journalist. Harding received 16 million popular votes to Cox's 9 million. Running for president from his prison cell, Socialist Eugene Debs polled nearly a million votes. Not even his closest backers considered Harding qualified for the White House, but as Lippmann said, the nation's "public spirit was exhausted" after the war years. The election of 1920 was "the final twitch" of America's "war mind."

CONCLUSION

The Great War disrupted the United States and much of the rest of the world. The initial American policy of neutrality yielded to sentimental and substantive links with the Allies and the pressure of German submarine warfare. Despite popular opposition. America joined the conflict when its leaders concluded that national interests demanded it. Using both military and diplomatic power, Woodrow Wilson sought to secure a more stable and prosperous world order, with an expanded role for the United States. But the Treaty of Versailles only partly fulfilled his hopes, and the Senate refused to ratify the treaty and its League of Nations. The postwar world order would be unstable and dangerous.

Participation in the war, moreover, had changed the American government, economy, and society. Some of these changes, including the centralization of the economy and an expansion of the regulatory role of the federal government, were already under way; some offered opportunities to implement progressive principles or reforms. Woman suffrage and prohibition gained decisive support because of the war spirit. But other consequences of the war betrayed both progressive impulses and the democratic principles the war was allegedly fought to promote. The suppression of civil liberties, manipulation of human emotions, repression of radicals and minorities, and exploitation of national crises by narrow interests helped disillusion the public. The repercussions of the Great War would linger for years, at home and abroad.

WHAT WAS the postwar backlash?

SUMMARY

Waging Neutrality Few Americans were prepared for the Great War that erupted in Europe in 1914; fewer still envisioned the United States becoming involved in the war. The Central Powers and the Allies were involved in mass slaughter and stalemate in Europe; America had no vital interest in the war, but it did not stay strictly neutral. The economy of America became closely tied with Britain and the Allies, the President sympathized with the Allied cause, and German submarine warfare tied the United States to the British war effort. The desire for peace determined the results of the 1916 election; in 1917 America entered the war as Germany decided to resume unrestricted submarine warfare and the contents of the Zimmermann Note, linking Germany to Mexico's recovering the Southwest, were exposed.

Waging War in America In addition to mobilizing for military invention, the government reorganized the economy to emphasize centralized management and developed policies to control public opinion and suppress dissent. In response to labor shortages women and minorities entered the work force, obtaining jobs which had previously been closed to them; individual citizens planted victory gardens and bought Liberty Bonds to help the war effort. Government propaganda to rally Americans painted the enemy as subhuman; dissent was viewed as unpatriotic; Americans were encouraged to spy on one another; basic civil rights were violated.

Waging War and Peace Abroad The American involvement in the Great War turned the tide and ensured Allied victory. Having stopped the German advance on the Western Front, the Allies, with fresh American troops, began a counteroffensive that ended the war with an armistice on November 11, 1918. President Wilson envisioned the postwar world based on the Fourteen Points and attended the Paris Peace Conference convinced of the righteousness of his peace plans. The Allied leaders were more interested in revenge and retribution than righteousness. The Treaty of Versailles imposed harsh restrictions on Germany; the specter of Bolshevism hung over the peace conference; fear of communism impacted decisions made by the delegates.

Waging Peace at Home While most Americans favored the Versailles treaty, the senators who had to vote on the treaty were largely opposed to it. The Irreconcilables opposed participation in the League of Nations, and the Reservationists feared the power of the League and the erosion of Congressional authority. The Treaty of Versailles was never approved by the United States. The vote in the Senate was not the only war casualty: An influenza epidemic, the reconversion to a peacetime economy, housing shortages, unemployment, labor unrest, and the Red Scare wearied Americans. By 1920, Americans wanted a return to "normalcy" and elected Warren Harding as president in a landslide victory.

REVIEW QUESTIONS

1. What were the major arguments for and against U.S. entry into the Great War?

2. How and why did the United States shape public opinion in World War I?

3. How did groups exploit the war crisis and the government's propaganda and repression?

4. What were the arguments for and against American ratification of the Treaty of Versailles?

KEY TERMS

Allies (p. 606)
Bolshevik (p. 617)
Central Powers (p. 606)
Committee on Public Information (CPI) (p. 614)
Declaration of London (p. 607)
Espionage Act (p. 614)

Irreconcilables (p. 621)
League of Nations (p. 620)
Liberty Bonds (p. 613)
Preparedness (p. 609)
Red Scare (p. 623)
Reservationists (p. 621)
Sedition Act (p. 614)

Selective Service Act of 1917 (p. 617)
Self-determination (p. 610)
Sussex **Pledge** (p. 609)
Treaty of Versailles (p. 620)
War Industries Board (WIB) (p. 611)

WHERE TO LEARN MORE

- **National Infantry Museum, Fort Benning, Georgia.** This sprawling collection of weapons, uniforms, and equipment includes exhibits on World War I. **www.benningmwr. com/index.cfm**

- **Fort George G. Meade Museum, Fort Meade, Maryland.** This museum contains unparalleled exhibits depicting U.S. military life during World War I, including artifacts, photographs, and French and American tanks designed for trench warfare.

- **General John J. Pershing Boyhood Home, Laclede, Missouri.** Maintained by the Missouri State Park Board, Pershing's restored nineteenth-century home exhibits some of his personal belongings and papers. **www.mostateparks.com/pershingsite.htm**

- **Sgt. Alvin C. York Homeplace and State Historic Site, Pall Mall, Tennessee.** The home of America's greatest military hero of World War I contains fascinating artifacts, including York's letters written in the trenches. **www.alvincyork.org**

- **Wisconsin Veterans Museum, Madison, Wisconsin.** The most stunning museum of its size in the United States, this large building combines impressive collections of artifacts ranging from uniforms to tanks, with substantive exhibits and video programs based on remarkable historical research. It both documents and explains the participation of Wisconsin soldiers in the nation's wars, including the Spanish-American War and World War I.

 For additional study resources for this chapter, go to:
www.prenhall.com/goldfield/chapter23

Happy times were here again.

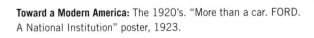

Toward a Modern America: The 1920's. "More than a car. FORD. A National Institution" poster, 1923.

24

TOWARD A MODERN AMERICA

THE 1920s

WHY WERE the 1920s referred to as the "Roaring Twenties?"

HOW DID big business shape the economy of the 1920s?

WHAT WAS the Great Migration, and how did it affect social life in the 1920s?

HOW DID new systems of distributing, marketing, and communication create culture?

WHAT CONFLICTS divided social groups in the 1920s?

WHAT WERE the reasons for U.S. involvement overseas in the 1920s?

CHAPTER 24

Happy times were here again. American industry, adopting Henry Ford's policy of mass production and low prices, was making it possible for everybody to have his share of everything. The newspapers, the statesmen, the economists, all agreed that American ingenuity had solved the age-old problem of poverty. There could never be another depression. . . .

The war had done something to Henry, it had taught him a new way to deal with his fellow men. . . . He became more abrupt in his manner, more harsh in his speech. "Gratitude?" he would say. "There's no gratitude in business. Men work for money." . . . From now on he was a business man, and held a tight rein on everything. This industry was his, he had made it himself, and what he wanted of the men he hired was that they should do exactly as he told them. . . .

Every worker had to be strained to the uttermost limit, every one had to be giving the last ounce of energy he had in his carcass. . . . They were tired when they started in the morning, and when they quit they were grey and staggering with fatigue, they were empty shells out of which the last drop of juice had been squeezed. . . .

Henry Ford was now getting close to his two million cars a year goal. . . . From the moment the ore was taken out of the ship at the River Rouge plant [in Detroit], through all the processes turning it into steel and shaping it into automobile parts with a hundred-ton press, and putting five thousand parts together into a car which rolled off the assembly line under its own power—all those processes were completed in less than a day and a half!

Some forty-five thousand different machines were now used in the making of Ford cars, in sixty establishments scattered over the United States. . . . Henry Ford was remaking the roads of America, and in the end he would remake the roads of the world—and line them all with filling stations and hot-dog stands of the American pattern.

Upton Sinclair, *The Flivver King: A Story of Ford–America*. (Chicago: Charles H. Kerr Publishing Company, 1999).

IMAGE KEY

for pages 628–629

a. Silent film star Gertrude Olmstead wears a ruffled flapper dress with a striped hat in 1925.

b. Toward A Modern America: The 1920's More than a car. FORD. A National Institution "poster", 1923.

c. A clarinet.

d. An old football.

e. Men are shown piecing together automobiles on an assembly line in the Rouge Plant of the Ford Motor Company.

f. The price of stocks through the 1920s and early 30s.

g. A Black family from the south arrives in Chicago, ca. 1910.

h. Campbell's Tomato Soup ad.

i. Women dressed in the white robes and hoods of the Ku Klux Klan in 1924.

UPTON SINCLAIR'S 1906 novel *The Jungle* graphically depicted the wretched conditions endured by Chicago's immigrant meatpacking workers. In *The Flivver King*, Sinclair portrayed the rise of the automobile industry and the revolutionizing vision of Henry Ford—the entrepreneur who symbolized modern America to the world.

"Machinery," proclaimed Henry Ford, "is the new Messiah." Ford had introduced the moving assembly line at his automobile factory on the eve of World War I, and, by 1925, it was turning out a Model T car every ten seconds. Mass production was becoming a reality; in fact, the term originated in Henry Ford's 1926 description of the system of flow production techniques popularly called "Fordism." The system symbolized the nation's booming economy: In the 1920s, Europeans used the word Fordize as a synonym for Americanize. Ford coupled machines and technology with managerial innovations. He established the "five-dollar day," twice the prevailing wage in Detroit's auto industry, and slashed the workweek from forty-eight to forty

---

CHRONOLOGY

1915	Ku Klux Klan is founded anew.		Country Club Plaza in Kansas City opens.
1919	Volstead Act is passed.	**1923**	Harding dies; Calvin Coolidge becomes president.
1920	Urban population exceeds rural population for the first time.	**1924**	National Origins Act sharply curtails immigration. Coolidge is elected president.
	Warren Harding is elected president. Prohibition takes effect. First commercial radio show is broadcast. Sinclair Lewis publishes *Main Street*.	**1925**	Scopes trial is held in Dayton, Tennessee. F. Scott Fitzgerald publishes *The Great Gatsby*
1921	Sheppard-Towner Maternity and Infancy Act is passed. Washington Naval Conference limits naval armaments.	**1927**	Charles A. Lindbergh flies solo across the Atlantic.
		1928	Kellogg-Briand Pact is signed. Herbert Hoover is elected president.
1922	Fordney-McCumber Act raises tariff rates. Sinclair Lewis publishes *Babbitt*.	**1929**	Ernest Hemingway publishes *A Farewell to Arms*.

---

hours. These changes, Ford argued, would reduce the costs of labor turnover and boost consumer purchasing power, leading to further profits from mass production.

The assembly line, however, alienated workers, and even Ford himself conceded that the repetitive operations of the assembly line were "so monotonous that it scarcely seems possible that any man would care to continue long at the same job." Ford first tried to adapt his mostly immigrant workers to these conditions through an Americanization program. His "Education Department" taught classes in English, sobriety, obedience, and industrial efficiency to the unskilled laborers entering the factory. After the course, they participated in a symbolic pageant: They climbed into a huge "melting pot," fifteen feet across and seven feet deep. After Ford managers stirred the pot with ten-foot ladles, the workers emerged wearing new clothes and waving American flags—new Americans made for the factory system.

When the labor market became more favorable to management in the early 1920s, Ford relied on discipline to control workers. To maximize profits and increase efficiency, he prohibited talking, whistling, sitting, or smoking on the job. Ford also banned unions and used spies to guard against their formation.

But Ford remained conflicted about the changes he saw and had helped facilitate. Cars and cigarettes were among the most intensively advertised goods in the 1920s, and for some they signaled rebellion and freedom. Women in short skirts and the rise of the Jazz Age—all contributed to what Ford saw as the evils of the "new America." Embracing nativism and protestantism, Ford, an ardent anti-Semite, blamed Jewish Americans for radicalism and labor organization and singled out the "International Jew" for allegedly controlling the financial community.

Henry Ford—and Fordism itself—thus reflected the complexity of the 1920s. Economic growth and technological innovation were paired with social conflict as traditions were destroyed, values displaced, and new people incorporated into a society increasingly industrialized, urbanized, and dominated by big business. Industrial production and national wealth soared, buoyed by new techniques and markets for consumer goods. Business values pervaded society and dominated government, which promoted business interests.

But not all Americans prospered. Many workers were unemployed, and the wages of still more were stagnant or falling. Farmers endured grim conditions and worse prospects. Social change brought pleasure to some and deep concern to others. City factories like the Ford Works attracted workers from the countryside, increasing urbanization; rapid suburbanization opened other horizons. Leisure activities flourished, and new mass media promoted modern ideas and stylish products. Workers would have to achieve personal satisfaction through consumption—and not production. But such experiences often proved unsettling, and some Americans sought reassurance by imposing their cultural or religious values on everyone around them. The tumultuous decade thus had many unresolved issues, much like the complex personality of Henry Ford himself. And Ford so dominated the age that when college students were asked to rank the greatest people of all time, Ford came in third—behind Christ and Napoleon.

THE ECONOMY THAT ROARED

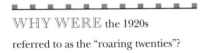

WHY WERE the 1920s referred to as the "roaring twenties"?

Following a severe postwar depression in 1920 and 1921, the American economy boomed through the remainder of the decade. Gross domestic product soared nearly 40 percent; output per worker-hour, or productivity, rose 72 percent in manufacturing; average per capita income increased by a third. Although the prosperity was not evenly distributed and some sectors of the economy were deeply troubled, most Americans welcomed the industrial expansion and business principles of the "New Era." (See American views, "The Cult of Business.")

BOOM INDUSTRIES

Many factors spurred the economic expansion of the 1920s. The huge wartime and postwar profits provided investment capital that enabled business to mechanize. Mass production spread quickly in American industry; machine-made standardized parts and the moving assembly line increased efficiency and production. Businesses steadily adopted the scientific management principles of Frederick W. Taylor. These highly touted systems, though often involving little more than an assembly-line "speed-up," also boosted efficiency. In factories, electric motors cut costs and improved manufacturing; in homes, electricity spurred demand for new products. Henry Ford was right: Mass production and consumption went hand in hand. Although not one in ten farm families had access to electric power, most other families did by 1929, and many bought electric sewing machines, vacuum cleaners, washing machines, and other labor-saving appliances.

The automobile industry drove the economy. Sales rose from about 1.9 million vehicles in 1920 to nearly 5 million by 1929. The automobile industry also employed one of every fourteen manufacturing workers and stimulated other industries from steel to rubber and glass. It created a huge new market for the petroleum industry and fostered oil drilling in Oklahoma, Texas, and Louisiana. It also encouraged the construction industry, a mainstay of the 1920s economy.

New industries also sprang up. The aviation industry grew rapidly, with government support. The U.S. Post Office subsidized commercial air service by providing air mail contracts to private carriers. Congress then authorized commercial passenger service over the mail routes, with regular traffic opening in 1927 between Boston and New York. By 1930, more than one hundred airlines criss-crossed America.

The Great War had stimulated the chemicals industry. The government confiscated chemical patents from German firms and transferred them to U.S. companies like Du Pont. With this advantage, Du Pont in the 1920s became a

W WHERE TO LEARN MORE

Henry Ford Museum and Greenfield Village, Dearborn, Michigan
www.hfmgv.org

· AMERICAN VIEWS ·

THE CULT OF BUSINESS

uring the 1920s, publicists and politicians joined manufacturers and merchants in proclaiming that business promoted not only material but also social and even spiritual well-being. In The Man Nobody Knows *(1924), advertising executive Bruce Barton portrayed Jesus Christ as the founder of modern business. The following excerpt from an article by Edward E. Purinton, a popular lecturer on business values and efficiency, makes even more extensive claims for business.*

HOW ACCURATE are Purinton's claims of great opportunity in the corporate world of the 1920s? Of occupational mobility in the factory economy? What does this view of business imply about the role of government? How might Protestant fundamentalists have viewed the cult of business?

Among the nations of the earth today America stands for one idea: Business. National opprobrium? National opportunity. For in this fact lies, potentially, the salvation of the world.

Through business, properly conceived, managed, and conducted, the human race is finally to be redeemed. How and why a man works foretells what he will do, think, have, give, and be. And real salvation is in doing, thinking, having, giving, and being—not in sermonizing and theorizing. . . .

What is the finest game? Business. The soundest science? Business. The truest art? Business. The fullest education? Business. The fairest opportunity? Business. The cleanest philanthropy? Business. The sanest religion? Business.

You may not agree. That is because you judge business by the crude, mean, stupid, false imitation of business that happens to be located near you.

The finest game is business. The rewards are for everybody, and all can win. There are no favorites—Providence always crowns the career of the man who is worthy. And in this game there is no "luck"—you have the fun of taking chances but the sobriety of guaranteeing certainties. The speed and size of your winnings are for you alone to determine. . . .

The soundest science is business. All investigation is reduced to action, and by action proved or disproved. The idealistic motive animates the materialistic method. . . . Capital is furnished for the researches of "pure science"; yet pure science is not regarded pure until practical. Competent scientists are suitably rewarded—as they are not in the scientific schools. . . .

The fullest education is business. A proper blend of study, work and life is essential to advancement. The whole man is educated. Human nature itself is the open book that all business men study; and the mastery of a page of this educates you more than the memorizing of a dusty tome from a library shelf. In the school of business, moreover, you teach yourself and learn most from your own mistakes. What you learn here you live out, the only real test.

The fairest opportunity is business. You can find more, better, quicker chances to get ahead in a large business house than anywhere else on earth. . . . Recognition of better work, of keener and quicker thought, of deeper and finer feeling, is gladly offered by the men higher up, with early promotion the rule for the man who justifies it. There is, and can be, no such thing as buried talent in a modern business organization. . . .

The sanest religion is business. Any relationship that forces a man to follow the Golden Rule rightfully belongs amid the ceremonials of the church. A great business enterprise includes and presupposes this relationship. I have seen more Christianity to the square inch as a regular part of the office equipment of famous corporation presidents than may ordinarily be found on Sunday in a verbalized but not vitalized church congregation. . . . You can fool your preacher with a sickly sprout or a wormy semblance of character, but you can't fool your employer. I would make every business house a consultation bureau for the guidance of the church whose members were employees of the house. . . .

The future work of the businessman is to teach the teacher, preach to the preacher, admonish the parent, advise the doctor, justify the lawyer, superintend the statesman, fructify the farmer, stabilize the banker, harness the dreamer, and reform the reformer.

Source: Edward E. Purinton, "Big Ideas from Big Business," *Independent,* April 16, 1921. National Weekly Corp., New York.

chemical empire producing plastics, finishes, dyes, and organic chemicals, which it developed into enamels, rayon, and cellophane.

The new radio and motion picture industries also flourished. Commercial broadcasting began in 1920. By 1927, there were 732 stations, and Congress created what became the Federal Communications Commission (FCC) to prevent wave band interference. Corporations dominated the new industry. Westinghouse, RCA, and General Electric began opening strings of stations in the early 1920s.

The motion picture industry became one of the nation's five largest businesses. Twenty thousand movie theaters sold 100 million tickets a week. Hollywood studios were huge factories, producing films on an assembly-line basis. While Americans watched Charlie Chaplin showcase his comedic genius in films like *The Gold Rush* (1925), corporations like Paramount were integrating production with distribution and exhibition to maximize control and profit and eliminate independent producers and theaters.

CORPORATE CONSOLIDATION

A wave of corporate mergers swept over the 1920s economy. Great corporations swallowed up thousands of small firms. Particularly significant was the spread of oligopoly—the control of an entire industry by a few giant firms. Three companies—Ford, General Motors, and Chrysler—produced 83 percent of the nation's cars. In the electric light and power industry, nearly four thousand local utility companies were merged into a dozen holding companies. By 1929, the nation's two hundred largest corporations controlled nearly half of all nonbanking corporate wealth.

Oligopolies also dominated finance and marketing. By 1929, a mere 1 percent of the nation's banks controlled half of its banking resources. In marketing, national chain stores like A&P and Woolworth's displaced local retailers.

The corporate consolidation of the 1920s provoked little public opposition. Americans mostly accepted that size brought efficiency and productivity.

OPEN SHOPS AND WELFARE CAPITALISM

Business also attacked labor. In 1921, the National Association of Manufacturers organized an **open shop** campaign to break union shop contracts, which required all employees to be union members. Denouncing collective bargaining as un-American, businesses described the open shop, in which union membership was not required and usually prohibited, as the "American plan." They forced workers to sign so-called **yellow dog contracts** that bound them to reject unions to keep their jobs. Business also used boycotts to force employers into a uniform antiunion front. Bethlehem Steel, for example, refused to sell steel to companies employing union labor. Where unions existed, corporations tried to crush them, using spies or hiring strikebreakers.

Some companies advocated a paternalistic system called **welfare capitalism** as an alternative to unions. Eastman Kodak, General Motors, U.S. Steel, and other firms provided medical services, insurance pensions and vacations for their workers to persuade workers to rely on the corporation. Welfare capitalism, however, covered scarcely 5 percent of the work force and often benefited only skilled workers who were already tied to the company through seniority. Moreover, it was directed primarily at men.

Corporations in the 1920s also promoted company unions, management-sponsored substitutes for labor unions. Company unions were usually forbidden to handle wage and hour issues. Their function was to implement company policies and undermine real unionism.

Open shop Factory or business employing workers whether or not they are union members; in practice, such a business usually refuses to hire union members and follows antiunion policies.

Yellow-dog contracts Employment agreements binding workers not to join a union.

Welfare capitalism A paternalistic system of labor relations emphasizing management responsibility for employee well-being.

Partly because of these pressures, membership in labor unions fell from 5.1 million in 1920 to 3.6 million in 1929. But unions also contributed to their own decline. Conservative union leaders neglected ethnic and black workers in mass production industries. Nor did they try to organize women, nearly one-fourth of all workers by 1930. The growing numbers of white-collar workers regarded themselves as middleclass and beyond the scope of union action.

With increasing mechanization and weak labor unions, workers suffered from job insecurity and stagnant wages. Real wages (purchasing power) did improve, but most of the improvement came before 1923 and reflected falling prices more than rising wages. After 1923, American wages stabilized. The failure to raise wages when productivity was increasing threatened the nation's long-term prosperity. In short, rising national income largely reflected salaries and dividends, not wages.

Overall, the gap between rich and poor widened during the decade. By 1929, 71 percent of American families earned less than what the U.S. Bureau of Labor Statistics regarded as necessary for a decent living standard. The maldistribution of income meant that eventually Americans would be unable to purchase the products they made.

The expansion of consumer credit, rare before the 1920s, offered temporary relief by permitting consumers to buy goods over time. General Motors introduced consumer credit on a national basis to create a mass market for expensive automobiles. By 1927, two-thirds of automobiles were purchased on the installment plan. However, installment loans simply added interest charges to the price of products.

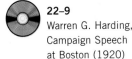

22–9
Warren G. Harding,
Campaign Speech
at Boston (1920)

SICK INDUSTRIES

Several "sick" industries dragged on the economy. Coal mining, textile and garment manufacturing, and railroads suffered from excess capacity (too many mines, factories and lines), shrinking demand, low returns, and management-labor conflicts. Unemployment in the coal industry approached 30 percent; by 1928, a reporter found "thousands of women and children literally starving to death" in Appalachia and the remaining miners held in "industrial slavery." The textile industry coped with overcapacity and declining demand by shifting operations from New England to the cheap-labor South, employing girls and young women for fifty-six-hour weeks at 18 cents an hour. Nevertheless, textile companies remained barely profitable.

American agriculture never recovered from the 1921 depression. Agricultural surpluses and shrinking demand forced down prices. After the war, foreign markets dried up, and demand for cotton slackened. Moreover, farmers' wartime expansion left them heavily mortgaged. Many small farmers lost their land and became tenants or farm hands. By the end of the 1920s, the average per capita income for people on the nation's farms was only one-fourth that of Americans off the farm.

THE BUSINESS OF GOVERNMENT

The Republican surge in national politics also shaped the economy. In the 1920 election, the Republican slogan was "Less government in business, more business in government." Under such direction, the federal government advanced business interests at the expense of other objectives.

HOW DID the big business
shape the economy of the 1920s?

REPUBLICAN ASCENDANCY

Republicans in 1920 had retained control of Congress and put Warren Harding in the White House. Harding was neither capable nor bright, but he had a genial touch that contrasted favorably with Wilson. He pardoned Eugene Debs, whom

WHERE TO LEARN MORE

Warren G. Harding House,
Marion, Ohio
www.ohiohistory.org/places/harding

WHERE TO LEARN MORE

George Norris Home,
McCook, Nebraska
**www.nebraskahistory.org/sites/
norris/index.htm**

Wilson had refused to release from prison, and he spoke out against racial violence. He also helped shape the modern presidency by supporting the Budget and Accounting Act of 1921, which gave the president authority over the budget and created the Budget Bureau and the General Accounting Office. Two of his cabinet appointees, Secretary of Commerce Herbert Hoover and Secretary of the Treasury Andrew Mellon, shaped economic policy throughout the 1920s.

Hoover made the Commerce Department the government's most dynamic office. He cemented its ties with the leading sectors of the economy, expanded its collection and distribution of industrial information, pushed to exploit foreign resources and markets, and encouraged innovation. Hoover's goal was to expand prosperity by making business efficient, responsive, and profitable. Andrew Mellon had a narrower goal. A wealthy banker and industrialist, he pressed Congress to reduce taxes on businesses and the rich. Despite the opposition of progressives, Mellon lowered maximum tax rates and eliminated wartime excess-profits taxes in 1921.

The Harding administration promoted business interests in other ways, too. The tariff of 1922 raised import rates to protect industry from foreign competition. Attorney General Harry Daugherty aided the business campaign for the open shop. And the Republicans also curtailed government regulation. By appointing advocates of big business to the Federal Trade Commission, the Federal Reserve Board, and other regulatory agencies established earlier by the progressives, Harding made government the collaborator rather than the regulator of business. Progressive Republican Senator George Norris of Nebraska angrily asked, "If trusts, combinations, and big business are to run the government, why not permit them to do it directly rather than through this expensive machinery which was originally honestly established for the protection of the people of the country against monopoly?"

Finally, Harding reshaped the Supreme Court into a still more aggressive champion of business. He named the conservative William Howard Taft as chief justice and matched him with three other pro-business justices. The Court struck down much of the government economic regulation adopted during the Progressive Era, invalidated restraints on child labor and a minimum wage law for women, and approved restrictions on labor unions.

GOVERNMENT CORRUPTION

The green light that Harding Republicans extended to private interests led to corruption and scandals. Harding appointed friends and cronies who saw public service as an opportunity for graft. The head of the Veterans Bureau went to prison for cheating disabled veterans of $200 million. Albert Fall, the secretary of the interior, leased the petroleum reserves set aside by progressive conservationists to oil companies in exchange for cash, bonds, and cattle for his New Mexico ranch. Exposed for his role in the Teapot Dome scandal, named after a Wyoming oil reserve, Fall became the first cabinet officer in history to go to jail. Attorney General Daugherty escaped a similar fate by destroying records and invoking the Fifth Amendment.

Harding was appalled as the scandals began to unfold. He died shortly thereafter, probably of a heart attack.

COOLIDGE PROSPERITY

On August 3, 1923, Vice President Calvin Coolidge was sworn in as president by his father while visiting his birthplace in rural Vermont, thereby reaffirming his association with traditional values. This image reassured Americans troubled by the Harding scandals.

QUICK REVIEW

The Teapot Dome Scandal

◆ Corruption and scandals plagued the Harding administration.

◆ Albert Hall, the secretary of the interior, leased petroleum reserves in exchange for cash and cattle.

◆ As a result of his part in the Teapot Dome scandal, Fall went to prison.

Coolidge supported business with ideological conviction and cultivated a deliberate inactivity calculated to lower expectations of government. He endorsed Secretary of the Treasury Mellon's ongoing efforts to reverse the progressive tax policies of the Wilson years and backed Secretary of Commerce Hoover's efforts on behalf of the business community (although he privately sneered at Hoover as the "Wonder Boy"). Coolidge continued, like Harding, to install business supporters in the regulatory agencies. To chair the Federal Trade Commission he appointed an attorney who had condemned the agency as "an instrument of oppression and disturbance and injury instead of help to business." The *Wall Street Journal* crowed, "Never before, here or anywhere else, has a government been so completely fused with business."

"Coolidge prosperity" determined the 1924 election. The Democrats, took 103 ballots to nominate the colorless, conservative Wall Street lawyer John W. Davis. A more interesting opponent for Coolidge was Robert La Follette, nominated by discontented farm and labor organizations that formed a new Progressive party. La Follette campaigned against "the power of private monopoly over the political and economic life of the American people." The Republicans, backed by immense contributions from business, denounced La Follette as an agent of Bolshevism. The choice, Republicans insisted, was "Coolidge or Chaos." Thus instructed, Americans chose Coolidge, though barely half the electorate bothered to vote.

THE FATE OF REFORM

The fate of women's groups illustrated the difficulties reformers faced in the 1920s. At first, the adoption of woman suffrage prompted politicians to champion women's reform issues. In 1920, both major parties endorsed many of the goals of the new **League of Women Voters**. Within a year, many states had granted women the right to serve on juries, several enacted equal pay laws, and Wisconsin adopted an equal rights law. Congress passed the **Sheppard-Towner Maternity and Infancy Act**, the first federal social welfare law, in 1921. It provided federal funds for infant and maternity care, precisely the type of protective legislation that the suffragists had described as women's special interest.

But thereafter women reformers gained little. As it became clear that women did not vote as a bloc but according to their varying social and economic backgrounds, Congress lost interest in "women's issues." In 1929, Congress killed the Sheppard-Towner Act. Nor could reformers gain ratification of a child labor amendment after the Supreme Court invalidated laws regulating child labor. Conservatives attacked women reformers as "Bolsheviks."

Disagreements among women reformers and shifting interests also limited their success. The National Woman's Party campaigned for an Equal Rights Amendment, but other reformers feared that such an amendment would nullify the progressive laws that protected working women. Reform organizations lost their energy, and many younger women rejected the public concerns of progressive feminists for what the president of the Women's Trade Union League called "cheap hopes and cheaper materialism."

CITIES AND SUBURBS

The 1920 census reported that, for the first time, more Americans lived in urban than in rural areas. The trend toward urbanization accelerated in the 1920s as millions of Americans fled the depressed countryside for the booming cities. This massive population movement interacted with technological innovations to reshape cities, build suburbs, and transform urban life (see Map 24–1).

WHERE TO LEARN MORE

Calvin Coolidge Homestead, Plymouth, Vermont
www.calvin-coolidge.org/ pages/homestead

League of Women Voters   League formed in 1920 advocating for women's rights, among them the right for women to serve on juries and equal pay laws.

Sheppard-Towner Maternity and Infancy Act   The first federal social welfare law, passed in 1921, providing federal funds for infant and maternity care.

WHAT WAS the Great Migration, and how did it affect social life in the 1920s?

MAP EXPLORATION

To explore this map, go to **http://www.prenhall.com/goldfield2/map24.1**

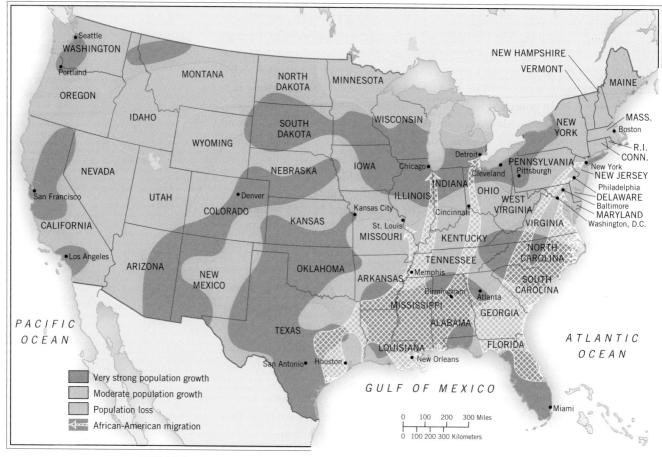

Very strong population growth
Moderate population growth
Population loss
African-American migration

MAP 24–1

Population Shifts, 1920–1930   Rural Americans fled to the cities during the 1920s, escaping a declining agricultural economy to search for new opportunities. African Americans in particular left the rural South for Eastern and Midwestern cities, but the urban population also jumped in the West and in the South itself.

WHY DID certain states and areas gain population during this period, and why did others see population decreases?

EXPANDING CITIES

Urbanization affected all regions of the country. The older industrial cities of the Northeast and Upper Midwest attracted migrants from the rural South and distressed Appalachia. Rural Southerners also poured into Atlanta, Birmingham, Memphis, and Houston. Little more than jungle before 1914, Miami became the fastest-growing city in the United States during the 1920s—"the Magic City." In the West, Denver, Portland, and Seattle (each a regional economic hub) and several California cities grew rapidly. By 1930 Los Angeles was the nation's fifth-largest city, with over 1.2 million people.

The population surge transformed the urban landscape. As land values soared, developers built skyscrapers. By the end of the decade, American cities had nearly four hundred skyscrapers taller than twenty stories. The tallest, New York's 102-story Empire State Building, symbolized the urban boom.

THE GREAT BLACK MIGRATION

A significant feature of the rural-to-urban movement was the **Great Migration** of African Americans from the South in search of job opportunities. Prosperity created jobs, and with the decline in European immigration, black workers filled the positions previously given to new immigrants. Though generally the lowest paid and least secure jobs, they were better than sharecropping in the rural South. Black men worked as unskilled or semiskilled laborers; black women became domestics in white homes. More than a million and a half African Americans moved to Northern cities in the 1920s.

Black ghettos developed in most Northern cities more because of prejudice than the wishes of the migrants. With thousands of newcomers limited to certain neighborhoods by racist restrictions, housing shortages developed. High rents and low wages forced black families to share inferior and unsanitary housing that threatened their health and safety. In Pittsburgh, only 20 percent of black houses had bathtubs and only 50 percent had indoor toilets.

However, the Great Migration also increased African Americans' racial consciousness and power. In 1928 black Chicagoans elected the first black man to Congress since the turn of the century. Mutual aid societies and fraternal orders proliferated. Churches were particularly influential.

Another organization also sought to appeal to poor black ghetto dwellers. The Universal Negro Improvement Association (UNIA), organized by Marcus Garvey, a Jamaican immigrant to New York, rejected the NAACP's goal of integration. A black nationalist espousing racial pride, Garvey exhorted African Americans to migrate to Africa to build a "free, redeemed, and mighty nation." UNIA organized many enterprises, including groceries, restaurants, laundries, a printing plant, and the Black Star Steamship Line. UNIA attracted half a million members, the first black mass movement in American history. When Garvey was convicted of mail fraud and deported, however, the movement collapsed.

Racial pride also found expression in the **Harlem Renaissance**, an outpouring of literature, painting, sculpture, and music. Inspired by African-American culture and black urban life, writers and artists created works of power and poignancy. The poetry of Langston Hughes reflected the rhythm and mood of jazz and the blues.

BARRIOS

Hispanic migrants also entered the nation's cities in the 1920s, creating their own communities, or *barrios*. Fifty thousand Puerto Ricans settled in New York, mostly in East ("Spanish") Harlem, where they found low-paying jobs. Far more migrants arrived from Mexico, usually settling in Western and Southwestern cities. The *barrios*, with their own businesses, churches, and cultural organizations, created a sense of permanency.

These communities enabled the newcomers to preserve their cultural values and build social institutions like *mutualistas* (mutual aid societies) that helped them get credit, housing, and health care. But the *barrios* also reflected the hostility that Hispanics encountered in American cities, for racism often restricted them to such districts. The number of Mexicans in Los Angeles tripled during the 1920s to nearly 100,000, but segregation confined them to East Los Angeles. Other areas of the city boasted of being "restricted to the white race."

Some Hispanics fought discrimination. *La Orden de Hijos de America* (The Order of the Sons of America), organized in San Antonio in 1921, campaigned against inequities in schools and the jury system. In 1929, it helped launch the larger League of United Latin American Citizens (LULAC), which would help advance civil rights for all Americans.

WHERE TO LEARN MORE

Smithsonian Institution, Washington, D.C.

23–1
F. J. Grimke, "Address of Welcome to the Men Who Have Returned from the Battlefront" (1919)

Great Migration   The mass movement of African Americans from the rural South to the urban North, spurred especially by new job opportunities during World War I and the 1920s.

Harlem Renaissance   A new African-American cultural awareness that flourished in literature, art, and music in the 1920s.

THE ROAD TO SUBURBIA

As fast as the cities mushroomed in the 1920s, the suburbs grew twice as fast. Automobiles created the modern suburb for it enabled people to live in formerly remote areas. A single-family house surrounded by a lawn became the social ideal, a pastoral escape from the overcrowded and dangerous city. Many suburbs excluded African Americans, Hispanics, Jews, and working-class people.

Suburbanization and the automobile brought other changes. In 1922, J.C. Nichols opened the Country Club Plaza, the first suburban shopping center, in Kansas City; it provided free, off-street parking. Department stores and other large retailers began leaving the urban cores for the suburbs, where both parking and more affluent customers were waiting. Drive-in restaurants began with Royce Hailey's Pig Stand in Dallas in 1921. Later in the decade, the first fast-food franchise chain, White Tower, appeared, with its standardized menu and building. To serve the automobile, governments spent more on road construction and maintenance. By 1930, road construction was the largest single item in the national budget.

MASS CULTURE IN THE JAZZ AGE

The White Tower chain symbolized a new society and culture. Urbanization and the automobile joined with new systems of distributing, marketing, and communications to mold a mass culture of standardized experiences and interests. Not all Americans participated equally in the new culture, however, and some attacked it.

ADVERTISING THE CONSUMER SOCIETY

Advertising and its focus on increasing consumption shaped the new society. Advertisers exhorted consumers via newspapers, billboards, streetcar signs, junk mail, radio, movies, and even skywriting. They sought to create a single market where everyone, regardless of region and ethnicity, consumed brand-name products. Advertisers attempted to stimulate new wants by ridiculing previous models or tastes as obsolete, acclaiming the convenience of a new brand, or linking the latest fashion with status or sex appeal.

The home became a focus of consumerism. Middle- and upper-class women purchased mass-produced household appliances, such as electric irons, toasters, vacuum cleaners, washing machines, and refrigerators. Working-class women bought packaged food, ready-made clothing, and other consumer goods to lighten their workload. Advertisers attempted to redefine the housewife's role as primarily that of a consumer, purchasing goods for her family.

A shifting labor market also promoted mass consumption. The increasing number of white-collar workers had more time and money for leisure and consumption. Women clerical workers, the fastest growing occupational group, found in the purchase of clothes and cosmetics a sign of social status and an antidote to workplace monotony.

Under the stimulus of advertising, consumption increasingly displaced the traditional virtues of thrift, prudence, and avoidance of debt. Installment buying became common. By 1928, 85 percent of furniture, 80 percent of radios, and 75 percent of washing machines were bought on credit. But with personal debt rising more than twice as fast as incomes, even aggressive advertising and credit could not indefinitely prolong the illusion of a healthy economy.

LEISURE AND ENTERTAINMENT

During the 1920s, Americans also spent more on recreation and leisure, important features of the new mass society. Millions of people packed into movie theaters whose ornate style symbolized their social importance. Movies helped set national trends in dress, language, and behavior. Studios made films to attract the largest audiences and fit prevailing stereotypes. Cecil B. De Mille titillated audiences while reinforcing conventional standards with religious epics, like *The Ten Commandments* (1923) or *The King of Kings* (1927).

Radio also helped mold national popular culture. The first radio network, the National Broadcasting Company (NBC), was formed in 1926. Soon it was charging $10,000 to broadcast commercials to a national market. Networks provided standardized entertainment, personalities, and news to Americans across the nation. Radio incorporated listeners into a national society. Rural residents welcomed the "talking furniture" for giving them access to the speeches, sermons, and business information available to city-dwellers.

The phonograph allowed families to listen to music of their choice in their own homes. Record companies promoted dance crazes, such as the Charleston, and developed regional markets for country, or "hillbilly," music in the South and West as well as a "race market" for blues and jazz among the growing urban population, black and white. The popularity of the trumpet player Louis Armstrong and other jazz greats gave the decade its nickname, the **Jazz Age**.

Jazz derived from African-American musical traditions. The Great Migration spread it from New Orleans and Kansas City to cities throughout the nation. Its improvisational and rhythmic characteristics differed sharply from older and more formal music and were often condemned by people who feared that jazz would undermine conventional restraints on behavior. But conductor Leopold Stokowski defended jazz as, "an expression of the times, of the breathless, energetic, superactive times in which we are living; it is useless to fight against it."

Professional sports also flourished and became more commercialized. Millions of Americans, attracted by the popularity of such celebrities as Babe Ruth of the New York Yankees, crowded into baseball parks to follow major league teams. Ruth treated himself as a commercial commodity, hiring an agent, endorsing Cadillacs and alligator shoes, and defending a salary in 1932 that dwarfed that of President Hoover by declaring, "I had a better year than he did."

Another celebrity who captured popular fascination was the aviator Charles Lindbergh, who flew alone across the Atlantic in 1927. In the *Spirit of St. Louis*, a tiny airplane built on a shoestring budget, Lindbergh fought bad weather and fatigue for thirty-four hours before landing to a hero's welcome in Paris. Named its first "Man of the Year" by *Time*, one of the new mass-circulation magazines, Lindbergh won adulation and awards from Americans who still valued the image of individualism.

THE NEW MORALITY

The promotion of consumption and immediate gratification weakened traditional self-restraint and fed a desire for personal fulfillment. The failure of wartime sacrifices to achieve promised glories deepened Americans' growing disenchantment

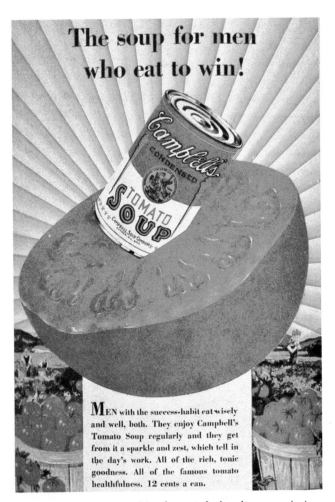

The soup for men who eat to win!

MEN with the success-habit eat wisely and well, both. They enjoy Campbell's Tomato Soup regularly and they get from it a sparkle and zest, which tell in the day's work. All of the rich, tonic goodness. All of the famous tomato healthfulness. 12 cents a can.

Advertisements for brand-name products, like this 1929 ad for Campbell's tomato soup, often tried to link simple consumption with larger issues of personal success and achievement.

By permission of Campbell Soup Company

Jazz Age The 1920s, so called for the popular music of the day as a symbol of the many changes taking place in the mass culture.

with traditional values. The social dislocations of the war years and growing urbanization accelerated moral and social change. Sexual pleasure became an increasingly open objective, as the growing availability of birth control information enabled women to enjoy sex with less fear of pregnancy; and movie stars like Clara Bow, known as "the It Girl," and Rudolph Valentino flaunted sexuality to mass audiences. Traditionalists worried as divorce rates, cigarette consumption, and hemlines went up while respect for parents, elders, and clergy went down.

Young people seemed to embody the new morality. Rejecting conventional standards, they embraced the era's frenzied dances, bootleg liquor, smoking, more revealing clothing, and sexual experimentation. They welcomed the freedom from parental control that the automobile afforded. The "flapper"—a frivolous young woman with short hair and a skimpy skirt who danced, smoked, and drank in oblivious self-absorption—was a major obsession.

But the new morality was neither as new nor as widespread as its advocates and critics believed. Signs of change had appeared before the war in new clothing fashions, social values, and public amusements among working-class and ethnic groups. But most Americans still adhered to traditional beliefs and values. Moreover, the new morality offered only a limited freedom. Women remained subject to traditional double standards, with marriage and divorce laws, property rights, and employment opportunities biased against them.

THE SEARCHING TWENTIES

Many writers rejected what they considered the materialism, conformity, and provincialism of the emerging mass culture. Their criticism made the postwar decade one of the most creative periods in American literature. The brutality and hypocrisy of the war stimulated their disillusionment and alienation. What Gertrude Stein called the **Lost Generation** considered, in the words of F. Scott Fitzgerald, "all Gods dead, all wars fought, all faiths in man shaken." Ernest Hemingway, wounded as a Red Cross volunteer during the war, rejected idealism in his novel *A Farewell to Arms* (1929), declaring that he no longer saw any meaning in "the words *sacred*, *glorious*, and *sacrifice*."

Novelists also turned their attention to American society. In *The Great Gatsby* (1925), Fitzgerald traced the self-deceptions of the wealthy. Sinclair Lewis ridiculed middle-class society and its narrow business culture in *Babbitt* (1922), whose title character provided a new word for the smug and shallow.

W WHERE TO LEARN MORE

⭐ F. Scott and Zelda Fitzgerald Museum, Montgomery, Alabama
www.alabamatravel.org/central/szfm.html

WHAT CONFLICTS

divided social groups in the 1920s?

CULTURE WARS

Despite the blossoming of mass culture and society in the 1920s, conflicts divided social groups. Some of these struggles involved reactions against the new currents in American life, including technological and scientific innovations, urban growth, and materialism. But movements to restrict immigration, enforce prohibition, prohibit the teaching of evolution, and even sustain the Ku Klux Klan did not have simple origins, motives, or consequences. The forces underlying the culture wars of the 1920s would surface repeatedly in the future (see the Overview table "Issues in the Culture Wars of the 1920s" on p. 644).

NATIVISM AND IMMIGRATION RESTRICTION

For years, many Americans, from racists to reformers, had campaigned to restrict immigration. In 1917, Congress required immigrants to pass a literacy test. But renewed immigration after the war revived the anti-immigration movement, and the propaganda of the war and Red Scare years generated public support for more restriction. Depicting immigrants as radicals, racial inferiors, religious subversives, or criminals, nativists clamored for congressional action.

The Emergency Quota Act of 1921 reduced immigration by about two-thirds and established quotas for nationalities on the basis of their numbers in the United States in 1910. Coolidge himself urged that America "be kept American," meaning white, Anglo-Saxon, and Protestant. Congress adopted this racist rationale in the **National Origins Act of 1924**, which proclaimed its objective to be the maintenance of the "racial preponderance" of "the basic strain of our population." This law restricted immigration quotas to 2 percent of the foreign-born population of each nationality as recorded in the 1890 census, which was taken before the mass immigration from southern and eastern Europe. Another provision excluded Japanese immigrants.

Other actions targeted Japanese residents in America. California, Oregon, Washington, Arizona, and other Western states prohibited them from owning or leasing land. In 1922, the Supreme Court ruled that, as nonwhites, they could never become naturalized citizens. Dispirited by the prejudice of the decade, Japanese residents hoped for fulfillment through their children, the **Nisei**, who were American citizens by birth.

Ironically, as a U.S. territory, the Philippines was not subject to the National Origins Act, and Filipino immigration increased ninefold during the 1920s. Similarly, because the law did not apply to immigrants from the Western Hemisphere, Mexican immigration also grew. Nativists lobbied to exclude Mexicans, but agribusiness interests in the Southwest blocked any restrictions on low-cost migrant labor.

THE KU KLUX KLAN

Nativism was also reflected in the popularity of the revived Ku Klux Klan, the goal of which, according to its leader, was to protect "the interest of those whose forefathers established the nation." Although founded in Georgia in 1915 and modeled on its Reconstruction predecessor, the new Klan was a national, not a Southern, movement and claimed several million members by the mid-1920s. Admitting only native-born white Protestants, the Klan embodied the fears of a traditional culture threatened by social change. Ironically, its rapid spread owed much to modern business and promotional techniques as hundreds of professional recruiters raked in hefty commissions selling Klan memberships to those hoping to defend their way of life.

In part the Klan was a fraternal order, providing entertainment, assistance, and community for its members. Its picnics, parades, charity drives, and other social and family-oriented activities—perhaps a half million women joined the Women of the Ku Klux Klan—sharply distinguished the organization from both the small, secretive Klan of the nineteenth century and the still smaller, extremist Klan of the later twentieth century.

But the Klan also exploited racial, ethnic, and religious prejudices, attacking African Americans in the South, Mexicans in Texas, Japanese in California, and Catholics and Jews everywhere. A twisted religious impulse ran through much of the Klan's organization and activities. It hired itinerant Protestant ministers to spread its message, erected altars and flaming crosses at its meetings, and sang Klan lyrics to the tunes of well-known hymns. The Klan also resorted to violence. In 1921, for example, a Methodist minister who belonged to the Klan murdered a Catholic priest on his own doorstep, and other Klansmen burned down Catholic churches.

National Origins Act of 1924   Law sharply restricting immigration on the basis of immigrants' national origins and discriminating against southern and eastern Europeans and Asians.

Nisei   U.S. citizens born of immigrant Japanese parents.

OVERVIEW

ISSUES IN THE CULTURE WARS OF THE 1920S

Issue	Proponent view	Opponent view
The new morality	Promotes greater personal freedom and opportunities for fulfillment	Promotes moral collapse
Evolutionism	A scientific advance linked to notions of progress	A threat to religious belief
Jazz	Modern and vital	Unsettling, irregular, vulgar, and primitive
Immigration	A source of national strength from ethnic and racial diversity	A threat to the status and authority of old-stock white Protestants
Great Migration	A chance for African Americans to find new economic opportunities and gain autonomy and pride	A threat to traditional white privilege, control, and status
Prohibition	Promotes social and family stability and reduces crime	Restricts personal liberty and increases crime
Fundamentalism	An admirable adherence to traditional religious faith and biblical injunctions	A superstitious creed given to intolerant interference in social and political affairs
Ku Klux Klan	An organization promoting community responsibility, patriotism, and traditional social, moral, and religious values	A group of religious and racial bigots given to violent vigilantism and fostering moral and public corruption
Mass culture	Increases popular participation in national culture; provides entertainment and relaxation	Promotes conformity, materialism, mediocrity, and spectacle
Consumerism	Promotes material progress and higher living standards	Promotes waste, sterility, and self-indulgence

The Klan also ventured into politics, with some success, but it eventually encountered resistance. In the North, Catholic workers disrupted Klan parades. In the South, too, Klan excesses provoked a backlash. After the Klan in Dallas flogged sixty-eight people in a "whipping meadow" along the Trinity River in 1922, respect turned to outrage. Newspapers demanded that the Klan disband, and district attorneys began to prosecute Klan thugs. Elsewhere the Klan was stung by revelations of criminal behavior and corruption. By 1930, the Klan had nearly collapsed.

PROHIBITION AND CRIME

Like the Klan, prohibition both reflected and provoked social tensions in the 1920s. In 1920 the Eighteenth Amendment, prohibited the manufacture, sale, or transportation of alcoholic beverages. Congress then passed the **Volstead Act**, which defined the forbidden liquors and established the Prohibition Bureau to enforce the law. But many social groups, especially among urban ethnic communities, opposed

Volstead Act The 1920 law defining the liquor forbidden under the Eighteenth Amendment and giving enforcement responsibilities to the Prohibition Bureau of the Department of the Treasury.

prohibition, and the government could not enforce the law where public opinion did not endorse it.

Evasion was easy. By permitting alcohol for medicinal, sacramental, and industrial purposes, the Volstead Act enabled doctors, priests, and druggists to satisfy their friends' needs. City dwellers made "bathtub gin," and rural people distilled "moonshine." Bootleggers often operated openly.

The huge profits encouraged organized crime—which had previously concentrated on gambling and prostitution—to develop elaborate liquor distribution networks. Crime "families" used violence to enforce contracts, suppress competition, and attack rivals. In Chicago, Al Capone's army of nearly a thousand gangsters killed hundreds.

Gradually, even many "drys"—people who had initially favored prohibition—dropped their support, horrified by the boost it gave organized crime and worried about a general disrespect for law that it promoted. In 1933, thirty-six states ratified an amendment repealing what Herbert Hoover had called a "noble experiment."

Indiana Klanswomen pose in their regalia in 1924. The Klan combined appeals to traditional family and religious values with violent attacks upon those who were not white, native-born Protestants.

Getty Image Inc./Image Bank

OLD-TIME RELIGION AND THE SCOPES TRIAL

Religion provided another fulcrum for traditionalists attempting to stem cultural change. Protestant fundamentalism, which emphasized the infallibility of the Bible, including the Genesis story of Adam and Eve, emerged at the turn of the century as a conservative reaction to religious modernism and the social changes brought by the mass immigration of Catholics and Jews; the growing influence of science and technology; and the secularization of public education. But the fundamentalist crusade to reshape America became formidable only in the 1920s.

Fundamentalist groups, colleges, and publications sprang up throughout the nation, especially in the South. The anti-Catholic sentiment exploited by the Klan was but one consequence of fundamentalism's insistence on strict biblical Christianity. A second was the assault on Darwin's theory of evolution which contradicted literal interpretations of biblical Creation. Fundamentalist legislators tried to prevent teaching evolution in public schools in at least twenty states. In 1925, Tennessee forbade teaching any idea contrary to the biblical account of human origins.

Social or political conservatism, however, was not an inherent part of old-time religion. The most prominent antievolution politician, William Jennings Bryan, feared that Darwinism promoted political and economic conservatism. The survival of the fittest, he complained, elevated force and brutality, ignored spiritual values and democracy, and discouraged altruism and reform. How could a person fight for social justice "unless he believes in the triumph of right?"

The controversy over evolution came to a head when the **American Civil Liberties Union (ACLU)** responded to Tennessee's violation of the constitutional separation of church and state by offering to defend any teacher who tested the anti-evolution law. John Scopes, a high school biology teacher in Dayton, Tennessee, did so and was arrested. Scopes's trial riveted national attention after Bryan agreed to assist the prosecution and Clarence Darrow, a famous Chicago lawyer and prominent atheist, volunteered to defend Scopes.

Millions of Americans tuned their radios to hear the first trial ever broadcast. Though the local jury took only eight minutes to convict Scopes, fundamentalists suffered public ridicule from reporters like H. L. Mencken, who sneered at the "hillbillies" and "yokels" of Dayton. But fundamentalism retained religious influence and would again challenge science and modernism in American life.

WHERE TO LEARN MORE (W)

Rhea County Courthouse and Museum, Dayton, Tennessee

23–2
The Sahara of the Bozart (1920)

FROM THEN TO NOW
The Culture Wars

Cultural conflict raged through American society in the 1920s as people reacted to great social changes, including new roles for women, increasing ethnic and racial diversity, rapid urbanization, and the "new morality." Nativists demanded immigration restriction; the Ku Klux Klan played on fears of racial, ethnic, and religious minorities; prohibitionists grappled with the minions of Demon Rum; and Protestant fundamentalists campaigned to prohibit the teaching of evolution in public schools.

Such conflicts are rooted in the moral systems that give people identity and purpose. As a result, the challenges of the Great Depression and World War II dampened but did not extinguish them. Beginning in the 1960s, fueled as before by challenges to traditional values and beliefs—African American demands for civil rights, opposition to the Vietnam War, the women's rights movement and women's growing presence in the workplace, a new wave of immigration (dominated this time by Asians and Latin Americans), the gay rights movement—cultural conflict flared again and continues to burn.

In the 1920s nativists succeeded in curtailing immigration with the passage of the National Origins Act of 1924. In 1994, the people of California approved Proposition 187, which barred undocumented aliens from public schools and social services. Again, as in the 1920s, fundamentalists are mounting an attack against the teaching of evolution in public schools, sometimes seeking to persuade local school boards to give equal time to the pseudoscience of creationism. And today rap and rock-and-roll provoke the same kind of worried condemnation that jazz provoked in the 1920s.

The central battleground of today's culture wars, however, is women's rights, and especially abortion rights. Ever since the Supreme Court ruled in *Roe v. Wade* in 1973 that women had a right to an abortion, opponents, primarily religious conservatives, have sought to curtail or abolish that right in the name of "family values." Antiabortion protests became increasingly violent in the 1980s and 1990s. Demonstrators have harassed women trying to enter abortion clinics, clinics have been bombed, and several abortion providers have been murdered. Although the Supreme Court has upheld *Roe* v. *Wade* and laws restraining demonstrations at abortion clinics, it has also upheld state laws imposing limits on abortion rights. Abortions have become harder to obtain in many parts of the country.

Gay rights is another new battleground in the culture wars. Religious conservatives, again in the name of "family values," have sought to counter efforts to extend civil rights protections to gays and lesbians. In 1992, for example, Colorado approved a measure (overturned by the Supreme Court in 1996) that prohibited local governments from passing ordinances protecting gays and lesbians from discrimination.

The hostility to the Catholic Church and Catholic immigrants that had long been characteristic of American nativism has been largely absent from the current culture wars. On the contrary, conservative Catholics have joined forces with evangelical Protestants on many fronts, particularly on abortion and gay rights.

According to one popular analysis, the antagonists in today's culture wars are, on one side, those who find authority in transcendent universal sources like those that religious traditions lay claim to, and, on the other, those who find authority in society and human reason. From this perspective, perhaps the most prominent recent engagement in the culture wars was the impeachment of President Clinton. Republican leader Tom DeLay of Texas, for example, declared in 1999 that the impeachment debate was "about relativism versus absolute truth." Polls, however, showed that most Americans were more tolerant and flexible, willing to separate the president's public performance from his personal morality. With the failure to convict Clinton, one Republican lamented. "We probably have lost the culture war." But given the deeply rooted convictions that motivate it, cultural conflict is likely to remain a persistent undercurrent in American life.

The packed courtroom for the Scopes Trial in 1925 illustrates the intense interest that Americans have persistently taken in conflicts stemming from differing cultural values and ethical visions.

Getty Images Inc.

A NEW ERA IN THE WORLD?

Abroad, as at home, Americans in the 1920s sought peace and economic order. Rejection of the Treaty of Versailles and the League of Nations did not foreshadow isolationism. Indeed, in the 1920s, the United States became more deeply involved in international matters than ever before in peacetime.

WAR DEBTS AND ECONOMIC EXPANSION

The United States was the world's dominant economic power in the 1920s, changed by the Great War from a debtor to a creditor nation. The loans that the United States had made to its allies during the war troubled the nation's relations with Europe throughout the decade. American insistence on repayment angered Europeans, who saw the money as a U.S. contribution to the joint war effort against Germany. Moreover, high American tariffs blocked Europeans from exporting goods to the United States and earning dollars to repay their debts. Eventually, the United States readjusted the terms for repayment, and American bankers extended large loans to Germany, which used the money to pay reparations to Britain and France, whose governments then used the same money to repay the United States. This unstable system depended on a constant flow of money from the United States.

America's global economic role expanded in other ways as well. By 1929, the United States was the world's largest exporter, responsible for one-sixth of all exports. American investment abroad more than doubled between 1919 and 1930. To expand their markets and avoid foreign tariffs, many U.S. companies became **multinational corporations**, establishing branches or subsidiaries abroad. Ford built assembly plants in England, Japan, Turkey, and Canada. American oil companies invested in foreign oil fields, especially in Latin America. The United Fruit Company developed such huge operations in Central America that it often dominated national economies.

The government worked to open doors for American businesses in foreign countries. Secretary of Commerce Hoover's Bureau of Foreign Commerce opened fifty offices around the world to boost American business. Secretary of State Charles Evans Hughes negotiated access to Iraqi oil fields for U.S. oil companies. The government also exempted bankers and manufacturers from antitrust laws to exploit foreign markets.

REJECTING WAR

Although government officials cooperated with business leaders to promote American strategic and economic interests, they had little desire to use force in the process. Popular reaction against the Great War, strengthened by a strong peace movement, constrained policymakers. Indeed, the State Department sought to restrict the buildup of armaments among nations.

At the invitation of President Harding, delegations from nine nations met at the Washington Naval Conference in 1921 to draft a treaty to reduce battleship tonnage and suspend the building of new ships for a decade. The terms virtually froze the existing balance of naval power, with the first rank assigned to Britain and the United States, followed by Japan and then France and Italy. The U.S. Senate ratified the treaty with only one dissenting vote. The United States made a more dramatic gesture in 1928 when it helped draft the **Kellogg-Briand Pact**. Signed by sixty-four nations, the treaty renounced aggression and outlawed war. Without provisions for enforcement, however, it was little more than symbolic.

Multinational corporations Firms with direct investments, branches, factories, and offices in a number of countries.

MANAGING THE HEMISPHERE

The United States continued to dominate Latin America to promote its own interests through investments, control of the Panama Canal, invocation of the Monroe Doctrine, and military intervention.

In response to American public opinion, the peace movement, and Latin American nationalism, the United States did retreat from the extreme gunboat diplomacy of the Progressive Era, withdrawing troops from the Dominican Republic and Nicaragua. But Haiti remained under U.S. occupation throughout the decade, American troops stayed in Cuba and Panama, and the United States directed the financial policies of other Latin American countries. Moreover, it sent the marines into Honduras in 1924 and back to Nicaragua in 1926. Such interventions provoked further Latin American hostility. "We are hated and despised," said one American businessman in Nicaragua. "This feeling has been created by employing American marines to hunt down and kill Nicaraguans in their own country."

The anger of Latin Americans prompted the State Department to draft the Clark Memorandum. This document, not published until 1930, receded from the Roosevelt Corollary and helped prepare the way for the so-called Good Neighbor Policy toward Latin America. Still, the United States continued to dominate the hemisphere.

HERBERT HOOVER AND THE FINAL TRIUMPH OF THE NEW ERA

As the national economy steamed ahead in 1928, the Republicans chose as their presidential candidate Herbert Hoover, a man who symbolized the policies of prosperity and the New Era. Hoover was not a politician—he had never been elected to office—but a successful administrator who championed rational and efficient economic development. Hoover's stiff managerial image was softened by his humanitarian record and his roots in rural Iowa.

The Democrats, in contrast, chose a candidate who evoked the cultural conflicts of the 1920s. Alfred E. Smith, four-term governor of New York, was a Catholic, an opponent of prohibition, and a Tammany politician tied to the immigrant constituency of New York City. His nomination plunged the nation into cultural strife. Rural fundamentalism, anti-Catholicism, prohibition, and nativism were crucial factors in the campaign. The fundamentalist assault was unrelenting. A Baptist minister in Oklahoma City warned his congregation: "If you vote for Al Smith, you're voting against Christ and you'll all be damned."

But Hoover was in fact the more progressive candidate. Sympathetic to labor, sensitive to women's issues, hostile to racial segregation, and favorable to the League of Nations, Hoover had always distanced himself from what he called "the reactionary group in the Republican party." By contrast, despite supporting state welfare legislation to benefit his urban working-class constituents, Smith was essentially conservative and opposed an active government. Moreover, he was as parochial as his most rural adversaries and never attempted to reach out to them. With the nation still enjoying the economic prosperity so closely associated with Hoover and the Republicans, the Democrats were routed.

But 1928 would be the Republicans' final triumph for a long time. The prosperity of the 1920s was ending, and the country faced a future dark with poverty.

(W) **WHERE TO LEARN MORE**

★ Herbert Hoover National Historic Site, West Branch, Iowa

American President Herbert Hoover in a color engraving.

The Granger Collection, New York

CONCLUSION

The New Era of the 1920s changed America. Technological and managerial innovations produced giant leaps in productivity, new patterns of labor, a growing concentration of corporate power, and high profits. Government policies from protective tariffs and regressive taxation to a relaxation of regulatory laws reinforced the triumphs of a business elite over traditional cautions and concerns.

The decade's economic developments stimulated social change, drawing millions of Americans from the countryside to the cities, creating an urban nation, and fostering a new ethic of materialism, consumerism, and leisure and a new mass culture based on the automobile, radio, the movies, and advertising. This social transformation swept up many Americans but left others unsettled by the erosion of traditional practices and values. The concerns of traditionalists found expression in campaigns for prohibition and against immigration, the revival of the Ku Klux Klan, and the rise of religious fundamentalism. Intellectuals denounced the materialism and conformity they saw in the new social order and fashioned new artistic and literary trends.

But the impact of the decade's trends was uneven. Mechanization increased the productivity of some workers but cost others their jobs; people poured into the cities while others left for the suburbs; prohibition, produced conflict, crime, and corruption; government policies advanced some economic interests but injured others. Even the notion of a "mass" culture obscured the degree to which millions of Americans were left out of the New Era. With no disposable income and little access to electricity, rural Americans scarcely participated in the joys of consumerism; racial and ethnic minorities were often isolated in ghettos and barrios; and many workers faced declining opportunities. Although living standards rose for many Americans and the rich expanded their share of national wealth, much of the population fell below the established poverty level. The unequal distribution of wealth and income made the economy vulnerable to a disastrous collapse.

SUMMARY

The Economy that Roared Following a postwar depression in 1920 and 1921, the American economy boomed through the rest of the decade. Mechanization of production, investment, new industries such as broadcasting and motion pictures and the automobile industry drove the economy. Oligopoly eliminated competition; Americans accepted the idea that size brought efficiency and productivity. While many businesses boomed, "sick" industries such as textiles, coal mining, agriculture and railroads dragged the economy down. Not all Americans shared in the economic boom; the gap between rich and poor widened.

The Business of Government The Republican surge in national politics also shaped the economy; a business government went hand in hand with a business country. Government regulation was curtailed, business supporters were installed in regulatory agencies, and the Supreme Court became a champion of business. While the Progressive party had little impact on politics, progressivism was not dead but had lost much of its energy and focus.

Cities and Suburbs By 1920 more Americans lived in urban than rural areas: the massive population movement interacted with technological innovations to reshape cities, build automobile-accessible suburbs, and transform urban life. The South was the most rapidly urbanizing region; however, African Americans left the South for job opportunities in Midwestern and Northern cities; increased racial pride found expression in the Harlem Renaissance. Puerto Ricans and Mexicans moved into U.S. cities creating their own communities. Suburbs grew more rapidly than cities as middle-class enclaves created by automobiles.

Mass Culture in the Jazz Age Fast food chains symbolized a new society and culture; advertising and its focus on increasing consumption shaped the new society. Brand-name goods, mass consumption, and buying on credit became hallmarks of the new American economy. People also spent more on recreation and leisure; radio, the phonograph, and the movies competed with college football, professional baseball, and boxing during the Jazz Age. The social dislocations and America's growing disenchantment with traditional values fueled the new morality among the young; writers of the Lost Generation criticized the new era.

Culture Wars Despite the new mass culture of the 1920's, conflicts divided social groups. Some of these struggles involved reactions against the new currents in American life, including technical and scientific innovation, urban growth, and materialism. Nativism, racism, religion, dislike of modernism and the expanding role of science, and the desire to return to and strengthen traditional rural values were all underlying issues in the culture wars.

A New Era in the World? The United States was changed by the Great War into a creditor nation. The loans made to the Allies troubled America's relations with Europe as America insisted on repayment; however, high tariffs blocked Europe exporting goods and earning money to repay those debts. America's global economic role expanded and companies became multinational corporations; Europe and Latin America resented this economic invasion. Reaction to the Great War resulted in America, along, with sixty-four other nations, outlawing war in 1928.

Herbert Hoover and the Triumph of the New Era Herbert Hoover's election as president in 1928 seemed the "final triumph over poverty"; in 1929, the Great Depression would begin.

REVIEW QUESTIONS

1. How did the automobile industry affect the nation's economy and society in the 1920s?

2. What factors characterized the "boom industries" of the 1920s? What factors characterized the "sick industries"?

3. What role did politics play in the public life of the 1920s?

4. How did the World War I experience shape the 1920s?

5. What was the U.S. level of involvement in world affairs in the 1920s?

KEY TERMS

Great Migration   (p. 639)
Harlem Renaissance   (p. 639)
Jazz Age   (p. 641)
League of Women Voters   (p. 637)
Multinational corporations   (p. 647)

National Origins Act of 1924   (p. 643)
Nisei   (p. 643)
Open shop   (p. 634)
Sheppard-Towner Maternity and Infancy Act   (p. 637)

Volstead Act   (p. 644)
Welfare capitalism   (p. 634)
Yellow-dog contracts   (p. 634)

WHERE TO LEARN MORE

F. Scott and Zelda Fitzgerald Museum, Montgomery, Alabama. The novelist and his wife lived a short while in this house in her hometown. **www.alabamatravel.org/central/szfm.html**

Smithsonian Institution, Washington, D.C. "From Farm to Factory," a permanent exhibition at the National Museum of American History, splendidly portrays the human side of the Great Migration.

Herbert Hoover National Historic Site, West Branch, Iowa. Visitors may tour Hoover's birth-place cottage, presidential library, and museum.

Henry Ford Museum and Greenfield Village, Dearborn, Michigan. Among many fascinating exhibits, "The Automobile in American Life" particularly and superbly demonstrates the importance of the automobile in American social history. **www.hfmgv.org**

George Norris Home, McCook, Nebraska. This museum, operated by the Nebraska State Historical Society, is dedicated to a leading progressive Republican of the 1920s. **www.nebraskahistory.org/sites/norris/index.htm**

Warren G. Harding House, Marion, Ohio. Harding's home from 1891 to 1921 is now a museum with period furnishings. **www.ohiohistory.org/places/harding**

Rhea County Courthouse and Museum, Dayton, Tennessee. The site of the Scopes Trial, the courtroom appears as it did in 1925; the museum contains memorabilia related to the trial.

Calvin Coolidge Homestead, Plymouth, Vermont. Operated by the Vermont Division of Historic Sites, the homestead preserves the exact interiors and furnishings from when Coolidge took the presidential oath of office there in 1923. **www.calvin-coolidge.org/pages/homestead** and **www.dhca.state.vt.us./HistoricSites/sites.htm**

 For additional study resources for this chapter, go to:
www.prenhall.com/goldfield/chapter24

Advertising and the Modern Woman

DURING the 1920s, for the first time in American history, consumer demand was the chief impetus to economic growth. As a direct consequence, the 1920s witnessed the emergence of advertising as a major industry. Most of the ads from this period promoted benefits that had little to do with product. Why? The simplest explanation is that the ad agency and the manufacturer believed that youth and feminine beauty would sell. By the late twenties, advertisements for all sorts of products touted the "modern young woman" as the arbiter of taste and beauty. In so doing, the advertisers signaled a deep shift in American culture. Which specific feminine characteristics are promoted in the advertisements shown here?

The image of a young, attractive woman in this Lucky Strike ad from the 1920s is much more prominent than the product she is promoting. How does the ad make the connection between cigarettes and femminine beauty? What is the underying message of the command to "reach for a Lucky—instead of a sweet?"

ADS-TOBACCO

"Reach for a Lucky – instead of a sweet"

LUCKY STRIKE "IT'S TOASTED"

CIGARETTES

"A flavor that completely satisfies"

Billie Burke
Billie Burke
Popular American Actress

"It's toasted"
No Throat Irritation-No Cough.

© 1928, The American Tobacco Co., Manufacturers

The Wonder of Creole Hair

CREOLE charm has been as much admired in aristocratic European circles as in America. Empress Josephine, wife of Napoleon, was a Creole. Queen Hortense of Holland and Prince Eugene, Viceroy of Italy, were Creoles. The glorious Creole hair has always been especially admired. The hair is a special pride and care of the Creoles and for generations La Creole Hair Dressing has been favorite among them. It preserves the youthful color and beauty of the hair even through advanced years.

La Creole Ends Gray Hair

La Creole not alone prevents gray hair. La Creole treatment will bring back to its youthful color and beauty, hair that has become gray, gray-streaked, or faded. La Creole contains no dyes. It promotes the youthfully vigorous healthy condition of hair and scalp which nature intended. Its effect on the hair is gradual but certain. Two to five weeks treatment is required to bring back any shade—lightest brown to deepest black—whatever the natural color was. After that an occasional application will preserve the vigorous healthy color permanently.

Good taste and good breeding approve the use of La Creole and there is no reason for making any secret of its use, though it can never be detected.

La Creole must not be confused with dyes—it can not give a dyed look and there is nothing to stain the scalp or to wash or rub off. It makes the hair soft, wavy, lustrous and beautiful. Eliminates dandruff.

Absolutely guaranteed to bring back the hair's color or money refunded.

Send coupon for booklet "La Creole—Hair Beautiful." Shows style of hair dressing best suited to each type of face.

At Drug Stores and Toilet Counters, Price $1.00
If your Dealer can't supply you, send his name and address.
We will see that you are supplied.

VAN VLEET-MANSFIELD LABORATORIES
132 Tenth Street, Memphis, Tenn.

Van Vleet-Mansfield Laboratories
132 Tenth St, Memphis, Tenn.

Please send booklet "La Creole—Hair Beautiful," teaching the hair dress most becoming to each individual.

Name ....

Address ....

City .... State ....

▲

Virtually all ads during this period, except those aimed explicitly at African Americans, avoided any ethnic or racial references. "La Creole" ads are exceptions. The product name itself referred to a specific Community of people in Louisiana, descendants of French settlers. But the term was also used to refer to individuals of mixed racial background. How does the "La Creole" ad deal with this? What does that suggest for how you might interpret the other ads?

This ad for a line of hair products created and manufactured by Madame C.J. Walker, one of the first African-American millionaires. The ad promises "fascinating beauty" to users of its product.
▼

You, too, may be a fascinating beauty

PERHAPS YOU ENVY the girl with irresistible beauty, whose skin is flawless and velvety, whose hair has a beautiful silky sheen, the girl who receives glances of undoubted admiration.

You need not envy her. Create new beauty for yourself by using Madam C. J. Walker's famous beauty preparations.

When Madam Walker and her associates started to develop her beauty preparations, which are now used all over the world, they perfected their toiletries step by step.

Each preparation was beyond the point of experiment before it was followed by another. Each preparation's wide use and high merit were always *proved*. Today they are unsurpassed.

Try these products and you won't have reason to envy another girl her lovely hair and her charming complexion.

You can obtain any of these marvelous preparations at your nearest druggist or from a Madam C. J. Walker agent (there's one near you) or write the company direct at Indianapolis.

Madam
C.J. WALKER'S
Beauty Preparations

COMPLEXION AND TOILET SOAP—A preservative of beauty—mild and safe for the most tender skin. Perfumed delightfully. 20 cents per large bar.

VEGETABLE OIL—ANTISEPTIC SOAP—A popular-priced household soap of purest vegetable oils. Lathers well in hardest water, removes grease and dirt, yet will not harm a baby's skin. A bargain at 10 cents a bar.

SUPERFINE FACE POWDER (Brown)—Clinging, velvety smooth, invisible and adorably perfumed. Imparts an olive tint to fair complexions and harmonizes bewitchingly with darker skins. Obtainable in rose-flesh and white. 50 cents per sealed box.

GLOSSINE—Oils and softens dry, brittle hair. Imparts a rich, healthy lustre. Indispensable for bobbed hair and unsurpassed in the opinion of social leaders and well-groomed gentlemen. 35 cents per long-lasting box.

THESE ARE BUT FOUR OF EIGHTEEN MADAM C. J. WALKER BEAUTY PREPARATIONS—AS FINE AS MONEY CAN BUY

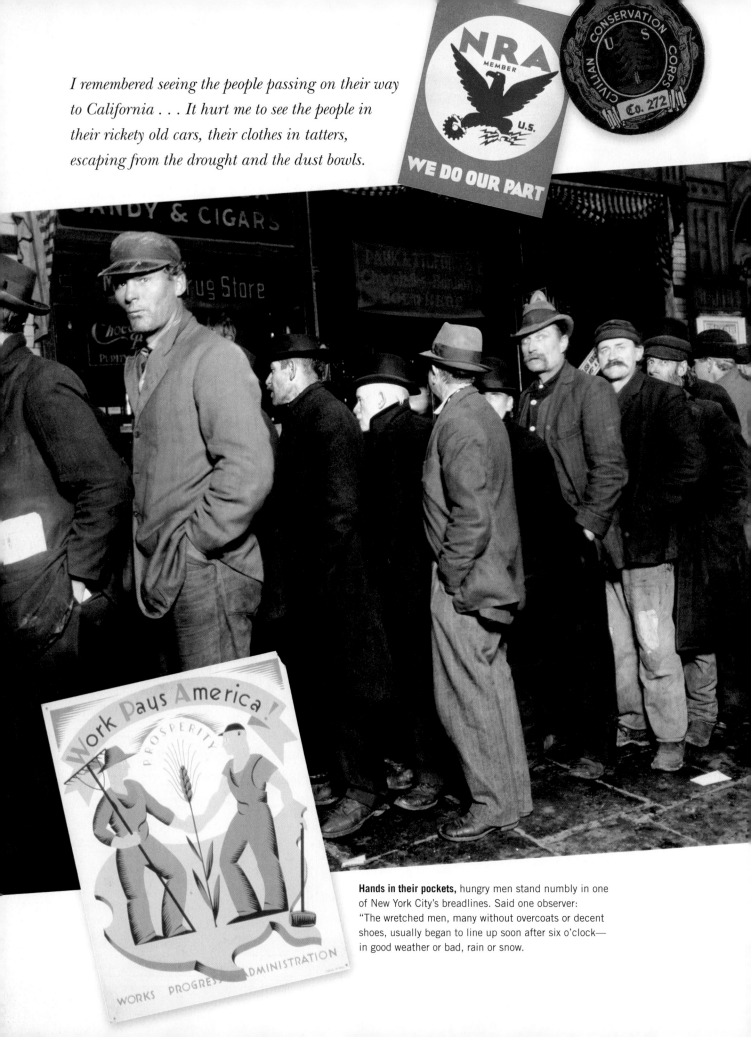

I remembered seeing the people passing on their way to California . . . It hurt me to see the people in their rickety old cars, their clothes in tatters, escaping from the drought and the dust bowls.

NRA
MEMBER
U.S.
WE DO OUR PART

CIVILIAN CONSERVATION CORPS
U S
Co. 272

Work Pays America!
PROSPERITY
WORKS PROGRESS ADMINISTRATION

Hands in their pockets, hungry men stand numbly in one of New York City's breadlines. Said one observer: "The wretched men, many without overcoats or decent shoes, usually began to line up soon after six o'clock— in good weather or bad, rain or snow.

25

THE GREAT DEPRESSION
AND THE NEW DEAL
1929–1939

WHAT TRIGGERED
the Great Depression?

WHY DID Herbert Hoover's actions
to resolve the Great Depression fail?

WHAT WERE
the main achievements
of the early New Deal?

YEARS OF DUST

RESETTLEMENT ADMINISTRATION
Rescues Victims
Restores Land to Proper Use

WHICH ECONOMIC
and social reforms made up
the "Second New Deal?"

WHAT IMPACT did New Deal
programs have on women and minorities?

WHY WERE late New Deal reforms unsuccessful?

1929 1939

My mother had two small babies on her hands. When I became sickly, Grandmother Josefa took me home with her, and I never returned to my parents. . . . My grandmother's house was located on the 'American' side of town, but there was nothing they could do about it because she was there before anybody else. . . . My grandmother worked very hard; I grew up in the Depression.

When it was time for me to go to school I was assigned to [the] Mexican side of town. We were segregated; [the] Anglo children were sent to Roosevelt and the Mexican children who lived closer to Roosevelt [still] had to go down to Harding. I'll admit, there was a lot of discrimination in those years.

During the Depression my grandmother sewed piecework for the WPA. My dad helped out when he could [and] Uncle Ernesto also worked. He used to dig graves.

The Depression years were very, very hard. I remember seeing the people passing on their way to California. . . . It hurt me to see the people in their rickety old cars, their clothes in tatters, escaping from the drought and the dust bowls.

—Oral Testimony,

Carlotta Silvas Martin
Star Route One
Albertville, Ala.

January 1, 1936

IMAGE KEY
for pages 654–655

a. The National Recovery Agency seal with an eagle holding a cog in one talon and lightning bolts in the other over the slogan "We Do Our Part."
b. The Civilian Conservation Corps Emblem.
c. Hungry men stand in a bread line in New York City.
d. A Works Progress Administration poster, depicting a farmer and a miner shaking hands.
e. An old fashioned radio in a wooden cabinet.
f. Anxious citizens crowd along Wall Street sidewalks while automobiles edge down the street on Black Tuesday October 29, 1929.
g. Mexican farm Workers, pecan shell homes that rent for 50 cents a week in San Antonio, TX.
h. Gov. Franklin D. Roosevelt shakes hands with a poor mine worker during campaign trip.
i. Ben Shahn, "Years of Dust," 1936. Poster for the Resettlement Administration.
j. Isaac Soyer, "Employment Agency." Oil on canvas, 34 1/2" × 45".

On April 27 [1933], according to the New York Times, *Paul Schneider, aged forty-four, a sick and crippled Chicago school teacher, shot himself to death. His widow, left with three children, stated that he had not been paid for eight months. . . . Less than a month after Paul Schneider's discouragement drove him to suicide, the militant action of Chicago teachers—patient no more . . . resulted in the payment of $12,000,000 due them for the last months of 1932. Their pay for the five months of 1933 is still owed them. Five hundred of them are reported to be in asylums and sanitariums as a result of the strain. . . .*

These are the conditions facing teachers fortunate enough to be employed. What of the unemployed? . . . "We are always hungry," wrote [one unemployed teacher]. "We owe six months' rent. . . . We live every hour in fear of eviction. . . . My sister, a typist, and I . . . have been out of work for two years. . . . We feel discouraged . . . and embittered. We are drifting, with no help from anyone."

—Eunice Langdon,

The Nation,
August 16, 1933

I am sitting in the city free employment bureau. It's the women's section. We have been sitting here now for hours. We sit here every day, waiting for a job. There are no jobs. . . .

. . . [W]e don't talk much. . . . There is a kind of humiliation. . . . We look away from each other. We look at the floor.

—*Meridel LeSeur,*

"Women on the Breadlines," 1932

Dear Mrs. Roosevelt,

I am now 15 years old and in the 10th grade. I have always been smart but I never had a chance as all of us is so poor. I hope to complete my education, but I will have to quit school I guess if there is no clothes can be bought. (Don't think that we are on the relief.) Mother has been a faithful servant for us to keep us togather. I don't see how she has made it.

Mrs. Roosevelt, don't think I am just begging, but that is all you can call it I guess. . . . Do you have any old clothes you have throwed back. You don't realize how honored I would feel to be wearing your clothes.

—*Your friend,*

M.I.

"Carlotta Silvas Martin: A Mexican American Childhood during the Depression" and "Meridel LeSeur: The Despair of Unemployed Women," both from Susan Ware, *Modern American Women: A Documentary History* (New York: McGraw-Hill Higher Education, 2002), pp. 162–165, 145–146, respectively; Letter to Eleanor Roosevelt, January 1, 1936, **http://www.newdeal.feri.org/eleanor/mi0136.htm**; Eunice Langdon, "The Teacher Faces the Depression," *The Nation* 137 (August 16, 1933): 182–187.

CARLOTTA SILVAS MARTINE, Eunice Langdon, and Meridel Le Seur convey some of the trauma of the Great Depression, but no one voice can capture its devastating effects. The American economy collapsed, leaving millions of people jobless, homeless, or in fear of foreclosure, eviction, and even starvation. Men, women, and children saw their families and dreams shattered and felt the humiliation of standing in bread lines or begging for clothes or food scraps. The winter of 1932–1933 was particularly cruel. Unemployment soared. Hunger was so widespread in Kentucky and West Virginia that one relief committee limited its handouts to those who were at least 10 percent below their normal weight for their height. In Chicago, half the people were without jobs. In the drought-stricken Great Plains families left their farms and took to the road to escape the darkened skies of the "Dust Bowl".

The election of Franklin D. Roosevelt, however, lifted spirits and hopes throughout the nation. Jobless Americans enthusiastically responded to his

New Deal, taking jobs with such programs as the Works Progress Administration (WPA). They also wrote to FDR and Eleanor Roosevelt, asking for advice and assistance and thanking the President and the First Lady for their compassionate support and leadership. Throughout all such letters ran the common theme: the belief among poor and unemployed Americans that for the first time there were people in the White House who cared about them.

The economic collapse hit hardest those industries dominated by male workers, leaving mothers and wives with new roles as the family breadwinners, sometimes straining family relationships and men's sense of purpose and respect.

Race and ethnicity further complicated the problems of both joblessness and relief. Southern states routinely denied African Americans relief assistance as did Southwestern states for Hispanic Americans. Despite some progress in assisting African Americans, the New Deal failed to overcome traditional attitudes and practices that targeted women and minorities and reinforced local prejudice and segregation.

Hard times, then, both united and divided the American people, and although the federal activism of the 1930s achieved neither full recovery nor systematic reform, it restored confidence to many Americans and transformed the nation's responsibilities for the welfare of its citizens. By the end of the decade, President Roosevelt was no longer worried that the economy—indeed society itself—teetered on the edge of catastrophe; his gaze now fixed abroad where even more ominous developments, he believed, threatened the nation's future and security.

New Deal The economic and political policies of the Roosevelt administration in the 1930s.

HARD TIMES IN HOOVERVILLE

WHAT TRIGGERED the Great Depression?

The prosperity of the 1920s ended in a stock market crash that revealed the flaws honeycombing the economy. As the nation slid into a catastrophic depression, factories closed, employment and incomes tumbled, and millions lost their homes, hopes, and dignity. Some protested and took direct action; others looked to the government for relief.

CRASH!

The buoyant prosperity of the New Era collapsed in October of 1929 when the stock market crashed. After peaking in September, the market suffered several sharp checks, and on October 29, "Black Tuesday," panicked investors dumped their stocks at any price. The slide continued for months, and then years. It hit bottom in July 1932. By then, the stock of U.S. Steel had plunged from 262 to 22, Montgomery Ward from 138 to 4.

The Wall Street crash marked the beginning of the **Great Depression**, but it did not cause it. The depression stemmed from weaknesses in the New Era economy. Most damaging was the unequal distribution of wealth and income. By 1929, the richest 0.1 percent of American families had as much total income as the bottom 42 percent (see Figure 25.1). With more than half the nation's people living at or below the subsistence level, there was not enough purchasing power to maintain the economy.

A second factor was that oligopolies dominated American industries. Their power led to "administered prices," prices kept artificially high and rigid rather than determined by supply and demand. By not responding to purchasing power, this

Great Depression The nation's worst economic crisis, extending through the 1930s, producing unprecedented bank failures, unemployment, and industrial and agricultural collapse.

system not only helped bring on economic collapse but also dimmed prospects for recovery.

Weaknesses in specific industries had further unbalanced the economy. Agriculture suffered from overproduction, declining prices, and heavy debt; so did the coal and textile industries. Poorly managed and regulated, banks had contributed to the instability of prosperity; they now threatened to spread the panic and depression.

International economic difficulties also contributed to the depression. Shut out from U.S. markets by high tariffs, Europeans had depended on American investments to manage their debts and reparation payments from the Great War. The stock market crash dried up the flow of American dollars to Europe, causing financial panics and industrial collapse and making the Great Depression global. In turn, European nations curtailed their imports of American goods and defaulted on their debts, further debilitating the U.S. economy. American exports fell by 70 percent from 1929 to 1932. As foreign markets shrank, so did hopes for economic recovery.

Government policies also bore some responsibility for the crash and depression. Failure to enforce antitrust laws had encouraged oligopolies and high prices; failure to regulate banking or the stock market had permitted financial recklessness. Reducing tax rates on the wealthy had also encouraged speculation and contributed to the maldistribution of income. Opposition to labor unions and collective bargaining helped keep workers' wages and purchasing power low. The absence of an effective agricultural policy and the high tariffs that inhibited foreign trade and reduced markets for agricultural products hurt farmers in the same way. In short, the same government policies that shaped the booming 1920s economy also pointed to economic disaster.

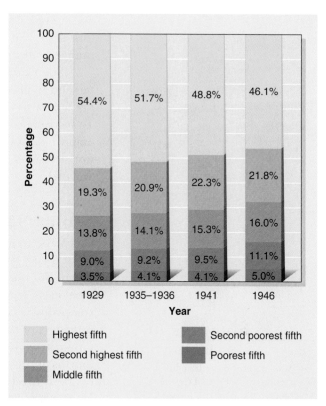

FIGURE 25.1
Distribution of Income in the United States, 1929–1946
An unequal distribution of income contributed to the Great Depression by limiting purchasing power. Only slight changes occurred until after World War II, but other factors gradually stabilized the national economy.

Source: U.S. Bureau of the Census

THE DEPRESSION SPREADS

By early 1930, factories had shut down or cut back, and industrial production plummeted; by 1932, it was scarcely 50 percent of its 1929 level. Steel mills operated at 12 percent of capacity, auto factories at 20 percent. Unemployment skyrocketed, as an average of 100,000 workers a week were fired in the first three years after the crash. By 1932, one-fourth of the labor force was out of work. Personal income dropped by more than half between 1929 and 1932; by 1933, industrial workers had average weekly wages of only $16.73. Moreover, the depression began to feed on itself in a vicious circle: Shrinking wages and employment cut into purchasing power, causing business to slash production again and lay off workers, thereby further reducing purchasing power.

The depression particularly battered farmers. Commodity prices fell by 55 percent between 1929 and 1932, stifling farm income. Unable to pay their mortgages, many farm families lost their homes and fields. "We have no security left," cried one South Dakota farm woman. "Foreclosures and evictions at the point of sheriff's guns are increasing daily."

Urban families were also evicted when they could not pay their rent. Some moved in with relatives; others lived in **Hoovervilles**—the name reflects the bitterness directed at the president—shacks where people shivered, suffered,

Hoovervilles Shantytowns, sarcastically named after President Hoover, in which unemployed and homeless people lived in makeshift shacks, tents, and boxes.

and starved. Oklahoma City's vast Hooverville covered 100 square miles; one witness described its hapless residents as squatting in "old, rusted-out car bodies," orange crates, and holes in the ground.

Soup kitchens became standard features of the urban landscape, but charities and local communities could not meet the massive needs, and neither state nor federal governments had welfare or unemployment compensation programs. To survive, people planted gardens in vacant lots and back alleys and tore apart empty houses or tapped gas lines for fuel. In immigrant neighborhoods, social workers found a "primitive communism" in which people shared food, clothing, and fuel.

"Women's Jobs" and "Men's Jobs"

Gender segregation had concentrated women in low-paid service, sales, and clerical jobs that shrank less than the heavy industries where men predominated. But traditional attitudes also reinforced opposition to female employment itself, especially that of married women. As one Chicago civic organization complained, "They are holding jobs that rightfully belong to the God-intended providers of the household." The city council of Akron, Ohio, resolved that public agencies and private employers should stop employing wives. Three-fourths of the nation's school systems refused to hire married women as teachers, and two-thirds dismissed female teachers who married. Many private employers, especially banks and insurance companies, also fired married women.

Few men sought positions in the fields associated with women, so firing women simply aggravated the suffering of families already reeling from the depression. Despite hostility, the proportion of married women in the work force increased in the 1930s as women took jobs to help their families survive.

Families in the Depression

"I have watched fear grip the people in our neighborhood around Hull House," wrote Jane Addams as the depression deepened in 1931 and family survival itself seemed threatened. Divorce declined because it was expensive, but desertion increased, and marriages were postponed. Birthrates fell. Husbands and fathers, the traditional breadwinners, were often humiliated and despondent when laid off from work. One social worker observed in 1931: "Like searing irons, the degradation, the sheer terror and panic which loss of job brings, the deprivation and the bitterness have eaten into men's souls."

The number of female-headed households increased. Not only did some women become wage earners, but to make ends meet, many women sewed their own clothing and raised and canned vegetables. Some also took on extra work at home. In San Antonio, one in every ten families had boarders, and in Alabama, housewives took in laundry at 10 cents a week.

Some parents sacrificed their own well-being to protect their children. One witness described "the uncontrolled trembling of parents who have starved themselves for weeks so that their children might not go hungry." In New York City, 139 people, most of them children, died of starvation and malnutrition in 1933. Many teenagers who left home so that younger children would have more to eat suffered from starvation, exposure, illness, and accidents. The California Unemployment Commission concluded that the depression had left the American family "morally shattered. There is no security, no foothold, no future."

"LAST HIRED, FIRST FIRED"

With fewer resources and opportunities, racial minorities were less able than other groups to absorb the economic pain. African Americans, reported a sociologist at Howard University in 1932, were "the last to be hired and the first to be fired." Black unemployment rates were more than twice the rate for white people. Jobless white workers now sought the menial jobs traditionally reserved for black workers, such as street cleaning and domestic service. Religious and charitable organizations often refused to care for black people. Local and state governments set higher requirements for black people than for white people to receive relief and provided them with less aid. The Urban League reported, "at no time in the history of the Negro since slavery has his economic and social outlook seemed so discouraging." African Americans were "hanging on by the barest thread."

Hispanic Americans also suffered. As mostly unskilled workers, they faced increasing competition for decreasing jobs paying declining wages. They were displaced even in the California agricultural labor force, which they had dominated. Other jobs were lost when Arizona, California, and Texas barred Mexicans from public works and highway construction jobs. Vigilantes threatened employers who hired Mexicans rather than white Americans. Economic woes and racism drove nearly half a million Mexican immigrants and their American-born children from the United States in the 1930s. Local authorities in the Southwest encouraged the federal government to deport Mexicans and offered free transportation to Mexico.

PROTEST

Bewildered and discouraged, most Americans responded to the depression with resignation. But others engaged in protests, ranging from small desperate gestures like stealing food and coal to more dramatic deeds. In Louisiana, women seized a train to call attention to the needs of their families; in New Jersey, in the "bloodless battle of Pleasantville," one hundred women held the city council hostage to demand assistance.

Communists organized the jobless into "unemployment councils" that staged hunger marches, demonstrated for relief, and blocked evictions. Mothers facing eviction in Chicago told their children: "Run quick and find the Reds." Socialists built similar organizations, including Baltimore's People's Unemployment League. However, local authorities often suppressed their protests. In 1932, police fired on the Detroit Unemployment Council as it marched to demand food and jobs, killing four marchers and wounding many more.

Rural protests also broke out. In the Midwest, the Farmers' Holiday Association stopped the shipment of produce to urban markets, hoping to drive up prices. A guerrilla war broke out as farmers blocked roads and halted freight trains, dumped milk in ditches, and fought bloody battles with deputy sheriffs. In Iowa, farmers beat sheriffs and mortgage agents and nearly lynched a lawyer conducting foreclosure proceedings.

HERBERT HOOVER AND THE DEPRESSION

The Great Depression challenged the optimism, policies, and philosophy of Herbert Hoover. The president took unprecedented steps to resolve the crisis but shrank back from the interventionist policies activists urged. His failures, personal as well as political and economic, led to his repudiation and opened the way to a new deal.

QUICK REVIEW

African-Americans and the Depression

- Black unemployment rates were twice the rate for white people.
- Blacks had less access to state and private aid and relief.
- Blacks faced a bleak economic outlook.

Many Mexican farm Workers lived in pecan shell homes that rented for 50 cents a week; this one in San Antonio, TX.

National Archives and Records Administration

WHERE TO LEARN MORE

Herbert Hoover National Historic Site, West Branch, Iowa
www.nps.gov/heho

WHY DID Herbert Hoover's actions to resolve the Great Depression Fail?

CHRONOLOGY

1929	Stock market crashes.
1932	Farmers' Holiday Association organizes rural protests in the Midwest. Reconstruction Finance Corporation is created to assist financial institutions. Bonus Army is routed in Washington, D.C. Franklin D. Roosevelt is elected president.
1933	Emergency Banking Act is passed. Agricultural Adjustment Administration (AAA) is created to regulate farm production. National Recovery Administration (NRA) is created to promote industrial cooperation and recovery. Federal Emergency Relief Act provides federal assistance to the unemployed. Civilian Conservation Corps (CCC) is established to provide work relief in conservation projects. Public Works Administration (PWA) is created to provide work relief on large public construction projects. Civil Works Administration (CWA) provides emergency winter relief jobs. Tennessee Valley Authority (TVA) is created to coordinate regional development.
1934	Securities and Exchange Commission (SEC) is established. Indian Reorganization Act reforms Indian policy. Huey Long organizes the Share-Our-Wealth Society. Democrats win midterm elections.
1935	Supreme Court declares NRA unconstitutional. National Labor Relations Act (Wagner Act) guarantees workers' rights to organize and bargain collectively.

Social Security Act establishes a federal social insurance system.
Banking Act strengthens the Federal Reserve.
Revenue Act establishes a more progressive tax system.
Resettlement Administration is created to aid dispossessed farmers.
Rural Electrification Administration (REA) is created to help provide electric power to rural areas.
Soil Conservation Service is established.
Emergency Relief Appropriation Act authorizes public relief projects for the unemployed.
Works Progress Administration (WPA) is created.
Huey Long is assassinated.

1936	Supreme Court declares AAA unconstitutional. Roosevelt is reelected president. Sit-down strikes begin.
1937	Chicago police kill workers in Memorial Day Massacre. FDR tries but fails to expand the Supreme Court. Farm Security Administration (FSA) is created to lend money to small farmers to buy and rehabilitate farms. National Housing Act is passed to promote public housing projects. "Roosevelt Recession" begins.
1938	Congress of Industrial Organizations (CIO) is founded. Fair Labor Standards Act establishes minimum wage and maximum hours rules for labor. Roosevelt fails to "purge" the Democratic party. Republicans make gains in midterm elections.

THE LIMITS OF VOLUNTARISM

Hoover fought economic depression more vigorously than any previous president, but he believed that voluntary, private action was preferable to federal intervention. In promoting voluntarism, Hoover first secured business leaders' pledges to maintain employment and wage levels. But most corporations soon repudiated these pledges, slashed wages, and laid off workers. Hoover complained, "You know, the only trouble with capitalism is capitalists; they're too damn greedy." Still, he rejected government action.

Hoover created the President's Organization for Unemployment Relief to help raise private funds for voluntary relief agencies. Charities and local authorities, he believed, should help the unemployed; direct federal relief would expand government power and undermine the recipients' character. He vetoed congressional attempts to aid the unemployed. "The American way of relieving distress," said Hoover, was through "the voluntary agencies of self help in the community."

But private programs to aid the unemployed scarcely existed. Private charitable groups like the Salvation Army, church associations, and ethnic societies quickly exhausted their resources. Nor could local governments cope. New York City provided relief payments of $2.39 a week for an entire family, and other cities much less. By 1932, more than one hundred cities made no relief appropriations at all, and the commissioner of charity in Salt Lake City reported that people were sliding toward starvation. Only eight state governments provided even token assistance.

Hoover blundered not in first relying on charities and local governments for relief but in refusing to admit that they were inadequate. As the depression worsened, Hoover adopted more activist policies. He persuaded Congress to cut taxes to boost consumers' buying power, and he increased the public works budget. The Reconstruction Finance Corporation (RFC), established in January 1932, lent federal funds to banks, insurance companies, and railroads so that their recovery could "trickle down" to ordinary Americans.

But these programs satisfied few Americans who saw Hoover as indifferent to their suffering and a reactionary protector of privileged business interests. (See American Views, "An Ohio Mayor on Unemployment and Relief.")

Bonus Marchers battling police in Washington, D.C., in 1932. Police and military assaults on these homeless veterans infuriated Americans and prompted Democratic Presidential nominee Franklin D. Roosevelt to declare, "Well, this will elect me."

National Archives and Records Administration

REPUDIATING HOOVER: THE 1932 ELECTION

Hoover's treatment of the **Bonus Army** symbolized his unpopularity and set the stage for the 1932 election. In 1932, unemployed veterans of World War I gathered in Washington, demanding payment of service bonuses not due until 1945. Hoover refused to meet with them, and Congress rejected their plan. But ten thousand veterans erected a shantytown at the edge of Washington and camped in vacant public buildings. General Douglas MacArthur disobeyed Hoover's cautious orders and on July 28 led cavalry, infantry, and tanks against the ragged Bonus Marchers. The troops cleared the buildings and assaulted the shantytown, dispersing the veterans and their families and setting their camp on fire.

"What a pitiful spectacle is that of the great American Government, mightiest in the world, chasing unarmed men, women, and children with army tanks," commented the *Washington News*. The administration tried to brand the Bonus Marchers as Communists and criminals, but official investigations refuted such claims. The incident confirmed Hoover's public image as harsh and insensitive.

In the summer of 1932, with no prospects for victory, Republicans renominated Hoover. Confident Democrats selected Governor Franklin D. Roosevelt of New York, who pledged "a new deal for the American people." Born into a wealthy family in 1882, FDR had been educated at Harvard, trained in the law, and schooled in politics, as a state legislator, assistant secretary of the navy, and the Democratic vice presidential nominee in 1920. In 1921, Roosevelt contracted polio, which paralyzed him from the waist down, leaving him dependent on braces or crutches. His continued involvement in politics owed much to his wife, Eleanor. A social reformer, she became a Democratic activist, organizing women's groups and campaigning across New York. In a remarkable political comeback, FDR was elected governor in 1928 and reelected in 1930.

The 1932 Democratic platform differed little from that of the Republicans, and Roosevelt spoke in vague or general terms. He knew that the election would

25–1
Herbert Hoover, Speech at New York City (1932)

QUICK REVIEW

The 1932 Election
- Republicans renominated Hoover.
- The Democratic platform differed little from the Republican platform.
- Franklin D. Roosevelt's victory was a repudiation of Hoover.

Bonus Army Unemployed veterans of World War I gathering in Washington in 1932 demanding payment of service bonuses not due until 1945.

• AMERICAN VIEWS •

AN OHIO MAYOR ON UNEMPLOYMENT AND RELIEF

Joesph Heffernan was the mayor of Youngstown, Ohio, when the nation sank into the Great Depression. Like other industrial cities, Youngstown soon confronted widespread unemployment and distress. In this document, written in 1932, Heffernan describes the obstacles he faced in responding to the suffering.

WHAT WOULD Heffernan think of President Hoover's belief that private charities and local authorities would provide unemployment relief? What did Heffernan see as obstacles to a public response to the depression? What did he fear would be the consequences of the failure to devise a rational and humane system of relief?

[In 1930] I asked for a bond issue of $1,000,000 for unemployment relief. Many leading business men went out of their way to show their disapproval. One of them . . . said to me: "You make a bad mistake in talking about the unemployed. Don't emphasize hard times and everything will be all right." An influential newspaper chastised me for "borrowing trouble"; the depression would be

over, the editor maintained, before relief would be needed. . . . The gravity of the situation was so deliberately misrepresented by the entire business community that when the bond issue finally came to a ballot, in November 1930, it was voted down.

Thus we passed into the early days of 1931–fourteen months after the first collapse—with no relief in sight except that which was provided by the orthodox charities. Not a single move had been made looking toward action by a united community.

Strange as it may seem, there was no way in which the city government could embark upon a program of its own. We had no funds available for emergency relief, and without specific authorization from the people we could not issue bonds. . . .

As time went on, business conditions showed no improvement. Every night hundreds of homeless men crowded into the municipal incinerator, where they found warmth even though they had to sleep on heaps of garbage. In January 1931, I obtained the cooperation of the City Council to convert an abandoned police station into a "flop

be a repudiation of Hoover more than an endorsement of himself. Indeed, FDR carried every state south and west of Pennsylvania.

In the months before his inauguration, the depression worsened, with rising unemployment, plunging farm prices, and spreading misery. When teachers in Chicago, unpaid for months, fainted in their classrooms from hunger, it symbolized the imminent collapse of the nation itself. The final blow came in February 1933 when desperate Americans rushed to withdraw their funds from the tottering bank system. State governments shut the banks to prevent their failure. Hoover concluded, "We are at the end of our string."

LAUNCHING THE NEW DEAL

WHAT WERE the main
achievements of the early New Deal?

In the midst of national anxiety, Franklin D. Roosevelt pushed forward an unprecedented program to resolve the crises of a collapsing financial system, crippling unemployment, and agricultural and industrial breakdown and to promote reform. The early New Deal achieved successes and attracted support, but it also had limitations and generated criticism that suggested the need for still greater innovations.

house." The first night it was filled, and it has remained filled ever since. I made a point of paying frequent visits to this establishment so that I could see for myself what kind of men these down-and-outers were, and I heartily wish that those folk who have made themselves comfortable by ignoring and denying the suffering of their less fortunate neighbors could see some of the sights I saw. There were old men gnarled by heavy labor, young mechanics tasting the first bitterness of defeat, clerks and white-collar workers learning the equality of misery, derelicts who fared no worse in bad times than in good, Negroes who only a short time before had come from Southern cotton fields, now glad to find any shelter from the cold, immigrants who had been lured to Van Dyke's "land of youth and freedom"— each one a personal tragedy, and all together an overwhelming catastrophe for the nation. . . .

This descent from respectability, frequent enough in the best of times, has been hastened immeasurably by two years of business paralysis, and the people who have been affected in this manner must be numbered in millions. This is what we have accomplished with our bread lines and soup kitchens. I know, because I have seen thousands of these defeated, discouraged, hopeless men and women, cringing and fawning as they come to ask for public aid. It is a spectacle of national degeneration. That is the fundamental tragedy for America. If every mill and factory in the land should begin to hum with prosperity to-morrow morning, the destructive effect of our haphazard relief measures would not work itself out of the nation's blood until the sons of our sons had expiated the sins of our neglect.

Even now there are signs of rebellion against a system so out of joint that it can only offer charity to honest men who want to work. Sometimes it takes the form of social agitation, but again it may show itself in a revolt that is absolute and final. Such an instance was reported in a Youngstown newspaper on the day I wrote these lines:—

Father Of Ten Drowns Self

. . . Out of work two years, Charles Wayne, aged 57, father of ten children, stood on the Spring Common bridge this morning. . . . He took off his coat, folded it carefully, and jumped into the swirling Mahoning River. Wayne was born in Youngstown and was employed by the Republic Iron and Steel Company for twenty-seven years as a hot mill worker. "We were about to lose our home," sobbed Mrs. Wayne. "And the gas and electric companies had threatened to shut off the service."

Source: Joseph L. Heffernan, "The Hungry City: A Mayor's Experience with Unemployment," *Atlantic Monthly,* May 1932, pp. 538–540, 546 5.

Action Now!

On March 4, 1933, Franklin Delano Roosevelt became president and immediately reassured the American people. He insisted that "the only thing we have to fear is fear itself—nameless, unreasoning, unjustified terror, which paralyzes needed efforts to convert retreat into advance." And he promised "action, and action now!" In the first three months of his administration, the famous Hundred Days of the New Deal, the Democratic Congress passed many important laws (see the Overview table "Major Laws of the Hundred Days" on p. 666).

Roosevelt's program reflected a mix of ideas, some from FDR himself, some from a diverse group of advisers, including academic experts dubbed the "brain trust," politicians, and social workers. It also incorporated principles from the progressive movement, precedents from the Great War mobilization, and even plans from the Hoover administration. FDR had set its tone in his campaign when he declared, "The country needs, and, unless I mistake its temper, the country demands bold, persistent experimentation. . . . Above all, try something."

On March 5, FDR proclaimed a national bank holiday, closing all remaining banks. Congress then passed his Emergency Banking Act, a conservative measure that extended government assistance to sound banks and reorganized the weak ones.

WHERE TO LEARN MORE

Center for the New Deal Studies, Roosevelt University, Chicago, Illinois

OVERVIEW

MAJOR LAWS OF THE HUNDRED DAYS

Law	Objective
Emergency Banking Act	Stabilized the private banking system
Agricultural Adjustment Act	Established a farm recovery program based on production controls and price supports
Emergency Farm Mortgage Act	Provided for the refinancing of farm mortgages
National Industrial Recovery Act	Established a national recovery program and authorized a public works program
Federal Emergency Relief Act	Established a national system of relief
Home Owners Loan Act	Protected homeowners from mortgage foreclosure by refinancing home loans
Glass-Steagall Act	Separated commercial and investment banking and guaranteed bank deposits
Tennessee Valley Authority Act	Established the TVA and provided for the planned development of the Tennessee River Valley
Civilian Conservation Corps Act	Established the CCC to provide work relief on reforestation and conservation projects
Farm Credit Act	Expanded agricultural credits and established the Farm Credit Administration
Securities Act	Required full disclosure from stock exchanges
Wagner-Peyser Act	Created a U.S. Employment Service and encouraged states to create local public employment offices

Fireside chats   Speeches broadcast nationally over the radio in which President Franklin D. Roosevelt explained complex issues and programs in plain language, as though his listeners were gathered around the fireside with him.

Federal Deposit Insurance Corporation (FDIC)   Government agency that guarantees bank deposits, thereby protecting both depositors and banks.

Securities and Exchange Commission (SEC)   Federal agency with authority to regulate trading practices in stocks and bonds.

Prompt government action, coupled with a reassuring **fireside chat** over the radio by the president, restored popular confidence in the banks. When they reopened on March 13, deposits exceeded withdrawals. "Capitalism," said Raymond Moley of the brain trust, "was saved in eight days." In June, Congress created the **Federal Deposit Insurance Corporation (FDIC)** to guarantee bank deposits up to $2,500.

The financial industry was also reformed. The Glass-Steagall Act separated investment and commercial banking to curtail risky speculation. The Securities Act reformed the sale of stocks to prevent the insider abuses that had characterized Wall Street, and in 1934, the **Securities and Exchange Commission (SEC)** was created to regulate the stock market. Two other financial measures in 1933 created the Home Owners Loan Corporation and the Farm Credit Administration, which enabled millions to refinance their mortgages.

CREATING JOBS

Roosevelt also provided relief for the unemployed. The Federal Emergency Relief Administration (FERA) furnished funds to state and local agencies. Directed by Harry Hopkins, FERA spent over $3 billion before it ended in 1935, and by then Hopkins and FDR had developed new programs that provided work relief to preserve both the skills and the morale of recipients. The Civil Works Administration (CWA) hired laborers to build roads, teachers to staff rural schools, and singers to give public performances. The Public Works Administration (PWA) provided work relief and stimulated the economy by building schools, hospitals, courthouses, airports, dams, and bridges. One of FDR's personal ideas, the Civilian Conservation Corps (CCC) employed 2.5 million young men to work on reforestation and flood control projects, build roads and bridges in national forests and parks, restore Civil War battlefields, and fight forest fires.

Helping Some Farmers

In May 1933, Congress established the Agricultural Adjustment Administration (AAA) to combat the depression in agriculture caused by crop surpluses and low prices. The AAA subsidized farmers who agreed to restrict production. The objective was to boost farm prices to parity, a level that would restore farmers' purchasing power to its 1914 level. In the summer of 1933, the AAA paid southern farmers to plow up 10 million acres of cotton and midwestern farmers to bury 9 million pounds of pork. Restricting production in hard times caused public outrage.

But agricultural conditions improved. Farm prices rose from 52 percent of parity in 1932 to 88 percent in 1935, and gross farm income rose by 50 percent. Not until 1941, however, would income exceed the level of 1929, a poor year for farmers. Moreover, some of the decreased production and increased prices stemmed from devastating droughts and dust storms on the Great Plains. The AAA itself harmed poor farmers while aiding larger commercial growers. As southern planters restricted their acreage, they dismissed tenants and sharecroppers, and with AAA payments, they bought new farm machinery, reducing their need for farm labor. Thus while big producers moved toward prosperity, many small farmers were forced into a pool of rural labor for which there was decreasing need or into the cities, where there were no jobs.

The Supreme Court declared the AAA unconstitutional in 1936, but new laws established the farm subsidy program for decades to come. Increasing mechanization and scientific agriculture kept production high and farmers dependent on government intervention.

The Flight of the Blue Eagle

The New Deal attempted to revive American industry with the National Industrial Recovery Act (NIRA), which created the National Recovery Administration (NRA). The NRA sought to halt the slide in prices, wages, and employment by suspending antitrust laws and authorizing industrial and trade associations to draft codes setting production quotas, price policies, wages and working conditions, and other business practices. The codes promoted the interests of business generally and big business in particular, but Section 7a of the NIRA guaranteed workers the rights to organize unions and bargain collectively.

Hugh Johnson became director of the NRA and persuaded business leaders to cooperate in drafting codes and the public to patronize participating companies, indicated by the NRA Blue Eagle insignia. Corporate leaders, however, used the NRA to advance their own goals and discriminate against small producers, consumers, and labor. Employers also violated Section 7a, even using violence to smother unions. The NRA did little to enforce Section 7a, and Johnson—strongly probusiness—denounced all strikes. Workers felt betrayed.

Roosevelt tried to reorganize the NRA, but it remained controversial until the Supreme Court declared it unconstitutional in 1935.

Critics Right and Left

Though the early New Deal had not ended the depression, its efforts to grapple with problems, its successes in reducing suffering and fear, and Roosevelt's own skills carried the Democratic party to victory in the 1934 elections. But New Deal policies also provoked criticism.

WHERE TO LEARN MORE

Civilian Conservation Corps Interpretive Center, Whidbey Island, Washington

QUICK REVIEW

The National Recovery Administration (NRA)

◆ Sought to halt the slide in prices, wages, and employment.

◆ Tended to help business, often at the expense of labor.

◆ Declared unconstitutional in 1935.

WHERE TO LEARN MORE

★ Labor Museum and Learning Center of Michigan, Flint, Michigan

QUICK REVIEW

Critique of the New Deal

◆ Conservative critics of the expansion of government gained little support.

◆ Many on the left saw the early New Deal as a "Raw Deal."

◆ Popular pressure mounted for more aggressive policies.

Conservatives complained that the expansion of government activity and its regulatory role weakened the autonomy of American business. They also condemned the efforts to aid nonbusiness groups as socialistic, particularly the "excessive" spending on unemployment relief and the "instigation" of labor organizing. By 1934, as *Time* magazine reported, "Private fulminations and public carpings against the New Deal have become almost a routine of the business day." These critics attracted little popular support, however.

More realistic criticism came from the left. In 1932, FDR had campaigned for "the forgotten man at the bottom of the economic pyramid," and some radicals argued that the early New Deal had forgotten the forgotten man. In Arkansas and Tennessee, socialists in 1934 helped organize sharecroppers into the Southern Tenant Farmers Union protesting the "Raw Deal" they had received from the AAA. A broader labor militancy in 1934 also pressed Roosevelt. Workers acted as much against the failure of the NRA to enforce Section 7a as against recalcitrant corporations. The number of workers participating in strikes leaped from 325,000 in 1932 (about the annual average since 1925) to 1.5 million in 1934. From dockworkers in Seattle and copper miners in Butte to streetcar drivers in Milwaukee and shoemakers in Boston, workers demanded their rights.

Employers moved to crush the strikes, often using complaisant police and private strikebreakers. In Minneapolis, police shot sixty-seven teamsters, almost all in the back as they fled an ambush arranged by employers; in Toledo, company police and National Guardsmen attacked autoworkers with tear gas, bayonets, and rifle fire. At times, the workers held their ground. But against such powerful opponents, they needed help to achieve their rights.

Popular discontent was also mobilized by four prominent individuals demanding government action to assist groups neglected by the New Deal. Representative William Lemke of North Dakota, an agrarian radical leader of the Nonpartisan League, objected to the New Deal's limited response to farmers crushed by the depression. The AAA's strategy of simply restricting production, he thundered, was an "insane policy in the midst of hunger, misery, want, and rags." He sought government financial aid for farmers and policies favoring inflation, a traditional rural demand.

Francis Townsend, a California physician, called for a government pension to all Americans over the age of 60, provided they retire from work and spend their entire pension. This promised to extend relief to the many destitute elderly, open jobs for the unemployed, and stimulate economic recovery. Over five thousand Townsend Clubs lobbied for government action to help the elderly poor.

Father Charles Coughlin, a Catholic priest in the Detroit suburb of Royal Oak, threatened to mobilize another large constituency against the limitations of the early New Deal. Thirty million Americans listened eagerly to his weekly radio broadcasts mixing religion with anti-Semitism and demands for social justice and financial reform. After concluding that FDR's policies favored "the virile viciousness of business and finance," Coughlin organized the National Union for Social Justice to lobby for his goals. With support among lower-middle-class, heavily Catholic, urban ethnic groups, Coughlin posed a real challenge to Roosevelt's Democratic party.

Senator Huey P. Long of Louisiana wanted more comprehensive social welfare policies, but he also wanted to be president. In 1934, he organized the Share-Our-Wealth Society. His plan to end poverty and unemployment called for confiscatory taxes on the rich to provide every family with a decent income, health coverage, education, and old-age pensions. Within months, Long's organization claimed more than 27,000 clubs and 7 million members.

These dissident movements raised complex issues and simple fears. They built on concerns about the New Deal, with programs often ill-defined or impractical. Nevertheless, their popularity warned Roosevelt that government action was needed to satisfy reform demands and assure his reelection in 1936.

CONSOLIDATING THE NEW DEAL

I n 1935, Roosevelt undertook economic and social reforms that some observers have called the Second New Deal. The new measures shifted the relative weights accorded to the constant objectives of recovery, relief, and reform. This new phase reflected the persisting depression, growing political pressures, and the progressive inclinations of key New Dealers, including FDR himself.

LIFTING UP AND WEEDING OUT

"In spite of our efforts and in spite of our talk," Roosevelt told the new Congress in 1935, "we have not weeded out the overprivileged and we have not effectively lifted up the underprivileged." To do so, he developed "must" legislation, to which his allies in Congress added. One of the new laws protected labor's rights to organize and bargain collectively. Drafted by Senator Robert Wagner of New York to replace Section 7a, the Wagner National Labor Relations Act, dubbed "Labor's Magna Carta," guaranteed workers' rights to organize unions and forbade employers to adopt unfair labor practices, such as firing union activists or forming company unions. The law also set up the National Labor Relations Board (NLRB) to enforce these provisions, protect workers from coercion, and supervise union elections.

Of greater long-range importance was the Social Security Act. It provided unemployment compensation, old-age pensions, and aid for dependent mothers and children and the blind. The conservative nature of the law appeared in its stingy benefit payments, its lack of health insurance, and its exclusion of more than a fourth of all workers, including many in desperate need of protection, such as farm laborers and domestic servants. Moreover, unlike in other nations, the old-age pensions were financed through a regressive payroll tax on both employees and employers rather than through general tax revenues. Thus the new system was more like a compulsory insurance program. Despite its weaknesses, however, the Social Security Act was one of the most important laws in American history. It provided, Roosevelt pointed out, "at least some measure of protection to the average citizen and to his family against the loss of a job and against poverty-ridden old age."

Among other reform measures, the Banking Act of 1935 increased the authority of the Federal Reserve Board over the nation's currency and credit system and decreased the power of the private bankers whose irresponsible behavior had contributed to the depression and the appeal of Father Coughlin. The Revenue Act of 1935 provided for graduated income taxes and increased estate and corporate taxes. Opponents called it the Soak the Rich Tax, but with its many loopholes, it was scarcely that. Nevertheless, it set a precedent for progressive taxation and attracted popular support.

The Second New Deal also responded belatedly to the environmental catastrophe that had turned much of the Great Plains into a "Dust Bowl" (see Map 25–1). Since World War I, farmers had stripped marginal land of its native grasses to plant wheat. When drought and high winds hit the plains in 1932, crops failed, and nothing held the soil. Dust storms blew away millions of tons of topsoil, despoiling the land and darkening the sky 1,000 miles away. Families abandoned their farms in droves.

WHICH ECONOMIC and social reforms made up the "Second New Deal"?

25–2
Share the Wealth

QUICK REVIEW

The Social Security Act

♦ Provided unemployment compensation, old-age pensions, and aid for dependent mothers and children and the blind.

♦ The law excluded more than a fourth of all workers and did not include health insurance.

♦ Funded by a regressive payroll tax.

A sullen mother stares vacantly between her two children in a migrant labor camp in Nipomo, California in 1936. This photograph, commissioned by the FSA, came to symbolize the Great Depression for many people.

Courtesy of the Library of Congress

MAP EXPLORATION
To explore an interactive version of this map, go to
http://www.prenhall.com/goldfield2/map25.1

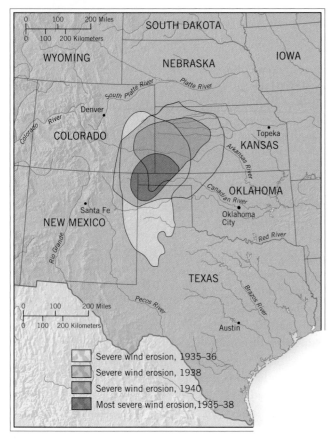

MAP 25–1
The Dust Bowl   Years of overcultivation, drought, and high winds created the Dust Bowl, which most severely affected the southern Great Plains. Federal relief and conservation programs provided assistance, but many residents fled the area, often migrating to California.

WHY WAS this drought particularly damaging to people in this region?

In 1935, Roosevelt established the Resettlement Administration to focus on land reform and help poor farmers. Under Rexford Tugwell, this agency initiated soil erosion projects and attempted to resettle impoverished farmers on better land, but the problem exceeded its resources. Congress moved to save the land, if not its people, by creating the Soil Conservation Service in 1935.

EXPANDING RELIEF
Relief remained critical in the Second New Deal. With millions still unemployed, Roosevelt pushed through Congress in 1935 the Emergency Relief Appropriation Act, authorizing $5 billion—at the time the largest single appropriation in history—for emergency public employment. Roosevelt created the Works Progress Administration (WPA) under Hopkins, who set up work relief programs to assist the unemployed and boost the economy. Before its end in 1943, the WPA gave jobs to 9 million people (more than a fifth of the labor force) and spent nearly $12 billion. Three-fourths of its expenditures went on construction projects that could employ manual labor: the WPA built 125,000 schools, post offices, and hospitals; 8,000 parks; nearly 100,000 bridges; and enough roads and sewer systems to circle the earth thirty times. From New York City's La Guardia Airport to Atlanta's sewer system to irrigation ditches in the Far West, the WPA laid much of the nation's basic infrastructure on which it still relies.

The WPA also developed work projects for unemployed writers, artists, musicians, and actors. "Why not?" said FDR. "They are human beings. They have to live." These WPA programs allowed people to use their talents while surviving the depression, increased popular access to cultural performances, and established a precedent for federal support of the arts.

The National Youth Administration (NYA), another WPA agency, gave part-time jobs to students, enabling 2 million high school and college students to stay in school, learn skills, and do productive work. Law student Richard M. Nixon earned 35 cents an hour doing research in the library. Lyndon Johnson, a Texas NYA official, believed that "if the Roosevelt administration had never done another thing, it would have been justified by the work of this great institution for salvaging youth."

THE ROOSEVELT COALITION AND THE ELECTION OF 1936
The 1936 election gave Americans an opportunity to judge FDR and the New Deal. Conservatives alarmed at the expansion of government, businesspeople angered by regulation and labor legislation, and well-to-do Americans furious with tax reform decried the New Deal. But they were a minority. Even the presidential candidate they supported, Republican Governor Alf Landon of Kansas, endorsed much of the New Deal, criticizing merely the inefficiency and cost of some of its programs. The reforms of 1935 had undercut the arguments of critics on the left, and the assassination of Huey Long in the same year had removed their ablest

FROM THEN TO NOW
Social Security

No politician will "ever scrap my social security program." So predicted FDR when he signed the Social Security Act in 1935. He based his confidence on the provisions in the act that linked benefits to payroll deductions. Because workers contributed to the program, they would feel a "right to collect their pensions and unemployment benefits." But Roosevelt could not have imagined just how successful the Social Security program would become. Expanded over the years since the 1930s, it now assists 44 million Americans, including the elderly, the disabled, and the survivors of contributors to the program. Certain poverty would confront half the nation's elderly without their monthly checks.

But the successful expansion of the program has also called its future into question. By 2030, the number of eligible recipients will double, but the number of employees paying Social Security taxes will increase by only 17 percent. Annual funding deficits of more than $100 billion loom ahead.

Still, as FDR predicted, no political leader dares to propose "scrapping" Social Security. Rather, proposals to solve this problem reflect conflicting views about the expansion of the federal government—and especially its efforts to promote social welfare—that began with the New Deal. No longer does the public overwhelmingly endorse federal responsibility for solving social problems as it did during the economic crisis of the 1930s. On the contrary, an increasingly intense backlash against "big government" emerged in the 1960s, ultimately finding its champion in the 1980s in Republican President Ronald Reagan, who declared, "Government is not the solution to our problems; government is the problem." Reagan's administration sought to reduce the size of government and curtail its regulatory oversight of American business. This "Reagan Revolution" appealed to those who never supported government responsibility for social welfare and to those who had lost trust in the government's ability to fulfill that role. By the 1990s, even Democratic President Bill Clinton declared an end to the era of "big government."

Support has grown for private initiatives to replace government programs, and now critics are pressing to "privatize" the Social Security system itself. They have proposed such sweeping changes as limiting benefits to contributors only and requiring contributors to invest their Social Security accounts themselves, including in the stock market. The predicted payoff would be larger earnings.

Opponents of these critics argue for reforming, not overturning, the current Social Security system. Privatization, they argue, would undermine Social Security's fundamental principle: to guarantee retirees a dependable income base. Investing retirement savings in the stock market subjects them to market volatility, which might benefit some people but could leave others with serious losses just when they were ready to retire. Privatization would also eliminate the special assistance that Social Security provides to large families, couples with one partner who has had no or limited earnings, and low-income earners.

Rather than scrap the current system, reformers propose other changes. They suggest taxing all workers for Social Security, many, especially in state and local governments, are now outside the system. Extending the age of eligibility to receive benefits, justified by the increasing life expectancy of Americans, would also bolster the Social Security funds. Another proposal would abandon the current investment strategy but have a quasi-private government entity manage the system's portfolio. Such changes would enable Social Security to continue meeting the needs of all citizens.

The current argument over Social Security echoes the disputes of the 1930s about the role and function of our government and reflects continuing differences over the degree to which the government should attempt to make American society more equitable. Finding a solution to funding Social Security in the new century will require addressing the issue of America's core values.

FDR signs the Social Security Act in 1935, establishing a program that would grow in size and importance in subsequent decades. To the left in a dark suit is Senator Robert F. Wagner; behind FDR is Secretary of Labor Frances Perkins. All three were influential in shaping an activist federal government that some Americans would later decry as unnecessary.

AP/Wide World Photos

W WHERE TO LEARN MORE

★ Franklin D. Roosevelt Home and
Presidential Library,
Hyde Park, New York
www.fdrlibrary.marist.edu

politician. They formed the Union party and nominated William Lemke for the presidency, but they were no longer a threat.

The programs and politicians of the New Deal had created an invincible coalition behind Roosevelt. The New Deal's agricultural programs reinforced the traditional Democratic allegiance of white Southerners while attracting many Western farmers. Labor legislation clinched the active support of the nation's workers. Middle-class voters, whose homes had been saved and whose hopes had been raised, also joined the Roosevelt coalition.

So did urban ethnic groups, who had benefited from welfare programs and received unprecedented recognition. FDR named the first Italian American to the federal judiciary, for example, and appointed five times as many Catholics and Jews to government positions as the three Republican presidents had during the 1920s. African Americans voted overwhelmingly Democratic for the first time. Women, too, were an important part of the Roosevelt coalition. As one campaigner said to a roaring crowd in 1936, "Many women in this country when they vote for Franklin D. Roosevelt will also be thinking with a choke in the throat of Eleanor Roosevelt!"

This political realignment produced a landslide. Roosevelt polled 61 percent of the popular vote and the largest electoral vote margin ever recorded, 523 to 8. Landon even lost Kansas, his own state, and Lemke received fewer than 900,000 votes. Democrats also won huge majorities in Congress.

THE NEW DEAL AND AMERICAN LIFE

The landslide of 1936 reflected the impact the New Deal had on Americans. Government programs changed daily life, and ordinary people often helped shape the new policies.

LABOR ON THE MARCH

The labor revival in the 1930s reflected both workers' determination and government support. Workers wanted not merely to improve their wages and benefits but also to gain union recognition and union contracts to limit arbitrary managerial authority and achieve some control over the workplace. The Wagner Act sparked a wave of labor activism. But if the government ultimately protected union rights, the unions themselves had to form locals, recruit members, and demonstrate influence in the workplace.

At first, the American Federation of Labor (AFL), with its reliance on craft-based unions and its reluctance to organize immigrant, black, and women workers, was unprepared for the rush of industrial workers seeking unionization. More progressive labor leaders formed the Committee for Industrial Organization (CIO) within the AFL. They campaigned to unionize workers in the steel, auto, and rubber industries, all notoriously hostile to unions. AFL leaders insisted that the CIO disband and then in 1937 expelled its unions. The militants reorganized as the separate **Congress of Industrial Organizations**.

The split roused the AFL to increase its own organizing activities, but it was primarily the new CIO that put labor on the march. It inspired workers previously neglected. The CIO's interracial union campaign in the Birmingham steel mills, said one organizer, was "like a second coming of Christ" for black workers, who welcomed the union as a chance for social recognition as well as economic opportunity. The CIO also employed new and aggressive tactics, particularly the sit-down strike, in which workers, rather than picketing outside the factory, simply sat inside the

---

WHAT IMPACT did New Deal programs have on women and minorities?

Congress of Industrial Organizations
An alliance of industrial unions that spurred the 1930s organizational drive among the mass-production industries.

plant, thereby blocking both production and the use of strikebreakers. Upton Sinclair said, "For seventy-five years big business has been sitting down on the American people, and now I am delighted to see the process reversed."

Sit-down strikes paralyzed General Motors in 1937 after it refused to recognize the United Auto Workers. GM tried to force the strikers out of its Flint, Michigan, plants by turning off the heat, using police and tear gas, and threatening strikers' families. The strikers held out, and after six weeks GM signed a contract with the UAW. Chrysler soon followed suit. Ford refused to recognize the union until 1941, often violently disrupting organizing efforts.

Steel companies also used violence against unionization. In the Memorial Day Massacre in Chicago in 1937, police guarding a plant of the Republic Steel Company fired on strikers and their families, killing ten people as they tried to flee. Scores more were wounded and beaten. A Senate investigation found that Republic and other companies "dominate their employees, deny them their constitutional rights, promote disorder and disharmony, and even set at naught the powers of the government itself." Federal court orders finally forced the companies to bargain collectively.

New Deal labor legislation, government investigations and court orders, and the federal refusal to use force against strikes helped the labor movement secure basic rights for American workers. Union membership leaped from under 3 million in 1932 to 9 million by 1939, and workers won higher wages, better working conditions, and more economic democracy.

WOMEN AND THE NEW DEAL

As federal programs proliferated in 1933, a Baltimore women's group urged the administration to "come out for a square and new deal for women." Although women did gain increased attention and influence, government and society remained largely bound by traditional values.

New Deal relief programs had a mixed impact on workingwomen. Formal government policy required "equal consideration" for women and men, but local officials so flouted this requirement that Eleanor Roosevelt urged Harry Hopkins to "impress on state administrators that the women's programs are as important as the men's. They are so apt to forget us!" Women on relief were restricted to "women's work"— more than half worked on sewing projects, regardless of their skills—and were paid scarcely half what men received. And although women constituted nearly a fourth of the labor force, they obtained only 19 percent of the jobs created by the WPA, 12 percent by the FERA, and 7 percent by the CWA. The CCC excluded women altogether. Still, relief agencies provided crucial assistance to women in the depression.

Other New Deal programs also had mixed benefits for women. Many NRA codes mandated lower wage scales for women than for men, which officials justified as reflecting "long-established customs." But by raising minimum wages, the NRA brought relatively greater improvements to women, who were concentrated in the lowest-paid occupations, than to male workers. The Social Security Act did not cover domestic servants, waitresses, and women who worked in the home but did help mothers with dependent children.

Women also gained political influence under the New Deal. Molly Dewson, the director of the Women's Division of the Democratic party, exercised considerable political power and helped shape the party's campaigns. Around Dewson revolved a network of women, linked by friendships and experiences in the National Consumers' League, Women's Trade Union League, and other progressive reform organizations. Appointed to positions in the Roosevelt administration, they helped develop and implement New Deal social legislation. Secretary of Labor Frances Perkins was the first

25–3
Mrs. Henry Weddington, Letter to President Roosevelt (1938)

QUICK REVIEW

Impact of the New Deal on Women

- Women received a smaller percentage than men of jobs created by New Deal programs.
- Increase in the minimum wage brought greater improvements to women than to men.
- Women gained political influence under the New Deal.

WHERE TO LEARN MORE

★ Eleanor Roosevelt National
Historic Site,
Hyde Park, New York
www.nps.gov/elro

woman cabinet member and a key member of the network; other women were in the Treasury Department, the Children's Bureau, and relief and cultural programs.

Eleanor Roosevelt roared across the social and political landscape of the 1930s, pushing for women's rights, demanding reforms, traveling across the country, writing newspaper columns and speaking over the radio, developing plans to help unemployed miners and abolish slums. FDR rebuffed her critics with a jaunty, "Well, that is my wife; I can't do anything about her." Indeed, Eleanor Roosevelt had become a symbol of the growing importance of women in public life.

MINORITIES AND THE NEW DEAL

Although Roosevelt deplored racial abuses, he never pushed for civil rights legislation, fearing to antagonize the influential Southern Democrats in Congress whose support he needed. For similar reasons, many New Deal programs discriminated against African Americans. The CCC segregated black workers; NRA codes so often specified lower wages and benefits for black workers relative to white workers or even excluded black workers from jobs that the black press claimed NRA stood for "Negro Run Around" or "Negroes Ruined Again."

However, African Americans did benefit from the New Deal's welfare and economic programs. W. E. B. Du Bois asserted that "large numbers of colored people in the United States would have starved to death if it had not been for the Roosevelt policies." And key New Dealers campaigned against racial discrimination. Eleanor Roosevelt, prodded FDR to appoint black officials, wrote articles supporting racial equality, and flouted segregationist laws. Attacked by white racists, she was popular in the black community. As black votes in Northern cities became important, more pragmatic New Dealers also began to pay more attention to black needs.

African Americans themselves pressed for reforms, and FDR took more interest in their economic and social problems. He prohibited discrimination in the WPA in 1935, and the NYA adopted enlightened racial policies. Roosevelt also appointed black people to important positions, including the first black federal judge. Many of these officials began meeting regularly at the home of Mary McLeod Bethune of the National Council of Negro Women. Dubbed the Black Cabinet, they worked with civil rights organizations, fought discrimination in government, influenced patronage, and stimulated black interest in politics.

WHERE TO LEARN MORE

★ Bethune Museum and Archives
National Historic Site,
Washington, D.C.

Under the New Deal, black illiteracy dropped because of federal education projects, and the number of black college students and graduates more than doubled, in part because the NYA provided student aid to black colleges. New Deal relief and public health programs reduced black infant mortality rates and raised life expectancy rates. Conditions for black people continued to lag behind those for white people, and discrimination persisted, but the black switch to the Roosevelt coalition reflected the New Deal's benefits.

Native Americans also benefited from the New Deal. The CCC particularly appealed to their interests and skills. More than eighty thousand Indians received training in agriculture, forestry, and animal husbandry, along with basic academic subjects. CCC projects, together with those undertaken by the PWA and the WPA, built schools, hospitals, roads, and irrigation systems on reservations.

New Deal officials also refocused government Indian policy, which had undermined tribal authority and promoted assimilation by reducing Indian landholding and attacking Indian culture. Appointed commissioner of Indian affairs in 1933, John Collier prohibited interference with Indian religious or cultural life, directed the Bureau of Indian Affairs to employ more Indians, and prevented Indian schools from suppressing native languages and traditions. The Indian Reorganization Act of 1934, often called the Indians' New Deal, guaranteed religious freedom, reestablished tribal self-government, and halted the sale of tribal lands. It also provided funds to expand Indian landholdings, support Indian students, and establish tribal businesses.

Hispanic Americans received less assistance from the New Deal. Its relief programs aided many Hispanics in California and the Southwest but ignored those who were not citizens. And by excluding agricultural workers, neither the Social Security Act nor the Wagner Act gave Mexican Americans much protection or hope. Farm workers remained largely unorganized, exploited, and at the mercy of agribusinesses.

THE NEW DEAL: NORTH, SOUTH, EAST, AND WEST

"We are going to make a country," President Roosevelt declared, "in which no one is left out." And with that statement along with his belief that the federal government must take the lead in building a new "economic constitutional order," FDR ensured that his New Deal programs and policies fanned out throughout the nation, bolstering the stock market and banking in New York, constructing public housing for poor immigrant families and African Americans in most major cities, and building schools, roads, and bridges in all regions of the United States. Ironically, the New Deal also offered special benefits to the South, traditionally averse to government activism, and to the West, which considered itself the land of rugged individualism.

The New Deal's agricultural program boosted farm prices and income more in the South than any other region. By controlling cotton production, it also promoted diversification; its subsidies financed mechanization. The resulting modernization helped replace an archaic sharecropping system with an emergent agribusiness. The rural poor were displaced, but the South's agricultural economy advanced.

The New Deal also improved Southern cities. FERA and WPA built urban sewer systems, airports, bridges, roads, and harbor facilities. Whereas Northern cities had already constructed such facilities themselves—and were still paying off their debts—the federal government largely paid for such modernization in the South, giving its cities an economic advantage.

Federal grants were supposed to be awarded to states in proportion to their own expenditures, but Southern politicians refused to contribute their share of the costs. Nationally, the federal proportion of FERA expenditures was 62 percent; in the South, it was usually 90 percent and never lower than 73 percent.

Federal money enabled Southern communities to balance their own budgets, preach fiscal orthodoxy, and maintain traditional claims of limited government. Even Southerners acknowledged the hypocrisy of the region's invocation of state's rights. "We recognize state boundaries when called on to give," noted the *Houston Press*, "but forget them when Uncle Sam is doing the giving."

The federal government had a particularly powerful impact on the South with the **Tennessee Valley Authority (TVA)**, launched in 1933 (see Map 25–2). Coordinating activities across seven states, the TVA built dams to control floods and generate hydroelectric power, produced fertilizer, fostered agricultural and forestry development, encouraged conservation, improved navigation, and modernized school and health systems. Its major drawback was environmental damage that only became apparent later. Over a vast area of the South, it provided electricity for the first time.

The New Deal further expanded access to electricity by establishing the Rural Electrification Administration (REA) in 1935. Private companies had refused to extend power lines into the countryside because it was not profitable, consigning 90 percent of the nation's farms to drudgery and darkness. The REA revolutionized farm life by sponsoring rural nonprofit electric cooperatives. By 1950, 78 percent of American farms had electricity.

American educator and activist Mary McLeod Bethune.
Courtesy of the Library of Congress

Tennessee Valley Authority (TVA)
Federal regional planning agency established to promote conservation, produce electric power, and encourage economic development in seven southern states.

MAP 25–2
The Tennessee Valley Authority By building dams and hydroelectric power plants, the TVA controlled flooding and soil erosion and generated electricity that did much to modernize a large region of the Upper South.

WHAT ECONOMIC and social impact did the Tennessee Valley Authority have on the Upper South?

The New Deal also changed the West. Westerners received the most federal money per capita in welfare, relief projects, and loans. Western farmers and cattle raisers were saved by federal payments, and even refugees from the Dust Bowl depended on relief assistance and medical care in federal camps.

The Bureau of Reclamation, established in 1902, built huge dams to control the Western river systems, promote large-scale development, prevent flooding, produce cheap hydroelectric power, and create reservoirs and canal systems to bring water to farms and cities. By furnishing capital and expertise, the government subsidized and stimulated western economic development, particularly the growth of agribusiness.

Westerners welcomed such assistance but rarely shared the federal goals of rational resource management. Instead, they often wanted to continue to exploit the land and resented federal supervision as colonial control. In practice, however, the government worked in partnership with the West's agribusinesses and timber and petroleum industries.

THE NEW DEAL AND PUBLIC ACTIVISM

Despite Hoover's fear that government responsibility would discourage local initiative, New Deal programs, in fact, often encouraged or empowered groups to shape public policy and social and economic behavior. Moreover, because the administration worried about centralization, some federal agencies fostered what New Dealers called "grass-roots democracy." The AAA set up committees totaling more than 100,000 people to implement agricultural policy and held referendums on crop controls; local advisory committees guided the various federal arts projects; federal management of the West's public grasslands mandated cooperation with associations of livestock raisers.

At times, federal programs allowed previously unrepresented groups to contest traditionally dominant interests. Often seeing greater opportunities for participation and influence in federal programs than in city and state governments, community groups even campaigned to expand federal authority. In short, depression conditions and New Deal programs actually increased citizen involvement in public affairs.

EBBING OF THE NEW DEAL

After his victory in 1936, Roosevelt committed himself to further reforms. "The test of our progress," he declared in his second inaugural address, "is not whether we add more to the abundance of those who have much; it is whether we provide enough for those who have too little." But determined opponents, continuing economic problems, and the president's own misjudgments blocked his reforms and deadlocked the New Deal.

WHY WERE late New Deal reforms unsuccessful?

CHALLENGING THE COURT

During Roosevelt's first term, the Supreme Court had declared unconstitutional several important measures. FDR complained that the justices held "horse-and-buggy" ideas about government that prevented the president and Congress from responding to changes. He decided to restructure the federal judiciary and, in early 1937, proposed legislation authorizing a new judge for each one serving past the age of 70. Additional judges, he said, would increase judicial efficiency, but his real goal was to appoint new judges more sympathetic to the New Deal.

His court plan led to a divisive struggle. The proposal was perfectly legal, but Republicans and conservative Democrats attacked the plan as a scheme to "pack" the Court and subvert the separation of powers among the three branches of government. Even many liberals expressed reservations. The Court itself undercut support for FDR's proposal by upholding the Social Security and Wagner Acts. Congress rejected Roosevelt's plan.

Roosevelt's challenge to the Court hurt the New Deal. It worried the public, split the Democratic party, and revived conservatives. Opponents promptly attacked other New Deal policies, from support for unions to progressive taxation. Henceforth, a conservative coalition of Republicans and Southern Democrats in Congress blocked FDR's reforms.

MORE HARD TIMES

A sharp recession beginning in August 1937 added to Roosevelt's problems. As the economy improved in 1936, Roosevelt decided to cut federal expenditures and balance the budget, but private investment and employment remained stagnant, and the economy plunged. A record decline in industrial production canceled the gains of the previous two years, and unemployment leaped from 7 million to 11 million. Republicans delighted in attacking the "Roosevelt recession," although it stemmed from retrenchment policies they themselves advocated.

In 1938, Roosevelt reluctantly increased spending, based on the principles of British economist John Maynard Keynes. As Marriner Eccles of the Federal Reserve Board explained, the federal government had to serve as the "compensatory agent" in the economy: It should use deficit spending to increase demand and production when private investment declined and raise taxes to pay its debt and cool the economy when business activity became excessive. New appropriations for the PWA and other government programs revived the faltering economy, but only the vast expenditures for World War II would bring full recovery.

POLITICAL STALEMATE

The recession interrupted the momentum of the New Deal and strengthened its opponents. In late 1937, their leaders in Congress issued a "conservative manifesto" decrying New Deal fiscal, labor, and regulatory policies. Holding seniority in a Congress malapportioned in their favor, they blocked most of Roosevelt's reforms. None of his "must" legislation passed a special session of Congress in December. In 1938, Congress rejected tax reforms and reduced corporate taxes. The few measures that passed were heavily amended. The Fair Labor Standards Act established maximum hours and minimum wages for workers but authorized so many exemptions that one New Dealer asked "whether anyone is subject to this bill."

To protect the New Deal, Roosevelt turned again to the public, with whom he remained immensely popular. In the 1938 Democratic primaries, he campaigned against the New Deal's conservative opponents. But FDR could not transfer his personal popularity to the political newcomers he supported. What his foes attacked as a "purge" failed. Roosevelt lost further political leverage when the Republicans gained seventy-five seats in the House and seven in the Senate and thirteen governorships.

The Democrats retained majorities in both houses of Congress, but the Republican revival and the survival of the conservative Southern Democrats guaranteed that the New Deal had gone as far as it ever would. With Roosevelt in the White House and his opponents controlling Congress, the New Deal ended in political stalemate.

GOOD NEIGHBORS AND HOSTILE FORCES

Even before FDR's conservative opposition derailed the New Deal, the President felt the impact of congressional limitations in foreign policy. Isolationists in Congress counseled against any U.S. involvement in world affairs. Republican Senator Gerald Nye established a committee in 1934 to investigate the origins of U.S. involvement in what many Americans termed the European War. The Nye Committee exposed the greed of big business and intimated that President Woodrow Wilson had gone to war to save profits for capitalists—and not democracy for the world. Jobless and homeless Americans reacted with anger to the committee's findings and public sentiment against fighting another "foreign" war hardened. Roosevelt himself believed that the gravity of the nation's economic depression warranted a primary focus on domestic recovery, and in the early years of his presidency, he took few international initiatives.

Those actions he did take related directly to salvaging America's desperate economy. In 1933, key business leaders informed FDR that they would welcome the opportunity to expand trade to the Soviet Union, and the President extended formal recognition of the Soviet Union in November 1933.

Enhancing trade opportunities also figured prominently in Roosevelt's policies in the Western hemisphere where he extended the Good Neighbor policy begun by President Herbert Hoover who had removed all U.S. troops from Latin America. Still, the Great Depression strained U.S.-Latin American relations, sending economic shock waves throughout Central and South America and helping propel to power ruthless dictators who ruled with U.S. support. In Cuba FDR supported a coup, which resulted in the coming to power of the infamous dictator Fulgencio Batista, whose domination lasted until it was overthrown by Fidel Castro in 1959.

FDR also worked to encourage trade by reducing tariffs. Between 1929 and 1933, the volume of trade worldwide had fallen by 40 percent and American exports had plummeted by 60 percent. Secretary of State Cordell Hull finalized trade agreements with Latin American nations that sharply increased U.S. exports to its southern neighbors. Good neighbors were also good trading partners.

NEUTRALITY AND FASCISM

During his first term as president, Roosevelt generally avoided involvement in Europe's problems, but the aggressive actions of Adolf Hitler in Germany ultimately led Roosevelt to try to educate the American public, still resentful of U.S. participation in World War I, about the fascist danger that was spreading in Europe. Hitler came to power in 1933, shortly before FDR entered the White House, and he pledged to restore German pride and nationalism in the aftermath of the Versailles Treaty. As the leader of the National Socialist Workers Party—the Nazis—Hitler established a **fascist government**—a one-party dictatorship—closely aligned with corporate interests, committed to a "biological world evolution," and determined to establish a new empire, the Third Reich. He vowed to destroy Bolshevik radicalism and purify the German "race" by eliminating those he deemed undesirable, especially Jews, whom Hitler blamed for most, if not all, Germany's ills.

Others aided the spread of fascism. Benito Mussolini, who had assumed power in Italy in 1922, attacked Ethiopia in 1935. The following year, a conservative military officer, Francisco Franco, led an uprising in Spain, and with the assistance of Italy and Germany, overthrew the Spanish Republic to create an authoritarian government. Meanwhile, Hitler remilitarized the Rhineland in 1936 and in 1938 he annexed Austria.

But the aggressive actions of Germany and Italy failed to eclipse American fears of being led into another European war. Congress passed four Neutrality Acts designed to continue America's trade with its world partners but prohibit the president from taking sides in the mounting European crisis. The first act, passed in 1935, prohibited Americans from traveling to a war zone, banned loans to belligerent nations, and instituted an embargo on armaments to belligerents. In 1937 Congress added a "cash-and-carry" provision that required belligerent nations to pay for American goods in advance of their shipment. President Roosevelt reluctantly signed the bill into law but continued to work to heighten public awareness of the dangers of Nazism.

In 1938, Hitler demanded the Sudetenland from Czechoslovakia. The French and British, following a policy of appeasement, met in Munich in September 1938, with Hitler and Mussolini and abandoned the Czechs, yielding the Sudetenland to Hitler in exchange for a weak promise of no more annexations.

In America, too, the sentiment was for peace at all costs, and Hitler did not regard the United States as a threat to his expansionist plan: He held FDR in low esteem and denounced America as a racially mixed nation of intellectual inferiors. "Transport a German to Kiev," Hitler declared, "and he remains a perfect German. But transplant him to Miami, and you make a degenerate out of him— in other words, an American." Isolationism also combined with anti-Semitism and with division among America's Jewish leadership to insure that the United States would not become a haven for Jews suffering under Nazi brutality. News of Nazi atrocities against Jews, particularly the violent pogrom, known as *Kristallnacht* (the Night of the Broken Glass) in November 1938, shocked the American Press. Although the United States recalled its ambassador from Berlin to protest the pogrom, the United States failed to alter its restrictive immigration quota system, the 1924 National Origins Act, to provide refuge for German Jews. Unchallenged,

Fascist government   A government subscribing to a philosophy of dictatorship that merges the interests of the state, armed forces, and big business.

On November 9, 1938 Nazi Germany launched an assault on Jews, destroying their businessess and burning their synagogues. This street scene in Berlin shows the shattered windows of Jewish businesses. Nazi leader Joseph Goebbels recorded the event, known as Kristallnacht, in his diary: "Yesterday: Berlin. There, all proceded fantastically. One fire after another. It is good that way. . . . 100 dead. But no German property damaged."

UPI/Corbis–Bettmann

Hitler pressed on with his campaign of terror, herding Jews, Slavs, homosexuals, and handicapped citizens into concentration camps.

As Europe edged closer to war, the relationship between the United States and Japan, periodically tense, became more strained. Japan resented U.S. economic interests in East Asia and was offended by American immigration policy which excluded Japanese immigrants. The United States regarded Japan's desires for empire as threatening but also needed Japan as a trading partner, especially in the economically depressed 1930s. Consequently in September 1931, when Japan seized Manchuria and then went to war with China, the United States merely condemned the actions, and although President Roosevelt denounced "the epidemic of world lawlessness", in 1937 and called for a "quarantine" of aggressors, he refused to risk war with Japan.

EDGING TOWARD INVOLVEMENT

After the Munich agreement, President Roosevelt moved away from domestic reform toward preparedness for war, fearful that conflict in Europe was unavoidable and determined to revise the neutrality laws. In his State of the Union address in January 1939, FDR explained that "our neutrality laws" might "actually give aid to an aggressor and deny it to the victim." By the fall of that year, he had won support for eliminating the prohibition of arms and adding armaments to the list of cash-and-carry items—a revision that would enable the United States to provide important assistance to Britain and France in the winter of 1939–1940. Hitler's defiance of the Munich agreement and his seizure of all of Czechoslovakia in March 1939 anticipated his next move toward Poland later that summer and also convinced the British and the French that war was imminent.

Conclusion

The Great Depression and the New Deal mark a major divide in American history. The depression cast doubt on the traditional practices, policies, and attitudes that underlay not only the nation's economy but its social and political institutions and relationships as well. The New Deal failed to restore prosperity, but it did bring partial economic recovery. Moreover, its economic policies, from banking and securities regulation to unemployment compensation, farm price supports, and minimum wages, created barriers against another depression. The gradual adoption of compensatory spending policies also expanded the government's role in the economy. Responding to the failures of both private organizations and state and local governments, the federal government also assumed the obligation to provide social welfare. "Better the occasional faults of a Government that lives in a spirit of charity," Roosevelt warned, "than the constant omission of a Government frozen in the ice of its own indifference."

The New Deal brought political changes, too. The role of the presidency expanded; the federal government, rather than state or local governments, became the focus of public interest and expectations; and the Roosevelt coalition made the Democrats the dominant national party for years to come. Political constraints limited some New Deal efforts, particularly to curtail racial discrimination or protect the rural and urban poor, but the New Deal did change American life. By 1939, as international relations deteriorated, FDR was already considering a shift, as he later said, from Dr. New Deal to Dr. Win-the-War.

Summary

Hard Times in Hooverville The prosperity of the 1920s ended in a stock market crash that revealed the flaws in the economy. As the nation slid into a catastrophic depression, factories closed, employment and incomes tumbled, and millions lost their homes, hopes, and dignity. Some protested and took direct action; others looked to the government for relief. The stock market crash of 1929 marked the beginning of the Great Depression but did not cause it. Contributing factors were the uneven distribution of wealth and income; industries dominated by oligarchies; overproduction in agriculture and other industries; declining prices; government policies; and European debts.

Herbert Hoover and the Depression President Hoover took unprecedented steps to resolve the growing economic crises, but he believed that voluntary private relief was preferable to federal intervention. The scope of the depression overwhelmed anything that private individuals and agencies could manage; Hoover blundered by refusing to admit a more activist approach was needed. The Reconstruction Finance Corporation lent funds that could "trickle down" to the public. The treatment of the Bonus Army symbolized Hoover's unpopularity and set the stage for the election of Franklin D. Roosevelt.

Launching the New Deal In the midst of national anxiety, Franklin D. Roosevelt pushed forward an unprecedented program to resolve the crises of a collapsing financial system, crippling unemployment, and agricultural and industrial breakdown and to promote reform. After initially addressing the banking crises, the New Deal went on to establish relief agencies and promote economic recovery. The New Deal achieved successes and attracted support but it also had limitations and generated criticism that suggested the need for still greater innovations.

Consolidating the New Deal In 1935 Roosevelt undertook additional economic and social reforms. Labor's right to organize and bargain collectively was addressed, the path-breaking Social Security Act was passed, and the Works Progress Administration was created. The administration also responded to the environmental crises that had turned the Great Plains into a dustbowl and driven the "Okies" to California. The 1936 election gave Americans an opportunity to judge the New Deal and Roosevelt. Political realignment resulted: Former Republican constituents voted Democratic and produced a landslide victory for the president.

The New Deal and American Life The election of 1936 revealed the impact the New Deal had on Americans. Industrial workers mobilized to secure their rights; women and minorities gained increased, if still limited, opportunities to participate in American society; and Southerners and Westerners benefited from government programs like the TVA that they turned to their own advantage. Government programs changed daily life, and ordinary people often helped shape the new policies.

Ebbing of the New Deal After his 1936 election, Roosevelt committed himself to further reforms, but his misjudgment blocked some efforts and deadlocked others. Regarding the Supreme Court as an adversary, Roosevelt attempted to restructure the federal judiciary; his attempt to "pack" the court hurt the New Deal. A 1937 recession caused by the New Deal's lack of aggressiveness caused the administration to adopt Keynesian economic theories and have the government use deficient spending to increase demand and production.

Good Neighbors and Hostile Forces While isolationists in Congress counseled against involvement in foreign affairs, fascism was spreading in Europe and Asia. In his first term Roosevelt followed a policy of neutrality; after the Munich crises, Hitler's intentions toward the world and Germany's Jewish citizens had become more defined and threatening. America's relationship with Japan continued to deteriorate; by 1939, the "epidemic of world lawlessness" was edging the United States toward involvement.

REVIEW QUESTIONS

1. Why did President Hoover's emphasis on voluntarism fail to resolve the Great Depression?

2. What were the relief programs of the New Deal, and what did they achieve?

3. What were the criticisms of the early New Deal?

4. What were the major issues between management and labor in the 1930s?

5. How did the role of the federal government change in the 1930s?

KEY TERMS

Bonus Army   (p. 663)
Congress of Industrial Organizations
(p. 672)
Fascist government   (p. 679)
Federal Deposit Insurance
Corporation (FDIC)   (p. 665)

Fireside chats   (p. 665)
Great Depression   (p. 658)
Hoovervilles   (p. 659)
New Deal   (p. 658)

**Securities and Exchange Commission
(SEC)**   (p. 665)
Tennessee Valley Authority (TVA)
(p. 675)

WHERE TO LEARN MORE

 Center for New Deal Studies, Roosevelt University, Chicago, Illinois. The center contains political memorabilia, photographs, papers, and taped interviews dealing with Franklin D. Roosevelt and the New Deal; it also sponsors an annual lecture series about the Roosevelt legacy.

Herbert Hoover National Historic Site, West Branch, Iowa. This 186-acre site contains the birthplace cottage and grave of Herbert Hoover as well as his presidential library and museum, which contains a reconstruction of Hoover's White House office. **www.nps.gov/heho**; **www.hoover.archives.gov**

Labor Museum and Learning Center of Michigan, Flint, Michigan. Exhibits trace the history of the labor movement, including the dramatic "Sit-Down Strike" of 1936–1937.

Franklin D. Roosevelt Home and Presidential Library, Hyde Park, New York. The Roosevelt home, furnished with family heirlooms, and the spacious grounds, where FDR is buried, personalize the president and provide insights into his career. The nearby library has displays and exhibitions about Roosevelt's presidency, and the Eleanor Roosevelt Wing is dedicated to the career of ER. **www.fdrlibrary.marist.edu**

Eleanor Roosevelt National Historic Site, Hyde Park, New York. These two cottages, where Eleanor Roosevelt worked and, after 1945, lived, contain her furniture and memorabilia. Visitors can also watch a film biography of ER and tour the grounds of this retreat where she entertained personal friends and world leaders. **www.nps.gov/elro**

Civilian Conservation Corps Interpretive Center, Whidbey Island, Washington. This stone and wood structure, built as a CCC project, now houses exhibits and artifacts illustrating the history of the CCC.

Bethune Museum and Archives National Historic Site, Washington, D.C. This four-story townhouse was the home of Mary McLeod Bethune, a friend of Eleanor Roosevelt and the director of the New Deal's Division of Negro Affairs, and the headquarters of the National Council of Negro Women, which Bethune founded in 1935. Exhibits feature the contributions of black activist women and activities of the civil rights movement.

For additional study resources for this chapter, go to:
www.prenhall.com/goldfield/chapter25

The event was not spectacular, no fuses burned, no lights flashed. But to us it meant that release of atomic energy on a large scale would be only a matter of time.

On June 6, 1944, American, British, and Canadian forces seized a beachhead in German-occupied France. The landings began the final phase of World War II in Europe, which ended eleven months later with German surrender to the U.S., Britain, the Soviet Union, and their allies.

WAR GARDENS
FOR
VICTORY

GROW VITAMINS AT
YOUR KITCHEN DOOR
Enter VICTORY GARDEN CONTEST
REGISTER 404 S. 8th ST.   MAY 1–15

26

WORLD WAR II
1939–1945

WHY WERE most Americans
reluctant to get involved in World War II?

WHY DID the United States
need a strategy for a two-front war?

HOW WAS the United States
transformed socially
and economically by the war?

HOW DID the Allies win the war?

December, 1942

The scene [under the stadium] at The University of Chicago would have been confusing to an outsider, if he could have eluded the security guards and gained admittance. He would have seen only what appeared to be a crude pile of black bricks and wooden timbers. . . .

Finally, the day came when we were ready to run the experiment. We gathered on a balcony about 10 feet above the floor of the large room in which the structure had been erected. Beneath us was a young scientist, George Weil, whose duty it was to handle the last control rod that was holding the reaction in check. . . .

Finally, it was time to remove the control rods. Slowly, Weil started to withdraw the main control rod. On the balcony, we watched the indicators which measured the neutron count and told us how rapidly the disintegration of the uranium atoms under their neutron bombardment was proceeding.

At 11:35 A.M., the counters were clicking rapidly. Then, with a loud clap, the automatic control rods slammed home. The safety point had been set too low.

It seemed a good time to eat lunch. During lunch everyone was thinking about the experiment but nobody talked much about it.

At 2:30, Weil pulled out the control rod in a series of measured adjustments. Shortly after, the intensity shown by the indicators began to rise at a slow but ever-increasing rate. At this moment we knew that the self-sustaining [nuclear] reaction was under way.

The event was not spectacular, no fuses burned, no lights flashed. But to us it meant that release of atomic energy on a large scale would be only a matter of time.

Enrico Fermi, in *The First Reactor* (Washington: U.S. Department of Energy, 1982), accessed at **http://hep.uchicago.edu/cp**; Laura Fermi, *Atoms in the Family* (Chicago: University of Chicago Press, 1954); Laura Fermi, "The Fermis' Path to Los Alamos," in Lawrence Badash, Joseph O. Hirschfelder, and Herbert P. Broida, eds. *Reminiscences of Los Alamos, 1943–45* (Boston and Dordrecht: D. Reidel Publishing Co.).

IMAGE KEY

for pages 684–685

a. A cloth patch with a yellow star of David that all Jews had to wear under the Nazi regime.

b. Victory Garden Poster.

c. All POWs had to carry identification (ID) tags with them at all times. These two came from the Oflag XVIIA and Stelag VI/A camps in Germany.

d. American soldiers landing on the coast of France at Normandy on 6 June 1944 (D-Day).

e. Unusually addressed letters to Winston Churchill.

f. The explosion of an atomic bomb.

g. Mpa of central Europe.

h. Pearl Harbor Attack, 7 December 1941. Motor launch rescues a man from the water, alongside the burning USS West Virginia (BB-48); USS Tennessee (BB-43) is inboard.

i. Wartime marriages, Chicago, IL, August 20, 1943.

j. D-Day invasion.

ENRICO FERMI was describing the first controlled nuclear chain reaction— the critical experiment from which atomic weapons and atomic power would soon develop. Fermi himself had emigrated to the United States to escape the growing repression of Fascist Italy in 1938. When the United States entered World War II, Fermi, other atomic scientists, and their families moved to Los Alamos, a science city that the government built in northern New Mexico, where isolation was supposed to ensure secrecy and help the United States win the race with Nazi Germany to develop atomic weapons.

The Fermis were not the only family to give Los Alamos a multinational flavor. Niels Bohr had fled Denmark to escape Nazi invasion. Edward Teller was a Hungarian who had studied in Germany. Hans Bethe had left Germany, and Stanislaus Ulam was the only member of his family to survive the Nazi conquest of Poland. Absent were scientists from the Soviet Union, which was bearing the worst of the fighting against Germany but was excluded from the secret of the atomic bomb.

The men and women racing to perfect the atomic bomb knew that victory was far from certain. Allied defeat in a few key battles could have resulted in stand-off or Axis victory. Not until 1944 did American economic power allow the United States and its allies to feel confident of victory. A new weapon might end the war more quickly or make the difference between victory and defeat.

The war's domestic impacts were as profound as its international consequences. The war highlighted racial inequalities, gave women new opportunities, and fostered growth in the South and West. By devastating the nation's commercial rivals, compelling workers to retrain and factories to modernize, World War II left the United States dominant in the world economy. It also increased the size and scope of the federal government and built an alliance among the armed forces, big business, and science that helped shape postwar America.

THE DILEMMAS OF NEUTRALITY

Opinion polls in the fall of 1941 showed that most voters still hoped to avoid war. President Roosevelt's challenge was to lead the United States toward rearmament and support for Great Britain and China without alarming a reluctant public.

THE ROOTS OF WAR

The roots of World War II can be found in the aftereffects of World War I. The peace settlement after that war created a set of small new nations in Eastern Europe that were vulnerable to aggression from large neighbors such as Germany and the Soviet Union. Italy and Japan thought that the Treaty of Versailles failed to recognize their stature as world powers. Many Germans were convinced that Germany had been betrayed rather than defeated in 1918. In the 1930s, economic crisis and political instability fueled the rise of right-wing dictatorships that offered territorial expansion by military conquest as the way to redress old rivalries, dominate trade, and gain access to raw materials.

Japanese nationalists believed that Japan should expel the French, British, Dutch, and Americans from Asia and create a **Greater East Asia Co-Prosperity Sphere**, in which Japan gave the orders and other Asian peoples complied. When war with China erupted in 1937, Japan took many of the key cities and killed tens of thousands of civilians in the "rape of Nanking" but failed to dislodge the government of Jiang Jieshi (Chi-ang Kai-shek) and settled into a war of attrition.

Italian aggression led to the conquest of Ethiopia in 1935 and intervention in Spain in support of General Francisco Franco's right-wing rebels.

In Germany, Adolf Hitler made himself the German Führer, or absolute leader in 1934. Proclaiming the start of a thousand-year Reich (empire), he combined the historic German interest in eastward expansion with a long tradition of German racial superiority. The Slavs of eastern Europe were to be pushed aside to provide more territory for a growing German population, and the Jews, who were prominent in German business and professional life, were to be driven from the country. In 1935, the "Nuremberg laws" denied civil rights to Jews and the campaign against them intensified. The Nazi government began expropriating Jewish property and excluded Jews from most employment.

Germany and Italy formed the Rome-Berlin Axis in October 1936 and the Tripartite Pact with Japan in 1940, leading to the term **Axis Powers** to describe the aggressor nations. Political dissidents in all three nations were suppressed in the but Hitler's Germany was the most repressive. The Nazi concentration camp was a device for political terrorism. Hitler decreed that opponents should disappear

WHY WERE most Americans reluctant to get involved in World War II?

Greater East Asia Co-Prosperity Sphere Japanese nationalists believed that Japan should expel the French, British, Dutch, and Americans from Asia and create this sphere in which Japan would give the orders and other Asian peoples would comply.

Axis Powers The opponents of the United States and its allies in World War II.

The raspy-voiced Adolf Hitler had a remarkable ability to stir the German people. He and his inner circle made skillful use of propaganda, exploiting German resentment over the country's defeat in World War I and, with carefully staged mass rallies, such as this event in 1938, inspiring an emotional conviction of national greatness.

Bildarchiv Preubisher Kulterbesitz, Berlin

26–2
Charles Lindbergh, Radio Address (1941)

Blitzkrieg   German war tactic in World War II ("lightning war") involving the concentration of air and armored firepower to punch and exploit holes in opposing defensive lines.

into "night and fog." The concentration camps would evolve into forced labor camps and then into hellish extermination camps.

HITLER'S WAR IN EUROPE

Germany invaded Poland on September 1, 1939. Western journalists covering the three-week conquest of Poland coined the term **Blitzkrieg**, or "lightning war," to describe the German tactics. Armored divisions with tanks and motorized infantry punched quick holes in defensive positions and raced forward 30 or 40 miles per day.

Striking from a central position against scattered enemies, Hitler chose the targets and timing of each new front: east to smash Poland in September 1939; north to capture Denmark and Norway in April and May 1940; west to defeat the Netherlands, Belgium, and France in May and June 1940; south into the Balkans, enlisting Hungary, Romania, and Bulgaria as allies and conquering Yugoslavia and Greece in April and May 1941. He also launched the Battle of Britain in the second half of 1940, sending bombers in an unsuccessful effort to pound Britain into submission.

In June 1941, having failed to knock Britain out of the war, Hitler invaded the Soviet Union (officially the Union of Soviet Socialist Republics, or USSR). The attack caught the Red Army off guard, because the Nazis and Soviets had signed a nonagression pact in 1939, and the USSR had helped dismember Poland. Nevertheless, from June until December 1941, more than 3 million Germans, Italians, and Romanians pushed eastward, encircling and capturing entire Soviet armies. Before desperate Soviet counterattacks and a bitter winter stopped the German tanks, the Axis powers had reached the outskirts of Moscow, and they expected to finish the job in the spring.

TRYING TO KEEP OUT

"We Must Keep Out!" shouted the September 7, 1939, *Chicago Daily News*. Most Americans wanted to avoid foreign quarrels. People who opposed intervention in the European conflict considered themselves realists. Drawing their lessons from 1914–1918, they assumed that the same situation applied in 1939. For more than two years after the invasion of Poland, strong isolationist sentiment shaped public debate and limited President Roosevelt's ability to help Britain and its allies.

Much of the emotional appeal of neutrality came from disillusionment with the American crusade in World War I, which had failed to make the world safe for democracy. Many opponents of intervention wanted the United States to protect its traditional spheres of interest in Latin America and the Pacific. Like George Washington, whose Farewell Address they quoted, they wanted to avoid becoming entangled in the perpetual quarrels of the European nations.

Noninterventionists spanned the political spectrum from left-leaning labor unions to such ultraconservative business tycoons as Henry Ford, from radicals who wanted the European nations to fight themselves into exhaustion to admirers of Hitler and Mussolini. Any move to intervene in Europe had to take these different views into account, meaning that Roosevelt had to move the United States slowly and carefully to the side of Britain.

MAP 26–1

Axis Europe, 1941, on the Eve of Hitler's Invasion of the Soviet Union   After almost two years of war, the Axis powers controlled most of Europe, from the Atlantic Ocean to the Soviet border through annexation, military conquest, and alliances. Failure to force Britain to make peace caused Hitler to look eastward in 1941 to attempt the conquest of the Soviet Union.

HOW WAS Germany's central location in Europe both a strength and a weakness?

CHRONOLOGY

1931	Japan invades Manchuria.
1933	Hitler takes power in Germany.
1935	Congress passes first of three Neutrality acts. Italy invades Ethiopia.
1936	Germany and Italy form the Rome Berlin Axis. Civil war erupts in Spain.
1937	Japan invades China.
1938	Germany absorbs Austria. Munich agreement between Germany, Britain and France.
1939	Germany and the Soviet Union sign a nonagression pact. Germany absorbs Czechoslovakia. Germany invades Poland; Great Britain and France declare war on Germany.
1940	Germany conquers Denmark, Norway, Belgium, the Netherlands, and France. Japan, Germany, and Italy sign the Tripartite Pact. Germany bombs England in the Battle of Britain. The United States begins to draft men into the armed forces. Franklin Roosevelt wins an unprecedented third term.
1941	The United States begins a lend-lease program to make military equipment available to Great Britain and later the USSR. The Fair Employment Practices Committee is established. Germany invades the Soviet Union. Roosevelt and Churchill issue the Atlantic Charter. Japan attacks U.S. military bases in Hawaii.
1942	American forces in the Philippines surrender to Japan. President Roosevelt authorizes the removal and internment of Japanese Americans living in four western states. Naval battles in the Coral Sea and off the island of Midway blunt Japanese expansion. U.S. forces land in North Africa. Soviet forces encircle a German army at Stalingrad. The first sustained and controlled nuclear chain reaction takes place at the University of Chicago.
1943	U.S. and British forces invade Italy, which makes terms with the Allies. Race conflict erupts in riots in Detroit, New York, and Los Angeles. The landing of Marines on Tarawa initiates the island-hopping strategy. U.S. war production peaks. Roosevelt, Churchill, and Stalin confer at Tehran.
1944	Allied forces land in Normandy. The U.S. Navy destroys Japanese sea power in the battles of the Philippine Sea and Leyte Gulf. The Battle of the Bulge is the last tactical setback for the Allies.
1945	Roosevelt, Stalin, and Churchill meet at Yalta to plan the postwar world. The United States takes the Pacific islands of Iwo Jima and Okinawa. Franklin Roosevelt dies; Harry S Truman becomes president. Germany surrenders to the United States, Great Britain, and the USSR. The United Nations is organized at an international meeting in San Francisco. Potsdam Conference. Japan surrenders after the detonation of atomic bombs over Hiroshima and Nagasaki.

EDGING TOWARD INTERVENTION

Because 85 percent of the American people agreed that the nation should fight only if directly attacked, Roosevelt had to chip away at neutrality. In October 1939, lawmakers reluctantly passed the Neutrality Act of 1939 allowing arms sales to belligerent nations on a "cash and carry" basis. In control of the Atlantic, France and Britain were the only expected customers.

26–2
Franklin Delano Roosevelt, Annual Message to Congress (1941)

Isolationism helps explain why the United States accepted only a few thousand Jewish refugees. Anti-Semitism at the State Department also contributed to tight enforcement of immigration quotas, and polls showed that the public supported restricted immigration.

The collapse of France in June 1940 scared Americans into rearming. In the summer of 1940, Congress voted to expand the army to 2 million men, build 19,000 new war planes, and add 150 ships to the navy. September brought the nation's first peacetime draft.

In the same month, the United States concluded a "destroyer deal" with Britain, trading fifty old destroyers for the use of bases on British territories in the Caribbean, Bermuda, and Newfoundland.

In the presidential election of 1940, the big campaign issue was therefore whether FDR's unprecedented try for a third term represented arrogance or legitimate concern for continuity in a time of peril. The voters gave Roosevelt 55 percent of their votes to defeat his Republican opponent, Wendell Wilkie. The president pledged that no Americans would fight in a foreign war, but if the United States were attacked, he said privately, the war would no longer be "foreign."

THE BRINK OF WAR

In January 1941, Roosevelt proposed the "lend-lease" program, which allowed Britain to "borrow" military equipment for the duration of the war. Roosevelt compared the program to lending a garden hose to a neighbor whose house had caught fire. Senator Robert Taft of Ohio countered that it was more like lending chewing gum—you wouldn't want it back after it was used. Behind the scheme was Britain's inability to go on paying for American goods.

The Committee to Defend America by Aiding the Allies argued the administration's position. In opposition, the America First Committee claimed that lend-lease would allow the president to declare anything a "defense article." Congress finally passed the measure in March 1941, giving Great Britain an unlimited line of credit.

FDR soon began an undeclared war in the North Atlantic. Roosevelt instructed the navy to report sightings of German submarines to the British. In September, the U.S. destroyer *Greer* clashed with a German submarine. Roosevelt proclaimed a "shoot on sight" policy for German subs and told the navy to escort British convoys to within 400 miles of Britain. In reply, German submarines torpedoed and damaged the destroyer *Kearny* on October 17 and sank the destroyer *Reuben James* with the loss of more than 100 lives on October 30. The United States was approaching outright naval war with Germany.

The **Atlantic Charter** of August 1941 provided a political umbrella for American involvement. Meeting off Newfoundland, Roosevelt and British prime minister Winston Churchill agreed that the first priority was to defeat Germany; Japan was secondary. Echoing Woodrow Wilson, Roosevelt also insisted on a commitment to oppose territorial change by conquest, to support self-government and promote freedom of the seas.

Some historians think that Roosevelt's goal in the North Atlantic was to support Britain short of war. Others believe that he accepted the inevitability of war but hesitated to outpace public opinion. In this second interpretation, FDR wanted to eliminate Hitler without going to war if possible, with war if necessary. "I am waiting to be pushed into the situation," he told his secretary of the treasury.

That final shove came in the Pacific rather than the Atlantic. In 1940, as part of its rearmament program, the United States decided to build a "two-ocean navy." This decision antagonized Japan. Japan had achieved roughly 70 percent of U.S. naval strength by late 1941. However, America's buildup promised to reduce that ratio to only 30 percent by 1944. Furthermore, the United States was gradually restricting Japan's vital imports of steel, iron ore, and aluminum. In July 1941, after Japan occupied French Indochina, Roosevelt froze Japanese assets in the United States, blocked petroleum shipments, and began to build up U.S. forces in the Philippines. Both militarily and economically, it looked in Tokyo as if 1942 was Japan's last chance for victory.

Japanese war planners never seriously considered an actual invasion of the United States or expected a decisive victory. They hoped that attacks on American Pacific bases would shock the United States into letting Japan have its way in Asia or at least win time to create impenetrable defenses in the central Pacific.

QUICK REVIEW

Undeclared War
- March 1941: Lend-lease program approved by Congress.
- FDR ordered navy to offer support to Britain.
- August 1941: Atlantic Charter lays out British and American war aims.

Atlantic Charter   Statement of common principles and war aims developed by President Franklin Roosevelt and British Prime Minister Winston Churchill at a meeting in August 1941.

DECEMBER 7, 1941

It now seems that Roosevelt wanted to restrain the Japanese with bluff and intimidation so that the United States could focus on Germany. FDR also recognized the possibility of a two-front war—at least a 20 percent chance, he told military advisers in January 1941. Because the United States cracked Japanese codes, it knew by November that Japanese military action was imminent but expected the blow to come in Southeast Asia.

Instead, the Japanese fleet sailed a 4,000-mile loop through the empty North Pacific, avoiding merchant shipping and American patrols. Before dawn on December 7, six Japanese aircraft carriers launched 351 planes in two unopposed bombing strikes on Pearl Harbor, Hawaii.

Americans counted their losses: eight battleships, eleven other warships, and nearly all military aircraft damaged or destroyed; and 2,403 people killed. Fortunately, dockyards, drydocks, and oil storage tanks remained intact because the Japanese admiral had refused to order a third attack. And the American carriers, at sea on patrol, were unharmed.

Speaking to Congress the following day, Roosevelt proclaimed December 7, 1941, "a date which will live in infamy." He asked for—and got—a declaration of war against the Japanese. Hitler and Mussolini declared war on the United States on December 11.

HOLDING THE LINE

WHY DID the United States

need a strategy for a two-front war?

In 1940, Admiral Isoroku Yamamoto, the chief of Japan's Combined Fleet, weighed the chances of victory against the United States and Great Britain: "If I am told to fight regardless of the consequences, I shall run wild for the first six months or a year, but I have utterly no confidence for the second or third year." The admiral was right. As it turned out, Japan's conquests reached their limit after six months, but in early 1942, it was far from clear that that would be so. In Europe, Allied fortunes went from bad to worse in the first half of 1942. Decisive turning points did not come until November 1942, a year after the United States had entered the war.

STOPPING GERMANY

In December 1941, the United States plunged into a truly global war that was being fought on six distinct fronts. In North Africa, the British battled Italian and German armies that were trying to seize the Suez Canal. On the **Eastern Front**, Soviet armies held defensive positions. In the North Atlantic, merchant ships dodged German submarines. In China, Japan controlled the most productive provinces but could not crush Chinese resistance, which was supported by supplies airlifted from British India. In Southeast Asia, Japanese troops attacked the Philippines, the Dutch East Indies, New Guinea, Malaya, and Burma. In the central Pacific, the Japanese fleet faced the U.S. Navy.

Despite the popular desire for revenge against Japan, the United States decided to defeat Germany first, as Germany was far stronger than Japan. Defeat of Japan would not assure the defeat of Germany, especially if it crushed the Soviet Union or starved Britain into submission. In contrast, a strategy that helped the Soviets and British survive and then destroyed German military power would doom Japan.

The strategy recognized that the Eastern Front held the key to Allied hopes. In 1941, Germany had seized control of 45 percent of the Soviet population, 47 percent of its grain production, and more than 60 percent of its coal, steel, and

Eastern Front The area of military operations in World War II located east of Germany in eastern Europe and the Soviet Union.

aluminum industries. Hitler next sought to destroy Soviet capacity to wage war. He targeted southern Russia, an area rich in grain and oil. The German thrust was also designed to eliminate the British from the Middle East.

The German offensive opened with stunning success. Every day's advance, however, stretched supply lines. Tanks ran out of fuel and spare parts. The horses that pulled German supply wagons died for lack of food.

Disaster came at Stalingrad (present-day Volgograd), an industrial center on the western bank of the Volga River. In September and October, 1942, German, Italian, and Romanian soldiers fought their way house by house into the city.

The Red Army delivered a counterstroke on November 18 that cut off 330,000 Axis soldiers. Airlifts kept the Germans fighting for two more months, but they surrendered in February 1943.

THE SURVIVAL OF BRITAIN

In 1940 and 1941, from bases in France, German submarines (greatly improved since World War I) intercepted shipments of oil from Nigeria, beef from Argentina, minerals from Brazil, and weapons from the United States. Through the end of 1941, German "tonnage warfare" sank merchant vessels faster than they could be replaced.

The **Battle of the Atlantic** forced the British to reduce their reliance on the Atlantic supply lines. Between 1939 and 1944, planning and rationing cut Britain's need for imports in half. The British also organized protected convoys. Grouping the merchant ships into convoys with armed escorts "hardened" the targets and made them more difficult to find in the wide ocean. Roosevelt's destroyer deal of 1940 and U.S. naval escorts in the western Atlantic in 1941 thus contributed directly to Britain's survival.

Nevertheless, German submarines (known as U-boats from *Unterseeboot*) operated as far as the Caribbean and the Carolinas in 1942. In June, U-boats sank 144 ships; drowned sailors washed up on Carolina beaches. Only the extension of the convoy system to American waters forced the subs back toward Britain. Meanwhile, Allied aircraft began to track submarines with radar, spot them with searchlights as they maneuvered on the surface, and attack them with depth charges. New sonar systems allowed escort ships to measure submarines' speed and depth. By the spring of 1943, American shipyards were also launching ships faster than the Germans could sink them.

British ground fighting in 1942 centered in North Africa. By October 1942, Field Marshal Erwin Rommel's German and Italian forces were within striking distance of the Suez Canal. At **El Alamein** between October 23 and November 5, 1942, however, General Bernard Montgomery, with twice Rommel's manpower and tanks, forced the enemy to retreat and lifted the danger to the Middle East.

RETREAT AND STABILIZATION IN THE PACIFIC

Striking the Philippines a few hours after Hawaii, the Japanese gained another tactical surprise (see Map 26–2), destroying most American air power on the ground and isolating U.S. forces. Between February 27 and March 1, Japan brushed aside a combined American, British, Dutch, and Australian fleet in the Battle of the Java Sea, and a numerically inferior Japanese force had seized Singapore.

In the spring Japan pushed the British out of Burma and overwhelmed Filipino and U.S. defensive positions on the Bataan peninsula. On May 6, the last American bastion, the island fortress of Corregidor in Manila Bay, surrendered.

The first check to Japanese expansion came on May 7–8, 1942, in the Battle of the Coral Sea, where U.S. aircraft carriers halted a Japanese advance toward

Battle of the Atlantic The long struggle between German submarines and the British and U.S. navies in the North Atlantic from 1940 to 1943.

MAP 26–2

World War II in the Pacific, from Pearl Harbor to Midway   The first six months after the Japanese attack on Pearl Harbor brought a string of Japanese victories and conquests in the Pacific, the islands southeast of Asia, and the British colonies of Malaya and Burma. Japan's advance was halted by a standoff battle in the Coral Sea, a decisive U.S. naval victory at Midway, and the length and vulnerability of Japanese supply lines to its most distant conquests.

HOW WAS Japan able to mount a series of victories in the Pacific after their attack on Pearl Harbor?

Australia. In June, the Japanese struck at the island of Midway, 1,500 miles northwest of Honolulu. Their goal was to destroy American carrier forces. Having cracked Japanese radio codes, U.S. forces were aware of the plan for a diversionary invasion of the Aleutian Islands. On the morning of June 4, U.S. Navy dive bombers found the Japanese fleet and sank or crippled three aircraft carriers in five minutes; another Japanese carrier sank later in the day. The Battle of Midway ended Japanese efforts to expand in the Pacific.

MOBILIZING FOR VICTORY

News of the Japanese attack on Pearl Harbor shattered a bright Sunday afternoon. Elliott Johnson was eating in a Chinese restaurant in Portland, Oregon, when the proprietor burst from the kitchen with a portable radio; the line was two blocks long by the time he got to the marine recruiting office.

War changed the lives of most Americans. Millions of men and women served in the armed forces and millions more worked in defense factories. The number of civilian employees of the federal government quadrupled to 3.8 million. Meanwhile, youngsters saved tin foil, collected scrap metal, and followed the freedom-fighting stories of Wonder Woman in the comics. The war effort gave Americans a common purpose that softened the divisions of region, class, and national origin while calling attention to continuing inequalities of race.

ORGANIZING THE ECONOMY

The need to fight a global war brought a huge expansion of the federal government. The War Manpower Commission allocated workers among vital industries and the military. The War Production Board invested $17 billion for new factories and managed $181 billion in war-supply contracts, favoring big corporations with experience in large-scale production.

The Office of Price Administration (OPA) fought inflation with price controls and rationing that began with tires, sugar, and coffee and eventually included meat, butter, gasoline, and shoes. Consumers used ration cards and ration stamps to obtain scarce products. By slowing price increases, the OPA helped to convince Americans to buy the war bonds that financed half the war spending. Americans also felt the bite of the first payroll deductions for income taxes as the government secured revenues and soaked up some of the high wages that would have pushed inflation. By 1945 the federal budget was $98 billion, eleven times as large as in 1939, and the national debt had increased more than sixfold.

Industry had reluctantly begun to convert from consumer goods to defense production in 1940 and 1941. Although corporations hated to give up the market for toasters and automobiles just as Americans had more money, the last passenger car for the duration of the war rolled off the assembly line in February 1942. Existing factories retooled to make war equipment, and huge new facilities turned out thousands of planes and ships. The United States applied mass production technology to aircraft production at a time when Japan was still building warplanes one at a time and Germany in small batches.

Most defense contracts went to such established industrial states as Michigan, New York, and Ohio, but in the South and West, the war marked the takeoff of what Americans would later call the Sunbelt. Albuquerque, New Mexico more than doubled in population during the 1940s. War-boom cities, such as San Diego (up 92 percent in population in the 1940s) and Mobile (up 68 percent), bustled with activity and hummed with tension. Factories operated three shifts, movies ran around the clock, and workers filled the streets after midnight.

The hordes of war workers found housing scarce. Workers in Seattle's shipyards and Boeing plants scrounged for living space in offices, tents, chicken coops, and rooming houses where "hot beds" rented in shifts. The situation was similar in small towns.

The results of war production were staggering—an estimated 40 percent of the world's military production was coming from the United States by 1944. The productivity of U.S. workers increased 30 percent between 1939 and 1945. Surging

HOW WAS the United States transformed socially and economically by the war?

A wartime shopper uses ration coupons to purchase groceries.
©Bettmann/Corbis

QUICK REVIEW

Government and the Economy
- War brought a huge expansion of the federal government.
- Office of Price Administration (OPA): oversaw price controls and rationing.
- Under government pressure, industry shifted to defense production.

farm income pulled agriculture out of its long slump. The rich certainly got richer, but overall per capita income doubled, and the poorest quarter of Americans made up some of the ground lost during the Great Depression.

THE ENLISTMENT OF SCIENCE

"There wasn't a physicist able to breathe who wasn't doing war work," remembered Professor Philip Morrison. At the center of the scientific enterprise was Vannevar Bush, former dean at the Massachusetts Institute of Technology. As head of the newly established Office of Scientific Research and Development, Bush guided spending on research and development that dwarfed previous scientific work and set the pattern of massive federal support for science that continued after the war.

The biggest scientific effort was the drive to produce an atomic bomb. As early as 1939, Albert Einstein had written FDR about the possibility of such a weapon and the danger of falling behind the Germans. In late 1941, Roosevelt established what became known as the **Manhattan Project**. On December 2, 1942, scientists manipulated graphite rods inserted in a stack of uranium ingots until they were certain they could trigger and control a self-sustaining nuclear reaction.

The Manhattan Project moved from theory to practice in 1943. Physicist J. Robert Oppenheimer directed the young scientists at Los Alamos in designing a nuclear fission bomb. Engineers in other new science cities tried two approaches to producing the fissionable material. Richland, Washington, burgeoned into a sprawling metropolis that supported the creation of plutonium at the Hanford Engineer Works. Oak Ridge, Tennessee, near Knoxville, was built around gaseous diffusion plants.

Plutonium from Hanford fueled the first bomb tested at the Trinity site, 100 miles from Alamogordo, New Mexico, on July 16, 1945. The explosion astonished even the physicists; Oppenheimer quoted from Hindu scriptures as he tried to comprehend the results: "Now I am become death, destroyer of worlds."

MEN AND WOMEN IN THE MILITARY

By 1945, 8.3 million men and women were on active duty in the army and army air forces and 3.4 million in the navy and Marine Corps, totals exceeded only by the Soviet Union. In total, some 350,000 women and more than 16 million men served in the armed forces; 292,000 died in battle, 100,000 survived prisoner-of-war camps, and 671,000 returned wounded.

Twenty-five thousand American Indians served in the armed forces, most in racially integrated units. Because the Navajo were one of the few tribes that had not been studied by German anthropologists, their language was unknown to the Axis armies. More than three hundred Navajo were "code-talkers" who served in radio combat-communication teams in the Pacific theater.

Approximately 1 million African Americans also served in the armed forces during World War II. As it had since the Civil War, the army organized black soldiers in segregated units and often assigned them to the more menial jobs, excluding them from combat until manpower shortages forced changes in policy.

Black soldiers encountered discrimination on and off the base. Towns adjacent to army posts were sometimes off limits to blacks. At some Southern bases, German prisoners of war watched movies from the first rows along with white GIs while African-American soldiers watched from the back. Military courts were quick to judge and harsh to punish when black GIs were the accused. Despite the obstacles, all-black units, such as the 761st Tank Battalion and the 99th Pursuit Squadron, earned distinguished records. More broadly, the war experience helped

---

(W) **WHERE TO LEARN MORE**

★ Los Alamos County Historical Museum and Bradbury Science Museum, Los Alamos, New Mexico

25–5
A. Philip Randolph, "Why Should We March?" (1942)

Manhattan Project The effort, using the code name Manhattan Engineer District, to develop an atomic bomb under the management of the U.S. Army Corps of Engineers during World War II.

to invigorate postwar efforts to achieve equal rights, as had also been true after World War I.

The nation had a different—but also mixed—reaction to the women who joined the armed forces. The armed services tried not to change established gender roles. Many of the women in uniform hammered at typewriters, worked switchboards, inventoried supplies. Others, however, worked close to combat zones as photographers, code analysts, and nurses.

The greatest departure from expected roles was the work of the 1,074 members of the Women's Airforce Service Pilots (WASPS), a civilian auxiliary of the U.S. Army Air Forces. From 1942 to 1944, they ferried military aircraft across the United States, towed targets for antiaircraft practices, and tested new planes. Nevertheless, WASPS were not allowed to carry male passengers, and the unit was dissolved when the supply of male pilots caught up with the demand.

THE HOME FRONT

The war inexorably penetrated everyday life. Residents in war-production cities had to cope with throngs of new workers, many of whom were unattached males—young men waiting for their draft call and older men without their families. Military and defense officials worried about sexually transmitted diseases and pressured cities to shut down their vice districts.

Americans put their lives on fast forward. Couples who had postponed marriage because of the depression could afford to marry as the economy picked up. Altogether, the war years brought 1.2 million "extra" marriages, compared to the rate for the period 1920–1939.

The war's impact on families was gradual. The draft started with single men, then called up married men without children, and finally tapped fathers in 1943. Left at home were millions of "service wives," whose compensation from the government was $50 per month.

The war had mixed effects on children. "Latchkey children" of working mothers often had to fend for themselves, but middle-class kids whose mothers stayed home could treat the war as an interminable scout project, with salvage drives and campaigns to sell war bonds. Between the end of the school day and suppertime, children listened as Captain Midnight, Jack Armstrong, and Hop Harrigan ("America's ace of the airways") fought the Nazis and Japanese on the radio.

The federal government tried to keep civilians of all ages committed to the war. It encouraged scrap drives and backyard victory gardens. The government also managed news about the fighting. Censors screened soldiers' letters. Early in the war, they blocked publication of most photographs of war casualties, although magazines such as *Life* were full of haunting images. Censors also authorized photographs of enemy atrocities to motivate the public.

Government officials had a harder time controlling Hollywood. The Office of War Information wanted propaganda in feature films, but not so heavy-handed that it drove viewers from theaters. War films revealed the nation's racial attitudes, often drawing distinctions between "good" and "bad" Germans but uniformly portraying Japanese as subhuman and repulsive. The most successful films dramatized the courage of the Allies. *Mrs. Miniver* (1942) showed the British transcending class differences in their battle with the Nazis. *So Proudly We Hail* (1943) celebrated the heroism of navy nurses in the Pacific theater.

Dorie Miller, a mess attendant on the battleship West Virginia, received the Navy Cross for "extraordinary courage" during the Japanese attack on Pearl Harbor. Miller helped to pull the Arizona's captain to safety and then manned a machine gun and shot down several Japanese planes. The War Department used Miller on recruiting posters such as this one but neglected to point out that it continued to restrict black recruits mostly to kitchen and other service jobs.

Courtesy of the Library of Congress

Members of Women Fliers of America
examine an aircraft engine. The organization had been asked by the U.S. Army to identify women with more than 200 flying hours who might ferry planes, freeing military aviators for other duties.

Getty Image Inc./Hutton Archive Photos

QUICK REVIEW

Rosie the Riveter

◆ Demand for labor drew women into the workplace.

◆ Companies opened positions for women in nontraditional jobs.

◆ Government funded daycare programs to help women enter the workforce.

NEW WORKERS

As draft calls took men off the assembly line, women changed the composition of the industrial work force. The war gave them new job opportunities that were embodied in the image of Rosie the Riveter. The acute shortage of welders and other skilled workers, opened thousands of journeyman positions to women, work that was far more lucrative than waiting tables or sewing in a clothing factory. Aircraft companies, which compounded labor shortages by stubborn "whites only" hiring, developed new power tools and production techniques to accommodate the smaller average size of women workers, increasing efficiency for everyone along the production line.

By July 1944, fully 19 million women held paid jobs, up 6 million in four years. Women's share of government jobs increased from 19 to 38 percent and their share of manufacturing jobs from 22 to 33 percent. Some women worked out of patriotism. Many others, however, needed to support their families and already had years of experience in the work force. As one of the workers recalled of herself and a friend, "We both had to work, we both had children, so we became welders, and if I might say so, damn good ones."

Americans did not know how to respond to the growing numbers of working women. Many worried that their employment would undermine families. The federal government assisted female entry into the labor force by funding day-care programs that served 600,000 children. Employment recruitment posters showed strong, handsome women with rolled-up sleeves and wrenches in hand, but men and women assumed that women would want to return to the home after victory; they were to work when the nation needed them and quit when the need was past.

Mexican-American workers made special contributions to the war effort. As defense factories and the military absorbed workers, western farms and railroads faced an acute shortage of workers. In 1942, the United States and Mexico negotiated the *bracero* program, under which the Mexican government recruited workers to come to the United States on six-to-twelve month contracts. Although *bracero* workers still faced discrimination, the U.S. government tried to improve working conditions because it wanted to keep public opinion in Latin America favorable to the Allied cause.

The war was a powerful force for the assimilation of Native Americans. Forty thousand moved to off-reservation jobs; they were a key labor force for military supply depots throughout the West. The average cash income of Indian households tripled during the war. Many stayed in cities at its end. The experience of the war accelerated the fight for full civil rights. Congress had made Indians citizens in 1924, but several states continued to deny them the vote. Activists organized the National Congress of American Indians in 1944 and began the efforts that led the U.S. Supreme Court in 1948 to require states to grant voting rights.

African Americans, too, found economic advancement through war jobs. Early in the mobilization, labor leader A. Philip Randolph of the Brotherhood of Sleeping Car Porters worked with Walter White of the NAACP to plan a "Negro March on Washington" to protest racial discrimination by the federal government.

To head off a major embarrassment, Roosevelt issued Executive Order 8802 in June 1941, barring racial discrimination in defense contracts and creating the **Fair Employment Practices Committee (FEPC)**; the order coined a phrase that reverberated powerfully through the coming decades: "No discrimination on grounds of race, color, creed, or national origin."

But white resistance to black coworkers remained strong. In Mobile, New Orleans, and Jacksonville, agreements between shipyards and segregated unions blocked skilled black workers from high-wage jobs. Attempts to overturn discrimination could lead to violence. When the Alabama Dry Dock Company integrated its work force in May 1943, white workers rioted. Nevertheless, African-American membership in labor unions doubled, and wartime prosperity raised the average black income from 41 percent of the white average in 1939 to 61 percent by 1950.

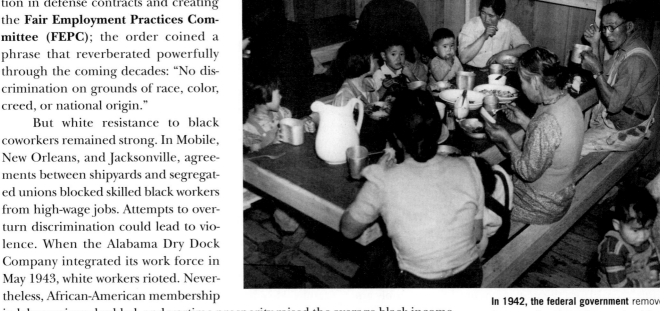

In 1942, the federal government removed Japanese Americans from parts of four western states and interned them in isolated camps scattered through the West.

AP/Wide World Photos

CLASHING CULTURES

As men and women migrated in search of work, they also crossed or collided with traditional boundaries of race and region. African-American migration out of the South accelerated in the early 1940s. Many of the migrants headed for well-established black neighborhoods in Northern cities. Others created new African-American neighborhoods in Western cities. White Southerners and black Northerners with different ideas of racial etiquette found themselves side by side in West Coast shipyards. In the Midwest, black migrants from the South and white migrants from Appalachia competed for the same high-wage jobs and scarce apartments.

Tensions between black and white residents exploded in at least fifty cities in 1943 alone. In June 1943, an argument over the use of Detroit's Belle Isle Park set off three days of violence: Twenty-five black people and nine white people died in the most serious racial riot of the war.

Tensions were simultaneously rising between Mexican Americans and Anglos. As the Mexican community in Los Angeles swelled to an estimated 400,000, newspapers published anti-Mexican articles. On June 6, 1943, off-duty sailors and soldiers attacked Latinos on downtown streets and invaded Mexican-American neighborhoods. The attacks dragged on for a week of sporadic violence against black people and Filipinos as well as Latinos.

INTERNMENT OF JAPANESE AMERICANS

On February 19, 1942, President Roosevelt issued Executive Order 9066, which authorized the secretary of war to define restricted areas and remove civilian residents who were threats to national security. The primary targets were 112,000 Japanese Americans in California and parts of Washington, Oregon, and Arizona. Japanese immigrants and their children in the Western states had experienced forty years of hostility and racial prejudice. The outbreak of war triggered anti-Japanese hysteria

Fair Employment Practices Committee (FEPC) Federal agency established in 1941 to curb racial discrimination in war production jobs and government employment.

·AMERICAN VIEWS·

THE INTERNMENT OF JAPANESE AMERICANS IN 1942

I*n the spring of 1942, the U.S. army ordered that Japanese Americans in four western states be relocated to internment camps distant from the Pacific Coast. Monica Itoe Stone describes the experience of her Seattle family as they were transferred to temporary quarters before they were moved again to Idaho.*

HOW DO the expectations of *issei* (immigrants who had been born in Japan) differ from those of *nisei* (their American-born children, including the author of this memoir)? Why did the U.S. army wait five months after Pearl Harbor before beginning the internment? Does the management of the assembly and internment suggest anything about stereotypes of Japanese Americans?

General DeWitt kept reminding us that E day, evacuation day, was drawing near. "E day will be announced in the very near future. If you have not wound up your affairs by now, it will soon be too late."

. . . On the twenty-first of April, a Tuesday, the general gave us the shattering news. "All the Seattle Japanese will be moved to Puyallup by May 1. Everyone must be registered Saturday and Sunday between 8 A.M. and 5 P.M.

Up to that moment, we had hoped against hope that something or someone would intervene for us. Now there

was no time for moaning. A thousand and one details must be attended to in this one week of grace. Those seven days sputtered out like matches struck in the wind, as we rushed wildly about. Mother distributed sheets, pillowcases and blankets, which we stuffed into seabags. Into the two suitcases, we packed heavy winter overcoats, plenty of sweaters, woolen slacks and skirts, flannel pajamas and scarves. Personal toilet articles, one tin plate, tin cup and silverware completed our luggage. The one seabag and two suitcases apiece were going to be the backbone of our future home, and we planned it carefully.

Henry went to the Control Station to register the family. He came home with twenty tags, all numbered "10710," tags to be attached to each piece of baggage, and one to hang from our coat lapels. From then on, we were known as Family #10710.

[On the day set for relocation] we climbed into the truck. . . . As we coasted down Beacon Hill bridge for the last time, we fell silent, and stared out at the delicately flushed, morning sky of Puget Sound. We drove through bustling Chinatown, and in a few minutes arrived on the corner of Eighth and Lane. This area was ordinarily lonely and deserted but now it was gradually filling up with silent, labeled Japanese. . . .

Finally at ten o'clock, a vanguard of Greyhound busses purred in and parked themselves neatly along

and gave officials an excuse to take action against both enemy aliens (immigrants who retained Japanese citizenship) and their American-born children. As the U.S. general commanding on the West Coast put it, "A Jap is a Jap. It makes no difference whether he is an American citizen or not."

At the end of April 1942, Japanese in the coastal states were given a week to organize their affairs and report to assembly centers, where they were housed before being moved to ten internment camps in isolated locations in the western interior (see American Views, "Internment of Japanese Americans: Life in Camp Harmony"). Here, they were housed in tar-paper barracks, hemmed in by barbed wire fences, and guarded by military police. The victims reacted to the hardship and stress in different ways. Several thousand second-generation Japanese Americans renounced their citizenship in disgust. But many others demonstrated their loyalty by cooperating with the authorities, finding sponsors who would help them move to the curb. The crowd stirred and murmured. The bus doors opened and from each, a soldier with rifle in hand stepped out and stood stiffly at attention by the door. The murmuring died. It was the first time I had seen a rifle at such close range and I felt uncomfortable. . . .

Newspaper photographers with flash-bulb cameras pushed busily through the crowd. One of them rushed up to our bus, and asked a young couple and their little boy to step out and stand by the door for a shot. They were reluctant, but the photographers were persistent and at length they got out of the bus and posed, grinning widely to cover their embarrassment. We saw the picture in the newspaper shortly after and the caption underneath it read, "japs good-natured about evacuation."

Our bus quickly filled to capacity. . . . The door closed with a low hiss. We were now the Wartime Civil Control Administration's babies.

About noon we crept into a small town. . . . and we noticed at the left of us an entire block filled with neat rows of low shacks, resembling chicken houses. Someone commented on it with awe, "Just look at those chicken houses. They sure go in for poultry in a big way here." Slowly the bus made a left turn, drove through a wire-fenced gate, and to our dismay, we were inside the over-sized chicken farm. . . .

The apartments resembled elongated, low stables about two blocks long. Our home was one room, about 18 by 20 feet, the size of a living room. There was one small window in the wall opposite the one door. It was bare except for a small, tinny wood-burning stove crouching in the center. The flooring consisted of two by fours laid directly on the earth, and dandelions were already pushing their way up through the cracks. . . .

I stared at our little window, unable to sleep. I was glad Mother had put up a makeshift curtain on the window for I noticed a powerful beam of light sweeping across it every few seconds. The lights came from high towers placed around the camp where guards with Tommy guns kept a twenty-four hour vigil. I remembered the wire fence encircling us, and a knot of anger tightened in my breast. What was I doing behind a fence like a criminal? If there were accusations to be made, why hadn't I been given a fair trial? Maybe I wasn't considered an American anymore. My citizenship wasn't real, after all. Then what was I? I was certainly not a citizen of Japan as my parents were. On second thought, even Father and Mother. . . . had little tie with their mother country. In their twenty-five years in America, they had worked and paid their taxes to their adopted government as any other citizen.

Of one thing I was sure. The wire fence was real. I no longer had the right to walk out of it. It was because I had Japanese ancestors. It was also because some people had little faith in the ideas and ideals of democracy.

Source: Monica Itoi Sone, *Nisei Daughter* (Seattle: University of Washington Press, 1979).

other parts of the country, or joining the 442nd Regimental Combat Team, the most decorated American unit in the European war.

Although the U.S. Supreme Court sanctioned the removals in *Korematsu v. United States* (1944), the nation officially recognized its liability with the Japanese Claims Act of 1948, for many internees had lost property that they had been powerless to protect. The nation acknowledged its broader moral responsibility in 1988, when Congress approved redress payments to each of the sixty thousand surviving evacuees.

By contrast Hawaii treated Japanese Americans much differently. Hawaii's long history as a multiethnic society made residents and officials disinclined to look for a racial scapegoat. Less than 1 percent of Hawaii's Japanese American population of 160,000 was interned. The treatment of mainland Japanese Americans also contrasted with the situation of German Americans and Italian Americans. Only tiny fractions of their total populations were interned or had their movements restricted.

THE END OF THE NEW DEAL

Roosevelt's New Deal had run out of steam in 1938. The war had reinvigorated his political fortunes by focusing national energies on foreign policy, over which presidents have the greatest power. After the 1942 election left Congress in the hands of Republicans, conservative lawmakers ignored proposals that war emergency housing be used to improve the nation's permanent housing stock, abolished the National Resources Planning Board, curtailed rural electrification, and crippled the Farm Security Administration.

For the presidential election of 1944, the Republicans nominated Governor Thomas Dewey of New York, who had made his reputation as a crime-fighting district attorney. The Democrats renominated Roosevelt for a fourth term. Missouri Senator Harry S Truman, a tough investigator of American military preparedness, replaced liberal New Dealer Henry Wallace as Roosevelt's running mate, which appeased Southern Democrats.

Roosevelt supporters argued that the nation could not afford to switch leaders in the middle of a war, but Dewey's vigor and relative youth (he was twenty years younger than FDR) pointed up the president's failing health and energy. Voters gave Roosevelt 432 electoral votes to 99, but the narrowing gap in the popular vote—54 percent for Roosevelt and 46 percent for Dewey—made the Republicans eager for 1948.

WAR AND PEACE

HOW DID the Allies win the war?

In January 1943, the U.S. War Department completed the world's largest office building, the Pentagon. The building housed 23,000 workers along 17.5 miles of corridors. The gray walls of the Pentagon symbolized an American government that was outgrowing its prewar roots.

GATHERING ALLIED STRENGTH

American and British landings in North Africa in 1942 and Italy in 1943 satisfied the British desire to secure Western influence in the Mediterranean and Middle East, but they pleased neither American policymakers nor the Soviet Union. U.S. leaders wanted to justify massive mobilization with a war-winning campaign and to strike across Europe to occupy the heart of Germany. Stalin needed a full-scale invasion of western Europe to divert German forces from the Eastern Front.

In fact, 1943 was the year in which the Allies gained the edge in quality of equipment, capacity for war production, and military sophistication. The United States poured men and equipment into Britain. The Soviets recruited, rearmed, and upgraded new armies, despite enormous losses in 1941 and 1942 and rebuilt munitions factories beyond German reach. As Soviet soldiers reconquered western Russia and the Ukraine, they marched in 13 million pairs of American-made boots and traveled in 51,000 jeeps and 375,000 Dodge trucks made available from U.S. lend-lease assistance.

Meeting in Casablanca in January 1943, Roosevelt and Churchill demanded the "unconditional surrender" of Italy, Germany, and Japan; the phrase meant no deals that kept the enemy governments or leaders in power. Ten months later, the Allied leaders huddled again. Roosevelt and Churchill met with China's Jiang in Cairo and then flew on to meet Stalin in Tehran. At Tehran, the United States and Britain promised to invade France within six months. "We leave here," said the three leaders, "friends in fact, in spirit, in purpose."

QUICK REVIEW

Allied Collaboration
- 1943: U.S. and Soviet leaders prepare for a full-scale invasion of Europe.
- Soviet advances made possible by U.S. equipment and materials.
- November 1943: Allied leaders leave Tehran with a time-table for invasion of Europe.

The superficial harmony barely survived the end of the war. Stalin and his generals scoffed at the small scale of early U.S. efforts. Roosevelt's ideal of self-determination for all peoples seemed naive to Churchill, who wanted the major powers to carve out realistic spheres of influence in Europe. It was irrelevant to Stalin, who wanted control of eastern Europe.

TURNING THE TIDE IN EUROPE

The United States had entered the ground war in Europe with Operation TORCH. Against little opposition, British and American troops under General Dwight Eisenhower landed in French Morocco and Algeria on November 8, 1942 (see Map 26–3). The puppet French government in place there, which had collaborated with the Nazis, now switched sides, giving the Allies footholds in North Africa.

German tanks in February 1943 counterattacked U.S. divisions at Kasserine Pass in the Atlas Mountains of Tunisia. Learning quickly from this tactical defeat, Allied troops forced the Axis in Africa to surrender in May. Eisenhower had already demonstrated his ability to handle the politics of military leadership, skills he perfected commanding a multinational army for the next two and a half years.

The central Mediterranean remained the focus of U.S. and British action for the next year. The British proposed strikes in southern Europe. U.S. Army Chief of Staff George Marshall and President Roosevelt agreed first to the action in North Africa and then to invade Italy in 1943. In July and August, Allied forces led by Montgomery and Patton overran Sicily. As Sicily fell, the Italian king and army forced Mussolini from power and began to negotiate peace with Britain and America (but not the Soviet Union). In September, the Allies announced an armistice with Italy, and Eisenhower's troops landed south of Naples. Germany responded by occupying the rest of Italy.

As American military planners had feared, the Italian campaign soaked up Allied resources. Week after week, the experience of GIs on the line was the same: "You wake up in the mud and your cigarettes are all wet and you have an ache in your joints and a rattle in your chest." Despite months of bitter fighting, the Allies controlled only two-thirds of Italy when the war there ended on May 1, 1945.

On the Eastern Front, the climactic battle of the German-Soviet war had erupted on July 5, 1943. The Germans sent three thousand tanks against the Kursk Salient. Soviet generals had prepared a defense in depth with three thousand tanks of their own. When the attack finally stalled, it marked the last great German offensive until December 1944.

OPERATION OVERLORD

On **D-Day**–June 6, 1944–the western Allies landed on the coast of Normandy in northwestern France. Six divisions went ashore from hundreds of attack transports carrying four thousand landing craft. Dozens of warships and twelve thousand aircraft provided support. One British and two American airborne divisions dropped behind German positions. When the sun set on the "longest day," the Allies had a tenuous toehold in France.

The Allies secured their beachheads and landed 500,000 men and 100,000 vehicles within two weeks. However, the German defenders kept the Allies along a narrow coastal strip. **Operation OVERLORD**, the code name for the entire campaign across northern France, met renewed success in late July and August. U.S. troops finally broke through German lines around the town of St.-Lô and then drew a ring around the Germans that slowly closed on the town of Falaise. The Germans lost a quarter of a million troops. The German command chose to regroup closer to Germany rather than fight in France. The Allies liberated Paris on August 25.

> **QUICK REVIEW**
>
> **The Beginning of the End**
> - Allies gained footholds in North Africa.
> - Allies took control of much of Italy.
> - German's last offensive in Russia turned back.

D-Day June 6, 1944, the day of the first paratroop drops and amphibious landings on the coast of Normandy, France, in the first stage of Operation OVERLORD during World War II.

Operation OVERLORD U.S. and British invasion of France in June 1944 during World War II.

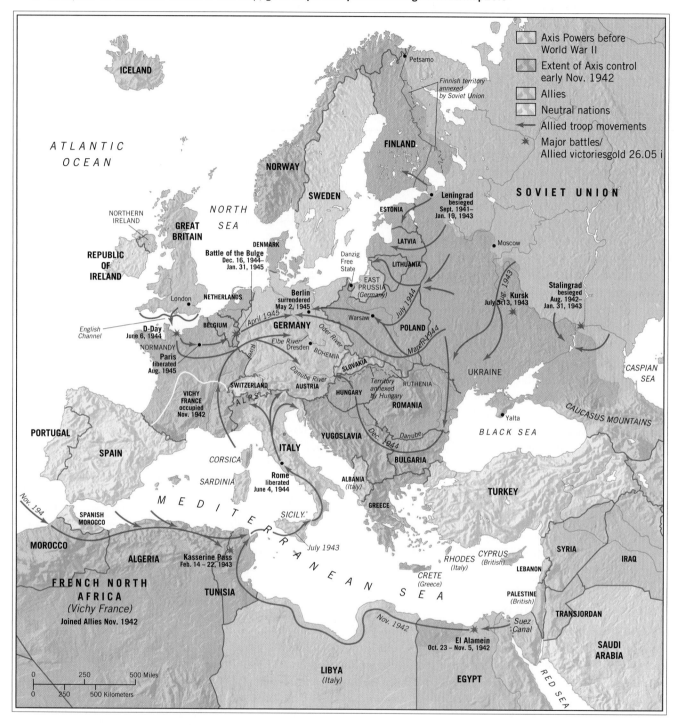

MAP 26-3

World War II in Europe, 1942–1945 Nazi Germany had to defend its conquests on three fronts. Around the Mediterranean, American and British forces pushed the Germans out of Africa and Southern Italy, while guerrillas in Yugoslavia pinned down many German troops. On the eastern front, Soviet armies advanced hundreds of miles to drive the German army out of the Soviet Union and eastern Europe. In June 1944, U.S. and British landings opened the western front in northern France for a decisive strike at the heart of Germany.

WHAT WERE the turning points in the war in Europe?

On the Eastern Front, by the end of 1944, the Red Army had entered the Balkans and reached central Poland. With the end in sight, the Soviets had suffered nearly 20 million casualties and sustained the heaviest burden in turning back Nazi tyranny.

VICTORY AND TRAGEDY IN EUROPE

In the last months of 1944, massive air strikes finally reduced German war production. The new American P-51 escort fighter helped B-17 bombers overfly Germany in relative safety after mid-1944. Thousand-bomber raids on railroads and oil facilities began to cripple the German economy. The raids also forced Germany to devote 2.5 million workers to air defense and damage repair. Politics rather than military need governed the final great action of the European air war. British and U.S. bombers in February 1945 staged a terror raid on the nonindustrial city of Dresden, packed with refugees, filled with great art, and undefended by the Germans; a firestorm fueled by incendiary bombs and rubble from blasted buildings killed tens of thousands of civilians without military justification.

Hitler struck a last blow on December 16, 1944. Stripping the Eastern Front of armored units, he launched twenty-five divisions against thinly held U.S. positions in the Ardennes Forest of Belgium. He hoped to split U.S. and British forces by capturing the Belgian port of Antwerp. Taking advantage of snow and fog that grounded Allied aircraft, the Germans drove a 50-mile bulge into U.S. lines. But the German thrust literally ran out of gas beyond the town of Bastogne. The Battle of the Bulge never seriously threatened the outcome of the war.

The Nazi empire collapsed in the spring of 1945. American and British divisions crossed the Rhine in March and enveloped Germany's industrial core. The Soviets drove through eastern Germany toward Berlin. On April 25, American and Red Army troops met on the Elbe River. Hitler committed suicide on April 30 in his concrete bunker deep under devastated Berlin, which surrendered to the Soviets on May 2. The Nazi state formally capitulated on May 8.

The defeat of Germany revealed appalling evidence of the evil at the heart of the Nazi ideology of racial superiority. The "final solution" to what Hitler thought of as the "Jewish problem" went far beyond slave labor. The elite SS, Hitler's personal army within the Nazi party, in 1942 set out to eliminate all of Europe's Jews. The evidence of genocide—systematic racial murder—is irrefutable. At Auschwitz and Treblinka, the SS organized the extermination of up to 6 million Jews and 1 million Poles, Gypsies, and others who failed to fit the Nazi vision of the German master race. Prisoners arrived by forced marches and cattle trains. Those who were not worked or starved to death were herded into gas chambers and then incinerated in huge crematoriums. Soviet troops could scarcely believe what they saw as they overran the death camps and freed the few survivors of what we now call the **Holocaust**.

THE PACIFIC WAR

Washington divided responsibilities in the Pacific theater. General Douglas MacArthur operated in the islands that stretched between Australia and the Philippines. Admiral Chester Nimitz commanded in the central Pacific. The Allies planned to isolate Japan from its southern conquests. The British moved from India to retake Burma. The Americans advanced along the islands of the southern Pacific to retake the Philippines. With Japan's army still tied down in China, the Americans then planned to bomb Japan into submission.

The Pacific campaigns of 1944, often called **island hopping**, were the American naval version of the *Blitzkrieg*. Planes from American carriers controlled the air, allowing the navy and land forces to isolate and capture the most strategically located Japanese-held islands while bypassing the rest (see Map 26–4).

Holocaust The systematic murder of millions of European Jews and others deemed undesirable by Nazi Germany.

Island hopping The Pacific campaigns of 1944 that were the American naval versions of the *Blitzkrieg*.

MAP 26–4

World War II in the Pacific, 1942–1945   The Allied strategy against Japan was to cut off Japan's southern conquests by retaking the central Pacific islands, the Philippines, and Burma and then to strike at the Japanese home islands. Submarine warfare and massive air attacks from November 1944 to August 1945 crippled Japan's capacity to wage war. The detonation of atomic bombs over Hiroshima and Nagasaki then forced surrender on August 15, 1945.

WHY WAS Japan unable to maintain its conquests in the Pacific?

Racial hatred animated both sides in the Pacific war and fueled a "war without mercy." Americans often characterized Japanese soldiers as vermin. In turn, the Japanese viewed Americans as racial mongrels and called them demons.

MacArthur used a version of the bypass strategy in the Solomon Islands and New Guinea, leapfrogging over Japanese strong points. The invasion of the Philippines repeated the approach by landing on Leyte, in the middle of the island chain. The Philippine campaign also destroyed the offensive capacity of the Japanese fleet. In the Battle of Leyte Gulf, the U.S. military sank four Japanese battleships, four carriers, and ten cruisers. The Japanese home islands were left with no defensive screen against an expected invasion.

During 1943 and 1944, submarines choked off food, oil, and raw materials bound for Japan and island bases. By 1945, imports to Japan were one-eighth of the 1940 level. Heavy bombing of Japan began in early 1944. A fire-bomb raid on Tokyo on the night of March 9, 1945, killed 124,000 people and left 1 million homeless. Overall, conventional bombing destroyed 42 percent of Japan's industrial capacity. By the time the United States captured the islands of Iwo Jima and Okinawa in fierce fighting (April–June 1945) and neared the Japanese home islands, Japan's position was hopeless.

SEARCHING FOR PEACE

At the beginning of 1945, the Allies sensed victory. Conferring from February 4 to 11 in the Ukrainian town of Yalta, Roosevelt, Stalin, and Churchill debated plans for the postwar world. The most important American goal was to enlist the USSR in finishing off the Pacific war. Americans hoped that a Soviet attack on Manchuria would tie down enough Japanese troops to reduce U.S. casualties in invading Japan. Stalin repeated his intent to declare war on Japan within three months of victory in Europe, in return for a free hand in Manchuria.

The most that Roosevelt could coax from Stalin were vague pledges to allow participation of non-Communists in coalition governments in eastern Europe. Stalin also agreed to join a new international organization, the United Nations.

Conservative critics later charged that the Western powers "gave away" eastern Europe at the **Yalta Conference**. In fact, the Soviet Union gained little that it did not already control. In East Asia as well, the Soviets could seize the territories that the agreements granted them.

On April 12, two months after Yalta, Roosevelt died of a cerebral hemorrhage. Harry Truman, the new president, was a shrewd politician, but his experience was limited; Roosevelt had not even told him about the Manhattan Project. Deeply distrustful of the Soviets, Truman first ventured into personal international diplomacy in July 1945 at a British-Soviet-American conference at Potsdam, near Berlin. Most of the sessions debated the future of Germany. The leaders endorsed the expulsion of ethnic Germans from eastern Europe and moved the borders of Poland 100 miles west into historically German territory. Truman also made it clear that the United States expected to dominate the occupation of Japan. Its goal was to democratize the Japanese political system and reintroduce Japan into the international community—a policy that succeeded. The **Potsdam Declaration** on July 26 summarized U.S. policy and gave Japan an opening for surrender. However, the declaration failed to guarantee that Emperor Hirohito would not be tried as a war criminal. The Japanese response was so cautious that Americans read it as rejection.

Secretary of State James Byrnes now urged Truman to use the new atomic bomb, tested just weeks earlier. Japan's ferocious defense of Okinawa and suicide missions by thousands of *kamikaze* pilots had confirmed American fears that the Japanese would fight to the death. In contrast, the bomb offered a quick end to the conflict, and it might intimidate Stalin (see the overview table "The Decision to Use the Atomic Bomb"). In short, a decision not to use atomic weapons was never a serious alternative.

In early August, the United States dropped two of three available nuclear bombs on Japan. On August 6 at Hiroshima the first bomb killed at least eighty thousand people and poisoned thousands more with radiation. A second bomb three days later at Nagasaki took another forty thousand lives. Japan ceased hostilities on August 14 and surrendered formally on September 2. The world has wondered ever since if the United States might have defeated Japan without resorting to atomic bombs, but recent research shows that the bombs were the shock that allowed the Emperor and peace advocates to overcome military leaders who wanted to fight to the death.

Yalta Conference   Meeting of U.S. President Franklin Roosevelt, British Prime Minister Winston Churchill, and Soviet Premier Joseph Stalin held in February 1945 to plan the final stages of World War II and postwar arrangements.

Potsdam Declaration   Statement issued by the United States during a meeting of U.S. President Harry Truman, British Prime Minister Winston Churchill, and Soviet Premier Joseph Stalin in which the United States declared its intention to democratize the Japanese political system and reintroduce Japan into the international community.

OVERVIEW

THE DECISION TO USE THE ATOMIC BOMB

Americans have long argued whether the use of atomic bombs on the Japanese cities of Hiroshima and Nagasaki was necessary to end the war. Several factors probably influenced President Truman's decision to use the new weapon:

Military necessity	Truman later argued that the use of atomic bombs was necessary to avoid an invasion of Japan that would have cost hundreds of thousand of lives. Military planners expected Japanese soldiers to put up the same kind of suicidal resistance in defense of the home islands as they had to American landings at the Philippines, Iwo Jima, and Okinawa. More recently, historians have argued that the Japanese military was near collapse and that an invasion would have met far less resistance than feared.
Atomic diplomacy	Some historians believe that Truman used atomic weapons to overawe the Soviet Union and induce it to move cautiously in expanding its influence in Europe and East Asia. Truman and his advisers were certainly aware of how the bomb might influence the Soviet leadership.
Domestic politics	President Roosevelt and his chief military advisers had spent billions on the secret atomic bomb project without the knowledge of Congress or the American public. The managers of the Manhattan Project may have believed that only proof of its military value would quiet critics and justify the huge cost.
Momentum of war	The United States and Britain had already adopted wholesale destruction of German and Japanese cities as a military tactic. Use of the atomic bomb looked like a variation on fire bombing, not the start of a new era of potential mass destruction. In this context, some historians argue, President Truman's choice was natural and expected.

CONCLUSION

World War II made and unmade families. It gave millions of women new responsibilities and then sent them back to the kitchen. It put money in pockets that had been emptied by the Great Depression and turned struggling business owners into tycoons.

Most of the 16 million men and women in uniform served in support jobs that keep the war machine going.

World War II adventure movies in which Americans always win leave the impression that triumph was necessary and inevitable. In fact, victory was the hard-fought result of public leadership and military effort. Under other leadership, for example, the United States might have stood aside until it was too late to reverse the Axis conquest of Europe and East Asia.

The war unified the nation in new ways while confirming old divisions. People of all backgrounds shared a common cause.

But nothing broke the barriers that separated white and black Americans. Unequal treatment in a war for democracy outraged black soldiers, who returned to fight for civil rights. The uprooting of Japanese Americans was another reminder of racial prejudice.

FROM THEN TO NOW
Nuclear Weapons

On May 11 and 12, 1998, India tested five nuclear weapons in its western desert. Two weeks later, Pakistan tested its own nuclear weapons. Neighbors and bitter rivals, the two became the sixth and seventh nations to publicly acknowledge the possession of a nuclear arsenal. Now the tensions between them, which had long fueled border clashes and twice erupted in open warfare, had become another factor in the delicate calculus of nuclear terror that has confronted the world since Hiroshima.

It has been a central goal of U.S. policy since 1945 to limit the number of nations with atomic weapons and place ceilings on the size of nuclear arsenals. The goal became more urgent when the Soviet Union deployed its own nuclear weapons after 1949, establishing the "balance of terror" that haunted the decades-long Cold War between the United States and the Soviet Union.

Two key steps toward reducing the nuclear threat were the Limited Test Ban Treaty of 1963—in which the United States, Britain, and the USSR outlawed atmospheric nuclear testing (see Chapter 30)—and the Nuclear Non-Proliferation Treaty, which was signed in 1968 and extended indefinitely in 1995. One hundred eighty nations have agreed not to acquire nuclear weapons, and five acknowledged nuclear powers—the United States, Russia, Britain, France, China—have agreed to eventual elimination of their own weapons.

The power of international opinion was clearly not enough to convince India and Pakistan to abandon their nuclear weapons programs, but it has been effective elsewhere in the 1990s. One justification of the Gulf War in 1991 (see Chapter 33) was to prevent Iraq from developing nuclear arms, and Iraqi interference with United Nations inspection teams triggered bombing raids on Iraq in 1998–1999. The United States also orchestrated pressure on North Korea to cancel a suspected nuclear weapons program and admit international inspectors.

The 1990s saw advances in efforts to reduce the huge nuclear stockpiles of the United States and Russia. The first Strategic Arms Limitation Treaty (START I) went into effect in 1994. The United States and Russia agreed to retain a maximum of eight thousand warheads each. START II, if implemented, would cut the total to three thousand each. The breakup of the Soviet Union and the economic challenges that have confronted its constituent republics have created fears about the diversion of warheads into the hands of terrorists. The United States, however, has helped to pay for dismantling of Russian warheads and their removal from Ukraine and Kazakhstan, both formerly parts of the Soviet Union.

The frightening proliferation and growth of nuclear arsenals that began with the Manhattan Project and continued into the 1980s may be ending. The 1990s, on the contrary, may have marked the beginning of a new era of shrinking nuclear capacity, despite reversals like those in India and Pakistan. South Africa, for example, announced in 1993 that it had destroyed six warheads that it had manufactured secretly. And planned reductions in the largest nuclear arsenals offer hope that the trend will continue in the new century.

The lessons of World War II influenced the thinking of presidents from Eisenhower in the 1950s to George H. W. Bush in the 1990s. Even though the United States ended 1945 with the world's mightiest navy, biggest air force, and only atomic bomb, the instability that had followed World War I made Western leaders nervous about the shape of world politics.

One result in the postwar era was conflict between the United States and the Soviet Union, which became the Cold War. At home, international tensions fed pressure for social and political conformity. Fifteen years of economic depression and sacrifice made the postwar generation sensitive to perceived threats to steady jobs and stable families. For the next generation, the unresolved business of World War II would haunt American life.

SUMMARY

The Dilemmas of Neutrality In the late 1930s President Roosevelt's challenge was to lead the United States toward rearmament and support nations at war with fascism without alarming the public. The roots of World War II were to be found in the after-effects of the first World War; as Germany marched from victory to victory from 1939 to 1941, strong isolationist sentiment in America shaped public debate and limited attempts to help Britain and the Soviet Union. The swift collapse of France and radio broadcasts describing the bombing of London frightened Americans; the Lend Lease Act, an undeclared naval war, and the Atlantic Charter drew America closer to war. The final shove came in the Pacific with the attack on Pearl Harbor; in December 1941 America entered World War II.

Holding the Line Despite the popular desire to defeat Japan, the Allies planned to defeat Germany first. The Soviet Union held the Eastern front in the Battle of Stalingrad; the British fought back in the Battle of the Atlantic; German troops in North Africa were forced to retreat; Japanese expansion came to a halt at the Battle of the Coral Sea and Battle of Midway. By the end of 1942 the tide was turning; in mid-1943 the Allies could begin to plan for victory with confidence.

Mobilizing for Victory The need to fight a global war brought a huge expansion of the federal government; price controls and rationing fought inflation, industry mobilized for defense production, and the Manhattan Project ushered in the age of atomic energy. The war penetrated every facet of everyday life; women and minorities changed the composition of the industrial work force. The government saw Japanese Americans as threats and interned them in camps throughout the West. The war required more than a thirtyfold expansion of the U.S. military; soldiers came from across the American spectrum. While women in the military received unequal treatment, African Americans fared worse.

War and Peace Plans for ending the war were drawn up at Casablanca and Tehran; Italy was invaded in 1943; Operation Overlord opened the second front in Europe; in 1944 Germany was being battered from the east and west. As Allied troops entered Germany and discovered the death camps, the extent of what is now called the Holocaust became clear. Through the island hopping campaign in the Pacific, American forces neared the Japanese home islands; in 1945 President Truman chose to use the atomic bomb to end the war with Japan. The postwar world would prove to be a challenge; the Yalta and Potsdam conferences divided Europe into spheres that would last for almost fifty years.

REVIEW QUESTIONS

1. What arguments did Americans make against involvement in the war in Europe? Why did President Roosevelt and many others believe it necessary to block German and Japanese expansion?

2. How did mobilization for World War II alter life in the United States? What opportunities did it open for women?

3. What factors were decisive in the defeat of Germany?

4. What was the U.S. strategy against Japan, and how well did it work?

5. What role did advanced science and technology play in World War II? How did the scientific lead of the United States affect the war's outcome?

KEY TERMS

Allies (p. 687)
Atlantic Charter (p. 691)
Axis Powers (p. 687)
Battle of the Atlantic (p. 693)
Blitzkrieg (p. 688)
D-Day (p. 703)

Eastern Front (p. 692)
Fair Employment Practices Committee (p. 699)
Greater East Asia Co-Prosperity Sphere (p. 687)
Holocaust (p. 705)

Island hopping (p. 705)
Manhattan Project (p. 696)
Operation OVERLORD (p. 703)
Postdam Declaration (p. 707)
Yalta Conference (p. 707)

WHERE TO LEARN MORE

Air Force Museum, Dayton, Ohio. Visitors can walk among World War II fighter planes and bombers, including the B-29 that dropped the atomic bomb in Nagasaki, and learn about the role of aviation in the war.

Museum of the Pacific War, Fredericksburg, Texas. In the birthplace of Admiral Chester Nimitz, this new museum is an excellent introduction to the war with Japan.

Los Alamos County Historical Museum and Bradbury Science Museum, Los Alamos, New Mexico. The museum traces the origins of atomic energy for military and civilian uses. Nearby is the Los Alamos County Historical Museum, which gives the feel of everyday life in the atomic town.

United States Holocaust Memorial Museum, Washington, D.C. The Holocaust Museum gives visitors a deeply moving depiction of the deadly impacts of Nazi ideas in the 1930s and 1940s. The museum's website at **http://www.ushmm.urlorg** also explores virtually every facet of the Holocaust experience for Jews during World War II.

 For additional study resources for this chapter, go to:
www.prenhall.com/goldfield/chapter26

To my mind we are in a situation no less dangerous than the one we were facing in 1939, and it is of the greatest importance that we realize it. We must realize . . . that democracy will not be saved by ideals alone.

As international tensions rose with the onset of the Cold War, Americans wondered how to prepare for a possible nuclear war. Many families stocked extra food and water and bought a battery-powered radio, but few actually installed backyard bomb shelters like the one being tested by this family in a Long Island suburb not far from Levittown.

I CERTIFY THAT the foregoing is a true copy of the North Atlantic Treaty signed at Washington on April 4, 1949 in the English and French languages, the signed original of which is deposited in the archives of the Government of the United States of America.

IN TESTIMONY WHEREOF, I, DEAN ACHESON, Secretary of State of the United States of America, have hereunto caused the seal of the Department of State to be affixed and my name subscribed by the Authentication Officer of the said Department, at the city of Washington, in the District of Columbia, this fourth day of April, 1949.

27

THE COLD WAR AT HOME AND ABROAD
1946–1952

WHAT WAS the catalyst
for the economic boom
that began in 1947?

HOW WAS Harry Truman
able to win the 1948
presidential election?

WHAT WERE
the origins of the Cold War?

WHAT WERE the major
conflicts of the early Cold War?

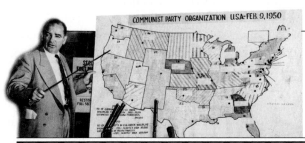

WHAT WAS the
"Second Red Scare?"

My eyes popped when I got to town hall because the lobby and the stairs leading up to the hearing room were loaded with people. The upstairs hallway was jammed and the room was packed. People were standing along the walls. I remember there were a lot of children, toddlers—some in strollers—and many babies held by men and women. We expected there would be quite a turnout. But the extent of the crowd was a big surprise to me. . . . The meeting itself was rather brief. There were some speeches. No screaming and yelling the way people do at town meetings today. Everyone was quiet, anxious. I remember one guy in uniform, holding a baby, made a strong statement. These people were desperate. It was very moving. When the decision was announced, the crowd broke into applause.

Levittown was the last place on the planet I thought I would be living. But, as it turned out, we moved there because the house was such a good buy. . . . We loved living there. I came into work and told [Newsday managing editor Alan] Hathway that I would be eating crow for the rest of my days.

Bernadette Rischer Wheeler, in "Levittown at Fifty: Long Island Voices," at **www.lihistory.com/specsec/hsvoices.htm**; originally published in *Newsday*.

IMAGE KEY
for pages 712–713

a. A man sitting reading "The Mirror" with a headline about Lucille Ball.
b. "The Cold War At Home and Abroad 1946-52." Photo of mother and father with 3 children in fallout shelter.
c. The North Atlantic Treaty Organization treaty with signature and seal.
d. "Fallout shelter" sign.
e. Unidentified model displaying a kitchen interior, photo 1950's.
f. American President Harry Truman shakes hands with supporters from a train car during a rally in the 1948 presidential campaign.
g. Civilians atop bombed out ruins of buildings watching American C-54 cargo plane fly overhead during Allied airlift to bring food & supplies to beseiged citizens of Soviet controlled Berlin.
h. Soldiers in Korea.
i. Senator Joseph McCarthy points to Oregon on an organizational map implying Communist Party organization in the United States.

Cold War The political and economic confrontation between the Soviet Union and the United States that dominated world affairs from 1946 to 1989.

BERNADETTE WHEELER was a reporter for *Newsday*, the daily newspaper for the Long Island suburbs of New York, who covered the birth of the new community of Levittown. She remembers the meeting on May 21, 1947, when the local governing board approved construction of the new subdivision. The size of the crowd indicates the severity of the housing shortage after World War II and the intense desire of Americans to return to normal life. After years of hardship, they defined American ideals in terms of economic opportunity and the chance to enjoy national prosperity. Over the next decade, the residents who moved to Levittown and thousands of other new subdivisions would start the baby boom and rekindle the economy with their purchases of automobiles, appliances, and televisions.

This yearning to enjoy the promise of American life after years of sacrifice helps to explain why Americans reacted so fiercely to new challenges and threats. They watched as congressional conservatives and President Truman fought over the fate of New Deal programs. More worrisome was the confrontation with the Soviet Union that was soon being called the **Cold War**. Triggered by the Soviet Union's imposition of communist regimes throughout eastern Europe, the Cold War grew into a global contest between the United States and the Soviets. By the time real war broke out in Korea in 1950, many Americans were venting their frustration by blaming international setbacks on internal subversion and by trying to root out suspected "reds."

The Cold War would shape the United States and the world for a generation. Massive rearmament allowed U.S. presidents to act as international policemen in the name of democratic values—a vast change from earlier American goals to remain disengaged from the problems of other nations. Defense spending also reshaped American industry and helped stimulate twenty-five years of economic growth. The Cold War narrowed the range of political discussion, making many of the left-wing ideas of the 1930s taboo by the 1950s. It also made racial segregation and limits on immigration into international embarrassments and thus nudged the nation to live up to its ideals.

LAUNCHING THE GREAT BOOM

When World War II ended, Americans feared that demobilization would bring a rerun of the inflation and unemployment that had followed World War I. In the first eighteen months of peace, rising prices, labor-management strife, and shortages of everything from meat to automobiles confirmed their anxiety. In 1947 and 1948, however, an economic expansion began that lasted for a quarter century. That prosperity would finance a military buildup and an activist foreign policy.

■ ■ ■ ■ ■ ■ ■ ■ ■ ■
WHAT WAS the catalyst
for the economic boom that began
in 1947?
■ ■ ■ ■ ■ ■ ■ ■ ■ ■

RECONVERSION CHAOS

Japan's sudden surrender took U.S. officials by surprise. They had planned on taking two years to phase out military spending and reintroduce veterans to the domestic economy. Now their plans were obsolete. The Pentagon, already scaling back defense spending, canceled $15 billion in war contracts in the first forty-eight hours after the victory over Japan. Public pressure demanded that the military release the nation's 12 million servicemen and servicewomen as rapidly as possible. GIs in Europe and the South Pacific waited impatiently for their discharge determined by length of time in uniform, service overseas, combat decorations, and number of children.

Veterans came home to shortages of both food in the grocery stores and consumer goods in the department stores. Automobiles were especially scarce; the number of vehicles registered in the United States had declined by 4 million during the war. For the privilege of spending a few hundred dollars on a junker, consumers sometimes had to pay used-car dealers for so-called accessories like $150 batteries and $100 lap robes.

Inflation squeezed factory workers, who had accepted wage controls during the war effort. Since 1941, prices had risen twice as fast as base wages. In the fall of 1945, more and more workers went on strike to redress the balance. By January 1946, some 1.3 million auto, steel, electrical, and packinghouse workers were off the job. Strikes in these basic industries shut other factories down for lack of supplies. Presidential committees finally crafted settlements that allowed steel and auto workers to make up ground lost during the war, but they also allowed corporations to pass on higher costs to consumers. One Republican senator complained of "unionists who fatten themselves at the expense of the rest of us." Bill Nation, who inspected window moldings at a GM plant in Detroit, wondered who the senator was talking about. The strike gave him an hourly raise of 18 cents, pushing his weekly income to $59. After paying for food, housing, and utilities, that left $13.44 for Bill, his wife, and their five children to spend on clothes, comic books, and doctor bills.

QUICK REVIEW

Post-war Economic Problems
◆ Military spending and military service came to an abrupt halt.
◆ Veterans came home to shortages in food and consumer goods.
◆ Inflation contributed to labor unrest.

ECONOMIC POLICY

The **Employment Act of 1946** and the **Taft-Hartley Act** of 1947 represented contradictory liberal and conservative approaches to the peacetime economy.

The Employment Act was an effort by congressional liberals to ward off economic crisis by fine-tuning government taxation and spending. It started as a proposal to ensure everyone's "right to a useful and remunerative job." Watered down in the face of business opposition, it still defined economic growth and high employment as national goals. It also established the **Council of Economic Advisers** to assist the president.

In fact, more than 2 million women provided some slack by leaving the labor force outright, so that unemployment rates were far lower than economists had predicted. Federal agencies hastened their departure by publishing pamphlets

Taft-Hartley Act Federal legislation of 1947 that substantially limited the tools available to labor unions in labor-management disputes.

Council of Economic Advisers Board of three professional economists established in 1946 to advise the president on economic policy.

American actors Dana Andrews and Virginia Mayo portray Fred and Marie Derry in the 1946 movie *The Best Years of Our Life*, a film about WWII soldiers returning from war and adjusting to their post-war lives.

RKO Radio Pictures/Hulton Archive

QUICK REVIEW

The Taft-Hartly Act (1947)

◆ Effort to reverse gains made by labor in the 1930s.

◆ Public anger over strikes made passage of the act possible.

◆ Many middle-class Americans believed labor had gone too far.

asking *men* the pointed question, "Do you want your wife to work after the war?" In addition, consumer spending from a savings pool of $140 billion in bank accounts and war bonds created a huge demand for workers to fill. Total employment rose rather than fell with the end of the war.

From the other end of the political spectrum, the Taft-Hartley Act climaxed a ten-year effort by conservatives to reverse the gains made by organized labor in the 1930s. The act passed in 1947 because of anger about continuing strikes. For many Americans, the chief culprit was John L. Lewis, head of the United Mine Workers. The burly, bushy-browed, and combative Lewis was instantly recognizable—loved by his workers and hated by nearly everyone else. In April 1946, a forty-day coal strike cut into industrial production. The coal settlement was only days old when the nation faced an even more crippling walkout by railroad workers. Many middle-class Americans were convinced that organized labor needed to be curbed.

In November 1946, Republicans capitalized on the problems of reconversion chaos, labor unrest, and dissatisfaction with Truman. Their election slogan was simple: "Had enough?" The GOP won control of Congress for the first time since the election of 1928.

Adopted by the now firmly conservative Congress, the Taft-Hartley Act was a serious counterattack by big business on the power of large unions. It barred the closed shop (the requirement that all workers hired in a particular company or plant be union members) and blocked secondary boycotts (strikes against suppliers or customers of a targeted business). The federal government could postpone a strike by imposing a "cooling-off period," which gave companies time to stockpile their output. Officers of national unions had to swear they were not Communists or Communist sympathizers, even though corporate executives had no similar obligation. The bill passed over Truman's veto.

THE GI BILL

Another landmark law for the postwar era passed Congress without controversy. Popularly known as the **GI Bill of Rights**, the Servicemen's Readjustment Act of 1944 was designed to ease veterans back into the civilian mainstream. Rather than pay cash bonuses to veterans, as after previous wars, Congress tied benefits to specific public goals. The GI Bill guaranteed loans for buying a house or farm or starting a business. The program encouraged veterans to attend college with money for tuition and books plus monthly stipends.

The GI Bill made college degrees accessible to men with working-class backgrounds. In the peak year of 1947, veterans made up half of all college students. "We're all trying to get where we would have been if there hadn't been a war," one vet attending Indiana University told *Time* magazine. Veterans helped convert the college degree—once available primarily to the socially privileged—into a basic business and professional credential.

An unfortunate side effect of the GI tide was to crowd women out of classrooms, although sixty thousand servicewomen did take advantage of educational benefits. Women's share of bachelor's degrees dropped from 40 percent in 1940 to 25 percent in 1950. The most common female presence on many campuses was working wives trying to make up the gap between Veterans Administration (VA) checks and the expenses of new families.

ASSEMBLY-LINE NEIGHBORHOODS

Americans faced a housing shortage after the war. In 1947, fully 3 million married couples were unable to set up their own household. Most doubled up with relatives while they waited for the construction industry to respond. Hunger for housing

GI Bill of Rights Legislation in June 1944 that eased the return of veterans into American society by providing educational and employment benefits.

was fierce. Eager buyers lined up for hours and paid admission fees to tour model homes or to put their names in drawings for the opportunity to buy.

The solution started with the federal government and its VA mortgage program. By guaranteeing repayment, the VA allowed veterans to get home purchase loans from private lenders without a down payment. Eyeing the mass market created by the federal programs, William Levitt, a New York builder who had developed defense housing projects, built two thousand rental houses for veterans on suburban Long Island in 1947. His basic house had 800 square feet of living space in two bedrooms, living room, kitchen, bath, and unfinished attic waiting for the weekend handyman. It gave new families a place to start. There were six thousand **Levittown** houses by the end of 1948 and more than seventeen thousand by 1951.

Other successful builders bought hundreds of acres of land, put in utilities for the entire tract, purchased materials by the carload, and kept specialized workers busy on scores of identical houses. Floor plans were square, simple, and easy for semiskilled workers to construct. For the first time, kitchens across America were designed for preassembled cabinets and appliances in standard sizes. "On-site fabrication" was mass production without an assembly line. Work crews at the Los Angeles suburb of Lakewood started a hundred houses a day as they moved down one side of the street and back up the other.

From 1946 through 1950, the federal government backed $20 billion in VA and New Deal era Federal Housing Administration (FHA) loans, approximately 40 percent of all home mortgage debt. Housing starts neared 2 million in the peak year of 1950. By the end of the 1940s, 55 percent of American households owned their homes. The suburban population grew much faster than the population of central cities, and the population outside the growing reach of metropolitan areas actually declined.

Unfortunately, the suburban solution to housing shortages also had costs. Vast new housing tracts tended to isolate women and children and did little to help African Americans. Discrimination excluded black workers and their families from new housing. Federal housing agencies and private industry worsened the problem by **redlining** older neighborhoods, which involved withholding home purchase loans and insurance coverage from innercity areas.

Public and private actions kept black people in deteriorating inner-city ghettos. When severe flooding in 1948 drove thousands of African Americans from wartime temporary housing in Portland, Oregon, for example, their only choice was to crowd into the city's small black neighborhood. Chicago landlords squeezed an estimated 27,000 black migrants per year into run-down buildings, subdividing larger apartments into one-room "kitchenette" units with sinks and hot plates but no private bathrooms. Families that tried to find new homes in white neighborhoods on the edge of black ghettos often met violence—rocks through windows, fire bombs, milling mobs of angry white people.

STEPS TOWARD CIVIL RIGHTS

A new generation of black leaders began working to reduce the gap between America's ideal of equality and its performance. At the same time, a wave of lynchings and racist violence surged across the South after the war; special targets were black veterans who tried to register to vote. However, many white people felt uneasy about the contradiction between a crusade for freedom abroad and racial discrimination at home.

Caught between pressure from black leaders and the fear of alienating Southern Democrats, President Truman in 1946 appointed the Committee on Civil Rights, whose report developed an agenda for racial justice that would take two

Levittown   Suburban Long Island community of postwar rental houses built by William Levitt for veterans of World War II.

Redlining   The withholding of home purchase loans and insurance coverage from inner-city older neighborhoods by federal housing agencies and private industry.

◆

CHRONOLOGY

1944	Servicemen's Readjustment Act (GI Bill) is passed.			Truman orders desegregation of the armed forces. Selective Service is reestablished. Truman wins reelection.
1945	United Nations is established.			
1946	Employment Act creates Council of Economic Advisers. George Kennan sends his "long telegram." Winston Churchill delivers his "iron curtain" speech.		**1949**	North Atlantic Treaty Organization is formed. Communist Chinese defeat Nationalists. Soviet Union tests an atomic bomb. Department of Defense is established.
1947	Truman Doctrine is announced. Truman establishes a federal employee loyalty program. Kennan explains containment policy in an anonymous article in *Foreign Affairs*. Marshall Plan begins providing economic aid to Europe. HUAC holds hearings in Hollywood. Taft-Hartley Act rolls back gains of organized labor. National Security Act creates the National Security Council and the Central Intelligence Agency.		**1950**	Senator McCarthy begins his Red hunt. Alger Hiss is convicted of perjury. NSC-68 is drafted and accepted as U.S. policy. Korean War begins.
			1951	Senate Internal Security Subcommittee begins hearings. Truman relieves MacArthur of his command. Julius and Ethel Rosenberg are convicted of conspiring to commit espionage. Truce talks begin in Korea.
1948	Communists stage coup in Czechoslovakia. Berlin airlift overcomes Soviet blockade.		**1952**	United States tests the hydrogen bomb. Eisenhower is elected president.

decades to put into effect. The Justice Department began to support antisegregation lawsuits filed by the NAACP.

The president also ordered "equality of treatment and opportunity" in the armed services in July 1948. The army in particular dragged its feet, hoping to limit black soldiers to 10 percent of enlistees. Manpower needs and the fighting record of integrated units in Korea from 1950 to 1953 persuaded the reluctant generals. Over the next generation, African Americans would find the military an important avenue for career opportunities.

More Americans were interested in the lowering of racial barriers in professional team sports. Individual black champions already included heavy-weight boxer Joe Louis and sprinter Jesse Owens. Jack Roosevelt (Jackie) Robinson, a proud and gifted African-American athlete, opened the 1947 baseball season as a member of the Brooklyn Dodgers. Robinson was the first African American to play for the modern major leagues. In the segregated society of the 1940s, Robinson also found himself a powerful symbol of racial change.

CONSUMER BOOM AND BABY BOOM

Americans celebrated the end of the war with weddings; the marriage rate in 1946 surpassed even its wartime high. By 1950, the median age at which women married would be just over 20 years—lower than at any previous time in the twentieth century. The United States ended the 1940s with 7 million more married couples than at the decade's start.

New marriages jump-started the "baby boom," as did already married couples who decided to catch up after postponing childbearing during the war. In the early 1940s, an average of 2.9 million children per year were born in the United States; in 1946–1950, the average was 3.6 million. Those 3.5 million "extra" babies needed diapers, swing sets, lunch boxes, bicycles, and school rooms. Fast-growing families also needed to stock up on household goods. Out of an average household income of roughly $4,000 in 1946 and 1947, a family of four had $300 to $400 a year for the furnishings and appliances that manufacturers were beginning to produce in growing volume. William Levitt tried to humorously capture the American satisfaction with the fruits of free enterprise when he said in 1948 that "no man who owns his house and lot can be a Communist; he has too much to do."

TRUMAN, REPUBLICANS, AND THE FAIR DEAL

From new radios to new homes to new jobs, the economic gains of the postwar years propelled Americans toward the political center. After fifteen years of economic crisis and world war, they wanted to enjoy prosperity. They wanted to keep the gains of the New Deal—but without risking new experiments.

Recognizing this attitude, Harry Truman and his political advisers tried to define policies acceptable to moderate Republicans as well as Democrats. This meant creating a bipartisan coalition to block Soviet influence in western Europe and defending the core of the New Deal's social and economic agenda at home.

This political package is known as the strategy of the "vital center," after the title of a 1949 book by Arthur Schlesinger Jr. The book linked anti-Communism in foreign policy with efforts to enact inclusive social and economic policies—to extend freedom abroad and at home at the same time. The vital center reflected the political reality of the Cold War years, when Democrats had to prove that they were tough on Communism before they could enact domestic reforms.

TRUMAN'S OPPOSITION

In his campaign for a full term as president in 1948, Truman faced not only the Republicans but also new fringe parties on the far right and far left that allowed him to position himself in the moderate center. The blunt, no-nonsense Missourian entered the campaign an underdog; he soon looked like the country's best option for steering a steady course.

Truman's formal opponents represented the American Progressive party (an amalgam of left-leaning political groups), the **Dixiecrats** (officially the States' Rights Democrats), and the Republicans. The president also ran against the Republican-controlled "donothing 80th Congress," which he used as a punching bag at every opportunity.

Progressive candidate Henry Wallace cast himself as the prophet for "the century of the common man." His background as a plant geneticist and farm journalist prepared him to deal with domestic policy but not world affairs. After Truman fired him from the cabinet in 1946 for advocating a conciliatory stance toward the Soviets, Wallace went to Europe to praise the USSR and denounced U.S. foreign policy. On his return, most liberal Democrats ran the other way when Wallace organized the Progressive party, leaving the Communist party to supply many of his campaign workers.

Wallace argued that the United States was forcing the Cold War on the Soviet Union and undermining American ideals by diverting attention from poverty and racism at home. He wanted to repeal the draft and destroy atomic weapons. His arguments had merit, for the United States was becoming a militarized society, but Wallace was the wrong person to change American minds. With his shy

HOW WAS Harry Truman able to win the 1948 presidential election?

WHERE TO LEARN MORE

Harry S Truman National Historical Site, Library, and Museum, Independence, Missouri
www.nps.gov/hstr/

Dixiecrats States' Rights Democrats.

personality, disheveled appearance, and fanaticism about health food, he struck most voters as a kook rather than a statesman.

At the other political extreme were the Southerners who walked out when the 1948 Democratic National Convention called for full civil rights for African Americans. Mayor Hubert Humphrey of Minneapolis challenged the Democratic party "to get out of the shadow of states' rights and walk forthrightly into the bright sunshine of human rights."

When the angry Southerners met to nominate their own candidate, however, the South's important politicians stayed away. Major Southern newspapers called the revolt futile and narrow-minded.

Tom Dewey, Truman's strongest opponent, had been an effective governor of New York and represented the moderate Eastern establishment within the Republican party. Fortunately for Truman, Dewey lacked the common touch. Smooth on the outside, he alienated people who should have been his closest supporters. He was an arrogant campaigner, refusing to interrupt his morning schedule to talk to voters. He acted like a snob and dressed like the groom on a wedding cake.

Dewey was also saddled with the results of the 80th Congress (1947–1948). Truman used confrontation with Congress to rally voters who had supported the New Deal. Vote for me, Truman argued, to protect the New Deal, or vote Republican to bring back the days of Herbert Hoover. After his nomination in July 1948, Truman called Congress back into session and dared Republicans to enact all the measures for which *their* party claimed to stand. Congress did nothing, and Truman had more proof that the Republicans were all talk and no show.

WHISTLE-STOPPING ACROSS AMERICA

In the 1948 presidential campaign, a major candidate crisscrossed the nation by rail for the last time and made hundreds of speeches from the rear platforms of trains. For the first time, national television broadcast the two party conventions. The Republican campaign issued a printed T-shirt that read "Dew-It With Dewey"—the earliest advertising T-shirt in the collections of the Smithsonian Institution.

Truman was a widely read and intelligent man who cultivated the image of a backslapper. "I'll mow 'em down . . . and I'll give 'em hell," he told his vice presidential running mate, Senator Alben Barkley of Kentucky. Crowds across the country greeted him with "Give 'em hell, Harry!" He covered 31,700 miles in his campaign train and gave ten speeches a day.

On the advice of political strategist Clark Clifford, Truman tied Dewey to inflation, housing shortages, and fears about the future of Social Security. In industrial cities, he hammered at the Taft-Hartley Act. In the West, he pointed out that Democratic administrations had built dams and helped turn natural resources into jobs. He called the Republicans the party of privilege and arrogance. The Democrats, he said, offered opportunity for farmers, factory workers, and small business owners.

Truman got a huge boost from Dewey's unwillingness to fight. Going into the fall with a huge lead in the public opinion polls, Dewey sought to avoid mistakes. He failed to counter Truman's attacks and packed his speeches with platitudes: "Our streams abound with fish." "You know that your future is still ahead of you." "Peace is a blessing that we all share." The results astounded the pollsters, who had stopped sampling opinion in mid-October—just as a swing to Truman gathered strength. Wallace and Thurmond each took just under 1.2 million votes. Dewey received nearly 22 million popular votes and 189 electoral votes, but Truman won more than 24 million popular votes and 303 electoral votes (see Map 27–1).

American President Harry Truman shakes hands with supporters from a train car during a rally in the 1948 presidential campaign.

AP/Wide World Photos

QUICK REVIEW

Truman's 1948 Presidential Campaign

- Truman campaigned from the back of a train.
- Truman tied Dewey to inflation, housing shortages, and fears about Social Security.
- Dewey's failure to campaign aggressively may have cost him the election.

TRUMAN'S FAIR DEAL

Truman hoped to build on the gains of the New Deal. In his State of the Union address in January 1949, he called for a **Fair Deal** for all Americans. He promised to extend the New Deal and ensure "greater economic opportunity for the mass of the people."

In the Housing Act of 1949, the federal government reaffirmed its concern about families who had been priced out of the private market. Passed with the backing of conservative Senator Robert Taft—"Mr. Republican" to his admirers—the act provided money for local housing agencies to buy, level, and resell land for housing. The intent was to level slums and replace them with affordable modern apartments. The program never worked as intended because of scanty appropriations and poor design of the replacement housing, but it established the goal of decent housing for all Americans.

In 1950, Congress revitalized the weak Social Security program. Benefits went up by an average of 80 percent, and 10.5 million additional people received old-age and survivors' insurance. Most of the new coverage went to rural and small-town people.

Congress rejected other Fair Deal proposals that would remain on the national agenda for decades. A plan to alter the farm subsidy system to favor small farmers rather than agribusiness went nowhere. A Senate filibuster killed a permanent Fair Employment Practices Commission to fight racial discrimination in hiring. The medical establishment blocked a proposal for national health insurance as "socialistic." The overall message from Truman's second term was clear: Americans liked what the New Deal had given them but were hesitant about new initiatives.

CONFRONTING THE SOVIET UNION

In 1945, the United States and the Soviet Union were allies, victorious against Germany and planning the defeat of Japan. By 1947, they were engaged in a diplomatic and economic confrontation and soon came close to war over the city of Berlin.

Over the next forty years, the United States and the USSR contested for economic, political, and military influence around the globe in a Cold War. The heart of Soviet policy was control of eastern Europe as a buffer zone against Germany. The centerpiece of American policy was to link the United States, western Europe, and Japan into an alliance of overwhelming economic power. Both sides spent vast sums on conventional military forces and atomic weapons that held the world in a balance of terror. They also competed for political advantage in Asia and Africa as newly independent nations replaced European colonial empires.

Americans and Soviets frequently interpreted each other's actions in the most threatening terms, turning miscalculations and misunderstandings into crises. At home, a U.S. public that had suffered through nearly two decades of economic depression and war reacted to international problems with frustration and anger.

MAP EXPLORATION

To explore an interactive version of this map, go to
http://www.prenhall.com/goldfield2/map27.1

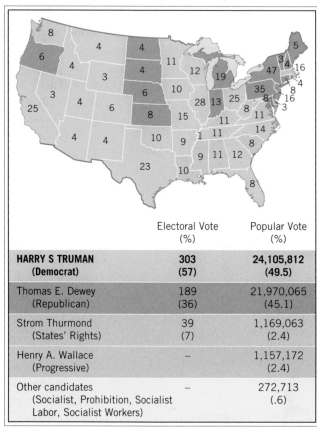

	Electoral Vote (%)	Popular Vote (%)
HARRY S TRUMAN (Democrat)	**303** **(57)**	**24,105,812** **(49.5)**
Thomas E. Dewey (Republican)	189 (36)	21,970,065 (45.1)
Strom Thurmond (States' Rights)	39 (7)	1,169,063 (2.4)
Henry A. Wallace (Progressive)	–	1,157,172 (2.4)
Other candidates (Socialist, Prohibition, Socialist Labor, Socialist Workers)	–	272,713 (.6)

MAP 27–1

The Election of 1948   Harry Truman won a narrow victory in the presidential election of 1948 by holding many of the traditionally Democratic states of the South and West and winning key industrial states in the Midwest. His success depended on the coalition of rural and urban interests that Franklin Roosevelt had pulled together in the 1930s.

WHY DO you think industrial states in the Midwest supported Harry S Truman in the 1948 presidential election?

WHAT WERE the origins of the Cold War?

THE END OF THE GRAND ALLIANCE

The Yalta Conference of February 1945 had recognized military realities by marking out rough spheres of influence. The Soviet defeat of Germany on the Eastern Front had made the USSR the only military power in eastern Europe. The American and British attacks through Italy and France had made the Western allies dominant in western Europe and the Mediterranean. The Soviets, Americans, British, and French shared control of defeated Germany, each with its own occupation zone of the country and its own sector of Berlin. The Western allies had the better of the bargain. Defeated Italy and Japan, whose reconstruction was firmly in Western hands, had far greater economic potential than Soviet-controlled Bulgaria, Romania, or Hungary.

The victorious powers argued bitterly about Germany and eastern Europe. For Poland, Truman and his advisers claimed that Yalta had assumed open elections on the American model. The Soviet Union saw Poland as the historic invasion route from the west; it claimed that Yalta had ensured that any Polish government would be friendly to Soviet interests and acted to guarantee that this would be so.

The United States tried to involve the USSR and eastern Europe in new international organizations, such as the United Nations (U.N.). The Washington-based **International Monetary Fund (IMF)** and the **World Bank** were designed to revive international trade. The IMF stabilized national currencies against the short-term pressures of international trade. The World Bank drew on the resources of member nations to make economic development loans to governments for such projects as new dams or agricultural modernization. These organizations ensured that a reviving world economy would revolve around the industrial and technological power of the United States.

In 1946, the United States also presented a plan in the United Nations to control atomic energy. Bernard Baruch suggested that an international agency should oversee all uranium production and research on atomic explosives, but this plan was unacceptable to the Soviets, who did not want to open their atomic energy program to outside control or inspection. On-site inspection would remain a problem in arms control negotiations for the next half-century.

American leaders were also becoming convinced of Soviet aggressiveness. In February 1946, George Kennan, a senior American diplomat in Moscow, sent a "long telegram" to the State Department. He depicted a USSR driven by expansionist Communist ideology. The Soviets, he argued, would constantly probe for weaknesses in the capitalist world. The best response was firm resistance to protect the western heartlands.

Lacking the strength to shape Europe on its own, Great Britain repeatedly nudged the United States into blocking Soviet influence. Speaking at Westminster College in Missouri in March 1946, Winston Churchill warned that the USSR had dropped an "iron curtain" across the middle of Europe and urged a firm Western response.

Truman's foreign policy advisers shared the belief in an aggressive Soviet Union. Administration leaders did not fear an immediate Soviet military threat to the United States itself, for they knew that World War II had exhausted the USSR, but they also knew that the Soviets were strong enough to brush aside the U.S. occupation forces in Germany. Added to military apprehension were worries about political and economic competition. Communist parties in war-ravaged Europe and Japan were exploiting discontent. In Asia and Africa, the allegiance of nationalists who were fighting for independence from France, Great Britain, and the Netherlands remained in doubt. America's leaders worried that much of the Eastern Hemisphere might fall under Soviet control and turn its back on North America.

WHERE TO LEARN MORE

★ United Nations Headquarters, New York, New York
www.un.org

27–1
George F. Kennan, "Long Telegram" (1946)

International Monetary Fund International organization established in 1945 to assist nations in maintaining stable currencies.

World Bank Designed to revive postwar international trade, it drew on the resources of member nations to make economic development loans to governments for such projects as new dams or agricultural modernization.

Truman and the "wise men" who made up his foreign policy circle ignored examples of Soviet caution and conciliation. The Soviets withdrew troops from Manchuria in northern China and acquiesced in America's control of defeated Japan. They allowed a neutral but democratic government in Finland and technically free elections in Hungary and Czechoslovakia (although it was clear that Communists would do well there). They demobilized much of their huge army and reduced their forces in eastern Europe while expecting a falling out between capitalist Britain and the United States.

However, the Soviet regime also did more than enough to justify American fears. The USSR pressured Turkey to give it partial control of the exit from the Black Sea. It retained troops in northern Iran until warned out by the United States. The Soviets were ruthless in support of Communist control in Bulgaria, Romania, and Poland. U.S. policymakers read these Soviet actions as a rerun of Nazi aggression and determined not to let a new totalitarian threat undermine Western power.

THE TRUMAN DOCTRINE AND THE MARSHALL PLAN

Early in 1947, Truman and his advisers decided on decisive action. The British could no longer afford to back the Greek government that was fighting Communist rebels, and U.S. officials feared that a Communist takeover in Greece would threaten the stability of Italy, France, and the Middle East. On March 12, he told Congress that the United States faced a "fateful hour." Taking the advice of Senator Arthur Vandenberg to "scare the hell out of the country," he said that only the appropriation of $400 million to fight Communism in Greece and Turkey could secure the free world. Congress agreed, and the United States became the dominant power in the eastern Mediterranean.

In a sweeping declaration that became known as the **Truman Doctrine**, the president pledged that "It must be the policy of the United States to support free peoples who are resisting attempted subjugation by armed minorities or by outside pressures. . . . I believe that our help should be primarily through economic and financial aid, which is essential to economic stability and orderly political processes."

Meanwhile, Europe was sliding toward chaos. Germany was close to famine after the bitter winter of 1946–1947. Western European nations were bankrupt and unable to import raw materials for their factories. Overstressed medical systems could no longer control diseases such as tuberculosis. Communist parties had gained in Italy, France, and Germany.

Secretary of State George C. Marshall announced the European Recovery Plan on June 5, 1947. What the press quickly dubbed the **Marshall Plan** committed the United States to help rebuild Europe. The United States invited Soviet and eastern European participation, but the Soviets refused, instead organizing their eastern European satellites in their own association for Mutual Economic Assistance, or Comecon, in 1949. In western Europe, the aid from the Marshall Plan totaled $13.5 billion over four years. It met many of Europe's economic needs and quieted class conflict. Because Europeans spent much of the aid on U.S. goods and machinery and because economic recovery promised markets for U.S. products, business and labor both supported it. In effect, the Marshall Plan created an "empire by invitation" in which Americans and Europeans jointly planned European recovery.

U.S. policy in Japan followed the pattern set in Europe. As supreme commander of the Allied Powers, General Douglas MacArthur acted as Japan's postwar dictator. He tried to change the values of the old war-prone Japan through social reform, democratization, and demilitarization. At the end of 1947, however,

QUICK REVIEW

Post-war Foreign Policy

- Truman launched the nation into a global battle against communism
- The U.S. pledged to help countries that faced external pressure or internal revolution.
- The U.S. played a decisive role in the rebuilding of Europe.

Truman Doctrine   President Harry Truman's statement in 1947 that the United States should assist other nations that were facing external pressure or internal revolution.

Marshall Plan   Secretary of State George C. Marshall's European Recovery Plan of June 5, 1947, committing the United States to help in the rebuilding of post-World War II Europe.

Berlin in 1948 was still a devastated city of gutted buildings and heaps of rubble. When the Soviet Union shut off ground access to Berlin's British, French, and American occupation zones, the city also became a symbol of the West's Cold War resolve. Allied aircraft lifted in food, fuel, and other essentials for West Berliners for nearly a year until the Soviets ended the blockade.

Getty Images/Time Life Pictures

Berlin blockade   Three-hundred-day Soviet blockade of land access to United States, British, and French occupation zones in Berlin, 1948–1949.

Central Intelligence Agency (CIA) Agency established in 1947 that co-ordinates the gathering and evaluation of military and economic information on other nations.

National Security Council   The for-mal policymaking body for national defense and foreign relations, creat-ed in 1947 and consisting of the president, the secretary of defense, the secretary of state, and others ap-pointed by the president.

North Atlantic Treaty Organization (NATO)   Organization of ten Euro-pean countries, Canada, and the United States whom together formed a mutual defense pact in April, 1949.

policymakers were fearful of economic collapse and political chaos, just as in Europe. The "reverse course" in occupation policy aimed to make Japan an economic magnet for other nations in East Asia, pulling them toward the American orbit and away from the Soviet Union. MacArthur reluctantly accepted the new policy of "eco-nomic crank-up" by preserving Japan's corporate giants and en-couraging American investment. At American insistence, the new Japan accepted American bases and created its own "self-defense force" (with no capacity for overseas aggression).

George Kennan summed up the new American policies in the magazine *Foreign Affairs* in July 1947. Writing anonymously as "X," Kennan warned that the emerging Cold War would be a long con-flict with no quick fixes.

SOVIET REACTIONS

The bold American moves in the first half of 1947 put the USSR on the defensive. East of the iron curtain, Hungarian Communists ex-pelled non-Communists from a coalition government. Bulgarian Communists shot opposition leaders. Romania, Bulgaria, and Hungary signed de-fense pacts with the Soviet Union.

In early 1948, the Soviets targeted Czechoslovakia. For three years, a neutral coalition government there based on the model of Finland had balanced trade with the West with a foreign policy friendly to the USSR. In February 1948, while Russ-ian forces assembled on the Czech borders, local communists pushed aside Czecho-slovakia's democratic leadership and turned the nation into a dictatorship and Soviet satellite within a week.

The climax of the Soviet reaction came on June 24, 1948, when Soviet troops blockaded surface traffic into Berlin, cutting off the U.S., British, and French sec-tors. The immediate Soviet aim was to block Western plans to merge their three occupation zones into an independent federal republic (West Germany). Rather than abandon 2.5 million Berliners or shoot their way through, the Western na-tions responded to the **Berlin blockade** by airlifting supplies to the city. Planes landed every two minutes at Berlin's Tempelhof Airport. Stalin decided not to in-tercept the flights. After eleven months, the Soviets abandoned the blockade, making the Berlin airlift a triumph of American resolve.

AMERICAN REARMAMENT

The coup in Czechoslovakia and the Berlin blockade shocked American leaders and backfired on the Soviets. Congress responded in 1948 by reinstating the mil-itary draft and increasing defense spending by 30 percent.

The United States had already begun to modernize and centralize its na-tional security apparatus. The National Security Act of July 1947 created the **Central Intelligence Agency (CIA)** and the **National Security Council (NSC)**. The CIA han-dled intelligence gathering and covert operations. The NSC assembled top diplo-matic and military advisers in one committee. In 1949, legislation also created the Department of Defense to oversee the army, navy, and air force (independent from the army since 1947).

In April 1949, ten European nations, the United States, and Canada signed the North Atlantic Treaty as a mutual defense pact. American commitments to the **North Atlantic Treaty Organization (NATO)** included military aid and the de-ployment of U.S. troops in western Europe. As Republican Senator Robert Taft warned in the ratification debate, NATO was the sort of "entangling alliance" that the United States had avoided for 160 years. It was also the insurance policy that western Europeans required if they were to accept the dangers as well as the benefits of a revived Germany, which was economically and militarily necessary for a strong Europe.

Two years later, the United States signed similar but less comprehensive agreements in the western Pacific: the ANZUS Pact with Australia and New Zealand and a new treaty with the Philippines. The alliances reassured Pacific allies who were nervously watching the United States negotiate a unilateral peace treaty with Japan (ignoring the Soviet Union). Taken together, peacetime rearmament and mutual defense pacts amounted to a revolution in American foreign policy.

COLD WAR AND HOT WAR

The first phase of the Cold War reached a crisis in the autumn of 1949. The two previous years had seen an uneasy equilibrium in which American success in southern and western Europe and the standoff over Berlin (the blockade ended in May 1949) balanced the consolidation of Soviet power in eastern Europe. Now, suddenly, two key events seemed to tilt the world balance against the United States and its allies. In September, Truman announced that the Soviet Union had tested its own atomic bomb. A month later, the Chinese Communists under Mao Zedong (Mao Tse-tung) took power in China. The following summer, civil war in Korea sucked the United States into a fierce war with communist North Korea and China. The United States government accelerated a forty-year arms race with the Soviet Union.

WHAT WERE the major conflicts of the early Cold War?

THE NUCLEAR SHADOW

Experts in Washington had known that the Soviets were working on an A-bomb, but the news shocked the average citizen. In 1946, advocates of civilian control had won a small victory when Congress gave control of atomic energy to the new Atomic Energy Commission (AEC). The AEC tried to balance research on atomic power with continued testing of new weapons. Now Truman told the AEC to double the output of fissionable uranium and plutonium for "conventional" nuclear weapons.

A more momentous decision soon followed. Truman decided in January 1950 to authorize work on the "super" bomb—the thermonuclear fusion weapon that would become the hydrogen bomb (H-bomb). As would be true in future nuclear defense debates, the underlying question was how much capacity for nuclear destruction was enough. (See American Views, "Deciding on a Nuclear Arms Race.")

Nuclear weapons proliferated in the early 1950s. The United States exploded the first hydrogen bomb in the South Pacific in November 1952. Releasing one hundred times the energy of the Hiroshima bomb, the detonation tore a mile-long chasm in the ocean floor. Great Britain became the third nuclear power in the same year. The Soviet Union tested its own hydrogen bomb only nine months after the U.S. test.

Under the guidance of the Federal Civil Defense Administration, Americans learned that they should always keep a battery-powered radio and tune to 640 or 1240 on the AM dial for emergency information when they heard air raid sirens. Schoolchildren learned to hide under their desks if they saw the blinding flash of a nuclear detonation.

Soldiers were exposed to posttest radiation with minimal protection. Nuclear tests in the South Pacific dusted fishing boats with radioactivity and forced islanders to abandon contaminated homes. Radioactive fallout from Nevada testing

QUICK REVIEW

Nuclear Weapons

◆ Truman ordered in the Atomic Energy Commission to double the production of materials for nuclear weapons.

◆ The U.S. began work on the hydrogen bomb.

◆ The U.S. tested the first hydrogen bomb in 1952.

•AMERICAN VIEWS•

DECIDING ON A NUCLEAR ARMS RACE

In 1950, the United States began work on a hydrogen (thermonuclear) bomb. The decision locked the United States and the Soviet Union into a nuclear arms race that lasted another forty years. In the first document reprinted here, an excerpt from a letter to President Truman written on November 25, 1949, Lewis Strauss, chairman of the Atomic Energy Commission, urged work on the H-bomb. In the second, scientist Edward Teller agreed. A refugee from Nazi-dominated Europe who had worked at Los Alamos, Teller remained an advocate of massive defense spending through the 1980s.

HOW DID memories of World War II affect this Cold War decision? How did U.S. policymakers evaluate the intentions of the Soviet Union?

Lewis Strauss,
November 1949:

Dear Mr. President:

As you know, the thermonuclear (super) bomb was suggested by scientists working at Los Alamos during the war. . . . I believe that the United States must be as completely armed as any possible enemy. From this, it follows that I believe it unwise to renounce, unilaterally, any weapon which an enemy can reasonably be expected to possess. I recommend that the President direct the Atomic Energy Commission to proceed with the development of the thermonuclear bomb, at highest priority. . . . Obviously the current atomic bomb as

well as the proposed thermonuclear weapon are horrible to contemplate. All war is horrible. Until, however, some means is found of eliminating war, I cannot agree with those of my colleagues who feel that an announcement should be made by the President to the effect that the development of the thermonuclear weapon will not be undertaken by the United States at this time. This is because I do not think the statement will be credited in the Kremlin . . . and because primarily until disarmament is universal, our arsenal must be not less well equipped than with the most potent weapons that our technology can devise.

Edward Teller,
March 1950:

President Truman has announced that we are going to make a hydrogen bomb. . . . The scientist is not responsible for the law of nature. It is his job to find out how these laws operate. . . . However, it is not the scientist's job to determine whether a hydrogen bomb should be constructed, whether it should be used, or how it should be used. This responsibility rests with the American people and their chosen representatives. Personally, as a citizen, I do not know in what other way President Truman could have acted. . . . To my mind we are in a situation no less dangerous than the one we were facing in 1939, and it is of the greatest importance that we realize it. We must realize. . . . that democracy will not be saved by ideals alone.

Source: Lewis L. Strauss, *Men and Decisions* (1962).

contaminated large sections of the West and increased cancer rates among "downwinders" in Utah. Weapons production and atomic experiments contaminated vast tracts in Nevada, Washington, and Colorado and left huge environmental costs for later generations.

THE COLD WAR IN ASIA

Communist victory in China's civil war was as predictable as the Soviet nuclear bomb but no less controversial. American military and diplomatic missions in the late 1940s pointed out that the collapse of Jiang Jieshi's Nationalist regime was nearly inevitable, given its corruption and narrow support. But advocates for Jiang, mostly conservative Republicans from the Midwest and West, were certain that

Truman's administration had done too little. "China asked for a sword," complained one senator, "and we gave her a dull paring knife." Critics looked for scapegoats. Foreign service officers who had honestly analyzed the weakness of the Nationalists were accused of Communist sympathies and hounded from their jobs. The results were damage to the State Department and tragedy for those unfairly branded as traitors.

NSC-68 AND AGGRESSIVE CONTAINMENT

The turmoil of 1949 led to a comprehensive statement of American strategic goals. In April 1950, the State Department prepared a sweeping report known as **National Security Council Paper 68 (NSC-68)**. The document described a world divided between the forces of "slavery" and "freedom" and assumed that the Soviet Union was actively and broadly aggressive, motivated by greed for territory and a "fanatic faith" in Communism. To defend civilization itself, said the experts, the United States should use as much force as needed to resist Communist expansion anywhere and everywhere.

Truman and his advisors in 1947 and 1948 had hoped to contain the Soviets by diplomacy and by integrating the economies of Europe and Japan with that of the United States. Now that the Soviets had the atomic bomb, NSC-68 argued that the United States needed to press friendly nations to rearm and to make its former enemies into military allies. It also argued the need for the nation to acquire expensive conventional forces to defend Europe. NSC-68 thus advocated nearly open-ended increases in the defense budget (which in fact tripled between 1950 and 1954).

Although it was not a public document, NSC-68's portrait of implacable Communist expansion would have made sense to most Americans; it certainly did to Harry Truman. The outbreak of war in Korea at the end of June 1950 seemed to confirm that Communism was a military threat. The thinking behind the report led the United States to approach the Cold War as a military competition and to view political changes in Africa and Asia as parts of a Soviet plan.

WAR IN KOREA, 1950–1953

The success of Mao and the Chinese Communists forced the Truman administration to define national interests in East Asia and the western Pacific. The most important U.S. interest was Japan, still an industrial power despite its devastating defeat. The United States had shaped a more democratic Japan that would be a strong and friendly trading partner. Protected by American armed forces, Japan would be part of a crescent of offshore strong points that included Alaska, the Philippines, Australia, and New Zealand.

Two questions remained unresolved at the start of 1950 (and were still troublesome at the turn of the century). One was the future of Taiwan and the remnants of Jiang's regime. The other question was Korea, whose own civil war would soon bring the world to the brink of World War III.

The Korean peninsula is the closest point on the Asian mainland to Japan. With three powerful neighbors—China, Russia, and Japan—Korea had always had to fight for its independence. As World War II ended, Soviet troops had moved down the peninsula from the north and American forces had landed in the south, creating a situation similar to that in Germany. The 38th parallel, which Russians and Americans set as the dividing line between their zones of occupation, became a de facto border. The United States in 1948 recognized an independent South Korea, with its capital at Seoul, under a conservative government led by Syngman Rhee. Rhee's support came from large landowners and a police force trained by

27–3
National Security Council Memorandum Number 68 (1950)

National Security Council Paper 68 (NSC-68)   Policy statement that committed the United States to a military approach to the Cold War.

MAP EXPLORATION

To explore an interactive version of this map, go to
http://www.prenhall.com/goldfield2/map27.2

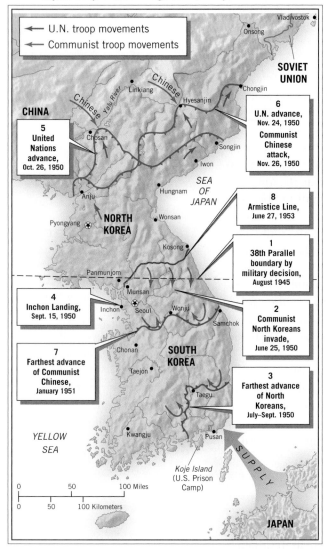

MAP 27–2

The Korean War   After rapid reversals of fortune in 1950 and early 1951, the war in Korea settled into stalemate. Most Americans agreed with the need to contain Communist expansion but found it deeply frustrating to fight for limited objectives rather than total victory.

WAS A stalemate the inevitable end to the Korean War? Why or why not?

Korean War   Pacific war started on June 25, 1950, when North Korea, helped by Soviet equipment and Chinese training, attacked South Korea.

the Japanese between 1910 and 1945. The Soviets recognized a separate North Korea, whose leader, Kim Il Sung, advocated radical social and political change. Both leaders hoped to unify all Koreans under their own rule, and each crushed political dissent and tried to undermine the other with economic pressure and commando raids.

United States military planners assumed that U.S. air power in Japan could neutralize unfriendly forces on the Korean peninsula. But Korea remained politically important as the only point of direct confrontation with the Soviet Union in Asia.

On June 25, 1950, North Korea, helped by Soviet equipment and Chinese training, attacked South Korea, starting the **Korean War**, which lasted until 1953 (see Map 27–2). Truman and Secretary of State Dean Acheson believed that Moscow lay behind the invasion. They worried that the attack was a ploy to suck America's limited military resources into Asia before a bigger war came in Europe or the Middle East. The war was really an intensification of an ongoing civil war that Stalin was willing to exploit. Kim originated the invasion plan and spent a year persuading Stalin to agree to it. Stalin hoped that the conquest of South Korea would force Japan to sign a favorable treaty with the USSR.

As the South Korean army collapsed, Truman committed American ground troops from Japan on June 30. The United States also had the diplomatic good fortune of securing an endorsement from the United Nations. Because the USSR was boycotting the UN, the Korean conflict remained officially a United Nations action, although U.S. Generals Douglas MacArthur, Matthew Ridgway, and Mark Clark ran the show as the successive heads of the U.N. command.

THE POLITICS OF WAR

The first U.S. combat troops were outnumbered, outgunned, and poorly trained. They could not stop the North Koreans. By early August, the Americans clung to a narrow toehold around the port of Pusan on the tip of the Korean peninsula. As reinforcements arrived from the United States, however, MacArthur transformed the war with a daring amphibious counterattack at Inchon, 150 miles behind North Korean lines. The North Korean army was already overextended and exhausted. It collapsed and fled north.

MacArthur and Washington officials disregarded warnings by China that it would enter the war if the United States tried to reunite Korea by force. U.S. and South Korean troops rolled north, drawing closer and closer to the boundary between North Korea and China.

Chinese forces attacked MacArthur's command in late October but then disappeared. MacArthur dismissed the attacks as a token gesture. But on November 26, the Chinese struck the overextended American columns. They had massed 300,000 troops without detection by American aviation. Their assault drove the U.N. forces into a two-month retreat that again abandoned Seoul.

In March 1951, with the U.N. forces again pushing north, Truman prepared to offer a cease-fire that would have preserved the separate nations of South and North Korea. MacArthur tried to preempt the president by demanding that China admit defeat or suffer the consequences. He then published a direct attack on the administration's policy of limiting the Asian war to ensure the security of Europe.

To protect civilian control of the armed forces, he was forced to relieve MacArthur of his commands on April 11, 1951. The general returned to parades and a hero's welcome when he addressed a joint session of Congress. He quoted a line from an old barracks song: "Old soldiers never die; they just fade away." But Truman remained in charge of the war.

In Korea itself, U.S. and South Korean forces stabilized a strong defensive line that cut diagonally across the 38th parallel. For two years, U.N. and Communist armies faced boredom that alternated with fierce inch-by-inch battles for territory with names like Heartbreak Ridge and Pork Chop Hill. In the air, the arrival of new F-86 Saberjets in 1952 allowed American pilots to clear the skies of Chinese aviators in Russian-made MIG 15s.

After 1950, the Chinese were careful to keep their war planes north of the ground combat zone, the Russians had stayed out of the war, and the United States was willing to accept a divided Korea.

Truce negotiations stalled over the political decision to turn free choice for Chinese POWs into a symbol of resistance to Communism. Nearly half of the 140,000 U.S. casualties came after the truce talks started. The war was a decisive factor behind the Republican victory in the November 1952 elections and dragged on until June 1953, when an armistice returned the peninsula roughly to its pre-war political division.

The blindly ambitious attack into North Korea was one of the great failures of intelligence and strategic leadership in American military history. Nearly everyone in Washington shared the blame for letting the excitement of battlefield victories obscure limited war aims. Civilian leaders couldn't resist the desire to roll back Communism. Truman hoped for a striking victory before the 1950 congressional elections. The Joint Chiefs of Staff failed to question a general with MacArthur's heroic reputation. MacArthur himself allowed ambition and wishful thinking to jeopardize his army.

The war in Korea was a preview of Vietnam fifteen years later. American leaders found themselves propping up an undemocratic regime to defend democracy. Both North Koreans and South Koreans engaged in savage political reprisals as the battlefront shifted back and forth. American emphasis on the massive application of firepower led U.S. forces to demolish entire villages to kill single snipers. General Curtis Le May estimated that Air Force bombings killed a million Koreans.

The Korean War helped to legitimize the United Nations. In Washington, it confirmed the ideas behind NSC-68, with its call for the United States to lead an anti-Communist alliance. Two days after the North Korean invasion, President Truman ordered the Seventh Fleet to protect the Nationalist Chinese on Taiwan, a decision that guaranteed twenty years of hostility between the United States and the People's Republic of China. In the same month, the United States began to aid France's struggle to retain control over its colony of Indochina, which included Laos, Cambodia, and Vietnam.

In Europe, the United States pushed to rearm West Germany as part of a militarized NATO and sent troops to Europe as a permanent defense force. It increased military aid to European governments and secured a unified command for the national forces allocated for NATO. The unified command made West German rearmament acceptable to France and the smaller nations of western Europe.

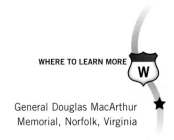

WHERE TO LEARN MORE

General Douglas MacArthur Memorial, Norfolk, Virginia

THE SECOND RED SCARE

WHAT WAS the "Second Red Scare"?

The Korean War reinforced the second Red Scare, an assault on civil liberties that stretched from the mid-1940s to the mid-1950s and dwarfed the Red Scare of 1919–1920. Legitimate concerns about espionage mixed with suspicions that Communist sympathizers in high places were helping Stalin and Mao (see the overview table "The Second Red Scare").

Efforts to root out suspected subversives operated on three tracks. National and state governments established loyalty programs to identify and fire suspect employees. The courts punished members of suspect organizations. Congressional and state legislative investigations followed the whims of committee chairs. Anti-Communist crusaders often relied on dubious evidence and eagerly believed the worst. They also threatened basic civil liberties.

THE COMMUNIST PARTY AND THE LOYALTY PROGRAM

The Communist party in the United States was actually in rapid decline after World War II. Many intellectuals had left the party over the Nazi-Soviet Pact in 1939. And the postwar years brought a series of failures. In 1946, Walter Reuther defeated a Communist for the presidency of the huge United Auto Workers union, and other large CIO unions froze Communists out of leadership positions.

Nevertheless, Republicans used red-baiting as a campaign technique in 1944 and 1946, setting the stage for a national loyalty program. Republicans in 1944 tried to frighten voters about "commydemocrats" by linking FDR, CIO labor unions, and Communism. Democrats slung their own mud by trying to convince voters that Hitler preferred the Republicans. Two years later, Republican campaigners told the public that the basic choice was "between Communism and Republicanism." The argument helped dozens of Republicans, including a young navy veteran named Richard Nixon, win congressional seats.

President Truman responded to the Republican landslide with a loyalty program for federal employees, initiated in March 1947 with Executive Order 9835. Order 9835 authorized the attorney general to prepare a list of "totalitarian, Fascist, Communist, or subversive" organizations and made membership or even "sympathetic association" with such groups grounds for dismissal. The loyalty program applied to approximately 8 million Americans working for the federal government or defense contractors; similar state laws affected another 5 million.

Many accusations were just malicious gossip, but allegations stayed in a worker's file even if refuted. Many New Dealers and people associated with presumably liberal East Coast institutions were targets. An Interior Department official boasted that he had been especially effective in squeezing out graduates of Harvard and Columbia.

Federal employees worked under a cloud of fear. Loyalty boards asked about religion, racial equality, and a taste for foreign films; they also tried to identify homosexuals, who were thought to be targets for blackmail by foreign agents. The loyalty program resulted in 1,210 firings and 6,000 resignations under Truman and comparable numbers during Dwight Eisenhower's first term from 1953 to 1956.

NAMING NAMES TO CONGRESS

The congressional hunt for subversives had its roots in 1938 when Congressman Martin Dies, a Texas Democrat, created the Special Committee on Un-American Activities. Originally intended to ferret out pro-Fascists, the Dies Committee evolved into the permanent **House Committee on Un-American Activities (HUAC)** in 1945. It investigated "un-American propaganda" that attacked constitutional government.

House Committee on Un-American Activities (HUAC) Originally intended to ferret out pro-Fascists, it later investigated "un-American propaganda" that attacked constitutional government.

OVERVIEW

THE SECOND RED SCARE

Type of Anti-Communist Effort	Key Tools	Results
Employee loyalty programs	U.S. attorney general's list of subversive organizations	Thousands of federal and state workers fired, careers damaged
Congressional investigations	HUAC McCarren Committee Army-McCarthy hearings	Employee blacklists, harassment of writers and intellectuals
Criminal prosecutions	Trials for espionage and conspiracy to advocate violent overthrow of the U.S. government	Convictions of Communist party leaders (1949), Rosenbergs (1951)

One of HUAC's juiciest targets was Hollywood. In 1946, Americans bought an average of 90 million tickets every *week*. But Hollywood's reputation for loose morals, high living, foreign-born directors, Jewish producers, and left-leaning writers aroused the suspicions of many congressmen. HUAC sought to make sure that no un-American messages were being peddled through America's most popular entertainment.

When the hearings opened in October 1947, studio executives assured HUAC of their anti-Communism. So did popular actors Gary Cooper and Ronald Reagan. In contrast, eight screenwriters and two directors—the Hollywood Ten—refused to discuss their past political associations, citing the free speech protections of the First Amendment to the Constitution. HUAC countered with citations for contempt of Congress. The First Amendment defense failed when it reached the Supreme Court, and the ten went to jail in 1950.

27–2
Ronald Reagan, Testimony Before the House Un-American Activities Committee (1947)

HUAC changed the politics of Hollywood. Before 1947, it had been fashionable to lean toward the left. After the hearings, it was imperative to tilt the other way. The government refused to let British-born Charlie Chaplin reenter the United States in 1952 because of his left-wing views. Other actors, writers, and directors found themselves on the Hollywood blacklist, banned from jobs where they might insert Communist propaganda into American movies.

At the start of 1951, the new Senate Internal Security Subcommittee joined the sometimes bumbling HUAC. The McCarran Committee, named for the Nevada senator who chaired it, targeted diplomats, labor union leaders, professors, and schoolteachers. The real point of the investigations was not to force personal confessions from witnesses but to badger them into identifying friends and associates who might have been involved in suspect activities.

The only sure way to avoid "naming names" was to respond to every question by citing the Fifth Amendment to the Constitution, which protects Americans from testifying against themselves. Many Americans wrongly assumed that citing the amendment was a sure sign of guilt, not a matter of principle, and talked about "Fifth Amendment Communists."

State legislatures imitated Congress by searching for "Reducators" among college faculty in such states as Oklahoma, Washington, and California. College presidents frequently fired faculty who took the Fifth Amendment. The experience of an economics professor fired from the University of Kansas City after testimony before the McCarran Committee was typical. He found it hard to keep any job once his name had been in the papers. A local dairy fired him because it thought its customers might be uneasy having a radical handle their milk bottles.

SUBVERSION TRIALS

In 1948, the Justice Department indicted the leaders of the American Communist party under the Alien Registration Act of 1940. Eleven men and women were convicted in 1949 of conspiring to advocate the violent overthrow of the United States government through their speech and publications. Some of the testimony came from Herbert Philbrick, an advertising manager and FBI informer who had posed as a party member. Philbrick parlayed his appearance into a bestseller titled *I Led Three Lives* and then into a popular television series on which the FBI foiled Communist spies every Friday night.

Then, in 1948, former Communist Whittaker Chambers named Alger Hiss as a Communist with whom he had associated in the 1930s. Hiss, who had held important posts in the State Department, sued Chambers for slander. As proof, Chambers gave Congressman Richard Nixon microfilms that he had hidden inside a pumpkin on his Maryland farm. Tests seemed to show that the "pumpkin papers" were State Department documents that had been copied on a typewriter that Hiss had once owned. The Justice Department indicted Hiss for perjury—lying under oath. A first perjury trial ended in deadlock, but a second jury convicted Hiss in January 1950.

The essence of the Hiss case has been a matter of faith, not facts. Even his enemies agreed that any documents he might have stolen were of limited importance. His smugness as a member of the East Coast establishment enraged them. To his opponents, Hiss stood for every wrong turn that the nation had taken since 1932. Many supporters believed that he had been framed. Both sides claimed support from Soviet records that became public in the 1990s.

In 1950, the British arrested nuclear physicist Klaus Fuchs, who confessed to passing atomic secrets to the Soviets when he worked at Los Alamos in 1944 and 1945. The "Fuchs spy ring" soon implicated Julius and Ethel Rosenberg, New York radicals of strong beliefs but limited sophistication. Convicted in 1951 of the vague charge of conspiring to commit espionage, they were sent to the electric chair in 1953 after refusing to buy a reprieve by naming other spies.

As in the case of Alger Hiss, the government had a plausible but not airtight case against the Rosenbergs. There is no doubt that Julius Rosenberg was a convinced Communist, and he was likely a minor figure in an atomic spy net, but it is likely that Ethel Rosenberg was charged with crimes to pressure her husband into confessing.

SENATOR MCCARTHY ON STAGE

The best-remembered participant in the second Red Scare was Senator Joseph McCarthy of Wisconsin. He burst into national prominence on February 9, 1950. In a rambling speech in Wheeling, West Virginia, he supposedly stated: "I have here in my hand a list of 205 that were known to the Secretary of State as being members of the Communist party and who, nevertheless, are still working and shaping the policy of the State Department." McCarthy's rise to fame climaxed with an incoherent six-hour speech to the Senate. He tried to document the charges by mixing previously exposed spies with people who no longer worked for the government or who never had worked for it. Over the next several years, his speeches were full of multiple untruths. He threw out so many accusations that the facts could never catch up.

Senators treated McCarthy as a crude outsider in their exclusive club, but voters in 1950 turned against his most prominent opponents. In 1951, McCarthy even called George Marshall, now serving as secretary of defense, an agent of Communism. The idea was ludicrous. Marshall was one of the most upright Americans of his generation, the architect of victory in World War II and a key contributor to the stabilization of Europe. Nevertheless, McCarthy was so popular that the Republicans featured him at their 1952 convention. That fall, the Re-

Senator Joseph McCarthy points to Oregon on an organizational map implying Communist Party organization in the United States.

UPI/Corbis/Bettmann

publicans' presidential candidate, Dwight Eisenhower, appeared on the same campaign platform with McCarthy and conspicuously failed to defend George Marshall—who was chiefly responsible for Eisenhower's fast-track career.

McCarthy's personal crudeness made him a media star but eventually undermined him. Given control of the Senate Committee on Government Operations in 1953, one of his investigations targeted the U.S. Army's promotion of an army dentist with a supposedly subversive background. Two months of televised hearings revealed the emptiness of the charges. The cameras also put McCarthy's style on trial. "Have you no decency?" asked the army's lawyer Joseph Welch at one point.

The end came quickly. McCarthy's "favorable" rating in the polls plummeted. The comic strip *Pogo* began to feature a foolishly menacing figure with McCarthy's face named Simple J. Malarkey. The U.S. Senate finally voted 67 to 22 in December 1954 to condemn McCarthy for conduct "unbecoming a Member of the Senate." When he died from alchoholism in 1957, he was repudiated by the Senate and ignored by the media.

UNDERSTANDING MCCARTHYISM

The antisubversive campaign now called **McCarthyism**, however, died a slower death. Legislation, such as the Internal Security Act (1950) and the Immigration and Nationality Act (1952), remained as tools of political repression. HUAC continued to mount investigations as late as the 1960s.

Fear of Communist subversion reached deep into American society. In the early 1950s, Cincinnati's National League baseball team tried out a new name. Harking back to its origins as the Red Stockings, the team was now the "Redlegs," not the "Reds," to avoid associations with Communism. Cities and states required loyalty oaths from their employees; Ohio even required oaths from recipients of unemployment compensation.

In retrospect, at least four factors made Americans afraid of Communist subversion. One was a legitimate but exaggerated concern about atomic spies. A second was an undercurrent of anti-Semitism and nativism, for many labor organizers and Communist party members (like the Rosenbergs) had Jewish and eastern European backgrounds. Third was Southern and Western resentment of the nation's Ivy League elite. Most general, finally, was that it was basically reassuring if Soviet and Chinese Communist successes were the result of American traitors rather than Communist strengths.

Partisan politics mobilized the fears and resentments into a political force. From 1946 through 1952, the conservative wing of the Republican party used the Red Scare to attack New Dealers and liberal Democrats. The Republican elite used McCarthy until they won control of the presidency and Congress in 1952 and then abandoned him.

McCarthyism Anti-Communist attitudes and actions associated with Senator Joe McCarthy in the early 1950s, including smear tactics and innuendo.

CONCLUSION

The Cold War stayed cool because each side achieved its essential goals. The Soviet Union controlled eastern Europe, while the United States built increasingly strong ties with the NATO nations and Japan. Though the result was a stalemate that would last through the 1980s, it nevertheless absorbed huge shares of Soviet and American resources and conditioned the thinking of an entire generation.

The shift from prewar isolationism to postwar internationalism was one of the most important changes in the nation's history. To many of its advocates, internationalism represented a commitment to spread political democracy to other nations. As the 1950s and 1960s would show, the results often contradicted the ideal when the United States forcibly imposed its will on other peoples. However, the new internationalism highlighted and helped change domestic racial attitudes.

The Truman years brought increasing stability. The economic chaos of 1946 faded quickly. By identifying liberalism at home with anti-Communism abroad, Truman's efforts to define a vital center helped protect the New Deal. If the Republicans had won in 1948, they might have dismantled the New Deal. By 1952, both presidential candidates affirmed the consensus that placed economic opportunity at the center of the national agenda. The suburban housing boom seemed to turn the dream of prosperity into reality for millions of families.

The United States emerged from the Truman years remarkably prosperous. It was also more secure from international threats than many nervous Americans appreciated. The years from 1946 to 1952 set the themes for a generation that believed that the United States could do whatever it set its mind to. As the world moved slowly toward greater stability in the 1950s, Americans were ready for a decade of confidence.

Summary

Launching the Great Boom Americans feared demobilization would bring inflation and unemployment, but the immediate postwar years ushered in an economic expansion that would last a quarter century; the resulting prosperity would finance a military buildup and activist foreign policy. Veterans benefited from VA mortgages and the GI Bill of Rights; the need for family housing fueled a boom and suburbs expanded; the housing boom was a product of the consumer and baby booms. The first steps toward civil rights for African Americans were taken; the crusade for freedom abroad had contrasted with the racial discrimination faced at home.

Truman, Republicans, and the Fair Deal The economic gains of the postwar years propelled Americans toward the political center; after depression and war they wanted prosperity. In his campaign for a full term as president in 1948, Truman faced third-party candidates in addition to Republican Thomas Dewey. Truman appealed to average Americans and his victory astounded the pollsters. The Fair Deal showed that Americans liked what the New Deal had given them but were hesitant about major new initiatives.

Confronting the Soviet Union By 1947 the former allies were involved in a conflict that came to be known as the Cold War. Both sides assumed the other's ill will, spent vast amounts on military forces and atomic weapons, and competed for political advantage around the globe. As the "iron curtain" divided Europe, the Marshall Plan committed the United States to aid European recovery. The announcement of the Truman Doctrine brought Soviet reactions climaxing in the Berlin blockade; the formation of the CIA, NSC, and signing mutual defense pacts such as NATO amounted to a revolution in American foreign policy.

Cold War and Hot War The news that the Soviet Union and China had developed nuclear bombs helped begin the "arms race" and the fear of nuclear war multiplied the apprehensions of the Cold War. America's strategic goals were outlined in NSC-68: America would use force to counter communist aggression: The first use of this policy was in Korea. North Korea, helped by Soviet equipment and Chinese training, attacked South Korea. The Korean War, which lasted until 1953, had global consequences and was a preview of another war to come.

The Second Red Scare The Korean War reinforced the second Red Scare, an assault on civil liberties that dwarfed the Red Scare of 1919–1920. The Cold War fanned fears of Communist subversion on American soil. Legitimate concerns about espionage mixed with suspicions that Communist sympathizers in high places were helping China and the Soviet Union. Loyalty programs and the Congressional hunt for subversives such as that by Senator Joseph McCarthy showed how deep the fear of Communists was in the country.

REVIEW QUESTIONS

1. What were the key differences between Harry Truman and congressional Republicans about the legacy of the New Deal?

2. How did the postwar years expand opportunity for veterans and members of the working class? How did they limit opportunities for women?

3. What foreign policy priorities did the United States set after 1945?

4. How did the Cold War change character in 1949 and 1950?

KEY TERMS

Berlin blockade (p. 724)
Central Intelligence Agency (p. 724)
Cold War (p. 714)
Council of Economic Advisers (p. 715)
Dixiecrats (p. 719)
GI Bill of Rights (p. 716)
House Committee on Un-American Activities (HUAC) (p. 730)

International Monetary Fund (p. 722)
Korean War (p. 728)
Levittown (p. 717)
Marshall Plan (p. 723)
McCarthyism (p. 733)
National Security Council (p. 724)
National Security Council Paper 68 (NSC-68) (p. 727)

North Atlantic Treaty Organization (NATO) (p. 724)
Redlining (p. 717)
Taft-Hartley Act (p. 715)
Truman Doctrine (p. 723)
World Bank (p. 722)

WHERE TO LEARN MORE

🗐 **Harry S Truman National Historical Site, Library, and Museum, Independence, Missouri.** The museum has exhibits on Truman's political career and U.S. history during his administration. Also in Independence is the Harry S Truman Courtroom and Office, with exhibits on his early career. **www.nps.gov/hstr/**

🗐 **General Douglas MacArthur Memorial, Norfolk, Virginia.** The MacArthur Memorial in downtown Norfolk commemorates the career of a key figure in shaping the postwar world.

🗐 **United Nations Headquarters, New York, New York.** A tour of the United Nations complex in New York is a reminder of the new organizations for international cooperation that emerged from World War II. **www.un.org**

 For additional study resources for this chapter, go to:
www.prenhall.com/goldfield/chapter27

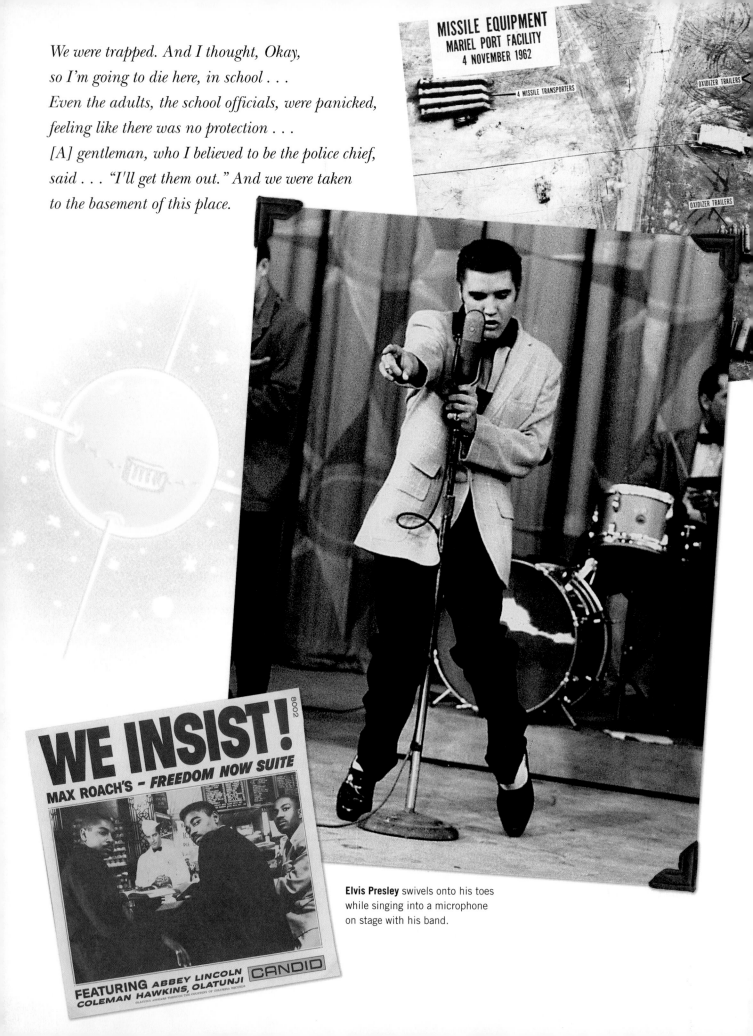

We were trapped. And I thought, Okay,
so I'm going to die here, in school . . .
Even the adults, the school officials, were panicked,
feeling like there was no protection . . .
[A] gentleman, who I believed to be the police chief,
said . . . "I'll get them out." And we were taken
to the basement of this place.

MISSILE EQUIPMENT
MARIEL PORT FACILITY
4 NOVEMBER 1962

4 MISSILE TRANSPORTERS

OXIDIZER TRAILERS

OXIDIZER TRAILERS

8002

WE INSIST!

MAX ROACH'S - FREEDOM NOW SUITE

CANDID

FEATURING ABBEY LINCOLN
COLEMAN HAWKINS, OLATUNJI

Elvis Presley swivels onto his toes
while singing into a microphone
on stage with his band.

28

THE CONFIDENT YEARS
1953–1964

HOW DID the "Decade of Affluence" alter social and religious life in America?

WHAT IMPACT did Dwight Eisenhower's foreign policy have on U.S. relations with the Soviet Union?

WHAT WAS John F. Kennedy's approach to dealing with the Soviet Union?

WHAT WAS the significance of *Brown* v. *Board of Education of Topeka?*

HOW DID Lyndon B. Johnson continue the domestic agenda inherited from the Kennedy administration?

1964

1953

The first day I was able to enter Central High School [in Little Rock, Arkansas, September 23, 1957], what I felt inside was terrible, wrenching, awful fear. On the car radio I could hear that there was a mob. I knew what a mob meant and I know that the sounds that came from the crowd were very angry. So we entered the side of the building, very, very fast. Even as we entered there were people running after us, people tripping other people. . . . There has never been in my life any stark terror or any fear akin to that.

I'd only been in the school a couple of hours and by that time it was apparent that the mob was just overrunning the school. Policemen were throwing down their badges and the mob was getting past the wooden sawhorses because the police would no longer fight their own in order to protect us. So we were all called into the principal's office, and there was great fear that we would not get out of this building. We were trapped. And I thought, Okay, so I'm going to die here, in school. . . . Even the adults, the school officials, were panicked, feeling like there was no protection. . . . [A] gentleman, who I believed to be the police chief, said . . . "I'll get them out." And we were taken to the basement of this place. And we were put into two cars, grayish blue Fords. And the man instructed the drivers, he said, "Once you start driving, do not stop." And he told us to put our heads down. "This guy revved up his engine and he came up out of the bowels of this building, and as he came up, I could just see hands reaching across this car, I could hear the yelling, I could see guns, and he was told not to stop. "If you hit somebody, you keep rolling, 'cause the kids are dead." And he did just that, and he didn't hit anybody, but he certainly was forceful and aggressive in the way he exited this driveway, because people tried to stop him and he didn't stop. He dropped me off at home. And I remember saying, "Thank you for the ride," and I should've said, "Thank you for my life."

Melba Patillo Beals in Henry Hampton and Steve Frayer, eds., *Voices of Freedom: An Oral History of the Civil Rights Movement from the 1950s through the 1980s* (New York: Bantam, 1990).

IMAGE KEY

for pages 736–737

a. Russian nuclear missiles photographed at Mariel Port facility in Cuba, with illustrative tags describing various equipment.

b. A drawing of the Sputnik satellite appears on a playing card from a card game about the space race.

c. Elvis Presley swivels onto his toes while singing into a microphone on stage with his band.

d. The album cover of "We Insist!" by Max Roach depicts African American men at a lunch counter during a sit-in.

e. 1960 Presidential candidates Richard Milhous Nixon and John F. Kennedy during a televised debate.

f. Suburban family standing in front of their 1948 Levittown house in 1950.

g. Children huddle below their desks in an elementary school classroom during an air raid drill.

h. President Kennedy's TV address on the Cuban Missile Crisis.

i. Elizabeth Eckford is heckled by a white student while integrating Central High School in Little Rock, Arkansas in 1957. Many other white students surround the girl.

j. LBJ takes the oath of office on the ride back to Washington, D.C. from Dallas, after the assassination of JFK.

MELBA PATTILLO was one of the nine African-American students who entered previously all-white Central High in 1957. Her enrollment in the high school, where she managed to last through a year of harassment, was a symbolic step in the journey toward greater racial equality in American society. School integration in Little Rock implemented the U.S. Supreme Court decision in the case of *Brown* v. *Board of Education* in 1954, which declared that racially segregated schools violated the mandate that all citizens receive equal protection of the law. The violence with which some white residents of Little Rock responded, and the courage of the students, was a key episode in the civil rights revolution that spanned roughly a decade from the *Brown* decision to the Voting Rights Act of 1965.

The struggle for full civil rights for all Americans was rooted in national ideals, but it was also shaped by the continuing tensions of the Cold War. President Dwight Eisenhower acted against his own inclinations and sent federal troops to keep the peace in Little Rock in part because he worried about public opinion in other nations. As the United States and the Soviet Union maneuvered for influence in Africa and Asia, domestic events sometimes loomed large in foreign relations. Few Americans questioned the necessity of the Cold War— or of America's ultimate triumph. This consensus gave U.S. policy an overarching goal of containment but also narrowed American options by casting issues at home and abroad in terms of the U.S.-Soviet rivalry.

Melba Pattillo's life after Little Rock also reflects the increasing economic opportunities available to most Americans. She eventually graduated from San Francisco State University, earned a master's degree from Columbia University, and become a television reporter and writer. San Francisco State, which was rapidly expanding, was itself part of the great expansion of higher education that helped millions of Americans move into middle-class jobs and neighborhoods. The prosperous years from 1953 to 1964 spread the economic promise of the 1940s across American society. Young couples could afford large families and new houses. Labor unions grew conservative because cooperation with big business offered immediate gains for their members.

Despite challenges at home and abroad, Americans were confident during the decade after the Korean War. They expected corporations to use scientific research to craft new products and medical researchers to conquer diseases. When the USSR challenged U.S. preeminence and launched the first artificial space satellite in 1957, Americans redoubled efforts to regain what they considered their rightful world leadership in science and technology.

A DECADE OF AFFLUENCE

Americans in the 1950s believed in the basic strength of the United States. Examples of self-assurance were everywhere. Television's *General Electric Theater* was third in the ratings in 1956–1957. Every week, its host, Ronald Reagan, a popular Hollywood lead from the late 1930s, stated, "At General Electric, progress is our most important product." Large, technologically sophisticated corporations were introducing new marvels: Orlon sweaters and Saran Wrap, long-playing records and Polaroid cameras.

Social and intellectual conformity assured a united front. National leaders argued that strong families were bulwarks against Communism and that churchgoing inoculated people against subversive ideas. Under the lingering cloud of McCarthyism, the range of political ideas that influenced government policy was narrower than in the 1930s and 1940s. Nevertheless, disaffected critics began to voice the discontents that exploded in the 1960s and 1970s.

HOW DID the "Decade of Affluence" alter social and religious life in America?

WHAT'S GOOD FOR GENERAL MOTORS

Dwight Eisenhower presided over the prosperity of the 1950s. Both Democrats and Republicans had courted him as a presidential candidate in 1948. Four years later, he picked the Republicans and easily defeated Democrat Adlai Stevenson, the moderately liberal governor of Illinois.

Publicists tried a variety of labels for Eisenhower's domestic views: "progressive moderation," "New Republicanism," "dynamic conservatism." Satisfied with postwar America, Eisenhower accepted much of the New Deal but saw little need for further reform. In a 1959 poll, liberals considered him a fellow liberal and conservatives thought him a conservative.

Eisenhower's first secretary of defense, "Engine Charlie" Wilson, had headed General Motors. At his Senate confirmation hearing, he proclaimed, "For years,

I thought what was good for the country was good for General Motors and vice versa." Wilson's statement captured a central theme of the 1950s.

The economy in the 1950s gave Americans much to like. Between 1950 and 1964, output grew by a solid 3.2 percent per year. Automobile production, on which dozens of other industries depended, neared 8 million vehicles per year in the mid-1950s; less than 1 percent of new car sales were imports.

In the 1950s American workers' productivity, or output per worker, increased steadily. Average wages rose faster than consumer prices in nine of eleven years between 1953 and 1964. The steel and auto industries gave their workers a middle-class way of life. In turn, labor leaders lost interest in radical changes in American society. In 1955, the older and politically more conservative American Federation of Labor absorbed the younger Congress of Industrial Organizations. The new AFL-CIO positioned itself as a partner in prosperity and foe of Communism at home and abroad.

Industrial cities offered members of minority groups factory jobs at wages that could support a family. African Americans worked through the Urban League, the National Association of Colored Women, and other race-oriented groups to secure fair employment laws and jobs with large corporations. Many Puerto Rican migrants to New York found steady work in the Brooklyn Navy Yard. Mexican-American families in San Antonio benefited from maintenance jobs at the city's military bases.

However, there were never enough family-wage jobs for all of the African-American and Latino workers who continued to move to Northern and Western cities. Many Mexican Americans were still migrant farm laborers and workers in nonunionized sweatshops. Minority workers were usually the first to suffer from the erosion of industrial jobs that began in the 1960s.

To cut costs and accelerate Native American assimilation, Congress pushed the policy of termination between 1954 and 1962. The government sold tribal land and assets, distributed the proceeds among tribal members, and terminated its treaty relationship with the tribe. Termination cut thousands of Indians adrift from the security of tribal organizations. The Bureau of Indian Affairs also encouraged Indians to move to large cities, but jobs were often unavailable.

RESHAPING URBAN AMERICA

If Eisenhower's administration opted for the status quo on many issues, it nevertheless reshaped American cities around an agenda of economic development. In 1954, Congress transformed the public housing program into urban renewal. Cities used federal funds to replace low-rent businesses and run-down housing on the fringes of their downtowns with new hospitals, civic centers, sports arenas, office towers, and luxury apartments.

Los Angeles demolished the seedy Victorian mansions of Bunker Hill, just northwest of downtown, for a music center and bank towers. A mile to the north was Chavez Ravine, whose Mexican-American population lived in substandard housing but maintained a lively community. When conservative opposition blocked plans for public housing, the residents were evicted, and Dodger Stadium was built. Here as elsewhere, urban showplaces rose at the expense of minority groups.

The Eisenhower administration also revolutionized American transportation. The **Federal Highway Act of 1956** created a national system of Interstate and Defense Highways. The legislation wrapped a program to build 41,000 miles of freeways in the language of the Cold War. The roads would be wide and strong enough for trucks hauling military hardware; they were also supposed to make it easy to evacuate cities in case of a Soviet attack.

QUICK REVIEW

America's Economy in the 1950s

- 1950–1964: U.S. economy grew at a rate of 3.2 percent per year.
- Productivity increased steadily.
- Wages rose faster than consumer prices.

Federal Highway Act of 1956
Measure that provided federal funding to build a nationwide system of interstate and defense highways.

Interstates halved the time of city-to-city travel. They were good for General Motors, the steel industry, and the concrete industry, requiring the construction equivalent of sixty Panama Canals. The highways promoted long-distance trucking at the expense of railroads. As with urban renewal, the bulldozers most often plowed through African-American or Latino neighborhoods.

The beltways or perimeter highways that began to ring most large cities made it easier and more profitable to develop new subdivisions and factory sites than to reinvest in city centers. Federal grants for sewers and other basic facilities further cut suburban costs. Continuing the pattern of the late 1940s, suburban growth added a million new single-family houses per year.

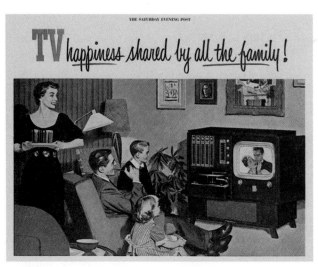

Television sets were major pieces of living room furniture in the 1950s. This 1951 Motorola ad from Woman's Home Companion emphasizes television as a source of family togetherness, a popular theme in the 1950s.

Gaslight Advertising Archives, Inc. NY

COMFORT ON CREDIT

The 1930s had taught Americans to avoid debt. The 1950s taught them to buy on credit. Families financed their new houses with 90 percent FHA mortgages and 100 percent VA mortgages. They filled the rooms by signing installment contracts at furniture and appliance stores and charging the drapes and carpeting on department store credit cards. The value of consumer debt, excluding home mortgages, tripled from 1952 to 1964.

New forms of marketing facilitated credit-based consumerism. The first large-scale suburban shopping center was Northgate in Seattle, which assembled all the pieces of the full-grown mall. By the end of the decade, developers were building malls with 1 million square feet of shopping floor. At the start of the 1970s, the universal credit card (Visa, MasterCard) made shopping even easier.

Where cities of the early twentieth century had been built around the public transportation of streetcars and subways, the 1950s depended on private automobiles. Interstate highways sucked retail business from small-town main streets to interchanges on the edge of town. Nationally franchised motels and fast-food restaurants sprang up along suburban shopping strips, pioneered by Holiday Inn (1952) and McDonald's (nationally franchised in 1955).

More extreme than the mall were entirely new environments for high-intensity consumption and entertainment that appeared in the Southwest, such as Las Vegas with its hotel-casinos. Opening in Orange County, California, in 1955, Disneyland was safe and artificial— a never-ending state fair without the smells and dust.

THE NEW FIFTIES FAMILY

Family life in the Eisenhower years departed from historic patterns. Prosperity allowed children to finish school and young adults to marry right after high school. Young women faced strong social pressure to pursue husbands rather than careers. The proportion of single adults reached its twentieth-century low in 1960. At all social levels, young people married quickly and had an average of three children spaced closely together. Family activities replaced the street corner for kids and the neighborhood tavern for men. Strong families, said experts, defended against Communism by teaching American values.

Television was made to order for the family-centered fifties. By 1960, fully 87 percent of households had sets. Popular entertainment was now enjoyed in the privacy of the home, rather than in a crowd. Situation comedies were the most popular programs. Successful shows depicted families who had northern European names and lived in single-family houses with friendly neighbors representing the 1950s ideal of American success.

28–1
Ladies Home Journal, "Young Mother" (1956)

QUICK REVIEW

Family Life
- Young women faced pressure to marry early and forego careers.
- Young people married young and had an average of three kids.
- Television took on a central role in family life.

Television programming helped limit women's roles by power of example. Women in the fifties had a smaller share of new college degrees and professional jobs. Despite millions of new electric appliances, the time spent on housework *increased*. Magazines proclaimed that proper families maintained distinct roles for dad and mom, who was urged to find fulfillment in a well-scrubbed house and children.

But in reality the number of employed women reached new highs. By 1960, nearly 35 percent of all women held jobs, including 7.5 million mothers with children under 17.

INVENTING TEENAGERS

Teenagers in the 1950s joined adults as consumers of movies, clothes, and automobiles. Advertisers tapped and expanded the growing youth market by promoting a distinct "youth culture," an idea that became omnipresent in the 1960s and 1970s. While psychologists pontificated on the special problems of adolescence, many cities matched their high schools to the social status of their students: college-prep curricula for middle-class neighborhoods, vocational and technical schools for future factory workers, and separate schools or tracks for African Americans and Latinos.

All teenagers shared rock-and-roll, a new music of the mid-1950s that adapted the rhythm-and-blues of urban blacks for a white mass market. Rock music drew vitality from poor white Southerners (Buddy Holly, Elvis Presley), Hispanics (Richie Valens), and, in the 1960s, the British working class (the Beatles). Record producers played up the association between rock music and youthful rebellion.

TURNING TO RELIGION

Leaders from Dwight Eisenhower to FBI Director J. Edgar Hoover advocated churchgoing as an antidote for Communism. Regular church attendance grew from 48 percent of the population in 1940 to 63 percent in 1960. Congress created new connections between religion and government when it added "under God" to the Pledge of Allegiance in 1954 and required currency to bear the phrase "In God We Trust" in 1955.

Radio and television preachers added a new dimension to religious life. Bishop Fulton J. Sheen brought vigorous anti-Communism and Catholic doctrine to millions of TV viewers who would never have entered a Catholic church. Norman Vincent Peale blended popular psychology with Protestantism. His book *The Power of Positive Thinking* (1952) told readers to "stop worrying and start living" and sold millions of copies.

Another strand in the religious revival was revitalized evangelical and fundamentalist churches. During the 1950s, the theologically and socially conservative Southern Baptists became the largest Protestant denomination. Evangelist Billy Graham continued the grand American tradition of the mass revival meeting. Graham was a pioneer in the resurgence of evangelical Christianity that stressed an individual approach to belief and social issues. "Before we can solve the economic, philosophical, and political problems in the world," he said, "pride, greed, lust, and sin are going to have to be erased."

African-American churches were community institutions as well as religious organizations. Black congregations in Northern cities swelled in the postwar years and often supported extensive social service programs. In Southern cities, churches were centers for community pride and training grounds for the emerging civil rights movement.

Boundaries between many Protestant denominations blurred as church leaders emphasized national unity. Supreme Court decisions sowed the seeds for later

QUICK REVIEW

Teenagers

- Teenagers became consumers in the 1950s.
- Advertisers directed their message at the youth market.
- Teenagers developed a shared culture.

CHRONOLOGY

1953	CIA-backed coup returns the Shah to power in Iran. USSR detonates hydrogen bomb.	**1961**	Bay of Pigs invasion fails. Kennedy establishes the Peace Corps. Vienna summit fails. Freedom rides are held in the Deep South. Berlin crisis leads to construction of the Berlin Wall.
1954	Vietnamese defeat the French. Geneva conference divides Vietnam. United States and allies form SEATO. Supreme Court decides *Brown* v. *Board of Education of Topeka* CIA overthrows the government of Guatemala. China provokes a crisis over Quemoy and Matsu.	**1962**	John Glenn orbits the earth. Cuban missile crisis brings the world to the brink. Michael Harrington publishes *The Other America.*
1955	Salk polio vaccine is announced. Black riders boycott Montgomery, Alabama, bus system. USSR forms the Warsaw Pact. AFL and CIO merge.	**1963**	Civil rights demonstrations rend Birmingham. Civil rights activists march in Washington. Betty Friedan publishes *The Feminine Mystique.* Limited Test Ban Treaty is signed. Ngo Dinh Diem is assassinated in South Vietnam. President Kennedy is assassinated.
1956	Interstate Highway Act is passed. Soviets repress Hungarian revolt. Israel, France, and Britain invade Egypt.	**1964**	Civil Rights Act is passed. Freedom Summer is organized in Mississippi. Office of Economic Opportunity is created. Gulf of Tonkin Resolution is passed. Wilderness Act launches the modern environmental movement.
1957	U.S. Army maintains law and order in Little Rock. Soviet Union launches *Sputnik.*		
1958	United States and USSR voluntarily suspend nuclear tests.	**1965**	Medical Care Act establishes Medicare and Medicaid. Elementary and Secondary Education Act extends direct federal aid to local schools. Selma-Montgomery march climaxes era of nonviolent civil rights demonstrations. Voting Rights Act suspends literacy tests.
1959	Fidel Castro takes power in Cuba. Nikita Khrushchev visits the United States.		
1960	U-2 shot down over Russia. Sit-in movement begins in Greensboro, North Carolina.		

political activism among evangelical Christians. In *Engel* v. *Vitale* (1962), the Court said that public schools could not require children to start the school day with group prayer. *Abington Township* v. *Schempp* (1963) prohibited devotional Bible reading in the schools. Such decisions alarmed many evangelicals.

The Gospel of Prosperity

Writers and intellectuals often marveled at the prosperity of Eisenhower's America. William H. Whyte Jr. searched American corporations for the changing character of the United States in *The Organization Man* (1956). Historian David Potter brilliantly analyzed Americans in *People of Plenty* (1954), contending that their national character had been shaped by the abundance of natural resources. In *The Affluent Society* (1958), economist John Kenneth Galbraith predicted that the challenge of the future would be to ensure the fair distribution of national wealth.

Officially, the American message was that abundance was a natural by-product of a free society. In fact, it was easy to present prosperity as a goal in itself, as Vice President Richard Nixon did when he represented the United States at a technology exposition in Moscow in 1959. The American exhibit included a complete six-room ranch house. In its "miracle kitchen," Nixon engaged Soviet Communist party chairman Nikita Khrushchev in a carefully planned "kitchen debate." The vice president claimed that the "most important thing" for Americans was "the right to choose": "We have so many different manufacturers and many different kinds of washing machines so that the housewives have a choice."

THE UNDERSIDE OF AFFLUENCE

The most basic criticism of the ideology of prosperity was the simplest— that affluence concealed vast inequalities. Michael Harrington wrote *The Other America* (1962) to remind Americans about the "underdeveloped nation" of 40 to 50 million poor people who had missed the last two decades of prosperity.

C. Wright Mills found dangers in the way that the Cold War distorted American society at the top. *The Power Elite* (1956) described an interlocking alliance of big government, big business, and the military. The losers in a permanent war economy, said Mills, were economic and political democracy.

Other critics targeted the alienating effects of consumerism and the conformity of homogeneous suburbs. Sociologist David Riesman saw suburbia as the home of "other-directed" individuals who lacked inner convictions.

There was far greater substance to increasing dissatisfaction among women. In 1963, Betty Friedan's book *The Feminine Mystique* followed numerous articles in *McCall's*, *Redbook*, and the *Ladies' Home Journal* about the unhappiness of college-educated women who were expected to find total satisfaction in kids and cooking. What Friedan called "the problem that has no name" was a sense of personal emptiness. "I got up one morning," remembered Geraldine Bean, "and I got my kids off to school. I went in to comb my hair and wash my face, and I stood in front of the bathroom mirror crying . . . because at eight-thirty in the morning I had my children off to school. I had my housework done. There was absolutely nothing for me to do the rest of the day." She went on to earn a Ph.D. and win election to the board of regents of the University of Colorado.

FACING OFF WITH THE SOVIET UNION

Americans got a reassuring new face in the White House in 1953, but not new policies toward the world. The United States pushed ahead in an arms race with the Soviet Union, stood guard on the borders of China and the Soviet empire, and judged political changes in Latin America, Africa, and Asia for their effect on the global balance of power.

WHY WE LIKED IKE

In the late twentieth century, few leaders were able to master both domestic policy and foreign affairs. Some presidents, such as Lyndon Johnson, were more adept at social problems than diplomacy. In contrast, Richard Nixon and George H.W. Bush were more interested in the world outside the United States.

Dwight Eisenhower was one of these "foreign policy presidents." He had helped hold together the alliance that defeated Nazi Germany and built NATO into an effective force in 1951–1952. He then sought the Republican nomination, he said, to ensure that the United States kept its international commitments. He sealed his victory in 1952 by emphasizing foreign policy expertise, telling a Detroit campaign audience that "to bring the Korean war to an early and honorable end . . . requires a personal trip to Korea. I shall make that trip . . . I shall go to Korea."

Many of the Eisenhower administration's accomplishments were things that didn't happen. Eisenhower refused to dismantle the social programs of the New Deal. He exerted American political and military power around the globe but avoided war.

It helped Eisenhower's political agenda if Americans thought of him as a smiling grandfather. The "Ike" who gave rambling, incoherent answers at White House press conferences was controlling information and keeping the opposition

QUICK REVIEW

Critique of the Ideology of Prosperity

◆ Some critics argued that affluence concealed inequality.

◆ Others were concerned about the alienating effects of consumerism.

◆ Many women became dissatisfied with their assigned role in society.

WHAT IMPACT did Dwight Eisenhower's foreign policy have on U.S. relations with the Soviet Union?

guessing. When his press secretary advised him to duck questions at one press conference, Ike replied, "Don't worry, I'll just confuse them." He was easily re-elected in 1956.

A BALANCE OF TERROR

The backdrop for U.S. foreign policy was the growing capacity for mutual nuclear annihilation. The old balance of power had become a balance of terror.

The Eisenhower administration's doctrine of massive retaliation took advantage of superior American technology while economizing on military spending. Eisenhower compared uncontrolled military spending to crucifying humankind on a "cross of iron." "Every gun that is fired," he warned, "every warship launched, every rocket fired signifies . . . a theft from those who hunger and are not fed, those who are cold and not clothed." The administration concentrated military spending where the nation already had the greatest advantage—on atomic weapons, instead of attempting to match the land armies of the Soviet Union and China. In response to any serious attack, the United States would direct maximum force against the homeland of the aggressor. The National Security Council in 1953 made reliance on "massive retaliatory damage" by nuclear weapons official policy.

The doctrine grew even more fearful as the Soviet Union developed its own hydrogen bombs. The chairman of the Atomic Energy Commission terrified the American people by mentioning casually that the Soviets could now obliterate New York City. Signs for air raid shelters posted on downtown buildings, air raid drills in schools, and appearance of radioactivity in milk supplies in the form of the isotope strontium 90 carried by fallout made the atomic threat very immediate.

The USSR added to worries about atomic war by launching the world's first artificial satellite. On the first Sunday of October 1957, Americans discovered that *Sputnik*— Russian for "satellite"— was orbiting the earth. The Soviets soon lifted a dog into orbit while U.S. rockets fizzled on the pad. Soviet propagandists claimed that their technological "first" showed the superiority of Communism, and Americans wondered if the United States had lost its edge. The new **National Aeronautics and Space Administration (NASA)** took over the satellite program in 1958.

The crisis was more apparent than real. The combination of Soviet rocketry and nuclear capacity created alarm about a missile gap. The USSR was said to be building hundreds of intercontinental ballistic missiles (ICBMs) to overwhelm American air defenses designed to intercept piloted bombers. Although there was no such gap, Eisenhower was unwilling to reveal secret information that might have allayed public anxiety.

CONTAINMENT IN ACTION

Someone who heard only the campaign speeches in 1952 might have expected sharp foreign policy changes under Eisenhower, but there was more continuity than change. John Foster Dulles, Eisenhower's secretary of state, had attacked the Democrats as defeatists and appeasers. He demanded that the United States liberate eastern Europe from Soviet control and encourage Jiang Jieshi to attack Communist China. In 1956, Dulles proudly claimed that tough-minded diplomacy had repeatedly brought the United States to the verge of war: "We walked to the brink and looked it in the face. We took strong action."

In fact, Eisenhower viewed the Cold War in the same terms as Truman. Caution replaced campaign rhetoric about "rolling back" Communism. Around the periphery of the Communist nations, from eastern Asia to the Middle East to Europe, the United States accepted the existing sphere of Communist influence but attempted to block its growth, a policy most Americans accepted.

WHERE TO LEARN MORE

Kansas Cosmosphere, Hutchinson, Kansas
www.cosmo.org

WHERE TO LEARN MORE

National Air and Space Museum, Washington, D.C.
www.nasm.edu

National Aeronautics and Space Administration (NASA)   Federal agency created in 1958 to manage American space flights and exploration.

The American worldview assumed both the right and the need to intervene in the affairs of other nations, especially in Latin America, Asia, and Africa. Policymakers saw these nations as markets for U.S. products and sources of vital raw materials. When political disturbances arose in these states, the United States blamed Soviet meddling to justify U.S. intervention. If Communism could not be rolled back in eastern Europe, the CIA could still undermine anti-American governments in the third world. The Soviets themselves took advantage of local revolutions even when they did not instigate them.

Twice during Eisenhower's first term, the CIA subverted democratically elected governments that seemed to threaten U.S. interests. In Iran, which had nationalized British and U.S. oil companies in an effort to break the hold of western corporations, the CIA in 1953 backed a coup that toppled the government and helped the young Shah, or monarch, gain control. The Shah then cooperated with the United States until his overthrow in 1979. In Guatemala, the leftist government was upsetting the United Fruit Company. When the Guatemalans accepted weapons from the Communist bloc in 1954, the CIA imposed a regime friendly to U.S. business (see Map 28–1).

For most Americans in 1953, democracy in Iran was far less important than ending the war in Korea and stabilizing relations with China. Eisenhower declined to escalate the Korean War by blockading China and sending more U.S. ground forces. Instead he shifted atomic bombs to Okinawa, only 400 miles from China. The nuclear threat, along with the continued cost of the war on both sides, brought the Chinese to a truce that left Korea divided into two nations.

In Vietnam, on China's southern border, France was fighting to maintain its colonial rule against rebels who combined Communist ideology with fervor for national independence under the leadership of Ho Chi Minh. The United States picked up three-quarters of the costs, but the French military position collapsed in 1954. The French had had enough, and Eisenhower was unwilling to join another Asian war. A Geneva peace conference in 1954 "temporarily" divided Vietnam into a Communist north and a non-Communist south and scheduled elections for a single Vietnamese government.

The United States then replaced France as the supporter of pro-Western Vietnamese in the south. Washington's client was Ngo Dinh Diem, an anti-Communist from South Vietnam's Roman Catholic elite. U.S. officials encouraged Diem to put off the elections and backed his efforts to construct an authoritarian South Vietnam. Ho meanwhile consolidated the northern half as a Communist state that claimed to be the legitimate government for all Vietnam. The United States further reinforced containment in Asia by creating the **Southeast Asia Treaty Organization (SEATO)** in 1954.

Halfway around the world, there was a new crisis when three American friends—France, Britain, and Israel—ganged up on Egypt, each for its own reasons. On October 29, 1956, Israel attacked Egypt. A week later, British and French forces attempted to seize the canal. The United States forced a quick cease-fire, partly to maintain its standing with oil-producing Arab nations. The war left Britain and France dependent on American oil that Eisenhower would not provide until they left Egypt.

In Europe, Eisenhower accepted the status quo because conflicts there could result in nuclear war. In 1956, challenges to Communist rule arose in East Germany, Poland, and Hungary and threatened to break up the Soviet empire. The Soviets replaced liberal Communists in East Germany and Poland with hard-liners. In Hungary, however, open warfare broke out. Hungarian freedom fighters in Budapest used rocks and fire bombs against Soviet tanks while pleading in vain for Western aid. NATO would not risk war with the USSR. Tens of thousands of Hungarians died and 200,000 fled when the Soviets crushed the resistance.

QUICK REVIEW

U.S. Intervention Abroad

◆ Many Americans assumed the U.S. had a right to intervene abroad.

◆ Eisenhower used the CIA to subvert democratically elected governments in Iran and Guatemala.

◆ The U.S. replaced France as the supporter of pro-Western Vietnamese in the south.

Southeast Asia Treaty Organization (SEATO)   Mutual defense alliance signed in 1954 by the United States, Britain, France, Thailand, Pakistan, the Philippines, Australia, and New Zealand.

MAP EXPLORATION

To explore an interactive version of this map, go to **http://www.prenhall.com/goldfield2/map28.1**

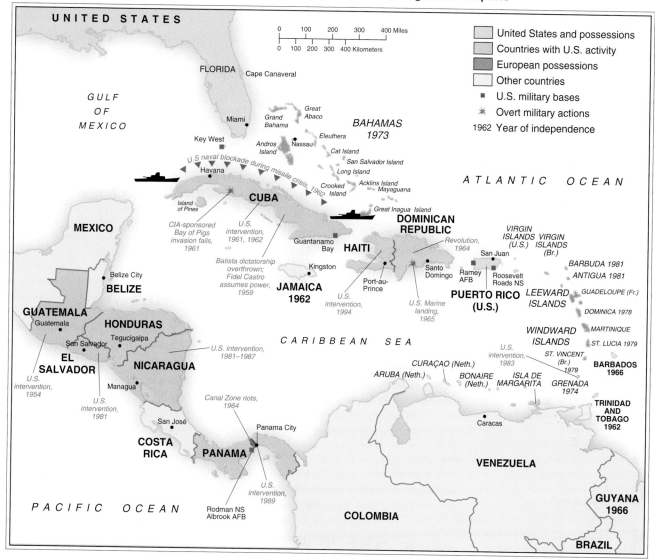

MAP 28–1

U.S. Intervention around the Caribbean since 1954   The United States has long kept a careful eye on the politics of neighboring nations to its south. In the second half of the twentieth century, the United States has frequently used military assistance or force to influence or intervene in Caribbean and Central American nations. The most common purpose has been to counter or undermine left-leaning governments; some interventions, as in Haiti, have been intended to stabilize democratic regimes.

WHAT WAS the effect of U.S. involvement in the Caribbean?

GLOBAL STANDOFF

As documents from both sides of the Cold War become available, historians have realized what dangerously different meanings the two sides gave to confrontations between 1953 and 1964.

A good example was the U-2 affair of 1960, which derailed progress toward nuclear disarmament. Both countries voluntarily suspended nuclear tests in 1958 and prepared for a June 1960 summit meeting in Paris, where Eisenhower intended to negotiate a test ban treaty.

But on May 1, 1960, Soviet air defenses shot down an American U-2 spy plane over the heart of Russia and captured the pilot, Francis Gary Powers. Designed to soar above the range of Soviet antiaircraft missiles, U-2s had assured American officials that there was no missile gap.

When Moscow trumpeted the news of the downing, Eisenhower took personal responsibility in hopes that Khrushchev would accept the U-2 as an unpleasant reality of international espionage. Unfortunately, the planes meant something very different to the Soviets, touching their festering sense of inferiority. They had stopped protesting the flights in 1957 because complaints were demeaning. The Americans thought that silence signaled acceptance. When Eisenhower refused to apologize in Paris, Khrushchev stalked out. Disarmament was set back for years.

The most important aspect of Eisenhower's foreign policy was continuity. The administration pursued containment as defined under Truman. The Cold War consensus, however, prevented the United States from seeing the nations of the developing world on their own terms. By viewing every independence movement and social revolution as part of the competition with Communism, American leaders created unnecessary problems.

JOHN F. KENNEDY AND THE COLD WAR

John Kennedy was a man of contradictions. A Democrat, he presided over policies whose direction was set under Eisenhower. Despite stirring rhetoric about leading the nation toward a **New Frontier** of scientific and social progress, he recorded his greatest failures and successes in the continuing Cold War. (See American Views, "Two Presidents Assess the Implication of the Cold War.")

THE KENNEDY MYSTIQUE

Kennedy won the presidency over Richard Nixon in a cliffhanging 1960 election that was more about personality and style than substance (see Map 28–2). Both candidates were determined not to yield another inch to Communism. The charming and eloquent Kennedy narrowly skirted scandal in his personal life. Well publicized as a war hero from World War II, he tempered ruthless ambition with respect for public service. His forthright campaigning allayed voter concern about his Roman Catholicism. Nixon had wider experience and was a shrewd tactician, but he was also self-righteous and awkward.

Television was crucial to the outcome. The campaign featured the first televised presidential debates. In the first session, Nixon actually gave better replies, but his nervousness and a bad makeup job turned off millions of viewers who admired Kennedy's energy. Nixon never overcame the setback. Kennedy's televised inauguration was the perfect setting for his impassioned plea for national unity: "My fellow Americans," he challenged, "ask not what your country can do for you— ask what you can do for your country."

Kennedy brought dash to the White House. His beautiful and refined wife, Jackie, outshined previous first ladies. Kennedy's staff and large family played touch football, not golf. No president had shown such verve since Teddy Roosevelt. People began to talk about Kennedy's "charisma," his ability to lead by sheer force of personality.

KENNEDY'S MISTAKES

Talking tough to satisfy more militant countrymen, Kennedy and Khrushchev pushed each other into corners, continuing the problems of mutual misunderstanding. When Khrushchev promised in January 1961 to support "wars of national liberation,"

WHAT WAS John F. Kennedy's approach to dealing with the Soviet Union?

WHERE TO LEARN MORE

John F. Kennedy Library and Museum, Boston, Massachusetts
www.cs.umb.edu/jfklibrary/

New Frontier   John F. Kennedy's domestic and foreign policy initiatives, designed to reinvigorate a sense of national purpose and energy.

he was really fending off Chinese criticism. But Kennedy over-reacted in his first State of the Union address by asking for more military spending.

Three months later, Kennedy fed Soviet fears of American aggressiveness by sponsoring an invasion of Cuba. At the start of 1959, Fidel Castro replaced another Cuban dictator, Fulgencio Batista.

When fourteen hundred anti-Castro Cubans landed at Cuba's **Bay of Pigs** on April 17, 1961, they were following a plan from the Eisenhower administration. The CIA had trained and armed the invaders and convinced Kennedy that the landing would trigger spontaneous uprisings. But when Kennedy refused to commit American armed forces to support them, Cuban forces captured the attackers.

Kennedy followed the Bay of Pigs debacle with a hasty and ill-prepared summit meeting with Khrushchev in Vienna in June that left the Soviets with the impression that the president was weak. To exploit Kennedy's perceived vulnerability, the USSR renewed tension over Berlin, deep within East Germany. The divided city served as an escape route from Communism for hundreds of thousands of East Germans. Khrushchev now threatened to transfer the Soviet sector in Berlin to East Germany, which had no treaty obligations to France, Britain, or the United States. If the West had to deal directly with East Germany for access to Berlin, it would have to recognize a permanently divided Germany. Kennedy sounded the alarm; he doubled draft calls, called up reservists, and warned families to build fallout shelters. Boise, Idaho, families paid $100 for a share in a community shelter with its own power plant and hospital.

Rather than confront the United States directly, however, the Soviets and East Germans on August 13, 1961, built the **Berlin Wall** around the western sectors of Berlin while leaving the access route to West Germany open. In private, Kennedy accepted the wall as a clever way to stabilize a dangerous situation: "A wall," he said, "is a hell of a lot better than a war."

GETTING INTO VIETNAM

American involvement in Vietnam dated from the mid-1950s when the United States replaced France, the former colonial power there, as the supporter of the anti-Communist Vietnamese who had established a government in the southern part of Vietnam. North Vietnam was ruled by Communists under the leadership of Ho Chi Minh who had defeated the French in 1954.

An international conference that negotiated the French withdrawal had called for elections for a single Vietnamese government. The Eisenhower administration, however, encouraged its client in the south, Ngo Dinh Diem from the country's Catholic elite, to put off elections and to establish an independent South Vietnam. Meanwhile, Ho's Communist state in the north claimed to be the legitimate government for all Vietnam.

Kennedy saw U.S. support for Diem as an opportunity to reassert America's commitment to containment. Although Diem's forces controlled the cities with the help of a Vietnamese elite that had also supported the French, Communist insurgents,

MAP EXPLORATION

To explore an interactive version of this map, go to
http://www.prenhall.com/goldfield2/map28.2

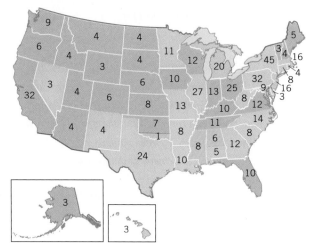

	Electoral Vote (%)	Popular Vote (%)
JOHN F. KENNEDY (Democrat)	**303 (56)**	**34,226,731 (49.9)**
Richard M. Nixon (Republican)	219 (41)	34,108,157 (49.7)
Other	15 (3)	197,029 (.4)

Note: Fifteen electors voted for Harry Byrd, although he had not been an active candidate. Minor party candidates took a tiny percentage of the popular vote.

MAP 28–2
The Election of 1960 The presidential election of 1960 was one of the closest in American history. John Kennedy's victory depended on his appeal in Northern industrial states with large Roman Catholic populations and his ability to hold much of the traditionally Democratic South. Texas, the home state of his vice presidential running mate Lyndon Johnson, was vital to the success of the ticket.

WHY DID most Western states not support Kennedy?

Bay of Pigs Site in Cuba of an unsuccessful landing by fourteen hundred anti-Castro Cuban refugees in April 1961.

Berlin Wall Wall erected by East Germany in 1961 that isolated West Berlin from the surrounding areas in Communist-controlled East Berlin and East Germany.

•AMERICAN VIEWS•

TWO PRESIDENTS ASSESS THE IMPLICATIONS OF THE COLD WAR

*I*n speeches two days apart in January 1961, outgoing President Dwight Eisenhower and incoming President John Kennedy offered contrasting interpretations of America's Cold War crusade. Eisenhower spoke with concern about the effects of defense spending on American society. Kennedy promised an unlimited commitment of resources to achieve national goals.

WHY DID Kennedy define the American mission to the world so broadly? Why did Eisenhower warn about the dangers of pursuing that mission? Do the selections show basic agreement or disagreement about the goals of national policy?

Dwight D.Eisenhower
Farewell Address,
January 18, 1961

Our military organization today bears little relation to that known by any of my predecessors in peacetime. . . . This conjunction of an immense military establishment and a large arms industry is new in the American experience. The total influence— economic, political, even spiritual—is felt in every city, every State house, every office of the federal government. We recognize the imperative need for this development. Yet we must not fail to comprehend its grave implications. . . .

In the councils of government, we must guard against the acquisition of unwarranted influence, whether sought or unsought, by the military-industrial complex. The potential for the disastrous rise of misplaced power exists and will persist.

We must never let the weight of this combination endanger our liberties or democratic processes. We should take nothing for granted. Only an alert and knowledgeable citizenry can compel the proper meshing of the huge industrial and military machinery of defense with our peaceful methods and goals.

John F. Kennedy
Inaugural Address,
January 20, 1961

Let the word go forth from this time and place, to friend and foe alike, that the torch has been passed to a new generation of Americans—born in this century, tempered by war, disciplined by a hard and bitter peace, proud of our ancient heritage—and unwilling to witness or permit the slow undoing of those human rights to which this nation has always been committed, and to which we are committed today at home and around the world.

Let every nation know, whether it wishes us well or ill, that we shall pay any price, bear any burden, meet any hardship, support any friends, oppose any foe to assure the survival and the success of liberty.

known as the **Viet Cong**, were gaining strength in the countryside. The United States sent Diem more weapons and increasing numbers of civilian and military advisors.

U.S. aid did not work. Despite overoptimistic reports and sixteen thousand American troops, Diem's government was losing the loyalty—"the hearts and minds"—of many South Vietnamese. North Vietnam's support for the Viet Cong offset the effect of U.S. assistance. Diem further weakened his position by crushing opposition from Vietnamese Buddhists. In frustration, Kennedy's administration tacitly approved a coup that killed Diem and his brother on November 1, 1963 and replaced them with an ineffectual military junta.

MISSILE CRISIS: A LINE DRAWN IN THE WAVES

On October 15, 1962 reconnaissance photos revealed Soviets at work on launching sites in Cuba from which Soviet-operated nuclear missiles could hit the United States. Top officials spent five exhausting and desperate days sorting through options. Doing nothing meant political disaster. Full-scale invasion of Cuba was

Viet Cong Communist rebels in South Vietnam who fought the pro-American government established in South Vietnam in 1954.

infeasible on short notice, and "surgical" air strikes were technically impossible. Secretary of Defense Robert McNamara suggested demanding removal of the missiles and declaring a naval "quarantine" against the arrival of further offensive weapons. A blockade would buy time for diplomacy.

Kennedy imposed the blockade in a terrifying speech on Monday, October 22. He emphasized the "deceptive" deployment of the Soviet missiles and raised the specter of nuclear war. Americans would have been even more afraid had they known that some of the missiles were operational and that Soviets in Cuba were authorized to use them in self-defense. On Friday, Khrushchev offered to withdraw the missiles in return for an American pledge not to invade Cuba. On Saturday, a second communication raised a new complaint about American missiles on the territory of NATO allies. The letter was the result of pressure by Kremlin hard-liners and Khrushchev's own wavering. Kennedy decided to accept the first letter and ignore the second. The United States pledged not to invade Cuba and secretly promised to remove obsolete Jupiter missiles from Turkey.

Why did Khrushchev risk the Cuban gamble? One reason was to protect Castro as a symbol of Soviet commitment to anti-Western regimes in the developing world. Kennedy had tried to preempt Castroism in 1961 by launching the **Alliance for Progress**, an economic development program for Latin America that tied aid to social reform. However, the United States had also orchestrated the Bay of Pigs invasion and funded a CIA campaign to sabotage Cuba and assassinate its leaders. Castro and Khrushchev had reason to fear the worst.

Khrushchev also hoped to redress the strategic balance. Intermediate-range rockets gave the USSR a nuclear club over western Europe, but in October 1962, the USSR had fewer than fifty ICBMs to aim at the United States and China. The United States was creating a defensive triad of a thousand land-based Minuteman missiles, five hundred long-range bombers, and six hundred Polaris missiles on nuclear submarines targeted on the USSR. The strategic imbalance had sustained NATO during the Berlin confrontation, but forty launchers in Cuba with two warheads each would have doubled the Soviet capacity to strike at the United States.

Soviet missiles in Cuba thus flouted the Monroe Doctrine and posed a real military threat. In the end, both sides were cautious. Khrushchev backed down rather than fight. Kennedy fended off hawkish advisers who wanted to destroy Castro. The world had trembled, but neither nation wanted war over "the missiles of October." In the long run, the crisis accelerated the global arms race. Never again, Soviet leaders vowed, would they submit to American nuclear superiority.

SCIENCE AND FOREIGN AFFAIRS

The two superpowers competed through science as well as diplomacy. A Russian, Yuri Gagarin, was the first human to orbit the earth, on April 12, 1961. American John Glenn did not match Gagarin's feat until February 1962. Kennedy committed the United States to placing an American astronaut on the moon by 1970.

The Soviet Union and the United States were also fencing about nuclear weapons testing. After the three-year moratorium, tests resumed in 1961–1962. Both nations worked on multiple targetable warheads, antiballistic missiles, and other innovations that might destabilize the balance of terror.

After the missile crisis showed his toughness, however, Kennedy had enough political maneuvering room to respond to pressure from liberal Democrats and groups like Women Strike for Peace and the Committee for a Sane Nuclear Policy by giving priority to disarmament. In July 1963, the United States, Britain, and the USSR signed the **Limited Test Ban Treaty**, which outlawed nuclear testing in the atmosphere, in outer space, and under water, and invited other nations to join in. A more comprehensive

The Kennedy family in Hyannis Port in August of 1962.

Cecil Soughton, White House/John Fitzgerald Kennedy Library, Boston

QUICK REVIEW

The Cuban Missile Crisis
- October 15, 1962: U.S. acquires evidence of construction of missile launching sites in Cuba.
- In response, Kennedy imposed a blockade.
- The Soviets removed the launchers in exchange for removal of U.S. missiles from Turkey and a U.S. promise not to invade Cuba.

28–2
John F. Kennedy, Cuban Missile Address (1962)

Alliance for Progress   Program of economic aid to Latin America during the Kennedy administration.

Limited Test Ban Treaty   Treaty, signed by the United States, Britain, and the Soviet Union, outlawing nuclear testing in the atmosphere, in outer space, and under water.

treaty was impossible because the Soviet Union refused on-site inspections. France and China, the other nuclear powers, refused to sign, and the treaty did not halt weapons development, but it was the most positive achievement of Kennedy's foreign policy and a step toward later disarmament treaties.

RIGHTEOUSNESS LIKE A MIGHTY STREAM: THE STRUGGLE FOR CIVIL RIGHTS

WHAT WAS the significance of *Brown* v. *Board of Education of Topeka?*

Linda Brown of Topeka, Kansas, was a third-grader whose parents were fed up with sending her past an all-white public school to attend an all-black school a mile away. The Browns volunteered to help the NAACP challenge Topeka's school segregation by trying to enroll Linda in their neighborhood school, beginning a legal challenge that reached the Supreme Court. Three years later, on May 17, 1954, in ***Brown v. Board of Education of Topeka***, the justices reversed the 1896 case of *Plessy* v. *Ferguson* by ruling that sending black children to "separate but equal" schools denied them equal treatment under the Constitution.

GETTING TO THE SUPREME COURT

The *Brown* decision climaxed a twenty-five-year campaign to reenlist the federal courts on the side of equal rights. The work began in the 1930s when Charles Hamilton Houston, dean of Howard University's law school, trained a corps of civil rights lawyers. Working on behalf of the NAACP, he hoped to erode *Plessy* by suits focused on interstate travel and professional graduate schools (the least defensible segregated institutions because states seldom provided alternatives). In 1938, Houston's student Thurgood Marshall, a future Supreme Court justice, took over the NAACP job.

The *Brown* case combined lawsuits from Delaware, Virginia, South Carolina, the District of Columbia, and Kansas. In each instance, students and families braved community pressure to demand equal access to a basic public service. Viewing public education as central for the equal opportunity that lay at the heart of American values, the Court weighed the *consequences* of segregated school systems and concluded that separate meant unequal.

Brown also built on efforts by Mexican Americans in the Southwest to assert their rights of citizenship. In 1946, the federal courts had prohibited segregation of Mexican-American children in California schools. Eight years later, the Supreme Court forbade Texas from excluding Mexican Americans from juries.

DELIBERATE SPEED

Racial segregation by law was largely a Southern problem, the legacy of Jim Crow laws from early in the century. At first, Americans elsewhere thought of racial injustice as a regional issue.

Southern responses to *Brown* emphasized regional differences. Few Southern communities desegregated schools voluntarily. Their reluctance was bolstered in 1955 when the Supreme Court allowed segregated states to carry out the 1954 decision "with all deliberate speed" rather than immediately. The following year, 101 Southern congressmen and senators issued the **Southern Manifesto**, which asserted that the Court decision was unconstitutional. President Eisenhower privately deplored the desegregation decision, which violated his sense of states' rights and upset Republican attempts to gain southern votes.

The first crisis came in Little Rock, Arkansas, in September 1957. The city school board admitted nine African Americans to Central High, only to be upstaged by Governor Orval Faubus. Claiming to fear violence, he surrounded Central with

Brown v. Board of Education of Topeka Supreme Court decision in 1954 that declared that "separate but equal" schools for children of different races violated the Constitution.

Southern Manifesto A document signed by 101 members of Congress from Southern states in 1956 that argued that the Supreme Court's decision in *Brown* v. *Board of Education of Topeka* itself contradicted the Constitution.

the National Guard and turned the new students away. Meanwhile, segregationists stirred up white fears. Under intense national pressure, Faubus withdrew the
Guard, and a howling crowd surrounded the school. When the black students entered anyway, the mob threatened to storm the building. The police had to sneak
them out after two hours. Fuming at the governor's defiance of federal authority,
which bordered on insurrection, Eisenhower reluctantly nationalized the National
Guard and sent in the 101st Airborne Division to keep order. Eight of the students endured a year of harassment in the hallways of Central.

The breakthrough in school integration did not come until the end of the
1960s, when the courts rejected further delays and federal authorities threatened
to cut off education funds. As late as 1968, only 6 percent of African-American children in the South attended integrated schools. By 1973, the figure was 90 percent.

PUBLIC ACCOMMODATIONS

Most Southern states separated the races in bus terminals and movie theaters.
They required black riders to take rear seats on buses. They labeled separate restrooms and drinking fountains for "colored" users. Hotels denied rooms to black
people, and restaurants refused them service.

The struggle to end segregated facilities started in Montgomery, Alabama.
On December 1, 1955, Rosa Parks, a seamstress who worked at a downtown department store, refused to give up her bus seat to a white passenger and was arrested. Parks acted spontaneously, but she was part of a network of civil rights
activists who wanted to challenge segregated buses and was the secretary of the
Montgomery NAACP. As news of her action spread, the Women's Political Council, a group of college-trained black women, initiated a mass boycott of the privately
owned bus company. Martin Luther King Jr., a twenty-six-year-old pastor, galvanized a mass meeting with a speech that quoted the biblical prophet Amos: "We
are determined here in Montgomery to work and fight until justice runs down
like water, and righteousness like a mighty stream."

A car pool substituted for the buses despite police harassment. As the boycott
survived months of pressure, the national media began to pay attention. After nearly
a year, the Supreme Court agreed that the bus segregation law was unconstitutional.

Victory in Montgomery depended on the steadfastness of African-American
involvement. Participants cut across the class lines that had divided black Southerners. Success also revealed the discrepancy between white attitudes in the Deep
South and national opinion. For white Southerners, segregation was a local concern best defined as a legal or constitutional matter. For other Americans, it was
increasingly an issue of the South's deviation from national moral norms.

The Montgomery boycott won a local victory and made King famous. King
formed the **Southern Christian Leadership Conference (SCLC)**, but four African-
American college students in Greensboro, North Carolina, started the next phase
of the struggle. On February 1, 1960, they sat down at the segregated lunch counter
in Woolworth's, waiting through the day without being served. Their patient
courage brought more demonstrators; within two days, eighty-five students packed
the store. Nonviolent sit-ins spread throughout the South.

In a comparatively sophisticated border city like Nashville, Tennessee, sit-
ins integrated lunch counters. Elsewhere they precipitated white violence and
mass arrests. Like soldiers on a battlefield, nervous participants in sit-ins and
demonstrations drew strength from one another. "If you don't have courage," said
one young woman in Albany, Georgia, "you can borrow it." SCLC leader Ella Baker
helped the students form a new organization, the **Student Nonviolent Coordinating Committee (SNCC)**.

WHERE TO LEARN MORE   **W**

National Afro-American Museum
and Cultural Center,
Wilberforce, Ohio
www.ohiohistory.org/places/afroam/

**Southern Christian Leadership Confer-
ence (SCLC)**   Black civil rights organization founded in 1957 by Martin
Luther King Jr., and other clergy.

**Student Nonviolent Coordinating Com-
mittee (SNCC)**   Black civil rights organization founded in 1960 and
drawing heavily on younger activists
and college students.

The year 1961 brought "freedom rides" to test the segregation of interstate bus terminals. The idea came from James Farmer of the **Congress of Racial Equality (CORE)**. Two buses carrying black and white passengers met only minor problems in Virginia, the Carolinas, and Georgia, but Alabamians burned one of the buses and attacked the riders in Birmingham, where they beat demonstrators senseless and clubbed a Justice Department observer. The governor and police refused to protect the freedom riders. The riders traveled into Mississippi under National Guard protection but were arrested at the Jackson bus terminal. Freedom rides continued through the summer.

MARCH ON WASHINGTON, 1963

John Kennedy was a tepid supporter of the civil rights movement and entered office with no civil rights agenda. He appointed segregationist judges to mollify Southern congressmen and would have preferred that black protestors stop disturbing the fragile Democratic party coalition.

In the face of slow federal response, the SCLC concentrated for 1963 on rigidly segregated Birmingham. April began with sit-ins and marches that aimed to integrate lunch counters, restrooms, and stores and secure open hiring for some clerical jobs. Birmingham's commissioner of public safety, Bull Connor, used fire hoses to blast demonstrators against buildings and roll children down the streets. When demonstrators fought back, his men chased them with dogs. Continued marches brought the arrest of hundreds of children. King's own "Letter from Birmingham City Jail" stated the case for protest: "We have not made a single gain in civil rights without determined legal and nonviolent pressure. . . . Freedom is never voluntarily given by the oppressor; it must be demanded by the oppressed."

The events in Alabama had forced President Kennedy to board the freedom train with an eloquent June 11 speech and to send a civil rights bill to Congress. "Are we to say . . . that this is the land of the free, except for Negroes, that we have no second-class citizens, except Negroes . . . ? Now the time has come for the nation to fulfill its promise."

On August 28, 1963, a quarter of a million black and white people marched to the Lincoln Memorial. The day gave Martin Luther King Jr. a national pulpit. His call for progress toward Christian and American goals had immense appeal. Television cut away from afternoon programs for his "I Have a Dream" speech. The March on Washington demonstrated the mass appeal of civil rights and its identification with national values.

"LET US CONTINUE"

The optimism of the March on Washington shattered with the assassination of John Kennedy in November 1963. In 1964 and 1965, however, President Lyndon Johnson pushed through Kennedy's legislative agenda and much more.

DALLAS, 1963

In November 1963, President Kennedy visited Texas to patch up feuds among Texas Democrats. On November 22, the president's motorcade took him near the Texas School Book Depository building in Dallas, where Lee Harvey Oswald had stationed himself at a window on the sixth floor. When Kennedy's open car swung into the sights of his rifle, Oswald fired three shots that wounded Texas Governor John Connally and killed the president. As doctors vainly treated the president in a hospital emergency room, Dallas police arrested Oswald. Vice President Lyndon Johnson took the oath of office as president on Air Force One while the blood-spattered Jacqueline Kennedy looked

---

28-3
John Lewis, Address at the March on Washington (1963)

Congress of Racial Equality (CORE)
Civil rights group formed in 1942 and committed to nonviolent civil disobedience.

HOW DID Lyndon Johnson continue the domestic agenda inherited from the Kennedy administration?

on. Two days later, as Oswald was being led to a courtroom, Texas nightclub owner Jack Ruby killed Oswald with a handgun, in full view of TV cameras.

Lee Oswald was a twenty-four-year old misfit. He had served in the Marines and worked maintaining U-2 spy planes before defecting to the Soviet Union. He returned to the United States after three years with a fervent commitment to Fidel Castro's Cuban revolution. He visited the Soviet and Cuban embassies in Mexico City in September trying to drum up a job, but neither country thought him worth hiring.

Some Americans believe there is more to the story. Why? One possibility is that Oswald seems too insignificant to be responsible on his own for the murder of a charismatic president. The sketchy job done by the Warren Commission, appointed to investigate the assassination, calmed fears in the short run but left loose ends that have fueled conspiracy theories.

All of the theories remain unproved. Logic holds that the simplest explanation for cutting through a mass of information is usually the best. Oswald was a social misfit with a grievance against American society. Ruby was an impulsive man who told his brother on his deathbed that he thought he was doing the country a favor.

WAR ON POVERTY

Five days after the assassination, Lyndon Johnson claimed Kennedy's progressive aura for his new administration. "Let us continue," he told the nation, promising to implement Kennedy's policies. Lyndon Johnson was a professional politician who had reached the top through Texas politics and congressional infighting. Johnson's presence on the ticket in 1960 had helped elect Kennedy by attracting Southern voters, but he lacked Kennedy's polish and easy relations with the Eastern elite. He had entered public life with the New Deal in the 1930s and believed in its principles. Johnson, not Kennedy, was the true heir of Franklin Roosevelt.

Johnson inherited a domestic agenda that the Kennedy administration had defined but not enacted. Initiatives in education, medical insurance, tax reform, and urban affairs had stalled or been gutted by conservatives in Congress.

When Michael Harrington's study *The Other America* became an unexpected bestseller, Kennedy had taken notice. As poverty captured public attention, Kennedy's economic advisers devised a community action program that emphasized education and job training, a national service corps, and a youth conservation corps.

Johnson made Kennedy's antipoverty package his own. Adopting Cold War rhetoric, he declared "unconditional war on poverty." The core of Johnson's program was the **Office of Economic Opportunity (OEO)**. Established under the direction of Kennedy's brother-in-law R. Sargent Shriver in 1964, the OEO operated the Job Corps for school dropouts, the Neighborhood Youth Corps for unemployed teenagers, the Head Start program to prepare poor children for school, and VISTA (Volunteers in Service to America), a domestic Peace Corps. OEO's biggest effort went to Community Action Agencies. By 1968, more than five hundred such agencies provided health and educational services. Despite flaws, the **War on Poverty** improved life for millions of Americans.

CIVIL RIGHTS, 1964–1965

In Johnson's view, segregation not only deprived African Americans of access to opportunity but also distracted Southern white people from their own poverty and underdevelopment.

One solution was the **Civil Rights Act of 1964**, which Kennedy had introduced but Johnson got enacted. The law prohibited segregation in public accommodations, such as hotels, restaurants, gas stations, theaters, and parks, and outlawed employment discrimination on federally assisted projects. It also created

WHERE TO LEARN MORE

Sixth Floor Museum, Dallas, Texas
www.jfk.org

WHERE TO LEARN MORE

National Civil Rights Museum, Memphis, Tennessee
http://www.civilrightsmuseum.org

Office of Economic Opportunity (OEO) Federal agency that coordinated many programs of the War on Poverty between 1964 and 1975.

War on Poverty Set of programs introduced by Lyndon Johnson between 1963 and 1966 designed to break the cycle of poverty by providing funds for job training, community development, nutrition, and supplementary education.

Civil Rights Act of 1964 Federal legislation that outlawed discrimination in public accommodations and employment on the basis of race, skin color, sex, religion, or national origin.

the Equal Employment Opportunity Commission (EEOC) and included gender in a list of categories protected against discrimination, a provision whose consequences were scarcely suspected in 1964.

Even as Congress was debating the 1964 law, **Freedom Summer** moved political power to the top of the civil rights agenda. Organized by SNCC, the Mississippi Summer Freedom Project was a voter registration drive that sent white and black volunteers to the small towns and back roads of Mississippi. The target was a Southern political system that used rigged literacy tests and intimidation to keep black people from voting. In Mississippi in 1964, only 7 percent of eligible black people were registered voters. Freedom Summer gained sixteen hundred new voters and taught two thousand children in SNCC-run Freedom Schools at the cost of beatings, bombings, church arson, and the murder of three project workers.

Another outgrowth of the SNCC effort was the Mississippi Freedom Democratic Party (MFDP), a biracial coalition that bypassed Mississippi's all-white Democratic party, followed state party rules, and sent its own delegates to the 1964 Democratic convention. To preserve party harmony, President Johnson refused to expel the "regular" Mississippi Democrats and offered instead to seat two MFDP delegates and enforce party rules for 1968. The MFDP walked out. Fannie Lou Hamer, a MFDP delegate, remembered, "We learned the hard way that even though we had all the law and all the righteousness on our side— that white man is not going to give up his power to us. We have to build our own power."

Lyndon Johnson and Martin Luther King Jr. agreed on the need for federal voting legislation when King visited the president in December 1964 after winning the Nobel Peace Prize. For King, power at the ballot box would help black Southerners take control of their own communities. For Johnson, voting reform would fulfill the promise of American democracy. It would also benefit the Democratic party by replacing with black voters the white Southerners who were drifting toward anti-integration Republicans.

The target for King and the SCLC was Dallas County, Alabama, where only 2 percent of eligible black voters were registered, compared with 70 percent of white voters. Peaceful demonstrations started in January 1965. By early February, jails in the county seat of Selma held 2,600 black people whose offense was marching to the courthouse to demand the vote. The campaign climaxed with a march from Selma to the state capital of Montgomery. SNCC leader John Lewis remembered, "I don't know what we expected. I think maybe we thought we'd be arrested and jailed, or maybe they wouldn't do anything to us. I had a little knapsack on my shoulder with an apple, a toothbrush, toothpaste, and two books in it: a history of America and a book by [Christian theologian] Thomas Merton."

On Sunday, March 7, five hundred marchers crossed the bridge over the Alabama River to meet a sea of state troopers. The troopers gave them two minutes to disperse and then attacked on foot and horseback "as if they were mowing a big field." The attack drove the demonstrators back in bloody confusion while television cameras rolled.

As violence continued, Johnson addressed a joint session of Congress to demand a voting rights law: "Our mission is at once the oldest and the most basic of this country: to right wrong, to do justice, to serve man." He ended with the refrain of the civil rights movement: "We shall overcome."

Johnson signed the **Voting Rights Act** on August 6, 1965. The law outlawed literacy tests and provided for federal voting registrars in states where registration or turnout in 1964 was less than 50 percent of eligible population. It applied initially in seven southern states. Black registration in these states jumped from 27 percent to 55 percent within the first year. In 1975, Congress extended coverage to Hispanic voters in the Southwest. By the end of 1992, Virginia had elected a black governor, and nearly

Freedom Summer   Voter registration effort in rural Mississippi organized by black and white civil rights workers in 1964.

Voting Rights Act   Legislation in 1965 that overturned a variety of practices by which states systematically denied voter registration to minorities.

every southern state had sent black representatives to Congress. Less obvious but just as revolutionary were the thousands of African Americans and Latinos who won local offices and the new moderation of white leaders who had to satisfy black voters.

WAR, PEACE, AND THE LANDSLIDE OF 1964

Johnson had maintained Kennedy's commitment to South Vietnam. On the advice of Kennedy hold-overs like Defense Secretary Robert McNamara, he stepped up commando raids and naval shelling of North Vietnam. On August 2, North Vietnamese torpedo boats attacked the U.S. destroyer *Maddox* in the Gulf of Tonkin while it was eavesdropping on North Vietnamese military signals. Two days later, the *Maddox* and the *C. Turner Joy* reported another torpedo attack (probably false sonar readings). Johnson ordered a bombing raid and asked Congress to authorize "all necessary measures" to protect American forces and stop further aggression. Congress passed the **Gulf of Tonkin Resolution** with only two nay votes.

Johnson's Republican opponent, Senator Barry Goldwater of Arizona, a former Air Force pilot, wanted aggressive confrontation with Communism. Campaign literature declared that "extremism in the defense of liberty is no vice," raising visions of vigilantes and mobs. Goldwater's campaign made Johnson look moderate. Johnson pledged not "to send American boys nine or ten thousand miles from home to do what Asian boys ought to be doing for themselves" while Goldwater proposed an all-out war.

Johnson's 61 percent of the popular vote was the greatest margin ever recorded in a presidential election. Democrats racked up two-to-one majorities in Congress. For the first time in decades, liberal Democrats could enact their domestic program without begging votes from conservative Southerners or Republicans, and Johnson could achieve his goal of a **Great Society** based on freedom and opportunity for all.

The result in 1965 was a series of measures that Johnson rushed through Congress before his political standing began to erode and Vietnam distracted national attention. The National Endowment for the Humanities, National Endowment for the Arts, and highway beautification were part of the Great Society for the middle class. The Wilderness Act (1964), an early success of the modern environmental movement, preserved 9.1 million acres from all development.

More central to Johnson's vision were efforts to increase opportunity for all. As he told a July 1965 news conference, "When I was young, poverty was so common that we didn't know it had a name. An education was something that you had to fight for. . . . It is now my opportunity to help every child get an education, to have every family get a decent home, and to help bring healing to the sick and dignity to the old." The Elementary and Secondary Education Act was the first general federal aid program for public schools, allocating $1.3 billion for textbooks and special education. The Higher Education Act funded low-interest student loans and university research facilities. The Medical Care Act created federally funded health insurance for the elderly (**Medicare**) and helped states offer medical care to the poor (**Medicaid**). The Appalachian Regional Development Act funded economic development in the depressed mountain counties of twelve states from Georgia to New York and proved a long-run success.

The United States came closer to winning the war on poverty than the war in Vietnam. New or expanded social insurance and income support programs, such as Medicare, Medicaid, Social Security, and food stamps, cut the proportion of poor people from 22 percent of the American population in 1960 to 13 percent in 1970. Infant mortality dropped by a third because of improved nutrition and better access to health care for mothers and children. Taken together, the political results of the 1964 landslide moved the United States far toward Lyndon Johnson's vision of an end to poverty and racial injustice.

WHERE TO LEARN MORE

Birmingham Civil Rights Institute Museum, Birmingham, Alabama
www.bcri.bham.al.us

WHERE TO LEARN MORE

Martin Luther King, Jr., National Historical Site, Atlanta, Georgia
http://www.nps.gov/malu/

Gulf of Tonkin Resolution   Request to Congress from President Lyndon Johnson in response to North Vietnamese torpedo boat attacks in which he sought authorization for "all necessary measures" to protect American forces and stop further aggression.

Great Society   Theme of Lyndon Johnson's administration, focusing on poverty, education, and civil rights.

Medicare   Basic medical insurance for the elderly, financed through the federal government; program created in 1965.

Medicaid   Supplementary medical insurance for the poor, financed through the federal government; program created in 1965.

CONCLUSION

From 1953 to 1964, consistent goals guided American foreign policy including vigilant anti-Communism and the confidence to intervene in trouble spots around the globe. At home, the Supreme Court's *Brown* decision introduced a decade-long civil rights revolution. However, many patterns of personal behavior and social relations remained unchanged. Women faced similar expectations from the early fifties to the early sixties. Churches showed more continuity than change.

In retrospect, it is remarkable how widely and deeply the Cold War shaped U.S. society. Fundamental social institutions, such as marriage and religion, got extra credit for their contributions to anti-Communism. The nation's long tradition of home-grown radicalism was virtually silent in the face of the Cold War consensus. Even economically meritorious programs like more money for science and better roads went down more easily if linked to national defense.

SUMMARY

A Decade of Affluence President Eisenhower presided over the prosperity of the 1950s. He claimed the "political middle" and accepted much of the New Deal but saw little need for further reform. Under Eisenhower, workers had more disposable income and credit-based consumerism expanded; suburbs and the "car culture" grew. Families were seen as part of the anti-Communist crusade. The "youth culture" emerged, but religious affiliation, the belief in prosperity, and social conformity characterized the era. Vast inequalities were concealed; many had missed out on "affluent America" and many women were unhappy in their "perfect" world.

Facing Off with the Soviet Union The actions of the United States and Soviet Union created a bipolar world: Each was a magnetic pole with countries aligning themselves or attempting to remain neutral. The Soviet launching of the *Sputnik* satellite concerned Americans who thought they were technologically superior; America's worldview of the right and need to intervene in areas that were possible Communist takeover targets resulted in an expansion of containment. "Brinksmanship" characterized this period in the Cold War.

John F. Kennedy and the Cold War John F. Kennedy won over Richard Nixon in a close election in 1960; television was a critical element. Kennedy's administration dealt with the Bay of Pigs invasion, a new Berlin crisis and the building of the Berlin Wall, growing American involvement in Vietnam, and the Cuban Missile crisis. Kennedy supported science as well as diplomacy; he committed the United States to placing an American astronaut on the moon and signed the Limited Test Ban Treaty which was a step toward later disarmament treaties.

Righteousness Like a Mighty Stream: The Struggle for Civil Rights The Supreme Court's *Brown* decision made the growing effort to secure equal legal treatment for African Americans a challenge to American society. The first phase of the civil rights struggle built from the Supreme Court's decision in 1954 to a vast gathering at the Lincoln Memorial in 1963. In between African Americans chipped away at racial segregation of schools, universities, and public facilities with boycotts, sit-ins, and lawsuits, forcing segregationists to choose between integration and violent defiance.

"Let Us Continue" After President Kennedy's assassination, Lyndon Johnson inherited a domestic agenda that was based on the knowledge that poverty was a widespread American problem. Johnson's passionate commitment to economic betterment accompanied a commitment to civil rights. War on Poverty and Great Society measures were passed before Johnson's enlargement of the Vietnam War eroded his political standing; the United States moved closer to addressing the effects of poverty and racial injustice than ever before.

REVIEW QUESTIONS

1. What were the sources of prosperity in the 1950s and 1960s? How did prosperity shape cities, family life, and religion?
2. What did American leaders think was at stake in Vietnam, Berlin, and Cuba?
3. Who initiated and led the African-American struggle for civil rights?
4. In what new directions did Lyndon Johnson take the United States?
5. Why was school integration the focus of such strong conflict?

KEY TERMS

Alliance for Progress (p. 751)
Bay of Pigs (p. 749)
Berlin Wall (p. 749)
Brown v. *Board of Education of Topeka* (p. 752)
Civil Rights Act of 1964 (p. 755)
Congress of Racial Equality (CORE) (p. 754)
Federal Highway Act of 1956 (p. 740)
Freedom Summer (p. 756)

Great Society (p. 757)
Gulf of Tonkin Resolution (p. 757)
Limited Test Ban Treaty (p. 751)
Medicaid (p. 757)
Medicare (p. 757)
National Aeronautics and Space Administration (NASA) (p. 745)
New Frontier (p. 748)
Office of Economic Opportunity (OEO) (p. 755)

Southeast Asia Treaty Organization (SEATO) (p. 746)
Southern Christian Leadership Conference (SCLC) (p. 753)
Southern Manifesto (p. 752)
Student Nonviolent Coordinating Committee (SNCC) (p. 753)
Viet Cong (p. 750)
Voting Rights Act (p. 756)
War on Poverty (p. 755)

WHERE TO LEARN MORE

- **National Air and Space Museum, Washington, D.C.** Part of the Smithsonian Institution's complex of museums in Washington, the Air and Space Museum is the richest source for artifacts and discussion of the American space program. **www.nasm.edu**

- **Kansas Cosmosphere, Hutchinson, Kansas.** A rich collection of artifacts and equipment from the U.S. space program. **www.cosmo.org**

- **Sixth Floor Museum, Dallas, Texas.** Occupying the sixth floor of the former Texas School Book Depository building, exhibits examine the life, death, and legacy of John F. Kennedy. **www.jfk.org**

- **Birmingham Civil Rights Institute Museum, Birmingham, Alabama.** This museum and archive deal with the background of Southern racial segregation, civil rights activism, and the 1963 demonstrations in Birmingham. **www.bcri.bham.al.us.**

- **Martin Luther King, Jr., National Historical Site, Atlanta, Georgia.** The birthplace and grave of Reverend King are the nucleus of a park set in the historic black neighborhood of Auburn. **http://www.nps.gov/malu/**

- **National Civil Rights Museum, Memphis, Tennessee.** Located in the Lorraine Motel, where Martin Luther King, Jr., was killed, the museum traces the participants, background, and effects of key events in the civil rights movement. **http://www.civilrightsmuseum.org**

- **National Afro-American Museum and Cultural Center, Wilberforce, Ohio.** The exhibit "From Victory to Freedom: Afro-American Life in the Fifties" looks at home, family, music, and religion. **www.ohiohistory.org/places/afroam/**

- **John F. Kennedy Library and Museum, Boston, Massachusetts.** Exhibits offer a sympathetic view of Kennedy's life and achievements. **www.cs.umb.edu/jfklibrary/**

 For additional study resources for this chapter, go to:
www.prenhall.com/goldfield/chapter28

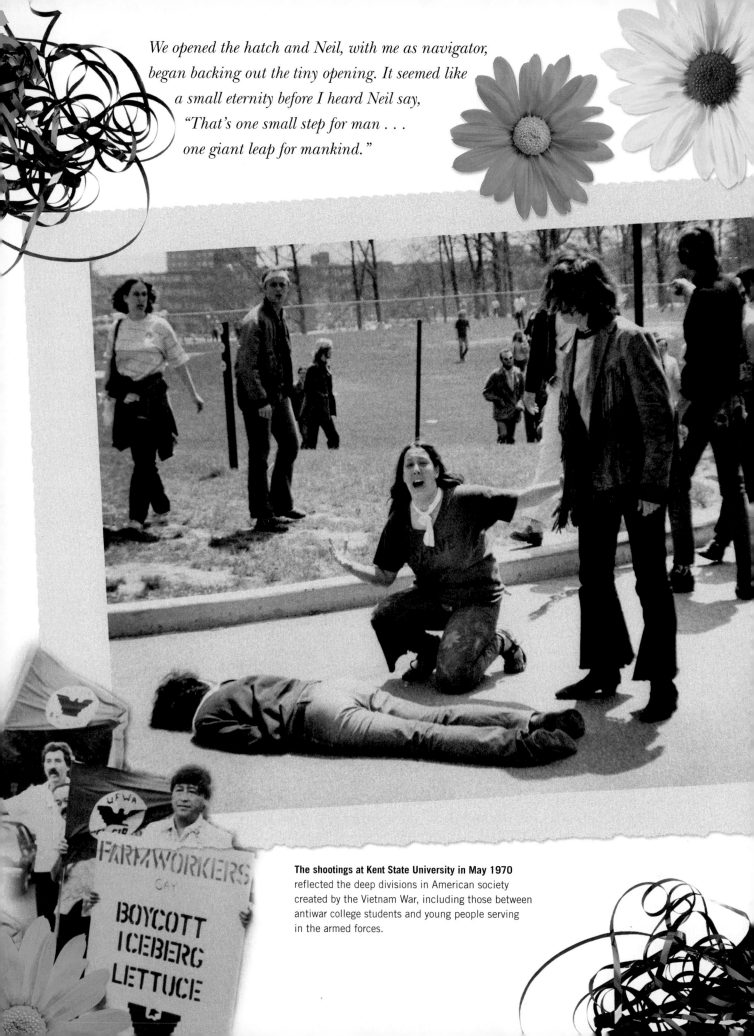

*We opened the hatch and Neil, with me as navigator,
began backing out the tiny opening. It seemed like
a small eternity before I heard Neil say,
"That's one small step for man . . .
one giant leap for mankind."*

The shootings at Kent State University in May 1970
reflected the deep divisions in American society
created by the Vietnam War, including those between
antiwar college students and young people serving
in the armed forces.

FARMWORKERS

BOYCOTT
ICEBERG
LETTUCE

29

MAKE LOVE NOT WAR

SHAKEN TO THE ROOTS
1965–1980

HOW DID the national consensus of the 1950s and early 1960s unravel?

WHAT CHALLENGES did American cities face in the late 1960s and 1970s?

WHY DID America's view of the war in Vietnam change in 1968?

WHAT WAS the legacy of Richard Nixon's presidency?

HOW WAS Jimmy Carter's idealism a frustration to his success as president?

Contact light! O.K., engine stop. . . . Houston, Tranquility Base here. The Eagle has landed! . . .

We opened the hatch and Neil, with me as navigator, began backing out of the tiny opening [in the Lunar Module Eagle]. It seemed like a small eternity before I heard Neil say, "That's one small step for man. . . . one giant leap for mankind." In less than fifteen minutes I was backing awkwardly out of the hatch and onto the surface to join Neil, who, in the tradition of all tourists, had his camera ready to photograph my arrival.

I took off jogging to test my maneuverability. The exercise gave me an odd sensation and looked even more odd when I later saw the films of it. With bulky suits on, we seemed to be moving in slow motion. . . . At one point, I re-marked that the surface was "Beautiful, beautiful. Magnificent desolation." I was struck by the contrast between the starkness of the shadows and the desert-like barrenness of the rest of the surface. It ranged from dusty gray to light tan and was unchanging except for one startling sight: our LM sitting there with its black, silver and bright yellow-orange thermal coating shining brightly in the otherwise colorless landscape.

During a pause in experiments, Neil suggested we proceed with the flag. . . . To our dismay the staff of the pole wouldn't go far enough into the lunar surface. . . . I dreaded the possibility of the American flag collapsing into the lunar dust in front of the television camera.

Edgar Cortright, ed., *Apollo Expeditions to the Moon* (Washington: NASA SP 350, 1975).

IMAGE KEY
for pages 760–761

a. Damaged cassette tape evocative of the Watergate scandal.

b. Daisies represent the "Flower Power" mindset.

c. A weeping young woman kneels beside the body of a protester during the 1970 riots at Kent State University in Ohio.

d. Caeser Chávez.

e. Anti war peace button.

f. Crowds gather to hear Martin Luther King, Jr. speak.

g. Vietnamese refugees.

h. President Nixon announces he will resign effective noon Friday in this Thursday, August 8, 1974 file photo shown during a broadcast from the Oval Room of the White House.

i. Egyptian president Anwar el-Sadat, US President Jimmy Carter, and Israeli Prime Minister Menachem Begin share a three-way handshake after signing an Arab-Israeli peace treaty on March 26, 1979. The three leaders agreed on the terms of the treaty at Camp David in September 1978.

BUZZ ALDRIN AND NEIL ARMSTRONG, on July 20, 1969, complet-ed the longest journey that any person had yet taken. Landing the Apollo 11 lunar module on the moon climaxed a five-day trip across the quarter million miles sep-arating the earth from the moon. Six and a half hours after the landing, Arm-strong and Aldrin were the first humans to walk on the moon's surface.

The Apollo 11 expedition combined science and Cold War politics. The American flag waving on the lunar surface was a symbol of victory in one phase of the space race between the United States and Soviet Union. NASA had been working since 1961 to meet John F. Kennedy's goal of a manned trip to the moon before the end of the decade. After Apollo II, American astronauts made five more trips to the moon between 1969 and 1972, which helped to restore the na-tion's standing as the world's scientific and technological leader.

Despite Apollo's success, however, the United States was increasingly shak-en in the later 1960s and 1970s. The failure to win an easy victory in Vietnam erod-ed the nation's confidence and fueled bitter divisions. Most Americans had agreed about the goals of the Cold War, the benefits of economic growth, and the value of equal opportunity. Stalemate in Southeast Asia, political changes in third world countries, and an oil supply crisis in the 1970s challenged U.S. influence in the world. Frustrated with slow progress toward racial equality, many minority Amer-icans advocated separation rather than integration, helping to plunge the nation's cities into crisis, while other Americans began to draw back from some of the ob-jectives of racial integration.

Political scandals, summarized in three syllables as "Watergate," undercut faith in government. Fifteen years of turmoil forced a grudging recognition of limits to American military power, economic capacity, governmental prerogatives, and even the ideal of a single American dream.

THE END OF CONSENSUS

Pleiku is a town in Vietnam 240 miles north of Saigon (now Ho Chi Minh City). In 1965, Pleiku was the site of a South Vietnamese army headquarters and American military base. At 2 A.M. on February 7, Viet Cong attacked the U.S. base, killing eight Americans and wounding a hundred. The national security adviser, McGeorge Bundy, in Saigon on a fact-finding visit; Ambassador Maxwell Taylor; and General William Westmoreland, the commander of U.S. forces South Vietnam recommended a retaliatory air strike against North Vietnam. President Johnson concurred, and navy bombers roared off aircraft carriers. A month later, Johnson ordered a full-scale air offensive.

The attack at Pleiku triggered plans that were waiting to be put into effect since the Gulf of Tonkin resolution the previous summer. The official reason for the bombing was to pressure North Vietnam to negotiate an end to the war. As the South Vietnamese government lost control of the countryside, air strikes on North Vietnam looked like an easy way to redress the balance. In the back of President Johnson's mind were the need to prove his toughness and the mistaken assumption that China was aggressively backing North Vietnam.

The air strikes pushed the United States over the line from propping up the South Vietnamese government to leading the war effort. A president who desperately wanted a way out of Southeast Asia kept adding American forces. The war in Vietnam would distract the United States from the goals of the Great Society, drive Johnson from office, set back progress toward global stability, and divide the American people.

DEEPER INTO VIETNAM

Advisers persuaded Lyndon Johnson that controlled military escalation—a middle course between withdrawal and all-out war—could secure Vietnam (see Map 29–1). They failed to understand the extent of popular opposition to the official government in Saigon and the willingness of North Vietnam to sacrifice to achieve national unity.

The air war required ground troops to protect bases in South Vietnam. Marines landed on March 8. More bombs, a pause, an offer of massive U.S. aid—nothing brought North Vietnam to the negotiating table. Johnson dribbled in new forces and expanded their mission from base security to combat. On July 28, he finally gave General William Westmoreland, the commander of U.S. forces in Vietnam, doubled draft calls and an increase in U.S. combat troops from 75,000 to 275,000 by 1966.

Secretary of Defense Robert McNamara was clear about the change: "We have relied on South Vietnam to carry the brunt. Now we would be responsible for a satisfactory military outcome." American forces in South Vietnam reached their maximum of 543,000 in August 1969. In all, more than 2 million Americans served in Vietnam.

The U.S. strategy on the ground was **search and destroy**. As conceived by Westmoreland, it used sophisticated surveillance and heavily armed patrols to locate enemy detachments, which could then be destroyed by air strikes, artillery, and reinforcements carried in by helicopter.

HOW DID the national consensus of the 1950s and early 1960s unravel?

WHERE TO LEARN MORE

Vietnam Veterans Memorial, Washington, D.C.
www.nps.gov/vive/

search and destroy   U.S. military tactic in South Vietnam, using small detachments to locate enemy units and then massive air, artillery, and ground forces to destroy them.

MAP EXPLORATION
To explore an interactive version of this map, go to
http://www.prenhall.com/goldfield2/map29.1

MAP 29–1

The War in Vietnam The United States attacked North Vietnam with air strikes but confined large-scale ground operations to South Vietnam and Cambodia. In South Vietnam, U.S. forces faced both North Vietnamese army units and Viet Cong rebels, all of whom received supplies by way of the so-called Ho Chi Minh Trail, named for the leader of North Vietnam. The coordinated attacks on cities and towns throughout South Vietnam during the Tet Offensive in 1968 surprised the United States.

WHAT WERE the shortcomings of American military strategy in Vietnam?

CHRONOLOGY

1962 Rachel Carson publishers *Silent Spring*
Port Huron Statement launches Students for a Democratic Society.

1965 Congress approves Wilderness Act.
Malcolm X is assassinated. Residents of Watts neighborhood in Los Angeles riot.

1967 African Americans riot in Detroit and Newark.

1968 Viet Cong launches Tet Offensive.
James Earl Ray kills Martin Luther King Jr.
Lyndon Johnson declines to run for reelection.
SDS disrupts Columbia University.
Sirhan Sirhan kills Robert Kennedy.
Peace talks start between the United States and North Vietnam.
Police riot against antiwar protesters during the Democratic National Convention in Chicago.
Richard Nixon is elected president.

1969 Neil Armstrong and Buzz Aldrin walk on the moon.

1970 United States invades Cambodia.

National Guard units kill students at Kent State and Jackson State Universities.

Earth Day is celebrated.

Environmental Protection Agency is created.

1971 *New York Times* publishes the secret "Pentagon Papers."
President Nixon freezes wages and prices.
"Plumbers" unit is established in the White House.

1972 Nixon visits China.
United States and Soviet Union adopt SALT I.

Operatives for Nixon's reelection campaign break into Democratic headquarters in the Watergate complex in Washington, D.C.

1973 Paris accords end direct U.S. involvement in South Vietnamese war.
United States moves to all-volunteer armed forces.
Watergate burglars are convicted.
Senate Watergate hearings reveal the existence of taped White House conversations.
Spiro Agnew resigns as vice president, is replaced by Gerald Ford.
Arab states impose an oil embargo after the third Arab-Israeli War.

1974 Nixon resigns as president, is succeeded by Gerald Ford.

1975 Communists triumph in South Vietnam.
United States, USSR, and European nations sign the Helsinki Accords.

1976 Jimmy Carter defeats Gerald Ford for the presidency.

1978 Carter brings the leaders of Egypt and Israel to Camp David for peace talks.

1979 SALT II agreement is signed but not ratified.
OPEC raises oil prices.
Three Mile Island nuclear plant comes close to disaster.
Iranian militants take U.S. embassy hostages.

1980 Iranian hostage rescue fails.
Soviet troops enter Afghanistan.
Ronald Reagan defeats Jimmy Carter for the presidency.

However, most opponents were South Vietnamese guerrillas forcing the United States to make repeated sweeps through farms and villages. The enemy were difficult for Americans to recognize among farmers and workers, making South Vietnamese society itself the target. Massive American firepower killed thousands of Vietnamese and made millions refugees.

Pilots dropped tons of bombs on the "Ho Chi Minh Trail," a network of supply routes from North Vietnam to South Vietnam through the mountains of neighboring Laos. Despite the bombing, thousands of workers converted rough paths into roads that were repaired as soon as they were damaged. Air assault on North Vietnam itself remained "diplomatic," intended to force North Vietnam to stop intervening in the South Vietnamese civil war. Since Ho Chi Minh considered North and South to be one country, the American goal was unacceptable. Attacking North Vietnam's poorly developed economy, the United States soon ran out of targets.

VOICES OF DISSENT

At home, protest against the war quickly mounted. In the 1950s, McCarthyism had intimidated dissenters on the left. Now antiwar activists and college students challenged the "Cold Warriors."

"Realists," such as Senator William Fulbright, the chairman of the Senate Foreign Relations Committee, argued that the war was a dangerous distraction from the country's vital interests in regions such as Europe, and a waste of American lives and resources. More radical critics saw the roots of the war in basic flaws in the American character and system. Some called it an example of economic imperialism that revealed the power of multinational corporations to control American foreign policy. A generation later, some of the same criticisms would reappear in arguments against the North American Free Trade Agreement (NAFTA) and the World Trade Organization.

In 1966 and 1967, antiwar activity accelerated into direct confrontation. Protesters blocked munitions trains. Peace organizations sent representatives to North Vietnam to explore possible solutions. Religious groups condemned the war.

Much of the anger was directed against the military draft administration, the **Selective Service System**. Draft deferral criteria favored the middle class and helped make Vietnam a working-class conflict. Full-time college enrollment was grounds for a deferment; so was the right diagnosis from the right doctor. As a result, enlistees and draftees tended to be small-town or innercity working-class youths. They were also young. In World War II, the average GI had been in his midtwenties. The typical soldier in Vietnam was 19 or 20. Women who served as military nurses tended to come from the same background. The resentment the draft created eroded the alliance between working-class Americans and the Democratic party.

Military service also deepened the racial gap. In 1965 African Americans made up 11 percent of the nation's population but were 24 percent of the soldiers killed in Vietnam. This disparity forced the Defense Department to revise its combat assignments. Martin Luther King Jr. joined the protest in 1967. King called the war a moral disaster and a new form of colonialism whose costs weighed most heavily on the poor.

As protests mounted, draft resistance provided a direct avenue to attack the war. Young men burned their draft cards, fled to Canada, or applied for conscientious objector status on moral or religious grounds. A few were jailed for refusing to cooperate in any way with the Selective Service System. And a handful of activists invaded draft-board offices and tried to destroy files. By 1969, over half the men drafted in California were refusing to show up, and thousands were prosecuted for draft evasion.

The popular media portrayed the conflicting visions of the war. While antiwar songs climbed the charts, an aging John Wayne portrayed a heroic American soldier saving South Vietnam in the movie *The Green Berets*, and country singer Merle Travis spoke for many small-town Americans who supported the war in "Okie from Muskogee" (where they didn't burn draft cards).

NEW LEFT AND COMMUNITY ACTIVISM

The antiwar movement was part of a growing grass-roots activism that took much of its tone from the university-based **Students for a Democratic Society (SDS)**. The group was important for its ideas, not its size. Its Port Huron Statement, adopted in 1962, called for grass-roots action and "participatory democracy." SDS tried to harness youthful disillusionment about consumerism, racism, and imperialism. It thought of itself as a "New Left" that was free from the doctrinal squabbles that hampered the old left of the 1930s and 1940s.

Many of the original SDS leaders were also participants in the civil-rights movement. The same was true of Mario Savio, founder of the **Free Speech Movement (FSM)** at the University of California at Berkeley in 1964. Savio hoped to build a

Selective Service System Federal agency that coordinated military conscription before and during the Vietnam War.

Students for a Democratic Society (SDS) The leading student organization of the New Left of the early and mid-1960s.

Free Speech Movement (FSM) Student movement at the University of California, Berkeley, formed in 1964 to protest limitations on political activities on campus.

multi-issue "community of protest" around the idea of "a free university in a free society." FSM protests climaxed with a December sit-in that led to 773 arrests and stirred protest on other campuses.

What SDS wanted to do with its grass-roots organizing resembled the federal community-action programs associated with the war on poverty. The **Model Cities Program** (1966) invited residents of poor neighborhoods to write their own plans for using federal funds to improve local housing, education, health services, and job opportunities. Model Cities assemblies challenged the racial bias in programs like urban renewal and helped train community leaders.

The lessons of grass-roots reform strengthened democracy from the bottom up. Activists staffed food cooperatives, free clinics, women's health groups, and drug counseling centers. Community-based organization was a key element in self-help efforts by African Americans, Asian Americans, and Latinos. Neighborhood associations and community-development corporations that provided affordable housing and jobs extended the "backyard revolution" into the 1980s and beyond. Social conservatives, such as antiabortionists, used the same techniques on behalf of their own agendas.

THE FEMINIST CRITIQUE

A revived feminism was another result of the ferment of the 1960s. Important steps in this revival included the Presidential Commission on the Status of Women in 1961; the addition of gender as one of the categories protected by the Civil Rights Act of 1964 (see Chapter 28); and creation of the National Organization for Women (NOW) in 1966.

Mainstream feminism targeted unequal opportunity in the job market. College-educated baby boomers encountered "glass ceilings" and job discrimination, in which companies hired less qualified men who "needed the job" rather than more qualified women who supposedly did not. Throughout the mid-1960s and 1970s, activists battled to open job categories to women, who proved that they could indeed use tools or pick stocks on Wall Street. They also battled for equal pay for everyone with equal qualifications and responsibilities.

Changes in sexual behavior paralleled efforts to equalize treatment in the workplace. More reliable methods of contraception, especially birth-control pills introduced in the early 1960s, gave women greater control over childbearing. A new sexual revolution eroded the double standard that expected chastity of women but tolerated promiscuity among men. One consequence was a singles culture that accepted sexual activity between unmarried men and women.

Women's liberation took off as a social and political movement in 1970 and 1971 as influential books probed the roots of inequality between men's and women's opportunities. Women shared their stories and ideas in small "consciousness-raising" sessions. Within a few years, millions of women had recognized events and patterns in their lives as discrimination based on gender. The feminist movement, and specific policy measures related to it, put equal rights

Antiwar protests were simultaneously symbolic and disruptive. Some activists dumped jars of animal blood over draft-board records. Others tried to block munitions trains. In October 1967, a hundred thousand people marched on the Pentagon and surrounded it with the light of burning draft cards. Some in front stuck flowers in the rifle barrels of the soldiers ringing the building; others kicked and spat. The troops and police cleared the grounds with tear gas and clubs.

Corbis–Bettman

 29–4
National Organization for Women, Statement of Purpose (1966)

Model Cities Program Effort to target federal funds to upgrade public services and economic opportunity in specifically defined urban neighborhoods between 1966 and 1974.

A hippie gestures the peace sign while standing in a meadow.

Getty Images, Inc.–Taxi

Counterculture   Various alternatives to mainstream values and behaviors that became popular in the 1960s, including experimentation with psychedelic drugs, communal living, a return to the land, Asian religions, and experimental art.

and the fight against sexism (a word no one knew before 1965) on the national agenda and changed how Americans thought about the relationships between men and women. Feminists highlighted rape as a crime of violence and called attention to the burdens the legal system placed on rape victims. In the 1980s and 1990s, they also challenged sexual harassment in the workplace, gradually refining the boundaries between acceptable and unacceptable behavior.

YOUTH CULTURE AND COUNTERCULTURE

Millions of young people in the second half of the 1960s expressed their alienation from American society by sampling drugs or chasing the rainbow of a youth culture. Some just smoked marijuana, grew long hair, and listened to psychedelic rock. Others plunged into ways of life that scorned their middle-class backgrounds. The middle aged and middle class ignored the differences and dubbed the rebellious young "hippies." A high point of the youth culture was the 1969 Woodstock rock festival in New York State, a weekend of "sex, drugs, and rock-and-roll" for 400,000 young people.

But within the youth culture was a smaller and more intense **counterculture** that added Eastern religion, social radicalism, and evangelistic belief in the drug LSD. The Harvard professor Timothy Leary and the writer Aldous Huxley claimed that hallucinogenic or psychedelic drugs, such as mescaline and LSD, would swing open the "doors of perception." Rock lyrics began to reflect the drug culture, and young people talked about Leary's advice to "tune in, turn on, and drop out." The mecca of the dropouts was San Francisco's Haight-Ashbury district, but hippie neighborhoods sprang up around university campuses across the country.

The cultural rebels of the late 1950s and early 1960s had been trying to combine personal freedom with new social arrangements. Many hippies were more interested in drugs than with politics or poetry. Serious exploration of societal alternatives was left for the minority who devoted themselves to the political work of the New Left, communal living, women's liberation, and other movements.

SOUNDS OF CHANGE

The youth culture was shaped by films and philosophers, by pot and poets, but above all by music. Many changes in American society are mirrored in the abrupt shift from the complacent rock-and-roll of the early 1960s to the more provocative albums of mid-decade: Bob Dylan's *Highway 61 Revisited* (1965), the Beatles *Rubber Soul* (1965) and *Sergeant Pepper's Lonely Hearts Club Band* (1967), the Jefferson Airplane's *Surrealistic Pillow* (1967). Musicians were increasingly self-conscious of themselves as artists and social critics.

At the start of the decade, the African-American roots of rock-and-roll were unmistakable, but there was no social agenda. Elvis Presley and the Everly Brothers kept the messages personal. Music that criticized American society initially found a much smaller audience through the folk-music revival. Folk singers, such as Pete Seeger and Joan Baez, drew on black music, white country music, and old labor-organizing songs to keep alive dissenting voices.

Then, in an artistic revolution, the doors opened to a new kind of rock music. The Beatles' immense popularity opened the way for such hard-edged British bands as the Rolling Stones and The Who to introduce social criticism and class consciousness into rock lyrics. San Francisco's new psychedelic-rock scene included performers such as the Jefferson Airplane, the Grateful Dead, Buffalo Springfield and Janis Joplin.

Bob Dylan transformed the music scene. His music was musically exciting and socially critical in a way that expressed much of the discontent of American young people. Dylan paved the way for later singers like Bruce Springsteen and Kurt Cobain.

The transformation of rock in the mid-1960s invited far more explicit treatment of sex and illegal drugs than was previously accepted in pop music. Jim Morrison and The Doors, Lou Reed and the Velvet Underground, and Jimi Hendrix exploded onto the scene in 1967. Their driving rhythms and sexually aggressive stage personalities blended the tensions of big cities with influences from white rock and roll and black rhythm and blues. By 1972, both Morrison and Hendrix were dead of hard living and drug abuse. Meanwhile, *Rolling Stone* magazine had published its first issue in November 1967, giving the new sounds a forum for serious analysis.

COMMUNES AND CULTS

Thousands of Americans in the late 1960s and 1970s formed "intentional communities" or "communes." Their members usually tried to combine individual freedom and spontaneity with cooperative living. Rural communes usually located on marginal land too poor to support commercial farming; members pored over *The Whole Earth Catalog* (1968) to figure out how to live on the land. Members of urban communes occupied large old houses and tried to pursue experiments in socialism, environmentalism, or feminism.

Communes were artificial families, financed by inheritances, food stamps, and handicraft sales, and they suffered from the same inequality between men and women that was fueling the feminist revolt. Like natural families, they were emotional hothouses; most collapsed because their members had incompatible goals.

Far more organized were exotic religious communities. Following an American tradition, they have offered tightly knit group membership and absolute answers to basic questions of human life. One of the most successful has been the Holy Spirit Association for the Unification of World Christianity (Unification Church), which Sun Myung Moon brought from Korea to the United States in 1973. Converts ("Moonies") have never numbered more than a few tens of thousands, but Moon amassed a huge fortune and dabbled in conservative politics.

Americans usually hear about cults only if they clash with authorities or end in disaster. Most tragic was the case of Jim Jones, who founded the People's Temple in California on a program of social justice but became dictatorial and abusive. He moved nearly a thousand followers to Guyana in South America and violently resisted efforts to penetrate his walls of secrecy. An investigation of abuses within the colony led to the murder of Congressman Leo Ryan and mass suicide by nine hundred of Jones's followers, who drank cyanide-laced punch on November 18, 1978.

At the Newport (Rhode Island) Jazz Festival in 1963, Joan Baez and Bob Dylan performed as folksingers who worked in the tradition of protest songs. Two years later in Newport, Dylan shocked the popular music world by replacing his acoustic instrument with an amplified guitar and backup and jump-starting a fruitful blending of folk, country, and rock music into radical new sounds.

AP/Wide World Photos

CITIES UNDER STRESS

In the confident years after World War II, big cities had an upbeat image. The typical movie with a New York setting opened with a shot of the towering Manhattan skyline and plunged into the bustling business or theater districts. By the 1970s, however, slums and squalid back streets dominated popular imagery.

The message in films and and on television was that cities had become places of random and frequent violence.

WHAT CHALLENGES
did American cities face in the late 1960s and 1970s?

DIAGNOSING AN URBAN CRISIS

Central cities had a special burden in caring for the domestic poor. Baltimore had 27 percent of the Maryland population in 1970 but 66 percent of the state's welfare recipients. Boston had 14 percent of the Massachusetts population but 32 percent of the welfare clients. Impoverished, and often fragmented, families needed schools to serve as social-work agencies as well as educational institutions. Poor people with no other access to health care treated city hospital emergency rooms as the family doctor.

Many urban problems were associated with the "second ghettos" created by the migration of 2.5 million African Americans from Southern farms to Northern and Western cities in the 1950s and 1960s. At the start of World War II, black Americans had been much more rural than white Americans. By 1970, they were more urban. One-third of all African Americans lived in the twelve largest cities, crowding into ghetto neighborhoods.

Postwar black migrants found systems of race relations that limited their access to decent housing, to the best schools, and to many unionized jobs. Many black families also had to face industrial layoffs and plant closures in the 1970s and 1980s. Already unneeded in the South because of the mechanization of agriculture, the migrants found themselves equally unwanted in the industrial North, caught in decaying neighborhoods and victimized by crime.

Because ghettos grew block by block, middle-class black families had to pioneer as intruders into white neighborhoods and then see ghetto problems crowd in behind them. Their children faced the seductions of the street, which became increasingly violent with the spread of handguns and illegal drugs.

Central cities faced additional financial problems unrelated to poverty and race. Much of their infrastructure was 50 to 100 years old by the 1960s and 1970s, and it was wearing out. This decay of urban utility and transportation systems was a by-product of market forces and public policy. Private developers often borrowed money saved through Northeastern bank accounts, insurance policies, and pension funds to finance new construction in the suburbs. The defense budget pumped tax dollars from the old industrial cities into the South and West.

High local taxes in older cities was one result, for the American system of local government demands that cities and the poor help themselves. By the early 1970s, the average resident of a central city paid roughly twice the state and local taxes per $1,000 of income as the average suburbanite. As Mayor Moon Laundreau of New Orleans commented, "We've taxed everything that moves and everything that stands still; and if anything moves again, we tax that, too."

RACIAL RIOTING

African Americans and Hispanics who rioted in city streets in the mid-1960s were fed up with lack of job opportunities, and with substandard housing and crime in their neighborhoods. Prominent black writers, such as James Baldwin in *The Fire Next Time* (1963), had warned of mounting anger. Suddenly the fires were real. Before they subsided, the riots scarred most big cities and killed two hundred people, most of them African Americans.

The explosion of the Watts neighborhood in Los Angeles fixed the danger of racial unrest in the public mind. Trouble started on August 11, 1965, when a white highway-patrol officer arrested a young African American for drunken driving. Loud complaints drew a crowd, and the arrival of Los Angeles police turned the bystanders into an angry mob that attacked passing cars. Rioting, looting, and arson spread through Watts until the National Guard occupied the neighborhood on August 14 and 15.

QUICK REVIEW

Urban Problems

◆ Minorities and the poor were concentrated in urban centers.

◆ Postwar black migrants to the north found themselves with limited access to better houses, schools, and jobs.

◆ Cities faced decaying infrastructure and high taxes.

28–2
Stokely Carmichael and Charles Hamilton, from Black Power (1968)

The outburst frightened white Americans. In most previous race riots, whites had used violence to keep blacks "in their place." In Watts, blacks were the instigators. The primary targets were the police and ghetto businesses that had reputations for exploiting their customers. The National Advisory Commission on Civil Disorders concluded in 1968 that most property damage was the "result of deliberate attacks on white-owned businesses characterized in the Negro community as unfair or disrespectful." In short, the riots were protests about the problems of ghetto life.

After Watts, Americans expected "long hot summers" and got them. Scores of cities suffered riots in 1966, including one by Puerto Ricans in Chicago that protested the same problems blacks faced. In 1967, the worst violence was in Newark, New Jersey, and in Detroit, where forty-three deaths and blocks of blazing buildings stunned television viewers.

Few politicians wanted to admit that African Americans and Hispanics had serious grievances. Their impulse was to blame riffraff and outside agitators—"lawbreakers and mad dogs," to quote California Governor Ronald Reagan. This theory was wrong. Almost all participants were younger neighborhood residents who were representative of the African-American population. Their violence came from the frustration of rising expectations. Despite the political gains of the civil rights movement, unemployment remained high, and the police treated all black people as potential criminals. The urban riots were political actions to force the problems of African Americans onto the national agenda.

MINORITY SEPARATISM

Minority separatism tapped the same anger. The phrase **"Black Power"** challenged the central goal of the civil rights movement, which sought full participation in American life. The term came from frustrated SNCC leader Stokely Carmichael in 1966: "We've been saying freedom for six years—and we ain't got nothing. What we're going to start saying now is 'Black Power'!"

Black power translated many ways—control of one's own community through the voting machine, celebration of the African-American heritage, creation of a parallel society that shunned white institutions. At the personal level, it was a synonym for black pride.

Black Power also meant increased interest in the **Nation of Islam**, or Black Muslims, who combined a version of Islam with radical separatism. It was strongest in Northern cities, where it offered an alternative to the life of the ghetto streets.

In the early 1960s, Malcolm X emerged as a leading Black Muslim. Growing up as Malcolm Little, he was a streetwise criminal until he converted to the Nation of Islam in prison. After his release, Malcolm preached that blacks should stop letting whites set the terms by which they judged their appearance, communities, and accomplishments. He emphasized the African cultural heritage and economic self-help and proclaimed himself an extremist for black rights. Rivals within the movement assassinated him in February 1965, but his ideas lived on in *The Autobiography of Malcolm X*.

The **Black Panthers** pursued similar goals. Bobby Seale and Huey Newton saw African-American ghettos as internal colonies in need of self-determination. They created the Panthers in 1966 and recruited Eldridge Cleaver as the group's chief publicist.

The Panthers shadowed police patrols to prevent mistreatment of African Americans and carried weapons into the California State Legislature in May 1967 to protest gun control. They also promoted community-based self-help efforts, and ran political candidates. Unlike the rioters in Watts, the Panthers

Black Power Philosophy emerging after 1965 that real economic and political gains for African Americans could come only through self-help, self-determination, and organizing for direct political influence.

Nation of Islam Religious movement among black Americans that emphasizes self-sufficiency, self-help, and separation from white society.

Black Panthers Political and social movement among black Americans, founded in Oakland, California, in 1966 and emphasizing black economic and political power.

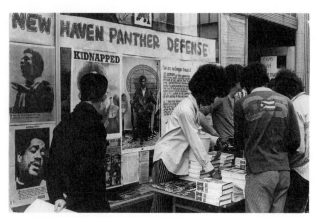

Some members of the Black Panther party raised funds to pay for the legal fees of those arrested and charged with various offenses, such as Bobby Seale and Ericka Huggins. The Panthers advocated a radical economic, social, and educational agenda that made the group the target of a determined campaign of suppression by the police and the FBI.

Magnum Photos Inc.

American Indian Movement (AIM)
Group of Native-American political activists who used confrontations with the federal government to publicize their case for Indian rights.

had a political program, if not the ability to carry it through. The movement was shaken when Newton was convicted of manslaughter for killing a police officer, Cleaver fled to Algeria, and a police raid killed Chicago Panther leader Fred Hampton.

Latinos in the Southwest developed a their own "Brown Power" movement in the late 1960s, but the best-known Hispanic activism combined social protest with the crusading spirit of earlier labor union organizing campaigns. César Chávez organized the multiracial United Farm Workers (UFW) among Mexican-American agricultural workers in California in 1965. UFW demands included better wages and safer working conditions. Because farm workers were not covered by the National Labor Relations Act of 1935, the issue was whether farm owners would recognize the union as a bargaining agent and sign a contract. Chávez supplemented work stoppages with national boycotts against table grapes, lettuce, and brands of wine, making *la huelga* ("the strike") into *la causa* for urban liberals. Although the UFW had only limited success, Chávez's toughness and self-sacrifice gave both Chicanos and the country a new hero.

Latino political activism had strong appeal for young people. Many rejected assimilation and began to talk about *la raza* ("the people"), whose language and heritage descended from centuries of Mexican history. "Chicano" itself was a slang term with insulting overtones that was now adopted as a badge of pride and cultural identity.

Native Americans also fought both for equal access to American society and to preserve cultural traditions through tribal institutions. Some Native American used media-oriented protest, such as seizing the abandoned Alcatraz Island (1969–1971) to assist "Red Power." Indians in Minneapolis created the **American Indian Movement (AIM)** in 1968 to increase economic opportunity, stop police mistreatment and to assert their distinctiveness within American society.

Black Power, Brown Power, and Red Power were all efforts by minorities to define themselves through their own heritage, not simply by looking in the mirror of white society. They thus questioned the American assumption that everyone wanted to be part of the same homogeneous society.

SUBURBAN INDEPENDENCE: THE OUTER CITY

The 1970 census found more people living in the suburban counties of metropolitan areas (37 percent) than in central cities (31 percent) or in small towns and rural areas (31 percent). By the late 1960s, these suburbs were becoming "outer cities," whose inhabitants had little need for the old central city and felt no personal connection to, or responsibility for, old city neighborhoods. For them, suburban malls and shopping strips were the new American Main Street and suburban communities the new Middle America.

Suburbs captured most new jobs, leaving the urban poor with fewer opportunities for employment. In the fifteen largest metropolitan areas, the number of central city jobs fell by 800,000 in the 1960s, while the number of suburban jobs rose by 3.2 million. The shift from rail to air for business travel accentuated suburban job growth. Sales representatives and executives could arrive at airports on the edge of town, and transact business without ever going downtown. Around many cities, suburban retailing, employment, and services fused into so-called "edge cities." Suburban rings also gained a growing share of public facilities including colleges and major league sports franchises.

Suburban political power grew along with economic clout. In 1962, the Supreme Court in the case of **Baker v. Carr** overturned laws that treated counties or other political subdivisions as the units to be represented in state legislatures. The Court said that legislative seats should be apportioned on the basis of population. This principle of "one person, one vote" broke the stranglehold of rural counties on state governments, but the big beneficiaries were fast-growing suburbs. By 1975, suburbanites held the largest block of seats in the House of Representatives—131 suburban districts, 130 rural, 102 central city, and 72 mixed.

School integration controversies in the 1970s reinforced a tendency for suburbanites to separate themselves from city problems. In *Swann v. Charlotte-Mecklenburg Board of Education* (1971), the U.S. Supreme Court held that crosstown busing was an acceptable solution to the *de facto* segregation that resulted from residential patterns within a single school district. When school officials around the country failed to achieve racial balance, federal judges ordered their own busing plans. Some white people resented the practice and for many Americans, the image of busing for racial integration was fixed in 1975, when white citizens in Boston resisted busing black students to largely white high schools. The goal of equal opportunity clashed with equally strong values of neighborhood, community, and ethnic solidarity.

Because the Supreme Court also ruled that busing programs normally stopped at school-district boundaries, suburbs with independent districts escaped school integration. One result was to make busing self-defeating, for it caused white families to move out of the integrating school district or place their children in private academies. Busing also caused suburbanites to defend their political independence fiercely. In Denver, for example, a by-product of court-ordered busing included incorporation or expansion of several large suburbs and a state constitutional amendment that blocked further expansion of the city boundaries (and thus of the Denver school district).

Baker v. Carr   U.S. Supreme Court decision in 1962 that allowed federal courts to review the appointment of state legislative districts and established the principle that such districts should have roughly equal populations ("one person, one vote").

Swann v. Charlotte-Mecklenburg Board of Education   U.S. Supreme Court decision in 1971 that upheld cross-city busing to achieve the racial integration of public schools.

THE YEAR OF THE GUN, 1968

In 1968, mainstream Americans turned against the war in Vietnam, student protest and youth counter-culture turned ugly, and political consensus shattered.

WHY DID America's view of the war in Vietnam change in 1968?

THE TET OFFENSIVE

The longer the Vietnam War continued and the less interest that China or the Soviet Union showed in it, the less valid the conflict seemed to the American people. It looked more and more like a war for pride, not national security.

At the end of 1967, U.S. officials were overconfidently predicting victory. They also fell for a North Vietnamese feint by committing U.S. forces to the defense of Khe Sanh, a strongpoint near the North-South border. The defense was a tactical success for the United States but thinned its forces elsewhere in South Vietnam. Then, at the beginning of Tet, the Vietnamese New Year on January 30, 1968, the Viet Cong attacked cities across South Vietnam. In the capital, Saigon, they even hit the U.S. embassy. U.S. and South Vietnamese troops repulsed the attacks, but the offensive was a psychological blow that convinced the American public that the war was quicksand.

Images from Vietnam went direct to the evening television news; it was a "living room war." A handful of images stayed in people's memories—a Buddhist monk burning himself to death in protest; a child with flesh peeled off by napalm; a South Vietnamese official executing a captive on the streets of Saigon.

In the wake of the Tet crisis, General Westmoreland's request for 200,000 more troops forced a political and military reevaluation. Clark Clifford, the new secretary of defense, as well as twenty "wise men"—the big names of the Cold War—told the president that the war was unwinnable. The best option was disengagement.

LBJ's Exit

Minnesota's liberal Senator Eugene McCarthy had decided to challenge Johnson in the presidential primaries. Because he controlled the party organizations in two-thirds of the states, Johnson ignored the first primary in New Hampshire. Enthusiastic college students staffed McCarthy's campaign. McCarthy won a startling 42 percent of the popular vote and twenty of twenty-four delegates in the March 16 election. The vote proved that the political middle ground would no longer hold.

By showing Johnson's vulnerability, New Hampshire also drew Robert Kennedy into the race. Younger brother of the former president, Kennedy inspired both fervent loyalty and strong distaste. In the 1950s, he had worked for Senator Joe McCarthy and had been a reluctant supporter of civil rights during his brother's administration. More than other mainstream politicians of the 1960s, however, he touched the hearts of Hispanic and African-American voters as well as the white working class.

Facing political challenges and an unraveling war, on March 31, 1968, Johnson announced a halt to most bombing of North Vietnam, opening the door for negotiations. He then astounded the country by withdrawing from the presidential race. As he told an aide, the war made him feel like a hitchhiker in a hailstorm: "I can't run, I can't hide, and I can't make it stop." Hoping to save his domestic program, he served out his term with few friends and little credit for his accomplishments.

Red Spring

In the months that followed the Tet crisis, grass-roots rebellion shook the Soviet grip on eastern Europe. University students in Poland protested the stifling of political discussion. Alexander Dubèek, the new leader of the Czech Communist party, brought together students and the middle class around reforms that caused people to talk about "Prague Spring"—a blossoming of democracy inside the iron curtain. In August, the Soviets sent in their tanks to crush the reforms and bring Czechoslovakia back into line.

Students protested across Europe. In Paris, student demonstrations against the Vietnam War turned into attacks on the university system and the French government. Students fought police in the Paris streets in the first days of May. Radical industrial workers called a general strike. The government nearly toppled.

At Columbia University in New York, African-American students and its SDS chapter had several grievances. One was the university's cooperation with the Pentagon-funded Institute for Defense Analysis. Another was its plan to build a gymnasium on park land that might better serve the residents of Harlem. Some students

WHERE TO LEARN MORE

★ Lyndon B. Johnson National Historic Park, Johnson City, Texas
www.nps.gov/lypo/

wanted changes in university policy, others a confrontation that would recruit new radicals. They occupied five university buildings, including the library and the president's office, for a week in April until police evicted them. The "battle of Morningside Heights" (the location of Columbia) gave Americans a glimpse of the gap that divided radicalized students from national institutions.

VIOLENCE AND POLITICS

On April 4, 1968, ex-convict James Earl Ray shot and killed Martin Luther King Jr. as he stood on the balcony of a Memphis motel. King's death triggered a climactic round of violence in black ghettos. Fires devastated the West Side of Chicago and downtown Washington, D.C. The army guarded the steps of the Capitol, ready to protect Congress from its fellow citizens.

The shock of King's death was still fresh when another political assassination stunned the nation. On June 5, Robert Kennedy won California's primary election. He was still behind Vice President Hubert Humphrey in the delegate count but coming on strong. As Kennedy walked out of the ballroom at his headquarters in the Ambassador Hotel in Los Angeles, a Jordanian immigrant named Sirhan Sirhan put a bullet in his brain.

Kennedy's death ensured the Democratic nomination for Humphrey, a liberal who had loyally supported Johnson's war policy. After his nomination, Humphrey faced Republican Richard Nixon and Independent George Wallace. Nixon positioned himself as the candidate of the political middle and claimed he had a secret plan for winning the war. Wallace appealed to white Southerners and working-class Northerners who feared black militancy and hated "the ivory-tower folks with pointed heads."

Both got great help from the Democratic Convention, held in Chicago on August 26–29. While Democrats feuded among themselves, Chicago Mayor Richard Daley and his police department monitored antiwar protesters. Leaders of the National Mobilization Committee to End the War in Vietnam were experienced peace activists—people who had long fought against nuclear weapons in the 1950s and the Vietnam War. They wanted to embarrass the Johnson-Humphrey administration by marching to the convention hall on nomination night. Mixed in were the **Yippies**. The term supposedly stood for Youth International Party. The Yippies planned to attract young people to Chicago with a promise of street theater, media events, and confrontation that would puncture the pretensions of the power structure.

On August 28, the same night that Democratic delegates were nominating Humphrey, protesters and Yippies had congregated in Grant Park, across Michigan Avenue from downtown hotels. Undisciplined police waded into the crowds with clubs and tear gas. Young people fought back with rocks and bottles. Television caught the hours of violence that ended when the National Guard separated police from demonstrators. On the convention floor, Senator Abraham Ribicoff of Connecticut decried "Gestapo tactics" on the streets of Chicago. Mayor Daley shouted back obscenities. For Humphrey, the convention was a catastrophe, alienating liberal Democrats.

Election day gave Wallace 13.5 percent of the popular vote, Humphrey 42.7 percent of the popular vote and 191 electoral votes, and Nixon 43.4 percent of the popular vote and 301 electoral votes. The national media saw Wallace in terms of bigotry and backlash against civil rights. But many of Wallace's northern backers were unhappy with both parties.

Dr. Martin Luther King, Jr.
Corbis/Bettmann

QUICK REVIEW

The 1968 Democratic Convention
◆ August 26–29: Democrats meet to nominate Hubert Humphrey.
◆ Antiwar protesters march on the convention hall.
◆ Undisciplined police helped precipitate violence between the police and the protesters.

WHAT WAS the legacy of
Richard Nixon's presidency?

NIXON AND WATERGATE

The new president was an unlikely politician. After losing a 1962 race for governor of California, he announced that he was quitting politics and that the press would no longer have Dick Nixon "to kick around." In 1968, he skillfully sold a "new Nixon" to the media. Seven years later, the press was his undoing as it uncovered the Watergate scandal.

GETTING OUT OF VIETNAM, 1969–1973

Nixon had no secret plan to end the war. Protests culminated in 1969 with the Vietnam Moratorium on October 15, when 2 million protesters joined rallies across the country. Disaffection also mounted in Vietnam. Nurses found their idealism strained as they treated young men maimed in thousands of nasty skirmishes in the jungles and mountains. Racial tensions sapped morale on the front lines. Troops lost discipline, took drugs, and hunkered down waiting for their tours of duty to end. Soldiers "fragged" (killed) their own gung-ho or racist officers, and the high command had to adapt its code of justice to keep an army on the job.

Nixon and Vice President Spiro Agnew responded by trying to isolate the antiwar opposition, but Nixon also reduced the role of U.S. ground forces. He claimed that his policies represented "the great silent majority of my fellow Americans." Agnew blamed bad morale on journalists and intellectuals—on "nattering nabobs of negativism" and "an effete corps of impudent snobs."

The New Left had already split into factions. About a hundred angry SDS members declared themselves the Weather Underground in 1969, taking their name from a Bob Dylan lyric. They tried to disrupt Chicago and Washington with window-smashing "days of rage." Three Weatherpeople blew themselves up with a homemade bomb in New York in 1970. Others bombed a University of Wisconsin building and killed a student.

Nixon's secretary of defense, Melvin Laird, responded to the antiwar sentiment with "Vietnamization," withdrawing U.S. troops as fast as possible without undermining the South Vietnamese government. In July 1969, the president announced the "**Nixon Doctrine**." The policy substituted weapons and money for men. Americans rearmed and expanded the South Vietnamese army and surreptitiously bombed Communist bases in neutral Cambodia.

The secret war against Cambodia culminated on April 30, 1970 with an invasion. Americans who had hoped that the war was fading away were outraged. Students shut down hundreds of colleges. At Kent State University in Ohio, the National Guard was called in to maintain order. On May 4, one unit fired on a group of nonthreatening students and killed four of them. At Jackson State University in Mississippi, two students were also killed when troops fired on their dormitory.

The Cambodian "incursion" extended the military stalemate in Vietnam to United States policy. In December 1970, Congress repealed the Gulf of Tonkin Resolution and prohibited use of U.S. ground troops outside South Vietnam. Cambodia, however, was already devastated. The U.S. invasion had opened the way for the bloodthirsty Khmer Rouge, who killed millions of Cambodians in the name of working-class revolution. Only ninety thousand U.S. ground troops were still in Vietnam by early 1972. A final air offensive in December smashed much of Hanoi into rubble and helped force four and a half years of peace talks to a conclusion.

The cease-fire began on January 27, 1973. The United States promised not to increase its military aid to South Vietnam. Immediately after coming to terms with North Vietnam, Nixon suspended the draft in favor of an all-volunteer military.

QUICK REVIEW

The Nixon Doctrine
- Nixon responded to antiwar protesters by reducing the role of U.S. ground forces in Vietnam.
- "Vietnamization": The withdrawal of U.S. troops as fast as possible without undermining the South Vietnamese government.
- The Nixon Doctrine substituted weapons and money for troops.

Nixon Doctrine President Nixon's new American policy (1969) toward Asia in which the United States would honor treaty commitments but would gradually disengage and expect Asian nations to handle military defense on their own.

NIXON AND THE WIDER WORLD

To his credit, Richard Nixon took American foreign policy in new directions even while he was struggling to escape from Vietnam and Cambodia. He hoped to distract the American people from frustration in Southeast Asia with more important accomplishments elsewhere.

Nixon's first foreign policy success was a gift from Kennedy and Johnson. NASA had been working since 1961 to meet Kennedy's goal of a manned trip to the moon before the end of the decade. On July 20, 1969 the lunar lander *Eagle* detached from the command module circling the moon and landed on the level plain known as the Sea of Tranquillity. Six hours later, Armstrong was the first human to walk on the moon.

For Nixon and Henry Kissinger, his national security adviser (and later secretary of state), foreign policy was about the balance of world economic and military power and securing the most advantageous agreements, alliances, and military positions. In particular, they hoped to trade improved relations with China and the USSR for help in settling the Vietnam War.

China was increasingly isolated within the Communist world. In 1969, it almost went to war with the USSR. Nixon was eager to take advantage of Chinese-Soviet tension. In April 1971 secret talks led to an easing of the American trade

WHERE TO LEARN MORE

Richard Nixon Library and Birthplace, Yorba Linda, California
www.nixonfoundation.org/index.shtml

WHERE TO LEARN MORE

★ Titan Missile Museum,
Green Valley, Arizona
www.pimaair.org/titan_0.1.htm

SALT (Strategic Arms Limitation Treaty)   Treaty signed in 1972 by the United States and the Soviet Union to slow the nuclear arms race.

détente   (French for "easing of tension") Used to describe the new U.S. relations with China and the Soviet Union in 1972.

New Federalism   President Richard Nixon's policy to shift responsibilities of government programs from the federal level to the states.

Organization of Petroleum Exporting Countries (OPEC)   Cartel of oil-producing nations in Asia, Africa, and Latin America that gained substantial power over the world economy in the mid-to late-1970s by controlling the production and price of oil.

embargo begun in 1950 and a tour of China by a U.S. table tennis team. Kissinger then arranged for Nixon's startling visit to Mao Zedong in Beijing in February 1972.

Playing the "China card" helped improve relations with the Soviet Union. The Soviets needed increased trade with the United States and a counterweight to China, the United States was looking for help in getting out of Vietnam, and both countries wanted to limit nuclear armaments. Protracted negotiations led to arms agreements known as **SALT**—the **Strategic Arms Limitation Treaty**—that Nixon signed in Moscow in May 1972. The agreements blocked creation of extensive antiballistic missiles (ABM) systems but failed to limit bombers, cruise missiles, or multiple independently targeted warheads on single missiles.

Diplomats used the French word *détente*, meaning easing of tension, to describe the new U.S. relations with China and the Soviet Union. It facilitated travel between the United States and China. It allowed U.S. farmers to sell wheat to the Soviets. More broadly, détente implied that the United States and China recognized mutual interests in Asia and that the United States acknowledged the Soviet Union as an equal in world affairs.

COURTING MIDDLE AMERICA

Nixon designed domestic policy to help him win reelection. His goal was to solidify his "Middle American" support; the strategy targeted the suburbs and the South. The Nixon White House preferred not to deal with troubled big cities. Spokesmen announced that the "urban crisis" was over and then dismantled the urban initiatives of Johnson's Great Society. Instead, Nixon tilted federal assistance to the suburbs. The centerpiece of his **New Federalism** was General Revenue Sharing (1972). By 1980, it had transferred more than $18 billion from the federal treasury to the states and more than $36 billion to local governments. Revenue sharing grants supplemented the general funds of every full-service government, whether a city of 2 million or a suburban town of five hundred.

Nixon pursued the southern strategy through Supreme Court nominations of Southerners Clement Haynsworth of Florida and G. Harrold Carswell of Alabama. Although the Senate rejected both as unqualified, the nominations nonetheless gave Nixon a reputation as a champion of the white South. He hoped to move cautiously in enforcing school desegregation, but a task force led by Secretary of Labor George Shultz crafted an approach that allowed substantial desegregation.

OIL, OPEC, AND STAGFLATION

More troublesome was inflation, one of Lyndon Johnson's unpleasant legacies. One of the causes was LBJ's decision to fight in Vietnam without tax increases until 1968. An income tax cut in 1969, supported by both parties, made the situation worse. Inflation eroded the value of savings and pensions. It also made U.S. goods too expensive for foreign buyers and generated a trade deficit.

After the 1972 election, inflation came roaring back. The main cause was sharp increases in the cost of energy. Angry at American support for Israel in the Arab-Israeli War of October 1973, Arab nations imposed an embargo on oil exports that lasted from October 1973 to March 1974. Gasoline and heating oil became scarce and expensive. The shortages eased when the embargo ended, but the **Organization of Petroleum Exporting Countries (OPEC)** had challenged the ability of the industrial nations to dictate world economic policy.

Americans switched off unused lights, turned down thermostats, and put on sweaters. Congress required states to enforce a highway speed limit of 55 miles per hour to get federal highway funds and enacted the first fuel economy standards for automobiles. More efficient imports captured a third of the U.S. car market by 1980.

After thirty years at the top, the United States could no longer dominate the world economy by itself. Germany and Japan now had economies as modern as that of the United States. In 1971, stagflation was the new term to describe the painful combination of inflation, high unemployment, and flat economic growth that matched no one's economic theory but everyone's daily experience.

AMERICANS AS ENVIRONMENTALISTS

In the turbulent 1970s, resource conservation grew into a multifaceted environmental movement. Environmentalism dealt with serious problems. It was broad enough for both scientific experts and activists, for both Republican Richard Nixon and Democrat Jimmy Carter.

After the booming 1950s, Americans had started to pay attention to the damage that advanced technologies and industrial production did to natural systems. Rachel Carson's *Silent Spring* in 1962 described the side effects of DDT and other pesticides on animal life. In her imagined future, spring was silent because all the birds had died of pesticide poisoning. Meanwhile, an offshore oil well polluted the beaches of Santa Barbara, California, in 1969. Fire danced across the Cuyahoga River in Cleveland when industrial discharges ignited.

On April 22, children in ten thousand schools and 20 million other people took part in Earth Day, an occasion first conceived by Wisconsin Senator Gaylord Nelson. Earth Day gained a grass-roots following in towns and cities across the country.

The mainstream media discovered the ravaged planet; so did a politically savvy president. Nixon had already signed the National Environmental Policy Act on January 1, 1970, and later in the year created the **Environmental Protection Agency (EPA)** to enforce environmental laws. The rest of the Nixon years brought legislation on clean air, clear water, pesticides, hazardous chemicals, and endangered species that made environmental management and protection part of governmental routine.

Americans began to realize that low-income and minority communities had more than their share of environmental problems. Residents near the Love Canal in Buffalo, New York, discovered in 1978 that an entire neighborhood was built on land contaminated by decades of chemical dumping. Activists sought to understand the health effects and force compensation, paving the way for the **Superfund** cleanup legislation. (See American View, "Grassroots Community action.") African Americans often lived downstream and downwind of heavily polluting industries. Landfills and waste disposal sites were frequently located near minority neighborhoods. Efforts to fight environmental racism became important in many minority communities.

FROM DIRTY TRICKS TO WATERGATE

Subordinates learned during his first administration that Richard Nixon would condone dishonest actions—"dirty tricks"—if they stood to improve his political position. In 1972 and 1973, dirty tricks grew from a scandal into a constitutional crisis when Nixon abused the power of his office to cover up wrongdoing and hinder criminal investigations.

The chain of events that undermined Nixon's presidency started with the **Pentagon Papers**. In his last year as secretary of defense, Robert McNamara had

Environmental Protection Agency (EPA) Federal agency created in 1970 to oversee environmental monitoring and cleanup programs.

Pentagon Papers Classified Defense Department documents on the history of the United States' involvement in Vietnam, prepared in 1968 and leaked to the press in 1971.

·AMERICAN VIEWS·

Grassroots Community Action

*I*n the 1950s, a major chemical company closed a waste dump in Niagara Falls, New York. The site, known as Love Canal, was soon surrounded by a park, school, and hundreds of modest homes. Residents put up with noxious odors and seepage of chemical wastes until 1978, when they learned that the State Health Department was concerned about the health effects on small children and pregnant women. Over the next two years, residents battled state and federal bureaucracies and reluctant politicians for accurate information about the risks they faced and then for financial assistance to move from the area (often their homes represented their only savings). In October, 1980, President Carter signed a bill to move all families permanently from the Love Canal area.

One of the leaders of the grassroots movement was housewife Lois Gibbs. The following excerpts from her story show her increasing sophistication as a community activist, starting by ringing doorbells in 1978 and ending with national television exposure in 1980. Although the Love Canal case itself was unusual, community based organizations in all parts of the country learned the tactics of effective action in the 1960s and 1970s.

WHAT PUBLIC programs in the 1960s and 1970s gave citizens experience in grassroots action? How might the Internet change the tactics of community organizing?

Knocking on Doors

I decided to go door-to-door with a petition. It seemed like a good idea to start near the school, to talk to the mothers nearest it. I had already heard that a lot of the residents near the school had been upset about the chemicals for the past couple of years. I thought they might help me. I had never done anything like this. . . . I was afraid a lot of doors would be slammed in my face, that people would think I was some crazy fanatic. But I decided to do it anyway. . . . and knocked on my first door. There was no answer. I just stood there, not knowing what to do. It was an usually warm June day and I was perspiring. I thought: What am I doing here? I must be crazy. People are going to think I am. Go home, you fool! And that's just what I did.

It was one of those times when I had to sit down and face myself. I was afraid of making a fool of myself, I had scared myself, and I had gone home. When I got there, I sat at the kitchen table with my petition in my hand, thinking. Wait. What if people do slam doors in your face? People may think you're crazy. But what's more important—what people think or your child's health? Either you're going to do something or

---

commissioned a report on America's road to Vietnam. The documents showed that the country's leaders had planned to expand the war even while they claimed to be looking for a way out. In June 1971, one of the contributors to the report, Daniel Ellsberg, leaked it to the *New York Times*. Its publication infuriated Nixon.

In response, the White House compiled a list of journalists and politicians who opposed Nixon. As White House staffer John Dean put it, the president's men could then "use the available federal machinery [Internal Revenue Service, FBI] to screw our political enemies." Former CIA employees E. Howard Hunt and G. Gordon Liddy became the chief "plumbers," as the group was known because its job was to prevent leaks of information. The plumbers cooked up schemes to embarrass political opponents and ransacked the office of Ellsberg's psychiatrist.

Early in 1972, Hunt went to work for CREEP—the Committee to Re-Elect the President—while Liddy took another position on the presidential staff. CREEP had already raised millions from corporations and was hatching plans to undermine Democrats with rumors and pranks. Then, on June 17, 1972, five inept burglars hired with CREEP funds were caught breaking into the Democratic National Committee office in Washington's **Watergate** apartment building. Nixon initiated

Watergate A complex scandal involving attempts to cover up illegal actions taken by administration officials and leading to the resignation of President Richard Nixon in 1974.

you're going to have to admit you're a coward and not do it. . . .

The next day, I went out on my own street to talk to people, I knew. It was a little easier to be brave with them. If I could convince people I knew—friends— maybe it would be less difficult to convince others. . . . I went to the back door, as I always did when I visited a neighbor. Each house took about twenty or twenty-five minutes. . . .

Phil Donahue and Political Action

The *Phil Donahue Show* called. They wanted us to appear on their June 18 show. The reaction in the office was different this time, compared to the show in October 1978. In October, everyone was excited. "Phil Donahue—wow!" Now, residents reacted differently. "Donahue. That's great press. Now we'll get the politicians to move!" . . . Now our people looked at the show as a tool to use in pushing the government to relocate us permanently. By this time we understood how politicians react to public pressure, how to play the political game. We eagerly agreed to go, and found forty other residents to go with us. . . .

[After arriving in Chicago] We then planned how we would handle the *Phil Donahue Show*. . . . We had to get the real issues across. Each resident was assigned an issue. One told of the chromosome tests. Another was to concentrate on her multiple miscarriages. Another was to ask for telegrams from across the country to the White House in support of permanent relocation. I coached them to get their point in, no matter the question asked. For example, if Donahue asked what you thought of the mayor, and your assignment was to discuss miscarriages, you should answer: "I don't like the mayor because I have had three miscarriages and other health problems, and he won't help us." Or; "My family is sick, and the mayor won't help us. That's why we need people to send telegrams to the White House for permanent relocation." . . . The residents were great! Each and every one followed through with our plan.

In July, I went on a speaking tour of California arranged by Jane Fonda and Tom Hayden. I visited many sites with problems similar to ours. I was able to give advice, based on our experiences. I told the leaders of each community that it wasn't hopeless that they could win. "Stick with it. We are!"

Source: Lois Marie Gibbs, as told to Murray Levine, *Love Canal: My Story* (Albany: State University of New York Press, 1982), pp. 12–13, 161–64.

a coverup. On June 23, he ordered his assistant H. R. Haldeman to warn the FBI off the case with the excuse that national security was involved. Nixon compounded this obstruction of justice by arranging a $400,000 bribe to keep the burglars quiet. The coverup worked in the short run.

Nixon's opponent in the 1972 election was South Dakota Senator George Mc-Govern, an impassioned opponent of the Vietnam War. McGovern was honest, intelligent, and well to the left on issues like the defense budget and legalization of marijuana. He did not appeal to the white Southerners and blue-collar Northerners. An assassination attempt that took George Wallace out of national politics also helped Nixon win in a landslide.

The coverup began to come apart with the trial of the Watergate burglars in January 1973. Federal Judge John Sirica used the threat of heavy sentences to pressure one burglar into a statement that implied that higher-ups had been involved. Meanwhile, the *Washington Post* was linking Nixon's people to dirty tricks and illegal campaign contributions. The White House scrambled to find a defensible story. Nixon now began to coach people on what they should tell investigators, claimed his staff had lied to him, and tried to set up John Dean to take the fall.

In the late spring and early summer, attention shifted to the televised hearings of the Senate's Select Committee on Presidential Campaign Activities. Its chair was Sam Ervin of North Carolina. A parade of White House and party officials described their own pieces in the affair, often accusing each other and revealing the plumbers and the enemies list. The real questions, it became obvious, were what the president knew and when he knew it. It seemed to be John Dean's word against Richard Nixon's.

A bombshell turned the scandal into a constitutional crisis. A mid-level staffer told the committee that Nixon made tape recordings of his White House conversations. Both the Senate and the Watergate special prosecutor, Archibald Cox, subpoenaed the tapes. Nixon refused to give them up. In late October, after he failed to cut a satisfactory deal, he fired his attorney general and the special prosecutor. Many Americans thought that these actions proved that Nixon had something to hide. In April 1974, he finally issued *edited* transcripts of the tapes, with foul language deleted and key passages missing. Finally, on July 24, 1974, the U.S. Supreme Court ruled unanimously that Nixon had to deliver sixty-four tapes to the new special prosecutor.

In Congress, Republicans joined Democrats in voting three articles of impeachment: for hindering the criminal investigation of the Watergate breakin, for abusing the power of the presidency by using federal agencies to deprive citizens of their rights, and for ignoring the committee's subpoena for the tapes. Before the full House could vote on the articles of impeachment, Nixon delivered the tapes containing direct evidence that he had participated in the coverup on June 23, 1972, and had been lying ever since. On August 8 he announced his resignation, effective the next day.

Watergate was two separate but related stories. On one level, it was about individuals, Nixon and his cronies who wanted to win so badly they repeatedly broke the law. Nixon paid for his overreaching ambition with the end of his political career; more than twenty others paid with jail terms.

On another level, the crisis was a lesson about the Constitution. The separation of powers allowed Congress and the courts to rein in a president who had spun out of control.

THE FORD FOOTNOTE

Gerald Ford was the first president who had been elected neither president nor vice president. Ford was Nixon's appointee to replace Spiro Agnew, who resigned and pleaded no contest to charges of bribery and income tax evasion in 1973. On September 8, Ford pardoned Richard Nixon for "any and all crimes" committed while president. Since Nixon had not yet been indicted, the pardon saved him from future prosecution. He also offered clemency to thousands of draft resisters.

Détente continued. American diplomats joined the Soviet Union and thirty other European nations in the capital of Finland to sign the **Helsinki Accords**, which called for increased commerce between the Eastern and Western blocs and human rights guarantees. They also legitimized the national boundaries that had been set in eastern Europe in 1945.

At home the economy slid into recession; unemployment climbed above 10 percent; inflation diminished the value of savings and wages.

Ford was the Republican presidential candidate in the 1976 election. His Democratic opponent was a political enigma. James Earl Carter Jr. had been a navy officer, a farmer, and governor of Georgia. Carter and other new style Southern politicians left race-baiting behind to talk like modern New Dealers. He appealed to Democrats as someone who could reassemble LBJ's political coalition and return the South to the Democratic party. In his successful campaign, Carter presented himself as an alternative to party hacks and Washington insiders.

Helsinki Accords   Agreement in 1975 among NATO and Warsaw Pact members that recognized European national boundaries as set after World War II and included guarantees of human rights.

JIMMY CARTER: IDEALISM AND FRUSTRATION IN THE WHITE HOUSE

As an outsider in Washington's political establishment, Carter had one great advantage: freedom from the narrow mind-set of experts who talk only to each other. However, he lacked both the knowledge of key political players and the experience to resolve legislative gridlock.

HOW WAS Jimmy Carter's idealism a frustration to his success as president?

CARTER, ENERGY, AND THE ECONOMY

Carter was refreshingly low-key. After his inauguration, he walked from the Capitol to the White House as Jefferson had. He signed official documents "Jimmy." He tended to tell the public what he thought rather than what pollsters said the people wanted to hear.

Carter's approach to politics reflected his training as an engineer. He was analytical, logical, and given to breaking a problem into its component parts. He filled his cabinet with experts rather than political operators. He didn't seem to understand the basic rules of Washington politics. For example, he and his cabinet officers developed policies and made appointments without consulting key congressional committee chairs.

The biggest domestic problem remained the economy, which slid into another recession in 1978. Another jump in petroleum prices helped make 1979 and 1980 the worst years for inflation in the postwar era. Carter himself was a fiscal conservative whose impulse was to cut federal spending. This worsened unemployment and alienated liberal Democrats, who wanted to revive the Great Society.

CLOSED FACTORIES AND FAILING FARMS

Ford and Carter both faced massive problems of economic transition that undercut their efforts to devise effective government programs.

Industrial decay stalked such "gritty cities" as Allentown, Pennsylvania; Trenton, New Jersey; and Gary, Indiana. Communities whose workers had made products in high volume for mass markets found that technological revolutions made them obsolete. Critics renamed the old manufacturing region of the Northeast and Midwest the Rustbelt in honor of its abandoned factories.

Plant closures were only one facet of business efforts to increase productivity by substituting machinery for employees. Between 1947 and 1977, American steelmakers doubled output while cutting their work force from 600,000 to 400,000. Lumber companies used economic recession in the early 1980s to automate mills and rehired only a fraction of their workers when the economy picked up. High interest rates in the early 1980s, the result of a ballooning federal deficit (see Chapter 30), attracted foreign investors and strengthened the dollar.

Carter simultaneously proposed a comprehensive energy policy. He asked Americans to make energy conservation the moral equivalent of war—to accept individual sacrifices for the common good. Congress created the Department of Energy but refused to raise taxes on oil and natural gas to reduce consumption. However, the Energy Policy and Conservation Act (1978) did encourage alternative energy sources to replace foreign petroleum. Big oil companies poured billions of dollars into western Colorado to squeeze a petroleum substitute from shale. Solar energy research prospered. Breezy western hillsides sprouted "wind farms" to wring electricity out of the air.

29–3
Jimmy Carter, The "Malaise" Speech (1979)

However, antinuclear activism blocked one obvious alternative to fossil fuels. In the late 1970s, activists staged sit-ins at the construction sites of nuclear plants. A near-meltdown at the Three Mile Island nuclear plant in Pennsylvania in March 1979 stalemated efforts to expand nuclear power capacity.

When the OPEC price hikes undermined the inflation-fighting effort in the summer of 1979, Carter proposed new steps to solve the energy crisis. A cabinet reshuffle a few days later was supposed to show that he was firmly in charge, but instead conveyed the message that he was erratic. By 1979, opinion leaders had decided that Carter was not capable of leading the nation and then interpreted every action as confirming that belief.

BUILDING A COOPERATIVE WORLD

Despite troubles on the home front, Carter's first two years brought foreign policy success that reflected a new vision of a multilateral world. He appointed Andrew Young—a fellow Georgian with long experience in the civil rights movement—as ambassador to the United Nations, where he worked effectively to build bridges to third-world nations.

Carter's moral convictions were responsible for a new concern with human rights around the globe. He criticized the Soviet Union for preventing free speech and denying its citizens the right to emigrate, angering Soviet leaders, who didn't expect the human rights clauses of the Helsinki Accords to be taken seriously. Carter also withheld economic aid from South Africa, Guatemala, Chile, and Nicaragua, which had long records of human rights abuses. In Nicaragua, the change in policy helped left-wing Sandinista rebels topple the Somoza dictatorship.

The triumph of the new foreign policy was the **Camp David Agreement** between Egypt and Israel. Carter risked his reputation and credibility in September 1978 to bring Egyptian President Anwar el-Sadat and Israeli Prime Minister Menachem Begin together at Camp David, the presidential retreat. A formal treaty signed in Washington on March 26, 1979 normalized relations between Israel and its most powerful neighbor and led to Israeli withdrawal from the Sinai Peninsula.

NEW CRISES ABROAD

The Soviets ignored the human rights provisions of the Helsinki Accords. Soviet advisers or Cuban troops intervened in African civil wars. At home, Cold Warriors who had never accepted détente found it easier to attack Carter than Nixon.

Carter inherited negotiations for SALT II—a strategic arms limitation treaty that would have reduced both the American and Soviet nuclear arsenals—from the Ford administration. SALT II met stiff resistance in the Senate. Opponents claimed it would create a "window of vulnerability" in the 1980s that would invite the Soviets to launch a nuclear first strike. Carter tried to counter criticism by stepping up defense spending, starting a buildup that would accelerate under Ronald Reagan.

Hopes for SALT II vanished on January 3, 1980, when Soviet troops entered Afghanistan. Muslim tribespeople unhappy with modernization had attacked Afghanistan's pro-Communist government, which invited Soviet intervention. The situation resembled the American involvement in South Vietnam. In the end, it took the Soviets a decade to find a way out.

The final blow to Carter's foreign policy came in Iran. Since 1953, the United States had strongly backed Iran's monarch, the Shah. The Shah modernized

Camp David Agreement Agreement to reduce points of conflict between Israel and Egypt, hammered out in 1977 with the help of U.S. President Jimmy Carter.

Iran's economy but jailed political opponents. U.S. aid and oil revenues helped him build a vast army, but the Iranian middle class despised his authoritarianism, and Muslim fundamentalists opposed modernization. Revolution toppled the Shah at the start of 1979.

The upheaval installed a nominally democratic government, but the Ayatollah Ruhollah Khomeini, a Muslim cleric who hated the United States, exercised real power. Throughout 1979, Iran grew increasingly anti-American. After the United States allowed the exiled Shah to seek medical treatment in New York, a mob stormed the U.S. embassy in Tehran on November 4, 1979, and took more than sixty Americans hostage. They demanded that Carter surrender the Shah.

Television brought pictures of blindfolded hostages and anti-American mobs burning effigies of Uncle Sam and wrapping American flags around garbage. The administration tried economic pressure and diplomacy, but Khomeini had no desire for accommodation. When Iran announced in April 1980 that the hostages would remain in the hands of the militants rather than be transferred to the government, Carter ordered an airborne rescue. The attempt misfired when three of eight helicopters malfunctioned and one crashed in the Iranian desert. The fiasco added to the national embarrassment. The United States and Iran finally reached agreement on the eve of the 1980 election. The hostages gained their freedom after 444 days at the moment Ronald Reagan took office as the new president.

The hostage crisis consumed Jimmy Carter the way that Vietnam had consumed Lyndon Johnson. It gripped the public and stalemated other issues. For weeks, Carter's tragedy was that "his" Iranian crisis was the fruit of policies hatched by the Eisenhower administration and pursued by every president since then, all of whom overlooked the Shah's despotic government because of his firm anti-Communism.

After thirty years in which the United States had viewed the entire world as a Cold War battlefield, Carter was willing to accept the developing world on its own terms. His human rights efforts showed that evangelical religious convictions could be tied to progressive aims. Iranian rage at past policies of the sort Carter hoped to change destroyed his ability to direct a new course.

CONCLUSION

A period of remarkable prosperity ended in 1974. Long lines at gas stations suggested that prosperity was fragile. Cities and regions began to feel the costs of obsolete industries. Environmental damage caused many Americans to reconsider the goal of economic expansion.

American withdrawal from Vietnam in 1973 and the collapse of the South Vietnamese government in 1975 were defeats; the United States ended up with little to show for a long and painful war. SALT I stabilized the arms race, but it also recognized that the Soviet Union was an equal. The American nuclear arsenal might help deter a third world war, but it could not prevent the seizure of hostages in Iran.

The nation finished the 1970s more egalitarian than it had been in the early 1960s but also more divided. More citizens had the opportunity to advance economically and to seek political power, but there were deepening fissures between social liberals and cultural conservatives, old and new views about roles for women, rich and poor, white and black people.

SUMMARY

The End of Consensus The failure to win an easy victory in Vietnam eroded the nation's confidence and fueled bitter division about the nation's goals. Operation Rolling Thunder in the air and search and destroy missions on the ground were not "wining" the war; protest against the war at home quickly followed America's decision to use combat forces. The tone of the debate over Vietnam turned nastier, much of the anger directed at the draft. The antiwar movement reflected a growing grass-roots activism on college campuses, among women, and the Woodstock generation counterculture.

Cities Under Stress Exploding metropolitan areas needed money for streets, schools, and sewers. Many urban problems were associated with the creation of "second ghettos" due to immigration in the 1950s and 1960s. A series of riots scarred most big cities during the 1960s; the riots were protests about the problems of ghetto life but were often blamed on "outsiders." Minority separatism tapped into the same anger that caused the riots. The Black Power movement, Hispanic activism in the Southwest, and the American Indian Movement all questioned the American assumption that everyone wanted to be a part of the same homogeneous society, a society increasingly becoming "suburbanized."

The Year of the Gun, 1968 1968 was a watershed year that forced American society to rethink the role of government. Mainstream Americans began questioning the war in Vietnam after the Tet Offensive; President Johnson was advised that the war was unwinnable on acceptable terms. Facing political challenges, Johnson announced a halt to the bombing of North Vietnam and his withdrawal from the presidential race. The assassinations of Martin Luther King Jr. and Robert Kennedy and the riots at the Democratic National Convention captured America's attention. Richard Nixon captured the presidency in 1968 with a secret plan to end the war and an appeal to middle America.

Nixon and Watergate President Nixon had no plan to end the Vietnam War and antiwar sentiment grew; while the Nixon Doctrine and "Vietnamization" made it appear the United States was withdrawing from Southeast Asia, the bombing of Cambodia intensified. The 1973 ceasefire confirmed American withdrawal from Vietnam; in 1975 South Vietnam collapsed. To his credit, Nixon took American foreign policy in new directions, improving relations with the Soviet Union and China, and the administration passed numerous laws relating to environmental issues. Nixon abused the power of his office in the Watergate scandal and resigned before he could be impeached; Gerald Ford, who had been appointed vice president, succeeded him.

Jimmy Carter: Idealism and Frustration in the White House Washington outsider Jimmy Carter's major domestic challenge was the economy. A recession, an energy crisis, the deindustrization of America, and the transformation of the family farm to agribusiness challenged the president upon his election. Carter's moral convictions brought attention to human rights issues abroad. The signing of the Camp David Agreement between Egypt and Israel was a high point; hopes for reducing nuclear arsenals ended when the Soviet Union invaded Afghanistan. The Iranian hostage crisis consumed the Carter administration and helped contribute to Ronald Reagan's 1980 victory.

REVIEW QUESTIONS

1. Why did the United States fail in Vietnam? What factors limited President Johnson's freedom of action there?

2. How did racial relations change between 1965 and 1970?

3. Why was 1968 a pivotal year for American politics and society?

4. What were the implications of détente? How and why did U.S. influence over the rest of the world change during the 1970s?

5. How did the backgrounds of Presidents Johnson, Nixon, and Carter shape their successes and failures as national leaders?

6. Why was the "space race" important for the United States?

KEY TERMS

American Indian Movement (AIM) (p. 772)
Baker v. *Carr* (p. 773)
Black Panthers (p. 771)
Black Power (p. 771)
Camp David Agreement (p. 784)
Counterculture (p. 768)
Détente (p. 778)
Environmental Protection Agency (p. 779)

Free Speech Movement (FSM) (p. 776)
Helsinki Accords (p. 782)
Model Cities Program (p. 767)
Nation of Islam (p. 771)
New Federalism (p. 778)
Nixon Doctrine (p. 776)
Organization of Petroleum Exporting Countries (OPEC) (p. 778)

Pentagon Papers (p. 779)
SALT (Strategic Arms Limitation Treaty) (p. 778)
Search and destroy (p. 763)
Selective Service System (p. 766)
Students for a Democratic Society (SDS) (p. 766)
Swann v. *Charlotte-Mecklenburg Board of Education* (p. 773)
Watergate (p. 780)

WHERE TO LEARN MORE

 Lyndon B. Johnson National Historical Park, Johnson City, Texas. Johnson's ranch, southwest of Austin, gives visitors a feeling for the open landscape in which Johnson spent his early years. **www.nps.gov/lypo/**

Vietnam Veterans Memorial, Washington, D.C. A simple wall engraved with the names of the nation's Vietnam War dead is testimony to one of the nation's most divisive wars. **www.nps.gov/vive/**

Richard Nixon Library and Birthplace, Yorba Linda, California. Exhibits trace Nixon's political career and related world events with a sympathetic interpretation. **www.nixonfoundation.org/index.shtml**

Titan Missile Museum, Green Valley, Arizona. The Green Valley complex near Tucson held eighteen Titan missiles. They were deactivated after SALT I, and the complex is now open to visitors. **www.pimaair.org/titan_01.htm**

For additional study resources for this chapter, go to:
www.prenhall.com/goldfield/chapter29

Iconic Images of the Vietnam Era

PRESIDENTS HAVE their picture taken shaking hands with visitors countless times. Usually they are of interest only to the visitors. What do you think made the photograph of President Nixon with Elvis Presley of interest to so many? During the late 1960s and early 1970s violence at home and overseas was distressingly commonplace. What do you think made the photographs of Mary Vecchio and Kim Phuk so memorable?

Television famously brought the Vietnam War "into the living room." Nonetheless some of the most memorable images of the era were photographs. What is it about particular images that turn them into iconic representations of a moment of history? Pictured here are three such photographs. The first shows Richard Nixon and Elvis Presley in the Oval Office. Fifteen years earlier, Presley had scandalized the "older generation" with his uninhibited gyrations. Nixon, then and later, always campaigned for "family values." Next is a photograph of a student reacting to the killing of a classmate on May 4, 1970 at Kent State University in Ohio. The preceeding week Nixon had ordered U.S. troops into Cambodia to destroy North Vietnamese supply routes and command centers. Campuses across the country erupted and in Ohio, the governor called in the National Guard to quell the demonstrations at Kent State. Guard soldiers fired on the students, killing the young man shown this photograph. The third photograph shows the impact on an American napalm attack upon the children of a South Vietnamese village.

◄ **This is the single most requested item in the National Archives which contain, among other national treasures, originals of the Declaration of Independence, the Constitution, and the Bill of Rights.** President Nixon and Elvis Presley met at the singer's request. He had volunteered to work in the administration's anti-drug crusade. The president, looking for a way to reach out to young people, readily agreed. He appointed Presley a "deputy" in the anti-drug war. Presley was, at the time, addicted to a variety of uppers, downers, and other medications.

This Pulitzer Prize-winning photo-graph of 9-year-old Kim Phuc, cen-ter, running after an aerial napalm attack on her village in 1972 was taken by Associated Press photog-rapher Nick Ut (Cong Ut). Kim suffered burns over 65% of her body. She survived and is now a peace activist. ►

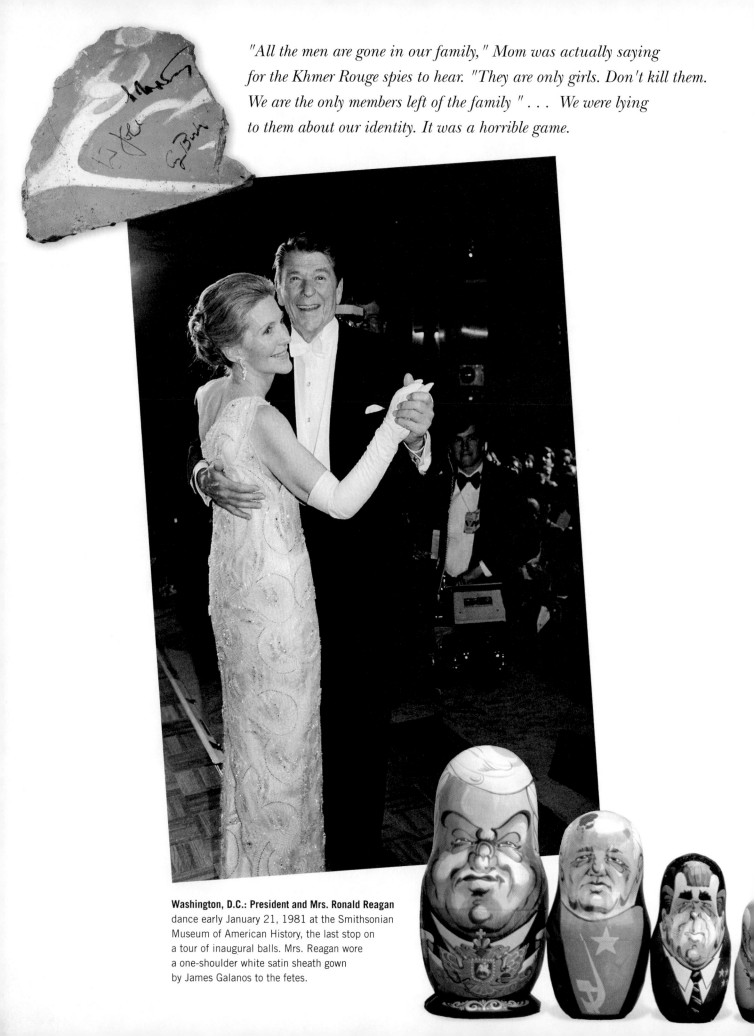

"All the men are gone in our family," Mom was actually saying
for the Khmer Rouge spies to hear. *"They are only girls. Don't kill them.
We are the only members left of the family "* . . . *We were lying
to them about our identity. It was a horrible game.*

Washington, D.C.: President and Mrs. Ronald Reagan
dance early January 21, 1981 at the Smithsonian
Museum of American History, the last stop on
a tour of inaugural balls. Mrs. Reagan wore
a one-shoulder white satin sheath gown
by James Galanos to the fetes.

30

THE REAGAN REVOLUTION AND A CHANGING WORLD

1981–1992

1992

1981

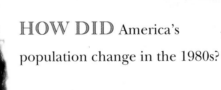

WHAT ECONOMIC

and social changes occurred during the Reagan administration?

WHAT foreign policy measures did Ronald Reagan employ in dealing with the Soviet Union and the Middle East?

HOW DID America's population change in the 1980s?

WHAT WERE the culture wars?

IMAGE KEY

for pages 790–791

a. A piece of the fallen Berlin Wall.

b. President Ronald Reagan and First Lady Nancy Reagan dance at his first inaugural at the Smithsonian on January 21, 1981.

c. Nesting dolls of Communist or Russian leaders Boris Yeltsin, Mikhail Gorbechev, Leonid Brezhnev, Nikita Khruschev, Joseph Stalin, Vladimir Lenin, and Czar Nicholas II.

d. The black flying wing design of the stealth bomber resembles a bat.

e. Traders on the floor of the new York Stock Exchange work frantically as panic selling swept Wall Street, Monday, October 19, 1987. The Dow Jones Industrial average plunged more than 500 points for the biggest one-day loss in history.

f. Mikhail Gorbachev and Reagan sign INF treaty at the White House.

g. Hispanic female student raises her hand in class.

h. Abortion rights advocate Inga Coulter stands next to pro life protester Elizabeth McGee during clashing demonstrations outside the Supreme Court building.

The Khmer Rouge marched into the city [Phnom Penh, the capital of Cambodia], dressed in black. . . . Young Khmer Rouge [Marxist revolutionary] soldiers, eight or ten years old, were dragging their rifles, which were taller than them. . . . The whole city, more than two million people was forced out of their homes into the streets. My family walked until we reached Mao Tse-Tung Boulevard, the main boulevard in Phnom Penh. All the population of the city was gathered there. The Khmer Rouge were telling everyone to leave the city.

Although my two middle children were safe in France, my oldest and youngest daughters were close beside me. Parika was only seven. Mealy, who was nineteen, carried her infant son. I kept my children huddled together. As soon as a parent let go, a child would be lost in the huge crowd. . . . And the Khmer Rouge kept ordering everybody, "You must go forward." They shot their guns in the air. Even during the middle of the night the procession was endless. The Khmer Rouge kept shooting and we kept moving forward. . . .

Recently I saw the movie Doctor Zhivago, *about the Russian Revolution. If you compare that to what happened in Phnon Penh, the movie is only on a very small scale. Even* Killing Fields *only gives you part of the idea of what happened in Cambodia. The reality was much more incredible. . . .*

Each night, when we came back to the village from working in the fields, Mom would say, "Children, let's all go to sleep." She would quietly warn me that the wood had eyes and ears. She'd say, "It's nine o'clock now. Go to sleep. . . . There is nothing else to do but work. All the men are gone in our family." Mom was actually saying for the Khmer Rouge spies to hear, "They are only girls. Don't kill them. We are the only members left of the family." . . . We were lying to them about our identity. It was a horrible game.

If you hid your identity, that meant you wanted your past forgotten. We had changed from people who were intellectual, who used to think independently. . . . You became humiliated, allowed to live only as a slave. . . . We were accepted into the United States thanks to my husband's military service. . . . My daughters and I flew to the United States on July 4, 1979. . . . As we landed, I thought, "This is real freedom." . . .

I've found that America is a country where people have come from all over the world. You do your job, you get paid like anybody else, and you're accepted. But Cambodians I know in France, like my sister, feel differently. People are not accepted if they are not French. But in America you're part of the melting pot. . . . In 1983, I came to Los Angeles for my daughter Monie's wedding. I decided to stay. . . . Long Beach has the largest concentration of Cambodians in the country. I called the community center in Long Beach. They said they had no job openings. So I decided to get involved in running a store. . . . Donut shops are very American. . . .

All that refugees have is our work, our dreams. Do I still hurt from what happened in the past? When I opened my mouth to tell you my story, I don't know where my tears came from. . . . My daughters don't like to talk

about the past in Cambodia. They want to forget and think about their fu-
ture. They ask me why I would talk about the past with anybody. I said, "The
past cannot be erased from my memory."

Celia Noup in Al Santoli, *New Americans: An Oral History* (New York, 1988).

CELIA NOUP taught school for twenty years in Cambodia, which borders on
South Vietnam. In 1975, after a long civil war, the Communist Khmer Rouge insurgents took over Cambodia's capital, Phnom Penh, and forced its inhabitants into
the countryside to work in the fields. Four years later, Noup managed to make
her way to a refugee camp in neighboring Thailand and then to the United States.
Here she joined hundreds of thousands of other refugees who arrived in the later
1970s and 1980s from war-devastated nations such as Cambodia, Vietnam, Laos,
Ethiopia, and Afghanistan. Within a decade, she was working from 5:00 A.M. to
7:00 P.M. in her own donut shop near Los Angeles airport and worrying about
helping her children buy houses.

Celia Noup's life shows some of the ways that new waves of immigration
from Asia, Latin America, and Africa have changed the United States over the
last generation. Immigrants fueled economic growth in the 1980s and 1990s
with their labor and their drive to succeed in business. They revitalized older
neighborhoods in cities from coast to coast and changed the ethnic mix of
major cities. And they created new racial tensions that found their way into national political debates about immigration and into open conflict in places such
as Miami and Los Angeles.

Noup's story is also a reminder of the drawn-out consequences of the U.S.
involvement in Vietnam and the long shadow of the Cold War. The Cambodian
civil war was fueled by the Vietnamese war and the American invasion of Cambodia in 1969. American refugee policy was humanitarian, but also political, opening the door to people fleeing Communist regimes but holding it shut against
refugees from right-wing dictatorships. In Washington, foreign policy decisions
in the 1980s started with the desire of a new administration to reaffirm American
toughness after failures in Vietnam and ended with the astonishing evaporation
of the Cold War.

By the end of Ronald Reagan's presidency (1981–89), new rules governed
domestic affairs as well as international relations. Since World War II, politics had
followed a well-thumbed script. Lessons about full employment and social services that were accepted in 1948 still applied in 1968 or 1972. In the 1980s, however, Americans decided to reverse the growth of federal government
responsibilities that had marked both Republican and Democratic administrations since the 1930s. By the 1990s, the center of U.S. politics had shifted substantially to the right, and even a "liberal" Democrat like Bill Clinton would
sound like an Eisenhower Republican. The backdrop to the political changes was
massive readjustments in the American economy that began in the 1970s with
the decline of heavy industry and then continued to shift employment from factory jobs to service jobs in the 1980s. The ideology of unregulated markets celebrated economic success and made "yuppies" or young urban professionals the
center of media attention. But behind the lifestyle stories was a troubling reality: a widening gap between the rich and poor. The result by 1992 was a nation
that was much more secure in the world than it had been in 1980, but also more
divided against itself.

REAGAN'S DOMESTIC REVOLUTION

WHAT ECONOMIC and social changes occurred during the Reagan administration?

WHERE TO LEARN MORE

Ronald Reagan Boyhood Home, Dixon, Illinois

Political change began in 1980, when Ronald Reagan and running mate George H. W. Bush rode American discontent to a decisive victory in the presidential election (see Map 30–1). Building on a conservative critique of American policies and developing issues that Jimmy Carter had placed on the national agenda, Reagan presided over revolutionary changes in American government and policies. He was a "Teflon president" who managed to take credit for successes but avoid blame for problems, and he rolled to a landslide reelection in 1984 and set the stage for George H. W. Bush's victory in 1988. The consequences of his two terms included an altered role for government, powerful but selective economic growth, and a shift of domestic politics away from bread-and-butter issues toward moral or lifestyle concerns.

An unresolved question is whether Ronald Reagan planned an economic revolution, or simply presided over changes initiated by others. Most memoirs by White House insiders and books by journalists suggest the latter. But even if Reagan was acting out a role that was scripted by others, he was a hit at the polling place. Americans voted *against* Jimmy Carter in 1980, but they enthusiastically voted *for* Reagan in 1984.

REAGAN'S MAJORITY

Ronald Reagan reinvented himself several times on the way to the White House. A product of small-town Illinois, he succeeded in Hollywood in the late 1930s as a romantic lead actor while adopting the liberal politics common at the time. After World War II, he moved to the political right as a spokesman for big business. In two terms as governor of California, he spoke for a state and then a nation that were drifting toward more conservative values and expectations.

Reagan tapped into nostalgia for a simpler America. Although he was 69 when elected, his Hollywood background made it easy for him to use popular films to make his points. He once threatened to veto legislation by challenging Congress with Clint Eastwood's "Make my day." Many blockbuster movies reinforced two of Reagan's messages. One was the importance of direct confrontation with bad guys. The second was the incompetence of government bureaucracies, whose elitist mistakes could only be set right by tough individuals, like the movie heroes Dirty Harry and Rambo.

Some of Reagan's most articulate support came from anti-Communist stalwarts who feared that the United States was losing influence in the world. Despite Jimmy Carter's tough actions in 1979 and 1980 and increased defense spending, such conservatives had not trusted him to do enough. The inability to free the hostages in Iran grated. The Panama Canal and SALT II treaties seemed to give away American power. Soviet military buildup, charged the critics, was creating a "window of vulnerability."

Other Reagan voters directed their anger at government bureaucracies. Christian conservatives worried that social activists were using the federal courts to alter traditional values. Wealthy entrepreneurs from the fast-growing South and West believed that Nixon-era federal offices such as the Environ-

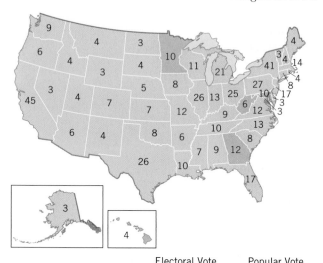

	Electoral Vote (%)	Popular Vote (%)
RONALD REAGAN (Republican)	**489** **(91)**	**43,201,220** **(50.9)**
Jimmy Carter (Democrat)	49 (9)	34,913,332 (41.2)
John B. Anderson (Independent)	–	5,581,379 (6.6)
Other candidates (Libertarian)	–	921,299 (1.1)

MAP 30–1

The Election of 1980   Ronald Reagan won in a landslide in 1980. Independent candidate John Anderson took more votes from Jimmy Carter than from Reagan, but Reagan's personal magnetism was a powerful political force. His victory confirmed the shift of the South to the Republican Party.

WHAT DID Reagan's victory tell about voters' desire for change in 1980?

CHRONOLOGY

1973	Roe v. Wade: Supreme Court struck down state laws banning abortion in the first trimester of pregnancy.
1980	Ronald Reagan is elected president.
1981	Economic Recovery and Tax Act, reducing personal income tax rates, is passed. Reagan breaks strike by air traffic controllers. AIDS is recognized as a new disease
1982	Nuclear freeze movement peaks. United States begins to finance Contra rebels against the Sandinista government in Nicaragua. Equal Rights Amendment fails to achieve ratification.
1983	241 Marines are killed by a terrorist bomb in Beirut, Lebanon. Strategic Defense Initiative introduced. U.S. invades Grenada.
1984	Reagan wins reelection.
1985	Mikhail Gorbachev initiates economic and political reforms in the Soviet Union.
1986	Tax Reform Act is adopted.

1987	Congress holds hearings on the Iran-Contra scandal. Reagan and Gorbachev sign the Intermediate Nuclear Force treaty.
1988	George Bush is elected president.
1989	Communist regimes in eastern Europe collapse; Germans tear down Berlin Wall. Financial crisis forces federal bailout of many savings and loans. United States invades Panama to capture General Manuel Noriega.
1990	Iraq invades Kuwait; and United States sends forces to the Persian Gulf. West Germany and East Germany reunite. Americans with Disabilities Act is adopted.
1991	Persian Gulf War: Operation Desert Storm drives the Iraqis from Kuwait. Soviet Union dissolves into independent nations. Strategic Arms Reduction Treaty (START) is signed.
1992	Acquittal of officers accused of beating Rodney King triggers Los Angeles riots.

mental Protection Agency and the Occupational Safety and Health Administration, were choking their businesses in red tape.

The key to Reagan's reforms, however, was disaffected blue-collar and middle-class voters who deserted the Democrats. Reagan's campaign hammered on the question; "Are you better off than you were four years ago?" Many white blue-collar voters were alienated by affirmative action and busing for school integration. They also worried about inflation and blamed their difficulties on runaway government spending.

30-1
Ronald Reagan, First Inaugural Address (1981)

Reagan also made the Republicans seem exciting. In the mid 1980s young people in their twenties and early thirties saw the Republicans as the party of energy and new ideas, leaving the Democrats to the middle-aged and elderly.

In the election of 1984, Democrats sealed their fate by nominating Walter Mondale, who had been vice president under Carter. Mondale was earnest, honest, and dull. Reagan ran on the theme, "It's Morning in America," with the message that a new age of pride and prosperity had begun. He won reelection with 98 percent of the electoral votes. His election confirmed that the American public found conservative ideas increasingly attractive.

THE NEW CONSERVATISM

Reagan's approach to public policy drew on conservative intellectuals who offered a critique of the New Deal-New Frontier approach to American government. Some of the leading figures were journalists and academics who feared that the antiwar movement had undermined the anti-Communist stance and that social changes were corrupting mainstream values. *Commentary* and The Public Interest magazines became platforms for these neoconservative arguments.

Edward Banfield's radical ideas about the failures of the Great Society set the tone of the neoconservative analysis. In *The Unheavenly City* (1968), he argued that

Ronald Reagan and his wife Nancy celebrate Reagan's inauguration as president.

Corbis–Bettman

QUICK REVIEW

The Conservative Critique

◆ Free markets work better than government programs.

◆ Government intervention does more harm than good.

◆ Government assistance saps the initiative of the poor.

 30–2
Ronald Reagan, Speech to the House of Commons (1982)

Economic Recovery and Tax Act of 1981 (ERTA) A major revision of the federal income tax system.

Deregulation Reduction or removal of government regulations and encouragement of direct competition in many important industries and economic sectors.

liberal programs failed because inequality is based on human character and rooted in the basic structure of society; government action can solve only the problems that require better engineering, such as pollution control, better highways, or the delivery of explosives to military targets. Government's job was to preserve public order, not to right wrongs or encourage unrealistic expectations.

Other conservative writers elaborated Banfield's ideas. Charles Murray's 1984 book, *Losing Ground*, argued that welfare assistance encouraged dependency and discouraged individual efforts at self-improvement. The editorial page of the *Wall Street Journal* became a national forum for outspoken versions of neoconservatism.

The common themes of the conservative critique were simple: Free markets work better than government programs; government intervention does more harm than good; government assistance may be acceptable for property owners, but it saps the initiative of the poor. In 1964, three-quarters of Americans had trusted Washington "to do what is right." By 1980, three-quarters were convinced that the federal government wasted tax money. The neoconservatives offered the details to support Reagan's own summary: "Government is not the solution to our problems; government is the problem." The cumulative effect of the neoconservative arguments was to trash the word "liberal" and convince many Americans that labor unions and minorities were "special interests" but that oil tycoons, defense contractors, and other members of Reagan's coalition were not.

The conservative cause found support in new "think tanks" and political lobbying organizations, such as the Manhattan Institute, the Heritage Foundation, and the American Enterprise Institute, where conservative analysts could develop policy proposals and opinion pieces for newspapers. The cumulative effect shifted political discussion in a conservative direction between 1975 and 1990.

Conservatives promoted their ideology with new political tactics. Targeted mailings raised funds and mobilized voters. Radio talk shows spread the conservative message.

REAGANOMICS: DEFICITS AND DEREGULATION

The heart of the 1980s revolution was the **Economic Recovery and Tax Act of 1981 (ERTA)**, which reduced personal income tax rates by 25 percent over three years. The explicit goal was to stimulate business activity by lowering taxes overall and slashing rates for the rich. Cutting the government's total income by $747 billion over five years, ERTA meant less money for federal programs and more money in the hands of consumers and investors to stimulate economic growth.

Reagan's first budget director, David Stockman, later revealed a second goal. Because defense spending and Social Security were politically untouchable, Congress would find it impossible to create and fund new programs without cutting old ones. The first year's tax reductions were accompanied by cuts of $40 billion in federal aid to mass transit, school lunches, and similar programs. If Americans still wanted social programs, they could enact them at the local or state level.

The second part of the economic agenda was to free eager capitalists from government regulations to increase business initiative, innovation, and efficiency. The **deregulation** revolution built on a head start from the 1970s. A federal antitrust case had split the unified Bell System of AT&T and its subsidiaries into seven regional telephone companies and opened long-distance service to competition.

Congress also deregulated air travel in 1978. The result has been cheaper and more frequent air service for major hubs and poorer and more expensive service for small cities. The transformation of telecommunications similarly meant more choices for sophisticated consumers but higher prices for basic phone service.

Corporate America used the Reagan administration to attack environmental legislation as "strangulation by regulation." Vice President George Bush headed the White House Task Force on Regulatory Relief, which delayed or blocked regulations on hazardous wastes, automobile emissions, and exposure of workers to chemicals on the job.

Most attention, however, went to the instantly controversial appointment of Colorado lawyer James Watt as Secretary of the Interior. He was sympathetic to a Western movement known as the **Sagebrush Rebellion**, which wanted the vast federal land holdings in the West transferred to the states for more rapid economic use. He blamed air pollution on natural emissions from trees and compared environmentalists to both Nazis and Bolsheviks. Federal resource agencies sold trees to timber companies at a loss to the Treasury, expanded offshore oil drilling, and expedited exploration for minerals.

The early 1980s also transformed American financial markets. Individual Retirement Accounts (IRAs), a creation of the 1981 tax act, made millions of households into new investors. Dollars poured from savings accounts into higher-paying money market funds. Savings and loans had traditionally been conservative financial institutions that funneled individual savings into safe home mortgages. Under new rules, they began to compete for deposits by offering high interest rates and reinvested the money in much riskier commercial real estate. By 1990, the result would be a financial crisis in which bad loans destroyed hundreds of S&Ls, especially in the Southwest.

Corporate raiders snapped up "cash cows," profitable and cash-rich companies that could be milked of profits and assets. Dealmakers brought together often mismatched companies into huge conglomerates. They raised money with "junk bonds," high-interest, high-risk securities that could be paid off only in favorable conditions. The merger mania channeled capital into paper transactions rather than investments in new equipment and products. Another effect was to damage the economies of small and middle-sized communities by transferring control of local companies to outside managers.

CRISIS FOR ORGANIZED LABOR

The flip side of the economic boom was another round in the Republican offensive against labor unions. Reagan set the tone when he fired more than eleven thousand members of the Professional Air Traffic Controllers Organization for violating a no-strike clause in their hiring agreements. He claimed to be enforcing the letter of the law, but the message to organized labor was clear. Over the next eight years, the National Labor Relations Board and other federal agencies also weakened the power of collective bargaining.

As union membership declined and unions struggled to cope with the changing economy, corporations demanded wage rollbacks and concessions on working conditions as trade-offs for continued employment. Workers faced the threat that employers might move a factory overseas or sell out to a new owner, who could close a plant, and reopen without a union contract.

Another cause for shrinking union membership was the decline of blue-collar jobs, from 36 percent of the American work force in 1960 to roughly 25 percent at the end of the 1990s. Although unions made up part of the loss from manufacturing by recruiting government workers, such as police officers, teachers,

Sagebrush Rebellion   Political movement in the Western states in the early 1980s that called for easing of regulations on the economic issue of federal lands and the transfer of some or all of those lands to state ownership.

and bus drivers, many white-collar jobs in the private sector were in small firms and offices that were difficult to organize.

The corporate merger mania of the 1980s added to unions' woes. Takeover specialists loaded old companies with new debt, triggering efforts to cut labor costs, sell off plants, or raid pension funds for cash to pay the interest. Manufacturing employment in the 1980s declined by nearly 2 million jobs, with the expansion of high-tech manufacturing concealing much higher losses in traditional industries. In sum, while corporate merger specialists steered their BMWs along the fast lane to success, displaced mill hands drove battered pickups along potholed roads to nowhere.

AN ACQUISITIVE SOCIETY

The national media in the early 1980s discovered "yuppies," or young urban professionals, who were both a marketing category and a symbol of social change. These upwardly mobile professionals supposedly defined themselves by elitist consumerism and flocked to such upscale retailers as Neiman-Marcus and Bloomingdale's.

Far richer than yuppies were wheeler-dealers who made themselves into media stars of finance capitalism. *Forbes* magazine began to publish an annual list of the nation's 400 richest people. Before he admitted to violating the law against profiting from insider information, the corporate-merger expert Ivan Boesky had told a business-school audience; "Greed is all right. . . . You shouldn't feel guilty," epitomizing an era of big business takeovers driven by paper profits rather than underlying economic fundamentals. The superficial glamour of this era of acquisitiveness and corporate greed had its underside of loneliness and despair. Young novelists in the 1980s like Bret Easton Ellis and Jay McInerny explored the emptiness of life among the privileged. Tom Wolfe's bestselling novel *The Bonfire of the Vanities* (1987), depicted a New York where the art dealers and stockbrokers of glitzy Manhattan meet the poor of the devastated South Bronx only through an automobile accident to their mutual incomprehension and ruin.

New movements in popular music reacted to the acquisitive 1980s. Punk rock lashed out at the emptiness of 1970s disco sounds and the commercialization of youth culture. Grunge bands expressed alienation from consumerism. Hip-Hop originated among African Americans and Latinos in New York, soon adding the angry and often violent lyrics of rap. Rap during the 1980s was about personal power and sex, but it also dealt with social inequities and deprivation and tapped some of the same anger and frustration that had motivated black power advocates in the 1960s. It crossed into the mainstream culture with the help of MTV, which had begun broadcasting in 1981, but its hard-edged "attitude" undercut any sense of complacency about an inclusive American society.

POVERTY AMID PROSPERITY

Federal tax and budget changes had different effects on the rich and poor. (see Figure 30.1) The 1981 tax cuts came with sharp increases in the Social Security tax, which hit lower-income workers the hardest. The tax changes meant that the average annual income of households in the bottom 20 percent declined and that many actually paid higher taxes, while those in the top fifth increased their share of after-tax income at the expense of everyone else.

Cities and their residents absorbed approximately two-thirds of the cuts in the 1981–1982 federal budget. Provisions for accelerated depreciation (tax write-offs) of factories and equipment in the 1981 tax act encouraged the abandon-

ment of center-city factories in favor of
new facilities in the suburbs. One result
was a growing jobs-housing mismatch.
There were often plenty of jobs in the
suburbs, but the poorer people who
most needed the jobs were marooned
in city slums and dependent on public
transit that seldom served suburban
employers.

Federal tax and spending policies
in the 1980s decreased the security of
middle-class families. As the economy
continued to struggle through deindustrialization, average wage rates fell
in the 1980s when measured in real purchasing. The squeeze put pressure on
traditional family patterns and pushed
into the workforce women who might

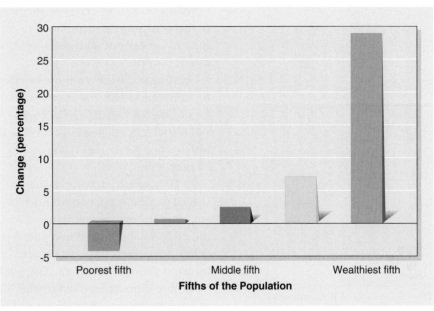

otherwise have stayed home. Even with two incomes, many families found it hard
to buy a house because of skyrocketing prices in urban markets and sky-high interest
rates. The national home ownership rate actually fell for the first time in almost fifty
years, from 66 to 64 percent of American households. Many Americans no longer
expected to surpass their parents' standard of living.

Corporate downsizing and white-collar jobs.   Corporate "downsizing" meant
that lower-paying office jobs fell under the same pressures as factory jobs. Companies increasingly computerized and automated their operations and replaced full-
time employees with "temps" who shifted from job to job and were not eligible for
company benefits. Takeovers sometimes eliminated even more white-collar jobs. A
targeted company could lose its entire management and support staff. The expectation for a college graduate who joined a large corporation of a "job for life" (often
true in the 1950s and 1960s) became dubious.

The chill of corporate "downsizing" hit white-collar families most heavily toward the end of the 1980s. Big business consolidations delivered improved profits by squeezing the ranks of middle managers as well as assembly-line workers. With
fewer workers to supervise and with new technologies to collect and distribute information, companies could complete their cost cutting by trimming administrators. Takeovers sometimes meant the elimination of the entire management and
support staff of target companies. In the 1950s, a college graduate could sign on
with a large corporation like IBM or General Motors, advance through the ranks,
and expect to retire from the same company. Now the expectation of a "job for
life" looked dubious; AT&T, for one example, eliminated 76,000 jobs— one-fifth
of its total— between 1985 and 1989. Those white-collar workers whose jobs survived clung to them more firmly than ever. The combined result was to clog the
ladder of economic opportunity for college graduates, making the cab-driving
Ph.D. and the *barrista* with the B.A. popular clichés.

Increase in the poverty rate.   At the lower end of the economic ladder, the
proportion of Americans living in poverty increased. After declining steadily from
1960 to a low of 11 percent in 1973, the poverty rate climbed back to the 13 to 15
percent range. Although the economy in the 1980s created lots of new jobs, half
of them paid less than poverty-level wages. Conservative critics began to talk about
an underclass of Americans permanently outside the mainstream economy because

FIGURE 30.1
**Changes in Real Family Income,
1980–1990**
In the 1980s, the poor got poorer, the
middle class made slight gains, and the
most affluent 20 percent of the American people did very well. Tax changes
that helped well-off households were one
factor. Another factor was the erosion of
"family-wage jobs" in manufacturing.

of poor education, drug abuse, or sheer laziness. In fact, most of the nation's millions of poor people lived in households with employed adults. In 1992, fully 18 percent of all full-time jobs did not pay enough to lift a family of four out of poverty.

Most women, even those working full time, did not earn as much as men. In the 1960s and 1970s, the average working woman earned just 60 percent of the earnings of the average man. Only part of the wage gap could be explained by measurable factors, such as education or experience. The gap narrowed in the 1980s, with women's earnings rising to 74 percent of men's by 1996 but falling back to 72 percent in 2000.

Despite a narrowing of the income gap between working men and women (which was the result of both a decline in men's earnings and the success of better-educated younger women), women constituted nearly two-thirds of poor adults at the end of the 1980s. While only 6 percent of married-couple households were below the poverty level, 32 percent of households headed by a woman without a husband present were poor. The feminization of poverty and American reliance on private support for child rearing also meant that children had a higher chance of living in poverty than adults and that poor American children were worse off than their peers in other advanced nations.

Falling below even the working poor were growing numbers of homeless Americans. In the 1980s, a new approach to the treatment of the mentally ill reduced the population of mental hospitals from 540,000 in 1960 to only 140,000 in 1980. Deinstitutionalized patients were supposed to receive community-based treatment, but many ended up on the streets and in overnight shelters. New forms of self-destructive drug abuse, such as crack addiction, joined alcoholism. A boom in downtown real estate destroyed old skid-row districts with their bars, missions, and dollar-a-night hotels.

These factors tripled the number of permanently homeless people during the early and middle 1980s, from 200,000 to somewhere between 500,000 to 700,000. For every person in a shelter on a given night, two people were sleeping on sidewalks, in parks, in cars, and in abandoned buildings.

CONSOLIDATING THE REVOLUTION: GEORGE H.W. BUSH

In 1988 George H.W. Bush, Reagan's vice president for eight years, won the presidential election with 56 percent of the popular vote and 40 out of 50 states. As someone who had survived twenty years of bureaucratic infighting, his watchword was prudence. Using a comparison from baseball, Bush described himself as the sort of guy who would play the averages and "bunt 'em over" rather than go for the big inning.

Michael Dukakis, the Democratic nominee in 1988, was a dry, by-the-numbers manager who offered the American people "competence." The Bush campaign director, Lee Atwater, looked for "hot-button" issues and found that Dukakis as governor of Massachusetts had delayed cleanup of Massachusetts Bay, favored gun control, and had vetoed a bill requiring schoolchildren to recite the Pledge of Allegiance (arguing correctly that it would be overturned in the courts). Even more damaging, Massachusetts officials had allowed a murderer named Willie Horton a weekend furlough from prison, during which he had committed a brutal rape. Pro-Bush advertisements tapped into real worries among the voters—fear of crime, racial tension (Horton was black), worry about eroding social values. George Bush,

WHERE TO LEARN MORE

The Causes of Homelessness in America
http://www.stanford.edu/class/
e297c/poverty_prejudice/soc_sec/
hcauses.htm

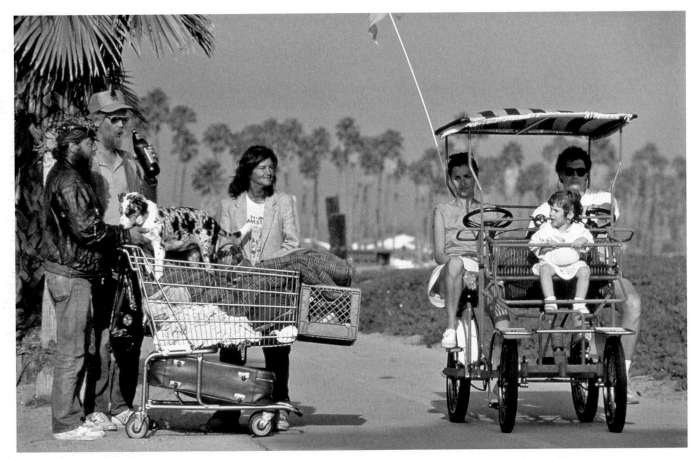

despite his background in prep schools and country clubs, came out looking tough as nails, while the Democrats looked inept.

The ads locked Bush into a rhetorical war on crime and drugs. Americans had good cause to be worried about public safety, but most were generally unaware that the likelihood of becoming the target of a violent crime had leveled off and would continue to fall in the 1990s or that crime was far worse in minority communities than elsewhere.

The Bush administration stepped up the fight against illegal drugs. By 1990, 50 percent of federal prison inmates were in jail for drug offenses.

Bush believed that Americans wanted government to leave them alone. The major legislation from his administration was a transportation bill that shifted federal priorities from highway building toward mass transit and the **Americans with Disabilities Act** (1990) to prevent discrimination against people with physical handicaps. In the areas of crime and health care, however, Bush's lack of leadership left continuing problems.

The same attitude produced weak economic policies. The massive budget deficits of the 1980s combined with growing trade deficits swelled the national debt and turned the United States from an international creditor to a debtor nation. Despite pledging "no new taxes" in his campaign, Bush backed into a tax increase in 1990. Voters found it hard to forget the president's waffling and attempts to downplay the importance of this decision.

The "Rodney King riot" of April 1992 in Los Angeles was a reminder of the nation's inattention to the problems of race and poverty. Rodney King was a black motorist who had been savagely beaten by police officers while being arrested after a car chase on March 3, 1991. A nearby resident captured the beating on

An affluent family pedals by a group of homeless people in Santa Barbara, California. In the 1980s a combination of rising housing prices and the closure of most mental hospitals pushed increasing numbers of Americans onto the streets. Estimates of the number of homeless Americans in the late 1980s ranged from 300,000 to 3 million, depending on the definition of homelessness and the political goals of the estimator.

P. F. Bentley, Time Magazine © TimePix

Americans with Disabilities Act Legislation in 1992 that banned discrimination against physically handicapped persons in employment, transportation, and public accommodations.

videotape from his apartment. Within two days, the tape was on national television. It confirmed the worst black fears about police behavior. Early the next year, the four officers stood trial for unjustified use of force before a suburban jury. The unexpected verdict of not guilty on April 29 stirred deep anger that escalated into four days of rioting that left fifty-eight people dead, mostly African Americans and Latinos.

The disorder was far more complex than the Watts outbreak of 1965. Central American and Mexican immigrants accounted for about one-third of the 12,000 arrests. As in 1965, some targets were white passers-by and symbols of white authority. But angry black people also targeted hundreds of Korean-owned and Vietnamese-owned shops as symbols of economic discrimination.

THE SECOND (SHORT) COLD WAR

Ronald Reagan considered the Soviet Union not a coequal nation with legitimate world interests but an "evil empire," like something from the *Star Wars* movies. After the era of détente, global tensions had started to mount in the late 1970s. They were soon higher than they had been since the 1960s.

CONFRONTING THE USSR

Who renewed the Cold War after Nixon's diplomacy of détente and Carter's early efforts at negotiation? The Soviets had pursued military expansion in the 1970s, and in 1980 were supporting Marxist regimes in civil wars in Angola, Ethiopia, Nicaragua, and especially Afghanistan. Given the aging Soviet leadership and the economic weaknesses revealed in the late 1980s, however, it makes more sense to see the Soviets as muddling along rather than executing a well-planned global strategy.

The new Reagan administration reemphasized central Europe as the focus of superpower rivalry. To counter improved Soviet armaments, the United States began to place cruise missiles and midrange Pershing II missiles in Europe in 1983. NATO governments approved the action, but it frightened millions of their citizens.

The controversy over the new missile systems was part of new thinking about nuclear weaponry. Multiple warheads on U.S. missiles already allowed Washington to target 25,000 separate places in the Soviet Union. National Security Directive D-13 (1981) stated that a nuclear war might be winnable, despite its enormous costs. All Americans needed for survival, said one administration official, were "enough shovels" to dig fallout shelters.

The nuclear freeze campaign caught the imagination of many Americans in 1981 and 1982. Drawing on the experience of the antiwar movement, it sought to halt the manufacture and deployment of new atomic weapons by the great powers. The movement gained urgency when a group of distinguished scientists argued that the smoke and dust thrown up by an atomic war would devastate the ecology of the entire globe by triggering "nuclear winter." Nearly a million people turned out for a nuclear freeze rally in New York in 1982.

In response, Reagan announced the **Strategic Defense Initiative (SDI)** or "Star Wars" program in March 1983. SDI would deploy new defenses that could intercept and destroy ballistic missiles as they rose from the ground and arced through space. Ideas included superlasers, killer satellites, and clouds of projectiles to rip missiles to shreds before they neared their targets. Few scientists thought that SDI could work. Nevertheless, President Reagan found SDI appealing, for it offered a way around the balance of terror.

WHAT FOREIGN policy measures did Reagan employ in dealing with the Soviet Union and the Middle East?

Strategic Defense Initiative (SDI) President Reagan's program, announced in 1983, to defend the United States against nuclear missile attack with untested weapons systems and sophisticated technologies.

RISKY BUSINESS: FOREIGN POLICY ADVENTURES

Reagan kept the United States out of a major war and backed off in the face of serious trouble. Foreign interventions were designed to achieve symbolic victories rather than the global balance of power. The exception was the Caribbean and Central America.

Lebanon was the model for Reagan's small-scale military interventions. Israel invaded Lebanon in 1982 to clear Palestinian guerrillas from its borders. The Israeli army found itself bogged down in civil war. Reagan sent U.S. Marines to preserve the semblance of a Lebanese state and provide a face-saving exit for Israel. But the Marines were on an ill-defined "presence mission" that angered Arabs. In October 1983, a car bomb killed 241 Marines. The remainder were soon gone, confirming the Syrian observation that Americans were "short of breath" when it came to Middle East politics.

The administration had already found an easier target. Only days after the disaster in Beirut, U.S. troops invaded the small independent Caribbean island of Grenada. A left-leaning government had invited Cuban help in building an airfield, which the U.S. feared would turn into a Cuban military base. Two thousand American troops overcame Cuban soldiers who were thinly disguised as construction workers, "rescued" American medical students, and put a more sympathetic and locally popular government in power.

The Caribbean was also the focus of a secret foreign policy operated by the CIA and then by National Security Council staff. The target was Nicaragua, the Central American country where leftist Sandinista rebels had overthrown the Somoza dictatorship in 1979. Reagan and his people were determined to prevent Nicaragua from becoming "another Cuba," especially when Sandinistas helped left-wing insurgents in neighboring El Salvador. The CIA organized perhaps ten thousand "Contras" from remnants of Somoza's national guard. From bases in Honduras, they harassed the Sandinistas with sabotage and raids. Reagan called the Contras "freedom fighters."

Constitutional trouble started when an unsympathetic Congress blocked U.S. funding for the Contras. Under the direction of CIA director William Casey, Lieutenant Colonel Oliver North flouted the law by organizing aid from private donors while serving on the staff of the National Security Council.

Even shadier were arms-for-hostages negotiations with Iran. The United States in 1985 joined Israel in selling five hundred antitank missiles to Iran. The deal followed stern public pronouncements that the United States would never negotiate with terrorists, and it violated this nation's official trade embargo against Iran. Iran helped in securing the release of several Americans held hostage in Lebanon by pro-Iranian radicals, but other hostages were soon taken. Colonel North funneled proceeds from the arms sales to the Contras, in a double evasion of the law.

Like Watergate, the Iran-Contra affair was a two-sided scandal. First was the blatant misjudgment of operating a secret and bumbling foreign policy that depended on international arms dealers and ousted Nicaraguan military officers. Second was a concerted effort to cover up the actions. North shredded relevant documents and lied to Congress. In his final report in 1994, Special Prosecutor Lawrence Walsh found that President Reagan and Vice President Bush participated in efforts to withhold information and mislead Congress.

American policy in Asia was a refreshing contrast with Central America and the Middle East. In the Philippines, American diplomats helped push corrupt President Ferdinand Marcos out and opened the way for a popular uprising to put Corazon Aquino in office. Secretary of State George Shultz made sure that the

QUICK REVIEW

Small-scale Military Intervention

◆ Marines were sent into Lebanon to help stabilize the Lebanese state and allow the Israelis to withdraw.

◆ The U.S. invaded Grenada to prevent the possible creation of a Cuban military base.

◆ Nicaragua and El Salvador were the targets of secret foreign policy operated by the CIA and later the National Security Council staff.

United States supported popular democracy while reassuring the Philippine military. In South Korea, the United States similarly helped ease out an unpopular dictator by firmly supporting democratic elections that brought in a more popular but still pro-U.S. government.

EMBRACING PERESTROIKA

Thaw in the Cold War started in Moscow. Mikhail Gorbachev became general secretary of the Communist party in 1985. Gorbachev was the picture of vigor compared to his three sick or elderly predecessors, Leonid Brezhnev, Yuri Andropov, and Constantin Chernenko. He was a master of public relations who charmed western Europe's leaders and public. Gorbachev startled Soviet citizens by urging *glasnost*, or political openness and free discussion of issues. He followed by setting the goal of *perestroika*, or restructuring of the painfully bureaucratic Soviet economy.

Gorbachev also decided that he needed to reduce the crushing burden of Soviet defense spending if the USSR was to have any chance of modernizing. During Reagan's second term, the Soviets offered one concession after another in a relentless drive for arms control.

Reagan cast off decades of belief in the dangers of Soviet Communism and took Gorbachev seriously. He was willing to abandon many of his most fervent supporters. He frightened his own staff when he met Gorbachev in Iceland in the summer of 1986 and accepted the principle of deep cuts in strategic forces. Reagan explained that when he railed against the "evil empire," he had been talking about Brezhnev and the bad old days; Gorbachev and *glasnost* were different.

In the end, Reagan negotiated the **Intermediate Nuclear Force (INF)** agreement over the strong objections of the CIA and the Defense Department but with the support of Secretary of State Shultz. Previous treaties had only slowed the growth of nuclear weapons. The new pact matched Soviet SS-20s with American cruise missiles as an entire class of weapons that would be destroyed, with on-site inspections for verification.

CRISIS AND DEMOCRACY IN EASTERN EUROPE

As a believer in personal diplomacy, George Bush based much of his foreign policy on his changing attitudes toward Mikhail Gorbachev. He started lukewarm, talking tough to please the Republican right wing. Before 1989 was over, however, the president had decided that Gorbachev was OK. For the next two years, the United States pushed reform in Europe while being careful not to damage Gorbachev's position at home.

The people of eastern Europe overcame both American and Soviet caution. Gorbachev had urged his eastern European allies to emulate *perestroika*. Poland and Hungary were the first satellite nations to eject their Communist leadership in favor of democracy in mid-1989. When East Germans began to flee westward through Hungary, the East German regime bowed to mounting pressure and opened the Berlin Wall on November 9. By the end of 1989, there were new governments in Czechoslovakia, Romania, Bulgaria, and East Germany. These largely peaceful revolutions destroyed the military and economic agreements that had harnessed the satellites to the Soviet economy. The USSR swallowed hard, accepted the loss of its satellites, and slowly withdrew its army from eastern Europe.

Events in eastern Europe left German reunification as a point of possible conflict. West German Chancellor Helmut Kohl removed one obstacle when he reassured Poland and Russia that Germany would seek no changes in the boundaries drawn after World War II. By July 1990, the United States and USSR had agreed that a reunited Germany would belong to NATO. The decision satisfied France and Britain

---

W WHERE TO LEARN MORE

The Intermediate Nuclear Force Agreement (INF)
http://www.state.gov/www/global/arms/treaties/infl.html

Glasnost Russian for "openness" applied to Mikhail Gorbachev's encouragement of new ideas and easing of political repression in the Soviet Union.

Perestroika Russian for "restructuring," applied to Mikhail Gorbachev's efforts to make the Soviet economic and political systems more modern, flexible, and innovative.

Intermediate Nuclear Force Agreement (INF) Disarmament agreement between the United States and the Soviet Union under which an entire class of missiles would be removed and destroyed and on-site inspections would be permitted.

that a stronger Germany would still be under the influence of the Western allies. In October, the two Germanies completed their political unification, although it would be years before their mismatched economies functioned as one.

Throughout these events, the Bush administration proceeded cautiously. Bush tried not to push the Soviet Union too hard and infuriate Russian hard-liners. "I don't want to do something that would inadvertently set back the progress," he said.

The final act in the transformation of the USSR began with an attempted coup against Mikhail Gorbachev in August, 1991 of old-line Communist bureaucrats. But they turned out to be bumblers and drunks who hadn't secured military support and even failed to take over radio and television stations. Boris Yeltsin, president of the Russian Republic, organized the resistance. Within three days, the plotters themselves were under arrest.

Before the month was out, the Soviet parliament banned the Communist party. By December, Gorbachev had resigned, and all of the fifteen component re-publics of the Soviet Union had declared their independence. The superpower Union of Soviet Socialist Republics ceased to exist. Russia remained the largest and strongest of the new states followed by Ukraine and Kazakhstan.

Analysts agree that the relentless pressure of American defense spending helped bankrupt and undermine the USSR. It is an open question whether this same American defense spending also weakened the United States' economy and its ability to compete in the world marketplace. Some scholars see the demise of the Soviet empire as ultimate justification for forty years of Cold War. Dissenters argue the opposite— that the collapse of European Communism shows that American leaders had magnified its threat.

A more definitive answer may lie in what scholars learn about Soviet Cold War policy when they explore the Russian archives.

THE FIRST PERSIAN GULF WAR

On August 2, 1990, President Saddam Hussein of Iraq seized the neighboring coun-try of Kuwait. The conquest gave Iraq control of 20 percent of the world's oil pro-duction and reserves. Bush demanded unconditional withdrawal, enlisted European and Arab allies in an anti-Iraq coalition, and persuaded Saudi Arabia to accept sub-stantial U.S. forces for its protection against Iraqi invasion. Within weeks, the Saud-is were host to tens of thousands of U.S. soldiers and hundreds of aircraft.

Iraq was a dictatorship that had just emerged from an eight-year war with Iran. Saddam Hussein had depended on help from the United States and Arab nations in this war, but Iraq was now economically exhausted. Kuwait itself was a small, rich nation whose ruling dynasty enjoyed huge oil royalties. The U.S. State Department had signaled earlier in 1990 that it might support some concessions by Kuwait to Iraq. Saddam Hussein read the signal as an open invitation to do what he wanted.

The Iraqis gave Bush a golden opportunity to assert America's world influ-ence. The importance of Middle Eastern oil helped enlist France and Britain as military allies and secure billions of dollars from Germany and Japan. A short-term oil glut also meant that the industrial nations could boycott Iraqi production. The collapse of Soviet power and Gorbachev's interest in cooperating with the United States meant that the Soviets would not interfere with U.S. plans.

President Bush and his advisers offered a series of justifications for Ameri-can actions. First and most basic were the desire to punish armed aggression and the need to protect Iraq's other neighbors, although there was scant evidence of Iraqi preparations against Saudi Arabia. Sanctions and diplomatic pressure might also have brought withdrawal from most or all of Kuwait. However, additional

WHERE TO LEARN MORE

A Concrete Curtain: The Life and Death of the Berlin Wall
http://www.wall-berlin.org/ gb/berlin.htm

QUICK REVIEW

The Fall of Gorbachev and the Soviet Union

◆ August 1991: old-line communists attempt a coup against Gorbachev.

◆ Boris Yeltsin organized the successful resistance to the plotters.

◆ Gorbachev resigned and all fifteen Soviet republics declared their independence.

30–3
George Bush, Address to the Nation Announcing Allied Military Action in the Persian Gulf (1991)

First Persian Gulf War War (1991) between Iraq and a U.S.-led coali-tion that followed Iraq's invasion of Kuwait and resulted in the expulsion of Iraqi forces from that country.

WHERE TO LEARN MORE

★ The Gulf War
http://www.pbs.org/wgbh/pages/
frontline/gulf/

Operation Desert Storm Code name for the successful offensive against Iraq by the United States and its allies in the Persian Gulf War (1991).

HOW DID America's population change in the 1980s?

Sunbelt The states of the American South and Southwest.

American objectives— to destroy Iraq's capacity to create atomic weapons and to topple Saddam's regime— would require direct military action.

The Persian Gulf itself offered an equally golden opportunity to the American and allied armed forces. The United States could try out the tactics of armored maneuver and close land-air cooperation that the Pentagon had devised to protect Germany against Soviet invasion.

In October, Bush decided to increase the number of American troops in Saudi Arabia to 580,000. The United States also secured a series of increasingly tough United Nations resolutions that culminated in November 1990 with Security Council Resolution 678, authorizing "all necessary means" to liberate Kuwait. The president convinced Congress to agree to military action under the umbrella of the U.N.

War began one day after the U.N.'s January 15 deadline for Iraqi withdrawal from Kuwait. **Operation Desert Storm** opened with massive air attacks on command centers, transportation facilities, and Iraqi forward positions. The air war also seriously hurt Iraqi civilians by disrupting utilities and food supplies.

Americans watched CNN's live transmission of Baghdad under bombardment in fascination. The forty-day rain of bombs was the prelude to a ground attack. On February 24, 1991, U.S. and allied forces swept into Iraq and advanced directly to liberate Kuwait. A cease-fire came one hundred hours after the start of the ground war. Allied forces suffered only 240 deaths in action, compared to perhaps 100,000 for the Iraqis. Militarily, overwhelming the Iraqis turned out to be easy.

The United States hoped to replace Saddam Hussein without disrupting Iraqi society. Instead, the hundred-hour war incited armed rebellions against Saddam by Shi'ite Muslims in southern Iraq and by Kurds in the north. Since Bush and his advisers were unwilling to get embroiled in a civil war, they stood by while Saddam crushed the uprisings. Saddam Hussein became a hero to many in the Islamic world simply by remaining in power. But Bush had accomplished exactly what he wanted— the restoration of the status quo.

In 2003, however, his son, President George W. Bush, was to launch the second Gulf War with the explicit purpose of toppling Saddam's regime (see Chapter 31).

GROWTH IN THE SUNBELT

The rise in the military and defense spending from the late 1970s through the early 1990s and the Persian Gulf War, were two of the most powerful sources of growth in the **Sunbelt**, the Southern and Western regions of the United States. Americans had discovered this "new" region in the 1970s. Kevin Phillips's book *The Emerging Republican Majority* (1969) first popularized the term "Sunbelt." Phillips pointed out that people and economic activity had been flowing southward and westward since World War II, shifting the balance of power away from the Northeast.

The Sunbelt was a region of conservative voting habits where Republicans solidified their status as a majority party, a process continuing to the present. In the 1990s, the region's economic power was reflected in a conservative tone in both the Republican and Democratic parties and in the prominence of Southern political leaders. (see Map 30–2).

The rise of the Sunbelt, which is anchored by Florida, Texas, and California, reflected the leading economic trends of the 1970s and 1980s, including military spending, immigration from Asia and Latin America, and recreation and retirement spending. Corporations liked the business climate of the South, which had weak labor laws, low taxes, and lower costs of living and doing business.

MAP EXPLORATION

To explore an interactive version of this map, go to **http://www.prenhall.com/goldfield2/map30.2**

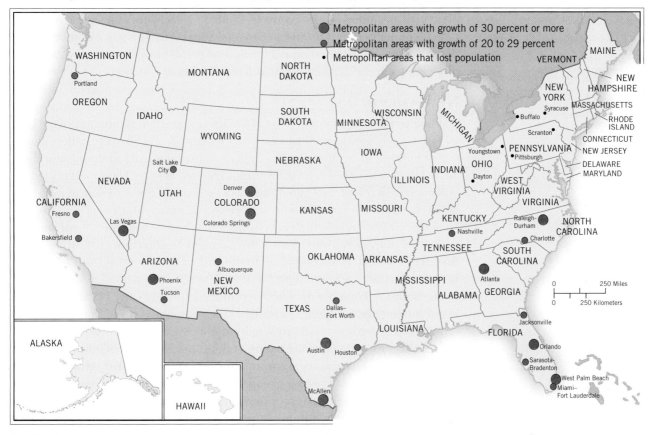

MAP 30–2

Fast-Growing and Shrinking Metropolitan Areas, 1900–2000   In the 1990s, boom cities were found in the Southeast, Southwest, and on the West Coast. In contrast, all of the large metropolitan areas that lost population were in Ohio, New York, or Pennsylvania, the area hardest hit by the decline of jobs in established manufacturing industries.

WHAT ECONOMIC forces contributed to the growth of some cities and the decline of others?

THE DEFENSE BOOM

The Vietnam buildup and reinvestment in the military during the Carter (1977–1981) and Reagan (1981–1989) administrations fueled the growth of the Sunbelt. Over the forty years from the Korean conflict to the first Persian Gulf War, the United States made itself the mightiest military power ever known. Military bases and defense contractors remolded the economic landscape, as mild winters and clear skies for training and operations helped the South and West attract more than 75 percent of military payrolls.

Big cities and small depended on defense spending. Southern California thrived on more than 500,000 jobs in the aircraft industry. Visitors to Colorado Springs could drive past sprawling Fort Carson and visit the new Air Force Academy, opened in 1958. Sunk deep from view was the North American Air Defense command post beneath Cheyenne Mountain. Malmstrom Air Force Base transformed Great Falls, Montana, from a manufacturing and transportation center into a coordinating center for Minuteman missiles targeted at Moscow and Beijing.

Defense spending underwrote the expansion of American science and technology. Nearly one-third of all engineers worked on military projects. Large universities, such as MIT, Michigan, CalTech, and Stanford, were leading defense contractors. The modern electronics business started in New York, Boston and the San Francisco Bay Area with research and development for military uses, such as guided-missile controls. California's Silicon Valley grew with military sales long before it turned to consumer markets. The space component of the aerospace industry was equally reliant on the defense economy. NASA's centers were scattered across the South from Florida to Houston.

NEW AMERICANS

The **Immigration and Nationality Act of 1965**, transformed the ethnic mix of the United States and helped to stimulate the Sunbelt boom. It abolished the national quota system in effect since 1924 that had favored immigrants from western Europe and limited those from other parts of the world. The old law's racial bias contradicted the self-proclaimed role of the United States as a defender of freedom. The new law gave preference to family reunification and welcomed immigrants from all nations. The United States also accepted refugees from communism outside the annual limits.

Immigration reform opened the doors to Mediterranean Europe, Latin America, and Asia. Legal migration to the United States surged from 1.1 million in 1960–1964 to nearly 4 million for 1990–1994. Nonlegal immigrants may have doubled the total number of newcomers in the 1970s and early 1980s. Meanwhile, over 2 million nonlegal immigrants had taken advantage of the Immigration Reform and Control Act of 1986 to legalize their presence in the United States.

Immigration changed the nation's ethnic mix. Members of officially defined ethnic and racial minorities accounted for 30 percent in 2000. Asians and Hispanics were the fastest growing group. (See Table 30.1)

The largest single group of new Americans came from Mexico. Mexican Americans are the largest minority group in many Southwestern and Western states. They were also transforming neighborhoods in Chicago and other midwestern cities and changing everything from politics to the Catholic church.

The East Coast has meanwhile welcomed migrants from the West Indies and Central America. Many Puerto Ricans, who hold U.S. citizenship, came to Philadelphia and New York in the 1950s and 1960s. Other countries sending large numbers of immigrants include Haiti, the Dominican Republic, Guatemala, Honduras, Nicaragua, El Salvador, and Jamaica. Cuban refugees from Castro's regime concentrated in Miami and in major cities such as Chicago and New York.

Another great immigration has occurred eastward across the Pacific. Chinese, Filipinos, Koreans, Samoans, and other Asians and Pacific Islanders constituted only 6 percent of newcomers to the United States in 1965, but nearly half of all arrivals in 1990. The numbers of ethnic Chinese in the United States jumped from a quarter of a million in 1965 to 1,645,000 in 1990.

The most publicized Asian immigrants were refugees from Indochina after Communist victories in 1975. Many settled on the West Coast. The San Francisco Bay area, for example, had more than a dozen Vietnamese-language newspapers, magazines, and cable television programs.

Recent immigrants have found both economic possibilities and problems. On the negative side, immigration has added to the numbers of nonunion workers. But immigrants also added to the pool of talent and ambition in the expanding economy of the mid-1980s and 1990s. The 130,000 Vietnamese immigrants of 1975 now have an average adjusted income above the national average. Asians and Pacific islanders by 2000 constituted 22 percent of students in California's public universities. Many newcomers have opened groceries, restaurants, and other businesses. Juan Fernandez found it easier to set up a successful car repair

QUICK REVIEW

Immigration

- Immigration changed the country's ethnic mix.
- The single largest group of new Americans came from Mexico.
- In 1990 nearly half of all new arrivals were Asians and Pacific islanders.

Immigration and Nationality Act of 1965 Federal legislation that replaced the national quota system for immigration with new limits for each hemisphere.

TABLE 30.1
Major Racial and Ethnic Minorities in the United States

1960 Population (in millions)	Percentage of total	2000 Population (in millions)	Percentage of total
American Indians	0.5	0.3	2.5 0.9
Asians and Pacific Islanders	1.1	0.6	10.6 3.7
African Americans	18.9	10.5	34.7 12.3
Hispanics	Not available		35.3 12.5

shop in Gary, Indiana, than in Guadalajara, Mexico, because his fellow immigrants prefer a Spanish-speaking mechanic. Asian-born business owners have filled retail vacuums in central city neighborhoods abandoned by chain stores.

OLD GATEWAYS AND NEW

The new immigration had its most striking effects in coastal and border cities. New York again became a great mixing bowl of the American population. By 1990, some 28 percent of the population of New York City was foreign-born, compared to 42 percent at the height of European immigration in 1910. ZIP code 11373 in North Queens was reportedly the most diverse neighborhood in the world.

Southern and Western cities became gateways for immigrants from Latin America and Asia. Los Angeles emerged as "the new Ellis Island." As *Time* magazine put it in 1983, the arrival of more than 2 million immigrants altered "the collective beat and bop of L.A." In 1960, a mere 1 percent of the Los Angeles County population was Asian and 11 percent was Hispanic. By 2000, the figures for a population of 9.5 million were 12 percent Asian and 45 percent Hispanic. The sprawling neighborhoods of East Los Angeles make up the second-largest Mexican city in the world. One hundred languages are spoken among students entering Los Angeles schools.

New York and Los Angeles are world cities as well as immigrant destinations. Like London and Tokyo, they are capitals of world trade and finance, with international banks and headquarters of multinational corporations. The deregulation of international finance and the explosive spread of instant electronic communication in the 1980s confirmed their importance as global decision centers.

Similar factors turned Miami into the economic capital of the Caribbean. Half a million Cuban businessmen, white-collar workers, and their families moved to the United States between 1959 and 1980 to escape Castro's government. Most of the newcomers stayed in South Florida. Their success in business made Miami and helped to attract two million Latin American tourists and shoppers during the 1980s. Miami also has hundreds of offices for corporations engaged in U.S.-Latin American trade.

Cross-border communities in the Southwest, such as El Paso, Texas and Juarez, Mexico, or San Diego, California and Tijuana, Mexico, are "Siamese twins joined at the cash register." Employees with work permits commute from Mexico to the United States. American popular culture flows southward. Bargain hunters and tourists pass in both directions.

Both nations have promoted the cross-border economy. The Mexican government in the mid-1960s began to encourage a "platform economy" by allowing companies on the Mexican side of the border to import components and inputs duty-free as long as 80 percent of the items were reexported and 90 percent of the workers were Mexicans. The intent is to encourage American corporations to locate assembly plants south of the border. Such *maquila* industries can employ lower-wage workers and avoid strict antipollution laws (leading to serious threats to public health on both sides of the border). From the Gulf of Mexico to the Pacific Ocean, eighteen hundred *maquiladora* plants employed half a million workers. North of the border, U.S. factories supplied components under laws that meshed with the Mexican regulations.

THE GRAYING OF AMERICA

Retirees were another factor contributing to the growth of the Sunbelt. Between 1965 and 2000, the number of Americans aged 65 and over jumped from 18.2 million to 35 million, or 12.4 percent of the population. For the first time, most Americans could expect to survive into old age. The "young old" are people in their sixties and seventies who remain sharp, vigorous, and financially secure because of better private pensions, Social Security, and Medicare. The "old old" are the 9 million people in their eighties and nineties who often require daily assistance, although data show that improved medical services have made such Americans healthier and more self-sufficient than they were ten or twenty years ago.

Older Americans have become a powerful voice in public affairs. They tend to vote against local taxes but fight efforts to slow the growth of Social Security, even though growing numbers of the elderly are being supported by a relatively smaller proportion of working men and women. By the 1990s, observers noted increasing resentment among younger Americans, who fear that public policy is biased against the needs of men and women in their productive years. In turn, the elderly fiercely defend the programs of the 1960s and 1970s that have kept many of them from poverty. Protecting Medicare and Social Security was one of the Democrats' best campaign issues in 1996 and 2000, after Republicans suggested cuts in spending growth.

Retired Americans changed the social geography of the United States. Much growth in the South and Southwest has been financed by money earned in the Northeast and Midwest and transferred by retirees. Florida in the 1980s absorbed nearly 1 million new residents aged sixty or older. California, Arizona, Texas, the Carolinas, and the Ozark Mountains of Missouri and Arkansas have all attracted retirees, many of them in age-segregated communities such as Sun City near Phoenix.

VALUES IN COLLISION

In 1988, two very different religious leaders sought a presidential nomination. Pat Robertson's campaign for the Republican nomination tapped deep discontent with the changes in American society since the 1960s. A television evangelist, Robertson used the mailing list from his 700 Club program to mobilize conservative Christians and pushed the Republican Party further to the right on family and social issues. Jesse Jackson, a civil-rights leader and minister from Chicago, mounted a grassroots campaign with the opposite goal of moving the Democratic Party to the left on social and economic policy. Drawing on his experience in the black civil-rights movement, he assembled a "Rainbow Coalition" that included labor unionists, feminists, and others whom Robertson's followers feared. Both Jackson and Robertson used their powerful personalities and religious convictions to inspire support from local churches and churchgoers.

In diagnosing social ills, Robertson pointed to the problems of individual indulgence, while Jackson pointed to racism and economic inequality. Their sharp divergence expressed differences in basic values that divided Americans in the 1980s and beyond. In substantial measure, the conflicts were rooted in the social and cultural changes of the 1960s and 1970s that had altered traditional institutions, especially the 1950s ideal of a "Ward and June Cleaver" family. Changes in roles and expectations among women and new openness about gay and lesbian sexuality were particularly powerful in dividing American churches and politics.

In Swann v. Charlotte-Mecklenburg Board of Education (1971), the U.S. Supreme Court held that crosstown busing was an acceptable solution to de facto segregation that resulted from residential patterns within a single school district. When school officials failed to achieve racial balance, federal judges ordered their own busing plans. For many Americans, the image of busing for racial integration was fixed in 1975 when white people in Boston reacted with violence against black students who were bused to largely white high schools in the South Boston and Charlestown neighborhoods. The goal of equal opportunity clashed with equally strong values of neighborhood, community, and ethnic solidarity.

Busing was self-defeating, for it caused white families to move out of the integrating school district or to place their children in private academies, as happened frequently in the South. Busing also caused suburbanites to defend their political independence fiercely.

Zoning was another powerful tool of suburban self-defense. Restrictive building codes, requirements for large lots, and expensive subdivision fees could price all but the rich out of the local housing market. Many suburbs refused to zone land for apartments. As one Connecticut suburbanite put it, for a moderate-income family to hope to move into one of the state's most exclusive suburbs was "like going into Tiffany and demanding a ring for $12.50. Tiffany doesn't have any rings for $12.50. Well, Greenwich is like Tiffany."

However, as continued decentralization pushed the suburban share of the U.S. population toward 50 percent in the 1990s, most suburban rings displayed the full range of American society with the same economic, traffic, and pollution problems as the central cities.

NEW MEANINGS FOR AMERICAN FAMILIES

The political and social changes of the 1960s altered the patterns and meaning of family life. Americans began to rethink ideas about families and to emphasize personal identities in addition to traditional family roles. Women redefined themselves as individuals and workers as well as wives and mothers. Gays and lesbians asserted that their sexual orientations were not aberrations from "normal" family patterns but were valid in their own right. As average life spans lengthened, older Americans found personal satisfaction and political influence as members of their own communities and interest groups.

WHAT WERE the culture wars?

If one result of changing family patterns was new political groupings and new policies, another was deep confusion. In 1992, Vice 'President Dan Quayle earned headlines, and some derision, by criticizing the television comedy *Murphy Brown* for a positive and unrealistic portrayal of its lead character as a single mother. In the same year, however, 98 percent of Americans agreed that the label "family" applied to a married couple living with their children and 81 percent also applied "family" to the *Murphy Brown* scenario of an unwed mother living with her child. More than a quarter were even comfortable using "family" for two lesbian women or two gay men living together and raising children.

THE FEMINIST CRITIQUE

The growing dissatisfaction of many women with the domestic role expected of them in the 1950s helped set the stage for a revived feminism. Important steps in this revival included the Presidential Commission on the Status of Women in 1961;

the addition of gender as one of the categories protected by the Civil Rights Act of 1964; and creation of the National Organization for Women (NOW) in 1966.

Throughout the 1970s, activists battled to open one job category after another to women who proved that they could indeed use tools, run computers, or pick stocks on Wall Street. They also battled for equal pay for everyone with equal qualifications and responsibilities.

Changes in sexual behavior paralleled efforts to equalize treatment in the workplace. More reliable methods of contraception, especially birth control pills introduced in the early 1960s, gave women greater control over child-bearing. In some ways a replay of ideas from the 1920s, a new sexual revolution eroded the double standard that expected chastity of women but tolerated promiscuity among men. One consequence was a singles culture that accepted sexual activity between unmarried men and women.

Feminist radicals caught the attention of the national media with a demonstration against the 1968 Miss America pageant. Protesters crowned a sheep as Miss America and set out barrels for women who wanted to make a statement by tossing their bras and makeup in the trash.

Women's liberation took off as a social and political movement in 1970 and 1971. Within a few years, millions of women had recognized events and patterns in their lives as discrimination based on gender.

WOMEN'S RIGHTS AND PUBLIC POLICY

Congress wrote key goals of the feminist movement into law in the early 1970s. Title IX of the Educational Amendments (1972) to the Civil Rights Act prohibited discrimination by sex in any educational program receiving federal aid. In the same year, Congress sent the Equal Rights Amendment (ERA) to the states for ratification. The amendment read, "Equal rights under the law shall not be denied or abridged by the United States or by any state on account of sex." More than twenty states ratified quickly in the first few months and another dozen after increasingly tough battles in state legislatures. The ERA then stalled, three states short, when the time limit for ratification expired in 1982.

In January 1973, the U.S. Supreme Court expanded the debate about women's rights with the case of *Roe v. Wade*. Voting 7 to 2, the Court struck down state laws forbidding abortion in the first three months of pregnancy and set guidelines for abortion during the remaining months. Drawing on the earlier decision of *Griswold v. Connecticut,* which dealt with access to information about birth control, the justices held that the Fourteenth Amendment includes a right to privacy that blocks states from interfering with a woman's right to terminate pregnancy.

The feminist movement and specific policy measures related to it put equal rights and the fight against sexism (a word no one knew before 1965) on the national agenda and gradually changed how Americans thought about the relationships between men and women. Feminists focused attention on rape as a crime of violence, calling attention to the burdens the legal system placed on rape victims. In the 1980s and 1990s, they also challenged sexual harassment in the workplace, gradually refining the boundaries between acceptable and unacceptable behavior.

These changes came in the context of increasingly sharp conflict over the feminist agenda. Both the ERA and *Roe* stirred impassioned support and equally passionate opposition. Opponents of the ERA worried about unisex restrooms (not a problem on commercial airliners) and women in the military (not a problem in the Persian Gulf War). Also fueling the debate was a deep split between the mainstream feminist view of women as fully equal individuals and the contrary belief that women had a special role as anchors of families, an updating of the nineteenth-century idea of separate spheres.

Roe v. Wade   U.S. Supreme Court decision (1973) that disallowed state laws prohibiting abortion during the first three months (trimester) of pregnancy and established guidelines for abortion in the second and third trimesters.

The most sweeping change in the lives of American women did not come from federal legislation or court cases but from the growing likelihood that a married woman would work outside the home. In 1960, some 32 percent of married women were in the labor force; forty years later, 69 percent were working or looking for work (along with 69 percent of single women). Federal and state governments slowly responded to the changing demands of work and family with new policies such as a federal child care tax credit.

One reason for more working women was inflation in the 1970s and declining wages in the 1980s, both of which eroded the ability of families to live comfortably on one income. Between 1979 and 1986, fully 80 percent of married households saw the husband's income fall in constant dollars. The result, headlined the *Wall Street Journal* in 1994: "More Women Take Low-Wage Jobs Just So Their Families Can Get By." One young woman juggled community college courses and full-time work as an insurance company clerk, earning more than her husband brought home as a heavy equipment operator. Another worked at the drive-up window of a shopping center bank and cleaned offices on Saturdays to help pay the mortgage on a house purchased before her husband's employer imposed pay cuts.

A second reason for the increase in working women from 29 million in 1970 to 66 million in 2000 was increasing need for "women's jobs" like data entry clerks, reservation agents, and nurses. Indeed, the American economy still divides job categories by sex. Despite some movement toward gender-neutral hiring in the 1970s job types were more segregated by sex than by race in the early 1990s.

COMING OUT

New militancy among gay men and lesbians drew on several of the social changes of the late 1960s and 1970s. Willingness to acknowledge nonstandard sexual behavior was part of a change in public values. Tactics of political pressure came from the antiwar and civil rights movements. The timing, with a series of key events from 1969 to 1974, coincided with that of women's liberation.

Gay activism spread from the biggest cities to smaller communities, from the coasts to Middle America. New York police had long harassed gay bars and their customers. When police raided Manhattan's Stonewall Inn in June 1969, patrons fought back in a weekend of disorder. The **"Stonewall Rebellion"** was a catalyst for homosexuals to assert themselves as a political force. San Francisco also became a center of gay life. By the late 1970s, the city had more than three hundred business and social gathering places identified as gay and lesbian.

With New Yorkers and San Franciscans as examples, more and more gay men and lesbians "came out," or went public about their sexual orientation. They published newspapers, organized churches, and lobbied politicians for protection of basic civil rights such as equal access to employment, housing, and public accommodations. They staged "gay pride" days and marches. In 1974, the American Psychiatric Association eliminated homosexuality from its official list of mental disorders.

Life in gay communities took an abrupt turn in the 1980s when a new worldwide epidemic began to affect the United States. Scientists first identified a new disease pattern, **acquired immune deficiency syndrome (AIDS)**, in 1981. The name described the symptoms resulting from the human immunodeficiency virus (HIV), which destroys the body's ability to resist disease. HIV is transferred through blood and semen. In the 1980s, the most frequent American victims were gay men and intravenous drug users.

A decade later, it was clear that HIV/AIDS was a national and even global problem. By the end of 1998, AIDS had been responsible for 411,000 deaths in the United States, transmission to heterosexual women was increasing, and HIV infection had spread to every American community.

AIDS quilt, Washington, D.C., October, 1992

Lisa Quinones/Black Star

Stonewall Rebellion On June 27, 1969, patrons fought back when police raided the gay Stonewall Inn in New York.

Acquired Immune Deficiency Syndrome (AIDS) A complex of deadly pathologies resulting from infection with the human immunodeficiency virus (HIV).

FROM THEN TO NOW
Women and Work in American Offices

At the end of the twentieth century, women filled the majority of America's office-based jobs. More women than men worked as office managers, receptionists, library administrators, bank tellers, travel agents, administrative assistants, insurance agents, bookkeepers, and other desk-and-computer occupations.

In 1997, women made up 46 percent of the American labor force. Seven out of ten of these women worked in professional, managerial, technical, administrative support, and sales positions. They ranged from corporate CEOs and college professors to clerks in state motor vehicle offices and the voices that take your orders and reservations when you dial 800.

This employment pattern, which most Americans now take for granted, is the product of 140 years of gradual change that began with, and was triggered by, the Civil War. Before the Civil War, American women found employment as domestic servants, sometimes as mill operatives, and increasingly as schoolteachers, but not as office workers. Clerks were men—sometimes settled into lower-status white-collar careers and sometimes learning a business from the inside before rising into management. Their jobs consisted of copying letters and documents by hand, tracing orders and correspondence, and keeping financial records.

The Civil War, however, sharply increased the flow of government paperwork while diverting young men into military service. The U.S. Treasury Department in Washington responded in 1862 by hiring women to sort and package federal bonds and currency. Treasury officials fretted about the moral implications of mixing men and women in offices but overcame these concerns when they found that women were both cheap and reliable workers. By 1870, several hundred women worked in Washington's federal offices, enough for a character in a novel about the Hayes administration (1877–1881) to comment that he could learn from a glance to "single out the young woman who supported her family upon her salary and the young woman who bought her ribbons with it; the widow who fed half-a-dozen children."

As the national economy grew in the late nineteenth century, it generated ever-increasing flows of information. New technologies such as telephones and typewriters routinized clerical work. These trends increased the need for desk workers, a need largely filled by middle-class women, whose literacy was often guaranteed by the high school diplomas that went disproportionately to women in the later nineteenth century. As women workers filled new downtown skyscrapers, the central districts of large cities lost some of their rough edges and grew more respectable as centers of shopping and entertainment.

By 1900, the division of labor that would characterize the first half of the twentieth century was in place. Women comprised 76 percent of the nation's stenographers and typists and 29 percent of its cashiers, bookkeepers, and accountants. For the most part, however, they occupied the lower echelons of the office hierarchy. It was men who determined what was to be said; women who transcribed, transmitted, recorded, and filed their messages. Only in recent decades have women begun successfully to challenge that established order.

By the 1990s, Americans were accustomed to open discussion of gay sexuality, if not always accepting of its reality. Television stars and other entertainers could "come out" and retain their popularity. So could politicians in selected districts. On the issue of gays in the military, however, Congress and the Pentagon were more cautious, accepting a policy that made engaging in homosexual acts, though not sexual orientation itself, grounds for discharge.

CHURCHES IN CHANGE

Americans take their search for spiritual grounding much more seriously than do citizens of other industrial nations. Roughly half of privately organized social activity (such as charity work) is church related. In the mid-1970s, 56 percent of Americans said that religion was "very important" to them, compared to only 27 percent of Europeans.

However, mainline Protestant denominations that traditionally defined the center of American belief struggled after 1970. The United Methodist Church, the Presbyterian Church U.S.A., the United Church of Christ, and the Episcopal Church battled internally over the morality of U.S. foreign policy, the role of women in the ministry, and the reception of gay and lesbian members. While they were strengthened by the ecumenical impulse, which united denominational branches that had been divided by ethnicity or regionalism, they gradually lost their predominant position among American churches, perhaps because ecumenism diluted the certainty of their message.

By contrast, evangelical Protestant churches have benefited from the direct appeal of their message and from strong roots in the booming Sunbelt. Members of evangelical churches (25 percent of white Americans) now outnumber the members of mainline Protestant churches (20 percent). Major evangelical denominations include Baptists, the Church of the Nazarene, and the Assemblies of God. Fundamentalists, defined by a belief in the literal truth of the Bible, are a subset of evangelicals. So are 8 to 10 million Pentecostals and charismatics, who accept "gifts of the spirit," such as healing by faith and speaking in tongues.

Outsiders know evangelical Christianity through "televangelists." Spending on religious television programming rose from $50 to $600 million by 1980. By the 1970s, it reached 20 percent of American households. (See American Views, "The Religious Imperative in Politics.")

Behind the glitz and hype of the television pulpit, evangelical churches emphasized religion as an individual experience focused on personal salvation. They also offered communities of faith to stabilize fragmented lives in a changing society.

Another important change in national religious life has been the continuing "Americanization" of the Roman Catholic church following the Second Vatican Council in 1965, in which church leaders sought to respond to postwar industrial society. In the United States, Roman Catholicism moved toward the center of American life, while Asian and Latino immigrants brought new vigor to many parishes and many inner-city churches have been centers for social action. Yet, modernization also sparked a conservative backlash in the church and Catholics disagree about whether priests should be allowed to marry and other adaptations to American culture.

Culture Wars

In the 1950s and 1960s, Americans argued most often over foreign policy, racial justice, and the economy. Since the 1980s, they have also quarreled over beliefs and values, especially as the patterns of family life have become more varied. In these quarrels, religious belief has heavily influenced politics as individuals and groups try to shape America around their particular, and often conflicting, ideas of the godly society. Americans who are undogmatic in religion are often liberal in politics as well, while religious and political conservatism also tend to go together.

The division on social issues is related to theological differences within Protestantism. The "conservative" emphasis on personal salvation and the literal truth of the Bible also expresses itself in a desire to restore "traditional" social patterns. Conservatives worry that social disorder occurs when people follow personal impulses and pleasures. In contrast, the "liberal" or "modern" emphasis on the universality of the Christian message restates the Social Gospel with its call to build the Kingdom of God through social justice and may recognize divergent pathways toward truth. Liberals worry that greed in the unregulated marketplace creates disorder and injustice.

The cultural conflict also transcends the historic three-way division of Americans among Protestants, Catholics, and Jews. Catholic reformers, liberal Protestants, and Reform Jews may agree on issues of cultural values. The same may be true of conservative Catholics, fundamentalist Protestants, and Orthodox Jews.

•AMERICAN VIEWS•

THE RELIGIOUS IMPERATIVE IN POLITICS

The strong religious faith of many Americans can drive them to different stands on political issues. The letter below written by Jerry Falwell in 1987 to potential supporters of the Moral Majority, reflects the politically conservative outlook of many evangelical Christians. Falwell is pastor of the Thomas Road Baptist Church in Lynchburg, Virginia. He founded the Moral Majority, a conservative religious lobbying and educational organization, in 1979 and served as its president until 1987. The second document, from an open letter issued by the Southside United Presbyterian Church in Tucson in 1982, expresses the conviction of other believers that God may sometimes require civil disobedience to oppose oppressive government actions. The letter explains the church's reasons for violating immigration law to offer sanctuary to refugees from repressive Central American regimes supported by the United States.

HOW DO Falwell and the Southside Presbyterian Church define the problems that demand a religious response? Are there any points of agreement? How does each statement balance the claims of God and government?

From the Reverend Jerry Falwell:
I believe that the overwhelming majority of Americans are sick and tired of the way that amoral liberals are trying to corrupt our nation from its commitment to freedom, democracy, traditional morality, and the free enterprise system.

And I believe that the majority of Americans agree on the basic moral values which this nation was founded upon over 200 years ago.

Today we face four burning crises as we continue in this Decade of Destiny the 1980s loss of our freedom by giving in to the Communists; the destruction of the family unit; the deterioration of the free enterprise system; and the crumbling of basic moral principles which has resulted in the legalizing of abortion, widespread pornography, and a drug problem of epidemic proportions.

That is why I went to Washington, D.C., in June of 1979, and started a new organization The Moral Majority.

Right now you may be wondering: "But I thought Jerry Falwell was the preacher on the Old-Time Gospel Hour television program?"

You are right. For over twenty-four years I have been calling the nation back to God from the pulpit on radio and television.

But in recent months I have been led to do more than just preach. I have been compelled to take action.

I have made the commitment to go right into the halls of Congress and fight for laws that will save America. . . .

I will still be preaching every Sunday on the Old-Time Gospel Hour and I still must be a husband and father to my precious family in Lynchburg, Virginia.

But as God gives me the strength, I must do more. I must go into the halls of Congress and fight for laws that will protect the grand old flag . . . for the sake of our children and grandchildren.

From Southside United Presbyterian Church.

We are writing to inform you that Southside Presbyterian Church will publicly violate the Immigration and Nationality Act, Section 274 (A). . . .

We take this action because we believe the current policy and practice of the United States Government with regard to Central American refugees is illegal and immoral. We believe our government is in violation of the 1980 Refugee Act and international law by continuing to arrest, detain, and forcibly return refugees to the terror, persecution, and murder in El Salvador and Guatemala.

We believe that justice and mercy require the people of conscience actively assert our God-given right to aid anyone fleeing from persecution and murder. . . .

We beg of you, in the name of God, to do justice and love mercy in the administration of your office. We ask that "extended voluntary departure" be granted to refugees from Central America and that current deportation proceedings against these victims be stopped.

Until such time, we will not cease to extend the sanctuary of the church. . . . Obedience to God requires this of us all.

Sources: Gary E. McCuen, ed., *The Religious Right* (G. E. McCuen Publishers, 1989); Ann Crittenden, *Sanctuary* (Weidenfeld and Nicolson, 1988).

Conservatives have initiated the culture wars, trying to stabilize what they fear is an American society spinning out of control because of sexual indulgence. In fact, the evidence on the sexual revolution is mixed. Growing numbers of teenagers reported being sexually active in the 1970s, but the rate of increase tapered off in the 1980s. The divorce rate began to drop after 1980. Births to teenagers dropped after 1990, and the number of two-parent families increased. Most adults remain monogamous, according to data from 1994.

There was, however, an astonishing eagerness to talk about sex in the 1990s and this set the stage for religiously rooted battles over two sets of issues. One cluster revolves around so-called family values, questioning the morality of access to abortion, the acceptability of homosexuality, and the roles and rights of women. A second set of concerns has focused on the supposed role of public schools in undermining morality through sex education, unrestricted reading matter, nonbiblical science, and the absence of prayer. Opinion polls show clear differences among religious denominations on issues such as censorship of library books, acceptability of racially segregated neighborhoods, freedom of choice in terminating pregnancy, and homosexuality, and efforts to restrict legal access to abortion mobilized thousands of "right to life" advocates in the late 1980s and early 1990s.

A culturally conservative issue with great popular appeal in the early 1990s was an effort to prevent states and localities from protecting homosexuals against discrimination. Under the slogan "No special rights," antigay measures passed in Cincinnati, Colorado, and Oregon in 1993 and 1994, only to have the Supreme Court overturn the Colorado law in *Romer* v. *Evans* (1996). Public support for lesbian and gay civil rights varies with different issues (strong support for equal employment opportunity, much less for granting marriage rights to same-sex couples) and whether the issues are framed in terms of specified rights for gays or in terms of the right of everyone, including gays, to be free from government interference with personal decisions, such as living arrangements and sexual choices.

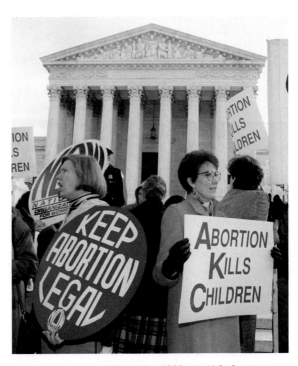

In December 1993, the U.S. Supreme Court heard arguments on whether states could require protesters to remain a certain distance from abortion clinics. These anti-abortion and pro-abortion protesters revealed the deep divisions over this and other issues in the culture wars.

AP/Wide World Photos

CONCLUSION

Americans entered the 1980s searching for stability. The 1970s had brought unexpected and uncomfortable change. America's global postwar dominance seemed to recede even as traditional values appeared under siege in the U.S. itself. Ronald Reagan's presidential campaign played to these insecurities by promising to revitalize the older ways of life and restore the United States to its former influence.

Taken as a whole, it is fair to call the years from 1981 through 1992 the era of the Reagan revolution. The astonishing collapse of the Soviet Union ended forty years of Cold War. The fifty-year expansion of federal government programs to deal with economic and social inequities was reversed. Prosperity alternated with recessions that shifted the balance between regions. Economic inequality increased after narrowing for a generation at the same time that more and more leaders proclaimed that unregulated markets could best meet social needs. Middle-class Latinos and African Americans made substantial gains while many other minority Americans sank deeper into poverty.

Every revolution has its precursors. Intellectuals had been clarifying the justifications for Reagan administration actions since the 1960s. The Reagan-Bush years extended changes that had begun in the 1970s, particularly the conservative economic policies and military buildup of the troubled Carter administration. In retrospect, the growing weakness of the USSR should also have been apparent in the same decade, had not the United States been blinded by its fear of communist power. Intervention in the Persian Gulf amplified American policies that had been in place since the CIA intervened in Iran in 1953. The outbreak of violence in Los Angeles after the Rodney King verdict showed that race relations were as tense as they had been in the 1960s.

In 1992, the United States was the undisputed world power. Its economy was poised for a surge of growth. It was the leader in scientific research and the development of new technologies. Its military capacities far surpassed those of any rival and seemed to offer a free hand in shaping the world— capacities that would be tested and utilized in the new century.

SUMMARY

Reagan's Domestic Revolution Political change began in 1980, when Ronald Reagan and his running mate George H.W. Bush, rode American discontent to a decisive victory in the presidential election. Building on a neoconservative critique of American public policies and issues from the Carter administration, Reagan presided over revolutionary changes in American government and policies. The consequences of his two terms included an altered role for government, powerful but selected economic growth, and a shift of domestic policy toward lifestyle concerns. Reaganomics and a new prosperity contrasted with corporate "downsizing" and an increase in the poverty rate.

The Second (Short) Cold War Reagan regarded the Soviet Union as an "evil empire." By the end of 1991 the Soviet Union was gone, Communist regimes had ended in Eastern Europe, and the Berlin Wall had come down. The Cold War had finally ended with the help of the relentless pressure of American spending on defense helping bankrupt the Soviet Union. Reagan's foreign policy was marked by the invasion of Granada, the overthrowing of a Panamanian strong man, assistance to Nicaraguan Contras, and the revelation of the Iran-Contra affair. In 1991, President George H.W. Bush intervened in the Persian Gulf in response to Iraq's invasion of Kuwait; the war fascinated millions who watched it live on television; America won the war but not the peace.

Growth in the Sunbelt The emergence of the Sunbelt as a center of population and source of conservative voting strength, the immigration "boom," the demographic and ethnic changes in American cities, and the graying of America are all characteristics of America since 1981. Much of the Sunbelt growth has come from retired Americans and new job seekers. Older Americans have now become a powerful voice in public affairs. Immigration has significantly changed the American ethnic mix; while the largest single group of immigrants is Hispanic, immigrants from Asia, Russia, Eastern Europe, and the Middle East are reflected in the 10.4 percent of the population that is foreign-born.

Values in Collision In the 1950s and 1960s Americans argued most often about foreign policy, racial injustice, and the economy. Since that time, they have also quarreled over beliefs and values, especially as patterns in family life have become more varied. In substantial measure these conflicts were rooted in the social and cultural changes of the 1960s and 1970s that had altered traditional institutions. Changes in roles and expectations among women and new openness about gay and lesbian sexuality were particularly powerful in dividing American churches and politics. Abortion rights and the conservative backlash, the increase of women in the work force, and the new "culture wars" were part of modern America.

REVIEW QUESTIONS

1. Was there a Reagan revolution in American politics? Did Reagan's presidency change the economic environment for workers and business corporations?

2. How did American ideas about the proper role of government change during the 1980s?

3. What caused the breakup of the Soviet Union and the end of the Cold War?

4. How did immigration from other nations affect different regions in America?

5. What changes in family roles and sexual behavior became divisive political issues?

KEY TERMS

Acquired immune deficiency syndrome (AIDS)   (p. 813)
Americans with Disabilities Act (p. 801)
Deregulation   (p. 796)
Economic Recovery and Tax Act of 1981 (ERTA)   (p. 796)

Glasnost   (p. 804)
Immigration and Nationality Act of 1965   (p. 808)
Intermediate Nuclear Force Agreement   (p. 804)
Operation Desert Storm   (p. 806)
First Persian Gulf War   (p. 805)

Perestroika   (p. 804)
Roe v. *Wade*   (p. 812)
Sagebrush Rebellion   (p. 797)
Stonewall Rebellion   (p. 813)
Strategic Defense Initiative (SDI) (p. 802)
Sunbelt   (p. 806)

WHERE TO LEARN MORE

📖 **Ronald Reagan Boyhood Home, Dixon, Illinois.** The home where Reagan lived from 1920 to 1923 tells relatively little about Reagan himself but a great deal about the small-town context that shaped his ideas.

📖 **The Causes of Homelessness in America.** Social and political policies since the 1980s that have contributed to the gap between rich and poor and the rise of homelessness. **http://www.stanford.edu/class/e297c/poverty_prejudice/soc_sec/bcauses.htm**

📖 **The Intermediate Nuclear Force Agreement (INF).** The full text document of the INF agreement between the United States and the Soviet Union, the first true nuclear disarmament treaty. **http://www.state.gov/www/global/arms/treaties/infl.html**

📖 **The Gulf War.** Read about the Persian Gulf War commanders, see testimony of American combat soldiers, and learn about the events leading up to the invasion. **http://www.pbs.org/wgbh/pages/frontline/gulf/**

📖 **A Concrete Curtain: The Life and Death of the Berlin Wall.** Traces the wall from creation in the 1960s to its destruction after the collapse of communist East Germany. **Http:www.wall-berlin.org/gb/berlin.htm**

 For additional study resources for this chapter, go to:
www.prenhall.com/goldfield/chapter30

. . . the looks on the faces of the people
coming out of the city that day will haunt me forever . . .
everyone was the same color . . . dust white . . .
women crying . . . men crying . . . we must never forget
the men and women that died that day . . .

Black smoke billows through lower Manhattan during the collapse of the World Trade Center.

31

COMPLACENCY AND CRISIS
1993–2003

HOW DID Bill Clinton dominate the politics of the "center?"

WHAT IMPACT did information technologies have on the economy in the 1990s?

HOW DID the make-up of the American population change in the 1990s?

WHAT WERE the policies of George W. Bush during his first two years in office?

HOW DID 9/11 affect American views on security and affairs?

IMAGE KEY

for pages 820–821

a. Black smoke billowing through lower Manhattan during the collapse of the World Trade Center.

b. A cell phone like those used by many in the stricken World Trade Center Towers to call for help or give their families their last goodbyes.

c. Computer chips have come to symbolize the boom of the 1990s.

d. A paper voting card like those used in Florida in the contentious 2000 presidential election.

e, f. Computer chips.

g. A gas mask used as protection from a chemical or biological attack.

h. Bill Clinton campaigning in 1992; shown surrounded by a crowd.

i. S.V. Marshall High School students join other Mississippi teens in building more than 125 new high-speed multimedia computers during a Computer Blitz Build at Jackson State University e-Center.

j. A pie chart showing the population shifts of the 1990s.

k. A soldier stops to watch the sunset during military exercises in Kuwait, November 18, 2002.

I'm a firefighter for the FDNY [Fire Department New York]. I had gotten off the night before. . . . My friend woke me up early that morning to borrow my car to take his sick cat to the vet. . . . I was up so I went to my local bagel store for my coffee and paper. . . . when I heard a lady scream a plane had hit the Trade Center. . . . I thought since it was a beautiful day that perhaps a Cessna with the pilot having a heart attack had accidentally done this. . . . I ran home to put the TV on. . . . as soon as I saw what damage was done I knew this wasn't any Cessna. . . . my god people were jumping . . . phone rang it was a fellow from my station and he hadn't turned his TV on yet. . . . I screamed to him to turn his #*#* TV on. . . .

When the second plane hit. . . . I said goodbye and told him I was going in. . . . I jumped in my car and was off to the races. . . . the highway was closed. . . . but open for us. . . . I had the gas pedal to the floor as I headed toward the city looking out my window I see both towers burning. . . . when I hear a rumble and see the south tower #2 fall. . . . I have to get my gear so I pull off the highway going down the on ramp. . . . arriving at the firehouse everyone's in shock and we know we gotta get there now to help. . . . as we're getting ready to leave the 2nd tower fell. . . . we commandeer a bus and we're off. . . .

We arrived at a staging area and then finally got the ok to go in. . . . who's in charge? . . . Shoes, papers, and dust are everywhere. . . . we wait til [building] 7 collapses. . . . chief gets us into the site by going thru the financial center and bam there we are. . . . pieces of the outside wall sticking out of the highway. . . . cars on fire . . . buses gutted. . . . I saw numerous acts of courage that day both civilian and uniformed. . . . the looks on the faces of the people coming out of the city that day will haunt me forever . . . everyone was the same color. . . . dust white. . . . women crying. . . . men crying. . . . we must never forget the men and women that died that day. . . . their sacrifice will live on for generations to come. . . .

Source: John McNamara Story #400, The September 11 Digital Archive, 13 April, 2002, **http://911digitalarchive.org/stories/details/400**

JOHN MCNAMARA was one of the many off-duty New York City fire fighters who rushed to the World Trade Center after the terrorist attack on September 11, 2001. Hijacking four commercial jetliners, the terrorists crashed one plane into the Pentagon and one into each of the twin towers of the World Trade Center, 110-story buildings that housed 50,000 workers at the peak of the workday. Millions of Americans watched in horror as television showed first one tower and then the other burned and disintegrated. September 11 was an occasion for terror and courage. Passengers on the fourth plane fought the hijackers and made sure that it crashed in a Pennsylvania field rather than hit a fourth target. Altogether, 479 police officers, fire fighters, and other emergency workers died in the collapse of the towers. Thousands of volunteers rushed to help. The total confirmed death toll was 2,795 in New York, 184 at the Pentagon, and 40 in Pennsylvania.

The attacks, masterminded by the Al-Qaeda network of Muslim extremists, ended a decade of prosperity at home and complacency about the place of the United States in the world. In their aftermath, as Americans became aware of millions of Muslim neighbors and tried to balance civil liberties against national security, they realized how diverse the nation had become. For most of the 1990s, prosperity allowed politics to focus on social issues, such as health care and education, as well as on bitterly partisan but often superficial battles over personalities and presidential behavior. However, the terrorists attacked buildings that were symbols of the nation's economic and military power. The aftermath of the attacks deepened a business recession that had followed a decade of growth spurred by new technologies. The vulnerability of the targets also undermined Americans' sense of security and isolation from world problems, underscored the global reach of terrorism, and made understanding its sources more necessary than ever.

THE POLITICS OF THE CENTER

In Bill Clinton's race for president in 1992, the "war room" was the decision center where Clinton and his staff planned tactics and countered Republican attacks. On the wall was a sign with a simple message: "It's the economy, stupid." It was a reminder that victory lay in emphasizing everyday problems that George H.W. Bush had neglected.

The message also revealed an insight into the character of the United States in the 1990s. What mattered most were down-to-earth issues, not the distant problems of foreign policy.

POLITICAL GENERATIONS

Every fifteen to twenty years, a new group of voters and leaders comes to power, driven by the desire to fix the mess that the previous generation left behind. The leaders who dominated the 1980s believed that the answer was to turn the nation's social and economic problems over to the market while asserting America's influence and power around the world.

In the mid-1990s the members of "Generation X" came of voting age with deep worries about the foreclosing of opportunities. They worried that previous administrations had neglected social problems and let the competitive position of the United States deteriorate.

Young and successful but not widely known as governor of Arkansas, Democrat Bill Clinton's campaign for the 1992 nomination overcame minimal name recognition and his use of a student deferment to avoid military service in Vietnam. Clinton made sure that the Democrats fielded a full baby boomer (and Southern) ticket by choosing the equally youthful Tennessean Albert Gore Jr. as his running mate.

Bush won renomination by beating back archconservative Patrick Buchanan. The party platform conformed to the beliefs of the Christian right. At the Republican National convention in Houston, Pat Buchanan called for a crusade against unbelievers. His startling speech was a reminder of how religious belief was reshaping American politics.

The wild card was Texas billionaire Ross Perot, whose independent campaign started with an appearance on a television talk show. Perot also tried to claim the political center, appealing to the middle of the middle-class—to small business owners, middle managers, and professionals who had approved of Reagan's antigovernment rhetoric but distrusted his corporate cronies. But, Perot's behavior became increasingly erratic.

HOW DID Bill Clinton dominate the politics of the center?

QUICK REVIEW

Candidates for President in 1992
- Republican George H.W. Bush: Ronald Reagan's vice president.
- Democrat Bill Clinton: little known governor of Arkansas.
- Independent Ross Perot: Texas billionaire and political maverick.

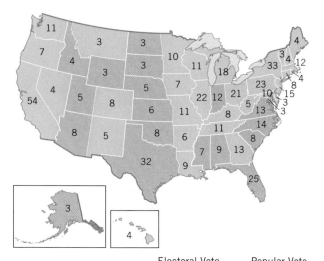

	Electoral Vote (%)	Popular Vote (%)
BILL CLINTON (Democrat)	**370** **(69)**	**43,728,275** **(43.2)**
George Bush (Republican)	168 (31)	38,167,416 (37.7)
H. Ross Perot (United We Stand, America)	–	19,237,247 (19.0)

MAP 31–1
The Election of 1992 Bill Clinton defeated George H.W. Bush in 1992 by reviving the Democratic Party in the industrial Northeast and enlisting new Democratic voters in the western states, where he appealed both to Hispanic immigrants and to people associated with fast-growing high-tech industries. He won reelection in 1996 with the same pattern of support. However, the coalition was an unstable combination of "Old Democrats," associated with older industries and labor unions, and "New Democrats," favoring economic change, free trade, and globalization.

WHAT FACTOR'S led to George H.W. Bush's downfall in the election of 1992?

Bosnia A nation in southeast Europe that split off from Yugoslavia and became the site of bitter civil and religious war, requiring NATO and U.S. intervention in the 1990s.

Kosovo Province of Yugoslavia where the United States and NATO intervened militarily in 1999 to protect ethnic Albanians from expulsion.

Bush campaigned as a foreign policy expert, but he ignored anxieties about the nation's direction at home. In fact, voters in November ranked the economy first as an issue, the deficit second, health care third, and foreign policy eighth. Clinton hammered away at economic concerns and the need for change from the Reagan-Bush years. He presented himself as a new, pragmatic, and livelier Democrat.

Election day gave the Clinton-Gore ticket 43 percent of the popular vote, Bush 38 percent, and Perot 19 percent. Millions who voted for Perot were casting a protest vote for "none of the above" and against "politics as usual" rather than hoping for an actual Perot victory. Clinton ran best among voters over 65, who remembered FDR and Harry Truman, and voters under 30.

POLICING THE WORLD

Clinton inherited an expectation that the United States could keep the world on an even keel. U.S. diplomats helped broker an Israel-PLO accord that gave Palestinians self-government in Gaza and the West Bank, only to watch extremists on both sides undermine the accords and plunge Israel into a near-civil war by 2002. The United States in 1994 used diplomatic pressure to persuade North Korea to promise to suspend building nuclear weapons. The world also benefited from a gradual reduction of nuclear arsenals and from a 1996 treaty to ban the testing of nuclear weapons.

Given the national distaste for overseas entanglements, Clinton used military power with caution. He inherited a U.S. military presence in Somalia (in northeastern Africa) but withdrew American forces when their humanitarian mission of guarding food relief to starving Somalis was overshadowed by the need to take sides in a civil war. In Haiti he restored an elected president.

Clinton also reluctantly committed the United States to a multinational effort to end bloody civil war in ethnically and religiously divided **Bosnia** in 1995.

The American military revisited the same part of Europe in 1999, when the United States and Britain led NATO's intervention in **Kosovo**. The majority of people in this Yugoslav province were ethnic Albanians who chafed under the control of the Serb-controlled Yugoslav government. When a Kosovar independence movement began a rebellion, the Yugoslavs responded with brutal repression. To protect the Kosovars, NATO began a bombing campaign that targeted Yugoslav military bases and forces in Kosovo. In June, Yugoslavia agreed to withdraw its troops and make way for a multinational NATO peacekeeping force, marking a measured success for U.S. policy.

To satisfy Russia, the peacekeeping force that entered Kosovo in June was technically a U.S. operation, but it was a reinvented NATO that negotiated with Yugoslavia.

The new NATO is a product of the new Europe of the 1990s. A key step was expansion into the former Soviet sphere in eastern Europe. In 1999, NATO formally admitted Poland, Hungary, and the Czech Republic. Three years later, NATO agreed to give Russia a formal role in its discussions further eroding the barriers of the Cold War.

CLINTON'S NEOLIBERALISM

Domestic policy attracted Clinton's greatest interest, and his first term can be divided into two parts. In 1993–1994, he worked with a slim Democratic majority in Congress to modernize the American economy, taking advantage of an economic upturn that lasted for most of the decade. In 1995 and 1996, however he faced solid Republican majorities, the result of a Republican sweep in the November 1994 elections.

The heart of Clinton's agenda was efforts to make the United States economy more equitable domestically and more competitive internationally; these goals marked Clinton as a **neoliberal** who envisioned a partnership between a leaner government and a dynamic private sector. Steps to "reinvent" government cut federal employment below Reagan administration levels. A new tax bill increased taxes on the top 1.2 percent of households. The Earned Income Tax Credit, a Nixon-era program that helped lift working Americans out of poverty, was expanded. In early 1993, Clinton pushed through the Family and Medical Leave Act, which provided up to twelve weeks of unpaid leave for workers with newborns or family emergencies and had been vetoed twice by George H.W. Bush.

Clinton's biggest setback was the failure of comprehensive health-care legislation. The goals seemed simple at first: containment of health-care costs and extension of basic medical insurance to all Americans under age 65. In the abstract, voters agreed that something needed to be done. So did individuals like the twenty-five-year-old photographer's assistant who found herself facing cancer surgery without savings or health insurance: "I work full-time, and because it's a very small business, we don't get any benefits. . . . It just devastated everybody financially. And that shouldn't happen. That's the American dream that's lost."

Unfortunately the plan that emerged from the White House ran to 1,342 pages of complex regulations, with something for everyone to dislike. Senior citizens worried about limits on Medicare spending. Insurance companies did not want more regulations. Businesses did not want the costs of insuring their workers. Taxpayers did not want to pay for wider medical insurance coverage through higher taxes or rationing of medical services. The reform effort went nowhere.

If Reagan avoided blame for mistakes, Clinton in his first two years in office seemed to avoid credit for successes despite his legislative accomplishments. Both the president and his wife attracted bitter hatred from the far right, of a sort previously reserved for Franklin and Eleanor Roosevelt and the Kennedy family. Indeed, Hillary Rodham Clinton became a symbol of discomfiting changes in American families.

CONTRACT WITH AMERICA AND THE ELECTION OF 1996

Conservative political ideology and personal animosity against the Clintons were part of an extraordinary off-year election in 1994, in which voters defeated dozens of incumbents and gave Republicans control of Congress. For most of 1995, the new Speaker of the House, Newt Gingrich of Georgia, dominated political headlines as he pushed the **Contract with America**, the official Republican campaign platform for the 1994 elections, which called for a revolutionary reduction in federal responsibilities.

Clinton laid low and let the new Congress attack environmental protections, propose cuts in federal benefits for the elderly, and try to slice the capital-gains tax to help the rich. As Congress and president battled over the budget, congressional Republicans forced the federal government to shut down for more than three weeks between November 1995 and January 1996. Democrats painted Gingrich and his congressional allies as a radical fringe who wanted to gut core values and programs that most Americans wanted to protect.

After the budget confrontations, 1996 brought a series of measures to reward work—a centrist position acceptable to most Americans. The minimum wage increased.

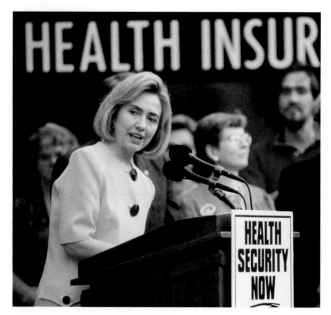

Hillary Rodham Clinton's mastery of policy details seemed to some critics to be inappropiate for a first lady, but it helped her be an effective senator from New York beginning in 2001.

SIPA Press

![W] **WHERE TO LEARN MORE**

★ Oklahoma City National Memorial Center Museum, Oklahoma City, OK
www.oklahomacitynationalmemorial.org

Temporary Assistance for Needy Families (TANF)   Federal program, utilizing work requirements for and time limits on benefits, created in 1996 to replace earlier welfare programs to aid families and children.

Congress made pension programs easier for employers to create and made health insurance portable when workers changed jobs. Clinton signed bi-partisan legislation to "end welfare as we know it." The new program of **Temporary Assistance to Needy Families (TANF)** replaced Aid to Families with Dependent Children (AFDC). Aid recipients had to seek work or be enrolled in schooling, and there was a time limit on assistance. By 2001, the number of public-assistance recipients had declined 58 percent from its 1994 high, but there are doubts that many of the former recipients have found jobs adequate to support their families.

Clinton's reelection in 1996 was a virtual replay of 1992. His opponent, Robert Dole, represented an earlier political generation. The Republican party was uncertain whether to stress free markets or morality. The party tried to paper over its uneasy mix of traditional probusiness and socially moderate country-club Republicans, radical proponents of unregulated markets, and religious conservatives affiliated with the Cristian Coalition. The Republicans thus displayed many of the internal fractures that characterized American society as a whole.

Because the nation was prosperous and at peace, and because Clinton had claimed the political center, Clinton became the first Democratic president to be elected to a second term since Franklin Roosevelt. The Clinton-Gore ticket easily won the Northeast, the industrial Midwest, and the Far West; Hispanic voters alienated by anti-immigrant rhetoric from the Republicans helped Clinton also take usually Republican Florida and Arizona.

The election confirmed that voters liked the pragmatic center. They wanted to continue the reduction of the federal role in domestic affairs that began in the 1980s without damaging social insurance programs.

THE DANGERS OF EVERYDAY LIFE

Part of the background for the sometimes vicious politics of the mid-1990s was a sense of individual insecurity and fear of violence that coexisted with an economy that was booming in some sectors but still leaving many Americans behind. The solutions, however, seemed inadequate. Neither the liberal response of tighter gun controls or the conservative response of harsher and mandatory prison terms could prevent irrational actions.

Headlines and news flashes proclaimed terrifying random acts of violence. In April 1999, two high-school students in Littleton, Colorado took rifles and pipe bombs into Columbine High School to kill twelve classmates, a teacher, and themselves.

The greatest losses of life came in Waco, Texas, and in Oklahoma City. On April 19, 1993, federal agents raided the fortified compound of the Branch Davidian cult outside Waco after a fifty-one day siege. A fire, probably set from inside, killed more than eighty people. On the second anniversary of the Waco raid, Timothy McVeigh detonated a truck packed with explosives in front of the federal office building in downtown Oklahoma City. The blast killed 169 people, presumably as revenge against what McVeigh considered an oppressive government.

The Brady Handgun Violence Prevention Act, passed in 1994, set up a waiting period and background checks for purchases of firearms. But gun control was political dynamite. Americans have drastically differing understandings of the Second Amendment, which states: "A well regulated militia, being necessary to the security of a free State, the right of the people to keep and bear arms, shall not be infringed." The National Rifle Association argued that the amendment establishes an absolute individual right. Until the 1980s, in contrast, federal courts consistently interpreted the amendment to apply to citizen service in a government-organized militia, and federal courts have yet to strike down any gun control law for violating the Second Amendment.

Conservatives, including many gun-ownership absolutists, put their faith in strict law enforcement as the best route to public security. Many states adopted "three strike" measures that drastically increased penalties for individuals convicted of a third crime. One result was an explosive growth of the prison industry. States diverted funds from education and health care to build and staff more prisons. The number of people serving sentences of a year or longer in state and federal prisons grew from 316,000 in 1980 to 1,305,000 in 1999.

The war on drugs, begun in the 1980s, was the biggest contributor to the prison boom. Aggressive enforcement of domestic laws against drug possession or sales filled American prison cells and fell most heavily on minorities. In Connecticut, for example, minority offenders arrested on drug charges were nine times more likely than white offenders to end up in jail.

In fact, crime fell steadily after peaking in 1991. The rate of violent crime (murder, rape, robbery, aggravated assault) fell by 31 percent from 1991 to 1999, including a 37 percent drop in number of murders. The rate of major property crimes (burglary, larceny-theft, and motor vehicle theft) fell by 27 percent over the same period. Easing fears and escalating costs caused some states to soften sentencing laws.

MORALITY AND PARTISANSHIP

If the economy was the fundamental news of the later 1990s, Bill Clinton's personal life was the hot news. In 1998 and 1999, the United States was riveted by revelations about the president's sex life, doubts about his integrity, and debates about his fitness for high office. Years of rumors, and law suits, culminated in 1999 in the nation's second presidential impeachment trial.

Clinton's problems began in 1994 with the appointment of a special prosecutor to investigate possible fraud in the **Whitewater** development, an Arkansas land promotion in which Bill and Hillary Clinton had invested in the 1980s. The probe by Kenneth Starr, the independent counsel, however, expanded into a wide-ranging investigation that eventually encompassed the sexual behavior of the president. Meanwhile, Paula Jones had brought a lawsuit claiming sexual harassment by then-governor Clinton while she was a state worker in Arkansas. The investigation of Whitewater brought convictions of several friends and former associates of the Clintons, but no evidence pointing directly at either Bill or Hillary Clinton themselves.

The legal landscape changed in January 1998, when allegations surfaced about an affair between the president and Monica Lewinsky, a former White House intern. Lewinsky admitted to the relationship privately and then to Starr's staff after the president had denied it in a sworn deposition for the Paula Jones case. This opened Clinton to charges of perjury and obstruction of justice. Although a federal judge dismissed Jones's suit in April, the continued unfolding of the Lewinsky affair treated the nation to a barrage of personal details about Bill Clinton. The affair certainly revealed deep flaws in Clinton's character and showed his willingness to shade the truth. Newspaper, radio talk shows, and politicians debated whether such flaws were relevant to his ability to perform his Constitutional duties.

In the fall of 1998, the Republican leaders who controlled Congress decided that Clinton's statements and misstatements justified the Constitutional process of impeachment. In December, the Republican majority on the House Judiciary Committee recommended four articles of impeachment, or specific charges against the president, to the House of Representatives. By a partisan vote, the full House

Whitewater   Arkansas real estate development in which Bill and Hillary Clinton were investors; several fraud convictions resulted from investigations into Whitewater, but evidence was not found that the Clinton's were involved in wrongdoing.

OVERVIEW

PRESIDENTIAL IMPEACHMENT

Andrew Johnson, 1868	Charges:	Failure to comply with Tenure of Office Act, requiring Congressional approval to fire cabinet members.
	Political Lineup:	Radical Republicans against Johnson; Democrats and moderate Republicans for him.
	Actions:	Tried and acquitted by Senate.
	Underlying Issues:	Johnson's opposition to Republican plans for reconstruction of southern states after the Civil War.
Richard Nixon, 1974	Charges:	Obstruction of justice in Watergate investigation; abuse of power of federal agencies for political purposes; refusal to recognize Congressional subpoena.
	Political Lineup:	Democrats and many Republicans against Nixon.
	Actions:	Charges approved by House committee; Nixon resigned before action by the full House of Representatives.
	Underlying Issues:	Nixon's construction of a secret government and his efforts to undermine integrity of national elections.
Bill Clinton, 1999	Charges:	Perjury and obstruction of justice in the investigation of sexual misconduct allegations by Paula Jones.
	Political Lineup:	Conservative Republicans against Clinton; Democrats and some moderate Republicans for him.
	Actions:	Tried and acquitted by Senate.
	Underlying Issues:	Republican frustration with Clinton's ability to block their agenda; deep concern about Clinton's character and moral fitness for presidency.

approved two of the charges and forwarded them to the Senate. The formal trial of the charges by the Senate began in January 1999 and ended on February 12. Moderate Republicans joined Democrats to assure that the Senate would fall far short of the two-thirds majority required for conviction and removal from office. Article 1, charging that the president had perjured himself, failed by a vote of 45 to 55. Article 2, charging that he had obstructed justice, failed by a vote of 50 to 50.

Why did Congressional Republicans pursue impeachment to the bitter end? It was clear that most Americans disapproved of Clinton's conduct but did not think that merited removal from office. The 1998 election, which reduced the Republican majority in the House and resulted in the resignation of Newt Gingrich, confirmed the opinion polls. At the same time, 25 to 30 percent of Americans remained convinced that Clinton's presence in the White House demeaned the nation. In other words, although impeachment was certainly motivated by politics, it was also another battle in America's culture wars.

A NEW ECONOMY?

WHAT IMPACT did information technologies have on the economy in the 1990s?

By the year 2000 the American economy had changed. More than ever, it was a global economy. And, unlike any time in the past, it was an economy that depended on electronic computing to manage and transmit vast quantities of data. The impacts of the electronic revolution are still being absorbed into the structures and routines of everyday life.

THE PROSPEROUS 1990S

From 1992 through 2000, Americans enjoyed nine years of continuous economic expansion. Unemployment dropped from 7.2 percent in 1992 to 4.0 percent at the start of 2000 as American businesses created more than 12 million new jobs. Key states like California experienced new growth driven by high-tech industries, entertainment, and foreign trade. The stock market soared; rising demand for shares in established blue-chip companies and new **Internet** firms swelled the value of individual portfolios, IRA accounts, and pension funds. The rate of home-ownership rose after declining for fifteen years. The proportion of Americans in poverty dropped to 12 percent in 1999, and the gap between rich and poor began to narrow (slightly) for the first time in two decades.

The economic boom was great news for the federal budget. Perennial deficits formed into surpluses for 1998, 1999, and 2000. Both political parties anticipated a growing surplus for the next decade and debated whether to offer massive tax cuts, buy down the national debt, or shore up Social Security and Medicare.

By the end of the decade the productivity of U.S. manufacturing workers was increasing more than 4 percent per year, the highest rate in a generation. Part of the gain was the payoff from the painful business restructuring and downsizing of the 1970s and 1980s. Another cause was improvements in efficiency from the full incorporation of personal computers and electronic communication into everyday life and business practice.

THE SERVICE ECONOMY

At the beginning of the twenty-first century, the United States was an economy of services. The service sector includes everyone not directly involved in producing and processing physical products, and by the 1990s, it included more than 70 percent of American jobs.

Service jobs vary greatly. At the bottom of the scale are minimum-wage jobs held mostly by women, immigrants, and the young such as cleaning people, child-care workers, hospital orderlies, and fast-food workers. In contrast, many of the best new jobs are in information industries. Teaching, research, government, advertising, mass communications, and professional consulting depend on producing and manipulating information. These fields add to national wealth by creating and applying new ideas rather than by supplying standardized products and services.

Another growth industry was health care. Spending on medical and health services amounted to 12 percent of the gross domestic product in 1990, up from 5 percent in 1960. The need to share this huge expense fairly was the motivation for Medicare and Medicaid in the 1960s and the search for a national health insurance program in the 1990s.

THE HIGH-TECH SECTOR

The epitome of the "sunrise" economy was electronics, which grew hand-in-glove with the defense budget. The first computers in the 1940s were derived in part from wartime code-breaking efforts. In the 1950s, IBM got half its revenues from air defense computers and guidance systems for B-52 bombers.

Invention of the microprocessor in 1971 kicked the industry into high gear. The farmlands of Santa Clara County, California, became a "silicon landscape" of neat one-story factories and research campuses. In 1950, the county had 800 factory workers. In 1980, it had 264,000 manufacturing workers and 3,000 electronics firms. Related hardware and microchip factories spread the industry throughout the West, creating "silicon prairies," "silicon forests," and "silicon deserts" to complement California's original **Silicon Valley**.

QUICK REVIEW

Boom Times

- U.S. enjoyed nine years of economic expansion between 1992 and 2000.
- Unemployment fell to 4.0 percent in 2000.
- The economic boom resulted in increased government revenues.

Internet The system of interconnected computers and servers that allows the exchange of email, posting of Web sites, and other means of instant communication.

Silicon Valley The region of California between San Jose and San Francisco that holds the nation's greatest concentration of electronics firms.

·AMERICAN VIEWS·

CREATING AND WORKING IN THE NEW ECONOMY

ike many other American industries, the booming information technology sector that employed millions of workers by the 1990s started with a few key ideas and innovators. Bill Gates and Paul Allen, the founders of software giant Microsoft Corporation, talk about their early encounters with computers as high school students and the origins of Allen's idea of a "wired world" in the early 1970s. Following their interview a worker reflects on the high-tech industry at the end of the 1990s.

WHAT DO the experiences suggest about the pace of technological innovation and industrial change? How do high-tech workers cope with the pace of change in their industry, and what are the implications for their jobs?

Bill Gates, Paul Allen, and the Seeds of the Personal Computer Revolution

GATES:

Our friendship started [in high school] after the mothers' club paid to put a computer terminal in the school in 1968. The notion was that, of course, the teachers would figure out this computer thing and then teach it to the students. But that didn't happen. It was the other way around. There was a group of students who kind of went nuts.

ALLEN:

The teletype room was full of rolled-up paper-tape programs and manuals and everything else. Between classes, or when-

ever any of us hard-core computer types had a spare period, we would congregate there.

GATES:

We were always scrounging free computer time. One year a student's mother arranged for us to go downtown to a new commercial center. We didn't have to pay for the time as long as we could find bugs in their system and report them. . . .

ALLEN:

At the end of every school day, a bunch of us would take our little leather satchel briefcases and ride the bus downtown to the computer center. Bill and I were the guys that stayed the latest, and afterward we'd eat pizza at this hippie place across the street. . . .

GATES:

The event that started everything for us business-wise was when Paul found an article in 1971 in an electronics magazine. . . . about Intel's 4004 chip, which was the world's first microprocessor. Paul comes up and says "Whoa" and explains that this microprocessor thing's only going to get better and better. . . .

ALLEN:

I remember having pizza at Shakey's in Vancouver, Washington, in 1973, and talking about the fact that eventually everyone is going to be online and have access to newspapers

The computer industry generated an accompanying software industry as a major component of information technology employment (see American Views, "Creating and Working in the New Economy"). Every computer needed a complexly coded operating system, word-processing programs, spreadsheet programs, file-reading programs, Internet browsers, and, of course, games. Seattle-based Microsoft parlayed an alliance with IBM into a dominant position that eventually triggered federal antitrust action. Other software firms rose and fell with innovative and then outmoded programs. Software writing skills also spawned a new world of multimedia entertainment.

and stuff and wouldn't people be willing to pay for information on a computer terminal.

Source: "Bill Gates and Paul Allen Talk," *Fortune*, 132, October 2, 1995, pp 69–72. Copyright © 1995 *Fortune* reprinted by permission.

Susie Johnson, Computer Chip Layout Designer

I design the layout of computer chips for Cirrus Logic in Austin, Texas. We're what they call a "chip solutions company." . . . [Laughs] Right now, we're laying out audio chips that go into computers and improve the sound of the speakers. I saw a demo of them recently. They had a regular PC with those regular little speakers and it sounded very weak. Then they put our chip in there, and the speakers sounded like this huge stereo. It was pretty wild.

My job is I'm given a schematic of the chip by the engineers, and it's basically just a bunch of symbols-triangles and rectangles with lines going in and out of them. Each symbol represents a device on the chip that hooks up to something else, and each of these little devices is designed to perform some function electronically. . . . I translate this technical information into the way the chip will actually look—how all this information will be contained in this tiny space. I draw it out using a computer program. It's mostly an automated process. In the past. I'd draw the devices by hand, but the chips I'm working on now are too complicated for that. . . .

I did lots of different jobs before—I was a waitress and I worked in a bunch of stores. . . . So I was wanting to change. . . . I certainly didn't think that I could do this, but one night I came into work with my ex-husband and he let me do some simple layout, and I thought, this is really cool, I want to try it. So I took a couple of classes at Austin Community College—an electrical design class and an integrated circuit layout class—so I'd understand a little more of the theory angle. . . . I've been doing this for three years. I have no plans to stop. I love it. . . .

There is some art to it. You could take one of these audio chips and give it to five different layout people and it would probably come back five different ways, you know? It's not all automated. Different people will put different things next to each other.

The way I think of it is I'm making little tiny highways for electrons. Some people say it's like New York City on a postage stamp. And it is! I mean, there are so many devices that I have to put into a tiny space. The one I was working on last week had over a hundred thousand. . . .

Sometimes there's problems that the computer catches and can't fix. I'm not sure why that happens, but it's the toughest part of the job. The computer will tell you what area of the chip the problem's in, but you have to go within that area yourself and find the problem and correct it. Like if something is too close to something else, then it needs to be moved over. . . . I think it's kind of fun. You have to figure it out, you have to be a detective. . . .

Source: John Bowe, Marisa Bowe, and Sabin Streeter, *Gig: Americans Talk about Their Jobs at the Turn of the Millenium* (New York: Crown Publishers, 2000), pp. 86–88, 305–308.

Personal computers and consumer electronics became part of everyday life in the 1990s. In 2000, 45 percent of adults reported that they had Internet access at home or work, up from around 14 percent in 1996. Children aged 10–14 used computers more frequently than any other age group, and nine out of ten could access the Internet at home or at school.

The electronics boom was part of a larger growth of "high-technology" industries. If "high tech" is applied to industries that devote a substantial portion of their income to research and development, it also covers chemicals, synthetic materials, cosmetics, aircraft and space satellites, drugs, measuring instruments, and

S.V. Marshall High School students Shawn Harris (left), 17, and Michael Clark, 17, join other Mississippi teens in building more than 125 new high-speed multimedia computers during a Computer Blitz Build at Jackson State University e-Center.

Barbara Gauntt/The Clarion-Ledger

QUICK REVIEW

Cable Television, the Internet, and Cell Phones

◆ Cable television reflected the fragmentation of American society and the increasing dependence on instant communication.

◆ The World Wide Web expanded dramatically in the 1990s.

◆ Cell phone subscribers reached 86 million by 2000.

World Wide Web A part of the Internet designed to allow easier navigation of the network through the use of graphical user interfaces and hypertext links between different addresses.

many other products. Pharmaceuticals, medical imaging and diagnosis, bioengineering, and genetic engineering were all areas of rapid advance in the 1990s with momentum for the future.

AN INSTANT SOCIETY

On June 1, 1980, CNN Cable News Network gave television viewers their first chance to watch news coverage twenty-four hours a day. A decade later, CNN had hundreds of millions of viewers in more than seventy-five countries.

Fourteen months after CNN went on the air, another new cable channel, MTV: Music Television, started broadcasting round-the-clock music videos. It then created a new form of popular art and advertising, aimed at viewers aged 18 to 34.

CNN, MTV, and the rest of cable television reflected both the fragmentation of American society in the 1980s and 1990s and the increasing dependence on instant communication. As late as 1980, ordinary Americans had few shared choices for learning about their nation and world: virtually identical newscasts on NBC, CBS, and ABC and similar stories in *Time* and *Newsweek*. Fifteen years later, they had learned to surf through dozens of cable channels in search of specialized programs and were beginning to explore the Internet. Hundreds of magazines for niche markets had replaced the general-circulation periodicals of the postwar generation. Vast quantities of information were more easily available, but much of it was packaged for a subdivided marketplace of specialized consumers.

The electronic society in the 1990s also learned to communicate by email and to look up information on the **World Wide Web**. No longer did messages need the delays of the postal system or the costs of long-distance telephone calls. Students could avoid inconvenient trips to the library because information was so much quicker to search on the Web. The United States was increasingly a society that depended on instant information and expected instant results.

The Internet grew out of concerns about defense and national security. Its first form in 1969 was ARPANet (for Advanced Research Projects Administration, part of the Defense Department), intended to be a communication system to survive nuclear attack. As the Internet evolved to connected universities and national weapons laboratories, the Pentagon gave up control in 1984. The World Wide Web, created in 1991, expanded the Internet's uses by allowing organizations and companies to create Web sites that placed information only a few clicks away from wired consumers. The equally rapid expansion of bandwidth and modem capacities allowed Web pages filled with pictures and graphics to replace the text-only sites of the 1980s. By the start of the new century, Web surfers could find vast quantities of material, from Paris hotel rates to pornography, from song lyrics to stock prices. Although many of the dot-com companies crashed in 2001, they can be viewed as extensions of ongoing trends in retailing and services. Americans in 2000 spent 48 cents on meals out for every 52 cents spent on food to eat at home, paying for the convenience of quick meals without preparation and clean up time. Automatic-teller machines had become a necessity. Americans expected to be able to pull cash from their bank accounts 168 hours a week rather than finding a bank open perhaps 30 hours a week.

Mobile telephones or "cell phones" were part of the same instant society. The 5 million cell phone subscribers of 1990 had exploded to 86 million before the end of the decade.

IN THE WORLD MARKET

Instant access to business and financial information accelerated the globalizing of the American economy. With the help of national policy and booming economies overseas, the value of American imports and exports more than doubled, from 7 percent of the gross domestic product in 1965 to 16 percent in 1990. Americans in the 1970s began to worry about a "colonial" status, in which the United States exported food and raw materials and imported manufactured goods. By the 1980s, foreign economic competitiveness and trade deficits, especially with Japan, became issues of national concern.

The effects of international competition were more complex than "Japan-bashers" acknowledged. Mass-production industries, such as textiles and aluminum, suffered from cheaper and sometimes higher-quality imports, but many specialized industries and services such as Houston's oil equipment and exploration firms thrived. Globalization also created new regional winners and losers. In 1982, the United States began to do more business with Pacific nations than with Europe.

More recent steps to expand the global reach of the American economy were the **North American Free Trade Agreement (NAFTA)** in 1993 and a new world wide General Agreement on Tarriffs and Trade (GATT) approved in 1994. Negotiated by Republican George H. W. Bush and pushed through Congress in 1993 by Democrat Bill Clinton, NAFTA combined 25 million Canadians, 90 million Mexicans, and 250 million U.S. consumers in a single "common market" similar to that of western Europe. GATT cut tariffs among 100 nations. NAFTA may have been a holdover from the Bush years, but it matched Clinton's ideas about reforming the American economy.

It was, however, a hard pill for many Democrats to swallow. Support was strongest from professional businesses and industries that sought foreign customers, including agriculture and electronics. Opponents included organized labor, communities already hit by industrial shutdowns, and environmentalists worried about industrial pollution in Mexico.

The **World Trade Organization (WTO)** which replaced GATT in 1996, became the unexpected target of a global protest movement. Thousands of protesters converged on its meetings in Geneva, Switzerland, Seattle, and Genoa, Italy. They were convinced that the WTO is a tool of transnational corporations that tramples on local labor and environmental protections in the name of "free trade" and benefits only the wealthy nations and their businesses. WTO defenders argued that open trade raised net production in the world economy and thereby made more wealth available for developing nations.

North American Free Trade Agreement (NAFTA) Agreement reached in 1993 by Canada, Mexico, and the United States to substantially reduce barriers to trade.

World Trade Organization (WTO) International organization that sets standards and practices for global trade, and the focus of international protests over world economic policy in the late 1990s.

BROADENING DEMOCRACY

Closely related to the changes in the American economy were the changing composition of the American people and the continued emergence of new participants in American government. In both the Clinton and George W. Bush administrations, the prominence of women and minorities in the cabinet and national government followed years of growing success in cities and states.

HOW DID the makeup of the American population change in the 1990s?

AMERICANS IN 2000

The federal census for the year 2000 found 281,400,000 Americans in the 50 states, District of Columbia, and Puerto Rico. The increase from 1990 was 13.2 percent, or 32,700,000, the largest ten-year population rise in U.S. history.

TABLE 31.1

States with Highest Proportions of Minority Residents in 2000 (percent of total population)

Hispanic

New Mexico	42%
California	32
Texas	32
Arizona	35
Nevada	20

Asian and Pacific Islander

Hawaii	51%
California	11
Washington	6
New Jersey	6
New York	6

Black

Mississippi	36%
Louisiana	33
South Carolina	30
Georgia	29
Maryland	28

American Indian

Alaska	16%
New Mexico	10
South Dakota	8
Oklahoma	8
Montana	6

One-third of all Americans lived in four states: California, Texas, New York, and Florida. Their regulations and consumer preferences conditioned national markets for products ranging from automobiles to textbooks.

No state lost populations, but the West grew the fastest. The super boom states were Nevada (66 percent growth), Arizona (40 percent), Colorado (31 percent), Utah (30 percent), and Idaho (29 percent).

In contrast, rural counties continued to empty out in Appalachia and across the Great Plains as fewer Americans were needed for mining and farming or for the small towns associated with those industries.

Another important trend was increasing ethnic and racial diversity (Table 3.1). Hispanics were the fastest-growing group in the American population. Indeed, the number of Hispanics in 2000 (35.2 million) matched the number of African Americans. Both Asians and Hispanics who had been in the United States for some time showed substantial economic success. Non-Hispanic whites are now a minority in California, the District of Columbia, Hawaii, and New Mexico. Over the coming decades, the effects of ethnic change will be apparent in schools, the workplace, popular culture, and politics.

WOMEN FROM THE GRASS ROOTS TO CONGRESS

The increasing prominence of women and family issues in national politics was a steady, quiet revolution that bore fruit in the 1990s, when the number of women in Congress more than doubled. In 1981, President Reagan had appointed Sandra Day O'Connor to be the first woman on the United States Supreme Court. In 1984, Walter Mondale chose Geraldine Ferraro as his vice presidential candidate. In 1993 Clinton appointed the second woman to the Supreme Court, Ruth Bader Ginsburg. Clinton appointee Janet Reno was the first woman to serve as Attorney General and Madeleine K. Albright, the first to serve as Secretary of State. In 2001, George W. Bush named Condoleezza Rice as his National Security Advisor.

Political gains for women at the national level reflected their importance in grass-roots politics. The spreading suburbs of postwar America were "frontiers" that required concerted action to solve immediate needs such as adequate schools and decent parks. They offered numerous opportunities for women to engage in civic work, learn political skills, and run for local office. Moreover, new cities and suburbs had fewer established political institutions, such as political machines and strong parties; their politics were open to energetic women.

Important support and training grounds are the League of Women Voters, which does nonpartisan studies of basic issues, and the National Women's Political Caucus, designed to support women candidates of both parties.

In 1991, the nomination of Judge Clarence Thomas, an African American, to the U.S. Supreme Court ensured that everyone knew that the terms of American politics were changing. His conservative positions on social and civil-rights issues, made Thomas a controversial nominee. Controversy deepened when law professor Anita Hill accused Thomas of harassing her sexually while she had served on his staff at the U.S. Civil Rights Commission. Critics tried to discredit Hill with vicious attacks on her character, but failed to dispute her story. The public was left with Hill's unproved allegations and Thomas's equally unproved denials. The Senate confirmed Thomas to the Supreme Court.

Hill's badgering by skeptical senators angered millions of women. In the shadow of the hearings, women made impressive gains in the 1992 election, when the number of women in the U.S. Senate jumped from two to six (and grew further to nine Democrats and four Republicans after November 2000, including Hillary Rodham Clinton from New York).

Since the 1980s, voting patterns have shown a widening gender gap. Women in the 1990s identified with the Democratic party and voted for its candidates at a higher rate than men. This gender gap has helped keep Democrats competitive and dampened the nation's conservative swing.

As leadership opportunities for African Americans have increased in recent decades, they have gained positions of influence in a growing range of activities. In the field of foreign policy, for example, President George W. Bush chose Colin Powell as Secretary of State and Condolezza Rice as National Security Advisor. Here Powell (2nd from left) and Rice (right) observe a White House meeting between Bush and United Nations Secretary General Kofi Annan.

© AFP/Corbis Photo by Stephen Jaffe

MINORITIES AT THE BALLOT BOX

The changing makeup of the American populace also helped black and Latino candidates for public office to increased success. After the racial violence of the 1960s, many black people had turned to local politics to gain control of their own communities. The first black mayors of major twentieth-century cities included Carl Stokes in Cleveland in 1967 and Tom Bradley in Los Angeles in 1973. By 1983, three of the nation's four largest cities had black mayors. In 1989, Virginia made Douglas Wilder the first black state governor since Reconstruction.

MAP EXPLORATION

To explore an interactive version of this map, go to **http://www.prenhall.com/goldfield2/map31.2**

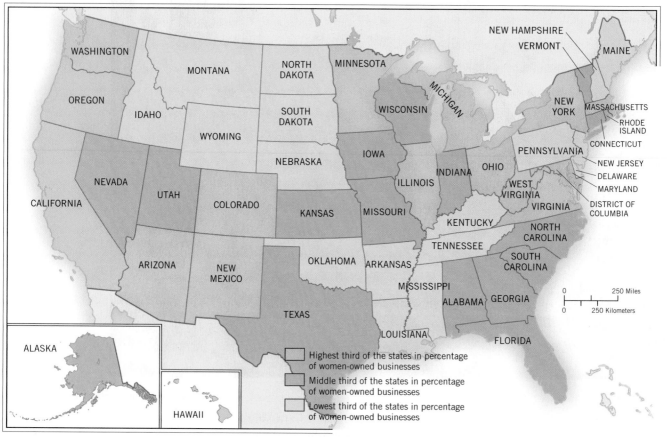

Highest third of the states in percentage of women-owned businesses

Middle third of the states in percentage of women-owned businesses

Lowest third of the states in percentage of women-owned businesses

MAP 31–2

Women as Business Owners, 1997   Some parts of the nation are more inviting to women-owned businesses than are others. The western and Great Lakes states, with histories of innovative politics, stand out as supportive of business opportunities for women.

U.S. Census Bureau, 1997 Economic Census

WHICH region of the country had the lowest percentage of women-owned businesses in 1997?

Most mid-sized cities had stopped electing city councils by wards or districts during the first half of the twentieth century. In the 1970s, minority leaders and community activists realized that a return to district voting could convert neighborhood segregation from a liability to a political resource. As amended in 1975, the federal Voting Rights Act allowed minorities to use the federal courts to challenge at-large voting systems that diluted the impact of their votes. African Americans and Mexican Americans used the act to reestablish city council districts in the late 1970s and early 1980s in city after city across the South and Southwest.

Young Hispanic and African-American politicians such as Henry Cisneros in San Antonio, Federico Peña in Denver, Dennis Archer in Detroit and Andrew Young in Atlanta, won elections, on positive platforms of growth and equity and mended fences with business leaders. Meanwhile, Washington state elected a Chinese American as governor, and Hawaii elected Japanese-American, native Hawaiian, and Filipino-American governors.

At the national level, minorities gradually increased their representation in Congress. Ben Nighthorse Campbell of Colorado, a Cheyenne, brought a Native American voice to the U.S. Senate in 1992. The number of African Americans in the House of Representatives topped forty after 1992, while the number of Latino members rose to 22 by 2003.

RIGHTS AND OPPORTUNITIES

The increasing presence of Latinos and African Americans in public life high-lighted a set of troublesome debates that replayed many of the questions that Eu-ropean immigration had raised at the beginning of the twentieth Century.

One issue has been the economic impact of illegal immigration. Advo-cates of tight borders assert that illegal immigrants take jobs away from legal res-idents and eat up public assistance. Many studies, however, find that illegal immigrants fill jobs that nobody else wants. Over the long run, high employment levels among immigrants mean that their tax contributions more than pay for their use of welfare, food stamps, and unemployment benefits, which illegal immigrants are often afraid to claim. Nevertheless, high immigration can strain local government budgets. Partly for this reason, 60 percent of California vot-ers approved **Proposition 187** in 1994, cutting off access to state-funded pub-lic education and health care for illegal immigrants. The mostly white supporters of the measure said that it was about following the rules; Hispanic opponents saw it as racism.

A symbolic issue was the degree to which American institutions should accommodate non-English speakers. Twenty-six states declared English their official language. California voters in 1998 banned bilingual public educa-tion, a system under which children whose first language was Spanish or an-other "immigrant" tongue were taught for several years in that language before shifting to English-language classrooms. Advocates of bilingual education claimed that it eased the transition into American society, while opponents said that it blocked immigrant children from fully assimilating into American life.

A more encompassing issue was a set of policies that originated in the 1960s as **affirmative action**. The initial goal was to require businesses that received fed-eral contracts to "take affirmative action to ensure that employees are treated with-out regard for their race, creed, color, or national origin." By the 1970s, many states and cities had adopted similar policies for hiring their own employees and choosing contractors and extended affirmative action to women as well as mi-norities. Colleges and universities used affirmative action policies to recruit faculty and admit students.

As these efforts spread, the initial goal of nondiscrimination evolved into expectations and requirements for active ("affirmative") efforts to achieve greater diversity. Government agencies began to set aside a small percentages of contracts for woman-owned or minority-owned firms. Cities worked to hire more minority police officers and fire fighters. Colleges made special efforts to attract minority students. The landmark court case about affirmative action was *University of Cal-ifornia* v. *Bakke* (1978). Allan Bakke, an unsuccessful applicant to the medical school at the University of California at Davis, argued that the university by re-serving 16 of 100 places in its entering class for minority students, had engaged in reverse discrimination against white applicants. The U.S. Supreme Court ordered Bakke admitted because the only basis for his rejection had been race, but the Court also stated that race or ethnicity could legally be one of several factors con-sidered in university admissions as long as a specific number of places were not re-served for minorities.

In 1996, California voters approved a ballot measure to eliminate state-sponsored affirmative action. One effect was to prohibit state-funded schools from using race or ethnicity as a factor in deciding which applicants to admit. In the same year, the Supreme Court let stand a lower-court ruling in *Hopwood* v. *Texas*, that had forbidden the University of Texas to consider race in admission decisions.

QUICK REVIEW

Divisive Issues

- The proper response to illegal immigration.
- Degree of accommodation of non-English speakers in U.S. schools.
- Affirmative action.

Proposition 187 California legisla-tion adopted by popular vote in Cali-fornia in 1994, which cuts off state-funded health and education benefits to undocumented or illegal immigrants.

Affirmative action A set of policies to open opportunities in business and education for members of mi-nority groups and women by allow-ing race and sex to be factors included in decisions to hire, award contracts, or admit students to high-er education programs.

University of California* v. *Bakke
U.S. Supreme Court case in 1978 that allowed race to be used as one of several factors in college and uni-versity admission decisions but made rigid quotas unacceptable.

The number of black freshmen in the University Texas dropped by half in 1997 and the number of black and Hispanic first-year law students by two-thirds. The results were similar at the University of California at Berkeley.

Affirmative action is a lightning rod for disagreements about American society. The goal of diversity seems to conflict with the fundamental American value of individual opportunity. Most Americans believe that individual merit and qualifications should be the sole basis for getting into school or getting a job, and that SAT scores and civil-service exams can measure those qualifications. Others argue that the merit system is severely flawed and that affirmative action helps to level the field. Nevertheless, many minorities worry that affirmative action suggests that they received jobs or contracts by racial preference rather than merit.

Edging into a New Century

On the evening of November 7, 2000, CBS-TV made a mistake that journalists dread. Relying on questions put to a sample of voters after they cast their ballots in the presidential contest between Albert Gore Jr. and George W. Bush, the CBS newsroom first projected that Gore would win Florida and likely the election, then reversed itself and called the election for Bush, only to find that it would be weeks before the votes in several pivotal states, including Florida, could be certified.

The inability to predict the outcome in 2000 was an indication of the degree to which Americans were split down the middle in their political preferences and their visions for the future. The United States entered the twenty-first century both divided and balanced, with extremes of opinion revolving around a center of basic goals and values.

THE ELECTION OF 2000

On November 8, 2000, the day after their national election, Americans woke up to the news that neither Republican George W. Bush nor Democrat Albert Gore Jr., had secured a majority of votes in the electoral college. Although Gore held a lead in the popular vote (about 340,000 votes out of more than 100 million cast), both candidates needed a majority in Florida to secure its electoral votes and the White House. After protracted protests and an on-again off-again recount in key counties, the U.S. Supreme Court ordered a halt to recounting on December 12 by the politically charged margin of 5 to 4. The result made Bush the winner in Florida by a few hundred votes and the winner nationwide by 271 electoral votes to 267.

It is difficult to know who "really" won Florida. African-American voters, who strongly favored Gore, were turned away in disproportionate numbers because of technical challenges to their registration. In one county, a poorly designed ballot probably caused several thousand mistaken votes for a minor candidate rather than Gore. Overseas absentee ballots, likely to favor Bush, were counted despite their frequent failure to meet the criteria for legitimate votes. But recounts by newspaper reporters came to different conclusions about who might have won, depending on what criteria were used to accept or reject disputed punch card ballots.

The election showed a nation that was paradoxically divided around a strong center. Gore appealed especially to residents of large cities, to women, to African

WHAT WERE the policies of George W. Bush during his first two years in office?

QUICK REVIEW

Election Controversy
- Al Gore secured a majority of the popular vote.
- Both sides needed Florida's contested electoral votes to secure election.
- The U.S. Supreme Court voted 5–4 to end the recount in Florida, making George W. Bush the new president.

Americans, and to families struggling to make it economically. Bush appealed to people from small towns, to men, and to members of households who had benefited the most from the prosperity of the Clinton era. These divisions had marked the two parties since the 1930s, and their persistence was a reminder of the nation's diversity of opinions and values. The nation also divided regionally, with Gore strong in the Northeast, upper Midwest, and Pacific Coast, Bush in the South, Ohio Valley, Great Plains, and Rocky Mountain states.

Both Bush and Gore targeted their campaigns at middle Americans. Each offered to cut taxes, reduce the federal government, and protect Social Security. Voters also shaved the Republican control of Congress to razor-thin margins, further undermining any chance of radical change in either a conservative or a liberal direction. To those on the political left and right, it looked like a formula for paralysis; for most Americans, it looked like stability.

REAGANOMICS REVISITED

Nevertheless, the Bush administration tilted domestic policy abruptly to the right. It decided it had a mandate for change and acted boldly to implement its goals. Following the example of Ronald Reagan, Bush made massive tax cuts

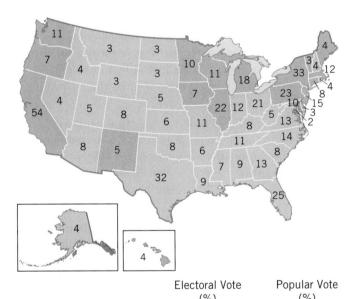

	Electoral Vote (%)	Popular Vote (%)
GEORGE W. BUSH (Republican)	**271 (50.4)**	**50,459,624 (47.9)**
Albert Gore (Democrat)	266 (49.4)	51,003,328 (48.4)
Ralph Nader (Green)	–	2,882,985 (2.7)

MAP 31–3

The Election of 2000   In the nation's closest presidential election, Democrat Al Gore was most successful in the Northeast and Far West, while George W. Bush swept the South and won most of the Great Plains states. Green Party candidate Ralph Nader took most of his votes from Gore, and, in a twist of irony, helped to swing the election to Bush.

WHAT DO the 2000 election results reveal about the divisions that separate Americans today?

George W. Bush awaits the results of the 2000 Presidential Election recount at his ranch in Texas. The controversial Florida recount was part of the closest election in U.S. history, finally granting Bush the presidency one month after election day.

Corbis/Bettmann

the centerpiece of his first months in office. By starting with proposals for ten-year cuts so large that two generations of federal programs were threatened, Bush and congressional Republicans forced the Democrats to "compromise" on reductions far higher than the economy could probably support. The resulting cuts to income taxes and estate taxes were projected to total $1,350 billion over the decade, with one-third of the benefits going to families earning more than $200,000. By 2003, officials were forecasting a budget deficit of at least $300 billion for the coming year, undoing the fiscal discipline of the Clinton administration. Nevertheless, the administration seemed likely to achieve its goal of making the tax cuts permanent after the 2002 elections confirmed a Republican majority in Congress.

The Bush team also moved to deregulate the economy. It opened many of the environmental and business regulations of the last two decades to reconsideration—from arsenic standards in drinking water to protections for wetlands to the pollution controls required of electric utilities. In many cases, the administration proposed to rely on the market through voluntary compliance and incentives to replace regulations. Vice President Dick Cheney developed a new production-oriented energy policy in consultation with energy companies but not with environmental or consumer groups. The administration failed to secure congressional approval for oil drilling in the Arctic National Wildlife Refuge in the far north of Alaska but crafted development-friendly policies for other federal lands. Collapse of the energy-trading company Enron in a hailstorm of deceptive accounting and shady market manipulations to create an energy crisis in California in early 2000 slowed the push to deregulate. In turn, Enron proved to be the first of many companies that had to restate earnings in 2002, depressing the stock market and raising questions about the ethics of big business and business accounting practices. Stock market declines and the evaporation of retirement savings for many workers raised doubts about the solidity of the 1990s boom and helped to hold down economic growth.

Education policy, a centerpiece of Bush's image as an innovator from his service as governor of Texas, was another legislative front. Tough battles with Congress resulted in compromise legislation, reminiscent of the 1990s, that included national testing standards, as Bush wanted, balanced by more federal funding. More important for both education and religion was the narrow decision by the Supreme Court in Zelman v. Simmons-Harris (2002) to uphold the use of taxpayer-funded assistance, or vouchers, to help students attend religious schools. By declaring that both religious and secular institutions can compete for government money as long as it is channeled through individuals who decided how to spend it, the court continued a two-decade trend to narrow the constitutional prohibition on the "establishment of religion."

DOWNSIZED DIPLOMACY

Conservatives had long criticized subordinating U.S. authority and freedom of action to international agreements. The new Bush administration repeatedly adopted unilateral or bilateral policies in preference to the complexities of negotiations with an entire range of nations.

In his first eighteen months, Bush opted out of a series of treaties and negotiations on global issues. The goal in each case was to reduce restrictions on U.S. business and the military. The administration undercut efforts to implement the Convention on Biological Warfare. It refused to sign on to efforts to reduce the international trade in armaments, declined to acknowledge a new International Criminal Court to try war criminals, and ignored an international compact on the rights of women. Most prominently, it refused to accept the Kyoto Agreement, aimed at combating the threat of massive environmental change through global warming resulting from the carbon dioxide released by fossil fuels, dismissing a growing scientific consensus on the problem.

Bush also ended the 1972 treaty that had limited the deployment of antimissile defenses by the United States and Russia. In its place he revived Ronald Reagan's idea of a Strategic Defense Initiative with proposals for new but unproven technologies to protect the United States against nuclear attacks by "rogue states." This argument was supported in 2002 by North Korea's revelation that it was pursuing a nuclear weapons program, even though it had agreed not to do so in 1994. A new U.S. policy that explicitly claimed the right to act militarily to preempt potential threats confirmed the go-it-alone approach.

PARADOXES OF POWER

The United States in the twenty-first century faced the paradox of power: The enormous economic, military, and technological capacity, that allowed it to impose its will on other nations could not prevent anti-American actions by enraged individuals.

In the 1990s, the U.S. economy had surged while Japan stagnated, Europe marked time, and Russia verged on economic collapse. The American military budget exceeded the total military spending of the next dozen nations.

But the United States remained vulnerable. Terrorist attacks by Islamic radicals killed nineteen American soldiers at military housing in Saudi Arabia in 1996 and seventeen sailors on the destroyer *Cole* while in port in the Arab nation of Yemen in 2000. Bombs at the U.S. embassies in Kenya and Tanzania in 1998 killed more than 200 people. These bombings followed the detonation of explosives in the basement garage of the World Trade Center in New York in February 1993. Terrorism remained a constant threat—realized in an appalling manner on September 11, 2001.

After September 11, there were reports of information-gathering failures by the FBI and CIA, to be investigated by a commission appointed by President Bush at the end of 2002. However, it is always easier to read the warnings after an event has occurred than to pick out the essential data before the unexpected happens—something as true about the attack on Pearl Harbor, for example, as about the attack of 9/11.

HOW DID 9/11 affect American views on security and foreign affairs?

SECURITY AND CONFLICT

On September 12, President George W. Bush called the Pentagon and World Trade Center attacks "acts of war." Three days later, Congress passed a Joint Resolution that gave the president sweeping powers "to use all necessary and appropriate force against those nations, organizations, or persons he determines planned, authorized, committed, or aided the terrorist attacks that occurred on September 11, 2001."

FROM THEN TO NOW
Loyalty in 2001 and 1917

In mid-October of 2001, Congress completed work on anti-terrorism legislation that President George W. Bush and Attorney General John Ashcroft had demanded in the aftermath of the September 11 tragedy. The Patriot Act gave federal authorities substantial new capacity to conduct criminal investigations, in most provisions for the next three to five years. These included the power to request "roving" wiretaps of individuals rather than single telephones; to obtain nationwide search warrants; to tap information in computerized records; and to detain foreigners without filing charges for up to a week.

These measures raised a number of concerns about the protection of civil liberties, as noted by the several dozen members of Congress who voted against the act. In historical perspective, however, it is comparatively restrained. Congress deliberated for several weeks rather than instantly ratifying the administration's request. And it seemed as if some history lessons had sunk in, for numerous lawmakers and commentators raised the painful memory of the unnecessary internment of Japanese Americans during World War II.

Perhaps the most useful historical comparison—and contrast—is not World War II but World War I. (see Chapter 23). When Americans plunged into war in April 1917, the nation's political and economic leaders took the occasion to muffle dissent in the name of unity. Congress rushed through an Espionage Act that set prison terms for obstructing the war effort and quickly became a tool for squashing dissenting voices. The Sedition Act of 1918 was even broader, establishing penalties for speaking or writing against the draft, bond sales, or war production.

Federal authorities in the Justice Department cooperated with the private, reactionary American Protective League and with tens of thousands of local councils of defense. Neighbors spied on each other and reported suspicious conversations. The "loyalty" efforts targeted African Americans and Asian Americans as well as German Americans. The Post Office censored mail. Schools stopped teaching German, and immigrants spoke the language at their peril. Workers who failed to buy war bonds were fired. Loyalty became an excuse for crushing working class organizing. Socialist Party leader Eugene Debs was put in jail for noting, accurately, that it was now hard to exercise free speech. Authorities and their allies raided labor union offices and used the war emergency as an excuse for violent strike breaking.

The anti-radical vigilantism of 1917–18 segued into the Red Scare of 1919–20, when federal and local authorities targeted immigrants and labor organizers as potential revolutionaries. The Wilson administration kept wartime political prisoners in jail and arrested thousands more before the nation got tired of fighting off a revolution that never came.

In contrast to the 1910s, Americans in 2001 and 2002 were careful on the homefront. The leaders and supporters of the War on Terrorism have reacted to dissenting voices, particularly those from a pacifist tradition, with caustic remarks rather than repression. Censorship to date consists of careful management of the news and stonewalling of requests under the Freedom of Information Act rather than direct censorship of speech and the press. Violations of civil liberties have affected individuals rather than entire groups. Ethnic profiling has resulted in heightened suspicion and surveillance of Muslims, selective enforcement of immigration laws on visitors from twenty Muslim nations, and detention of several hundred U.S. residents of middle eastern origin, rather than incarceration of entire ethnic groups. Because a number of the detainees have been held without formal charges for periods of many months, a close analogy is the suspension of the writ of habeas corpus by President Lincoln during the Civil War rather than the wholesale constriction of freedom during World War I.

The different reactions can be linked to the far greater sense of national identity at the start of the twenty-first century than early in the twentieth century. Americans in the twenty-first century worry about the challenges of racial and ethnic variety and the stresses of immigration, but mass media and easy travel have helped to promote a shared sense of "being American." There are small fringe groups that advocate or practice violent preservation of a "white nation," but the middle and upper classes do not fear immigration or working class revolution in the way that was common a hundred years ago. Despite a number of individual hate crimes, the formal effort to recognize the Americanness of most of the nation's six million Muslims and Arab Americans stands in contrast to the demonizing of Japanese-Americans in the 1940s and discrimination against German-Americans in 1917–1918. Through the second half of the twentieth century, Americans seem to have learned at least something about tolerance, diversity, and the value of civil liberties.

The government response in the United States was a hodge-podge of security measures and arrests. Air travelers found endless lines and stringent new screening procedures, watched over by army reservists called to duty by the president. Members of Congress and journalists received letters containing potentially deadly anthrax spores, heightening fears of biological warfare (the source of the letters is still a mystery). Federal agents detained more than one thousand terrorist suspects, mostly men from the Middle East, releasing some but holding hundreds without charges, evidence, or legal counsel. President Bush also declared that "enemy combatants" could be tried by special military tribunals, although domestic and international protest caused the administration to agree to more legal safeguards than originally planned. Congress passed the **Patriot Act** in late October. The legislation tries to bring surveillance and information gathering into the electronic age.

In November 2002, Congress approved a massive reorganization of the federal government to improve security at home. The new Department of Homeland Security with 170,000 employees is the second-largest federal agency, after the Defense Department, but it leaves unsolved the problem of an ineffective FBI and CIA.

In the months after 9/11, the military response overseas focused on Afghanistan, where the ruling Taliban regime was harboring Bin-Laden. Afghanistan had been wracked by civil war since it had been invaded by the Soviet Union in 1979. The Taliban, who came to power after Soviet withdrawal and civil war, were repressive rulers with few international friends. American bombing attacks on Taliban forces began in early October 2001, and opposition groups within Afghanistan threw the Taliban out of power by December. Bin-Laden, however, escaped, leaving the U.S. with an uncertain commitment to rebuild a stable Afghanistan. The Al-Qaeda network and its sympathizer remained active around the world.

Patriot Act Federal legislation adopted in 2001, in response to the terrorist attacks of September 11, intended to facilitate antiterror actions by federal law enforcement and intelligence agencies.

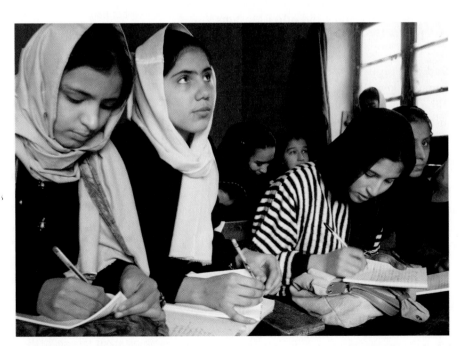

The overthrow of the Taliban regime in Afghanistan reopened many opportunities for women, including access to education as called for in Muslim scriptures. These young women are among 600 who were studying at the Cheva school for girls in Kabul by December 2002.

AP/Wilde World Photos

Saddam Hussein upon capture by U.S. troops in Iraq in December 2003.

Corbis/Bettmann

IRAQ AND CONFLICTS IN THE MIDDLE EAST

Even while the United States was intervening in Afghanistan, the administration was expanding its attention to other nations. George Bush named North Korea, Iran, and Iraq as an "axis of evil" for supporting terrorism and bearing weapons of mass destruction focused on Iraq. After the first Gulf War, Iraq had grudgingly accepted a United Nations requirement that it eliminate such weapons but had gradually made U.N. inspections impossible. Such resistance caused Bush to make the overthrow of Iraq's ruthless dictator, Saddam Hussein, the center of foreign policy. In effect, he declared one small, and possibly dangerous, nation to be the greatest menace that the United States faced. In the meantime, North Korea created a further crisis by actively pursuing its atomic weapons program with the threat of additional war.

In addition to the direct fallout from the first Gulf War, U.S. support of Israel in its worsening of relations with Arab Palestinians in territories occupied by Israel since 1967 also increased tensions in the Middle East. The United States has consistently backed Israel since the 1960s. The cornerstones of American policy have been the full endorsement of Israel's right to exist with secure borders and agreement on the right of Palestinians to a national state—in effect, a policy of coexistence. The United States had helped to broker an Israel-Egypt peace agreement in 1977 and agreements pointing toward an independent Palestinian state in the 1990s, but hardline Israeli governments have repeatedly taken advantage of U.S. support.

In 2001–2002, the United States watched from the sidelines as the Israeli-Palestinian agreements for transition to a Palestinian state fell apart. Palestinian extremists and suicide bombers and an Israeli government that favored military responses locked each other into a downward spiral that turned anti-Israel demonstrations into civil war. As a result, many Arabs regard the United States as an enemy of Arab nations and peoples, despite formal U.S. policy. The deep and seemingly unsolvable Israel-Palestinian conflict helps to explain anti-American terrorism among Arabs and other Muslims.

In the spring and summer of 2002, the administration began preparations for a second war in the Persian Gulf. On October 10, Congress authorized preemptive military action against Iraq. However, the prospect of war dismayed key allies, such as France and Germany. Together with Russia and China, they refused to support a war without U.N. backing and demanded that Bush allow more time for U.N. inspectors to search out and destroy any Iraqi weapons of mass destruction. Nonetheless, despite these objections and massive peace demonstrations in cities in the United States and around the world, American and British forces invaded Iraq in March 2003 and occupied Baghdad within two weeks, toppling Saddam's government. The United States was now faced with the possibility of a long-term occupation of Iraq and the difficult problems of rebuilding the country and trying to establish a democratic and pro-Western regime there.

CONCLUSION

If there was a dominant theme that ran through the changes and challenges of the 1990s and early 2000s, it was interconnection. The Internet, email, and cell phones brought instant communication. The national economy was more and more deeply engaged with the rest of the world through trade, investment, travel, and immigration. Corporate mismanagement affected far more people than before because of pensions and savings invested in the stock market.

The nation's growing diversity—closely connected to its internationalized economy—was reflected in the political gains of African Americans and Hispanics, as well as women. The same diversity fueled battles over affirmative action and language politics. It underlay the effort to increase security against terrorism without endangering the civil liberties of Muslim Americans.

Despite what some might have wished, Americans also found that they could not always isolate the nation from the world's problems and conflicts. The Clinton administration joined international peacekeeping efforts in Bosnia and Kosovo. The Bush administration adopted a "go it alone" policy.

The events of September 11 sparked a renewed sense of national unity, at least in the short run. There were inspiring acts of heroism and an outpouring of volunteers and contributions for rescue and relief efforts. However, the question that remained was whether Americans could sustain a new sense of unity and inclusiveness under the pressures of economic uncertainty, threats of terrorism, and war.

Summary

Politics of the Center In 1992 voters ranked the economy as their first concern, and Bill Clinton hammered at this in his campaign messages. His elections in 1992 and 1996 showed a move toward the political center; Clinton emerged as a neoliberal. Conservative political ideology and animosity toward the Clintons dominated the headlines; the Contract with America, the budget battle that shut down the federal government, Whitewater, the Clinton scandals, and impeachment filled the political headlines. Domestic terrorism (Waco, Oklahoma City, and Columbine) also grabbed the national spotlight. In foreign affairs, the United States became involved in a multinational effort to restore peace in Bosnia and Kosovo.

A New Economy? At the end of the millennium, America had a new worry, the "Y2K" problem, that did not materialize. Americans enjoyed nine years of continuous economic expansion; services became the new underpinning of the economy; and an instant society based on twenty-four hour access gave people immediate satisfaction. The American economy also expanded internationally. The controversial North American Free Trade Act went into effect and protestors took on the World Trade Organization in the streets of Seattle which demonstrated part of a larger worldwide debate over free trade and the role of transnational corporations.

Broadening Democracy The changing composition of the American people is related to the changes in the economy. The growing West, the concentration of one-third of the population in four states, the largest ten-year population increase in history, and racial and ethnic diversity, are all significance trends. As women have become more influential in national politics, so have minorities; both have contributed to a political rebalancing. Questions about equal rights and equal opportunities (Proposition 187, bilingual education, and affirmative action) have become part of the American dialogue.

REVIEW QUESTIONS

1. Was the American political system more polarized and divided in 1992 than in 1980? How did religiously conservative and liberal Americans differ over foreign relations and economic policy? What was the gender gap in national politics in the 1990s? Why were Republicans unable to appeal to most black and Hispanic voters in 1992?

2. What were Bill Clinton's major policy accomplishments? Do these represent "liberal," "moderate," or "conservative" positions?

3. How was a conservative political trend evident in the 1990s?

4. What issues were involved in Clinton's impeachment? How does the impeachment compare with the challenges to presidents Andrew Johnson and Richard Nixon?

5. How did the American economy change in the 1990s? What has been the impact of the computer revolution?

6. What new directions did George W. Bush establish for U.S. domestic and foreign policy?

7. How did the terrorist attacks of September 11, 2001 change life inside the United States?

KEY TERMS

Affirmative action   (p. 837)
Bosnia   (p. 824)
Contract with America
(p. 825)
Internet   (p. 829)
Kosovo   (p. 824)
Neoliberal   (p. 825)

North American Free Trade
Agreement (NAFTA)   (p. 833)
Patriot Act   (p. 843)
Proposition 187   (p. 837)
Silicon Valley   (p. 829)
Temporary Assistance for Needy
Families (TANF)   (p. 826)

University of California vs. *Bakke*
(p. 837)
Whitewater   (p. 827)
World Trade Organization
(WTO)   (p. 833)
World Wide Web   (p. 832)

WHERE TO LEARN MORE

Oklahoma City National Memorial Center Museum, Oklahoma City, OK. Exhibits about the federal building bombing and its impacts on the community. **www.oklahomacitynationalmemorial.org**

U.S. Census Bureau. Explore the demographic composition of the United States through the use of statistics concerning such topics as age, population distribution, income, education, and race. **http://www.census.gov/**

Computer History Museum. Trace the evolution of computers from 1945 through the present day with one of the largest collections of artifacts, photographs, documents, and film found anywhere in the world. **http://www.computerhistory.org**

Clinton Presidential Center. Showcases the legacy of the Clinton years and functions as the first virtual presidential library. The William J. Clinton Presidential Center in Little Rock, Arkansas opens November 2004. **http://www.clintonpresidentialcenter.com**

Republican Contract with America. Read the full text document of the official Republican campaign platform for the 1994 election. **http://www.house.gov/house/Contract/CONTRACT.html**

 For additional study resources for this chapter, go to:
www.prenhall.com/goldfield/chapter31

APPENDIX

The Declaration of Independence

When in the course of human events it becomes necessary for one people to dissolve the political bands which have connected them with another and to assume, among the powers of the earth, the separate and equal station to which the laws of nature and of nature's God entitle them, a decent respect to the opinions of mankind requires that they should declare the causes which impel them to the separation.

We hold these truths to be self-evident, that all men are created equal; that they are endowed by their Creator with certain unalienable rights; that among these are life, liberty, and the pursuit of happiness. That, to secure these rights, governments are instituted among men, deriving their just powers from the consent of the governed; that, whenever any form of government becomes destructive of these ends, it is the right of the people to alter or to abolish it, and to institute a new government, laying its foundation on such principles, and organizing its powers in such form, as to them shall seem most likely to effect their safety and happiness. Prudence, indeed, will dictate that governments long established should not be changed for light and transient causes; and, accordingly, all experience hath shown that mankind are more disposed to suffer, while evils are sufferable, than to right themselves by abolishing the forms to which they are accustomed. But when a long train of abuses and usurpations, pursuing invariably the same object, evinces a design to reduce them under absolute despotism, it is their right, it is their duty, to throw off such government and to provide new guards for their future security. Such has been the patient sufferance of these colonies, and such is now the necessity which constrains them to alter their former systems of government. The history of the present King of Great Britain is a history of repeated injuries and usurpations, all having, in direct object, the establishment of an absolute tyranny over these States. To prove this, let facts be submitted to a candid world:

He has refused his assent to laws the most wholesome and necessary for the public good.

He has forbidden his governors to pass laws of immediate and pressing importance, unless suspended in their operation till his assent should be obtained; and, when so suspended, he has utterly neglected to attend to them.

He has refused to pass other laws for the accommodation of large districts of people, unless those people would relinquish the right of representation in the legislature, a right inestimable to them and formidable to tyrants only.

He has called together legislative bodies at places unusual, uncomfortable, and distant from the depository of their public records, for the sole purpose of fatiguing them into compliance with his measures.

He has dissolved representative houses, repeatedly for opposing, with manly firmness, his invasions on the rights of the people.

He has refused, for a long time after such dissolutions, to cause others to be elected; whereby the legislative powers, incapable of annihilation, have returned to the people at large for their exercise; the state remaining, in the meantime, exposed to all the danger of invasion from without and convulsions within.

He has endeavored to prevent the population of these States; for that purpose, obstructing the laws for naturalization of foreigners, refusing to pass others to encourage their migration hither, and raising the conditions of new appropriations of lands.

He has obstructed the administration of justice by refusing his assent to laws for establishing judiciary powers.

He has made judges dependent on his will alone for the tenure of their offices and the amount and payment of their salaries.

He has erected a multitude of new offices and sent hither swarms of officers to harass our people and eat out their substance.

He has kept among us, in time of peace, standing armies, without the consent of our legislatures.

He has affected to render the military independent of, and superior to, the civil power.

He has combined with others to subject us to a jurisdiction foreign to our Constitution and unacknowledged by our laws, giving his assent to their acts of pretended legislation—

For quartering large bodies of armed troops among us;

For protecting them by mock trial, from punishment for any murders which they should commit on the inhabitants of these States;

For cutting off our trade with all parts of the world;

For imposing taxes on us without our consent;

For depriving us, in many cases, of the benefit of trial by jury;

For transporting us beyond seas to be tried for pretended offences;

For abolishing the free system of English laws in a neighboring province, establishing therein an arbitrary government, and enlarging its boundaries, so as to render it at once an example and fit instrument for introducing the same absolute rule into these colonies;

For taking away our charters, abolishing our most valuable laws, and altering, fundamentally, the powers of our governments.

For suspending our own legislatures and declaring themselves invested with power to legislate for us in all cases whatsoever.

He has abdicated government here by declaring us out of his protection and waging war against us.

He has plundered our seas, ravaged our coasts, burnt our towns, and destroyed the lives of our people.

He is, at this time, transporting large armies of foreign mercenaries to complete the works of death, desolation, and tyranny already begun with circumstances of cruelty and perfidy scarcely paralleled in the most barbarous ages, and totally unworthy the head of a civilized nation.

He has constrained our fellow citizens, taken captive on the high seas, to bear arms against their country, to become the executioners of their friends and brethren, or to fall themselves by their hands.

He has excited domestic insurrections amongst us and has endeavored to bring on the inhabitants of our frontiers, the merciless Indian savages, whose known rule of warfare is an undistinguished destruction of all ages, sexes, and conditions.

In every stage of these oppressions, we have petitioned for redress in the most humble terms; our repeated petitions have been answered only by repeated injury. A prince whose character is thus marked by every act which may define a tyrant is unfit to be the ruler of a free people.

Nor have we been wanting in attention to our British brethren. We have warned them, from time to time, of attempts made by their legislature to extend an unwarrantable jurisdiction over us. We have reminded them of the circumstances of our emigration and settlement here. We have appealed to their native justice and magnanimity, and

we have conjured them, by the ties of our common kindred, to disavow these usurpations, which would inevitably interrupt our connections and correspondence. They, too, have been deaf to the voice of justice and consanguinity. We must, therefore, acquiesce in the necessity which denounces our separation, and hold them, as we hold the rest of mankind, enemies in war, in peace, friends.

We, therefore, the representatives of the United States of America, in general Congress assembled, appealing to the Supreme Judge of the world for the rectitude of our intentions, do, in the name and by the authority of the good people of these colonies, solemnly publish and declare, that these united colonies are, and of right ought to be, free and independent states: that they are absolved from all allegiance to the British Crown, and that all political connection between them and the state of Great Britain is, and ought to be, totally dissolved; and that, as free and independent states, they have full power to levy war, conclude peace, contract alliances, establish commerce, and to do all other acts and things which independent states may of right do. And, for the support of this declaration, with a firm reliance on the protection of Divine Providence, we mutually pledge to each other our lives, our fortunes, and our sacred honor.

THE ARTICLES OF CONFEDERATION AND PERPETUAL UNION*

Between the states of New Hampshire, Massachusetts-bay Rhode Island and Providence Plantations, Connecticut, New York, New Jersey, Pennsylvania, Delaware, Maryland, Virginia, North Carolina, South Carolina, and Georgia.

ARTICLE 1
The Stile of this Confederacy shall be "The United States of America."

ARTICLE 2
Each state retains its sovereignty, freedom, and independence, and every power, jurisdiction, and right, which is not by this Confederation expressly delegated to the United States, in Congress assembled.

ARTICLE 3
The said States hereby severally enter into a firm league of friendship with each other, for their common defense, the security of their liberties, and their mutual and general welfare, binding themselves to assist each other, against all force offered to, or attacks made upon them, or any of them, on account of religion, sovereignty, trade, or any other pretense whatever.

ARTICLE 4
The better to secure and perpetuate mutual friendship and intercourse among the people of the different States in this Union, the free inhabitants of each of these States, paupers, vagabonds, and fugitives from justice excepted, shall be entitled to all privileges and immunities of free citizens in the several States; and the people of each State shall have free ingress and regress to and from any other State, and shall enjoy therein all the privileges of trade and commerce, subject to the same duties, impositions, and restrictions as the inhabitants thereof respectively, provided that such restrictions shall not extend so far as to prevent the removal of property imported into any State, to any other State of which the owner is an inhabitant; provided also that no imposition, duties or restriction shall be laid by any State, on the property of the United States, or either of them.

If any person guilty of, or charged with, treason, felony, or other high misdemeanor in any State, shall flee from justice, and be found in any of the United States, he shall, upon demand of the Governor or executive power of the State from which he fled, be delivered up and removed to the State having jurisdiction of his offense.

Full faith and credit shall be given in each of these States to the records, acts, and judicial proceedings of the courts and magistrates of every other State.

ARTICLE 5
For the most convenient management of the general interests of the United States, delegates shall be annually appointed in such manner as the legislatures of each State shall direct, to meet in Congress on the first Monday in November, in every year, with a power reserved to each State to recall its delegates, or any of them, at any time within the year, and to send others in their stead for the remainder of the year.

No State shall be represented in Congress by less than two, nor by more than seven members; and no person shall be capable of being a delegate for more than three years in any term of six years; nor shall any person, being a delegate,

---

*Agreed to in Congress November 15, 1777; ratified March 1781.

be capable of holding any office under the United States, for which he, or another for his benefit, receives any salary, fees or emolument of any kind.

Each State shall maintain its own delegates in a meeting of the States, and while they act as members of the committee of the States.

In determining questions in the United States in Congress assembled, each State shall have one vote.

Freedom of speech and debate in Congress shall not be impeached or questioned in any court or place out of Congress, and the members of Congress shall be protected in their persons from arrests or imprisonments, during the time of their going to and from, and attendence on Congress, except for treason, felony, or breach of the peace.

ARTICLE 6

No State, without the consent of the United States in Congress assembled, shall send any embassy to, or receive any embassy from, or enter into any conference, agreement, alliance or treaty with any King, Prince or State; nor shall any person holding any office of profit or trust under the United States, or any of them, accept any present, emolument, office or title of any kind whatever from any King, Prince or foreign State; nor shall the United States in Congress assembled, or any of them, grant any title of nobility.

No two or more States shall enter into any treaty, confederation or alliance whatever between them, without the consent of the United States in Congress assembled, specifying accurately the purposes for which the same is to be entered into, and how long it shall continue.

No State shall lay any imposts or duties, which may interfere with any stipulations in treaties, entered into by the United States in Congress assembled, with any King, Prince or State, in pursuance of any treaties already proposed by Congress, to the courts of France and Spain.

No vessel of war shall be kept up in time of peace by any State, except such number only, as shall be deemed necessary by the United States in Congress assembled, for the defense of such State, or its trade; nor shall any body of forces be kept up by any State in time of peace, except such number only, as in the judgement of the United States in Congress assembled, shall be deemed requisite to garrison the forts necessary for the defense of such State; but every State shall always keep up a well-regulated and disciplined militia, sufficiently armed and accoutered, and shall provide and constantly have ready for use, in public stores, a due number of filed pieces and tents, and a proper quantity of arms, ammunition and camp equipage.

No State shall engage in any war without the consent of the United States in Congress assembled, unless such State be actually invaded by enemies, or shall have received certain advice of a resolution being formed by some nation of Indians to invade such State, and the danger is so imminent as not to admit of a delay, till the United States in Congress assembled can be consulted; nor shall any State grant commissions to any ships or vessels of war, nor letters of marque or reprisal, except it be after a declaration of war by the United States in Congress assembled, and then only against the Kingdom or State and the subjects thereof, against which war has been so declared, and under such regulations as shall be established by the United States in Congress assem-

bled, unless such State be infested by pirates, in which case vessels of war may be fitted out for that occasion, and kept so long as the danger shall continue, or until the United States in Congress assembled shall determine otherwise.

ARTICLE 7

When land forces are raised by any State for the common defense, all officers of or under the rank of colonel, shall be appointed by the legislature of each State respectively, by whom such forces shall be raised, or in such manner as such State shall direct, and all vacancies shall be filled up by the State which first made the appointment.

ARTICLE 8

All charges of war, and all other expenses that shall be incurred for the common defense or general welfare, and allowed by the United States in Congress assembled, shall be defrayed out of a common treasury, which shall be supplied by the several States in proportion to the value of all land within each State, granted to or surveyed for any person, as such land and the buildings and improvements thereon shall be estimated according to such mode as the United States in Congress assembled, shall from time to time direct and appoint.

The taxes for paying that proportion shall be laid and levied by the authority and direction of the legislatures of the several States within the time agreed upon by the United States in Congress assembled.

ARTICLE 9

The United States in Congress assembled, shall have the sole and exclusive right and power of determining on peace and war, except in the cases mentioned in the sixth article; of sending and receiving ambassadors; entering into treaties and alliances, provided that no treaty of commerce shall be made whereby the legislative power of the respective States shall be restrained from imposing such imposts and duties on foreigners, as their own people are subjected to, or from prohibiting the exportation or importation of any species of goods or commodities whatsoever; of establishing rules for deciding in all cases, what captures on land or water shall be legal, and in what manner prizes taken by land or naval forces in the service of the United States shall be divided or appropriated; of granting letters of marque and reprisal in times of peace; appointing courts for the trial of piracies and felonies committed on the high seas and establishing courts for receiving and determining finally appeals in all cases of captures, provided that no member of Congress shall be appointed a judge of any of the said courts.

The United States in Congress assembled shall also be the last resort on appeal in all disputes and differences now subsisting or that hereafter may arise between two or more States concerning boundary, jurisdiction or any other causes whatever; which authority shall always be exercised in the manner following. Whenever the legislative or executive authority or lawful agent of any State in controversy with another shall present a petition to Congress stating the matter in question and praying for a hearing, notice thereof shall be given by order of Congress to the legislative or executive authority of the other State in controversy, and a day assigned for the appearance of the parties by their lawful agents, who shall then be directed to appoint by joint consent, commissioners or judges to constitute a court for hearing and determining the matter in question: but if they cannot agree, Congress shall name three persons out of each of the United States, and from the list of such persons each party shall alternately strike out one, the petitioners beginning, until the number shall be reduced to thirteen; and from that number not less than seven, nor more than nine names as Congress shall direct, shall in the presence of Congress be drawn out by lot, and the persons whose names shall be so drawn or any five of them, shall be commissioners or judges, to hear and finally determine the controversy, so always as a major part of the judges who shall hear the cause shall agree in the determination: and if either party shall neglect to attend at the day appointed, without showing reasons, which Congress shall judge sufficient, or being present shall refuse to strike, the Congress shall proceed to nominate three persons out of each State, and the secretary of Congress shall strike in behalf of such party absent or refusing; and the judgement and sentence of the court to be appointed, in the manner before prescribed, shall be final and conclusive; and if any of the parties shall refuse to submit to the authority of such court, or to appear or defend their claim or cause, the court shall nevertheless proceed to pronounce sentence, or judgement, which shall in like manner be final and decisive, the judgement or sentence and other proceedings being in either case transmitted to Congress, and lodged among the acts of Congress for the security of the parties concerned: provided that every commissioner, before he sits in judgement, shall take an oath to be administered by one of the judges of the supreme or superior court of the State, where the cause shall be tried, "well and truly to hear and determine the matter in question, according to the best of his judgement, without favor, affection or hope of reward:" provided also, that no State shall be deprived of territory for the benefit of the United States.

All controversies concerning the private right of soil claimed under different grants of two or more States, whose jurisdictions as they may respect such lands, and the States which passed such grants are adjusted, the said grants or either of them being at the same time claimed to have originated antecedent to such settlement of jurisdiction, shall on the petition of either party to the Congress of the United States, be finally determined as near as may be in the same manner as is before prescribed for deciding disputes respecting territorial jurisdiction between different States.

The United States in Congress assembled shall also have the sole and exclusive right and power of regulating the alloy and value of coin struck by their own authority, or by that of the respective States; fixing the standards of weights and measures throughout the United States; regulating the trade and managing all affairs with the Indians not members of any of the States; provided that the legislative right of any State within its own limits be not infringed or violated; establishing or regulating post offices from one State to another, throughout all the United States, and exacting such postage on the papers passing through the same as may be requisite to defray the expenses of the said office; appointing all officers of the land forces in the service of the United States, excepting regimental officers; appointing all the officers of the naval forces, and commissioning all officers whatever in the service of the United States; making rules for the government and regulation of the said land and naval forces, and directing their operations.

The United States in Congress assembled shall have authority to appoint a committee, to sit in the recess of Congress, to be denominated "A Committee of the States," and to consist of one delegate from each State; and to appoint such other committees and civil officers as may be necessary for managing the general affairs of the United States under their direction; to appoint one of their members to preside, provided that no person be allowed to serve in the office of president more than one year in any term of three years; to ascertain the necessary sums of money to be raised for the service of the United States, and to appropriate and apply the same for defraying the public expenses; to borrow money, or emit bills on the credit of the United States, transmitting every half year to the respective States an account of the sums of money so borrowed or emitted; to build and equip a navy; to agree upon the number of land forces, and to make requisitions from each State for its quota, in proportion to the number of white inhabitants in such State; which requisition shall be binding, and thereupon the legislature of each State shall appoint the regimental officers, raise the men and cloath, arm and equip them in a soldierlike manner, at the expense of the United States; and the officers and men so cloathed, armed and equipped shall march to the place appointed, and within the time agreed on by the United States in Congress assembled; but if the United States in Congress assembled shall, on consideration of circumstances judge proper that any State should not raise men, or should raise a smaller number of men than the quota thereof, such extra number shall be raised, officered, cloathed, armed and equipped in the same manner as the quota of each State, unless the legislature of such State shall judge that such extra number cannot be safely spared out in the same, in which case they shall raise, officer, cloath, arm and equip as many of such extra number as they judge can be safely spared. And the officers and men so cloathed, armed, and equipped, shall march to the place appointed, and within the time agreed on by the United States in Congress assembled.

The United States in Congress assembled shall never engage in a war, nor grant letters of marque or reprisal in time of peace, nor enter into any treaties or alliances, nor coin money, nor regulate the value thereof, nor ascertain the sums and expenses necessary for the defense and welfare of the United States, or any of them, nor emit bills, nor borrow money on the credit of the United States, nor appropriate money, nor agree upon the number of vessels of war, to be built or purchased, or the number of land or sea forces to be raised, nor appoint a commander in chief of the army or navy, unless nine States assent to the same: nor shall a question on any other point, except for adjourning from day to day be determined, unless by the votes of the majority of the United States in Congress assembled.

The Congress of the United States shall have power to adjourn to any time within the year, and to any place within the United States, so that no period of adjournment be for a longer duration than the space of six months, and shall publish the journal of their proceedings monthly, except such parts thereof relating to treaties, alliances or military operations, as in their judgement require secrecy; and the yeas and nays of the delegates of each State on any question shall be entered on the journal, when it is desired by any delegates of a State, or any of them, at his or their request shall be furnished with a transcript of the said journal, except such parts as are above excepted, to lay before the legislatures of the several States.

ARTICLE 10

The Committee of the States, or any nine of them, shall be authorized to execute, in the recess of Congress, such of the powers of Congress as the United States in Congress assembled, by the consent of the nine States, shall from time to time think expedient to vest them with; provided that no power be delegated to the said Committee, for the exercise of which, by the Articles of Confederation, the voice of nine States in the Congress of the United States assembled is requisite.

ARTICLE 11

Canada acceding to this confederation, and adjoining in the measures of the United States, shall be admitted into, and entitled to all the advantages of this Union; but no other colony shall be admitted into the same, unless such admission be agreed to by nine States.

ARTICLE 12

All bills of credit emitted, monies borrowed, and debts contracted by, or under the authority of Congress, before the assembling of the United States, in pursuance of the present confederation, shall be deemed and considered as a charge against the United States, for payment and satisfaction whereof the said United States, and the public faith are hereby solemnly pledged.

ARTICLE 13

Every State shall abide by the determination of the United States in Congress assembled, on all questions which by this confederation are submitted to them. And the Articles of this Confederation shall be inviolably observed by every State, and the Union shall be perpetual; nor shall any alteration at any time hereafter be made in any of them; unless such alteration be agreed to in a Congress of the United States, and be afterwards confirmed by the legislatures of every State.

These articles shall be proposed to the legislatures of all the United States, to be considered, and if approved of by them, they are advised to authorize their delegates to ratify the same in the Congress of the United States; which being done, the same shall become conclusive.

THE CONSTITUTION OF THE UNITED STATES OF AMERICA

We the people of the United States, in order to form a more perfect union, establish justice, insure domestic tranquillity, provide for the common defense, promote the general welfare, and secure the blessings of liberty to ourselves and our posterity, do ordain and establish this Constitution for the United States of America.

ARTICLE I

SECTION 1. All legislative powers herein granted shall be vested in a Congress of the United States, which shall consist of a Senate and House of Representatives.

SECTION 2. 1. The House of Representatives shall be composed of members chosen every second year by the people of the several States, and the electors in each State shall have the qualifications requisite for electors of the most numerous branch of the State legislature.

2. No person shall be a representative who shall not have attained to the age of twenty-five years, and been seven years a citizen of the United States, and who shall not, when elected, be an inhabitant of that State in which he shall be chosen.

3. Representatives and direct taxes[1] shall be apportioned among the several States which may be included within this Union, according to their respective numbers, which shall be determined by adding to the whole number of free persons, including those bound to service for a term of years, and excluding Indians not taxed, three fifths of all other persons.[2] The actual enumeration shall be made within three years after the first meeting of the Congress of the United States, and within every subsequent term of ten years, in such manner as they shall by law direct. The number of representatives shall

not exceed one for every thirty thousand, but each State shall have at least one representative; and until such enumeration shall be made, the State of New Hampshire shall be entitled to choose three, Massachusetts eight, Rhode Island and Providence Plantations one, Connecticut five, New York six, New Jersey four, Pennsylvania eight, Delaware one, Maryland six, Virginia ten, North Carolina five, South Carolina five, and Georgia three.

4. When vacancies happen in the representation from any State, the executive authority thereof shall issue writs of election to fill such vacancies.

5. The House of Representatives shall choose their speaker and other officers; and shall have the sole power of impeachment.

SECTION 3. 1. The Senate of the United States shall be composed of two senators from each State, chosen by the legislature thereof,[3] for six years; and each senator shall have one vote.

2. Immediately after they shall be assembled in consequence of the first election, they shall be divided as equally as may be into three classes. The seats of the senators of the first class shall be vacated at the expiration of the second year, of the second class at the expiration of the fourth year, and of the third class at the expiration of the sixth year, so that one third may be chosen every second year; and if vacancies happen by resignation, or otherwise, during the recess of the legislature of any State, the executive thereof may make temporary appointments until the next meeting of the legislature, which shall then fill such vacancies.[4]

3. No person shall be a senator who shall not have attained to the age of thirty years, and been nine years a citizen of the

---

[1] See the Sixteenth Amendment.
[2] See the Fourteenth Amendment.

[3] See the Seventeenth Amendment.
[4] See the Seventeenth Amendment.

United States, and who shall not, when elected, be an inhabitant of that State for which he shall be chosen.

4. The Vice President of the United States shall be President of the Senate, but shall have no vote, unless they be equally divided.

5. The Senate shall choose their other officers, and also a president pro tempore, in the absence of the Vice President, or when he shall exercise the office of the President of the United States.

6. The Senate shall have the sole power to try all impeachments. When sitting for that purpose, they shall be on oath or affirmation. When the President of the United States is tried, the chief justice shall preside: and no person shall be convicted without the concurrence of two thirds of the members present.

7. Judgment in cases of impeachment shall not extend further than to removal from office, and disqualification to hold and enjoy any office of honor, trust or profit under the United States: but the party convicted shall nevertheless be liable and subject to indictment, trial, judgment and punishment, according to law.

SECTION 4. 1. The times, places, and manner of holding elections for senators and representatives, shall be prescribed in each State by the legislature thereof; but the Congress may at any time by law make or alter such regulations, except as to the places of choosing senators.

2. The Congress shall assemble at least once in every year, and such meeting shall be on the first Monday in December, unless they shall by law appoint a different day.

SECTION 5. 1. Each House shall be the judge of the elections, returns and qualifications of its own members, and a majority of each shall constitute a quorum to do business; but a smaller number may adjourn from day to day, and may be authorized to compel the attendance of absent members, in such manner, and under such penalties as each House may provide.

2. Each House may determine the rules of its proceedings, punish its members for disorderly behavior, and, with the concurrence of two thirds, expel a member.

3. Each House shall keep a journal of its proceedings, and from time to time publish the same, excepting such parts as may in their judgment require secrecy; and the yeas and nays of the members of either House on any question shall, at the desire of one fifth of those present, be entered on the journal.

4. Neither House, during the session of Congress, shall, without the consent of the other, adjourn for more than three days, nor to any other place than that in which the two Houses shall be sitting.

SECTION 6. 1. The senators and representatives shall receive a compensation for their services, to be ascertained by law, and paid out of the Treasury of the United States. They shall in all cases, except treason, felony, and breach of the peace, be privileged from arrest during their attendance at the session of their respective Houses, and in going to and returning from the same; and for any speech or debate in either House, they shall not be questioned in any other place.

2. No senator or representative shall, during the time for which he was elected, be appointed to any civil office under the authority of the United States, which shall have been cre-

ated, or the emoluments whereof shall have been increased, during such time; and no person holding any office under the United States shall be a member of either House during his continuance in office.

SECTION 7. 1. All bills for raising revenue shall originate in the House of Representatives; but the Senate may propose or concur with amendments as on other bills.

2. Every bill which shall have passed the House of Representatives and the Senate, shall, before it become a law, be presented to the President of the United States; If he approves he shall sign it, but if not he shall return it, with his objections, to that House in which it shall have originated, who shall enter the objections at large on their journal, and proceed to reconsider it. If after such reconsideration two thirds of that House shall agree to pass the bill, it shall be sent, together with the objections, to the other House, by which it shall likewise be reconsidered, and if approved by two thirds of that House, it shall become a law. But in all such cases the votes of both Houses shall be determined by yeas and nays, and the names of the persons voting for and against the bill shall be entered on the journal of each House respectively. If any bill shall not be returned by the President within ten days (Sundays excepted) after it shall have been presented to him, the same shall be a law, in like manner as if he had signed it, unless the Congress by their adjournment prevent its return, in which case it shall not be a law.

3. Every order, resolution, or vote to which the concurrence of the Senate and the House of Representatives may be necessary (except on a question of adjournment) shall be presented to the President of the United States; and before the same shall take effect, shall be approved by him, or being disapproved by him, shall be repassed by two thirds of the Senate and House of Representatives, according to the rules and limitations prescribed in the case of a bill.

SECTION 8. 1. The Congress shall have the power

1. To lay and collect taxes, duties, imposts, and excises, to pay the debts and provide for the common defense and general welfare of the United States; but all duties, imposts, and excises shall be uniform throughout the United States.

2. To borrow money on the credit of the United States;

3. To regulate commerce with foreign nations, and among the several States, and with the Indian tribes;

4. To establish a uniform rule of naturalization, and uniform laws on the subject of bankruptcies throughout the United States;

5. To coin money, regulate the value thereof, and of foreign coin, and fix the standard of weights and measures;

6. To provide for the punishment of counterfeiting the securities and current coin of the United States;

7. To establish post offices and post roads;

8. To promote the progress of science and useful arts, by securing for limited times to authors and inventors the exclusive right to their respective writings and discoveries;

9. To constitute tribunals inferior to the Supreme Court;

10. To define and punish piracies and felonies committed on the high seas, and offenses against the law of nations;

11. To declare war, grant letters of marque and reprisal, and make rules concerning captures on land and water;

12. To raise and support armies, but no appropriation of money to that use shall be for a longer term than two years;

13. To provide and maintain a navy;

14. To make rules for the government and regulation of the land and naval forces;

15. To provide for calling forth the militia to execute the laws of the Union, suppress insurrections and repel invasions;

16. To provide for organizing, arming, and disciplining the militia, and for governing such part of them as may be employed in the service of the United States, reserving to the States respectively, the appointment of the officers, and the authority of training the militia according to the discipline prescribed by Congress;

17. To exercise exclusive legislation in all cases whatsoever, over such district (not exceeding ten miles square) as may, by cession of particular States, and the acceptance of Congress, become the seat of the government of the United States, and to exercise like authority over all places purchased by the consent of the legislature of the State in which the same shall be, for the erection of forts, magazines, arsenals, dockyards, and other needful buildings; and

18. To make all laws which shall be necessary and proper for carrying into execution the foregoing powers, and all other powers vested by this Constitution in the government of the United States, or any department or officer thereof.

SECTION 9. 1. The migration or importation of such persons as any of the States now existing shall think proper to admit, shall not be prohibited by the Congress prior to the year one thousand eight hundred and eight, but a tax or duty may be imposed on such importation, not exceeding ten dollars for each person.

2. The privilege of the writ of habeas corpus shall not be suspended, unless when in cases of rebellion or invasion the public safety may require it.

3. No bill of attainder or ex post facto law shall be passed.

4. No capitation, or other direct, tax shall be laid, unless in proportion to the census or enumeration hereinbefore directed to be taken.[5]

5. No tax or duty shall be laid on articles exported from any State.

6. No preference shall be given by any regulation of commerce or revenue to the ports of one State over those of another: nor shall vessels bound to, or from, one State be obliged to enter, clear, or pay duties in another.

7. No money shall be drawn from the treasury, but in consequence of appropriations made by law; and a regular statement and account of the receipts and expenditures of all public money shall be published from time to time.

8. No title of nobility shall be granted by the United States: and no person holding any office of profit or trust under them, shall, without the consent of the Congress, accept of any present, emolument, office, or title, of any kind whatever, from any king, prince, or foreign State.

SECTION 10. 1 No State shall enter into any treaty, alliance, or confederation; grant letters of marque and reprisal; coin money; emit bills of credit; make any thing but gold and silver coin a tender in payment of debts; pass any bill of attainder, ex post facto law, or law impairing the obligation of contracts, or grant, any title of nobility.

2. No State shall, without the consent of the Congress, lay any imposts or duties on imports or exports, except what may be absolutely necessary for executing its inspection laws: and the net produce of all duties and imposts laid by any State on imports or exports, shall be for the use of the treasury of the United States; and all such laws shall be subject to the revision and control of the Congress.

3. No State shall, without the consent of the Congress, lay any duty of tonnage, keep troops, or ships of war in time of peace, enter into any agreement or compact with another State, or with a foreign power, or engage in war, unless actually invaded, or in such imminent danger as will not admit of delay.

ARTICLE II

SECTION 1. 1. The executive power shall be vested in a President of the United States of America. He shall hold his office during the term of four years, and, together with the Vice President, chosen for the same term, be elected, as follows:

2. Each State shall appoint, in such manner as the legislature thereof may direct, a number of electors, equal to the whole number of senators and representatives to which the State may be entitled in the Congress: but no senator or representative, or person holding any office of trust or profit under the United States, shall be appointed an elector.

The electors shall meet in their respective States, and vote by ballot for two persons, of whom one at least shall not be an inhabitant of the same State with themselves. And they shall make a list of all the persons voted for, and of the number of votes for each; which list they shall sign and certify, and transmit sealed to the seat of the government of the United States, directed to the president of the Senate. The president of the Senate shall, in the presence of the Senate and House of Representatives, open all the certificates, and the votes shall then be counted. The person having the greatest number of votes shall be the President, if such number be a majority of the whole number of electors appointed; and if there be more than one who have such majority, and have an equal number of votes, then the House of Representatives shall immediately choose by ballot one of them for President; and if no person have a majority, then from the five highest on the list the said House shall in like manner choose the President. But in choosing the President, the votes shall be taken by States, the representation from each State having one vote; a quorum for this purpose shall consist of a member or members from two thirds of the States, and a majority of all the States shall be necessary to a choice. In every case after the choice of the President, the person having the greatest number of votes of the electors shall be the Vice President. But if there should remain two or more who have equal votes, the Senate shall choose from them by ballot the Vice President.[6]

3. The Congress may determine the time of choosing the electors, and the day on which they shall give their votes; which day shall be the same throughout the United States.

4. No person except a natural born citizen, or a citizen of the United States, at the time of the adoption of this Constitution, shall be eligible to the office of President; neither shall any person be eligible to the office who shall not have attained to the

---

[5]See the Sixteenth Amendment.

[6]Superseded by the Twelfth Amendment.

age of thirty-five years, and been fourteen years a resident within the United States.

5. In case of the removal of the President from office, or of his death, resignation, or inability to discharge the powers and duties of the said office, the same shall devolve on the Vice President, and the congress may by law provide for the case of removal, death, resignation or inability, both of the President and Vice President, declaring what officer shall then act as President, and such officer shall act accordingly until the disability be removed, or a President shall be elected.

6. The President shall, at stated times, receive for his services a compensation which shall neither be increased nor diminished during the period for which he shall have been elected, and he shall not receive within that period any other emolument from the United States, or any of them.

7. Before he enter on the execution of his office, he shall take the following oath or affirmation:—"I do solemnly swear (or affirm) that I will faithfully execute the office of President of the United States, and will to the best of my ability, preserve, protect and defend the Constitution of the United States."

SECTION 2.   1. The President shall be commander in chief of the army and navy of the United States, and of the militia of the several States, when called into the actual service of the United States; he may require the opinion in writing, of the principal officer in each of the executive departments, upon any subject relating to the duties of their respective offices, and he shall have power to grant reprieves and pardons for offenses against the United States, except in cases of impeachment.

2. He shall have power, by and with the advice and consent of the Senate, to make treaties, provided two thirds of the senators present concur; and he shall nominate, and by and with the advice and consent of the Senate, shall appoint ambassadors, other public ministers and consuls, judges of the Supreme Court, and all other officers of the United States, whose appointments are not herein otherwise provided for, and which shall be established by law; but the Congress may by law vest the appointment of such inferior officers, as they think proper, in the President alone, in the courts of laws, or in the heads of departments.

3. The President shall have power to fill up all vacancies that may happen during the recess of the Senate, by granting commissions which shall expire at the end of their next session.

SECTION 3.   He shall from time to time give to the Congress information of the state of the Union, and recommend to their consideration such measures as he shall judge necessary and expedient; he may, on extraordinary occasions, convene both Houses, or either of them, and in case of disagreement between them with respect to the time of adjournment, he may adjourn them to such time as he shall think proper; he shall receive ambassadors and other public ministers; he shall take care that the laws be faithfully executed, and shall commission all the officers of the United States.

SECTION 4.   The President, Vice President, and all civil officers of the United States, shall be removed from office on impeachment for, and conviction of, treason, bribery, or other high crimes and misdemeanors.

ARTICLE III

SECTION 1. The judicial power of the United States shall be vested in one Supreme Court, and in such inferior courts as the Congress may from time to time ordain and establish. The judges, both of the Supreme and inferior courts, shall hold their offices during good behavior, and shall, at stated times, receive for their services, a compensation, which shall not be diminished during their continuance in office.

SECTION 2.   1. The judicial power shall extend to all cases, in law and equity, arising under this Constitution, the laws of the United States, and treaties made, or which shall be made, under their authority;—to all cases of admiralty and maritime jurisdiction;—to controversies to which the United States shall be a party;[7]—to controversies between two or more States;—between a State and citizens of another State;—between citizens of different States;—between citizens of the same State claiming lands under grants of different States, and between a State, or the citizens thereof, and foreign States, citizens or subjects.

2. In all cases affecting ambassadors, other public ministers and consuls, and those in which a State shall be party, the Supreme Court shall have original jurisdiction. In all the other cases before mentioned, the Supreme Court shall have appellate jurisdiction, both as to law and fact, with such exceptions, and under such regulations as the Congress shall make.

3. The trial of all crimes, except in cases of impeachment, shall be by jury; and such trial shall be held in the State where the said crimes shall have been committed; but when not committed within any State, the trial shall be such place or places as the congress may by law have directed.

SECTION 3.   1. Treason against the United States shall consist only in levying war against them, or in adhering to their enemies, giving them aid and comfort. No person shall be convicted of treason unless on the testimony of two witnesses to the same overt act, or on confession in open court.

2. The Congress shall have power to declare the punishment of treason, but no attainder of treason shall work corruption of blood, or forfeiture except during the life of the person attained.

ARTICLE IV

SECTION 1. Full faith and credit shall be given in each State to the public acts, records, and judicial proceedings of every other State. And the Congress may by general laws prescribe the manner in which such acts, records and proceedings shall be proved, and the effect thereof.

SECTION 2.   1. The citizens of each State shall be entitled to all privileges and immunities of citizens in the several States.[8]

2. A person charged in any State with treason, felony, or other crime, who shall flee from justice, and be found in another State, shall on demand of the executive authority of the State from which he fled, be delivered up to be removed to the State having jurisdiction of the crime.

3. No person held to service or labor in one State under the laws thereof, escaping into another, shall, in consequence of any law or regulation therein, be discharged from

---

[7]See the Eleventh Amendment.
[8]See the Fourteenth Amendment, Sec. 1.

such service or labor, but shall be delivered up on claim of the party to whom such service or labor may be due.[9]

SECTION 3.   1. New States may be admitted by the Congress into this Union; but no new State shall be formed or erected within the jurisdiction of any other State, nor any State be formed by the junction of two or more States, or parts of States, without the consent of the legislatures of the States concerned as well as of the Congress.

2. The Congress shall have power to dispose of and make all needful rules and regulations respecting the territory or other property belonging to the United States; and nothing in this Constitution shall be so construed as to prejudice any claims of the United States, or of any particular State.

SECTION 4.   The United States shall guarantee to every State in this Union a republican form of government, and shall protect each of them against invasion; and on application of the legislature, or of the executive (when the legislature cannot be convened) against domestic violence.

ARTICLE V

The Congress, whenever two thirds of both Houses shall deem it necessary, shall propose amendments to this Constitution, or, on the application of the legislatures of two thirds of the several States, shall call a convention for proposing amendments, which in either case shall be valid to all intents and purposes, as part of this Constitution, when ratified by the legislatures of three fourths of the several States, or by conventions in three fourths thereof, as the one or the other mode of ratification may be proposed by the Congress; Provided that no amendment which may be made prior to the year one thousand eight hundred and eight shall in any manner affect the first and fourth clauses in the ninth section of the first article; and that no State, without its consent, shall be deprived of its equal suffrage in the Senate.

ARTICLE VI

1. All debts contracted and engagements entered into, before the adoption of this Constitution, shall be as valid against the United States under this Constitution, as under the Confederation.[10]

2. This Constitution, and the laws of the United States which shall be made in pursuance thereof; and all treaties made, or which shall be made, under the authority of the United States, shall be the supreme law of the land; and the judges in every State shall be bound thereby, any thing in the Constitution or laws of any State to the contrary notwithstanding.

3. The senators and representatives before mentioned, and the members of the several State legislatures, and all executive and judicial officers, both of the United States and of the several States, shall be bound by oath or affirmation to support this Constitution; but no religious test shall ever be required as a qualification to any office or public trust under the United States.

ARTICLE VII

The ratification of the conventions of nine States shall be sufficient for the establishment of this Constitution between the States so ratifying the same.

Done in Convention by the unanimous consent of the States present the seventeenth day of September in the year of our Lord one thousand seven hundred and eighty-seven, and of the independence of the United States of America the twelfth. In witness whereof we have hereunto subscribed our names.

[Signatories' names omitted]

Articles in addition to, and amendment of, the Constitution of the United States of America, proposed by Congress, and ratified by the legislatures of the several States, pursuant to the fifth article of the original Constitution.

Amendment I

[First ten amendments ratified December 15, 1791]
Congress shall make no law respecting an establishment of religion, or prohibiting the free exercise thereof; or abridging the freedom of speech, or of the press; or the right of the people peaceably to assemble, and to petition the government for a redress of grievances.

Amendment II

A well regulated militia, being necessary to the security of a free State, the right of the people to keep and bear arms, shall not be infringed.

Amendment III

No soldier shall, in time of peace be quartered in any house, without the consent of the owner, nor in time of war, but in a manner to be prescribed by law.

Amendment IV

The right of the people to be secure in their persons, houses, papers, and effects, against unreasonable searches and seizures, shall not be violated, and no warrants shall issue, but upon probable cause, supported by oath or affirmation, and particularly describing the place to be searched, and the persons or things to be seized.

Amendment V

No person shall be held to answer for a capital or otherwise infamous crime, unless on a presentment or indictment of a grand jury, except in cases arising in the land or naval forces, or in the militia, when in actual service in time of war or public danger; nor shall any person be subject for the same offense to be twice put in jeopardy of life or limb; nor shall be compelled in any criminal case to be a witness against himself, nor be deprived of life, liberty, or property, without due process of law; nor shall private property be taken for public use, without just compensation.

Amendment VI

In all criminal prosecutions, the accused shall enjoy the right to a speedy and public trial, by an impartial jury of the State and district wherein the crime shall have been committed, which district shall have been previously ascertained by law, and to be informed of the nature and cause of the accusation; to be confronted with the witnesses against him; to have compulsory process for obtaining witnesses in his favor, and to have the assistance of counsel for his defense.

---

[9]See the Thirteenth Amendment.
[10]See the Fourteenth Amendment, Sec. 4.

Amendment VII

In suits at common law, where the value in controversy shall exceed twenty dollars, the right of trial by jury shall be preserved, and no fact tried by a jury shall be otherwise reexamined in any court of the United States, than according to the rules of the common law.

Amendment VIII

Excessive bail shall not be required, nor excessive fines imposed, nor cruel and unusual punishments inflicted.

Amendment IX

The enumeration in the Constitution of certain rights shall not be construed to deny or disparage others retained by the people.

Amendment X

The powers not delegated to the United States by the Constitution, nor prohibited by it to the States, are reserved to the States respectively, or to the people.

Amendment XI [January 8, 1798]

The judicial power of the United States shall not be construed to extend to any suit in law or equity, commended or prosecuted against one of the United States by citizens of another State, or by citizens or subjects of any foreign State.

Amendment XII [September 25, 1804]

The electors shall meet in their respective States, and vote by ballot for President and Vice President, one of whom, at least, shall not be an inhabitant of the same State with themselves; they shall name in their ballots the person voted for as President, and in distinct ballots, the person voted for as Vice President, and they shall make distinct lists of all persons voted for as President and of all persons voted for as Vice President, and of the number of votes for each, which lists they shall sign and certify, and transmit sealed to the seat of the government of the United States, directed to the President of the Senate;—The President of the Senate shall, in the presence of the Senate and House of Representatives, open all the certificates and the votes shall then be counted;—The person having the greatest number of votes for President, shall be the President, if such number be a majority of the whole number of electors appointed; and if no person have such majority, then from the persons having the highest numbers not exceeding three on the list of those voted for as President, the House of Representatives shall choose immediately, by ballot, the President. But in choosing the President, the votes shall be taken by States, the representation from each State having one vote; a quorum for this purpose shall consist of a member or members from two thirds of the States, and a majority of all the States shall be necessary to a choice. And if the House of Representatives shall not choose a President whenever the right of choice shall devolve upon them, before the fourth day of March next following, then the Vice President shall act as President, as in the case of the death or other constitutional disability of the President. The person having the greatest number of votes as Vice President shall be the Vice President, if such number be a majority of the whole number of electors appointed, and if no person have a majority, then from the two highest numbers on the list, the Senate shall choose the Vice President; a quorum for the purpose shall consist of two thirds of the whole number of Senators, and a majority of the whole number shall be necessary to a choice. But no person constitutionally ineligible to the office of President shall be eligible to that of Vice President of the United States.

Amendment XIII [December 18, 1865]

Section 1.   Neither slavery nor involuntary servitude, except as a punishment for crime whereof the party shall have been duly convicted, shall exist within the United States, or any place subject to their jurisdiction.

Section 2.   Congress shall have power to enforce this article by appropriate legislation.

Amendment XIV [July 28, 1868]

Section 1.   All persons born or naturalized in the United States, and subject to the jurisdiction thereof, are citizens of the United States and of the State wherein they reside. No State shall make or enforce any law which shall abridge the privileges or immunities of citizens of the United States; nor shall any State deprive any person of life, liberty, or property, without due process of law; nor deny to any person within its jurisdiction the equal protection of the laws.

Section 2.   Representatives shall be apportioned among the several States according to their respective numbers, counting the whole number of persons in each State, excluding Indians not taxed. But when the right to vote at any election for the choice of electors for President and Vice President of the United States, representatives in Congress, the executive and judicial officers of a State, or the members of the legislature thereof, is denied to any of the male inhabitants of such State, being twenty-one years of age, and citizens of the United States, or in any way abridged, except for participating in rebellion, or other crime, the basis of representation there shall be reduced in the proportion which the number of such male citizens shall bear to the whole number of male citizens twenty-one years of age in such State.

Section 3.   No person shall be a senator or representative in Congress, or elector of President and Vice President, or hold any office, civil or military, under the United States, or under any State, who having previously taken an oath, as a member of Congress, or as an officer of the United States, or as a member of any State legislature, or as an executive or judicial officer of any State, to support the Constitution of the United States, shall have engaged in insurrection or rebellion against the same, or given aid or comfort to the enemies thereof. But Congress may by a vote of two thirds of each House, remove such disability.

Section 4.   The validity of the public debt of the United States, authorized by law, including debts incurred for payment of pensions and bounties for services in suppressing insurrection or rebellion; shall not be questioned. But neither the United States nor any State shall assume or pay any debt or obligation incurred in aid of insurrection or rebellion against the United States, or any claim for the loss or emancipation of any slave; but all such debts, obligations, and claims shall be held illegal and void.

SECTION 5.   The Congress shall have the power to enforce, by appropriate legislation, the provisions of this article.

Amendment XV [March 30, 1870]

SECTION 1. The right of citizens of the United States to vote shall not be denied or abridged by the United States or by any State on account of race, color, or previous condition of servitude.

SECTION 2. The Congress shall have power to enforce this article by appropriate legislation.

Amendment XVI [February 25, 1913]

The Congress shall have power to lay and collect taxes on incomes, from whatever source derived, without apportionment among the several States, and without regard to any census or enumeration.

Amendment XVII [May 31, 1913]

The Senate of the United States shall be composed of two senators from each State, elected by the people thereof, for six years; and each senator shall have one vote. The electors in each State shall have the qualifications requisite for electors of the most numerous branch of the State legislature.

When vacancies happen in the representation of any State in the Senate, the executive authority of such State shall issue writs of election to fill such vacancies: Provided, That the legislature of any State may empower the executive thereof to make temporary appointments until the people fill the vacancies by election as the legislature may direct.

This amendment shall not be so construed as to affect the election or term of any senator chosen before it becomes valid as part of the Constitution.

Amendment XVIII11 [January 29, 1919]

After one year from the ratification of this article, the manufacture, sale, or transportation of intoxicating liquors within, the importation thereof into, or the exportation thereof from the United States and all territory subject to the jurisdiction thereof for beverage purposes is thereby prohibited.

The Congress and the several States shall have concurrent power to enforce this article by appropriate legislation.

This article shall be inoperative unless it shall have been ratified as an amendment to the Constitution by the legislatures of the several States, as provided in the constitution, within seven years from the date of the submission hereof to the States by Congress.

Amendment XIX [August 26, 1920]

The right of citizens of the United States to vote shall not be denied or abridged by the United States or by any State on account of sex.

Congress shall have the power to enforce this article by appropriate legislation.

Amendment XX [January 23, 1933]

SECTION 1.   The terms of the President and Vice President shall end at noon on the 20th day of January and the terms of Senators and Representatives at noon on the 3d day of January, of the years in which such terms would have ended if this article had not been ratified; and the terms of their successors shall then begin.

SECTION 2.   The Congress shall assemble at least once in every year, and such meeting shall begin at noon on the 3d day of January, unless they shall by law appoint a different day.

SECTION 3.   If, at the time fixed for the beginning of the term of President, the President-elect shall have died, the Vice President-elect shall become President. If a President shall not have been chosen before the time fixed for the beginning of his term, or if the President-elect shall have failed to qualify, then the Vice President-elect shall act as President until a President shall have qualified; and the Congress may by law provide for the case wherein neither a President-elect nor a Vice President-elect shall have qualified, declaring who shall then act as President, or the manner in which one who is to act shall be selected, and such person shall act accordingly until a President or Vice President shall have qualified.

SECTION 4. The Congress may by law provide for the case of the death of any of the persons from whom, the House of Representatives may choose a President whenever the right of choice shall have devolved upon them, and for the case of the death of any of the persons from whom the Senate may choose a Vice President whenever the right of choice shall have devolved upon them.

SECTION 5.   Sections 1 and 2 shall take effect on the 15th day of October following the ratification of this article.

SECTION 6.   This article shall be inoperative unless it shall have been ratified as an amendment to the Constitution by the legislatures of three-fourths of the several States within seven years from the date of its submission.

Amendment XXI [December 5, 1933]

SECTION 1.   The Eighteenth Article of amendment to the Constitution of the United States is hereby repealed.

SECTION 2.   The transportation or importation into any State, Territory, or possession of the United States for delivery or use therein of intoxicating liquors in violation of the laws thereof, is hereby prohibited.

SECTION 3.   This article shall be inoperative unless it shall have been ratified as an amendment to the Constitution by conventions in the several States, as provided in the Constitution, within seven years from the date of the submission thereof to the States by the Congress.

Amendment XXII [March 1, 1951]

No person shall be elected to the office of the President more than twice, and no person who has held the office of President, or acted as President, for more than two years of a term to which some other person was elected President shall be elected to the office of the President more than once.

But this article shall not apply to any person holding the office of President when this article was proposed by the Congress, and shall not prevent any person who may be holding the office of President, or acting as President, during the term within which this article becomes operative from holding the office of President or acting as President during the remainder of such term.

This article shall be inoperative unless it shall have been ratified as an amendment to the Constitution by the legislatures of three-fourths of the several States within seven years from the date of its submission to the States by the Congress.

Amendment XXIII [March 29, 1961]

SECTION 1. The District constituting the seat of Government of the United States shall appoint in such manner as the Congress may direct.

A number of electors of President and Vice President equal to the whole number of Senators and Representatives in Congress to which the District would be entitled if it were a State, but in no event more than the least populous State; they shall be in addition to those appointed by the States, but they shall be considered, for the purposes of the election of President and Vice President, to be electors appointed by a State; and they shall meet in the District and perform such duties as provided by the twelfth article of amendment.

SECTION 2. The Congress shall have power to enforce this article by appropriate legislation.

Amendment XXIV [January 23, 1964]

SECTION 1. The right of citizens of the United States to vote in any primary or other election for President or Vice President, for electors for President or Vice President, or for Senator or Representative in Congress, shall not be denied or abridged by the United States or any State by reason of failure to pay any poll tax or other tax.

SECTION 2. The Congress shall have power to enforce this article by appropriate legislation.

Amendment XXV [February 10, 1967]

SECTION 1. In case of the removal of the President from office or of his death or resignation, the Vice President shall become President.

SECTION 2. Whenever there is a vacancy in the office of the Vice President, the President shall nominate a Vice President who shall take office upon confirmation by a majority of both Houses of Congress.

SECTION 3. Whenever the President transmits to the President pro tempore of the Senate and the Speaker of the House of Representatives his written declaration that he is unable to discharge the powers and duties of his office, and until he transmits to them a written declaration to the contrary, such powers and duties shall be discharged by the Vice President as Acting President.

SECTION 4. Whenever the Vice President and a majority of either the principal officers of the executive departments or of such other body as Congress may by law provide, transmit

to the President pro tempore of the Senate and the Speaker of the House of Representatives their written declaration that the President is unable to discharge the powers and duties of his office, the Vice President shall immediately assume the powers and duties of the office as Acting President.

Thereafter, when the President transmits to the President pro tempore of the Senate and the Speaker of the House of Representatives his written declaration that no inability exists, he shall resume the powers and duties of his office unless the Vice President and a majority of either the principal officers of the executive departments or of such other body as Congress may by law provide, transmit within four days to the President pro tempore of the Senate and the Speaker of the House of Representatives their written declaration that the President is unable to discharge the powers and duties of his office. Thereupon Congress shall decide the issue, assembling within forty-eight hours for that purpose if not in session. If the Congress, within twenty-one days after receipt of the latter written declaration, or, if Congress is not in session, within twenty-one days after Congress is required to assemble, determines by two-thirds vote of both Houses that the President is unable to discharge the powers and duties of his office, the Vice President shall continue to discharge the same as Acting President; otherwise, the President shall resume the powers and duties of his office.

Amendment XXVI [June 30, 1971]

SECTION 1. The right of citizens of the United States who are eighteen years of age or older to vote shall not be denied or abridged by the United States or by any State on account of age.

SECTION 2. The Congress shall have power to enforce this article by appropriate legislation.

Amendment XXVII[12] [May 7, 1992]

No law, varying the compensation for services of the Senators and Representatives, shall take effect until an election of Representatives shall have intervened.

---

[12]James Madison proposed this amendment in 1789 together with the ten amendments that were adopted as the Bill of Rights, but it failed to win ratification at the time. Congress, however, had set no deadline for its ratification, and over the years—particularly in the 1980s and 1990s—many states voted to add it to the Constitution. With the ratification of Michigan in 1992 it passed the threshold of 3/4ths of the states required for adoption, but because the process took more than 200 years, its validity remains in doubt.

PRESIDENTIAL ELECTIONS (CONTINUED)

Year	Number of States	Candidates	Party	Popular Vote*	Electoral Vote†	Percentage of Popular Vote
1789	11	GEORGE WASHINGTON	No party designations		69	
		John Adams			34	
		Other Candidates			35	
1792	15	GEORGE WASHINGTON	No party designations		132	
		John Adams			77	
		George Clinton			50	
		Other Candidates			5	
1796	16	JOHN ADAMS	Federalist		71	
		Thomas Jefferson	Democratic-Republican		68	
		Thomas Pinckney	Federalist		59	
		Aaron Burr	Democratic-Republican		30	
		Other Candidates			48	
1800	16	THOMAS JEFFERSON	Democratic-Republican		73	
		Aaron Burr	Democratic-Republican		73	
		John Adams	Federalist		65	
		Charles C. Pinckney	Federalist		64	
		John Jay	Federalist		1	
1804	17	THOMAS JEFFERSON	Democratic-Republican		162	
		Charles C. Pinckney	Federalist		14	
1808	17	JAMES MADISON	Democratic-Republican		122	
		Charles C. Pinckney	Federalist		47	
		George Clinton	Democratic-Republican		6	
1812	18	JAMES MADISON	Democratic-Republican		128	
		DeWitt Clinton	Federalist		89	
1816	19	JAMES MONROE	Democratic-Republican		183	
		Rufus King	Federalist		34	
1820	24	JAMES MONROE	Democratic-Republican		231	
		John Quincy Adams	Independent-Republican		1	
1824	24	JOHN QUINCY ADAMS	Democratic-Republican	108,740	84	30.5
		Andrew Jackson	Democratic-Republican	153,544	99	43.1
		William H. Crawford	Democratic-Republican	46,618	41	13.1
		Henry Clay	Democratic-Republican	47,136	37	13.2
1828	24	ANDREW JACKSON	Democrat	647,286	178	56.0
		John Quincy Adams	National Republican	508,064	83	44.0
1832	24	ANDREW JACKSON	Democrat	687,502	219	55.0
		Henry Clay	National Republican	530,189	49	42.4
		William Wirt	Anti-Masonic	} 33,108	7	} 2.6
		John Floyd	National Republican		11	

* Percentage of popular vote given for any election year may not total 100 percent because candidates receiving less than 1 percent of the popular vote have been omitted.

† Prior to the passage of the Twelfth Amendment in 1904, the electoral college voted for two presidential candidates; the runner-up became Vice-President. Data from Historical Statistics of the United States, Colonial Times to 1957 (1961), pp. 682–683, and The World Almanac.

PRESIDENTIAL ELECTIONS (CONTINUED)

Year	Number of States	Candidates	Party	Popular Vote	Electoral Vote	Percentage of Popular Vote
1836	26	MARTIN VAN BUREN	Democrat	765,483	170	50.9
		William H. Harrison	Whig		73	
		Hugh L. White	Whig	739,795	26	
		Daniel Webster	Whig		14	49.1
		W. P. Mangum	Whig		11	
1840	26	WILLIAM H. HARRISON	Whig	1,274,624	234	53.1
		Martin Van Buren	Democrat	1,127,781	60	46.9
1844	26	JAMES K. POLK	Democrat	1,338,464	170	49.6
		Henry Clay	Whig	1,300,097	105	48.1
		James G. Birney	Liberty	62,300		2.3
1848	30	ZACHARY TAYLOR	Whig	1,360,967	163	47.4
		Lewis Cass	Democrat	1,222,342	127	42.5
		Martin Van Buren	Free Soil	291,263		10.1
1852	31	FRANKLIN PIERCE	Democrat	1,601,117	254	50.9
		Winfield Scott	Whig	1,385,453	42	44.1
		John P. Hale	Free Soil	155,825		5.0
1856	31	JAMES BUCHANAN	Democrat	1,832,955	174	45.3
		John C. Frémont	Republican	1,339,932	114	33.1
		Millard Fillmore	American ("Know Nothing")	871,731	8	21.6
1860	33	ABRAHAM LINCOLN	Republican	1,865,593	180	39.8
		Stephen A. Douglas	Democrat	1,382,713	12	29.5
		John C. Breckinridge	Democrat	848,356	72	18.1
		John Bell	Constitutional Union	592,906	39	12.6
1864	36	ABRAHAM LINCOLN	Republican	2,206,938	212	55.0
		George B. McClellan	Democrat	1,803,787	21	45.0
1868	37	ULYSSES S. GRANT	Republican	3,013,421	214	52.7
		Horatio Seymour	Democrat	2,706,829	80	47.3
1872	37	ULYSSES S. GRANT	Republican	3,596,745	286	55.6
		Horace Greeley	Democrat	2,843,446	*	43.9
1876	38	RUTHERFORD B. HAYES	Republican	4,036,572	185	48.0
		Samuel J. Tilden	Democrat	4,284,020	184	51.0
1880	38	JAMES A. GARFIELD	Republican	4,453,295	214	48.5
		Winfield S. Hancock	Democrat	4,414,082	155	48.1
		James B. Weaver	Greenback-Labor	308,578		3.4
1884	38	GROVER CLEVELAND	Democrat	4,879,507	219	48.5
		James G. Blaine	Republican	4,850,293	182	48.2
		Benjamin F. Butler	Greenback-Labor	175,370		1.8
		John P. St. John	Prohibition	150,369		1.5
1888	38	BENJAMIN HARRISON	Republican	5,447,129	233	47.9
		Grover Cleveland	Democrat	5,537,857	168	48.6
		Clinton B. Fisk	Prohibition	249,506		2.2
		Anson J. Streeter	Union Labor	146,935		1.3

Because of the death of Greeley, Democratic electors scattered their votes.

PRESIDENTIAL ELECTIONS   (CONTINUED)

Year	Number of States	Candidates	Party	Popular Vote	Electoral Vote	Percentage of Popular Vote
1892	44	GROVER CLEVELAND	Democrat	5,555,426	277	46.1
		Benjamin Harrison	Republican	5,182,690	145	43.0
		James B. Weaver	People's	1,029,846	22	8.5
		John Bidwell	Prohibition	264,133		2.2
1896	45	WILLIAM MCKINLEY	Republican	7,102,246	271	51.1
		William J. Bryan	Democrat	6,492,559	176	47.7
1900	45	WILLIAM MCKINLEY	Republican	7,218,491	292	51.7
		William J. Bryan	Democrat; Populist	6,356,734	155	45.5
		John C. Woolley	Prohibition	208,914		1.5
1904	45	THEODORE ROOSEVELT	Republican	7,628,461	336	57.4
		Alton B. Parker	Democrat	5,084,223	140	37.6
		Eugene V. Debs	Socialist	402,283		3.0
		Silas C. Swallow	Prohibition	258,536		1.9
1908	46	WILLIAM H. TAFT	Republican	7,675,320	321	51.6
		William J. Bryan	Democrat	6,412,294	162	43.1
		Eugene V. Debs	Socialist	420,793		2.8
		Eugene W. Chafin	Prohibition	253,840		1.7
1912	48	WOODROW WILSON	Democrat	6,296,547	435	41.9
		Theodore Roosevelt	Progressive	4,118,571	88	27.4
		William H. Taft	Republican	3,486,720	8	23.2
		Eugene V. Debs	Socialist	900,672		6.0
		Eugene W. Chafin	Prohibition	206,275		1.4
1916	48	WOODROW WILSON	Democrat	9,127,695	277	49.4
		Charles E. Hughes	Republican	8,533,507	254	46.2
		A. L. Benson	Socialist	585,113		3.2
		J. Frank Hanly	Prohibition	220,506		1.2
1920	48	WARREN G. HARDING	Republican	16,143,407	404	60.4
		James M. Cox	Democrat	9,130,328	127	34.2
		Eugene V. Debs	Socialist	919,799		3.4
		P. P. Christensen	Farmer-Labor	265,411		1.0
1924	48	CALVIN COOLIDGE	Republican	15,718,211	382	54.0
		John W. Davis	Democrat	8,385,283	136	28.8
		Robert M. La Follette	Progressive	4,831,289	13	16.6
1928	48	HERBERT C. HOOVER	Republican	21,391,993	444	58.2
		Alfred E. Smith	Democrat	15,016,169	87	40.9
1932	48	FRANKLIN D. ROOSEVELT	Democrat	22,809,638	472	57.4
		Herbert C. Hoover	Republican	15,758,901	59	39.7
		Norman Thomas	Socialist	881,951		2.2
1936	48	FRANKLIN D. ROOSEVELT	Democrat	27,752,869	523	60.8
		Alfred M. Landon	Republican	16,674,665	8	36.5
		William Lemke	Union	882,479		1.9
1940	48	FRANKLIN D. ROOSEVELT	Democrat	27,307,819	449	54.8
		Wendell L. Willkie	Republican	22,321,018	82	44.8

PRESIDENTIAL ELECTIONS (CONTINUED)

Year	Number of States	Candidates	Party	Popular Vote	Electoral Vote	Percentage of Popular Vote
1944	48	FRANKLIN D. ROOSEVELT	Democrat	25,606,585	432	53.5
		Thomas E. Dewey	Republican	22,014,745	99	46.0
1948	48	HARRY S. TRUMAN	Democrat	24,105,812	303	49.5
		Thomas E. Dewey	Republican	21,970,065	189	45.1
		J. Strom Thurmond	States' Rights	1,169,063	39	2.4
		Henry A. Wallace	Progressive	1,157,172		2.4
1952	48	DWIGHT D. EISENHOWER	Republican	33,936,234	442	55.1
		Adlai E. Stevenson	Democrat	27,314,992	89	44.4
1956	48	DWIGHT D. EISENHOWER	Republican	35,590,472	457*	57.6
		Adlai E. Stevenson	Democrat	26,022,752	73	42.1
1960	50	JOHN F. KENNEDY	Democrat	34,227,096	303†	49.9
		Richard M. Nixon	Republican	34,108,546	219	49.6
1964	50	LYNDON B. JOHNSON	Democrat	42,676,220	486	61.3
		Barry M. Goldwater	Republican	26,860,314	52	38.5
1968	50	RICHARD M. NIXON	Republican	31,785,480	301	43.4
		Hubert H. Humphrey	Democrat	31,275,165	191	42.7
		George C. Wallace	American Independent	9,906,473	46	13.5
1972	50	RICHARD M. NIXON‡	Republican	47,165,234	520	60.6
		George S. McGovern	Democrat	29,168,110	17	37.5
1976	50	JIMMY CARTER	Democrat	40,828,929	297	50.1
		Gerald R. Ford	Republican	39,148,940	240	47.9
		Eugene McCarthy	Independent	739,256		
1980	50	RONALD REAGAN	Republican	43,201,220	489	50.9
		Jimmy Carter	Democrat	34,913,332	49	41.2
		John B. Anderson	Independent	5,581,379		
1984	50	RONALD REAGAN	Republican	53,428,357	525	59.0
		Walter F. Mondale	Democrat	36,930,923	13	41.0
1988	50	GEORGE BUSH	Republican	48,901,046	426	53.4
		Michael Dukakis	Democrat	41,809,030	111	45.6
1992	50	BILL CLINTON	Democrat	43,728,275	370	43.2
		George Bush	Republican	38,167,416	168	37.7
		H. Ross Perot	United We Stand, America	19,237,247		19.0
1996	50	BILL CLINTON	Democrat	45,590,703	379	49.0
		Robert Dole	Republican	37,816,307	159	41.0
		H. Ross Perot	Reform	7,866,284		8.0
2000	50	GEORGE W. BUSH	Republican	50,459,624	271	47.9
		Albert Gore, Jr.	Democrat	51,003,328	266	49.4
		Ralph Nader	Green	2,882,985		2.7

* Walter B. Jones received 1 electoral vote.

† Harry F. Byrd received 15 electoral votes.

‡ Resigned August 9, 1974: Vice President Gerald R. Ford became President.

SUPREME COURT JUSTICES

Name*	Years on Court	Appointing President
JOHN JAY	1789–1795	Washington
James Wilson	1789–1798	Washington
John Rutledge	1790–1791	Washington
William Cushing	1790–1810	Washington
John Blair	1790–1796	Washington
James Iredell	1790–1799	Washington
Thomas Jefferson	1792–1793	Washington
William Paterson	1793–1806	Washington
JOHN RUTLEDGE†	1795	Washington
Samuel Chase	1796–1811	Washington
OLIVER ELLSWORTH	1796–1800	Washington
Bushrod Washington	1799–1829	J. Adams
Alfred Moore	1800–1804	J. Adams
JOHN MARSHALL	1801–1835	J. Adams
William Johnson	1804–1834	Jefferson
Brockholst Livingston	1807–1823	Jefferson
Thomas Todd	1807–1826	Jefferson
Gabriel Duvall	1811–1835	Madison
Joseph Story	1812–1845	Madison
Smith Thompson	1823–1843	Monroe
Robert Trimble	1826–1828	J. Q. Adams
John McLean	1830–1861	Jackson
Henry Baldwin	1830–1844	Jackson
James M. Wayne	1835–1867	Jackson
ROGER B. TANEY	1836–1864	Jackson
Philip P. Barbour	1836–1841	Jackson
John Cartron	1837–1865	Van Buren
John McKinley	1838–1852	Van Buren
Peter V. Daniel	1842–1860	Van Buren
Samuel Nelson	1845–1872	Tyler
Levi Woodbury	1845–1851	Polk
Robert C. Grier	1846–1870	Polk
Benjamin R. Curtis	1851–1857	Fillmore
John A. Campbell	1853–1861	Pierce
Nathan Clifford	1858–1881	Buchanan
Noah H. Swayne	1862–1881	Lincoln
Samuel F. Miller	1862–1890	Lincoln
David Davis	1862–1877	Lincoln
Stephen J. Field	1863–1897	Lincoln
SALMON P. CHASE	1864–1873	Lincoln
William Strong	1870–1880	Grant
Joseph P. Bradley	1870–1892	Grant
Ward Hunt	1873–1882	Grant
MORRISON R. WAITE	1874–1888	Grant
John M. Harlan	1877–1911	Hayes
William B. Woods	1881–1887	Hayes
Stanley Matthews	1881–1889	Garfield
Horace Gray	1882–1902	Arthur
Samuel Blatchford	1882–1893	Arthur

SUPREME COURT JUSTICES (CONTINUED)

Name*	Years on Court	Appointing President
Lucious Q. C. Lamar	1888–1893	Cleveland
MELVILLE W. FULLER	1888–1910	Cleveland
David J. Brewer	1890–1910	B. Harrison
Henry B. Brown	1891–1906	B. Harrison
George Shiras, Jr.	1892–1903	B. Harrison
Howell E. Jackson	1893–1895	B. Harrison
Edward D. White	1894–1910	Cleveland
Rufus W. Peckham	1896–1909	Cleveland
Joseph McKenna	1898–1925	McKinley
Oliver W. Holmes	1902–1932	T. Roosevelt
William R. Day	1903–1922	T. Roosevelt
William H. Moody	1906–1910	T. Roosevelt
Horace H. Lurton	1910–1914	Taft
Charles E. Hughes	1910–1916	Taft
EDWARD D. WHITE	1910–1921	Taft
Willis Van Devanter	1911–1937	Taft
Joseph R. Lamar	1911–1916	Taft
Mahlon Pitney	1912–1922	Taft
James C. McReynolds	1914–1941	Wilson
Louis D. Brandeis	1916–1939	Wilson
John H. Clarke	1916–1922	Wilson
WILLIAM H. TAFT	1921–1930	Harding
George Sutherland	1922–1938	Harding
Pierce Butler	1923–1939	Harding
Edward T. Sanford	1923–1930	Harding
Harlan F. Stone	1925–1941	Coolidge
CHARLES E. HUGHES	1930–1941	Hoover
Owen J. Roberts	1930–1945	Hoover
Benjamin N. Cardozo	1932–1938	Hoover
Hugo L. Black	1937–1971	F. Roosevelt
Stanley F. Reed	1938–1957	F. Roosevelt
Felix Frankfurter	1939–1962	F. Roosevelt
William O. Douglas	1939–1975	F. Roosevelt
Frank Murphy	1940–1949	F. Roosevelt
HARLAN F. STONE	1941–1946	F. Roosevelt
James F. Brynes	1941–1942	F. Roosevelt
Robert H. Jackson	1941–1954	F. Roosevelt
Wiley B. Rutledge	1943–1949	F. Roosevelt
Harold H. Burton	1945–1958	Truman
FREDERICK M. VINSON	1946–1953	Truman
Tom C. Clark	1949–1967	Truman
Sherman Minton	1949–1956	Truman
EARL WARREN	1953–1969	Eisenhower
John Marshall Harlan	1955–1971	Eisenhower
William J. Brennan, Jr.	1956–1990	Eisenhower
Charles E. Whittaker	1957–1962	Eisenhower
Potter Stewart	1958–1981	Eisenhower
Byron R. White	1962–1993	Kennedy
Arthur J. Goldberg	1962–1965	Kennedy

SUPREME COURT JUSTICES   (CONTINUED)

Name*	Years on Court	Appointing President
Abe Fortas	1965–1970	L. Johnson
Thurgood Marshall	1967–1991	L. Johnson
WARREN E. BURGER	1969–1986	Nixon
Harry A. Blackmun	1970–1994	Nixon
Lewis F. Powell, Jr.	1971–1987	Nixon
William H. Rehnquist	1971–1986	Nixon
John Paul Stevens	1975–	Ford
Sandra Day O'Connor	1981–	Reagan
WILLIAM H. REHNQUIJST	1986–	Reagan
Antonin Scalia	1986–	Reagan
Anthony Kennedy	1988–	Reagan
David Souter	1990–	Bush
Clarence Thomas	1991–	Bush
Ruth Bader Ginsburg	1993–	Clinton
Stephen Breyer	1994–	Clinton

* Capital letters designate Chief Justices

† Never confirmed by the Senate as Chief Justice

ADMISSION OF STATES INTO THE UNION

State	Date of Admission	State	Date of Admission
1. Delaware	December 7, 1787	26. Michigan	January 26, 1837
2. Pennsylvania	December 12, 1787	27. Florida	March 3, 1845
3. New Jersey	December 18, 1787	28. Texas	December 29, 1845
4. Georgia	January 2, 1788	29. Iowa	December 28, 1846
5. Connecticut	January 9, 1788	30. Wisconsin	May 29, 1848
6. Massachusetts	February 6, 1788	31. California	September 9, 1850
7. Maryland	April 28, 1788	32. Minnesota	May 11, 1858
8. South Carolina	May 23, 1788	33. Oregon	February 14, 1859
9. New Hampshire	June 21, 1788	34. Kansas	January 29, 1861
10. Virginia	June 25, 1788	35. West Virginia	June 20, 1863
11. New York	July 26, 1788	36. Nevada	October 31, 1864
12. North Carolina	November 21, 1789	37. Nebraska	March 1, 1867
13. Rhode Island	May 29, 1790	38. Colorado	August 1, 1876
14. Vermont	March 4, 1791	39. North Dakota	November 2, 1889
15. Kentucky	June 1, 1792	40. South Dakota	November 2, 1889
16. Tennessee	June 1, 1796	41. Montana	November 8, 1889
17. Ohio	March 1, 1803	42. Washington	November 11, 1889
18. Louisiana	April 30, 1812	43. Idaho	July 3, 1890
19. Indiana	December 11, 1816	44. Wyoming	July 10, 1890
20. Mississippi	December 10, 1817	45. Utah	January 4, 1896
21. Illinois	December 3, 1818	46. Oklahoma	November 16, 1907
22. Alabama	December 14, 1819	47. New Mexico	January 6, 1912
23. Maine	March 15, 1820	48. Arizona	February 14, 1912
24. Missouri	August 10, 1821	49. Alaska	January 3, 1959
25. Arkansas	June 15, 1836	50. Hawaii	August 21, 1959

DEMOGRAPHICS OF THE UNITED STATES

POPULATION GROWTH

Year	Population	Percent Increase
1630	4,600	
1640	26,600	478.3
1650	50,400	90.8
1660	75,100	49.0
1670	111,900	49.0
1680	151,500	35.4
1690	210,400	38.9
1700	250,900	19.2
1710	331,700	32.2
1720	466,200	40.5
1730	629,400	35.0
1740	905,600	43.9
1750	1,170,800	29.3
1760	1,593,600	36.1
1770	2,148,100	34.8
1780	2,780,400	29.4
1790	3,929,214	41.3
1800	5,308,483	35.1
1810	7,239,881	36.4
1820	9,638,453	33.1
1830	12,866,020	33.5
1840	17,069,453	32.7
1850	23,191,876	35.9
1860	31,443,321	35.6
1870	39,818,449	26.6
1880	50,155,783	26.0
1890	62,947,714	25.5
1900	75,994,575	20.7
1910	91,972,266	21.0
1920	105,710,620	14.9
1930	122,775,046	16.1
1940	131,669,275	7.2
1950	151,325,798	14.5
1960	179,323,175	18.5
1970	203,302,031	13.4
1980	226,542,199	11.4
1990	248,718,301	9.8
2000	281,421,906	13.1

Source: *Historical Statistics of the United States* (1975); *Statistical Abstract by the United States* (2001).
Note: Figures for 1630–1780 include British colonies within limits of present United States only; Native American population included only in 1930 and thereafter.

WORK FORCE

Year	Total Number Workers (1000s)	Farmers as % of Total	Women as % of Total	% Workers in Unions
1810	2,330	84	(NA)	(NA)
1840	5,660	75	(NA)	(NA)
1860	11,110	53	(NA)	(NA)
1870	12,506	53	15	(NA)
1880	17,392	52	15	(NA)
1890	23,318	43	17	(NA)
1900	29,073	40	18	3
1910	38,167	31	21	6
1920	41,614	26	21	12
1930	48,830	22	22	7
1940	53,011	17	24	27
1950	59,643	12	28	25
1960	69,877	8	32	26
1970	82,049	4	37	25
1980	106,940	3	43	23
1990	125,840	3	45	16
2000	140,863	2	47	12

Source: *Historical Statistics of the United States* (1975); *Statistical Abstract of the United States* (2001).

VITAL STATISTICS (IN THOUSANDS)

Year	Births	Deaths	Marriages	Divorces
1800	55	(NA)	(NA)	(NA)
1810	54.3	(NA)	(NA)	(NA)
1820	55.2	(NA)	(NA)	(NA)
1830	51.4	(NA)	(NA)	(NA)
1840	51.8	(NA)	(NA)	(NA)
1850	43.3	(NA)	(NA)	(NA)
1860	44.3	(NA)	(NA)	(NA)
1870	38.3	(NA)	9.6 (1867)	0.3 (1867)
1880	39.8	(NA)	9.1 (1875)	0.3 (1875)
1890	31.5	(NA)	9.0	0.5
1900	32.3	17.2	9.3	0.7
1910	30.1	14.7	10.3	0.9
1920	27.7	13.0	12.0	1.6
1930	21.3	11.3	9.2	1.6
1940	19.4	10.8	12.1	2.0
1950	24.1	9.6	11.1	2.6
1960	23.7	9.5	8.5	2.2
1970	18.4	9.5	10.6	3.5
1980	15.9	8.8	10.6	5.2
1990	16.7	8.6	9.8	4.7
1997	14.6	8.6	8.9	4.3

Source: *Historical Statistics of the United States* (1975); *Statistical Abstract of the United States* (1999).

RACIAL COMPOSITION OF THE POPULATION

(IN THOUSANDS)

Year	White	Black	Indian	Hispanic	Asian/Pacific Islander
1790	3,172	757	(NA)	(NA)	(NA)
1800	4,306	1,002	(NA)	(NA)	(NA)
1820	7,867	1,772	(NA)	(NA)	(NA)
1840	14,196	2,874	(NA)	(NA)	(NA)
1860	26,923	4,442	(NA)	(NA)	(NA)
1880	43,403	6,581	(NA)	(NA)	(NA)
1900	66,809	8,834	(NA)	(NA)	(NA)
1910	81,732	9,828	(NA)	(NA)	(NA)
1920	94,821	10,463	(NA)	(NA)	(NA)
1930	110,287	11,891	(NA)	(NA)	(NA)
1940	118,215	12,866	(NA)	(NA)	(NA)
1950	134,942	15,042	(NA)	(NA)	(NA)
1960	158,832	18,872	(NA)	(NA)	(NA)
1970	178,098	22,581	(NA)	(NA)	(NA)
1980	194,713	26,683	1,420	14,609	3,729
1990	208,727	30,511	2,065	22,372	2,462
2000	211,461	34,658	2,476	35,306	10,642

Source: U.S. Bureau of the Census, U.S. *Census of Population: 1940*, vol. II, part 1, and vol. IV, part 1; *1950*, vol. II, part 1; *1960*, vol. I, part 1; *1970*, vol. I, part B; and *Current Population Reports*, P25-1095 and P25-1104; *Statistical Abstract of the United States* (2001).

THE ECONOMY AND FEDERAL SPENDING

Year	Gross National Product (GNP) (in billions)	Foreign Trade (in millions)			Federal Budget (in billions)	Federal Surplus/Deficit (in billions)	Federal Debt (in billions)
		Exports	Imports	Balance of Trade			
1790	(NA)	$ 20	$ 23	$ −3	$ 0.004	$ +0.00015	$ 0.076
1800	(NA)	71	91	−20	0.011	+0.0006	0.083
1810	(NA)	67	85	−18	0.008	+0.0012	0.053
1820	(NA)	70	74	−4	0.018	−0.0004	0.091
1830	(NA)	74	71	+3	0.015	+0.100	0.049
1840	(NA)	132	107	+25	0.024	−0.005	0.004
1850	(NA)	152	178	−26	0.040	+0.004	0.064
1860	(NA)	400	362	−38	0.063	−0.01	0.065
1870	$ 7.4	451	462	−11	0.310	+0.10	2.4
1880	11.2	853	761	+92	0.268	+0.07	2.1
1890	13.1	910	823	+87	0.318	+0.09	1.2
1900	18.7	1,499	930	+569	0.521	+0.05	1.2
1910	35.3	1,919	1,646	+273	0.694	−0.02	1.1
1920	91.5	8,664	5,784	+2,880	6.357	+0.3	24.3
1930	90.7	4,013	3,500	+513	3.320	+0.7	16.3
1940	100.0	4,030	7,433	−3,403	9.6	−2.7	43.0
1950	286.5	10,816	9,125	+1,691	43.1	−2.2	257.4
1960	506.5	19,600	15,046	+4,556	92.2	+0.3	286.3
1970	992.7	42,700	40,189	+2,511	195.6	−2.8	371.0
1980	2,631.7	220,783	244,871	+24,088	590.9	−73.8	907.7
1990	5,524.5	394,030	494,042	−101,012	1,251.8	−220.5	3,233.3
2000	9,958.7	1,068,397	1,438,086	−369,689	1,788.8	+236.4	5,629.0

Source: *U.S. Office of Management and Budget, Budget of the United States Government, annual; Statistical Abstract of the United States*, 2001.

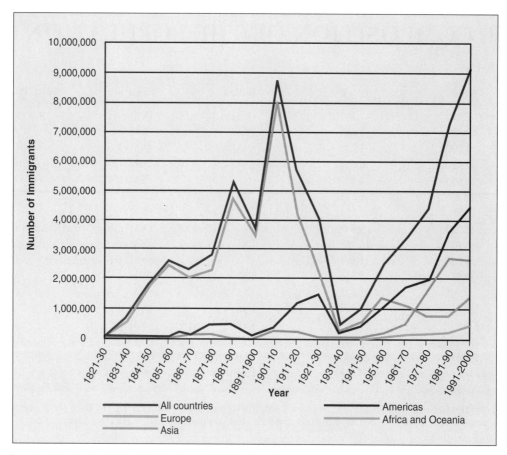

Immigration to the United States since 1820, by decade
Source: *Statistical Yearbook of the Immigration and Naturalization Service,* 2001.

GLOSSARY

Acquired Immune Deficiency Syndrome (AIDS) A complex of deadly pathologies resulting from infection with the human immunodeficiency virus (HIV).

Act for Religious Toleration The first law in America to call for freedom of worship for all Christians.

Actual Representation The practice whereby elected representatives normally reside in their districts and are directly responsive to local interests.

Affirmative action A set of policies to open opportunities in business and education for members of minority groups and women by allowing race and sex to be factors included in decisions to hire, award contracts, or admit students to higher education programs.

Age of Enlightenment Major intellectual movement occurring in Western Europe in the late seventeenth and early eighteenth centuries.

Agricultural Wheel One of several farmer organizations that emerged in the South during the 1880s. It sought federal legislation to deal with credit and currency issues.

Alamo Franciscan mission at San Antonio, Texas that was the site in 1836 of a siege and massacre of Texans by Mexican troops.

Albany Plan of Union Plan put forward in 1754 calling for an intercolonial union to manage defense and Indian affairs. The plan was rejected by participants at the Albany Congress.

Albany Regency The tightly disciplined state political machine built by Martin Van Buren in New York.

Alien and Sedition Acts Collective name given to four acts passed by Congress in 1798 that curtailed freedom of speech and the liberty of foreigners resident in the United States.

Alliance for Progress Program of economic aid to Latin America during the Kennedy administration.

Allies In World War I, Britain, France, Russia, and other belligerent nations fighting against the Central Powers but not including the United States.

American Anti-Slavery Society The first national organization of abolitionists, founded in 1833.

American Colonization Society Organization, founded in 1817 by antislavery reformers, that called for gradual emancipation and the removal of freed blacks to Africa.

American Federation of Labor (AFL) Union formed in 1886 that organized skilled workers along craft lines and emphasized a few workplace issues rather than a broad social program.

American Indian Movement (AIM) Group of Native-American political activists who used confrontations with the federal government to publicize their case for Indian rights.

American System of Manufacturing A technique of production pioneered in the United States in the first half of the nineteenth century that relied on precision manufacturing with the use of interchangeable parts.

American System The program of government subsidies favored by Henry Clay and his followers to promote American economic growth and protect domestic manufacturers from foreign competition.

Americans with Disabilities Act Legislation in 1992 that banned discrimination against physically handicapped persons in employment, transportation, and public accommodations.

Anarchists Persons who believe that all government interferes with individual liberty and should be abolished by whatever means necessary.

Anglican Of or belonging to the Church of England, a Protestant denomination.

Anglo-American Accords Series of agreements reached in the British-American Conventions of 1818 that fixed the western boundary between the United States and Canada, allowed for joint occupation of Oregon, and restored American fishing rights.

Annapolis Convention Conference of state delegates at Annapolis, Maryland, that issued a call in September 1786 for a convention to meet at Philadelphia to consider fundamental changes.

Antifederalists Opponents of the Constitution in the debate over its ratification.

Anti-Masons Third party formed in 1827 in opposition to the presumed power and influence of the Masonic order.

Appeal to the Colored Citizens of the World Written by David Walker, a published insistence that "America is more our country, than it is the whites'—we have enriched it with our blood and tears."

Articles of Confederation Written document setting up the loose confederation of states that comprised the first national government of the United States.

Atlanta Compromise Booker T. Washington's policy accepting segregation and disenfranchisement for African Americans in exchange for white assistance in education and job training.

Atlantic Charter Statement of common principles and war aims developed by President Franklin Roosevelt and British Prime Minister Winston Churchill at a meeting in August 1941.

Australian ballot Secret voting and the use of official ballots rather than party tickets.

Axis Powers The opponents of the United States and its allies in World War II.

Aztecs A warrior people who dominated the Valley of Mexico from 1100–1521.

Bacon's Rebellion Violent conflict in Virginia (1675–1676), beginning with settler attacks on Indians but culminating in a rebellion led by Nathaniel Bacon against Virginia's government.

Baker v. Carr U.S. Supreme Court decision in 1962 that allowed federal courts to review the appointment of state legislative districts and established the principle that such districts should have roughly equal populations ("one person, one vote").

Bank War The political struggle between President Andrew Jackson and the supporters of the Second Bank of the United States.

Battle of New Orleans Decisive American War of 1812 victory over British troops in January 1815 that ended any British hopes of gaining control of the lower Mississippi River Valley.

Battle of Put-in-Bay American naval victory on Lake Erie in September 1813 in the War of 1812 that denied the British strategic control over the Great Lakes.

Battle of the Atlantic The long struggle between German submarines and the British and U.S. navies in the North Atlantic from 1940 to 1943.

Battle of the Little Bighorn Battle in which Colonel George A. Custer and the Seventh Cavalry were defeated by the Sioux and Cheyennes under Sitting Bull and Crazy Horse in Montana in 1876.

Battles of Lexington and Concord The first two battles of the American Revolution which resulted in a total of 273 British soldiers dead, wounded, and missing and nearly one hundred Americans dead, wounded, and missing.

Bay of Pigs Site in Cuba of an unsuccessful landing by fourteen hundred anti-Castro Cuban refugees in April 1961.

Beaver Wars Series of bloody conflicts, occurring between 1640s and 1680s, during which the Iroquois fought the French for control of the fur trade in the east and the Great Lakes region.

Benevolent empire Network of reform associations affiliated with Protestant churches in the early nineteenth century dedicated to the restoration of moral order.

Berlin blockade Three-hundred-day Soviet blockade of land access to United States, British, and French occupation zones in Berlin, 1948–1949.

Berlin Wall Wall erected by East Germany in 1961 that isolated West Berlin from the surrounding areas in Communist-controlled East Berlin and East Germany.

Bill of Rights A written summary of inalienable rights and liberties.

Black codes Laws passed by states and municipalities denying many rights of citizenship to free black people before the Civil War.

Black Hawk's War Short 1832 war in which federal troops and Illinois militia units defeated the Sauk and Fox Indians led by Black Hawk.

Black Panthers Political and social movement among black Americans, founded in Oakland, California, in 1966 and emphasizing black economic and political power.

Black Power Philosophy emerging after 1965 that real economic and political gains for African Americans could

come only through self-help, self-determination, and organizing for direct political influence.

"Bleeding Kansas" Violence between pro- and antislavery forces in Kansas Territory after the passage of the Kansas-Nebraska Act in 1854.

Blitzkrieg German war tactic in World War II ("lightning war") involving the concentration of air and armored firepower to punch and exploit holes in opposing defensive lines.

Bolshevik Member of the Communist movement in Russia that established the Soviet government after the 1917 Russian Revolution.

Bonus Army Unemployed veterans of World War I gathering in Washington in 1932 demanding payment of service bonuses not due until 1945.

Bosnia A nation in southeast Europe that split off from Yugoslavia and became the site of bitter civil and religious war, requiring NATO and U.S. intervention in the 1990s.

Boston Massacre After months of increasing friction between townspeople and the British troops stationed in the city, on March 5, 1770, British troops fired on American civilians in Boston.

Boston Tea Party Incident that occurred on December 16, 1773, in which Bostonians, disguised as Indians, destroyed £9,000 worth of tea belonging to the British East India Company in order to prevent payment of the duty on it.

British Constitution The principles, procedures, and precedents that governed the operation of the British government.

Brook Farm A utopian community and experimental farm established in 1841 near Boston.

Brown v. Board of Education of Topeka Supreme Court decision in 1954 that declared that "separate but equal" schools for children of different races violated the Constitution.

Bureau of Reclamation Federal agency established in 1902 providing public funds for irrigation projects in arid regions.

Cahokia One of the largest urban centers created by Mississippian peoples, containing 30,000 residents in 1250.

Californios Californians of Spanish descent.

Camp David Agreement Agreement to reduce points of conflict between Israel and Egypt, hammered out in 1977 with the help of U.S. President Jimmy Carter.

Carpetbaggers Northern transplants to the South, many of whom were Union soldiers who stayed in the South after the war.

Central Intelligence Agency (CIA) Agency established in 1947 that coordinates the gathering and evaluation of military and economic information on other nations.

Central Powers Germany and its World War I allies in Austria, Turkey, and Bulgaria.

Chain migration Process common to many immigrant groups whereby one family member brings over other family members, who in turn bring other relatives and friends and occasionally entire villages.

Charles River Bridge v. *Warren Bridge* Supreme Court decision of 1837 that promised economic competition by ruling that the broader rights of the community took precedence over any presumed right of monopoly granted in a corporate charter.

Cherokee War Conflict (1759–1761) on the southern frontier between the Cherokee Indians and colonists from Virginia southward.

Chesapeake **incident** Attack in 1807 by the British ship *Leopard* on the American ship *Chesapeake* in American territorial waters.

Chisholm Trail The route followed by Texas cattle raisers driving their herds north to markets at Kansas railheads.

Church of Jesus Christ of Latter-day Saints (Mormon Church) Church founded in 1830 by Joseph Smith and based on the revelations in a sacred book he called the Book of Mormon.

Civil Rights Act of 1964 Federal legislation that outlawed discrimination in public accommodations and employment on the basis of race, skin color, sex, religion, or national origin.

Claims clubs Groups of local settlers on the nineteenth-century frontier who banded together to prevent the price of their land claims from being bid up by outsiders at public land auctions.

Coercive Acts Legislation passed by Parliament in 1774; included the Boston Port Act, the Massachusetts Government Act, the Administration of Justice Act, and the Quartering Act of 1774.

Cold War The political and economic confrontation between the Soviet Union and the United States that dominated world affairs from 1946 to 1989.

Collective Bargaining Representatives of a union negotiating with management on behalf of all members.

Colored Farmer's Alliance An organization of Southern black farmers formed in Texas in 1886 in response to the Southern Farmer's Alliance, which did not accept black people as members.

Columbian Exchange The transatlantic exchange of plants, animals, and diseases that occurred after the first European contact with the Americas.

Committee of Safety Any of the extralegal committees that directed the revolutionary movement and carried on the functions of government at the local level in the period between the breakdown of royal authority and the establishment of regular governments.

Committee on Public Information (CPI) Government agency during World War I that sought to shape public opinion in support of the war effort through newspapers, pamphlets, speeches, films, and other media.

Committees of Correspondence Committees formed in Massachusetts and other colonies in the pre-Revolutionary period to keep Americans informed about British measures that would affect the colonies.

Communism A social structure based on the common ownership of property.

Compromise of 1850 The four-step compromise which admitted California as a free state, allowed the residents of the New Mexico and Utah territories to decide the slavery issue for themselves, ended the slave trade in the District of Columbia, and passed a new fugitive slave law to enforce the constitutional provision stating that a slave escaping into a free state shall be delivered back to the owner.

Compromise of 1877 The Congressional settling of the 1876 election which installed Republican Rutherford B. Hayes in the White House and gave Democrats control of all state governments in the South.

Conciliatory Proposition Plan whereby Parliament would "forbear" taxation of Americans in colonies whose assemblies imposed taxes considered satisfactory by the British government.

Confederate States of America Nation proclaimed in Montgomery, Alabama, in February 1861, after the seven states of the Lower South seceded from the United States.

Confiscation Act Second confiscation law passed by Congress, ordering the seizure of land from disloyal Southerners and the emancipation of their slaves.

Congress of Industrial Organizations An alliance of industrial unions that spurred the 1930s organizational drive among the mass-production industries.

Congress of Racial Equality (CORE) Civil rights group formed in 1942 and committed to nonviolent civil disobedience.

Congressional Reconstruction Name given to the period 1867–1870 when the Republican-dominated Congress controlled Reconstruction era policy.

Conservation The efficient management and use of natural resources, such as forests, grasslands, and rivers, as opposed to preservation or controlled exploitation.

Constitution of the United States The written document providing for a new central government of the United States.

Constitutional Convention Convention that met in Philadelphia in 1787 and drafted the Constitution of the United States.

Constitutional Union Party National party formed in 1860, mainly by former Whigs, that emphasized allegiance to the Union and strict enforcement of all national legislation.

Continental Army The regular or professional army authorized by the Second Continental Congress and commanded by General George Washington during the Revolutionary War.

Continental Association Agreement, adopted by the First Continental Congress in 1774 in response to the Coercive Acts to cut off trade with Britain until the objectionable measures were repealed.

Contract Theory of Government The belief that government is established by human beings to protect certain rights—such as life, liberty, and property—that are theirs by natural, divinely sanctioned law and that when government protects these rights, people are obligated to obey it.

Contract with America Platform proposing a sweeping reduction in the role and activities of the federal government on which many Republican candidates ran for Congress in 1994.

Copper-heads A term Republicans applied to Northern war dissenters and those suspected of aiding the Confederate cause during the Civil War.

Council of Economic Advisers Board of three professional economists established in 1946 to advise the president on economic policy.

Counterculture Various alternatives to mainstream values and behaviors that became popular in the 1960s, including experimentation with psychedelic drugs, communal living, a return to the land, Asian religions, and experimental art.

Country (Real Whig) Ideology Strain of thought (focusing on the threat to personal liberty and the taxation of property holders) first appearing in England in the late seventeenth century in response to the growth of governmental power and a national debt.

Coureur de Bois French for "woods runner," an independent fur trader in New France.

Covenant A contract with God, binding settlers to meet their religious obligations in return for God's favor.

Coxey's Army A protest march of unemployed workers, led by Populist businessman Jacob Coxey, demanding inflation and a public works program during the depression of the 1890s.

Cult of domesticity The belief that women, by virtue of their sex, should stay home as the moral guardians of family life.

Currency Act Law passed by Parliament in 1764 to prevent the colonies from issuing legal tender paper money.

Dartmouth College v. Woodward Supreme Court decision of 1819 that prohibited states from interfering with the privileges granted to a private corporation.

Dawes Act An 1887 law terminating tribal ownership of land and allotting some parcels of land to individual Indians with the remainder opened for white settlement.

D-Day June 6, 1944, the day of the first paratroop drops and amphibious landings on the coast of Normandy, France, in the first stage of Operation OVERLORD during World War II.

Declaration of Independence The document by which the Second Continental Congress announced and justified its decision to renounce the colonies' allegiance to the British government.

Declaration of London Statement drafted by an international conference in 1909 to clarify international law and specify the rights of neutral nations.

Declaration of Rights and Grievances Resolves asserting that the Stamp Act and other taxes imposed on the colonists without their consent were unconstitutional.

Declaration of Sentiments The resolutions passed at the Seneca Falls Convention in 1848 calling for full female equality, including the right to vote.

Deism Religious orientation that rejects divine revelation and holds that the workings of nature alone reveal God's design for the universe.

Democratic Party Political party formed in the 1820s under the leadership of Andrew Jackson; favored states' rights and a limited role for the federal government.

Denmark Vesey's Conspiracy The most carefully devised slave revolt in which rebels planned to seize control of Charleston in 1822 and escape to freedom in Haiti, a free black republic, but they were betrayed by other slaves, and seventy-five conspirators were executed.

Deregulation Reduction or removal of government regulations and encouragement of direct competition in many important industries and economic sectors.

Détente (French for "easing of tension") Used to describe the new U.S. relations with China and the Soviet Union in 1972.

Disnfranchisement The use of legal means to bar individuals or groups from voting.

Dixiecrats States' Rights Democrats.

Dollar diplomacy The U.S. policy of using private investment in other nations to promote American diplomatic goals and business interests.

Dominion of New England James II's failed plan of 1686 to combine eight northern colonies into a single large province, to be governed by a royal appointee with no elective assembly.

Dred Scott Decision Supreme Court ruling, in a lawsuit brought by Dred Scott, a slave demanding his freedom based on his residence in a free state, that slaves could not be U.S. citizens and that Congress had no jurisdiction over slavery in the territories.

Eastern Front The area of military operations in World War II located east of Germany in eastern Europe and the Soviet Union.

Economic Recovery and Tax Act of 1981 (ERTA) A major revision of the federal income tax system.

Emancipation Proclamation Decree announced by President Abraham Lincoln in September 1862 and formally issued on January 1, 1863, freeing slaves in all Confederate states still in rebellion.

Embargo Act of 1807 Act passed by Congress in 1807 prohibiting American ships from leaving for any foreign port.

Empresarios Agents who received a land grant from the Spanish or Mexican government in return for organizing settlements.

Encomienda In the Spanish colonies, the grant to a Spanish settler of a certain number of Indian subjects, who would pay him tribute in goods and labor.

Enumerated Products Items produced in the colonies and enumerated in acts of Parliament that could be legally shipped from the colony of origin only to specified locations.

Environmental Protection Agency (EPA) Federal agency created in 1970 to oversee environmental monitoring and cleanup programs.

Era of Good Feelings The period from 1817 to 1823 in which the disappearance of the Federalists enabled the Republicans to govern in a spirit of seemingly nonpartisan harmony.

Espionage Act Law whose vague prohibition against obstructing the nation's war effort was used to crush dissent and criticism during World War I.

Fair Employment Practices Committee (FEPC) Federal agency established in 1941 to curb racial discrimination in war production jobs and government employment.

Farmers' Alliance A broad mass movement in the rural South and West during the late nineteenth century, encompassing several organizations and demanding economic and political reforms.

Fascist Government A government subscribing to a philosophy of dictatorship that merges the interests of the state, armed forces, and big business.

Federal Deposit Insurance Corporation (FDIC) Government agency that guarantees bank deposits, thereby protecting both depositors and banks.

Federal Highway Act of 1956 Measure that provided federal funding to build a nationwide system of interstate and defense highways.

Federal Reserve Act The 1913 law that revised banking and currency by extending limited government regulation through the creation of the Federal Reserve System.

Federal Trade Commission Government agency established in 1914 to provide regulatory oversight of business activity.

Federalism The sharing of powers between the national government and the states.

Federalists Supporters of the Constitution who favored its ratification.

Field Order No. 15 Order by General William T. Sherman in January 1865 to set aside abandoned land along the southern Atlantic coast for forty-acre grants to freedmen, rescinded by President Andrew Johnson later that year.

Fifteenth Amendment Passed by Congress in 1869, guaranteed the right of American men to vote, regardless of race.

Fireside Chats Speeches broadcast nationally over the radio in which President Franklin D. Roosevelt explained complex issues and programs in plain language, as though his listeners were gathered around the fireside with him.

First Continental Congress Meeting of delegates from most of the colonies held in 1774 in response to the Coercive Acts. The Congress endorsed the Suffolk Resolves, adopted the Declaration of Rights and Grievances, and agreed to establish the Continental Association.

First Persian Gulf War War (1991) between Iraq and a U.S.-led coalition that followed Iraq's invasion of Kuwait and resulted in the expulsion of Iraqi forces from that country.

Fletcher v. *Peck* Supreme Court decision of 1810 that overturned a state law by ruling that it violated a legal contract.

Fort Sumter A fort located in Charleston, South Carolina, where President Lincoln attempted to provision federal troops in 1861, triggering a hostile response from onshore Confederate forces, opening the Civil War.

Fourteenth Amendment Passed by Congress in 1866, guaranteed every citizen equality before the law by prohibiting states from violating the civil rights of their citizens, thus outlawing the black codes.

Frame of Government William Penn's constitution for Pennsylvania which included a provision allowing for religious freedom.

Franco-American Accord of 1800 Settlement reached with France that brought an end to the Quasi-War and released the United Sates from its 1778 alliance with France.

Free Silver Philosophy that the government should expand the money supply by purchasing and coining all the silver offered to it.

Free Speech Movement (FSM) Student movement at the University of California, Berkeley, formed in 1964 to protest limitations on political activities on campus.

Freedmen's Bureau Agency established by Congress in March 1865 to provide social, educational, and economic services, advice, and protection to former slaves and destitute whites; lasted seven years.

Freedom Summer Voter registration effort in rural Mississippi organized by black and white civil rights workers in 1964.

French and Indian War The last of the Anglo-French colonial wars (1754–1763) and the first in which fighting began in North America. The war ended with France's defeat.

Fugitive Slave Act Law, part of the Compromise of 1850, that required the authorities in the North to assist Southern slave catchers and return runaway slaves to their owners.

Fundamental Constitutions of Carolina A complex plan for organizing the colony of Carolina, drafted in 1669 by Anthony Ashley Cooper and John Locke.

Gabriel Prosser's Rebellion Slave revolt that failed when Gabriel Prosser, a slave preacher and blacksmith, organized a thousand slaves for an attack on Richmond, Virginia, in 1800.

Gag Rule A procedural device whereby antislavery petitions were automatically tabled in Congress with no discussion.

Gang System The organization and supervision of slave field hands into working teams on Southern plantations.

Gentlemen's Agreement A diplomatic agreement in 1907 between Japan and the United States curtailing but not abolishing Japanese immigration.

GI Bill of Rights Legislation in June 1944 that eased the return of veterans into American society by providing educational and employment benefits.

Gibbons v. *Ogden* Supreme Court decision of 1824 involving coastal commerce that overturned a steamboat monopoly granted by the state of New York on the grounds that only Congress had the authority to regulate interstate commerce.

Gilded Age Term applied to late-nineteenth-century America that refers to the shallow display and worship of wealth characteristic of that period.

Glasnost Russian for "openness" applied to Mikhail Gorbachev's encouragement of new ideas and easing of political repression in the Soviet Union.

Glorious Revolution Bloodless revolt that occurred in England in 1688 when parliamentary leaders invited William of Orange, a Protestant, to assume the English throne.

Gospel of Wealth Thesis that hard work and perseverance lead to wealth, implying that poverty is a character flaw.

Grand Settlement of 1701 Separate peace treaties negotiated by Iroquois diplomats at Montreal and Albany that marked the beginning of Iroquois neutrality in conflicts between the French and the British in North America.

Grandfather Clause Rule that required potential voters to demonstrate that their grandfathers had been eligible to vote; used in some Southern states after 1890 to limit the black electorate.

Grange The National Grange of the Patrons of Husbandry, a national organization of farm owners formed after the Civil War.

Granger Laws State laws enacted in the Midwest in the 1870s that regulated rates charged by railroads, grain elevator operators, and other middlemen.

Great Awakening Tremendous religious revival in colonial America striking first in the Middle Colonies and New England in the 1740s and then spreading to the southern colonies.

Great Compromise Plan proposed at the 1787 Constitutional Convention for creating a national bicameral legislature in which all states would be equally represented in the Senate and proportionally represented in the House.

Great Depression The nation's worst economic crisis, extending through the 1930s, producing unprecedented bank failures, unemployment, and industrial and agricultural collapse.

Great Migration The mass movement of African Americans from the rural South to the urban North.

Great Migration The mass movement of African Americans from the rural South to the urban North, spurred especially by new job opportunities during World War I and the 1920s.

Great Society Theme of Lyndon Johnson's administration, focusing on poverty, education, and civil rights.

Great Uprising Unsuccessful railroad strike of 1877 to protest wage cuts and the use of federal troops against strikers; the first nationwide work stoppage in American history.

Greater East Asia Co-Prosperity Sphere Japanese nationalists believed that Japan should expel the French, British, Dutch, and Americans from Asia and create this sphere in which Japan would give the orders and other Asian peoples would comply.

Greenback Party A third party of the 1870s and 1880s that garnered temporary support by advocating currency inflation to expand the economy and assist debtors.

Gulf of Tonkin Resolution Request to Congress from President Lyndon Johnson in response to North Vietnamese torpedo boat attacks in which he sought authorization for "all necessary measures" to protect American forces and stop further aggression.

Halfway Covenant Plan adopted in 1662 by New England clergy to deal with the problem of declining church membership, allowing children of baptized parents to be baptized whether or not their parents had experienced conversion.

Harlem Renaissance A new African-American cultural awareness that flourished in literature, art, and music in the 1920s.

Headright System Instituted by the Virginia Company in 1616, this system gave fifty acres to anyone who paid his own way to Virginia and an additional fifty for each person (or "head") he brought with him.

Helsinki Accords Agreement in 1975 among NATO and Warsaw Pact members that recognized European national boundaries as set after World War II and included guarantees of human rights.

Holocaust The systematic murder of millions of European Jews and others deemed undesirable by Nazi Germany.

Homestead Act Law passed by Congress in May 1862 providing homesteads with 160 acres of free land in exchange for improving the land within five years of the grant.

Hoovervilles Shantytowns, sarcastically named after President Hoover, in which unemployed and homeless people lived in makeshift shacks, tents, and boxes.

Horizontal Integration The merger of competitors in the same industry.

House Committee on Un-American Activities (HUAC) Originally intended to ferret out pro-Fascists, it later investigated "un-American propaganda" that attacked constitutional government.

House of Burgesses The legislature of colonial Virginia. First organized in 1619, it was the first institution of representative government in the English colonies.

Hull House Chicago settlement house that became part of a broader neighborhood revitalization project led by Jane Addams.

Immigration and Nationality Act of 1965 Federal legislation that replaced the national quota system for immigration with new limits for each hemisphere.

Imperialism The policy and practice of exploiting nations and peoples for the benefit of an imperial power either directly through military occupation and colonial rule or indirectly through economic domination of resources and markets.

Indentured servants Individuals who contracted to serve a master for a period of four to seven years in return for payment of the servant's passage to America.

Independent Treasury System Fiscal arrangement first instituted by President Martin Van Buren in which the federal government kept its money in regional vaults and transacted its business in hard money.

Indian Removal Act President Andrew Jackson's measure that allowed state officials to override federal protection of Native Americans.

Initiative Procedure by which citizens can introduce a subject for legislation, usually through a petition signed by a specific number of voters.

Intermediate Nuclear Force Agreement (INF) Disarmament agreement between the United States and the Soviet Union under which an entire class of missiles would be removed and destroyed and on-site inspections would be permitted.

International Monetary Fund International organization established in 1945 to assist nations in maintaining stable currencies.

Internet The system of interconnected computers and servers that allows the exchange of email, posting of Web sites, and other means of instant communication.

Interstate Commerce Act The 1887 law that expanded federal power over business by prohibiting pooling and discriminatory rates by railroads and establishing the first federal regulatory agency, the Interstate Commerce Commission.

Intolerable Acts American term for the Coercive Acts and the Quebec Act.

Irreconcilables Group of U.S. senators adamantly opposed to ratification of the Treaty of Versailles after World War I.

Island Hopping The Pacific campaigns of 1944 that were the American naval versions of the *Blitzkrieg*.

Jay's Treaty Treaty with Britain negotiated in 1794 in which the United States made major concessions to avert a war over the British seizure of American ships.

Jazz Age The 1920s, so called for the popular music of the day as a symbol of the many changes taking place in the mass culture.

Jim Crow Laws Segregation laws that became widespread in the South during the 1890s.

John Brown's Raid New England abolitionist John Brown's ill-fated attempt to free Virginia's slaves with a raid on the federal arsenal at Harper's Ferry, Virginia, in 1859.

Joint-stock company Business enterprise in which a group of stockholders pooled their money to engage in trade or to fund colonizing expeditions.

Judicial Review A power implied in the Constitution that gives federal courts the right to review and determine the constitutionality of acts passed by Congress and state legislatures.

Judiciary Act of 1789 Act of Congress that implemented the judiciary clause of the Constitution by establishing the Supreme Court and a system of lower federal courts.

Kansas-Nebraska Act Law passed in 1854 creating the Kansas and Nebraska Territories but leaving the question of slavery open to residents, thereby repealing the Missouri Compromise.

King George's War The third Anglo-French war in North America (1744–1748), part of the European conflict known as the War of the Austrian Succession.

King Phillip's War Conflict in New England (1675–1676) between Wampanoags, Narragansetts, and other Indian peoples against English settlers; sparked by English encroachments on native lands.

King William's War The first Anglo-French conflict in North America (1689–1697), the American phase of Europe's War of the League of Augsburg.

Knights of Labor Labor union founded in 1869 that included skilled and unskilled workers irrespective of race or gender.

Know-Nothing Party Anti-immigrant party formed from the wreckage of the Whig Party and some disaffected Northern democrats in 1854.

Korean War Pacific war started on June 25, 1950, when North Korea, helped by Soviet equipment and Chinese training, attacked South Korea.

Kosovo Province of Yugoslavia where the United States and NATO intervened militarily in 1999 to protect ethnic Albanians from expulsion.

Ku Klux Klan Perhaps the most prominent of the vigilante groups that terrorized black people in the South during Reconstruction era, founded by the Confederate veterans in 1866.

Land Grant College Act Law passed by Congress in July 1862 awarding proceeds from the sale of public lands to the states for the establishment of agricultural and mechanical colleges.

Land Ordinance of 1785 Act passed by Congress under the Articles of Confederation that created the grid system of surveys by which all subsequent public land was made available for sale.

League of Nations International organization created by the Versailles Treaty after World War I to ensure world stability.

League of Women Voters League formed in 1920 advocating for women's rights, among them the right for women to serve on juries and equal pay laws.

Lecompton Constitution Proslavery draft written in 1857 by Kansas territorial delegates elected under questionable circumstances; it was rejected by two governors, supported by President Buchanan, and decisively defeated by Congress.

Levittown Suburban Long Island community of postwar rental houses built by William Levitt for veterans of World War II.

Liberty Bonds Interest-bearing certificates sold by the U.S. government to finance the American World War I effort.

Liberty party The first antislavery political party, formed in 1840.

Limited Test Ban Treaty Treaty, signed by the United States, Britain, and the Soviet Union, outlawing nuclear testing in the atmosphere, in outer space, and under water.

Lincoln-Douglas Debates Series of debates in the 1858 Illinois senatorial campaign during which Douglas and Lincoln staked out their differing opinions on the issue of slavery.

Lost Cause The phrase many white Southerners applied to their Civil War defeat. They viewed the war as a noble cause but only a temporary setback in the South's ultimate vindication.

Lynching Execution, usually by a mob, without trial.

Mahanism The ideas advanced by Alfred Thayer Mahan, stressing U.S. naval, economic, and territorial expansion.

Manhattan Project The effort, using the code name Manhattan Engineer District, to develop an atomic bomb under the management of the U.S. Army Corps of Engineers during World War II.

Manifest Destiny Doctrine, first expressed in 1845, that the expansion of white Americans across the continent was inevitable and ordained by God.

Marbury v. *Madison* Supreme Court decision of 1803 that created the precedent of judicial review by ruling as unconstitutional part of the Judiciary Act of 1789.

Marshall Plan Secretary of State George C. Marshall's European Recovery Plan of June 5, 1947, committing the United States to help in the rebuilding of post-World War II Europe.

McCarthyism Anti-Communist attitudes and actions associated with Senator Joe McCarthy in the early 1950s, including smear tactics and innuendo.

Medicaid Supplementary medical insurance for the poor, financed through the federal government; program created in 1965.

Medicare Basic medical insurance for the elderly, financed through the federal government; program created in 1965.

Mercantilism Economic system whereby the government intervenes in the economy for the purpose of increasing national wealth.

Mexican Cession of 1848 The addition of half a million square miles to the United States as a result of victory in the 1846 war between the United States and Mexico.

Middle Passage The voyage between West Africa and the New World slave colonies.

Minute Men Special companies of militia formed in Massachusetts and elsewhere beginning in late 1744.

Missouri Compromise Sectional compromise in Congress in 1820 that admitted Missouri to the Union as a slave state and Maine as a free state and prohibited slavery in the northern Louisiana Purchase territory.

Model Cities Program Effort to target federal funds to upgrade public services and economic opportunity in specifically defined urban neighborhoods between 1966 and 1974.

Monroe Doctrine Declaration by President James Monroe in 1823 that the Western Hemisphere was to be closed off to further European colonization and that the United States would not interfere in the internal affairs of European nations.

Monroe Doctrine In December 1823, Monroe declared to Congress that Americans "are henceforth not to be considered as subjects for future colonization by any European power."

Muckraking Journalism exposing economic, social, and political evils, so named by Theodore Roosevelt for its "raking the muck" of American society.

Mugwumps Elitist and conservative reformers who favored sound money and limited government and opposed tariffs and the spoils system.

Multinational corporations Firms with direct investments, branches, factories, and offices in a number of countries.

Nat Turner's Rebellion Uprising of slaves in Southampton County, Virginia, in the summer of 1831 led by Nat Turner that resulted in the death of fifty-five white people.

Nation of Islam Religious movement among black Americans that emphasizes self-sufficiency, self-help, and separation from white society.

National Aeronautics and Space Administration (NASA) Federal agency created in 1958 to manage American space flights and exploration.

National American Woman Suffrage Association The organization, formed in 1890, that coordinated the ultimately successful campaign to achieve women's right to vote.

National Association for the Advancement of Colored People (NAACP) Interracial organization co-founded by W. E. B. DuBois in 1910 dedicated to restoring African-American political and social rights.

National Origins Act of 1924 Law sharply restricting immigration on the basis of immigrants' national origins and discriminating against southern and eastern Europeans and Asians.

National Security Council Paper 68 (NSC-68) Policy statement that committed the United States to a military approach to the Cold War.

National Security Council The formal policymaking body for national defense and foreign relations, created in 1947 and consisting of the president, the secretary of defense, the secretary of state, and others appointed by the president.

Nationalists Group of leaders in the 1780s who spearheaded the drive to replace the Articles of Confederation with a stronger central government.

Nativism Favoring the interests and culture of native-born inhabitants over those of immigrants.

Nativist Organizations Joined by American-born artisans in the 1840s which sought to curb mass immigration from Europe and limit the political rights of Catholic immigrants.

Natural Rights Political philosophy that maintains that individuals have an inherent right, found in nature and preceding any government or written law, to life and liberty.

Neoliberal Advocate or participant in the effort to reshape the Democratic party for the 1990s around a policy emphasizing economic growth and competitiveness in the world economy.

New Deal The economic and political policies of the Roosevelt administration in the 1930s.

New Federalism President Richard Nixon's policy to shift responsibilities of government programs from the federal level to the states.

New Freedom Woodrow Wilson's 1912 program for limited government intervention in the economy to restore competition by curtailing the restrictive influences of trusts and protective tariffs, thereby providing opportunities for individual achievement.

New Frontier John F. Kennedy's domestic and foreign policy initiatives, designed to reinvigorate sense of national purpose and energy.

New Harmony Short-lived utopian community established in Indiana in 1825, based on the socialist ideas of Robert Owen, a wealthy Scottish manufacturer.

New Jersey Plan Proposal of the New Jersey delegation for a strengthened national government in which all states would have an equal representation in a unicameral legislature.

New Lights People who experienced conversion during the revivals of the Great Awakening.

New Nationalism Theodore Roosevelt's 1912 program calling for a strong national government to foster, regulate, and protect business, industry, workers, and consumers.

Niagara Movement African-Ameri-can group organized in 1905 to promote racial integration, civil and political rights, and equal access to economic opportunity.

Nineteenth Amendment Constitutional revision that in 1920 established women citizens' right to vote.

Nisei U.S. citizens born of immigrant Japanese parents.

Nixon Doctrine President Nixon's new American policy (1969) toward Asia in which the United States would honor treaty commitments but would gradually disengage and expect Asian nations to handle military defense on their own.

Nonimportation Movement A tactical means of putting economic pressure on Britain by refusing to buy its exports to the colonies.

North American Free Trade Agreement (NAFTA) Agreement reached in 1993 by Canada, Mexico, and the United States to substantially reduce barriers to trade.

North Atlantic Treaty Organization (NATO) Organization of ten European countries, Canada, and the United States whom together formed a mutual defense pact in April, 1949.

Northwest Ordinance of 1787 Legislation that prohibited slavery in the Northwest Territories and provided the model for the incorporation of future territories into the union as co-equal states.

Nullification A constitutional doctrine holding that a state has a legal right to declare a national law null and void within its borders.

Nullification Crisis Sectional crisis in the early 1830s in which a states' rights party in South Carolina attempted to nullify federal law.

Office of Economic Opportunity (OEO) Federal agency that coordinated many programs of the War on Poverty between 1964 and 1975.

Olive Branch Petition adopted by the Second Continental Congress as a last effort of peace that avowed America's loyalty to George III and requested that he protect them from further aggressions.

Omaha Platform The 1892 platform of the Populist party repudiating laissez-faire and demanding economic and political reforms to aid distressed farmers and workers.

Oneida Community Utopian community established in upstate New York in 1848 by John Humphrey Noyes and his followers.

Open Door American policy of seeking equal trade and investment opportunities in foreign nations or regions.

Open shop Factory of business employing workers whether or not they are union members; in practice, such a business usually refuses to hire union members and follows antiunion policies.

Operation Desert Storm Code name for the successful offensive against Iraq by the United States and its allies in the Persian Gulf War (1991).

Operation OVERLORD U.S. and British invasion of France in June 1944 during World War II.

Oregon Trail Overland trail of more than two thousand miles that carried American settlers from the Midwest to new settlements in Oregon, California, and Utah.

Organization of Petroleum Exporting Countries (OPEC) Cartel of oil-producing nations in Asia, Africa, and Latin America that gained substantial power over the world economy in the mid- to late-1970s by controlling the production and price of oil.

Panic of 1857 Banking crisis that caused a credit crunch in the North; it was less severe in the South, where high cotton prices spurred a quick recovery.

Pan-Indian Resistance Movement Movement calling for the political and cultural unification of Indian tribes in the late eighteenth and early nineteenth centuries.

Parson's Cause Series of developments (1758–1763) that began when the Virginia legislature modified the salaries of Anglican clergymen, who complained to the crown and sued to recover damages. British authorities responded by imposing additional restrictions on the legislature. Virginians, who saw this as a threat, reacted by strongly reasserting local autonomy.

Patriot Act   Federal legislation adopted in 2001, in response to the terrorist attacks of September 11, intended to facilitate antiterror actions by federal law enforcement and intelligence agencies.

Peace of Paris   Treaties signed in 1783 by Great Britain, the United States, France, Spain, and the Netherlands that ended the Revolutionary War.

Pendelton Civil Service Act   A law of 1883 that reformed the spoils system by prohibiting government workers from making political contributions and creating the Civil Service Commission to oversee their appointment on the basis of merit rather than politics.

Pentagon Papers   Classified Defense Department documents on the history of the United States' involvement in Vietnam, prepared in 1968 and leaked to the press in 1971.

Pequot War   Conflict between English settlers and Pequot Indians over control of land and trade in eastern Connecticut.

Perestroika   Russian for "restructuring," applied to Mikhail Gorbachev's efforts to make the Soviet economic and political systems more modern, flexible, and innovative.

Pilgrims   Settlers of Plymouth Colony, who viewed themselves as spiritual wanderers.

Platt Amendment   A stipulation the United States had inserted into the Cuban constitution in 1901 restricting Cuban autonomy and authorizing U.S. intervention and naval bases.

Plessy v. *Ferguson*   Supreme Court decision holding that Louisiana's railroad segregation law did not violate the Constitution as long as the railroads or the state provided equal accommodations.

Pogroms   Government-directed attacks against Jewish citizens, property, and villages in tsarist Russia beginning in the 1880s; a primary reason for Russian Jewish migration to the United States.

Poll Taxes   Taxes imposed on voters as a requirement for voting.

Pontiac's Rebellion   Indian uprising (1763–1766) led by Pontiac of the Ottawas and Neolin of the Delawares.

Popular Sovereignty   A solution to the slavery crisis suggested by Michigan senator Lewis Cass by which territorial residents, not Congress, would decide slavery's fate.

Populist Party   A major third party of the 1890s formed on the basis of the Southern Farmer's Alliance and other reform organizations.

Populist Party   A major third party of the 1890s, formed on the basis of the Southern Farmers' Alliance and other organizations, mounting electoral challenges against Democrats in the South and the Republicans in the West.

Potsdam Declaration   Statement issued by the United States during a meeting of U.S. President Harry Truman, British Prime Minister Winston Churchill, and Soviet Premier Joseph Stalin in which the United States declared its intention to democratize the Japanese political system and reintroduce Japan into the international community.

Predestination   The belief that God decided at the moment of Creation which humans would achieve salvation.

Preparedness   Military buildup in preparation for possible U.S. participation in World War I.

Proclamation Line   Boundary, decreed as part of the Proclamation of 1763, that limited British settlements to the eastern side of the Appalachian Mountains.

Proclamation of 1763   Royal proclamation setting the boundary known as the Proclamation Line.

Progressive Era   An era in the United States (roughly between 1900 and 1917) in which important movements challenged traditional relationships and attitudes.

Prohibition   A ban on the production, sale, and consumption of liquor, achieved temporarily through state laws and the Eighteenth Amendment.

Prohibition Party   A venerable third party still in existence that has persistently campaigned for the abolition of alcohol but has also introduced many important reform ideas into American politics.

Proposition 187   California legislation adopted by popular vote in California in 1994, which cuts off state-funded health and education benefits to undocumented or illegal immigrants.

Proprietary Colony   A colony created when the English monarch granted a huge tract of land to an individual or group of individuals, who became "lords proprietor."

Protestant Fundamentalists   Religious conservatives who believe in the literal accuracy and divine inspiration of the Bible.

Protestants   All European supporters of religious reform under Charles V's Holy Roman Empire.

Pueblo Revolt   Rebellion in 1680 of Pueblo Indians in New Mexico against their Spanish overlords, sparked by religious conflict and excessive Spanish demands for tribute.

Puritans   Individuals who believed that Queen Elizabeth's reforms of the Church of England had not gone far enough in improving the church. Puritans led the settlement of Massachusetts Bay Colony.

Putting-out System   System of manufacturing in which merchants furnished households with raw materials for processing by family members.

Quakers   Members of the Society of Friends, a radical religious group that arose in the mid-seventeenth century. Quakers rejected formal theology, focusing instead on the Holy Spirit that dwelt within them.

Quartering Acts   Acts of Parliament requiring colonial legislatures to provide supplies and quarters for the troops stationed in America.

Quasi-War   Undeclared naval war of 1797 to 1800 between the United States and France.

Quebec Act   Law passed by Parliament in 1774 that provided an appointed government for Canada, enlarged the boundaries of Quebec, and confirmed the privileges of the Catholic Church.

Queen Anne's War   American phase (1702–1713) of Europe's War of the Spanish Succession.

Radical Republicans   A shifting group of Republican congressmen, usually a substantial minority, who favored the abolition of slavery from the beginning of the Civil War and later advocated harsh treatment of the defeated South.

Recall   The process of removing an official from office by popular vote, usually after using petitions to call for such a vote.

Reconquista   The long struggle (ending in 1492) during which Spanish Christians reconquered the Iberian peninsula from Muslim occupiers.

Red Scare   Post-World War I public hysteria over Bolshevik influence in the United States directed against labor activism, radical dissenters, and some ethnic groups.

Redemptioner   Similar to an indentured servant, except that a redemptioner signed a labor contract in America rather than in Europe.

Redlining   The withholding of home purchase loans and insurance coverage from inner-city older neighborhoods by federal housing agencies and private industry.

Referendum   Submission of a law, proposed or already in effect, to a direct popular vote for approval or rejection.

Reformation   Martin Luther's challenge to the Catholic Church, initiated in 1517, calling for a return to what he understood to be the purer practices and beliefs of the early church.

Regulators   Vigilante groups active in the 1760s and 1770s in the western parts of North and South Carolina. The South Carolina Regulators attempted to rid the area of outlaws; the North Carolina Regulators were more concerned with high taxes and court costs.

Repartimiento   In the Spanish colonies, the assignment of Indian workers to labor on public works projects.

Republican (Jeffersonian) Party   Party headed by Thomas Jefferson that formed in opposition to the financial and diplomatic policies of the Federalist party; favored limiting the powers of the national government and placing the interests of farmers over those of financial and commercial groups.

Republican Party   Party that emerged in the 1850s in the aftermath of the bitter controversy over the Kansas-Nebraska Act, consisting of former Whigs, some Northern Democrats, and many Know-Nothings.

Republicanism   A complex, changing body of ideas, values, and assumptions, closely related to country ideology, that influenced American political behavior during the eighteenth and nineteenth centuries.

Rescate   Procedure by which Spanish colonists would pay ransom to free Indians captured by rival natives.

Reservationists   Group of U.S. senators favoring approval of the Treaty of Versailles, after amending it to incorporate their reservations.

Roe v. Wade   U.S. Supreme Court decision (1973) that disallowed state laws prohibiting abortion during the first three months (trimester) of pregnancy and established guidelines for abortion in the second and third trimesters.

Roosevelt Corollary   President Theodore Roosevelt's policy asserting U.S. authority to intervene in the affairs of Latin American nations; an expansion of the Monroe Doctrine.

Rush-Bagot Agreement   Treaty of 1817 between the United States and Britain that effectively demilitarized the Great Lakes by sharply limiting the number of ships each power could station on them.

Sabbatarian Movement   Reform organization founded in 1828 by Congregationalist and Presbyterian ministers that lobbied for an end to the delivery of mail on Sundays and other Sabbath violations.

"Sack of Lawrence"   Vandalism and arson committed by a group of proslavery men in Lawrence, the free-state capital of Kansas Territory.

Sagebrush Rebellion   Political movement in the Western states in the early 1980s that called for easing of regulations on the economic issue of federal lands and the transfer of some or all of those lands to state ownership.

SALT (Strategic Arms Limitation Treaty)   Treaty signed in 1972 by the United States and the Soviet Union to slow the nuclear arms race.

Sand Creek Massacre   The near annihilation in 1864 of Black Kettle's Cheyenne band by Colorado troops under Colonel John Chivington's orders to "kill and scalp all, big and little."

Santa Fe Trail   The 900-mile trail opened by American merchants for trading purposes following Mexico's liberalization of the formerly restrictive trading policies of Spain.

Scalawags   Southern whites, mainly small landowning farmers and well-off merchants and planters, who supported the Southern Republican party during Reconstruction.

Search and Destroy   U.S. military tactic in South Vietnam, using small detachments to locate enemy units and then massive air, artillery, and ground forces to destroy them.

Second Bank of the United States   A national bank chartered by Congress in 1816 with extensive regulatory powers over currency and credit.

Second Great Awakening   Series of religious revivals in the first half of the nineteenth century characterized by great emotionalism in large public meetings.

Second Party System   The national two-party competition between Democrats and Whigs from the 1830s through the early 1850s.

Second Treaty of Fort Laramie   The treaty acknowledging U.S. defeat in the Great Sioux War in 1868 and supposedly guaranteeing the Sioux perpetual land and hunting rights in South Dakota, Wyoming, and Montana.

Securities and Exchange Commission (SEC) Federal agency with authority to regulate trading practices in stocks and bonds.

Sedition Act Broad law restricting criticism of America's involvement in World War I or its government, flag, military, taxes, or officials.

Segregation A system of racial control that separated the races, initially by custom but increasingly by law during and after Reconstruction.

Selective Service Act of 1917 The law establishing the military draft for World War I.

Selective Service System Federal agency that coordinated military conscription before and during the Vietnam War.

Self-determination The right of a people or a nation to decide on its own political allegiance or form of government without external influence.

Seneca Falls Convention The first convention for women's equality in legal rights, held in upstate New York in 1848.

Separatists Members of an offshoot branch of Puritanism. Separatists believed that the Church of England was too corrupt to be reformed and hence were convinced they must "separate" from it to save their souls.

Seventeenth Amendment Constitutional change that in 1913 established the direct popular election of U.S. senators.

Shakers The followers of Mother Ann Lee, who preached a religion of strict celibacy and communal living.

Sharecropping Labor system that evolved during and after Reconstruction whereby landowners furnished laborers with a house, farm animals, and tools and advanced credit in exchange for a share of the laborers' crop.

Shays's Rebellion An armed movement of debt-ridden farmers in western Massachusetts in the winter of 1786–1787. The rebellion created a crisis atmosphere.

Sheppard-Towner Maternity and Infancy Act The first federal social welfare law, passed in 1921, providing federal funds for infant and maternity care.

Sherman Antitrust Act The first federal antitrust measure, passed in 1890; sought to promote economic competition by prohibiting business combinations in restraint of trade or commerce.

Silicon Valley The region of California including San Jose and San Francisco that holds the nation's greatest concentration of electronics firms.

Sixteenth Amendment Constitutional revision that in 1913 authorized a federal income tax.

***Slaughterhouse* Cases** Group of cases resulting in one sweeping decision by the U.S. Supreme Court in 1873 that contradicted the intent of the Fourteenth Amendment by decreeing that most citizenship rights remained under state, not federal, control.

Slave Codes A series of laws passed mainly in the Southern colonies in the late seventeenth and early eighteenth centuries to defend the status of slaves and codify the denial of basic civil rights to them.

Social Darwinism The application of Charles Darwin's theory of biological evolution to society, holding that the fittest and wealthiest survive, the weak and the poor perish, and government action is unable to alter this "natural" process.

Social Gospel Movement Movement created by reform-minded Protestant ministers seeking to introduce religious ethics into industrial relations and appealing to churches to meet their social responsibilities.

Socialism Political and economic theory advocating that land, natural resources, and the chief industries should be owned by the community as a whole.

Solid South The one-party (Democratic) political system that dominated the South from the 1890s to the 1950s.

Sons of Liberty Secret organizations in the colonies formed to oppose the Stamp Act.

Sound Money Misleading slogan that referred to a conservative policy of restricting the money supply and adhering to the gold standard.

Southeast Asia Treaty Organization (SEATO) Mutual defense alliance signed in 1954 by the United States, Britain, France, Thailand, Pakistan, the Philippines, Australia, and New Zealand.

Southern Christian Leadership Conference (SCLC) Black civil rights organization founded in 1957 by Martin Luther King Jr., and other clergy.

Southern Farmer's Alliance The largest of several organizations that formed in the post-Reconstruction South to advance the interests of beleaguered small farmers.

Southern Homestead Act Largely unsuccessful law passed in 1866 that gave black people preferential access to public lands in five southern states.

Southern Manifesto A document signed by 101 members of Congress from Southern states in 1956 that argued that the Supreme Court's decision in *Brown* v. *Board of Education of Topeka* itself contradicted the Constitution.

Southwest Ordinance of 1790 Legislation passed by Congress that set up a government with no prohibition on slavery in U.S. territory south of the Ohio River.

Specie Circular Proclamation issued by President Andrew Jackson in 1836 stipulating that only gold or silver could be used as payment for public land.

Spheres of Influence Regions dominated and controlled by an outside power.

Spoils System The awarding of government jobs to party loyalists.

Stamp Act Congress October 1765 meeting of delegates sent by nine colonies, held in New York City, that adopted the Declaration of Rights and Grievances and petitioned against the Stamp Act.

Stamp Act Law passed by Parliament in 1765 to raise revenue in America by requiring taxed, stamped paper for legal documents, publications, and playing cards.

States' Rights Favoring the rights of individual states over rights claimed by the national government.

Stonewall Rebellion On June 27, 1969, patrons fought back when police raided the gay Stonewall Inn in New York.

Stono Rebellion Uprising in 1739 of South Carolina slaves against whites; inspired in part by Spanish officials' promise of freedom for American slaves who escaped to Florida.

Strategic Defense Initiative (SDI) President Reagan's program, announced in 1983, to defend the United States against nuclear missile attack with untested weapons systems and sophisticated technologies.

Student Nonviolent Coordinating Committee (SNCC) Black civil rights organization founded in 1960 and drawing heavily on younger activists and college students.

Students for a Democratic Society (SDS) The leading student organization of the New Left of the early and mid-1960s.

Subtreasury Plan A program promoted by the Southern Farmer's Alliance in response to low cotton prices and tight credit. Farmers would store their crop in a warehouse until prices rose, in the meantime borrowing up to 80 percent of the value of the stored crops from the government at a low interest rate.

Suffolk Resolves Militant resolves adopted in 1774 in response to the Coercive Acts by representatives from the towns in Suffolk County, Massachusetts, including Boston.

Suffrage The right to vote in a political election.

Sugar Act Law passed in 1764 to raise revenue in the American colonies. It lowered the duty from 6 pence to 3 pence per gallon on foreign molasses imported into the colonies and increased the restrictions on colonial commerce.

Sunbelt The states of the American South and Southwest.

Sussex **Pledge** Germany's pledge during World War I not to sink merchant ships without warning, on the condition that Britain also observe recognized rules of international laws.

Swann v. *Charlotte-Mecklenburg Board of Education* U.S. Supreme Court decision in 1971 that upheld cross-city busing to achieve the racial integration of public schools.

Sweatshops Small, poorly ventilated shops or apartments crammed with workers, often family members, who pieced together garments.

Taft-Hartley Act Federal legislation of 1947 that substantially limited the tools available to labor unions in labor-management disputes.

Taos Revolt Uprising of Pueblo Indians in New Mexico that broke out in January 1847 over the imposition of American rule during the Mexican War; the revolt was crushed within a few weeks.

Tariff Act of 1789 Apart from a few selected industries, this first tariff passed by Congress was intended to raise revenue and not protect American manufacturers from foreign competition.

Tea Act of 1773 Act of Parliament that permitted the East India Company to sell through agents in America without paying the duty customarily collected in Britain, thus reducing the retail price.

Tejanos Persons of Spanish or Mexican descent born in Texas.

Teller Amendment A congressional resolution adopted in 1898 renouncing any American intention to annex Cuba.

Temperance Reform movement originating in the 1820s that sought to eliminate the consumption of alcohol.

Temporary Assistance for Needy Families (TANF) Federal program, utilizing work requirements for and time limits on benefits, created in 1996 to replace earlier welfare programs to aid families and children.

Tenements Four- to six-story residential dwellings, once common in New York, built on tiny lots without regard to providing ventilation or light.

Tennessee Valley Authority (TVA) Federal regional planning agency established to promote conservation, produce electric power, and encourage economic development in seven southern states.

Thirteenth Amendment Constitutional amendment ratified in 1865 that freed all slaves throughout the United States.

Tonnage Act of 1789 Duty levied on the tonnage of incoming ships to U.S. ports; tax was higher on foreign-owned ships to favor American shippers.

Tories A derisive term applied to Loyalists in America who supported the king and Parliament just before and during the American Revolution.

Townshend Duty Act Act of Parliament, passed in 1767, imposing duties on colonial tea, lead, paint, paper, and glass.

Trail of Tears The forced march in 1838 of the Cherokee Indians from their homelands in Georgia to the Indian Territory in the West.

Transcendentalism A philosophical and literary movement centered on an idealistic belief in the divinity of individuals and nature.

Trans-Continental Treaty of 1819 Treaty between the United States and Spain in which Spain ceded Florida to the United States, surrendered all claims to the Pacific Northwest, and agreed to a boundary between the Louisiana Purchase territory and the Spanish Southwest.

Transportation Revolution Dramatic improvements in transportation that stimulated economic growth after 1815 by expanding the range of travel and reducing the time and cost of moving goods and people.

Treaty of Ghent Treaty signed in December 1814 between the United States and Britain that ended the War of 1812.

Treaty of Greenville Treaty of 1795 in which Native Americans in the Old Northwest were forced to cede most of the present state of Ohio to the United States.

Treaty of Lancaster Negotiation in 1744 whereby Iroquois chiefs sold Virginia land speculators the right to trade at the Forks of the Ohio.

Treaty of Paris The formal end to British hostilities against France and Spain in February 1763.

Treaty of San Lorenzo (Pickney's Treaty) Treaty with Spain in 1795 in which Spain recognized the 31st parallel as the boundary between the United States and Spanish Florida.

Treaty of Tordesillas   Treaty negotiated by the pope in 1494 to resolve the territorial claims of Spain and Portugal.

Treaty of Versailles   The treaty ending World War I and creating the League of Nations.

Truman Doctrine   President Harry Truman's statement in 1947 that the United States should assist other nations that were facing external pressure or internal revolution.

Underground Railroad   Support system set up by antislavery groups in the Upper South and the North to assist fugitive slaves in escaping the South.

Underwood-Simmons Tariff Act   The 1913 reform law that lowered tariff rates and levied the first regular federal income tax.

Union Leagues   Republican party organizations in Northern cities that became an important organizing device among freedmen in Southern cities after 1865.

United States v. *Cruikshank*   Supreme Court ruling of 1876 that overturned the convictions of some of those responsible for the Colfax Massacre, ruling that the Enforcement Act applied only to violations of black rights by states, not individuals.

University of California v. *Bakke*   U.S. Supreme Court case in 1978 that allowed race to be used as one of several factors in college and university admission decisions but made rigid quotas unacceptable.

Valley Forge   Area of Pennsylvania approximately 20 miles northwest of Philadelphia where General George Washington's Continental troops were quartered from December 1777 to June 1778 while British forces occupied Philadelphia during the Revolutionary War.

Vertical Integration   The consolidation of numerous production functions, from the extraction of the raw materials to the distribution and marketing of the finished products, under the direction of one firm.

Viet Cong   Communist rebels in South Vietnam who fought the pro-American government established in South Vietnam in 1954.

Virginia Plan   Proposal calling for a national legislature in which the states would be represented according to population.

Virtual Representation   The notion that parliamentary members represented the interests of the nation as a whole, not those of the particular district that elected them.

Volstead Act   The 1920 law defining the liquor forbidden under the Eighteenth Amendment and giving enforcement responsibilities to the Prohibition Bureau of the Department of the Treasury.

Voting Rights Act   Legislation in 1965 that overturned a variety of practices by which states systematically denied voter registration to minorities.

Waltham System   During the industrialization of the early nineteenth century, the recruitment of unmarried young women for employment in factories.

War Hawks   Members of Congress, predominantly from the South and West, who aggressively pushed for a war against Britain after their election in 1810.

War Industries Board (WIB)   The federal agency that reorganized industry for maximum efficiency and productivity during World War I.

War of 1812   War fought between the United States and Britain from June 1812 to January 1815 largely over British restrictions on American shipping.

War on Poverty   Set of programs introduced by Lyndon Johnson between 1963 and 1966 designed to break the cycle of poverty by providing funds for job training, community development, nutrition, and supplementary education.

Watergate   A complex scandal involving attempts to cover up illegal actions taken by administration officials and leading to the resignation of President Richard Nixon in 1974.

Webster-Ashburton Treaty   Treaty signed by the United States and Britain in 1842 that settled a boundary dispute between Maine and Canada.

Welfare Capitalism   A paternalistic system of labor relations emphasizing management responsibility for employee well-being.

Whig Party   Political party, formed in the mid-1830s in opposition to the Jacksonian Democrats, that favored a strong role for the national government for promoting economic growth.

Whigs   The name used by advocates of colonial resistance to British measures during the 1760s and 1770s.

Whiskey Rebellion   Armed uprising in 1794 by farmers in western Pennsylvania who attempted to prevent the collection of the excise tax on whiskey.

Whitewater   Arkansas real estate development in which Bill and Hillary Clinton were investors; several fraud convictions resulted from investigations into Whitewater, but evidence was not found that the Clinton's were involved in wrongdoing.

Wilmot Proviso   The amendment offered by Pennsylvania Democrat David Wilmot in 1846 which stipulated that "as an express and fundamental condition to the acquisition of any territory from the Republic of Mexico . . . neither slavery nor involuntary servitude shall ever exist in any part of said territory."

Wobblies   Popular name for the members of the Industrial Workers of the World (IWW).

Women's Christian Temperance Union (WCTU)   Women's organization whose members visited schools to educate children about the evils of alcohol, addressed prisoners, and blanketed men's meetings with literature.

World Bank   Designed to revive postwar international trade, it drew on the resources of member nations to make economic development loans to governments for such projects as new dams or agricultural modernization.

World Trade Organization (WTO)   International organization that sets standards and practices for global trade, and the focus of international protests over world economic policy in the late 1990s.

World Wide Web   A part of the Internet designed to allow easier navigation of the network through the use of graphical user interfaces and hypertext links between different addresses.

Wounded Knee Massacre The U.S. Army's brutal winter massacre in 1890 of at least two hundred Sioux men, women, and children as part of the government's assault on the tribe's Ghost Dance religion.

Writs of Assistance Documents issued by a court of law that gave British officials in America the power to search for smuggled goods whenever they wished.

XYZ Affair Diplomatic incident in 1798 in which Americans were outraged by the demand of the French for a bribe as a condition for negotiating with American diplomats.

Yalta Conference Meeting of U.S. President Franklin Roosevelt, British Prime Minister Winston Churchill, and Soviet Premier Joseph Stalin held in February 1945 to plan the final stages of World War II and postwar arrangements.

Yellow press A deliberately sensational journalism of scandal and exposure designed to attract an urban mass audience and increase advertising revenues.

Yellow-dog Contracts Employment agreements binding workers not to join a union.

CREDITS

Chapter 1 Image Key: A, Corbis/Bettmann; B, The Granger Collection, New York; C, Robert Frerck, Odyssey Productions, Inc.; D, The Bridgeman Art Library International Ltd.; E, Getty Images Inc.-Hulton Archive Photos; F, The Granger Collection; G, The Granger Collection, New York.

Chapter 2 Image Key: A, Dorling Kindersley Media Library; B, The New York Public Library, Rare Book Division/Art Resource; C, Getty Images, Inc.–Photodisc; D, Getty Images, Inc.–Hutton Archive Photos; E, Pilgrim Society ; F, Fur traders and Indians; engraving, 1777. © The Granger Collection, New York; G Jonathan Carver, A TREATISE ON THE CULTURE OF THE TOBACCO PLANT (London, 1779), Manuscripts and Rare Book Division, Swem Library, College of William and Mary; H. Courtesy, American Antiquarian Society; I. The New York Public Library, Rare Book Division/Art Resource; J. The Granger Collection, New York.

Chapter 3 Image Key: A, The John Carter Brown Library, at Brown University; B, the Granger Collection, New York. C, Dorling Kindersley Media Library; D. Library of Congress; E, Courtesy, American Antiquarian Society, F. The Granger Collection, New York, G. Chronicles of Michoacan (by Beaumont); Collection Revillagigedo Historia; 18th-century manuscript (detail); Archivos General de la Nacion, Palacio Nacional.

Chapter 4 Image Key: A. Liz MacAulay, Dorling Kindersley/Worthing Museum; B. The Granger Collection, New York. C. David Murray, Dorling Kindersley Media Library; D. Frank Greenaway, Dorling Kindersley Media Library; E. © Judith Miller & Dorling Kindersley. F. Dorling Kindersley Media Library; G. Tina Chambers, Dorling Kindersley/National Maritime Museum; H. Robert Feke (1707–1752) Portrait of Benjamin Franklin (1706–1790), c. 1746. Oil on Canvas, 127 × 102 cm. Courtesy of the Harvard University Portrait Collection. Bequest of Dr. John Collins Warren, 1856. I. John Wollaston "George Whitefield" ca. 1770. By courtesy of the National Portrait Gallery, London. J. North Wind Picture Archvies; K. Benjamin West (1738–1820), "The Death of General Wolfe", 1770. Oil on canvas, 152.6 × 214.5 cm. Transfer from the Canadian War Memorials, 1921 (Gift of the 2nd Duke of Westminster, Eaton Hall, Cheshire, 1918). National Gallery of Canada, Ottawa, Ontari.

Chapter 5 Image Key: A. Dorling Kindersely Media Library; B. Steve Gorton, Dorling Kindersely Media Library; C. The Granger Collection, New York. D. Dave King, Dorling Kindersely Media Library; E. © Judith Miller & Dorling Kindersley; F. Museum of the Cherokee Indian, Cherokee, NC; G. © Christie's Images Inc. 2004; H. Getty Images, Inc. Hutton Archive Photos.

Chapter 6 Image Key: A. Courtesy of the Library of Congress; B. Corbis/Bettmann; C. Corbis/Bettmann; D. Photograph courtesy of the Concord Museum, Concord, MA and the archives of the Lexington Historical Society. David Bohl, photographer. E. Joseph Sohm, Corbis/Bettmann; F. "Mezzotint", 1780–1800. Size: H. 7 3/8″, W. 9 3/4″. Courtesy, Winterthur Museum. G. "Paul Jones Shooting a sailor", color engraving from the Olds Collection #366, no negative number. Collection of The New-York Historical Society. H. Benjamin West, 1783 "American Commissioners of Preliminary Negotiations". Courtesy, Winterthur Museum. I. Anne S.K. Brown Military Collection, John Hay Library, Brown University.

Chapter 7 Image Key: A. Harry N. Abrams, Inc.; B. Courtesy of The Historical Society of Pennsylvania Collection, Atwater Kent Museum of Philadeplhia. C. Corbis/Bettmann. D. Gallery of the Republic. E. the Granger Collection, New York. F. the Granger Collection, New York. G. Print and Picture Collection, The Free Library of Philadelphia. H. Courtesy of the Library of Congress.

Chapter 8 Image Key: A. Courtesy of the Library of Congress; B. Abby Aldrich Rockefeller Folk Art Museum, Colonial Williamsburg Foundation, Williamsburg, VA; C. Museum of American Political Life; D. Getty Images, Inc. Hutton Archive Photos. E. The Granger Collection, New York. F. "White House Historical Association (White House Collection)" (25).

Chapter 9 Image Key: A. Corbis/Bettmann; B. From the collection of Mac G. and Janelle C. Morris Collection; C. Getty Images–Hutton Archive Photos; D. Smithsonian Institution, Photo no. 95-3550. E. Corbis/Bettmann; F. The Granger Collection, New York. G. ©Bettmann/CORBIS; H. Getty Images Inc.-Hulton Archive Photos.

Chapter 10 Image key: A. National Numismatic Collection/Smithsonian Institution; B. Corbis/Bettmann; C. Courtesy of the Library of Congress. D. Getty Images, Inc.-Photodisc. E. Courtesy of the Library of Congress. F. The Bridgeman Art Library International Ltd. G. The Bridgeman Art Library International Ltd.

Chapter 11 Image Key A. Tina Chambers, Dorling Kindersley Media Library; B. Corbis/Bettmann; C. The Granger Collection, New York; D. Library of Congress; E. Dorling Kindersley Media Library; F. "Returning from the Cotton Fields in South Carolina", ca. 1860, stereograph by Barbard, negative number 47843. Collection of The New-York Historical Society. G. The Boston Athenaeum; H. William Gladstone; I. James Cameron (1817–1882), "Colonel and Mrs. James A. Whiteside, Son Charles and Servants", Oil on Canvas; c. 1858–1859. Hunter Museum of Art, Chattanooga, Tennessee, Gift of Mr. and Mrs. Whiteside. J. Courtesy of the Library of Congress.

Chapter 12 Image Key: A. Courtesy of the New-York Historical Society, New York City. B. The Granger Collection, New York. C. the Granger Collection; D. ©Bettmann/CORBIS. E. Courtesy of the Rhode Island Historical Society, negative number RHi ×5 22. F. Omni-Photo Communications, Inc. G. Omni-Photo Communications, Inc. H. Frederick Douglass (1817–95). Oil on canvas, c. 1844, attr. to E. Hammond. The Granger Collection.

Chapter 13 Image Key: A. Geoff Brightling; Dorling Kindersley Media Library; B. Getty Images Inc.-Hulton Archive Photos C. Albert Bierstadt (1830–1902), "The Oregon Trail" (oil on canvas). Private Collection/Bridgeman Art Library International Ltd., New York. D. Peter Anderson, Dorling Kindersley Media Library; E. Lynton Gardinier, Dorling Kindersely, Media Library; F. © Christie's Images Inc. 2004. G. Art Resource, NY. H. Nathaniel Currier, "General Winfield Scott at the Siege of Vera Cruz, March 1847", 1847. Lithograph. The Granger Collection. I. Alfred Jacob Miller, "The Interior of Fort Laramie", 1858–60. The Walters Art Museum, Baltimore.

Chapter 14 Image Key: A. Corbis NY; B. Courtesy of the Library of Congress. C. Corbis NY. D. Corbis/Bettmann; E. Courtesy of the Library of Congress; F. Courtesy of Library of Congress. G. Courtesy of Library of Congress. H. the Granger Collection, New York. I. Getty Images, Inc.-Photodisc.

Chapter 15 Image key: A. Getty Images, Inc.-Photodisc. B. National Archives and Records Administration; C. Dorling Kindersley Media Library; D. Dorling Kindersley Media Library. E. Dorling Kindersley Media Library. F. Corbis/Bettmann. G. Getty Images Inc.-Hulton Archive Photos. H. Center of Military History, U.S. Army. I. Corbis/Bettmann. J. Library of Congress.

Chapter 16 Image Key: A. William Gladstone; B. Rocks; C. Corbis/Bettmann; D. Courtesy of Specials Collection, Musselman Library, Gettysburg College, Gettysburg, PA. E. Thomas C. Roche, Courtesy of the Library of Congress; F. The Granger Collection, New York.G. Library of Congress; H. Corbis/Bettmann.

Chapter 17 Image Key: A. Courtesy of the Library of Congress. B. The Granger Collection, New York. C. Library of Congress; D. Prentice Hall School Division. E. SHOMBURG CENTER Center/Art Resource, NY. F. Courtesy of The North Carolina Division of Archives and History. G. Getty Images Inc.-Hulton Archive Photos. H. The Granger Collection, New York.

Chapter 18 Image Key: A. Courtesy of the Library of Congress. B. Lewis W. Hine, George Eastman House; C. Corbis/Bettmann; D. The Granger Collection, New York. E. Ford Motor Company; F. Courtesy of the Library of Congress.

Chapter 19 Image Key: A. Lynton Gardiner, Dorling Kindersley Media Library; B. The Granger Collection, New York; C. Dave King ©, Dorling Kindersley Media Library; D. Dorling Kindersley Media Library; E. Library of Congress; F. Chinese mining laborers, Idaho, 76-119.2/A, Idaho State Historical Society. G. Library of Congress.

Chapter 20 Image Key: A. Picture Research Consultants. B. Courtesy of the Library of Congress. C. The Granger Collection, New York. D. The Granger Collection, New York. E. Corbis/Bettmann; F. Corbis/Bettmann; G. the Granger Collection, New York. H. Courtesy of the Library of Congress; I. Courtesy of the Library of Congress; J. Culver Pictures, Inc. K. Corbis/Bettmann; I. Courtesy of the Library of Congress.

Chapter 21 Image Key: A. Corbis/Bettmann; B. the Granger Collection, New York; C. the Granger Collection, New York; D. Corbis/Bettmann; E. Indiana Historical Society, A70. F. Kheel Center, Cornell University, Ithaca, NY 14853-3901. G. Corbis/Bettmann; H. the Granger Collection, New York; I. The Granger Collection, New York.

Chapter 22 Image Key: A. Corbis/Bettmann; B. Corbis/Bettmann; C. The Granger Collection, New York; D. Corbis/Bettmann; E. Courtesy of Library of Congress; F. Jonathan Potter, Dorling Kindersley Media Library; G. Corbis/Bettmann; H. The Granger Collection, New York. I. © Stock Montage, 2004. J. Theodore Roosevelt Collection, Harvard College Library.

Chapter 23 Image Key: A. Corbis/Bettmann; B. Getty Images Inc.-Hulton Archive Photos; C. Corbis/Bettmann; D. Richard Ward, Dorling Kindersley Media Library; E. the Granger Collection, New York; F. National Archives and Records Administration. G. Corbis/Bettmann.

Chapter 24 Image Key: A. Getty Images Inc.-Hulton Archive Photos; B. Corbis/Bettmann; C. Getty Images–Photodisc. D. C. Squared Studios, Getty Images, Inc. Photodisc. E. Wisconsin Historical Society/WHi-5020; F. Prentice Hall Higher Education; G. Stock Montage, Inc./Historical Pictures Collection. H. By permission of Campbell Soup Company. I. Courtesy W. A. Swift Photograph Collection, Archives and Special Collections, Ball State University.

Chapter 25 Image Key: A. Corbis/Bettmann; B. Corbis/Bettmann; C. SuperStock, Inc.; D. Corbis/Bettmann; E. Getty Images, Inc.-Photodisc. F. Brown Brothers; G. National Archives and Records Administration; H.

Corbis/Bettmann; I. The Granger Collection/© Estate Of Ben Shahn/Liscensed By Vaga, New York, NY. J. Isaac Soyer, "Employment Agency". Oil on canvas, 34 1/2″ × 45″. The Whitney Museum of American Art.

Chapter 26 Image Key: A. Andy Crawford, Dorling Kindersley Media Library; B. Corbis/Bettmann; C. Andy Crawford, Dorling Kindersley Media Library; D. The Granger Collection, New York; E. Getty Images Inc.-Hulton Archive Photos; F. Corbis/Bettmann; G. Prentice Hall Higher Education; H. Rieger Communications, Inc. I. Corbis/Bettmann; J. The Granger Collection, New York.

Chapter 27 Image Key: A. Corbis/Bettmann; B. Getty Images/Time Life Pictures; C. Corbis/Bettmann; D. Getty Images Inc.-Hulton Archive Photos E. Corbis/Bettmann; F. AP/Wide World Photos; G. Getty Images/Time Life Pictures; H. National Archives and Records Administration; I. Corbis/Bettmann.

Chapter 28 Image Key: A. Corbis/Bettmann; B. Getty Images Inc.-Hulton Archive Photos; C. Dorling Kindersley Media Library; D. Getty Images, Inc.-Photodisc. E. Bernard Hoffman/Life Magazine/©1950 TimePix; F. Sondak, Getty Images, Inc.–Taxi; G. Ralph Crane, Getty Images/Time Life Pictures. H. AP/Wide World Photos; I. AP/Wide World Photos.

Chapter 29 Image Key: A. © Royalty-Free/CORBIS; B. © Royalty-Free/CORBIS C. ©John Paul Filo/Hulton/Archive; D. George Meany Memorial Archives; E. Corbis/Bettmann; F. AP/Wide World Photos; G. Philip Jones Griffith, Magnum Photos, Inc., H. AP/Wide World Photos; I. Wally McNamee, Corbis/Bettmann.

Chapter 30 Image key: A. Telepress Syndicate Agency, Corbis/Bettmann; B. Ron Edmonds, Corbis/Bettmann; C. Corbis/Bettmann; D. Dorling Kindersley Media Library; E. AP/Wide World Photos; F. Denis Paquin, Corbis/Bettmann; G. Jose L. Pelaez, Corbis/Stock Market; H. Joe Marquette, AP/Wide World Photos.

Chapter 31 Image Key: A. Doug Kanter, SIPA Press; B. Author supplied; C. Dorling Kindersley Media Library D. Dorling Kindersley Media Library; E. Dorling Kindersley Media Library; F. Dorling Kindersley Media Library; G. Dorling Kindersley Media Library; H. Ira Wyman, Corbis/Sygma; I. Barbara Gauntt/The Clarion-Ledger; J. Prentice Hall Higher Education; K. Stephen Crowley, New York Times Pictures.

INDEX

38th parallel, 727
"40 acres and a mule," 419
54th Massachusetts Regiment, 392
99th Pursuit Squadron, 696
101st Airborne Division, 753
442nd Regimental Combat Team, 701
700 Club, 810
761st Tank Battalion, 696

A

Abandoned Lands legislation,
    418–419, 431
Abbott, Robert, 487
ABC newscasts, 832
Abd (slave), 68
Abenaki Indians, 77
Abilene, Kansas, 510–511
Abington Township v. *Schempp*
    (1963), 743
Abolitionists
    attacks on slavery, 283
    opinion of poor whites, 281
    religion & politics, 370
    social reform in 19th century,
        315–317
    women's rights leaders
        disappointed, 424–426
Abolitionist tracts, 256
Abolition of alcohol. *See* Temperance
Abolition of slavery
    Union objectives, 381
Abortion
    legalized, 370
    opposition to, 817
    rights, 646
    Roe v. *Wade*, 812
Abortions, 559–560
Abruzzi, Italy, 485
Academies for wealthy, 311
Acadia, Nova Scotia, 100
Accelerated depreciation, 798
Accidents, *See also* Industrial accidents
    in mines, 509
Acheson, Dean, secretary of State, 728
Acquired immune deficiency
    syndrome (AIDS), 813
Acquisitive society, 798
Act for Religious Toleration, 39
"Action now" by FDR, 664–666
Actors, 670
Actual representation, 96
Adam and Eve in Bible, 645
Adams, Abigail, 158
Adams, Charles Francis Jr., 456
Adams, Henry, historian, 468
Adams, John, U.S. president
    American minister to London, 182
    on British constitutional conflict,
        117
    at First Continental Congress, 127
    First Federalist candidate, 210–211
    Fries's Rebellion, 212
    mentioned, 197
    named Jefferson to Declaration, 141
    named Washington to Continental
        Army, 138
    Peace of Paris, 156
Adams, John Quincy, U.S. president
    attempted fairness for Creeks, 249
    in election of 1828, 242
    political maneuvering around gag
        rule, 320
    as president, 246
    as Secretary of State, 232–233, 237
Adams, Samuel, 119, 124, 127,
    136, 190
Adamson Act, 574
Addams, Jane, social reformer
    on Great Depression, 660

helped start NAACP, 563
Hull House founder, 476
opposed military preparations, 609
opposed Treaty of Paris, 592
as radical agitator, 624
settlement houses, 557
Adena-Hopewell Indians, 10
Administered prices in Great
    Depression, 659
Administration of Justice Act,
    124–125
Admiralty judges, 94
Advanced Research Projects
    Administration (ARPANet), 832
Advertisers, 490–491
Advertising consumerism, 640–641,
    652–653
Advocate for Moral Reform, 309
Aerospace industry, 808
Aetna Insurance Company, 70
Affirmative action, 795, 837–838
Affluence, 743–744
Affluent Society, The (Galbraith), 743
Afghanistan, 784, 793, 802, 843
AFL-CIO, 740
African-American churches, 282, 742
African Americans, *See also* Black
    soldiers; Great Migration
    aspirations in 1865, 416–421
    and Battle of Gettysburg, 396
    in Congress, 836
    current population, 834
    disappointment after Great War, 622
    discrimination against, 358–359
    discrimination in housing, 717
    Evangelicalism empowerment, 245
    excluded from suburbs, 640
    FDR coalition, 672
    freedom in Britain, 156–157
    during Great Depression, 661
    imperialist debate, 592
    jobs in New South late 19th
        century, 445
    Klan attacks, 643
    migration in 1950s and 1960s, 770
    migration out of South, 699
    military career opportunities, 718
    millionaires, 653
    Modern woman advertising, 652
    native born by 1850s, 272
    and New Deal, 674
    party loyalty, 527
    racial discrimination during WWII,
        698–699
    racial pride in 1920s, 639
    reestablish city council districts, 836
    Revolutionary War effect on slavery,
        171–172
    rights during Progressive Era,
        563–564
    roles during Great War, 612–613
    view of Filipino-America War, 593
    during WWII, 696
African Methodist Episcopal (AME)
    Church, 276, 418, 420–421, 458
African practices, 72–74
Africans in Virginia, 35
African traditions, 275
Afro-American Council, 458
Age of Enlightenment, 90
Age-segregated communities and
    retirees, 810
Agnew, Spiro, vice president, 776, 782
Agrarian revolt in South, 446–450
Agrarian unrest
    crisis after Revolutionary War, 184
Agribusiness, 612, 676
Agricultural Adjustment
    Administration (AAA), 666–667,
    676–677

Agricultural colleges, 561
Agricultural depression, 225
Agricultural expansion, 513–517
Agricultural policy, 676–677
Agricultural press literature, 270
Agricultural program, New Deal, 675
Agricultural protest, 536–537
Agricultural reform, 270–271,
    446–450
Agricultural Wheel, 447
Agriculture
    in 1920s, 635
    in Africa c. 1500, 14–15
    on frontier, 327–333
    in Lower South, 267
    Native American before 1492, 6–11
    in Old Northwest, 329–331
    in Old Southwest, 331–333
    role in Great Depression, 659
    source of conflict in English
        colonies, 62
    in Upper South, 270–271
Aguinaldo, Emilio, Filipino
    leader, 593
Aid for dependent mothers and
    children, 669
Aid to Families with Dependent
    Children (AFDC), 826
Aircraft industry, 807
Aircraft production, 695, 698
Aircraft used to fight submarines, 693
Airplanes, military, 705, 729, 747,
    751, 755
Air pollution, 570, 797
Air raid shelters, 745
Air strikes in Vietnam, 763–765
Air travel deregulated in 1978, 797
Air war, Europe in World War II, 705
Akan Africans, 14
Akron, Ohio, 660
Alabama
    admitted to Union, 235, 332
    black voters, 427
    denied Indian rights, 249
    disfranchisement, 456
    freedom riders, 754
    losing migrants, 333
    Lower South in 1850, 267
    mentioned, 449, 455, 459
    mentioned, Redemption, 430
    Populist election, 539
    secession from Union, 369
    Slave Code of 1852, 273
    social policy during
        Reconstruction, 427
    state flag, 460
    voting requirements, 243
Alabama Dry Dock Company, 699
Alamo, 99, 340
Alamogordo, New Mexico, 696
Alaska, 6, 543, 572, 585
Albany, 51, 101, 292
Albany Congress, 102, 114
Albany Plan of Union, 103
Albany Regency, 246
Alben Barkley, Adolf, Kentucky
    senator, 720
Albright, Madeleine K., secretary of
    State, 834
Albuquerque, New Mexico, 695
Alcatraz Island, 772
Alcohol consumption, 307, 527
Alcoholic beverages, 644–645
Aldrich, Nelson, Rhode Island
    senator, 535, 572
Aldrin, Buzz, astronaut, 762
Aleutian Islands, 694
Aleut Indians, 7
Alexander II, Tsar of Russia, 389, 481
Algeria, 703

Algonquian Indians, 52, 59
Alien and Sedition Acts, 219
Alien Registration Act (1940), 732
Aliens, 700
Allen, brothers Ethan, Ira, and Levi,
    of Vermont, 182
Allen, Paul, 830
Allentown, Pennsylvania, 783
Alliance, Southern Farmers, 447–449
Alliance Democrats, 538
Alliance for Progress, 751
Allies, *See also* World War II
    in Great War (WWI), 605–607,
        610–611, 617–620
Alligator shoes, 641
"All men are created equal,"
    Declaration of
    Independence, 141
All Mexico movement, 345
All-volunteer military, 776
Almshouses, 451
Al-Qaeda network, 823, 843
Alta California, 339, 342, 346
Aluminum imports to Japan
    restricted, 691
Amalgamated Clothing Workers
    (1914), 554
Amendments to U.S. Constitution. *See*
    Constitutional Amendments
America First Committee, 691
American Ambulance in France, 604
American and Foreign Anti-Slavery
    Society (1840), 318
American Anti-Slavery Society (1833),
    316–317
American Association (AA)
    baseball, 492
American Bible Society (1816), 306
American Board of Commissioners
    for Foreign Missions (1810), 306
American Civil Liberties Union
    (ACLU), 645
American Colonization Society
    (1817), 315
American Communist Party, 623
American Enterprise Institute, 796
American Equal Rights Association,
    424, 426
American Expeditionary Force (AEF),
    617
American Federation of Labor (AFL),
    479, 554, 623, 672, 740
American Federation of Teachers
    (1916), 565
American Female Moral Reform
    Society (1839), 309
American Foreign Legion, 617
American Fur Company, 335
American Home Missionary Society
    (1826), 306
American Indian Movement
    (AIM), 772
American Iron and Steel
    Association, 528
Americanization
    of ethnic groups during Great
        War, 624
    of immigrants, 483–485, 562, 616
    of immigrants by Ford, 631
    of Indians, 503–506
American League to Limit
    Armaments, 609
American Legion, 623
American Missionary Association, 418
American Progressive Party, 719
American Protective Association
    (APA) (1887), 485
American Protective League, 615, 842
American Protective Tariff
    League, 528

American Psychiatric Association, 813
American Railway Union (ARU), 480
American Revenue Act, 116
Americans, *See also* Black Americans;
   German Americans; Hispanic
   Americans; Jewish Americans;
   Mexican Americans; Native
   Americans; White Southerners
as defined in 1782, 170
American Slavery As It Is (Weld),
   290, 317
American society, modernization
   of, 399
American Sugar Refining
   Company, 541
American Sunday School Union
   (1824), 306
Americans with Disabilities Act
   (1990), 801
American System, Clay, 237, 248, 260
American system of
   manufacturing, 301
American Temperance Society
   (1828), 307–308
American Tobacco Company,
   440, 443
American Tract Society (1825), 306
American Views
   appeal of female abolitionist,
      318–319
   Boston celebrates new king, 95
   business, cult of, 633
   Cherokee Nation memorial, 252
   Cold War implications, 750
   computers in new economy, 830
   de Vaca among Indians, 5
   disfranchisement, 457
   Federalist Antiwar Resolutions, 227
   grassroots community action,
      780–781
   Great War, mobilizing America, 616
   imperialist view of world, 584
   Japanese American internment,
      700–701
   letter from escaped slave, 278
   Lincoln on slavery, 380
   Little Turtle defends Miami
      lands, 209
   Mexican view of Texans, 341
   Miantonomo's plea for Indian
      unity, 53
   Mississippi's black codes, 423
   Mother Jones and child labor,
      560–561
   new republic observed, 170
   nonimportation movement, 122–123
   nuclear arms race, 726
   Populist view of government, 540
   religion in politics, 816
   Rowlandson among Indians, 66
   tenement life, 477
   unemployment and relief, 664–665
   Union soldier, 391
   Zitkala-Sa's view of
      Americanization, 504
American West
   agricultural expansion, 513–517
   between Appalachians and
      Mississippi, 179, 199–201
   cattle industry, 510–512
   center of farm machinery
      industry, 301
   homesteads of 160 acres, 362
   mining the mountains, 506–510
   Native Americans subjugated,
      499–506
   Ohio secured, 207–208
   population in 1780s, 199
   public grasslands, 677
   transformed, 497–521
American Woman's Home (Beecher and
   Stowe), 489
Amputations, 386
Amusement parks, 492
Anarchists, 317
Anasazi Indians, 9

Ancestor reverence in slave
   religion, 275
Anderson, Robert, Major, 373, 381
Andover South Parish Society for the
   Reformation of Morals, 306
Andrew, John, governor of
   Massachusetts, 390
Andropov, Yuri, Soviet Union general
   secretary, 804
Andros, Sir Edmund, 93–94
Anglican Church, 40, 41, 91, 173
Anglican clergy, 115, 125, 173
Anglo-American Accords, 233
Anglo-American forces in French &
   Indian War, 104
Anglo-American treaty of peace, 156,
   See also Peace of Paris,
   Revolutionary War
Anglo-Dutch wars, 52
Anglo-Mexican trade, 296
Anglo-Saxon superiority, 582
Anglo-Tejano relations, 340–342
Angola, 802
Animal by-products, 296
Animals in Columbian exchange, 23
Anna, Santa, president of Mexico, 340
Annapolis, Maryland, 184
Annapolis Convention, 184
Annexations
   of Hawaiian Islands, 345
   of Texas, 339–342
   of trade *vs.* territory, 583
Annual fairs for fur traders, 335–336
Annual income of households, 798
Annual Register, 160
Anthony, Susan B., 319, 424, 425, 529
Anthrax, 843
Antiabolitionist mobs, 317
Antiabortion organizations, 370
Antiabortion protests, 646
Anti-American riots in Tokyo, 594
Anti-American sentiments in
   Caribbean, 595–599
Antiballistic missiles (ABM), 751, 778
Antiblack race riots. *See* Race riots
Antiblack sentiment in California
   gold rush, 355
Anti-Bolshevik hysteria, 623
Anti-British sentiments, 261
Anti-Catholic sentiment, 93–94,
   362, 645
Anti-Communism, 620, 730–733, 742,
   794, 795
Anti-drug crusade, 788
Antietam, Battle of, 390
Anti-evolution law, 645
Antifederalists, 188–189, 202
Antiforeign sentiment, 484
Antigua, 45
Anti-immigrant legislation, 298
Anti-Imperialist League, 592, 593
Anti-imperialists, 592, 593
Anti-Loyalist legislation, 182
Anti-Masons Party, 257
Antin, Mary, 466–467, 491
Antinomian, 43
Antipiracy law, 610
Antipollution laws, 810
Anti-Saloon League, 562
Anti-Semitism, 574, 631, 668, 690, 733
Antislavery agitation, 251
Antislavery literature, 256, 316
Antislavery petitions, 317
Antislavery tracts, 290, 317
Antislavery white people, 315–317
Antislavery women, demands for
   equality, 317–319
Antisubversive campaign, 730–733
Antitemperance coalitions, 308
Antitrust actions
   Bell System of AT&T, 796
   Microsoft and IBM, 830
Antitrust laws, 535, 611, 647, 659, 667
Antitrust program, Taft, 571
Antiwar movement, 765–767, 795
Antiwar protests

at Democratic Convention
   (1968), 775
in Filipino-American War, 593
during Great War, 614–616
Vietnam War, 776
Antwerp, 705
ANZUS Pact, 725
Apache Indians, 64, 65–67, 339, 503
Apalachee Indians, 22
A&P in 1920s, 634
Apollo 11 lunar module, 762
Appalachian migration, 638
Appalachian Mountains, 98, 101,
   113, 441
Appalachian Regional Development
   Act, 757
Appeal to Reason, 555
*Appeal to the Colored Citizens of the
   World* (Walker), 316
Appeasement policy, 679
Appliances, household, 490, 632, 640,
   719, 741–742
Appomattox Court House,
   Virginia, 406
Apprentices, 87, 298–299
Apprentice system, 304–305
Appropriation bills for Mexican
   War, 353
Aquino, Corazon, president of
   Philippines, 803
Arab-Israeli War, 778
Arabs, 844
Arapaho Indians, 334, 500, 502, 503
Archaic period, 6
Archer, Dennis, mayor of Detroit, 836
Arctic National Wildlife Refuge, 840
Ardennes Forest of Belgium, 705
Argentina, 693
Argonne Forest, 618
Aridity of American West, 515–516
Arikara Indians, 334
Aristocracy not in America, 96
Aristocratic republic, 237
Arizona
   discrimination against Mexicans, 661
   discrimination of Japanese
      residents, 643
   internment of Japanese
      Americans, 699
   in Mexican War, 346
   population growth in 1990s, 834
   Populist election, 538
   retirees, 810
   women suffrage adopted, 564
Arkansas
   admitted to the Union, 332
   Border South in 1850, 270
   mentioned, 446
   retirees, 810
   secession from Union, 375, 384
   sharecroppers, 668
   slave population in 1860, 272
Armaments, 647, 802, 841
Armed forces in Constitution, 186
Armistice ending Great War, 618–620
Arms control negotiations, 722
Arms-for-hostages negotiations with
   Iran, 803
Arms race, 725, 744, 751, 778
Arms sales, 690
Armstrong, Jack, 697
Armstrong, Louis, trumpet player, 641
Armstrong, Neil, astronaut, 762, 777
Army of Northern Virginia, 388,
   401–402
Army of the Potomac, 388, 393, 402
Army of Tennessee, 406
Arnold, Benedict, 138, 143, 144
Arson, 277
Arthur, Chester A., U.S. president,
   530, 532–533
Articles of Confederation, 174–175,
   184, 186–187
Artisans, 298–299, 300
   in colonial times, 87
   skilled, 470, 472, 490

and workers, tariffs on British
   goods, 178
Artists, 670
Arts, 670, 677
Aruba, 45
Asante Africans, 14
Ashcroft, John, attorney general, 842
Ashley, William Henry, 335
Asia, 592–595, 726–729, 803
Asian Americans (see Chinese
   Americans; Japanese Americans)
Assemblies in colonies, 115–116
Assemblies of God, 815
Assembly centers for Japanese
   Americans, 700
Assembly line, 631–634
Assembly-line neighborhoods,
   716–717
Assembly plants, 809–810
Assimilation
   of immigrants in late 19th century,
      484, 485
   of Indians, 503, 506
Associational politics, 527–530
Astrolabe, 18
Asylums, 312
Atlanta, Georgia
   in Civil War, 402–404
   growth during 1920s, 638
   home missions, 450
   mentioned, 440, 488
   mentioned, race riots, 458
   race riot (1906), 461, 563
   railroad convergence, 441
   sewer system, 670
   unskilled laborers, 420
Atlanta Campaign, 402
Atlanta Compromise, 459
Atlanta Constitution newspaper, 534
Atlanta's Five Points, 489
Atlanta University, 458, 461
Atlantic, Battle of, 693
Atlantic Charter (1941), 691
Atlantic Magazine, 441
Atlantic seaports as commercial
   centers, 295–297
Atomic bomb, 696, 707–708, 725, *See
   also individual entries under
   Nuclear*
Atomic Energy Commission (AEC),
   725, 726, 745
Atomic energy program, 722
Atrocities, *See also* Indians, forced
   migrations; Massacres
   Alamo and Goliad, 340
   in Revolutionary War, 152, 160
AT&T, 796, 799
Attacks on towns and villages
   Algonquian Indians, 52
   Lawrence, Kansas, 361
   Pleiku, Vietnam, 763
   in Revolutionary War, 146, 150
   in Virginia, 37, 38
Atwater, Lee, 800
Augusta, Georgia, 152, 446
Austin, Stephen F, 339, 341
Austin, Texas, 341
Australia, 543, 694, 725
Australian ballot, 564
Austria, 150, 679
Austro-Hungarian Empire, 481,
   605, 620
Automobile factories, 659
Automobile industry, 630, 632,
   672, 740
Automobile production, 740
Automobiles, 640, 695, 715
Auto workers, 715
Aviation industry, 632
Axis Powers, 687
Aztec Indians, 4, 9, 20

B

B-17 bombers, 705
Babbitt (Lewis), 642
Baby boom, 718–719

Backcountry settlers and farmers, 98, 199
Bacon, Nathaniel, 65
Bacon's Rebellion, 64, 69
Badmen of Bodie, 508
Baez, Joan, folk singer, 768
Baghdad, Iraq, 806, 844
Baja California, 360
Baker, Ella, 753
Baker, Newton, secretary of War, 612
Baker, Ray Stannard, 555, 604–605
Baker v. *Carr*, 773
Bakke, Allan, 837
Balance of terror, 709, 721, 745, 802
Balboa, Vasco Núñez de, 20
Baldwin, Christopher Columbus, of Massachusetts, 292
Baldwin, James, writer, 770
Balkans, 688, 705
Ballard, Allan B., 396
Ballinger, Richard, 572
Ballots, 244, 526, 564
Ballou, Sullivan, 381
Baltimore, Cecilius Calvert, Lord, 39
Baltimore, Maryland
  in 19th century, 295
  Coxey's Army, 540
  harbor importance, 87
  slave population in 1860, 272
  urban crisis in 1970s, 770
  in War of 1812, 230
Baltimore & Ohio Railroad, 292, 478
Banfield, Edward, 795
Bank Bill of 1816, 231
Bank closures in 1893, 539
Bank holiday, 665
Banking
  in 1920s, 634
  closures in 1893, 539
  control in Latin America, 598–599
  farmer and urban markets, 561
  first commercial bank, 175
  funds withdrawn in 1933, 663
  government rules on credit, 537
  during Great War, 613
  and immigrant businesses, 484
  industry reformed, 665
  in New York, 675
  North *vs.* South in late 19th century, 442–443
  reform by Wilson, 573
  role in Great Depression, 659
  women's employment in Great Depression, 660
Banking Act of 1935, 669
Banking crisis in 1837, 254
Bank notes, 175, 253
Bank of America, 484
Bank of England and Panic of 1837, 254
Bank of Italy, 484
Bank of North America, 175
Bank of the United States
  charter expired, 230
  dechartered, 253–254, 255
  during Jefferson presidency, 220
  as a national bank, 204
  national bank supported by Clay, 259–260
  policy precipitated depression, 234
  Second Bank, 231
Bankruptcies, 235, 255
Bank War, 253–254
Bannock Indians, 343
Baptism, 64, 91, 275
Baptist ministers, opposition to WCTU, 451
Baptists
  colonial religion, 91, 92
  divided in 1845, 366
  financial ties to state governments, 173
  in late 20th century, 815
  in New England, 197
  Piedmont farmers in slave South, 199
  religious divisions in War of 1812, 229
Second Great Awakening, 244–245
  slave converts, 275
Barbados, 45
Barbary pirates, 220
Barbed wire, 516
Barnard College, 466
Barone, Francesco, 482
Barracoons, 71
Barré, Isaac, 116
Barrett, James, 446
Barrett, W.H., 453
Barrios, 639
Barrows, Reverend J.H., 582
Bartering farm produce, 177
Barton, Bruce, 633
Barton, Clara, 399
Baruch, Bernard, 611, 621, 722
Baseball, 491–492, 718
Baseball parks, 641
Bastogne, 705
Bataan peninsula, 693
Batavia, 51
Bathtub gin, 645
Batista, Fulgencio, Cuban dictator, 678, 749
Baton Rouge Daily Advocate, 449
Battle flag of Confederacy, 460
Battle of Morningside Heights, 775
Battle of Pleasantville, 661
Battle of San Jacinto, 340
Battles. *See* Battles of Civil War; Battles of Korean War; Battles of Revolutionary War; Battles of Vietnam War; Battles of War of 1812; Battles of World War II; Conflicts in colonies; Indian wars
Battleships, *See also* U.S. naval warships
  Roosevelt desired, 584
  tonnage reduction, 647
Battles of Civil War
  Antietam, 390
  Atlanta Campaign, 402
  Bleeding Kansas, 361
  Bull Run, First Battle, 385
  Bull Run, Second Battle, 388
  Chancellorsville, 393
  Cold Harbor, 402
  Fort Wagner, 392
  Franklin, 406
  Gettysburg, 393, 396, 413
  Glorieta Pass, 394
  Manassas, First, 385
  Manassas, Second, 388
  Nashville, 406
  Pea Ridge, 394
  Peninsula Campaign, 388
  Seven Days Battles, 388
  Seven Pines, 388
  Spotsylvania, 402
  the Wilderness, 402
Battles of Korean War
  Heartbreak Ridge, 729
  Pork Chop Hill, 729
Battles of Revolutionary War
  Breeds Hill, 138
  Brooklyn Heights, 147
  Bunker Hill, 138, 145
  Charleston, 152
  Concord, 136–137
  Cowpens, 155
  Kettle Creek, 152
  Lexington, 136–137
  Monmouth Court House, 145, 150
  overview, 154
  Princeton, 147
  Saratoga, 149
  Savannah, 143
  Trenton, 147
  White Plains, 147
Battles of Vietnam War
  Cambodian Incursion, 776
  Tet Offensive, 773–774
Battles of War of 1812
  Horseshoe Bend, 230

New Orleans, 230–231, 246
Plattsburgh, 230
Put-in-Bay, 229
Queenston Heights, 229
Tippecanoe, 225, 258
Battles of World War II
  the Atlantic, 693
  Britain, 688
  the Bulge, 705
  the Coral Sea, 693
  the Java Sea, 693
  Leyte Gulf, 706
  Midway, 694
Bay of Pigs, 749–751
Bayonets, 143–144
Bean, Geraldine, 744
Beardsley, D., 391
Beasley, David, South Carolina governor, 460
Beatles rock group, 742, 768
Beaufort, South Carolina, 457
Beauregard, P.G.T., Confederate general, 373, 385
Beaver fur, 33
Beaver pelts, 336
Beaver trapping by Sioux, 334–335
Beaver Wars, 60–61, 64, 67
Bee, Barnard, Confederate general, 385
Beecher, Catherine, 290, 489
Beecher, Reverend Lyman, 290, 306, 307, 353, 358
Begin, Menachem, Israeli Prime Minister, 784
Beijing, China, 594
Beirut, Lebanon, 803
Bejar, 341
Belgium, 606, 688, 705
Belk, William Henry, 445
Belknap, Jeremy, of New Hampshire, 173–174
Bell, Alexander Graham, 467
Bell, John, 369
Belle Boyd, 401
Belle Isle Park in Detroit, Michigan, 699
Bell System of AT&T, 796
Benevolent empire, 306–307, 310
Benevolent societies, 320, 509
Benin, 58
Benton, Jessie, 362
Benton, Thomas Hart, Missouri senator, 344, 359, 362
Beriberi among slaves, 273
Berkeley, William, Governor of colonial Virginia, 65
Berlin, Germany, 705, 722
Berlin airlift, 724
Berlin blockade, 724
Berlin Wall, 749, 804
Bermuda naval bases, 691
Bethe, Hans, 686
Bethlehem Steel, 634
Bethune, Mary McLeod, 674
Bible
  during Civil War, 386
  Farmers' Alliance qualification, 447
  prophet Amos, 753
  societies, 306–307
  study in colonial New England, 89
  used to justify slavery, 283
  used to maintain superiority, 245
Biblical Creation, 645–646
Bicameral legislatures, 174, 184
Bicycling, 491
Biddle, Nicholas, bank president, 253–254
Biddle Institute in Charlotte, Virginia, 418
Big government, 671
Bilingual education, 837
Bill of Rights
  added to Constitution, 190, 202
  included in state constitutions, 173
  in Northwest Ordinance of 1787, 181
  passed by Parliament, 94

Bimetallic system, 536
Bini Africans, 14
Bin-Laden, 843
Biological diversity, 236
Biological warfare, 843
Bipartisan coalition, 719
Biracial plantation society, 45–46
Birmingham, Alabama
  freedom riders, 754
  growth during 1920s, 638
  iron and steel industry, 440, 442, 443
Birth control information, 559–560, 642
Birth-control pills, 767, 812
Birth of a Nation movie, 456
Birthrates
  early 19th century, 304
  during Great Depression, 660
  post WWII, 718
Bison, 6
Bitter Cry of the Children, The (Spargo), 557
Black Americans, *See also* African Americans
  aspirations in 1865, 416–421
  barred entry to Missouri, 235
  disfranchisement of, 563, 565
  Evangelicalist empowerment, 245
  during Great Depression, 661
  officeholders, 427
  stole their freedom, 391–392
  workers, 305, 672
Black Ball Line, 295
Black Baptists, 458
Black Belt, 332
Black British dragoons, 145
Black business districts, 458
Black Cabinet, FDR appointees, 674
Black churches, 420, 742
Black codes, 281, 422–424
Black colleges, 674
Black communities, 514
Black Death, 16
Black ghettos, 639, 775
Black Hawk's War (1832), 250, 334
Black Hills, 502–503
Black immigrants, 298
Black inferiority, 456
Black institutions, 487
Black Kettle, 502
Black Legend, 22
Black Man's Burden Association, 592
Black middle class, 458
Black Migration, 639
Black militancy, 316
Black Muslims, 771
Black newspapers, 459
Black Northerners, formed protection associations, 357
Black Panthers, 771–772
Black Power, 771, 798
Black Pride, 461
Black rats in Columbian exchange, 23–24
Black Reconstruction (DuBois), 431
Black Republican party, 363
Black Sea, 723
Black soldiers
  in Civil War, 392
  in Great War, 617
  in Revolutionary War, 145, 171
  in WWII, 696
Black Southerners, status in late 19th century, 440
Black Star Steamship Line, 639
Black Tuesday, 658
Black voting rights. *See* Suffrage
Black women's clubs, 459
Black women's roles in South, 459
Blaine, James G., secretary of State, 533, 585–586, 595
Bland-Allison Act (1878), 536
Blankets and germ warfare, 114
Blatch, Harriot Stanton, 613
Bleeding Kansas, 361
Blitzkrieg, 688, 705

Blockades
  Berlin, 724
  Cuban, 751
  Union, 457
Bloomingdales, 798
Blue-collar jobs during Reagan
  years, 797
Blue Eagle insignia (NRA), 667
Blues music, 639, 641
Boarders, 660
Boarding schools, 505
Board of Trade, England, 94
Bodie, California, 508
Boeing plants, 695
Boesky, Ivan, 798
Bohemia, 484, 620
Bohr, Niels, 686
Boise City, Idaho, 506
Bolivia, 22
Bolshevik Russia, 619, 620
Bolsheviks, 617, 619
Bolshevism as derogatory term,
  623, 637
Bombing of federal office
  building, 826
Bombs mailed, 623
Bonds, 204, 384, 604, 613, 615, 664
Bondwoman's Narrative, The
  (Crafts), 266
"Bone and sinew of your country," 457
Bonfire of the Vanities, The (Wolfe), 798
Bon Homme Richard, John Paul Jones'
  ship, 151, 152
Bonus Army, 663
Bonus Marchers, 663
Book of Common Prayer, 40
Book of Mormon, The, 310
Boone, Daniel and James, 199
Booth, John Wilkes, 407
Bootleggers, 645
Border disputes
  between British Canada and Maine,
    260
  in British Guiana, 587
  between Texas and Mexico, 340, 344
Border South, 270, 272
Bosnia, 824
Boston, Massachusetts
  in 19th century, 295
  black protection associations, 357
  Coxey's Army, 540
  duties collected by British, 121
  founded, 42
  Jordan Marsh retail, 491
  passenger air service, 632
  in Revolutionary War, 138
  rich *vs.* poor, 88
  school busing violence, 811
  strike by police officers, 623
  temperance movement, 307
  urban crisis in 1970s, 770
Boston and Worcester Railroad, 292,
  296
Boston Associates, 299, 301
Boston Common elm trees, 87
Boston Globe, 607
Boston Massacre, 122–123
Boston News-Letter, 95
Boston Port Act, 124–125
Boston Post, 368
Boston Seamen's Aid Society, 309
Boston Tea Party, 111, 124, 135
Bow, Clara, movie star, 642
Bowdoin, James, Massachusetts
  governor, 168
Bowery, Charity, 274, 275
Boxer Rebellion, 594
Boycotts
  of British manufactured goods, 118
  prohibited by courts, 556
  secondary, 716
  of streetcar systems, 458
  of Townshend duties, 121–122
  used by business in 1920s, 634
Boys' Working Reserve, 612
Bozeman Trail, 502
Bracero program, 698

Braddock, Edward, major
  general, 103
Bradford, governor of Plymouth, 43
Bradley, Tom, mayor of Los
  Angeles, 835
Brady, Matthew V., photographer,
  412–413
Brady Company, 412–413
Brady Handgun Violence Prevention
  Act (1994), 826
Bragg, Braxton, Confederate
  general, 394
Brain trust, 665
Branch Davidian, 826
Brandeis, Louis, 574
Branding cattle, 512
Brandywine Creek, 149
Brazil, 24, 693
Brazos River, 340
Breadbasket, 198, 331
Bread lines, 665
Breckinridge, John C., 368
Breeds Hill, Battle of, 138
Brennan, William, Supreme Court
  justice, 433
Brent brothers from Missouri, 342
Brent's Old Fort on Arkansas River,
  342
"Brer Rabbit," 277
Brezhnev, Leonid, Soviet Union
  general secretary, 804
Bridges, 670
Britain, *See also* England; Great
  Britain
  abandoned Indian allies, 329
  after the War of 1812, 232–233
  boundary negotiations, 260
  control of Old Northwest, 229
  diplomatic settlement, Jay's Treaty,
    208–210, 211
  forts in Northwest, 209
  joint occupation of Oregon, 261
  Native American allis, 172
  neutrality in Civil War, 389–390
  and Panic of 1837, 254
  technology secrets guarded, 299
  textile mills and Southern cotton,
    268
  trade embargo in 1807, 223–225
  trade with U.S. after Revolutionary
    War, 176
  violations of Peace of Paris, 182
  War of 1812, 226–231
Britain, Battle of, 688
British American colonies
  assemblies, 115–116, 125–127
  Boston Massacre, 122–123
  Boston Tea Party, 111, 124, 135
  culture transformed, 88–90
  expansion west, 97–100
  Intolerable Acts, 124–125
  as members of British empire, 82–83
  political world, 93–97
  reactions to British taxes, 116–120
  religion, 90–93
  taxation, 116–122
  trade & economic development,
    83–88
  warfare, 100–104
British Canada, takeover of, 225
British Constitution, 117, 173
British East India Company, 124
British Guiana, 587
British India, 692
British-Indian alliance, 225
British investors in cattle industry, 511
British passenger liner, *Lusitania,* 608
Brocas, William, 39
Brook Farm, 314
Brookline, Massachusetts, 491
Brooklyn, New York, Coney Island,
  492
Brooklyn Dodgers, 718
Brooklyn Heights, Battle of, 147
Brooklyn Navy Yard, 740
Brothels, 508
Brothels and male patrons, 309

Brotherhood of Sleeping Car Porters,
  698
Brotherly love, 50
Brown, Henry "Box," 276
Brown, John, 124, 367–368
Brown, Linda, 752
Brown, Mather, artist, 141
Brown Bess musket, 143
Brown Power, 772
Brown University, 92
Brown v. Board of Education of Topeka
  (1954), 738, 752
Bryan, William Jennings, secretary of
  State
  appointed by Wilson, 599
  in election of 1896, 542–543
  in election of 1908, 571
  on evolution, 645
  during Great War, 606–609
  imperialist debate, 592
  silver policy, 541
Bubonic plague, 16
Buchanan, James, U.S. president,
  362–364, 371
Buchanan, Patrick, 823
Budapest, Hungary, 746
Budget and Accounting Act (1921),
  636
Budget Bureau, 636
Budget deficits, 801, 840
Buena Vista in Mexican War, 346
Buffalo, New York, 292, 296, 482, 550
Buffalo herds, 335, 339, 502
Buffalo Springfield rock band, 768
Buffington, Captain, 168
Builders, 717
Building codes, 557
Bulgaria, 606, 688, 722, 723, 724, 804
Bulge, Battle of the, 705
Bull Run, Battles of, 385, 388
Bunau-Varilla, Philippe, 597
Bundy, McGeorge, national security
  advisor, 763
Bunker Hill, Battle of, 138, 145
Bunker Hill (Los Angeles) urban
  renewal, 740
Bureaucrats, 212, 248
Bureau of Foreign Commerce, 647
Bureau of Indian Affairs, 335, 337,
  501, 503, 505, 506, 674, 740
Bureau of Labor Statistics, 635
Bureau of Reclamation, 568, 676
Bureau of Refugees, Freedmen, and
  Abandoned Lands, 418–419, 431
Buren, Martin Van, U.S. president,
  246–247, 254, 354
Burgess, John W., 582
Burials, *See also* Funerals
  of Archaic Indians, 6
  of Confederate soldiers, 451
Burial societies, 420
Burleson, Albert, Postmaster General,
  614
Burma, 692, 693, 705
Burnside, Ambrose E., Union
  general, 393
Burr, Aaron, 213, 223
Burroughs, Nannie H., 459
Bus boycott in Montgomery, Alabama,
  753
Buses and freedom riders, 754
Bush, George H.W. (elder), U.S.
  president
  on education standards, 159
  election of 1988, 800
  election of 1992, 823–824
  and environmental policies, 570
  foreign policy, 804–806
  mentioned, 744, 794, 825
  mislead Congress as vice president,
    803
  Reaganomics, 800–802
  regulatory relief as vice president,
    797
Bush, George W. (younger), U.S.
  president
  appointments, 835

  economy, 838–841
  foreign policy, 345, 845
  Lewis and Clark Bicentennial, 236
  national debt, 206
  terrorism and national security,
    841–844
  trade agreement, 833
Bush, Vannevar, 696
Business
  advertising consumer society, 640,
    652–653
  boom industries in 1920s, 632–634
  cult of, 633
  gains after WWII, 715–716
  of government, 635–637
  Henry Ford, 630–632
  war debts, 647
Business leaders
  in 1920s, 647
  after Great War, 623
  in American West, 235
  Blue Eagle companies, 667
  cheap labor promoted in South, 441
  in election of 1936, 670
  and government regulation, 568
  during Great War, 615
  monopoly support, 574
  and municipal reform, 565–566
  unemployment relief opposition,
    664
Business regulations, 840
Busing for school integration, 773,
  795, 811
Butler, Benjamin, Union general, 391,
  402
Butler, Nicholas Murray, 478
Butter rationed, 695
Buying on credit, 741
Byrnes, James, secretary of State, 707

C

Cabinet, presidential advisory body,
  202
Cabot, John, 25, 27
Caddos Indians, 99
Cadillacs, 641
Cahokia, British settlement, 150
Cahokia, city of mound-builders, 10
Cahuilla Indians, 500
Cairo, Egypt, 702
Calcutta, India, 476
Calendars in Mesoamerica, 7
Calhoun, John C.
  on annexation of Texas, 260
  creation of national bank, 231
  formation of Whig Party, 256
  nullification crises, 251
  Salary Act uproar, 243
  as Secretary of War, 237
  of South Carolina, 226
  South Carolina senator, 355
California
  discrimination against Mexicans, 661
  discrimination of Japanese residents,
    643
  expanding Spanish empire, 98–99
  future acquisitions, 233
  gold discovery, 355
  gold fields, 508
  immigrant workers, 483
  internment of Japanese Americans,
    699
  IWW trial, 616
  mentioned, 829
  Mexican rule ended, 342–343
  on Oregon Trail, 336
  population growth in 1990s, 834
  Populist election, 538
  progressives interests, 563
  protective legislation for women, 558
  protective tariffs, 533
  Red Scare, 731
  retirees, 810
  statehood granted, 355
  Sunbelt, 806
  women suffrage adopted, 564

California Unemployment Commission, 660
Californios, 342, 344
Call-and-response pattern, 275
Caltech University, 808
Calvert, Cecilius, Lord Baltimore, 39
Calvert, Rosalie E., 218–219
Calvert family, 94
Calvin, John, 17, 40
Calvinist doctrine, 304
Cambodia, 729, 776, 792–793
Cambridge University, 90
Camden, South Carolina, 152
Campaign
  contributions, 528
  finance reform laws, 528
  practices reformed, 565
  rallies in late 19th century, 525
  train, 720
Campbell, Ben Nighthorse, Colorado senator, 836
Camp David Agreement, 784
Camp fever during Civil War, 386
Camp Gordon, Georgia, 617
Canada
  British forces advance, 148–149
  development of New France, 33
  explored by France, 24–25
  freedom for slaves, 278
  in French and Indian War, 104
  French colonial expansion, 99–100, 102
  mentioned, Ford assembly plants, 647
  moratorium on fishing, 27
  patriots attempt to win, 138–139
  Peace of Paris, 156
  Quebec Act, 125
  U.S. attempt to conquer, 229
Canal networks, 292–295
Canals, *See also* Panama Canal; Suez Canal
  in Upper South, 271
Canal Zone, 597–598
Canaries, 515
Canary Islands, 18, 20
Candidates and party support, 528
Candler, Asa, 440
Cane Ridge, Kentucky, 245
Cannon, Uncle Joe, 572
Canton, South China, 482
Cape Breton Island, Fortress of Louisbourg, 102
Cape Horn, 342
Cape of Good Hope, 51
Cape Verde Islands, 19
Capitalists, 512, 796, *See also* Corporations
Capitals of world trade and finance, 809
Capone, Al, gangster, 645
Capoque Indians, 5
Caravan routes to Asia, 18
Card playing, 563
Caribbean
  CIA foreign policy, 803
  imperialist power, 595–599
  naval bases, 691
Caribbean islanders, 11
Caribbean naval bases, 585
Carib Indians, 11, 19, 20
Carmichael, Stokely, 771
Carnegie, Andrew, 471, 478, 479–480, 592
Carnegie Steel Company, 471
Carolina beaches, 693
Carolina Cherokee Indians, 60
Carolina Colony, 46–49, 48, 69
Carolina Piedmont, 440
Carolinas and retirees, 810
Carpenter, Helen, 337
Carpenter's Hall in Philadelphia, 125
Carpetbaggers, 426
Carranza, Venustiano, 599
Carson, Rachel, 779
Carswell, G. Harrold, Supreme Court nominee, 778

Carter, James Jr., U.S. president, 779, 780, 782, 783–785, 794, 802, 807, 818
Carter, Landon, 74
Carter, Robert, 77
Cartier, Jacques, 24
Casablanca, 702
Casey, William, CIA director, 803
Cash and carry arms sales, 690
Cash cows, 797
Cash crops, 198, 271, 295
Cashtown, Pennsylvania, 393
Casinos, 505
Cass, Lewis, Michigan senator, 354
Cassville, Georgia, 404
Castro, Fidel, 678, 749, 751
Casualties
  in Civil War, 381, 407
    at Battle of Antietam, 390
    at Battle of Gettysburg, 393
    in battles of 1864, 402
    of Continental Army, 157
    at Seven Days Battles, 388
    at Shiloh, 386
  in Cuba, 590
  of Great War, 618
  in Korean War, 729
  of Reagan revolution, 799–800
  in wars with Western Indians, 502
Catherine of Aragon, 25
Catherine the Great of Russia, 150
Catholic Church
  Americanization, 815
  anti-Communist churchgoing, 742
  challenged in 1690s, 93–94
  cultural attitude changes, 646
  in England, 25
  in Europe c. 1500, 16–18
  Indians forced to convert, 338
  landholding given up, 342
  Mexican Texas converts, 339–340
  recognized by Parliament in Canada, 125
  resisted school reform, 311
Catholic colonists
  in Maryland, 39
Catholic missionaries, 62–64
Catholics
  attacked by Klan, 643
  FDR coalition, 672
  German immigrants 1848-1860, 361
  immigrants, 305, 646
  immigration feared by Protestants, 298
  in New England, 197
  opposed prohibition, 562
  party loyalty, 527
  peasants from Ireland, 297
Catlin, George, 326
Cat-o'-ninetails, 144
Cato's Letters (Gordon and Trenchard), 118
Catt, Carrie Chapman, 564, 609
Cattle in Columbian exchange, 23
Cattle industry, 510–512
Cattle ranches, 342
Cayuga Indians, 60
Cayuse Indians, 337
CBS newscasts, 832
Cease-fire
  in Egypt, 746
  in Vietnam War, 776
Celibacy
  advocated for slaves, 266
  Shaker rule, 313
Cellophane, 634
Cell phones, 832
Cemetery Hill and Ridge, 393
Censorship
  artistic, 563
  current methods, 842
  during Great War, 614–616
  of war news, 593, 606
  during WWII, 697
Census
  of 1890, 643
  of 1900, 487

in 1920, 637
  of 1970, 772
  of 1990, 2000, 833–834
Centennial Exposition (1876), 467
Center politics, 823–828
Centers of cities, 489
Central America, 803
Central government, 186, 187
Central heating, 489
Central High School, 752
Central Intelligence Agency (CIA), 724, 746, 751, 803, 804, 841, 842
Centralization of government in New Deal, 676
Centralization of power, 531
Centralized power, Jackson, 251
Central Labor Council, 623
Central Pacific, 692
Central Pacific Railroad, 498–499
Central Powers, 606–607, 619
Ceuta, 15
Ceylon, 51
Chaco Canyon, New Mexico, 9
Chain migration, 482
Chamberlain, Daniel H., governor of South Carolina, 430
Chamber pots, 296
Chambers, Whittaker, 732
Champlain, Samuel de, 33
Chancellorsville, Battle of, 393
Chaplin, Charlie, 634, 731
Charismatics, 815
Charitable societies, 245
Charities, 660, 662
Charity for poor, 478
Charles I, king of England, 39, 41
Charles II, king of England, 46–48, 50, 52, 93
Charles River Bridge v. *Warren Bridge* (1837), 295
Charleston, Battle of, 152
Charleston, South Carolina
  black codes, 281
  captured by black troops, 406
  first church erected after War, 420
  girls boarding schools, 89
  library, 90
  mentioned, 268
  mulatto elite, 282
  railroads effect on, 441
  in Revolutionary War, 138, 152
  slave uprising, 74
  Vesey's Conspiracy, 276
Charleston dance craze, 641
Charleston Harbor, 373
Charlotte, North Carolina, 441
Charles V of Spain, 17
Charter generation of American slaves, 69–71
Charters for colonization, 53
Chattanooga, Tennessee, 394
Chávez, César, 772
Chavez Ravine (Los Angeles) urban renewal, 740
Cheek, Joel, 490
Chemicals industry, 632
Cheney, Dick, vice president, 840
Chernenko, Constantin, Soviet Union general secretary, 804
Cherokee Indians, 62, 146, 158–159, 394
  denied rights in Georgia, 249
  forced removal of, 252
Cherokee Nation v. *Georgia* (1831), 251
Cherokee War, 114
Cherry Valley, New York, 150
Chesapeake, U.S. frigate, 223
Chesapeake area, British threat, 175
Chesapeake Bay settlement, Jamestown, 34
Chesapeake campaign in War of 1812, 230
Chesapeake colonies, 69
Chesapeake incident (1807), 223
Chesapeake planters use of convicts, 75

Chester, Reverend John, 307
Chevalier, Michel, French traveler, 296
Cheyenne, Wyoming, 510
Cheyenne Indians, 334, 500, 502, 503
  railroad construction, 499
Cheyenne Mountain, 807
Chi-ang Kai-shek (Jiang Jieshi), 687, 726, 745
Chicago, Illinois, 622, 658
  black migration, 613
  black protection associations, 357
  Democratic Convention (1968), 775
  early 19th century, 296
  immigrant population, 550
  landlords, 717
  Marshall Field retail, 491
  mentioned, 454
  occupations for blacks, 486
  violence in strikes, 479
  in War of 1812, 229
Chicago American, 597
Chicago Daily News, 688
Chicago Defender newspaper, 486, 487, 622
Chicago Vice Commission, 474
Chicanos (see Mexican Americans)
Chickamauga Creek, 394
Chickasaw Indians, 249, 332
Child, Lydia Maria, 316, 318–319
Childbearing, 767
Child care, 529
Child care tax credit, 813
Child labor
  in early 20th century, 550
  exploited, 304–305
  in late 19th century, 473–474
  as mill workers, 300
  Mother Jones' efforts, 560–561
  in New England, 44, 76
  reform, 451–452, 557
  regulations struck down, 636
  in Southern textile mills, 443
  Supreme Court laws, 637
  Wilson non-support, 574
Children
  aid for dependent mothers and children, 669
  baby boom, 718
  early 19th century, 304
  in Great Depression, 660
  poverty in late 20th century, 800
  protective legislation, 557–559
  during WWII, 697
Chile, 587–588, 784
China
  civil war, 726–727
  easing of tensions, 777–778
  in Korean War, 728, 746
  open door, 593–594
  trade opportunities, 584–585
  war with Japan, 687, 692
Chinatowns, 482, 483, 509
Chinese
  immigrants, 482, 483–484, 485, 808
  miners, 508
  railroad workers, 499
Chinese Communists, 727–728
Chinese Consolidated Benevolent Association, 483
Chinese Exclusion Act (1882), 485
Chinook Indians, 7, 499
Chippewa Indians, 335
Chips, dried dung, 515
Chisholm Trail, 510
Chivington, John, 502
Choctaw Indians, 100, 249, 332
Cholera, 273, 296, 337, 501
Chopin, Kate, novelist, 474
Christian activism, 291
Christian Coalition, 370
Christian conservatives, 794
Christian Herald, 306
Christian Intelligencer, Universalist, 310
Christianity
  adopted by slaves, 73
  in business, 633
  converting Indians, 62–64

Christianity *(cont.)*
  in Europe c. 1500, 17
  failure to convert Indians, 337
  Fundamentalism, 645–646
  in Pueblo Revolt, 65–67
  Second Great Awakening, 244–245
  slave converts, 275
  and social reform, 552
  subverted by slavery, 358
  theological differences, 815
  vs. Native American religion, 12
Christianity and the Social Crisis
    (Rauschenbusch), 552
Christian palefaces, 504
Christian reformers, 306
Christian right, 823
Christians
  anarchists, 317
  ending of human bondage, 256
  owning slaves, 68
Chronology
  40,000 B.C. to 1598 A.D. early
    history, 10
  1440–1775 creating new worlds, 59
  1603–1681 establishing colonies, 36
  1651–1760 colonial development, 86
  1759–1774 British imperialism, 115
  1775–1783 Revolutionary War, 140
  1776–1788 first Republic, 172
  1789–1800 new republic, 201
  1790–1848 market revolution &
    social reform, 294
  1790–1857 slavery and Old
    South, 269
  1801–1825 Jeffersonian
    Republicanism, 222
  1803–1851 westward expansion, 331
  1826–1845 Jacksonian era, 247
  1846–1861 politics of
    Sectionalism, 356
  1858–1893 American West, 500
  1861–1865 Civil War, 382
  1861–1922 empire creation, 588
  1863–1877 Reconstruction, 421
  1867–1900 politics and
    government, 529
  1869–1898 Gilded Age, 469
  1872–1907 New South, 442
  1893–1920 Progressive Era, 552
  1914–1921 The Great War, 608
  1915–1929 modern America, 631
  1929–1938 Great Depression, 662
  1931–1945 World War II, 690
  1944–1952 Cold War, 718
  1953–1965 confident years, 743
  1962–1980 Vietnam War, 765
  1973–1992 Reagan years, 795
Chrysler Corporation, 634, 673
Churches, *See also specific church names*
  in 1920s, 639
  African-American, 282
  associations, 662
  changes in late 20th century,
    814–815
  and Farmers Alliance, 447–448
  fundamentalist, 742
  immigrant institutions, 482
  in postwar South, 418, 420
  social reform, 551–552
Churchgoing as antidote for
    Communism, 742
Churchill, Winston, British Prime
    Minister, 691, 702, 707, 722
Church membership in Second Great
    Awakening, 245
Church of England, 25, 40, 50, 91, *See
    also* Anglican Church
Church of God, 448
Church of Jesus Christ of Latter-day
    Saints, 310, 343
Church of Nazarene, 815
Cigarettes, 440, 443, 461, 471, 472,
    631, 642
Cincinnati, Ohio, 296, 317, 357,
    454, 525
Cincinnatus, Roman soldier, 156
Cirrus Logic in Austin, Texas, 831

Cisneros, Henry, mayor of San
    Antonio, Texas, 836
Cities
  in 1920s, 637–640
  black residents in South, 458
  in colonies, 87–88
  in early 19th century, 295–297
  and free blacks, 282
  freedmen migration to, 420
  in Gilded Age, 487–492
    centers and suburbs, 489–490
    middle class, 490–492
  minimal in Lower South, 268–269
  in New South late 19th century,
    439–441, 443–446
  poverty amid prosperity, 798–799
  Southern, 281
  under stress, 769–773
  in Upper South, 277
Citizen involvement in public
    affairs, 677
City commission, 565
City government, 662–664
City managers, 565
City transportation, 296
Civic Church, 555
Civilian Conservation Corps (CCC),
    666, 673, 674
Civilian workers in WWII, 698–699
Civilized peoples, 504
Civil liberties
  Jefferson support of, 219
  and Patriot Act, 842
  Red Scare assault, 730–733
  upheld by Lincoln, 397
  of whites, 320
Civil rights
  in 1830s, 316
  affirmative action, 837–838
  Compromise of 1877, 430
  of former slaves, 422–425
  for German Jews, 687
  lawyers, 752
  legislation, 674
  legislation to reverse legacy of
    slavery, 70
  Mississippi black codes, 423
  organizations, 674
  protection to gays and lesbians, 646
Civil Rights Act (1866), 423–424
Civil Rights Act (1875), 430
Civil Rights Act (1964), 755, 767,
    811, 812
Civil Rights Cases (1883), 433
Civil Rights movement
  after WWII, 717–718
  backed by white business, 284
  Black Power, 771
  Jackson experience, 810
  under Lyndon Johnson, 755–757
  school desegregation, 738–739
  struggle, 752–757
Civil Service Commission, 533
Civil service reform, 248, 429, 528,
    529, 532–533, 544
Civil War, 379–413, *See also* Battles of
    Civil War; Reconstruction
  Antietam, 390
  battles, early, 385–388
  battles, major, 408
  Confederacy collapses, 400–401
  effect on democratic governments
    around world, 384
  effect on Southern economy, 442
  Emancipation, 390–392
  foreign diplomacy, 389–390
  Gettysburg, 393–394, 396
  human toll, 386–388
  mobilization for war, 381–385
  naval blockade, 389
  North transformed, 397–399
  Second war, 440
  Sherman's march, 406
  war in East, 385–388, 390, 393–394,
    396, 401–407
  war in West, 385–387, 393–395
  and women office workers, 814

Civil war in England in 1642, 39
Civil Works Administration (CWA),
    666, 673
Claim clubs, 330
Clansman, The (Dixon), 456
Clark, George Rogers, 150
Clark, Mark, general, 728
Clark, William, 221, 335
Clark Memorandum, 648
Class divisions in colonies, 89
Classes in society, inequalities, 301–305
Class hierarchy, 484
Clay, Henry
  American Colonization Society, 315
  American System, 237, 248, 260
  Bank war, 253–254
  compromise of 1850, 355–356
  corrupt bargain, 246
  creation of national bank, 231
  in election of 1824, 237
  in election of 1844, 261
  of Kentucky, 226
  passed over as candidate, 258
  program of economic nationalism,
    259–260
  as Speaker of the House, 235
  Whig Party founder, 256
Clayton antitrust bill, 574
Clear-cutting trees, 443
Cleaver, Eldridge, 771–772
Clemenceau, Georges, of France,
    619, 620
Clerical office work, 474
Clermont steamboat, 292
Cleveland, Grover, U.S. president
  actions in 1893 depression, 539,
    541–542
  annexation of Hawaiian Islands, 345,
    584, 587
  boundary dispute over British
    Guiana, 587–588
  broke Pullman union, 567
  conservative president, 530, 543
  Pullman strike, 480
  tariff reduction, 533–534
Cleveland, Ohio, 296, 357, 454, 487
Clifford, Clark, secretary of Defense,
    720, 774
Clinton, Hillary Rodham, 825,
    827, 835
Clinton, Sir Henry, British
    commander in chief, 145,
    150, 152
Clinton, William, U.S. president
  appointments, 834
  in election of 1992, 370, 823
  end of big government, 671
  foreign policy, 345
  impeachment of, 646
  legacy of slavery, 70
  political center shift, 793
  prosperity of country, 839, 840
  reelection in 1996, 826
  trade agreement, 833
Clocks with interchangeable
    parts, 301
Closed shop, 716
Cloth factories, 299
Clothing for slaves, 273
Clothing industry. *See* Garment
    industry; Sweatshops
CNN Cable News Network, 806, 832
Coahuila, 339
Coalfields of western
    Pennsylvania, 296
Coal industry, 635, 659
Coalminer strikes, 567–568, 623, 716
Coal mines and child labor, 473, 550
Cobain, Kurt, singer, 769
Cobb, Howell, Confederate
    general, 406
Cobb, Thomas R. R., of Georgia, 273
Coca-Cola, 440, 451
Cockroaches in Columbian exchange,
    23–24
Code analysts, 697
Code-talkers, 696

Cod fishing off Grand Banks, 27
Coercive Acts, 124–125
Coeur d' Alene, Idaho, 510
Coffee rationed, 695
Coffin, Judith of Massachusetts, 97
Cohen, Maurice, 548
Coinage, 535
Cold Harbor, 402
Cold War, 712–735
  Civil Rights influences, 738–739
  Communist threat, 726–729
  economic boom in post-war years,
    715–719
  and Eisenhower, 744–748
  freeway construction, 740
  and Kennedy, 748–752
  and moon landings, 762
  national debt, 206
  nuclear arms race, 725–727
  and nuclear weapons, 709
  Red Scare, 730–733
  Second one, 802–806
  Soviet Union, confronting, 721–725
  Truman and Fair Deal, 719–721
Cold Warriors, 765, 784
Colfax, Louisiana, 428
Colfax Massacre, 432
Collective bargaining, 479, 622, 634,
    659, 667, 669, 673, 797
Collective liberty of New
    Englanders, 198
College degrees, 716, 742
College enrollment, 766
College of New Jersey (Princeton
    University), 92
College of Philadelphia, 87
College of Rhode Island (Brown
    University), 92
Colleges, *See also* Universities
  agricultural, 561
  campuses during Filipino-American
    War, 593
  coeducational, 475
  Land Grant College Act (1862),
    397–398
College students, 765
Collier, John, commissioner of Indian
    Affairs, 674
Colombia, 585, 597, 599
Colonial governors, 96–97
Colonialism
  of Cuba, 580–581, 590
  at Paris peace conference, 620
  of Philippines, 593
Colonial Wars, 100–104
Colonies in Great War peace
    terms, 621
Colonies in New World, *See also* British
    American colonies
  becoming more like England, 87
  cultural transformation, 88–90
  early English, 25–26
  early French, 24–25
  English in 17th century, 49
  Spanish, 20–23
Colonization
  of black Americans to Africa,
    315–326
  ended with Monroe Doctrine, 233
Colorado
  mentioned, 510, 511
  nuclear weapons testing, 726
  petroleum substitute, 783
  population growth in 1990s, 834
  Populist election, 538
  protested forest reserves, 568
  women suffrage, 529
Colorado Fuel and Iron Company,
    556
Colorado River, 338, 340
Colorado Springs, Colorado, 807
Colored Farmers Alliance, 448, 537
Colored Masons, 458
Colored Methodist Episcopal
    Church, 420
Colored Monitor Union, 426
Colored Odd Fellows, 458

Colored Orphan Asylum, 398
Colored schools, 418
Columbia, South Carolina, 406, 452, 460
Columbian exchange, 23–24
Columbia River, 236, 336
Columbia River Plateau, 7
Columbia University, 478, 484, 730, 739, 774–775
Columbine High School, 826
Columbus, Christopher, 6, 19
Columbus, Ohio, 551
Comanche Indians, 339, 342, 347, 500, 501, 503
Comecon, Soviet aid, 723
Comic strips, 491
Coming out, 813–814
Commerce, *See also* Business; Trade
  in large cities, early 19th century, 295–297
Commerce Department, 636
Commercial broadcasting, 634
Commercial Club, 565
Commercial growers, 667
Commercials, 641, *See also* Advertisers
Commercial treaty, U.S. and France, 150
Commission on Status of Women, 767
Committee for a Sane Nuclear Policy, 751
Committee for Industrial Organization (CIO), 672
Committee of Safety, 135, 136
Committee on American Interests in China, 594
Committee on Civil Rights, 717–718
Committee on Public Information (CPI), 614
Committees of correspondence, 124
Committee to Defend America by Aiding the Allies, 691
Committee to Re-Elect the President, 780
Commodity prices, 659
Common lands, 514
Common law, 171
Common man, 246, 259, 719
Common Sense, 140, 165
Common Sense (Paine), 345
Commonwealth, 142
Commonwealth v. *Hunt*, 305
Communal property of Native Americans, 500
Communes in 1960s and 1970s, 769
Communism
  contained in Cold War, 727, 745–746, 749
  in Greece, 723
  military threat, 727–729
  primitive in immigrant neighborhoods, 660
  Shaker communities, 313
Communist Khmer Rouge, 793
Communist parties in Europe and Japan, 722
Communist Party, 805
  after WWII, 730
  during Great Depression, 661
  helped Progressive Party, 719
  and Red Scare, 732
Communist regimes, 793
Communists, 617
Communitarianism of Mormons, 343
Communitarian living, 313–314
Community Action Agencies, 755
Community life
  blacks in South late 19th century, 458–459
  of slaves, 72–74
Commuter railroads, 296
Commuter travel, 489
Company unions, 634
Competency, 44, 299
Compromise of 1850, 355–359
Compromise of 1877, 430
Compromise Tariff (1833), 253
Compulsory insurance program, 669

Compulsory school attendance, 554, 559
Computer industry, 829–832
Comstock Lode in Nevada, 506
Concentration camps, 680, 687–688
Conciliatory Proposition from Parliament, 136
Concord, Battle of, 136–137
Concord, Massachusetts, 314
Concord North Bridge, 136
Conestogas, 114
Coney Island in Brooklyn, New York, 492
Confederate Army of Tennessee, 401–404
Confederate States of America, 371, *See also* Civil War
  after Civil War, 417
  battle flag, 460
  capital at Richmond, Virginia, 385
  collapse of, 400–401
  defensive strategy, 388
  objectives of war, 381, 384–385
  preserving memories, 451, 460
  resources during Civil War, 383–384
  strategy, 384–386, 388–389
Confederation Congress, 174–175
  Revolutionary War effects on, 172
  Superintendent of finance, 175
Conference on Negro Problems, 458
Confidence shaken, 760–789
  cities under stress, 769–773
  environmental pollution, 779–781
  hostage crisis, 785
  oil embargo, 778–779
  recession, 782, 783
  social activism, 765–769
  Vietnam War, 763–767, 773–774, 776, 788–789
  Watergate, 779–782
  year of gun 1968, 773–775
Confident years, 736–759
  Civil Rights, 752–757
  decade of affluence, 739–744
  Eisenhower and Cold War, 744–748
  Johnson, Lyndon, 754–757
  Kennedy and Cold War, 748–752
Confiscated property, 182
Confiscation Act, 390–391
Conflict-of-interest laws, 429
Conflicts in colonies, *See also* Indian wars
  after first hundred years, 64–67
  Bacon's Rebellion, 64, 69
  Beaver Wars, 60–61, 64, 67
  Boston Massacre, 122–123
  Cherokee War, 114
  European wars in America, 100–104
  French and Indian War, 102–104, 111–112
  Pontiac's Rebellion, 114
  Stono Rebellion, 74–75
Conformity of mass culture, 642
Congregational Churches, 90–91, 173, 197
Congregationalists, 229, 551–552
Congress, U.S.
  in 19th century
    Constitutional authority of, 232
    gag rule on antislavery petitions, 317
    Hispanic land grants, 514
    inefficient in late 19th century, 531
    nullification crisis, 253
    proviso debate, 354–356
  in 20th century
    80th, 719–720
    opposed New Deal reforms, 678
    and Theodore Roosevelt, 567
  after Revolutionary War
    checks and balances, 187
    control of American West, 179
    financial reports from Hamilton, 203–204
    upgrade of Navy and Army, 211
  during Revolutionary War
    commissioned privateers, 151

  fled to Baltimore, 147
  fled to York, Pennsylvania, 149
  Peace of Paris instructions, 156
  power to levy taxes, 145
  veterans' payments, 144–145
Congressional Reconstruction, 425–426
Congressional representatives to Confederation Congress, 174
Congress of Industrial Organizations (CIO), 672, 740
Congress of Racial Equality (CORE), 754
Connally, John, governor of Texas, 754
Connecticut, 96, 189, 197, 243
  women in majority, 197
Connecticut River Valley, 42
Connor, Bull, public safety commissioner, 754
Conquistadores, 20
Conscience Whigs, 354
Conscientious objector status in Vietnam War, 766
Conscription, 383, 398, 617, *See also* Draft
Conservation, 675
Conservationists, 568, 570
Conservation of natural resources, 568
Conservative Christians, 810
Conservative manifesto, 678
Conservatives
  Carter dissatisfaction, 794
  challenged by women, 834–835
  coalition blocked FDR's reforms, 677
  Constitutional support, 189
  crisis after Revolutionary War, 179
  critics of unemployment relief, 668
  critics of Yalta Conference, 707
  and Eisenhower, 739
  in election of 1936, 670
  ideas for Reagan, 795–796
  international agreements, 840–841
  in Kennedy administration, 755
  New Deal setbacks, 702
  opposed organized labor, 716
  opposed women reformers, 637
  social issues, 815–817
  writing state constitutions, 173
Conservative values of nativists, 562
Conspiracy in Continental Army, 144–145
Conspiracy theories, 755
Constantinople, 18
Constitution, U.S.
  adoption, 184
  citizenship guarantee violated, 235
  national bank bill, 204–205
  overview, 186–188
  separation of powers, 782
  support of National good, 222
Constitutional Amendments
  Bill of Rights, 202
  1st Amendment, religious & political freedom, 731
  2nd Amendment, right to bear arms, 826–827
  5th Amendment, rights of accused persons, 636, 731
  12th Amendment, election of executives, 213
  13th Amendment, slavery abolished, 405, 424
  14th Amendment, civil rights, 424, 430, 432, 454, 812
  15th Amendment, right to vote, 425, 428, 430, 432, 455
  16th Amendment, income tax, 571, 573
  17th Amendment, senatorial elections, 566
  18th Amendment, prohibition, 562, 613, 644
  19th Amendment, woman suffrage, 564, 613

Constitutional conflict between colonies & Britain, 117
Constitutional Convention, 184–186
Constitutional conventions in states, 243, 364
Constitutional limits of federal authority, 397
Constitutional Union party, 368–369
Construction industry, 632, 716–717
Constructionist views, 205
Construction projects of WPA, 670, 674, 675
Consumer boom, 718–719
Consumer credit, 635
Consumer debt, 741
Consumer goods, 303, 640, 695
Consumerism, 490, 640, 741–742, 744
Consumer prices, 740
Consumer prices, 740
Consumer society in 1920s, 640
Consumer spending, 715–716
Containment of Communism, 727, 745–746, 749
Continental Army
  casualty rate, 157
  disbanded, 156
  formation of, 137
  professional soldiers, 142–145
  troop needs, 135
  winter at Valley Forge, 149
Continental Association, 127, 135
Continental Congress, 137, 158, 169
Continental Dollars, 144, 160, 175, 182
Contrabands, 391
Contraception, 767, 812
Contraceptives, 559–560
Contract theory of government, 141
Contractual property rights, 232
Contract with America, 825
Contras, 803
Convention on Biological Warfare, 841
Conventions, black response to Fugitive Slave Act, 357
Conversion, religious, in colonies, 92
Convoys of merchant ships, 693
Conway, Massachusetts, 177
Coolidge, Calvin, U.S. president, 623, 624, 636–637, 643
Cooling-off period in strikes, 716
Cooper, Anna J., 438–439, 459
Cooper, Anthony Ashley, 48
Cooper, Gary, actor, 731
Cooperative living, 769
Copperheads, 397
Coral Sea, Battle of the, 693
Cordon sanitaire, 620
Corinth, Mississippi, 385–386
Corliss steam engine, 467
Corn, 267, 330, 333
Cornwallis, Lord, 152, 155
Coronado, Francisco Vásquez de, 22
Corporate downsizing, 799
Corporate farms in American West, 568
Corporate mergers in 1920s, 634
Corporate mismanagement, 840, 845
Corporate raiders, 797–798
Corporate Regulation, 568–567
Corporations
  and federal regulations, 534
  in late 19th century, 470–471
  mining industry, 509–510
  open-range ranching, 511–512
  research and development, 469
Corregidor in Manila Bay, 693
Corruption, 636
Cortés, Hernán, 4, 20
Cosmetics, 640
Cosmopolitan, 553
Cost of production, 540
Cotton
  in 1920s, 635
  in Archaic period, 6
  brokerages, 537
  exports, 383, 389
  exports required by expansion of economy, 583
  farming crises in late 19th century, 446

Cotton (cont.)
first permanent factory, 299
mills, textile, 297
mills and child labor, 550
in Old Southwest, 332–333
prices, 234–235, 254, 284, 332, 399, 446, 449
production, 267–268, 340, 441, 675
Subtreasury plan, 448
Cotton gin, 267, 300–301, 332
Coughlin, Father Charles, 668, 669
Council Bluffs, Iowa, 337
Council of Economic Advisers, 715
Council of National Defense, 611, 621
Council of the Indies, 20
Councils of defense, 615, 842
Counterculture, 768
Counter-Reconstruction, 427–429
Counter Reformation, 33
Counting coup, 334
Country club, 491
Country Club Plaza, first shopping center, 640
Country ideology, 101, 117–118, 142
Country Life, rural reforms, 560–561
Country Life Commission (1908), 560
Country music, 641
County agent system, 560–561
Coups
in Czechoslovakia, 724
in Iran, 746
in Vietnam, 750
Coureurs de bois fur traders, 34, 99
Court costs, 120
Courtesy books, 89
Courts, Vice-admiralty, 94
Court System established, 202–203
Covenant, 42
Covert operations, 724, See also
Central Intelligence Agency (CIA)
Cowboy independence, 512
Cowhands, 512
Cowpens, Battle of, 155
Cow towns, 510–511
Cox, Archibald, 782
Cox, George, Republican Party boss, 527
Cox, James, 625
Coxey, Jacob, Populist businessman, 539
Coxey's Army of unemployed, 539–540
Craft, Ellen, 276–277
Crafts, Hannah, 266
Craftsmen, 298–299
Craftwork, 87
Crawford, Medorum, 337
Crawford, William, secretary of Treasury, 237
Crazy Horse, Sioux leader, 503
Creationism, 646
Credit
from British merchants, 86–87
economic crisis after Revolutionary War, 176–177
farmers protest, 537
funding wars, 100
in New South late 19th century, 446
to Western farmers, 516–517
and Wilson's reforms, 573
Credit-based consumerism, 741
Credit cards (Visa, MasterCard), 741
Credit contraction, 254–255
Creditor nation from Great War, 647
Creditors
and money supply, 535
in new nation, 203
rights in Constitution, 186
Credit system, 669
Credit system of nation, 254
Cree Indians, 7
Creek Indians, 183, 230, 249
Creel, George, 614, 615
Creole slaves, 72
Crèvecoeur, J. Hector St. John, 170
Crime, 644–645, 826–827

Crime of 1873, 536
Criminal justice system, 450
Criminals used as slaves, 75
Criollos population group in Southwest, 338
Crisis, The, magazine, 564
Crisis atmosphere of 1786, 188
Crisis of confidence after Revolutionary War, 184
Crispus Attucks, Boston Massacre casualty, 123
Crittenden, John J., Kentucky senator, 371, 372
Crittenden Plan, 371
Croatoan Indians, 26
Croker, Richard, Democrat Party boss, 527
Cromwell, Oliver, 39
Crop controls, 677
Crop lien laws, 432
Crop rotation, 270
Crops, Native American before 1492, 6–11
Cross-border economy, 809
Cross-town busing, 811
Crow Indians, 334, 338
CSX Corporation, 70
Cuba
attempt to win as slave state, 360
Britain returned to Spain, 104, 112
coup supported by FDR, 678
future acquisitions, 233
invasion, 749, 750–751
and Latin America policy, 648
mentioned, 11, 584
military occupation, 580–581
Spanish-American War, 588–592
Spanish conquest, 20
as U.S. protectorate, 596–597, 599
Cuban missile crisis, 750–751
Cuban refugee immigrants, 808
Cuban Revolution, 588–589
Cuban soldiers, 803
Cult of domesticity, 304, 308
Cults in 1960s and 1970s, 769
Cultural differences between whites & Indians, 11–12, 500–501
Cultural expansionism, 581
Cultural traditions of immigrants, 482–483
Culture, colonial transformation, 88–90
Culture areas, 7
Culture wars, 815–817
Cumming, Kate, Confederate nurse, 386
Curaçao, 45
Currency, See also Continental Dollars; Money; Paper money
crisis after Revolutionary War, 178
"In God We Trust," 742
legal tender issued by colonial legislatures, 115–116
money question in late 19th century, 535
national, Populist demand, 538
from National Bank, 204
National Banking Act (1863), 398
reform, 447
reform by Wilson, 573
reform in New Deal, 669
state issued, 144
Currency Act (1764), 115–116, 120
Currency Act (1900), 543
Curtis, Edward S., 520, 521
Custer, George A., colonel, 502–503
Customs collectors, 116
Customs duties, nullification crisis, 251
Customs houses in Nicaragua, 598
Customs union, 585
Cuyahoga River in Cleveland, Ohio, 779
Cuzco, Inca capital, 20
Czech Communist party, 774
Czechoslovakia, 620, 679, 723, 724, 804
Czech Republic, 824

D

Dahomey Africans, 14
Daily Forward newspaper, 483
Dairy commission in Minnesota, 532
Dakotas, 511, 513
Daley, Richard, mayor of Chicago, 775
Dallas, Texas, 441, 488, 640, 754–755
Dallas County, Alabama, 756
Dalton, Georgia, 403
Dams, 675, 676
Dance, 275
Dance halls, 508
Danish West Indies, 584, 585
Dan River, 155
Dare, Virginia, 26
Darrow, Clarence, lawyer, 645
Dartmouth, tea ship, 124
Dartmouth College v. Woodward (1819), 232
Darwin's theory of evolution, 645–646
Daugherty, Harry, Attorney General, 636
Daughters of American Revolution, 562
Davenport, John, Puritan reverend, 43
Davis, Jefferson, Confederate president
Civil War actions, 404
end of war, 406–407
failure to create Confederate nationalism, 384, 400
as Mississippi senator, 354
sworn in, 371
taking Fort Sumter, 373
Davis, John W., Wall Street lawyer, 637
Dawes Act (1887), 506
Day, Thomas, North Carolina cabinet-maker, 282
Day-care centers/programs, 459, 563, 698
Dayton, Tennessee, 645
D-Day (June 6, 1944), 703
Dean, John, White House staffer, 780, 781, 782
Deaths in mines, 509
Debs, Eugene, socialist
in election of 1912, 573
in election of 1920, 625
imprisoned during Great War, 615, 842
pardoned from prison, 636
Pullman strike, 480
Socialism in Progressive Era, 555–556
Debts
abolition of imprisonment, 305
between citizens of Britain and U.S., 156
crisis after Revolutionary War, 176–177, 178
personal, 640
role in Great Depression, 659
unpaid, peace treaty violations, 182
Debt-stay laws, 426–427, 446–449
Decentralization, 811
Declaration of Independence, 139–141, 592
Declaration of London, 607
Declaration of Rights and Grievances, 119
Declaration of Sentiments, 319
Declaration of war against Japanese, 692
Declaratory Act, 119
Deep South resistance to Civil Rights, 752–754
Deere, John, 330
Defense contractors, 807, 808
Defense factories, 695
Defense of slavery, 282–284
Defense spending, 220, 695, 715, 724, 727, 745, 770, 784, 805, 807–808
Deficit spending, national debt, 206
Deindustrialization, 799
Deism, religious philosophy, 213

Delaware
election of 1864, 405
founding of colony, 50
mentioned, 752
ratification of Constitution, 189
slave population in 1860, 272
stayed in Union, 384
Upper South in 1850, 270
Delaware Indians, 50, 101, 103, 104
Delaware Prophet, 114
DeLay, Tom, of Texas, 646
Delegates to Confederation Congress, 174
"Deliberate speed," 752
Delta country, 332
DeMille, Cecil B., 641
Demobilization after WWII, 715–719
Democracy, 611, 804, 833–838
Democratic Convention in Chicago (1968), 775
Democratic National Committee, 780
Democratic National Convention of 1948, 720
Democratic Party
in 20th century, first half
in election of 1928, 648
election of 1932, 663
election of 1948, 719–721
Great War, 609–610
on Hawaiian annexation, 587
imperialist debate, 592, 596
opposed New Deal reforms, 677–678
and Progressive reform, 572–574
Treaty of Versailles, 619–621
Women's Division, 673
in 20th century, second half
in 1968 primaries, 774–775
during Clinton years, 825–826
conservative tone, 806
gender gap, 835
impeachment of Nixon, 782
during Reagan years, 795
social and economic policy, 810
in Vietnam War, 766
voting reform, 756
in Civil War years
counter-reconstruction, 427–431
in election of 1852, 359
in election of 1860, 365, 368
executive sanctions during Civil War, 397
federal reconstruction, 422, 424
issue of slavery, 354
politics of 1854–1858, 361–365
in late 19th century
congressional election of 1884, 524–525
disfranchisement of blacks, 455–456
election of 1896 and gold standard, 541–543
gold standard, 542–543
partisan politics, 524–525
protective traiff, 533–534
Redeemers in New South, 446–447
Southern agrarian revolt, 449–450
Southern opposition to Populists, 539
Southern politics, 439
pre-Civil War years
composition of, 258
formation of, 246–247
gag rule on antislavery petitions, 317
Manifest Destiny, 343–344
nullification crisis, 251, 253
role in Panic of 1837, 255
support in Old South, 280
vs. Whigs in early 1840s, 256–261
Democratic reform, 244
Democratic-Republican societies, 207–208
Democratic republic evolution, 237
Demon Rum, 646
Demonstrating, 549
Denmark, 150, 688

Denunciation of partisanship by G. Washington, 210
Denver, Colorado, 488, 506, 540, 638
Denver school district, 773
Department of Educational Propaganda and Patriotic Education, 614
Department stores, 491
Deportation of Mexicans, 661
Depressions, *See also Panic of . . .; Recessions*
  of 1819, 231
  of 1839–1843, 320
  in 1840s, 255
  in 1870s, 443
  in 1873 and 1893, 478
  in 1890s, 449, 539–543
  of 1890s, 585
  in 1920 and 1921, 632
  agricultural, early 1800s, 225
  economic crisis after Revolutionary War, 176–177
Deregulation, 796, 840
Desegregation, 454, 752, 778, *See also Segregation*
Deserters during Civil War, 398
Desertion of husbands in Great Depression, 660
Deskilling, 455, 478
Des Moines, Iowa, 565
Destroyer deal (1940), 691, 693
Destroyers. *See* U.S. naval warships
Détente, 778, 782, 784, 802
Detroit, Michigan
  Belle Isle Park, 699
  black districts, 486
  black migration, 613
  British post in Revolutionary War, 150
  early 19th century, 296
  race riots in 1967, 771
  in War of 1812, 229
Detroit Unemployment Council, 661
Dew, Thomas R., 283
Dewey, George, Navy commodore, 590
Dewey, John, philosopher, 559
Dewey, Thomas, governor of New York, 702, 720
DeWitt, John, general, 700
Dewson, Molly, 673
Diaries
  of Southern Civil War soldiers, 400
  women's, on Oregon Trail, 337
Dias, Bartolomeu, 18
Diaz, Porfirio, Mexican dictator, 599
Dickens, Charles, 313
Dickinson, John, 121
Dictators in Latin America, 678
Diem, Ngo Dinh, 746, 749–750
Diet of slaves, 273
Diggs, Annie, 537
Dime novels, 520
Dinwiddie, Emily, 482
Diplomacy weakness in 1780s, 181
Diplomatic nationalism, 231–232
Diplomatic War in Civil War, 389–390
Direct primaries in Wisconsin, 566
Direct Tax of 1798, 211, 212, 213
Dirty tricks, 779
Disarmament of nuclear weapons, 751–752
Discourse of Western Planting, 26
Discrimination, *See also See also Racial discrimination; Racial segregation; Racism*
  based on gender, 767, 812
  against Black troops, 392
  during Great Depression, 658
  during WWII, 696
Diseases, *See also specific types of diseases*
  among Slaves, 273
  during Civil War, 386
  in Columbian exchange, 23
  in crowded cities, 476
  epidemics of European, 99
  in Europe after WWII, 723
  in Great Plains, 335

HIV/AIDS, 813
  in Jamestown, 35
  killer on Oregon Trail, 337
  in Native Americans, 505
  in New York tenements, 477
  and Plains Indians, 501
  reduced Indian population, 60
  role in Aztec collapse, 20–21
Disfranchisement of black voters, 454, 455–456, 457, 563, 565
Disloyalty during Great War, 614
Disneyland, 741
Dissent suppressed in Great War, 614–616, 623
District of Columbia. *See* Washington, D.C.
Diversification, 446, 675
Diversity, 842
Divorce
  during Great Depression, 660
  laws, 198, 642
  rates, 642, 817
Dixiecrats (States' Rights Democrats), 719
Dixon, Thomas, 456
Djenné, 15
Doctor Zhivago movie, 792
Doctrine of nullification, 212
Dodge City, Kansas, 510
Dodger Stadium, 740
Dole, Robert, 826
Dollar diplomacy, 598
Domestic poor, 770
Domination of land by Europeans, 12
Dominican Republic, 222, 585, 598, 599, 648, 808
Dominion of New England, 93–94
Donahue, Phil, 781
Donothing 80th Congress, 719, 720
"Don't Tread on Me," 150, 164
Doolittle, Amos, engraver, 136
Doors, The, rock band, 769
Double standard for women, 309, 642, 812
Douglas, Stephen A., Illinois senator
  Compromise of 1850, 356
  in election of 1860, 368
  Lecompton Constitution, 364
  railroad proposal, 360–361
  support of Union, 382
Douglass, Frederick, black abolitionist
  on black troops' lower pay, 392
  called for political war against slavery, 320
  National Black Convention, 357–358
  race relations, 431
  warning to John Brown, 367
Downtown, 489
Draft, 383, 604, 617, 690, 724, 766, 776, *See also* Conscription
Draft resisters
  during Civil War, 398
  clemency, 782
  in Vietnam War, 766
Drago Doctrine, 598
Drake, Francis, 25
Drama clubs, 420
Drayton, William Henry, 122–123
Dreamland, 492
Dream songs, 338
Dred Scott Case, 363–364, 423
Dreiser, Theodore, novelist, 474, 487
Dresden, Germany, 705
Drive-in restaurants, 640
Droughts in mid-1880s, 511
Drug addiction, 562–563
Drug culture, 768
Drugs, 770
Drumbeats in slave religion, 275
Dry farming, 516
Dubček, Alexander, 774
Du Bois, W.E.B., 431, 458, 461, 563–564, 622, 674
Dudley, Thomas and Dorothy, 32–33
Dukakis, Michael, 800
Duke, James B., 440, 443, 471
Duke University, 443

Dulles, John Foster, secretary of State, 745
Dummer, William, 95
Dunning, William A., 456
Dunwich, England, 96
Du Pont Company, 469, 632
Durant, Dr., 498
Durham, North Carolina, 407, 440, 443, 458
Dust Bowl in Great Plains, 658, 669
Dust storms on Great Plains, 667
Dutch colonies in Caribbean, 45
Dutch East India Company, 51–52
Dutch East Indies, 692
Dutch fur trade, 60–61
Dutch Reformed Church, 92, 173
Dutch Republic, 51–52
Duties on imports, 121
Dyes, 632
Dylan, Bob, 768–769
Dysentery among slaves, 273

E
"Eagle has landed," 762
Earl, Ralph, painter, 136
Early, Jubal, Confederate general, 402
Earned Income Tax Credit, 825
Earth Day, 779
East Asia, 591, 592–595
Eastern and European capital in cattle industry, 511
Eastern Front, Europe, Great War, 617, 620
Eastern Front, Europe, WWII, 692, 702, 703, 705
Eastern Mediterranean, 723
Eastern State Penitentiary in Philadelphia, 313
Eastern Woodlands, 10–11
East Germany, 746, 749, 804
East India Company, 111
East Los Angeles, California, 639
Eastman Kodak, 634
East ("Spanish") Harlem, 639
East St Louis, Illinois, 613
East Timor, 51
Eastwood, Clint, 794
Eccles, Marriner, of Federal Reserve Board, 677
Ecology of Great Plains, 337
Economic boom, 829
Economic development
  in the British Colonies, 83–88
  of cities by Eisenhower administration, 740–741
  for Latin America, 751
  loans to foreign governments, 722
Economic expansion, 583–585
Economic imperialism in Vietnam War, 766
Economic independence of women, 558
Economic interests
  in China, 594
  in Cuba, 589
Economic legacy of slavery, 284
Economic nationalism, 231–232
Economic power in Caribbean, 598
Economic Recovery and Tax Act (ERTA) (1981), 796
Economic sanctions in Madison administration, 224–225
Economy
  of 1920s, 632–635
  after WWII, 715–716
  of British colonies, 84–88
  collapse of 1893, 539
  crisis of 1830s, 270–272
  current, 828–833, 839–840
  driven by automobile industry, 632
  of the Mid-Atlantic region economic crisis after Revolutionary War, 177
  mobilized for WWII, 695–696
  of Native Americans, 500, 505–506
  post WWII, 718–719

of Spain, 22–23
  state government involvement, 532
  of Western agriculture, 516–517
Ecosystem in North America, 236
Ecumenical churches, 815
E day, 700
Edge cities, 773
Edison, Thomas A., 467, 468
Education, *See also* Public education
  bilingual schools, 837
  for blacks, 282
  of black students in South late 19th century, 458–459
  Bush policy, 840
  in colonies, 89
  elementary, 306
  for former slaves, 416, 418
  funds, 753
  at primary level, 311
  reform, 311–312
  in New South late 19th century, 450–452
  rural, 561
  in South, 284
  supported by new Congress, 180
  used to Americanize Indians, 503–505
  for women in New England, 197–198
  women's in late 19th century, 475
Educational institutions, 420, *See also* Colleges; Schools; Universities
Efficiency
  in 1920s industry, 632, 634
  from computers and electronics, 829
  and industrial society, 553
  stressed by La Follette, 566
  supported by Theodore Roosevelt, 567
Egalitarian Policitics, 243–247
Egypt, 746, 784
Einstein, Albert, 696
Eisenhower, Dwight, U.S. president
  churchgoing advocacy, 742
  civil rights actions, 752–753
  farewell address, 750
  first term in office, 730
  foreign policy president, 744–748
  as general in WWII, 703
  as president, 752–754
  presidential candidate in 1952, 733
  prosperity of 1950s, 739
  school segregation, 738
El Alamein, 693
Elbe River, 705
Elder respect, 642
Election clerks and judges, 526
Election fraud, 524
Election laws, 528
Election reforms, 564–565
Elections
  annual norm for governors, 173
  disputed in 1876, 430
  landslide for FDR, 672
Elections, Congressional
  of 1865, 422
  of 1894, 542, 543
  of 1934, 667
  of 1938, 678
  of 1946, 716
  of 1994, 825
  of 1998, 828
Elections, Presidential
  of 1788, 201
  of 1792, 201, 205
  of 1796, 205, 210
  of 1800, 213
  of 1804, 224
  of 1808, 224
  of 1812, 229
  of 1820, 237
  of 1824, 233, 237, 246
  of 1828, 242, 247
  of 1832, 254
  of 1836, 257
  of 1840, 258–259
  of 1844, 261

Elections, Presidential (cont.)
of 1848, 354
of 1852, 359
of 1856, 362–364
of 1860, 365, 368–369
of 1864, 405–406
of 1868, 425
of 1872, 429
of 1876, 430
of 1880, 532
of 1884, 533
of 1888, 534
of 1892, 449, 539
of 1896, 450, 542–543, 589
of 1900, 543, 566, 592
of 1904, 570
of 1908, 571
of 1912, 572–573
of 1916, 609–610
of 1920, 624–625, 635
of 1924, 637
of 1928, 648
of 1932, 663
of 1936, 670, 672
of 1940, 691
of 1944, 702
of 1948, 719–720
of 1952, 732–733
of 1956, 745
of 1960, 748–749
of 1964, 757
of 1968, 774–775
of 1972, 778
of 1976, 782
of 1980, 794
of 1984, 794, 795
of 1988, 794, 810
of 1992, 206, 823–824
of 1996, 825–826
of 2000, 838–839
Electoral College, 186, 838
Electric Age, 468–470
Electric household appliances, 632, 640
Electric irons, 640
Electricity in South and rural areas, 675
Electric light bulb, 468
Electric lights, 489, 492, 634
Electric power, 632
Electric power generation, 443
Electric trolleys, 489, 491
Electronics
boom, 831
business, 808
communication, 809
revolution, 828
Elementary and Secondary Education Act (1965), 757
Elementary schools, 559
Elevated railroads, 489
Eliot, John, Puritan minister, 64
Elizabeth, queen of England, 25, 40
Ellis, Bret Easton, novelist, 798
Ellis Island, 809
Ellsberg, Daniel, 780
Ellsworth, Kansas, 510
El Paso, Texas, 809
El Salvador, 803, 808
Ely, Richard T., economist, 552
Email, 832
Emancipation of slaves, 320
abolitionists in 1830s, 256
agitation in Border South, 272
in Biblical terms, 420
constitutional amendment, 405
gradual, 315–316
racial arguments, 283
Emancipation Proclamation
from President Lincoln, 390–392
in Republic of Mexico (1829), 340
Embargo Act of 1807, 224, 225
Embargo on oil exports, 778
Emergency Banking Act, 665
Emergency Quota Act (1921), 643
Emergency relief, 664

Emergency Relief Appropriation Act (1935), 670
Emerging Republican Majority, The (Phillips), 806
Emerson, Ralph Waldo, 137, 314, 368
Empire creation, 578–601
beginnings, 585–588
East Asia, 592–595
Latin America, 595–599
origins of imperialism, 581–585
Spanish-American War and Cuba, 588–592
Empire State Building, 638
Employment, *See also* Jobs
of families in Southern textile mills, 443
of women in mining camps, 508
Employment Act of 1946, 715
Employment Practices Commission, 721
Emporia, Kansas, 525
Empresario, 339–340
Enamels, 634
Encomienda system, 59, 67
Endangered species, 570
Energy policy, 783
Energy Policy and Conservation Act (1978), 783
Enforcement Act (1870), 428, 432
Engel v. Vitale (1962), 743
Engineers for railroad surveys, 294
England, *See also* Britain; Great Britain; Parliament, British
in 1500, 16–18
Civil War in 1642, 39
colonial economic development, 83
colonies in 17th century, 49
colonies in Caribbean, 45
colonists in backcountry, 97
conflict with French, 67
convicts used as slaves, 75
displacing Indians, 61–62
expansion of state power, 101
Imperial reorganization, 111–114
Indian affairs, 114–115
New World exploration, 25–27
policies in colonies, 115–120
in Revolutionary War
army, 135
recruitment of blacks, 145
surrendered, 155
troops, 143–144
war in the North, 147–149
navy, 150, 151
southern strategy, 152
Townshend crisis, 121–125
wars in Europe and North America, 100–104
English as official language, 616, 837
English Civil War, 142
English-Indian marriages, 38
Enlightenment religious philosophy Deism, 213
Enlightenment thought, 90
Enlistments in Continental Army, 142
Enumerated products, 83, 116
Environmental issues
damage from Southern dams, 675
Dust Bowl catastrophe, 669
legislation attacked by Reagan, 797
nuclear weapons testing, 726
regulations, 840
Environmental movement, 568, 570, 757, 779
Environmental Protection Agency (EPA), 570, 779, 794–795
Ephrata settlement, 77
Epidemics
coastal New England in 1616, 40
in Columbian exchange, 23
in early 19th century, 296
in Great Plains, 335
influenza, 621
measles in 1847, 337
smallpox in Pequots, 42

Episcopal Church, 283, 815
Episcopalian clergymen, 173
Episcopalians, 275, 552
Equal Employment Opportunity Commission (EEOC), 756
Equality
for blacks, 316
of genders among Native Americans, 12
racial, 298
in Shaker life, 313
of white men, 244
Equal pay, 767, 812
Equal rights
for blacks, 752
for blacks after WWII, 697
"Remember the Ladies," 158
for women, 555
Equal Rights Amendment (ERA), 637, 812
Equal Rights Association, 424, 426
Equiano, Olaudah, 58
Era of Good Feelings, 231–233
Erie Canal, 292, 295, 296, 303, 330
Erskine, David, British minister in Washington, 224
Ervin, Sam, North Carolina senator, 782
Escaped slave, letter from, 278
Escape to freedom, 276
Eskimo Indians, 7
Espionage, 748
Espionage Act (1917), 614, 842
Establishment of religion, 840
Ethiopia, 687, 793, 802
Ethnic diversity, 198
Ethnic neighborhoods, 482–483
Ethnic prejudices, 551
Ethnic profiling, 842
Etiquette books, 303
Europe
immigrant backgrounds, 480–482
influence on progressivism, 555, 559
Reagan's view, 802
European Enlightenment, 310
European immigrants in colonies, 76
European nations, role in Great Depression, 659
European Recovery Plan, 723
Europeans, cultural differences, 12
European society in 1500, 16
Evangelical businessmen, 306–308
Evangelical Christianity, 245, 283, 303, 742
Evangelical Christians, 816
Evangelical ministers, 92
Evangelical Protestant churches, 815
Evangelical Protestants, 283, 361, 366, 370, 646
Evangelical reformers, 308, 358
Evangelical revivalists and slave converts, 275
Everly Brothers, 768
Everybody's, 553
Evictions during Great Depression, 659, 661
Evil empire, 802
Evolution theory opposed in schools, 645–646
Executive branch
authority of W. Wilson, 573
checks and balances, 187
duties set in Constitution Convention, 186
expansion of power, 567
powers consolidated by Jefferson, 224
Virginia Plan, 184
Executive Departments, 202
Executive Order 8802, 699
Executive Order 9066, 699
Executive Order 9835, 730
Exodus, black settlement movement, 514
Expansion of federal government, 695
Expansion of federal power, 574

Experts in state regulatory commissions, 566
Exploration, reasons for, 18
Explosives, war materiel, 607
Exports
in 1920s, 647
of colonies, 84–86
cotton from Lower South, 268
importance during Civil War, 389
required for overproduction, 585
Extermination, the Holocaust, 705
Extermination camps, 688

F

F-86 Saberjets, 729
Factories
closing, 783
early 19th century, 296
garment during Civil War, 398
in Great Depression, 659
minimal in Lower South, 268–269
poverty amid prosperity, 798–799
resources during Civil War, 383
in World War II, 695
Factory laborers, 305
Factory system of production, 299–301
Facts of Reconstruction, The (Lynch), 431
Fair Deal, 721
Fair Employment Practices Committee (FEPC), 699
Fair Labor Standards Act, 678
Falaise, France, 703
Fall, Albert, secretary of Interior, 636
Falwell, Jerry, 370, 816
Families
broken by slavery, 358
communes as family, 769
definitions, 811
in early 1800s, 304
in early New England, 43–45
in Great Depression, 659–660
of planters class, 278–280
of slaves, 72–74, 274–275
during WWII, 697
Family and Medical Leave Act, 825
Family issues, 810–811
Family life, 741–742, 811
Family reunification, 808
Family values, 646, 788, 817
Farewell to Arms, A (Hemingway), 642
Farm commodities, 516
Farm Credit Administration, 666
Farmer, Eliza, 110–111
Farmer, James, 754
Farmer-Paellmann, Deandria, 70
Farmers, *See also* Foreclosures
in 1920s, 635
in Africa c. 1500, 14–15
during and after Great War, 612, 615, 622, 624
and agribusiness in South, 675
agriculture credit in 1916, 574
in American West, 235
associational politics, 527–528
benefits from urbanization, 295
champion of demands, 668
complaints on corporations, 534
in Dust Bowl, 669–670
economic crisis after Revolutionary War, 176–177
funds for transportation, 231
in Great Depression, 659
income, 667
income during WWII, 695–696
Indians in Southwest, 338–339
land inheritance in East, 327–329
land ownership for freedmen, 419
local control over schools, 311
lost opportunity, 433
mill-working daughters in New England, 300
and monetary policy, 535
Native American before 1492, 6–11
new markets, 291
in new Republic Party, 205

in Old Northwest, 330–331
in Old Southwest, 331–333
production restrictions, 666–667
protests during Great Depression,
661
protests in late 19th century,
536–537
rural life reforms, 560–561
scalawags, 426
Southern agrarian revolt, 446–450
tenant, 284
Western, FDR coalition, 672
western farmers and cattle
raisers, 676
yeoman in Old South, 280–281,
332–333
Farmers Alliance, 447–449, 537
Farmers cooperatives, 447, 537
Farmers' Holiday Association, 661
Farm implements
in American West, 516
during Civil War, 398
with interchangeable parts, 301
iron production and plows, 330–331
Farm machinery industry, 301
Farm parity, 667
Farm prices, 225
Farms, *See also* Soil fertility exhaustion
corporate in American West, 568
in early New England, 43–45
on Great Plains, 513–517
in New South late 19th century,
443–446
Farm Security Administration, 702
Farm subsidy program, 667, 721
Farragut, David G., Union admiral,
386, 388
Fascist government, 679
Fashions, 491
Fastfood franchise chain, 640
Fast-food restaurants, 741
Faubus, Orval, governor of Arkansas,
752
Faulkner, William, 396
FDR. *See* Roosevelt, Franklin (FDR)
Federal aid
cuts, 796
program for public schools, 757
subsidies, 237
support for science, 696
and Title IX, 812
Federal appointment, 248
Federal arsenal at Harpers Ferry,
Virginia, 301, 367
Federal authority, Constitutional
limits, 397
Federal bureaucracy, 531
Federal Bureau of Investigation
(FBI), 841, 842
Federal Civil Defense
Administration, 725
Federal Communications
Commission (FCC), 634
Federal Council of Churches of
Christ in America, 552
Federal deficit, 783
Federal Deposit Insurance
Corporation (FDIC), 665
Federal Emergency Relief
Administration (FERA), 666,
673, 675
Federal employees, 258, 730
Federal Farm Loan Act, 574
Federal funding, 840
Federal government
peacefully relinquished control, 214
Federal grants, 675
Federal Highway Act (1956), 740
Federal Housing Administration
(FHA), 717
Federal Indian policy, 501
Federalism, 188, 231
Federalist, The, 190
Federalist Antiwar Resolutions, 227
Federalist Party, 188–190
amended the Constitution, 202
emergence as political party, 205

end of, 212–213
opposed war with Britain, 226
peaceful overthrow, 219
rise of parties, 196–197
vs. Antifederalists, 189
vs. Republicans, 207
XYZ Affair, 211
Federal jobs, 248
Federal judiciary, FDR restructuring
plan, 677
Federal law violated by
Postmasters, 256
Federal regulation, *See also*
Government, regulations
beginnings of, 534–535
Federal republic, 184
Federal Reserve Act (1913), 573
Federal Reserve banks, 573
Federal Reserve Board, 573, 636,
669, 677
Federal Trade Commission Act
(1914), 574
Federal Trade Commission
(FTC), 574, 636, 637
Federal troops, 478, 480
Federal *vs.* state interests, 428, 432
Felton, Dr. William H., 451
Felton, Rebecca Latimer, 450–451
Female-headed households, 660
Feminine Mystique, The (Friedan), 744
Feminism, 317–320, 744, 767–768
Feminist Alliance, 555
Feminist movement, 811–812
Feminists, 637
Feminization of poverty, 800
Feminized evangelicalism, 310
Fences, 511, 515, 516
Ferdinand, Franz, Archduke of
Austro-Hungary, 606
Ferdinand and Isabella of Spain,
16–17, 19
Ferguson, Clementia, seamstress, 88
Fermi, Enrico, 686
Fernandez, Juan, 808
Ferraro, Geraldine, 834
Ferris, George Washington, 492
Ferris, Warren A., 335–336
Ferris Wheel, 492
FHA mortgages, 741
Field hands in gang labor, 268, 273
Field Order No 15, 419
Fifth Amendment Communists, 731
Filipino-American War, 593
Filipino immigration, 643, 808
Fillmore, Millard, U.S. president,
355–356, 363
Films, 641
Filo, John, 789
Final solution to Hitler's Jewish
problem, 705
Finances for new federal
government, 203
Financial centers, New York City, 295
Financial crisis, 797
Financial Crisis during Revolutionary
War, 175–176
Financial industry, 665
Financial institutions, 797
Financial panic. *See* individual Panic of
Financial policy and Republicans, 220
Financial reforms, 527
Financial reports from Hamilton,
203–204
Financing of mining with Eastern or
British capital, 509
Finger Lakes region in New York, 150
Finishes, 632
Finland, 723, 782
Finley, James, 245
Finney, Charles G., 303–304
Fire at sewing company, 550, 554
Fire Next Time, The (Baldwin), 770
Fireside chat, 665
First Continental Congress, 125–127
First International American
Conference, 585

First Republic, 166–193, 195–215
American West, 179–181
Articles of Confederation, 174–175
Constitutional Convention, 183–190
diplomacy problems, 181–183
economic problems, 175–179
emergence of parties, 205–210
forming new government,
201–205
last Federalists, 210–213
republicanism, new order, 169–175
state constitutions, 172–174
Washington years, 197–201
Fishermen and Peace of Paris, 156
Fishing, 27, 177, 499
Fishing rights off Labrador and
Newfoundland, 233
Fisk Herald newspaper, 452
Fisk University in Nashville,
Tennessee, 418
Fitzgerald, F. Scott, 642
Five-dollar day, 630
Flapper girls, 642
FleetBoston Financial Corporation, 70
Fletcher v. Peck (1810), 232
Flint, Michigan, 673
Flivver King, The (Sinclair), 630
Flop houses, 664–665
Florida
admitted to Union, 332
election of 1876, 430
election of 2000, 838
Jefferson's failed bid, 223
Lower South in 1850, 267
Peace of Paris, 156
population growth in 1990s, 834
retirees, 810
secession from Union, 369
Sunbelt, 806
in Treaty of Paris, 104, 112
Foley, Margaret, 548
Folk singers, 768
Folktales, 279
Follen, Eliza Cabot, 352
Folwell, John, Philadelphia furniture
maker, 87
Fonda, Jane, 781
Food Administration, 611, 613
Food and drugs regulation, 571
Food preparation, 490
Food stamps, 757
Football, 491
Forbes magazine, 798
Force Act of 1833, 253
Forced labor camps, 688
Ford, Gerald, U.S. president, 782
Ford, Henry, 630–632, 688
Ford cars, 630
Fordism, 630–631
Ford Motor Company, 634, 647, 673
Ford Works, 632
Foreclosures
farm, 178
farmers protest, 537
of farms in New South late 19th
century, 446
during Great Depression, 659, 661
prohibited in Reconstruction, 427
restricted, 538
of western farms, 517
Foreign Affairs Magazine, 724
Foreign diplomacy in Civil War,
389–390
Foreign languages, 527, 616
Foreign markets, 647, 659
Foreign policy
of Bush (elder), 804–806
of Bush (younger), 840–841
of Carter, 784–785
of Clinton, 824
of Eisenhower, 744
of FDR, 678, 702
of Franklin Pierce, 359
and Manifest Destiny, 345
of Nixon and Kissinger, 777–778
and Panama Canal, 597
post WWII, 721–723

of Reagan, 803–804
Roosevelt, T.R., 584
Foreign trade, 583–585
Forest Management Act (1897), 568
Forest Reserve Act (1891), 568
Forest reserves, 568
Forestry development, 675
Forest Service, 568, 570
Forests east of Mississippi, 301
Forging passes, 269
Formosa, 51
Forts
Carson in Colorado, 807
Dearborn, 229
Donelson on Cumberland River, 385
Duquesne, 102–104
Henry on Tennessee River, 385
Laramie, Second Treaty, 502
Laramie Treaty (1851), 337
Necessity, 102
Orange, 51
Oswego, New York, 103
in peace treaty violations, 182
Sumter, 373–375, 381, 385
Ticonderoga, 138, 149
Wagner, 392
William Henry, New York, 103
Fortune, T. Thomas, 416–417
Forty-Niners, 355
Foster-home programs, 554
Fourteen Points, 619
Fox Indians, 250, 334
Frame of Government, 50
France, *See also* French colonialism;
New France
after French and Indian War, 112
Civil War neutrality, 389–390
German reunification, 804–805
in Great War, 605, 617, 620
Great War, war debts, 647
Louisiana Purchase, 220–222
and Panama Canal, 597
Quasi-War, 211
Revolutionary War assistance, 152,
155–157
Revolutionary War investment, 161
spheres of influence in China,
593–594
supported patriot cause, 149–150
trade embargo in 1807, 224–225
treaty of Paris, 156
treaty with Spain in 1800, 221
in WWII and later
collapse in June 1940, 690
D-Day, 703
early dealings with Hitler, 679–681
Egypt and Eisenhower, 746
mentioned, German invasion, 688
post WWII, 722
in Vietnam, 746
war in Iraq, 844
XYZ Affair, 211
Franciscan priests, 62–64, 67, 98, 338
Francis I, king of France, 24
Francis Marion "Swamp Fox," 155
Franco, Francisco, 679, 687
Franco-American Accord of 1800, 212
Franco-American alliance in
Revolutionary War, 149–150
Frankfurt, Germany, 492
Frankfurters, 492
Franklin, Battle of, 406
Franklin, Benjamin
and *Bon Homme Richard*, 151
colonial governor conflict, 97
on colonial religion, 92
designed national symbol, 164–165
as inventor, 90
on manufactures and prosperity, 89
and Paxton Boys, 114
Peace of Paris, 156
proposed Albany Plan, 102–103
secured French aid, 149
Franklin, John Hope, historian, 70, 432
Franklin stove, 90
Fraternal associations, 458
Fraternal orders, 643

Fraternal orders in 1920s, 639
Fraud, 514, 517
Fraunces Tavern, 156
Frederick, Maryland, 390
Fredericksburg, Virginia, 393
Free blacks, 199, 244, 281–282
Free coinage, 540
Freedmen's Bureau, 418–419, 431
Freedmen's schools, 418
Freedom
  at home and abroad, 719
  public consciousness of North, 391
  readmission to Union, 430
Freedom dues, 38
Freedom of contract, 556
Freedom of expression, 202
Freedom of Information Act, 842
Freedom of speech, 616
Freedom of the press, 173
Freedom of the seas, 619, 691
Freedom of worship, 39, 198
Freedom papers, 281
Freedom Riders, 460, 754
Freedom's Journal, 316
Freedom Summer, 756
Free labor, 272, 319
Freeman, 42
Freeport Doctrine, 365
Free silver, 536, 542
Free Society in Old South, 277–282
Free-Soil Party of 1848, 321, 354
Free speech, 256, 731
Free Speech Movement (FSM), 766
Free trade in Fourteen Points, 619
Freeways and urban renewal, 740–741
Free workers in Southern cities, 281
Frémont, John C., 362–363, 369
French, Benjamin Brown, 242
French and Indian War, 102–104, 111–112
French colonialism
  in 1500, 16–18
  colonies in Caribbean, 45
  conflict with British, 67
  expansion in heart of North America, 99–100
  explored Canada, 24–25
  fur trade, 60–61
  and Iroquois neutrality, 101–102, 104
  loss of empire in North America, 104
  New World empire, 33–34
  transatlantic trade, 83
  wars in Europe and North America, 100–104
French Indochina, 691
French Louisiana, colonial expansion, 99–100
French Morocco, 703
French Protestant immigrants, 77
French Revolution of 1789, 161, 205–207, 213
French ship *Sussex*, 609
Freud, Sigmund, 492
Frick, Henry Clay, 479–480
Friedan, Betty, 744
Fries, John, 212
Fries's Rebellion, 212
Frink, Margaret, 337
Frobisher, Martin, 25
From Then to Now
  African-American voting rights in South, 433
  cod off Grand Banks, 27
  Confederate Battle Flag, 460
  culture wars, 646
  economic legacy of slavery, 284
  environmental movement, 570
  Gettysburg, 396
  Hamilton's legacy and national debt, 206
  immigration, 298
  legacy of Indian Americanization, 505
  legacy of slavery, 70
  Lewis and Clark Expedition, 236

loyalty in 2001 and 1917, 842
Manifest Destiny and foreign policy, 345
  nuclear weapons, 709
  political parties, 528
  religion and politics, 370
  Social Security, 671
  teaching American history, 159
  women and work in American offices, 814
Frontier, 150, 225–226
Fuchs, Klaus, nuclear physicist, 732
Fuchs spy ring, 732
Fuel economy standards for automobiles, 779
Fugitive Slave Act (1850), 278, 352, 356–358
Fugitive slaves, 266, 276–277, 391
Fukien (Fujian), China, 593
Fulbright, William, senator, 766
Fulton, Robert, steamboats, 292
Fundamental Constitutions of Carolina, 48
Fundamentalist churches, 742
Fundamentalists, 645, 648, 815
Fundamental Orders, 42
Funded debt, 100
Funerals, *See also* Burials
  in Africa, 14
  of slaves, 73
Furnishings, 719, 741
Furniture, 313, 440, 640
Fur trade, 33, 51, 60–61, 114, 182
Fur traders, 59, 99, 333, 335–336

G

Gadsden, Christopher, 119, 127, 164
Gadsden flag, 164
Gagarin, Yuri, astronaut, 751
Gage, Margaret, 548
Gage, Thomas, British army general, 135, 136, 138, 147
Gag rule, 256, 317, 320
Gallatin, Albert, Treasury Secretary, 220, 230
Galveston, Texas, 478
Galvez, Jose de, 99
Gama, Vasco da, 18
Gambling, 505, 511, 563
Gangsters, 645
Gang system of labor in fields, 268, 273
Garden crops, 483
Garden plots, 273, 274
Gardiner, Lion, 53
Gardoqui, Don Diego de, 183
Garfield, James A., U.S. president, 526, 530, 532–533, 535, 585
Garment industry, 398, 473, 483, 484, 491
Garment worker unions, 554
Garrison, William Lloyd, abolitionist
  advocated racial equality, 358
  broke with Douglass, 320–321
  on John Brown, 368
  leader in early abolitionism, 316–317
  published *The Liberator*, 256
  supported women's rights, 315, 318
Garvey, Marcus, 639
Gary, Indiana, 783
Gaseous diffusion plants, 696
Gasoline rationed, 695
Gaspee, British revenue schooner, 123–124
Gates, Bill, 830
Gates, Horatio, Continental army general, 149, 152
Gay pride, 813
Gays and lesbians, 646, 811, 813–814, 817
Gender
  divided workers, 305
  gap, 835
  protected category, 767, 811
  protected class in 1964, 756
  segregation, 660

General Accounting Office, 636
General Agreement on Tariffs and Trade (GATT), 833
General Court, 42
General Electric, 634
General Electric Company, 469
General Electric Theater, 739
General Federation of Women's Clubs, 554
General Motors, 634, 635, 673, 739–740, 799
General Revenue Sharing, 778
General Union for Promoting Observance of Christian Sabbath (1828), 307
Generation X, 823
Genêt, Edmond, French ambassador, 205
Geneva, 17
Geneva peace conference, 746
Genocide, *See also* Indians
  Holocaust, 705
"Gentleman Johnny" Burgoyne, 149
Gentlemen's Agreement, Japanese immigration, 595
George, Henry, 479
George II, king of England, 95
George III, king of England, 111, 117, 137, 140, 141
Georgia
  agrarian revolt, 448, 449
  freedom riders, 754
  Lower South in 1850, 267
  mentioned, 125
  mentioned, in Civil War, 400, 406
  moves against Indians, 249
  in national symbol, 165
  ratification of Constitution, 189
  Reconstruction, 428
  secession from Union, 369
  slavery legalized, 69
  state flag, 460
  taken by General Clinton, 152
  Treaty of New Echota, 252
German Americans
  during Great War, 614–615
  Great War peace terms, 621
  party loyalty, 527
  targeted in Great War, 842
  in World War II, 701
German immigrants
  in 1848–1860, 361
  economic opportunities, 297, 298
  not warmly received, 484
  in Pennsylvania, 97–98
  Protestant redemptioners, 75–76
German Jews, refuge, 679
German master race, 705
German Mennonites, 516
German mercenaries, 143
German prisoners of war, 696
German Reformed churches, 91
Germany
  in 20th century
    interest in Philippines, 591
    mentioned, 584
    Persian Gulf War, 805–806
    reunification, 804–805
    spheres of influence in China, 593–594
    on war in Iraq, 844
    world economy, 779
  in Great War, 605–609
    propaganda, 606
    submarine warfare, 617
    terms of Treaty of Versailles, 620
    war debts, 647
  sent immigrants, 481
  states in 1500, 16–18
  in World War II
    early actions, 687–688
    Eastern Front, 692–693, 703
    post WWII, 722, 723
    unconditional surrender demanded, 702
Germ warfare, 114
Geronimo, Apache leader, 503

Gerry, Elbridge, antifederalist, 188
Gettysburg, Battle of, 393, 396, 413
Gettysburg National Military Park, 396
Ghettos, 420, 486, 717, 770–771, 775, *See also* Slums
Ghost Dance religion, 503
Ghosts, 275
Giannini, Amadeo Pietro, 484
Gibbons, Thomas, 294
Gibbons v. *Ogden* (1824), steamboats, 294
Gibbs, Lois, 780–781
GI Bill of Rights, 716
Giddings, Joshua R., 320
Gilbert, Sir Humphrey, 25
Gilded Age, 467, *See also* Immigrants; Industry in Gilded Age
Gilman, Charlotte Perkins, 609
Gilmer, John A, 374
Gingrich, Newt, Speaker of House, 825, 828
Ginsburg, Ruth Bader, Supreme Court justice, 834
Girard, Kansas, 555
Girls' boarding schools, 89
Gladden, Washington, 551–552
Glasnost, 804
Glass harmonica, 90
Glass production, in 19th century, 296
Glass-Steagall Act, 665
Glenn, John, astronaut, 751
Global economy, 828, 833
Global warming, 570, 841
Glorieta Pass, Battle of, 394
Glorious Revolution, 94–95
Gold
  discoveries, 355, 502, 543
  prospectors, 509
  rushes, 355, 506
  and silver coins, 253
  Spanish acquisition, 20, 22–23
  standard, 536, 542–543
  trade in Africa, 15
Gold Coast, 51
Golden Rule, 633
Gold Hill, Nevada, 508
Goldman, Emma, 624
Goldsboro, North Carolina, 406
Goldwater, Barry, Arizona senator, 757
Golf courses for men, 491
Goliad, 340
Gompers, Samuel, AFL leader, 479, 592
Good Neighbor Policy, 648, 678
Gorbachev, Mikhail, Soviet Union general secretary, 804
Gordon, Thomas, 118
Gore, Albert, Jr., vice president, 823, 838–839
Gore, Thomas, Oklahoma senator, 609
Gore-McLemore resolutions, 609
Gospel of efficiency, 553
Gospel of Wealth, 478
Government, *See also* Federal aid
  English institutions in colonies, 53
  establishing after Revolutionary War (*See* First Republic)
  expansion of power, 567
  forging a new, 201–205
  funding railroads & canals, 294
  intervention for farmers, 667
  jobs, 533, 698 (*See also* Civil Service)
  land sales, 254
  limits of, 530–532
  pensions, 668
  policies in Great Depression, 659
  regulations, 509, 553, 568–571, 636, 796
  regulatory agencies in Great War, 611–612
"Government is the problem," 796
Governors in state constitutions, 173
Gradual emancipation, 198, 235, 283, 315

Graham, Billy, evangelist, 742
Grain and canal networks, 292
Grain elevators, 516, 517, 527, 537
Grand Banks, 27
Grandfather clauses, 455
Grand Old Party (GOP), 527, 538
Grand Settlement of 1701, 101
Grange, 447, 527–528
Granger, Mrs. A. O., 451
Granger laws, 527, 534
Grant, Ulysses S., U.S. president
　Civil War general, 381, 385, 388,
　　393, 402–407
　in election of 1868, 425
　mentioned, 524
　presidency as weak institution, 530,
　　531
　refusal to help South Carolina, 430
　scandals in administration, 428, 429
Grant Park in Chicago, Illinois, 775
Grasslands, public lands in West, 677
Grass-roots activism, 766
Grass-roots democracy, 676
Grass-roots election committees, 247
Grass-roots movement, Farmers'
　Alliances, 537
Grass-roots politics as training for
　women, 834
Grateful Dead rock band, 768
Graying of America, 810
Grazing fees, 568
Great American Desert, 501
Great Awakening, 90–93, 142
Great Awakening, Second, 244–245,
　291, 306
Great Basin, 7, 343
Great Bridge, near Norfolk, 138
Great Britain, *See also* Britain;
　England
　boundary dispute over British
　　Guiana, 587–588
　in Great War, 605–609, 617–618
　war debts, 647
　mentioned, 584, 647, 805
　sent immigrants, 481
　since World War II
　　Egypt and Eisenhower, 746
　　German reunification, 804
　　nuclear power, 725
　　spread of Communism, 722
　spheres of influence in China,
　　593–594
　in World War II, 679–681, 688, 690,
　　705
Great Compromise, 185
Great Depression, 284, 654–678, *See
　also* New Deal; Roosevelt,
　　Franklin (FDR)
　beginnings, 658–660
　Dust Bowl, 669–670
　Hoover, 661–663
　jobs, 659–661, 666, 670
　recession in 1937, 677–678
Greater East Asia Co-Prosperity
　Sphere, 687
Great Falls of Missouri River, 236
Great Gatsby, The (Fitzgerald), 642
Great Khan of China, 19
Great Lakes, 233, 292, 296
Great Lakes basin, 100
Great Migration of African
　Americans, 486–487, 639, 641
Great Northern Railroad, 480
Great Plains, 9–10
　Dust Bowl, 658, 669
　economy and ecology, 337
Great Salt Lake, 343
Great Society, 757, 778, 783
Great Uprising, 478
The Great War, 603–627, 842
　heavy artillery, 618
　mobilizing for war, 609, 611–616,
　　665
　neutrality, 605–611
　peace abroad, 619–620
　peace at home, 620–625
　Treaty of Versailles, 619–621

war abroad, 617–618
war debts and economic expansion,
　647
Greece, 688, 723
Greeley, Horace, 369, 429
Greenback paper money, 384,
　535–536
Greenback Party, 527, 536, 537
Green Berets, The, movie, 766
Greene, Nathanael, Continental army
　leader, 152, 155
Green groups, 570
Greenhow, Rose O'Neal, 401
Greenpeace, 570
Green River in Wyoming, 336
Greensboro battle, North Carolina,
　155
Greensburg, Indiana, 458
Greenville, Ohio, 209
Gregory, Thomas, Attorney General,
　615
Grenada, 803
Grenville, George, British prime
　minister, 116
Grid system of surveys, 179
Griffith, D. W., 456
Grimké, Angelina Emily, 290, 317
Griswold v. *Connecticut*, 812
Guadaloupe, 45
Guadalupe Victoria, 341
Guam, Treaty of Paris, 591
Guanahatabey Indians, 11
Guatemala, 746, 784, 808
Guerrilla warfare
　in Cuba, 589
　during Great Depression, 661
　patriots in Revolutionary War, 143,
　　150, 155
　Seven Years' War, 103
Guilford Court House, 155
Gulf Coast defense, 230
Gulf of Mexico, 99–100, 156
Gulf of Tonkin, 757
Gulf of Tonkin Resolution, 757, 763,
　776
Gulf War (1991), 709
Gunboat diplomacy, 648
Gun control, 771, 800, 826–827
Guns
　Brown Bess, 143
　of Comanches, 339
　handguns, 770
　prevented slave revolts, 276
　of Spaniards, 20
　used by Sioux, 334
Guyana in South America, 769
Gypsies, 705

H

Habeas corpus suspended by Lincoln,
　397
Haight-Ashbury district, 768
Hair cuts of Indians, 504
Haiti, 45, 222, 585, 598, 599, 648, 808,
　824
Hakluyt, Richard, 26
Haldeman, H. R., White House
　staffer, 781
Hale, Sarah Josepha, 309
Halfway Covenant, 91
Halifax, Nova Scotia, 138
Hamburg-American Line (HAPAG),
　481
Hamer, Fannie Lou, 756
Hamilton, Alexander, secretary of
　Treasury
　crisis in 1786, 183
　end of Federalists, 212
　head of Treasury Department,
　　203–205
　killed by Burr, 223
　national debt, 206
　ratification of Constitution, 190
　role in first partisan election, 210
Hamilton, James Jr., South Carolina
　planter, 251

Hammond, James H., South Carolina
　senator, 269, 368, 389
Hammond, Lily, 450
Hampton, Fred, 772
Hampton Normal and Agricultural
　Institute, 459
Hancock, John, 121, 135, 136, 190
Hanford Engineer Works, 696
Hanna, Marcus A., 542–543
Hanoi, North Vietnam, 776
Harassment, racial, 738, 753
Harbors, 87, 362
Harding, Warren, U.S. president,
　624–625, 635, 647
Harding, W.L., governor of Iowa, 616
Hard money, economic crisis, 178
Hard rock mining, 509
Hariot, Thomas, 26
Harkness, Dr., 498
Harlan, John Marshall, 455
Harlem, New York, 774
Harlem Renaissance, 639
Harpers Ferry, Virginia, 301, 367
Harper's Illustrated Weekly, 412–413
Harpers Magazine, 441
Harrigan, Hop, 697
Harrington, Michael, 744, 755
Harris, George, 279
Harrison, Benjamin, U.S. president,
　530, 534, 539, 587
Harrison, William Henry, U.S.
　president, 225, 229, 243,
　257–259
Harrison Act (1914), 562
Hartford Convention, 226
Harvard College
　colonial training of ministers, 90
Harvard University, 461, 491, 730
Harvesting methods, 330–331
Hats, imports, 86
Havana harbor, 589
Hawaii, 586–587, 701, 836
Hawaiian Islands, 582–584, 590
Hawkers, paid party workers, 526
Hawkins, John, 25
Hawthorne, Nathaniel, 314
Hay, John, secretary of State, 583, 594
Hayden, Tom, 781
Hayes, Rutherford B., U.S. president,
　430, 478, 530, 532, 814
Haygood, Atticus G., 453
Haygood, Laura, 450
Haygood, Lucy, 450
Haymarket Square incident, 479
Haynsworth, Clement, Supreme
　Court nominee, 778
Hays, Mary Ludwig, 145
Hazardous waste, 570
Headright system, 35
Head Start, 755
Health care, 829
Health inspectors, 477
Health insurance, 559, 826, 829
Hearst, William Randolph, 490, 589
Heartbreak Ridge, 729
Hebrew Emigrant Aid Society, 514
Heffernan, Joseph, 664
Heinz electric sign, 490
Helena, Montana, 506
Helper, Hinton Rowan, 285
Helsinki Accords, 782, 784
Hemingway, Ernest, 642
Hemlines, 642
Henderson, Julia, examiner of
　accounts, 533
Hendrix, Jimi, rock singer, 769
Henry, Andrew, 335
Henry, O., writer, 474
Henry, Patrick, 118, 127
　crisis of confidence, 184
　lawyer, 115
Henry, prince of Portugal, 18
Henry VII, king of England, 16, 25
Henry VIII, king of England, 25
Hepburn Act (1906), 570
Heritage Foundation, 796
Hessian mercenaries, 143, 147

Hidatsa Indians, 334
Hide hunters, buffalo, 502
Hides, 342
Higher Education Act, 757
High Federalists, 212
High schools, 738–739, 742, 752–753
High-tech industry, 798, 829–832
Highway Act (1916), 574
Highway beautification, 757
Highway speed limit, 778
Hill, Anita, 835
Hillbilly music, 641
Hindu scriptures, 696
Hip-Hop music, 798
Hippies, 768
Hirohito, Emperor of Japan, 707
Hiroshima, Japan, 707, 708
Hispanic Americans, *See also* Mexican
　Americans
　activism in Southwest, 772
　in Congress, 836
　current population, 834
　excluded from suburbs, 640
　in Great Depression, 661
　migrants in 1920s, 639
　and New Deal, 675
　Populist election, 538
　Southwest lands lost, 514–515
Hiss, Alger, 732
History, teaching American, 159
Hitler, Adolf, German Führer,
　679–681, 687, 688, 692, 705
H.M.S. Serapis, Revolutionary War
　ship, 151
Ho Chi Minh, 746, 749, 765
Ho Chi Minh City (Saigon), Vietnam,
　763, 773
Ho Chi Minh Trail, 765
Hogs, 267, 296, 330
Hohokam Indians, 9
Holiness movement, 448
Holland colonies, 51–52
Holly, Buddy, 742
Hollywood, 697, 731
Hollywood, California, 794
Hollywood studios, 634
Hollywood Ten, 731
Holocaust, 705
Holy experiment, 50–51
Holy Roman Empire, 17
Home Front, 697
Homeless people, 800
Homemakers, 548
Home mission societies, 450
Home ownership, 799, 829
Home Owners Loan Corporation, 666
Home purchase loans, 717
Homespun clothes, 121
Homestead Act (1862), 397
Homestead Act of 1862, 513–515
Homesteaders, 513–517
Homesteads in West, 362
Homestead strike, 479–480
Homosexual rights, 370
Homosexuals, 813–814, 817
Honduras, 598, 648, 808
Honeybees in Columbian exchange,
　23–24
Hong Kong, 593
Hood, John Bell, Confederate
　general, 404, 406
Hooker, Joseph, Union major
　general, 393
Hooper, William, of North Carolina,
　174
Hoover, Herbert, U.S. president
　in election of 1928, 648
　in Great Depression, 661–663
　as head of Food Administration,
　　611–612
　mentioned, 641, 665, 678
　New Deal fears, 676
　on prohibition, 645
　as Secretary of Commerce, 636, 637,
　　647
Hoover, J. Edgar, FBI Director,
　623–624, 742

Hoovervilles, 659–660
Hope, Lugenia Burns, 459
Hopi Indians, 9, 64, 343, 500
Hopkins, Esek, of Rhode Island, 164
Hopkins, Harry, 666, 673
Hopwood v. *Texas*, 837
Horizontal integration, 471
Horse-drawn coaches, omnibuses, 296
Horse-drawn mechanical harvesters, 330
Horse-drawn wagons, 292
Horses
  in Columbian exchange, 23
  of Spaniards, 20
  used by Sioux, 334
  used by Southwest Indians, 339
Horseshoe Bend, Battle of, 230
Horton, Willie, 800
Hospitals, 670
Hostages
  in Iran, 785
  in Lebanon, 803
Hostility from Latin American, 648
Hot beds rented in shifts, 695
House, Edward, adviser to Wilson, 606
House Committee on Un-American
    Activities (HUAC), 730–731, 733
"House divided against itself," 374
Household appliances, 640
Household income, 718
Households, female-headed, 660
House of Burgesses, 36, 65, 82
House of Commons, 96, 117
House of Lords, 96
House of the Seven Gables, The
    (Hawthorne), 314
Houses
  colonial, 88–89
  of slaves, 73, 273
Housewife's role, 640
Housing Act (1949), 721
Housing reform, 477, 557
Housing shortages
  in 1920s, 639
  after Great War, 622
  after WWII, 714, 716–717
  goal of decent housing, 721
  war workers, 695
Houston, Charles Hamilton, dean of
    law school, 752
Houston, Sam, 340
Houston, Texas, 638
Houston, Tranquility Base, 762
Houston Press, 675
Howard University, 418, 661, 752
Howe, Richard, British admiral of
    navy, 147–149
Howe, Robert, Continental army, 146
Howe, Sir William, commander in
    chief of British forces, 147–149
How the Other Half Lives (Riis), 476, 477
Hudson, Henry, 51
Hudson River steamboats, 292
Hudson River Valley, 146
Hudson's Bay Company, 335, 336
Huerta, Victoriano, Mexican general,
    599
Hughes, Charles Evans, secretary of
    State, 610, 647
Hughes, Langston, 639
Huguenot immigrants, 77
Hull, Cordell, secretary of State, 679
Hull, William, general, 229
Hull House, 476, 557, 660
Human immunodeficiency virus
    (HIV), 813
Human origins, 645
Human rights, 345, 782, 784, 785
Human sacrifice, 7, 9
Humphrey, Hubert, vice president,
    720, 775
Hundred Days of New Deal, 664–667
Hundred Years' War, 16
Hungary, 688, 722, 723, 724, 746, 804,
    824
Hunger, *See also* Malnutrition;
    Starvation

in Kentucky during Great
    Depression, 657
marches during Great Depression,
    661
of teachers, 663
Hunt, E. Howard, 780
Hunter, Addie W., 486
Hunting and gathering, 6–7
Huron Indians, 12, 33–34, 59, 60–61
Hussein, Saddam, president of Iraq,
    805–806, 844
Hutchinson, Anne, 43
Hutchinson, Thomas, governor of
    Massachusetts, 118, 124, 135
Huxley, Aldous, writer, 768
Hydroelectric power, 675
Hydroelectric sites, 568
Hydrogen bomb, 725–726
Hymns, 245

I

IBM Corporation, 799, 829, 830
Ibo Africans, 14
ICBMs, 751
Idaho
  mentioned, 508, 514
  on Oregon Trail, 336
  population growth in 1990s, 834
  woman suffrage, 529, 538
"I Have a Dream" speeches, 541, 754
Illinois
  IWW trial, 616
  Northwestern Farmers' Alliance, 537
  in Old Northwest, 329
  voting requirements, 243
Illinois Woman's Alliance, 529
Immediate gratification, 641–642
Immediatism, 256
Immigrants, *See also* German
    immigrants; Japanese
    immigrants
  1848 to 1860, 361
  Catholic, 298, 305, 646
  in colonies, from Europe, 75–77
  in early 20th century, 550–551
  in Great War, 617
  Hispanic, 639
  Japanese, Filipinos, Mexicans in
    1920s, 643
  nativist restrictions, 642–643
  neighborhoods during Great
    Depression, 660
  workers, 631
  workers displaced slaves, 272
Immigrants in Gilded Age, 480–487
  Great Migration, 486–487
  jobs, 483–484
  nativism, 484–486
  neighborhoods, 482–483
  Old World backgrounds, 480–482
Immigration
  after mid-1840s, 295–297
  to American West, 514
  antiforeign sentiment, 484
  in colonies, 97
  decline in European, 639
  illegal in late 20th century, 837
  of Japanese, 595
  laws, 842
  literacy tests, 642
  in New South late 19th century, 442
  policy, 680
  quotas, 298, 679, 690
  racist limits, 562
  reform in 1960s, 808
  restriction of foreign, 485
  restrictions in 1920s, 642–643
  since 1965, 808–809
  to Texas, 339–341
  from Upper South to West, 270
  and urban manufacturing, 300
  as wage earners, 305
  of white people to trans-Mississippi
    region, 326–327
Immigration and Nationality Act
    (1952), 733

Immigration and Nationality Act
    (1965), 808
Immigration Reform and Control Act
    (1986), 808
Immigration Restriction League
    (IRL) (1894), 485, 562
Impeachment, 173, 187
  of Andrew Johnson, 425
  of Clinton, 646, 827–828
  of Johnson, 530
  of Nixon, 782
Impending Crisis of the South, (Helper),
    285
Imperialism, *See also* Empire creation;
    England
  after Great War, 620
  economic, in Vietnam War, 766
  of righteousness, 582
  of U.S., 581–585
Imports
  after War of 1812, 231
  from Britain reduced by colonists,
    121
  of colonies, 86–87, 88
Impost tax, 176
Impressment, 223, 226
Imprisonment during Civil War, 397
Inca empire, 20
Inchon, North Korea, 728
Income, unequal distribution of, 649,
    658–659
Income taxes
  early in Vietnam years, 778
  endorsed by Agricultural Wheel, 447
  endorsed by Democrats, 542
  first one, 573
  first used during Civil War, 384
  graduated, Populist demand, 538
  invalidated in 1895, 541
  rates, 796
  state in Wisconsin, 566
  supported by Taft, 571
  in World War II, 695
Incorporation, 294
In Defense of the Indians, 22
Indenture, 299
Indentured servants, 37–38, 68–69
Independence, *See also* Revolutionary
    War
  of job for immigrants, 483
  of New England millhands, 300
  Revolutionary War demands, 156
  second war for, 226
  of workers lost to industrial capital,
    471, 478
Independence, Missouri, 337
Independent candidates, 447, 528
Independent producers and theaters,
    634
Independent Treasury Act, 258
Independent Treasury System, 255,
    259–260
Independent Whig (Gordon and
    Trenchard), 118
India, 51, 705, 709
Indiana, 243, 526
  in Old Northwest, 329
Indian affairs of British, French and
    Indian War, 102–104, 111–112,
    114–116
Indiana Territory, 229
Indiana University, 716
Indian dance, 505
Indian Knoll, 6
Indian Removal Act (1830), 249, 334
Indian removal cases, Supreme Court,
    251
Indian Reorganization Act (1934),
    674
Indians, *See also* Indian wars; Native
    Americans
  abandoned land claims in West, 179
  Americanization on reservations,
    503–506
  in American West, 499–506
  British allies and peace treaty
    violations, 182

Civil War battles, 394
confederations in Southeast, 249
conquests by Jackson, 230
converted to Catholicism, 62–64
cultural differences, 12
displaced in backcountry, 98
displaced in English colonies, 61–62
effects of Revolutionary War,
    158–159
forced migrations
  in 1830s, 333–335
  removal by Jackson, 249–251, 252
  removal of Plains Indians, 501
  removals opened West, 329, 332
fur trade with French & Dutch,
    60–61
marriages with fur trappers, 335
in Mexican borderlands, 339
in Ohio Valley, 102
of Plains, 333–338
population group in Southwest, 338
recorded history and customs, 326
resistance in Indiana, 225–226
in Revolutionary War, 146, 150
Revolutionary War effects on, 172
as slaves, 68
societies before 1492, 6–11
in Spanish colonies, 98–99
tribal lands, 333–335, 339, 343
tribal meetings, 335, 337
tribes and cultures in West, 499–501
in Utah, 343
voting rights, 172
warfare and dispossession in West,
    501–503
in War of 1812, 229
whiskey corruption, 336
as workers for Spaniards, 59–60
Indian schools, 504, 674
Indian Territory, *See also* Tribal lands
  Civil War battles, 394
  railroad proposal, 360
Indian wars
  Black Hawk's War, 250, 334
  Fallen Timbers, 208, 209
  of Little Bighorn, 503
  of One Hundred Slain, 502
  with Plains Indians, 501–503
  of the Rosebud, 503
  Seminole Indians, 250
  warfare of Sioux Indians, 334–335
Indigo, colonial export, 85
Indios, 6
Individual Retirement Accounts
    (IRAs), 797
Individual rights and liberties in
    Constitution, 202
Indochina, 729, 808
Indonesia, 51
Indoor plumbing, 490
Industrial accidents, 472, 550, 557,
    562
Industrial capacity during Civil War,
    383
Industrial decay, 783
Industrialists, 528, 553
Industrialization
  in 1870s, 428–429
  led in North by New England, 297
  minimal in Lower South, 268–269
  in New South late 19th century,
    440–443
  North *vs.* South in 1860, 366
  and social reform, 552
  and state governments, 531
  in Upper South, 271–272
  U.S. as world leader, 291
Industrial production, 659
Industrial Revolution, 297–301
Industrial slaves, 274
Industrial towns in New England,
    296–297
Industrial Workers of the World
    (IWW), 554, 559, 612, 615–616,
    623
Industry
  in 1920s, 632–634

defense production, 695
  regulation of, 532
Industry in Gilded Age, 467–480
  child labor, 473–474
  corporations, 470–471
  Electric Age, 468–470
  poverty and wealth, 476–478
  union organizing, 478–480
  working conditions, 471–473
  working women, 474–476
Infant care, 637
Infant mortality, 476, 505, 674, 757
Inflation
  1780 and 1781, 175–176
  in 1970s sent women to work, 813
  in 1980, 783
  after Great War, 622
  during Civil War, 383–384
  L. Johnson legacy, 778
  post WWII, 715
  in Revolutionary War, 160
  supported by farmers, 668
  in World War II, 695
Inflation advocates, 535–536
Influence of Sea Power upon History, The
  (Mahan), 583
Influenza, 20, 23, 621
Information industries, 829
Infrastructure, 231, 488, 670, 770, *See
  also* Internal improvements
"In God We Trust," 742
Inheritance in Europe, 16
Inheritance taxes, 571
Initiative, 566
Injunctions, 541, 623
Inleheme, Endymion, 38
Inner-city ghettos, 717
Inner Light, 50
Insane asylums, 312
Installment buying, 640
Installment loans, 635
Instant communication, 832
Institute for Defense Analysis, 774
Institutions and social improvement,
  310–314
Instruments of slavery, 117
Insular Cases, Supreme Court (1901),
  595
Insurance
  compulsory, 669
  life, 458
  national health, 721
Intellectual life in colonies, 89–90
Intelligence gathering, 724, 729
Intendant, royal appointee, 34
Interchangeable parts, 301
Intercontinental ballistic missiles
  (ICBMs), 745
Intermediate Nuclear Force (INF), 804
Internal improvements, 248, 259–260,
  271, *See also* Infrastructure
Internal Revenue Service, 370
Internal Security Act (1950), 733
Internal taxes during Jefferson
  presidency, 220
International Criminal Court, 841
International inspectors, 709
International Jew, 631
International Ladies Garment
  Workers Union (1900), 554
International law, 598, 607, 609, 610
International Monetary Fund (IMF),
  722
International relations in Fourteen
  Points, 619
International trade, 722
Internet, 829, 831, 832
Internment of Japanese Americans,
  699–701, 842
Interstate and Defense Highways,
  740–741
Interstate Commerce Act (1887),
  534–535
Interstate Commerce Commission
  (ICC), 535, 570, 571
Interventionist government, 258
Intolerable Acts, 124–125

Invention of cotton gin, 267, 300–301
Investigative reporting, 553
Investment capital
  in mining industry, 509
  in Upper South, 272
  in Western ranches, 511
Investments
  in Caribbean, 598
  in Cuba, 589
  opportunities, 284
  role in Great Depression, 659
Iowa, 331, 334, 661
Iran, 723, 746, 805, 844
Iran-Contra affair, 803
Iranian hostage crisis, 784–785
Iraq, 647, 709, 844
Ireland, 25, 621
Irish Catholics during Great War, 614
Irish immigrants, 76, 297, 298, 300,
  361, 482–484
Iron
  exports, 85
  foundry in South, 274
  imports of ironware, 86
  ore imports to Japan restricted, 691
  production of, 296, 331
  and steel industry, 440, 442, 443
Iron curtain, 722
Iroquois Confederation
  lands encroached upon, 98
  of New York ceded territory, 179
  Revolutionary War effects on, 172
Iroquois Indians
  Beaver Wars, 60–61, 67
  and Dutch merchants, 51–52
  effects of Revolutionary War, 158–159
  enemies of French, 34
  matrilineal society, 12
  neutrality, 101, 104
  reprisals in Revolutionary War, 150
  saved early French, 24
  tobacco, 11–12
Iroquois League
  composition and purpose, 60
  neutrality in Imperial wars, 100,
  101–102
Irreconcilables, 621
Irrigation systems, 9, 343, 500, 568
Islam in West Africa, 14
Islam with radical separatism, 771
Island hopping in WWII, 705
Island peoples, 11
Isolationism, 585, 688, 690
Isolationists in Congress, 678
Israel, 746, 784, 803, 824, 844
Italian Americans, 672, 701
Italian immigrants, 482–484, 485–486
Italy
  Great War, 606, 620, 621
  World War II, 687, 702, 703, 722
It Girl, 642
Iveson, Alfred, Georgia planter, 272
Ivory, 652–653
Ivy League elite, 733
Iwo Jima, 707

J

Jackson, Andrew, U.S. president
  annexation of Texas, 260
  destruction of Bank of United
  States, 253–254, 255
  election of 1824, 237
  Gulf Coast defense, 230–231, 233
  Indian removal, 249–251, 252
  political opponents, 256–257
  presidency, 206, 242, 247–254
Jackson, Jesse, 810
Jackson, Mississippi, 394
Jackson, Thomas J. "Stonewall," 385,
  393
Jackson bus terminal, freedom riders,
  754
Jacksonian Democrats, 242, 246–247
Jacksonian Era, 241–263
  egalitarian politics, 243–247
  Jackson presidency, 247–254

transportation revolution, 292
Van Buren presidency, 254–256
Whig Party, 256–261
Jackson State University, 776
Jacksonville, Florida, 699
Jacobs, Charlotte Webb, 330
Jakarta, 51
Jamaica, 20, 45, 808
James, Duke of York, 52, 93
James, Jesse, 769
James I, king of England, 35, 37, 41
James River, 402
Jamestown, 34, 35, 65
Japan
  ambitions in China, 593–594
  in Great War, 606, 620
  interest in Philippines, 591
  under MacArthur, 723
  mentioned, Ford assembly plants,
  647
  opened to trade, 584–585
  post WWII, 722, 723, 725, 727
  relations with U.S. in early 1930s, 680
  support of Persian Gulf War, 805
  warning on immigration restrictions,
  485
  war with China, 687
  world economy, 779
  in World War II, 691, 692, 693–694,
  702, 705, 707
    Combined Fleet, 692
Japanese Americans, internment,
  699–701, 842
Japanese Americans attacked by Klan,
  643
Japanese Association of America, 483
Japanese immigrants, 482, 483–484,
  485, 643, 680
Japanese immigration, 562, 595
Java Sea, Battle of the, 693
Jay, John, Supreme Court chief
  justice, 208
  negotiating for U.S., 183
  Peace of Paris, 156
  ratification of Constitution, 190
  secretary for foreign affairs, 182
Jay-Gardoqui talks, 183, 184
Jay's Treaty, 208–210, 211, 213
Jazz Age, 641
Jazz music, 639, 641, 646
Jefferson, Thomas, U.S. president, 197
  advice to Lewis on Sioux, 335
  colonial intellectual, 90
  Declaration of Independence, 141
  election of 1800, 213
  etiquette of receptions for
  presidential visitors, 219
  naming of Republican party, 205
  on national debt, 204
  Ordinance of 1784, 179
  presidency, 219–224
  prohibition of slavery in Old
  Northwest, 353
  Republican candidate, 210
  states rights, 211
Jefferson Airplane, 768
Jeffersonian Republicanism, 217–239
  Era of Good Feelings, 231–233
  Jacksonian appeal, 248
  Jefferson presidency, 219–224
  Louisiana Purchase, 220–222, 236
  Madison presidency, 224–230
  unity breakdown, 233–237
  War of 1812, 226–231
Jeffersonian Republicans, 197
Jesuit missionaries, 33, 64, 112
Jesus Christ, 455, 633
Jewish Americans
  agricultural colonies, 514
  and anti-Semite H. Ford, 631
  appointed to Supreme Court, 574
  attacked by Klan, 643
  cultural values, 815
  excluded from suburbs, 640
  FDR coalition, 672
  immigrants, 361, 482
  opposed prohibition, 562

Jewish expulsion from Spain, 22
Jewish problem and Holocaust, 705
Jewish refugees, 690
Jiang Jieshi (Chi-ang Kai-shek), 687,
  726, 745
Jim Crow laws, 455, 752
Job Corps, 755
Job discrimination, 767
Jobs, *See also* Employment
  blacks' loss, immigrants' gain, 486
  categorized by sex, 813
  during Great Depression
  creation of, 666, 670
  lack of, 660
  for women, 673
  for immigrants, 483–484
  in New South late 19th century, 445
  during Reagan years, 797–800
  in suburbs *vs.* city, 772
Joffre, Joseph, French marshal, 617
John Brown's Raid, 367–368
Johnson, Andrew, U.S. president
  impeachment, 828
  nullified order for abandoned lands,
  419
  presidential Reconstruction, 417,
  422–425
  as Tennessee senator, 280
Johnson, Anthony, black plantation
  owner, 69
Johnson, Elliott, 695
Johnson, Hiram, California senator,
  613, 614, 621
Johnson, Hugh, 667
Johnson, Lyndon, U.S. president
  Civil Rights actions, 754–756
  end of term, 774
  Great Society, 757
  oil embargo, 778–779
  as president, 744
  Texas NYA official, 670
  Vietnam War, 763
Johnson, Richard M., of Kentucky, 243
Johnson, Susie, 831
Johnson C. Smith University in
  Charlotte, Virginia, 418
Johnston, Joseph E., Confederate
  general, 388, 401–404, 406–407
"Join, Or Die," national symbol,
  164–165
Joint Committee on Conduct of War,
  397
Joint-stock companies, 35, 100
  Oneida Community, 313–314
Jones, Charles Colcock, 283
Jones, Jim, 769
Jones, John Paul, naval hero, 151, 152
Jones, Mary Harris (Mother Jones),
  560–561
Jones, Paula, 827
Jones, Rosalie, 548
Jones, Sam, 445
Jones, Samuel "Golden Rule," 565
Joplin, Janis, rock singer, 768
Journeymen, 87, 298–299, 304–305
  positions to women in WWII, 698
  temperance movement, 307
Juarez, Benito, 389
Juarez, Mexico, 809
Judicial checks and balances, 187
Judicial nationalism, 232
Judicial review, 187, 220
Judicial system established, 202
Judiciary, Virginia Plan, 184
Judiciary Act (1789), 202
Judiciary Act (1801), 220
Jungle, The (Sinclair), 472, 553, 630
Junk bonds, 797
Jupiter missiles, 751
Justice Department, 623–624, 718, 842
Jute boycott, 448
Juvenile courts, 554

K

Kahnawake village, 77
Kamikaze pilots, 707

Kansas
  Bleeding, Battle of, 361
  IWW trial, 616
  mentioned, 511, 512, 513, 516, 752
  Populist control, 538, 539
  settlements, 514
  tribal lands, 334
  women suffrage adopted, 564
Kansas City, Kansas, 471, 509
Kansas City, Missouri, 640, 641
Kansas Farmer magazine, 513, 537
Kansas Indians, 334
Kansas-Nebraska Act, 360–361, 364
Kansas Pacific Railroad, 510
Kansas People's Party, 537
Kansas Territory, 360–361, 364
Kaskaskia settlement in Mississippi
  Valley, 150
Kasserine Pass, 703
Kazakhstan, 709, 805
Kearny, Stephen W. colonel, 346
Keating-Owen Act, 574
Kelley, Abby, Quaker abolitionist, 318
Kelley, Florence, 554
Kellie, Luna, 515, 516
Kellogg-Briand Pact (1928), 647
Kellor, Frances, 562
Kennan, George, diplomat in
  Moscow, 722, 724
Kennedy, Jacqueline, 748, 754
Kennedy, John F., U.S. president
  assassination, 754–755
  Civil Rights actions, 754
  and Cold War, 748–752
  inaugural address, 750
  moon landing goal, 762, 777
Kennedy, Robert, 774, 775
Kennesaw Mountain, 404
Kenneth Galbraith, John,
  economist, 743
Kensington, Pennsylvania, 560
Kent State University in Ohio, 776,
  788–789
Kentucky
  admitted as slave state, 235
  election of 1864, 405
  hunger during Great Depression,
    657
  losing migrants, 333
  in Old Northwest, 329
  political separation, 199–201
  problems after Revolutionary War,
    183
  in Revolutionary War, 150
  slave population in 1860, 272
  states rights, 211
  stayed in Union, 384
  Upper South in 1850, 270
  under Virginia control, 175
Kenya, 841
Kern-McGillicuddy Act, 574
Kettle Creek, Battle of, 152
Key, Francis Scott, 230
Keynes, John Maynard, British
  economist, 677
Key West, Florida, 441
Khan, Great, of China, 19
Khe Sanh, South Vietnam, 773
Khmer Rouge, 776, 792
Khomeini, Ayatollah Ruhollah, 785
Khrushchev, Nikita, 743, 748, 749, 751
Kickbacks to party machines, 527
Kieft, Willem, governor of New
  Netherland, 54
Killing Fields movie, 792
Kim II Sung, 728
Kindergartens
  created by black women, 563
  municipal reforms, 565
  proposed by women reformers, 554
  settlement workers, 557
  standard element in schools, 559
King, Martin Luther Jr., 753, 754, 756,
  766, 775
King, Rodney, 801–802
King George's War (War of the
  Austrian Succession), 102

King of Kings, The (DeMille film), 641
King Philip's War, 64–65
Kings Mountain, South Carolina, 152
King William's War, 100
Kinship ties, 72
Kiowa Indians, 338, 339, 501, 503
Kissinger, Henry, national security
  adviser, 777–778
Kitchen debate, 743
Kitchens standardized, 717
Kitchin, Claude, North Carolina
  representative, 611
Kivas, 9, 66, 339
Klan night riders, 428
Knights of Labor, 459, 478, 529
Know-Nothing party, 362–363
Kohl, Helmut, West German
  Chancellor, 804
Korea, 585, 594, 718
Korean immigrants, 808
Korean War, 727–730, 746
Korematsu v. United States (1944), 701
Kosciuszko, Tadeusz, Polish engineer,
  143
Kosovo, 824
Kowloon, 593
Kristallnacht, 679
Ku Klux Klan, 428, 456, 643–644
Ku Klux Klan Act (1871), 428
Kurds, 806
Kursk Salient, 703
Kuwait, 805–806
Kwakiutl Indians, 7
Kyoto Agreement, 841

L
La Bahía del Espiritu Santo, 341
Labor
  contracts between former slaves and
    masters, 419
  groups, 432
  Magna Carta, 669
  market in Upper South, 271–272
  migrant, 643
  needs in English colonies, 73, 75
Laborers. *See* Workers
Labor unions, *See also* Trade unions
  African-Americans, 699
  after Great War, 622, 624
  became conservative, 739
  demand for rights, 553–554
  disputes and Roosevelt, 567–568
  gains reversed after WWII, 716
  in Great Depression, 659
  during Great War, 612, 615
  in late 19th century, 478–480
  loyalty excuses during war, 842
  membership in 1920s, 634
  new labor movement in 1830s, 305
  opposed by business, 556
  organizing criticized by
    conservatives, 668
  during Reagan years, 797–798
  regulations struck down, 636
  revival in 1930s, 672–673
  right to organize, 669
  turmoil and strikes in 1894, 540–541
  Wilson's actions, 574
La Creole ads, 652
Ladies Association of Philadelphia, 158
Ladies' Home Journal Magazine, 744
Ladies Memorial Associations, 451
Lafayette, Marquis de, 143
La Follette, Robert, 566, 571, 572,
  621, 624
Lagos, Nigeria, 476
Laird, Melvin, secretary of Defense, 776
Laissez-faire, 530, 532, 538, 539, 552
Lake Champlain, 102, 182, 230
Lake Erie in War of 1812, 229
Lake Texcoco, 9
Lakewood, California, 717
Lakota Indians, 500, 502
Land
  allocated to individual Indians, 506
  development in colonies, 76

disputes between Indians & whites,
    61–62
  Indian concept of ownership, 500
  reform, 670
  scarcity in East, 327–329
  termination policy sold Indian
    lands, 740
  West public grasslands, 677
Land bridge from Siberia, 6
Land Grant College Act of 1862,
  397–398
Land grants
  in California, 342
  in Texas, 339–341
Landless states and Articles of
  Confederation, 175
Landless white people, 281
Landon, Alf, 670, 672
Land Ordinance of 1785, 179–180
Land ownership
  for freedmen, 419
  in Maryland colony, 39
  in Virginia colony, 37–38
  and voting, 96
Land redistribution, 419, 423, 429, 538
Landsmanshaften Jewish associations,
  482–484
Land speculation, 175, 178, 181, 199,
  329, 330
Land transportation, 292
Lane rebels, 317
Lane Theological Seminary, 317
Langdon, Eunice, 656–657
Language in schools, 616, 837
Languages, Indian native, 674
La Orden de Hijos de America (The
  Order of the Sons of America),
  639
Laos, 729, 793
Larkin, Thomas, 344
LaSalle, Robert sieur de, 34
Las Casas, Bartolomé de, 22
Las Gorras Blancas, 515
Last Hired, First Fired in Great
  Depression, 661
Las Vegas, Nevada, 741
Latchkey children during WWII, 697
Latin America
  in 1920s, 648
  imperial power, 595–599
  oil fields, 647
  rejected customs union, 585
  relations, 678–679
Latin Americans
  view of Americans, 588
Latino political activism, 772
Latino race riots during WWII, 699
Latinos. *See* Hispanic Americans; (see
  also Mexican Americans)
Laundreau, Moon, mayor of New
  Orleans, 770
Laurens, John, 134–135, 145
Lawes Divine, Morall and Martiall, 35
Lawrence, Kansas, 361
Laws, *See also specific legislation*
  anti-evolution, 645
  antitrust, 647
  of gravity, 90
Leadville, Colorado, 508
League of Armed Neutrality, 150
League of Freedom, 357
League of Nations, 345, 619, 620, 624
League of United Latin American
  Citizens (LULAC), 639
League of Women Voters, 637, 834
Leary, Timothy, Harvard professor, 768
Lease, Mary E., 537–538
Leaves of Grass (Whitman), 314
Lebanon, 803
Lecompton Constitution, 364
Lee, Ann, 313
Lee, Jason, 336
Lee, Jesse, 245
Lee, Richard Henry, of Virginia,
  140–141

Lee, Robert E., Confederate general
  abandoned Petersburg and
    Richmond, 406
  battled Grant in 1864, 401–403
  "Furl the flag, boys," 460
  in John Brown's raid, 367
  role in Lost Cause, 417
  war in East, 388
Legal aid for poor, 427
Legal nationalism, 232
Legislative checks and balances, 187
Legislative Reference Bureau, 566
Legislatures in states, 173, 243
Leisler, Jacob, 94
Leisure, 491, 641
Le May, Curtis, Air Force general, 729
Lemke, William, North Dakota
  representative, 668, 672
Lend-lease program, 691
Lenin, V.I., 617, 619
Leopard, British ship, 223
Lesbians. *See* Gays and lesbians
LeSeur, Meridel, 657
Letters from an American Farmer,
  (Crèvecoeur), 170
Letters home, D. Beardsley, 391
Levitt, William, New York builder,
  717, 719
Levittown houses in New York, 714,
  717
Lewelling, Lorenzo D., Populist
  governor of Kansas, 540
Lewinsky, Monica, 827
Lewis, John L., 716, 756
Lewis, Meriwether, 221, 335
Lewis, Sinclair, 642
Lewis and Clark expedition, 221, 236
Lewiston, Idaho, 506
Lexington, Battle of, 136–137
Leyte, Battle of, 706
Liberal Republicans, 427, 429
Liberals
  denounced by conservatives, 796
  and Eisenhower, 739
  Employment Act, 715–716
  protest of Vietnam War, 765–766
  social issues, 815–817
  students, 766–767, 776
Liberator, The, 256, 316, 368
Liberia, West Africa, 315, 458
Liberty, 197–198, 199, 527
Liberty Association, 357
Liberty Bonds, 613, 615
Liberty Party, 320
Libraries, 90, 509
Liddy, G. Gordon, 780
Life expectancy, 273, 671, 674
Life insurance, 458
Life Magazine, 697
Life spans, 811
Light bulbs, 468, 489, 492
Lighting rod experiments, 90
Liliuokalani, queen of Hawaii, 586
Lima, Peru, 20
Limbaugh, Rush, 159
Limited liability, 294, 470
Limited Test Ban Treaty (1963), 709,
  751
Lincoln, Abraham, U.S. president
  abolitionists support of, 370
  assassination, 407
  Civil War actions, 385, 388, 393
  debated Douglas, 364–365
  election of 1864, 404–405
  on immigration, 298
  issued Emancipation Proclamation,
    390–392
  readmission of Southern States,
    421–422
  secession of Lower South, 369–375
  suspended writ of habeas corpus, 842
  as Union president, 384
  use of executive authority, 397
  views on slavery, 374
Lincoln, Countess of, 32
Lincoln-Douglas Debates, 364–365
Lindbergh, Charles, aviator, 641

Linecum, Gideon, 332
Linn, William, Reverend, 213
Lippmann, Walter, journalist, 625
Liquor, 642, 645
Literacy
of Black Americans, 674
and educational qualifications for
voting, 455
and freedmen's schools, 418
laws for immigrants, 562
requirement, 485
of slaves, 273
in South late 19th century, 457
of women and office work, 814
Literacy rates
in colonies, 89–90
North *vs.* South in 1860, 366
Literacy tests, 455, 565, 642, 756
Literary Digest Magazine, 606, 613
Little Crow, Santee Sioux Indian, 335
Little Rock, Arkansas, 738, 752
Little Turtle, Miami chief, 208, 209
Livestock in Columbian exchange, 23
Livestock raisers' associations, 677
Living conditions, *See also*
Neighborhoods
of Civil War soldiers, 386–388
in early 19th century, 301
in ethnic neighborhoods, 482
in first slums, 296
for fur trappers, 335–336
in New York tenements, 477
of slaves, 273–274
in Virginia, 38–39
of Western homesteaders, 515
in Western settlements in 1780s, 199
Living standard in 1920s, 635
Livingston, Robert R., chancellor of
New York, 196
Lloyd George, David of Britain, 619,
620
Loans
from Great War, 647
for veterans, 716
Lobbying, 549
Lobbying groups, special-interest, 528
Local government, 770
Localism, 530
Lochner v. New York (1905), 556
Locke, John, 48, 90, 117, 141
Lode mining, 509
Lodge, Henry Cabot, Massachusetts
Senator
advocate of imperialism, 581, 583,
584
Cuban revolution, 589
opposition to Treaty of Versailles,
621
Log College in Neshaminy,
Pennsylvania, 92
Loggers, strikebreaking, 615
London, England, 318, 809
Lone Star (Texas) Federation, 451
Long, Huey P., Louisiana senator,
668, 670
Long, Stephen, 333
Long Beach, California, 792
Long drives of cattle, 510, 512
Longest day, 703
Long Island, New York, 52, 714, 717
Long-range bombers, 751
Lords of Trade, 93, 94
Los Alamos, New Mexico, 686, 696
Los Angeles, California
growth during 1920s, 638
immigrant workers, 483
immigration gateway, 809
mentioned, 488
Mexican Americans in WWII, race
riots, 699
race riots, 801–802
social control and moral reform, 563
urban renewal, 740
Losing Ground (Murray), 796
Lost Cause, 417, 420, 452, 460
Lost Generation, 642
Loudoun, Lord, 103

Louis, Joe, 718
Louisbourg fortress on Cape Breton
Island, 102, 104
Louisiana
admitted as slave state, 235
black voters, 426
election of 1876, 430
French colonies, 99–100
Lower South in 1850, 267
mentioned, 446, 454
oil drilling, 632
Redemption, 430
secession from Union, 369
train seized by women, 661
voters, 243
in War of 1812, 230
Louisiana Purchase, 220–222, 223, 236
Louisiana Territory, 233
Louis XI, king of France, 16–17
Louis XIV, king of France, 100
Louis XVI, king of France, 205
Lou Reed and Velvet Underground,
rock band, 769
L'Ouverture, Toussaint, 222
Love Canal in New York, 779,
780–781
Lovejoy, Elijah P, 317
Lowcountry planters, 199, 251
Lowell, Massachusetts, 297, 300
Lower Midwest, migration from
South, 330
Lower South, 267–269
first president from, 354
and public education, 312
secession from Union, 369
Loyalists
losses from Revolutionary War, 182
parted company with Whigs, 136
Southern militias, 152, 155
Loyalty programs, 730
LSD drug, 768
Ludlow, Colorado, 556
Lumber industry, 274, 443, 568, 783
Luna Park, 492
Lunar module Eagle, 762, 777
Lunch counter sit-ins, 753
Lüshun (Port Arthur), Manchuria,
593, 594
Lusitania, British passenger liner, 608
Luther, Martin, 17
Luther, Seth, 244
Lutherans, 91, 173
Lyman, Major, 168
Lynch, John R., Mississippi
congressman, 431
Lynchburg, Virginia, 816
Lynchings
of black men, 451
origins, 453–454
post WWII, 717
as racial control, 563
Lynn, Massachusetts, 624

M

MacArthur, Douglas, general
in Great Depression, 663
in Korean War, 728, 729
in World War II, 705, 706, 723
Macdonough, Thomas, Commodore,
230
Machine tool production, 301
MacIntosh, Ebenezer, Boston
shoemaker, 118
Maclay, William, Pennsylvania senator,
196
Macon's Bill No 2, 224
Macune, Charles W., 447–448
Madeira, 19
Madison, James, U.S. president
American Colonization Society, 315
constitution, 186
crisis in 1786, 183
leader in the House of
Representatives, 202
naming of the Republican party, 205
on national debt, 204

presidency, 224–230
ratification of Constitution, 190
states rights, 211
tariffs and tonnage duties, 203
Virginia Plan, 184
Madison-Erskine agreement, 224
Magazines, *See also individual titles*
and advertising, 652–653
banned from mail, 614
family messages in 1950s, 742
investigative reporting, 553, 555
for middle class, 491
for niche markets, 832
on Panama Canal issue, 597–598
Socialism, 555
for Southern readers, 441
Magnetic compass, 18
Mahan, Alfred Thayer, 582–583, 584
Mahanism, 583
Mahoning River, 665
Mail, *See also* U.S. Post Office
rural free delivery, 561
Maine, 94, 243
Maize, 6, 9, 23
Major leagues, 718
Major league sports, 773
Makah Tribal Museum, 505
Malaya, 692
Malcolm X, 771
Mallory, Stephen R., Florida senator,
359
Malmstrom Air Force Base in Great
Falls, Montana, 807
Malnutrition, 660, *See also* Hunger;
Starvation
Mammoths, 6
Managerial innovations, 630
Manassas, Battles of, 385, 388
Manassas Junction, 388
Manchester, England, 96
Manchuria, 593, 680, 707, 723
Mandan Indians, 9, 334
Manhattan Institute, 796
Manhattan Island, 51, 147
Manhattan Project, 696, 707, 708, 709
Manifest Destiny
in 1840s, 343–345
and foreign policy, 345
Hawaiian annexation, 587
navy policy, 583, 590
supported by Franklin Pierce, 359
white migration, 327
Manila, Philippines, 104, 591, 593
Manila Bay, Philippines, 590, 693
Mann, Horace, 311
Mann Act (1910), 563
Mann-Elkins Act (1910), 571
Man Nobody Knows, The (Barton), 633
Man of the Year, Time magazine, 641
Manufactures, imports in colonies, 88
Manufacturing, 284
economic crisis after Revolutionary
War, 177
in late 19th century, 470
in market revolution, 291
minimal in Lower South, 268–269
in New England, 298–301
new markets, 291
putting-out system, 297
in Upper South, 271–272
Manumissions of slaves, 199, 281
Mao Tse-tung (Mao Zedong), 725,
727
Mao Zedong, 778
Mapmakers, 18
Maps
20th century, first half
Axis Europe, 1941, 689
Caribbean interventions, 596
election of 1916, 610
election of 1948, 721
expansion in Pacific, 586
National Forests and National
Parks, 569
population shifts, 1920–1930, 638
Spanish-American War, 591

Western economic development,
507
Western front, 1918, 618
WWII, 1942–1945, 704
WWII in Pacific, 694, 706
20th century, last half
election of 1960, 749
election of 1980, 794
election of 1992, 824
election of 2000, 839
Korean War, 728
metropolitan areas, 1900–2000, 807
Tennessee Valley Authority, 676
U.S. in Caribbean since 1954, 747
War in Vietnam, 764
women as business owners, 836
Civil War
Atlanta Campaign and Sherman's
March, 404
Battle of Gettysburg, 394
Compromise of 1850, 357
Congressional Reconstruction, 425
election of 1860, 369
Grant and Lee in Virginia, 403
War in East, 1861–1862, 386
War in East, 1862–1863, 393
War in West, 395
War in West, 1861–1862, 387
late 19th century
election of 1896, 543
growth of America's cities,
1880–1900, 488
patterns of immigration,
1820–1914, 481
railroads in South, 444–445
two-party stalemate, 526
post-Revolutionary War
election of 1800, 213
election of 1824, 237
Indian land cessions, 1784–1800,
200
Land Ordinance of 1785, 180
Louisiana Purchase, Lewis and
Clark expedition, 221
Missouri Compromise of 1820, 234
War of 1812, 228
pre-Civil War
crops in South, 1860, 271
election of 1840, 259
growth of cities 1820–1860,
302–303
Indian removals, 250
Mexican War, 347
spread of slavery, 1800–1850, 270
Texas and Mexico after Texas
Revolt, 340
transportation revolution, 293
western Overland Trails, 336
westward shift of population,
1790–1850, 328
pre-Revolutionary War
African origins of slaves, 71
English and Dutch colonies, 35
English North American colonies
c. 1685, 47
ethnic populations in early
colonies, 77
European empires in North
America, 1750–1763, 105
European voyages in 16th century,
21
New France c. 1650, 33
North American culture areas c.
1500, 8
Proclamation Line of 1763, 113
Spanish and French missions in
17th century, 63
transatlantic commerce, 85
West Africa and Europe in 1492, 13
Revolutionary War
Battles of Lexington and Concord,
137
early fighting, 1775–1776, 139
North America after Peace of Paris,
1783, 157
war in North 1776–1777, 148
war in South, 1778–1781, 153

war on Frontier, 1778–1779, 151
Maquiladora plants, 810
Marbury v. *Madison,* 220
Marches
  gay pride in late 20th century, 813
Marches on Washington
  Civil Rights (1963), 698, 754
  unemployed (1893), 539–540
Marcos, Ferdinand, president of
    Philippines, 803
Marijuana, 768
Market revolution in 19th century
  immigration & cities, 295–297, 298
  industrial revolution, 297–301
  transportation advances, 292–295
  urbanization, 291–297
Marl (shell deposits), 270
Marriage
  in 1950s, 741
  boom after WWII, 718
  fur trappers & Indian women, 335
  during Great Depression, 660
  intermarriage in Spanish colonies,
    99
  laws in 1920s, 642
  plural in Oneida Community, 313
  to preserve plantations, 329
  of slaves, 274
  in Virginia, 38
  during WWII, 697
Married Women's Property Act
    (1860), 319
Marshall, George C., 703, 723,
    732–733
Marshall, John, Chief Justice, 220,
    232, 251, 294
Marshall, Thurgood, 752
Marshall Plan, 723–724
Martin, Carlota Silvas, 656–657
Martinique, 45
Maryland
  and Articles of Confederation, 175
  Catholic colonists, 39
  national debt payments, 176
  ratification of Constitution, 190
  slavery embraced, 69
  stayed in Union, 384
  Upper South in 1850, 270
Mason, George, antifederalist, 173,
    188
Mason-Dixon line, 442
Masonic lodges, 420
Masons, 257
Massachusetts
  Constitutional conventions, 243
  girls' elementary education, 198
  mentioned, 145, 454
  protective tariffs, 533
  ratification of Constitution, 189–190
  regulation of industry, 531
  state board of education, 311
  state-supported religion, 197
  Supreme Court, 305
  women in majority, 197
Massachusetts Bay, 800
Massachusetts Bay Company, 41–42
Massachusetts Bureau of Labor
    Statistics, 474
Massachusetts colony, 91, 94, 97
Massachusetts Constitution, 173
Massachusetts Government
    Act, 124–125
Massachusetts Institute of
    Technology, 696
Massachusetts Institute of Technology
    (MIT), 808
Massachusetts legislature, 135
Massachusetts Spy, revolutionary
    newspaper, 164
Massacre of Fort William Henry, 104
Massacres
  Boston, 122–123
  Colfax Massacre, 432
  of Conestoga Indians, 114
  of Fort William Henry, 104
  Memorial Day, Chicago, 1937, 673
  Sand Creek, Colorado, 502

Massaponax Church, Virginia, 405
Mass appeal of Whig Party, 257–258
Massasoit, Wampanoag leader, 41, 64
Mass consumption, 640
Mass conversions, 92
Mass culture in Jazz Age, 640–642
Massive retaliation, 745
Mass media, 567
Mass mobilization in 1800s, 247
Mass movement, temperance, 308
Mass politics in 1840, 259
Mass production, 630–632, 695, 717
Mass transit, 801
Master craftsmen, 304–305, 307
Mastodons, 6
Matamoros, Mexico, 394
Materialism of mass culture, 642
Maternity and Infancy Act, Sheppard-
    Towner (1921), 637
Maternity care, 637
Mathematics in Mesoamerica, 7
Mather, Reverend Cotton, colonial
    intellectual, 90
Matrilineal societies, 12, 14
Maverick, Maury, Lieutenant, 618
Maximillian, Archduke of Austria, 389
Maxwell House Hotel, 490
Mayan civilization, 7
Mayflower Compact, 41
Maynard, Lucy, 329
Maysville Road Bill, 248
McAdoo, William, 607, 611, 613
McCall's Magazine, 744
McCarran Committee, 731
McCarthy, Eugene, Minnesota
    senator, 774
McCarthy, Joseph, senator from
    Wisconsin, 732–733, 774
McCarthyism, 730–733, 739
McClellan, George B., Union general
  at Battle of Antietam, 390
  led Army of Potomac, 388, 402
  presidential candidate, 405
  replaced by Lincoln, 393
McClure, Samuel S., 553
McClure's Magazine, 553, 555
McCormick, Cyrus, 330
McCoy, Joseph, cattle shipper, 510
McCrae, Jane, fiancé of British officer,
    146
McCulloch v. *Maryland* (1819), 232
McDonald's Restaurant, 741
McDowell, Calvin, 453
McDowell, Irvin, Union general, 385
McGillivray, Alexander, Creek leader,
    183
McGovern, George, South Dakota
    senator, 781
McGuffey Readers, 312
McInerny, Jay, novelist, 798
McKinley, William, U.S. president
  assassination, 566
  on Cuban affairs, 589–590, 596
  as governor of Ohio, 542–543
  imperialist debate, 584, 592, 594
  and Panama Canal, 597
  on tariffs, 533–534
McKinley Tariff Act (1890), 534, 538,
    542–543, 586
McLemore, Jeff, Texas representative,
    609
McNamara, John, 822
McNamara, Robert, secretary of
    Defense, 751, 757, 779
McVeigh, Timothy, 826
Meade, George, Union general, 393,
    402
Measles, 20, 23, 337
Meat Inspection Act (1906), 571
Meatpacking center in Cincinnati,
    296
Meatpacking industry, 470–471, 553
Meatpacking workers, 630
Meat rationed, 695
Mechanicks, 122–123
Mechanics, 298–299, 300–301
Mechanic's Free Press, 299

Mechanization, 480, 667, 675
Mecklenburg County, North
    Carolina, 172
Medicaid, 757, 829
Medical care, 144, 427
Medical Care Act, 757
Medicare, 757, 810, 829
Mediterranean, 702, 703
Mediterranean tribute system, 220
Mellon, Andrew, secretary of
    Treasury, 636, 637
Melting pot, 631
Melville, Herman, 314, 492
Memorial Day Massacre, Chicago
    (1937), 673
Memphis, Tennessee, 386, 454, 482,
    638
Men
  changing roles in late 19th century,
    489
  division of labor
    in Africa, 14
    in Native America, 6, 9, 10, 12
    in New England, 44
    in New South in late 19th century,
      445
  office workers, 814
  on Oregon Trail, 337
  in Western Europe, 16
  employment opportunities in
    colonial cities, 87–88
  gender segregation during Great
    Depression, 660
  horses valued, 23
  image as protectors of family, 305
  on Indian reservations, 505
  manufacturing workers, 300
  in military in WWII, 696
  political rights, 169–172
  slave life, 274
  Southern planters, 279
  superiority over household, 310
  as wage earners, 305
Mencken, H. L., reporter, 645
Mendes Africans, 14
Menlo Park, New Jersey, 468
Mennonites, 91
Mental hospitals, 312, 800
Mercantilism, 83
Merchant marine, 223
Merchant vessels as privateers, 151
Merger mania, 797–798
Merrimack River, 297, 301
Mesoamerica, 7–9
Mestizos, 64, 77, 338
Metacom (King Philip), 64
Methodist Church
  financial ties to state governments,
    173
  religious divisions in War of 1812,
    229
  settlement houses, 450
  split over slavery in 1844, 283, 366
Methodist clergy, 451, 453
Methodists
  Second Great Awakening, 244–245
  and social reform, 552
Mexican Americans, *See also* Hispanic
    Americans
  agricultural workers, 772
  attacked by Klan, 643
  in Chavez Ravine, 740
  derogatory stereotypes of, 347
  immigrants, 639, 643, 808
  race riots in WWII, 699
  reestablish city council districts, 836
  workers during WWII, 698
Mexican Borderlands, 338–343
Mexican Cession of 1848, 343
Mexican cowboys, 512
Mexican deportations, 661
Mexican migrant labor, 483, 612, 643,
    740
Mexican War, 343, 344–346, 353
Mexico
  California and Southwest lost to
    U.S., 342–343

during Civil War, 389
cross-border economy, 809–810
and Germany, Zimmerman note, 610
slavery in territories, 353–354
Texas independence, 339–342
Wilson's actions, 599
Mexico City, 346
Mezzogiorno, Italy, 481–482
Miami, Florida, 638, 809
Miami Indians, 207, 209
Miantonomo, 53
Michigan, 330, 331, 454, 695
Michigan Liberty Party, 320
Michigan University, 808
Micmac Indians, 60
Microsoft Corporation, 830
Mid-Atlantic pluraism in 1800, 198
Middle class
  domesticity, 308
  early industrialization in 1800s,
    302–304
  in late 19th century, 490–492
  move to suburbs, 489
  and school reform, 312
  support of Nixon, 778
  voters in FDR coalition, 672
Middle East, 803
Middle Passage, 72
Midnight, Captain, 697
Midway Island, 585
Midway Island, Battle of, 694
MIG 15s, 729
Migrant labor, 483, 612, 643, 740
Migrations
  of African Americans, 639, 770
  to cities in 1920s, 638–640
  from New Jersey and Pennsylvania to
    old Northwest, 330
  from Old Southwest, 333
  from Upper South to West, 270
  urban crisis in 1970s, 770
  into West, 514
  of whites going West, 326–327
  of whites on Oregon Trail, 336–338
Milholland, Inez, 549
Militarized society after WWII, 719
Military aid to European
    governments, 729
Military airplanes, 705, 729, 747, 751,
    755
Military bases, 807
Military courts, 696
Military expansion in 1940, 690
Military life, 144
Military power
  European c. 1500, 16
  in Latin America, 595–599
  subjugating Indians, 501–505
Military practices in Europe, 103–104
Military Reconstruction Acts, 425
Military spending. *See* Defense
    spending
Military supply depots, 698
Militia. *See* State militias
Millenarian folk movement, 514
Miller, Jeff, 789
Milling machines, 301
Millionaires, African-American, 653
Mills, C. Wright, 744
Milwaukee, Wisconsin, 296, 454, 550
Mine inspectors, 509
Minerals, 568, 797
Miners' Union Library, 509
Mine safety legislation, 509
Mingo Indians, 199
Minimum wage law for women, 636
Minimum wages, 673
Mining, 274
Mining bonanza in American West,
    506–510
Mining camps, 506–508
Mining industry, 509–510
Mink brigade, 554
Minneapolis, Minnesota, 668, 772
Minnesota
  in election of 1860, 369
  grain elevator fraud, 517

mentioned, 513, 514
Northwestern Farmers' Alliance, 537
Populist election, 538
public safety committees, 615
state agencies established, 532
Minorities
    at ballot box, 835–836
    current population, 834
    defining their heritage, 772
    during Great Depression, 661
    jobs and housing in affluent years, 740–741
    and New Deal, 674–675
    roles during Great War, 612–613
Minority separatism, 771–772
Minor v. Happersett, 526
Minuteman missiles, 751, 807
Minute Men, 135, 137
Miranda, Francisco de, Spanish officer, 169
Mishikinakwa (Little Turtle), Miami chief, 208, 209
Missile Crisis in Cuba, 750–751
Missile gap, 745, 748
Missiles, weapons, 745, 751, 802, 803, 807
Missionaries, 336, 582
Missionary associations, 245
Missionary diplomacy, 599
Missionary schools, 504
Missions in California, 342
Mission system, 338
Mississippi
    admitted as slave state, 235
    admitted to Union, 332
    black codes of 1865, 423
    black voters, 426
    in Civil War, 394
    denied Indian rights, 249
    disfranchisement, 455
    freedom riders, 754
    losing migrants, 333
    Lower South in 1850, 267
    mentioned, during Reconstruction, 430
    primary election, 565
    refusal to ratify 13th Amendment, 422
    secession from Union, 369
    state flag, 460
    voter turnout, 456
    voting requirements, 243
Mississippian mound-building culture, 10
Mississippi Freedom Democratic Party (MFDP), 756
Mississippi River
    claimed by French, 34
    closed by Spain, 183
    demanded free and open navigation, 207
    mentioned, 332
    Peace of Paris, 156
    transit thru port of New Orleans, 210
    Union control during Civil War, 385–386, 394
Mississippi Summer Freedom Project, 756
Mississippi Valley
    American forces in, 221
    French colonies, 99–100
    mound-building society, 10–11
    Revolutionary War fighting, 150
    strategic corridor for French, 101
Missouri
    admitted to Union, 332
    on Oregon Trail, 336
    slave population in 1860, 272
    slavery issue, 235
    stayed in Union, 384
    Upper South in 1850, 270
    voting requirements, 243
Missouri Compromise, 235–236
    held as unconstitutional, 363–364
    plan to extend line, 371
    repealed, 360

Missouri River, 236
Mitchell, John, 567, 593
Mob government, 302
Mobile, Alabama, 268, 282, 695, 699
Mobilization for war, North and South, 381–385
Mob rule, 173
Mobs, antiabolitionist, 317
Moby Dick (Melville), 314
Moctezuma, Aztec king, 4, 20
Model Cities Program (1966), 767
Model T car, 630
Modern American in 1920s, 629–653
    business of government, 635–637
    cities & suburbs, 637–640
    culture wars, 642–646
    economy, 632–635
    mass culture in Jazz Age, 640–642
    world interests, 647–648
Modernization of American society, 399
Modern presidency, T. Roosevelt, 567
Modern Woman advertising, 652
Modoc Indians, 503
Mohawk Indians, 60, 77
Mohegan Indians, 42
Molasses, colonial export, 86
Molasses Act, 84
Moley, Raymond, 665
Mondale, Walter, vice president, 795, 834
Monetary policy in late 19th century, 535–537
Money, *See also* Currency; Paper money; Specie Circular (1836)
    economic crisis after Revolutionary War, 178
    gold or silver coin, 253
    limited supply in colonies, 120
    reduction of supply, 255
Money supply, 535
Monmouth Court House, Battle of, 145, 150
Monongahela River, 102
Monopolies, 535, 537, 574
Monroe, James, U.S. president, 231, 237, 315
Monroe, Sarah, of New York City, 305
Monroe Doctrine, 233, 587, 751
    and Roosevelt Corollary, 598, 648
Montana, 336, 508, 538
    mentioned, 502, 510, 511
Montauk Indians of Long Island, 53
Montcalm, Marquis de, 103, 104
Monterrey in Mexican War, 346
Montgomery, Alabama, 753
Montgomery, Bernard, general, 693, 703
Montgomery NAACP, 753
Montgomery Ward, 658
Montreal, 33, 101, 138, 230
Montserrat, 45
Moody, Dwight, 459
Moon, Sun Myung, 769
Moon landings, 762
Moonshine, 645
Moore, John Bassett, assistant secretary of State, 592
Moore's Creek Bridge in North Carolina, 138
Moral Majority, 370, 816
Moral order, 306–310
Moral reforms, 562–563
Moratorium on fishing, 27
Morgan, Daniel, general in Continental army, 155
Morgan, John, Alabama senator, 583
Morgan, J.P., 471, 542, 569, 572
Morgan, William, 257
Mormon Church, 310, 343
Mormons, 501, 514, 516
Morningside Heights, Battle of, 775
Morocco, 15
Morris, Robert, Philadelphia merchant, 175–176
Morrison, Jim, rock singer, 769
Morrison, Philip, professor, 696

Morristown, New Jersey, 147
Morse, Omar H., 327
Mortality rates
    among fur trappers, 336
    early 19th century, 296
    in early American West, 199
Mortgages, 666, *See also* Foreclosures
Moscow, 688
Moss, Tom, 453
Motels, 741
Motherhood, sanctified notion, 304
Mother Jones (Mary Harris Jones), 560–561
Mothers' pensions, 559
Motion picture industry, 634
Mott, Lucretia, 318–319
Mound-building societies, 10–11
Mountain men. *See* Fur traders
Mounted patrols of whites, 276
Mount Vernon, 82, 89
Movie "fan" magazines, 652
Movies, portrayal of cities, 769
Movie theaters, 641
Mrs. Miniver (1942), 697
MTV: Music Television, 798, 832
Muckraking, 553, 556
Mugwumps, 529, 532
Muir, John, 570
Mulatto elite, 282
Muller v. Oregon, 558
Multinational corporations, 647, 766, 809
Munich agreement, 679–681
Municipal elections, 528
Municipal reform, 565–566
Munitions plant during Civil War, 383
"Murder of," 125
Murder of slaves, 273
Murray, Charles, 796
Music
    in 1920s, 639, 641, 646
    in 1980s, 798
    rock-and-roll and folk, 768–769
    rock-and-roll and rhythm-and-blues, 742
    of slaves, 73
Musicians, 670
Muskets, manufacture, 301
Muslim extremists, 823
Muslim fundamentalists, 784–785
Muslims, 14, 68, 842, 844
Mussolini, Benito, 679, 688, 692, 703
Mutiny in Continental Army, 144
Mutual aid societies in 1920s, 639
Mutual defense pacts, 725
Mutual Economic Assistance, 723
Mutualistas (mutual aid societies), 639
Mutual misunderstanding, 747–749
Mystic River, 42

N

Nacogdoches, 341
Nagasaki, Japan, 707, 708
Naming names, 730–731
Nanking, China, 687
Napier, J. C., 458
Naples, 703
Napoleon Bonaparte, 221, 224, 229
Napoleon III, emperor of France, 389
Narcotics, 562–563
Narragansett Bay, 123–124
Narragansett Indians, 41, 42, 53
Narrative of Life of Frederick Douglass, an American Slave (Douglass), 320
Nash, Gary, 159
Nashville, Battle of, 406
Nashville, Tennessee, 420, 441, 753
Nast, Thomas, 432
Nation, Bill, 715
National Advisory Commission on Civil Disorders, 771

National Aeronautics and Space Administration (NASA), 745, 762, 777, 808
National Americanization Committee, 562
National American Woman Suffrage Association, 529, 564
National Association for Advancement of Colored People (NAACP), 460, 461, 563–564, 639, 718, 752
National Association of Colored Women, 459, 740
National Association of Manufacturers (1895), 556, 565, 634
National bank. *See* Bank of the United States
National Banking Act (1863), 398
National Birth Control League, 560
National Black Convention, 358
National Broadcasting Company (NBC), 641
National Child Labor Committee, 557
National Civil Service Reform League, 529
National Congress of American Indians (1944), 698
National Congress of Mothers, 554
National Conservation Commission, 568
National Consumers' League, 554, 673
National Council of Negro Women, 674
National culture, 202
National debt
    in 1781, 175, 176
    in 1789, 203–204
    in 1980s, 801
    of England after French and Indian War, 112
    through history, 206
    in World War II, 695
National Defense Act, 609
National Endowment for the Arts, 757
National Endowment for the Humanities, 757
National Environmental Policy Act (1970), 779
National Farmers Union (1902), 565
National Grange of Patrons of Husbandry, 447
National Guard, 623, 668, 753, 754, 770, 775, 776
National health insurance, 721
National History Standards, 159
National Housing Association in 1910, 557
National Industrial Recovery Act (NIRA), 667
Nationalists, 175–176, 183–184
National Labor Relations Act (1935), 772
National Labor Relations Board, 797
National Labor Relations Board (NLRB), 669
National League baseball, 492
National Mobilization Committee to End the War in Vietnam, 775
National Organization for Women (NOW) (1966), 767, 812
National Origins Act, 679
National Origins Act (1924), 643, 646
National Park Service, 396
National Progressive League, 572
National Reclamation Act, 568
National Recovery Administration (NRA), 667, 673, 674
National Republican party, 254
National Resources Planning Board, 702
National Rifle Association, 826–827
National Security Act (1947), 724
National Security Council (NSC), 724, 745, 803

National Security Council Paper 68 (NSC-68), 727, 729
National Socialist Workers Party (Nazis), 679
National symbol, rattlesnake, 164–165
National Trades Union, 305
National Union for Social Justice, 668
National War Labor Board, 612
National Woman's Party, 637
National Women's Political Caucus, 834
National Youth Administration (NYA), 670, 674
Nation of Islam, 771
Native American Graves Protection and Repatriation Act (1990), 505
Native American Religious Freedom Act (1978), 505
Native Americans, *See also* Indians
activism in 1960s, 1970s, 772
assimilation, 740
in Congress, 836
landholdings, 675
New Deal, 674–675
under New Deal, 674–675
religious freedom, 674–675
during WWII, 696, 698
Native Sons of Golden State, 485
Nativism
in 1920s, 642–643, 646
in election of 1928, 648
of H. Ford, 631
Japanese immigration limited, 562
in late 19th century, 484–486
and McCarthyism, 733
Nativist arguments, 298
Nativist organizations, 305
NATO, 729, 746
Nat Turner's Rebellion, 251, 276, 316
Naturalization Act (1870), 485
Naturalization law, 298
Natural resources management & T. Roosevelt, 568
Natural rights, 172
Nature as economic resource, 301
Nauvoo, Illinois, 343
Navajo Indians, 339, 343, 503, 696
Naval Advisory Board, 583
Naval bases
in Cuba, 596
in destroyer deal, 691
Gulf of St. Lawrence, 102
in Japan, 583
Naval blockades
British, during Great War, 607–608
by Union forces, 389
Naval Construction Act, 609
Naval stores
colonial export, 85
tar, pitch, and turpentine, 177
Naval War College, 582
Navigation Acts, 177
Navigation Acts of England, 83, 93, 94
Navy. *See* U.S. Navy
Nazi government, 687, 705
Nazis (National Socialist Workers Party), 679
Nazi-Soviet Pact, 730
NBC newscasts, 832
Nebraska
mentioned, 511, 512, 513
Northwestern Farmers' Alliance, 537
Populist election, 538
settlements, 514
Nebraska Territory
on Oregon Trail, 336
Pawnees driven out, 334
railroad proposal, 360
Needle trades, 473, 474
Negro improvement, 418
Negro March on Washington, 698, 754
Neighborhood Guild, 476
Neighborhoods
for African Americans, 486
decay, 770
ethnic, 482–483
middle class, 489
Neighborhood Union, 459, 563

Neighborhood Youth Corps, 755
Neiman-Marcus, 798
Nelson, Gaylord, Wisconsin senator, 779
Neoconservatives, 795–796
Neoliberalism of Clinton, 825
Neolin, Delaware Prophet, 114
Neshaminy, Pennsylvania, 92
Networks, broadcasting, 641
Neutrality
and fascism, 679–680
In French Revolution, 206–207
in Great War, 605–611
Neutrality Acts, 679, 690
Nevada
in Mexican War, 346
mining camps, 508
nuclear weapons tests, 725, 726
on Oregon Trail, 336
population growth in 1990s, 834
Nevis Island, 45
New Air Force Academy, 807
New Amsterdam, 51
Newark, New Jersey, 771
New Bern, North Carolina, 169
New Deal, 669–671
agricultural program, 675
and American Life, 672–677
beginnings, 664–667
benefits, 675–676
critics of, 667–669
and Eisenhower, 739, 744
and Lyndon Johnson, 755–757
and minorities, 674–675
political stalemate, 677–678
and Truman, 719–721
New Deal-New Frontier, 795
New Echota, 252
New England
colonial exports, 86
early family life, 43–45
economic crisis after Revolutionary War, 177
fish merchants, 76
industrial towns, 296–297
King Philip's War, 64–65
labor shortage, 76
land settlement system, 179
Massachusetts Bay Colony, 41–43
Pilgrims and settlements, 40–41
shipping industry, 83, 203
temperance movement, 308
uniformity in 1789, 197–198
New England Anti-Slavery Society (1831), 316
New England Non-Restant Society (1838), 317
New England Woman Suffrage Association, 426
New Era economy, 658
New Federalism, 778
Newfoundland naval bases, 691
New France
Beaver Wars, 60–61, 64, 67
development of, 33–34
forts established, 102
New Freedom, 573
New Frontier, 748
New Guinea, 692
New Hampshire, 190, 301, 774
New Harmony, Indiana, 314
New Haven, 43
New Israel, 344
New Jersey
Battle of Pleasantville, 661
Constitution defined suffrage, 171
Constitution of 1776, 244
Constitution ratification, 189
election of 1864, 405
national debt payments, 176
pluralism in 1800, 198
proprietary colony, 46–49, 52
slavery ended, 171
swing state, 526
tariff complaints, 178
New Jersey Plan, 185
New Lebanon, New York, 313

New Left, 766–767, 776
New Lights, religious converts, 92–93
New Mexico
American takeover of, 342–343
Battle of Glorieta Pass, 394
Franciscan priests & Pueblos, 98
Los Alamos science city, 686
in Mexican War, 346
Pancho Villa attacks, 599
Populist election, 538
in Spanish borderlands, 65–67
statehood granted, 355
New Morality, 641–642
New Nationalism, 573–574
New Orleans, Louisiana
acquisition by Jefferson, 221
Battle of, 230–231, 246
capture during Civil War, 386
commercial right of deposit, 183
discrimination of black workers, 699
free transit through port, 210
French colonial expansion, 99–100
Great Migration, 641
mentioned, 268, 441
mulatto elite, 282
Republican government overthrown, 430
slave rebellion, 276
in Treaty of Paris, 104
New Orleans *Crescent*, 269
New Republicanism, 739
Newsday newspaper, 714
New South, 437–463
agrarian revolt, 446–450
industrial and urban growth, 439–446
race issue, 452–461
women, 450–452
New Spain, 20
Newspapers
after Great War, 623
American Western, 502
banned from mail, 614
on civil rights, 720
covered housing shortages, 714
editors
Fortune, Thomas, 416–417
Greeley, Horace, 369
in election of 1896, 542
on Filipino-American War, 593
on immigrants, 484
Japanese American internments, 701
news for middle class, 490–491
party-subsidized in 1828, 247
supported Versailles Treaty, 620
tabloid exposes, 471
on unemployment in 1930, 664
Newsweek Magazine, 832
Newton, Huey, 771–772
Newton, Isaac, 90
Newtown, 32
New World, 20, 24–25
New York Bureau of Immigration, 562
New York City
antiblack race riots, 563
commerce in early 19th century, 295
during Great Depression, 660
as headquarters of British army, 147
immigrant population, 550
immigration gateway, 809
La Guardia Airport, 670
Levittown, 714, 717
library, 90
Lord & Taylor retail, 491
mentioned, 454, 632
police raid on gay bars, 813
poverty in late 19th century, 476–477
power station, 468
prostitution, 474
relief payments, 662–663
scandals in 1870s, 428
steamboats to Albany, 292
New York colony
governor's salary, 97
legislature, 120
proprietary colony, 46–49, 52
New York Daily Tribune, 382

New York Female Moral Reform Society (1834), 308
New York Journal, 490, 589
New York state
blocked national tariff, 176
Constitutional conventions, 243
Constitutional ratification, 190
gubernatorial race of 1804, 223
legislature financed Erie Canal, 295
Married Women's Property Act (1860), 319
pluralism in 1800, 198
population growth in 1990s, 834
slavery ended, 171
Socialist support, 555
swing state, 526
temperance movement, 308
warned Congress of peace treaty violations, 182
during WWII, 695
New York State Factory Commission, 554
New York Stock Exchange (1817), 295
New York Sun, 417, 590
New York Tenement House Law, 557
New York Times, 456, 484, 780
New York Tribune, 583
New York World, 399, 589
New York World newspaper, 490
New York Yankees, 741
New Zealand, ANZUS alliance, 725
Nez Percé Indians, 503
Niagara, 67
Niagara Falls, New York, 780–781
Niagara Movement, 563
Nicaragua, 360, 597, 598, 648, 784, 802, 803, 808
Nichols, J.C., 640
Nigeria, 693
Nimitz, Chester, Admiral, 705
Nisei, Japanese Americans, 643
Nixon, Richard, U.S. president
in 1960 election, 748
to China, 778
as Congressman, role in Red Scare, 732
in election of 1968, 775
and Elvis Presley, 788
and environmental policies, 570
impeachment, 828
as law student, 670
as president, 744, 802
prosperity message as Vice President, 743
as representative from California, 730
and Watergate, 776–782
Nixon Doctrine, 776
Nobel Peace Prize, 756
Nomadic bands in Great Basin, 7
Nomini Hall, Virginia plantation, 77
Nonaggression pact, 688
Nonexportation agreement, 127
Nonimportation movement, 118, 121, 122–123
militia exercise observed, 146
Nonintercourse Act, 224, 225
Noninterventionists, 688
Nonpartisan elections, 565
Nonpartisan League, 615
Nonresistants, Garrisonian, 317
Nonviolent sit-ins, 753
Norfolk, Virginia, 426, 441
Normandy, France, 703
Norris, Frank, 553
Norris, George, Nebraska senator, 636
The North, *See also* Civil War; Politics of sectionalism; The South; The Union
end of slavery, 171
Northern Republicans, 539
North-South differences, 366–367
North-South railroad transportation, 292
vs. South
abolition in 1830s, 256
nullification crisis, 251, 253
Texas annexation, 260
North, Lord, British Prime Minister, 124, 136, 155

North, Oliver, lieutenant colonel, 803
North Africa, 692, 693, 702, 703
North American Air Defense, 807
North American Free Trade Agreement (NAFTA), 766, 833
North American Indian, The (Curtis), 520
North Atlantic, 692
North Atlantic Treaty Organization (NATO), 724, 802, 804, 824
North Bridge in Concord, 136
North Carolina
  agrarian revolt, 449–450
  black voters, 427
  Border South in 1850, 270
  freedom riders, 754
  joined Union, 202
  mentioned, 120, 400, 428, 447, 448, 452, 458
  pine barrens, 177
  public education reform, 559
  ratification of Constitution, 190
  secession from Union, 375, 384
  tariff complaints, 178
North Carolina Mutual Life Insurance Company, 458
North Dakota, 514
Northern New Mexico Cowboys Union, 512
Northern Pacific Railroad, 502, 514
Northern Securities Company, 569
Northgate shopping center in Seattle, Washington, 741
North Korea, 709, 727–728, 729, 824, 844
North Platte, 336
Northrup, Solomon, 273
North Star, The, black abolitionist newspaper, 320
North Vietnam, 746, 749–750, 757, 763, 773, 776
Northwest Coast, home to Indians, 7
Northwestern Farmers' Alliance, 537
Northwest Ordinance of 1787, 181, 235, 353
Northwest Passage to Asia, 24, 25, 35
Norway, 688
Notes as legal tender, 115–116
Noup, Celia, 793
Nova Scotia, 100
Novelists, 642
Novels
  by female black slave, 266
  Uncle Tom's Cabin, 352, 358–359
Noyes, John Humphrey, 313
NSC-68, 727, 729
Nuclear. See also Atomic Energy Commission (AEC)
  arms race, 725–727
  arsenals, 709, 784
  bombs, 696, 707–709, 725–726
  chain reaction, 686
  freeze, 802
  reaction, 696
  superiority, 751
  threat in Korean War, 746
  war, 802
  weapons, 709, 725–726, 745, 802, 824
  weapons testing, 751–752
  winter, 802
Nuclear Non-Proliferation Treaty, 709
Nuclear power plants, 570
Nueces River, 340, 344
Nuevo León, 339
Nullification crisis, 251, 253
Nullification Doctrine, 212
Nullifiers, 251
Nuremberg laws, 687
Nurses, 697, 776
Nursing profession, 399, 401, 475
Nye, Gerald, senator, 678
Nye Committee, 678

O
Oahu, Hawaii, Pearl Harbor, 586
Oak groves, food for Indians, 7
Oakland, California, 540

Oak Ridge, Tennessee, 696
Obstruction of justice, 781
Occupational Safety and Health Administration, 795
Occupation zones in Germany, 722, 724
Ocean liners, 481
O'Connor, Sandra Day, Supreme Court justice, 834
October 29, 1929 (Black Tuesday), 658
Octopus, The (Norris), 553
Octoroon balls, 282
Office of Economic Opportunity (OEO), 755
Office of Price Administration (OPA), 695
Office of Scientific Research and Development, 696
Office of War Information, 697
Office workers, 814
Office work transformed by typewriter, 474
Official language, English, 616
Ogden, Aaron, and steamboats, 294
Oglala Sioux Indians, 503
Ohio, 329, 526, 540, 695
Ohio Company, 181
Ohio country open to white settlement, 208
Ohio Indians, 208
Ohio River, 100, 125
Ohio River Valley, 10, 101, 102, 114
Ohio River Valley canal networks, 292
Oil companies, 647, 746
Oil drilling, 632, 797, 840
Oil embargo, 778–779
Oil fields, 471
Oil from Nigeria, 693
Oil industry, 471
Oil price hikes by OPEC, 784
Oil production and reserves, 805
Oil refineries in Cleveland, 471
Oil spills, 570
Oil supply crisis in 1970s, 762
Okinawa, 707, 746
Oklahoma
  Indians imprisoned, 503
  oil drilling, 632
  Populist election, 538
  Red Scare, 731
  settled by land grab, 514
  Socialist support, 555
Oklahoma City, Oklahoma, 514, 648, 660, 826
Oklahoma territory
  Civil War battles, 394
  Indians destination, 249–250
  tribal lands, 334
Old-age pension, 559
Older Americans, 810
Old Guard Republican conservatives
  in election of 1920, 624
  and government regulation, 568
  opponents of reform, 556
  and Theodore Roosevelt, 567, 571
Old Northwest, 229, 327, 329–331
Old Southwest, 331–333
Old World backgrounds, 480–482
Oligopolies, 634, 659
Olive Branch Petition, 137, 140
Olmec Indians, 7
Olney, Richard, secretary of State, 587
Omaha, Nebraska, 471, 538
Omaha Indians, 334
Omaha Platform, 538
Omnibuses, horse-drawn coaches, 296
Oñate, Juan de, 22
Oneida Community, 313–314
Oneida Indians, 60, 146
"One man, one vote," 245
Onondaga Indians, 60
On-site fabrication of houses, 717
On-site inspections, 722, 752, 804
Opechancanough, 36–37, 38
Open Door policy, 593–595, 597
Open-range ranching, 511
Open shop campaign, 634, 636
Operation Desert Storm, 806

Operation Rescue, 370
Operations OVERLOAD & TORCH, 703
Oppenheimer, J. Robert, 696
Oral or "stand-up" voting, 244
Oral traditions of Native Americans, 12
Order of Freemasons, 257
Order of the Sons of America (La Orden de Hijos de America), 639
Orders in Council, 224, 226
Ordinance of 1784, 179
Oregon
  discrimination of Japanese residents, 643
  internment of Japanese Americans, 699
  joint occupation by U.S. and Britain, 261
  mentioned, 511
  on Oregon Trail, 336
  recall adopted, 566
  woman suffrage adopted, 564
Oregon Country, 336
Oregon Territory, 343, 344
Oregon Trail, 333, 336–338, 337, 342
Organic chemicals, 632
Organizational model for reformers, 307
Organization Man, The (Whyte), 743
Organization of Petroleum Exporting Countries (OPEC), 778, 784
Organized crime, 644–645
Organized labor. See Labor unions
Orlando, Vittorio, of Italy, 619
Orphanages, 312, 451
Orthodox Calvinists, 310
Orthodox party, 310
Osage Indians, 334
Osceola, Seminole leader, 250
Ostend, Belgium, 360
Ostend Manifesto, 360
O'Sullivan, John L., 343
Oswald, Lee Harvey, 754
Other America, The (Harrington), 744, 755
The other shore, Mexico, 342
Otis, James Jr., 117
Ottawa Indians, 67
Ottomans, Muslim rulers of Turkey, 18
Outcasts of society, 313
Outlaws, 120
Outlook journal, 456
Overgrazing by cattle, 511
Over mountain men, militia from Virginia, 152
Overseas expansion, 543
Overviews
  antislavery reform, 315
  Articles of Confederation vs. Constitution, 187
  atomic bomb decision, 708
  British Imperial trade regulations, 84
  British restraints and burdens on colonists, 126
  Civil War major battles, 408
  colonial wars, 101
  Columbian exchange, 23
  culture wars of 1920s, 644
  English colonies in 17th century, 49
  Federalists vs. Antifederalists, 189
  Federalists vs. Republicans, 207
  free society in South, 277
  government land policy, 513
  government wartime agencies, 612
  Hundred Days laws, 666
  imperialism rationalizations, 582
  presidential impeachment, 828
  Progressive era laws, 558
  progressive organizations, 551
  Reconstruction: President and Congress, 424
  reform impulse, 309
  Revolutionary War battles, 154
  second party system, 257
  Second Red Scare, 731
  Sectional crisis 1846–1861, 372
  South and North compared in 1860, 366
  tariff debates, 534

territorial expansion under Republicans, 232
westward expansion, 332
workers organize, 479
Overwork, extra factory work, 274
Owen, Robert, 314
Owens, Jesse, 718
Owens Valley, 338
Oyo Africans, 14
Oyster Bay, 561
Ozark Mountains of Missouri, 810
Ozone depletion, 570

P
P-51 escort fighter, 705
Pacific allies and ANZUS alliance, 725
Pacific Coast acquisitions, 233
Pacific Islander immigrants, 808
Pacific islands annexation, 583
Pacific Railroad, 498–499
Pacific sea otter, skins of, 336
Pacifists during Great War, 614–615
Packet ships, 295
Paddock, Adino, Boston artisan, 87
Paine, Thomas, 140, 165, 345
Paiute Indians, 338, 499, 500
Pakenham, Richard, British minister, 260
Pakistan, 709
Palace of Versailles, 619
Palace Sleeping Car Company, 480
Paleo-Indians, 6
Palestinians, 803, 824, 844
Palmer, Mitchell, Attorney General, 623–624
Panama, 585
Panama Canal, 583, 584, 597–599, 648, 794
Panama Canal Company, 597
Panama Railroad, 597
Panhandle Stock Association, 512
Panic of 1819, 233–235, 253
Panic of 1837, 254–255, 292, 344
Panic of 1857, 364
Panics. See Depressions; Recessions
Pan-Indian resistance movement, 225
Papal plot to undermine American freedom, 298
Papaw, African game, 73
Paper money. See also Continental Dollars; Currency; Money
  Continental dollars, 137, 144, 160
  crisis after Revolutionary War, 182
  demand of Agricultural Wheel, 447
  economic crisis after Revolutionary War, 178
  issued by colonial legislatures, 115–116
  Jackson's bank war, 253, 255
  money question in late 19th century, 535–536
  resources during Civil War, 384
Paramount Studios, 634
Parent respect, 642
Parent-teacher associations, 559
Paris, France, 703, 774
Paris, Peace of, 156
Paris Peace Conference, 619–620
Parity, 667
Parker, Alton B., 570
Parks, Rosa, 753
Parks built by WPA, 670
Parliament, British
  accepted defeat in Revolutionary War, 155
  appeal for peace, 137
  authority over colonies debated, 125–128
  barred exports from colonies, 140
  Coercive Acts, 124–125
  Conciliatory Proposition, 136
  crown's partner in governing England, 94
  granted former colonies full autonomy, 149–150
  taxes on Americans, 116
  trade regulation laws, 93
  unpopular policies in colonies, 117–119

Parochial schools, 311, 527
Parsons, Theophilus, of Massachusetts, 171
Parson's Cause, 115
Parties, political, *See also* Democratic Party; Republican Party; Third parties; Whig Party
 domination in late 19th century, 525–528
 election control moved to public officials, 564–565
 emergence in new nation, 205–210
 kickbacks to, 527
 party machines, 565–566
 realignment in North, 361
 workingmen, 305
Partisan elections, 210
Partisan politics
 denounced by G. Washington, 210
 in late 19th century, 526–527
 recent decline, 528
 during Red Scare, 733
Partnership, 470
Party bosses, 527
Party Caucus, 210
Party conventions on TV, 720
Party machines, 527, 528
Party of the people, 259
Passenger ship *Lusitania*, 608
Patented inventions, 300–301
Patents, 468
Paternalism in New England, 300, 310
Paterson, William, 185
Patriarchy, 16, 319
Patrilineal societies in Africa, 14
Patriot Act, 842, 843
Patriotism
 after Great War, 622–623
 Christian anti-British, 229
 during Civil War, 380–382
 in Confederacy, 400–401
 during Great War, 604, 614–615
 of women during WWII, 698
Patronage, 173, 429, 532–533, 544, 674
Patrons of Husbandry, 527
Pattillo, Melba, brave student, 738–739
Patton, George, general, 703
Pawnee Indians, 9, 334, 501
Paxton Boys, 114
Payroll deductions, 671
Pays des Illinois, French colonial expansion, 99–100
Peace activists at Democratic Convention, 775
Peace Corps, 755
Peace movement in 1920s, 647, 648
Peace of Paris, Revolutionary War, 156, 182
Peace organizations, 766
Peace rally, 609
Peace without victory, 610
Peach farming, 446
Peachtree Creek, 404
Peale, Charles Willson, 145
Peale, Norman Vincent, 742
Pea Ridge, Battle of, 394
Pearl Harbor, Hawaii, 586, 692, 695
Pearl River, 225
Peasants, 16, 299
Peddlers, paid party workers, 526
Peffer, William A., 537
Pellagra among slaves, 273
Pemberton, Dr. John, inventor of Coca Cola, 440
Pemberton, John, Confederate general, 394
Peña, Federico, mayor of Denver, 836
Pendleton Civil Service Act (1883), 528, 533
Peninsula Campaign, 388
Penitentiaries for criminals, 312–313
Penn, William, 50, 62, 91
Penn's Woods, 50
Pennsylvania
 child labor in coal mines, 473

Coxey's Army, 540
 founding as proprietary colony, 46–51
 labor strikes, 623
 national debt payments, 176
 pluralism in 1800, 198
 ratification of Constitution, 189
 state constitution development, 174
 Whiskey Rebellion, 208
Pennsylvania Assembly, 114
Pennsylvania Avenue, 549
Pensacola, Florida, 98, 230
Pension programs, 826
Pensions, old-age, 669
Pentagon, 702, 715, 822, 832, 841
Pentagon Papers, 779
Pentecostals, 815
People, defined for political rights, 169–172
People of Plenty (Potter), 743
People's Grocery lynchings, 453–454
People's Party, 449, 527, 537–539, 543
People's President, 248
People's Republic of China, 729
People's Temple in California, 769
People's Unemployment League, 661
Pequot Indians, 62
Pequot War, 42, 53
Per capita income, 301, 441, 696
Perdue, Sonny, Georgia governor, 460
Perestroika, 804
Perkins, Frances, secretary of Labor, 671, 673
Perot, Ross, 823
Perpetual Emigrating Fund Company, 514
Perry, Matthew, Commodore, 583
Perry, Oliver Hazard, Commodore, 229
Pershing, John J., general, 599, 617
Persian Gulf War, 805–806
Personal computers, 831
Personal freedom in Constitution, 190
Peru, 22
Pesticides, 570
Pet banks, 254, 255
Petersburg, Virginia, 392, 402, 406
Petition campaign of late 1830s, 320
Petroleum industry, 471, 568, 632, 676, *See also* Oil companies
Phelps-Dodge Company, 615
Philadelphia
 in 19th century, 295
 Centennial Exposition of 1876, 467
 colonial city, 87
 Congress fled to Baltimore, 147
 early libraries, 90
 occupied by Howe, 149
 religious freedom, 50
 rich *vs.* poor, 88
 Wanamaker & Brown retail, 491
Philadelphia Convention, 184–186
Philadelphia Inquirer, 590
Philadelphia Working Men's Committee, 311
Philanthropics, 478
Philbrick, Herbert, 732
Philip, King of Wampanoags, 64–65
Philippines
 Britain returned to Spain, 104, 112
 invasion in WWII, 706
 race riots during WWII, 699
 Spanish colony, 590
Philippines, Republic of
 Filipino-American War, 593
 Marcos out, Aquino in, 803–804
 treaty after WWII, 725
 in World War II, 691–693
Philippines Territory, 643
Phillips, Kevin, 806
Phnom Penh, Cambodia, 792, 793
Phonograph, 641
Photographers, 697
Photographs
 Civil War, 412–413
 of Vietnam Era, 788
 during WWII, 697

Photoplay magazine, 652
Phuc, Kim, 789
Physicians licensing standards, 553
Pickett, George, Confederate general, 393
Piedmont farmers, 199
Pierce, Franklin, U.S. president, 359–361, 362
Pike, Zebulon, 333
Pilgrims, 40–41
Pinchot, Gifford, 568, 572
Pinckney, Charles C., of South Carolina, 224
Pinckney, Thomas, of South Carolina, 210
Pinckney's Treaty, 210
Pine barrens of North Carolina, 177
Pitcher, Molly, 145
Pitt, William, British secretary of state, 104
Pittsburgh, Pennsylvania, 296, 472, 478, 639
Pizarro, Francisco, 20
Plague. *See* Black death
Plains Indians, 23, 333–338, 501, 503
Planned communities, 314
Plantations
 living conditions, 278–280
 in Lower South, 267–269
 in Old Southwest, 331–333
 slaves, 273–274
Plants in Columbian exchange, 23
Plastics, 632
Platform economy, 809
Platt Amendment, 596
Platte River Valley, 334, 336
Plattsburgh, Battle of, 230
Pleasantville, Battle of, 661
Pledge of abstinence, 308
Pledge of Allegiance, 742, 800
Pleiku attack, 763
Plessy, Homer, 454
Plessy v. Ferguson, 454–455, 752
Plows, 330
Plumbing, 303
Plural marriage, 313
Plutonium, 696
Plymouth Colony, 40–41, 94
Plymouth Company, 35, 40
Pocahontas, 36, 38
Pocket veto, 421
Poetry, 557, 614
Pogroms in Russia, 481
Poison gas in Great War, 618
Poland
 in Great War, 620, 621
 in WWII, 688, 705, 707, 722, 723
 since WWII, 746, 774, 804, 824
Polaris missiles, 751
Poles in European Holocaust, 705
Police in strikes and protests, 478, 661, 668, 673
Policy of appeasement, 679
Policy of termination, 740
Polio, 663
Polish immigrants, 480, 483–484
Political abolitionism, 320
Political action committees (PACs), 528
Political authority in Europe, 16
Political center, 719
Political culture in colonies, 93–97, 117–119
Political democracy, 243
Political generations, 823–824
Political lobbying organizations, 796
Political opportunities, 244
Political parties. *See* Parties, political
Political rights, 169–172, 432
Political separation
 Kentucky from Virginia, 199–201
 West Virginia, 400
Political violence, 427–429
Politics and religion, 370, 815
Politics of sectionalism, 351–377
 compromise of 1850, 355–359
 Lincoln, 371–375

North/South differences, 365–371
 political realignment, 359–365
 slavery in territories, 353–354
Polk, James K., U.S. president, 261, 320, 327, 343–346
Polls, 528, 720
Poll taxes, 455, 565
Pollution
 industrial in late 19th century, 472
 in late 20th century, 779–781
 in Pittsburgh, 296
 of waterways, 301
Polygamy among slaves, 72–73
Ponce de León, Juan, 20
Pontiac Rebellion, 114
Poor, legal and medical aid, 427
Poor, rural, 667, 675
Poor asylums, 312–313
Poor laborers and school reform, 311
Poor relief in colonies, 88
Poor whites in Southern cities, 281
Pope, Alexander, English poet, 118
Pope, John, Union general, 388
Popé, Pueblo leader, 66
Popular entertainment, 741
Popular sovereignty, 354–356, 360, 364–365
Population, *See also* Census
 in colonial years
  Cahokia city, 10
  Caribbean islands, 11
  in colonies in 1700s, 97
  English colonies, 61
  Indians & Spanish in California, 99
  Jamestown, 35
  Mexico, 20
  in New England cities, 87
  New England in 1660, 43
  New Netherland, 51
  New York in 1700, 52
  North & South America c. 1500, 6
  Pennsylvania colony, 50
  Virginia, 38
 post-Civil War
  of cities in 1900, 467
  density in New York's tenement district, 476
  of mining camps, 508
 pre-Civil War
  in 1800s, 327
  in 1860 in Old South, 268
  blacks in South Carolina, 251
  of cities in early 19th century, 295
  Indians in 1828, 249
  of Indians in Southwest, 338
  Native Americans in trans-Mississippi, 333
  of Oregon in 1840s, 261
  of slaves in South, 269, 272
  Texas in 1830s, 340
 pre-colonial years
  Mesoamerica, 9
  Timbuktu, West Africa, 12
 during Revolution years
  of Americans in 1787, 177
  American West in 1780s, 199
Populist Party, 449–450, 527, 537–539, 540–541, 566, 589
Pork, 333
Pork Chop Hill, 729
Porkopolis, Cincinnati meatpacking center, 296
Port Arthur (Lüshun), Manchuria, 593, 594
Port Hudson, Louisiana, 392
Port Huron Statement, 766
Portland, Oregon, 638, 717
Ports barred to British warships, 223
Portugal
 in 1500, 16–17
 League of Armed Neutrality, 150
 Treaty of Tordesillas, 24
Portuguese fleet, 18
Portuguese immigrants, 485
Portuguese traders, 15
Post, Louis, assistant secretary of Labor, 624

Postal law (1810), 307
Post Office. *See* U.S. Post Office
Potash, colonial export, 85
Potato blight, 297
Potato King, 483
Potsdam, Germany, 707
Potsdam Declaration, 707
Pottawatamie Indians, 209
Potter, David, historian, 743
Poverty
  in 1980s, 798–800
  in late 19th century, 476–478
  in Puerto Rico, 595
  and school reform, 311
Powderly, Terence V., 478
Powder River, 502, 503
Power, Tyrone, Irish visitor, 278–279
Power-driven industry, 301
Power Elite, The (Mills), 744
Power industry in 1920s, 634
Power of eminent domain, 294
Power of Positive Thinking, The (Peale), 742
Powers, Francis Gary, 747
Power station, first, 468
Powhatan Indians, 12, 36, 65, 67
Powwows, 505
Prague Spring, 774
Prairie grasslands, 236
Prayer in school, 370
Prayer meetings during Civil war, 386
Praying towns, 64
Preachers, radio and TV in 1950s, 742
Preachers to slaves, 275
Preaching as form of theater, 245
Preamble of Constitution, 186
Predestination, 17, 40, 245
Preemption Act (1841), 260, 329
Prejudice in 1920s, 643
Preparedness, 609
Presbyterian Banner, 592
Presbyterian Church, 283, 366, 815
Presbyterians, 91, 92, 173, 199, 275
Preservationists, 570
Preservation of the Union, 381, 384
President
  checks and balances, 187
  duties set in Constitution Convention, 186
  weak institution in late 19th century, 530
Presidential apology for slavery, 70
Presidential campaign covered by TV, 720
Presidential Commission on Status of Women, 811
Presidential debates, 748
Presidential electors, 186, 244
Presidential etiquette established, 201–202
Presidential Reconstruction, 422–425
Presidential vetoes, 423–424, 530
President's Organization for Unemployment Relief, 662
Presidios, 338
Presley, Elvis, 742, 768, 788
Prevost, George, general, 230
Price, Charles, 452
Price, Richard, 38
Price controls, 695
Primaries, 565
Primary elections, 528
Primitive communism, 660
Princeton, Battle of, 147
Princeton, New Jersey, 561
Princeton University, 92, 561, 573
Printing presses, 306, 308, 317
Prison boom, 827
Prison reform, 450, 451
Prisons, 312–313
Private enterprise in China, 594
Privateers and British shipping, 205
Privateers in Revolutionary War, 151
Private tutors, 311
Privatization of Social Security, 671
Privies, 296, 303
Privy Council, 93

Prizefighting, 563
Procedural rules in Congress, 531
Proclamation Line, 113
Proclamation of 1763, 112–114, 115
Productivity
  of corporate consolidation in 1920s, 634
  of workers, 829
  of workers in 1950, 740
Products, enumerated, 83
Professional Air Traffic Controllers Organization, 797
Professional team sports, 641, 718
Professions, nursing and women, 399
Profiteers, 399
Profit margin, 471
Profits of Slavery, 268–269
Progressive Era, 547–577
  children's protection, 557, 560–561
  electoral reform, 564–565
  labor demands, 553–554, 556
  muckrakers, 553, 556
  opponents, 556
  origins of progressivism, 550–551
  public education, 559, 561
  racism, 562–564
  regulations struck down by Supreme Court, 636
  Roosevelt's modern presidency, 566–572
  rural reform, 560–561
  social control, 562–563
  Social Gospel movement, 551–552, 556
  Socialism, 555–556
  state government reform, 566
  transatlantic influence, 555, 559
  urban reform, 557, 565–566
  Wilson and reform, 572–574
  women's rights, 548–549, 554–555, 557–560, 564
Progressive movement, 665
Progressive Party, 572, 610, 637, 719
Progressive reform
  in FDR's New Deal, 673–674
  of Irreconcilables, 621
Progressivism
  diversity of, 549–550
  in election of 1928, 648
  during Great War, 605, 611, 613, 624
  in New Deal, 673
Prohibition
  of alcoholic beverages, 304
  Constitutional amendment, 613
  and crime, 644–645
  in Great War, 617
  and immigrants, 562
  law in Maine (1851), 308
Prohibition Bureau, 644
Prohibition Party, 527
Promised Land, 337, 477
Promised Land, The (Antin), 466
Promontory, 499
Propaganda campaigns
  after Great War, 623
  of Germany during Great War, 606
  during Great War, 613–614
  promoted immigration restrictions, 643
  railroads on Western opportunity, 514
  of Reconstruction horrors, 430–431
  of secessionists, 371
  of temperance movement, 307–308
  white superiority, 456
  during WWII, 697
Property in common, 313–314
Property interests of plantation owners, 272
Property owners and political rights, 169
Property rights
  in Northwest Ordinance of 1787, 181
  in Whig ideology, 101
  of women, 427
Prophet's Town, 225

Prophet Tenskwatawa, 225
Proposition 187 in California, 646, 837
Proprietary colonies, 39, 46–50
Proslavery argument, 282–284
Prospectors. *See* Gold
Prosperity, *See also* Confident years
  in 1990s, 829
  after War of 1812, 233
  desired after WWII, 719
  ended in 1974, 785
  in English colonies, 82
  gospel of, 743–744
  and poverty in Reagan years, 798–799
Prosser, Gabriel, 276
Prosser's Rebellion (1800), 276
Prostitution, 308–309, 452, 474, 476, 508, 511, 562–563
Protective legislation
  children's, 557, 560–561
  restricted women's occupations, 475–476
  women's minimum wage law, 636
Protective tariffs, 204, 259–260
Protestant fundamentalists, 556
  in 1920s, 645
  support of prohibition, 562
Protestantism
  anti-Communist churchgoing, 742
  in England, 25
  mainline denominations, 815
Protestant ministers, 643
Protestant movement, 17–18
Protestant Reformation, 24
Protestants
  destruction of Indian religion, 503
  feared Catholic immigration, 298
  foreign missions, 582
  German immigrants 1848–1860, 361
  in Mexican Texas, 340
  missionaries, 64, 336
  party loyalty, 527
  Quebec Act general alarm, 125
  Scots-Irish immigrants, 76
  and social reform, 366–367, 551–552
Protests, *See also* Slave revolts
  American Indian Movement, 772
  antiabortion, 646
  Black Power and ghettos, 770–772
  Civil Rights March on Washington, 698, 754
  forest reserves opposition, 568
  Hispanic agriculture workers, 772
  Hispanics on land seizures, 515
  peace activists at Democratic Convention, 775
  peace movement in 1920s, 647–648
  repression of dissent during Great War, 614–616
  Revolutionary War demonstrations, 160
  unemployed march on Washington, 539–540
  of Vietnam War, 765–767
  woman suffrage parade, 548–549, 564
Providence, Rhode Island, 43, 299
Provident Hospital, 487
Provincial Congress, 135
Provincialism of mass culture, 642
Proviso debate on slavery, 353–356
Prussia, 150
Public accommodations, 430, 454, 753–754, 755
Public activism of New Deal, 676–677
Public affairs and citizen involvement, 677
Public assistance in colonies, 88
Public-assistance recipients, 826
Publications, printing revolution, 306
Public auction, 329
Public domain, 511
Public education, *See also* Education
  land set aside for schools, 180
  in New South late 19th century, 442
  in Reconstruction, 426, 427

reform around 1900, 559
  schools in North, 311
  schools in South, 563
  schools teaching morality, 817
  secularized, 645
  in South, 312
  supported by Whigs, 258
Public health, 553, 810
Public housing program, 675, 740
Public interest magazines, 795
Public lands, *See also* Homesteaders
  grid system of surveys, 179
  price in 1900s, 329
  sales, goals of Henry Clay, 259–260
Public opinion
  on European War (WWII), 688, 690, 691
  on gunboat diplomacy, 648
  in Latin America during WWII, 698
  manipulated in Great War, 614
  molded by T. Roosevelt, 567
  against slavery, 317
Public Opinion, 597
Public opinion polls, 720
Public playgrounds, 565
Public projects, 60
Public safety committees, 615
Public securities, 204
Public transit, 799
Public Works Administration (PWA), 666, 674, 678
Public works budget in Great Depression, 663
Public works program, 539
Pueblo Bonito in New Mexico, 9
Pueblo Indians
  in Archaic period, 7, 9, 12
  in Arizona & New Mexico in early 19th century, 339
  culture and economy, 500
  and European livestock, 23
  in Spanish borderlands, 59, 64
  in Spanish colonies, 98
  and Spanish conquistadores, 22
Pueblo Revolt, 64, 65–67
Puerto Ricans, 740, 771, 808
Puerto Rico
  gained during Spanish-American War, 590
  immigrations, 639
  Spanish conquest, 20
  Treaty of Paris, 591–592
  under U.S. rule, 595
Puget Sound, 700
Pulaski, Kazimierz, Polish cavalry commander, 143
Pulitzer, Joseph, 490, 589
Pullman, George, 480
Pullman strike, 480, 540–541, 567
Pumpkin papers, 732
Punishment of slaves, 273
Punk rock, 798
Purchasing power of dollar, 540
Pure Food and Drug Act (1906), 571
Purinton, Edward E., 633
Puritan faith as established religion, 90
Puritans
  heritage in New England, 197–198
  Manifest Destiny contribution, 344
  Massachusetts control, 94
  settling New England, 40, 41
  support of American Revolution, 142
  "Pursuit of happiness" in Declaration of Independence, 141
Pusan, South Koran, 728
Put-in-Bay, Battle of, 229
Putting-out system, 297
Puyallup, 700

Q
Quaker abolitionist, 318
Quakers, 50, 91, 173, 197, 276
Quartering Acts, 113, 120, 125
Quartz mining, 509
Quasi-War, 211
Quayle, Dan, vice president, 811

Quebec, 33–34, 100, 138–139
Quebec, Battle of, 104
Quebec Act, 125
Queen Anne's War, 100
Queens College (Rutgers University), 92
Queenston Heights, Battle of, 229
Quiberon Bay, Battle of, in France, 104
Quiet Period, 123–124
Quorum in Congress, 531
Quotas, immigration, 298

R

Race issue in South
 black community response, 458–461
 disfranchisement, 455–456
 lynchings, 453–454
 national consensus, 456, 458
 segregation, 454–455
 white backlash, 452–453
Race relations
 in 1600s, 69
 and Frederick Douglass, 431
 interbreeding, 315
 prejudice condemnation, 318–319
 rules of social interactions, 454
 in South late 19th century, 452–453
Race riots
 after Great War, 622
 Atlanta (1906), 461, 563
 in early 1900s, 458
 ghetto neighborhoods, 770–771
 in Northern cities, 613
 in Progressive Era, 563
 Rodney King in California, 801–802
 during WWII, 699
Racial component of Manifest Destiny, 344
Racial defense of slavery, 283–284
Racial discrimination
 and New Deal, 674
 post WWII, 717–718
 and voting rights, 433
 during WWII, 698–699
Racial equality, See also Civil Rights Movement
 responsibility of black people, 420
 views of Republican Party, 365
Racial gap in Vietnam War, 766
Racial groups, marketing music to, 641
Racial hatred, 706
Racial murder in Holocaust, 705
Racial preponderance, 643
Racial pride in 1920s, 639
Racial segregation
 formal end in South, 284
 during Great War, 617
 laws in late 19th century, 454–455
 Reconstruction failure, 431, 432
 in schools, 738–739, 752–754
Racial superiority
 of Germans, 687
 in Reconstruction, 416–417, 424, 427
 white man's burden, 582
Racial tensions
 in election of 1988, 800
 labor conflicts, 398
 in Southern industry, 274
Racial violence
 in Counter-Reconstruction, 427–428
 post WWII, 717
 turned minorities to local politics, 835
Racism
 in 1920s, 639
 after Great War, 622
 effect on Republican Party, 427
 effects of slavery, 70
 fear of racial interbreeding, 315
 of Filipino-America War, 593
 in mining camps, 508
 in popular entertainment, 487
 in postwar South, 420

of Progressive Era, 563–564
 during Washington years, 198
Radar, 693
Radical Reconstruction, 425–426
Radicals
 agitators, 624
 during Great War, 614–615
 writing state constitutions, 173
Radio broadcasts, 668, 674, 697
Radio codes, 694
Radio combat-communication teams, 696
Radio networks, 634, 641
Radios purchased on credit, 640
Radio talk shows, conservative message, 796
Rail hubs, early 19th century, 296
Railroad Administration, 611
Railroads, See also Trains
 in 20th century
 in 1920s, 635
 antitrust suit, 569
 farmer and urban markets, 561
 federal funds loaned, 663
 during Great War, 611
 lose to trucking firms, 741
 and Panama Canal, 597
 regulations in Wisconsin, 566
 regulations on rates, 570
 strikes, 574, 716
 during WWII, 698
 in Civil War period
 at Chattanooga, Tennessee, 394
 during Civil War, 398
 in Dalton, Georgia, 403
 expansive period in 1870s, 428–429
 Homestead Act (1862), 397
 land grants, 428–429
 resources during Civil War, 383
 in early 19th century
 construction in Upper South, 271–272
 in Lower South, 269
 replaced canals, 292–295
 serving Atlantic ports and Great Lakes, 296
 transcontinental, 360, 362
 in late 19th century
 and cattle industry, 510
 construction, 439
 elevated, 489
 employment numbers, 472
 expansion used against Indians, 502
 and federal regulations, 534–535
 government ownership, Populist demands, 538
 opening South, 440–441, 443–445
 opening West, 514
 overexpansion and 1893 depression, 539
 Pullman strike, 480
 rates charged, 527
 regulation of, 532
 segregated facilities, 454
 strike of 1877, 478
 Western farmers' protest, 516–517
Rainbow Coalition, 810
Rainfall, 511, 516
Raleigh, Sir Walter, 26
Rancheros, 342
Ranchers in West, 676, 677
Ranching, open-range, 511
Rancho era in California, 342
Randolph, Edmund, antifederalist, 188
Randolph, Philip, 698
Range cattle industry, 510–512
Rangnew, Gussie, 561
Rape as crime of violence, 768, 812
Rape laws, 530
Rape of Nanking, 687
Rapidan River, 402
Rap music, 646, 798
Rappahannock River, 393
Ration cards, 695
Rationing, 695

Rattlesnake flag, 150, 164–165
Rauschenbusch, Walter, 552, 556
Raw Deal, 668
Ray, James Earl, 775
Rayner, John, Populist leader, 449
Rayon, 634
RCA, 634
Readmission to the Union, 422, 426, 430
Ready-made clothing, 640
Reagan, Ronald, U.S. president
 as an actor, 731, 739
 defense spending, 784, 807, 841
 domestic revolution, 793–797
 end of big government, 671, 825
 and environmental policies, 570
 Iran hostage crisis, 785
 on race problems as California governor, 771
 Second Cold War, 802–804
Reagan revolution, 790–819
 Bush, 800–802
 Reaganomics, 794–800
 revisited, 839–840
 second Cold War, 820–806
 social issues, 810–817
 Sunbelt growth, 806–810
Reapers, 330
Rearmament program for WWII, 690, 691
Rebellions, See also Protests; Slave revolts
 Shays's Rebellion, 168–169
Rebel yell, 386
Recall, 566
Recessions, See also Depressions; Panic of . . .
 in 1937, 677
 in 1978, 783
 in 2002, 823
 mid 1970s, 782
 at start of Great War, 607
Reconcentration camps in Cuba, 589, 590
Reconquista, 17, 19, 20
Reconstruction, 415–435, See also Readmission to the Union
 African-American aspirations, 418–421
 counter-reconstruction, 427–429
 failure of, 431–433
 federal reconstruction, 421–427
 memories preserved, 460
 Redemption, 429–431
 Second, 433
Reconstruction Finance Corporation (RFC), 663
Record companies, 641
Recreation
 in 1920s, 641
 in late 19th century, 491–492
 space for, 476
Red Army, 688, 693, 705
Red-baiting, 730
Red Bird, 504
Redbook Magazine, 744
Redbook magazine, 653
Red Cloud, Oglala chief, 503
Redcoats, 144
Red Cross, 604, 642
Redeemer Democrats, 446–447
Redemption, 429–431
Redemptioner system, 75
Red light districts, 563
Red Light Saloon, 508
Redlining older neighborhoods, 717
Red Power, 772
Redress payments, 701
Red River in Arkansas Territory, 339
Red Scare, 623–624, 643, 842
Red Spring, 774–775
Reducators, 731
Reduction of armaments in Fourteen Points, 619
Referendum, 566
Reform, See also Social reform
 difficulties in 1920s, 637

by Jefferson presidency, 219–220
 in New South late 19th century, 450–452
Reformation, 17–18
Reformatories, 312
Reformed clergy, 91
Reformers
 goal with Indians, 503
 women, 554–555
Reform impulse, three phases, 291
Reform organizations, 306, 320, 362
Refrigerated railway cars, 471
Refrigerators, 640
Refugees from communism in 1960s, 808
Refuge for German Jews, 679
Regional differences
 Upper South *vs.* Lower South, 267
Regulation of commerce
 in Constitution, 186
 interstate, by national government, 294
 railroads, 534–535, 566, 570
 sectional clash in Constitution Convention, 185–186
 by state governments, 532
Regulators, 120
Regulatory agencies, 621
Regulatory commissions, 528, 566
Regulatory legislation and social reform, 552
Reich (empire), 687, See also Hitler, Adolf, German Führer
Reid, Whitelaw, 583
Relief agency jobs for women, 673
Relief for unemployed, 662–663, 666, 670
Religion
 changes in late 20th century, 814–815
 in colonies 1660–1760, 90
 consolation in Civil War, 386
 defense of slavery, 283
 denominations in 1820s, 244
 and government in 1950s, 742–743
 Great Awakening, 90–93, 142
 ideology of American expansion, 582
 in Ku Klux Klan, 643
 in New England in 1790, 197
 and politics, 370, 810, 815
 in postwar South, 420
 Scopes trial in 1920s, 645
 Second Great Awakening, 244–245
 under state constitutions, 173
 taxation for support of, 173
Religious beliefs
 of African slaves, 73
 colonial revival, 88
 European c. 1500, 17
 of Native Americans, 12, 500
 of Plains Indians suppressed, 503–506
 of slaves, 275
 in West Africa, 14
 of Yuman Indians, 338
Religious communities, 769
Religious conservatives, 646
Religious freedom
 in Bill of Rights, 202
 included in state constitutions, 173
 for Indians, 674–675
 in Pennsylvania, 50
 and political voting in colonies, 93
Religious oppression, 298
Religious persecution, 39, 41, 77, 98
Religious philosophy Deism, 213
Religious populism
 Great Awakening, 90–93, 142
 Second Great Awakening, 244–245
Religious presses, 306, 589
Religious refugees from Europe, 51
Religious revivals
 of 1820s and 1830s, 258
 inspired abolitionists, 256
Religious schools, 840
Religious sects, 313

Religious television, 815
Religious tolerance, 91, 94
"Remember Goliad," 340
"Remember the Alamo," 340
"Remember the Ladies," 158
Remington, Frederic, 520, 521
Renaissance, 16
Reno, Janet, attorney general, 834
Rensselaer, Stephen Van, general, 229
Reparations
  to former slaves, 70
  Great War, 620, 621, 647
  role in Great Depression, 659
Repartimiento, draft of Indian labor, 60
Representation
  in British House of Commons, 117
  in Great Compromise, 185
  proportional to population, 184
Representative government in
    Massachusetts Bay Colony, 42
Reproductive rights, 559–560
Republicanism
  colonists definition of, 169
  and Declaration of Independence, 142
  domestic policy, 219–220
  status of women in Revolutionary Era, 158
Republican National Convention in
    Houston, Texas, 823
Republican Party
  in 20th century, first half
    conservation shift, 570
    in control in 1920s, 635–637
    in election of 1928, 648
    election of 1932, 663
    election of 1948, 719–721
    Great War, 609–610
    on Hawaiian annexation, 587
    imperialist debate, 592
    and Mahanism, 583
    opposed New Deal reforms, 677–678
    post WWII, 715–716
    privilege and arrogance, 720
    progressive reform, 572–574
    scandals in 1920s, 636
  treaty of Versailles, 619–621
  in 20th century, second half
    Clinton impeachment, 827–828
    during Clinton years, 825–826
    conservative tone, 806
    critical of Chinese civil war, 726–727
    election of 1952, 729
    family and social issues, moved to right, 810
    gender gap, 835
    impeachment of Nixon, 782
    during Reagan years, 795
    Red Scare role, 730–733
  in Civil War years
    Civil War legislation and politics, 397
    counter-reconstruction, 427–430
    in election of 1860, 368
    federal reconstruction, 421–427
    formation in 1854, 362–364
    radicals, 407
    views on racial equality, 365
  early years
    economic nationalism after War of 1812, 231–232
    emergence as political party, 205
    as empire builders, 237
    in Jefferson administration, 219–224
    rise of during 1796–1801, 210–213
    voted to declare war on Britain, 226
    vs. Federalists, 207
  in late 19th century
    civil service reform, 532
    congressional election of 1884, 524–525

election of 1896 and gold standard, 542–543
  gold standard, 542–543
  Grand Old Party (GOP)
    defeats due to Populist Party, 538
    Northern opposition to Populists, 539
    partisan politics, 524–525
    protective tariffs, 533–534
    Southern agrarian revolt, 449–450
    Southern votes, 456, 458
Republic Iron and Steel Company, 665
Republic Steel Company, 673
Resaca, Georgia, 404
Rescate, ransom work, 60
Research and development, 468–469, 696
Reservationists, 621
Reservations for Indians, 503, 505
Resettlement Administration (1935), 670
Residential neighborhood, 489
Resistance, *See also* Protests; Slave revolts
  to authority in colonies, 93
  Pan-Indian movement, 225
  to slavery, 275–277, 358
Resource development, 568
Resource management, 676
Resources of North *vs.* South during
    Civil War, 383–384
Respect for parents and elders, 642
Retail palaces, 491
Retired Americans, 810
Retirement savings, 671
Retrenchment, 219–220
Reuther, Walter, 730
Revenue Act of 1935, 669
Revere, Paul, Boston silversmith, 87, 136, 164–165
Review of Reviews, 583
Revivals
  in 1820s, 303
  of 1820s, 1830s, 258
  in 1890s, 445
  in 1950s, 742
  and abolitionism, 317
  colonial religion, 92
  in Second Great Awakening, 245
  to win converts, 308
Revolts. *See* Slave revolts
Revolutionary War, 132–165
  American victory, 155–157
  assumption of war debt, 203–204, 206
  combatants, 142–146
  effect on African Americans, 171–172
  effect on Native Americans, 158–159, 172
  effect on Slavery, 158
  independece declared, 139–142
  investment by France, 161
  outbreak of war, 135–139
  problems after, 181–184
  rattlesnake national symbol, 164–165
  three phases of, 147
  war in the North, 147–149
  war widens, 149–155
  women at war, 158
Rhee, Syngman, 727
Rhineland remilitarization
    (Germany), 679
Rhode Island
  and A. Hutchinson, 43
  blocked national tariff, 176
  colonial governor conflict, 96
  Constitutional ratification, 190
  currency laws, 178–179
  Gaspee incident, 123–124
  joined Union, 202
  mentioned, 145, 184
  religion in colonies, 90
  Slater's mill, 299
  voters, 243
  women in majority, 197

Rhode Island system of family
    employment, 300
Rhythm-and-blues music, 742
Ribicoff, Abraham, Connecticut
    senator, 775
Rice, Condoleezza, national security
    advisor, 834
Rice, Thomas, 455
Rice as colonial export, 85
Rice plantations, 48, 251
Rice production, 177, 446
Richland, Washington, 696
Richmond, Virginia
  Civil War target, 388, 402, 406
  as Confederate capital, 385
  petitioned for democratic reform, 244
  Prosser's Rebellion, 276
  segregation laws in 1870s, 454
Rich *vs.* poor, *See also* Unequal
    distribution of wealth and
    income
  in 1920s, 635
  in 1950s, 743–744
  in 1980s, 798–800
  in 1990s, 829
  in colonial cities, 88
  early industrialization in 1800s, 301–305
  in late 19th century, 476–478
  Populist view of government, 540–541
Ridgway, Matthew, general, 728
Riesman, David, sociologist, 744
Rights, *See also* Civil rights; Gays and
    lesbians; Women's rights
  political, 169–172, 432
  of slaves, 273
Right to vote. *See* Suffrage
Right-wing dictatorships, 687, 793
Riis, Jacob A., 476, 477, 559
Riley, William, of Springfield, Ky, 278
Ring shout, 275
Rio Grande, 344
Riots, *See also* Race riots
  draft during Civil War, 398
River improvements favored by
    Northerns, 362
River Rouge plant in Detroit,
    Michigan, 630
Road construction in 1920s, 640
Roanoke Indians, 26
Roanoke Island, 26
Robertson, Pat, 370, 810
Robinson, Harriet Hanson, 300
Robinson, (Jackie) Jack, 718
Rochester, New York, 358, 485
Rock-and-roll music, 646, 742,
    768–769
Rockefeller, John D., 471, 478, 553, 556
Rockford (Illinois) College, 476
Rockingham, Lord, prime minister, 155
Rock Springs, Wyoming, 508
Rocky Mountain Fur Company, 335
Rocky Mountain News, 624
Rocky Mountains, 506
Rocque, Jean François de la, sieur de
    Roberval, 24
Rodney King riot in Los Angeles,
    California, 801–802
Roe v. *Wade*, 370, 646, 812
Rolfe, John, 36, 38
Rolling Stone magazine, 769
Rolling Stones rock band, 768
Romania, 620, 688, 722, 723, 724, 804
Rome-Berlin Axis, 687
Romer v. *Evans* (1996), 817
Rommel, Erwin, German field
    marshal, 693
Roosevelt, Eleanor, 657–658, 663,
    672–674
Roosevelt, Franklin (FDR), U.S.
    president
  background, 663
  coalition for 1936 election, 670, 672
  conservative opposition, 677–678
  died, 707

educated public on Nazi dangers, 679
  in election of 1944, 702
  foreign policy, 345
  foreign trade, 678–679, 680
  hope during Depression, 658
  isolationism and support for Britain, 687, 688, 690
  left no one out, 674–675
  mentioned, Johnson as heir, 755
  national debt, 206
  New Deal, end of, 702
  New Deal launched, 663
  Second New Deal, 669–671
  at summits, 702
  war preparations, 680, 691–692
  wartime Executive Orders, 699
Roosevelt, Theodore, Jr., governor of
    Puerto Rico, 595
Roosevelt, Theodore, U.S. president
  assistant secretary of navy, 589
  child labor reform, 561
  Country Life Commission created, 560
  debate over military policy, 609
  gospel of efficiency, 553
  imperialism, 583, 584, 592
  Maxwell House coffee, 490
  and New Nationalism, 573
  and Panama Canal, 597–598
  Progressive Era, 566–572
  Rough Riders, 581, 590
  and Russo-Japanese War, 594
Roosevelt coalition, 672
Roosevelt Corollary to Monroe
    Doctrine, 598, 648
Root, Elihu, secretary of State, 583,
    595, 598
Rosecrans, William S, Union general,
    394
Rosenberg, Julius and Ethel, 732, 733
Rosie the Riveter, 698
Ross, John, 252
Roughing It (Twain), 508
Rough Riders, 581, 590
Rowlandson, Mary, 66
Royal African Company, 69
Royal Navy, seized smugglers' ships,
    116
Royal Society of London, 90
Royce Hailey's Pig Stand, 640
Rubber industry, 672
Ruby, Jack, 755
Ruffin, Edmund, Virginia planter,
    270, 272
Rule of law, England, 94
Runaway slaves, 276–277
Rural electrification, 675, 702
Rural Electrification Administration
    (REA), 675
Rural life, 560–561
Rural overpopulation in East,
    327–329
Rural poor, 667, 675
Rural protests during Great
    Depression, 661
Rural South, migration from, 638
Rush-Bagot Agreement of 1817, 232
Russell, Andrew J., 498–499
Russell, Ella Gibson, 489
Russell, William, 489
Russia
  ambitions in China, 593–594
  formation after USSR, 805
  in Fourteen Points, 619, 620
  in Great War, 617
  immigrants, 481
  and NATO intervention in Kosovo,
    824
  Red Scare, 623
  revolution, 610–611
  sold Alaska, 585
  spheres of influence in China,
    593–594
  support of Union, 389
  treaty with Revolutionary U.S., 161
  Tsarist, in Great War, 605–606

Russian fur traders, 59
Russian Jews, 481, 614
Russo-Japanese war, 594
Rustbelt, 783
Rutgers University, 92
Ruth, Babe, 641
Rutledge, Edward, South Carolina
  delegate, 174
Ryan, Leo, Congressman, 769

S

Sabbatarian movement, 307
Sabine River in Louisiana, 339, 340
Sack of Lawrence, 361
Sacramento Delta, 483
Sacramento River Valley, 342
Sadat, Anwar el, Egyptian president,
  784
Sagebrush Rebellion, 570, 797
Saigon (Ho Chi Minh City), Vietnam,
  763, 773–774
Saint Dominque, 45
Sakhalin Island, 594
Salary Act of 1816, 243
Salem, Massachusetts, witchcraft, 94
Salish Indians of Montana, 336
Salmon, 499
Saloons, 492, 508
Saltillo, Texas, 339, 341
Salt Lake City, Utah, 663
Salutary neglect, 95
Salvation, 17, 50, 64, 245, 303, 367, 447
Salvation Army, 662
Samoan immigrants, 808
Samoset, 41
San Antonio, Texas, 99, 342
San Antonio de Valero (the Alamo), 99
Sánchez, Jose Maria, 341
Sanctions against Britain, 127
Sand Creek Massacre, Colorado, 502
San Diego, California, 695, 809
Sandinista rebels, 784, 803
San Francisco, California, 478, 488,
  540, 594–595
San Francisco Bay area (California),
  808
San Francisco Call, 592
San Francisco Examiner, 587
San Francisco State University, 739
Sanger, Margaret, 559–560
Sanitary police, 477
Sanitation systems, 557, 560, See also
  Waste disposal
San Jacinto, Battle of, 340
San Marcos de Apalachee, Spanish
  base, 98
Santa Barbara, California beaches, 779
Santa Clara County, California, 829
Santa Fe, New Mexico, 296, 342–343,
  343
Santa Fe Ring, 514
Santa Fe Trail, 296, 339, 342
Santee Sioux, 335
Saratoga, Battle of, 149
Saratoga, New York, 243
Satellite program, 745
Saturday Evening Post, 623
Saudi Arabia, 805
Sauk Indians, 250, 334
Savannah, Battle of, 143
Savannah, Georgia, 152, 406, 441
Savings and loans, 797
Savio, Mario, antiwar activist, 766
Scab workers, 480
Scalawags, 427
Scandalmongering, 533
Scandals
  in 1870s, 428–429
  among Republicans in 1920s, 636
  Kennedy, 748
  Teapot Dome, 636
  Watergate, 779–782
Scandinavian immigrants, 614
Scandinavian Immigration Society, 514
Scandinavian party loyalty, 527
Scarlet Letter, The (Hawthorne), 314

Schaw, Janet, visiting Scotswoman, 146
Schaw, Robert, North Carolina militia
  colonel, 146
Schenck, David, 452–453
Schlesinger, Arthur Jr, 719
Schneider, Paul, 656
Schofield, Martha, 418
School and Society, The (Dewey), 559
School desegregation, 778
School nurses, 559
Schools, See also Colleges; Educational
  institutions; High schools; Public
  education; Universities
  bilingual education, 837
  for blacks in Reconstruction, 432
  built by WPA, 670
  busing for racial integration, 773
  compulsory attendance, 529, 554
  consolidation, 561
  evolution teaching opposed,
    645–646
  Freedmen's, 418
  jobs for married women during
    Great Depression, 660
  parochial, 311, 527
  racial segregation, 738–739, 752
  reform in early 20th century, 559
  reform in New England, 311–312
Schurz, Carl, 592
Science and technology
  enlisted in WWII, 696
  expanded by defense spending, 807
  world leadership, 739
Scientific agriculture, 553
Scientific American Magazine, 484
Scientific management principles,
  553, 632
Scientific methods, 553
Scientific theory, 468
Scientists, 468
Scopes, John, 645
Scopes Trial, 645, 646
Scots-Irish Piedmont farmers, 199
Scots-Irish settlers in backcountry,
  97–98
Scott, Dred, 363
Scott, Winfield, general, 346
Scranton, Pennsylvania, 474
Scrap drives, 697
Scrooby separatists, 40
Scurvy, 24
Seale, Bobby, 771
Seamstresses strikes, 305
Sea of Tranquillity, 777
Seaports as commercial centers,
  295–297
Seaports of colonies, 87
Sea power and imperial expansion,
  582–583
Search and destroy, 763
Search warrants, 117
Sears, Roebuck catalogs, 461
Seattle, Washington, 540, 623, 638
Seattle's shipyards, 695
Secession
  British peace treaty violations, 182
  of Kentucky from Virginia, 199–201
  New England talk of, 226, 230
  propaganda campaign, 371
  of the South, 369–371
  vs. nullification, 251
  of West Virginia, 400
Secondary boycotts, 716
Second Bank of the United States,
  231
Second Civil War, 440
Second-class citizens, 456
Second Cold War, 802–806
Second Coming of Christ, 367
Second Continental Congress, 158
Second ghettos, 770
Second Great Awakening, 244–245,
  291, 306
Second New Deal, 669–671
Second party system, 256–257
Second Reconstruction, 433
Second Red Scare, 730–733

Secret ballot, 455, 538
Secret Six, 367
Secret voting, 564
Sectionalism, See also Politics of
  sectionalism
  abolition in 1830s, 256
  annexation of Texas, 260
  in Constitutional Convention,
    185–186
  Missouri Compromise, 235–236
  religious schisms, 283
  shift of issues, 262
  Upper South vs. Lower South, 267
Secular utopians, 314
Securities Act, 665
Securities and Exchange Commission
  (SEC), 665
Security measures, 843
Sedition Act, 211
Sedition Act (1918), 614, 842
Seeger, Pete, folk singer, 768
Segregated unions, 699
Segregation
  in 1920s, 639
  of Asian & white schoolchildren,
    594–595
  and crosstown busing, 811
  gender, 660
  by law, 454–455
  in Progressive Era, 563
  racial, 738–739, 752–754
  Reconstruction failure, 431
  in Southern public education, 559
  Wilson support of, 574
Select Committee on Presidential
  Campaign Activities, 782
Selective Service Act (1917), 617
Selective Service System, 766
Selectmen, 44
Self-determination, Wilson's Great
  War peace terms, 610, 619, 620,
  621
Self-government
  in Atlantic Charter, 691
  in English colonies, 36, 95
  of freedmen, 420
  of Indians, 675
  and Manifest Destiny, 345
  in new republic, 226
  republicanism ideal, 169
  republicanism in Declaration of
    Independence, 142
  for settlers, 179
Seminole Indians, 233, 249, 250
Senate Committee on Government
  Operations, 733
Senate Foreign Relations Committee,
  621, 766
Senate Internal Security
  Subcommittee, 731
Seneca Falls, New York, 319
Seneca Falls Convention, 319
Seneca Indians, 60, 67
Seneca-Iroquois Museum, 505
Seoul, South Korea, 727–728
Separate but equal, 752
Separate facilities for black people,
  455
Separation of church and state, 43,
  307, 361, 370, 645
Separation of powers, 677
Separation of work and home, 303
Separatists, 40
September 11, 2001, 822–823
Serapis, H.M.S., ship in Revolutionary
  War, 151
Serbia, 606
Serra, Junípero, Franciscan priest, 99
Servants, 303
Servants rights in Virginia colony, 38
Service economy, 829
Servicemen's Readjustment Act
  (1944), 716
Service wives during WWII, 697
Settlement houses, 450, 459, 476, 487,
  557, 563
Settlement of Great Plains, 513–517

Settlers, 179, 501
Seven Days, Battle of, 388
Seven Pines, Battle of, 388
Seven Years' War, 82, 103
Seward, William H., New York senator,
  257, 362, 369, 390, 585
Sewer systems, 670, 675, See also
  Sanitation systems; Waste
  disposal
Sewing company fire, 550, 554
Sewing machines, 301, 398, 474, 632
Sexism, 768, 812
Sexual abuse of slaves, 274, 279
Sexual behavior, 642, 812, 813–814
Sexual crimes, 453–454
Sexual harassment, 476, 768
Sexually transmitted diseases, 697
Sexual orientation, 811, 813–814, 817
Sexual revolution, 817
Shah of Iran, 746, 784–785
Shakers, 313
Shandong Peninsula, 593
Sharecropping, 284, 431–432, 446,
  537, 639, 667, 668, 675
Share-Our-Wealth Society, 668
Sharpsburg, Maryland, 390
Shaw, Albert, 583
Shawnee Indians, 103, 104
Shaw vs. Reno, 433
Shays, Daniel, 168
Shays's Rebellion, 168–169, 178, 184
Sheen, Bishop Fulton J., 742
Shelburne, Lord, British prime
  minister at Peace of Paris, 156
Shelling in Great War, 618
Shenandoah Valley, 271, 401–402
Shepard, William, militia commander,
  168
Sheppard-Towner Maternity and
  Infancy Act (1921), 637
Sheridan, Philip, general, 501, 502
Sherman, Roger of Connecticut, 185
Sherman, William T., Union general
  control of Chattanooga, 401–404
  Field Order No 15, 419
  fighting Indians in West, 502
  march to the sea, 406–407
  prediction of war's length, 381
Sherman Antitrust Act (1890),
  534–535, 541
Sherman Silver Purchase Act (1890),
  536, 538, 541
Sherman's March to the Sea, 406–407
Shiite Muslims, 806
Shiloh Church, 385–386
Shima, George, 483
Shipbuilding in New England, 44
Shipping industry, 177, 203
Shipyards, 693, 699
Shipyard workers, 623
Shirley, William, governor of
  Massachusetts, 102
Shoddy aristocracy, 399
Shoes rationed, 695
Shopping centers, 640, 741
Shopping malls, 772
Shortages after WWII, 715
Short Hills, New Jersey, 489
Shoshone Indians, 7, 339, 500, 505
"Shot heard around the world," 137,
  161
Shriver, R. Sargent, 755
Shultz, George, secretary of Labor and
  State, 778, 803, 804
Siberia, 6
Sicily, 150, 703
Siege of Quebec, 139
Sierra Club, 570
Sierra Leone, 158
Silent Spring (Carson), 779
Silesia, 620
Silicon Valley, 808, 829
Silk mills, 474
Silliman, Mary, 158
Silver
  coinage, 535–536, 538
  mines, 68, 506

production, 536
  Spanish acquisition, 22–23
  standard, 536, 541–543
Simpson, Sockless Jerry, 537
Sinclair, Upton, 472, 553, 555, 630, 673
Singapore, 693
Single, Peter, 299
Sin taxes in cow towns, 511
Sioux Indians
  in Black Hawk's War, 250
  culture and economy, 500
  held off white invaders, 334–335, 347
  Indian Wars and Americanization, 502–504
  railroad construction, 499
  treaty rights to Platte lands, 338
Sirhan, Sirhan, 775
Sirica, John, federal justice, 781
Sister Carrie (Dreiser), 474
Sit-down strike, 672–673
Sitting Bull, Sioux leader, 500, 503
Situation comedies, 741
Six Sermons on Temperance (Beecher), 307
Skilled trades, 282
Skyscrapers, 638
Slater, Samuel of Rhode Island, 299
Slaughterhouse cases (1873), 432
Slave catchers, 357, 391
Slave codes, 48, 69–71, 273, 317
Slaveholders, 278–280
Slave patrols, 280
Slave Power, 320–321, 364, 373
Slave reparations, 70
Slave revolts
  in early colonial period, 74–75
  incited by abolitionists, 317
  John Brown's Raid, 367–368
  resistance, 275–277, 358
  Turner's Rebellion, 251, 276, 316
  uprisings in early 1800s, 276
  in Virginia in 1831, 251
Slavery
  before Civil War
    abolished in District of Columbia, 256
    abolished in New England, 197
    call to abolish in District of Columbia, 355
    challenged by Evangelicalism, 245
    controversy in 1819, 231
    cotton and slaves, 267–268
    critism stifled by white mobs, 282
    danger to Union of slavery question, 233
    decline of, 272
    economic legacy of, 284
    emancipation in Mid-Atlanic region, 198
    fear of race war, 315
    free society, 277–282
    importation banned, 235
    incentives for work, 274
    living conditions of slaves, 273–274
    Lower South, 267–269
    profits, 268–269
    prohibited in West, 179, 181
    proslavery argument, 282–284
    Revolutionary War effects, 158, 171–172
    sectional clash in Constitutional Convention, 185–186
    slave life & culture, 272–277
    in South in 1780, 199
    in Texas, 340–341
    Texas question, 262
    unresolved in Constitution, 188
    Upper South, 270–272
  during Civil War years
    Compromise of 1850, 355–359
    in Confederacy, 401
    Confederate plan to abandon, 406
    Emancipation Proclamation, 390–392
    Lincoln's views, 374

in Mexican territories, 353–354
    moral perceptions, 352, 358–359, 365
    North-South differences, 366–369
    outlawed, 405
    political alignments, 359–365
    popular sovereignty, 360
    proviso debate, 353–356
  before Revolutionary War
    from Africa to New World, 71–72
    conditions in Caribbean sugar plantations, 45–46
    early history in New World, 68–71
    early labor in colonies, 68–71
    and family life, 72–74
    importance to New England, 86
    rice plantations in South Carolina, 48
    sugar plantations on Atlantic islands, 19
    in West African societies, 15
Slaves
  count of, 185
  families, 268, 274–275, 279
  fugitives, 276–277, 316
  letter from escaped slave, 278
  manumit (free), 199
  moved to Old Southwest, 331–333
  native born by 1850s, 272
  religions of, 275
  skills of survival, 274
  as soldiers in Revolutionary War, 145
Slave trade
  in Africa, 71–72
  ended in District of Columbia, 256, 355
  internal trade, 272
    among Upper South plantations, 268
  not in Declaration of Independence, 141
  not in Peace of Paris, 156
  professional traders, 268
  sales, 268, 274
  suppression of African trade, 260
Slidell, John L., 346
Slums, *See also* Ghettos
  Fair Deal plan, 721
  first appeared, 296
  housing reform in early 20th century, 557
  overcrowding in tenement apartments, 476
Smallpox
  affect on Plains Indians, 335–336
  in Columbian exchange, 20, 23
  germ warfare, 114
  vaccinations for Sioux, 335
Smalls, Robert, 456, 457
Smelting plants, 509
Smiley, Carrie, of Jacksonville, Florida, 317
Smith, Alfred E., 648
Smith, Anna, leader of Coxey's Army, 540
Smith, Captain John, 35–36
Smith, Hoke, governor of Georgia, 563
Smith, John, 40
Smith, Joseph, 310, 343
Smith, Peg-Leg, 336
Smith-Lever Act (1914), 561
Smuggling, 112, 117, 118, 121, 123–124
Soak the Rich Tax, 669
Social conservatives grass-roots activism, 767
Social control, 556, 562–563
Social Darwinism, 478, 484, 581–582
Social Gospel movement, 551–552, 555–556, 555
Social housekeepers, 554–555
Social improvement, 310–314
Socialism, 555–556
Social issues in late 20th century, 810–817
Socialist Party of America, 555, 615

Socialists, 623, 661, 668
Social justice, 135, 552, 556
Social mother, 308
Social policy during Reconstruction, 427
Social reform, *See also* Progressive Era; Reform organizations
  in 19th century
    abolitionism, 315–321
    institutions, 310–314
    moral order, 306–310
    new classes, 301–305
    women's rights, 315, 317–320
  Eleanor Roosevelt, 663
  by Whigs, 258
Social Security, 677, 721, 757, 798, 810
Social Security Act, 669, 673
Social service organizations and child care, 529
Social status of Southern planters, 278–280
Social welfare
  associations, 432
  first federal law, 637
  legislation, 418
  policies, 668
  and Social Security, 671
  state government involment, 532
  and Woodrow Wilson, 573
Social workers in ethnic neighborhoods, 482
Social work profession, 475
Society of Friends, 50
Sod houses, 515
Software industry, 830
Soil Conservation Service, 670
Soil erosion projects, 670
Soil fertility exhaustion, 267, 270–271, 327
Soil loss in Dust Bowl storms, 669
Solar energy research, 783
Soldiers, *See also* Black soldiers; Continental army
  in Civil War, 386–388
  Civil War pay, 392
  colonial in French and Indian War, 103–104
  Confederate, 400–401
  of fortune, 143
  in Great War, 617, 621–622
  letters home, 391
  nuclear weapons tests, 725
  in Revolutionary War, 142–145
  in Vietnam War, 766, 776
Solid South, 439
Solomon Islands, 706
Somalia, 824
Somoza dictatorship, 784, 803
Songhai empire in Africa, 14
Sonoran Desert, 342
Sons of Confederate Veterans, 460
Sons of Liberty, 116, 118–119, 124
So Proudly We Hail (1943), 697
Sorghum, 511
Souls of Black Folk, The (Du Bois), 461
Sound money policy, 535, 543
Soup kitchens, 660, 665
The South, *See also* Civil War; New South; The North
  Church of England, 91
  immigration, 97
  mobilizing for war, 381–385
  New Deal benefits, 675–676
  public education, 559
  Revolutionary War, 139, 147, 149, 152–155, 158
  secession from Union, 369–375
  slavery in the new republic, 198–199
South Africa, 543, 709, 784
Southampton County, Virginia, 276
South Carolina
  black voters, 426–427
  colonial exports, 85

Confederate battle flag, 460
  disfranchisement, 456
  freedom riders, 754
  Lower South in 1850, 267
  mentioned, 120, 446, 752
  nullification crisis, 251
  political violence in election of 1876, 430
  presidential electors, 244
  public education in 1900s, 559
  ratification of Constitution, 190
  Reconstruction Constitution, 457
  secession from Union, 369, 371
  secession ordinance, 422
  social policy during Reconstruction, 427
  state constitution development, 174
  Whig *vs.* Loyalist militias, 152
South Dakota, 659
Southeast Asia, 692
Southeast Asia Treaty Organization (SEATO) (1954), 746
Southern Baptists, 742
Southern Christian Leadership Conference (SCLC), 753–754
Southern Democrats
  election of 1912, 572
  opposed New Deal reforms, 677–678
  opposition to Populists, 539
  political violence during Redemption, 429–430
  use of racism, 427
Southern economy
  during Civil War, 400–401
  land ownership for freedmen, 419
  legacy of slavery, 284
Southerners
  evangelicals justified slavery, 283
  migration to lower Midwest, 330
Southern Farmers Alliance, 447–449, 537
Southern Homestead Act, 419
Southern industry, 274
Southern loyalists, 152, 155
Southern Manifesto, 752
Southern Pacific Railroad, 553
Southern Republican governments after Civil War, 426–427
Southern states
  economic crisis after Revolutionary War, 177
  segregation and desegregation, 753–754
Southern Tenant Farmers Union, 668
Southern women, 439–440
South Korea, 727–728, 804
South Vietnam, 746, 749–750, 757, 773, 776
Southwest
  Indians & white settlements, 338–339
  Mexican rule ended, 342–343
Southwest Ordinance (1790), 181, 235, 333
Soviet Union
  balance of terror, 745
  ceased to exist, 805
  Cold War, 725–729
  Cold War beginnings, 721–725
  Czech resistance, 774
  easing of tension, 777–778
  and Eisenhower, 744–748
  end of Grand Alliance, WWII, 722
  excluded from bomb research, 686
  formal recognition, 678
  human rights violations, 784
  Hungarian resistance, 746
  independence of republics, 805
  invaded by Hitler, 688
  and Kennedy, 748–749
  nuclear power, 725
  weapons agreement, 804
  in World War II, 702
  in World War II, under German control, 692–693
Space satellite, 739

Spain
 after French and Indian War, 112
 after War of 1812, 233
 conquest and colonization, 20–23
 declared war on Britain, 150
 entered Revolutionary War, 152
 loss of Florida, 104
 mentioned, 584
 negotiations after Revolutionary
  War, 183
 Peace of Paris, 156
 proposed treaty in 1786, 183
 selling of West Florida, 223
 Spanish-American War, 588–592
 support for Columbus, 19
 treaties with, 208–210
 Treaty of Tordesillas, 24
 before WWII, 687
Spaniards as population group in
  Southwest, 338
Spanish-American War, 580–581,
  588–592, 596, 597
Spanish Armada, 26
Spanish colonies
 expanding in Texas & California,
  98–99
 and Indian workers, 59
 and Pueblo Revolt, 65–67
Spanish Florida, 98, 210, 225, 233
Spanish missionaries, 62–64, 67
Spanish missions, 338
Spanish Republic, 679
Spargo, John, 557
Speaker of the House, 531
Special Committee on Un-American
  Activities, 730
Special interests, 796
Special privilege, assault on, 248
Specie Circular (1836), 255
Specie payments (1837), 254–255
Speculative capital for cattle industry,
  511
Speculators during Civil War, 400
Spheres of influence
 in Caribbean, 597
 in China, 593–594
 Communist growth blocked,
  745–746
 Roosevelt vs. Churchill, 703
 in Yalta Conference, 722
Spice Islands, 51
Spice trade, 18
Spies for Confederacy, 401
Spirit of St. Louis, Lindbergh's
  airplane, 641
Spirituals, 275
Split tickets, 528
Spoils system, 248, 531, 532–533
Spontaneous creativity, 314
Sporting goods, 491
Sports
 major leagues, 773
 professional teams, 718
 spectator, in late 19th century,
  491–492
Spotsylvania, Battle of, 402
Springfield, Illinois, 458, 563
Springfield, Massachusetts, 178
Springfield, Ohio, 458
Springsteen, Bruce, singer, 769
Sputnik, 745
Squanto, 41
"Square deal" by Roosevelt, 568
Squatters, 179, 180, 199, 260, 329
Sri Lanka, 51
St. Augustine, Florida, 22, 77, 98
St. Christopher, 45
St. Domingue Island, 222
St. Eustasius, 45
St. Joseph, Missouri, 337
St. Lawrence River, 33, 99–100
St. Louis, Missouri, 272, 296, 474, 509
St. Martin, 45
Stagflation, 779
Stalin, 702, 707, 728
Stalingrad (Volgograd), 693
Stamp Act, 116, 118–119, 120

Stamp Act Congress, 119, 121
Stamp distributors, 119
Standard, gold vs. silver, 542–543
Standard of living, 799
Standard Oil Company, 469, 471, 478,
  535, 542, 553, 556
Stanford University, 562, 808
Stanton, Edwin M., Secretary of War,
  425
Stanton, Elizabeth Cady, 318–319,
  425–426
Starr, Kenneth, independent counsel,
  827
Star Spangled Banner, 230
Starvation, See also Hunger;
  Malnutrition
 during Civil War, 400
 in Germany, 723
 in Jamestown, 35
 in New York City, 660
 in New York tenements, 477
Star Wars defense program, 802
State board of education in
  Massachusetts, 311
State conservation commissions, 568
State constitutions, 172–174, 455, 457
State courts, 203
State Department, 202, 727
State governments
 external restraints on central
  government, 187–188
 during Great Depression, 663
 in late 19th century, 531–532
 reform of, 566
 representation of populations, 773
 social legislation, 427
Statehood, requirements & process,
  181
State income taxes in Wisconsin, 566
State laws on seduction and adultery,
  309
State legislatures, 173, 294, 295
State militias
 in Civil War, 381
 in Revolutionary War, 142, 146, 152
 used to break strikes, 480, 510
States, redistricting for Congressional
  elections, 433
States admitted to Union, 331, 332
States rights, 211, 251, 253, 384, 400,
  432
State's rights in New Deal, 675
State-supported schools, 311
State vs. federal powers, 424, 425
Stay laws, 426–427
Stead, William T., 555
Steal their freedom, 391–392
Steamboats, 292
 Gibbons v. Ogden (1824), 294
Steam engines, stationary, 301
Steam power, 301
Steamship companies in Europe, 481
Steel as war resource, 607, 691
Steel industry
 in 1950s, 740
 consolidated in Carnegie Steel, 471
 in Great Depression, 659
 post WWII, 715
 substituted machinery for
  employees, 783
 and unions, 673
 workers unionized, 672
Steelworkers, 550, 623
Steelworker's strike, 479–480
Steeplechase Park, 492
Steffens, Lincoln, 553, 555
Stein, Gertrude, 642
Stephens, Major, 168
Stereotypes
 of blacks, 487
 of immigrants, 483
 of women, 476
Steuben, Baron von, Prussian
  drillmaster, 143, 149
Stevens, John, minister of Hawaii, 587
Stevens, Thaddeus of Pennsylvania,
  422–423

Stevenson, Adlai, 739
Stewart, T. McCants, 452
Stewart, William, 453
St-Lô, France, 703
Stockman, David, budget director,
  796
Stock market
 crash of 1929, 658–659
 and New Deal, 675
 scandals of 1870s, 428
 soared in 2000, 829
 and Social Security, 671
Stock market regulation, 571
Stockmen-hunters, 332–333
Stockton and Darlington Railroad,
  292
Stokes, Carl, mayor of Cleveland,
  Ohio, 835
Stokowski, Leopold, conductor, 641
Stone, Monica Itoe, 700
Stonewall Inn (New York), 813
"Stonewall" Jackson. See Jackson,
  Thomas J. "Stonewall"
Stonewall Rebellion, 813
Stono Rebellion in South Carolina, 75
Stowe, Harriet Beecher, author,
  352–353, 358, 489
Strategic Arms Limitation Treaty
  (SALT), 709, 778, 784–785, 794
Strategic balance, 751
Strategic Defense Initiative (SDI),
  802, 841
Strauss, Lewis, 726
Strikebreakers
 blocked, 673
 during Civil War, 398
 in Great Depression, 668
 in Pennsylvania steelworkers' strike,
  623
 used during Great War, 615
 used in 1920s, 634
 war emergency excuse, 842
Strikes
 after Great War, 622–623
 coalminers in 1902, 567–568
 by cowboys, 512
 garment workers, 554
 in Great Depression, 668
 in late 19th century, 478–480
 of New England millhands, 300
 post WWII, 715–716
 Pullman, 540–541
 against Pullman in 1894, 567
 railroad, 574
 by seamstresses, 305
 shipyard workers, 623
 sit-down, 672–673
Strip-mining, 570
Strontium 90, 745
Student jobs, 670
Student Nonviolent Coordinating
  Committee (SNCC), 753, 756,
  771
Student protests
 in Europe, 774
 Kent State University, 776
 Vietnam War, 765–767, 776
Students for a Democratic Society
  (SDS), 766–767, 776
Stuyvesant, Peter, governor of New
  Netherland, 52
Submarine warfare, 608–611, 617,
  691, 693
Subtreasury plan, 448
Subtreasury system, 537, 538
Suburban growth, 741
Suburbanization, 632, 640
Suburban population after WWII, 717
Suburbs
 in 1920s, 637, 640
 federal assistance at expense of
  cities, 778
 and feminine mystique, 744
 location of factories vs. workers,
  798–799
 as outer cities, 772–773

preferred by middle class after 1870,
  489
 urban crisis in 1970s, 770
 zoning defense, 811
Subversion, 624
Subversion Trials, 732
Subversives, 730–733
Sudetenland, 679
Suez Canal, 692, 693, 746
Suffolk Resolves, 127
Suffrage, See also Voting; Woman
  suffrage movement
 15th Amendment, 425, 432
 African-American voting rights, 422,
  433
 of black men, 172
 Compromise of 1877, 430
 of former slaves, 422–425
 of Indians, 172, 698
 New Jersey constitution, 171
 under republicanism, 169–172
 Susan B. Anthony, 424–426
 universal manhood suffrage, 425,
  426
 Voting Rights Act (1965), 433
 from wealth and status to race and
  gender, 244
Sugar, court ruling, 541
Sugar Act, 116, 118–119
Sugar beet fields, 515
Sugar Creek, Illinois, 330
Sugar imports, 86
Sugar interests, Hawaiian-Californian,
  592
Sugar islands, 104, 222
Sugar plantations
 on Atlantic islands, 19
 in Brazil, 24
 in Caribbean, 22, 45
 in Hawaii, 586
 use of slaves, 68
Sugar planters, Parliament lobby, 84
Sugar production in Puerto Rico, 595
Sugar rationed, 695
Suicide
 during Great Depression, 656, 665
 legacy of Indian Americanization,
  505
 mass suicide in cult, 769
 missions, 707
Sumatra, 51
Summit meetings
 in Paris, 747
 in Vienna (1961), 749
Sumner, Charles, of Massachusetts,
  422–423, 430
Sunbelt, 695, 806–810, 815
Sun City near Phoenix, Arizona, 810
Sun Dance, 503
Sunday, Billy, evangelist, 556
Sunday interdenominational schools,
  306
Sunni Ali, 14
Superfund cleanup, 779
Supply and demand, 659
Surveys, grid system adopted, 179–181
Susquehannock Indians, 52, 65, 67, 101
Sussex Pledge, 609
"Swamp Fox" Francis Marion, 155
Swan, James of Massachusetts, 176
Swann v. Charlotte-Mecklenburg Board of
  Education (1971), 773, 811
Sweatshops, 473, 474, 550, 554
Sweden, 16–18, 150
Swift, Gustavus, 470–471
Swing states in late 19th century, 526
Swiss Protestant immigrants, 77
Syphilis in Columbian exchange, 23

T
Table tennis team, 778
Tabloids, 490–491
Taft, Alphonso, in Grant's cabinet,
  524
Taft, Horace, 524–525

Taft, Robert, Ohio senator, 691, 721, 724
Taft, William Howard, U.S. president
  Chief Justice of Supreme Court, 636
  dollar diplomacy in Caribbean, 598, 599
  early years, 524–525
  in election of 1912, 573
  first governor general of Philippines, 593
  inaction on tariffs, 572
  as president, 571
Taft family, 524
Taft-Hartley Act (1947), 715–716, 720
Taino Indians, 11–12, 19, 20
Taiwan, 51, 593, 727, 729
Taliban regime, 843
Tallmadge, James, of New York, 235
Tallmadge Amendment, 235
Tallow, 342
Tammany Hall politicians, 428, 648
Taney, Roger B., Supreme Court chief justice, 294, 363
Tanzania, 841
Taos, 342
Taos Revolt, 346
Tappan, Arthur and Lewis, 317
Tarbell, Ida, 553
Tariff Act (1789), 203
Tariff Act (1816), 231
Tariff of Abominations, 251
Tariff reductions, 533–534
Tariffs
  attempt to establish, 176
  during Civil War, 398
  complaints, 178
  favored by Northerns, 362
  FDR foreign trade, 679
  on imported goods, 203, 533–534
  law of 1922, 636
  laws, 528
  McKinley Tariff, 538
  protective, 251
  reductions, Taft inaction, 572
  reductions, Wilson, 573
  role in Great Depression, 659
Tarleton, Banastre, British colonel, 152, 155
Taverns, 492
Taxation
  years 1600–1774
    for Anglican ministers, 115
    in colonies, 93
    English vs. colonists, 112
    to pay for England's wars, 101
    Sugar and Stamp Acts, 116–120
    Townshend Duty Act, 121–122, 124
  years 1774–1850
    Congress granted power to levy, 145
    power to tax, 176, 185
    slave assessments in Great Compromise, 185
    for support of religion, 173
    on whiskey, 204, 205, 208, 220
  years 1850–1900
    Civil War resources, 383–384
    in South, 457
  years 1900–1950
    confiscatory on rich, 668
    income tax, 571, 573, 695
    laws of 1917 and 1918, 613
    poll tax, 565
    rates on wealthy, role in Great Depression, 659
    reduction on business and wealthy, 636
    in Second New Deal, 669
    tax cuts in Great Depression, 663
  years 1950–2000
    in 1996, 825
    cuts by Bush, 839–840
Tax-exempt status of religious groups, 370
Tax-supported schools, 311
Taylor, Frederick W., 553, 632
Taylor, Maxwell, ambassador to Vietnam, 763

Taylor, Zachary, U.S. president, 344, 346, 354–355
Taylorization, 553
Tea Act of 1773, 124
Teachers, 312, 475, 660, 663
Teaching American history, 159
Teapot Dome scandal, 636
Tear gas used in strikes, 673
Technological developments
  after European plague, 16
  industrial revolution, 297–301
  ocean navigation, 18
  used against Indians, 502
Technology
  agricultural advances in American West, 515–517
  exposition in Moscow (1959), 743
  late 19th century, 468–470
  secrets guarded by Britain, 299
Tecumseh, Shawnee chief, 225, 229
Teenagers, 660, 742
Teflon president, 794
Tehran, Iran, 702, 785
Tejanos (Texans of Mexican descent), 260, 340–342
Telecommunications, 797
Telegrams, 397
Telegraph companies, 532, 538, 571
Telegraphs, 467
Telephone companies, 538, 571
Telephones, 467, 561, 615
Televangelists, 815
Television
  covered party conventions & campaigns, 720
  hostages in Iran, 785
  news of Vietnam War, 774
  and political candidates, 528
  popularity in 1950s, 741–742
  portrayal of cities, 769
  presidential debates, 748
  religious, 815
Teller, Edward, 686, 726
Teller Amendment, 590, 596
Tempelhof Airport, 724
Temperance, 450–451, 527, 530, 644–645
Temperance groups, 420
Temperance movement, 304, 307–308
Temperance Recorder, 308
Temporary Assistance to Needy Families (TANF), 826
Tenancy, 432, 433
Tenant farmers, 76, 284, 446
Ten Commandments, 370
Ten Commandments, The (DeMille film), 641
Tenement apartments, 476, 477
Tennent, William Sr, evangelist, 92
Tennessee
  admitted to Union, 235, 332
  Border South in 1850, 270
  disfranchisement, 455
  evolution in school law (1925), 645
  formation of Church of God, 448
  losing migrants, 333
  migrants in 1780s, 199
  problems after Revolutionary War, 183
  secession from Union, 375, 384
  sharecroppers, 668
Tennessee Valley Authority (TVA), 675
Tennis courts for women, 491
Tenochtitlán, 4, 9
Ten Percent Plan, 421
Tenure of Office Act, 425
Teoti-huacán in Mexico, 7
Termination policy, Native Americans, 740
Territorial aggrandizement and Manifest Destiny, 344
Territory of Oregon, 261
Terrorism, 822–823, 841–844
Terry, Randall, 370
Timber, 676
Texan army, 340
Texas

admitted to Union, 320, 332
annexation of, 260, 344
in Civil War, 394
discrimination against Mexicans, 661
expanding Spanish empire, 98–99
future acquisitions, 233
Lower South in 1850, 267
mentioned, 447, 449, 512
from Mexico to independence, 339–342
oil drilling, 632
Pancho Villa attacks, 599
population growth in 1990s, 834
Populist Party, 449
question on slavery, 262
refusal to ratify 13th Amendment, 422
retirees, 810
secession from Union, 369
Sunbelt, 806
Texas and Pacific Railway, 441
Texas longhorns, 510
Texas Rangers and cowboy strike, 512
Texas Republic, 342
Texas School Book Depository, 754
Textile employees, 550
Textile industry
  in 1920s, 635
  in England, 235
  role in Great Depression, 659
  in South late 19th century, 443
Textile mills, 297, 440
Textiles, 583
Textile workers, 299–300, 305
Thames River in Ontario, 229
Thanksgiving, 41
The Liberator, abolitionist paper, 256
Theological differences, 815
Theory of evolution, 645–646
Think tanks, 796
Third International, 623
Third parties
  American Communist Party, 623
  American Progressive Party, 719
  Anti-Masons, 257
  Communist Party (See Communist Party)
  Constitutional Union party, 368–369
  Free-Soil party, 321, 354
  Greenback Party, 527, 536, 537
  Kansas People's Party, 537
  Know-Nothing party, 362–363
  National Woman's Party, 637
  People's Party, 449, 527, 537–539, 543
  Populist Party, 449–450, 527, 537–539, 540–541, 566, 589
  Progressive Party, 572, 610, 637, 719
  Prohibition Party, 527
  Socialist Party of America, 555, 615
  in South late 19th century, 455–456
  Union Party, 672
  Woman's Peace Party, 609
Third Reich, 679
Third World, 746
Thistles in Columbian exchange, 24
Thomas, Clarence, Supreme Court justice, 834
Thompson, Cyrus, of North Carolina, 448
Thompson, Waddy, 344
Thomson, Elihu, 468
Thoreau, Henry David, 314, 368
Three Mile Island nuclear plant, 784
Thurmond, Strom, 720
Tidewater planters, 199
Tijuana, Mexico, 809
Tilden, Samuel J., 430
Tillamook Indians, 499
Tilyou, George C., 492
Timber, 676
Timber companies, 797
Timberlands, 568
Timber-processing industry, 440
Timbuktu, West Africa, 12–15
Time Magazine, 641, 668, 716, 832
Tippecanoe, Battle of, 225, 258

Tippecanoe River, 225
Tires rationed, 695
Title IX of Educational Amendments (1972), 812
Toasters, 640
Tobacco
  in Chesapeake Bay region, 34
  colonial export, 85
  French explorers' first taste, 11–12
  market, 271
  price collapse in 1785, 177
  shift out of production, 272
  in Virginia colony, 37–39
Tobacco industry, 440, 443, 471
Tobacco planters, 182
  credit reliance, 86
  early use of slaves, 68–71
Tobin, Brian, 27
Todd, Mary, 364
Tokyo, Japan, 594, 691, 706, 809
Toledo, Ohio, 208, 565, 668
Tolerance, 842
Toltec Indians, 7
Tomasito, Pueblo chieftain, 346
Tompkins County, New York, 391
Tonnage Act of 1789, 203
Tonnage duties, 203
Tonnage warfare by Germany, 693
Toombs, Robert, 354
Topsoil, 669
Tories, 128
Toronto, Canada, 230
Towns
  in early New England, 43–45
  Lower South stifled growth, 268
Townsend, Francis, California physician, 668
Townsend Clubs, 668
Townshend, Charles, 121
Townshend Duty Act, 121–122, 124
Toxic waste, 570
Trade, *See also* Boycotts
  years 1400–1774
    in Africa c. 1500, 14–15
    among Native Americans, 6–7, 9
    British regulations, 116, 118, 121
    colonial exports, 84–86
    colonial imports, 86–87
    in early New England, 44
    Europe and Asia, 18–19
    French fur traders, 34
    in Pennsylvania colony, 50
    regulated by British Parliament, 83–84
    Spain's economy, 22–23
    undermining self-sufficiency, 60–61
  years 1774–1850
    American merchants c.1800, 223
    Britain's retaliatory policies, 182
    to California in 1830s, 342
    deficit with Britain, 176
    embargo as substitute for war, 223–225
    European powers and U.S., 150
    fur trade in Wyoming, 335–336
    interregional, transportation revolution, 292
    in large cities, early 19th century, 295–297
    legislative sectional clash in Constitution Convention, 185
    in Old Northwest, 330–331
    revenue for new federal government, 203, 206
  years 1850–1900
    protective tariffs, 533
  years 1900–1950
    with China, 593–594
    with Cuba, 580–581
    economic expansion, 583–585
    foreign, FDR actions, 678–679
    reduction proposal to barriers, 585
    to Soviet Union, 678
    treaty with China, 583
    war materiel during Great War, 607
  years 1950–2000
    CIA in Third World, 746
    deficits, 801
    global economy, 833

Trade unions, 305, 420, *See also* Labor unions
  during Civil War, 398
  exclusion of African Americans, 455
Traditionalists in 1920s, 645
Traditional values, 556, 641–642, 673
Trail of Tears, 249–250
Trains, *See also* Railroads
  seized in Great Depression, 661
Traitors, 144
Transatlantic exchange, 23
Transcendentalism, 314
Transcontinental railroad, 360, 362, 498–499
Trans-Continental Treaty (1819), 233, 333
Trans-Mississippi West, 104, 249–250, 327, 333
Transportation
  canals and railroads, 292–295
  grid in Upper South, 271
  projects, Federal subsidies, 231
  public transit, 799
  revolution, 291–295
  and suburban growth, 772–773
  system decay in 1960s and 1970s, 770
  urban renewal, 740–741
Travel time between cities, 291
Travis, Joseph, 276
Travis, Merle, country singer, 766
Treason
  of Aaron Burr, 223
  of John Brown, 368
  in New England, 226
Treasury Department, 202, 203–204
Treasury System. *See* Independent Treasury System
Treaties
  with Indians, 334, 337–338
  with Indians enforced, 505
  with Indians in American West, 501
  international, Bush non-support of, 840–841
  between Texas & Mexico, 340
Treaty, Jay's, 208–210, 211, 213
Treaty of Fort McIntosh, 179
Treaty of Fort Stanwix, 179
Treaty of Ghent, 230–231
Treaty of Greenville (1795), 208, 225
Treaty of Guadalupe Hidalgo (1848), 346
Treaty of Iroquois with English & French, 67
Treaty of Lancaster (1744), 102
Treaty of New Echota (1835), 252
Treaty of Paris, 591–592, 593, 595
Treaty of Paris (1763), 104
Treaty of Paris (1783), 27, 147, 159, 179, 182
Treaty of Portsmouth, 594
Treaty of San Lorenzo (1795), 210
Treaty of Tordesillas, 24
Treaty of Versailles, 619–621, 679, 687
Treaty of Vincennes (1804), 225
Tredegar Iron Works Company in Richmond, 274, 383
Trenchard, John, 118
Trenton, Battle of, 147
Trenton, New Jersey, 783
Trial by jury, 173
Triangle Shirtwaist Company, 550
Tribal councils, 503
Tribal institutions, 772
Tribal lands
  in Mexican borderlands, 339
  Plains Indians, 333–335
  in Utah, 343
Tribal meetings, 335, 337
Tribal museums, 505
Tribal organizations, 740
Tribute system in Mediterranean, 220
Trickle down economics, 663
Trinity River, 644
Trinity site, 696
Tripartite Pact, 687
Trolley lines, 489, 491

Troops stationed in colonies, 112–114
Truck farmers, 483, 485
Trujillo, Jesús, 346
Truman, Harry S., U.S. president
  and bipartisan coalition, 719–721
  civil rights actions, 717–718
  Cold War, 725–729, 730
  decision on dropping atomic bomb, 708
  demobilization, 716
  in election of 1944, 702
  fighting Communism, 722–723, 748
  mentioned, 824
  as new president, 707
Truman Doctrine, 723
Trumbull, John, artist, 183
Trusts, 568, 569, 571
Truth, Sojourner, 274
T-shirt advertising, 720
Tuberculosis, 723
Tucson, Arizona, 346
Tugwell, Rexford, 670
Tulsa, Oklahoma, 615
Tunisia, 703
Turkey, 606, 620, 647, 723, 751
Turkey Red winter wheat, 516
Turner, Henry McNeal, AME bishop, 420, 458
Turner, Nat, 256
Turner's Rebellion, 251, 276, 316
Turnover in Congress and Federal government, 531
Turret lathes, 301
Tuscarora Indians, 62, 146
Tuskegee Institute, 459
Tuttle, F.A., of Nevada, 498
Twain, Mark, 417, 467, 492, 508, 567, 592
Tweed, William M., New York City mayor, 428
Two-ocean navy, 691
Two-party system, 528
Two Penny Act, 115
Tyler, John, U.S. president, 243, 258, 259–260, 261, 320, 371, 372, 373
Typewriters, 474
Typhoid, 386, 476
Typhus, 20, 23, 296

U

U-2 spy planes, 747, 755
U-boats (Unterseeboot), 691, 693
Ukraine, 709, 805
Ulam, Stanislaus, 686
Ulysses S. Grant, U.S. president
  in election of 1872, 429
  Union general, 385, 402–407
  at Vicksburg, 393–395
U.N. inspectors, 844
Uncle Tom's Cabin, 352, 358–359
Unconditional surrender, 702
"Under God" in Pledge of Allegiance, 742
Underground Railroad, 276
Underwood-Simmons Tariff Act (1913), 573
Unemployed, March on Washington (1893), 539–540
Unemployment
  in 1893, 539
  in 1990s, 829
  after Great War, 622
  during Great Depression, 661–666
  in Great Depression, 659
  in Panic of 1837, 255
  post WWII, 715–716
Unemployment compensation programs, 660, 669
Unemployment councils, 661
Unemployment relief, 662–663, 666, 668, 670, 673
Unequal distribution of wealth and income, 649, *See also* Rich *vs.* poor
  and Great Depression, 658–659
Unfair labor practices, 669

Unheavenly City, The (Banfield), 795
Unicameral legislature in state constitutions, 174
Unification Church, 769
Uniforms as war materiel, 607
Uniforms of soldiers in Civil War, 383
Unilateral peace treaty with Japan, 725
Unincorporated territory, 595
The Union, *See also* Civil War
  economy during Civil War, 398–399
  freedom goals, 390–392
  mobilizing for war, 381–385
  North transformed, 397–399
  objectives in Civil War, 381, 384–385
  resources during Civil War, 383–384
  strategy, 384–386, 388–389
Union leaders in 1920s, 635
Union Leagues, 426
Union of Soviet Socialist Republics (USSR). *See* Soviet Union
Union Pacific Railroad, 498–499
Union Party, 672
Unions, labor, 305
  after Great War, 622
  during Civil War, 398
  coalminers strike, 567–568
  collective bargaining, 622, 669, 673
  contracts, 672
  gains reversed after WWII, 716
  in Great Depression, 659
  during Great War, 612
  in late 19th century, 478–480
  membership, 673
  organized, 554
  racially mixed, 282
  recognition, 677
  shop contracts in 1920s, 634
  Southern Tenant Farmers Union, 668
  strikebreakers, 623
  Western miners, 509
  workers organized, 177
United Auto Workers, 673, 730
United Church of Christ, 815
United Daughters of Confederacy (UDC), 451, 460
United Farm Workers (UFW), 772
United Fruit Company, 647, 746
United Methodist Church, 815
United Mine Workers Union, 567–568, 716
United Nations Resolution 678, 806
United Nations (U.N.), 707, 722, 728, 729, 784
  and Manifest Destiny, 345
United Presbyterian Church, 816
United States Investor, 591
United States v. Cruikshank, 432–433
United States v. E. C. Knight Company, 541
Universalist *Christian Intelligencer*, 310
Universal manhood suffrage, 425, 426
Universal Negro Improvement Association (UNIA), 639
Universities, *See also* Colleges; Education; Public education
  affirmative action, 837–838
  colonial training of ministers, 90
  in colonies, 87
  as defense contractors, 807–808
  established for former slaves, 418
University of California at Berkeley, 766, 838
University of California at Davis, 837
University of California v. Bakke (1978), 837
University of Chicago, 562, 686
University of Colorado, 744
University of Georgia, 451
University of Kansas City, 731
University of Michigan, 593
University of Pennsylvania, 87
University of Texas, 837–838
University of Wisconsin, 776
University Settlement in New York City, 557
Unrestricted development, 570

Unskilled laborers, 420
Unthinking decision, 45
Upper Canada, 230
Upper class in late 19th century, 491
Upper houses, 173
Upper Midwest, Yankee migration to Old Northwest, 329–330
Upper South
  in 1800s before Civil War, 270–272
  poor agricultural management, 270, 278
  secession from Union, 371–373, 375
  slave families separated, 268, 274
"Uprising of 20,000," 554
Uprisings. *See* Slave revolts
Up-river shipments by steamboat, 292
Upshur, Abel P., proannexationist Virginian, 260
Uranium production, 722
Urban crisis in 1970s, 770, 778
Urban ethnic groups, FDR coalition, 672
Urban-industrial core, 487
Urbanization
  in 1920s, 632, 637
  of American West, 511
  in early 19th century, 291–301
  led in North by New England, 297
  minimal in Lower South, 268–269
  in New South late 19th century, 440–446
  North *vs.* South in 1860, 366
  in Upper South, 271–272
Urban League, 661, 740
Urban manufacturing reliance on immigration, 300–301
Urban reform, 557, 565–566
Urban renewal, 740–741
Urban rich, 302
Urban slaves, 269
Urban workers in Southern cities, 281
U.S. aircraft carriers, 693
U.S. Army, 510, 718, 733
U.S. Army Air Force, 697
U.S. Asiatic squadron, 590
U.S. as world leader in industrialization, 291
U.S. Chamber of Commerce (1912), 565
U.S. Civil Rights Commission, 835
U.S. Defense Department, 832, 843
U.S. Department of Agriculture, 560–561
U.S. Department of Defense, 724
U.S. Department of Energy, 783
U.S. Department of Homeland Security, 843
U.S. Department of Labor, 474
U.S. Division of Forestry, 568
U.S. embassy in Tehran, Iran, 785
U.S. Marines in John Brown's raid, 367
U.S. naval warships
  C. Turner Joy, 757
  Cole, 841
  Greer, 691
  Kearny, 691
  Maddox, 757
  Maine, 584, 589
  Reuben James, 691
U.S. Navy, *See also* Naval bases
  creation of, 137, 164
  in Cuba, 590
  expedition to Oregon, 261
  naval power, 582–583, 647
  naval war
    in Civil War, 389–390
    with Germany, 691, 693
    in Mexican War, 346
    in Philippines, 593
    in Revolutionary War, 150–151
    in War of 1812, 229
  occupation of Midway Islands in 1867, 585
  protection of American shipping, 220
U.S. Post Office, 632

censorship during Great War, 614
established, 137
mail censored during war, 842
offices built by WPA, 670
Postal law (1810), 307
postmasters violation of Federal law, 256
rural free delivery of mail, 561
U.S. Rubber Company, 469
U.S. Sanitary Commission, 386
U.S. Steel Company, 443, 471, 472, 634, 658
U.S. Supreme Court
abortion rights, 646
business and government rulings in 1895, 541
champion of business, 636
checks and balances, 187
in Constitution, 186
crosstown busing, 811
as defined by the Constitution, 202
election of 2000, 838
farm program and recovery, 667
first Jewish-American on court, 574
first woman justice, 834
gay rights, 817
Indian removal cases, 251
Japanese removals, 701
Japanese residents, 643
judicial nationalism, 235
nominations, 778
Northern Securities Company antitrust suit, 569
opened economy to competition, 294
overturned Civil Rights Act, 430
racial segregation upheld, 432–433
regulation of interstate commerce, 535
restructuring plan by FDR, 677
school segregation, 738, 752
on segregated accommodations, 454–455
separation of church and state, 742–743
status of Puerto Rico, 595
voting rights of Indians, 698
Wilson activist government nomination, 574
woman suffrage, 526
U.S. Treasury Department, 542
U.S. War Department, 202, 231, 702
Used-car dealers post WWII, 715
Ut, Nick, 789
Utah
dry farming practices, 516
mentioned, 510, 514
in Mexican War, 346
nuclear weapons testing, 726
on Oregon Trail, 336
population growth in 1990s, 834
settled by Mormons, 342–343
woman suffrage, 529
Ute Indians, 7, 343, 503
Utility companies
in 1920s, 634
public ownership, 565
Utility systems, 770
Utopian communities and socialism, 313–314

V

Vaca, Cabeza de, 5, 22
Vaccinations of Sioux against smallpox, 335
Vacuum cleaners, 632, 640
Vagrant Laws, 423
Valens, Richie, 742
Valentino, Rudolph, movie star, 642
VA mortgages, 717, 741
Van Buren, Martin, U.S. president, 257, 261
Vance, Zebulon, North Carolina governor, 406
Vancouver Island in Puget Sound, 344

Vandenberg, Arthur, senator from Michigan, 723
Vardaman, James (White Chief), governor of Mississippi, 563
Vecchio, Mary, 789
Veiller, Lawrence, 557
Venereal disease, 388, 617
Venezuela, 587–588
Vera Cruz, Mexico, 599
Verger, Jean-Baptiste-Antoine de, 160
Vermont, 149, 182
Verrazano, Giovanni de, 24
Vesey, Denmark, 276
Vesey's Conspiracy, 276
Vest, George, Missouri senator, 587
Veterans
and GI Bill of Rights, 716
of Great War, 663, 667
payments, 144–145
post WWII, 715
Veterans Administration, 716
Veterans Bureau, 636
Vetoes, presidental, 530
Vice-admiralty courts, 94
Vice trade, 508
Vicksburg, Mississippi, 385–386, 393–395
Victory gardens, 697
Viet Cong, 750, 773
Vietnam, 729, 746, 749–750, 793
Vietnamese Buddhists, 750
Vietnamization, 776
Vietnam Moratorium, 776
Vietnam War, 763–767, 773–774, 776, 788–789
Vigilante groups, 120
Villa, Francisco "Pancho," 599
Villages of dead, 501
Vincennes settlement in Mississippi Valley, 150
Violence
anti-Asian, 485
against blacks in housing shortage, 717
Civil Rights movement, 756
Columbine High School, 826
in cow towns, 511
by Klan, 643
against miners' unions, 510
in mining camps, 508
racial (whites against blacks), 416–417, 424, 427–428, 429–430
railroad strike, 478
Trinity River, 644
Whipping meadow, 644
Virginia
Border South in 1850, 270
freedom riders, 754
John Brown's raid, 367–368
Lee's army in Civil War, 406
mentioned, 752
ratification of Constitution, 190
secession from Union, 375, 384
slave population in 1860, 272
states rights, 211
tobacco industry, 440
voters, 243
Virginia City, Nevada, 506
Virginia colony
Bacon's Rebellion, 65
conflict with French in Ohio Valley, 102–103
settlement, 34–37
slavery embraced, 69
tobacco, 37–39
Virginia Company, 35
Virginia Declaration of Rights, 173
Virginia Methodists condemned slavery, 171
Virginia Plan, 184
Virginia Tidewater, 270
Virtual representation, 96, 116
Vital center politics, 719
Voice from the South, A (Cooper), 438
Volga River, 693
Volgograd (Stalingrad), 693

Volstead Act, 644
Voluntarism, 662–663
Volunteers in Civil War, 382
Volunteers in Service to America (VISTA), 755
Voter registration, 756
Voters
in colonies, 96
in election of 2000, 838
Voter turnout
in 1800s, early, 261
in 1828, 247
in 1840, 259
in 1852, 359
in 1876–1900 elections, 526
in 1920, 565
in 1924, 637
current trends, 528
in election of 1896, 543
in South late 19th century, 456
Voting
law in colonies, 94
and officeholding property requirements, 243
oral or "stand-up," 244
Voting qualifications, 455, 457
Voting reform, 756
Voting rights. See Suffrage; Woman suffrage movement
Voting Rights Act, amended (1975), 836
Voting Rights Act (1965), 433, 738, 756

W

Wabash, St Louis, and Pacific Railway Company vs. Illinois, 535
Wabash Indians, 209
Wabash River, 225
Waco, Texas, 826
Wade-Davis Bill, 421
Wages
in 1905, 550
in 1920s, 635
in 1950s, 740
in 1980s, 799, 813
during Civil War, 398–399
coalminers strike, 567–568
economic crisis after Revolutionary War, 177
of freedmen, 420
gender gap in late 20th century, 800
minimum, 673
minimum in 1996, 825
in New South late 19th century, 441–442
protective legislation, 557–558
regulations struck down, 636
rollbacks in Reaganomics, 797
for women in 1836, 309
women vs. men late 19th century, 474–476
worker demands, 553
Wagner, Robert F., New York senator, 669, 671
Wagner National Labor Relations Act, 669, 672, 677
Wagon trains, 337
Waite, Morrison, Supreme Court chief justice, 526
Wald, Lillian, 548
Walden, or Life in the Woods (Thoreau), 314
Walden Pond, 314
Walker, David, 316
Walker, Madame C.J., 653
Walker, Robert, 364
Walker, William, "General," 360
Walking cities, 296
Wallace, George, 775, 781
Wallace, Henry, New Dealer, 702, 719–720
Wallace, Mary, seamstress, 87–88
Wall Street, 542
stock market crash of 1929, 658–659
Wall Street Journal, 637, 796, 813

Walsh, Lawrence, special prosecutor, 803
Waltham, Massachusetts, 299
Waltham system, 300
Wampanoag Indians, 12, 41, 64–65, 67
Wanamaker & Brown in Philadelphia, 491
War against Cambodia, 776
War bonds, 695
War contracts after WWII, 715
War criminals, 841
Ward, Lester, 552
War debts, 175, 647
Ward elections, 565
War economy, 744
Warehouse Act (1916), 574
War for Independence. See Revolutionary War
War Hawks, 225–226
War hysteria during Great War, 614–615
War Industries Board (WIB), 611, 621
War Manpower Commission, 695
War materiel, 607
War of 1812
against Britain, 226–231
cotton & woolen mills started, 299
end of war opened West, 329, 332
events leading to, 223–226
War of attrition, 383
War of the Austrian Succession (King George's War), 102
War of the League of Augsburg, 100
War of the Spanish Succession, 100
War on crime and drugs, 801
War on drugs, 827
War on Poverty, 755, 757, 767
War on radicalism, 623
War on Terrorism, 842–844
War outlawed, 647
War production, 695
War Production Board, 695
Warren Commission, 755
War resolution, 611
Wars. See Battles; Civil War; Conflicts in colonies; Great War; Indian wars; Revolutionary War; War of 1812; World War II
War-supply contracts, 695
Wartime Civil Control Administration's, 701
Wartime economy, 611–612, 621
Wasatch Mountains, 343
Washing machines, 632, 640
Washington, Booker T., 459, 559
Washington, D.C., 752
abolition of slavery, 256
march of unemployed (1893), 539–540
Negro March on Washington, 698, 754
Shantytown, 663
torched, 230
Washington, George, U.S. president, 105
colonial planter, 89
convention presiding officer, 184
credit reliance, 86
as English gentleman, 82
established presidential etiquette, 201–202
expected to be the president, 186
Farewell Address, 161, 210, 688
in French and Indian War, 104
as head of Continental Army, 142, 156
inauguration of, 196
John Jay correspondence, 183
land speculation, 98
as Lieutenant Colonel defending Virginia, 102
reelected to presidency, 205
selected as Commander in Chief, 138
speech to army discontents, 145
Whiskey Rebellion, 208
Washington, Martha Custis, 82

Washington Naval Conference (1921), 647
Washington News, 663
Washington Post, 549, 624, 781
Washington state
  discrimination of Japanese residents, 643
  internment of Japanese Americans, 699
  mentioned, 511
  minority governor elected, 836
  nuclear weapons testing, 726
  Populist election, 538
  Red Scare, 731
  women suffrage adopted, 564
Washington Temperance Societies, 308
Waste disposal, *See also* Sanitation systems
  in early large cities, 296
Watch parts manufactured with interchangeable parts, 301
Watergate scandal, 779–782
Water pollution, 570
Water scarcity in American West, 515–516
Water systems in early large cities, 296
Watson, Tom, Populist leader, 449
Watt, James, secretary of Interior, 797
Watts neighborhood in Los Angeles, 770
Wave band interference, 634
Wayne, Anthony, general, 208
Wayne, Charles, 665
Wayne, John, actor, 766
Wealth
  in late 19th century, 476–478
  unequal distribution of wealth and income, 649, 658–659
Weapons, *See also* Guns
  of mass destruction, 844
  missiles, 745, 751
  from U.S., German tonnage warfare, 693
Weather Underground, 776
Weaver, James B., Populist candidate, 538, 542
Webster, Daniel
  Compromise of 1850, 355
  election of 1836, 257
  formation of Whig Party, 256
  secretary of state, 259–260
Webster-Ashburton Treaty (1842), 260
Weed, Thurlow, 257
Weeds in Columbian exchange, 23
Weil, George, 686
Welch, Joseph, Army lawyer, 733
Welch, Mary Josephine, 508
Weld, Theodore Dwight, abolitionist, 290, 317
Welfare, 552, 660
Welfare capitalism, 634
Welfare programs, lack of in 1893, 539
Welfare recipients, 770
Welfare state, 559
Wells, Ida B., 454, 459, 563
Wesley, John, 450
Wesley Houses, 450
West African colony, Liberia, 315
West African societies, 12–16
Western allies after WWII, 722
Western Europe c. 1500, 16
Western expansion to American West, *See also* American West
  agriculture frontier, 326–333
  California, 342–343
  Manifest Destiny, 343–345
  Mexican borderlands, 338–343
  and Mexican War, 344–346
  Plains Indians, 333–338
  Texas annexation, 339–342
Western farms
  and cattle ranches, 676
  worker shortage in WWII, 698
Western Federation of Miners, 510
Western front in Great War, 617

Western markets via Erie Canal, 292
Western newspapers on Indian extermination, 502
Western Pennsylvania coalfields, 296
Western settlers, 207
West Florida, 223, 233
West Germany, 724, 729
West India Company, 51–52
West Indian colonies, 316
West Indies sugar, 45–46, 104
Westinghouse, 634
Westminster College in Missouri, 722
Westmoreland, William, Vietnam commander, 763, 774
West Point, 144
West Roxbury, Massachusetts, 314
West Springfield, Massachusetts, 174
West Virginia
  formation of, 400
  hunger during Great Depression, 657
  stayed in Union, 384
Whale oil market, 177
Whale products, colonial export, 86
Wheat
  exports, 85
  Mid-Atlantic region, 198
  production, 330–331
  in Virginia in 1800s, 271, 272
  war materiel, 607
Wheatley, Phillis, African-American poet, 172
Wheeler, Bernadette, 714
Wheeler, John Hill, of North Carolina, 266
Whig militia
  Battle of Kettle Creek, 152
  skirmish in Vermont, 149
Whig Party
  Country ideology, 101
  finished as a national party, 359
  formation of, 242–243, 255
  issue of slavery, 354
  rise of, 256–261
  and school reform, 311–312
  support in Old South, 280
Whigs, 128
  patriotic anti-British, 135, 136, 140, 142, 152
  reaction to black soldiers, 145
Whipper, W.J., 456
Whipping meadow, 644
Whippings of slaves, 273
Whiskey and corruption of Plains Indians, 336
Whiskey Rebellion, 208
Whistle-stopping campaign, 720
White, Hugh Lawson, 257
White, John, 26
White, Walter, of NAACP, 698
White, William Allen, 624
White Caps, 515
White Cliffs in Montana, 236
White-collar jobs, 799
White-collar workers, 640
Whitefield, George, charismatic evangelist, 92
White House Task Force on Regulatory Relief, 797
White Indians, 98
White League, 430
White male democracy, 243–244
White man's burden, 582, 593
White migration onto Great Plains, 501
White mobs, 282, 453
White nation, fringe groups, 842
White overseers, 268
White paramilitary groups, 428
White people backlash on blacks' rights, 452–453
White Plains, Battle of, 147
White prejudice, 282
White solidarity, 282–284
Whites only hiring during WWII, 698

Whites only in California gold rush, 355
White Southerners
  after Civil War, 417, 422
  belief in black inferiority, 424
  defeated Populists, 539
  FDR coalition, 672
  in New South late 19th century, 445–446
  party loyalty, 527
  Redemption, 429–430
  slavery and moral condemnation, 367
  state governments, 426–427
  support of George Wallace, 775
  united on slavery, 367
White supremacy, 439, 449, 450, 455, 456, 460, 461
White Tower fastfood franchise chain, 640
Whitewater development, 827
Whitman, Marcus and Narcissa, 337
Whitman, Walt, poet, 295, 314
Whitney, Eli, inventor of cotton gin, 300–301, 332
Whitney, Jackson, 278
Who, The, rock band, 768
Whole Earth Catalog, The, 769
Whyte, William H., Jr., 743
Wichita, 511
Wichita, Kansas, 510
Widows employed in colonies, 88
Wildcat operations, 253
Wilder, Douglas, Virginia governor, 835
Wilderness, Battle of the, 402
Wilderness Act (1964), 757
Wildlife refuges, 568
Wild West, 520
Wilhelm II, German Kaiser, 605
Wilkes-Barre, Pennsylvania, 474
Wilkie, Wendell, 691
Wilkinson, Eliza, of South Carolina, 171
Wilkinson, James, Louisiana Territory governor, 223
Willamette Valley, 261, 336
Willard, Frances, 529–530
William Byrd, colonial intellectual, 90
William of Orange, king of England, 93–94, 100
Williams, Daniel Hale, 487
Williams, Fannie Barrier, 486
Williams, Roger, of Rhode Island, 42–43, 62
Williamsburg, Virginia, 82, 89
Wilmington, North Carolina, 458
Wilmington Herald, 371
Wilmot, David, Pennsylvania Democrat, 353
Wilmot Proviso, 353–354
Wilson, Edith Galt, 621
Wilson, "Engine Charlie," secretary of Defense, 739–740
Wilson, James, Pennsylvania lawyer, 128
Wilson, Woodrow, U.S. president
  in Caribbean and Mexico, 599
  county agent system, 561
  foreign policy, 345
  Great War
    Fourteen Points, 619–620
    mobilizing America, 613–614
    neutrality, 606–611
  immigrant prejudice, 551
  mentioned, in FDR administration, 678, 691
  mentioned, women's parader, 549
  as professor of history and government, 530
  progressive reform, 572–574
  Red Scare, 842
  suffered stroke, 621
Windmills, 511, 516
Window of vulnerability, 794
Wingina, chief of Roanokes, 26
Winston, North Carolina, 443

Winter quarters
  at Morristown, New Jersey, 147
  at Valley Forge, Pennsylvania, 149
Winter wheat, 516
Winthrop, John, governor of Massachusetts Bay colony, 41–42, 43
Wisconsin
  admitted to Union, 331
  adopted equal rights law, 637
  Bob La Follette, 566
  in Old Northwest, 330
  Socialist support, 555
  workers' compensation, 559
Witchcraft in Salem, 94
Wobblies. *See* Industrial Workers of the World (IWW)
Wolfe, James, British general, 104
Wolfe, Tom, novelist, 798
Woman, modern, 652
Woman Rebel magazine, 559–560
Woman's Christian Temperance Union (WCTU), 529–530
Woman's Committee of the Council of National Defense, 614
Woman's Land Army, 612
Woman's Peace Party, 609
Woman suffrage movement
  in 1920s, 637
  amendment, 613
  black women's clubs, 459
  demanded, 319
  gaining right to vote, 564
  in late 19th century, 526
  momentum lost, 637
  in New South late 19th century, 450–452
  Populist support, 538
  questioned at antislavery convention, 318
  in Reconstruction, 424–426
  in states, 529
  suffrage parade, 548–549, 564
  Wilson non-support, 574
Women
  advertising, 652
  aid for dependent mothers and children, 669
  in Alliance, 448
  in associational politics, 529
  camp followers in wars, 145, 386–388
  changing roles, 811
  church membership, 245
  civil rights bus boycott, 753
  during Civil War, 399, 401
  in Civil War armies, 383
  clubs, 554
  department store shoppers, 491
  with dependent children, 673
  division of labor
    in Africa, 14
    in Native America, 6–7, 10, 12
    in New England, 44
    office workers, 814
    in Old Northwest, 330
    in Western Europe, 16
  division of labor in New South, 445
  economic independence, 558
  employment opportunities in colonial cities, 87–88
  in farmers protest, 537–538
  in FDR administration, 673–674
  FDR coalition, 672
  feminine mystique, 744
  in government job opportunities, 533
  from grass roots to Congress, 834–835
  Great Depression gender segregation, 660
  Great Depression protests, 661
  Great War, jobs lost after, 622
  Great War, roles during, 612–613
  in higher education, 716
  homesteaders on Great Plains, 515
  horses valued, 23

housewife's role, 640
immigrant workers, 484
on Indian reservations, 505
isolation in suburbia, 717, 744
Jazz Age freedoms, 642
jobs after WWII, 715–716
legal protections in Second
    Continental Congress, 158
manufacturing and factory
    workforce, 299–300
in military in WWII, 696
moral superiors of men, 304
New Deal jobs, 673–674
on Oregon Trail, 337
political opportunities, 244
political rights, lack of, 169–171
public role in social reform, 308–309
reformers, 554–555
slave life, 274
social pressures in 1950s, 741–742
Southern, in late 19th century, 439–440
Southern planters, 279
Southern white virtue and purity,
    450–452
status in New England in 1789,
    197–198
subordination to men, 304, 310
teaching profession, 312
in temperance movement, 308
in Vietnam War, 766
as wage earners, 305
wage gap in late 20th century, 800
in Western mining camps, 508
workers in late 19th century,
    474–476
workers in late 20th century, 813
work force in WWII, 698
Women of Ku Klux Klan, 643, 645
Women's Air Force Service Pilots
    (WASPS), 697
Women's Christian Temperance
    Union (WCTU), 450–451, 459
Women's clubs, 451–452
Women's groups
    criticized male employers, 309
    Eleanor Roosevelt, 663
Women's liberation, 767–768,
    811–812
Women's Political Council, 753
Women's rights, *See also* Woman
    suffrage movement
    abolitionist support, 315
    abortion rights, 646
    break with abolitionists, 425–426
    current culture wars, 646
    Elizabeth Cady Stanton, 425–426
    in late 20th century, 811–814
    in New Deal, 673–674
    opposition from religious
        conservatives, 817

property, 427
protective legislation, 557–559, 636
reproductive rights, 559–560
Susan B. Anthony, 424–426
women's issues in 1920s, 637
Women's Rights Movement, 317–320
Women's Trade Union League
    (WTUL), 554, 558, 637, 673
Women's trail diaries, 337
Women Strike for Peace, 751
Women's war, during Revolution, 158
Wonder Woman, 695
Wood, Jethro, 330
Wood, Leonard, military governor of
    Cuba, 581, 596
Woodlands region, 10–11
Woodmason, Charles, 98
Woods runners, fur traders, 99
Woodstock rock festival, 768
Wood used in early 19th century, 301
Woolen mills, 299, 301
Woolworth's, 634, 753
Worcester v. *Georgia* (1832), 251
Workday
    coalminers strike, 567–568
    eight hour day won, 479
    of factory workers in late 19th
        century, 472
    for Federal employees, 258
    Roosevelt support, 571
    in Southern textile mills, 443
    ten-hour, 305
Workers
    blacks, 672
    demanded rights, 668
    farm, 675
    freedom of contract, 556
    immigrant, 631
    meatpacking, 630
    Mexican, during Great War, 612
    organizing unions in late 19th
        century, 478–480
    propertyless, 244
    during Reagan years, 797
    rights for, 673
    rights to organize unions, 667
    textile, 305
    in textile mills, 299–300
    unemployment councils, 661
    union organizing, 177
    United Mine Workers Union,
        567–568
    white-collar, 640
Workers' compensation, 559, 566, 574
Work hours
    in early 20th century, 550
    protective legislation for women,
        557–558
    worker demands, 553
Workhouses, 88, 312

Working class
    excluded from suburbs, 640
    industrialization in early 1800s,
        304–305
    and municipal reform, 565
Working-class men, 492
Working conditions
    in late 19th century, 471–473
    worker demands, 553
Workingmen's movement in Eastern
    cities, 311
Workload of slaves, 273–274
Work projects, 670
Works Progress Administration (WPA),
    658, 670, 673, 674, 675
Workweek, 630
World Anti-Slavery Convention
    (1840), 318
World Bank, 722
World market, 833
World Trade Center, 822–823, 841
World Trade Organization (WTO),
    766, 833
World War I. *See* Great War
World War II, 684–711
    Allies and end of Grand Alliance,
        722–723
    Allies strength gathered in 1943, 702
    civilian work force, 698–699
    demobilization, 715–719
    economy mobilized, 695–696
    home front, 697
    Japanese internment, 699–701
    mobilizing for war, 695–702
    neutrality, 687–691
    nuclear fission bomb, 696,
        707–709
    peace conference, 707
    Pearl Harbor attack, 692
    soldiers, men and women, 696–697
    two-front strategy, 692–694
    war in Europe, 702–705
    war in Pacific, 705–707
World War III, 727
Worldwide conflicts
    Revolutionary War, 149
    Seven Years' War, 103
World Wide Web, 832
Worth, Jonathan, 400
Wounded Knee, South Dakota, 503,
    505
Writers, 670
Writing in Mesoamerica, 7
Writ of habeas corpus, 842
    suspended by Lincoln, 397
Writs of assistance, 117
Wyandot Indians, 67
Wyoming, 335–336, 502,
    511, 529
Wyoming Valley, Pennsylvania, 150

X
XYZ Affair, 211

Y
Yale University, 90, 491
Yalta Conference, 707, 722
Yamamoto, Isoroku, Japanese
    admiral, 692
Yamasee Indians, 62
Yankees
    farm children to mills, 300
    migration to Old Northwest,
        329–330
Yaquis Indians, 23
Yarn factories, 299
Yazoo River, 332
Year of the Hangman, 147–149
Yellow dog contracts, 634
Yellow fever, 597
Yellow press, 589
Yeltsin, Boris, president of Russian
    Republic, 805
Yemen, 841
Yeoman farmers, 280–281, 426, 433
Yippies, 775
Yorktown, Virginia, 155
Young, Andrew, mayor of Atlanta,
    784, 836
Young, Brigham, 343
Young America, 359–360
Young Citizens' Club, 476
Young Men's Christian Association
    (YMCA), 458, 487, 604
Youngstown, Ohio, 664
Young Women's Christian Association
    (YWCA), 451, 459, 487
Youth
    in 1920s, 642
    as selling tool, 652–653
Youth culture, 742, 768, 798
Yucatan, 7
Yugoslavia, 688, 824
Yuman Indians, 338, 342
Yuppies, 798

Z
Zelman v. *Simmons-Harris* (2002), 840
Zero concept in Mesoamerica, 7
Zimmermann, Arthur, German
    foreign minister, 610
Zimmermann note, 610
Zitkala-Sa, 504
Zoning, 811
Zuni Indians, 9, 64, 500

U.S. HISTORY DOCUMENTS CD-ROM

Over 300 Primary Source Documents

Part 1 Meeting of Three Cultures:

1–1 Marco Polo Recounts His Travels Through Asia (1324)
1–2 Christopher Columbus, Letter to Ferdinand and Isabella of Spain (1494)
1–3 Alvar Núñez Cabeza de Vaca, "Indians of the Rio Grande" (1528–1536)
1–4 Jacques Cartier: First Contact with the Indians (1534)
1–5 Bartolomé de Las Casas, "Of the Island of Hispaniola" (1542)
1–6 Thomas Mun, from England's Treasure by Foreign Trade (1664)
1–7 Don Juan de Oñate, Plaus: A Settlement in New Mexico (1599)
1–8 The Founding of St. Augustine, 1565
1–9 The Columbian Exchange (1590)
1–10 Thomas Harriot, The Algonquian Peoples of the Atlantic Coast (1588)
1–11 Jose de Acosta, A Spanish Priest Speculates on the Origins of the Indians (1590)

Part 2 Colonizing the New World

2–1 John White, The Lost Colony (1590)
2–2 Samuel de Champlain's Battle With the Iroquois, July 1609
2–3 An Act Concerning Servants and Slaves
2–4 Reasons for the Plantation in New England (1629)
2–5 John Winthrop, "A Model of Christian Charity" (1630)
2–6 The Taking of the Fort at Mystic: A Brief History of the Pequot War
2–7 The Trial of Anne Hutchinson (1638)
2–8 A Jesuit Priest Describes New Amsterdam (1642)
2–9 George Alsop, The Importance of Tobacco (1660)
2–10 The Examination and Confession of Ann Foster at Salem Village (1692)
2–11 Onandogas and Cayugas: Iroquois Chiefs Address the Governors of New York and Virginia (1684)
2–12 James Oglethorpe: The Stono Rebellion (1739)
2–13 Gottlieb Mittelberger, The Passage of Indentured Servants (1750)

Part 3 Colonial America

3–1 Navigation Act of September 13, 1660
3–2 Nathaniel Bacon's Challenge to William Berkeley and the Governor's Response (1676)
3–3 Early French Explorations of the Mississippi River (1673)
3–4 Edward Randolph Describes King Philip's War (1685)
3–5 Excerpt from Cotton Mather's "Memorable Providences, Relating to Witchcrafts and Possessions" (1689)
3–6 William Penn's Charter of Privileges (1701)
3–7 William Byrd II, Diary (1709)
3–8 Manners and Etiquette in the Eighteenth Century
3–9 "The Storm Arising in the West," George Washington Delivers a Warning to the French (1753)
3–10 The Closing of the Frontier (1763)
3–11 The Adventures of Daniel Boone (1769)
3–12 Alexander Falconbridge, The African Slave Trade (1788)
3–13 Olaudah Equiano, The Middle Passage (1788)

Part 4 Prelude to Revolution

4–1 John Peter Zenger and the Responsibility of the Press (1734)
4–2 Declaration of the Injured Frontier Inhabitants [of Pennsylvania] (1764)
4–3 Benjamin Franklin, Testimony Against the Stamp Act (1766)
4–4 "Letters From a Farmer in Pennsylvania" (1767)
4–5 John Dickinson, from Letters from a Farmer in Pennsylvania (1768)
4–6 The Boston "Massacre" or Victims of Circumstance? (1770)
4–7 John Andrews to William Barrell, Letter Regarding the Boston Tea Party (1773)
4–8 Address of the Inhabitants of Anson County to Governor Martin (1774)
4–9 J. Hector St. John Crèvecoeur, "What Is an American?" (1782)

Part 5 The American Revolution

5–1 Benjamin Franklin, "Observations Concerning the Increase of Mankind, Peopling of Countries, & c." (1751)
5–2 James Otis, The Rights of the British Colonies Asserted and Proved (1763)
5–3 The Crisis Comes to a Head: April 19, 1775
5–4 A Freelance Writer Urges His Readers To Use Common Sense (1776)
5–5 Abigail Adams and John Adams Letters; Abigail Adams Letter to Mercy Otis Warren
5–6 Petition of "A Grate Number of Blackes of the Province" to Governor Thomas Gage and the Members of the Massachusetts General Court (1774)
5–7 Joseph Warren, "Account of the Battle of Lexington" (1775)
5–8 Thomas Jefferson, "Original Rough Draught" of the Declaration of Independence (1776)
5–9 Rights of Women in an Independent Republic
5–10 The Rise of Partisan Warfare in the South (1778)

Part 6 Forging a Constitution

6–1 Constitution of Pennsylvania (1776)
6–2 A Declaration of the Rights of the Inhabitants of the Commonwealth of Massachusetts (1780)
6–3 George Washington, The Newburgh Address (1783)
6–4 Henry Knox, Letter to George Washington (1786)
6–5 Marquis de Chastellux, Travels in North America (1786)
6–6 Shays's Rebellion: Letters of Generals William Shepard and Benjamin Lincoln to Governor James Bowdoin of Massachusetts (1787)
6–7 Divergent Reactions to Shays's Rebellion
6–8 The "Distracting Question" in Philadelphia (1787)
6–9 Patrick Henry Speaks Against Ratification of the Constitution (1788)
6–10 Benjamin Banneker, Letter to Thomas Jefferson (1791)
6–11 James Wilson, An Introductory Lecture To a Course of Law Lectures (1791)
6–12 Molly Wallace, Valedictory Oration (1792)

Part 7 The Federalist Era

7–1   James Madison Defends the Constitution (1788)
7–2   [William Maclay], "For the Independent Gazetteer" (1790)
7–3   Alexander Hamilton, Final Version of "An Opinion on the Constitutionality of an Act to Establish a Bank" (1791)
7–4   Questions Concerning the Constitutionality of the National Bank (1791)
7–5   Opposing Visions for the New Nation (1791)
7–6   An African American Calls for an End to Slavery (1791)
7–7   Backcountry Turmoil Puts the New Government to the Test (1794)
7–8   George Washington, Farewell Address (1796)
7–9   The Alien and Sedition Acts (1798)
7–10 Questions of Constitutionality and the Roots of Nullification (1798)
7–11 Reverend Peter Cartwright on Cane Ridge and the "New Lights" (1801)
7–12 Marbury v. Madison (1803)

Part 8 Jefferson and the Republic

8–1   Memoirs of a Monticello Slave, as Dictated to Charles Campbell by Isaac (1847)
8–2   Thomas Jefferson, "First Inaugural Address" (1801)
8–3   Margaret Bayard Smith Meets Thomas Jefferson (1801)
8–4   Constitutionality of the Louisiana Purchase (1803)
8–5   The United States Navy and the Bombardment of Tripoli (1803)
8–6   A Matter of Honor or Vengeance? (1804)
8–7   Fisher Ames, "The Republican. No. II" (1804)
8–8   Sacagawea Interprets for Lewis and Clark (1804)
8–9   An "Uncommon Genius" Advocates Indian Unity (1809)
8–10 Indian Hostilities (1812)
8–11 The British Attack Baltimore (1814)
8–12 Report and Resolutions of the Hartford Convention (1814)
8–13 Davy Crockett, Advice to Politicians (1833)

Part 9 Economic and Social Change

9–1   The Western Country, Extracts from Letters Published in Niles' Weekly Register (1816)
9–2   The Cherokee Treaty of 1817
9–3   The Case for the Erie Canal
9–4   John Marshall Affirms the Power of the Federal Government
9–5   Thomas Jefferson Reacts to the "Missouri Question" (1820)
9–6   The Monroe Doctrine and a Reaction (1823)
9–7   Henry Clay, "Defense of the American System" (1832)
9–8   Imminent Dangers to the Free Institutions of the United States through Foreign Immigration (1835)
9–9   The Harbinger, Female Workers of Lowell (1836)
9–10 James F. Cooper, Notions of the Americans (1840)
9–11 Resolutions of the Boston Carpenters' Strike (1845)
9–12 The Trials of a Slave Girl

Part 10 Jacksonian Democracy

10–1 Joseph Smith and the Beginnings of Mormonism (1823)
10–2 A "Corrupt Bargain" or Politics as Usual? (1824)
10–3 A Disaffected Mason Speaks Out Against the Order (1826)
10–4 The "Commoner" Takes Office (1828)
10–5 Andrew Jackson, First Annual Message to Congress (1829)
10–6 "Memorial of the Cherokee Nation" (1830)
10–7 Andrew Jackson, Veto of the Bank Bill (1832)
10–8 President Andrew Jackson's Proclamation Regarding Nullification (1832)
10–9 The Force Bill (1833)
10–10 Black Hawk, "Life of Black Hawk" (1833)
10–11 A French Traveler Reports on American Society (1835)
10–12 Female Industry Association, from the New York Herald (1845)

Part 11 Reforming the Nation

11–1 Joshua and Sally Wilson Letters to George Wilson (1823)
11–2 Lyman Beecher, Six Sermons on Intemperance (1828)
11–3 "Early Habits of Industry," The Mother's Magazine (1834)
11–4 Charles Finney, "What a Revival of Religion Is" (1835)
11–5 Temperance and the Washingtonians (1836)
11–6 A Lowell Mill Girl Tells Her Story (1836)
11–7 "Petition of the Catholics of New York" (1840)
11–8 Ralph Waldo Emerson, "Self-Reliance" (1841)
11–9 Ja Norcom, Letter to Mary Matilda Norcom (1846)
11–10 Declaration of Sentiments and Resolutions, Woman's Rights Convention, Seneca Falls, New York (1848)
11–11 Horace Mann on Education and National Welfare
11–12 John Humphrey Noyes and Bible Communism (1845 and 1849)
11–13 Sojourner Truth, Address to the Woman's Rights Convention, Akron, Ohio (1851)

Part 12 Manifest Destiny

12–1 The Treaties of Velasco (May 14, 1836)
12–2 The Aroostook War (1839)
12–3 Across the Plains With Catherine Sager Pringle in 1844
12–4 John L. O'Sullivan, "The Great Nation of Futurity" (1845)
12–5 Thomas Corwin, Against the Mexican War (1847)
12–6 Chief Seattle, Oration (1854)

Part 13 Antebellum South

13–1 State v. Boon (1801)
13–2 A Black Abolitionist Speaks Out (1829)
13–3 Nat Turner, Confession (1831)
13–4 An Abolitionist Defends the Amistad Mutineers (1839)
13–5 De Bow's Review, "The Stability of the Union," (1850)
13–6 Benjamin Drew, Narratives of Escaped Slaves (1855)
13–7 George Fitzhugh, "The Blessings of Slavery" (1857)

Part 14 The Sectional Crisis

14–1 William Lloyd Garrison, from The Liberator (1831)
14–2 Harriet Beecher Stowe, from Uncle Tom's Cabin
14–3 National Convention of Colored People, Report on Abolition (1847)

14–4 A Dying Statesman Speaks out Against the Compromise of 1850

14–5 Frederick Douglass, Independence Day Speech (1852)

14–6 Kansas Begins to Bleed (1856)

14–7 A White Southerner Speaks Out Against Slavery (1857)

14–8 Dred Scott v. Sanford (1857)

14–9 Abraham Lincoln, "A House Divided" (1858)

Part 15 The Civil War

15–1 Jefferson Davis, Address to the Provisional Congress of the Confederate States of America (1861)

15–2 The "Cornerstone Speech" (1861)

15–3 Mary Boykin Chesnut, A Confederate Lady's Diary (1861)

15–4 Why They Fought (1861)

15–5 A Confederate General Assesses First Bull Run (1861)

15–6 Charles Harvey Brewster, Three Letters from the Civil War Front (1862)

15–7 Clara Barton, Medical Life at the Battlefield (1862)

15–8 James Henry Gooding, Letter to President Lincoln (1863)

15–9 Abraham Lincoln, Gettysburg Address (1863)

15–10 John Dooley, Passages from a Journal (1863)

15–11 A Firsthand Account of the New York Draft Riots (1863)

15–12 Susie King Taylor, Reminiscences of an Army Laundress (1902)

15–13 General William Tecumseh Sherman on War (1864)

Part 16 Reconstruction

16–1 "Address from the Colored Citizens of Norfolk, Virginia, to the People of the United States" (1865)

16–2 Carl Schurz, Report on the Condition of the South (1865)

16–3 Clinton B. Fisk, Plain Counsels for Freedmen (1865)

16–4 Mississippi Black Code (1865)

16–5 James C. Beecher, Report on Land Reform in the South Carolina Islands (1865, 1866)

16–6 The Memphis Riot (1866)

16–7 The Fourteenth Amendment (1868)

16–8 Albion W. Tourgee, Letter on Ku Klux Klan Activities (1870)

16–9 The Nation, "The State of the South" (1872)

16–10 Susan B. Anthony and the "New Departure" for Women (1873)

16–11 James T. Rapier, Testimony Before U.S. Senate Regarding the Agricultural Labor Force in the South (1880)

16–12 A Sharecrop Contract (1882)

Part 17 New South, Expanding West

17–1 Edward Gould Buffum, Six Months in the Gold Mines (1850)

17–2 Lydia Allen Rudd, Diary of Westward Travel (1852)

17–3 Horace Greeley, An Overland Journey (1860)

17–4 Joseph G. McCoy, Historic Sketches of the Cattle Trade of the West and Southwest (1874)

17–5 Helen Hunt Jackson, from A Century of Dishonor (1881)

17–6 Congressional Report on Indian Affairs (1887)

17–7 Tragedy at Wounded Knee (1890)

17–8 Benjamin Harrison, Report on Wounded Knee Massacre and the Decrease in Indian Land Acreage (1891)

17–9 The Omaha Platform of the Populist Party (1892)

17–10 From Plessy v. Ferguson (1896)

17–11 W. E. B. Du Bois, from "Of Mr. Booker T. Washington and Others" (1903)

Part 18 Industrializing America

18–1 Charles Loring Brace, "The Life of the Street Rats" (1872)

18–2 Progress and Poverty (1879)

18–3 The Gilded Age (1880)

18–4 Richard K. Fox, from Coney Island Frolics (1883)

18–5 Address by George Engel, Condemned Haymarket Anarchist (1886)

18–6 Edward Bellamy, from Looking Backward (1888)

18–7 The Assassination of President Garfield (1889)

18–8 Ida B. Wells-Barnett, from A Red Record (1895)

18–9 Booker T. Washington, Atlanta Exposition Address (1895)

18–10 United States Sanitary Commission, Sketch of Its Purposes (1864)

18–11 Lincoln Steffens, from The Shame of the Cities (1904)

18–12 Etiquette for the Upper Classes (1919)

18–13 Scientific Management (1919)

Part 19 Immigrant and Urban Nation

19–1 Memorial of the Chinese Six Companies to U.S. Grant, President of the United States (1876)

19–2 Plain Facts for Old and Young (1884)

19–3 Anglo-Saxon Culture Under Siege (1885)

19–4 How the Other Half Lives (1890)

19–5 The People's Party Platform (1892)

19–6 The Secret Oath of the American Protective Association (1893)

19–7 Adna Weber, The Growth of Cities in the Nineteenth Century (1899)

19–8 Lee Chew, Life of a Chinese Immigrant (1903)

19–9 Lincoln Steffens, from The Shame of the Cities (1904)

19–10 William T. Riordon, from Plunkitt of Tammany Hall (1905)

19–11 John Spargo, From The Bitter Cry of Children (1906)

19–12 Mary Antin, The Promised Land (1912)

Part 20 America Around the Globe

20–1 Josiah Strong, from Our Country (1885)

20–2 Henry Cabot Lodge, "The Business World vs. the Politicians" (1895)

20–3 Albert Beveridge, "The March of the Flag" (1898)

20–4 The Spanish-American War (1898)

20–5 William McKinley, "Decision on the Philippines" (1900)

20–6 The Boxer Rebellion (1900)

20–7 Theodore Roosevelt, Third Annual Message to Congress (1903)

20–8 Mark Twain, "Incident in the Philippines" (1924)

Part 21 The Progressive Era

21–1 Frederick Winslow Taylor, "A Piece-Rate System" (1896)

21–2 William Graham Sumner, What the Social Classes Owe to Each Other (1883)
21–3 Eugene V. Debs, "The Outlook for Socialism in the United States" (1900)
21–4 Platform Adopted by the National Negro Committee (1909)
21–5 James H. Patten, Chairman of the National Legislative Committee of the American Purity Federation, Testimony Before Congress (1910)
21–6 Jane Addams, Twenty Years at Hull House (1910)
21–7 Theodore Roosevelt, from The New Nationalism (1910)
21–8 Walker Percy, "Birmingham under the Commission Plan" (1911)
21–9 Helen M. Todd, "Getting Out the Vote" (1911)
21–10 Louis Brandeis, Other People's Money and How the Bankers Use It (1913)
21–11 Woodrow Wilson, from The New Freedom (1913)
21–12 Herbert Croly, Progressive Democracy (1914)

Part 22 World War One
22–1 The Great War
22–2 Boy Scouts of America from, "Boy Scouts Support the War Effort" (1917)
22–3 Letters from the Great Migration (1917)
22–4 American Troops in the Trenches (1918)
22–5 Eugene Kennedy, A "Doughboy" Describes the Fighting Front (1918)
22–6 Newton D. Baker, "The Treatment of German-Americans" (1918)
22–7 An Official Report
22–8 Woodrow Wilson, The Fourteen Points (1918)
22–9 Warren G. Harding, Campaign Speech at Boston (1920)
22–10 Edward Earle Purinton, "Big Ideas from Big Business" (1921)

Part 23 The 1920s and Modern America
23–1 J. Grimke, "Address of Welcome to the Men Who Have Returned from the Battlefront" (1919)
23–2 The Sahara of the Bozart (1920)
23–3 National Origins Quota Act, 1924
23–4 Advertisements (1925, 1927)
23–5 Family Planning 1926
23–6 Bartolomeo Vanzetti, Court Statement (1927)

Part 24 Depression and New Deal
24–1 Herbert Hoover, Speech at New York City (1932)
24–2 FDR's First Inauguration Speech (1932)
24–3 Franklin Delano Roosevelt, Speech at San Francisco (1932)
24–4 Share the Wealth
24–5 The Victims of the Ku Klux Klan (1935)
24–6 Father Charles E. Coughlin, "A Third Party" (1936)
24–7 Mrs. Henry Weddington, Letter to President Roosevelt (1938)

Part 25 World War Two
25–1 Albert Einstein, Letter to President Roosevelt (1939)
25–2 Charles Lindbergh, Radio Address (1941)
25–3 Franklin D. Roosevelt, The Four Freedoms (1941)
25–4 Franklin Delano Roosevelt, Annual Message to Congress (1941)
25–5 A. Philip Randolph, "Why Should We March?" (1942)
25–6 Japanese Relocation Order, February 19, 1942
25–7 Sterling A. Brown, "Out of Their Mouths" (1942)

Part 26 Cold War
26–1 George F. Kennan, "Long Telegram" (1946)
26–2 Kenneth MacFarland, "The Unfinished Work" (1946)
26–3 George Marshall, The Marshall Plan (1947)
26–4 Containment (1947)
26–5 Harry S Truman, The Truman Doctrine (1947)
26–6 Ronald Reagan, Testimony Before the House Un-American Activities Committee (1947)
26–7 Joseph R. McCarthy, from Speech Delivered to the Women's Club of Wheeling, West Virginia (1950)
26–8 National Security Council Memorandum Number 68 (1950)
26–9 Senator Joseph McCarthy's telegram to President Truman following the 'Wheeling [W. Va.] Speech,' February 11, 1950

Part 27 Consensus and Conformity
27–1 The Kinsey Report (1948)
27–2 Brown v. Board of Education(1954)
27–3 Ladies Home Journal, "Young Mother" (1956)
27–4 Student Nonviolent Coordinating Committee, Statement of Purpose (1960)

Part 28 The Changing Liberal State
28–1 Dwight D. Eisenhower, Decision Not to Intervene at Dien Bien Phu (1954)
28–2 Charles Sherrod, Student Nonviolent Coordinating Committee Memorandum (1961)
28–3 John F. Kennedy, Cuban Missile Address (1962)
28–4 Students for a Democratic Society, The Port Huron Statement (1962)
28–5 John Lewis, Address at the March on Washington (1963)
28–6 The Civil Rights Act of 1964
28–7 The Tonkin Gulf Incident (1964)
28–8 Lyndon B. Johnson, Commencement Address at Howard University (1965)
28–9 Stokely Carmichael and Charles Hamilton, from Black Power (1967)
28–10 Donald Wheeldin, "The Situation in Watts Today" (1967)
28–11 Vietnamization (1969)

Part 29 The Struggle For Social Change
29–1 John F. Kennedy, Inaugural Address (1961)
29–2 The Feminist Mystique (1963)
29–3 Lyndon Johnson, The War on Poverty (1964)
29–4 National Organization for Women, Statement of Purpose (1966)
29–5 The Gay Liberation Front, Come Out (1970)
29–6 Swann v. Charlotte-Mecklenburg Board of Education (1971)
29–7 Roe v. Wade (1973)
29–8 Ione Malloy, Southie Won't Go (1975)
29–9 Jimmy Carter, The "Malaise" Speech (1979)

Part 30 America at the Millennium

30–1 House Judiciary Committee, Conclusion on Impeachment Resolution (1974)

30–2 Ronald Reagan, First Inaugural Address (1981)

30–3 Ronald Reagan, Speech to the House of Commons (1982)

30–4 Ronald Reagan, Address to the National Association of Evangelicals (1983)

30–5 T. Boone Pickens, "My Case for Reagan" (1984)

30–6 Paul Craig Roberts, The Supply-Side Revolution (1984)

30–7 Bill Chappell, Speech to the American Security Council Foundation (1985)

30–8 Patricia Morrisroe, "The New Class" (1985)

30–9 George Bush, Address to the Nation Announcing Allied Military Action in the Persian Gulf (1991)

SINGLE PC LICENSE AGREEMENT AND LIMITED WARRANTY

READ THIS LICENSE CAREFULLY BEFORE OPENING THIS PACKAGE. BY OPENING THIS PACKAGE, YOU ARE AGREEING TO THE TERMS AND CONDITIONS OF THIS LICENSE. IF YOU DO NOT AGREE, DO NOT OPEN THE PACKAGE. PROMPTLY RETURN THE UNOPENED PACKAGE AND ALL ACCOMPANYING ITEMS TO THE PLACE YOU OBTAINED THEM.

1. GRANT OF LICENSE AND OWNERSHIP: THE ENCLOSED COMPUTER PROGRAMS <<AND DATA>> ("SOFTWARE") ARE LICENSED, NOT SOLD, TO YOU BY PEARSON EDUCATION, INC. PUBLISHING AS PEARSON PRENTICE HALL ("WE" OR THE "COMPANY") AND IN CONSIDERATION OF YOUR PURCHASE OR ADOPTION OF THE ACCOMPANYING COMPANY TEXTBOOKS AND/OR OTHER MATERIALS, AND YOUR AGREEMENT TO THESE TERMS. WE RESERVE ANY RIGHTS NOT GRANTED TO YOU. YOU OWN ONLY THE DISK(S) BUT WE AND/OR OUR LICENSORS OWN THE SOFTWARE ITSELF. THIS LICENSE ALLOWS YOU TO USE AND DISPLAY YOUR COPY OF THE SOFTWARE ON A SINGLE COMPUTER (I.E., WITH A SINGLE CPU) AT A SINGLE LOCATION FOR ACADEMIC USE ONLY, SO LONG AS YOU COMPLY WITH THE TERMS OF THIS AGREEMENT. YOU MAY MAKE ONE COPY FOR BACK UP, OR TRANSFER YOUR COPY TO ANOTHER CPU, PROVIDED THAT THE SOFTWARE IS USABLE ON ONLY ONE COMPUTER.

2. RESTRICTIONS: YOU MAY NOT TRANSFER OR DISTRIBUTE THE SOFTWARE OR DOCUMENTATION TO ANYONE ELSE. EXCEPT FOR BACKUP, YOU MAY NOT COPY THE DOCUMENTATION OR THE SOFTWARE. YOU MAY NOT NETWORK THE SOFTWARE OR OTHERWISE USE IT ON MORE THAN ONE COMPUTER OR COMPUTER TERMINAL AT THE SAME TIME. YOU MAY NOT REVERSE ENGINEER, DISASSEMBLE, DECOMPILE, MODIFY, ADAPT, TRANSLATE, OR CREATE DERIVATIVE WORKS BASED ON THE SOFTWARE OR THE DOCUMENTATION. YOU MAY BE HELD LEGALLY RESPONSIBLE FOR ANY COPYING OR COPYRIGHT INFRINGEMENT THAT IS CAUSED BY YOUR FAILURE TO ABIDE BY THE TERMS OF THESE RESTRICTIONS.

3. TERMINATION: THIS LICENSE IS EFFECTIVE UNTIL TERMINATED. THIS LICENSE WILL TERMINATE AUTOMATICALLY WITHOUT NOTICE FROM THE COMPANY IF YOU FAIL TO COMPLY WITH ANY PROVISIONS OR LIMITATIONS OF THIS LICENSE. UPON TERMINATION, YOU SHALL DESTROY THE DOCUMENTATION AND ALL COPIES OF THE SOFTWARE. ALL PROVISIONS OF THIS AGREEMENT AS TO LIMITATION AND DISCLAIMER OF WARRANTIES, LIMITATION OF LIABILITY, REMEDIES OR DAMAGES, AND OUR OWNERSHIP RIGHTS SHALL SURVIVE TERMINATION.

4. LIMITED WARRANTY AND DISCLAIMER OF WARRANTY: COMPANY WARRANTS THAT FOR A PERIOD OF 60 DAYS FROM THE DATE YOU PURCHASE THIS SOFTWARE (OR PURCHASE OR ADOPT THE ACCOMPANYING TEXTBOOK), THE SOFTWARE, WHEN PROPERLY INSTALLED AND USED IN ACCORDANCE WITH THE DOCUMENTATION, WILL OPERATE IN SUBSTANTIAL CONFORMITY WITH THE DESCRIPTION OF THE SOFTWARE SET FORTH IN THE DOCUMENTATION, AND THAT FOR A PERIOD OF 30 DAYS THE DISK(S) ON WHICH THE SOFTWARE IS DELIVERED SHALL BE FREE FROM DEFECTS IN MATERIALS AND WORKMANSHIP UNDER NORMAL USE. THE COMPANY DOES NOT WARRANT THAT THE SOFTWARE WILL MEET YOUR REQUIREMENTS OR THAT THE OPERATION OF THE SOFTWARE WILL BE UNINTERRUPTED OR ERROR-FREE. YOUR ONLY REMEDY AND THE COMPANY'S ONLY OBLIGATION UNDER THESE LIMITED WARRANTIES IS, AT THE COMPANY'S OPTION, RETURN OF THE DISK FOR A REFUND OF ANY AMOUNTS PAID FOR IT BY YOU OR REPLACEMENT OF THE DISK. THIS LIMITED WARRANTY IS THE ONLY WARRANTY PROVIDED BY THE COMPANY AND ITS LICENSORS, AND THE COMPANY AND ITS LICENSORS DISCLAIM ALL OTHER WARRANTIES, EXPRESS OR IMPLIED, INCLUDING WITHOUT LIMITATION, THE IMPLIED WARRANTIES OF MERCHANTABILITY AND FITNESS FOR A PARTICULAR PURPOSE. THE COMPANY DOES NOT WARRANT, GUARANTEE OR MAKE ANY REPRESENTATION REGARDING THE ACCURACY, RELIABILITY, CURRENTNESS, USE, OR RESULTS OF USE, OF THE SOFTWARE.

5. LIMITATION OF REMEDIES AND DAMAGES: IN NO EVENT, SHALL THE COMPANY OR ITS EMPLOYEES, AGENTS, LICENSORS, OR CONTRACTORS BE LIABLE FOR ANY INCIDENTAL, INDIRECT, SPECIAL, OR CONSEQUENTIAL DAMAGES ARISING OUT OF OR IN CONNECTION WITH THIS LICENSE OR THE SOFTWARE, INCLUDING FOR LOSS OF USE, LOSS OF DATA, LOSS OF INCOME OR PROFIT, OR OTHER LOSSES, SUSTAINED AS A RESULT OF INJURY TO ANY PERSON, OR LOSS OF OR DAMAGE TO PROPERTY, OR CLAIMS OF THIRD PARTIES, EVEN IF THE COMPANY OR AN AUTHORIZED REPRESENTATIVE OF THE COMPANY HAS BEEN ADVISED OF THE POSSIBILITY OF SUCH DAMAGES. IN NO EVENT SHALL THE LIABILITY OF THE COMPANY FOR DAMAGES WITH RESPECT TO THE SOFTWARE EXCEED THE AMOUNTS ACTUALLY PAID BY YOU, IF ANY, FOR THE SOFTWARE OR THE ACCOMPANYING TEXTBOOK. BECAUSE SOME JURISDICTIONS DO NOT ALLOW THE LIMITATION OF LIABILITY IN CERTAIN CIRCUMSTANCES, THE ABOVE LIMITATIONS MAY NOT ALWAYS APPLY TO YOU.

6. GENERAL: THIS AGREEMENT SHALL BE CONSTRUED IN ACCORDANCE WITH THE LAWS OF THE UNITED STATES OF AMERICA AND THE STATE OF NEW YORK, APPLICABLE TO CONTRACTS MADE IN NEW YORK, EXCLUDING THE STATE'S LAWS AND POLICIES ON CONFLICTS OF LAW, AND SHALL BENEFIT THE COMPANY, ITS AFFILIATES AND ASSIGNEES. THIS AGREEMENT IS THE COMPLETE AND EXCLUSIVE STATEMENT OF THE AGREEMENT BETWEEN YOU AND THE COMPANY AND SUPERSEDES ALL PROPOSALS OR PRIOR AGREEMENTS, ORAL, OR WRITTEN, AND ANY OTHER COMMUNICATIONS BETWEEN YOU AND THE COMPANY OR ANY REPRESENTATIVE OF THE COMPANY RELATING TO THE SUBJECT MATTER OF THIS AGREEMENT. IF YOU ARE A U.S. GOVERNMENT USER, THIS SOFTWARE IS LICENSED WITH "RESTRICTED RIGHTS" AS SET FORTH IN SUBPARAGRAPHS (A)-(D) OF THE COMMERCIAL COMPUTER-RESTRICTED RIGHTS CLAUSE AT FAR 52.227-19 OR IN SUBPARAGRAPHS (C)(1)(II) OF THE RIGHTS IN TECHNICAL DATA AND COMPUTER SOFTWARE CLAUSE AT DFARS 252.227-7013, AND SIMILAR CLAUSES, AS APPLICABLE.

SHOULD YOU HAVE ANY QUESTIONS CONCERNING THIS AGREEMENT OR IF YOU WISH TO CONTACT THE COMPANY FOR ANY REASON, PLEASE CONTACT IN WRITING: LEGAL DEPARTMENT, PRENTICE HALL, 1 LAKE STREET, UPPER SADDLE RIVER, NJ 07450 OR CALL PEARSON EDUCATION PRODUCT SUPPORT AT 1-800-677-6337.